Introduction to Learning and Behavior

Fourth Edition

RUSSELL A. POWELL

Grant MacEwan University

P. LYNNE HONEY

Grant MacEwan University

DIANE G. SYMBALUK

Grant MacEwan University

WADSWORTH
CENGAGE Learning·

Australia • Brazil • Japan • Korea • Mexico • Singapore • Spain • United Kingdom • United States

WADSWORTH
CENGAGE Learning·

Introduction to Learning and Behavior, Fourth Edition
Russell A. Powell,
P. Lynne Honey and Diane G. Symbaluk

Publisher: Jon-David Hague

Editorial Assistant: Travis Holland

Assistant Editor: Jessica Alderman

Media Editor: Noel Mary

Marketing Manager: Sean Foy

Marketing Communications Manager: Janay Pryor

Design Direction, Production Management and Composition: PreMediaGlobal

Art Director: Vernon Boes

Manufacturing Planner: Karen Hunt

Rights Acquisition Specialist: Roberta Broyer

Cover Designer: Andy Norris

Cover Image: Vicky Kasala, Getty Images

For product information and technology assistance, contact us at **Cengage Learning Customer & Sales Support, 1-800-354-9706**.

For permission to use material from this text or product, submit all requests online at **www.cengage.com/permissions**. Further permissions questions can be e-mailed to **permissionrequest@cengage.com**.

Library of Congress Control Number: 2012931528

ISBN-13: 978-1-111-83430-2

ISBN-10: 1-111-83430-X

Wadsworth
20 Davis Drive
Belmont, CA 94002-3098
USA

Cengage Learning is a leading provider of customized learning solutions with office locations around the globe, including Singapore, the United Kingdom, Australia, Mexico, Brazil, and Japan. Locate your local office at: **www.cengage.com/global**.

Cengage Learning products are represented in Canada by Nelson Education, Ltd.

To learn more about Wadsworth, visit **www.cengage.com/wadsworth**.

Purchase any of our products at your local college store or at our preferred online store **www.cengagebrain.com**.

Printed in the United States of America
2 3 4 5 6 7 16 15 14 13 12

To parents, mentors, and students who shaped our behavior so well as to make this book a reality.

Brief Contents

Contents

CHAPTER 4 Classical Conditioning: Basic Phenomena and Various Complexities 134

CHAPTER 5 Classical Conditioning: Underlying Processes and Practical Applications 174

CHAPTER 6 Operant Conditioning: Introduction 222

CHAPTER 7 Schedules and Theories of Reinforcement 269

CHAPTER 8 Extinction and Stimulus Control 308

CHAPTER 9 Escape, Avoidance, and Punishment 350

CHAPTER 10 Choice, Matching, and Self-Control 391

CHAPTER 11 Observational Learning and Rule-Governed Behavior 434

CHAPTER 12 Biological Dispositions in Learning 472

CHAPTER 13 Comparative Cognition 508

Preface

"I wouldn't do this to my budgie," a student once muttered following a lecture in which I (the senior author of this text) had discussed the process of reinforcement. She apparently saw the use of reinforcement as manipulative and reprehensible. I can't remember how I responded (probably with something a bit more diplomatic than what follows), but I could have said that she actually does "this" to her budgie all the time and is simply not aware of it. Moreover, because she's not aware of it, she may be reinforcing her budgie's behavior quite erratically, with the result that the two of them are having a much less fulfilling relationship than they could be having. Unfortunately, this student's negative reaction to behavioral principles of conditioning is not uncommon, and most instructors who teach such courses can probably recount similar instances. Thus, one goal of this text is to help convince students that conditioning is not some dangerous form of manipulation, but rather a natural process that we do far better to understand and apply wisely than to ignore and apply carelessly.

Another opinion sometimes voiced is that the principles of conditioning, many of which have been derived from research with animals, are largely irrelevant to important aspects of human behavior. After all, how can studies of lever-pressing rats or key-pecking pigeons say anything meaningful about what truly matters to us? This was the very conclusion that I (the senior author again) came to when, as an undergraduate, I first encountered a demonstration of operant conditioning in my introductory psychology class. We were shown a film in which pigeons were taught to peck a little plastic disk (which I later learned is called a "response key") to earn food. The whole endeavor struck me as so completely artificial—not to mention mind-numbingly boring—that I couldn't understand why any psychologist would waste his or her time on it. Little did I know that some years later I would find myself sitting in a pigeon lab, thrilled that I had been given an opportunity to study something so interesting and important! What I had learned in the interim was that: (1) you have to be careful what you criticize (fate has a way of making us pay for our arrogance) and (2) many of the principles derived from conditioning experiments with animals are among the most useful principles ever discovered by psychologists. Thus, a second goal of this text is to help convince students that the principles derived from behavioral research are far from irrelevant, and that they often have useful and provocative things to say about human behavior.

An even more basic goal of this text is to provide students with a clear introduction to the basic principles of learning and behavior that would be both accessible and engaging, especially for those who may have had only limited prior exposure to these principles (such as in an introductory psychology course). Those students who later proceed to a higher-level course in the subject matter (one that might utilize, for example, Domjan's *The Principles of Learning and Behavior* as a text) will then have a solid foundation on which to build. Students who do not proceed to a higher-level course will nevertheless have gained an appreciation for the behavioral perspective and learned much that may be of relevance to their everyday lives and future careers.

Key Characteristics

The following summarizes some key characteristics of this text:

- **It emphasizes basic principles of learning and behavior rather than theory.** To the extent that theory is discussed, it is either because the theory itself has something meaningful and provocative to say about human behavior (e.g., melioration theory as discussed in Chapter 10) or because a general overview of certain theories (e.g., the Rescorla-Wagner theory, as presented in Chapter 5) can help prepare students for a more in-depth discussion of those theories in a higher-level course.
- **It attempts to strike an appropriate balance between basic research findings, many of which are derived from animal research, and the application of those findings to important and interesting aspects of human behavior.** Although many texts make this claim, we feel that this text represents a truly concerted effort in that direction. Wherever possible, examples from research paradigms with rats or pigeons are juxtaposed with everyday examples with humans. And although some of the applications to humans are highly speculative, they nevertheless represent the type of speculation that behaviorists themselves often engage in and that many students find entertaining and memorable.
- **Following from the above, this text is especially innovative in the many examples given of the application of behavioral principles to understanding certain aspects of romantic relationships.** In particular, scattered throughout the text are *Advice for the Lovelorn* columns in which hypothetical students are given behavioral-type advice concerning their

relationship difficulties. Personal relationships are, of course, a key concern for many students, who are often fascinated by the notion that behavioral principles may be helpful in understanding and resolving problematic relationships. These columns have thus proven to be an effective way to maintain students' interest in the material, enhance their grasp of certain concepts, and provide them with a sense of what it means to think like a behaviorist. (Students are of course given due warning that the advice in these columns is quite speculative and not to be taken too seriously.)

- **This text contains numerous pedagogical features designed to facilitate students' ability to study and understand the material.** These features are described later in the section on learning aids.
- **The text contains many interesting and thought-provoking topics not normally found in textbooks on learning and behavior.** This includes such topics as the meaning of life, what it means to have "willpower", and the controversy over the inadvertent creation of multiple personalities during therapy, all discussed from a behavioral perspective. Many of these topics are presented in special boxed inserts entitled *And Furthermore*, which are intended to expand on material presented in the preceding section.

Changes to the Fourth Edition

It is not easy to do yet another revision of a textbook that seems to be working so well. Students have almost overwhelmingly endorsed it as one of the most interesting and student-friendly textbooks they have encountered. Several professors have likewise contacted us to say how much they and their students enjoyed the text. But some have also told us to be careful when revising the text, and in particular to be vigilant against the dreaded textbook disease of becoming gradually longer with each subsequent edition. Unfortunately, we have been only partially successful in this regard. We have resisted making changes simply for the sake of change; the changes that we have made have been directed toward creating a clearer, more coherent, and more informative text. We have been somewhat less successful in holding down the length, particularly in this latest edition in which we have added a new chapter. But we feel that this too is more than justified.

The new chapter that we have added covers the topic of comparative cognition, which we had only touched upon in previous editions, and which several reviewers and users of previous editions had indicated was a significant omission. This is especially the case given the many interesting findings in this area in recent years, ranging from tool-using crows to problem-solving parrots. Hence, this new chapter covers such topics as numerical ability, categorization, relational decision making, and tool-use and tool-making across a range of species. It also includes some topics that were previously (and somewhat awkwardly) incorporated into other chapters, namely, the use of delayed matching-to-sample procedures for studying memory in pigeons and language learning in animals (which we had previously combined with observational learning and rule-governed behavior, but which many reviewers said was a poor fit). Note as well that there has been a slight reordering of chapters: The previous Chapter 12 (which included observational learning and rule-governed behavior) is now Chapter 11, and the previous Chapter 11 (which discussed biological dispositions in learning) is now Chapter 12, where it can more easily flow into the comparative cognition material in Chapter 13.

As for those who preferred the length and range of topics covered in the last edition, please be aware that you can closely replicate that edition simply by assigning only the memory and language learning sections from Chapter 13. In fact, across the last three chapters in particular, different sections of each chapter can readily be omitted or combined in a variety of ways to match instructors' preferences. (The only drawback is that students will have to be careful to skip irrelevant items in the end-of-chapter material and exercises, as well as in the online quizzes, that pertain to the omitted sections—though the effort of having to do so may itself be a good learning exercise.)

Most other changes in this new edition have been in the realm of tightening up definitions, clarifying concepts, and updating references. Among the more substantive changes are the following: Chapter 2 now includes a short section on assessing reliability, while Chapter 5 includes a discussion of evidence that calls into question the recent claim that the true identity of Watson's Little Albert has now been discovered. In Chapter 8, we have added an And Furthermore discussion of the ability of dogs and giant African pouched rats to detect landmines and discriminate the presence of cancer and tuberculosis in human patients. As well, DRI (differential reinforcement of incompatible behavior) has been omitted from the main text discussion of DRO (differential reinforcement of other behavior) procedures and relegated to brief mention in a footnote. The self-control section of Chapter 10 now includes, in an And Furthermore box, a discussion of the popular *strength model* of self-control, which may be seen as juxtaposed against behavioral approaches to self-control. In Chapter 11 (formerly Chapter 12), we have incorporated a discussion of Acceptance and Commitment Therapy (ACT), a topic that had been included in the second edition but which was removed from the third edition when the observational learning section of that chapter was substantially revised and lengthened. It is, however, covered more briefly than before and is included in an And Furthermore box, making it relatively easy to omit for those who wish to do so. Finally, for those who are detail oriented, be aware that the text now informs students that S^{R+} and S^{R-} are regarded by many as acceptable symbols for positive and negative reinforcers, respectively, and that S^{Dp} can be used as the symbol for a discriminative stimulus for punishment.

Learning Aids

This text contains many pedagogical features designed to facilitate students' reading and comprehension of the material. These include the following:

- **Quick Quizzes.** Scattered throughout each chapter are many fill-in-the-blank quizzes. The purpose of these quizzes is to help students actively work with the material as they read it. Although an early reviewer of the first edition commented that such frequent quizzing might frustrate students by interrupting their reading, actual use of the material in class revealed quite the opposite. Students uniformly commented that the quizzes were extremely beneficial in helping them engage with and process the material. They especially appreciated the *Quick Quizzes* embedded within sections that they perceived as quite technical, simply because the quizzes broke the material up into short chunks that they were better able to assimilate. Students therefore demanded more quizzes, not fewer, and the authors duly complied.

- **Study Questions.** A focused set of about 15 to 20 study questions is included at the end of each chapter. These study questions cover the most basic concepts discussed in that chapter. Because these questions are quite focused and require a relatively short answer—varying from a sentence to a paragraph in length—students are likely to incorporate them into their studying (as opposed to the standard, comprehensive list of learning objectives found in many texts, which many students unfortunately often ignore). Students can be further motivated to answer the study questions if instructors inform them that some of these questions may appear as short-answer items on exams. In fact, the senior author's own strategy is to utilize a random sample of these questions for weekly chapter tests. Students are required to answer five of the study questions, but do not know which five will be presented.

- **Concept Reviews.** Each chapter is followed by a concept review, which lists all key terms and definitions in the chapter. These key terms and definitions are then reiterated in the glossary at the end of the text.

- **Chapter Tests.** Each chapter ends with a chapter test, consisting mostly of fill-in-the-blank items. This test provides comprehensive coverage of the material presented in the chapter. It differs from the *Quick Quizzes* in that more items are of a conceptual, rather than factual, nature, thereby encouraging students to think more deeply about the material. These test items are numbered in random order, so that students can immediately look up the answer to any particular question without having to worry about inadvertently seeing the answer to the next question.

- **Opening Vignettes.** Each chapter begins with a chapter outline, followed by either a quotation or a vignette related to the material presented in that chapter. The vignettes usually consist of a short, fictional scenario illustrating a particular concept. The exact concept involved is not immediately revealed, however, thus encouraging students to actively ponder how the material they are reading may be related to the scenario. (An explanation of the concept each scenario is intended to illustrate can be found in the instructor's manual.)

Web Site Materials and Alternative Course Delivery

Accompanying this text is a well-designed student resource Web site that contains additional information, practice tests (including multiple-choice, short-answer, and fill-in-the-blank), answers to all Quick Quiz items in the text, and interesting Web links designed to enhance students' learning experience. This material will prove especially useful for instructors who are considering offering a learning and behavior course (especially a Web-based course) in a nonlecture, alternative delivery format. In fact, this text, with its many pedagogical features, was explicitly designed to function as a student-friendly, independent learning tool, and the senior author himself has used it as such for an independent study, computer-based, alternative delivery course.

Instructor's Manual

The instructor's manual includes a thoroughly revised, comprehensive test bank containing a large number of multiple-choice items per chapter, many of which are new or revised for this edition. Many of these items are conceptual in nature. They are organized by textbook headings and subheadings. A portion of the test bank items are drawn from the practice test items at the student resource Web site (and are clearly marked as such); thus, by including some of these items on exams and quizzes, instructors will be able to motivate students to access and work through these ancillary materials. The instructor's manual also contains answers to all of the *Quick Quiz* and study question items for each chapter, as well as a set of annotated Web links where students will find information of interest. In response to a clever suggestion from certain students and instructors, the manual also contains a description of how the *Advice for the Lovelorn* column can be adapted as a student assignment (along with additional examples of such columns that can be provided to students to facilitate their own efforts).

Sniffy™ the Virtual Rat Lite, Version 2.0: An Available Option

Sniffy, the Virtual Rat Lite provides every student with hands-on experience in applying, either at home or in school, the principles of operant and classical conditioning. Sniffy is a computer-generated rat that can be taught to press a lever to earn food, a protocol that is then used to demonstrate many aspects of both operant and classical conditioning. Students purchasing Sniffy receive a laboratory manual with instructions, and a hybrid CD-ROM that operates on Mac OS Version 8.6 or later and Windows 95 SE, ME, 2000, or XP.

The Lite version of Sniffy includes 16 exercises that cover the essential phenomena of learning psychology. The stimulant operant phenomena covered include magazine training; shaping; primary and secondary reinforcement; variable-interval, variable-ratio, fixed-interval, and fixed-ratio schedule effects; and the partial-reinforcement effect. The classical conditioning phenomena covered include acquisition, extinction, and spontaneous recovery.

Students enjoy working with Sniffy and report that these exercises greatly enhance their understanding of the basic principles. We do not, of course, propose that Sniffy can fully substitute for the actual experience of working with live animals. Unfortunately, for various reasons, most institutions are no longer able to offer this valuable opportunity to their undergraduates. Sniffy was created precisely to fill this void. Additionally, some schools use Sniffy as a warm-up before allowing students to work with real animals. For more information about Sniffy, the Virtual Rat Lite, Version 2.0, visit academic.cengage.com or obtain a 6-minute videotape by calling Wadsworth at 1-877-999-2350. Sniffy's creators discuss on the tape how they use Sniffy in their classes, and students describe their experiences working with Sniffy.

Acknowledgments

We wish to thank "Dr. Dee," Ally McBeal (who was all the rage on television when this text was first conceived), and all the other people (real and fictional) who originally inspired the Advice to the Lovelorn features. We also thank the following reviewers for their comments and suggestions which contributed greatly to the improvements made in this edition: Matthew Bell, Santa Clara University; Rita Rodriguez, San Francisco State University; Cathleen Hunt, The Pennsylvania State University; Brady Phelps, South Dakota State University; Mimi Phan, Rutgers University; Terry Pettijohn, Ohio State University; and Cedric Williams, University of Virginia. We also wish to thank James Todd from Eastern Michigan University, whom we never properly thanked in the third edition for many helpful suggestions he made for that edition. Unfortunately, due to some miscommunication and tight timelines, we were unable to utilize him as a reviewer for this edition; hopefully we can rectify that omission for the fifth edition. And a special thanks to James Radiker from Mercer University who, with the help of one of his students, keenly spotted a couple of errors in our discussion of the Tolman and Honzik (1930) study in Chapter 1, including an error in our drawing of the maze that was used in that study (our version had two solutions!).

In addition, we thank the great people at Cengage, including Jon-David Hague, Jessica Alderman, Vernon Boes, Mary Noel, Sharmila Krishnamurthy, Roberta Broyer, and Janay Pryor, for all their support in helping to create this edition.

Finally, a special thanks to Dr. Suzanne E. MacDonald, who served as a coauthor on earlier editions of the text and whose influence can still be seen within certain chapters.

Russ Powell
Lynne Honey
Diane Symbaluk

About the Authors

Russell A. Powell

Russ Powell completed his Ph.D. in psychology under the stimulating supervision of the late Frank Epling and his research partner, David Pierce, at the University of Alberta, and now serves as the Chair of the Department of Psychology at Grant MacEwan University, in Edmonton, Alberta. He has a wide range of academic experiences, the influence of which can be seen throughout this text. He has taught a variety of courses over the years, including social psychology, experimental psychology, and theories of personality. More importantly, he has almost 30 years of experience in teaching undergraduate students the basic course in principles of behavior. In keeping with this diverse teaching background, Russ has also conducted research and published articles on such varied topics as operant conditioning, sleep paralysis nightmares, Freud's influence on the false versus recovered memory debate, and the controversy over the nature and causes of dissociative identity disorder. His present research endeavors focus upon behavioral models of self-regulation (or self-control) and on the psychological and behavioral effects of meal patterns and meal frequency.

P. Lynne Honey

Lynne Honey considers herself an "evolutionary behaviorist." She completed a Ph.D. in experimental psychology in Jeff Galef's lab at McMaster University, studying the role of social learning on alcohol consumption in rats. She has published a number of papers on this topic and considers social learning to be one of the most powerful adaptations available to our species and others. At McMaster, Lynne was inspired and influenced not only by her supervisor, a leading theorist in social learning, but also by the work of

Shepard Siegel (on compensatory responses and conditioned drug tolerance) as well as Martin Daly and Margo Wilson (on evolution and human behavior). Lynne joined the Department of Psychology at Grant MacEwan University in 2003, because of its focus on teaching and student engagement. Lynne is currently conducting research on human social behavior in an evolutionary context, including studies of dominance, attraction, and cooperation. In addition to these research interests, Lynne is a committed teacher and mentor to her students and on any given day can be found in her office, the classroom, or the lab, chatting with and working alongside students, trying to find new ways to demonstrate to them the beauty and elegance of the science of psychology.

Diane G. Symbaluk

Diane Symbaluk received her Ph.D. in sociology from the University of Alberta in 1997, with a specialization in criminology and social psychology. Much of her training, however, was in behavior analysis under the mentorship of David Pierce, Judy Cameron, and the late Frank Epling. She is currently a faculty member in the Department of Sociology at Grant MacEwan University in Edmonton, Alberta. Diane's student-centered approach to teaching is evident in her many publications, which include several study guides and resource manuals as well as Web-course tools and interactive Web sites. Her research background includes the investigation of self-control and impulsiveness in sex offenders, tendencies toward activity anorexia in male athletes (discussed in Chapter 12 of this text), and the effect of social modeling and self-efficacy on pain perception and tolerance.

CHAPTER 1

Introduction

CHAPTER OUTLINE

A review of Gerald Zuriff's *Behaviorism: A Conceptual Reconstruction* (1985) … begins with a story about two behaviorists. They make love and then one of them says, "That was fine for you. How was it for me?" The reviewer, P. N. Johnson-Laird, insists that [this story has a ring of truth about it]. Behaviorists are not supposed to have feelings, or at least to admit that they have them. Of the many ways in which behaviorism has been misunderstood for so many years, that is perhaps the commonest.… [In fact,] how people feel is often as important as what they do.

B. F. SKINNER, 1989, p. 3

Of all contemporary psychologists, B. F. Skinner is perhaps the most honored and the most maligned, the most widely recognized and the most misrepresented, the most cited and the most misunderstood.

A. CHARLES CATANIA, 1988, p. 3

Imagine that while flipping through a new textbook you see that it spends a lot of time discussing experiments with rats and pigeons. Pretty boring, huh? But what if the principles of behavior discussed in those experiments could help you improve your study habits, understand your eating disorder, and overcome your fear of spiders? In fact, what if those same principles could help you improve your romantic relationships and be a more effective parent? Hmm, perhaps not so boring after all. Well, this volume might be just such a book. Let's consider a few of these claims in more detail.

Improving study habits. Many of our behaviors, including study behaviors, are strongly influenced by their consequences. Chapter 6 discusses the basic processes by which consequences influence behavior, and Chapter 10 demonstrates how these processes can be directly applied to the development of self-control. As well, specific information about improving study habits through the use of "stimulus control" procedures can be found toward the end of Chapter 8.

Understanding eating disorders. Contrary to popular belief, eating disorders are not necessarily indicative of a psychological problem. For example, through a simple manipulation of a rat's feeding schedule, the rat can be induced to stop eating and to engage in extreme levels of exercise. Chapter 11 discusses how similar processes might account for the development of a clinical disorder in humans known as anorexia nervosa.

Overcoming fears and phobias. Whether you fear spiders, snakes, or exams, this textbook will provide you with insight into how these fears develop. You will learn how the principles of classical conditioning and negative reinforcement underlie many fears and anxieties, and how these same principles suggest effective means for treating problematic symptoms.

Improving relationships with others. In this text, we often use relationship issues to illustrate basic principles of learning and behavior. As well, each chapter contains an *Advice for the Lovelorn* column, in which relationship problems are discussed from a behavioral perspective. Although the advice given is necessarily speculative—and as such should not be taken too seriously—these columns highlight the manner in which behavioral principles have the potential to enrich our understanding of human relationships.

Raising children. Our students sometimes comment that "no one should be allowed to have children until they have taken a course like this." Although this is admittedly an exaggeration, it is nevertheless the case that many of the principles discussed in this text are directly applicable to many common parenting problems.

In general, a proper grounding in the basic principles of learning and behavior will help you understand why you behave the way you do and how your behavior can often be changed for the better. This knowledge can make you a better parent, a better teacher, and a better friend or partner. In a very real sense, the principles described in this text have the potential to enrich both your life and the lives of others—even though many of these principles have been derived from research with rats and pigeons!

Let's begin with a brief outline of what this textbook is about. Simply put, *behavior* is any activity of an organism that can be observed or somehow measured. As we will discuss in Chapter 2, the activity may be internal or external and may or may not be visible to others. *Learning* is a relatively permanent change in behavior that results from some type of experience. For example, reading this text is an example of a behavior, and any lasting change in your behavior as a result of reading this text (e.g., a change in your ability to speak knowledgeably about the subject matter) is an example of learning. Note that the change in behavior does not have to be immediate, and in some circumstances the change might not become evident until long after the experience has occurred.

This text emphasizes two fundamental processes of learning: classical and operant conditioning. Although these will be discussed in more detail later, a brief description of each is useful at this point. At its most basic level, *classical conditioning* (also known as Pavlovian or respondent conditioning) is the process by which certain inborn behaviors come to be produced in new situations. The behaviors involved are often what the average person regards as reflexive or "involuntary," such as sneezing in response to dust or salivating in response to food. A familiar example of classical conditioning, which is often presented in introductory psychology textbooks, is that of a dog learning to salivate in response to a bell that has been paired with food. This process can be diagrammed as follows:

Bell: Food → *Salivation*
Bell → *Salivation*

(See "Notation for Conditioning Diagrams" in the And Furthermore box.)

And Furthermore

Notation for Conditioning Diagrams

In this text, you will encounter many diagrams of conditioning procedures. In these diagrams, a colon separating two events indicates that the two events occur in sequence. For example, the term "Bell: Food" means that the sound of a bell is followed by the presentation of food. An arrow between two events also indicates that the two events occur in sequence, but with an emphasis on the fact that the first event *produces* or *causes* the second. For example, "Food → *Salivation*" means that the presentation of food causes the dog to salivate. Thus, with respect to a standard classical conditioning procedure, the term:

Bell: Food → *Salivation*

means that the bell is presented just before the food, and the food in turn causes salivation. This is followed by:

Bell → *Salivation*

which indicates that the presentation of the bell itself now causes the dog to salivate (because of the bell's previous pairing with food). For clarity, we usually italicize the behavior that is being conditioned (which is often called the "target behavior"). In writing out your notes, however, you may find it easier to indicate the target behavior by underlining it. For example:

Bell: Food → <u>Salivation</u>
Bell → <u>Salivation</u>

As you will learn in this text, classical conditioning underlies many of our emotional responses and contributes to the development of our likes and dislikes. It can even lead to the development of debilitating fears and powerful feelings of sexual attraction.

In contrast to classical conditioning, *operant conditioning* involves the strengthening or weakening of a behavior as a result of its consequences. The behaviors involved are often those that the average person usually regards as goal-directed or "voluntary." A common experimental example is that of a rat that has learned to press a lever (the behavior) to obtain food (the consequence), the effect of which is an increase in the rat's tendency to press the lever. This can be diagrammed as follows:

Lever press → **Food pellet**
The effect: Likelihood of lever pressing increases

Because the lever press produced a food pellet, the rat is subsequently more likely to press the lever again. In other words, the consequence of the behavior (the food pellet) has served to strengthen future occurrences of that behavior. Many of the behaviors that concern us each day are motivated by such consequences: we hit the remote button to turn on a favorite television show, compliment a loved one because it produces a smile, and study diligently to obtain a passing grade. The consequences can be either immediate, as in the first two examples, or delayed, as in the last example—though, as we will later discuss, the effect of delayed consequences on behavior can involve certain complexities. Because of its importance for humans, operant conditioning is the type of learning most strongly emphasized in this text.

Although the text concentrates on classical and operant conditioning, other types of behavioral processes are also discussed. For example, in *observational learning*, the act of observing someone else's behavior facilitates the development of similar behavior in oneself. Certain types of non-learned, inherited behavior patterns, such as *fixed action patterns*, are also discussed, as is the effect of inherited dispositions in either facilitating or inhibiting certain types of learning. Let's begin, however, with a brief overview of the historical background to the study of learning and behavior.

While reading the text, you will frequently encounter fill-in-the-blank quizzes like this one. Students report that these quizzes greatly facilitate the task of reading by dividing the material into manageable chunks and encouraging them to be actively involved with the reading. For many of the items, we have provided helpful hints, usually in the form of the initial letter or two of the word that should be inserted into the blank. But we have not provided an answer key here, partly because most of the answers can be easily found in the text and partly because a certain amount of uncertainty can actually facilitate the process of learning (Schmidt & Bjork, 1992). Nevertheless, if you "just have to know" the answer to a particular item, the answers for all of the Quick Quiz items can be found at the textbook companion Web site at http://www.academic.cengage.com/psychology/powell.[1]

1. The term *behavior* refers to any activity of an organism that can be o̲b̲s̲e̲r̲v̲e̲d̲ or somehow m̲e̲a̲s̲u̲r̲e̲d̲, whereas the term *learning* refers to a relatively p̲e̲r̲m̲a̲n̲e̲n̲t̲ change in what an organism does as a result of some type of ex̲p̲e̲r̲i̲e̲n̲c̲e̲.

2. In C̲l̲a̲s̲s̲i̲c̲a̲l̲ conditioning, behaviors that the average person typically regards as (voluntary/involuntary) i̲n̲v̲o̲l̲u̲n̲t̲a̲r̲y̲ come to be elicited in new situations.

3. In o̲p̲e̲r̲a̲n̲t̲ conditioning, a behavior produces some type of consequence that strengthens or weakens its occurrence. Such behaviors are typically those that are generally regarded as "g̲o̲a̲l̲-directed" and which the average person often perceives as being "v̲o̲l̲u̲n̲t̲a̲r̲y̲" in nature.

4. Feeling anxious as you enter a dentist's office is an example of a behavior that has most likely been learned through o̲p̲e̲r̲a̲n̲t̲ conditioning.

5. Speaking with a loud voice in a noisy environment so that others will be able to hear you is an example of a behavior that has most likely been learned through C̲l̲a̲s̲s̲i̲c̲a̲l̲ conditioning.

6. According to the notational system to be used in this text, the term "A: B" means that event A (produces/is followed by) i̲s̲ ̲f̲o̲l̲l̲o̲w̲e̲d̲ ̲b̲y̲ event B, and the term "X → Y" means that event X (produces/is followed by) p̲r̲o̲d̲u̲c̲e̲s̲ event Y.

[1]If you are concerned that this type of exercise will simply produce a superficial form of "rote learning," research has shown that repeated attempts to recall information just studied (i.e., self-quizzing) can have powerful effects on learning (Roediger & Karpicke, 2006), including on one's ability to apply that information in new ways (Karpicke & Bunt, 2011).

Historical Background

Just as it is impossible to outline all of the experiences that have made you who you are, it is impossible to outline all of the historical events that have contributed to the modern-day study of learning and behavior. Some particularly important contributions, however, are discussed in this section.

Aristotle: Empiricism and the Laws of Association

Aristotle was a Greek philosopher who lived between 384 and 322 B.C. Aristotle's teacher, Plato, believed that everything we know is inborn (which he conceived of as "residing in our soul"); thus, learning is simply a process of inner reflection to uncover the knowledge that already exists within. Aristotle, however, disagreed with Plato and argued that knowledge is not inborn but instead is acquired through experience.

Aristotle's disagreement with Plato is an early example of the classic debate between nativism and empiricism, or nature and nurture. The *nativist (nature)* perspective assumes that a person's abilities and tendencies are largely inborn, whereas the *empiricist (nurture)* perspective assumes that a person's abilities and tendencies are mostly learned. Plato is thus an early example of a nativist and Aristotle is an early example of an empiricist.[2]

Aristotle also suggested that ideas come to be connected or associated with each other via four laws of association (well, actually three, but he also hinted at a fourth that later philosophers expanded upon).

1. **The Law of Similarity.** According to this law, events that are similar to each other are readily associated with each other. For example, cars and trucks are readily associated because they are similar in appearance (wheels, doors, headlights, etc.) and function (both are used to carry passengers and materials along roadways). These similarities enable us to learn to view cars and trucks as instances of a larger category of objects known as automobiles.

2. **The Law of Contrast.** Just as events that are similar to each other are readily associated, so too events that are opposite from each other are readily associated. For example, on a word association test the word *black* often brings to mind the word *white*, and the word *tall* often brings to mind the word *short*. Likewise, the sight of your unwashed car reminds you of how nice it would look if you washed it, and an evening of work reminds you of how enjoyable it would be to spend the evening not working.

---

[2]In philosophy, the term *empiricism* usually refers to the mentalistic notion that *knowledge* can be gained only through sensory experience rather than through heredity or by pure reasoning. In psychology, the term has a slightly altered meaning, which is that a certain *behavior* or *ability* is the result of experience rather than heredity. Thus, the notion that great musicians have inherited a "gift" for music is a nativist viewpoint, whereas the notion that almost anyone can become a great musician given the right kind of experiences (as will be discussed later in this chapter) is an empiricist viewpoint. But the word *empiricism* can also be used in a methodological sense to refer to the gathering of information through systematic observation and experimentation, as in, "behavioral psychology is an empirical approach to the study of behavior."

3. **The Law of Contiguity.** According to this law, events that occur in close proximity to each other in time or space are readily associated (*contiguity* means "closeness"). For example, a child quickly learns to associate thunder and lightning because the sound of thunder soon follows the flash of lightning. Thunder and lightning are also perceived as coming from the same direction, meaning that there is a certain degree of spatial proximity between them. Imagine how difficult it would be to associate thunder and lightning if the thunder occurred several minutes after the lightning flash and was perceived to have come from a different direction.

combining things that happen close in time and space

4. **The Law of Frequency.** In addition to the three preceding laws, Aristotle mentioned a supplement to the law of contiguity, which is that the more frequently two items occur together, the more strongly they are associated. You will more strongly associate a friend with a certain perfume the more frequently you smell that perfume upon meeting her. Likewise, you will more strongly associate a term (such as the law of frequency) with its definition the more frequently you practice saying that definition whenever you see the term (as when using flash cards to help memorize basic terminology).

combing things that happen together frequently

Aristotle's laws of association are not merely of historical interest. As you will read later, *the laws of contiguity and frequency are still considered important aspects of learning.* After all, how well could a dog learn to salivate to the sound of a bell if the bell preceded the presentation of food by several minutes, or if there was only one pairing of bell and food?

QUICK QUIZ B

1. The nativist position, as exemplified by the Greek philosopher _Plato_ , emphasizes the role of (learning/heredity) _heredity_ .

2. The empiricist position, as exemplified by the Greek philosopher _Aristotle_, emphasizes the role of (learning/heredity) _learning_ .

3. Nativist is to (nature/nurture) _nature_ as empiricist is to (nature/nurture) _nurture_.

4. The law of _Contrast_ states that we associate events that are opposite to each other, whereas the law of _Contiguity_ states that we associate events that occur in close proximity to each other.

5. According to the law of _Similarity_, we easily associate events that resemble each other. According to the law of _Frequency_, the more often two events occur together, the stronger the association.

6. Animals that have fur, four legs, a tail, and can bark are quickly perceived as belonging to the same species. This is an example of the law of _Similarity_.

7. The fact that the words *full* and *empty* are easily associated with each other is an example of the law of _Contrast_ .

8. The *more often* one practices a particular move in wrestling, the more likely one is to perform that move in a real match. This is an example of the law of _Contiguity_

9. After once encountering a snake in her garage, Lisa is now quite nervous each time she is in the garage. This is an example of Aristotle's law of _Contiguity_ This is also an example of (classical/operant) _Classical_ conditioning.

Descartes: Mind–Body Dualism and the Reflex

René Descartes
(1596–1650)

Bettmann/CORBIS

René Descartes (1596–1650) is the French philosopher who wrote the famous line "I think, therefore I am." Fortunately for psychology, this was not his only contribution. In Descartes' time, many people assumed that human behavior was governed entirely by free will or "reason." Descartes disputed this notion and proposed a dualistic model of human nature. On the one hand, he claimed, we have a body that functions like a machine and produces involuntary, reflexive behaviors in response to external stimulation (such as sneezing in response to dust). On the other hand, we have a mind that has free will and produces behaviors that we regard as voluntary (such as choosing what to eat for dinner). Thus, Descartes' notion of *mind–body dualism* proposes that some human behaviors are reflexes that are automatically elicited by external stimulation, while other behaviors are freely chosen and controlled by the mind. Descartes also believed that only humans possess such a self-directing mind, while the behavior of nonhuman animals is entirely reflexive.

Descartes' dualistic view of human nature was a major step in the scientific study of learning and behavior because it suggested that at least some behaviors—namely, reflexive behaviors—are mechanistic and could therefore be scientifically investigated. It also suggested that the study of animal behavior might yield useful information about the reflexive aspects of human behavior.

The British Empiricists

Although Descartes believed that the human mind has free will, he also assumed, like Plato, that some of the ideas contained within it (e.g., the concepts of time and space) are inborn. This notion was disputed by a group of British philosophers, known as the *British empiricists*, who maintained that almost all knowledge is a function of experience. For example, one of the major proponents of British Empiricism, John Locke (1632–1704), proposed that a newborn's mind is a *blank slate* (in Latin, *tabula rasa*) upon which environmental experiences are written—an empiricist concept that had earlier been promoted by Aristotle. The British empiricists also believed that the conscious mind is composed of a finite set of basic elements (specific colors, sounds, smells, etc.) that are combined through the principles of association into complex sensations and thought patterns—a sort of psychological version of the notion that all physical matter consists of various combinations of the basic elements.

[handwritten margin notes:]
Dualism
Some behaviors are governed by external stimuli
Others are by free will (self-direction)

Blank slate
– nature debate

By "principles of association" we have our senses.

1. Descartes' dualistic model proposed that human behavior has two aspects: an involuntary aspect that functions like a machine and a voluntary aspect governed by free will . By contrast, the behavior of animals was believed to be entirely _____.

2. The British empiricist , such as John locke , maintained that knowledge was largely a function of experience and that the mind of a newborn infant is a (in Latin) tabula r asa (which means blank slate).

3. They also believed that the mind is composed of a finite set of basic elements that are then combined through the principles of association to form our conscious experiences.

Structuralism: The Experimental Study of Human Consciousness

The British empiricists did not conduct any experiments to test their notion that the mind consists of various combinations of basic elements; their conclusions were instead based upon logical reasoning and the subjective examination of their own conscious experience. Realizing the deficiencies in this approach, the German philosopher Wilhelm Wundt (1832–1920) proposed using the scientific method to investigate the issue. This approach was then strongly promoted by an American student of Wundt's, Edward Titchener (1867–1927), and became known as structuralism. *Structuralism* assumes that it is possible to determine the structure of the mind by identifying the basic elements that compose it.

Edward B. Titchener
(1867–1927)

Psychology Archives/The University of Akron

Structuralists made great use of the method of *introspection*, in which the subject in an experiment attempts to accurately describe his or her conscious thoughts, emotions, and sensory experiences. To get a feel for how difficult this is, try to describe your conscious experience as you listen to the ticking of a clock (and just saying, "I'm bored" doesn't cut it). One thing you might report is that the ticks seem to have a certain rhythm, with a series of two or three clicks being clustered together. You might also report a slight feeling of tension (is it pleasant or unpleasant?) that builds or decreases during each series of ticks. As you can see, an accurate report of what we introspectively observe can be quite difficult.

Although this approach to psychology died out by the early 1900s (for reasons described shortly), its emphasis on systematic observation helped establish psychology as a scientific discipline. More importantly, its extreme emphasis on conscious experience as the proper subject matter for psychology resulted in a great deal of frustration and dissatisfaction—which laid the groundwork for the later establishment of a more objective approach to psychology, known as behaviorism.

William James
(1842–1910)

Adaptation to help us live in our surroundings.

Functionalism: The Study of the Adaptive Mind

William James (1842–1910), often regarded as the founder of American psychology, helped establish the approach to psychology known as functionalism. *Functionalism* assumes that the mind evolved to help us adapt to the world around us and that the focus of psychology should be the study of those adaptive processes. This proposition was partially derived from Darwin's theory of evolution, which proposes that adaptive characteristics that enable a species to survive and reproduce tend to increase in frequency across generations while nonadaptive characteristics tend to die out. Thus, according to a functionalist perspective, characteristics that are highly typical of a species, such as the characteristic of consciousness in humans, must have some type of adaptive value.

Based on such reasoning, functionalists believed that psychologists should not study the structure of the mind, but instead study the adaptive significance of the mind. Learning, as an adaptive process, was therefore a topic of great interest to the functionalists. Moreover, although functionalists still made use of introspection and still emphasized the analysis of conscious experience (in this manner, being similar to the structuralists), they were not opposed to the study of animal behavior. Again following from Darwin, they believed that humans evolved in the same manner as other animals, and that much of what we learn from studying other animals might therefore be of direct relevance to humans. Not surprisingly, two of the most important figures in the early history of behaviorism, E. B. Thorndike (discussed in Chapter 6) and John B. Watson (discussed later in this chapter), were students of functionalist psychologists.

QUICK QUIZ D

1. The (functionalist/structuralist) _____ approach proposed that the goal of psychology should be to identify the basic elements of the mind. The primary research method used for accomplishing this was the method of i_____.

2. In contrast to the above, those who adopted the (functionalist/structuralist) _____ approach to psychology emphasized the adaptive processes of the mind and were thus very interested in the study of learning.

3. The functionalist approach was strongly influenced by Darwin's theory of _____. As such, these psychologists viewed animal research as (relevant/irrelevant) _____ to the study of human behavior in that humans were assumed to have evolved in a (similar/dissimilar) _____ way to other animals.

4. The functionalists were similar to the structuralists in that they still emphasized the study of c_____ experience and in doing so often used the method of i_____.

5. William James was a (functionalist/structuralist) _____, and Edward Titchener was a _____.

The Theory of Evolution: Humans as Animals

As we have seen, the theory of evolution had a profound influence on the development of behaviorism, which continues today. We should therefore take some time to discuss this theory more fully. Charles Darwin published the theory of evolution in 1859 in his book, *On the Origin of Species by Means of Natural Selection* (often simply called *The Origin of Species*). It describes how species, including humans, change across generations in response to environmental pressures. The basis of this theory is the principle of **natural selection**, which is the concept that individuals or species that are capable of adapting to environmental pressures are more likely to reproduce and pass along their adaptive characteristics than those that cannot adapt.

Charles Darwin
(1809–1882)

Philip Gendreau/Bettmann/CORBIS

There are three main components to the principle of natural selection. The first is that *traits vary, both within a species* (e.g., some dogs are larger than other dogs) *and between species* (e.g., humans have a slower metabolism than hummingbirds). The second is that *many traits are heritable,* meaning that they have a genetic basis and can be inherited by offspring. The third component of natural selection is that *organisms must compete for limited resources* (bearing in mind, however, that being an effective competitor might sometimes involve cooperation as much as conflict).

Now let us put all three of these ideas together. Some individuals will acquire more resources than others based on certain, inherited traits that give them an advantage. These individuals are therefore better able to survive—which, of course, is commonly referred to as "survival of the fittest." But here is where a lot of people misunderstand evolutionary theory. The real driving force behind evolution is not survival of the fittest, but the *reproductive advantage that accrues to those individuals possessing traits that are best suited to the environment.* In other words, successful individuals are more likely to have offspring who, when they inherit the successful traits from their parents, are also more likely to survive and have offspring. As this process continues through each succeeding generation, the proportion of individuals possessing the successful traits increases while the proportion of individuals possessing the unsuccessful traits decreases. Eventually, the changed population might differ so much from the source population that it becomes a new species.

A trait that evolves as a result of natural selection is referred to as an **evolutionary adaptation**. We usually think of such adaptations as physical characteristics (e.g., the trunk of an elephant), but adaptations can also be behaviors. For example, as you will learn in Chapter 3, if you inadvertently place your hand over a flame, a *flexion reflex* will cause you automatically to pull your hand away from the damaging fire even before you consciously feel pain. You can imagine how an inborn reflex like this would help an individual live long enough to reproduce, compared to an individual who lacked such reflexes.

A particularly important evolutionary adaptation, which is the focus of this text, is the ability to learn. From an evolutionary perspective, the ability to learn evolved because it conferred significant survival advantages on those who had this ability. Thus, the distinction between nature and nurture can be seen as highly simplistic, since the ability to learn (nurture) is itself inherited (nature).

In this text, you will learn about features of learning that are common across a wide variety of species. These common features suggest that the ancestors of these species faced similar environmental pressures that resulted in the evolution of similar features. Nevertheless, you will also learn (especially in Chapters 11 and 13) about certain differences between species in learning ability. These cross-species variations suggest that the ancestors of these species faced different environmental pressures, which in turn resulted in the evolution of differences in learning ability.

As noted, Darwin's theory of evolution had a profound effect on the early development of behaviorism, especially through its influence on the functionalist school of psychology out of which behaviorism developed. It continues to have an effect through the increased attention given these days to the role of genetic factors in learning, and through the recent establishment of "evolutionary psychology" as a major area of specialization within psychology.

1. An ev_____ ad_____ is a trait that has evolved through n_____ s_____.

2. The three main components to the theory of natural selection are:

   a.

   b.

   c.

3. To say that a trait is h_____ means that it has a genetic basis and can be inherited by offspring.

4. The real driving force behind evolution is not survival of the fittest, but rather the r_____ advantage held by those individuals who possess adaptive traits.

5. It is simplistic to assume that one can draw a clear distinction between n_____ and n_____ because the way we learn is itself an i_____ trait.

John B. Watson
(1878–1958)

Behaviorism: The Study of Observable Behavior

In 1913, a flamboyant young psychologist by the name of John B. Watson published a paper titled "Psychology as the Behaviorist Views It." In it, he lamented the lack of progress achieved by experimental psychologists up to that time, particularly the lack of findings that had any practical significance. A major difficulty, Watson believed, was the then-current emphasis on the study of conscious experience, especially as promoted by the structuralists.

Focus on the study of environmental influence on observable behavior.

Historical Background | **13**

In particular, the method of introspection was proving to be highly unreliable. Researchers frequently failed to replicate each other's findings, which often led to bitter squabbles. Watson mockingly described the types of arguments that often ensued:

> If you fail to reproduce my findings, it is not due to some fault in your apparatus or in the control of your stimulus, but it is due to the fact that your introspection is untrained. … If you can't observe 3–9 states of clearness in attention, your introspection is poor. If, on the other hand, a feeling seems reasonably clear to you, your introspection is again faulty. You are seeing too much. Feelings are never clear. (Watson, 1913, p. 163)

The difficulty, of course, is that we are unable to directly observe another person's thoughts and feelings. We therefore have to make an *inference* that the person's verbal reports about those thoughts and feelings are accurate.[3] It is also the case that many of the questions being tackled by the structuralists were essentially unanswerable, such as whether sound has the quality of "extension in space" and whether there is a difference in "texture" between an imagined perception of an object and the actual perception of the object (Watson, 1913, p. 164). In a very real sense, experimental psychology seemed to be drowning in a sea of vaguely perceived images and difficult-to-describe mental events. Moreover, the notion that the proper subject matter of psychology was the study of consciousness was so strongly entrenched that it affected even those who studied animal behavior. As Watson exclaimed,

> On this view, after having determined our animal's ability to learn, the simplicity or complexity of its methods of learning, the effect of past habit upon present response … we should still feel that the task is unfinished and that the results are worthless, until we can interpret them by analogy in the light of consciousness. [In other words,] we feel forced to say something about the possible mental processes of the animal. (Watson, 1913, p. 160)

Watson reasoned that the only solution to this dilemma was to make psychology a purely "objective science" based solely on the study of directly observable behavior and the environmental events that surround it. All reference to internal processes, such as thoughts and feelings that could not be objectively measured by an outside observer, were to be stricken from

---

[3] An *inference* is a supposition or guess based on logical deduction rather than on observation. For example, if you describe to me a dream that you had last night, your report is based on your direct observation of a subjective experience. But if I accept that description (because there seems to be no reason for you to lie about it), I am making an inference that your report is accurate. Now suppose I interpret the dream as indicating that you have some unresolved, unconscious conflict, and you accept that interpretation as true. We are now both making an inference that this unconscious conflict exists, because neither you nor I have directly observed it. Needless to say, inferences about unconscious processes are even more problematic than inferences about conscious processes, because not even the person in whom the unconscious process exists is able to directly observe it.

analysis. By objectifying psychology in this manner, Watson hoped that psychology could then join the ranks of the *natural sciences*—biology, chemistry, and physics—which had traditionally emphasized the study of observable phenomena. In Watson's now-classic words,

> Psychology as the behaviorist views it is a purely objective experimental branch of natural science. Its theoretical goal is the prediction and control of behavior. Introspection forms no essential part of its methods, nor is the scientific value of its data dependent upon the readiness with which they lend themselves to interpretation in terms of consciousness. (Watson, 1913, p. 154)

Thus, as originally defined by Watson, ***behaviorism*** is a natural science approach to psychology that focuses on the study of environmental influences on observable behavior.

Watson also believed strongly in the value of animal research. In keeping with his functionalist background—in turn following from Darwin's theory of evolution—he believed that the principles governing the behavior of nonhuman species might also be relevant to the behavior of humans. Thus, traditional behavioral research is often conducted using nonhuman animals, primarily rats and pigeons. As many of the examples in this text illustrate, the results obtained from such research are often highly applicable to human behavior.

Behavioral psychology also adheres to the ***law of parsimony***, which proposes that simpler explanations for a phenomenon are generally preferable to more complex explanations. One version of this law—which strongly influenced Watson—is known as *Morgan's Canon* (*canon* means "principle"). Conway Lloyd Morgan was a nineteenth century British physiologist/psychologist who became concerned about the manner in which many scientists of his era were attributing human characteristics to nonhuman animals. Morgan (1894) argued that, whenever possible, one should interpret an animal's behavior in terms of lower, more primitive processes (e.g., reflex or habit) rather than higher, more mentalistic processes (e.g., decision or imagination). Watson essentially took this one step further by arguing that psychologists should avoid interpreting even human behavior in terms of mentalistic processes.

It is worth noting that Watson was not the first psychologist to recommend a more objective, natural science approach to psychology. He reflected a growing sentiment among many researchers at that time that such a move was necessary. Watson's arguments, however, were the most clearly stated and therefore had a strong effect. Thus, while his 1913 paper (which later became known as the "Behaviorist Manifesto") did not have an immediate impact, its influence slowly grew until, by the 1920s, the behaviorist revolution was well under way. (For a brief discussion of Watson's personal life, see "John B. Watson: Behaviorism's Controversial Founder" in the And Furthermore box.)

And Furthermore

John B. Watson: Behaviorism's Controversial Founder

John B. Watson was a charismatic and aggressive individual and as such was perhaps ideally suited for lifting psychology out of the mentalistic quagmire in which it had become immersed. Unfortunately, those same traits led to a life of conflict. The most infamous story concerns the manner in which Watson was forced to resign from his university position. One commonly-told version has it that he and a female student were caught conducting intimate experiments on human sexual responding, and he was forced to resign over the resultant scandal. There is, however, little evidence for this (see Benjamin, Whitaker, Ramsey, & Zeve, 2007, for a description of how this rumor became established), and the real events appear to be as follows.

In 1920, at the height of his academic career, Watson began an affair with Rosalie Rayner, a graduate student whose family was both well connected and powerful. Catching wind of the affair, Watson's wife entered Rosalie's room during a social visit to the Rayners and stole the letters Watson had written to his young lover. Watson's wife then filed for divorce and used the letters to help win a lucrative settlement. Meanwhile, the university told Watson to end his affair with Rosalie. Watson refused and, when given an ultimatum, immediately tendered his resignation. Soon after, news of Watson's divorce and of the affair found its way into the national media, with one of Watson's love letters even appearing in several newspapers. In the space of a few months, his academic career was ruined.

Cast adrift, Watson married Rayner and obtained a job with a New York advertising firm. In his new position, he attempted to promote a more scientific approach to the discipline of advertising—though the extent to which he had any significant influence on the industry is questionable (Coon, 1994). He also continued to publish books and magazine articles promoting his behavioristic views. In fact, Watson was very much the pop psychologist of his era, much like the present-day Dr. Phil. Unfortunately, as with pop psychology today, some of his advice was based more on personal opinion than on well-established principles. For example, Watson believed that children should be trained to act like adults and even recommended giving them a handshake, rather than a hug or a kiss, when sending them to bed! In fact, the only time he ever showed affection to his own children was when his wife died in 1935. Teary eyed, Watson lightly put his arms around his children as he told them that their mother had passed away, then never again mentioned her name. Not surprisingly, his children retained bitter memories of their upbringing, and one son later committed suicide.

It has been suggested that Watson had an underlying fear of emotions, as though fearful of losing control. In his love relationships (and he had numerous affairs throughout his life) he was extremely impulsive and amorous; yet in a group setting he would reportedly flee the room when the discussion turned to emotional issues. Thus, although Watson's proposal to banish thoughts and feelings from psychology helped establish it as a more objective science, it may also have reflected some of his personal difficulties.

In his later years, Watson became something of a recluse, living in the country and raising animals. He had always been fond of animals—sometimes claiming that he preferred their company to that of humans—which may account for his early interest in animal research. He died in 1958 at the age of 80. (See Buckley, 1989, for a comprehensive biography of Watson.)

1. Watson noted that a major problem with the method of _____ was that the results obtained were often unreliable.

2. A basic problem with relying on someone's report about his or her thoughts and feelings is that we are making a(n) _____ that the report is accurate. This term is defined in the footnote as a supposition or guess based on logical d_____ rather than direct o_____.

3. The notion that the proper subject matter of psychology should be the study of consciousness was so strong that even those who studied _____ behavior felt compelled to make inferences about possible mental processes in their subjects.

4. Watson argued that psychology needed to become a n_____ science (like biology, chemistry, and physics) based solely on the study of directly ob_____ events.

5. According to the law of p_____, the (simple/complex) _____ explanation is generally the preferable explanation.

6. One version of the above law, known as M_____ C_____, holds that it is preferable to interpret animal behavior in terms of lower, more primitive processes, such as reflex or habit, than higher, more mentalistic processes, such as reasoning.

Different ways of how to study the influence of environment on behavior.

Five Schools of Behaviorism

Many people believe that behaviorism is some monolithic entity, with Watson's views being the same views held by other behaviorists. In fact, there are several schools of behaviorism, each based on a somewhat different set of assumptions about how best to study environmental influences on behavior. In this section, we describe five of these schools, beginning with Watson's original brand of behaviorism, which is sometimes referred to as methodological behaviorism (e.g., O'Donohue & Ferguson, 2001).[4]

Watson's Methodological Behaviorism

Among the most extreme versions of behaviorism is the one originally proposed by Watson (1913). As previously noted, Watson believed that psychologists should study only publicly observable behavior. All reference to internal events—that is, events that can only be subjectively perceived (such as our inner thoughts and feelings) or that are assumed to exist on an

---

[4]Be aware that the names of the different schools presented here are not at all standardized. For example, a quick search of scholarly postings on the Internet will soon reveal alternative names for Watson's approach, such as *classical behaviorism* and even *radical behaviorism* (which is usually reserved for Skinner's version of behaviorism). And the term *methodological behaviorism* is sometimes applied to any approach that rejects the value of data gathered through introspection, including many cognitive approaches to psychology. This inconsistency in terminology has arisen not only from the adoption of different labels by different writers, but also from subtle distinctions between the different schools of behaviorism that are still being debated among behaviorists and philosophers.

FIGURE 1.1   In the methodological behaviorism, internal events, such as consciously perceived thoughts and feelings and unconscious drives and motives, are excluded from the analysis of behavior. Instead, one studies the direct relationship between changes in the environment and changes in observable behavior.

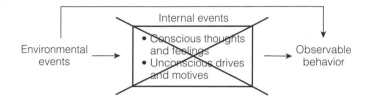

unconscious level (e.g., a mother's unconscious hatred of her unwanted child)—were to be stricken from scientific analysis (see Figure 1.1).

Thus, *methodological behaviorism* asserts that, for methodological rea- *Only behaviors* sons, psychologists should study only those behaviors that can be directly *that can be* observed. Subjectively perceived activities, such as thinking, are methodo- *directly seen.* logically too difficult to assess to be of much use in a scientific analysis of behavior. Such activities can be included for analysis only if they can, in some way, be directly measured. Watson, for example, hypothesized that thinking involves minute movements of the vocal cords in the larynx—and he enjoyed goading his critics by referring to his own thoughts as "laryngeal activity" (Buckley, 1989). If this were true, and if such movements could be precisely measured, then the act of thinking could be subjected to scientific analysis. (As it turns out, laryngeal activity is not a reliable measure of thinking.)

It is important to emphasize that Watson's behavioristic proposal to ignore thoughts and feelings in scientific analysis was not simply an attempt to dehumanize people or to pretend that thoughts and feelings do not exist (whatever his own personal biases may have been); rather, it was in part a logical response to a crisis. If the discipline of psychology was to survive, it *Believed all* would need to break free from the extreme mentalism of the time and adopt *behavior is* a much different perspective. Watson's behavioristic call to arms, though *reflexive* extreme, accomplished just that.

From a theoretical perspective, Watson's specific view of learning was rather mechanistic. Drawing from Pavlov's work on classical conditioning, he came to believe that all behavior, both animal and human, is essentially reflexive. He also believed that learning involves the development of a simple connection between an environmental event (the "stimulus") and a specific behavior (the "response"). Watson's theory of learning is therefore regarded as a type of *S-R theory*, in which learning is believed to involve the establishment of a connection between a specific stimulus (S) and a specific response (R). Complex behavior is presumed to involve extremely long chains of these S-R connections.

specific stimulus directly effects response

Over time, Watson also became something of an extremist regarding the nature–nurture issue. In his original 1913 article, he had emphasized the influence of *both* heredity and environment on behavior. In fact, he was one of the first individuals to systematically study inborn behavior patterns in animals (he spent several strenuous summers engaged in field research with a type of seabird). Later, however, following extensive observations of human infants, he came to the conclusion that humans inherit only a few fundamental reflexes along with three basic emotions (love, rage, and fear). Everything else, he believed, is learned. This led Watson, in 1930, to make one of his most famous claims:

> Give me a dozen healthy infants, well-formed, and my own specified world to bring them up in and I'll guarantee to take any one at random and train him to become any type of specialist I might select—doctor, lawyer, artist, merchant-chief, and, yes, even beggar-man and thief, regardless of his talents, penchants, tendencies, abilities, vocations, and race of his ancestors. (p. 104)

Unfortunately, many textbooks quote only this passage and omit the very next sentence, which reads, "I am going beyond my facts, but so have the advocates of the contrary and they have been doing it for many thousands of years" (p. 104). And this was precisely Watson's point: The supposition that a person's abilities are largely inherited has been strongly promoted throughout history (and has often been used to justify acts of discrimination and racism). Watson was one of the first to issue a strong challenge to this assumption, arguing instead that there is at least as much evidence suggesting that human abilities are mostly learned. For this reason, Watson's behavioral model became quite popular among the reformists of his day who were attempting to combat racism. (For some recent evidence on the importance of learning as opposed to heredity, see "Deliberate Practice and Expert Performance" in the And Furthermore box.)

As we previously noted, many people mistakenly equate behaviorism with Watson's rather extreme version. In fact, few behaviorists were this extreme; instead, they developed approaches that were considerably more moderate. One of the most influential of these was Hull's neobehaviorism, which we discuss next.[5]

---

[5]While reading about these different schools of behaviorism, bear in mind that behavioristic assumptions are just that—assumptions. They do not necessarily reflect some type of absolute truth, nor do they necessarily reflect the private beliefs of the scientist. Thus, one can adopt these assumptions as a useful way of looking at behavior without abandoning other assumptions, such as certain religious beliefs about the existence of free will. After all, even if free will does exist, the environment still has a major impact on our behavior, and it would be foolish for us not to learn the principles by which the environment influences behavior. In this regard, the first author recalls a seminary student he once taught who could always be seen carrying around his two favorite textbooks—his behavior analysis text and the Bible.

1. Watson's brand of behaviorism is often referred to as _____ behaviorism.

2. According to this type of behaviorism, psychologists should study only those behaviors that can be _____ _____.

3. Watson believed that all reference to _____ events should be eliminated from the study of behavior.

4. Watson proposed a(n) _____-_____ theory of learning which hypothesizes that learning involves the formation of a direct connection between a st_____ and a r_____.

5. In his 1913 article on behaviorism, Watson emphasized the role of both h_____ and e_____ in the development of human behavior. In his later theorizing, however, he downplayed the role of _____.

6. In his later theorizing, Watson proposed that humans inherit (many/a few) _____ basic reflexes, along with three basic emotions: _____, _____, and _____.

And Furthermore

Deliberate Practice and Expert Performance

Watson's emphasis on the importance of nurture over nature in determining human behavior is often viewed with a great deal of skepticism. This is especially the case when it comes to behaviors that are indicative of exceptional ability. Most people, including many psychologists (e.g., Gardner, 1993), assume that, unless a person is born with a certain amount of talent, there are limits in how far he or she will be able to progress in a particular endeavor. Indeed, the notion that a Babe Ruth, Albert Einstein, or Wolfgang Amadeus Mozart is to a large extent born, and not made, is part of the mystique surrounding these individuals.

But consider the following:

- Expert performers in almost all fields of endeavor, ranging from music to athletics to chess, require a minimum of 10 years of intensive training before achieving a high level of performance. Even Mozart, who started composing at age 4, did not compose world-class music until his late teens. Mozart's father was also a professional musician who published the first book on violin instruction and provided his children with intensive musical training from an early age. (Mozart's reputation has also benefitted from certain dubious claims: for example, the notion that Mozart could compose entire works in memory and then write them down with little or no editing is based on a single passage in a supposed letter of his that is now believed to be a forgery [Colvin, 2008]).
- As an experiment, a Hungarian educator, Polgar, set out to systematically train his daughters to become expert chess players. All three daughters have achieved high rankings in international chess, and one daughter, Judit, at one point held the record for becoming the youngest grand master ever, at 15 years of age.

(continued)

- The superlative abilities shown by experts are almost always specific to their field of endeavor. For example, chess experts have the ability to memorize the exact positions of all the chess pieces in a game after only a few seconds' glance at the chessboard. But they perform no better than non–chess players at memorizing chess pieces randomly distributed around the board in a non–game pattern. As well, their performance on standard memory tests is typically no better than that of the average person.
- Almost all of the remarkable feats displayed by *savants*—individuals of low intellectual ability who nevertheless possess some remarkable skill—have been taught to normal individuals. For example, the ability of some savants to name the day of the week for any arbitrary date (e.g., "What day of the week was June 30, 1854?") has been duplicated by ordinary college students after only a few weeks of training.
- Excellent musicians often have perfect pitch, which many people assume is something a person is born with. Researchers, however, have been able to systematically train this ability in some adults. More importantly, people who display perfect pitch have almost always had considerable exposure to music at an early age. This suggests that, as with language development, there may be a critical period in childhood during which perfect pitch can be more readily acquired.

Based on findings such as these, Ericsson, Krampe, and Tesch-Römer (1993; see also Ericsson & Charness, 1994) argued that the most critical factor in determining expert performance is not innate ability but deliberate practice. Deliberate practice is practice that is not inherently enjoyable and does not involve mere repetition; it instead involves intense concentration and considerable effort with a view toward improving one's performance. More than any other variable, the accumulated amount of deliberate practice in an activity is strongly predictive of an individual's level of performance.

For example, Ericsson et al. (1993) compared student violinists who were the "best" with those who were merely "good" and with those who were in training to become music teachers. The best students had accumulated about 7400 hours of deliberate practice by the age of 18, compared to 5300 hours for the good students and 3400 hours for the teachers-in-training. Such differences account for why elite performers so often report having begun their training at an early age. An early start enables one to accumulate the huge number of practice hours needed to outperform others. Those who begin at a later age are simply unable to catch up.

Because deliberate practice is so effortful, the amount that can be tolerated each day is necessarily limited. For this reason, elite performers often practice about 4 hours per day. Ericsson et al. (1993), for example, found that the best violin students engaged in solitary practice (which was judged to be the most important type of practice) for approximately 3.5 hours per day, spread out across two to three sessions, each session lasting an average of 80 minutes. Note that this did not include time spent receiving instruction, giving performances, or playing for enjoyment. The students also devoted about 3.5 hours a day to rest and recreation and obtained more than average amounts of sleep.

Top-level performers in intellectual pursuits display similar characteristics. Novelists typically write for about 3 to 4 hours each day, usually in the morning. Eminent scientists likewise write for a few hours each morning—the writing of articles arguably being the most important activity determining their success—and then devote the rest of the day to other duties.

B. F. Skinner is especially instructive in this regard. In his later life, he would rise at midnight and write for 1 hour, then rise again at 5:00 A.M. and write for another 2 hours. The remainder of the morning was devoted to correspondence and other professional tasks, while much of the afternoon was devoted to leisure activities such as tinkering in his workshop and listening to music. He deliberately resisted any urge to engage in serious writing at other times of the day, feeling that this often resulted in poor-quality writing the next morning. However, the limited amount of writing he did each day was more than compensated for by the consistency with which he wrote, resulting in a steady stream of influential articles and books throughout his career (Bjork, 1993). Skinner (1987) recommended that students adopt a similar approach to improve the quality of their writing. Congruent with this, effective college students are more likely to describe themselves as utilizing a *balanced* approach to studying, involving reg-ular study sessions with frequent breaks, than a *driven* approach, involving few breaks and studying to the point of exhaustion (Bouvier & Powell, 2008).

Of course, Ericsson et al. (1993) do not completely discount the role of heredity in expert performance. Heredity might well affect the extent to which one becomes interested in an endeavor, as well as one's ability to endure the years of hard work needed to become an elite performer. Nevertheless, the obvious importance of deliberate practice suggests that we should not be too quick to discount our ability to acquire a certain skill. Although many of us might not have the desire, time, or resources to become elite athletes, excellent musicians, or famous scientists, this does not rule out the possibility of becoming better tennis players, learning how to play the guitar, or significantly improving our math skills. After all, the best evidence available suggests that it is largely a matter of practice. (See Ericsson, 2009, for a recent exposition of research on the acquisition of expert performance.)

Utilizes interviewing variables, in the form of hypothesized Psychological processes, to explain behavior.

Hull's Neobehaviorism

One of the first major challenges to methodological behaviorism came from Clark Hull (1884–1952), who claimed that Watson's rejection of unobservable events was scientifically unsound. Hull noted that both physicists and chemists make inferences about events that have never been directly observed but that can nevertheless be *operationalized* (that is, defined in such a way that they can be measured). For example, gravity cannot be directly observed, but its effect on falling objects can be precisely measured. Hull believed that it might likewise be useful for psychologists to infer the existence of internal events that might *mediate* (draw a connection) between the environment and behavior.

Clark L. Hull
(1884–1952)

Deane Keller, "Dr. Clark Leonard Hull (1884–1952), M. A. (Hon.) 1929" Yale University Art Gallery, Gift of Colleagues, friends and students of the sitter

The mediating events that Hull incorporated into his theory consisted largely of physiological-type reactions, for example a "hunger drive" that can be operationalized as number of hours of food deprivation. Such mediating events are formally called *intervening variables,* meaning that they intervene *(hunger, tiredness...)*

Environment ⟶ Intervening variables ⟶ behavior.

FIGURE 1.2 In Hull's neobehaviorism, theorists make use of intervening variables, in the form of hypothesized physiological processes, to help explain the relationship between the environment and behavior.

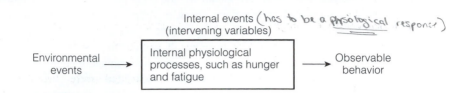

Internal events (has to be a physiological response)
(intervening variables)

Environmental events → Internal physiological processes, such as hunger and fatigue → Observable behavior

between a cause (such as food deprivation) and an effect (such as speed of running toward food). Thus, Hull's *neobehaviorism* is a brand of behaviorism that utilizes intervening variables, in the form of hypothesized physiological processes, to help explain behavior (see Figure 1.2).

It is important to note that Hull's use of intervening variables did not mean that he advocated a return to mentalism. Like Watson, he strongly opposed the use of introspection as a scientific tool, believing that subjective experiences are too vague and unreliable to be of much use. Thus, whether the organism actually experienced a feeling of hunger was of no concern to him. What did concern him was whether the *concept of hunger*, as defined in some measurable way (such as number of hours of food deprivation), was scientifically useful and led to testable hypotheses.

Hull's theory was also a pure S-R theory because it assumed that learning consists of the establishment of connections between specific stimuli and specific responses. Thus, like Watson, he viewed behavior in a very mechanistic fashion. Lest this seem dehumanizing, recognize that it is not far removed from some modern-day cognitive approaches, which view humans as analogous to computers that process bits of information from the environment (input) to produce responses (output). This is actually quite similar to Hull's model of behavior: Specific stimuli (input) yield specific responses (output), with certain internal events mediating the process. In fact, some versions of modern-day cognitive psychology can even be considered an outgrowth of Hull's neobehaviorism.[6]

Hull was the most influential experimental psychologist of the 1940s and 1950s. Unfortunately, it turned out that major aspects of his theory (which are beyond the scope of this text) were very difficult to test. As well, the theory was highly mathematical and grew increasingly complex as

---

[6]Interestingly, people seem less critical of the cognitive information-processing approach to psychology, which draws an analogy between humans and computers, than they are of the traditional behavioral approach, which draws an analogy between humans and animals such as rats. Perhaps this is because we are impressed by the ability of computers to perform certain human-like tasks (e.g., play chess), and we are insulted by the notion that humans and rats have anything in common. Yet, outside their specialized abilities, computers are quite inferior to rats. Imagine, for example, that a man, a rat, and a computer are washed up on a deserted island. To the extent that the man emulates the rat (if he is capable of it), he will likely survive; to the extent that he emulates the computer, he will sit on the beach and rot. Rats have a marvelous ability to learn and adapt; present-day computers do not. Fortunately for us, humans are far more rat-like than computer-like.

equations were expanded and modified. Many of these modifications were forced on Hull by his critics, the most famous of whom was Edward C. Tolman. (For a major overview of Hull's theory, as well as to gain a sense of its complexity, see Hull, 1943.)

1. Hull believed that it might be useful to incorporate internal events into one's theorizing so long as they can be op_____ by defining them in such a way that they can be measured.

2. In Hull's approach, the internal events he included were hypothetical ph_____ processes.

3. Such internal events are called i_____ variables in that they are presumed to m_____ between the environment and behavior.

4. Hull's theory was a pure _____-_____ theory in that it assumed that the process of learning involves the creation of connections between specific s_____ and specific r_____.

Tolman's Cognitive Behaviorism

Hull's S-R theory of learning is often categorized as a "molecular" theory because it viewed behavior as consisting of a long chain of specific responses connected to specific stimuli. Edward Tolman (1886–1959) disagreed with this approach and believed that it would be more useful to analyze behavior on a "molar" (i.e., broader) level. For example, he felt that we can understand a rat's behavior in a maze more accurately as a goal-directed attempt to obtain food than as a long chain of distinct stimulus-response connections that, in machine-like fashion, lead to food (e.g., Tolman, 1932). This molar approach to learning is similar to the gestalt approach to perception (Kohler, 1947), from which Tolman drew much of his inspiration. To the gestalt psychologists, perception is not simply the summation of different bits of conscious experience but is instead a "holistic" process resulting in an organized, coherent, perceptual experience. We perceive a house as more than just a combination of bricks and boards; it is bricks and boards plus something more. As the classic gestalt saying goes, "the whole is more than the sum of the parts." Similarly, for Tolman, behavior was more than just a chain of discrete responses attached to discrete stimuli. It was instead an overall pattern of behavior directed toward particular outcomes, and it can be properly analyzed only on that level.

Edward C. Tolman
(1886–1959)

Psychology Archives /The University of Akron

Shift focus on broader cognitive reasons "molar"

More goal-oriented

Although Tolman disagreed with much of Hull's theorizing, he did agree that intervening variables may be useful in a theory of learning (in fact, it was Tolman who first suggested this). However, while Hull's intervening variables were physiological-type processes like hunger and fatigue, Tolman's were more mentalistic. The Tolmanian rat, as well as the Tolmanian person,

FIGURE 1.3   In Tolman's cognitive behaviorism, theorists make use of intervening variables, in the form of hypothesized cognitive processes, to help explain the relationship between environment and behavior.

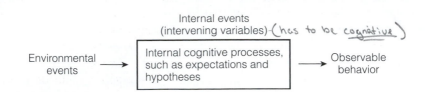

Internal events
(intervening variables) *(has to be cognitive)*

Environmental events → Internal cognitive processes, such as expectations and hypotheses → Observable behavior

was not simply motivated by drives and habits but also had "expectations" and "hypotheses." Thus, Tolman's *cognitive behaviorism* (sometimes called "purposive behaviorism") utilizes intervening variables, usually in the form of hypothesized cognitive processes, to help explain behavior (see Figure 1.3).

We have mental representations of our surroundings   Tolman's (1948) most famous intervening variable is the *cognitive map*, which is a mental representation of one's spatial surroundings. Evidence for this concept was provided by a study on "latent learning" by Tolman and Honzik (1930). This experiment was conducted in an attempt to disprove Hull's notion that behavior must be rewarded for learning to take place; that is, in the absence of some type of reward, nothing can be learned. To test this notion, Tolman and Honzik trained three groups of rats on a complex maze task (see Figure 1.4).

FIGURE 1.4   Maze used by Tolman and Honzik (1930) in their study of latent learning. (Adapted from M. H. Elliott, *The Effect of Change of Reward on the Maze Performance of Rats.* University of California, Publications in Psychology, Volume 4, 1928.).

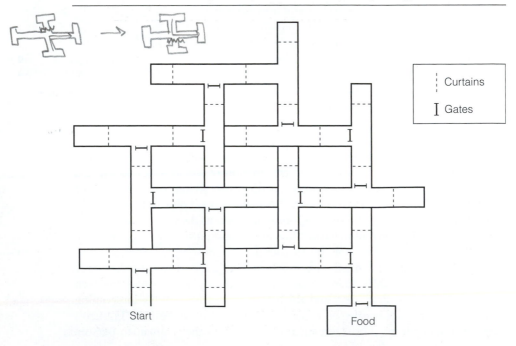

Curtains

I Gates

Start

Food

The rats in a continuous-reward group always found food when they reached the goal box, but the rats in the two other groups found no food when they reached the goal box (they were simply removed from the maze and then fed several hours later). Training proceeded at the rate of one trial per day for 10 consecutive days. As expected, the rewarded group learned to run quickly to the goal box, whereas the two nonrewarded groups took much longer to do so.

Following this initial phase of training, on day 11 of the study the rats in one of the nonrewarded groups also began receiving food when they reached the goal box. According to Hull, the rats in that group should only then have started to learn their way through the maze, which would have been demonstrated by a gradual improvement in their performance. What Tolman and Honzik found instead was a dramatic improvement in the rats' performance on the very next trial. In fact, on day 12 of the study, the newly rewarded group slightly outperformed the group that had been receiving a reward from the outset (see Figure 1.5).

FIGURE 1.5 Errors made by the different groups of rats in Tolman and Honzik's (1930) latent learning experiment. The vertical axis represents the average number of wrong turns the rats in each group made before reaching the goal box. Group NR are those rats that never received a reward for reaching the goal box. Group R are those rats that always received a reward for reaching the goal box. Group NR-R received no reward for the first 10 days of the study, then began receiving a reward on day 11. Note that this group was run for a few days longer than the other two groups to see if there would be any additional change in their performance. (Adapted from Tolman, E. C., & Honzik, C. H. (1930). *Degrees of hunger, reward and nonreward, and maze learning in rats.* University of California Publications in Psychology, 4, 241–275.)

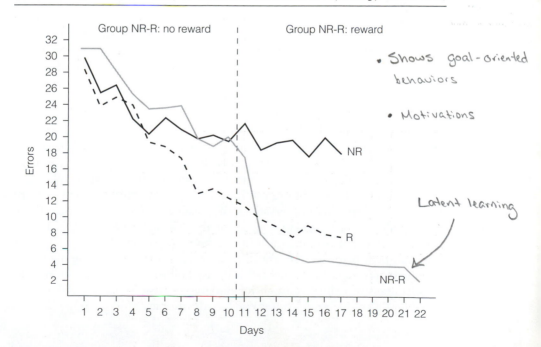

And Furthermore

How to Read Graphs

A graph is a concise way of conveying information. It has two axes: the horizontal or x-axis, which is formally called the abscissa, and the vertical or y-axis, which is formally called the ordinate. The vertical axis is usually a measure of the target behavior in which we are interested; in Figure 1.5 this is the number of errors the rats made while running through a maze. The horizontal axis usually indicates some aspect of the experimental manipulation, in this case the days on which the rats were run through the maze. The broken line between days 10 and 11 indicates that there was a change in conditions at this time, which is described by the labels on each side of the broken line (namely, that group NR-R switched from receiving no reward to receiving a reward). The three lines within the graph therefore indicate the average number of errors made by each group of rats on each day of the experiment.

Tolman interpreted these results as indicating that the initially non-rewarded rats had in fact learned the maze during the first 10 trials of the experiment, and that they had learned it at least as well as the group that had been receiving food. He would later interpret these findings as indicating the development of a "cognitive map" (Tolman, 1948), which only became apparent when the rats finally began to receive food. Thus, this experiment is regarded as a classic demonstration of *latent learning*, in which learning occurs despite the absence of any observable indication of learning and only becomes apparent under a different set of conditions. The experiment also demonstrates the distinction between *learning and performance*, because learning was apparently taking place even when the subjects showed no evidence of such learning in their performance at that time. (See, however, Jensen, 2006, for a more detailed exposition and critique of these findings and how they have been interpreted.)

Although Tolman believed that it was theoretically useful to incorporate cognitive variables, he remained in many other ways a standard behaviorist. For example, like Hull and Watson, he believed that introspective reports of thoughts and feelings are so unreliable as to be of little scientific value. He maintained that his own theoretical inferences about cognitive processes were based entirely on direct observations of behavior and were thus objectively based. Tolman once even apologized for the "shameful necessity" of having to discuss conscious experience in a text he was writing (Tolman, 1932)—a reflection perhaps of how frustrated psychologists had been by the old introspectionist approach. Like other behaviorists, Tolman also believed strongly in the usefulness of animal research for discovering basic processes of learning, and almost all of his research was conducted with rats.

P. BYRNES.

*"Bathroom? Sure, it's just down the hall to the left, jog
right, left, another left, straight past two more lefts, then right,
and it's at the end of the third corridor on your right."*

Much of Tolman's research was directly aimed at refuting Hull's theory of learning. Hull responded by modifying his theory, in increasingly complex ways, to account for many of Tolman's findings.[7] As a result, during Tolman's life, his cognitive approach never achieved the same popularity as Hull's neobehavioral approach. With the advent of the cognitive revolution in psychology, however, many of Tolman's research methods and concepts have been adopted by modern researchers. Cognitive behaviorism is now a flourishing field of study, and the study of cognitive processes in nonhuman animals is now known as "animal cognition" or "comparative cognition."

---

[7]Roughly speaking, Hull (1943) tried to account for the results of Tolman and Honzik's latent learning experiment by hypothesizing that the rats in the non-rewarded conditions found the mere act of being removed from the maze when they reached the empty goal box to be slightly rewarding. This slight reward was sufficient to ensure that the rats learned the pathway to the goal box, but not sufficient to motivate them to greatly reduce the number of errors they were making. Only when the incentive to get to the goal box was increased by the availability of food did the number of errors drop significantly and the degree of learning become evident. Alternatively, Jensen (2006) has recently pointed to evidence indicating that the rats in the nonrewarded group may have found the act of entering a blind alley punishing, thereby reducing their tendency to make incorrect responses. This would again argue against interpreting these particular results as strong evidence of latent learning.

1. Tolman's approach is known as _____ behaviorism because it utilizes mentalistic concepts, such as "expectations," to explain behavior. This approach is also sometimes called p_____ behaviorism.

2. A _____ _____ is an internal representation of one's surroundings.

3. The experiment by Tolman and Honzik (1930) has traditionally been regarded as a demonstration of _____ learning, in which learning appears to take place in the absence of any reward. The experiment has also been regarded as a demonstration of the distinction between learning and _____.

4. Tolman believed that introspectively observed thoughts and feelings are (useless/useful) _____ in the analysis of behavior. As well, almost all of Tolman's research was conducted using _____ as subjects.

5. The modern-day study of cognitive processes in nonhuman animals is known as a_____ c_____ or com_____ c_____.

Albert Bandura
(b. 1925)

Linda A. Cicero/Stanford News Service

Bandura's Social Learning Theory

If Tolman's use of cognitive concepts seems to represent a partial return to mentalism, Albert Bandura's social learning theory is an even stronger step in that direction. The roots of social learning theory can be partially traced to Hull's neobehaviorism in that Bandura had considerable exposure to Hullian theorists during his graduate training. In fact, the term *social learning theory* was first used by followers of Hull who were attempting to apply Hullian concepts to human social behavior, particularly to the process of imitation (Miller & Dollard, 1941). Bandura was very much interested in imitation, which he referred to as observational learning, and he eventually became the dominant researcher in the field. His most famous investigations concern the influence of observational learning on aggressive behavior (Bandura, 1973).

Although Bandura's interests were partially influenced by Hullian psychologists, his interpretation of the learning process is more closely aligned with that of Tolman. Like Tolman, Bandura focuses on broad behavior patterns (i.e., he uses a molar approach) and emphasizes the distinction between learning and performance. He also gives internal events, such as expectations, a primary role in the learning process. Bandura's approach differs from that of Tolman, however, in that these internal events are viewed as more than just theoretically useful; they are viewed as actual events occurring within us that strongly influence our behavior. Additionally, these internal events include *self-referent thoughts* about our abilities and accomplishments, a distinctly human form of cognition that Bandura believes has significant impact on our behavior. This means that, unlike the other behaviorists we have discussed, Bandura does not dismiss the value of

FIGURE 1.6 Bandura's model of reciprocal determinism, in which observable behavior, environmental events, and international events are all viewed as interacting with each other.

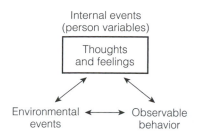

Internal events
(person variables)

Thoughts
and feelings

Environmental ⟷ Observable
events   behavior

introspectively observed subjective experience in explaining behavior. Thus, *social learning theory* is a cognitive-behavioral approach that strongly emphasizes the importance of observational learning and cognitive variables in explaining human behavior (Bandura, 1977, 1997).[8]

Observing + learning from our environment

Social learning theory also has a distinct view of determinism (the notion that each behavior has a cause). More specifically, Bandura has proposed the concept of *reciprocal determinism*, in which environmental events, observable behavior, and "person variables" (including thoughts and feelings) are seen as having a reciprocal influence on each other (see Figure 1.6). Reciprocal determinism can be contrasted with the deterministic models proposed by other behaviorists in which internal events, if they are included, simply mediate between the environment and behavior (Environment → Internal events → Behavior).

Thoughts, emotion that are observable

Self-referent thoughts

As an illustration of reciprocal determinism, imagine that you are out on a date with someone to whom you are very attracted. Trying to impress this individual, you start the evening off by telling a joke (thus, an aspect of your environment—namely, the person you are dating—has affected your behavior). Unfortunately, your off-color sense of humor is not appreciated, and your date reacts to the joke with a look of horror (your behavior has affected your environment). The look of horror in turn elicits feelings of anxiety (your environment has affected your feelings), which then causes you to stammer as you speak (your feelings have affected your behavior). Observing yourself stammer then leads you to conclude that your date must think you are an idiot (your behavior has affected your beliefs), which in turn leads you to interpret your date's smile as a smile of pity (your beliefs have affected the environment—or, more precisely, the environment as you perceive it). Needless to say, the evening turns out to be a complete disaster, with the environment, behavior, and person variables (thoughts and feelings) all interacting to conspire against you. (No wonder life is rough!)

"help improve or disprove abilities"

↓

"lift or put down yourself"

↓

Self confidence

---

[8]Bandura (e.g., 1997) has more recently referred to this approach as "social-cognitive" theory, so as to emphasize the importance of cognitive variables.

Social learning theory has stimulated a lot of research, particularly in the area of observational learning. It has also stimulated the development of *cognitive-behavior therapy*, in which psychological disorders are treated by altering both environmental variables and cognitive processes. For example, a cognitive-behavioral treatment for an irrational fear of spiders might involve some type of safe exposure to spiders (an environmental manipulation) along with instructions to replace fearful thoughts with certain types of calming thoughts (a cognitive manipulation). Cognitive-behavioral treatments have become very popular in recent years. It (along with its cousin, animal cognition) has become a dominant force in behavioral psychology and is rivaled by only one other school of thought—B. F. Skinner's radical behaviorism.

1. Bandura's _____ _____ theory emphasizes the importance of o_____ learning and c_____ variables.

2. The concept of _____ _____ proposes that three variables: e_____, b_____, and p_____ variables, all interact with each other.

3. Bandura's work has influenced the development of a type of therapy known as _____-_____ therapy, in which an attempt is made to change behavior by altering both environmental and c_____ factors.

Skinner's Radical Behaviorism

Burrhus Frederick Skinner
(1904–1990)

Yvonne Hemsey/Getty Images

From Watson to Bandura, we see a steady increase in the use of internal events to help explain behavior. Not everyone has agreed with this trend. Burrhus Frederick Skinner argued for a return to a stricter form of behaviorism. Skinner's version of behaviorism, known as *radical behaviorism*, emphasizes the influence of the environment on observable (overt) behavior, rejects the use of internal events to explain behavior, and views thoughts and feelings as behaviors that themselves need to be explained. Thus, unlike Watson's methodological behaviorism, radical behaviorism does not completely reject the inclusion of internal events in a science of behavior; it merely rejects the use of these events as explanations for behavior (Skinner, 1953, 1974). We explain this notion more fully in the following section.

Skinner's View of Internal Events Skinner viewed internal events, such as sensing, thinking, and feeling, as "covert" or private behaviors that are subject to the same laws of learning as "overt" or publicly observable behaviors. Thus, internal events can be included in an analysis of behavior,

All internal events may be private but are influenced by Environment.

Covert → internal thoughts
Overt → public behavior

but only as behaviors that themselves need to be explained. For example, whereas a social learning theorist might say that a student studies because she expects that studying will result in a high mark, Skinner would say that both the act of studying and the thoughts about achieving a high mark by studying are the result of some experience, such as a history of doing well on exams when the student did study.

For several reasons, Skinner was loath to consider internal events as explanations for behavior. First, he agreed with Watson's concern that, since we do not have direct access to the internal events of others, we must rely on their verbal reports of such events. Our assessments of internal thoughts and feelings thus are often unreliable. Skinner further noted that such unreliability is to be expected, given the manner in which people learn to label their internal events. More specifically, young children need to be taught by their caretakers to describe their internal experiences. Because these caretakers (usually parents) cannot directly observe internal events in their children, they must infer their occurrence from the children's observable behaviors.

Consider, for example, the task of teaching a young boy to correctly label the feeling of pain. The parent must wait until the child is displaying some observable behavior that typically accompanies pain, such as crying in response to a stubbed toe. Based on this behavior, the parent then infers that the child is experiencing pain and says something like, "My, your toe must really hurt!" After a few experiences like this, the child will himself begin using the word *hurt* to describe what he is feeling in such circumstances.

Pain is probably one of the easier feelings to teach, given that the observable behaviors accompanying it are usually quite distinct (although even here, there may be considerable variability across individuals in the intensity of sensation required before something is called painful). Consider how much more difficult it is to teach a child to accurately describe subtle emotions such as contentment or discomfort, for which the observable behaviors are often much less distinct. Because the parents have less reliable information on which to base their inferences about such states, the labels they provide to the child are likely to be only crude approximations of the child's actual feelings. As a result, the labels people learn to use to describe their feelings may be only crude approximations of what they actually feel. For this reason, Skinner was uninterested in using a person's description of an internal emotional state as an explanation for behavior; he was, however, quite interested in how people come to label their internal states.

A second problem with using internal events to explain behavior is that it is often difficult to determine the actual relationship of thoughts and feelings to behavior. Do the thoughts and feelings precede the behavior, follow the behavior, or simply occur parallel to the behavior? Take, for example, the act of providing help in an emergency. Do you provide help because you feel concern for the person involved (Figure 1.7a)? Or do you provide help and feel concerned at the same time, with no necessary link between the two (Figure 1.7b)? After all, people often take action in an emergency quite quickly, without reflecting upon how they feel.

Or do your feelings of concern for someone sometimes arise after you have tried to help them (Figure 1.7c)? Lest this notion seem rather strange to you, consider that people's "feelings" about an event can often be altered simply by manipulating their behavior toward the event. For example, people can often be induced to change their opinion about a certain issue—such as whether capital punishment should be abolished—by asking them to write an essay promoting a certain point of view. If they do not already hold a strong opinion about that issue and do not feel that they are being forced to write the essay, they may alter their opinion to be consistent with what they have written (Cialdini, 1993). In similar fashion, the concern you feel for others might sometimes result from, or at least be strengthened by, the act of helping them.

FIGURE 1.7 Three ways in which feelings of concern can be associated with the behavior of helping.

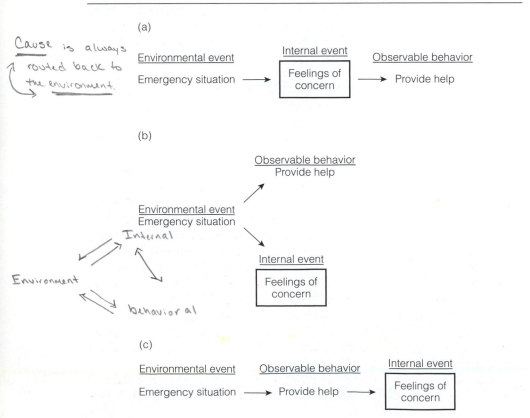

Handwritten annotations:
Cause is always routed back to the environment.

Environment

Internal

behavioral

A third difficulty with using internal events to explain behavior is that we do not have any means of directly changing these internal events. Our only means of changing both internal events and external behavior is to change some aspect of the environment. For example, if I instruct a client to think calm, relaxing thoughts whenever he or she is in an anxiety-arousing situation, and this effectively reduces the anxiety, a radical behaviorist would say that the effective treatment is not the calm, relaxing thoughts but the instructions I have given the person about thinking calm, relaxing thoughts. And since exposing the client to these instructions is really a manipulation of the client's environment, then it is really a change in the environment that is ultimately responsible for reducing the level of anxiety. Therefore, if changing the environment is the only manner in which behavior can be influenced, then why not emphasize the environment as the ultimate cause of behavior?

A fourth problem with using internal events to explain behavior is that (as with explanations based on instinct) such explanations are sometimes only pseudo-explanations. For example, if I say that I "feel like going to the movies," am I referring to a bodily condition of some sort, or am I simply making a prediction about my future behavior? Perhaps all I am really saying is that I am quite likely to go to the movies under these particular circumstances (which may or may not include a certain bodily state), given that nothing prevents me from doing so. Thus, my "feeling" statement is more a statement about potential behavior than about a bodily feeling of some sort. For this reason, saying that I am going to the movies because I "feel like going" is really no explanation at all.

For reasons such as these, Skinner rejected internal events as explanations for behavior; instead, he focused on the environment—in particular, the environmental consequences of our behavior—as the ultimate cause of both observable behavior (overt behavior) and internal events (covert behavior). But neither did he believe that we are helpless pawns of our environment. He assumed that once we understand the manner in which the environment affects us, we can change the environment so that it will exert a more beneficial influence on our behavior. Skinner referred to this process as *countercontrol,* which is the deliberate manipulation of environmental events to alter their impact on our behavior. Nevertheless, in Skinner's view, even such acts of countercontrol can ultimately be traced to environmental influence. Suppose, for example, that Jamie decides to improve her study habits by rearranging her study environment. On one level of analysis, Jamie's decision (the thoughts she has had about this issue) is the cause of the improvement in her study habits. On another level, however, Jamie would not have made this decision unless she had first been exposed to information about its usefulness. The source of this information is an environmental influence and is, in Skinner's view, the ultimate cause of the improvement in Jamie's study habits.

Thus, Skinner might be seen as agreeing with some aspects of Bandura's notion of reciprocal determinism, in the sense that environmental events,

FIGURE 1.8 A diagrammatic representation of Skinner's view of the relationship between environmental events, internal events, and observable behavior. Although all three components are capable of influencing each other, the emphasis is on environmental events as the ultimate cause of both observable behavior and internal events (as indicated by the solid arrows).

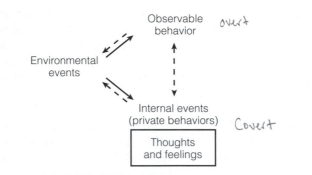

internal events, and observable behavior are seen as capable of interacting with each other. Where Skinner differs, however, is in his assumption that the environment ultimately determines both external behavior and internal events. A diagrammatic depiction of Skinner's approach might therefore look something like that depicted in Figure 1.8. (See Skinner [1953, 1987, 1989] for a discussion of his perspective on private events; also see Anderson, Hawkins, Freeman, and Scotti [2000] for the many issues involved in incorporating private events into a science of behavior.)

QUICK QUIZ K

1. Skinner's _____ behaviorism emphasizes both internal and external behaviors as resulting from e_____ influences.

2. Skinner views thoughts and feelings as pr_____ behaviors that themselves need to be explained. These can also be called _____ behaviors.

3. In teaching children to label their thoughts and feelings, parents first have to make an inf_____ about what the child is feeling.

4. In determining the relationship of thoughts and feelings to behavior, it is sometimes difficult to know if the internal event pr_____, f_____, or occurs pa_____ to the behavior.

5. Yet another issue with respect to using internal events to explain behavior is that we (can/cannot) _____ directly change such events.

6. Saying that you are feeling "happy" to explain why you are always smiling and laughing is, from Skinner's perspective, an example of using feelings as a ps_____ explanation for your behavior.

7. Altering the environment so as to control our own behavior is referred to as c_____control. However, in Skinner's view, even this type of behavior is ultimately the result of some type of e_____ influence.

Skinner's Approach as Molar Although Skinner disagreed with Tolman about the value of using internal events to help explain behavior, he agreed with Tolman in emphasizing a molar rather than a molecular approach. Critics are thus incorrect in referring to Skinner as an S-R psychologist who held a mechanistic view of behavior. He did not believe, as Watson and Hull did, that all behaviors consist of long chains of S-R connections that propel the animal forward in a robotic, step-by-step fashion. Skinner (1938) instead believed that only reflexive behaviors—those that can be classically conditioned, such as salivating in response to food—are automatically elicited by the stimuli that precede them. Such behaviors need to be distinguished from operant behaviors—behaviors that are controlled by their consequences—which have a more flexible, less predictable quality to them. Therefore, for both Skinner and Tolman, the rat's behavior of running through the maze is a behavior that is controlled by the consequence of obtaining food in the goal box. The difference is that the Tolmanian rat is running through the maze because it *expects* that doing so will lead to food, whereas the Skinnerian rat is running through the maze because such behavior has *in the past* resulted in food. Tolman was comfortable with hypothesizing the existence of a mental event inside the animal to help explain its present behavior—a mental event that was, of course, based on the rat's past experience—whereas Skinner preferred to explain the behavior by simply referring to past experience.

Skinner's View of Genetic Factors What about the role of genetic influences on behavior? In discussing these various schools of behaviorism, we have focused on the role of the environment; but we have done so simply because that is what behaviorists generally do—they study the effects of environmental experiences on behavior. Traditionally, they have left it to other disciplines, such as ethology (a subfield of zoology that studies instinctive behavior patterns in animals), to study the role of genetic influences. But this does not mean that behaviorists discount the role of heredity. As we noted earlier, Darwin's theory of evolution played a strong role in the eventual establishment of behaviorism, and many behaviorists clearly recognize that heredity can profoundly influence animal and human behavior. Skinner (e.g., 1953, 1987, 1989), in fact, repeatedly acknowledged that behavior was fundamentally the result of the interaction between genes and the environment. Moreover, far from being dismayed by research indicating genetic limitations on operant conditioning (some of which is discussed in Chapter 12), Skinner (1987) was quite fascinated by it and even initiated some early research along these lines.

Skinner also noted that operant conditioning bears a striking resemblance to the evolutionary principle of natural selection. As earlier discussed, according to the principle of natural selection, members of a species that inherit certain adaptive characteristics are more likely to survive and propagate, thereby passing those characteristics on to their offspring.

Thus, over many generations, the frequency of those adaptive characteristics within the population increases and becomes well established. In a similar fashion, according to the principle of operant conditioning, behaviors that lead to reinforcing consequences are more likely to be repeated, whereas those that do not lead to reinforcing consequences are less likely to be repeated. In other words, operant conditioning is sort of a mini-evolution in which behaviors that are adaptive (that lead to reinforcers) increase in frequency while behaviors that are nonadaptive (that do not lead to reinforcers) decrease in frequency. The processes of natural selection and operant conditioning are therefore very similar. The basic difference is that natural selection is concerned with the evolution of inherited characteristics within a species, whereas operant conditioning is concerned with the evolution of learned behavior patterns within an individual.

Skinner (1953) was more accepting of the effects of heredity on behavior than was Watson, but he nevertheless remained wary about placing too much emphasis on such factors. Genetic factors are largely unmodifiable, and to assume that a behavior pattern has a strong genetic basis is to assume also that little can be done to alter it (except perhaps through some type of physiological intervention). When dealing with maladaptive characteristics such as learning difficulties or aggressive tendencies in children, this assumption can have serious implications. Think about it: If you had a son who was having difficulty in math, would you want his teacher to be a strong empiricist (who emphasizes the role of experience in determining behavior), or a strong nativist (who emphasizes the role of genetics and heredity)? Almost certainly, you would want a teacher who is a strong empiricist and who believes the child's math problems are the result of poor learning experiences, which can then be corrected by providing better experiences. Thus, a strong empiricist approach, such as that exemplified by Skinner and other behaviorists, tends to be more optimistic about the possibility of changing behavior for the better. Behaviorists nevertheless have a growing appreciation for the influence of genetic factors on learning and behavior, and in the future we will no doubt see a significant increase in research in this area.

QUICK QUIZ L

1. Skinner is most similar to (Hull/Watson/Tolman) _____ in arguing that behavior is best viewed from a m_____ perspective.

2. For Skinner, an S-R interpretation can best be applied to behavior that is r_____ and can be _____ conditioned. It cannot be applied to _____ behavior that is under the control of its c_____ and has a more fl_____ quality about it.

3. The Tolmanian rat runs through the maze because it e_____ that doing so will result in food; the Skinnerian rat runs through the maze because, in its p_____ exp_____, doing so resulted in food.

4. Although he emphasized the role of the environment, Skinner also believed that behavior was fundamentally the result of the interaction of g_____ and the environment. He was in fact quite interested in evidence indicating g_____ limitations on _____ conditioning.

5. Skinner believed that the processes of ev_____ and op_____ conditioning were quite similar in that both involved the selection of what was beneficial from what was not beneficial.

6. On a practical level, Skinner was (enthused/cautious) _____ about genetic explanations for behavior because he believed that such explanations tend to be (optimistic/pessimistic) _____ about the possibility of change.

Behavior Analysis and Applied Behavior Analysis More so than other behaviorists, Skinner was careful to distinguish between the philosophical aspect of his approach and the experimental science that grew out of that approach. The term *radical behaviorism* refers to the philosophical aspect of Skinner's approach, consisting of the set of assumptions, which we discussed earlier, upon which his behavioral science is based. The basic science that grew out of radical behaviorism was originally called the ***experimental analysis of behavior***, but is now more commonly referred to as ***behavior analysis***. Behavior analysts, following the lead of Skinner, have especially concentrated on researching the various principles of operant conditioning (which are discussed in Chapters 6 through 10).

Like Watson, Skinner was concerned that the principles discovered through research should have practical application. In this regard, he did not disappoint. His work directly led to the establishment of ***applied behavior analysis***, a technology of behavior in which basic principles of behavior are applied to solving real-world issues. These applications range from helping people with clinical disorders (such as phobias and schizophrenia), to improving educational practices, to implementing programs that encourage communities to stop polluting and conserve energy. Applied behavior analysis is particularly well established as the treatment of choice for children with developmental disabilities, including autism, and many graduates from behavior analysis programs find work in this field. (See Miltenberger, 2012, for a more extensive list of areas of application.) Applied behavior analysis is also sometimes referred to as *behavior modification* or *behavior therapy*, though the latter term can also refer to more cognitive-behavioral approaches to treatment than would be found in pure applied behavior analysis.

1. Skinner's philosophy of behaviorism (meaning the set of basic assumptions for how best to conduct a science of behavior) is called _____ behaviorism.

2. The science that grew out of that philosophy is called the e_____ a_____ of behavior or, more briefly, _____ _____.

3. The technology that has grown out of that science is known as _____ _____ _____.

ADVICE FOR THE LOVELORN

While reading this text you will occasionally encounter advice columns, like this one, in which behavioral concepts are applied to relationship problems. Bear in mind that the advice given is often quite speculative and that real relationship difficulties are too complex to be properly assessed and dealt with through simplistic advice columns. Nevertheless, these columns will, in a fun manner, give you a sense for how behavioral concepts can offer a unique perspective on important aspects of human behavior.

Dear Dr. Dee,

I have very strong feelings for my new girlfriend, but I can't tell if these are feelings of infatuation or love. My friends tell me I am in love, but my parents tell me I am infatuated. How can I tell the difference?

So Confused

Dear So,

The distinction between love and infatuation is a tough one, and many people find it difficult to differentiate between the two. Interestingly, Skinner (1989) suggested that the more subtle an emotional state (and, presumably, the more subtle the differences between emotional states), the more value there is in analyzing that emotion in terms of the circumstances that surround it. In what circumstance, for example, are we most likely to use the term *infatuation*? For starters, are we not more likely to use that term when the level of attachment seems to greatly exceed the total rewards available in the relationship? In particular, isn't it the case that we often apply the word *infatuation* to a relationship that is driven by short-term sexual rewards with few long-term prospects? By contrast, the word *love* is typically applied to a relationship in which a strong level of attachment seems to properly match the available rewards. The relationship seems to have good long-term prospects and is not driven merely by short-term sexual rewards. Thus, for many people, the word *infatuation* implies an "unhealthy" relationship that is doomed to failure, whereas the word *love* implies a "healthy" relationship that has the potential to prosper.

A little thought will likely reveal other differences between infatuation and love. Nevertheless, our brief analysis suggests that if you wish to determine whether you are "in love" or "merely infatuated," you might do well to ponder the rewards offered by that relationship and forget about trying to detect minute differences in feelings.

Behaviorally yours,

Dr. Dee

And Furthermore

The Life of B. F. Skinner

Though quieter and less colorful than Watson, Skinner was nevertheless also the focus of much controversy. As such, it may be worthwhile to briefly describe his life, especially since he is viewed by many as the prototypical behaviorist. Indeed, in a survey of psychology department chairpersons, Skinner was voted the most influential psychologist of the twentieth century (Haggbloom et al., 2002).

Burrhus Frederick Skinner was born in Susquehanna, Pennsylvania, in 1904. Raised in a traditional Presbyterian household, Skinner had a relatively normal childhood, though it was not without difficulties. For example, although he was never physically punished as a child (apart from once having his mouth washed out with soap for saying a bad word), he was taught through reprimands and warnings "to fear God, the police, and what people will think" (Skinner, 1967, p. 407). Interestingly, as a behaviorist, he would later conclude that punishment is an ineffective means for managing behavior, often creating more problems than it solves.

One of Skinner's strongest traits, even in childhood, was his love of building and inventing.

> I made slingshots, bows and arrows, blow guns and water pistols from lengths of bamboo, and from a discarded water boiler a steam cannon with which I could shoot plugs of potato and carrot over the houses of our neighbors. ... I tried again and again to make a glider in which I might fly. (Skinner, 1967, p. 388)

This inventiveness served Skinner well in later years when he was able to build unique devices for studying the behavior of animals, most notably the "Skinner box" (see Chapter 6). Without these inventions, it is conceivable that many of the principles discussed in this text would have remained undiscovered.

Skinner's personality was also characterized by a strange mixture of objectivity and sentimentality (Bjork, 1993). For example, when his younger brother Ebbie suddenly died of a cerebral hemorrhage, Skinner observed the death in a surprisingly detached fashion. Nevertheless, he was greatly distressed by the incident and felt pangs of guilt when he later recalled how he had once injured his brother in play. Skinner's objectivity was also apparent in everyday settings. For example, in describing a family friend, Skinner once wrote:

> The doctor and his dog are becoming more than idle amusement. ... He becomes a fool in the eyes of everyone but me when he attempts to justify the dog's actions. ... [Pep] comes up to us wagging his tail—"He says 'throw me a stick,'" says the doctor. ... Lately I've got the habit too. It's quite fun to make up mental processes to fit a dog's every move. (as quoted in Bjork, 1993, p. 63)

As a radical behaviorist, Skinner would later argue that mentalistic terms are often mere inferences derived from observable behavior.

Skinner graduated from a small liberal arts college and, with some encouragement from the famous poet Robert Frost, spent a year trying to establish himself as a writer. Although

(continued)

quite disciplined about it, he completed only a few stories and poems and eventually gave up in despair. He sometimes claimed that he had failed as a writer because he had nothing important to say; but he also speculated that his writing was simply too "objective" to interest the average reader, with too few references to thoughts and feelings (Bjork, 1993, p. 56). Years later Skinner would publish a novel called *Walden Two*, but it was an "objective" novel about a utopian community founded on behavioral principles.

Following his failure at becoming a writer, Skinner came to the conclusion that his real interests lay in the study of behavior. Impressed by the writings of John B. Watson, he entered graduate studies at Harvard in 1928. He thrived in that environment. Much of his graduate and postdoctoral training was surprisingly unstructured, and he was often left to his own devices to study whatever he wished. In later years, he would write that he had no sense of ever devising a theory or testing a hypothesis; he simply followed his interests. He discounted the notion of science as a formal system of theory building and hypothesis testing, asserting that real science is much less structured than most scientists describe it to be (Skinner, 1956).

Skinner eventually became a major figure in behaviorism, in a league with the likes of Tolman and Hull. During World War II, he also had an opportunity to apply the principles of conditioning to national defense. While contemplating the widespread destructiveness of bombing attacks, it occurred to him that it might be possible to train pigeons to guide missiles toward specific targets. The basic notion was first to train a pigeon to peck at a moving picture of, say, a ship in order to receive a food reward. The pigeon would then be placed in the nose cone of a missile that was being launched toward a ship. A lens would project the seascape in front of the missile onto a glass screen in front of the pigeon. As the pigeon pecked at the image of the ship, the position of the pecks on the screen would provide feedback to the missile's guidance system. Skinner and his coworkers envisioned squadrons of "kamikaze" pigeons being trained to attack different kinds of targets. After obtaining some funding, they were in fact able to demonstrate that such a device was feasible. Nevertheless, the scientists and military personnel who viewed the demonstration withdrew their support. The sight of a pigeon tracking a military target across a screen with such accuracy was simply too bizarre, and too amusing, for them to give it serious consideration.

Like Watson before him, Skinner was sometimes the target of false rumors. For example, when Skinner's wife, Eve, did not adjust well to the "joys" of motherhood, Skinner built an "aircrib" (or "baby tender") to ease the burden of raising their youngest daughter, Deborah. The crib was a large, enclosed space with an unbreakable glass window. The baby, wearing only a diaper, lay on a woven plastic sheet (the surface of which felt like linen), while the surrounding air was carefully filtered and maintained at a precise temperature (Figure 1.9). Skinner believed the aircrib to be far superior to the jail-like bars, uncertain temperature fluctuations, and loose bedding of the standard crib. It was also much easier to keep clean. Enthused by his invention and by the way Deborah seemed to thrive, Skinner wrote an article on the device for *Ladies' Home Journal* and set out to market it. Unfortunately, a story arose that Skinner was isolating his daughter in an "operant conditioning chamber" and experimenting on her. According to one version of the story, the daughter eventually went insane and killed herself. The reality is that she

FIGURE 1.9 Skinner's daughter, Deborah, seemed to thrive in the "aircrib" or "baby tender" her father had built for her, so Skinner set out to market it as an improvement over the standard crib with its jail-like bars and poor hygiene. Unfortunately, it led to the completely false rumor that he was conducting conditioning experiments on his daughters, and that they developed severe psychological disorders as a result.

Bettmann/CORBIS

had a happy childhood, spent no more time in the aircrib than other children do in a regular crib, and grew up to be quite normal. Nevertheless, the damage was done, and relatively few aircribs were ever sold.[9]

In the early 1970s, Skinner was severely criticized by numerous intellectuals and politicians for his book, *Beyond Freedom and Dignity*. In the book, Skinner (1971) rejected the concept of free will and argued that we must instead "engineer" society to more effectively control human behavior. He had hoped the book would encourage people to devise better programs for eliminating pollution, preventing crime, and so on, and he became quite depressed over the criticism he received. Skinner received a more favorable reaction for his invention of the "teaching machine" and programmed

[9]Unfortunately, the myth that Skinner had experimented on his daughter still makes the rounds today. A notable example is a book by Laura Slater (2004) entitled *Opening Skinner's Box: Great Psychological Experiments of the Twentieth Century*, in which she repeats the rumors of Deborah's insanity. This prompted an angry response from Skinner's daughter, entitled "I Was Not a Lab Rat," in which she demands that people stop spreading these vicious rumors (Skinner-Buzan, 2004).

(continued)

instruction—although in later years, he lamented that this notion too had been largely ignored and never utilized to its full potential. The recent popularity of personal computers, which are ideally suited for programmed instruction, could well change that.

Throughout his later years, Skinner remained intellectually active, carefully engineering his environment to compensate for the effects of aging. He even wrote a book, *Enjoy Old Age*, offering behavioral advice on self-management for the elderly (Skinner & Vaughan, 1983). His final public appearance was on August 10, 1990, when he was presented with a Lifetime Contribution Award by the American Psychological Association. Terminally ill, but with little fear of death and as independent as ever, Skinner used his acceptance speech to lambaste the psychological community for its return to mentalistic explanations of behavior. Eight days later he passed away from leukemia at the age of 86. (See Vargas, 1990, for a touching description of Skinner's final days.)

SUMMARY

This text introduces the basic principles of learning and behavior. It particularly emphasizes the principles of classical conditioning—in which reflexive behaviors come to be elicited in new situations, and operant conditioning—in which the strength of a behavior is influenced by its consequences.

Individuals of historical significance in the study of learning include Aristotle, who assumed that knowledge is gained largely from experience (as opposed to being inborn) and believed that learning is based on four laws of association: similarity, contrast, contiguity, and frequency. Descartes proposed that involuntary behaviors, which occur in both humans and animals, are automatically elicited by external stimulation, whereas voluntary behaviors, which occur only in humans, are controlled by free will. The British empiricists argued that all knowledge is a function of experience, and they strongly emphasized the laws of association in their study of learning. Structuralists, such as Titchener, assumed that the mind is composed of a finite number of basic elements that can be discovered using the method of introspection. Darwin's theory of evolution established the notion that adaptive characteristics, including the ability to learn, evolve through the process of natural selection. This influenced the functionalists, such as William James, who believed that psychologists should study the adaptive processes of the mind. Functionalism eventually led to the establishment of behaviorism, with its emphasis on the study of publicly observable behavior and the environmental events that influence it.

There are several schools of behaviorism. Watson's methodological behaviorism rejects all references to internal events, such as thoughts and feelings, that cannot be directly observed. Hull's neobehaviorism includes references to hypothetical internal events, usually of a physiological nature (such as fatigue or hunger), that are presumed to mediate between the environment and behavior. Tolman's cognitive behaviorism differs from Hull's approach in that the hypothesized intervening variables are of a mentalistic nature, such as expectations and cognitive maps. This approach eventually led to Bandura's social learning theory, which emphasizes the importance of observational learning as well as the reciprocal interaction of internal events, environment, and behavior. By contrast, Skinner's radical behaviorism views internal events as private behaviors subject to the same laws of learning as publicly observable behaviors. Skinner's perspective is molar rather than molecular and does not discount the influence of genetic factors on learning. The science that has grown out of radical behaviorism is called the experimental analysis of behavior, or simply behavior analysis. This science has in turn led to a technology of behaviorism, known as applied behavior analysis, in which basic principles of learning are applied to solving real-world problems. The chapter ends with a brief biography of Skinner, whom many consider to be the prototypical behaviorist.

SUGGESTED READINGS

Watson, J. B. (1913). Psychology as the behaviorist views it. *Psychological Review*, 20, 154–177. The article that started it all.

Skinner, B. F. (1953). *Science and human behavior*. New York: Macmillan. A book that many regard as the bible of radical behaviorism.

Skinner, B. F. (1974). *About behaviorism*. New York: Knopf. For the average undergraduate, this introduction to radical behaviorism is probably more accessible than *Science and Human Behavior*.

Barash, D. P. (1982). How it works: Evolution as a process. In *Sociobiology and behavior* (2nd ed.). New York: Elsevier Science. A good introduction to evolution and behavior.

Hergenhahn, B. R. (2009). *An introduction to theories of learning* (8th ed.). Englewood Cliffs, NJ: Prentice-Hall. Contains extensive descriptions of the different approaches to learning and behavior, such as those by Hull and Tolman.

Buckley, K. W. (1989). *Mechanical man: John Broadus Watson and the beginnings of behaviorism*. New York: Guilford Press. A well-written biography of John B. Watson and the various controversies that swirled around him.

Bjork, D. W. (1993). *B. F. Skinner: A life*. New York: Basic Books. A very readable biography of Skinner's life.

STUDY QUESTIONS

Because many students tend to ignore long lists of broad study questions (or learning objectives) that attempt to cover all the material in a chapter, the end-of-chapter study questions in this text focus on the most basic information. To determine if you have a grasp of this information, see if you can write out a clear answer to each of these questions. Be aware, however, that obtaining an excellent mark in this course will require more than just a simple reiteration of this basic material.

1. Name and briefly describe the two fundamental forms of learning emphasized in this textbook.
2. Describe the nativist versus empiricist approaches to knowledge. How would a nativist versus an empiricist explain how Picasso became such a great artist?
3. Name and briefly describe the four laws of association.
4. Outline Descartes' dualistic model of human behavior. In his view, what is a basic distinction between the behavior of humans and the behavior of other animals?
5. How did the British empiricists view the acquisition of knowledge and the composition of the conscious mind?
6. Describe the structuralist approach to psychology. Name and define the basic method by which the structuralists gathered data.
7. Describe the functionalist approach to psychology. Where did functionalists stand on the issue of animal experimentation, and what was their reasoning behind this?
8. Describe Darwin's principle of natural selection. What are the three main components of the principle of natural selection?
9. Define the law of parsimony and Morgan's Canon.
10. Describe Watson's methodological behaviorism. How did Watson's position on the nature–nurture debate change over time?
11. Describe Hull's neobehaviorism. How does Tolman's cognitive behaviorism differ from it?
12. Describe Bandura's social learning theory. Outline or diagram his concept of reciprocal determinism.
13. Describe Skinner's radical behaviorism. How does his approach to determinism differ from that of Bandura's?
14. In what way is operant conditioning similar to Darwin's principle of natural selection? Why was Skinner cautious about placing too much emphasis on genetic factors in behavior?
15. What is the distinction between radical behaviorism, behavior analysis, and applied behavior analysis?

CONCEPT REVIEW

applied behavior analysis. A technology of behavior in which basic principles of behavior are applied to solving real-world issues.

behavior. Any activity of an organism that can be observed or somehow measured.

behavior analysis (or experimental analysis of behavior). The behavioral science that grew out of Skinner's philosophy of radical behaviorism.

behaviorism. A natural science approach to psychology that traditionally focuses on the study of environmental influences on observable behavior.

British empiricism. A philosophical school of thought which maintains that almost all knowledge is a function of experience.

cognitive behaviorism. A brand of behaviorism that utilizes intervening variables, usually in the form of hypothesized cognitive processes, to help explain behavior. Sometimes called "purposive behaviorism."

cognitive map. The mental representation of one's spatial surroundings.

countercontrol. The deliberate manipulation of environmental events to alter their impact on our behavior.

empiricism. In psychology, the assumption that behavior patterns are mostly learned rather than inherited. Also known as the *nurture* perspective (or, on rare occasion, as *nurturism*).

evolutionary adaptation. An inherited trait (physical or behavioral) that has been shaped through natural selection.

functionalism. An approach to psychology which proposes that the mind evolved to help us adapt to the world around us, and that the focus of psychology should be the study of those adaptive processes.

introspection. The attempt to accurately describe one's conscious thoughts, emotions, and sensory experiences.

latent learning. Learning that occurs in the absence of any observable indication of learning and only becomes apparent under a different set of conditions.

law of contiguity. A law of association, according to which events that occur in close proximity to each other in time or space are readily associated with each other.

law of contrast. A law of association, according to which events that are opposite from each other are readily associated with each other.

law of frequency. A law of association, according to which the more frequently two items occur together, the more strongly they are associated with each other

law of parsimony. The assumption that simpler explanations for a phenomenon are generally preferable to more complex explanations.

law of similarity. A law of association, according to which events that are similar to each other are readily associated with each other.

learning. A relatively permanent change in behavior that results from some type of experience.

methodological behaviorism. A brand of behaviorism which asserts that, for methodological reasons, psychologists should study only those behaviors that can be directly observed.

mind–body dualism. Descartes' philosophical assumption that some human behaviors are bodily reflexes that are automatically elicited by external stimulation, while other behaviors are freely chosen and controlled by the mind.

nativism. The assumption that a person's characteristics are largely inborn. Also known as the *nature* perspective.

natural selection. The evolutionary principle according to which organisms that are better able to adapt to environmental pressures are more likely to reproduce and pass along those adaptive characteristics than those that cannot adapt.

neobehaviorism. A brand of behaviorism that utilizes intervening variables, in the form of hypothesized physiological processes, to help explain behavior.

radical behaviorism. A brand of behaviorism that emphasizes the influence of the environment on overt behavior, rejects the use of internal events to explain behavior, and views thoughts and feelings as behaviors that themselves need to be explained.

reciprocal determinism. The assumption that environmental events, observable behavior, and "person variables" (including internal thoughts and feelings) reciprocally influence each other.

social learning theory. A brand of behaviorism that strongly emphasizes the importance of observational learning and cognitive variables in explaining human behavior. It has more recently been referred to as "social-cognitive theory."

S-R theory. The theory that learning involves the establishment of a connection between a specific stimulus (S) and a specific response (R).

structuralism. An approach to psychology which assumes that it is possible to determine the structure of the mind by identifying the basic elements that compose it.

CHAPTER TEST

Chapter tests typically contain fewer hints than quick quizzes do—for example, there is usually only a single blank for an answer, even though the answer may require more than a single word. Unlike the quick quizzes, however, an answer key has been provided at the end. Note too that the question numbers have been scrambled (e.g., the first question on this list is number 9). This allows you to look up the answer to a question immediately without having to worry about inadvertently seeing the answer to the next question. Finally, do not worry if you are initially unable to answer some of the items without having to look back through the chapter. Fill-in-the-blank items can be difficult, and this test is designed to be a learning experience more than a form of self-assessment. You may find it difficult to recall some of the information because it is still relatively unfamiliar to you.

9. When Tara saw the lush green lawn, it reminded her of just how dry the lawn had been the previous year. Among the four laws of association, this is best described as an example of the law of _____.

29. Deanna often gets lost when she drives around the city that she lives in. Tolman would say that she has a faulty _____.

17. When Janelle first saw a video of the pop singer Britney Spears, she immediately thought back to an old video she had seen of Paula Abdul, because the two performers seemed to have a common style of performance. Among the four laws of association, this is best described as an example of the law of _____.

 1. Jordan once became terribly ill while visiting Chicago. As a result, whenever he visits Chicago, he thinks of the illness he suffered at that time. Among the four laws of association, this is best described as an example of the law of _____.

10. After struggling unsuccessfully to completely eliminate his test anxiety, Andres finally accepts that there are some aspects of himself that he can control and some that he cannot. This conclusion is similar to that of the French philosopher _____ and his theory of _____ dualism.

12. In trying to understand her feelings for Juan, Alisha pays close attention to the sensations she feels each time she sees him. This is an example of the method of _____. This was a favorite method of research by psychologists who adhered to the approach known as _____.

27. Hull's theory is a (molar/molecular) _____ type of theory, whereas Tolman's theory is a _____ type.

 7. When Anastasia once visited Vancouver, it rained *every day for a month*. As a result, whenever she is trapped in a rainstorm, it reminds her of her trip to Vancouver. Among the four laws of association, this is best described as an example of the law of _____.

20. The law of _____ is the proposition that simpler explanations are usually preferable explanations.

15. "My cat never gets lost. It's like she has a blueprint in her mind of the exact layout of the entire town." This statement fits best with (name the behaviorist) _____'s brand of behaviorism, known as _____.

11. "Babies know nothing," Kristie pronounced when her sister commented on how intelligent her new baby seemed to be. Kristie obviously believes that the mind of a newborn is a _____ slate (or, in Latin, _____), a notion that was promoted by a group of philosophers known as the _____.

31. Although Roberta just sits there throughout the lecture, she can afterward repeat everything the professor said. This is an example of _____ learning, which illustrates the distinction between learning and _____.

16. Ava tells her friend Trish that she believes that her husband kept yawning during their anniversary dinner because he was subconsciously trying to punish her for having become pregnant. Trish tells Ava to quit being paranoid and that he was probably just tired.

Conway Lloyd Morgan would have leaned toward accepting (Ava/Trish) _____'s explanation as more likely correct.

25. Recall the opening vignette to the chapter where, after making love, one behaviorist comments, "That was fine for you, how was it for me?" This joke is most descriptive of which school of behaviorism? _____.

23. Shira emphasizes environmental explanations for behavior and believes that thoughts and feelings should be regarded as private behaviors that also need to be explained. As such, she is most likely a _____ behaviorist. To the extent that Shira also conducts research into basic principles of behavior, she can be called a(n) _____. To the extent that she applies such principles to developing better methods for coaching basketball, she can be called a(n) _____.

2. Aristotle was a(n) (nativist/empiricist) _____, whereas Plato was a(n) _____.

32. Learning is a relatively _____ change in behavior that results from some type of _____.

22. When I haven't eaten for several hours, I feel a strong sense of hunger and therefore walk quickly as I head to the cafeteria. This statement fits best with (name the behaviorist) _____'s brand of behaviorism, known as _____.

5. Neal was recently stung by a wasp and is now quite fearful of wasps. This is best seen as an example of _____ conditioning.

30. John's therapist tells him that, although she cares about what he feels, she is more interested in what he did and in the circumstances that affected both his behavior and his feelings. This therapist's approach fits best with _____'s brand of behaviorism, known as _____.

19. Descartes believed that the behavior of (animals/humans/both) _____ is entirely reflexive.

14. Mandy found a five-dollar bill when she took out the trash one day. As a result, she now often volunteers to take out the trash. This is an example of _____ conditioning.

26. A middleman in a business transaction is analogous to what Tolman and Hull referred to as a(n) _____ variable.

33. As originally defined by Watson, behaviorism is a _____ approach to psychology that emphasizes the study of _____ influences on _____ behavior.

3. After Jasmine saw her sister talk back to the sassy kid next door, she herself did likewise. This is an example of _____ learning.

36. Learning how to swing a bat by watching others is an example of (observable/ observational) _____ learning. Actually swinging the bat is an example of (observable/observational) _____ behavior.

18. Ally's therapist tells her that he doesn't care what she thinks and feels; he is concerned only about what she did and about the circumstances that affected her behavior. This therapist's approach fits best with (name the behaviorist) _____'s brand of behaviorism, known as _____.

8. In considering the process of dreaming, a researcher who followed the approach to psychology known as _____ would have been most concerned with understanding how dreaming facilitates our ability to adapt to the world around us.

35. Lynne persists in teaching her daughter music despite the insistence of her husband that the child "was born tone deaf." Which of these two has an attitude most similar to that of a behaviorist? _____.

24. Sal claims that the neglect he suffered as a child resulted in low self-esteem, which in turn resulted in his long history of criminal activity. His parole officer tells him that such an explanation is too simplistic, that it ignores the complex manner in which the various facets of life interact with each other, and that Sal needs to acknowledge that his own attitude played a role in creating his difficulties. Among the theorists in this chapter, the one who would most appreciate this statement is _____, because it agrees with his concept of _____ determinism.

4. "Great musicians are born, not made" is an example of the (nativist/empiricist) _____ perspective on behavior, and "practice makes perfect" is an example of the _____ perspective.

28. (Hull/Watson/both) _____ assumed that behavior consists of a long chain of specific stimulus-response connections. This approach is known as a(n) _____ theory of behavior.

13. William James was a (structuralist/functionalist) _____, and Titchener was a _____.

6. The defining characteristic of behaviorism, as originally proposed by Watson, is the emphasis on _____ behavior.

21. Removing the television set from your room so you won't be distracted while studying each evening is an example of what Skinner called _____.

34. Skinner's approach to the study of behavior is a (molar/molecular) _____ approach. In this sense, Skinner is quite similar to (Watson/Tolman/Hull) _____.

Visit the book companion Web site at http://www.academic.cengage.com/ psychology/powell for additional practice questions, answers to the Quick Quizzes, practice review exams, and additional exercises and information.

ANSWERS TO CHAPTER TEST

1. contiguity
2. empiricist; nativist
3. observational
4. nativist (or nature); empiricist (or nurture)
5. classical
6. observable
7. frequency
8. functionalism ("evolutionary psychology" would also be correct)
9. contrast
10. Descartes; mind–body
11. blank; *tabula rasa*; British empiricists
12. introspection; structuralism
13. functionalist; structuralist
14. operant
15. Tolman's; cognitive (or purposive) behaviorism
16. Trish's
17. similarity
18. Watson's; methodological behaviorism
19. animals
20. parsimony
21. countercontrol
22. Hull's; neobehaviorism
23. radical; behavior analyst; applied behavior analyst
24. Bandura; reciprocal
25. methodological behaviorism
26. intervening variable
27. molecular; molar
28. both; S-R
29. cognitive map
30. Skinner's; radical behaviorism
31. latent; performance
32. permanent; experience
33. natural science; environmental; observable
34. molar; Tolman
35. Lynne
36. observational; observable

Research Methods

CHAPTER OUTLINE

Based on an actual conversation that took place between a "relationship expert" and a caller on a radio call-in show:

"Hi Dr. Kramer. I need some advice. I'm wondering if I should get married or break off my engagement and finish university first."

"How old are you?"

"Twenty-one."

"Break off your engagement. Statistically, your marriage has a much better chance of surviving if you don't get married until your late 20s."

"Oh, okay."

This chapter introduces you to the basic methods of behavioral research. Once a researcher has developed a hypothesis or has decided on a specific area of interest, such as the effect of reward size on speed of learning, he or she will employ a research method to obtain some behavioral data. Some of the methods for obtaining data include naturalistic observation, case studies, control group designs, and single-subject designs.

The methods used in behavioral research are in many ways similar to those used in other fields of psychology. For example, much behavioral research involves comparisons between "experimental" groups that receive some kind of manipulation (or treatment) and "control" groups that do not receive that manipulation. In some cases, however, the methods are quite distinctive. For example, behavior analysts (as discussed in Chapter 1, these are behaviorists who adhere to Skinner's philosophy of radical behaviorism) have a strong preference for conducting experiments that require only one or, at most, a few subjects. These types of experimental designs, known as *single-subject designs (or single-case)*, have several advantages (as well as disadvantages), which we discuss later in the chapter. Let's begin, however, with an overview of some basic terms and definitions.

Basic Terms and Definitions

Independent and Dependent Variables

All scientific research involves the manipulation and/or measurement of certain variables. A *variable* is a characteristic of a person, place, or thing that can change (vary) over time or from one situation to another. Temperature is an example of a variable; temperature varies from day to day, season to season, and place to place. Height and weight are also examples of variables—people come in many different sizes and shapes. Until a person reaches maturity, his or her height will change over a period of time. Weight is even less consistent and can fluctuate endlessly, often in directions we do not particularly like.

A characteristic that can change

Almost anything can be considered a variable. Consider the following singles ad:

Brown-haired, S, M, 25, seeks S, F, aged 20–26, for fun and friendship.

The *S* in this ad stands for "single," which is one category of the variable *marital status*, which can range from single, to common-law married, to married, to divorced, and even to widowed. The *M* stands for "male," which is part of the dichotomous (meaning "two categories") variable *gender* (i.e., male and female). *Age*, *hair color*, and preference for *fun and friendship* are examples of other variables represented in this ad.

Two types of variables are particularly important in setting up an experiment. The ***independent variable*** is the aspect of an experiment that systematically varies across the different conditions in the experiment. In other words, the independent variable is what is *manipulated* in an experiment. For example, we may be interested in whether the size of a reward (or "reinforcer") can affect the efficiency of learning. To test this notion, we might conduct a maze learning experiment with rats. Each rat is given 10 trials in which it is placed in a maze and allowed to find its way to the goal box. Depending on the "experimental condition" to which the rat has been randomly assigned, it receives one, two, or three pellets of food each time it reaches the goal box. Thus, the independent variable in this experiment is the number of food pellets the rats in each group receive when they reach the goal box.

[margin note: What is manipulated (environment)]

The ***dependent variable*** is the aspect of an experiment that is allowed to vary freely to see if it is affected by changes in the independent variable. In other words, the dependent variable is what is measured in an experiment. In a psychology experiment, this is always some type of behavior. Changes in the dependent variable are *dependent upon* changes in the independent variable (which is a useful phrase to remember to help you distinguish between the dependent and independent variables in an experiment). In the rat experiment, the dependent variable could be the total number of errors (i.e., number of wrong turns) the rat makes while trying to find its way to the goal box. Alternatively, we might simply look at the speed with which the rat reaches the goal box. Either way, a significant difference between groups on this measure will indicate whether the number of food pellets found in the goal box affects the rat's efficiency in learning the maze. In turn, this will provide supportive evidence for our more general notion—which is what we are really interested in—that the size of a reinforcer affects the efficiency of learning.

[margin note: Freely open to manipulation (behavior)]

Functional Relationships

In behavioral research, the dependent variable is almost always some behavior, and the independent variable is some environmental event that is presumed to influence the behavior. The relationship between changes in an independent variable and changes in a dependent variable is known as a

Change in one
Variable Causes
Change in the
other.

functional relationship. Thus, behaviorists are typically interested in discovering functional relationships between environmental events and behavior. A functional relationship can also be thought of as a cause-and-effect relationship, with changes in the independent variable being the cause and changes in the dependent variable being the effect.

QUICK QUIZ A

1. A researcher is interested in studying the effects of viewing television violence on aggression in children. She shows one group of participants an extremely violent movie, another group a moderately violent movie, and a third group a nonviolent movie. In this case, the level of movie violence shown to the children would be considered the _dependent_ variable, and the children's subsequent level of aggressive behavior would be the _independent_ variable.

2. A change in the dependent variable is considered to be the (cause/effect) _effect_ in an experiment, whereas a change in the independent variable is considered to be the _cause_.

3. A _functional_ relationship is the relationship between a change in an independent variable and an associated change in a dependent variable. Behaviorists are typically concerned with discovering the relationship between changes in _environmental_ events and changes in b_ehavior_.

Stimulus and Response

Stimulus → cause

Response → action

Two terms commonly encountered in behavioral textbooks are *stimulus* and *response*. A **stimulus** is any event that can potentially influence behavior, whereas a **response** is a particular instance of a behavior. For example, food is a stimulus that elicits the response of salivation when presented to a hungry dog. Similarly, loud music (a stimulus) might cause your neighbor to bang on the wall (a response), and a high mark on a test (a stimulus) might cause you to grin with delight (a response).

The plural for the word *stimulus* is *stimuli*. Thus, a red light is a stimulus, and a red light and a green light are stimuli. A stimulus is sometimes also

Stimulus
Signal

referred to as a *cue* in that it serves as a signal for the occurrence of a certain behavior, such as when a red traffic light serves as a cue for stopping and a green traffic light serves as a cue for proceeding.

Note that the response of one organism can act as a stimulus that influences the response of another organism. For example, when one rat bites another, the bite is a stimulus that might elicit a retaliatory response from the other rat. In turn, this retaliatory response might then act as a stimulus that induces the first rat to retreat. Likewise, a smile from Shane is a stimulus that encourages Nav to say hello; Nav's hello is in turn a stimulus that encourages Shane to introduce himself. Thus, social interactions generally consist of a chain of alternating responses, with each response acting as a stimulus for the next response from the other person.

Overt and Covert Behavior

It is also important to distinguish between overt and covert behavior. ==*Overt*== *Diactly* ==*behavior*== is behavior that has the potential for being directly observed by an *observable* individual other than the one performing the behavior. In other words, it is behavior that could be publicly observed if others were present. A person's response of saying hello and a rat's response of pressing a lever are both instances of overt behavior. As noted in Chapter 1, behaviorists traditionally have emphasized the study of overt behavior.

Skinner, however, maintained that internal events such as thoughts, feelings, and even sensory experiences (e.g., seeing and hearing) should also be classified as behaviors. Skinner referred to such behaviors as "private behaviors" or "private events," although they are more commonly referred to as covert behaviors (or covert events). Thus, ==*covert behavior*== is behavior that *Subjectively* can be perceived only by the person performing the behavior. In other words, *Percieved* it is behavior that is *subjectively* perceived and is not publicly observable. Dreaming, thinking about your next chess move, visualizing how your date will go on the weekend, and feeling anxious are all examples of covert behavior. Of course, some covert behaviors have components that could be made publicly observable. A feeling of anxiety, for example, is likely to involve increases in heart rate and muscle tension, both of which could be electronically measured. If such measurements are made, then those particular components of anxiety can be considered overt—which from a traditional behavioral perspective is much preferred over a purely subjective report of anxiety.

Just as the behavior of one person can serve as a stimulus for the behavior of another, covert and overt behaviors within the same person can act as stimuli for each other. For example, thinking about one's next move in chess (a covert behavior) is a stimulus that influences which chess piece you actually move (an overt behavior), while accidentally moving the wrong chess piece (an overt behavior) is a stimulus that induces you to think unpleasant thoughts about yourself (a covert behavior). As behavior analysts put it, the environment does not stop with the skin: events both outside the skin and inside the skin can influence our behavior—though behavior analysts maintain that the ultimate cause of the behavior is often to be found outside the skin. (For example, what might a behavior analyst consider to be the ultimate cause of a person thinking about a certain chess move and then making that move?)

Appetitive and Aversive Stimuli

Something Many stimuli, both internal and external, can be classified as appetitive or *worth* aversive. An ==*appetitive stimulus*== is an event that an organism will seek out. *going for* Food is an appetitive stimulus when we are hungry; water is an appetitive stimulus when we are thirsty. An ==*aversive stimulus*== is an event that an organ- *Something to* ism will avoid. Electric shock and extreme heat are examples of aversive *avoid* stimuli. (Note that the word ***is*** *aversive* and not *adversive*.)

Calvin and Hobbes

by Bill Watterson

Appetitive and aversive stimuli might also be defined as those events that people usually describe as pleasant or unpleasant. Such descriptions are often quite accurate, but one has to be careful not to rely on them too much. As the *Calvin and Hobbes* cartoon illustrates, people can vary widely in the types of events they regard as appetitive versus aversive—a point that many parents overlook when they attempt to reinforce or punish a child's behavior. As well, a person may claim that a certain experience is unpleasant, yet work actively to obtain it. For example, someone might describe her pack-a-day smoking habit as "disgusting," yet move heaven and earth to make it to the store in time to buy another pack. Despite what she says, tobacco is clearly an appetitive stimulus for her. The moral of the story is that talk is cheap— or, as behavior analysts sometimes put it, "just verbal behavior." It may or may not accurately reflect the nonverbal behavior it presumably describes.

1. A(n) _stimulus_ is any event that can potentially influence behavior; a(n) _response_ is a specific instance of behavior.

2. A tone is a _stimulus_ and a tone and a bell are _stimuli_ .

3. One person's response can be another person's _stimulus_.

4. Julie dislikes Jake, one of the sales personnel who works in her department. Because Julie avoids Jake like the plague, Jake can be considered an _aversive_ stimulus. For example, Julie closes her office door when Jake is nearby, which is an example of a(n) (overt/covert) _Overt_ behavior.

5. Julie also thinks unkind thoughts about Jake and feels anxious when she sees him in the hallway, both of which are examples of _Covert_ behavior.

6. Jake is strongly attracted to Julie and often hangs around her office just to get a glimpse of her. Julie is thus an _appetitive_ stimulus for Jake.

7. If we think before we act, then our (covert/overt) _Covert_ behavior serves as a stimulus that influences our (covert/overt) _Overt_ behavior. If we act first and then feel regret later, then our _Overt_ behavior serves as a stimulus that influences our _Covert_ behavior.

Establishing Operations: Deprivation and Satiation

You may have noticed in some of the preceding examples that the appetitiveness or aversiveness of an event depends on a particular state or condition. For example, food is an appetitive stimulus to a hungry rat but might not be an appetitive stimulus to a rat that has just eaten. A procedure that affects the appetitiveness or aversiveness of a stimulus is called an *establishing operation* (Michael, 1982). Deprivation and satiation are two types of establishing operations. *Deprivation* is the prolonged absence of an event, which often increases the appetitiveness of that event. If the event is being used as a reinforcer (reward) for some behavior—such as food being used as a reinforcer for lever pressing—then we could also define deprivation as a procedure that increases the reinforcing value of an event. Going without food for a long period of time obviously increases the appetitiveness of food, thereby increasing its ability to serve as a reinforcer for some behavior. Less obviously, deprivation of many other events might also increase their appetitiveness. If you have ever gone without television for a while (as did the first author, when he was a poor, starving graduate student), you may have found it quite interesting when you finally had an opportunity to watch it again. Likewise, lack of social contact for several days (i.e., social deprivation) will usually result in a strong desire for social contact.

[margin note: Absence of events]

In contrast to deprivation, *satiation* refers to the prolonged exposure to (or consumption of) an event, which often decreases the appetitiveness of that event. Food is much less effective as a reinforcer for lever pressing if a rat has just eaten a large meal and is thus "satiated" on food. Similarly, if you hear a favorite piece of music too often, you may grow tired of hearing it. In fact, you might even become "sick of it" and avoid it, meaning the song has become aversive.[1]

[margin note: Consumed by an event]

Although the general rule is that deprivation increases the appetitiveness of an event while satiation decreases its appetitiveness, exceptions can occur. For example, people (and rats, as you will discover in a later chapter) who undertake severe diets sometimes acquire a disorder known as anorexia nervosa. In these cases, severe food deprivation seems to decrease the appetitive value of food rather than increase it, and these individuals begin to eat even less food than the diet allows. People (and rats) who become anorexic also engage in extremely high levels of activity yet seem to find the activity more, not less, reinforcing—that is, they do not seem to "satiate" on the activity. These processes are discussed more fully in Chapter 11.

Contiguity and Contingency

Two terms that are often confused are *contiguity* and *contingency*. Although they sound similar, they actually refer to very different conditions. *Contiguity*, as mentioned in the opening chapter, means "closeness or nearness." Thus,

---

[1]If you are uncertain how to pronounce *satiation*, or any other word in this text, audio examples of pronunciation can often be found on the Internet, such as at the Merriam-Webster site: http://www.merriam-webster.com/help/audiofaq.htm.

temporal contiguity is the extent to which events occur close together in time. Thunder and lightning are temporally contiguous—we see the lightning and shortly afterwards hear the thunder. Temporal contiguity is an important aspect of learning. A rat will more readily learn to press a lever for food if the food immediately follows the lever press than if it appears several seconds later. Likewise, a child will more readily learn to throw a tantrum for candy if he is immediately given candy each time he throws a tantrum.

Spatial contiguity is the extent to which events are situated close to each other in space. This type of contiguity also affects learning (though perhaps not as strongly as temporal contiguity). It is easier for a rat to learn to press a lever for food if the food dispenser is close to the lever as opposed to being several feet away. Likewise, it may take a young child (or a young puppy) some-what longer to learn that a doorbell, as opposed to a knock, indicates that some-one is at the front door. The sound of the knock is spatially contiguous with the door (the sound comes from the door), whereas the sound of the doorbell is not (the sound usually comes from a box located elsewhere in the house).

The term *contingency* has a quite different meaning from contiguity. A *contingency* is a predictive (or functional) relationship between two events, such that the occurrence of one event predicts the probable occurrence of another. If a rat receives a food pellet whenever it presses a lever, then a contingency exists between lever pressing and food. We then say that the presentation of food is contingent on lever pressing. Likewise, if a child receives a big balloon every time she goes to the dentist, then a contingency exists between visiting the dentist and receiving the balloon. In other words, receiving the balloon is contingent upon visiting the dentist. As you will see later, contingency is an extremely important aspect of learning.

QUICK QUIZ C

1. An establishing operation is a procedure that affects the appetitiveness or aversiveness of a stimulus.

2. Farah has been working out of town and has not seen a movie for over a year. It is likely that the reward value of going to a movie has (increased/decreased) increases as a function of (satiation/deprivation) deprivation

3. The term contiguity means "closeness or nearness."

4. Erin says that she once experienced a strong pain in her leg at the precise moment that her son, who was away on a mountain-climbing expedition, broke his leg. Because of the temporal contiguity between her feeling of pain and her son's injury, Erin now claims that she has some type of psychic ability.

5. People who live close to each other are more likely to date and fall in love. Thus, spatial contiguity seems to have a strong effect on the development of romantic relationships.

6. Sasha obtains a high mark on her exams only when she studies diligently. For Sasha, there is a contingency between studying diligently and doing well on her exams.

7. If a dog receives a dog biscuit only when it begs, then receiving the dog biscuit is contiguity upon the behavior of begging.

Measurement of Behavior

Behavioral Definitions

When we study the effects of certain variables on a behavior, it is important that we properly define the behavior. Such behavioral definitions should be *objective* in the sense that they refer to some observable aspect of the individual's behavior. For example, yelling and striking are observable aspects of aggressive behavior, but feelings of anger are not. Therefore, defining aggression in terms of the physical characteristics of yelling and striking is more precise than defining it as feelings of anger.

Behavioral definitions should also be clearly defined, that is, *unambiguous*. For example, we might define yelling as a loud vocalization that continues for more than 5 seconds and can be heard outside a closed door. Striking might be defined as a rapid arm or leg movement that results in physical contact. From a scientific perspective, an unambiguous definition will ensure that our measurements of the behavior are relatively consistent over time and across settings. What counts as an aggressive incident today will also count as an aggressive incident tomorrow. Further, if we are investigating various treatments to reduce the number of aggressive incidents (e.g., by rewarding the child for acting nonaggressively), we can be more certain that any observed change in the aggressive behavior is the result of our treatment as opposed to an unconscious shift in our definition of aggression. Finally, an unambiguous behavioral definition will make it easier for other researchers to replicate our results.

Clear definitions of behavior are also beneficial outside the research setting, particularly in tasks such as child-rearing (the ultimate challenge in behavior management). A major problem faced by many children is that parents often shift their standards as to what constitutes appropriate behavior. For example, a parent might constantly tell a child that eating in the living room is wrong, but then allow eating in the living room when visitors arrive or when the family is watching a movie. A clearer definition of what behaviors are appropriate versus inappropriate would be far less confusing to the child and would reduce the probability of the child violating the rules. One highly effective parent we know of uses a "three-warning" rule for situations that require compliance. For example, if one of the children is asked to get ready to go swimming with her aunt, she must comply by the third warning or else suffer a negative consequence (e.g., she will not be allowed to go swimming that day). Because the rule is so well defined and allows the child a certain amount of time "to get mobilized," negative consequences rarely have to be imposed. And even when the child does not comply and does suffer the consequences, she rarely makes a fuss about it because she was well aware of the contingencies from the outset. (This does not mean that the children in this family are rigidly controlled. In fact, one's first impression upon entering the household is that it is quite chaotic, with children running everywhere, laughing and playing. Within clearly defined limits, the children are allowed a great deal of freedom, which they very much appreciate.)

Recording Methods

Depending on how we define a behavior, there are several ways in which we can go about measuring it. Let's look at a few of these methods.

Rate of Response   One of the most popular measures in behavioral research is *rate of response*, which is the frequency with which a response occurs in a certain period of time. Rate measurements are most appropriate when the response is of brief duration, with a well-defined start and finish (i.e., onset and offset). The number of cigarettes smoked per day, the number of words written in a 1-hour writing session, and the number of body stomps in a half-hour broadcast of professional wrestling are all rate measures of behavior. (When defining or giving examples of rate, be sure to include the time aspect. For example, *number of lever presses per hour* is a rate measure of behavior, but *number of lever presses* alone is not.)

[handwritten: Frequency within a specific time period.]

Certain experimental procedures have been explicitly designed to facilitate measuring behavior in terms of rate. For example, operant conditioning experiments often involve rats pressing levers to earn food. The lever press is a very definable response because once the lever is pressed sufficiently for the microswitch to be activated, a response is electronically recorded. Number of lever presses per session thus provides a precise measure of the rat's food-directed behavior. Rate is a particularly favored measure among some behaviorists (especially radical behaviorists), because it tends to be highly sensitive to the influence of other variables. For example, the rate at which a rat presses a lever for food will vary closely with the number of hours of food deprivation, the type of food being delivered (preferred or non-preferred), and the amount of effort required to press the lever. Likewise, the rate at which you can say aloud the definitions of the concepts in this text (e.g., the number of terms you are able to define per minute while sorting through your flash cards) may be a good indicator of the extent to which you are now fluent enough with the concept to begin applying it to different situations. In fact, such fluency measures of learning are a basic aspect of a behavioral approach to instruction known as *precision learning* (e.g., Lindsley, 1991; Binder, 1996).

A *cumulative recorder* is a classic device that measures the total number of responses over time and provides a graphic depiction of the rate of behavior. This instrument consists of a roll of paper that unravels at a slow, constant pace and a movable pen that makes tracks across it (see Figure 2.1). If there are no responses for a period of time, the pen remains stationary while the paper unrolls beneath it. This results in a flat, horizontal line along the paper, with longer lines indicating longer periods of no responding. When a response occurs (e.g., the rat presses the lever), electronic equipment registers the response and produces a slight upward movement of the pen. Thus, a low rate of response produces a line that slopes upward at a shallow angle (because the pen is slowly moving upward while the paper passes beneath it), whereas a high rate of response produces a line that slopes

FIGURE 2.1 Illustration of a cumulative recorder. This device consists of a roll of paper that unravels at a slow, constant pace. If no response is made, the pen remains stationary, resulting in a horizontal line. A high rate of response produces a steep line, and a low rate of response produces a shallow line. The short diagonal slashes indicate the points at which reinforcers were delivered, for example, food pellets delivered to a rat for making a certain number of lever presses. (*Source:* Malone, 1990.)

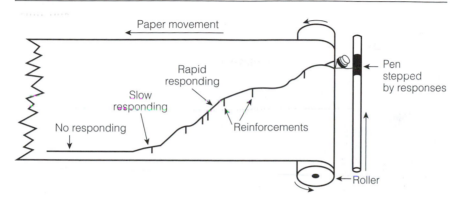

upward at a steep angle. *The important thing to remember is that the steeper the line, the higher the rate of response.* A cumulative record thereby provides an easily read, graphic depiction of changes in the organism's rate of response over time. (Needless to say, these days, response rates are more often recorded by computer software programs. This allows for the generation of various types of descriptive records, including cumulative records, and facilitates various complex analyses of the data.)

Intensity Responding can also be measured in terms of intensity. The ~~force or magnitude~~ *intensity* of a behavior is the force or magnitude of the behavior. For exam- ~~of the behavior~~ ple, in Pavlov's classical conditioning procedure with dogs, a tone was asso- ciated with food, such that the tone itself eventually came to elicit salivation.

 Tone: Food → *Salivation*
 Tone → *Salivation*

The strength of conditioning was typically measured as the amount (magni- tude) of saliva produced whenever the tone was sounded by itself. More saliva indicated stronger conditioning. Another intensity measure of behavior is the force with which a rat presses a lever to obtain food. Likewise, it is intensity that we are concerned with when we teach a child to speak softly and to print firmly.

Duration *Duration* is the length of time that an individual repeatedly or ~~how long~~ continuously performs a certain behavior. This measure is appropriate ~~behavior took~~ when we are concerned with either increasing or decreasing the length of time the behavior occurs. For example, a student may attempt to increase the amount of time he spends studying each week, as well as decrease the amount of time spent watching television.

Speed Although duration measures are sometimes useful, they are problematic in the sense that they do not indicate certain qualities of the behavior. You may run for an hour, but the speed at which you run (as indicated by the amount of distance you cover during that hour) will be a much more accurate indicator of your fitness level. Thus, *speed* is a measure of how quickly or slowly a behavior occurs, or the rapidity with which one progresses through some type of distance. The length of time it takes for a rat to run through a maze from the start box to the goal box is a measure of speed. (See Figure 2.2 for examples of the different types of mazes that have been used in psychological research.) We are also concerned with speed when we teach a child to eat more quickly (if he tends to dawdle at the dinner table) or more slowly (if he tends to fling food everywhere in a rush to get finished). Studies on activity levels in rats often measure both the duration of running (the amount of time the

How quickly a behavior occurs

FIGURE 2.2 Three types of mazes used in behavioral research. Although the Hampton Court type of maze was often used by researchers in the early 1900s, it was later largely supplanted by the T-maze and the straight-alley "maze," which, because of their simplicity, proved more useful for investigating basic principles of behavior. (*Source:* Lieberman, 2000.)

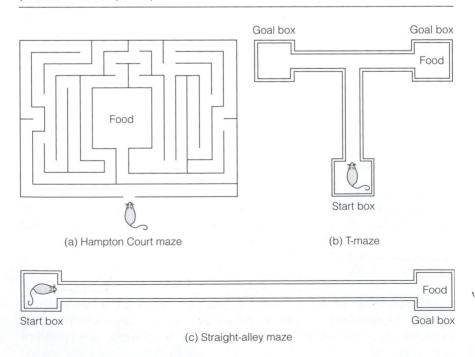

(a) Hampton Court maze

(b) T-maze

(c) Straight-alley maze

*the quicker you engage in something
the faster you'll learn something

rats spend in a running wheel) as well as the speed of running (the amount of distance covered during that time). (Note, however, that we could also use a rate measure for wheel running, that is, the number of wheel turns per minute.)

Latency   The *latency* of a behavior is the length of time required for the behavior to begin. With respect to classical conditioning of salivation, the strength of conditioning can be measured not only in terms of the amount of saliva, but in terms of how soon the dog begins salivating after it hears the tone. Likewise, the amount of time it takes for a student to sit down and begin studying following her evening meal might be a useful measure of the extent to which she finds studying aversive (unpleasant). TV game shows that require contestants to press buzzers when they believe they have the right answer are using a latency measure of the contestants' performance.

how long before behavior begins

(time between stimulus + response)

   Latency, speed, and duration are often confused because they all involve some type of time measurement. To help distinguish between them, consider the behavior of an athlete who specializes in the 100-meter sprint. The amount of time it takes for her to commence running when she hears the starting pistol—which is only a fraction of a second—is a measure of latency, whereas the amount of time it takes for her to complete the race is a measure of speed. The amount of time she trains each day is a measure of duration.

Interval Recording   A particularly efficient way of measuring behavior, often utilized in applied settings, is *interval recording*: the measurement of whether or not a behavior occurs during each interval within a series of continuous intervals. For example, if we wish to measure the amount of aggressive behavior in a classroom, we might videotape several hours of class time. We would then have observers view the videotape and record whether or not an aggressive incident occurred within each successive 10-minute interval. The proportion of intervals in which at least one incident occurred would be our overall measure of aggression. For instance, imagine that we videotape 3 hours (180 minutes) of class time. We then have observers view the videotape and record whether at least one aggressive incident occurred within each successive 10-minute interval. Note that we are not concerned with how many aggressive incidents occurred in each interval, only with whether at least one aggressive incident occurred in each interval. The percentage of intervals during which at least one incident occurred is our measure of the behavior. For example, if at least one act of aggression occurred in 12 of the 18 intervals, then 12/18 × 100 = 66.7%.

Does a behavior happen within a time period.

3/6 = 1/2

   A major advantage of interval recording is that one does not have to record every single response, which may be difficult if responses occur at a very high rate or where it may be difficult to count separate responses (e.g., an argument that consists of a rapid exchange of aggressive vocalizations). Interval recording is also useful if it is difficult to determine the point at which the behavior starts and stops. Aggressive incidents are a good example of this in that they sometimes build slowly, and trying to determine the exact moment when the aggression begins may be difficult.

Time–Sample Recording A variant of interval recording is time-sample recording. In *time-sample recording*, one measures whether or not a behavior occurs during each interval within a series of discontinuous intervals (intervals that are spaced apart). For example, to assess the level of aggression in a classroom, we might have an observer unobtrusively enter the classroom for a 10-minute interval at the start of each half-hour and record whether at least one aggressive incident occurred during that interval. The behavior of the students is thus intermittently sampled, and the percentage of these sampled intervals in which an aggressive incident occurred is our overall measure of aggression. Imagine, for example, that over the course of 6 hours we are able to sample 12 ten-minute intervals. If one or more aggressive incidents occurred in nine of those intervals, then the overall level of aggression is calculated as $9/12 \times 100 = 75\%$. Although we will not have observed every act of aggression using such a method, and we may even have missed a few whoppers, we will nevertheless have obtained a fairly good assessment of the amount of aggression in that setting. As well, this method of recording is very time efficient for our observer, who can spend most of the day working on other tasks or making observations in other classrooms. *(To reemphasize, remember that for both interval and time-sample recording, we do not measure the number of responses that occur in each interval, but rather the number of intervals in which at least one response occurs.)*

Topography Sometimes we are concerned with the behavior's *topography*, which is the actual physical form of the behavior. For example, rather than record the rate at which a rat presses a lever, we might observe *how* it presses the lever, such as whether it uses its left paw or right paw. Similarly, it is the topography of the behavior that we are concerned with when we teach a child how to dress appropriately, write neatly, and brush his teeth properly. Training a dolphin (or your pet goldfish) to swim through a hoop to obtain a food reward is yet another example in which the topography of the behavior is the focus of concern.

Number of Errors Any behavior in which responses can be categorized as right or wrong can be assessed in terms of the number of errors. For example, the number of wrong turns a rat takes before it finds its way through a maze to the goal box is one measure of how well the rat has learned the maze. Likewise, the number of errors a student makes on an exam is the traditional method for determining how well the student knows the material.

TABLE 2.1	Recordings of aggressive behavior by two independent observers in each of 12 intervals. A ✓ indicates that at least one aggressive incident was judged to have occurred in that interval. The observers were in disagreement only in intervals 4 and 5, yielding an interobserver reliability measure of 10/12=83.3%.

INTERNAL	1	2	3	4*	5*	6	7	8	9	10	11	12
Observer A	✓		✓		✓	✓		✓	✓		✓	
Observer B	✓		✓	✓		✓		✓	✓		✓	

Assessing Reliability

One thing you may have wondered about in reading some of the preceding examples is the reliability or trustworthiness of the data that we are gathering using these methods. This is a particularly important issue when the data is being gathered by observers who might vary widely in their judgments as to whether or not a particular behavior has occurred. For this reason, whenever possible, researchers attempt to utilize two or more independent observers for at least part of the assessment period, and then calculate the extent to which the observers agree versus disagree on their observations. For example, in an interval recording procedure in which two observers independently record the occurrence of aggression in each of 12 consecutive intervals, they may agree on whether or not an incident occurred in 10 of the intervals and disagree in two of the intervals (see Table 2.1). Our measure of *interobserver reliability* in this case is calculated as the number of intervals during which the observers agree divided by the total number of intervals, that is, 10/12 = 83.3%. There are no hard and fast rules about what constitutes adequate reliability, but 80% is often regarded as the minimum acceptable level and 90% as the preferred level. If reliability is considered to be inadequate, then our behavioral definition may need to be revised or our observers may need further training in identifying aggressive incidents. (For more complete information on assessing reliability, see Kazdin, 2011.)

1. Behavioral definitions should be objective_____ and unambiguous.

2. The force with which a person can squeeze a device that measures grip strength is a measure of intensity____.

3. How quickly a musician plays a musical piece from beginning to end is a measure of _speed____ whereas the number of hours the musician practices each week is a measure of duration____. The amount of time it takes the musician to commence playing following the conductor's cue to begin is a measure of _latency_.

4. The exact manner in which Jana lifts a dumbbell and presses it overhead is called the topography____ of the behavior.

5. The time it takes before a response begins is a measure of <u>latency</u>.

6. The number of fish a person catches in a 1-hour period is a measure of <u>rate of response</u>

7. Recording whether Ashley hiccups during a continuous series of 5-minute time periods is an example of <u>interval</u> recording, whereas recording whether hiccupping occurs during a 5-minute period at the start of each hour throughout the day is an example of <u>time</u> - <u>sampling</u> recording.

8. A device commonly used to measure the ongoing rate of a behavior is a <u>cumlative</u> <u>recorder</u>. On this device, a flat line indicates (no/slow/fast) <u>NO</u> responding, a steep line indicates <u>fast</u> responding, and a shallow line indicates <u>slow</u> responding.

9. Which of the following is an example of a rate measure of writing? (a) number of words written (b) the number of words written per hour.

10. In an interval recording procedure, our two observers agreed on whether Mika was being disruptive in class during 15 of the 20 observed intervals. The level of interobserver reliability in this example is <u>75</u>%, which is generally considered (adequate/inadequate) <u>adequate</u>.

Research Designs

Deciding how to measure a behavior is only part of the problem. We must also determine which method to use to assess the impact of certain variables on that behavior. Several methods are available, and they can be divided into two general types: descriptive methods and experimental methods.

Descriptive Research

Descriptive research involves simply describing the behavior and the situation within which it occurs. Descriptive methods do not involve the manipulation of any variables. Two commonly used descriptive methods are naturalistic observation and case studies.

Naturalistic Observation   *Naturalistic observation* involves the systematic observation and recording of behavior in its natural environment. Note the word *systematic*. We are not talking here about casual observations, which may be strongly biased by the researcher's preconceptions about behavior. Behavioral scientists have as many preconceptions about behavior as the average person does—perhaps even more, because it is their job to study behavior—and are therefore quite susceptible to viewing behavior from a biased perspective. To avoid, or at least minimize, such biases, researchers attempt to define their variables objectively and unambiguously and make their observations in a consistent and uniform manner.

Jane Goodall's systematic study of chimpanzee behavior in the wild is a classic example of naturalistic observation. Through her detailed observations, we now know that chimpanzees eat meat (they sometimes kill and devour monkeys), use primitive tools (they sometimes dip a twig into a termite hill to capture termites for food), and engage in warfare (chimpanzees from one group have been observed stalking, attacking, and killing members of a neighboring group; see Goodall, 1990).

Naturalistic observation is a commonly used approach in ethology, a branch of zoology that focuses on the study of inherited behavior patterns in animals. Such patterns have presumably evolved to help the animal cope with certain aspects of its natural environment. For this reason, inherited behavior patterns are usually best studied within the natural environment (or at least a close approximation to it), because the behavior may not occur when the animal is removed from that environment. Displays of dominance and submission, for example, may not be evident unless an animal is allowed to freely interact with members of its own species. If such displays do occur in other situations, they may be difficult to identify. For example, a dog's gesture of rolling over on its back and displaying its underbelly can be more clearly seen as a submissive gesture when dogs interact with each other than when they interact with us. One of the authors first realized this when he witnessed the family dog being attacked by a much larger dog. Following a brief skirmish, Trixie rolled over on her back and displayed her underside, the same behavior she often displayed toward us. What had always seemed like a simple request for a tummy scratch also functioned as an inborn gesture of subordination.

Although naturalistic observation is ideal for studying inherited behavior patterns, it also contributes to our understanding of learning. A famous example of this is the "cultural adoption" of food-washing behavior among a troop of macaque monkeys off the coast of Japan. When one monkey acquired the habit of washing sand off a sweet potato by dipping it in lake water (the researchers had left the potatoes on a sandy beach to attract the monkeys to that area), other monkeys in the troop soon imitated this behavior. Interestingly, the oldest monkeys in the troop never adopted this "newfangled way" of cleaning food (Kawamura, 1963).

The naturalistic approach is excellent for gaining rich, detailed information about a behavior and the circumstances in which it typically occurs. A major problem with this approach is that it often leaves us uncertain as to which variables are most important in determining the behavior. For example, if you study childhood aggression by observing children interacting on a playground, you may see many displays of aggressive behavior (e.g., grabbing a toy away from another child, pushing, yelling, etc.). However, it will be difficult to determine *why* these behaviors are occurring. As a naturalistic observer, you cannot intervene or ask the participants any questions for clarification. It will also be difficult to know if an aggressive child has a long history of aggression, is experiencing considerable frustration that day, or has had frequent exposure to violence in the home. In a sense, the natural environment is a vast sea of variables, and sorting out which variables are responsible for which behavior can be a daunting task. Thus, the naturalistic observation approach is often insufficient for gaining a full understanding of a behavior and the variables that influence it.

Case Studies Another type of descriptive method is the *case study approach*, which involves the intensive examination of one or a few individuals. Case studies can be done in natural settings (as a form of naturalistic observation), or they may involve detailed examination in a more structured setting such as a clinic. Case studies are especially prevalent in medical research. Individuals who have suffered certain types of neurological damage often provide us with insight into which areas of the brain control which functions. Similarly, examining the lives of highly gifted individuals, such as Albert Einstein and Judit Polgar (the famous young chess player described in Chapter 1), can sometimes yield important information as to how exceptional skills can be acquired.

The case study approach is frequently employed in some areas of clinical psychology, especially with respect to relatively rare disorders—for example, *fugue states*, in which a person suddenly moves away from home and assumes a different identity—for which the few case studies available constitute our only source of information. Some clinical case studies have become quite famous. Consider, for example, the case of Anna O., which was reported by Sigmund Freud and his colleague Joseph Breuer (1895/1955). Anna O. is the pseudonym given to a young woman Breuer treated for symptoms of hysteria—a common psychiatric disorder in the latter part of the nineteenth century. A major characteristic of the disorder was various neurological symptoms, such as limb paralysis, that seemed to have no actual neurological basis, though psychological symptoms, such as "dual" personality and hallucinations, were also common. Breuer and Freud reported that most of Anna O.'s symptoms disappeared when she was encouraged to talk about upsetting events that had occurred to her and that seemed to be related to the onset of her symptoms. This case is generally regarded as the first clear demonstration of the therapeutic effectiveness of *catharsis* (that is, the release of tension that is assumed to automatically result from expressing pent-up thoughts and emotions).

As with naturalistic observations, it is important to ensure that case studies are based on systematic observation and that researcher bias has been reduced to a minimum. Unfortunately, these criteria are sometimes lacking. For example, scholars have recently discovered that the case of Anna O. actually had a far different outcome than that reported by Breuer and Freud. Following her "successful" treatment, Anna O. quickly relapsed and needed to be institutionalized. It was in fact several years before she finally recovered from her hysterical illness, a fact that Breuer and Freud were aware of but never publicly acknowledged. Nevertheless, Breuer and Freud's false report of Anna O.'s recovery helped establish psychoanalysis as the dominant school of psychotherapy in the first half of the twentieth century.[2] (For these and other examples of how Freud may have misled people with his reported case studies—which has evolved into quite a controversy—see Esterson, 1993, and Webster, 1995.)

In addition to the problem of researcher bias, case studies are limited in the extent to which the results can be generalized to other people, places, and times. For example, Anna O.'s case history, even if it had been accurate, may not have been at all representative of how most cases of hysteria at that time could best be treated. Because case studies often involve only one person, we have no way of knowing if the case being described is the norm or the exception. The major limitation, however, for both case studies and other descriptive approaches, is that it is usually difficult to determine which variables are responsible for which behavior. Nevertheless, despite these limitations, the case study method of research, just like the naturalistic observation method, often provides a valuable starting point for further investigations.

1. Two common descriptive methods are n*aturalistic observations* and c*ase studies*.

2. Both approaches are susceptible to the problem of researcher b*ias*, in which the opinions and beliefs of the researcher can unduly influence his or her observations.

3. The major limitation of both approaches is that it is often (easy/difficult) *difficult* to specify which variables influence which behavior.

4. Because the case study approach often involves only one person, the results may be limited in the extent to which they can be *general* to other people, places, and times.

Experimental Research

Although descriptive research methods such as naturalistic observations and case studies often provide detailed information about behavior, they usually do not allow us to draw firm conclusions about the causes of a behavior. If, for example, we observe that children who read a lot tend to have higher marks in school, is it the case that reading leads to higher marks, or do "bright" children simply like to read? To answer this question, it is necessary to conduct an experiment. In general, in their quest to discover cause-and-effect relationships (that is, functional relationships) between

---

[2]By contrast, behavioral methods of therapy are usually subjected to rigorous experimentation before being widely adopted by practitioners (although informative case studies are also published). Thus, it is not surprising that in a 1995 list of "empirically validated therapies"—that is, therapies for which there is good research evidence demonstrating their effectiveness—a large majority of the therapies listed were either behavioral or cognitive-behavioral in orientation (Task Force on Promotion and Dissemination of Psychological Procedures, 1995; see also Wilson, 1997).

QUICK QUIZ E

environmental events and behavior, behavioral researchers have a strong preference for the experimental approach to research.

In an experiment, one or more independent variables are systematically varied to determine their effect on a dependent variable (the behavior you suspect will change as a result of changes in the independent variable). Any differences in behavior across the different conditions of the experiment are presumed to be caused by the differences in the independent variable.

Behavioral researchers use two main types of experimental designs: control group designs and single-subject designs. As will be seen, each type of design has its advantages and disadvantages, and the decision to employ one method or the other largely has to do with the nature of the particular issue being investigated.

Control Group Designs   The most common type of experimental design is the *control group design*. In the simplest form of this design, individuals are randomly assigned to either an experimental (or treatment) group or a control group; individuals assigned to the experimental group are exposed to a certain manipulation or treatment, whereas those assigned to the control group are not. Imagine, for example, that 20 rats are randomly assigned to either an experimental group or a control group. Rats in the experimental group are individually placed in an experimental chamber for 30 minutes, during which time they receive a free food pellet every minute. The rats in the control group are treated exactly the same except they receive no food during the 30-minute session. They are simply allowed to snoop around the chamber. The rats in each group receive one session per day for 10 consecutive days. On day 11, a mechanical lever is placed in each chamber, and the rats must learn to press the lever to obtain food. The question of interest is whether the rats that previously received free food will learn to press the lever more readily or less readily than the rats that did not receive free food. Thus, the *independent variable* in this experiment is the presence versus absence of free food during the initial phase of the experiment, and the *dependent variable* is the average amount of time it takes for the rats in each group to learn to press the lever for food. (By the way, research has shown that animals that receive free food subsequently have more difficulty learning how to respond for food [Welker, 1976; Wheatley, Welker, & Miles, 1977]. This suggests that exposure to free reinforcers can sometimes impair an organism's ability to learn how to respond for reinforcers.)

Control group designs are often considerably more complicated than the simple experiment we have described. For example, we might wonder if the damaging effects of free food on ability to learn are dependent on age. Thus, we might rerun this experiment with groups of old rats, middle-aged rats, and young rats. This approach would yield what is known as a 2×3 *factorial design*, in which there are two independent variables (food and age), the first of which has two levels (free food versus no food) and the second of which has three levels (old age versus middle age versus young age). This experiment would therefore involve a total of six groups (old with free food, old

TABLE 2.2 Six experimental conditions (groups of participants) in a 2 × 3 factorial experiment involving two levels of a "food" variable and three levels of an "age" variable

	YOUNG (Y)	MIDDLE–AGED (M)	OLD (O)
No food (NF)	NFY	NFM	NFO
Free food (FF)	FFY	FFM	FFO

with no food, middle-aged with free food, middle-aged with no food, young with free food, and young with no food; see Table 2.2). If free food affects learning ability only in rats of a certain age, then we say that there is an *interaction* between the effects of free food and age. Such interaction effects give us a much finer understanding of the variables in which we are interested, and a lot of research is designed to search for such effects.

A particular type of control group design, often used in certain types of animal research, is a comparative design. A ***comparative design*** is a type of control group design in which different species constitute one of the independent variables. It is often used to test an evolutionary hypothesis regarding the differences in selective pressures for a particular trait between species. Comparative designs can be simple or factorial, and they can involve more than one independent or dependent variable. The main distinction between comparative designs and standard control group designs (other than the use of more than one species) is that in a comparative design you do not have a pure control group that receives no treatment.

For example, if you hypothesize that rats have evolved to deal with small, enclosed environments better than dogs have (or that dogs have evolved to deal with larger, more open environments better than rats have), you could examine how quickly dogs and rats learn to find a target in an enclosed maze versus a large open area. This is a 2 × 2 factorial design in which there are two independent variables (species and environment), where each independent variable has two levels (rat versus dog; maze versus open area). (Of course, you would not use exactly the same apparatus for a rat that you would for a dog. Rather, you would attempt to equate the equipment for the particular size and other important traits of each species.) You will note, however, that in no condition does a group receive no treatment. Instead, the control comes in the form of providing each group with the same treatments so that the changes in the dependent variable (speed of learning) can be isolated to the changes in the independent variables (species or type of environment, or an interaction between the two).

Control group designs are excellent for assessing the general effects of certain variables. Cause-and-effect statements are possible due to the strict control over the environment that allows the experimenter to rule out alternative explanations. Because all subjects receive identical experiences except for the independent variable that is being manipulated, we can be fairly confident that differences between groups in performance are the result of differences in the independent variable. Random assignment of subjects to each condition also ensures that various characteristics of the subjects in each group are likely to be evenly distributed across the experimental and control conditions. Thus, the two groups will be pretty much alike at the onset of the experiment, and any differences found at the end of the experiment are most likely due to our manipulation of the independent variable.

Control group designs, however, are not without their drawbacks. To begin with, this type of design usually requires a large number of subjects (often 10 or more per group). In fact, for statistical reasons, the larger the number of subjects in a group, the more trustworthy the results. But what if you wished to conduct research on the effectiveness of a behavioral treatment for one individual? It would be impractical to conduct an experiment with a large number of subjects just to determine if a certain treatment might be effective for one person. Control group designs are therefore not well suited for investigating the effect of a certain treatment on a particular individual.

A second difficulty with control group designs is that they typically focus on the *average* performance of all subjects in each group. Little attention is given to the performance of individual subjects, even if some subjects differ markedly from the average. For example, going back to our rat study, suppose that 2 out of the 10 rats previously given free food learned to press the lever almost immediately, while the others took much longer. Even if, on average, the rats in this free-food group learned more slowly than the rats in the no-food group, what about the two quick learners? Should we regard them as mere aberrations ("I guess some rats are just brighter than others"), or is it the case that exposure to free food actually facilitates subsequent learning in some individuals? Using similar reasoning, one behavior analyst (himself a victim of brain cancer) has questioned the heavy reliance on large-scale clinical trials to determine the efficacy of new drugs in treating cancer, his argument being that a drug that appears ineffective for the average patient might nevertheless be effective for a subset of patients (Williams, 2010). By ignoring individual data, we might never consider such a possibility. In other words, group data is combined to produce a statistical average, but the scores of some individuals within the group may deviate markedly from this average; therefore, average results may have little relevance to certain individuals. (Question: What implication does this have for the value of the advice given during the radio call-in show in the vignette presented at the start of this chapter?)

A third limitation of control group designs is that the results are often analyzed and interpreted only at the end of the experiment, rather than during the experiment. In some situations, this may be undesirable. If, for example, we are treating a child for self-injurious behavior, we need to be aware throughout whether our treatment is having a positive effect. If the effect is positive, we can maintain the treatment; if the effect is negative, we should immediately halt our treatment and try something different. By contrast, control group designs that measure effects only at the end of the study usually do not provide us with this type of flexibility.

Finally, a weakness *specific* to the comparative type of control group design is that species can differ in more ways than just their learning capacity or style. This limits the type of study that can be conducted, or the species that can be compared. For example, if we were comparing cats and hedgehogs for escape learning, we might find that cats learn to escape relatively quickly when they see a cue related to the onset of electric shock, whereas hedgehogs tend not to run away from this potentially dangerous situation. Is this because hedgehogs cannot learn? No. It is more likely that hedgehogs employ a different defensive behavior when threatened (rolling into a ball and freezing) than do cats, so the choice of dependent variable (running to escape) in this situation is not appropriate for the species in question.

In conclusion, control group designs are excellent for assessing general relationships between independent and dependent variables. There are drawbacks, however; these designs are inefficient when we are interested in relating the findings to a particular individual, when the focus on average effects results in the neglect of unusual effects displayed by certain individuals, and when there is a need to monitor the individual's progress throughout the study. Alternative designs that do not suffer from these limitations—but have their own—are called single-subject designs.

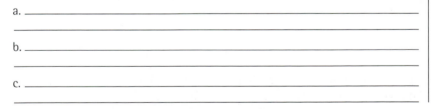

1. In an experiment, a(n) independent variable is systematically varied (manipulated) to determine its effects on the dependent variable.

2. In the simplest form of a control group design, individuals are randomly assigned to either an experimental (or treatment) group and a control group.

3. Control group designs that are used to assess behavioral differences between species are referred to as comparitive designs.

4. Briefly stated, three problems with control group designs are:

a. _____

_____

b. _____

_____

c. _____

_____

QUICK QUIZ F

Single-Subject Designs Unlike control group designs, ***single-subject designs*** require only one or a few subjects to conduct an entire experiment. Also known as *single-case* or *small n* designs, there are several types of such designs, four of which are described here.

Simple-Comparison (AB) Design In a ***simple-comparison design***, behavior in a baseline condition is compared to behavior in a treatment condition. Suppose, for example, that Cory wishes to cut down on smoking (as a first step toward quitting) and wonders if he might be able to do so by punishing himself. In a *self-punishment* procedure, people apply an aversive consequence to themselves each time they engage in an unwanted target behavior. Self-punishment of smoking might consist of Cory giving his buddy 25 cents for each cigarette he smokes. (Another way of looking at this is that Cory has implemented a fine or tax on himself to try to reduce the amount he smokes.)

The first step in the program would be for Cory to take a baseline measure of the number of cigarettes he typically smokes each day. The **baseline** of a behavior is the normal frequency of the behavior that occurs before some intervention. Cory could, for example, keep an index card tucked inside the flap of his cigarette pack and make a check mark on it for each cigarette he smokes prior to his self-punishment program.

The baseline period should last several days to provide a good assessment of the typical frequency of Cory's smoking. If it appears that there is a gradual upward or downward trend in the amount smoked during baseline (sometimes the mere act of closely monitoring a behavior can result in some improvement, a process known as *reactivity*), Cory should continue the baseline period until the behavior stabilizes. Following the baseline, he should then institute the self-punishment procedure for several days. If the treatment is effective, the frequency of smoking during the treatment period should be consistently lower than it was during the baseline period (see Figure 2.3).

In this type of study, the baseline period is often called the A phase, and the treatment period is called the B phase. Thus, this design is sometimes

FIGURE 2.3 Simple-comparison (AB) design. Hypothetical results using a simple-comparison design to assess the effectiveness of a treatment (self-punishment) on number of cigarettes smoked. The dashed vertical line divides the baseline condition from the treatment condition. Results are consistent with, but do not provide strong evidence for, the notion that the treatment was effective.

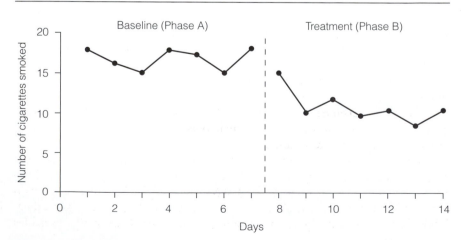

referred to as an AB design. (Students sometimes think the baseline phase is the B phase because the word *baseline* starts with a B. Do not think that way. The *baseline phase is the A phase* because that is the phase we start with, and the treatment phase is the B phase because it follows the A phase. The letters A and B simply indicate the order in which the conditions occur.)

A major problem with the simple-comparison design is that it does not control for the possibility that some other event occurred at the same time that the treatment was implemented, and it was this other event that caused the change in the behavior. For example, perhaps Cory caught a cold at the same time that he began self-punishment, and it is actually the cold that accounts for the reduction in smoking. The simple-comparison design does not allow us to assess this possibility and thus constitutes a poor experimental design. In other words, it does not clearly demonstrate a functional relationship between the independent variable (self-punishment) and the dependent variable (smoking). At best, it provides only suggestive evidence that the treatment is effective. If you have limited resources and time for investigating a treatment effect, however, and you are simply interested in seeing whether there is some type of improvement, then a simple-comparison design may be sufficient.

Reversal Design A much better design is the reversal design, which is sometimes also called an ABA or ABAB design (depending on the number of reversals carried out). The **reversal design** is a type of single-subject design that involves repeated alternations between a baseline period and a treatment period. If the behavior systematically changes each time the treatment is instituted and later withdrawn, then a functional relationship has been demonstrated between the treatment and the behavior. In Cory's case, he would begin with the baseline phase, then institute a self-punishment phase, then revert to baseline, and then revert to self-punishment. If the results are something like those depicted in Figure 2.4, with smoking decreasing each time the treatment is implemented and increasing each time the treatment is withdrawn, then we have obtained fairly strong evidence that the treatment is the cause of the improvement. It is extremely unlikely that some other event, such as illness, coincided precisely with each application of the treatment to produce such systematic changes in behavior.

The reversal design has many strengths. First, unlike the control group design, it allows an entire experiment to be conducted with a single subject. As such, the reversal design is often ideal for determining the effectiveness of a behavioral intervention for a particular person. Second, some behaviorists argue that statistical tests are not needed to determine if the changes in behavior are meaningful (Sidman, 1960). One can often just "eyeball" the graph to see if the treatment is working. The underlying logic is that if the results are not clear enough to be judged meaningful by visual inspection alone, then the treatment should be altered to produce a stronger effect. This forces the investigator to attain precise control over the variables

FIGURE 2.4 Reversal (ABAB) design. Hypothetical results using a reversal design to assess the effectiveness of a treatment (self-punishment) on number of cigarettes smoked. The systematic change in smoking across the alternating conditions provides strong *evidence* that the treatment is the cause of the improvement.

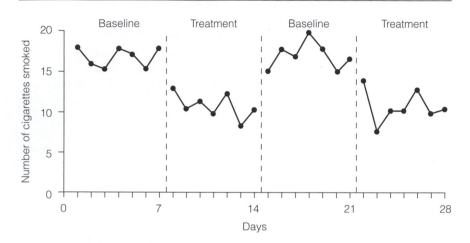

influencing the target behavior and to strive for powerful treatments that produce large effects.

You might be wondering whether results from a reversal design can be generalized to other subjects, since we have demonstrated the effect with only one subject. This is an important question, because in science we are concerned with finding effects that have generality. With single-subject designs, this issue is easily dealt with by conducting the study with more than one subject. Since each subject in the study constitutes an entire experiment, each additional subject constitutes a replication of that experiment. If we find the same pattern of results for all of the subjects exposed to these procedures, the findings are likely to have good generality. For example, if we tried the self-punishment treatment with three additional individuals and they too showed consistent decreases in smoking, then it is quite likely that this treatment will be effective for many individuals (although the nature of the punishing consequence might have to be tailored to each individual; what is punishing for one person might not be punishing for another). Thus, studies that utilize reversal (as well as other single-subject) designs are often conducted with four or more individuals to ensure that the results do have good generality.

It is also possible to use a reversal design to assess the effectiveness of more than one treatment. For example, imagine that Cory's initial treatment turns out to be relatively ineffective and results in little if any improvement. Rather than withdrawing the treatment and returning to baseline, a better strategy would be to implement a new treatment and see if it produces a stronger effect. In Cory's case, he might decide that the 25-cent fine for

FIGURE 2.5 Two-treatment reversal design. Hypothetical results in which a reversal design was used to assess the effectiveness of two treatment procedures on the number of cigarettes smoked. When the first treatment (B) produced little improvement, a second treatment (C) was immediately implemented. This treatment was then alternated with a baseline period to confirm its effectiveness. This would therefore be called an ABCAC design.

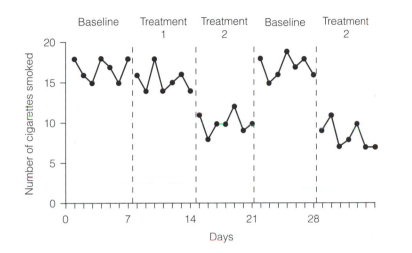

each cigarette smoked is insufficiently punishing and that he should instead fine himself a dollar. The implementation of this larger punisher constitutes a new phase of treatment, phase C. If after a week that treatment appears to be successful, Cory can revert to the baseline for a week and then return again to the treatment to confirm its effectiveness. This would then be called an ABCAC design (see Figure 2.5).

Reversal designs have some advantages, but they also have some disadvantages. One disadvantage is that if the behavior doesn't revert to its original baseline level when the treatment is withdrawn, we will be left wondering if the treatment was effective. If, for example, the results for Cory's study looked something like those depicted in Figure 2.6, in which smoking does not return to its pretreatment level during the reversal to baseline, we would be in no better situation than if we had run a simple-comparison design. Although the rate of smoking dropped when Cory first instituted the self-punishment procedure, it did not climb back up when the procedure was halted; therefore, we cannot be sure that self-punishment was the actual cause of the initial decrease. Although we may be pleased that Cory is now smoking less than he used to, from a scientific perspective of demonstrating the effectiveness of self-punishment, these results are less than ideal.

A second, related disadvantage is that the design is inappropriate for situations in which the treatment is intended to produce a long-lasting effect. For example, a student who is exposed to a new method of teaching math will

FIGURE 2.6 Reversal (ABAB) design. Hypothetical results in which a reversal design was used to assess the effectiveness of a self-punishment treatment on smoking. In this case, the behavior did not revert to its baseline level when the treatment was withdrawn. Thus, although it is possible that the treatment was the cause of the improvement, these results do not provide strong evidence in this regard.

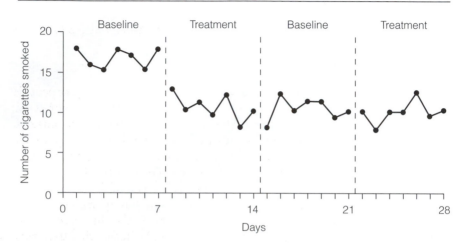

hopefully experience a permanent increase in his or her math ability. A reversal design would not be appropriate for assessing the effect of such an intervention, because the improvement should remain evident long after the intervention has ended.

A third disadvantage with a reversal design is that it may be ethically inappropriate to remove a treatment once some improvement has been obtained. If, for example, the implementation of a treatment results in the elimination of a person's severe drug addiction, is it reasonable for us to temporarily withdraw the treatment in the hope that the addictive behavior will reappear? Although from a scientific perspective withdrawing the treatment would help confirm its effectiveness, such withdrawal would not be ethical. In such cases, we must instead look for another method of demonstrating a functional relationship between the implementation of the treatment and the improvement in behavior. One alternative is to use a multiple-baseline design.

1. In a simple-comparison design, behavior in a _baseline_ condition is compared to behavior in a _treatment_ condition.

2. A simple-comparison design (does/does not) _does not_ allow us to determine if there is a _functional_ relationship between the independent and dependent variables.

3. A reversal design (also called an _ABA_ design) involves repeated alternations between a _baseline_ period and a _treatment_ period.

4. What type of result do we need to see during the second baseline phase to determine whether our treatment is the cause of the change in the behavior? _____

_____.

5. A reversal design is inappropriate for an experiment in which the treatment is expected to produce a (temporary/permanent) *temporary* change in the behavior.

6. A reversal design is also inappropriate when the act of withdrawing a successful treatment would lead to *effective* problems.

Multiple-Baseline Design In a **multiple-baseline design**, a treatment is instituted at successive points in time for two or more persons, settings, or behaviors. As an example of a *multiple baseline-across-persons* design, imagine that we have three people who wish to try a self-punishment program for smoking. We begin by taking a baseline measurement of smoking for each person. At the end of the first week, we have one person begin the treatment, while the other two carry on with the baseline. At the end of the second week, we have a second person begin the treatment while the third person carries on with the baseline. Finally, at the end of the third week, the third person also begins the treatment. Thus, across the three individuals, the treatment is implemented at different points in time. If the improvement in smoking coincides with the implementation of the treatment for each individual, then a functional relationship between the treatment and the improvement in behavior has been demonstrated (see Figure 2.7).

As an example of a *multiple-baseline-across-settings* design, imagine that the three graphs in Figure 2.7 represent Cory's rate of smoking in three different settings: at work, at home, and at the coffee shop. After a week of baseline, Cory begins self-punishing his smoking, but only at work. After the second week, he begins self-punishing smoking at home while continuing to punish it at work. Finally, after the third week, he also starts punishing his smoking behavior at the coffee shop. If his rate of smoking in each setting drops only at the point when the self-punishment procedure is implemented, then the procedure is highly likely to be the cause of the improvement.

As an example of a *multiple-baseline-across-behaviors* design, imagine that the three graphs in Figure 2.7 represent three of Cory's problem behaviors—for example, smoking, swearing, and nail-biting. In this case, we implement the treatment at different times for each behavior. If each behavior shows improvement only when the treatment is implemented, then we have again demonstrated a functional relationship between the treatment and behavior.

The multiple-baseline design is a good alternative to the reversal design in that we do not have to worry about withdrawing the treatment to determine that it is effective. This design is therefore appropriate for situations in

FIGURE 2.7 Multiple-baseline design. Hypothetical results using a multiple-baseline-across-persons design to assess the effectiveness of a treatment (self-punishment) on number of cigarettes smoked. The three graphs represent the data for three different persons. For each person, the improvement in behavior coincides with the point at which the treatment was implemented. This result shows a functional relationship between the treatment and the improvement in behavior.

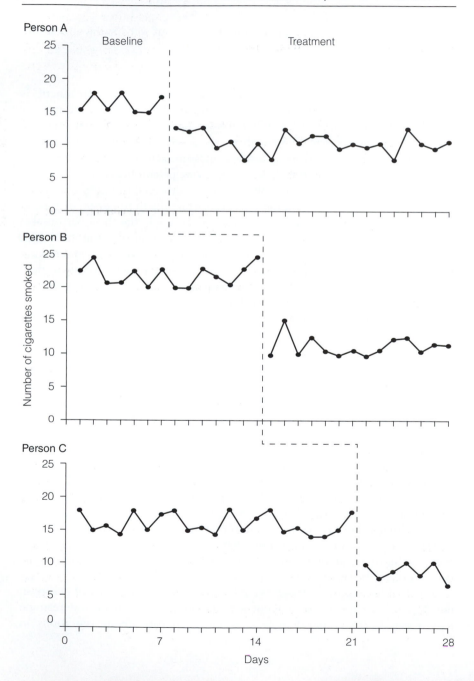

which the treatment is likely to produce a permanent change in behavior, or in which it may be unethical to withdraw the treatment once some improvement has been achieved. Nevertheless, this design is limited because we need to have more than one person, setting, or behavior to which the treatment can be applied. Another limitation is that the treatment effect might generalize across the different settings or behaviors before the treatment is instituted within those settings or behaviors. For example, as Cory begins to exert more control over his smoking at work, this effect might generalize to his smoking patterns at home and at the coffee shop even before the treatment is applied in those settings. Under such circumstances, it would be difficult to determine whether the treatment was in fact the cause of the improvement.

1. With a multiple-baseline design, the treatment is instituted at different points in time _____ for one or more persons _____, settings _____, or behaviors _____.

2. A key advantage of the multiple-baseline design is that we do not have to watch _____ the treatment to determine if it is effective.

3. It is therefore a preferable design for situations in which the treatment might result in a (temporary/permanent) _permanent_ change in behavior, or where it might be un ethical _____ to withdraw the treatment.

QUICK QUIZ H

Changing-Criterion Design In some circumstances, the treatment is not intended to produce a large, immediate change in behavior but rather a gradual change over time. A useful design for measuring such changes is a ***changing-criterion design***, in which the effect of the treatment is demonstrated by how closely the behavior matches a criterion that is being systematically altered.

Imagine, for example, that Cory decides to use self-punishment to gradually reduce his smoking behavior. Following a baseline period, he sets a certain criterion for an allowable number of cigarettes that is only slightly less than the average number of cigarettes he smoked during the baseline. If he successfully meets this criterion for 3 consecutive days, he reduces the allowable limit by two cigarettes. If he meets that criterion for 3 successive days, he reduces the limit by two more cigarettes. He repeats this process until the eventual goal of no smoking has been achieved. The self-punishment procedure consists of tearing up a dollar bill for every cigarette that is smoked over the allowable limit (see Axelrod, Hall, Weiss, & Rohrer, 1974, for a case report of such a procedure).

Hypothetical results for this program are displayed in Figure 2.8. Cory was generally successful in meeting each criterion, with the number of cigarettes smoked per day either matching or falling below the criterion for that day. The three exceptions occurred on days 29, 33, and 34. Because Cory exceeded the criterion on these days, he would have implemented the self-punishment contingency of tearing up a dollar bill.

FIGURE 2.8 Changing-criterion design. Hypothetical data illustrating use of a changing-criterion design to assess the effectiveness of self-punishment to gradually reduce smoking. The dashed horizontal lines indicate the changing criterion for maximum allowable number of cigarettes smoked per day.

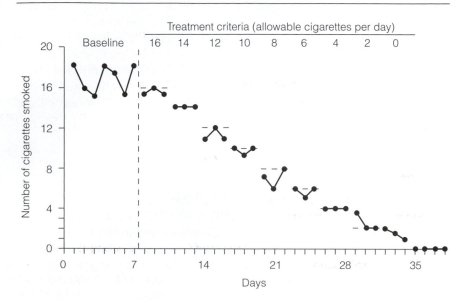

As noted previously, the changing-criterion design is especially appropriate for situations in which the behavior is intended to change gradually by some specific amount. Thus, it would be an appropriate design for gradually increasing the amount of time one studies each day or decreasing the amount of time spent playing computer games. It is important, however, that the behavior closely match the changing criteria; otherwise, it will be difficult to determine if the change in behavior is the result of the treatment or of some other factor. The design can, however, be greatly strengthened by including periods in which the criteria suddenly change in the opposite direction (for example, in the case of Cory, the number of cigarettes allowed would sometimes be raised). If the behavior continues to track the criteria closely even when they change direction, then we will have obtained strong evidence for the effectiveness of the treatment. In a sense, we have created a changing-criterion design that incorporates certain aspects of a reversal design.

The reversal design and multiple-baseline design are the most basic single-subject designs, with the changing-criterion design being less often utilized. Other types of single-subject designs have also been devised, each having its advantages and disadvantages (see Kazdin, 2011). Most of these designs have been developed for use in applied settings. In experimental research, the reversal design (or some variation of it) is often employed in studies of operant conditioning, whereas the control group design is often employed in studies of classical conditioning.

ADVICE FOR THE LOVELORN

Dear Dr. Dee,

I am suspicious that my boyfriend is having an affair with his old girlfriend. Whenever she is in town, he phones me significantly less often. For example, between May and August, when I know for a fact that she was in town, he phoned me an average of 5.8 times per week, while between September and December, when she was out of town, he phoned an average of 6.4 times per week. I worked it out, and sure enough, this is a statistically significant difference! But when I confronted him with this hard evidence of his unfaithfulness, he denied it and said that I'm being paranoid.

Am I Being Paranoid?

Dear Am I,

Given the evidence that you have presented, I would have to say yes, you are being paranoid. Worse than that, you are being a poor scientist. For example, you have neglected to consider other factors that might account for the observed difference. Quite apart from his old girlfriend being in town, your boyfriend may be calling less frequently between May and August for several other reasons, such as spending more time in outdoor activities or visiting with relatives. Such other possibilities need to be assessed before you can draw any conclusions about your boyfriend's unfaithfulness.

You also need to recognize that statistically significant differences do not provide hard evidence of anything. What they provide is *supportive* evidence for a certain possibility. Thus, even with a highly significant difference between two sets of scores, there is still a slight possibility that the difference is actually due to chance variation. As well, you need to consider that a difference that is *statistically* significant may not be *meaningfully* significant. In fact, the difference you have described seems quite small. I bet that if you chart the number of phone calls week by week, as in a simple-comparison design, you will have a hard time spotting much of a difference between the May–August period and the September–December period. And in this particular case, if you can't see much of a difference by eyeballing the data, then maybe there isn't much of a difference.

Behaviorally yours,

Dr. Dee

In general, the value of any experimental design is that it enables us to make causal statements about the effects of independent variables on dependent variables. Control over the environment enables the researcher to isolate the effects of the independent variables while controlling for extraneous influences. Despite this advantage, experimental methods also have a major disadvantage. Because of the need to strictly control the environment, experimental settings are sometimes quite artificial, with the result that the findings may have limited applicability to the real world. However, the precise control over the environment that can be obtained with experimental research lends itself to replication, and with each replication across new subjects and new settings, we gain confidence that our findings do have generality.

QUICK QUIZ I

1. In a changing-criterion design, the question of interest is whether the changes in behavior match changes in a c̲r̲i̲t̲e̲r̲i̲o̲n̲ for the behavior that is being systematically al̲t̲e̲r̲e̲d̲.

2. A changing-criterion design is most appropriate for assessing the effect of programs designed to produce a (sudden/gradual) g̲r̲a̲d̲u̲a̲l̲ change in behavior.

3. In using this type of design, it is important that the level of behavior closely r̲e̲f̲l̲e̲x̲e̲s̲ the changes in the criterion for that behavior.

4. The changing-criterion design can be strengthened by including periods in which the criterion suddenly _____.

Use of Animals in Behavioral Research

Animal research has greatly contributed to our understanding and treatment of serious diseases and illnesses, as well as to our understanding of basic physiological processes. Similarly, many of the basic principles of behavior have been discovered through research with animals, especially rats and pigeons. But if the ultimate goal of such research is to discover principles of behavior that are applicable to humans, why use animals at all? In this section we outline some of the advantages and disadvantages of animal research that may help inform your opinion in this highly controversial debate.

Two advantages of using animals in research are the ability to control their genetic makeup and their learning history. Knowledge of an animal's genetic makeup may help us eliminate, or assess, the effects of inherited differences on learning and behavior. Rats, for example, can be bred so that entire batches of research subjects are genetically identical or highly similar. We can try to control for genetic differences in humans by studying identical twins, but the number of people we can obtain for such research is necessarily quite limited. Similarly, animals bred for research have had somewhat identical experiences during their upbringing, along with a fairly limited learning history. It is impossible to control for the learning histories of humans who volunteer for psychological research. If we are conducting experiments designed to assess basic principles of learning, then the learning histories of one's subjects could critically influence the outcome of the experiment.

A *third advantage to using animals as subjects is that researchers are often able to more strictly control the experimental environment for animals than for humans.* This advantage is especially important in behavioral research, in which we are attempting to isolate and manipulate certain aspects of the environment to determine their effect on behavior. For example, if we are interested in the effect of food deprivation on activity level in rats (as discussed in Chapter 11), then it is highly advantageous to strictly control the rat's feeding schedule—to a degree that would be impossible in humans. Human subjects participating in ongoing research also have an unfortunate tendency to discuss the research task with their friends when they leave the lab each day, even when they are asked not to do so. These conversations can easily lead to a significant change in the person's behavior during the next experimental session. By contrast, rats and mice tend not to give each other suggestions while lounging about in their home cages following a hard day of lever pressing. Their behavior therefore tends to be more consistent from day to day. In general, because animals are more easily insulated from extraneous influences during the course of the experiment, their behavior is more likely to reflect the true influence of the independent variable.

A *fourth reason for using animals in behavioral research is that some research cannot ethically be conducted with humans.* This is particularly the case with experimental manipulations that are potentially aversive or harmful. For example, rats have been used to investigate the manner in which classical conditioning might account for unusual instances of drug overdose (this finding is discussed in Chapter 5). Investigations using such an *animal model* of drug addiction have the potential to save lives but would be impossible to conduct with human subjects. (An *animal model* is a procedure that uses animals to mimic a particular human characteristic or symptom, such as drug addiction or obesity, which can then be systematically investigated to a greater extent than would be possible with humans.)

In reaction to these claimed benefits of animal research, critics have offered several counterarguments. One criticism is that because animals are not humans, the findings from animal research necessarily have limited applicability to humans. The physiological processes, genetic tendencies, and learning histories of animals are simply too different for research with animals to be of much relevance to humans. In this text we hope to convince you of the opposite, but the argument should not be dismissed out of hand. Despite the demonstrated benefits of animal research, some research with animals almost certainly does have little applicability to humans. Unfortunately, determining ahead of time which research findings are likely to be applicable to humans is a difficult task. Some of the most applicable findings from animal research, such as basic research on schedules of reinforcement (discussed in Chapter 7), initially would have struck some people as trivial and unimportant. (In fact, some people opposed to behaviorism still regard these findings as trivial and unimportant.)

Perhaps the most fundamental criticism of animal research is that it is morally wrong and that animals have rights similar to humans. Animal rights activists oppose "inhumane" research practices, such as confining animals to cages, subjecting them to electric shock, depriving them of food, and so on. From this perspective, even the reported benefits of animal research for saving lives and improving the human condition are insufficient to justify submitting animals to such morally reprehensible practices. (See the And Furthermore box: Cruel Starvation or a Healthy Diet.)

Beginning in the 1800s, researchers have reacted to such criticism by developing guidelines that weigh the benefits of research against the injurious or aversive nature of the procedures. The first guidelines were formulated in 1876, with the introduction of the British Cruelty to Animals Act.

And Furthermore

Cruel Starvation or a Healthy Diet: The Ethics of Food Restriction

In many of the animal studies described in this text, food is used as a reward (reinforcer) for performing certain behaviors. As such, the animals are typically food deprived to ensure that they are well motivated to work for food. Pigeons, for example, are typically placed on a diet until their weight is about 80 to 85% of their *free-feeding weight* (which is the amount they weigh when food is constantly available). Some people regard such food restriction procedures as inhumane. But is this really the case?

First, we have to remember that the 80 to 85% level is calculated based on the pigeon's weight when food is freely available. Free food is an unnatural state of affairs for a pigeon, which in its natural environment must constantly forage for food. The result is that the weight of a pigeon on free food is well beyond its natural weight. Poling, Nickel, and Alling (1990), for example, found that wild pigeons placed on free food for 42 days experienced an average weight increase of 17%, with some pigeons gaining as much as 30%. (This latter figure is equivalent to a 160-pound individual who, with little to do but eat, balloons up to 208 pounds!) Thus, the weight of a pigeon at 80% of its free-feeding weight may be quite close to what it would be if it were foraging for food in its natural environment.

A second point to bear in mind is that a certain amount of food restriction can be quite healthy. In fact, calorie restriction is the most reliable means known for slowing the aging process. Almost all species tested, ranging from spiders to monkeys, have shown significant increases in both health status and life span when raised on diets that provide 30 to 50% fewer calories than normal (e.g., Weindruch, 1996; Koubova, 2003). (Of course, the animals growing up on these diets are also significantly smaller than normal.) This longevity effect has yet to be confirmed in humans, and sometimes the diet produces negative results when it is suddenly imposed later in life. Nevertheless, sufficient evidence exists to suggest that a certain degree of calorie restriction, or intermittent calorie restriction, might be a healthy regimen for people as well as animals (e.g., Varady & Hellerstein, 2008). (But see also the discussion on activity anorexia in Chapter 12 for a warning of what can happen when calorie restriction is taken too far.)

It was in the 1960s, however, that animal care committees and review boards became strongly established. Today, researchers in most professional organizations, including the American Psychological Association, are regulated by ethical standards that provide strict guidelines for the care and use of animals.

It is also worth noting that animal researchers are themselves concerned about the welfare of their animals. Skinner, for example, disliked shocking rats and therefore conducted few studies of punishment (Bjork, 1993). Many researchers also acknowledge that the animal rights movement has served a valuable purpose by ensuring the development of strict standards of ethical conduct. They likewise recognize that the extent to which animal research is justified is a difficult question that individuals must answer for themselves. The important thing, however, is to make it an informed decision. (For a discussion of these issues, see Smoo & Resnick, 2009.)

1. Two advantages to using animals for behavioral research is that one can more strictly control an animal's g*enetic* makeup and *Learning* history.

2. A third advantage to using animals is that the *experimental* environment can more easily be controlled for animals than for humans.

3. A fourth advantage to using animals for research is that it would be *unethical* to conduct certain types of studies with humans, such as examining the effects of brain lesions on learning ability.

4. Two arguments against the use of animals in research are:

   a. *No relavance to humans*

   b. *Inhumain practices*

QUICK QUIZ J

SUMMARY

Behavioral research involves the manipulation and measurement of variables. The independent variable is that aspect of an experiment that is systematically varied across conditions in an experiment and is believed to affect the dependent variable, which is the behavior being measured. Appetitive stimuli are events that are sought out by an organism, whereas aversive stimuli are events that are avoided. Establishing operations are conditions that affect the appetitiveness or aversiveness of an event. Deprivation is one such condition, which tends to increase the appetitiveness of an event, whereas satiation tends to decrease the appetitiveness of an event. A contingency exists if there is a conditional relationship between two events such that the occurrence of one event predicts the likely occurrence of another. This is often the case in experimental research where changes in an independent variable produce changes in a dependent variable.

Behavioral researchers strive to employ objective, unambiguous definitions of behavior. Depending on the research question, there are several ways to measure behavior. Rate of response indicates the frequency with which a response occurs within a certain period of time, and intensity is the force or magnitude of a behavior. Duration is the length of time an ongoing behavior is performed, speed is the time required to perform a complete episode of behavior, and latency is the amount of time it takes for the behavior to commence. Interval recording measures whether a behavior occurs within each of a series of continuous intervals, and time-sample recording measures whether a behavior occurs within a series of discontinuous intervals. Other behavioral measures include topography (the physical form of a behavior) and number of errors. The interobserver reliability of behavioral measures is often assessed by calculating the extent to which two or more independent observers agree in their observations.

In addition to selecting a measure of behavior, researchers need to determine the most appropriate method for conducting research. Research methods can be classified as descriptive or experimental. Two descriptive methods are naturalistic observation and the case study approach. Descriptive methods provide rich, detailed information but do not demonstrate causal relationships. Experimental methods do demonstrate causal relationships and generally take the form of control group or single-subject designs. Control group designs generally involve the random assignment of participants to experimental and nonexperimental (control) conditions. However, control group designs have certain drawbacks, such as requiring large numbers of participants. In contrast, single-subject designs can be used to demonstrate cause-and-effect relationships using only one or a few individuals. Types of single-subject designs include the simple-comparison design, reversal design, multiple-baseline design, and changing-criterion design, each of which has its strengths and weaknesses.

Advantages of using animals as subjects in behavioral research include enhanced control over learning history, genetic background, and experimental environment relative to human participants. Also, animals can be used in studies that cannot ethically be conducted on humans. Disadvantages of using animals are the possibility that findings may have limited application to humans and the notion that animals have the same rights as humans. Ethics committees have been established to weigh the costs and benefits of proposed research involving animals.

SUGGESTED READINGS

Skinner, B. F. (1956). *A case history in scientific method. American Psychologist, 11,* 221–233. Skinner's interesting and sometimes irreverent view of what the "scientific method" *really* involves, at least from the perspective of his own experience.

Sidman, M. (1960). *Tactics of scientific research: Evaluating experimental data in psychology*. New York: Basic Books. The classic text on single-subject research designs. Although this book is a bit beyond most undergraduates, a quick perusal will give you a sense for the radical behaviorist approach to research.

Kazdin, A. E. (2011). *Single-case research designs* (2nd ed.). New York: Oxford University Press. Contains an extensive discussion of research methods in applied behavior analysis, including additional types of single-subject designs.

Martin, D. W. (2008). *Doing psychology experiments* (7th ed.). Belmont, CA: Wadsworth. A very readable introductory textbook on research methods in psychology.

STUDY QUESTIONS

1. Distinguish between independent and dependent variables. What is a functional relationship?
2. Define stimulus and response. Differentiate between the terms *stimulus* and *stimuli*.
3. Distinguish between overt and covert behavior. Distinguish between appetitive and aversive stimuli.
4. Define establishing operation. Name and describe two types of establishing operations.
5. Distinguish between contiguity and contingency. Name and define two types of contiguity.
6. Define rate of response. Why is rate of response a particularly favored measure of behavior among radical behaviorists (include an example)?
7. How does one distinguish a high rate of response versus a low rate of response versus a period of no response on a cumulative record?
8. Define speed, duration, and latency measures of behavior, and give a clear example of each.
9. Define the intensity and topography of a behavior, and give a clear example of each.
10. Define interval recording and time-sample recording, and give a clear example of each. Specify how the overall measure of behavior is calculated.
11. How does one calculate the reliability of observations conducted with an interval recording procedure? Illustrate your answer with an example.
12. Name and describe two types of descriptive research methods. What is the major limitation of descriptive research methods?
13. Describe the simplest form of a control group design. How are subjects assigned to the different conditions, and why is this done?
14. What is a comparative design?
15. What are three limitations of control group designs?

16. What are single-subject designs? Describe a simple-comparison design. In what sense is it a "flawed" design?
17. Describe a reversal design. What are three disadvantages with this type of design?
18. Describe a multiple-baseline design. What are two limitations of this type of design?
19. Describe a changing-criterion design. How can it be strengthened? For what types of situations is this design appropriate?
20. List four advantages and two disadvantages of using animals as subjects in behavioral research.

CONCEPT REVIEW

appetitive stimulus. An event that an organism will seek out.

aversive stimulus. An event that an organism will avoid.

baseline. The normal frequency of a behavior before some intervention.

case study approach. A descriptive research approach that involves intensive examination of one or a few individuals.

changing-criterion design. A type of single-subject design in which the effect of the treatment is demonstrated by how closely the behavior matches a criterion that is systematically altered.

comparative design. A type of control group design in which different species constitute one of the independent variables.

contingency. A predictive relationship between two events such that the occurrence of one event predicts the probable occurrence of the other.

control group design. A type of experiment in which, at its simplest, subjects are randomly assigned to either an experimental (or treatment) group or a control group; subjects assigned to the experimental group are exposed to a certain manipulation or treatment, while those assigned to the control group are not.

covert behavior. Behavior that can be subjectively perceived only by the person performing the behavior. Thoughts and feelings are covert behaviors. Also known as *private events* or *private behavior*.

cumulative recorder. A device that measures total number of responses over time and provides a graphic depiction of the rate of behavior.

dependent variable. That aspect of an experiment that is allowed to freely vary to determine if it is affected by changes in the independent variable.

deprivation. The prolonged absence of an event that tends to increase the appetitiveness of that event.

descriptive research. Research that focuses on describing the behavior and the situation within which it occurs.

duration. The length of time that an individual repeatedly or continuously performs a certain behavior.

establishing operation. A procedure that affects the appetitiveness or aversiveness of a stimulus.

functional relationship. The relationship between changes in an independent variable and changes in a dependent variable; a cause-and-effect relationship.

independent variable. That aspect of an experiment that is made to systematically vary across the different conditions in an experiment.

intensity. The force or magnitude of a behavior.

interval recording. The measurement of whether or not a behavior occurs within a series of continuous intervals. (Note that the number of times that the behavior occurs within each interval is irrelevant.)

latency. The length of time required for a behavior to begin.

multiple-baseline design. A type of single-subject design in which a treatment is instituted at successive points in time for two or more persons, settings, or behaviors.

naturalistic observation. A descriptive research approach that involves the systematic observation and recording of behavior in its natural environment.

overt behavior. Behavior that has the potential for being directly observed by an individual other than the one performing the behavior.

rate of response. The frequency with which a response occurs in a certain period of time.

response. A particular instance of a behavior.

reversal design. A type of single-subject design that involves repeated alternations between a baseline period and a treatment period.

satiation. The prolonged exposure to (or consumption of) an event that tends to decrease the appetitiveness of that event.

simple-comparison design. A type of single-subject design in which behavior in a baseline condition is compared to behavior in a treatment condition.

single-subject design. A research design that requires only one or a few subjects in order to conduct an entire experiment. Also known as *single-case* or *small n* designs.

spatial contiguity. The extent to which events are situated close to each other in space.

speed. The amount of time required to perform a complete episode of a behavior from start to finish.

stimulus. Any event that can potentially influence behavior. (The plural for stimulus is *stimuli*.)

temporal contiguity. The extent to which events occur close together in time.

time-sample recording. The measurement of whether or not a behavior occurs within a series of discontinuous intervals. (The number of times that it occurs within each interval is irrelevant.)

topography. The physical form of a behavior.

variable. A characteristic of a person, place, or thing that can change (vary) over time or from one situation to another.

CHAPTER TEST

12. Using a(n) _____ recording procedure, we find that during each successive 10-minute observation, Erik chewed his nails only during the first and second minute, as well as during the fourth, seventh, ninth, and tenth minutes.

27. Being quite addicted to computer games, James decides to implement a program to *gradually* reduce the amount of time that he spends playing these games. A useful design for determining if his program is successful would be a _____ design.

18. The reversal design is also known as a(n) _____ design.

3. Each time it rains, I see an increased number of umbrellas being carried. There appears to be a _____ relationship between the weather and the appearance of umbrellas.

8. You have just eaten a large pizza. It is likely that the reward value of eating a pizza has now (increased/decreased) _____ as a function of (which type of establishing operation) _____.

23. The amount of time it takes Robert to read a chapter is a _____ measure of behavior, and the amount of time it took him to begin reading the chapter is a _____ measure of behavior. The total amount of time he spends reading each day is a _____ measure of behavior.

15. In a _____ design, subjects are randomly assigned to a treatment or nontreatment condition.

11. Number of cigarettes smoked each week is a _____ measure of smoking.

19. Animals are often used in behavioral research because this practice allows for greater _____ over learning history, genetic influences, and experimental environment than is possible with humans. As well, animals are often used when the use of humans would be _____ questionable.

10. In measuring the force with which a boxer delivers a blow, we are measuring the _____ of the behavior.

26. I wish to test a new drug that I believe will permanently remove the symptoms of a rare neurological disorder. Unfortunately, only three patients who suffer from the disorder have volunteered to take the drug. What would be a useful type of design to demonstrate the effectiveness of this drug? _____.

16. An experiment that utilizes a type of _____ design requires only one or a few subjects.

4. A flash of light is called a _____, and two flashes of light are called _____. A specific eyeblink that is elicited by a flash of light can be called a _____.

20. After Trish told Jen that Ryan was the most popular guy in school, Jen became extremely interested in him. Trish's statement about Ryan apparently functioned as an _____ that increased Ryan's value as an _____ stimulus.

7. You have not had a pizza in four months. It is likely that the reward value of eating a pizza has (increased/decreased) _____ as a function of (which type of establishing operation) _____.

24. When people feel confident, they tend to stand straight. In this case, we are using a _____ measure of behavior as an index of confidence.

1. Any characteristic of a person, place, or thing that can change is called a _____.

9. Robbie is afraid of spiders, but Naseem finds them interesting. A spider is a(n) _____ stimulus to Robbie, and a(n) _____ stimulus to Naseem.

6. A knife and spoon are placed side by side in a dinner setting, creating spatial (contiguity/contingency) _____ between the two utensils.

28. Dr. Takeuchi wonders whether the crows that he is studying can solve certain types of problems as well as dogs can. In testing this notion, he would use a type of experimental design known as a _____ design.

13. Using a(n) _____ recording procedure, a school psychologist drops into a classroom for a 20-minute period four times each day and notes whether some type of disruption occurs during the time that he is there.

17. The _____ approach is a descriptive method of research often used by psychiatrists who encounter a rare type of clinical disorder.

2. In a classical conditioning experiment, one group of dogs first hears a tone and then receives food, while another group of dogs receives food and then hears a tone. Following this, the researcher measures how much the dogs in each group salivate when they simply hear the tone. In this experiment, the order in which tone and food are presented is the _____ variable, and the amount of salivation to the tone is the _____ variable.

22. On a cumulative recorder, a gradually sloping line indicates a _____ rate of response, and a steep line indicates a _____ rate of response. By contrast, a _____ line indicates no response.

14. Two main approaches to behavioral research are the _____ approach and the _____ approach.

29. Using an interval recording procedure, two independent observers agree on whether the target behavior occurred during seven of the observed

intervals and disagree on whether it occurred during three of the observed intervals. Interobserver reliability is therefore calculated as _____%, which is (below/at/above) _____ the generally acceptable minimum for reliability.

5. Blinking is a(n) _____ behavior, but thinking about blinking is a(n) _____ behavior.

25. Dr. Ross studies the effects of schizoid personality disorder by sitting in the park each day and observing the behavior of street people who are known to be suffering from the disorder. Dr. Ross is using a descriptive research method known as _____.

21. To determine whether drinking coffee in the evening keeps me awake at night, I observe my sleep patterns for a 2-week period in which I drink coffee each evening, followed by a 2-week period in which I do not drink coffee in the evening. I am using a _____ design to conduct this study, which will likely give me (strong/questionable) _____ evidence concerning how coffee affects my sleep patterns.

Visit the book companion Web site at http://www.academic.cengage.com/ psychology/powell for additional practice questions, answers to the Quick Quizzes, practice review exams, and additional exercises and information.

ANSWERS TO CHAPTER TEST

1. variable
2. independent; dependent
3. functional
4. stimulus; stimuli; response
5. overt; covert (or private)
6. contiguity
7. increased; deprivation
8. decreased; satiation
9. aversive; appetitive
10. magnitude (or intensity)
11. rate
12. interval
13. time sample
14. descriptive; experimental
15. control group
16. single-subject (or single-case)
17. case study
18. ABA (or ABAB)
19. control; ethically
20. establishing operation; appetitive
21. simple comparison or AB; questionable (or weak)
22. low (or slow); high (or fast); flat
23. speed; latency; duration
24. topography (or topographical)
25. naturalistic observation
26. multiple-baseline (across persons)
27. changing-criterion
28. comparative
29. 70%; below

CHAPTER 3

Elicited Behaviors and Classical Conditioning

CHAPTER OUTLINE

At a friend's party, Uma witnessed her boyfriend flagrantly flirting with another woman. She was initially quite angry, but when he later apologized for his actions and was very attentive to her, she experienced unusually strong feelings of attraction toward him. Still, she somehow felt manipulated by the whole affair. After all, her friends had warned her that he had a terrible reputation for playing "mind games."

Elicited Behaviors

Involuntary, automatic response

The word *elicit* means "to draw out or bring forth." Thus, an elicited behavior is one that is automatically drawn out by a certain stimulus. (Note that the word is *elicit* and not *illicit*, which refers to something illegal, such as an illicit drug.) A sneeze produced by a particle of dust or a startle reaction to the sound of a gunshot are examples of elicited behaviors. They are elicited in the sense that they are automatically drawn out by the stimuli that produce them. In this sense, many elicited behaviors are behaviors that we consider to be involuntary. For example, you do not choose to be startled by a gunshot; your startle reaction is an involuntary response to the gunshot. Similarly, you do not choose to salivate when you bite into a lemon; salivating is an involuntary response to the lemon.

In this chapter, we begin by describing different types of elicited behaviors as well as some simple mechanisms by which they can be modified. This will include a discussion of the opponent-process theory of emotion, an intriguing theory that explains a wide variety of emotional phenomena ranging from symptoms of drug withdrawal to the sense of loss you feel following the breakup of a relationship. The remainder of the chapter will then be devoted to introducing the concept of classical conditioning, the first major type of learning to be discussed in this text.

Reflexes

Simple, automatic response

Reflexes are the most basic form of elicited behavior. A *reflex* is a relatively simple, automatic response to a stimulus. (It can also be defined as the *relationship* between such a response and the stimulus that elicits it.) Some reflexes involve only one gland or set of muscles, such as when you salivate in response to a drop of lemon juice or blink in response to a puff of air. Other reflexes are more general in scope, involving the coordinated action of several body parts. For example, the *startle response*—a defensive reaction to a sudden, unexpected stimulus—involves the automatic tightening of skeletal muscles as well as various hormonal and visceral (internal organ) changes. Similarly, the *orienting response*—in which we automatically position ourselves to facilitate attending to a stimulus—can involve a relatively major body movement, such as when we automatically turn in response to an unfamiliar noise behind us.

Defensive response to a sudden unexpected stimulus

automatic positioning to attend to a stimulus (toast)

Many reflexes are closely tied to survival. For example, food consumption involves a chain of reflexes including salivation, peristalsis (wave-like actions that push food down the esophagus and through the digestive system), and secretion of digestive juices in the stomach. Conversely, the vomiting reflex serves a protective function by expelling potentially poisonous substances from the digestive system. Other protective reflexes include the *flexion response*, in which we automatically jerk our hand or foot away from a hot or sharp object that we have inadvertently contacted, and the aforementioned startle reaction—designed to ready us for fight or flight if an unexpected stimulus should prove dangerous.

[margin note: Immediate pull away from a negative stimuli (hot oven)]

Newborns come "prepackaged" with a host of reflexes that facilitate their survival. For example, if you touch a baby's cheek with your finger, the baby will automatically turn his or her head in that direction. This reflex action is designed to facilitate taking a nipple into the mouth. Once the nipple is in the mouth, the baby's sucking reflex is activated (which in turn elicits a "milk letdown" reflex in the mother). Many of these reflexes disappear within a few years (e.g., the sucking reflex), but others, such as salivating and vomiting, remain with us throughout life.

Many of the simpler reflexes are activated through a reflex arc. A *reflex arc* is a neural structure that underlies many reflexes and consists of a sensory neuron, an interneuron, and a motor neuron. For example, when you quickly jerk your hand away from an open flame, you are exhibiting a flexion response. Upon touching the flame, receptors in the hand stimulate sensory neurons that carry a danger message (in the form of a burst of nerve impulses) toward the spinal cord. Within the spinal cord, interneurons receive this message and immediately pass it on to the motor neurons. These motor neurons then activate the muscles in the arm that pull the hand away from the flame. Simultaneous with this process, pain messages are also sent up the spinal cord to the brain; but by the time they are received and you consciously feel the pain, the hand is already being withdrawn from the flame. Thus, we do not withdraw our hand from the flame because of the pain; we actually begin withdrawing our hand before feeling any pain. Because the flexion response utilizes a simple reflex arc through the spinal cord, we are able to withdraw our hand from the flame much quicker than if the message had to be routed all the way through the brain and then back down to the arm muscles (see Figure 3.1).

1. A simple, involuntary response to a stimulus is called a __reflex__.

2. Reflexes are e__licit__ in the sense that they are drawn out by stimuli that precede their occurrence.

3. A s__tartle__ response is an automatic defensive response to a sudden, unexpected stimulus; the o__rienting__ response is an elicited set of movements designed to facilitate attending to a stimulus.

4. Many simple reflexes are activated through a r__eflex__ a__rc__ that consists of a(n) __sensory__ neuron, a(n) __interneuron__ neuron, and a(n) __motor__ neuron (in that order).

5. Quickly jerking your hand or foot away from contact with an open flame or sharp object is a reflexive action known as a fl__exion__ response. In such cases, the perception of pain generally (precedes/follows) __follows__ the response.

FIGURE 3.1 The reflex arc underlying a flexion response. Upon touching the flame, receptors in the finger stimulate sensory neurons that carry the message via nerve impulses toward the spinal cord. Interneurons within the spinal cord receive the message and pass it directly to motor neurons. The motor neurons in turn activate muscles in the arm that pull the finger away from the flame. At the same time this action is occurring within the reference arc, a pain message is sent to the brain. (*Source:* Nairne, 2000.)

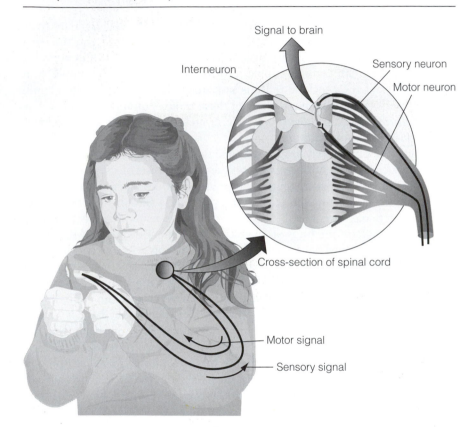

Fixed Action Patterns

Fixed sequence
of responses
elicited by a
specific stimulus
(girl flipping hair)

Some types of elicited behaviors are more complex than simple reflexes. A *fixed action pattern* is a fixed sequence of responses elicited by a specific stimulus. Fixed action patterns are also sometimes called "modal action patterns" (Domjan, 2010). Examples include web building by spiders, V-shaped formation flying by ducks, and nut burying by some species of squirrels. Dogs and cats display numerous fixed action patterns. Cats compulsively scratch the ground to cover up urine and feces (effective in a litter box but completely ineffective

FIGURE 3.2   Fixed action pattern for play. A dog will indicate its desire for play by stretching out its front legs and lowering its head to the ground.

WilleeCole/Shutterstock.com

on your carpet) and rub up against the legs of visitors to "mark" them as belonging to their territory. Dogs indicate their desire to play by wagging their tails, stretching out their front legs, and lowering their heads to the ground (see Figure 3.2). In fact, by adopting this posture (and looking completely foolish in front of any visitors), you can effectively ask your dog if it wishes to play (which of course it will not, given that it now has you looking like an idiot).

For many fixed action patterns, we are able to identify a specific stimulus that sets it in motion. The specific stimulus that elicits a fixed action pattern is called a ***sign stimulus* or *releaser*.** For example, a male *Betta splendens*, better known as a Siamese fighting fish, immediately takes an aggressive posture at the sight of another male (the releaser), with both fish spreading out their brilliant red or blue fins and gills. If introduced into the same tank, the two fish will attack each other. Similarly, during mating season, a male stickleback fish displays a fixed sequence of aggressive actions when another male enters its territory (Tinbergen, 1951). Interestingly, the sign stimulus for the stickleback's aggressive actions is not the presence of the other male but the sight of its red underbelly. If the red belly is covered up or painted a different color, the intruder will not be attacked. On the other hand, if a pie-shaped or cigar-shaped piece of wood with a red patch on the bottom is introduced into the tank, it will be attacked.

Fixed action patterns tend to be unique to certain species and are therefore sometimes called *species-specific behaviors*. They can also be called instincts, but some researchers dislike this term because it implies that the behavior is more rigid and inflexible than is actually the case. For example, if two rats are subjected to a painful stimulus, such as an electric shock, they will automatically attack each other (Ulrich & Azrin, 1962). In fact, many species will become aggressive in reaction to pain, but in rats it often takes the form of a fixed action pattern in which the two combatants rear up on their hind legs and essentially box by striking out at each other with their front paws. Interestingly, this aggression is more likely to occur in rats that had previously been trained to be aggressive than in those that had not been trained to be aggressive (Baeninger & Ulm, 1969). Thus, the rats' fixed action pattern of aggression is actually somewhat variable and can be significantly modified by experience.

Fixed action patterns are adaptive responses that have evolved to help animals cope with consistent aspects of their environment. The difficulty with such inherited behavior patterns is that a sudden, large-scale change in the environment may render the pattern useless—or even harmful. For example, deer have an inborn tendency to run a zigzag pattern when being pursued by a predator. This action, which confuses the predator, greatly increases the deer's chances of survival in the wild; however, this same action greatly reduces its chances of survival when it is being pursued down the highway by an automobile. The inborn tendency to zigzag is a maladaptive way of responding to the modern threat of automobiles. By comparison, an animal that can modify its behavior patterns through learning can better adapt to a changing environment, which is why the ability to learn was such an important evolutionary advancement.

QUICK QUIZ B

1. A ___fixed___ ___action___ ___response___ is a fixed sequence of responses that occurs in reaction to a specific stimulus.

2. The specific stimulus that elicits a fixed action pattern is called a s___igned___ stimulus or r___eleaser___.

3. Different species of spiders spin different kinds of webs. Web spinning of this sort can thus be considered a sp___ecies___-sp___ecific___ behavior. Such behaviors used to be called i___nstincts___, but some researchers dislike this term because it implies that the behavior is more (flexible/inflexible) ___inflexible___ than is actually the case.

Simple Mechanisms of Learning

Habituation and Sensitization

The repeated presentation of an eliciting stimulus can alter the strength of the elicited behavior. *Habituation* is a decrease in the strength of an elicited behavior following repeated presentations of the eliciting stimulus. For example, we quickly stop attending to low-intensity background noises such as the

Adaptation to repeated presentations of a elicited stimulus, repeated presentations

ticking of a clock or the distant noise of traffic. Similarly, a sudden, unexpected tap on the shoulder may elicit a startle response, whereas any additional taps might have no such effect.

By contrast, *sensitization* is an increase in the strength of an elicited behavior following repeated presentations of the eliciting stimulus. For example, soldiers under attack generally do not habituate to the sound of artillery shells exploding nearby. Instead, their startle reaction grows stronger. Needless to say, this greatly contributes to the stress they experience and the inevitable breakdown virtually all soldiers will suffer after too much exposure to battle conditions (though Hollywood would often have you think otherwise).

[handwritten margin note: Increase in behavior due to eliciting Stimulus (phobias)]

The effects of habituation and sensitization usually disappear when the stimulus is not presented for a period of time, meaning that the strength of the behavior goes back to its original level. For example, you might habituate to the sound of a neighbor's stereo one evening, only to be once more bothered by it when she first turns it on the next morning. In the few hours since you last heard the music, your habituation to it disappeared and you again responded to the noise like you normally would. But some forms of habituation last for longer periods of time. For example, if you move into an apartment from which you hear the sound of a train each morning, your reaction to the noise will probably be most intense on the first day and then decrease slowly thereafter. Moreover, once you become fully habituated to the noise, you would have to be away from your apartment for several weeks or even months before your reaction to the noise would return to its original level. This type of habituation is known as long-term habituation, as opposed to short-term habituation. Thus, in *long-term habituation*, the response *slowly* decreases as a result of repeated stimulation, and one's ability to respond to the stimulus then *slowly* recovers in the absence of repeated stimulation. In *short-term habituation*, the response *quickly* decreases as a result of repeated stimulation and one's ability to respond then *quickly* recovers in the absence of stimulation. Moreover, long-term habituation tends to occur when presentations of the stimulus are widely spaced (e.g., a train going by your apartment each morning), whereas short-term habituation tends to occur when presentations of the stimulus are narrowly spaced or continuous (e.g., a child next door repeatedly banging on a drum). Also, repeated sessions of short-term habituation, spread out over time, can gradually lead to long-term habituation. The outside traffic noise that you had to habituate to each time you came home in the evening eventually becomes largely unnoticeable even when you first walk in the door.

Note that sensitization often generalizes to other stimuli. A shell-shocked soldier is likely to jump not only in response to artillery explosions but also to any sudden stimulus. By contrast, habituation tends to be more stimulus specific, such that even small changes in the stimulus may result in the reappearance of the response. Thus, many people suddenly become aware of the sound of their car when the motor sounds a bit different or when the car has a slightly different feel to it as they are driving along. Only a minor change is needed to alert the driver that something is potentially wrong (and hopefully, inexpensive to fix). One version of this process is known as the *Coolidge effect*, based on an old joke about former U.S. president Calvin Coolidge. The story has it that he and his wife were once being separately escorted around a chicken farm. When Mrs. Coolidge was informed that the resident rooster was capable of mating several times a day, she replied, "You should tell that to the president." Informed about this, the president asked whether the repeated matings occurred with the same chicken or different chickens. When told that it was different chickens, he replied, "You should tell that to my wife." The Coolidge effect therefore is the enhanced sexual arousal displayed by the males of some species when presented with different sexual partners as opposed to the same sexual partner to whom it has habituated.

Response happens again from an irrelevant stimulus (cookie jar, cat)

Habituated responses can also reappear following the presentation of a seemingly irrelevant novel stimulus, a phenomenon called ***dishabituation.*** For example, Sherri might quickly habituate to the sound of gunshots at a shooting range. If, however, a handsome stranger approaches and stands nearby, she might again be startled when the next shot is fired. Likewise, couples can sometimes rekindle their romance by traveling to a new and different environment— or even just by treating themselves to a night in a hotel room rather than staying at home.

QUICK QUIZ C

1. An increase in the strength of a behavior following repeated presentations of the eliciting stimulus is called __Sensitization__

2. A decrease in the strength of a behavior following repeated presentations of the eliciting stimulus is called __habituation__

3. Learning to ignore the sound of dripping water is an example of habituation; becoming increasingly aware of the sound of a jackhammer on the street below your apartment is an example of _____.

4. The fact that it has been several months since you noticed the sound of the fan in your home computer is an example of __Long__-t__erm__ habituation. Such habituation tends to build up (quickly/slowly) __quickly__ and disappear (quickly/slowly) __Slowly__.

5. In general, sensitization is (less/more) __More__ stimulus specific than habituation.

6. The presentation of a novel stimulus during a period of habituation can sometimes result in dishabituation, in which the habituated response (reappears/disappears) __disappears__

Why does repeated exposure to certain stimuli sometimes result in habituation and sometimes in sensitization? One factor is the intensity of the eliciting stimulus. A *low-intensity stimulus*, such as the ticking of a clock, typically results in habituation, while a *high-intensity stimulus*, such as exploding artillery shells, typically results in sensitization. A *stimulus of intermediate intensity* often results in an initial period of sensitization, followed by habituation. For example, at a shooting range, the first few shots you hear might

Low intensity ⟶ habituation
High intensity ⟶ sensitization
Mid intensity ⟶ sensitization ⟶ habituation

Simple Mechanisms of Learning | **103**

produce an increasingly strong startle reaction. But you then begin to habituate to the shots, and after a while you hardly notice them.

Another factor that influences habituation versus sensitization, which can often override the intensity factor, is the evolutionary (adaptive) significance of the stimulus. For example, which of the following would be easier to habituate to at night: the constant sound of locomotives shuttling railcars back and forth in the rail yard nearby or the sound of a wasp buzzing in your bedroom? The buzzing of the wasp is a much less intense stimulus than the sound of the trains, and yet many people will find it much easier to habituate to the sound of the trains. Now consider other sensory modalities. Think of smells associated with foods. Most people quickly habituate to the smell of onions and spices, even if quite strong, but become increasingly bothered by the smell of something rancid, even if relatively weak. Likewise with touch: we habituate easily to firm pressure on our body, such as our body weight pressing down on a chair, whereas we do not habituate to tickling or a gentle caress. (See Provine, 2004, for an interesting discussion of the evolutionary and social significance of tickling.)

So what is happening here? Habituation and sensitization are processes that we see across species, even in very simple organisms like worms and snails (e.g., Wicks & Rankin, 1997). From an evolutionary perspective, this suggests that these processes probably have tremendous survival advantages. In a sense, they help us sort stimuli into two basic categories: currently relevant and currently irrelevant (Eisenstein, Eisenstein, & Smith, 2001). If a stimulus is currently irrelevant, we tend to habituate to it; if a stimulus is currently relevant—that is, it provides some sort of useful or at least novel information—we tend not to habituate to it. And if a stimulus is extremely relevant, perhaps even dangerous, we may become sensitized to it. It therefore makes sense to become sensitized to the buzzing sound of insects that sting and the smell of something rotten that could poison us. It also makes sense not to habituate to the caress of a lover, since such touching has, throughout our evolutionary history, been associated with possible reproductive opportunities. This perspective also explains why stimulus intensity can make a difference: low-intensity stimuli are often insignificant while high-intensity stimuli are often very significant and sometimes potentially dangerous.

Of course, we do not always get it right, and we sometimes become sensitized to things that are really of no danger to us. Wouldn't you love to be able to habituate quickly to the sound of the barking dog next door or the car alarms that go off in the middle of the night? Unfortunately (or fortunately), organisms behave in ways that increase their likelihood of survival and reproduction, which often means erring on the side of caution. The result is that we often fail to habituate to stimuli that are not actually dangerous, and that we would really do better to ignore. Add to that the fact that there are individual differences in the tendency to habituate and sensitize (LaRowe, Patrick, Curtin, & Kline, 2006), and sleepless nights due to barking dogs are an unfortunate reality for many of us.

1. In general, repeated presentations of a low-intensity stimulus result in _habituation_ and repeated presentations of a high-intensity stimulus result in _sensitization_

2. A stimulus of intermediate intensity will initially result in a period of _sensitization,_ which is then followed by _habituation_

3. From an evolutionary standpoint, if a stimulus is irrelevant or "safe," we tend to _habituate_ to it, whereas if a stimulus is potentially dangerous we become _sensitized_ to it.

4. We often fail to _habituate_ to stimuli (even if they are not actually dangerous) because our nervous system tends to "err on the side of caution" to keep us safe.

Opponent-Process Theory of Emotion

Habituation and sensitization represent two opposing tendencies: weaker reactivity to a stimulus versus stronger reactivity. Solomon (1980; see also Solomon & Corbit, 1974) has proposed an intriguing theory of emotion that involves a similar dual mechanism. Known as the opponent-process theory, it is particularly good at explaining the aftereffects of strong emotional responses. Consider, for example, the following anecdote:

> My neighbor's son was struck by lightning as he was returning from a golf course. He was thrown to the ground. His shorts were torn to shreds and he was burned across his thighs. When his companion sat him up, he screamed "I'm dead, I'm dead." His legs were numb and blue and he could not move. By the time he reached the nearest hospital he was *euphoric* [italics added]. (Taussig, as quoted in Solomon, 1980, p. 691)

In one sense, the boy's euphoria is logical in that he was lucky to be alive. But in another sense, it is illogical because he was injured and decidedly worse off than before the incident. Should he not have remained at least somewhat distressed about the incident?

Consider, too, the following scenario. Suppose you purchase a lottery ticket during a visit home. Next weekend, your mom phones to tell you the winning numbers—and lo and behold, you discover that you have won $50,000! Wow! You are absolutely elated. Unfortunately, an hour later you receive another call from your mom informing you that she made a mistake on the numbers. It turns out that you won $50. You are now extremely disappointed even though you are still $50 better off than when you climbed out of bed that morning. Within a day, however, your disappointment wears off and you carry on with your impoverished lifestyle as usual.

Now consider an experiment in which a dog is exposed to electric shock (e.g., Katcher et al., 1969). During the shock, the dog's heart rate quickly rises to a peak, decreases slightly, and then stabilizes at a relatively high level. Now guess what happens when the shock is turned off. Does the dog's heart rate return to normal? No, it does not. When the shock is

FIGURE 3.3 Heart rate changes accompanying the application and withdrawal of shock. Our emotional responses often follow a similar pattern, with the onset of the emotional event followed by one type of response and the offset of the event followed by an opposite response.

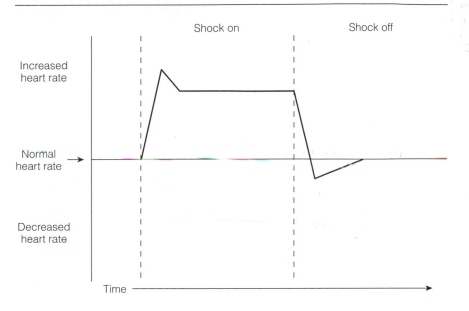

removed, the dog's heart rate plunges to *below* normal and then after a few minutes moves back up to normal (see Figure 3.3). In fact, the pattern of changes in heart rate during and after the shock—an index of the dog's emotional response to shock—is very similar to the emotional pattern displayed in the preceding lottery scenario. In both cases, an event elicits a strong emotional response; but when the event is withdrawn, an opposite response is elicited and then gradually disappears. In fact, this pattern of emotional changes is relatively common.

An explanation for these emotional changes is provided by the opponent-process theory of emotion. The ==opponent-process theory== proposes that an emotional event elicits two competing processes: (1) an a-process (or primary process) that is directly elicited by the event, and (2) a b-process (or opponent process) that is elicited by the a-process and serves to counteract the a-process. For example, the presentation of shock directly elicits a tendency for the dog's heart rate to increase, which is the a-process. This increase in heart rate in turn elicits a compensatory reaction that tries to decrease heart rate, which is the b-process. The purpose of this compensatory b-process is to counter the sudden increase in heart rate, thereby maintaining a state of internal balance (known as homeostasis). In other words, the b-process tries to prevent the increase in heart rate from becoming too extreme, which could be damaging or even fatal. The actual heart rate elicited by shock is therefore the net result of the tendency for heart rate to increase in the presence of shock (the a-process), minus the compensatory tendency for heart rate to decrease (the b-process; see Figure 3.4). Similarly, in the lottery example, the feeling of elation you experience when you think you have won the lottery is the amount of elation directly elicited by the thought of winning (the a-process) minus the compensatory reaction to this elation (the b-process), which is trying to keep your elation from becoming too extreme.

1. The opponent-process theory of emotion accounts for why a strong emotional response is often followed by a(n) (similar/opposite) _opposite_ emotional response.

2. The _A_ _process_ is directly elicited by the emotional event; this in turn elicits the _B_ _-process_, the purpose of which is to maintain a relatively balanced internal state known as _homeostasis_.

3. The a-process is also known as the _primary_ process, and the b-process is also known as the _opponent_ process.

The a- and b-processes have some important characteristics:

1. **The a-process correlates closely with the presence of the emotional event**. As shown in Figure 3.4, the tendency for the heart rate to increase in response to shock is directly tied to the presence of the shock. When the shock is presented, heart rate immediately increases; when the shock is removed, heart rate immediately decreases. Similarly, you immediately become elated when you think you have won the lottery, and your elation immediately disappears when you discover that you have not.

2. **The b-process is slow to increase and slow to decrease**. The slow buildup in the b-process accounts for why our emotional response to an event is often strongest at the outset. If you look again at Figure 3.4, you can see that when the shock is first turned on, the dog's heart rate quickly peaks and then declines slightly before stabilizing. The immediate peak happens during the early moments of shock because the b-process is not yet strong enough to counteract the a-process, thereby allowing the a-process free rein to increase heart rate. After a few moments, though, the b-process becomes strong enough to moderate the a-process, causing a slight decrease in heart rate before stabilizing. When the shock is removed, the a-process immediately disappears; but the b-process only slowly declines. For this reason, when the shock is turned off, the dog's heart rate plunges to well below normal, because all that remains is the b-process that has been trying to pull heart rate down. (It is as though, in a tug-of-war, the other team suddenly let go of the rope, sending your team flying backward in the direction you were pulling.) Similarly, when you discover that you have not won the lottery, you immediately feel depressed because the counter-reaction to the

FIGURE 3.4 Opponent-process mechanisms that underlie changes in heart rate due to the onset and offset of shock. During the shock, as the b-process acquires strength, it pulls heart rate down from its initial peak and stabilizes it at a moderately high level. Following shock, when the a-process is no longer active, the b-process pulls heart rate to below normal, then gradually disappears, allowing the heart rate to return to normal.

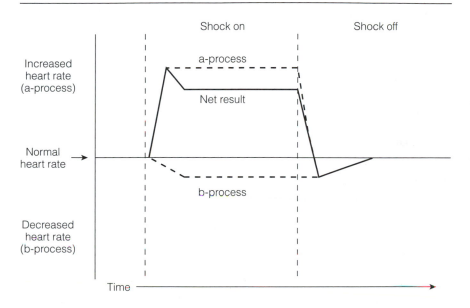

elation you have been feeling is all that remains. As the b-process gradually weakens, however, your emotional response slowly returns to normal, just as the dog's heart rate slowly returns to normal.

3. **With repeated presentations of the emotional event, the b-process increases in both strength and duration.** This is the most interesting part of the theory. For example, what happens to the dog's heart rate if it is repeatedly shocked? As it turns out, the increase in heart rate during each shock becomes less and less extreme. Additionally, each time the shock is turned off, the dog's heart rate plunges more and more deeply and takes increasingly longer to return to normal (see Figure 3.5). The dog's overt emotional response matches these changes in heart rate. Whereas in the early sessions the dog shows considerable distress in response to the shock, in later sessions it appears more annoyed than distressed. More surprising, though, is the change in the dog's emotional response following the shock. Whereas in the early sessions the dog appears somewhat relieved when the shock is turned off, in the later sessions it shows signs of extreme pleasure and euphoria, jumping about and greeting the experimenter with enthusiasm.

FIGURE 3.5   Effects of repeated stimulus presentations on primary and opponent processes. With repeated stimulation, the b-process (opponent process) becomes stronger and takes longer to disappear. The result is that the heart rate rises only slightly above normal during the shock, then drops considerably below normal following the shock and takes a relatively long time to return to normal.

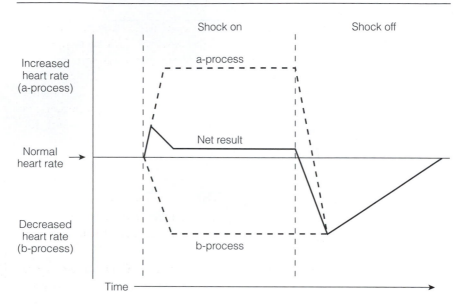

Similar emotional patterns have been found in humans. For example, S. Epstein (1967) found that military parachutists became less and less terrified with repeated jumps and became more and more elated following each jump. This sense of elation can last several hours among veteran jumpers and probably accounts, at least partially, for the strong attraction some people feel toward parachuting and other high-risk activities.[1]

The opponent-process theory of emotion also has implications for a phenomenon known as revictimization (van der Kolk, 1989). Some people repeatedly become involved in abusive relationships or have great difficulty leaving such relationships. A contributing factor in some cases may be that the person has become hooked on the powerful feelings of pleasure that occur during the "honeymoon period" of forgiveness that often follows

---

[1]Note, however, that emotional changes during skydiving can be a bit more complex than this. Veteran skydivers experience a peak of anxiety just before leaving the plane, followed by a strong sense of elation during the free fall, another peak of anxiety when the chute is being deployed (a high-risk moment), and then a sense of elation after they land. The strong sense of elation that occurs during free fall may be a contributing factor to accidents because veteran jumpers may be tempted to delay deploying the chute until the last possible moment (Delk, 1980).

an intense period of abuse. This intense pleasure is the compensatory after-reaction (the b-process), which has become greatly strengthened during repeated episodes of abuse. As suggested in the opening vignette to this chapter, a weaker version of this honeymoon effect might even occur in relationships in which one is exposed to a period of emotional distress rather than actual abuse.

It must be remembered that the opponent-process theory, however intriguing, is still a theory; and some of the research fails to support it (e.g., Fanselow, DeCola, & Young, 1993). Furthermore, as you will see in Chapter 5, classical conditioning might often play an important role in the elicitation of opponent processes, especially processes associated with drug use. Nevertheless, opponent-process theory has stimulated a considerable amount of research and has proven extremely useful for enhancing our understanding of emotional responses.

1. With repeated presentations of the emotional event, the b-process (increases/ decreases) _increase_ in both s_trength_ and d_uration_ .

2. The _A_-_process_ is directly tied to the presence of the emotional event, whereas the _B_-_process_ is (slow/quick) _slow_ to increase and (slow/quick) _slow_ to decrease.

3. Feeling elated while talking on the phone to someone with whom you are in love is an example of the _A_-_Process_. Feeling lovesick after you finally hang up for the night is an example of the _B_-_process_.

Classical Conditioning

We have so far discussed those situations in which a certain stimulus (e.g., lemon juice) elicits a particular response (e.g., salivation). We have also noted that repeated presentations of a stimulus can sometimes change the nature of the response, either strengthening it (sensitization), weakening it (habituation), or by eliciting a compensatory reaction (the opponent process). But these are relatively simple means of adaptation. Insofar as the world is a complex place filled with a vast array of stimuli, we often need to anticipate whether an event is about to occur and to recognize whether certain events are meaningfully related to other events. For example, when we are first stung by a wasp, it is adaptive for us to associate the pain with the sight and sound of the wasp. It is also adaptive for us to be wary of insects that resemble wasps, because many of them (e.g., honeybees and hornets) also sting. Thus, the ability to relate one event to another allows us to better anticipate the future, thereby greatly facilitating our chances of survival.

Classical conditioning is a process in which one stimulus that does not elicit a certain response is associated with a second stimulus that does; as a

ADVICE FOR THE LOVELORN

Dear Dr. Dee,

Several months ago I broke up with my boyfriend when he took a job in another city. We were together 5 years, and it had turned into a pretty monotonous relationship by the time it ended. But it sure is taking me a long time to get over it. My friend tells me that I must have some kind of "unresolved dependency issue" for me to be this depressed. She recently broke up with her boyfriend—she went out with him for only a month but claims that she was madly in love—and got over it in a week. Is there something wrong with me, or is my friend just superficial?

Still Depressed

Dear Still,

There may be several reasons why some people take longer than others to recover from a breakup. The opponent-process theory, however, might be particularly applicable in your case. Remember that our primary emotional response to an event typically weakens with repeated exposure, while the emotional after-reaction typically strengthens. Solomon (1980) suggested that these processes are as applicable to love relationships as they are to other emotional events. Couples that have been together for only a short time usually have much stronger feelings of affection for each other than do couples that have been together for a long time. In other words, the emotional response of affection generally decreases over time. When relationships end, however, couples that have been together for a long time experience a much deeper and longer-lasting sense of loss than do couples that have been together for a short time. According to opponent-process theory, this sense of loss is the compensatory reaction to the relationship, which should be much stronger in those couples that have been together longer. For this reason, it will naturally take more time for you to get over your long-term "monotonous" relationship than for your friend to get over her brief "madly-in-love" relationship.

Behaviorally yours,

Dr. Dee

result, the first stimulus also comes to elicit a response. Classical conditioning is also known as *Pavlovian conditioning*, after Pavlov, who discovered many of the basic principles of classical conditioning. However, behavior analysts who follow Skinner's approach to behaviorism often refer to this type of conditioning as *respondent conditioning*, in which case the elicited behaviors are called *respondent behaviors* or simply *respondents*.

Pavlov's Discovery of Classical Conditioning

Ivan P. Pavlov (1849–1936), a Russian physiologist, is generally credited with the first systematic investigations into classical conditioning.[2] Beginning in the late 1800s, Pavlov conducted important research on digestive secretions as well as the neural mechanisms that control them. He is, in fact, responsible for much of what we now know about digestion, and he won the Nobel Prize for his discoveries.

Ivan P. Pavlov
(1849–1936)

As part of this research enterprise, Pavlov also investigated salivation, the initial step in the digestive process. By this time, Pavlov was well aware that salivation could be initiated by psychic factors such as the sight of food (visual perception being regarded as a psychic, meaning a psychological, process). He was nevertheless surprised at the amount of control exerted by these factors. He noted, for instance, that different substances affected both the quantity and quality of saliva produced. For example, a moist, edible substance such as meat elicited a small amount of slimy saliva whereas a dry, inedible substance such as sand elicited a large amount of watery saliva (to facilitate spitting it out). These differences existed both when the substances were actually placed in the

Pavlov with his research team. If the assistants seem more tense than the dog, this is not surprising. Pavlov was very demanding of his assistants, but quite concerned about the welfare of his dogs.

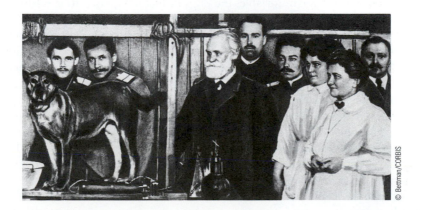

---

[2]At about the same time, an American graduate student by the name of E. B. Twitmyer also conducted experiments on this type of conditioning, and even reported his results at the 1904 conference of the American Psychological Association (Hothersall, 1984). However, his report generated little interest, and he abandoned the topic, which is fortunate because the term "Twitmyerian conditioning" is a mouthful.

dogs' mouths and, later, when the dogs were merely shown these substances. Subsequent research confirmed that these psychic secretions exhibited a great deal of regularity and lawfulness, and Pavlov began to devote more and more resources to their investigation. By 1907, classical conditioning, as it would come to be known, had become the sole focus of his research efforts.

In the decades that followed, Pavlov discovered most of the basic principles of classical conditioning and explored their application in such diverse areas as personality, hypnosis, sleep, and psychopathology. The epitome of the devoted scientist, Pavlov could be a tough taskmaster with students and assistants (once refusing to accept an assistant's excuse that he was late because he had to avoid the revolutionary battles going on in the streets). Yet in other ways he was a devoted humanitarian. When the Soviet regime took control—fortunately, the regime continued to support his research endeavors—he was openly critical of its denial of basic rights and religious freedoms. Pavlov also showed great concern for the welfare of his dogs. He invested considerable effort in devising surgical procedures that allowed for the accurate observation of internal mechanisms of digestion while minimizing the animals' discomfort and ensuring a full postoperative recovery.

Basic Procedure and Definitions

We will illustrate the process of classical conditioning using one of Pavlov's basic procedures in which a dog was trained to salivate to the sound of a metronome. During these experiments, the dog was restrained in a harness, and a tube was inserted into an incision that had been made in its cheek. Whenever the dog salivated, the saliva would run down the tube into a container where it could be precisely measured (see Figure 3.6). Although the apparatus appears uncomfortable, the dogs in fact habituated to it readily.

Pavlov's basic procedure worked as follows. Before conditioning, the dogs would automatically salivate in response to the taste of food. Because salivation to food occurs naturally and does not require prior training (conditioning), it is called an **unconditioned response** (UR), and the food is called an *unconditioned stimulus* (US). The sound of a metronome, however, does not elicit salivation and is therefore said to be a *neutral stimulus* (NS) with respect to salivation. During conditioning, the sound of the metronome is presented just before the food, which of course continues to elicit salivation. After conditioning, as a result of having been paired with the food, the metronome itself now elicits salivation. Because salivating to the metronome requires prior training (conditioning), it is called a *conditioned response* (CR), and the sound of the metronome is called a *conditioned stimulus* (CS)[3] (see Figure 3.7).

---

[3]Note that the Russian terms used by Pavlov were originally translated as "conditioned" and "unconditioned." They are, however, more precisely translated as "conditional" and "unconditional." In this text, we will continue to use the former terms because they remain more commonly used.

FIGURE 3.6 Pavlov's conditioning apparatus. In some of Pavlov's early experiments, a dog was trained to salivate to the sound of a metronome. The dog was restrained in a harness, and a tube was inserted into an incision in its cheek. Whenever the dog salivated, the tube carried the saliva to a container that activated a recording device. (*Source:* Coon, 1998.)

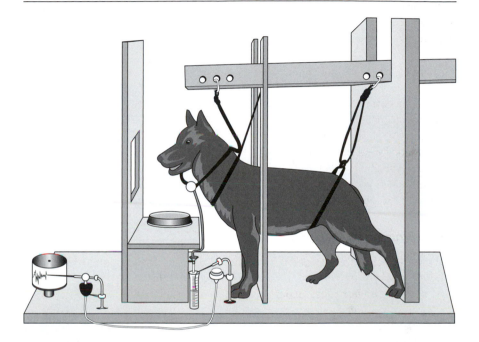

This procedure can be schematically diagrammed as follows.

Before conditioning:
Food → *Salivation*
  US   **UR**
Metronome → No salivation
    NS   —

During conditioning:
Metronome: Food → *Salivation*
 NS (or CS)   US   UR

(During conditioning, the metronome can be labeled either an NS or a CS, because during this phase it begins as an NS and then becomes a CS.)

After conditioning:
Metronome → *Salivation*
    CS   CR

FIGURE 3.7 Classical conditioning of salivation. Before conditioning, the dog automatically salivates to the taste of food. During conditioning, the sound of a metronome is presented just before the presentation of food. After conditioning, the metronome itself now elicits salivation. (*Source:* Nairne, 2000.)

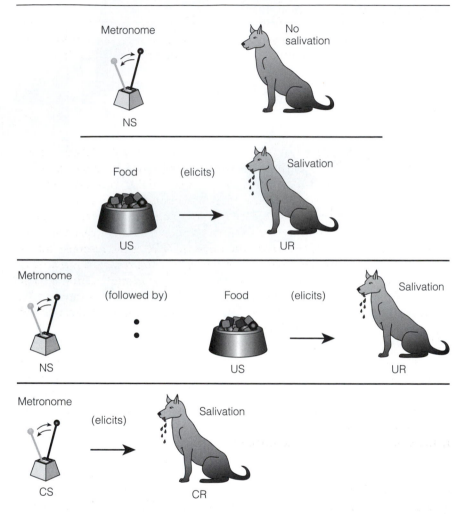

Each pairing of the NS and US during conditioning is called a *conditioning trial*.[4] Several conditioning trials are often needed before the NS becomes established as a CS. Measuring the level of conditioning can be done in various ways. The most common procedure is to intersperse the conditioning trials with an occasional *test trial* in which the NS is presented by

---

[4]It is also sometimes referred to as a *reinforcement trial*, but in this text we will reserve the term *reinforcement* for certain operant conditioning procedures, as discussed in the last half of this text.

itself. For example, every once in a while, the metronome can be presented alone to see if it elicits salivation. Alternatively, one can continue to pair the metronome with the food and simply observe whether salivation occurs in the short interval between the start of the metronome and the presentation of food.

As an everyday example of classical conditioning, let us suppose that a child is bitten by a dog and subsequently develops a fear of dogs. This process can be diagrammed as follows (omitting the "before conditioning" phase):

Dog: Bite → *Fear*
  NS   **US**   **UR**
Dog → *Fear*
 CS   **CR**

The bite can be considered an unconditioned stimulus that elicits an unconditioned response of fear (actually more pain than fear, but we will simplify matters a bit). As a result of the bite, the sight of the dog becomes a conditioned stimulus that elicits in the child a conditioned response of fear.

Let us now look more closely at each component of the classical conditioning procedure. The ***unconditioned stimulus (US)*** is a stimulus that naturally elicits a response, and the ***unconditioned response (UR)*** is the response that is naturally elicited by the US. When we say here that the response is *naturally* elicited by the US, we mean that it is an *unlearned* or *innate* reaction to that stimulus. For example, food naturally elicits the response of salivation, and a bite naturally elicits the response of fear (and pain). (Note that the US and UR are sometimes given the abbreviations of UCS and UCR.)

The ***conditioned stimulus (CS)*** is any stimulus that, although initially neutral, comes to elicit a response because it has been associated with an unconditioned stimulus. The metronome is initially neutral with respect to salivation in that it does not naturally elicit salivation.[5] After the metronome has been associated with food, however, it does elicit salivation. The ***conditioned response (CR)*** is the response, often similar to the UR, that is elicited by the CS. Note that the conditioned response is at most only similar to the unconditioned response. It is never identical (a fact that is overlooked in many introductory psychology textbooks). Even when the UR and CR appear identical, as in the case of salivation elicited by the food (US) and by the metronome (CS), there are always some differences. For example, the CR is usually weaker or less intense than the UR. Thus, the dog will salivate less to the metronome than it will to the food. The CR is also sometimes quite different from the UR. For example, as noted earlier, the unconditioned response elicited by a dog bite is actually somewhat different from the conditioned response elicited by the sight of the dog that bit us.

---

[5]Although the sound of the metronome is neutral with respect to salivation, it might not be neutral with respect to other types of responses. For example, the sound will very likely function as a US for an orienting response (turn on the metronome, and the dog will naturally prick up its ears and turn toward it).

Fortunately, Pavlov realized that the value of such experiments lay in their ability to reveal basic principles of behavior, not in their ability to simply make a dog salivate.

"PERHAPS, DR. PAVLOV, HE COULD BE TAUGHT TO SEAL ENVELOPES."

For simplicity, we labeled both responses as fear responses; however, the response to the bite is mostly what we would describe as a pain reaction ("Yeow!"), whereas the subsequent response to the dog is one that is more clearly identified as fear (e.g., freezing). The extent to which the CR can differ from the UR is discussed more fully in Chapter 5.

QUICK QUIZ G

1. Classical conditioning is also known as P<u>avlonian</u> conditioning or r<u>espondent</u> conditioning.

2. In the latter case, the behaviors themselves are called <u>respondent</u> behaviors or simply <u>respondants</u>

3. In the metronome example, the metronome is initially a(n) <u>Nuetral</u> stimulus because it (does/does not) <u>does not</u> elicit salivation. The food, however, is a(n) <u>uncondition</u> stimulus that elicits a(n) <u>unconditional</u> response of salivation.

4. During conditioning, the metronome can be labeled as either a(n) <u>Nuetral</u> stimulus or a(n) <u>Conditioned</u> stimulus.

5. Following conditioning, the metronome is a(n) <u>Conditioned</u> stimulus, and the salivation elicited by the metronome is a(n) <u>Conditional</u> response.

6. Each pairing of the metronome and the food is called a <u>conditioning</u> tr<u>ial</u> _____.

7. Write out the term indicated by each of the following abbreviations:

CS: _____
UR: _____
NS: _____
US: _____
CR: _____

8. In the basic classical conditioning procedure, the (CS/US/NS) _____ is paired with the (CS/US/NS) _____, which in turn elicits the (CR/UR) _____. As a result, the first stimulus becomes a (CS/US/NS) _____, which elicits a (CR/UR) _____.

9. Using the appropriate abbreviations, label each component in the following diagram of a classical conditioning procedure:

Wasp: Painful sting → *Fear*

Wasp → *Fear*

10. Using the format in question 9, diagram a classical conditioning procedure involving the stimuli of "nurse" and "painful injection," and the response of "anxiety." Label each component using the appropriate abbreviations.

11. The CR is (often/always) _____ (similar/identical) _____ to the UR.

12. A CR that appears identical to the UR is almost always (less/more) _____ intense.

13. Define each of the following terms (do not worry if at this point you are forced to go back and look at the definitions).

Unconditioned stimulus:

Unconditioned response:

Conditioned stimulus:

Conditioned response:

Appetitive and Aversive Conditioning

Most classical conditioning procedures can be divided into two categories based on whether the US is pleasant or unpleasant. In *appetitive conditioning*, the US is an event that an organism will generally approach or seek out; in mentalistic terms, it is something that one would usually regard as pleasant. Examples include food (if the organism is hungry), water (if the organism is thirsty), or addictive drugs (especially if the organism is a drug addict). Sexual stimuli too are regarded as appetitive stimuli, and there is good evidence that sexual responses can be classically conditioned. For example, Rachman and Hodgson (1968) took seven male volunteers and presented them with conditioning trials in which a picture of black, knee-length boots was followed by a picture of a nude woman. After about 30 trials, five of the males became sexually aroused by the sight of the boots. (Don't worry. The researchers later eliminated the conditioning by repeatedly presenting the picture of the boots without the picture of the nude—this process, known as *extinction*, is discussed later.)

In *aversive conditioning*, the US is an event that an organism generally avoids; that is, in mentalistic terms, it is something that one would usually regard as unpleasant. Examples of aversive USs include an electric shock, a painful bite, and an unpleasant odor. Aversive conditioning often occurs rapidly, especially when the aversive stimulus is quite strong, and sometimes requires only one or two pairings of the NS and the US. This reflects the close relationship between aversive conditioning and survival; to survive, we have evolved in such a way as to quickly learn to dislike those events that cause pain or illness.

Given how easily aversive conditioning can occur, it is not surprising that this type of conditioning helps account for many of our fears and anxieties. When the fear is appropriate—as in learning to fear a vicious dog that has bitten us—such conditioning is beneficial. When the fear is inappropriate— as when we begin to fear all dogs—such conditioning can be problematic. Therefore, a great deal of effort has gone into the study of fear conditioning, as well as into how such fears can be eliminated. This research has yielded important information on how real-world fears and anxieties can be treated (we discuss this topic more fully in Chapter 5).

When conducting research on fear conditioning in animals, measuring the level of fear can be problematic. Changes in certain physiological responses, such as heart rate, that might indicate fear are difficult to record, especially in small experimental animals such as rats. An ingenious solution to this problem was developed by Estes and Skinner (1941); it is known as the *conditioned suppression* or *conditioned emotional response (CER) paradigm*. In the basic paradigm, the rat is first trained to engage in an ongoing behavior in the form of lever pressing to obtain food (with many lever presses being required to obtain a single pellet). When a steady rate of lever pressing has been established, a fear-conditioning procedure is introduced in which, say, a 30-second tone is presented followed by a 1-second shock. Thus:

30 Tone: 1 Shock → *Fear*
    NS   **US**   **UR**

(In a proper conditioning procedure, each of these conditioning trials is separated by an interval of time, perhaps 30 minutes.) In the initial phase, the rat will become emotionally upset (fearful) whenever it receives a shock and will stop pressing the lever for food. As conditioning proceeds, however, the tone too will come to elicit fear, and the rat will stop pressing the lever when it hears the tone.

30 Tone → *Fear*
   CS   **CR**

Thus, the degree to which lever pressing for food is suppressed in the presence of the 30-second tone can be used as an indirect measure of the extent to which the tone elicits fear. Think of the procedure as similar to a gunfighter walking in and out of a saloon. The extent to which the saloon patrons fear the gunfighter can be accurately measured by the extent to which they stop talking to each other when he is in the saloon (you can hear a pin drop!) and resume talking when he leaves. Similarly, the rat's level of fear can be assessed by the extent to which it stops lever pressing for food when the tone is sounding and resumes lever pressing for food when the tone is not sounding.

On a more formal level, conditioned suppression is measured in the form of a suppression ratio. A *suppression ratio* is the number of responses emitted during the CS period divided by the total number emitted during the CS period and the same length period immediately preceding the CS. Thus,

$$\textbf{Suppression Ratio} = \frac{\textbf{\# of CS responses}}{\textbf{\# of CS responses + \# of pre-CS responses}}$$

For example, imagine that a rat emits 20 responses during the 30-second pre-CS period followed by 0 responses during a 30-second CS period. In other words, there is total suppression of responding during the CS period. The suppression ratio would be:

$$\frac{0}{0+20} = 0$$

Thus, a suppression ratio of 0 indicates total suppression of responding. But what if instead there was only a partial suppression of responding during the CS? For example, what if the rat emitted 10 responses during the CS period? In this case, the suppression ratio would be:

$$\frac{10}{10+20} = \frac{10}{30} = .33$$

And if there was no suppression of responding—that is, the rat emitted the same number of responses during the CS period as during the pre-CS period—the suppression ratio would be:

$$\frac{20}{20+20} = \frac{20}{40} = .5$$

Note how the suppression ratio will generally vary between 0 and .5, with a lower ratio indicating greater suppression and more effective conditioning than a higher ratio. A ratio of 0 indicates greater suppression and stronger fear conditioning than a ratio of .33, which in turn indicates greater suppression and stronger fear conditioning than a ratio of .5. Students often find this confusing since the stronger conditioning is indicated by the lower number, which is opposite to the way most ratios work. To keep it straight, simply remember that *a lower ratio indicates less responding, and less responding indicates greater suppression.*

The CER paradigm has proven to be a useful method for investigating fear conditioning in animals and is, in fact, commonly used to study classical conditioning processes. But be careful to remember that the CR in this type of procedure is the covert response of fear; it is *not* the reduction in lever pressing, which simply serves as the indirect measure of the covert response of fear.

Note that classical conditioning can transform a normally aversive stimulus into an appetitive stimulus. Pavlov found that if a dog received a shock to one of its paws and then received food, the dog would eventually begin to salivate in response to the shock. The dog's overt reactions to the shock, such as tail wagging, further indicated that the shock had lost its aversiveness. Interestingly, if the shock was then applied to a different paw, the dog would not salivate but would instead react with discomfort. The perception of shock as pleasurable appeared to be quite specific to the body part involved in the conditioning.

As you may already have guessed, this same process might partially account for the development of masochistic tendencies (the tendency to perceive painful stimulation as pleasurable) in humans. The painful stimulation from being whipped, for example, has for some people become associated with feelings of sexual arousal, as a result of which the painful stimulation itself can now elicit arousal. Interestingly, as with Pavlov's dogs, people who are masochistic do not perceive all pain as pleasurable; rather, it is only the type of pain that is connected with their erotic experiences (e.g., being whipped) that is perceived as pleasurable. The pain they feel from accidentally stubbing a toe or banging a shin is as aversive for them as it is for anyone else (Rathus, Nevid, & Fichner-Rathus, 2000).

QUICK QUIZ H

1. In _adverse_ conditioning, the US is an event that is usually considered unpleasant and that the organism avoids.

2. In _appetitive_ conditioning, the US is an event that is usually considered pleasant and that the organism seeks out.

3. Learning to associate the corner bar with the happy times you experience in that bar is an example of _appetitive_ conditioning.

4. Learning to associate your refrigerator with the nauseating smell of spoiled food is an example of _aversive_ conditioning.

5. In a _conditional emotional_ response (CER) paradigm, the level of fear elicited by a CS is indicated by the degree to which the rat's rate of lever pressing for food (decreases/increases) _decreases_ in the presence of that stimulus.

6. The CER paradigm is also known as a _conditioned supression_ procedure.

7. The suppression ratio is the number of (pre-CS/CS/post-CS) _CS_ responses divided by the number of _post-CS_ responses plus the number of _pre-CS_ responses.

8. Intense fear in a CER procedure will result in a suppression ratio of (.5/0) _.5_, whereas no fear will result in a suppression ratio of around _0_.

And Furthermore

Classical Conditioning and Interpersonal Attraction

Classical conditioning may play an important role in interpersonal attraction. According to the reinforcement-affect model of attraction (Byrne & Clore, 1970; see also Baron Byrne, 1997), the extent to which we are attracted to someone can be significantly affected by the degree to which the person is associated with events that elicit positive emotions. For this reason, we are generally attracted to people who say and do the kinds of things that make us feel good. Eventually, we feel good just being around such people.

Interestingly, the model also predicts that we can become attracted to a person who is only incidentally associated with positive events. Experiments have revealed that events as innocuous as pleasant background music or a positive news story on the radio can heighten the extent to which a person we are meeting is perceived as attractive. Of course, this means that associating ourselves with pleasant stimuli—pleasant music, attractive clothing, and even a clean car—during an initial date can greatly facilitate the possibility of a second date.

The reinforcement-affect model also suggests that we are less attracted to someone who is associated with aversive events. Obviously, dressing like a slob or drinking to the point of vomiting during a first date is probably not a good idea. Less obviously, inadvertently hearing bad news on the radio or really annoying music may also undermine your prospects for a second date. On the other hand, there may be times when you *want* to be perceived as less attractive. A letter once appeared in a newspaper advice column in which a woman described how she finally managed to dissuade a persistent acquaintance from continually asking her out. She agreed to a date and then ate plenty of garlic beforehand! Her suitor was apparently not a big garlic fan, and she had no further difficulties with him.

Excitatory and Inhibitory Conditioning

In all of the examples so far, and as it is traditionally defined, the NS is associated with the presentation of a US. The metronome is associated with the presentation of food, the dog is associated with a painful bite, and the tone is associated with shock. Conditioning in which the NS is associated with the presentation of a US is known as *excitatory conditioning*. The result of excitatory conditioning is that the CS comes to elicit a certain response, such as salivation or fear.

But what if a stimulus is associated with the absence of the US rather than its presentation? What if, for example, a vicious dog always bites you except when its owner is present? The owner then is a sort of safety signal that indicates the absence of a painful bite. Conditioning in which the NS is associated with the absence or removal of a US is known as ***inhibitory conditioning***. The result of inhibitory conditioning is that the CS comes to inhibit the occurrence of a certain response—that is, the response is less likely to occur when that stimulus is present. Thus, although the dog is an excitatory CS for fear, the owner is an inhibitory CS for fear, and your fear of the dog will be suppressed when the owner is present. Similarly, if a rat is consistently shocked when a tone is presented, the tone will become an excitatory stimulus for fear. But if the rat is never shocked when a tone and a light are presented together, the light will become an inhibitory CS for fear because it explicitly signals the absence of shock. In such procedures, the excitatory CS is usually labeled a CS+, and the inhibitory CS is labeled a CS−.

Traditionally, researchers have focused on the study of excitatory conditioning, and most of the basic principles of classical conditioning have been established using excitatory procedures. For this reason, most of the examples in this text are examples of excitatory conditioning. In recent years, however, the study of inhibitory conditioning has begun to attract a good deal of attention (Domjan, 2010).

QUICK QUIZ I

1. Conditioning associated with the removal of a US is known as _Inhibitory_ conditioning, whereas conditioning associated with the presentation of a US is known as _Excititory_ conditioning.

2. Your grandmother always cooks great meals except when your vegetarian sister is present. As a result, you usually salivate a great deal when sitting at your grandmother's table for a meal, but not when your sister is present. Your grandmother's table is an _excititory_ CS for salivation, while your vegetarian sister is an _inhibitory_ CS for salivation.

3. Most of the basic principles of classical conditioning have been established using procedures that involve _excititory_ conditioning.

4. A conditioned excitatory stimulus (an excitatory CS) is one that is associated with the (presentation/removal) _presentation_ of a US; a conditioned inhibitory stimulus (an inhibitory CS) is one that is associated with the (presentation/removal) _removal_ of a US.

5. An excitatory CS for fear is one that will (elicit/suppress) _suppresses_ a fear response; an inhibitory CS for fear is one that will (elicit/suppress) _elicits_ a fear response.

6. For the residents of Berlin and London during World War II, an air-raid siren would have been a (CS+/CS−) _CS−_ for anxiety, while the all-clear siren would have been a (CS+/CS−) _CS+_ for anxiety.

7. A click is followed by food, while a click and a buzzing noise is never followed by food. In this case, the click will become a (CS+/CS−) _CS+_ for salivation and the buzzing noise will become a (CS+/CS−) _CS−_.

Temporal Arrangement of Stimuli

In the classical conditioning examples discussed to this point, the NS was always presented before the US. This temporal arrangement, though, is only one of several ways to arrange the NS and US. In this section, we outline four such arrangements and note the effectiveness of each for producing a conditioned response.

1. **Delayed Conditioning.** In *delayed conditioning*, the onset of the NS precedes the onset of the US, and the two stimuli overlap. For example, if we want a rat to associate a tone with a brief shock, we first present the tone and then, while the tone is still on, present a shock. As shown in Figure 3.8a, the onset of the tone precedes the onset of the shock and the tone is still on when the shock is presented. (Note that it is the point at which the two stimuli are turned on, rather than turned off, that is critical.) A delayed conditioning procedure is often the best arrangement for conditioning, especially if the time between the onset of the NS and the onset of the US (known as the *interstimulus interval* or ISI) is relatively short. When conditioning certain autonomic responses (responses controlled by the autonomic nervous system), such as salivation, the optimal ISI is generally in the range of a few seconds. When conditioning skeletal responses (responses controlled by skeletal muscles), such as the eyeblink reflex, the optimal ISI is about a half second. Thus, conditioning generally works best when the onset of the NS more or less immediately precedes the onset of the US; this fact is consistent with the notion that the NS generally serves as a predictor of the US, a notion that is discussed further in Chapter 5. (Nevertheless, some forms of classical conditioning do not require a close temporal pairing between the NS and US. One such form, known as taste aversion conditioning, is described in Chapter 12.)

2. **Trace Conditioning.** In *trace conditioning*, the onset and offset of the NS precede the onset of the US. In other words, the NS occurs before the US, and the two stimuli do not overlap. For example, a tone is turned on and then off, and this is then followed by the presentation of a shock (see Figure 3.8b). The time between the offset of the NS and the onset of the US (e.g., between the point when the tone was turned off and the shock was turned *on*) is called the *trace interval*. Because the tone is no longer present when the shock occurs, you might say that the organism has to "remember" the occurrence of the tone (or, in cognitive parlance, have some "memory trace" of it) to be able to associate the two. Trace conditioning can be almost as effective as delayed conditioning if the trace interval is relatively short (no more than a few seconds). If the trace interval is longer than that, conditioning is, in most cases, much less likely to occur.

FIGURE 3.8 Four ways in which presentation of the NS and US can be temporally arranged.

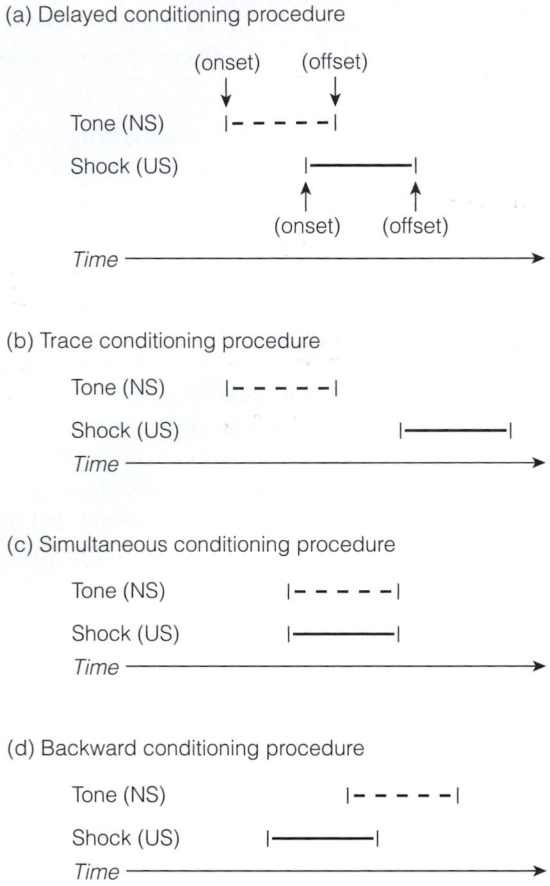

(a) Delayed conditioning procedure

(onset)   (offset)

Tone (NS) |- - - - -|

Shock (US) |————————|

(onset)   (offset)

Time ————————————————————→

(b) Trace conditioning procedure

Tone (NS) |- - - - -|

Shock (US) |————————|

Time ————————————————————→

(c) Simultaneous conditioning procedure

Tone (NS) |- - - - -|

Shock (US) |————————|

Time ————————————————————→

(d) Backward conditioning procedure

Tone (NS) |- - - - -|

Shock (US) |————————|

Time ————————————————————→

3. **Simultaneous Conditioning.** In *simultaneous conditioning*, the onset of the NS and the onset of the US occur simultaneously. For example, a tone and a shock are turned on at the same time (see Figure 3.8c). Although simultaneous conditioning involves the closest possible contiguity between the NS and the US, this procedure usually results in poor conditioning. One reason for this is that if the NS occurs at the same time as the US, the NS is no longer a good predictor of the US.

4. **Backward Conditioning.** In *backward conditioning*, the onset of the NS follows the onset of the US. In other words, the US is presented

FIGURE 3.9   A potentially effective backward conditioning procedure in which the NS is a biologically relevant stimulus for a conditioned fear response.

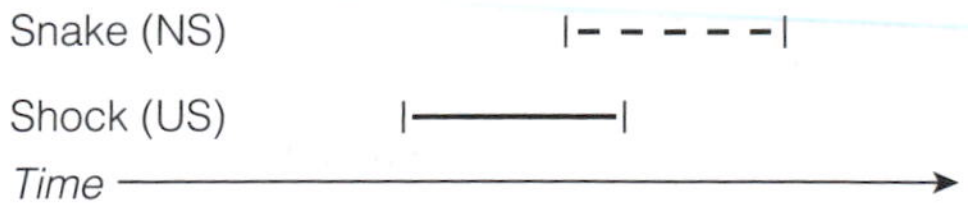

```
Snake (NS)                          |- - - - -|

Shock (US)              |————————|

Time  ——————————————————————————————————————>
```

first and the NS is presented later. For example, the rat receives a shock and then hears a tone (see Figure 3.8d). Backward conditioning is traditionally considered the least effective procedure for conditioning. This is especially true for conditioning of an excitatory response like salivation. Nevertheless, under some circumstances, backward excitatory conditioning can be achieved, such as when the NS is a "biologically relevant" stimulus for fear (Keith-Lucas & Guttman, 1975). For example, if instead of using a tone as the NS for shock, we use the sight of a snake, then backward conditioning might occur (see Figure 3.9).

Why does backward conditioning work with the snake but not the tone? Some researchers (e.g., Seligman, 1971) have proposed that many species of animals (including people) have an inherited predisposition to fear certain types of events. From this perspective, rats have an inherited predisposition to fear snakes, because poisonous snakes have constituted a significant threat to rats throughout their evolutionary history. This predisposition is so strong that even if the snake is presented after the shock, the fear elicited by the shock still becomes associated with the snake. (Needless to say, such predispositions would also facilitate conditioning using a delayed, trace, or simultaneous procedure.)

Backward conditioning can also result in inhibitory conditioning. For example, if a tone sounds just before a shock is *terminated*, then the tone reliably predicts the removal of shock. The tone in this case can become a safety signal (CS–) that inhibits the occurrence of fear. Similarly, if a child suffers from severe asthma attacks, but feels relief when the doctor gives him an injection, the doctor's presence will become a safety signal that effectively inhibits the child's sense of distress. Whenever this doctor is nearby, the child will feel especially safe and comfortable.

Thus, although delayed conditioning is traditionally thought of as the most effective arrangement, conditioning can occur with other arrangements as well. Although beyond the scope of this text, recent evidence in fact indicates that each type of arrangement can have an impact on behavior (see Domjan, 2010).

1. The most successful temporal arrangement for conditioning is delayed conditioning, in which the onset of the NS (precedes/follows) _Precedes_ the onset of the US, and the two stimuli (overlap/do not overlap) _overlap_.

2. In delayed conditioning, the time between the onset of the NS and the onset of the US is called the _interstimulus_ interval (abbreviated _ISI_).

3. In trace conditioning, the (onset/offset) _onset_ and _offset_ of the NS precedes the _onset_ of the US.

4. In trace conditioning, the time between the _offset_ of the NS and the _onset_ of the US is called the _trace_ interval. Trace conditioning can be effective if this interval is relatively (long/short) _short_.

5. In simultaneous conditioning, the _onset_ of the NS occurs at the same time as the _onset_ of the US. Simultaneous conditioning usually results in (good/poor) _poor_ conditioning.

6. In backward conditioning, the (US/NS) _US_ is presented first and the (US/NS) _NS_ is presented later. Backward conditioning is generally considered to result in (good/poor) _poor_ conditioning.

7. Backward conditioning can result in excitatory conditioning of fear when the NS is a b_iologically_ relevant stimulus for fear. Backward conditioning can also result in inhibitory conditioning when the NS signals the (presentation/removal)_removal_ of the US.

8. Suppose that we attempt to condition a reflex response of sneezing using a flower as the NS and pollen as the US. Name each of the four NS–US arrangements listed below.

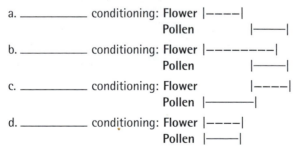

a. _____ conditioning: **Flower** |————|
                             Pollen |———|

b. _____ conditioning: **Flower** |—————————|
                             Pollen |———|

c. _____ conditioning: **Flower** |————|
                             Pollen |————————|

d. _____ conditioning: **Flower** |————|
                             Pollen |———|

SUMMARY

In general, elicited behaviors are involuntary reactions to specific stimuli. Examples of elicited behaviors include reflexes and fixed action patterns. Repeated presentations of the same stimulus may decrease the strength of a behavior (known as habituation) or increase the strength of a behavior (known as sensitization), depending on the intensity and evolutionary significance of the eliciting stimulus. A similar dual mechanism is evident in the opponent-process theory of emotion, in which an event elicits an emotional response (the a-process) that in turn elicits a compensatory response (the b-process).

In classical conditioning, a neutral stimulus is associated with some other stimulus that naturally elicits a response; as a result, the neutral stimulus also comes to elicit a response. In Pavlov's basic procedure, the unconditioned stimulus (US) is the stimulus that naturally elicits a response, and the unconditioned response (UR) is the response that is naturally elicited by the US. The conditioned stimulus (CS) is the stimulus that, although initially a neutral stimulus (NS), comes to elicit a response because it has been associated with the US. The conditioned response (CR) is the response that is elicited by the CS.

In appetitive conditioning, the US is an appetitive stimulus such as food; in aversive conditioning, the US is an aversive stimulus such as a shock. Studies of aversive conditioning are often carried out using a conditioned suppression procedure in which a rat stops lever pressing for food in the presence of a tone that has been paired with a shock. In excitatory conditioning the NS is associated with the presentation of the US, whereas in inhibitory conditioning the NS is associated with the removal of the US.

There can be various temporal arrangements of the NS and US in classical conditioning. In delayed conditioning, the onset of the NS precedes the onset of the US and overlaps with it. In trace conditioning, the onset and offset of the NS precede the onset of the US. In simultaneous conditioning, the NS and US are presented at the same time. Finally, in backward conditioning, the onset of the NS follows the onset of the US. Delayed conditioning and trace conditioning are usually the most effective procedures, with backward conditioning being the least effective. However, backward conditioning can occur under some circumstances, such as when the NS is a biologically relevant stimulus for fear and the US is an aversive stimulus.

SUGGESTED READINGS

Babkin, B. P. (1949). *Pavlov: A biography*. Chicago, IL: University of Chicago Press. An excellent biography of Pavlov by a former student of his.

Pavlov, I. P. (1927). *Conditioned reflexes* (G. V. Anrep, Trans.). London: Oxford University Press. The best of Pavlov's own books on classical conditioning.

Windholz, G. (1997). Ivan P. Pavlov: An overview of his life and psychological work. *American Psychologist*, 52, 941–946. The commemorative issue of *American Psychologist* in which this article appears also contains several other articles on Pavlov's work and on the modern-day status of classical conditioning.

STUDY QUESTIONS

1. What is a reflex? Describe the startle response, orienting response, and flexion response.
2. Describe, or diagram, the sequence of events in a reflex arc.
3. Define fixed action pattern. What is a sign stimulus or releaser?
4. Define habituation and sensitization.
5. What is the effect of high versus low versus moderate stimulus intensity on habituation and sensitization?
6. Distinguish between long-term and short-term habituation and give an example of each.
7. Describe the evolutionary significance of habituation and sensitization.
8. Describe the phenomenon of dishabituation.
9. Define the opponent-process theory of emotion.
10. List three main characteristics of opponent processes.
11. Define classical conditioning.
12. Diagram an example of a classical conditioning procedure. Be sure to label each component using the appropriate abbreviations.
13. Define the terms unconditioned stimulus and unconditioned response.
14. Define the terms conditioned stimulus and conditioned response.
15. Distinguish between appetitive and aversive conditioning.
16. Describe the conditioned suppression (or CER) procedure. How does one calculate a suppression ratio?
17. Distinguish between excitatory and inhibitory conditioning.
18. Name and diagram four temporal arrangements of the NS and US. Which two temporal arrangements of the NS and US are traditionally considered to be most effective?

CONCEPT REVIEW

appetitive conditioning. Conditioning procedure in which the US is an event that an organism approaches or seeks out.

aversive conditioning. Conditioning procedure in which the US is an event that an organism avoids.

backward conditioning. Conditioning procedure in which the onset of the NS follows the onset of the US.

classical conditioning. A process whereby one stimulus that does not elicit a certain response is associated with a second stimulus that does; as a result, the first stimulus also comes to elicit a response.

conditioned response (CR). The response, often similar to the unconditioned response, that is elicited by the conditioned stimulus.

conditioned stimulus (CS). Any stimulus that, although initially neutral, comes to elicit a response because it has been associated with an unconditioned stimulus.

delayed conditioning. Conditioning procedure in which the onset of the NS precedes the onset of the US, and the two stimuli overlap.

dishabituation. The reappearance of a habituated response to a stimulus following the presentation of another, seemingly irrelevant novel stimulus.

excitatory conditioning. Conditioning procedure in which the NS is associated with the *presentation* of a US.

fixed action pattern. A fixed sequence of responses elicited by a specific stimulus.

flexion response. The automatic response of jerking one's hand or foot away from a hot or sharp object.

habituation. A decrease in the strength of an elicited behavior following repeated presentations of the eliciting stimulus.

inhibitory conditioning. Conditioning procedure in which the NS is associated with the *absence* or *removal* of a US.

opponent-process theory. A theory proposing that an emotional event elicits two competing processes: (1) an a-process (or primary process) directly elicited by the event, and (2) a b-process (or opponent process) that is elicited by the a-process and serves to counteract the a-process.

orienting response. The automatic positioning of oneself to facilitate attending to a stimulus.

reflex. A relatively simple, involuntary response to a stimulus.

reflex arc. A neural structure that underlies many reflexes and consists of a sensory neuron, an interneuron, and a motor neuron.

sensitization. An increase in the strength of an elicited response following repeated presentations of the eliciting stimulus.

sign stimulus (or releaser). A specific stimulus that elicits a fixed action pattern.

simultaneous conditioning. Conditioning procedure in which the onset of the NS and the onset of the US are simultaneous.

startle response. A defensive reaction to a sudden, unexpected stimulus, which involves automatic tightening of skeletal muscles and various hormonal and visceral changes.

trace conditioning. Conditioning procedure in which the onset and offset of the NS precede the onset of the US.

unconditioned response (UR). The response that is naturally elicited by the unconditioned stimulus without any prior learning.

unconditioned stimulus (US). A stimulus that naturally elicits a response without any prior learning.

CHAPTER TEST

4. A sudden loud noise is likely to elicit a(n) _____ reaction, which is a reflexive defensive response to a sudden stimulus.

13. With repeated presentations of the emotional event, the b-process (increases/decreases) _____ in both _____ and _____.

23. Seeing a wasp land on your arm and then watching it as it stings you is an example of a _____ conditioning procedure; noticing the wasp at the same moment that you feel the sting is an example of a _____ conditioning procedure.

6. When a subordinate dog submits to a threatening display from a dominant dog, it will often roll over on its back and display its belly. This type of action sequence is called a _____, and the threatening display from the dominant dog is called the _____ stimulus or _____ for these actions.

14. Classical conditioning is also known as P_____ conditioning or _____ conditioning. In the latter case, the elicited behaviors are referred to as _____.

9. The faint sound of a jackhammer several blocks away will likely result in _____, but the extremely loud sound of a jackhammer right outside your window may result in _____. The moderately loud sound of a jackhammer half a block away may result in a period of _____ followed by _____.

26. In general, aversive conditioning occurs (more/less) _____ readily than appetitive conditioning.

2. The most basic type of elicited behavior is the _____, which is a simple, involuntary response to a stimulus.

12. According to the opponent-process theory of emotion, b-processes are (slow/quick) _____ to increase and (slow/quick) _____ to decrease.

18. Imagine an eyeblink conditioning procedure in which the sound of a click is paired with a puff of air to the eye. Each pairing of the click and air puff during conditioning is referred to as a(n) _____.

11. In the opening scenario to this chapter, Uma witnessed her boyfriend flirting with another woman. First, she experienced intense anger. Later, however, when he apologized for his actions and was very attentive to her, she experienced unusually strong feelings of attraction toward him. An explanation for this pattern of emotional changes is provided by the _____ theory of emotion. In this case, Uma's feelings of anger are an example of the _____ process, and her feelings of affection following his apology are an example of the _____ process.

1. Behaviors that are automatically drawn out by the stimuli that precede them are referred to as _____ behaviors.

20. When you opened the refrigerator yesterday, the putrid smell of rotten eggs made you feel extremely nauseous. Today, when you are about to open the refrigerator again, you find yourself becoming nauseous, even though the refrigerator has been thoroughly cleaned. In classical conditioning terms, the refrigerator has become a(n) _____ stimulus that now elicits a(n) _____ response of nausea. In this case, the nausea produced by the sight of the refrigerator is likely to

be (less/more) _____ severe than the nausea produced by the smell of rotten eggs.

5. The reflexive action of pulling your hand away from a hot plate is activated through a _____: a neural structure underlying simple reflexes that consists of a (in correct order) _____
_____.

25. Feeling a bite and then seeing the snake that bit you is an example of a _____ conditioning procedure, which in this case may be (effective/ineffective) _____ because the CS is a _____ for a fear response.

10. You finally habituate to the faint sound of a jackhammer half a block away, such that you cease to notice it. The lights in your house then go out, at which point you again notice the sound of the jackhammer. This is an example of the process of _____.

15. Imagine an eyeblink conditioning procedure in which the sound of a click is paired with a puff of air to the eye. The puff of air is called the _____ stimulus (abbreviated _____), and the eyeblink that it elicits is called the _____ response (abbreviated _____).

30. In general, long-term habituation is most likely to occur when the stimulus is presented at (narrowly/widely) _____ spaced intervals; in this case, the ability to respond tends to recover (slowly/quickly) _____ when the stimulus is no longer presented.

19. When you opened the refrigerator one evening, the putrid smell of rotten eggs made you feel extremely nauseous. In classical conditioning terms, the putrid smell is a(n) _____ stimulus that elicits a(n) _____ response of nausea.

28. Inadvertently touching a hot object is likely to elicit a(n) _____ response; the sound of a gunshot is likely to elicit a(n) _____ response; the sound of someone talking behind you may elicit a(n) _____ response.

7. Fixed action patterns are sometimes called _____ behaviors because they are often unique to a certain species.

3. The reflexive action of a dog pricking up its ears in response to a sound is an example of a(n) _____ response, which consists of movements designed to facilitate _____.

31. How does one calculate a suppression ratio? _____
_____.

17. Imagine an eyeblink conditioning procedure in which the sound of a click is paired with a puff of air to the eye. After conditioning, the click becomes a(n) _____ stimulus (abbreviated _____) because it now elicits an eyeblink. The eyeblink elicited by the click is called the _____ response (abbreviated _____).

27. Dana always feels very relaxed when she takes her large dog for a walk, even though the neighborhood is relatively dangerous. This appears to

be an example of _____, with the dog functioning as an _____ CS (abbreviated _____).

21. When you opened the refrigerator one evening, the putrid smell of rotten eggs made you feel extremely nauseous. The subsequent response of nausea to the sight of the refrigerator is an example of (aversive/appetitive) _____ conditioning as well as (excitatory/inhibitory) _____ conditioning.

16. Imagine an eyeblink conditioning procedure in which the sound of a click is paired with a puff of air to the eye. Before conditioning, the sound of the click does not elicit an eyeblink; it is therefore considered a(n) _____ stimulus.

24. In an experiment involving the conditioning of an eyeblink response to the sound of a click, hearing the click and then a second later feeling the puff of air in your eye is an example of a _____ conditioning procedure. Conversely, feeling the puff of air and then hearing the click is an example of a _____ conditioning procedure. In general, the (former/latter) _____ procedure is likely to produce more effective conditioning.

8. In a restaurant, the parents of a very noisy child hardly notice the commotion. This is an example of _____. However, the customers at neighboring tables are becoming increasingly annoyed by the child. This is an example of _____.

22. Brett is allergic to bee stings. He eats and drinks heartily when he is inside the restaurant, but not when he is seated on the outdoor patio surrounded by flowers. This circumstance is similar to the _____ paradigm, which is also known as the _____ (CER) procedure.

29. In a conditioned suppression ratio, a score of _____ indicates total suppression of the behavior, while a score of around _____ indicates no suppression.

Visit the book companion Web site at http://www.academic.cengage.com/psychology/powell for additional practice questions, answers to the Quick Quizzes, practice review exams, and additional exercises and information.

ANSWERS TO CHAPTER TEST

1. elicited
2. reflex
3. orienting; attending to a stimulus
4. startle
5. reflex arc; sensory neuron; interneuron; motor neuron
6. fixed action pattern; sign; releaser
7. species-specific

8. habituation (or long-term habituation); sensitization
9. habituation; sensitization; sensitization; habituation
10. dishabituation
11. opponent-process; primary (or a-) process; opponent (or b-) process
12. slow; slow

13. increases; strength; duration
14. Pavlovian; respondent; respondents
15. unconditioned stimulus (US); unconditioned response (UR)
16. neutral
17. conditioned; CS; conditioned; CR
18. conditioning trial
19. unconditioned; unconditioned
20. conditioned; conditioned; less
21. aversive; excitatory
22. conditioned suppression; conditioned emotional response
23. delayed; simultaneous
24. trace; backward; former
25. backward; effective; biologically relevant stimulus
26. more
27. inhibitory conditioning; inhibitory; CS–
28. flexion; startle; orienting
29. 0; .5
30. widely; slowly
31. using equal CS and pre-CS periods (e.g., 30 sec.), divide the number of CS responses by the number of CS responses plus the number of pre-CS responses

CHAPTER 4

Classical Conditioning: Basic Phenomena and Various Complexities

CHAPTER OUTLINE

Jana enjoys being wildly unpredictable in her relationships, believing that most men find unpredictable women quite exciting. She cancels dates at the last minute, shows up on the guy's doorstep at odd hours of the day or night, and tries as much as possible to be completely spontaneous. Once, she stole a man's bowling trophy and cheese grater, just to see if he would notice. Unfortunately, many of the guys she goes out with seem to be rather stressed out and neurotic, though it usually takes a while before this becomes apparent. She is starting to wonder if there are any good men around these days.

Some Basic Conditioning Phenomena

Acquisition

In classical conditioning, *acquisition* is the process of developing and strengthening a conditioned response through repeated pairings of a neutral stimulus (NS) with an unconditioned stimulus (US). In general, acquisition proceeds rapidly during early conditioning trials, then gradually levels off. The maximum amount of conditioning that can take place in a particular situation is known as the *asymptote* of conditioning (see Figure 4.1).

Process that strengths CR with repetition

The asymptote of conditioning, as well as the speed of conditioning, is dependent on several factors. In general, *more intense USs produce stronger and more rapid conditioning than do less intense USs.* For example, we can obtain stronger conditioning of a salivary response when the US consists of a large

FIGURE 4.1   A typical acquisition curve in which strength of conditioning increases rapidly during the first few trials and then gradually levels off over subsequent trials.

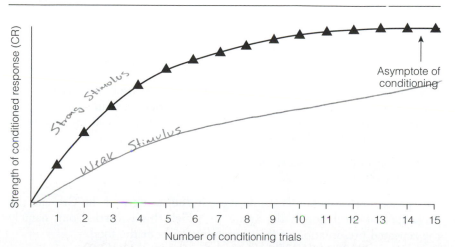

amount of food or a highly preferred food than if it consists of a small amount or less preferred food. Likewise, a severe bite from a dog will result in a stronger conditioned fear response than a minor bite will. Similarly, *more intense* NSs *result in stronger and more rapid conditioning than do less intense* NSs. For example, a loud metronome that has been paired with food produces a stronger response of salivation than a faint metronome that has been paired with food. And, not surprisingly, conditioned fear responses to dogs are more readily acquired if the person is bitten by a large dog than by a small dog.

1. The process of strengthening a conditioned response through repeated pairings of an NS with a US is known as <u>aquisition</u>. In general, conditioning proceeds more (rapidly/slowly) <u>rapidly</u> during the early trials of a conditioning procedure.

2. The maximum amount of learning (or conditioning) that can take place in a given situation is known as the <u>asymptote</u> of learning.

3. In general, a (more/less) <u>More</u> intense US produces better conditioning.

4. In general, a (more/less) <u>More</u> intense NS produces better conditioning.

Extinction, Spontaneous Recovery, and Disinhibition

CR is eliminated when CS is shown without US

"extinction trial"

Given that a certain stimulus now elicits a conditioned response, is there any way to eliminate the response? In a *process* known as **extinction**, a conditioned response is weakened or eliminated when the conditioned stimulus (CS) is repeatedly presented in the absence of the US. The term *extinction* also applies to the *procedure* whereby this happens, namely the repeated presentation of the CS in the absence of the US.

Suppose, for example, that a metronome has been paired with food such that it now elicits a conditioned response of salivation:

Metronome: Food → *Salivation*
    NS   US   UR
Metronome → *Salivation*
    CS   CR

If we now continue to present the metronome by itself and never again pair it with food (each presentation of the metronome being known as an "extinction trial"), the conditioned response of salivation will eventually die out—that is, the CR of salivation will have been *extinguished*.

Metronome → **No salivation**
  "NS"   —

The process of extinction is the decrease in the strength of the CR, and the procedure of extinction is the means by which this is carried out, namely the repeated presentation of the metronome without the food.

In a similar manner, if a dog that once bit me never again bites me, my fear response to the dog should eventually extinguish. Unfortunately, some people who were once bitten by a dog continue to fear that dog as well as other dogs, in which case we might say that they have a "phobia" about dogs. But if the person has never again been bitten by the dog, why is his or her fear so persistent? One reason is that people who fear dogs tend to avoid them, and to the extent that they avoid them, their fear response cannot be extinguished. As you will see in later chapters, this tendency to avoid a feared event is a major factor in the development and maintenance of a phobia, and treatment procedures for phobias are often based on preventing this avoidance response from occurring.

Once a CR has been extinguished, one should not assume that the effects of conditioning have been completely eliminated. For this reason, in the above diagram the "NS" following extinction has been placed in quotation marks, since it is no longer a pure neutral stimulus. For one thing, *a response that has been extinguished can be reacquired quite rapidly when the CS (or NS) is again paired with the US.* If we again pair the metronome with food following an extinction procedure, it may take only a few pairings before we achieve a fairly strong level of conditioning. Likewise, if I somehow manage to overcome my phobia of dogs, I might rapidly reacquire that phobia if I again have a frightening experience with dogs.

As further evidence that extinction does not completely eliminate the effects of conditioning, an extinguished response can reappear even in the absence of further pairings between the CS and US. Suppose, for example, that we do extinguish a dog's conditioned salivary response to a metronome by repeatedly presenting the metronome without food. By the end of the extinction session, the metronome no longer elicits salivation. However, if we come back the next morning and sound the metronome, the dog will very likely salivate. In everyday terms, it is almost as if the dog has forgotten that the metronome no longer predicts food. As a result, we are forced to conduct another series of extinction trials, repeatedly sounding the metronome without the food. After several trials, the response is again extinguished. The next day, however, the dog again starts salivating when we first present the metronome. At this point, we might be tempted to conclude that we have an awfully dumb dog on our hands. The dog, however, is simply displaying a phenomenon known as spontaneous recovery.

Spontaneous recovery is the reappearance of a conditioned response to a CS following a rest period after extinction. Fortunately, spontaneous recovery does not last forever. In general, each time the response recovers it is somewhat weaker and is extinguished more quickly than before (see Figure 4.2). Therefore, after several extinction sessions, we should be able to sound the metronome at the start of the session and find little or no salivation.

The phenomenon of spontaneous recovery is particularly important to remember when attempting to extinguish a conditioned fear response.

Reappearance of a CR to a CS after Extinction

FIGURE 4.2 Hypothetical results illustrating a decline in spontaneous recovery across repeated sessions of extinction.

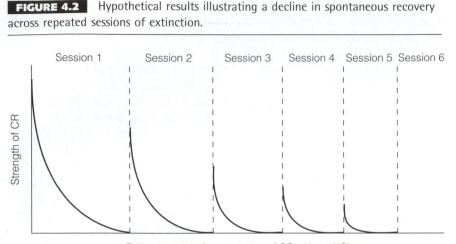

For example, we might arrange for a dog-phobic child to spend several hours with a dog. At the end of that time, the child's fear of the dog might seem to have been totally eliminated. Nevertheless, it is quite possible that the fear will at least partially recover the next time the child is confronted with a dog, and that several sessions of extinction may be needed before the fear is completely eliminated. Similarly, if you feel terribly anxious with a new date at the start of the evening but more at ease after a couple of hours, do not be disappointed if you again find yourself becoming anxious at the start of your next date. It may take several dates with that person before you feel comfortable right from the outset. Likewise, following a breakup, it may take a while before your feelings of attraction to the other person are finally extinguished, and even then they may intermittently reappear for a considerable period of time.

To Pavlov (1927), the phenomenon of spontaneous recovery indicated that extinction is not simply a process of unlearning the conditioning that has taken place. Rather, extinction involves learning something new, namely, to inhibit the occurrence of the CR in the presence of the CS. For example, rather than unlearning the response of salivation to the metronome during extinction, the dog learns to inhibit the response of salivation to the metronome, with the connection between the metronome and salivation still remaining intact on some underlying level. Spontaneous recovery may therefore represent the partial weakening of this inhibition during the rest period between extinction sessions.

Support for the notion that extinction involves a buildup of inhibition is also provided by a phenomenon known as disinhibition. **Disinhibition** is the sudden recovery of a response during an extinction procedure when a novel stimulus is introduced. For example, if we are in the process of extinguishing

Sudden recovery of a CR during extinction because of a type of change in environment

conditioning to a metronome but then present a novel humming noise in the background, the sound of the metronome may again elicit a considerable amount of salivation. In diagram form:

(**Step 1:** First condition the metronome as a CS for salivation)

> **Metronome: Food** → *Salivation*
>   **NS**   **US**   **UR**
> **Metronome** → *Salivation*
>   **CS**   **CR**

(**Step 2:** Begin extinction trials by repeatedly presenting the metronome by itself, as a result of which the CR is greatly weakened)

> **Metronome** → *Weak salivation* (Partial extinction)
>   **CS**   **CR**

(**Step 3:** Present a novel humming noise in background during the extinction procedure, as a result of which the CR recovers in strength)

> **(Novel humming noise) Metronome** → *Salivation*
>   **CS**   **CR**

Similarly, if your anxiety while giving a speech in class gradually fades, it may suddenly recover when a noisy ceiling fan starts up or someone walks in late. (Note that the phenomenon of disinhibition is similar to dishabituation, discussed in Chapter 3, in which the presentation of a novel stimulus results in the reappearance of a habituated response. To distinguish these concepts, it may help to remember that *dishabituation* involves the reappearance of a *habituated* response, and *disinhibition* involves the recovery of a response that has become partially *inhibited* due to extinction.)[1]

---

1. In the *process* of extinction, a conditioned response grows weaker because __A CS is presented without a US__.

2. The *procedure* of extinction involves __presenting a CS in the absence of a US__.

3. Once a CR has been extinguished, reacquisition of that response tends to occur (more/less) _____ rapidly than the original conditioning.

4. The sudden recovery of an extinguished response following some delay after extinction is known as __spontaneous recovery__.

QUICK QUIZ B

---

[1]Another reason that extinction of CRs can be difficult or incomplete is that we might not identify all of the stimuli that are helping to elicit the response. For example, in the case of a dog phobia, stimuli other than the dog—such as the sound of growling or worried looks on the faces of others—may also be involved. Those stimuli may also need to be incorporated into the extinction procedure.

5. With repeated sessions of extinction, each time a response recovers, it is usually somewhat (weaker/stronger) ___Stronger___ and extinguishes more (slowly/quickly) ___slowly___

6. Pavlov believed that this phenomenon indicates that extinction involves the (inhibition/unlearning) ___unlearning___ of a conditioned response.

7. The sudden recovery of a response during an extinction procedure when a novel stimulus is introduced is called ___dishinabition___

Stimulus Generalization and Discrimination

Classical conditioning would not be very useful if it only enabled us to learn about relationships between particular stimuli. For example, if we are bitten by a spider, it would not be very helpful for us to fear only that particular spider (which, in any case, we probably obliterated the moment it bit us). From an evolutionary perspective, it would be far more adaptive to learn to fear other spiders as well, particularly those spiders that look similar to the one that bit us. Fortunately, this is precisely what happens, through a process known as stimulus generalization.

[margin note: CR responds to similar things like original CS]

In classical conditioning, ==*stimulus generalization*== is the tendency for a CR to occur in the presence of a stimulus that is similar to the CS. In general, the more similar the stimulus is to the original CS, the stronger the response. For example, if a dog is conditioned to salivate to a tone that has a pitch of 2000 Hz, it will salivate to similar tones as well. But it will salivate more strongly to a 1900-Hz tone or a 2100-Hz tone than it will to a 1000-Hz tone or a 3000-Hz tone. In other words, tones that are most similar in pitch to the original CS will elicit the strongest response. Similarly, after being bitten by a dog, a child will probably fear not only that particular dog but other dogs as well. And the child is particularly likely to fear dogs that closely resemble the dog that bit him.

[margin note: - Vision is stro...]

The process of generalization is most readily apparent when the stimuli involved are physically similar and vary along a continuum. Tones of varying pitch or loudness and lights of varying color or brightness are examples of such stimuli. However, generalization can also occur across nonphysical dimensions, particularly in humans who use language. ==*Semantic generalization*== is the generalization of a conditioned response to verbal stimuli that are similar in *meaning* to the CS. For example, if humans are exposed to a conditioning procedure in which the sight of the word *car* is paired with shock, that word eventually becomes a CS that elicits a fear response. When participants are shown other words, generalization of the fear response is more likely to occur to those words that are similar in meaning to *car*, such as *automobile* or *truck*, than to words that look or sound similar, such as *bar* or *tar*. Thus, the meaning of the word is the critical factor in semantic generalization. For this reason, words that have similar meaning for an individual—for example, *Jennifer Lopez* and *J-Lo*—are likely to generate the same conditioned emotional response.

[margin note: Meaning over appearance]

tendency for a response to happen from one stimuli over another

The opposite of stimulus generalization is **_stimulus discrimination_**, the tendency for a response to be elicited more by one stimulus than another. For example, if the dog salivates in the presence of the 2000-Hz tone but not in the presence of a 1900-Hz tone, then we say that it is able to *discriminate*, or has *formed a discrimination*, between the two stimuli. Such discriminations can be deliberately trained through a procedure known as *discrimination training*. If we repeatedly present the dog with one type of trial in which a 2000-Hz tone is always followed by food and another type of trial in which a 1900-Hz tone is never followed by food, the dog will soon learn to salivate in the presence of the 2000-Hz tone and not in the presence of the 1900-Hz tone.

Step 1: Conditioning phase (with the two types of trials presented several times in random order)

> **2000-Hz tone: Food → *Salivation***
>   **NS**   **US**   **UR**
> **1900-Hz tone: No food**
>   **NS**   —

Step 2: Test phase

> **2000-Hz tone → *Salivation***
>   **CS+**   **CR**
> **1900-Hz tone → No salivation**
>   **CS−**   —

As a result of training, the 2000-Hz tone has become an excitatory CS (or CS+) because it predicts the presentation of food, and the 1900-Hz tone has become an inhibitory CS (or CS−) because it predicts the absence of food. The discrimination training has, in effect, countered the tendency for generalization to occur. (Note that the two types of trials were presented in random order during the conditioning phase. If they were instead presented in alternating order, the dog might associate the presentation of food with every second tone rather than with the tone that has a pitch of 2000 Hz.)

As you may have already guessed, discrimination training is a useful means for determining the sensory capacities of animals. For example, by presenting an animal with a CS+ tone and a CS− tone that are successively more and more similar, we can determine the animal's ability to discriminate between tones of different pitch. If it salivates to a CS+ of 2000 Hz and does not salivate to a CS− of 1950 Hz, then it has shown us that it can distinguish between the two. But if it salivates to both the 2000-Hz tone and the 1950-Hz tone, then it cannot distinguish between the two.

Generalization and discrimination play an important role in many aspects of human behavior. Phobias, for example, involve not only the classical conditioning of a fear response but also an overgeneralization of that fear response to inappropriate stimuli. For example, a woman who has been through an abusive relationship may develop feelings of anxiety and apprehensiveness toward all men. Eventually, however, through repeated interactions with men, this tendency will decrease and she will begin to adaptively discriminate between men who are potentially abusive and those who are not. Unfortunately, such discriminations are not always easily made, and further bad experiences could greatly strengthen her fear. Moreover, if the woman begins to avoid all men, then the tendency to overgeneralize may remain, thereby significantly impairing her social life. As noted earlier, if we avoid that which we are afraid of, it is difficult for us to overcome our fears.

1. Stimulus generalization is the tendency for a (CR/UR) __CR__ to occur in the presence of stimuli that are similar to the original (CS/US) __CS__. In general, the more (similar/different) __similar__ the stimulus, the stronger the response.

2. The generalization of a conditioned response to stimuli that are similar in meaning to a verbal CS is called s__emantic__ generalization.

3. The opposite of stimulus generalization is stimulus __discrimination__. This can be defined as _____

_____

_____ .

4. Feeling anxious around all objects that look like a rattlesnake is an example of stimulus __generalization__, whereas feeling anxious only around rattlesnakes is an example of stimulus __discrimination__.

5. Suppose Cary disliked his physics instructor and, as a result, came to dislike all science instructors. This example illustrates the process of over-__generalization__

Discrimination Training and Experimental Neurosis

Overgeneralization is not the only way that processes of discrimination versus generalization influence the development of psychological disorders. For example, Pavlov (1927, 1928) reported an interesting discovery made by a colleague, Shenger-Krestovnikova, that arose during a discrimination training procedure. In this experiment, an image of a circle signaled the presentation of food and an ellipse signaled no food (see Figure 4.3). In keeping with normal processes of discrimination, the dog duly learned to salivate when it

FIGURE 4.3 Discrimination training procedure used by Shenger-Krestovnikova in which the picture of a circle functioned as the CS+ and the picture of the ellipse functioned as the CS−.

○ : Food ⟶ *Salivation*
⬯ : No food

Experiment neurosis
—Disorder from unpredictable exposure

saw the circle (a CS+) and not to salivate when it saw the ellipse (a CS–). Following this, the ellipse was gradually made more circular, making it more difficult for the dog to determine when food was about to appear. When the ellipse was almost completely circular, the dog was able to make only a weak discrimination, salivating slightly more in the presence of the circle than in the presence of the ellipse. Interestingly, continued training with these stimuli did not result in any improvement. In fact, after several weeks, the discrimination was lost. More interestingly, however, the hitherto well-behaved dog became extremely agitated during each session—squealing, wriggling about, and biting at the equipment. It acted as though it was suffering a nervous breakdown.

Pavlov called this phenomenon **experimental neurosis,** an experimentally produced disorder in which animals exposed to unpredictable events develop neurotic-like symptoms. Pavlov hypothesized that human neuroses might develop in a similar manner. Situations of extreme uncertainty can be stressful, and prolonged exposure to such uncertainty might result in the development of neurotic symptoms. Thus, in the opening vignette to this chapter, it is not surprising that Jana's boyfriends often display increasing symptoms of neuroticism as the relationship progresses. A little uncertainty in one's romantic relationships can be exciting, but extreme uncertainty might eventually become aversive.

In carrying out their studies of experimental neurosis, Pavlov and his assistants also discovered that different dogs displayed different symptoms. Some dogs displayed symptoms of anxiety when exposed to the procedure, while others became catatonic (rigid) and acted almost hypnotized. Additionally, some dogs displayed few if any symptoms and did not have a nervous breakdown. Pavlov speculated that such differences reflected underlying differences in temperament. This was an extension of one of Pavlov's earlier observations that some dogs condition more easily than others. Shy, withdrawn dogs seem to make the best subjects, conditioning easily, whereas active, outgoing dogs are more difficult to condition (which is quite the opposite of what Pavlov had originally expected).

Based on results such as these, Pavlov formulated a theory of personality in which inherited differences in temperament interact with classical conditioning to produce certain patterns of behavior. This work served to initiate the study of the biological basis of personality (Gray, 1999). For example, Eysenck (1957) later utilized certain aspects of Pavlov's work in formulating his own theory of personality. A major aspect of Eysenck's theory is the distinction between introversion and extroversion. In very general terms, introverts are individuals who are highly reactive to external stimulation (hence, cannot tolerate large amounts of stimulation and tend to withdraw from such stimulation), condition easily, and develop anxiety-type symptoms in reaction to stress. By contrast, extroverts are less reactive to external stimulation (hence, can tolerate, and will even seek out, large amounts of stimulation), condition less easily, and develop physical-type symptoms in reaction to stress. Eysenck's theory also proposes that psychopaths, individuals who engage in antisocial behavior, are extreme extroverts who condition very poorly. As a result, they experience little or no conditioned anxiety when harming or taking advantage of others, such anxiety being the underlying basis of a conscience.

Both Pavlov's and Eysenck's theories of personality are considerably more complicated than presented here, involving additional dimensions of personality and finer distinctions between different types of conditioning, especially excitatory and inhibitory conditioning. Thus, extroverts do not always condition more poorly than introverts, and additional factors are presumed to influence the development of neurotic symptoms (Clark, Watson, & Mineka, 1994; Eysenck, 1967; Monte, 1999). Nevertheless, processes of classical conditioning interacting with inherited differences in temperament could well be major factors in determining one's personality.

The experimental neurosis paradigm also indicates that prolonged exposure to unpredictable events can sometimes have serious effects on our well-being. We will explore this topic in more detail in Chapter 9.

QUICK QUIZ D

1. In Shenger-Krestovnikova's experiment the animal suffered a nervous breakdown when exposed to a CS+ and a CS− that were made progressively (more/less) ___More___ similar.

2. Pavlov referred to this nervous breakdown as e_xprimental_ n_urosis_, an experimentally produced disorder in which animals exposed to unp_leasent_ events develop n_urotic_ -like symptoms.

3. Pavlov and his assistants noted that the dogs displayed two general patterns of symptoms. Some dogs became ___introverts___ while other dogs became ___extroverts___. In addition, (all / not all) _not all_ dogs developed symptoms.

4. Pavlov believed that these differences between dogs reflected (learned/ inherited) _inherited_ differences in t_emporement_

5. In Eysenck's theory, introverts are (more/less) ___more___ reactive to external stimulation than extroverts are, and they therefore (can/cannot) ___cannot___ tolerate large doses of stimulation.

6. Introverts also condition (more/less) ___less___ easily than extroverts.

7. Introverts seem to develop a_nxiety_-type symptoms in reaction to stress, whereas extroverts develop p_hysical_-type symptoms.

8. Psychopaths are extreme (introverts/extroverts) _____ who condition (very easily / very poorly) _____. They therefore feel little or no conditioned _____ when harming or manipulating others.

Two Extensions to Classical Conditioning

The normal classical conditioning procedure involves associating a single neutral stimulus with a US. But stimuli rarely exist in isolation. For example, a neighborhood bully does not exist as an isolated element in a child's world. The bully is associated with a variety of other stimuli, such as the house he lives in, the route he takes to school, and the kids he hangs around with. If a child is assaulted by the bully and learns to fear him, will he also fear the various objects, places, and people with which the bully is associated? In more technical terms, can classical conditioning of a CS also result in the development of a conditioned response to various stimuli that have been, or will be, associated with the CS? The processes of higher-order conditioning and sensory preconditioning indicate that it can.

Higher-Order Conditioning

Suppose you are stung by a wasp while out for a run one day and, as a result, develop a terrible fear of wasps. Imagine, too, that following the development of this fear, you notice a lot of wasps hanging around the trash bin outside your apartment building. Could the trash bin also come to elicit a certain amount of fear, or at least a feeling of edginess or discomfort? In a process known as ***higher-order conditioning***, a stimulus that is associated with a CS can also become a CS. Thus, the trash bin could very well come to elicit a fear response through its association with the wasps. This process can be diagrammed as follows:

S that can be associated with CS becomes a CS.

(**Step 1:** Basic conditioning of a fear response to wasps. As part of a higher-order conditioning procedure, this first step is called "first-order conditioning," and the original NS and CS are respectively labeled NS_1 and CS_1.)

Wasp: Sting → *Fear*
  NS_1 US   UR
Wasp → *Fear*
  CS_1 CR

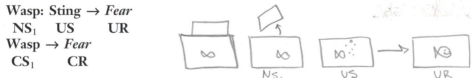

(**Step 2:** Higher-order conditioning of the trash bin through its association with wasps. This second step is sometimes also called "second-order conditioning," and the new NS and CS are labeled NS_2 and CS_2.)

Trash bin: Wasp → *Fear*
  NS_2 CS_1 CR
Trash bin → *Fear*
  CS_2 CR

Note that the CS_2 generally elicits a weaker response than the CS_1 (which, as noted in Chapter 3, generally elicits a weaker response than the US). Thus, the fear response produced by the trash bin is likely to be much weaker than the fear response produced by the wasps. This is not surprising given that the trash bin is only *indirectly* associated with the unconditioned stimulus (i.e., the wasp sting) upon which the fear response is actually based.

FIGURE 4.4 In this example of higher-order conditioning, a metronome is paired with food and becomes a CS_1 for salivation, following which a light paired with the metronome becomes a CS_2 for salivation. (*Source*: Nairne, 2000.)

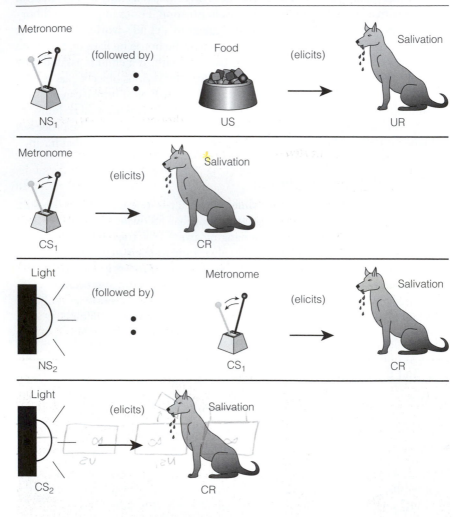

An experimental example of higher-order conditioning might involve pairing a metronome with food so that the metronome becomes a CS_1 for salivation, and then pairing a light with the metronome so that the light becomes a CS_2 for salivation (see Figure 4.4). In diagram form:

(**Step 1:** First-order conditioning)

    Metronome: Food → *Salivation*
       NS_1   **US**   **UR**
    Metronome → *Salivation*
       CS_1   **CR**

(**Step 2:** Second-order, or higher-order, conditioning)

Light: Metronome $\rightarrow$ *Salivation*
NS_2 $\quad\;\;$ CS_1 $\qquad\qquad\quad$ **CR**
Light $\rightarrow$ *Salivation*
CS_2 $\qquad$ **CR**

The light now elicits salivation although it has never been directly paired with food. (For consistency, we will continue to use Pavlov's salivary conditioning procedure as the basic experimental example throughout much of this chapter. In reality, however, modern researchers use other procedures to study classical conditioning, such as the conditioned emotional response [CER] procedure discussed in Chapter 3.)

We could also attempt *third-order conditioning* by pairing yet another stimulus, such as the sound of a tone, with the light. However, third-order conditioning is difficult to obtain, and when it is obtained, the conditioned response to a third-order conditioned stimulus (the CS_3) is likely to be very weak.

Higher-order conditioning is commonly used in advertising. Advertisements often pair a company name or product with objects, events, or people (usually attractive people) that have been conditioned to elicit positive emotional responses. For example, the advertisement in Figure 4.5

FIGURE 4.5 An example of higher-order conditioning in advertising. The advertiser assumes that the positive emotional response elicited by the sight of the attractive model will be associated with the clothes, increasing the probability that some readers of the ad will purchase the clothes.

presents an attractive woman in conjunction with a certain product. The assumption is that the sight of the woman elicits a positive emotional response, partly conditioned through various cultural experiences, that will be associated with the product and thereby increase the probability that readers of the ad will wish to purchase that product. (Of course, readers who are concerned about sexism in advertising would likely find the advertisement offensive, in which case they might be less likely to purchase that product.)

QUICK QUIZ E

1. In _higher_ _order_ conditioning, an already established CS is used to condition a new CS.

2. In general, the CS_2 elicits a (weaker/stronger) _weaker_ response than the CS_1.

3. In higher-order conditioning, conditioning of the CS_1 is often called _First_-order conditioning, while conditioning of the CS_2 is called _third_-order conditioning.

4. In a higher-order conditioning procedure in which a car is associated with an attractive model, the attractive model is the (CS_1/CS_2) _CS_1_ and the car is the (CS_1/CS_2) _CS_2_.

Sensory Preconditioning

We have seen that an event that is *subsequently* associated with wasps, such as trash bins, can become a CS for fear. What about an event that was *previously* associated with wasps, such as a toolshed that once had a wasps' nest hanging in it? Will walking near the shed now also elicit feelings of anxiety?

In *sensory preconditioning,* when one stimulus is conditioned as a CS, another stimulus with which it was previously associated can also become a CS. If you previously associated the toolshed with wasps and then acquired a fear of wasps as a result of being stung, you might also feel anxious when walking near the toolshed. This process can be diagrammed as follows:

2 Stimuli Conditioned as a CS

(**Step 1:** Preconditioning phase in which the toolshed is associated with wasps)

> **Toolshed: Wasps**
> NS_2 NS_1

(**Step 2:** Conditioning of wasps as a CS_1)

> **Wasp: Sting → *Fear***
> NS_1 US   UR
> **Wasp → *Fear***
> CS_1 CR

(*Step 3*)

> Toolshed → Fear
> NS_2 CR

And Furthermore

When Celebrities Misbehave

As mentioned, advertisers are aware that we are more likely to buy products that are associated with celebrities ... but will any celebrity do? Some companies will shy away from a celebrity who has been convicted of a crime or implicated in some sort of scandal. For example, when basketball star Kobe Bryant was accused of sexual assault in 2003 (a case that was eventually dismissed), he lost his endorsement deal with McDonald's. When Mary-Kate Olsen checked into a treatment facility in 2004 because of an eating disorder, "Got Milk?" ads featuring the Olsen twins were no longer used by the California Milk Processor Board (CMPB). Companies like McDonald's and CMPB are particularly sensitive to indiscretions by their celebrity endorsers, because their corporate image is aimed at being "wholesome" and "family oriented."

kate moss

Do all advertisers react this way to celebrity scandal? Not necessarily. When photos were published in 2005 by the *Daily Mirror* (a British tabloid) that showed model Kate Moss allegedly using cocaine, she immediately lost some lucrative endorsements with fashion companies, including H & M and Burberry, as well as several modeling contracts. Interestingly, this short-term loss was not sustained; according to Forbes.com (a leading business and finance news site), not only did Burberry re-sign Moss to an endorsement deal, but other high-end clients were quick to sign her to new contracts. Why would companies want their products associated with a drug-using model?

The fashion industry thrives on what is "edgy," and many designers and retailers want their products to be associated with things that are dark and dangerous, as well as sexy. While some companies (like H & M, which made statements about its antidrug stance in the wake of the Moss cocaine scandal) try to maintain a clean image, others are comfortable being associated with the darker side of life. Thus, if consumers associate a product with the dangerous and less-than-pure image of Kate Moss, then they are making exactly the association the retailer was hoping for. (And they can put on that eyeliner, and feel a little bit dangerous, without having to resort to cocaine use of their own!)

(Step 3: Presentation of the toolshed)

> **Toolshed → *Fear***
>   **CS$_2$**   **CR**

The toolshed now elicits a fear response, although it was never directly associated with a wasp sting.

An experimental example of sensory preconditioning with dogs involves first presenting several pairings of two neutral stimuli such as a light and a metronome. The metronome is then paired with food to become a CS for salivation. As a result of this conditioning, the light, which has never been directly paired with the food but has been associated with the metronome, also comes to elicit salivation (see Figure 4.6). This process can be diagrammed as follows:

(Step 1: Preconditioning phase, in which the light is repeatedly associated with the metronome)

> **Light: Metronome** (10 presentations of light followed by metronome)
> **NS$_2$**   **NS1**

(Step 2: Conditioning of the metronome as a CS$_1$)

> **Metronome: Food → Salivation**
>   **NS$_1$**   **US**   **UR**
> **Metronome → *Salivation***
>   **CS$_1$**   **CR**

(Step 3: Presentation of the light)

> **Light → *Salivation***
> **CS$_2$**   **CR**

As with higher-order conditioning, the response elicited by the light (CS$_2$) is generally weaker than the response elicited by the metronome (CS$_1$). Likewise, the fear response elicited by the toolshed (CS$_2$) is likely to be weaker than the fear response elicited by the wasps (CS$_1$).

Although it was once believed necessary to pair the neutral stimuli hundreds of times in the preconditioning phase (e.g., Brogden, 1939), it is now known that this type of conditioning works best if the stimuli are paired relatively few times (R. F. Thompson, 1972). This prevents the animal from becoming overly familiar with the stimuli prior to conditioning. (As you will see in a later section on *latent inhibition,* familiar stimuli are more difficult to condition as CSs than unfamiliar stimuli.) Another unusual finding with sensory preconditioning is that the procedure is sometimes more effective when the two stimuli in the preconditioning phase are presented simultaneously as opposed to sequentially (Rescorla, 1980). This result is unusual because it contradicts what we find with NS-US pairings, in which simultaneous presentation of the two stimuli is relatively ineffective.

Sensory preconditioning is significant because it demonstrates that stimuli can become associated with each other in the absence of any identifiable

FIGURE 4.6   In this example of sensory preconditioning, a dog is presented with several pairings of a light and a metronome. The metronome is then paired with food and becomes a conditioned stimulus for salivation. As a result, the light that was previously paired with the metronome also becomes a conditioned stimulus for salivation. (*Source*: Nairne, 2000.)

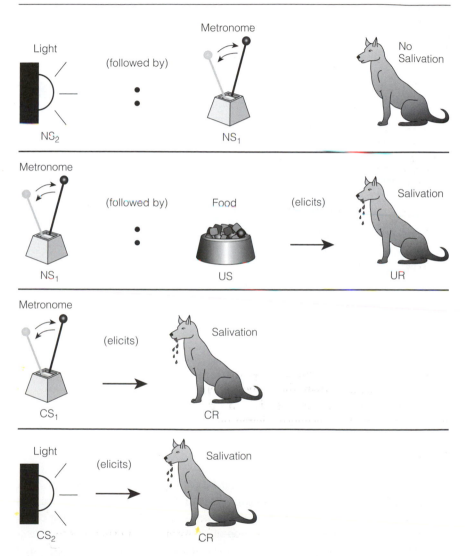

response (other than an orienting response). In this sense, sensory preconditioning can be viewed as a form of *latent learning*, which was first discussed in Chapter 1. Just as Tolman's rats learned to find their way around a maze even when it seemed as if there were no significant consequences for doing so (i.e., food had not yet been introduced into the goal box), animals will

Is this scenario more likely an example of higher-order conditioning or of sensory pre-conditioning? (You will find the answer when you complete the end-of-chapter test.)

"HE'S BEEN AT IT TOO LONG. NOW, WHEN THE BELL RINGS, DR. PAVLOV SALIVATES."

associate stimuli with each other even when those stimuli seem to have little significance for them.

1. Suppose you suddenly developed a strong fear of dogs after being severely bitten. As a result, you are also anxious about in-line skating because, on several occasions in the past, you witnessed people walking their dogs on the in-line skating paths. This example illustrates the phenomenon of _Sensory_ _Preconditioning_.

2. In the above example, the in-line skating paths will probably elicit a (stronger/weaker) _weaker_ fear response than will the sight of the dogs.

3. Sensory preconditioning often works best when the two neutral stimuli are paired (relatively few / hundreds of) _____ times in the preconditioning phase.

4. Unlike NS-US pairings in normal conditioning, NS-NS pairings in sensory preconditioning can produce stronger conditioning when the two stimuli are presented (sequentially/simultaneously) _Simultaneously_.

Three Examples of Specificity in Classical Conditioning

In the preceding section, we examined two ways in which the classical conditioning process can be extended to conditioning of additional CSs. In this section, we discuss three procedures—overshadowing, blocking, and latent inhibition—in which conditioning occurs to specific stimuli only, despite close pairing of other stimuli with the US. Two of these procedures (overshadowing and blocking) involve the presentation of what is known as a compound stimulus. A *compound stimulus* consists of the simultaneous presentation of two or more individual stimuli (e.g., the sound of a metronome is presented at the same time as a light).

Presentation of 2 S at the same time [handwritten]

Overshadowing

If you were stung by a wasp during a walk in the woods, would it make sense to develop a conditioned fear response to every stimulus associated with that event (e.g., the trees surrounding you, the butterfly fluttering by, and the cloud formation in the sky)? No, it would not. Rather, it would make more sense to develop a fear of those stimuli that were most salient (that really stood out) at the time of being stung, such as the sight of the wasp.

In *overshadowing*, the most salient member of a compound stimulus is more readily conditioned as a CS and thereby interferes with conditioning of the least salient member. In the wasp example, you are likely to develop a conditioned fear response to the most distinctive stimuli associated with that event, such as the sight of the wasp and perhaps the buzzing sound it makes.

Stronger CS promotes a higher % of a CR [handwritten]

An experimental example of overshadowing might involve first pairing a compound stimulus, such as a bright light and a faint-sounding metronome, with food. After several pairings, the compound stimulus becomes a CS that elicits salivation. However, when each member of the compound is tested separately, the bright light elicits salivation while the faint metronome elicits little or no salivation (see Figure 4.7). In diagram form:

(**Step 1:** Conditioning of a compound stimulus as a CS. Note that the compound stimulus consists of the simultaneous presentation of the two bracketed stimuli.)

$$[\text{Bright light} + \text{Faint metronome}]: \text{Food} \rightarrow \textit{Salivation}$$
$$\text{NS} \qquad\qquad \text{US} \qquad \text{UR}$$
$$[\text{Bright light} + \text{Faint metronome}] \rightarrow \textit{Salivation}$$
$$\text{CS} \qquad\qquad \text{CR}$$

(**Step 2:** Presentation of each member of the compound separately)

$$\text{Bright light} \rightarrow \textit{Salivation}$$
$$\text{CS} \qquad\quad \text{CR}$$
$$\text{Faint metronome} \rightarrow \textbf{No salivation}$$
$$\text{NS} \qquad\qquad\quad —$$

FIGURE 4.7 In this example of overshadowing, a bright light and a faint-sounding metronome are simultaneously presented as a compound stimulus and paired with food. After several pairings, the compound stimulus becomes a CS that elicits salivation. However, when each member of the compound is tested separately, the bright light elicits salivation but the faint-sounding metronome does not. (*Source*: Nairne, 2000.)

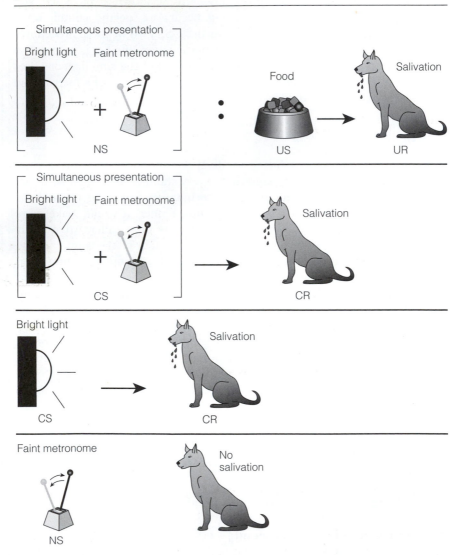

Due to the presence of the bright light during the conditioning trials, no conditioning occurred to the faint metronome. This is not because the faint metronome is unnoticeable. If it had been paired with the food by itself, it could easily have become an effective CS. Only in the presence of a more salient stimulus does the less salient stimulus come to elicit little or no response.

Head managers make use of the overshadowing effect when they assign an assistant to announce an unpopular decision. Although the employees might recognize that the head manager is mostly responsible, the assistant is the most salient stimulus and will, as a result, bear the brunt of the blame. It is thus the assistant who is likely to become most disliked by the employees. On the other hand, head managers often make a point of personally announcing popular decisions, thereby attracting most of the positive associations to themselves even if they have been only minimally involved in those decisions. Similarly, the positive feelings generated by the music of a rock band will be most strongly associated with the most salient member of that band (e.g., the lead singer)—a fact that often leads to problems when other band members conclude that they are not receiving their fair share of the accolades.

Bell → salivate

Light → No salivate

Blocking

The phenomenon of overshadowing demonstrates that, in some circumstances, mere contiguity between a neutral stimulus and a US is insufficient for conditioning to occur. An even clearer demonstration of this fact is provided by a phenomenon known as blocking. In **blocking,** the presence of an established CS interferes with conditioning of a new CS. Blocking is similar to overshadowing, except that the compound consists of a neutral stimulus and a CS rather than two neutral stimuli that differ in salience. For example, suppose that a light is first conditioned as a CS for salivation. If the light is then combined with a metronome to form a compound, and this compound is then paired with food, little or no conditioning occurs to the metronome (see Figure 4.8). In diagram form:

An established CS blocks the learning of a new CS

(**Step 1:** Conditioning of the light as a CS)

    Light: Food → *Salivation*
      NS   US   UR
    Light → *Salivation*
      CS   CR

(**Step 2:** Several pairings of a compound stimulus with the US)

    [Light + Metronome]: Food → *Salivation*
      CS +   NS   US   UR

(**Step 3:** Presentation of each member of the compound separately. The question at this point is whether conditioning occurred to the metronome.)

    Light → *Salivation*
      CS   CR
    Metronome → **No salivation**
       NS   —

FIGURE 4.8 In this example of blocking, a light is first conditioned as a CS for salivation. When the light is then combined with a metronome to form a compound stimulus, and this compound stimulus is paired with food, the metronome does not become a conditioned stimulus. The presence of the already established CS blocks conditioning to the metronome. (*Source*: Nairne, 2000.)

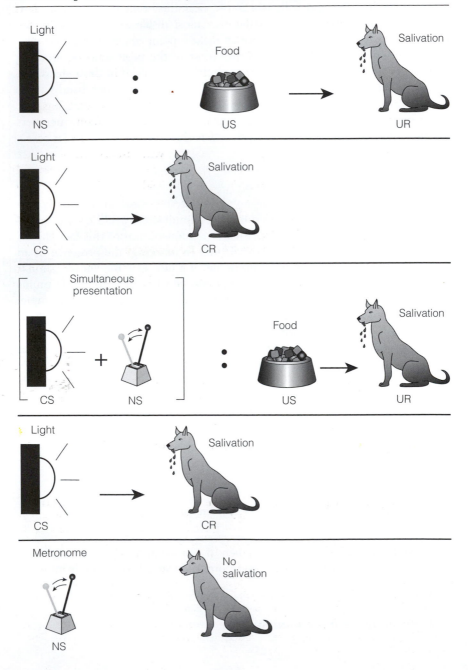

In step 2, the presence of the light blocked conditioning to the metronome. An everyday (but overly simplistic) way of thinking about what is happening here is that the light already predicts the food, so the dog pays attention only to the light. As a result, the metronome does not become an effective CS despite being paired with the food.

For a real-life example of the blocking effect, imagine that you have to make an unpopular announcement to your employees. The phenomenon of blocking suggests that you would do well to make it a joint announcement with another manager who is already disliked by the employees (one who is already an aversive CS). The employees might then attribute most or all of the bad news to the unpopular manager, and you will be left relatively unscathed.

The phenomenon of blocking garnered a lot of attention when it was first demonstrated (Kamin, 1969). It clearly indicates that mere contiguity between an NS and a US is insufficient to produce conditioning. Rather, it seems that a more crucial factor in conditioning is the extent to which the NS comes to act as a signal or predictor of the US. In more cognitive terms (Tolman would have loved blocking), the act of conditioning can be said to produce an "expectation" that a particular event is about to occur. When the light is conditioned as a CS, the dog comes to expect that food will follow the light. Later, when the metronome is presented at the same time as the light, the metronome provides no additional information about when food will occur; hence, no conditioning occurs to it. We will again encounter this notion of expectations when we discuss the Rescorla-Wagner theory of conditioning in Chapter 5.[2]

(before)   1500 × S = condition to laugh

Latent Inhibition

Familiar stimulus
is more difficult to
condition than a
novel S

Do we condition more readily to stimuli that are familiar or unfamiliar? You might think that familiar stimuli are more readily conditioned; if we already know something about a topic, it seems easier to learn more about it. In fact, in what is known as *latent inhibition*, a familiar stimulus is more difficult to condition as a CS than is an unfamiliar (novel) stimulus.[3] Or, stated the other way around, *an unfamiliar stimulus is more readily conditioned as a CS than a familiar stimulus.* For example, if, on many occasions, a dog has heard the sound of a metronome prior to conditioning, then a standard number of

---

[2]A different way of thinking about this (again, popular with researchers who have a preference for cognitive interpretations of such matters) is that increases in conditioning can occur only to the extent that a US is unexpected or surprising. Once a US is fully expected, such as when a light by itself reliably predicts the occurrence of food, no further conditioning can occur. In more general terms, we learn the most about something when we are placed in a position of uncertainty and must then strive to reduce that uncertainty. Once the uncertainty has been eliminated, learning ceases to occur. Thus, in blocking, no conditioning (no new learning) occurs to the neutral stimulus, because the presence of the CS that it has been combined with ensures that the animal is not surprised when the US soon follows.

[3]Latent inhibition is also known as the CS pre-exposure effect. A related phenomenon, known as the US pre-exposure effect, holds that conditioning is slower with familiar, as opposed to unfamiliar, USs.

FIGURE 4.9 In latent inhibition, familiar stimuli are more difficult to condition as CSs than novel stimuli. If a dog has, on many occasions, heard the sound of a metronome prior to conditioning being implemented, then it will be difficult to obtain conditioning to the metronome using a standard number of conditioning trials. (*Source*: Nairne, 2000.)

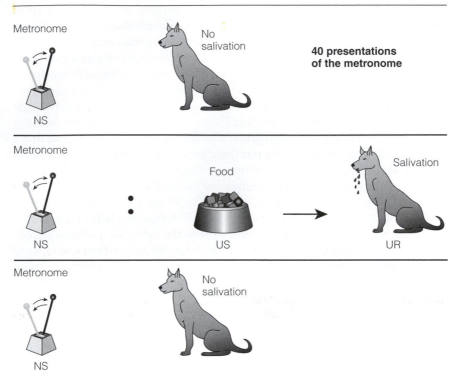

conditioning trials might result in little or no conditioning to the metronome (see Figure 4.9). In diagram form:

(**Step 1:** Stimulus pre-exposure phase in which a metronome is repeatedly presented alone)

    Metronome (40 presentations)
        NS

(**Step 2:** Conditioning trials in which the pre-exposed metronome is now paired with food)

    Metronome: Food → *Salivation* (10 trials)
        NS   **US**   **UR**

(**Step 3:** Test trial to determine if conditioning has occurred to the metronome)

    Metronome → **No salivation**
        NS   —

If the dog had not been pre-exposed to the metronome and it had been a novel stimulus when first paired with food, then the 10 conditioning trials would have resulted in significant conditioning to the metronome. Because of the pre-exposure, however, no conditioning occurred. It will take many more pairings of metronome and food before the metronome will reliably elicit salivation.

Latent inhibition prevents the development of conditioned associations to redundant stimuli in the environment. Such stimuli are likely to be relatively inconsequential with respect to the conditioning event. For example, if a rabbit in a grassy field is attacked by a coyote and then escapes, it will be much more adaptive for the rabbit to associate the attack with the novel scent of the coyote than with the familiar scent of grass. The scent of the coyote is a good predictor of a possible attack, and a conditioned fear response to that scent will help the rabbit avoid such attacks in the future. A conditioned fear response to grass, however, will be completely maladaptive because the rabbit is surrounded by grass day in and day out. It is the novel stimuli preceding the presentation of a US that are most likely to be meaningfully related to it.

Problems concerning latent inhibition are evident in people who have schizophrenia (Lubow & Gewirtz, 1995). These individuals often have great difficulty attending to relevant stimuli in their environment and are instead distracted by irrelevant stimuli, such as various background noises or people passing nearby. Experiments have revealed that people with schizophrenia display less latent inhibition than is normal—that is, they condition more easily to familiar stimuli—indicating that the disorder partly involves an inability to screen out redundant stimuli. Experiments have also revealed that drugs used to treat schizophrenia tend to increase levels of latent inhibition, thereby normalizing the person's attentional processes.

1. A compound stimulus consists of the (simultaneous/successive) Simultaneous presentation of two or more separate stimuli.

2. In Overshadowing the most salient member of a compound stimulus is more readily conditioned as a CS and thereby interferes with conditioning of the less salient member.

3. In blocking, the presence of an established CS interferes with conditioning of another stimulus.

4. In latent Conditioning a familiar stimulus is more difficult to condition as a CS than is an unfamiliar stimulus.

5. In a(n) _____ procedure, the compound stimulus consists of a neutral stimulus and a CS, whereas in a(n) _____ procedure, the compound stimulus consists of two neutral stimuli that differ in salience or intensity.

6. Latent inhibition (prevents/promotes) _____ the development of conditioned associations to redundant stimuli.

7. Because Jez has a history of getting into trouble, he often catches most of the blame when something goes wrong, even when others are also responsible for what happened. This is most similar to the phenomenon of _____.

QUICK QUIZ G

ADVICE FOR THE LOVELORN

Dear Dr. Dee,

My friend has started dating someone who is quite aggressive toward her. I am worried for her safety, yet she says she's known him for years and he is not that frightening. To the rest of us, it is obvious that the guy is dangerous. Is she blinded by love?

Deeply Concerned

Dear Deeply,

On the one hand, your friend is more familiar with this person than you are, so it may be that her judgment is indeed more accurate. On the other hand, her increased familiarity with him might also mean that it will take longer for her to become fearful of him. This is in keeping with the process of latent inhibition, in which we condition less readily to familiar stimuli than to unfamiliar stimuli. This is yet another factor that might contribute to people remaining in an abusive relationship even though the people around them clearly recognize the danger signals. So it may be that she is blinded by latent inhibition, not love.

Behaviorally yours,

Dr. Dee

Additional Phenomena

In this section, we briefly cover some additional ways in which the process of classical conditioning can be affected by modifications in the typical conditioning procedure.

the CS in the passage of time *Waking up before Alarm clock*

Temporal Conditioning

In all of the preceding examples, the CS is a distinctive, external stimulus of some sort, such as a light, a metronome, or a dog. But this need not always be the case. *Temporal conditioning* is a form of classical conditioning in which the CS is the passage of time. For example, if a dog is given a bite of food every 10 minutes, it will eventually salivate more strongly toward the end of each 10-minute interval than at the start of the interval. The end of the 10-minute interval is the effective CS for salivation. Similarly, residents of a city who experience a bombing attack

heroin *HR BP* *A* *B* *Occasion setting* *HR BP*

each night at 2:00 a.m. for several nights in a row will likely start feeling anxious as 2:00 a.m. approaches, even in the absence of any clock indicating the time. The various cues that we use to estimate time, some of which are internal, are sufficient to elicit the feelings of anxiety.

Environment that triggers a respons

Occasion Setting

As we have learned, classical conditioning involves establishment of an association between two events, such as between the sound of a metronome and the taste of food or between the sight of a wasp and the feel of its sting. To date, however, we have largely ignored the fact that these two events do not exist in isolation but instead occur within a certain context. This context often comes to serve as an overall predictor of the relationship between these two events. Imagine, for example, that presentations of the metronome are followed by food, but only when a background light is on. When the background light is off, presentations of the metronome are not followed by food. The conditioning procedure would look something like this (with presentation of light-on and light-off phases in random order):

(Background light on) Metronome: Food → *Salivation*
(Background light off) Metronome: No food

As a result, we are likely to find that the metronome elicits salivation only when the background light is on and not when it is off:

(Background light on) Metronome → *Salivation*
(Background light off) Metronome → No salivation

The background light in this instance is referred to as an *occasion setter* because it predicts the occasions on which the metronome is followed by food. Its presence therefore comes to control the extent to which the metronome serves as a CS for salivation. Thus, ***occasion setting*** is a procedure in which a stimulus (an *occasion setter*) signals that a CS is likely to be followed by the US with which it is associated. The presence of this stimulus then facilitates the occurrence of the CR in response to the CS.

An occasion setter can be associated not only with the presentation of a US but also with a change in the intensity of the US. Imagine, for example, that an abused child receives his worst beatings from his parents whenever they are drinking alcohol. Thus:

(Alcohol absent) Parents: Mild abuse → Mild *anxiety*
(Alcohol present) Parents: Severe abuse → *Strong anxiety*

Although the child typically feels a mild amount of anxiety around his parents, the sight or smell of alcohol in the presence of his parents greatly increases his anxiety. Thus:

(Alcohol absent) Parents → *Mild anxiety*
(Alcohol present) Parents → *Strong anxiety*

The conditioned response of anxiety to the parents is intensified by the presence of alcohol. The alcohol is therefore an occasion setter that alters the child's level of anxiety in the presence of the parents.

Because the real world consists of a complex mixture of stimuli, occasion setting is an important factor in many instances of classical conditioning. Women are typically more anxious about being harassed while walking by a construction worker at a construction site than while walking by a construction worker in an office complex. And hikers are more anxious around bears with cubs than they are around bears without cubs. The additional stimuli present in these circumstances (construction site and bear cubs) indicate a higher probability of certain events (harassment and bear attack).

QUICK QUIZ H

1. In temporal conditioning, the (NS/US) _NS_____ is presented at regular intervals, with the result that the end of each interval becomes a (CS/US) _CS_____ that elicits a (CR/UR) _CR_____.

2. In classical conditioning, o_ccasion__ s_etting_____ is a procedure in which a stimulus signals that a CS is likely to be followed by the _CR_____. This stimulus is called a(n) _occasion__ _setter_____, and serves to (facilitate/retard) _facilitate_ the occurrence of the (UR/CR) _CR_____.

3. Kessler became very accustomed to having a snack at about 4:00 p.m. each afternoon. As a result, he now finds that he automatically starts thinking about food at about 4:00 p.m. each afternoon, even before he notices the time. These automatic thoughts of food seem to represent an example of _____ conditioning.

4. Brandon notices that the doctor gives him an injection only when a nurse is present in the examining room. As a result, he feels more anxious about the medical exam when the nurse is present than when the nurse is absent. In this case, the nurse functions as an o_____ s_____ for his conditioned feelings of anxiety.

Novel s + CS = decrease strength of CR

External Inhibition

Remember how the presentation of a novel stimulus during an extinction procedure can result in a sudden recovery of the conditioned response? According to Pavlov, the presentation of the novel stimulus at the same time as the CS seems to disrupt the buildup of inhibition that was occurring during extinction; therefore, this process is known as *disinhibition*. The process of external inhibition is the mirror opposite of disinhibition. In ***external inhibition***, the presentation of a novel stimulus at the same time as the conditioned stimulus produces a decrease in the strength of the conditioned response. In other words, the presence of the novel stimulus inhibits the occurrence of the CR.

Burger → salivation

Car crash + Burger → probably no salivation

Suppose, for example, that the sound of the metronome has been strongly associated with food so that it reliably elicits salivation:

Metronome: Food → *Salivation*
       NS   **US**   **UR**
Metronome → *Salivation*
     CS   **CR**

If we now turn on a novel background light, then the metronome will elicit considerably less salivation.

(Novel background light on) Metronome → *Weak salivation*
                        CS   **Weak CR**

A simple way of thinking about this is that the dog has been distracted by the background light and therefore doesn't react to the metronome.

In a similar fashion, if you happen to be feeling anxious because some wasps are buzzing around your table at an outdoor cafe, you may find that the occurrence of an unusual event, such as the sound of a violinist who begins entertaining the patrons, will somewhat alleviate the anxiety. In fact, this process works well enough that people in anxiety-arousing situations sometimes deliberately create a distracting stimulus. For example, on a popular television morning show, one of the hosts once described how he used to sometimes jab himself with a darning needle just before the start of his segments to alleviate some of the anxiety he was experiencing!

US Revaluation

Presenting US at different intensity alters the strength of CS.

At the beginning of this chapter, we mentioned how more intense stimuli produce stronger conditioning than do less intense stimuli. For example, a strong shock will produce stronger fear conditioning than a weak shock does. But what would happen if we conducted our conditioning trials with one level of shock and then presented a different level of shock by itself on a subsequent noncon-ditioning trial? In other words, would changing the intensity or value of the US after the conditioning of a CS also change the strength of response to the CS?

Imagine, for example, that the sound of a metronome is followed by a small amount of food, with the result that the metronome comes to elicit a small amount of saliva.

Metronome: Small amount of food → *Weak salivation*
     NS   **US**   **UR**
Metronome → *Weak salivation*
     CS   **CR**

Once this conditioning has been established, we now present the dog with a large amount of food, which elicits a large amount of saliva.

Large amount of food → *Strong salivation*
      US   **UR**

What type of response will now be elicited by the metronome? As it turns out, the dog may react to the metronome as though it predicts a large amount of food rather than a small amount of food.

Metronome → *Strong salivation*
    CS   **CR**

Note that the metronome was never directly paired with the large amount of food; the intervening experience with the large amount by itself produced the stronger CR of salivation.

Therefore, **US revaluation** is the postconditioning presentation of the US at a different level of intensity, thereby altering the strength of response to the previously conditioned CS. It is called US *revaluation* because the *value* or magnitude of the US is being changed. Depending on whether the US is increased or decreased in strength, this procedure can also be called *US inflation or US deflation*. The preceding scenario is an example of US inflation. As an example of US deflation, imagine that you salivate profusely when you enter Joe's restaurant because you love their turkey gumbo. You then get a new roommate, who, as it turns out, is a turkey gumbo fanatic and prepares turkey gumbo meals five times a week. Needless to say, so much turkey gumbo can become monotonous (an instance of long-term habituation), and you finally reach a point where you have little interest in turkey gumbo. As a result, when you next enter Joe's restaurant, you salivate very little. The value of turkey gumbo has been markedly reduced in your eyes, which in turn affects your response to the restaurant that has been associated with it.

In everyday terms, it seems like what is happening in US revaluation is that the animal has learned to expect the US whenever it sees the CS. The intensity of its response is thus dependent on the animal's most recent experience with the US. On a more theoretical level, as with blocking, US revaluation suggests that conditioning generally involves the creation of an association between the CS and the US (i.e., a stimulus-stimulus, or S-S, association) as opposed to an association between the NS and the UR (i.e., a stimulus-response, or S-R, association). These theoretical issues are more fully discussed in Chapter 5. (You will also see that US revaluation might play a role in the development of some human phobias.)

QUICK QUIZ I

1. In external inhibition the presentation of a (novel/familiar) novel stimulus at the same time as the conditioned stimulus produces a (n) (increase/decrease) decrease in the strength of the conditioned response.

2. The (US/CS) US revaluation procedure involves the (pre/post) post conditioning presentation of the (CS/US) US at a different level of intensity.

3. Shahid usually salivates when he enters Joe's restaurant because he loves their turkey gumbo. One time, however, when the waiters were all dressed like clowns and bagpipes were playing in the background, he salivated much less. This appears to be an instance of _____ _____.

4. Nikki feels all excited when she sees her father arrive home each evening because he always brings her some licorice. One day her mother bought her a lot of licorice earlier in the day, and Nikki had no desire for licorice when evening came around. As a result, she was not as excited when her father came home that evening. In this example, her father is a (CS/US) _____ through his association with licorice. Being satiated with licorice therefore reduced the value of the (CS/US) _____ that typically followed her father's arrival home. As a result, her (CR/UR) _____ of excitement on seeing her father was greatly reduced. This process is known as _____ _____.

Pseudoconditioning

Response believed to be CR is actually, because of Sensitization rather then conditioning (Jump at things in general)

We hope you are now pretty familiar with the basic classical conditioning procedure and some of the phenomena associated with it. Be aware, however, that determining whether classical conditioning has occurred is not always as straightforward as it might seem. A phenomenon known as *pseudoconditioning* poses a particular problem. In ***pseudoconditioning***, an elicited response that appears to be a CR is actually the result of sensitization rather than conditioning. Suppose, for example, that we try to condition a leg withdrawal reflex (leg flexion) in a dog by presenting a light flash followed by a slight shock to its foot.

Light flash: Shock → *Leg flexion*

After a few pairings of the light with the shock, we now find that a fairly strong flexion response occurs immediately when the light is flashed.

Light flash → *Leg flexion*

On the surface, it seems that the light flash has become a CS and that we have successfully conditioned a flexion response. But have we? What if instead of flashing a light, we sound a beep and find that, lo and behold, it too elicits a response?

Beep *Leg → flexion*

What is going on here?

Remember the process of sensitization in which the repeated presentation of an eliciting stimulus can sometimes increase the strength of the elicited response? Well, sensitization can result in the response being elicited by other stimuli as well. For example, soldiers with war trauma exhibit an enhanced startle response, not just to the sound of exploding mortar shells but to certain other stimuli as well, including doors slamming, cars backfiring, or even an unexpected tap on the shoulder. Similarly, if a dog has been shocked in the paw a couple of times, it would not be at all surprising if any sudden stimulus in that setting could make the dog quickly jerk its leg up. Therefore, although we thought we had established a CR—which is the result of a CS having been paired with a US—in reality we have simply produced a hypersensitive dog that automatically reacts to almost any sudden stimulus.

Pseudoconditioning is a potential problem whenever the US is some type of emotionally arousing stimulus. Fortunately, there are ways of determining the extent to which a response is the result of pseudoconditioning rather than real conditioning. One alternative is to employ a control condition in which the NS and US are presented separately. For example, while subjects in the experimental group receive several pairings of the light flash and the shock, subjects in the control group receive light flashes and shocks that are well separated in time.

Experimental group   *Control group*
Light flash: Shock → *Leg flexion*   **Light flash // Shock** → *Leg flexion*

(The symbol / / for the control group means that the light flash and the shock are *not* paired together and are instead presented far apart from each other.) When the animals in each group are then exposed to the light flash presented on its own, we find the following:

Experimental group   *Control group*
Light flash → *Leg flexion*   **Light flash** → *Weak leg flexion*

The level of responding shown by the control group is presumed to reflect the amount of sensitization (pseudoconditioning) due to the use of an upsetting stimulus such as a shock. However, because the response shown by the experimental group is stronger than that shown by the control group, conditioning is assumed to have occurred, with the difference between the two groups indicating the strength of conditioning. Classical conditioning experiments typically utilize one or more control groups like this to assess how much actual conditioning has taken place versus how much the subject's responses are the result of nonconditioning factors such as sensitization.

QUICK QUIZ J

1. When an elicited response that appears to be a CR is actually the result of sensitization, we say that ~~Pseudocondition~~ has taken place.

2. The above phenomenon is a potential problem whenever the US produces a strong ~~emotional~~ response.

3. An appropriate control procedure to test for this phenomenon involves presenting a control group of subjects with the NS and US (close together / quite separate) ~~seperate~~. Whatever responding is later elicited by the NS in this group is assumed to be the result of ~~sensitization~~ rather than real conditioning.

SUMMARY

Strengthening a conditioned response by pairing a CS (or NS) with a US is known as acquisition. In general, early conditioning trials produce more rapid acquisition than do later trials. Weakening a conditioned response by repeatedly presenting the CS by itself is known as extinction. Spontaneous recovery is the reappearance of a previously extinguished response after a rest period, and disinhibition is the sudden recovery of an extinguished response following introduction of a novel stimulus.

In stimulus generalization, we learn to respond similarly to stimuli that resemble an original stimulus. One version of stimulus generalization, known as semantic generalization, involves generalization of a response to verbal stimuli that are similar in meaning to the original stimulus. In stimulus discrimination, we respond to one stimulus more than another, a process that is established through discrimination training. Pavlov discovered that dogs that were exposed to a difficult discrimination problem often suffered from nervous breakdowns, a phenomenon that he called experimental neurosis.

In higher-order conditioning, a previously conditioned stimulus (CS_1) is used to condition a new stimulus (CS_2). The CS_2 elicits a weaker response than the CS_1 does because there is only an indirect association between the CS_2 and the US. In sensory preconditioning, when one stimulus is conditioned as a CS, another stimulus with which it was previously associated also becomes a CS.

Certain situations can also interfere with the process of conditioning. For example, overshadowing occurs when the most salient member of a compound stimulus is more readily conditioned as a CS and thereby interferes with the conditioning of a less salient member. Blocking occurs when the presence of an established CS during conditioning interferes with conditioning of a new CS. Familiar stimuli are also more difficult to condition than unfamiliar stimuli, a phenomenon known as latent inhibition.

In temporal conditioning, the effective CS is the passage of time between USs that are presented at regular intervals. With occasion setting, an additional stimulus (an occasion setter) indicates whether a CS will be followed by a US; the CS therefore elicits a CR only in the presence of the occasion setter. External inhibition occurs when the presentation of a novel stimulus at the same time as the CS reduces the strength of the CR. US revaluation involves exposure to a stronger or weaker US following conditioning, which then alters the strength of response to the previously conditioned CS. Pseudoconditioning is a false form of conditioning in which the response is actually the result of sensitization rather than classical conditioning.

SUGGESTED READINGS

Eysenck, H. J. (1967). *The biological basis of personality*. Springfield, IL: Charles C Thomas. Indicates the extent to which Pavlov's work influenced Eysenck's theory of personality and, hence, many other theories of personality.

Lieberman, D. A. (2000). *Learning: Behavior and cognition* (3rd ed.). Belmont, CA: Wadsworth. For students who may find it helpful to read alternative descriptions of these various classical conditioning phenomena.

STUDY QUESTIONS

1. Define acquisition. Draw a graph of a typical acquisition curve (remember to properly label each axis), and indicate the asymptote of conditioning.
2. Define the processes of extinction and spontaneous recovery.
3. Define disinhibition. How does it differ from dishabituation?
4. Describe stimulus generalization and semantic generalization.
5. What is stimulus discrimination? Diagram an example of a discrimination training procedure. (For both this question and ones that follow, when asked to diagram a conditioning procedure, be sure to label each component with the appropriate abbreviations, e.g., CS, US, etc.)
6. Define experimental neurosis, and describe Shenger-Krestovnikova's procedure for producing it.
7. Define higher-order conditioning, and diagram an example.
8. Define sensory preconditioning, and diagram an example.
9. Define overshadowing, and diagram an example.
10. Define blocking, and diagram an example.
11. Define latent inhibition, and diagram an example.
12. What is temporal conditioning? Describe an example.
13. Define occasion setting, and diagram an example.
14. Define external inhibition, and diagram an example.
15. Define US revaluation, and diagram an example.
16. How does pseudoconditioning differ from classical conditioning? How can one experimentally determine whether a response is the result of classical conditioning or pseudoconditioning?

CONCEPT REVIEW

acquisition. The process of developing and strengthening a conditioned response through repeated pairings of an NS (or CS) with a US.

blocking. The phenomenon whereby the presence of an established CS interferes with conditioning of a new CS.

compound stimulus. A complex stimulus that consists of the simultaneous presentation of two or more individual stimuli.

disinhibition. The sudden recovery of a response during an extinction procedure when a novel stimulus is introduced.

experimental neurosis. An experimentally produced disorder in which animals exposed to unpredictable events develop neurotic-like symptoms.

external inhibition. A decrease in the strength of the conditioned response due to the presentation of a novel stimulus at the same time as the conditioned stimulus.

extinction. The process whereby a conditioned response can be weakened or eliminated when the CS is repeatedly presented in the absence of the US; also, the procedure whereby this happens, namely, the repeated presentation of the CS in the absence of the US.

higher-order conditioning. The process whereby a neutral stimulus that is associated with a CS (rather than a US) also becomes a CS.

latent inhibition. The phenomenon whereby a familiar stimulus is more difficult to condition as a CS than is an unfamiliar (novel) stimulus.

occasion setting. A procedure in which a stimulus (known as an occasion setter) signals that a CS is likely to be followed by the US with which it is associated.

overshadowing. The phenomenon whereby the most salient member of a compound stimulus is more readily conditioned as a CS and thereby interferes with conditioning of the least salient member.

pseudoconditioning. A situation in which an elicited response that appears to be a CR is actually the result of sensitization rather than conditioning.

semantic generalization. The generalization of a conditioned response to verbal stimuli that are similar in meaning to the CS.

sensory preconditioning. In this phenomenon, when one stimulus is conditioned as a CS, another stimulus with which it was previously associated can also become a CS.

spontaneous recovery. The reappearance of a conditioned response to a CS following a rest period after extinction.

stimulus discrimination. The tendency for a response to be elicited more by one stimulus than another.

stimulus generalization. The tendency for a CR to occur in the presence of a stimulus that is similar to the CS.

temporal conditioning. A form of classical conditioning in which the CS is the passage of time.

US revaluation. A process that involves the postconditioning presentation of the US at a different level of intensity, thereby altering the strength of response to the previously conditioned CS.

CHAPTER TEST

12. In higher-order conditioning, the CS_2 generally elicits a (stronger/weaker) _____ response than does the CS_1.

5. The fact that you learned to fear wasps and hornets, as well as bees, after being stung by a bee is an example of _____. On the other hand, if you fear only poisonous snakes and not nonpoisonous snakes, that would be an example of _____.

8. During an eyeblink conditioning procedure, you blinked not only in response to the sound of the click but also when someone tapped you on the shoulder. Your response to the tap on the shoulder may be indicative of _____ conditioning, which means that the elicited response is likely the result of _____ rather than classical conditioning.

18. While playing tennis one day, you suffer a minor ankle sprain. Two weeks later you severely twist your ankle while stepping off a curb. The next time you play tennis, you find yourself surprisingly worried about spraining your ankle. This is an example of _____.

23. According to Eysenck, psychopaths tend to be extreme (extroverts/introverts) _____ who condition (easily/poorly) _____.

20. Midori feels anxious whenever the manager walks into the store accompanied by the owner because the manager always finds fault with the employees when the owner is there. This is best seen as an example of _____ with the owner functioning as the _____.

14. Two examples of specificity in conditioning, known as _____ and _____, involve pairing a compound stimulus with a US. They both provide evidence that contiguity between the NS and the US (is/is not) _____ a critical factor in conditioning.

2. Following an experience in which you were stung by a bee and subsequently developed a fear of bees, you are hired for a 1-day job in which your task is to catch bees for a biologist. During the day, you never once get stung by a bee. As a result, your fear of bees will likely (decrease/increase) _____, a process known as _____.

10. The researcher feels that you have done such a fine job catching bees that she hires you for another day. At the start of the next day, you will likely find that your fear of bees has (completely disappeared / partially returned) _____, a phenomenon known as _____.

22. By the end of the second day, your fear of bees has mostly disappeared. However, you then hear thunder in the distance and become a bit worried about whether you should immediately head back to the lab. You decide first to catch one more bee, but find that your fear of bees is now somewhat stronger. The sudden recovery of your fear response is an example of a process known as _____.

15. Marty once played in an all-star game alongside Bobby Orr (a famous and talented hockey player). Marty scored two goals and an assist, as did Orr. Orr was later voted the game's most valuable player, while Marty's name was barely mentioned. This situation seems analogous to the _____ effect in classical conditioning.

25. Remember the cartoon of Pavlov learning to salivate to the bell after watching the dogs being trained to salivate to the sound of a bell? This situation might have arisen during conditioning if the dogs were being fed bites of juicy steak, the sight of which for most humans is probably a (CS_1/CS_2) _____ for salivation. The bell would then become a (CS_1/CS_2) _____ through its association with the sight of the steak. Thus, of the two types of extensions to classical conditioning, this is most similar to the process of _____.

19. Jared's parents always start arguing at about midnight each night. As a result, he wakes up feeling anxious each night just before midnight. This seems to be an example of _____ conditioning.

3. Consider the following example in which the sight of different people comes to elicit feelings of anger:

    (**Step 1**)
    John: Rude behavior → *Anger*
    John → *Anger*

    (**Step 2**)
    Amir: John → *Anger*
    Amir → *Anger*

    This is an example of _____ conditioning.

11. In higher-order conditioning, conditioning of the CS_1 is sometimes called _____ conditioning, and conditioning of the CS_2 is called _____ conditioning.

6. The *procedure* of extinction involves the _____; whereas the process of extinction involves the _____ _____.

24. The gradual strengthening of a classically conditioned fear response by repeated pairings of a tone with a shock is an example of the process of _____. During this process, early pairings of tone and shock are likely to produce (larger/smaller) _____ increments in conditioning compared to later pairings.

1. The maximum amount of conditioning that can take place in a particular situation is known as the _____ of conditioning.

9. Consider the following example in which feelings of tension toward your former friend, Yoshi, are also elicited by a restaurant where you often used to meet up with him:

(**Step 1:** Repeated experiences in restaurant)
Restaurant: Yoshi

(**Step 2:** Not in restaurant)
Yoshi: Argument → *Tension*
Yoshi → *Tension*

(**Step 3**)
Restaurant → *Tension*

This process is best interpreted as an example of _____.

4. Based partially on Pavlov's work on experimental neurosis, Eysenck concluded that people who are _____ tend to be highly reactive to external stimulation, condition easily, and develop anxiety-type symptoms in reaction to stress. By contrast, people who are _____ are less reactive, condition less easily, and develop physical-type symptoms in reaction to stress.

17. You once played in an all-star game alongside Antonio, an unknown basketball player just like you. Antonio, however, is a very tall and noticeable player on the court. Although you both played equally well, almost all the credit for the win went to _____, which seems analogous to the _____ effect in classical conditioning.

13. If the scent of ammonia and the ticking of a clock are combined to form a compound stimulus, then the two stimuli are being presented (simultaneously/successively) _____.

26. Alan finds that he can lessen his hunger pangs while waiting for dinner by watching an exciting television show. This is most similar to the concept of _____.

21. Rasheed had never experienced a more difficult multiple-choice test. Virtually every alternative for every question looked equally correct. By the end of the exam, he felt extremely anxious. Rasheed's experience is somewhat analogous to a phenomenon discovered by Pavlov's associates, which they called _____.

16. A student has great difficulty ignoring irrelevant material sometimes mentioned in class and is easily distracted. This student might also display (stronger/weaker) _____ evidence of _____ inhibition compared to the average student.

7. A person who fears dogs also feels anxious when he hears the word canine. This is an example of _____.

![www icon] Visit the book companion Web site at http://www.academic.cengage. com/psychology/powell for additional practice questions, answers to the Quick Quizzes, practice review exams, and additional exercises and information.

ANSWERS TO CHAPTER TEST

1. asymptote
2. decrease; extinction
3. higher-order
4. introverts; extroverts
5. stimulus generalization; stimulus discrimination
6. repeated presentations of the CS without the US; resultant decrease in the strength of the conditioned response.
7. semantic generalization
8. pseudo; sensitization
9. sensory preconditioning
10. partially returned; spontaneous recovery
11. first-order; second-order
12. weaker
13. simultaneously
14. blocking; overshadowing; is not
15. blocking (with Orr being analogous to an established CS)
16. weaker; latent
17. Antonio; overshadowing
18. US revaluation (or US inflation)
19. temporal
20. occasion setting; occasion setter
21. experimental neurosis
22. disinhibition
23. extroverts; poorly
24. acquisition; larger
25. CS_1; CS_2; higher-order conditioning
26. external inhibition

Advertising

- Takes advantage of higher-order conditioning
- Who you are ← what it does

Phobias

- Specific phobias followed by social anxiety disorder + agraphobia

    Situation or stimulus = Ns /Cs
    Fear = UR

- Ns immediatly → Cs → strong CR
- Fear increases over time

    Incubation → Presentation of Ns w/o US in natural setting often does not cause the CR to become instinct.

- Possible observationally learned
    - dentist
- Temperament

Phobia Treatment

- Extinction
    - Systematic desensitization (gradual exposure to fear)
    - Exposure therapy (Direct exposure)

- Genetic predeposition

- Selective sensitization — unrealated stress causes an (car crash, deer crash) increase in phobic response

CHAPTER 5

Classical Conditioning: Underlying Processes and Practical Applications

[handwritten notes:]

Addiction Treatments

Exposure therapy - focused on coping in the presense of triggers

Aversion therapy - Creating negative relations to replace positive relations

Agonist therapy - apply another stimulus to help withdrawl from happening

CHAPTER OUTLINE

[handwritten notes left column:]

Addiction

Craving - cosistent desire

Tolerance - increased amounts to get the same effect.

Withdrawl - symptoms related with absence of the substance, often opposite effects

Continuem Disorder - Experimentation, abuse, dependence

3C's
- Compulsive engagment
- Loss of control
- Continued use despite negative consequences

[handwritten notes right column:]

learning Principles
1 - Opponent process theory 
2 - Classical Conditioning
3 - Spontaneous Recovery

① Tolerance = OP↑
Withdrawl = O
Craving = ↗

② Rituals use (Sensory preconditioning)
- Preparing sub. = NS(cs)   NS + US = VR
- Subst. use = US
- Phys. effect = UR   CS = CR

Absesense of CS could cause Overdose

③

Estella thought Juan looked a bit tipsy as he left the picnic to drive home. She wondered if she should tell him that the supposedly nonalcoholic punch he had been drinking was actually spiked with vodka. On the other hand, he had only had a single glass. Surely, he couldn't be drunk.

Underlying Processes in Classical Conditioning

By now, you probably realize that classical conditioning is not as simple a process as it first seems. It is a complex phenomenon that is only slowly yielding its secrets to researchers. The following sections discuss major theoretical notions concerning the underlying processes of classical conditioning. You will then learn how some of these theories have resulted in findings of great practical importance.

S–S Versus S–R Learning

There are two basic ways to conceptualize the type of learning that occurs in classical conditioning. One way, which conforms to the general S-R approach promoted by Watson and Hull, is to view classical conditioning as a process of directly attaching a reflex response to a new stimulus. According to this *S-R (stimulus-response) model* of conditioning, the neutral stimulus (NS) becomes directly associated with the unconditioned response (UR) and therefore comes to elicit the same response as the UR. For example, when bitten by a dog, a child directly associates the dog with the pain and fear that were elicited by the bite and therefore experiences fear when he or she next encounters the dog. Similarly, if I can somehow cause you to salivate in the presence of a tone (such as by presenting food immediately after the tone), then the response of salivation will become connected to the tone, and you will subsequently salivate whenever you hear the tone. In each case, the purpose of the unconditioned stimulus (US) is simply to elicit the UR so that it occurs in close proximity to the NS, thereby allowing a connection to be created between the NS and the UR (see Figure 5.1).

Another way of conceptualizing classical conditioning is the *S-S (stimulus-stimulus) model* of conditioning, in which the NS becomes

FIGURE 5.1   According to the S-R model of conditioning, the NS is directly associated with the UR.

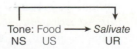

Tone: Food ⟶ *Salivate*
NS   US   UR

FIGURE 5.2 According to the S-S model of conditioning, the NS is directly associated with the US.

Tone: Food ⟶ *Salivate*
   NS   US   UR

directly associated with the US and, because of this association, comes to elicit a response that is related to the US. Thus, a child who is bitten by a dog associates the dog with the bite, and because of that association the child comes to fear the dog. Likewise, pairing a tone with food results in the tone being associated with food, as a result of which the tone comes to elicit salivation. An everyday mentalistic way of thinking about it is that the tone makes the dog think of the food, and because it is thinking of food, it now salivates (see Figure 5.2). Although the S-R and S-S models might seem mutually exclusive (i.e., it seems as though both cannot be correct) and have often been pitted against each other by theorists, many researchers now believe that both types of processes may be involved in conditioning. Many basic conditioning procedures do seem to cause an association to develop between the NS and the US (an S-S association)—as shown, for example, by the phenomena of blocking and US revaluation that were discussed in the last chapter. Other instances of conditioning, however, seem to involve the establishment of an S-R association (see Domjan, 2010, for further details). Nevertheless, modern theories of conditioning have generally emphasized the establishment of S-S associations. In particular, they have attempted to specify how the NS and US become associated during the conditioning process—a problem that Pavlov himself grappled with.

QUICK QUIZ A

1. In the Stimulus - Response model of classical conditioning, conditioning is viewed as a process of directly attaching a reflex response to a new stimulus.

2. In the Stimulus - Stimulus model of classical conditioning, conditioning involves establishing a direct connection between an NS and a US.

3. Tyrell was once bitten by Rover, the neighbor's dog, and as a result he developed a strong fear of the dog. However, when he heard that Rover had to have all his teeth removed, Tyrell's fear of the dog completely disappeared. This suggests that Tyrell's fear response was based on an _____-_____ association. (Think: Was Tyrell's fear based on associating Rover with the response of fear or with the possibility of being bitten?)

Stimulus–Substitution Versus Preparatory-Response Theory

An early S-S theory of conditioning was introduced by Pavlov (1927). According to Pavlov's *stimulus-substitution theory*, the CS acts as a substitute for the US. For example, pairing a tone with food results in the tone becoming a substitute for the food, eliciting salivation just as the food does.

Pavlov was a physiologist who believed that classical conditioning was an effective, though indirect, way of studying neurological processes in the brain. Thus, he often made inferences about the kinds of neurological processes that are activated during conditioning. He claimed that presentation of a US, such as food, activates an area of the cerebral cortex (the outermost layer of the brain) that is responsible for sensing the occurrence of that event. Activation of this "food center" in the brain in turn activates another part of the cortex (the "salivation center") that produces the unconditioned response of salivation.

Food → *Activates food center in cortex* → *Activates salivation center in cortex* → **Salivation**

Pavlov also believed that the presentation of a neutral stimulus, such as a light, activates another area of the cortex responsible for detecting that type of stimulus. According to Pavlov, when the light is presented just before the food during conditioning, a connection is formed between the area of the cortex activated by the light and the area activated by the food. As a result, activation of the light center of the cortex also activates the food center of the cortex, resulting in salivation. In other words, Pavlov believed that the presentation of the light set in motion the following sequence of events:

Light → *Activates light center in cortex* → *Activates food center in cortex* → *Activates salivation center in cortex* → **Salivation**

Pavlov's notions about the kinds of neurological processes underlying classical conditioning are now considered to be incorrect. The actual processes involved are known to be considerably more complex than he presumed. Nevertheless, this does not negate all aspects of Pavlov's theory. For example, consider the notion that the conditioned stimulus (CS) is somehow a direct substitute for the US. In at least some cases, it seems as though animals do react to the CS as if it were the US. The dog salivates to the light just as it does to food. More importantly, the dog may even approach the light and start to lick it, as though pairing the light with the food resulted in the light being perceived as edible (Pavlov, 1941). This sort of phenomenon, now known as sign tracking, is discussed more fully in Chapter 11.

Pavlov's theory can be classified as a type of S-S theory because it involves the formation of a neurological association between an NS and a US. Nevertheless, on a behavioral level, it is similar to an S-R theory insofar as it predicts that the conditioned response (CR) will be the same, or at least highly similar, to the UR. Although this is often the case, the major problem with this theory is that it sometimes is not the case. In fact, sometimes the CR and the UR differ substantially. For example, a rat that receives a foot shock (the US) will probably jump (the UR). However, if it sees a light (CS) that has been paired with a foot shock, it will freeze (the CR).

Why would the rat jump in one instance and freeze in the other? An examination of the rat's natural response to danger gives us a clue. If a rat is attacked by a snake, jumping straight up (and rats can really jump!) may cause the snake to miss. On the other hand, if a rat detects a snake in the vicinity, tensing its muscles and freezing will minimize the possibility of being detected or, if the rat is attacked, will enable it to jump quickly. This suggests that the purpose of the CR, rather than merely being a version of the UR, is to ready the organism for the occurrence of the US.

Thus, according to ***preparatory-response theory***, the purpose of the CR is to prepare the organism for the presentation of the US (Kimble, 1961, 1967). The dog salivates to the tone to get ready for food, and the rat freezes in response to the light to get ready for the shock. Note that in one case, the preparatory response is highly similar to the UR, whereas in the other case it is quite different. Thus, unlike stimulus-substitution theory, preparatory-response theory allows for situations in which the CR and the UR are different. In some cases, conditioning can even result in a CR that appears to be the opposite of the original UR. We examine this possibility in the next section, in which we discuss a version of preparatory-response theory known as the compensatory-response model.

QUICK QUIZ B

1. According to ___Stimulus___ - ___Substitution___ theory, the CS acts as a substitute for the US.

2. According to ___Preparatory___ - ___response___ theory, the purpose of the CR is to prepare the organism for the occurrence of the US.

3. According to ___Stimulus___ - ___Response___ theory, the CR and UR should always be the same or at least highly similar. As it turns out, this is (true/false) ___false___.

Compensatory–Response Model

An interesting example of preparatory-response theory involves cases in which conditioning eventually results in a CR that appears to be the opposite of the original UR. This type of conditioning often occurs with drug reactions, so we will illustrate it using the example of heroin. Imagine that a heroin addict always injects heroin in the presence of certain environmental cues, such as a particular room or with certain friends. Heroin has several effects on the body, but we will focus on just one of them for now, which is a decrease in blood pressure. Shooting up with heroin involves the following sequence of events:

> **Heroin-related cues**: Heroin → *Decreased blood pressure*
>   **NS**   **US**   **UR**

If this was a normal conditioning procedure, one might expect that the heroin-related cues will eventually become a CS that will itself elicit a decrease in blood pressure. But in reality, quite the opposite occurs. With repeated drug use, the presence of the heroin-related cues elicit not a decrease in blood pressure, but an increase in blood pressure!

Heroin-related cues → *Increased blood pressure*
CS   **CR**

How can this be? Remember the opponent-process theory of emotion that we learned about in Chapter 3. Recall how certain stimuli can elicit both a primary response (the a-process) and a compensatory response (the b-process). According to the *compensatory-response model,* a CS that has been repeatedly associated with the primary response (a-process) to a US will eventually come to elicit a compensatory response (b-process).

To help clarify this, let us examine the heroin example in more detail. Repeatedly injecting heroin does not simply elicit a response, but instead sets in motion a chain of events. The heroin directly elicits an immediate decrease in blood pressure (the a-process) that in turn elicits a compensatory increase in blood pressure (the b-process).

Heroin → *Decreased blood pressure* → *Increased blood pressure*
          (a-process)   *(b-process)*

In terms of stimuli and responses, the heroin is a US that naturally elicits a decrease in blood pressure, and the decrease in blood pressure is itself a US that naturally elicits an increase in blood pressure. Therefore, the decrease in blood pressure is both an unconditioned response (UR) to heroin and an unconditioned stimulus (US) that elicits a compensatory increase in blood pressure.

Heroin → *Decreased blood pressure* → *Increased blood pressure*
 US   UR/US   UR

Notice that there are two USs in this sequence that the cues in the environment could potentially become associated with: the heroin and the decrease in blood pressure that results from the heroin.

What happens in compensatory conditioning is that the heroin-related cues, such as being in a certain room, become associated not with the heroin but with the primary response to heroin—that is, with the decrease in blood pressure. As a result, these cues eventually come to elicit the compensatory reaction to that response. So the actual conditioning that takes place with heroin is as follows:

Heroin-related cues: Decreased blood pressure → *Increased blood pressure*
          NS   **US**   **UR**
Heroin-related cues → *Increased blood pressure*
          CS   **CR**

Why would this type of compensatory conditioning occur? Remember how, in the opponent-process theory, the compensatory reactions to a US serve to maintain a state of homeostasis (internal balance). If these compensatory reactions start occurring before the US is presented, they will be even more effective in minimizing the disturbance produced by the US. For example, if the compensatory reaction to the heroin (an increase in blood pressure) can be elicited just before the injection of heroin, then the immediate physical reaction to the heroin (the decrease in blood pressure) will be effectively moderated. In this sense, a conditioned compensatory response allows the body to prepare itself *ahead of time* for the onslaught of the drug. Conditioned compensatory responses therefore constitute an extreme form of preparatory response to certain environmental events.

1. According to the Compensatory response model of drug conditioning, a CS that has been associated with (a drug / primary response to a drug) _____ will eventually come to elicit a c_____ reaction.

2. Another way of looking at it is that the CS has become associated with the (a-process/b-process) _____ and therefore eventually comes to elicit the (a-process/b-process) _____.

3. Diagram the *actual* events involved in the conditioning of an increase in blood pressure in response to a hypodermic needle that has been consistently associated with heroin administration (*hint*: the US in this conditioning is not heroin):

   Needle: _____ → _____
      NS   US   UR
   Needle → _____
      CS   CR

4. Shock naturally elicits an increase in heart rate. In this case, shock is the (NS/CS/US) _____ and the increase in heart rate is the (CR/UR) _____.

5. Following from question 4, an increase in heart rate naturally elicits a compensatory decrease in heart rate. For this sequence of events, the increase in heart rate is the (NS/CS/US) _____ and the decrease in heart rate is the (CR/UR) _____.

6. Following from question 5, a tone that is repeatedly paired with shock will eventually come to elicit a compensatory decrease in heart rate. Diagram the actual events involved in this type of conditioning (paying particular attention to what the actual US consists of).

   Tone: _____ → _____
      NS   US   UR
   Tone → _____
      CS   CR

The compensatory-response model obviously has important implications for *drug addiction*. Drug addictions are partly motivated by a tendency to avoid the symptoms of withdrawal, which are essentially the compensatory responses to the effect of the drug. For example, heroin produces a decrease in blood pressure as well as a combination of other effects, which the drug user experiences as pleasant feelings of relaxation and euphoria. This relaxing effect of heroin in turn elicits compensatory reactions that, on their own, would be experienced as unpleasant feelings of tension. Repeated heroin use therefore results in the following process of conditioning:

Heroin-related cues: Relaxing effect → *Compensatory tension*
                           of heroin   *reaction*
           NS   **US**   **UR**
Heroin-related cues → *Compensatory tension reaction*
           CS   **CR**

Thus, a heroin addict will, after repeated heroin use, begin to experience unpleasant symptoms of tension and agitation simply by being in the presence of cues associated with heroin use. These symptoms are what the drug addict interprets as symptoms of withdrawal.

The presence of drug-related cues is therefore one of the strongest reasons why people continue to battle cravings long after they have stopped using a drug. Think of an individual who always uses heroin in a particular environment, goes into a rehab program, and then returns home to her usual environment. When she returns to the environment in which she had previously used heroin, she will very likely become tense and agitated, which she will interpret as withdrawal symptoms and a craving for heroin. And to escape from these symptoms, she will be sorely tempted to once more take heroin.

To the extent that withdrawal symptoms are elicited by cues associated with drug use, then removing those cues should weaken the withdrawal symptoms and make it easier to remain abstinent. This possibility is supported by anecdotal evidence. Many American soldiers became heroin users during their tour of duty in Vietnam, leading to fears that they would remain addicted when they returned home. These fears, however, did not materialize (Robins, 1974). One explanation for this is that the drastic change in environment when the soldiers returned home removed many of the cues associated with heroin use, thereby alleviating the symptoms of withdrawal and making it easier for them to remain heroin free.

Unfortunately, for many people trying to kick a habit, whether it is alcohol, cigarettes, or heroin, it is often not possible to completely avoid all cues associated with the drug. For this reason, modern treatments for drug addiction often include procedures designed to extinguish the power of drug-related cues. For example, someone attempting to quit smoking may be required to remain in the presence of cigarettes for a long period of time without smoking. Repeated presentations of the CS (the sight of the cigarettes) in the absence of the US (nicotine ingestion) should result in weaker and weaker CRs (cravings for a smoke). Of course, this process can initially be very difficult—and in the case of severe alcoholism, even dangerous due to the severity of withdrawal symptoms. It therefore requires careful management, but once accomplished it can significantly reduce the possibility of a relapse.

(See also Sokolowska, Siegel, & Kim, 2002, for a discussion of how some CSs can be internal, such as feelings of stress that lead to smoking, and how the effect of these internal cues may also need to be extinguished.)

The compensatory-response model also has implications for *drug tolerance* (Siegel, 1983, 2005). For example, if you have a habit of always drinking in a particular setting, then the various cues in that setting—people greeting you as you walk in the front door of the bar; the stool you always sit on—become CSs for the effect of alcohol. The presence of these CSs will initiate physiological reactions that compensate for the alcohol you are about to consume. As a result, in the presence of these CSs, you should have greater tolerance for alcohol than you would in their absence.

Research has confirmed this association. In a study by McCusker and Brown (1990), participants consumed alcohol in either an "alcohol expected" environment (i.e., alcohol was consumed in a simulated lounge during the evening with pub noises playing in the background) or an "alcohol unexpected" environment (i.e., alcohol was consumed during the day in an office environment). Those who consumed alcohol in the expected environment performed significantly better on various measures of cognitive and motor functioning compared to those who consumed alcohol in the unexpected environment. They also showed smaller increases in pulse rate. This suggests that the alcohol-related cues in the expected condition (evening, lounge setting) elicited compensatory reactions that partially compensated for the effects of the alcohol (see also Bennett & Samson, 1991).

On the other side of the coin, this also means that if you consume alcohol in an environment where you typically do not drink (e.g., a business luncheon), the alcohol could have a much stronger effect on you than if you consumed it in an environment where you typically do drink (e.g., a bar). This means that your ability to drive safely could be significantly more impaired following a lunchtime martini than after an evening drink at a bar. Worse yet, even if you do consume the drink at a bar, consider what happens when you leave that setting. Your compensatory reactions might be significantly reduced because you have now removed yourself from the alcohol-related cues that elicit those reactions. As a result, you may become more intoxicated during the drive home from the bar than you were in the bar (Linnoila, Stapleton, Lister, Guthrie, & Eckhardt, 1986). This means that the amount of alcohol you consume is not, by itself, a reliable gauge for determining how intoxicated you are. (Thus, going back to the opening vignette for this chapter, why should Estella be especially concerned about Juan's ability to drive?)[1]

It should be noted that there are exceptions to the typical compensatory reactions to a CS. Stimuli associated with drug use sometimes elicit drug-like

---

[1]The type of alcohol consumed can also have an effect. People become significantly more intoxicated following consumption of an unusual drink (such as a strange liqueur) rather than a familiar drink (such as beer). The familiar drink can be seen as a CS for alcohol that elicits compensatory reactions to the alcohol (Remington, Roberts, & Glautier, 1997).

reactions rather than drug-compensatory reactions. In other words, the stimuli become associated with the primary response to the drug rather than the compensatory response. For example, in one study, rats became more sensitive to cocaine when it was administered in the usual cocaine administration environment than in a different one (Hinson & Poulos, 1981). The CSs for cocaine administration apparently elicited reactions that mimicked the drug, thereby strengthening its effect. There is also evidence that stimuli associated with drug use sometimes elicit both drug compensatory responses in one system of the body and drug-like responses in another. For example, a cup of decaffeinated coffee (which is a cue for coffee/caffeine consumption) produces a caffeine-like increase in alertness and a caffeine-compensatory decrease in salivation in moderate caffeine users (Rozen, Reff, Mark, & Schull, 1984; see also Eikelboom & Stewart, 1982; Lang, Ross, & Glover, 1967). Thus, the circumstances in which conditioning results in drug-like reactions versus drug-compensatory reactions are complex and not entirely understood (Siegel, 1989). (See also "Conditioned Compensatory Responses and Drug Overdose" in the And Furthermore box.)

And Furthermore

Conditioned Compensatory Responses and Drug Overdose

The compensatory-response model has also been used to explain incidents of *drug overdose*. Many "overdose" fatalities do not, in fact, involve an unusually large amount of the drug. For example, heroin addicts often die after injecting a dosage that has been well tolerated on previous occasions. A critical factor appears to be the setting within which the drug is administered. As we have seen, if a heroin addict typically administers the drug in the presence of certain cues, those cues become CSs that elicit compensatory reactions to the drug. An addict's tolerance to heroin therefore is much greater in the presence of those cues than in their absence. Anecdotal evidence supports this possibility. Siegel (1984) interviewed 10 survivors of heroin overdose, 7 of whom reported that the overdose had been preceded by an unusual change in the setting or drug administration procedure. For example, one woman reported that she overdosed after hitting a vein on the first try at injecting the drug, whereas she usually required several tries. Further evidence comes from studies with rats that had become addicted to heroin. When the cues usually associated with heroin were absent, the rats' ability to tolerate a large dose was markedly reduced to the point that many of the rats died. Thus, heroin-tolerant rats who were administered a very strong dose of heroin in a novel setting were more likely to die than those who received the dose in the setting previously associated with the drug (Siegel, Hinson, Krank, & McCully, 1982).

(continued)

Siegel (1989) describes two cases that clearly illustrate the dangers of drug overdose resulting from conditioning effects.

> The respondent (E. C.) was a heavy user of heroin for three years. She usually self-administered her first, daily dose of heroin in the bathroom of her apartment, where she lived with her mother. Typically, E. C. would awake earlier than her mother, turn on the water in the bathroom (pretending to take a shower), and self-inject without arousing suspicion. However, on the occasion of the overdose, her mother was already awake when E. C. started her injection ritual, and knocked loudly on the bathroom door telling E. C. to hurry. When E. C. then injected the heroin, she immediately found that she could not breathe. She was unable to call her mother for help (her mother eventually broke down the bathroom door and rushed E. C. to the hospital, where she was successfully treated for heroin overdose). (pp. 155–156)

Siegel goes on to explain that the mother knocking on the bathroom door was an unusual cue that may have disrupted the environmental CSs that would normally have elicited compensatory reactions to the heroin. In other words, the knocking was a novel stimulus that resulted in *external inhibition* of the compensatory CRs that would normally have occurred in that setting.

The second example described by Siegel involves administration of a drug to a patient to alleviate the pain of pancreatic cancer.

> The patient's [17-year-old] son, N. E., regularly administered the [morphine] in accordance with the procedures and dosage level specified by the patient's physician...The patient's condition was such that he stayed in his bedroom which was dimly lit and contained much hospital-type apparatus necessary for his care. The morphine had always been injected in this environment. For some reason, on the day that the overdose occurred, the patient dragged himself out of the bedroom to the living room. The living room was brightly lit and different in many ways from the bedroom/sickroom. The patient, discovered in the living room by N. E., appeared to be in considerable pain. Inasmuch as it was time for his father's scheduled morphine injection, N. E. injected the drug while his father was in the living room. N. E. noticed that his father's reaction to this injection was atypical; his pupils became unusually small, and his breathing shallow...The father died some hours later. (pp. 156–157)

Two years later, N. E. took a class in which conditioning effects on drug tolerance were discussed, at which point he realized the implications of these effects for his own experience.

1. According to the compensatory-response model of drug addiction, symptoms of withdrawal are likely to be (stronger/weaker) _____ in the presence of drug-related cues. This is because the drug-related cues tend to elicit (primary/compensatory) _____ responses to the drug that are experienced as cravings.

2. In keeping with the compensatory-response model, modern treatments for drug addiction often recommend (exposure to / removal of) _____ drug-related cues to allow (conditioning/extinction) _____ of the cravings to take place.

3. We tend to have (higher/lower) _____ tolerance for a drug in the presence of cues associated with taking the drug.

4. Suppose an addict always injects heroin in her bedroom at home, but one time stays overnight at a friend's house and decides to take an injection there. The addict will likely experience a(n) (increased/decreased) _____ reaction to the drug at her friend's house.

5. A person who drinks a glass of wine in a fine restaurant is likely to be (more/less) _____ affected by the alcohol than if she drank the same amount of wine in a courtroom.

Rescorla–Wagner Theory

One of the most influential theories of classical conditioning was proposed by Rescorla and Wagner (1972). Their theory attempted to explain the effect of each conditioning trial on the strength, or what might be called the "associative value," of the CS in its relationship to the US. The *Rescorla-Wagner theory* proposes that a given US can support only so much conditioning, and this amount of conditioning must be distributed among the various CSs that are present. Another way of saying this is that there is only so much associative value available to be distributed among the various cues associated with the US.

One assumption of this theory is that *stronger USs support more conditioning than do weaker USs.* For example, the use of a highly preferred food as the US produces a stronger conditioned response of salivation than does a less preferred food. Imagine, for example, that a tone paired with a highly preferred food (say, steak) elicits a maximum of 10 drops of saliva, while a tone paired with a much less preferred food (say, dog food) elicits only 5 drops of saliva. If we regard each drop of saliva as a unit of associative value, then we could say that the highly preferred food supports a maximum associative value of 10 units, while the less preferred food supports a maximum associative value of 5 units.

We can use the following format to diagram the changes in the associative value (we will assume the highly preferred food is the US):

Tone $(V = 0)$: **Food** (*Max = 10*) → *Salivation*
Tone $(V = 10)$ → *Salivation*

The letter V will stand for the associative value of the CS (which at the start of conditioning is 0). The term *Max* will stand for the maximum associative value that can be supported by the US once conditioning is complete. In our example, imagine V as the number of drops of saliva the tone elicits—0 drops of saliva to begin with and 10 drops once the tone is fully associated with the food—and Max as the maximum number of drops of saliva that the tone can potentially elicit if it is fully associated with the food. (If this is starting to look a bit mathematical to you, you are correct. In fact, the model can be expressed in the form of an equation. For our purposes, however, the equation is unnecessary.)[2]

Now suppose that a compound stimulus consisting of a tone and a light are repeatedly paired with the food, to the point that the compound stimulus obtains the maximum associative value.

[Tone + Light] (V = 0): **Food** (*Max* = 10) → *Salivation*
[Tone + Light] (V = 10) → *Salivation*

This associative value, however, must somehow be distributed between the two component members of the compound. For example, if the tone is a bit more salient than the light, then the tone might have picked up 6 units of associative value while the light picked up only 4 units. In other words, when tested separately, the tone elicits 6 drops of saliva while the light elicits 4.

Tone (V = 6) → *Salivation*
Tone (V = 4) → *Salivation*

If the tone was even more salient than the light—for example, it was a very loud tone and a very faint light—then *overshadowing* might occur, with the tone picking up 9 units of associative value and the light only 1 unit:

[Loud tone + Faint light] (V = 0): **Food** (*Max* = 10) → *Salivation*
Loud tone (V = 9) → *Salivation*
Faint light (V = 1) → *Salivation*

The loud tone now elicits 9 drops of saliva (a strong CR) while the faint light elicits only 1 drop of saliva (a weak CR). Thus, the Rescorla-Wagner explanation for the overshadowing effect is that there is only so much associative value available (if you will, only so much spit available) for conditioning, and if the more salient stimulus in the compound picks up most of the associative value, then there is little associative value left over for the less salient stimulus.

As can be seen, the Rescorla-Wagner theory readily explains conditioning situations involving compound stimuli. Take, for example, a *blocking* procedure. One stimulus is first conditioned to its maximum associative value:

Tone (V = 0): **Food** (*Max* = 10) → *Salivation*
Tone (V = 10) → *Salivation*

---

[2]The equation for the Rescorla-Wagner model is $\Delta V = k(\lambda - V)$, where V is the associative value of the CS, λ ("lambda") represents the maximum associative value that the CS can hold (i.e., the asymptote of learning), and k is a constant that represents the salience of the CS and US (with greater salience supporting more conditioning). For additional information on the use of this equation, see the additional information for this chapter that is posted at the textbook Web site.

This stimulus is then combined with another stimulus for further conditioning trials:

[Tone + Light] (V = 10 + 0 = 10): **Food** (*Max* = 10) → *Salivation*

But note that the food supports a maximum associative value of only 10 units, and the tone has already acquired that much value. The light can therefore acquire no associative value because all of the associative value has already been assigned to the tone. Thus, when the two stimuli are later tested for conditioning, the following occurs:

Tone (V = 10) → *Salivation*
Light (V − 0) → **No salivation**

So far we have described the Rescorla-Wagner theory in relation to changes in associative value. The theory has also been interpreted in more cognitive terms. To say that a CS has high associative value is similar to saying that it is a strong predictor of the US, or that the subject strongly "expects" the US whenever it encounters the CS. Thus, in the previous example, to say that the tone has high associative value means that it is a good predictor of food and that the dog "expects" food whenever it hears the tone. In the case of blocking, however, the tone is such a good predictor of food that the light with which it is later paired becomes redundant, and the presence of the light does not affect the subject's expectations about food. As a result, no conditioning occurs to the light. In general, then, conditioning can be viewed as a matter of building the subject's expectations that one event will follow another.

The Rescorla-Wagner theory also leads to some counterintuitive predictions. Consider what happens if you first condition two CSs to their maximum associative value and then combine them into a compound stimulus for further conditioning. For example, suppose we condition a tone to its maximum associative value, as follows:

Tone (V = 0): **Food** (*Max* = 10) → *Salivation*
Tone (V = 10) → *Salivation*

and then do the same for the light:

Light (V = 0): **Food** (*Max* = 10) → *Salivation*
Light (V = 10) → *Salivation*

We now combine the tone and the light into a compound stimulus and conduct further conditioning trials:

[Tone + Light] (V = 10 + 10 = 20): **Food** (*Max* = 10) → *Salivation*

Note that the tone and the light together have 20 units of associative value (10 for the tone and 10 for the light). However, the maximum associative value that can be supported by the food at any one moment is only 10 units. This means that the associative value of the compound stimulus must decrease to match the maximum value that can be supported by the US. Thus, according to the Rescorla-Wagner theory, after several pairings of the compound stimulus with food, the total associative value of the compound stimulus will be reduced to 10:

[Tone + Light] (V = 10) → *Salivation*

This in turn means that when each member in the compound is tested separately, its value also will have decreased. For example:

Tone (V = 5) → *Salivation*
Light (V = 5) → *Salivation*

ADVICE FOR THE LOVELORN

Dear Dr. Dee,

My friend says that if you are deeply and madly in love with someone, then you will necessarily be much less interested in anyone else. I think my friend is wrong. There is no reason why someone can't be deeply in love with more than one person at a time. So who is right?

The Wanderer

Dear Wanderer,

I honestly do not know who is right. But your friend's hypothesis seems somewhat consistent with the Rescorla-Wagner theory. If feelings of love are to some extent classically conditioned emotional responses, then the more love you feel for one person (meaning that he or she is a distinctive CS that has strong associative value), the less love you should feel for alternative partners who are simultaneously available (because there is little associative value left over for those other CSs). In other words, there is only so much love (so much associative value) to go around, and strong romantic feelings for one person will likely result in weak romantic feelings for others. In keeping with this, you can occasionally encounter people who report being so "in love" with someone—at least in the early stages of a relationship—that they are attracted to no one else. (I remember a male movie star some years ago commenting on this, remarking that he had never thought it possible that he could so completely lose interest in other women.) It is the case, however, that some people are strongly attracted to many different partners, though perhaps what is attracting them in such cases is some quality that those partners have in common, such as a high degree of physical attractiveness. But would we then define such attraction as love?

Behaviorally yours

Dr. Dee

Thus, even though the tone and light were subjected to further pairings with the food, the associative value of each decreased (i.e., each stimulus elicited less salivation than it originally did when it had been conditioned individually).

The effect we have just described is known as the ***overexpectation effect***, which is the decrease in the conditioned response that occurs when two separately conditioned CSs are combined into a compound stimulus for further pairings with the US. It is as though presenting the two CSs together leads to an "overexpectation" about what will follow. When this expectation is not fulfilled, the subject's expectations are modified downward. As a result, each CS in the compound loses some of its associative value.

Although the Rescorla-Wagner model has been a source of inspiration for researchers, not all of its predictions have been confirmed. As a result, revisions to the model have been proposed along with alternative models. Some behaviorists have also criticized the common practice of interpreting the Rescorla-Wagner model in cognitive terms by arguing that the concept of associative value, which can be objectively measured by the strength of the CR, makes inferences about mentalistic processes, such as expectations, unnecessary (e.g., Pierce & Epling, 1995). Despite these debates, however, few models have been as productive in furthering our understanding of the underlying processes of classical conditioning.

1. The Rescorla-Wagner theory proposes that a given _US_ can support only so much conditioning, and this amount of conditioning must be distributed among the various _CS_ available.

2. In general, stronger USs support (more/less) _____ conditioning than weaker USs.

3. According to the Rescorla-Wagner theory, overshadowing occurs because the more salient CS picks up (most/little) _____ of the associative value available in that setting.

4. According to the Rescorla-Wagner theory, blocking occurs because the (CS/NS) _____ in the compound has already picked up all of the available associative value.

5. Suppose a compound stimulus has an associative value of 25 following conditioning. According to the Rescorla-Wagner theory, if one CS has acquired 15 units of associative value, the other CS must have acquired _10_ units of associative value.

6. Suppose a tone and a light are each conditioned with food to a maximum associative value of 8 units. If the tone and light are combined into a compound stimulus for further conditioning trials, the associative value of each stimulus must necessarily (decrease/increase) _____. This is known as the o_____ effect.

QUICK QUIZ E

Practical Applications of Classical Conditioning

Understanding Phobias

Phobia

Strong, persistant unwarrented fear of specific object or situation

Excessive

A particularly salient way that classical conditioning affects our lives is through its involvement in the development of fears and anxieties. As already noted, a conditioned fear response can be elicited by a previously neutral stimulus that has been associated with an aversive stimulus. In most cases, this sort of fear conditioning is a highly adaptive process because it motivates the individual to avoid a dangerous situation. A person who is bitten by a dog and learns to fear dogs is less likely to be bitten in the future simply because he or she will tend to avoid dogs.

This process, however, occasionally becomes exaggerated, with the result that we become very fearful of events that are not at all dangerous or only minimally dangerous. Such extreme, irrational fear reactions are known as phobias. In many cases, these phobias seem to represent a process of *overgeneralization*, in which a conditioned fear response to one event has become overgeneralized to other harmless events. Thus, although it may be rational to fear a mean-looking dog that once bit you, it is irrational to fear a friendly-looking dog that has never bitten you.

Watson and Rayner's "Little Albert"   The importance of classical conditioning and overgeneralization in the development of phobias was first noted by John B. Watson and his student (and wife-to-be) Rosalie Rayner. In 1920, Watson and Rayner published a now-famous article in which they described their attempt to condition a fear response in an 11-month-old infant named Albert. Albert was a very healthy, well-developed child, whose mother worked as a wet nurse in the hospital where the tests were conducted. Albert was described as "stolid and unemotional," almost never cried, and had never been seen to display rage or fear. In fact, he seemed to display an unusual level of emotional stability.

The researchers began the experiment by testing Albert's reactions to a variety of objects. These included a white rat, a rabbit, a dog, some cotton wool, and even a burning newspaper. None of the objects elicited any fear, and in fact Albert often attempted to handle them. He was, however, startled when the experimenters made a loud noise by banging a steel bar with a hammer. The experimenters thus concluded that the loud noise was an unconditioned stimulus that elicited a fear response (or, more specifically, a startle reaction), whereas the other objects, such as the rat, were neutral stimuli with respect to fear:

Loud noise → *Fear* (as indicated by startle reaction)
   US   **UR**
Rat → **No fear**
NS   —

In the next part of the experiment, Watson and Rayner (1920) paired the loud noise (US) with the white rat (NS). The rat was presented to Albert, and just as his hand touched it, the steel bar was struck with the hammer. In this first conditioning trial, Albert "jumped violently and fell forward, burying his face in the mattress. He did not cry, however" (p. 4). He reacted similarly when the trial was repeated, except that this time he began to whimper. The conditioning session was ended at that point.

The next session was held a week later. At the start of the session, the rat was handed to Albert to test his reaction to it. He tentatively reached for the rat, but quickly withdrew his hand after touching it. Since, by comparison, he showed no fear of some toy blocks that were handed to him, it seemed that a slight amount of fear conditioning to the rat had occurred during the previous week's session. Albert was then subjected to further pairings of the rat with the noise, during which he became more and more fearful. Finally, at one point, when the rat was presented without the noise, Albert "began to crawl so rapidly that he was caught with difficulty before reaching the edge of the table" (Watson & Rayner, 1920, p. 5). Albert's reaction was interpreted by Watson and Rayner as indicating that the rat had indeed become a conditioned fear stimulus as a result of its association with the noise. This process can be diagrammed as follows:

Rat: Loud noise → *Fear*
NS   US   UR
Rat → *Fear* (as indicated by crying and crawling away from the rat)
CS   CR

In subsequent sessions (during which Albert occasionally received further pairings of the rat with the noise to "freshen" the conditioning), Albert appeared to show not only a fear of the rat but also of objects that were in some way similar to the rat, such as a rabbit, a fur coat, a dog, and even a Santa Claus mask. In other words, Albert's fear response seemed to have generalized to objects that were similar to the original CS. His apparent fear of the rat, and his generalized fear of similar objects, persisted even following a 30-day break, although the intensity of his reactions was somewhat diminished. At that point, Albert left the hospital, so further tests could not be conducted. Watson and Rayner were therefore unable to carry out their stated plan of using behavioral procedures to eliminate Albert's newly acquired fear response.[3]

Although the Little Albert experiment is often depicted as a convincing demonstration of phobic conditioning in a young infant, this is actually

---

[3]If all this seems terribly unethical, well, by today's standards, it is. The lack of established ethical guidelines for psychological research at that time no doubt played a role. But it is also interesting to note that the Little Albert study hardly raised an eyebrow when it was published. In fact, Watson received far more criticism for his research with rats (from animal rights activists of that era) than he ever did for his research with Albert (Buckley, 1989). Although mistreatment of children was a concern at that time, people have since become much more worried about potential long-term problems resulting from adverse childhood experiences.

Watson and Rayner with Little Albert. (The white rat is beside Albert's left arm.)

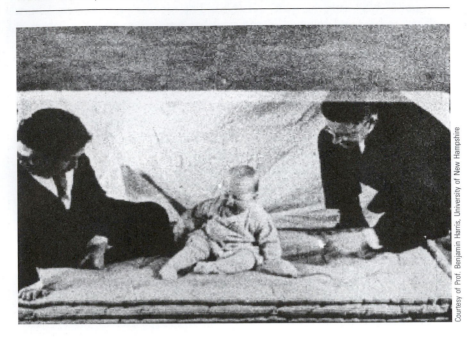

debatable (Harris, 1979). For example, it took several pairings of the loud noise with the rat before the rat elicited a fear reaction; additionally, Albert's fear reaction diminished considerably following a 30-day rest period. By contrast, real-life phobias usually require only one pairing of the US with the CS to become established, and they often grow stronger over time. Watson and Rayner (1920) also noted that Albert displayed no fear so long as he was able to suck his thumb, and the experimenters had to repeatedly remove his thumb from his mouth during the sessions to enable a fear reaction to be elicited. This suggests that any fear conditioning that did occur was relatively weak since it was easily countered by the pleasure derived from thumb sucking.

Thus, although Watson and Rayner (1920) speculated about the possibility of Albert growing up to be a neurotic individual with a strange fear of furry objects, it is quite likely that he did not develop a true phobia and soon got over any aversion he may have acquired to furry objects. In fact, more recent evidence suggests that additional factors are often involved in the development of a true phobia. Some of these factors are discussed in the next section.[4] (See also "Little Albert: Lost or Found?" in the And Furthermore box.)

---

[4]It has been noted that the Little Albert study can also be interpreted as an example of operant conditioning (e.g., Goodwin, 2005). More specifically, because the loud noise occurred when Albert reached for the rat—meaning that the noise followed the reaching response and served to punish that response—the process can be described as an example of "positive punishment" (which is discussed in Chapter 6).

1. A phobia is an extreme, irrational fear reaction to a particular event. From a classical conditioning perspective, it seems to represent a process of over- _generalization_

2. In the Little Albert experiment, the rat was originally a(n) _Nuetral_ stimulus, while the loud noise was a(n) _Unconditio_ stimulus.

3. Albert's startle response to the noise was a(n) _fear_ response, while his crying in response to the rat was a(n) _____ response.

4. One difference between Albert's fear conditioning and conditioning of real-life phobias is that the latter often require (only one / more than one) _____ conditioning trial.

5. Unlike real-life phobias, Albert's fear of the rat seemed to grow (stronger/ weaker) _weaker_ following a 30-day break.

6. Albert's fear response was (present/absent) _absent_ whenever he was suck- ing his thumb, which suggests that the fear conditioning was actually relatively (strong/weak) _weak_ .

And Furthermore

Little Albert: Lost or Found?

As you may recall, Watson and Rayner (1920) reported that Little Albert left the hospital before they were able to remove the phobia that they believed they had created in him. As a result, over the years, the question of what happened to Albert has intrigued many a psychologist. Did he grow up with a fear of furry objects, as Watson and Rayner specu- lated that he might, or did he remain unaffected by his experiences? Unfortunately, all attempts to track him down have failed—that is, until recently.

In a clever bit of detective work, Beck, Levinson, and Irons (2009) used U.S. census records to identify a woman, Arvilla Merritte, who apparently (like Albert's mother) worked as a wet nurse in the hospital at the time that Watson and Rayner were conducting research there. Hospital records revealed that Arvilla gave birth to a son, Douglas, in the hospital several months earlier, with the child's age closely matching the reported age of Albert at the time of the recorded baseline session. Based largely on these congruencies, the authors concluded that Douglas very likely was Albert, with the published name, Albert B, having been a pseudonym. (Other evidence included a facial comparison between a photo of Douglas and film images of Albert, but this was judged to be inconclusive, partly because the film images are so blurry and also because of inherent difficulties in doing facial comparisons with infants.)

Needless to say, the purported discovery of Little Albert's real identity resulted in a great deal of fanfare—the *APA Monitor* proclaiming that "one of psychology's greatest mysteries appears to have been solved" (DeAngelis, 2010, p. 10)—as well as a tinge of

(*continued*)

sadness insofar as Douglas Merritte had died at the age of 6 (which nullified any speculation about what had happened to "Albert" when he grew up). Unfortunately, possible weaknesses in the case for Douglas being Albert also soon emerged (Powell, 2010; Reese, 2010; Harris, 2011). For example, in summarizing their investigation, Beck et al. (2009) had commented that "none of the folktales [about Albert] we encountered during our inquiry had a factual basis. [For example] he was not adopted by a family north of Baltimore" (p. 613). This is in reference to the fact that Douglas had remained with his mother after they left the hospital. It turns out, however, that the adoption story is not a simple folktale, but is actually based on a direct quote from Watson (1924/25): "No further tests could be made upon Albert B ... *because he was shortly adopted by an out-of-town family* [emphasis added]" (p. 167). In reply to this criticism, Beck (2010) argued that Watson over the years was often careless in his descriptions of the Albert case, and may have used the word *adoption* loosely in reference to Albert and his mother moving in with another family (Douglas' mother having left the hospital to work as a live-in maid). This is indeed possible, but if Watson did not use the word *adoption* loosely or incorrectly, then Douglas Merritte is almost certainly not Little Albert.

Questions have also arisen about the purported match in age between Douglas and Albert at the time of the baseline session (Powell, 2011). (The details of this are a bit intricate, but those who enjoy puzzles might find it interesting). Beck et al. (2009) had estimated the approximate date of the baseline session based on a note from Watson (1919) to university president, Frank Goodnow, thanking him for funding to purchase film to make a movie of his research with infants:

> Thank you very much for your note concerning the movies. I am only waiting for a warm spell to start in on the work. The laboratory is so cold that I am a little afraid to expose the babies for so long a time.

Although the letter is dated December 5, Beck et al. speculated that it might have been dictated up to a week earlier and then typed up and sent some days later, due to Watson's secretary often being overworked. They therefore proposed a two week interval, November 28 to December 12, during which the baseline session with Albert (which was filmed) likely occurred. Significantly, Douglas Merritte's age exactly matches the reported age of Albert at baseline (8 months 26 days) in the middle of this interval, December 5, the very date that appears on Watson's note to Goodnow.

Given the importance of the timelines in this case, Powell (2011) attempted to more accurately date when the letter was dictated, and thereby the time at which the baseline session might have occurred. In fact, a search of the hospital archives revealed a note from Goodnow to Watson, dated December 3, which Watson's note of December 5 appears to have been written in reply to. This means that Watson's note almost certainly *was* dictated on or around December 5, and not up to a week earlier as Beck et al. (2009) had speculated. Powell also checked the historical weather records for the Baltimore region, since Watson's note had indicated that he was not yet ready to begin filming because of the cold temperature. As it turns out, the first cold spell of the season had started on December 2 and then abruptly ended on December 7. If Watson had indeed waited for a warm spell before starting to film, this means that the baseline session would likely have occurred no earlier than December 7, or, more likely, December 8 given that December 7 was a Sunday. But this then creates a problem for Douglas Merritte being Albert, since, on December 7, Douglas is already two days older than the reported age of Albert at the time of the baseline film session. On top of this, there is no evidence that Watson began his movie project by filming the baseline session with Albert (the Albert scenes constituting only 5 minutes of the 15 minutes of research activity presented in the movie [Watson, 1923]). This means that the baseline session with Albert could very well have been filmed several days after December 7, thereby further increasing the potential discrepancy in age between Douglas and Albert.

In conclusion, some of the known facts about Douglas—for example, his age at what would have been the most likely time for the baseline session to have occurred and the fact that he was not given up for adoption—do not match the reported information about Albert. Thus, while it remains possible that Douglas Merritte was Albert (they were potentially at least close in age and they do have some similar facial characteristics), it is also possible that he was not Albert, and that the real Albert has yet to be identified. Hopefully, more information will soon be uncovered to help solve this puzzle. (See also Harris, 2011, for an interesting description of his futile attempts over several years to put an end to the many myths and inaccuracies surrounding Little Albert.)

Additional Factors in Phobic Conditioning   Not all phobias are acquired through a direct process of classical conditioning. Indeed, many people with phobias are unable to recall any particular conditioning event before the development of their symptoms (Marks, 1969). Additionally, most people are surprisingly resilient when exposed to extremely frightening events, and do not develop chronic fear reactions such as phobias and posttraumatic stress disorder (PTSD, which typically includes phobia as one of its symptoms). For example, the vast majority of people exposed to air raids during the World War II endured them rather well, developing only short-term fear reactions that quickly disappeared (Rachman, 1977). Researchers have therefore suggested several additional variables that, singly or in combination, may be involved in the development of phobic symptoms. These include observational learning, temperament, preparedness, history of control, incubation, US revaluation, and selective sensitization.

Observational Learning.   Many phobias are acquired when observing fearful reactions in others. For example, in World War II a major predictor of whether children developed a fear of air raids was whether their mothers displayed such fears. As well, airmen who became phobic of combat often developed their symptoms after witnessing fear reactions in a crewmate (Rachman, 1977).

This tendency to acquire conditioned fear reactions through observation may be inherited (Mineka, 1987). If so, a display of fear by another person may be conceptualized as an unconditioned stimulus that elicits an unconditioned fear response in oneself:

Display of fear by others → *Fear* (in oneself)
         US   **UR**

A neutral stimulus that is associated with this display might then become a conditioned stimulus for fear:

Snake: Display of fear by others → *Fear*
   NS   **US**   **UR**
Snake → *Fear*
   CS   **CR**

The result is that a person who has had no direct confrontation with snakes may indirectly acquire a conditioned fear of snakes. (The other way in which observational learning of a fear response can occur is through higher-order conditioning, which is discussed in the section on observational learning in Chapter 12.)

Temperament.   **Temperament** is an individual's base level of emotionality and reactivity to stimulation which is to a large extent genetically determined. Temperament seems to affect how easily a conditioned response can be acquired. As noted in Chapter 4, Pavlov found that dogs that were shy and withdrawn conditioned more readily than dogs that were active and outgoing. Similarly, individuals with certain temperaments may be more genetically susceptible than others to the development of conditioned fears (Clark, Watson, & Mineka, 1994).

Even Watson, who made a career out of downplaying the role of genetic influences in human behavior, acknowledged the possible influence of temperament. Watson and Rayner (1920) deliberately chose Albert as a subject under the assumption that his emotional stability would grant him a good deal of immunity against the harmful effects of their procedures. They also noted that "had he been emotionally unstable probably both the directly conditioned response [to the rat] and those transferred [to similar stimuli] would have persisted throughout the month unchanged in form" (p. 12), when in fact his fears had somewhat diminished following the 30-day break. Thus, they believed that Albert did not have the sort of temperament that would facilitate acquiring a phobia.

Preparedness. The concept of **preparedness** refers to a genetically based predisposition within a species to learn certain kinds of associations more easily than others (Seligman, 1971). Thus, we may have an inherited predisposition to develop fears to certain types of objects or events. This notion was initially proposed by Valentine (1930), who attempted to replicate Watson and Rayner's experiment with his 1-year-old daughter by blowing a loud whistle whenever she touched certain objects. When the object she touched was a pair of opera glasses, she displayed no fear, even to the sound of the whistle. When the object was a caterpillar, however, some fear was elicited. By contrast, Valentine observed a 2-year-old who became fearful of dogs "at slight provocation." He concluded that people may have an innate tendency to fear certain kinds of events (such as insects and certain other animals) and that Watson had been able to successfully condition Albert to fear rats because of this tendency.

More recent evidence for the role of preparedness in fear conditioning includes a study by Cook and Mineka (1989). They exposed laboratory-raised rhesus monkeys to videotapes edited to show another monkey reacting either fearfully or non-fearfully to either a fear-relevant stimulus (toy snake or toy crocodile) or a fear-irrelevant stimulus (flowers or toy rabbit). Only those monkeys who observed the model reacting fearfully to the fear-relevant stimulus acquired a conditioned fear reaction to that stimulus. Similarly, Soares and Öhman (1993) found that human subjects displayed physiological signs of anxiety in reaction to certain subliminal stimuli— pictures presented so briefly that subjects were consciously unaware of the content—that had been paired with uncomfortable levels of electric shock. This reaction occurred when the pictures were of fear-relevant stimuli (snakes and spiders) as opposed to fear-irrelevant stimuli (flowers and mushrooms). This result supports the notion that humans, too, may be predisposed to learn to fear certain types of objects and events. (The concept of preparedness is more fully discussed in Chapter 11.)

Students often confuse the concepts of temperament and preparedness. In people, temperament refers to differences between people in how emotionally reactive they are, which in turn affects how easily they can develop a phobia. Preparedness (as it relates to phobias) refers to differences between the types of phobias in how easily they can be acquired. Thus, temperament refers to how easily a particular person can acquire a phobia, while preparedness refers to how easily a particular type of phobia can be acquired. For example, the fact that Jason more easily develops phobias than does Samantha reflects the role of temperament; the fact that, for both of them, a phobia of snakes is more easily acquired than a phobia of toasters reflects the role of preparedness.

1. From a conditioning perspective, viewing a display of fear in others can be conceptualized as a(n) _____ stimulus that elicits a(n) _____ response of fear in oneself. The event the other person is reacting to might then become a(n) _____ stimulus that elicits a(n) _____ response of fear in oneself.

2. The term _____ refers to an individual's genetically determined level of emotionality and reactivity to stimulation. It (does / does not) _____ seem to affect the extent to which responses can be classically conditioned.

3. The concept of p_____ holds that we are genetically programmed to acquire certain kinds of fears, such as fear of snakes and spiders, more readily than other kinds.

4. Travis rolled his pickup truck, yet he had no qualms about driving home afterwards; Cam was in a minor fender bender last week and remained petrified of driving for several days afterward. These different outcomes may reflect inherited differences in t_____ between the two individuals.

5. The fact that many people are more petrified of encountering snakes than they are of being run over by cars, even though the latter is a far more relevant danger in the world in which they live, reflects differences in _____ for acquiring certain kinds of fears.

History of Control. Another factor that may influence susceptibility to fear conditioning is a history of being able to control important events in one's environment. For example, in one study, young monkeys who had a history of controlling the delivery of food, water, and treats (such as by pulling a chain) were considerably less fearful of a mechanical toy monster than were monkeys who had simply been given these items regardless of their behavior (Mineka, Gunnar, & Champoux, 1986). Living in an environment where they had some degree of control over important events seemed to effectively immunize them against the traumatic effects of encountering a strange and frightening object. Presumably, these monkeys would also have been less susceptible to classical conditioning of fear responses, although this prediction was not directly tested. The harmful effects of prolonged exposure to uncontrollable events, and the beneficial effects of prior exposure to controllable events, are further examined in Chapter 9 under the topic of learned helplessness.

Incubation. When a phobia develops through a direct process of classical conditioning, an important question must be asked: Why does the conditioned fear not extinguish with subsequent exposures to the CS? To some extent, extinction does not occur, because the person tends to avoid the feared stimulus (the CS) so that repeated exposure to the CS in the absence of the US does not take place. Additionally, however, because of this tendency to move away from the feared stimulus, any exposures that do occur are likely to be very brief. According to Eysenck (1968), such brief exposures may result in a phenomenon known as "incubation."

Incubation refers to the strengthening of a conditioned fear response as a result of brief exposures to the aversive CS. For example, a child who is bitten by a dog and then runs away each time he encounters a dog may find that his fear of dogs grows worse even though he is never again bitten. As a result, what may have started off as a moderate fear of dogs may evolve over time into a severe fear. In fact, this process might even result in a conditioned fear that is actually stronger than the unconditioned fear that was originally elicited when the child was bitten. Thus, the CR would be stronger than the UR, which contradicts the general rule that a CR is weaker than the UR. It also contradicts the general rule that the presentation of the CS without the US will result in extinction. Note, too, that covert exposures to the feared stimulus—as in worrying about it—might also result in incubation (Wells & Papageorgiou, 1995). Incubation is, of course, the reason for the old adage that if you fall off a horse you should immediately get back on. If you wait, you might later become too fearful to get back on. Note, however, that some researchers believe that the process of incubation has yet to be convincingly demonstrated (Levis & Brewer, 2001).[5]

US Revaluation.   As noted in Chapter 4, exposure to a US of a different intensity (i.e., a different *value*) than that used during conditioning can alter the strength of the response to a previously conditioned CS. This process could play a major role in human phobias (Davey, 1992). Consider, for example, a skateboarder who experiences a minor injury as a result of a fall:

Skateboarding: Minor injury → *Slight anxiety*
Skateboarding → *Slight anxiety*

Because the injury was relatively minor, skateboarding elicits only a slight amount of conditioned anxiety, most of which will likely extinguish as the skateboarder continues the activity. But imagine that this person later is in a car accident and suffers a severe injury:

Severe injury → *Strong anxiety*

What might happen is that he might now display a strong degree of anxiety, not only to cars, but also to skateboarding:

Skateboarding → *Strong anxiety*

It is as though the skateboarder finally realizes just how painful an injury can be. And given that skateboarding is associated with being injured, it now elicits strong feelings of anxiety.

The preceding example involves direct exposure to a US of different intensity; however, the process of US revaluation can also occur through observational learning. A student of one of the authors reported that she

---

[5]The term incubation has also been used to refer to the increased strength of a fear response that can sometimes occur following a rest period after fear conditioning, even *without* brief exposures to the CS (e.g., Corsini, 2002).

developed a phobia about snowboarding after first spraining her leg in a minor snowboarding accident—which resulted in only minor anxiety about snowboarding—and then witnessing someone else suffer a severe snowboarding accident. In this circumstance, observational learning may have resulted in US inflation, which then led to the phobia. Note that this differs from pure observational learning to the extent that her earlier minor snowboarding accident set the stage for her strong reaction when witnessing someone else's major snowboarding accident.

US inflation can also occur through verbally transmitted information. Consider the following case described by Davey, de Jong, and Tallis (1993):

> M. F. (male, aged 29 yr) worked as a bank employee. On one occasion the bank was robbed, and during the robbery M. F. was threatened with a gun. He had not been particularly anxious at the time and returned to work the next day without complaining of any residual fear symptoms. However, 10 days after the robbery he was interviewed by the police, and during this interview he was told that he was very lucky to be alive because the bank robber was considered to be a dangerous man who had already killed several people. From this point on M. F. did not return to work and developed severe PTSD symptoms. (p. 496)

This latter example suggests that we have to be particularly careful about the sort of information we convey to people who have suffered potentially traumatic events because that information itself might induce a traumatic reaction. Indeed, research has shown that individuals who have been exposed to a traumatic event and are then given a *psychological debriefing* (also known as *critical incident stress debriefing*)—which is a structured form of counseling designed to prevent the development of posttraumatic stress disorder (PTSD)—are sometimes *more* likely to develop symptoms of PTSD than those who do not receive such debriefings (e.g., Mayou & Ehlers, 2000; Sijbrandij, Olff, Reitsma, Carlier, & Gersons, 2006). It seems that the debriefing itself sometimes heightens the effect of the trauma, perhaps by giving victims the impression that the trauma was more severe than they would otherwise have thought. Although the use of psychological debriefings is still being promoted by some psychologists, more empirically-based procedures have now been developed that are more respectful of a person's own coping style and are less likely to inadvertently do harm (Gist & Devilly, 2010).

Selective Sensitization. Yet another process that could influence the development of a phobia is **selective sensitization**, which is an increase in one's reactivity to a potentially fearful stimulus following exposure to an unrelated stressful event. For example, people with *agoraphobia* (fear of being alone in a public place) often report that the initial onset of the disorder occurred during a period in which they were emotionally upset or suffered from some type of physical illness (Rachman, 1977). Similarly, an individual going through a stressful divorce might find that her previously minor anxiety about driving in heavy traffic suddenly develops into severe anxiety.

The stressful circumstance surrounding the divorce affects her reactions not only to the divorce but to other potentially aversive events as well. Therefore, during turbulent times in one's life, minor fears and anxieties may become exacerbated into major fears and anxieties (Barlow, 1988).

1. We will probably be (more/less) _____ susceptible to acquiring a conditioned fear response if we grow up in a world in which we experience little or no control over the available rewards.

2. Brief exposures to a feared CS in the absence of the US may result in a phenomenon known as _____ in which the conditioned fear response grows (stronger/weaker) _____. This runs counter to the general principle that presentation of the CS without the US usually results in e_____.

3. According to the concept of _____ revaluation, phobic behavior might sometimes develop when the person encounters a (more/less) _____ intense version of the (CS/US) _____ than was used in the original conditioning. This process can also occur through o_____ l_____ or through v_____ transmitted information.

4. The process of s_____ s_____ refers to an increase in one's reactivity to a potentially fearful stimulus following exposure to a stressful event, even though the stressful event is (related/unrelated) _____ to the feared stimulus.

Treating Phobias

Perhaps more than any other disorder, phobias are highly susceptible to treatments based on behavioral principles of classical conditioning. In this section, we discuss the two basic types of treatment: systematic desensitization and flooding.

Systematic Desensitization   Recall how Watson and Rayner had intended to use behavioral procedures to eliminate Albert's fears but were unable to do so because his mother suddenly moved away. A few years later, Mary Cover Jones (1924) did carry out such a treatment (under Watson's supervision) with Peter, a 2-year-old boy who had an extreme fear of rabbits. Jones's treatment strategy consisted of first feeding Peter cookies while presenting a rabbit at a considerable distance. It was assumed that the positive emotional response elicited by the cookies would overcome the mild anxiety elicited by the distant rabbit. Over successive sessions, the rabbit was gradually brought closer to Peter as he continued to eat cookies. Within a few months, Peter was holding the rabbit in his lap while munching on cookies. As a result of this gradual conditioning procedure, Peter's fear of the rabbit was eliminated.

Although Jones's treatment procedure, carried out in 1924, seemed to have effectively eliminated a phobia, it languished in obscurity until Joseph

Wolpe (1958) essentially rediscovered it 30 years later. As a graduate student, Wolpe conducted research on fear conditioning in cats exposed to electric shocks. The cats displayed a strong fear of both the experimental chamber in which they had been shocked and the room containing the chamber. A major indication of this fear was the cats' refusal to eat while in the room (an example of conditioned suppression). Wolpe then devised a treatment plan to eliminate the fear. He began by feeding the cats in a room that was quite dissimilar from the original "shock" room. Then, over a period of days, the cats were fed in rooms that were made progressively similar to the shock room. Eventually they were able to eat in the original room and even in the experimental cage in which they had been shocked. This procedure effectively eliminated the conditioned fear response in all 12 cats that Wolpe studied.

Wolpe (1958) interpreted the cats' improvements to be the result of *counterconditioning*, in which a CS that elicits one type of response is associated with an event that elicits an incompatible response. In Wolpe's study, the experimental room originally elicited a fear response because of its association with shock. Later, it elicited a positive emotional reaction after it had become associated with food. Wolpe proposed that the underlying process in counterconditioning is *reciprocal inhibition*, in which certain responses are incompatible with each other, and the occurrence of one response necessarily inhibits the other. Thus, the positive emotional response elicited by food inhibited the cats' anxiety because the two responses countered each other.

As a result of his success, Wolpe (1958) began to ponder ways of applying this treatment procedure to human phobias. Although both he and Jones had successfully used food to counter feelings of anxiety, Wolpe felt that this approach would be impractical for most treatment situations involving humans. He toyed with other types of responses that might counter anxiety, such as anger and assertiveness (i.e., the client was taught to act angry or assertive in situations that were normally associated with fear), but then he finally hit upon the use of deep muscle relaxation. Deep muscle relaxation is largely incompatible with the experience of anxiety (Jacobson, 1938), making it ideal from Wolpe's perspective as a tool for counterconditioning.

Wolpe (1958) also realized that real-life exposure to a phobic stimulus was impractical in some treatment scenarios. For example, it would be extremely difficult to expose a person with a fear of thunderstorms to a succession of storms that are made progressively frightening. To solve this dilemma, Wolpe decided to have the patient simply visualize the feared stimulus. A series of visualized scenarios could then be constructed that would represent varying intensities of the feared event. For example, the person could imagine a storm some distance away that had only a mild amount of thunder and lightning, then a storm that was somewhat closer with a bit more thunder and lightning, and so on. One drawback to this procedure is that the counterconditioning occurs only to the visualized event, and it will then have to generalize to the real event. Nevertheless, if the visualization is fairly vivid, the amount of generalization to the real world should be considerable.

Thus, three basic aspects of Wolpe's (1958) treatment procedure, which is generally known as *systematic desensitization*, are as follows:

1. **Training in relaxation.** An abbreviated version of Jacobson's (1938) deep muscle relaxation procedure is commonly employed for inducing relaxation, but other methods such as meditation or hypnosis have also been used.

2. **Creation of a hierarchy of imaginary scenes that elicit progressively intense levels of fear.** Experience has shown that about 10 to 15 scenes are sufficient, starting with a scene that elicits only a minor degree of fear (e.g., for a dog-phobic individual, it might be visualizing a friendly poodle tied to a tree at a distance of several yards) and finishing with a scene that elicits a tremendous amount of anxiety (e.g., visualizing standing beside a large dog that is barking).

3. **Pairing of each item in the hierarchy with relaxation.** Starting with the least fearful scene in the hierarchy, the person is asked to visualize the scene for about 10 to 30 seconds and then engage in a short period of relaxation. This process is repeated until the first scene no longer elicits anxiety, at which point the process is carried out using the next scene. By the time the top item in the hierarchy is reached, most of the person's conditioned fear will have been eliminated, leaving only a residual amount of fear to what was once an intensely fearful scene. The fear response to this final scene is also eliminated, at which point it is quite likely that the person will now feel significantly less anxious when confronted with the phobic stimulus in real life.

Thus, *systematic desensitization* is a behavioral treatment for phobias that involves pairing relaxation with a succession of stimuli that elicit increasing levels of fear. Although Wolpe (1958) emphasized, mostly for convenience, the use of imaginary stimuli (the procedure then being referred to as *imaginal desensitization*), the treatment can also be carried out with real phobic stimuli. This version of desensitization is sometimes referred to as *in vivo desensitization*. Mary Cover Jones's (1925) treatment of Peter's rabbit phobia is an example of *in vivo* desensitization. As with imaginal desensitization, *in vivo* desensitization usually makes use of relaxation to counter the person's fear response. For example, a dog-phobic client might move gradually closer to a real dog, pausing after each step and relaxing for several seconds. Additionally, the process might first be carried out with a very small dog and then gradually progress to a very large dog. *In vivo* desensitization has an obvious advantage in that one does not have to worry about whether the treatment effect will generalize to a real-life stimulus because one is already working with a real-life stimulus. As previously noted, however, it is often difficult or impossible to arrange such systematic real-life exposures. Additionally, in severely phobic clients, the real stimulus might elicit a tremendous amount of anxiety. In such cases, it might be wiser to first use imaginal desensitization to eliminate much of the fear, and then switch to *in vivo* desensitization to complete the process. More detailed information on systematic desensitization can be found in behavior modification texts such as Miltenberger (2012) and Spiegler and Guevremont (2010).

Considerable research has been carried out on systematic desensitization. The procedure has proven to be highly effective in certain circumstances. For example, systematic desensitization tends to be quite effective with patients who have relatively few phobias that are quite specific in nature (e.g., a fear of dogs and spiders). By contrast, people who suffer from social phobias tend to experience a general fear of many different social situations and do not respond as well to this form of treatment. Additionally, when using imaginal desensitization, the client must be able to clearly visualize the feared event and experience anxiety while doing so. Unfortunately, some individuals are unable to visualize clearly, or they feel no anxiety even with clear visualization. In these cases, *in vivo* desensitization is the better alternative.

Wolpe (1958) assumed that systematic desensitization is a counterconditioning procedure that works through the process of reciprocal inhibition. Not everyone agrees. Some researchers (e.g., Eysenck, 1976) have claimed that systematic desensitization is really just a simple matter of extinction, in which a CS is repeatedly presented in the absence of the US. From this perspective, systematic desensitization for a dog-phobic individual works because it involves repeated presentations of dogs (or images of dogs) in the absence of anything bad happening. Evidence for the extinction explanation comes from the fact that relaxation is not always needed for the treatment to be effective; gradual exposure to the feared stimulus is by itself often sufficient. On the other hand, in support of the counterconditioning explanation, severe phobias respond better to treatment when relaxation is included (Wolpe, 1995). The exact mechanism by which systematic desensitization produces its effects is, however, still unknown, and it could well be that both extinction and counterconditioning are involved.

QUICK QUIZ I

1. Associating a stimulus that already elicits one type of response with an event that elicits an incompatible response is called c_____. Wolpe believed that the underlying process is r_____ i_____ in which certain types of responses are (compatible/incompatible) _____ with each other, and the occurrence of one type of response necessarily i_____ the other.

2. Mary Cover Jones used the stimulus of _____ to counter Peter's feelings of anxiety, while Wolpe, in his s_____ d_____ procedure, used _____.

3. The three basic components of Wolpe's procedure are:

   a. _____

   b. _____

   c. _____

4. A version of Wolpe's procedure that uses real-life rather than imaginary stimuli is called _____ _____ _____. A major advantage of this procedure is that there is less worry about whether the treatment effect will g_____ to the real world.

5. Wolpe's procedure is very effective with people who have (few/many) _____ phobias that are highly (general/specific) _____. Thus, this procedure (does / does not) _____ work well with people who have a social phobia.

6. One bit of evidence against the counterconditioning explanation for this type of treatment is that relaxation (is / is not) _____ always necessary for the treatment to be effective. On the other hand, in keeping with the counterconditioning explanation, relaxation does seem to facilitate treatment when the phobia is (nonspecific/severe) _____.

Flooding   Consider a rat that continues to avoid a goal box in which it was once shocked, even though no further shocks will ever be delivered. One straight forward way to eliminate this phobic behavior is to place the rat in the goal box and insert a barrier that prevents it from leaving. Forced to remain in the box, the rat will initially show considerable distress, but this distress will disappear as time passes and no shock is delivered. By simply preventing the avoidance response from occurring, we can quickly eliminate the rat's irrational fear.

The treatment procedure that makes use of this response-prevention principle is *flooding therapy:* a behavioral treatment that involves prolonged exposure to a feared stimulus, thereby providing maximal opportunity for the conditioned fear response to be extinguished (Spiegler & Guevremont, 2010). This method can be contrasted with systematic desensitization, in which exposure to the feared stimulus not only occurs gradually but also involves pairing the feared event with a response that will counteract the fear (such as relaxation). Flooding is more clearly based on the principle of extinction as opposed to counterconditioning.

As with systematic desensitization, there are two basic types of flooding procedures. In *imaginal flooding*, the client is asked to visualize, as clearly as possible, a scenario involving the feared event. For example, an individual who is spider phobic might imagine waking up at night to find a large, hairy spider on the pillow beside her. A person with a fear of heights might imagine having to climb down a fire escape from a 10th-floor apartment. The greater the level of fear induced by the visualized scenario, the better.

The client first visualizes the scenario in the therapist's office and then practices visualizing it at home. Although the level of fear during visualization may initially increase, it should eventually begin to decrease and finally will be extinguished. Once the fear response to one scenario has been extinguished, the fear response to other scenarios (e.g., having to remove a spider from the kitchen sink) can be similarly extinguished. After extinction has occurred in several scenarios, the client will likely experience considerably less fear when encountering the feared event in the real world.

In vivo flooding is an alternative to imaginal flooding. *In vivo* flooding consists of prolonged exposure to the actual feared event. Consider, for example, a woman who is extremely fearful of balloons (perhaps because someone once burst a balloon in her face when she was a young child). An *in vivo* flooding procedure might involve filling a room with balloons and then having the woman enter the room, close the door, and remain inside for an hour or more. After a few sessions of this, her fear of balloons might well be eliminated.

Of course, flooding is something that people have been intuitively aware of for centuries. The famous German poet and philosopher Goethe described how, as a young man, he had cured himself of a fear of heights by climbing the tower of the local cathedral and standing on the ledge. He repeated this procedure until his fear was greatly alleviated (Lewes, 1965). As with *in vivo* desensitization, *in vivo* flooding is advantageous because it does not require the treatment effect to generalize from an imagined encounter to a real encounter. It is also not dependent on a person's visualization ability. Unfortunately, *in vivo* flooding can be highly aversive. It is also not a realistic alternative with some types of feared events, such as house fires, which are impossible to replicate in the therapy setting.

One concern with any type of flooding therapy is that the stress involved may result in medical complications. As well, clients who have a history of other psychiatric disorders may experience an exacerbation of their fears as a result of this type of treatment. One must be particularly cautious about using flooding to treat clients suffering from posttraumatic stress disorder (a severe stress reaction produced by a traumatic event such as an accident or wartime experience). It is also important that the duration of each exposure, whether *in vivo* or imaginal, be sufficiently long (at least 30 to 45 minutes); otherwise the fear may not be extinguished or, worse yet, may grow more intense. In this sense, flooding is a riskier procedure than systematic desensitization (Spiegler & Guevremont, 2010). (See also "Was Sigmund Freud a Behavior Analyst?" in the And Furthermore box.)

Hybrid Approaches to the Treatment of Phobias Systematic desensitization and flooding are the most basic behavioral approaches to the treatment of phobic behavior. Several variations of these approaches have been devised, which often combine aspects of each along with additional processes such as observational learning. Such approaches are generally known as *exposure-based treatments* or *exposure therapies* and are now considered the treatment of choice for phobic disorders (Spiegler & Guevremont, 2010).

For example, Öst (1989) described a method for rapidly eliminating specific phobias, such as a specific fear of injections or spiders, in a single session. The major component of the treatment package was an *in vivo exposure* procedure in which clients were encouraged to approach the feared object as

And Furthermore

Was Sigmund Freud a Behavior Analyst?

Students sometimes wonder how, if conditioning principles are so effective in treating certain disorders, other therapeutic systems that use decidedly different methods for treating such disorders could have become so well established. One possibility is that these other systems might sometimes make use of behavioral principles but have neglected to advertise the fact. For example, few people are aware that Sigmund Freud, the founder of psychoanalysis, very much appreciated the therapeutic value of direct exposure to one's fears. This is apparent in the following description of Freud and his followers on a holiday outing in 1921 (Grosskurth, 1991). During an excursion in the mountains, they climbed a tower to a platform that was surrounded by an iron railing at hip level.

> Freud suggested that they all lean forward against the railing with their hands behind their backs, their feet well back, and imagine that there was nothing there to prevent them from falling. This was an exercise Freud had devised for overcoming the fear of heights, from which he had suffered as a young man. Jones [one of Freud's most devoted followers] teased him that it didn't seem very psychoanalytic. (p. 21)

Despite Jones's opinion, Freud (1919/1955) was so impressed with the effectiveness of direct exposure to one's fears that he explicitly recommended it as an adjunct to standard psychoanalysis:

> One can hardly master a phobia if one waits till the patient lets the analysis influence him to give it up. He will never in that case bring into the analysis the material indispensable for a convincing resolution of the phobia. One must proceed differently. Take the example of agoraphobia; there are two classes of it, one mild, the other severe. Patients belonging to the first class suffer from anxiety when they go into the streets by themselves, but they have not yet given up going out alone on that account; the others protect themselves from the anxiety by altogether ceasing to go about alone. With these last, one succeeds only when one can induce them by the influence of the analysis to behave like phobic patients of the first class—that is to go into the street and to struggle with the anxiety while they make the attempt. One starts, therefore, by moderating the phobia so far; and it is only when that has been achieved at the physician's demand that the associations and memories [of childhood trauma and unconscious conflicts] come into the patient's mind which enable the phobia to be resolved. (pp. 165–166)

Of course, one can only wonder how Freud could have determined that the final resolution of the phobia was due to the retrieval of childhood memories rather than the cumulative effects of further exposure. (See also Thyer, 1999, for an example of how Carl Jung, another psycho-dynamic therapist, used an exposure-based procedure to treat a case of railroad phobia.)

closely as possible, remain there until the anxiety faded away, and then approach the object even more closely. This process continued until the client had approached the object closely and her reported level of fear toward the object had been reduced by 50% or more. Note that this exposure procedure is similar to systematic desensitization in that it is somewhat gradual, and similar to flooding in that the client is encouraged to endure a fairly intense level of anxiety each step of the way.

Öst's (1989) treatment package included several additional components. For example, throughout the procedure, most clients were accompanied by a person (the therapist) who acted as a model to demonstrate to the client how to interact with the feared object (such as how to use a jar to capture a spider). The therapist also helped the client physically contact the feared object—for example, by first touching the object while the client touched the model's hand, then touching the object while the client also touched the object, and then gradually removing his hand while the patient continued touching the object. The therapeutic use of modeling in this manner is called *participant modeling, contact desensitization,* or *guided participation,* and it has been shown to greatly facilitate fear reduction (Bandura, 1975; Bandura, Blanchard, & Ritter, 1969).

Öst (1989) reported that out of 20 female patients who had been treated with this method (interestingly, men rarely volunteer for such treatment), 19 showed considerable improvement following an average session length of only 2.1 hours. As well, 18 of the clients remained either much improved or completely recovered at long-term follow-up (follow-up information was gathered an average of 4 years after treatment). Needless to say, these results are quite encouraging, especially because most of the clients had suffered from their phobia for several years before treatment. (Question: Although the results are encouraging, what is a major weakness of this study in terms of its methodology [which the author himself readily acknowledged]?)

1. In flooding therapy, the avoidance response is (blocked/facilitated) _____, thereby providing maximal opportunity for the conditioned fear to _____.

2. Two types of flooding therapy are _____ flooding in which one visualizes the feared stimulus, and _____ flooding in which one encounters a real example of the feared stimulus.

3. For flooding therapy to be effective, the exposure period must be of relatively (long/short) _____ duration.

4. Modern-day therapies for phobias are often given the general name of e_____-b_____ treatments.

5. Öst's single-session procedure combines the gradualness of s_____ d_____ with the prolonged exposure time of f_____. This procedure also makes use of p_____ m_____, in which the therapist demonstrates how to interact with the feared object.

A convincing example of animal intelligence.

Aversion Therapy for Eliminating Problem Behaviors

Some behavior problems stem from events being overly enticing rather than overly aversive. For example, nicotine and alcohol can be highly pleasurable, with the result that many people become addicted to these substances. Similarly, pedophiles have inappropriate feelings of sexual attraction to young children. Obviously, one way to counter these problem behaviors is to directly reduce the attractiveness of the relevant stimuli.

Aversion therapy is a treatment procedure that reduces the attractiveness of a desired event by associating it with an aversive stimulus (Spiegler & Guevremont, 2010). An ancient version of this treatment was suggested by the Roman writer Pliny the Elder, who recommended treating overindulgence in wine by secretly slipping the putrid body of a large spider into the bottom of the wine drinker's glass. The intention was that the feelings of revulsion elicited by a mouthful of spider would become associated with the wine, thereby significantly reducing the person's desire for wine (Franks, 1963). More recent versions of this therapy are somewhat less primitive. For example, the taste of alcohol has sometimes been paired with painful electric shocks. An alternative version—which is more similar to Pliny's treatment in that it makes use of stimuli associated with ingestion—involves pairing the taste of alcohol with nausea. In this case, the client is first given an *emetic*, which is a drug that produces nausea. As the nausea develops, the client takes a mouthful of alcohol. This procedure is repeated several times; as well, the type of alcohol is varied across trials to ensure generalization. Research has shown that such nausea-based treatments are more effective than shock-based treatments, presumably because we have a biological tendency to quickly associate nausea with substances that we ingest (Baker & Cannon, 1979; Masters, Burish, Hollon, & Rimm, 1987). This tendency, known as taste aversion conditioning, is discussed more fully in Chapter 11.

Aversion therapy has also been used with smoking, with similar results. Early attempts to pair smoking and electric shock were relatively ineffective, possibly because physical pain is not a biologically relevant response to smoking. A more effective procedure has been to pair smoking with nicotine-induced nausea. This procedure, known as "rapid smoking," involves having the client smoke continuously, inhaling every 6 to 10 seconds (Danaher, 1977). Within a few minutes, extreme feelings of nausea are elicited and the person will be unable to continue. One session is usually sufficient to produce at least temporary abstinence. This is especially the case with smokers who do not yet have a strong physical addiction to smoking and who smoke more for the pleasure of smoking—which the aversive conditioning counteracts—than for the avoidance of withdrawal symptoms (Zelman, Brandon, Jorenby, & Baker, 1992). Long-term abstinence is much less certain but can be facilitated through the use of additional treatment procedures (such as *relapse prevention training*, in which the person learns to identify and cope with situations in which there is a high risk of resuming the problematic behavior [Marlatt & Gordon, 1985]). Rapid smoking is, however, very stressful, usually resulting in extreme increases in heart rate. Thus, this type of treatment must be employed cautiously, particularly if the client has a history of medical difficulties (Lichtenstein & Glasgow, 1977). (In other words, do not try this at home!)

Aversion therapy has also been used to treat sex offenders (Hall, Shondrick, & Hirschman, 1993). In the case of pedophiles, photographic images of unclothed children may be paired with drug-induced nausea or a powerfully unpleasant scent such as ammonia. As part of a comprehensive treatment package, such procedures help reduce the risk that the individual will reoffend following release from prison.[6]

Aversion therapy is sometimes carried out with the use of imaginal stimuli rather than real stimuli. This version of the treatment is usually called *covert sensitization*. For example, a person addicted to smoking might imagine experiencing extreme illness and vomiting each time she tries to smoke. Alternatively, she might visualize being forced to smoke cigarettes that have been smeared with feces. As with imaginal desensitization, the effectiveness of this procedure is dependent on the client's ability to visualize images clearly and to experience strong feelings of revulsion in response to these images. The treatment effect also has to generalize from the visualized event to the real event, which, as in imaginal versus *in vivo* desensitization and flooding, is likely to result in some loss of effectiveness. Thus, covert sensitization will likely be somewhat less effective than aversion therapy, which utilizes exposure to the actual stimulus.

QUICK QUIZ K

1. In _____ therapy, one attempts to reduce the attractiveness of an event by associating that event with an unpleasant stimulus.

2. A standard treatment for alcoholism is to associate the taste of alcohol with feelings of n_____ that have been induced by consumption of an e_____.

3. A highly effective procedure for reducing cigarette consumption, at least temporarily, is r_____ s_____.

---

[6]Although aversion therapy for pedophiles does reduce the likelihood that they will reoffend, be aware that these treatments have not been demonstrated to be a "cure" for most offenders (Kirsch & Becker, 2006).

4. In general, aversion therapy is (more/less) _____ effective when the unpleasant response that is elicited is biologically relevant to the problematic behavior.

5. Aversion therapy is sometimes carried out using _____ stimuli rather than real stimuli. This type of treatment procedure is known as _____ sensitization.

Medical Applications of Classical Conditioning

There is a growing body of evidence indicating that processes of classical conditioning have significant medical implications. For example, Russell et al. (1984) were able to condition guinea pigs to become allergic to certain odors by pairing those odors with an allergy-inducing protein. People who have allergies may suffer from a similar process, in which their allergic reaction is elicited not only by the substance that originally caused the allergy but also by stimuli associated with that substance. Thus, for a person who is allergic to pollen, even the mere sight of flowers might elicit an allergic reaction.

Flowers: Pollen → *Allergic reaction*
  NS   US   UR
Flowers → *Allergic reaction*
  CS   CR

Other studies have shown that various aspects of the immune system can be classically conditioned. For example, Ader and Cohen (1975) exposed rats to an immunosuppressive drug paired with saccharin-flavored water. These rats were then given an injection of foreign cells, followed by a drink of either saccharin-flavored water or plain water. The rats that drank the saccharin-flavored water produced fewer antibodies in reaction to the foreign cells than did the rats that drank the plain water. The flavored water had apparently become a CS for immunosuppression.

In a real-world extension of this study, Bovbjerg et al. (1990) found that women who received chemotherapy in a hospital setting displayed evidence of immunosuppression when they later returned to the hospital. The hospital environment had become associated with the immunosuppressive effect of the chemotherapy and was now a CS for a conditioned immunosuppressive response. Thus:

Hospital: Chemotherapy → *Immunosuppression*
  NS   US   UR
Hospital → *Immunosuppression*
  CS   CR

Other studies have shown that classical conditioning can be used to strengthen immune system functioning. For example, one team of researchers gave human subjects a taste of sherbet followed by shots of adrenaline

(Buske-Kirschbaum, Kirschbaum, Stierle, Jabaij, & Hellhammer, 1994). Adrenaline tends to increase the activity of natural killer cells, which are an important component of the body's immune system. After pairing the sweet sherbet with the adrenaline, the sweet sherbet itself elicited an increase in natural killer cell activity. Hence:

> **Sweet sherbet: Adrenaline** → *Increased natural killer cell activity*
>   **NS**   **US**   **UR**
> **Sweet sherbet** → *Increased natural killer cell activity*
>   **CS**   **CR**

(See also Solvason, Ghanta, & Hiramoto, 1988.)

The medical implications of such findings are significant. Obviously, many patients would benefit considerably from enhanced immune functioning during the course of their illness. Other patients, however—namely those who suffer from autoimmune diseases, such as arthritis, in which the immune system seems to be overactive—would benefit from a procedure that could reliably weaken their immune system. (See Exton et al., 2000, for a review of research into this issue; also Ader, 2003.)

As the preceding discussion suggests, classical conditioning has important implications for our understanding of the *placebo effect* (Siegel, 2002). In drug research, a placebo is an inert substance that appears to be a drug but in reality has no pharmacological value. In double-blind control studies, placebos are given to a control group to assess the effects of "expectancy" upon the patient's symptoms, such effects being known as placebo effects. Only when the drug effect is stronger than the placebo effect is the drug considered effective.

In classical conditioning terms, the placebo effect can be seen as the result of pairing the appearance of the drug (originally an NS) with the active ingredients of the drug (the US). Thus, conditioning a placebo effect for aspirin, in which the active ingredient is acetylsalicylic acid, would involve the following:

> **White pill: Acetylsalicylic acid** → *Headache removal*
>   **NS**   **US**   **UR**
> **White pill** → *Headache removal*
>   **CS**   **CR**

The possibility that this type of process underlies the placebo effect is supported by the fact that such effects are much more likely to occur following a period of treatment with the active drug (e.g., Kantor, Sunshine, Laska, Meisner, & Hopper, 1966). Also supportive of a conditioning interpretation is the finding that repeated administration of a placebo by itself tends to reduce its effectiveness, which suggests that a process of extinction is taking place (Lasagna, Mosteller, von Felsinger, & Beecher, 1954).

If conditioning processes do underlie placebo effects, research into this process might allow us to better control such effects. Placebos could then be used, for example, to reduce the frequency with which a patient has to take the real drug, thereby possibly reducing some of the side effects associated with that drug. Additionally, we may be able to devise ways in which the placebo effect can be combined with the effect of the real drug to produce an enhanced form of treatment (see Siegel, 2002).

And Furthermore

Classical Conditioning, Gulf War Syndrome, and Multiple Chemical Sensitivity

Processes of classical conditioning may be implicated in the controversial disorder known as Gulf War syndrome. Many veterans returning home from that war in 1991 began suffering from a wide array of symptoms—nausea, headaches, sleep problems, and rashes—which they attributed to their experiences in the war. The precise cause of these symptoms has been difficult to determine. Based on a conditioning model, Ferguson and Cassaday (1999) have proposed that the cluster of symptoms displayed by these veterans is virtually identical to that induced by interleukin-1, a small protein produced by the immune system during periods of stress or illness that causes inflammatory reactions in the body. They suggested that the chronic stresses and chemical agents the veterans were exposed to during the war produced an increase in interleukin-1 production and its resultant symptoms. These symptoms then became associated with the sights, sounds, and smells of the war zone. At home, these symptoms were again elicited when the veterans encountered stimuli that were similar to those encountered in the war zone.

One veteran reported that he experienced a headache any time he smelled petroleum, which had been a particularly prevalent smell in the war zone at that time. According to the Ferguson and Cassaday (1999) model, this veteran had presumably been exposed to toxic levels of petroleum fumes, which elicited an increase in interleukin-1 and its perceived symptoms, such as a headache. Through the process of conditioning, the smell of petroleum became a conditioned stimulus that by itself elicited interleukin-1 symptoms:

Petroleum smell: Toxic petroleum fumes → *Interleukin-1 symptoms*

      NS   US   UR

Petroleum smell → *Interleukin-1 symptoms*

      CS   CR

If this conditioning explanation of Gulf War syndrome is accurate, it suggests two possible treatment strategies: (1) administration of drugs to block the effect of interleukin-1 and

(*continued*)

(2) delivery of cognitive-behavioral treatments designed to eliminate the conditioned associations (see also Ferguson, Cassaday, & Bibby, 2004).

Similar conditioning processes may account for a type of environmental illness known as multiple chemical sensitivity or MCS (Bolla-Wilson, Wilson, & Bleecker, 1988). People with MCS develop symptoms in response to low levels of common odorous substances. As with the Gulf War veteran, MCS patients sometimes report that the onset of their illness was preceded by exposure to toxic levels of an odorous substance. From a conditioning perspective, it may be that the toxic substance served as a US that elicited a variety of symptoms. The odor of that substance then became a CS, with the symptoms (the CRs) generalizing to a variety of odors. Consistent with this interpretation, MCS patients do not report developing their symptoms following exposure to toxic levels of a substance that has no odor.

Both Gulf War syndrome and MCS have been controversial diagnoses, with some physicians maintaining that these illnesses are "merely psychological." A classical conditioning interpretation, however, allows us to interpret these illnesses as psychological in the sense of being conditioned but quite real in the sense of involving true physiological reactions over which the patient has little or no control.

QUICK QUIZ L

1. When Christopher entered his friend's house, he noticed a dog dish beside the door. He soon began experiencing symptoms of asthma and assumed that the house was filled with dog dander (particles of fur or skin), to which he is allergic. Only later did he discover that his friend's children had placed the dish by the door in anticipation of soon owning a dog. In fact, no dog had yet been in the house. Assuming that Christopher's reaction is an example of higher-order conditioning, diagram the conditioning process that resulted in Christopher's allergic reaction. Label each component using the appropriate abbreviations.

2. Diagram the classical conditioning process in Ader and Cohen's (1975) study of immunosuppression. Label each component using the appropriate abbreviations.

3. Supporting the possibility that placebo effects are classically conditioned responses, such effects are more likely to occur (following/preceding) _____ a period of treatment with the real drug. As well, repeated presentations of the placebo by itself tends to (reduce/increase) _____ its effectiveness, which suggests that e_____ may be taking place.

SUMMARY

According to the S-S approach to classical conditioning, conditioning involves the formation of an association between the NS and the US. In contrast, the S-R approach claims that conditioning involves the formation of an association between the NS and a reflex response. Pavlov's stimulus-substitution theory was an early S-S approach in which the CS is presumed to act as a substitute for the US. The fact that the CR is sometimes different from the UR does not support this theory; rather, it seems like the CR often serves to prepare the organism for the onset of the US (in keeping with the preparatory-response theory of conditioning). In one version of preparatory-response theory, known as the compensatory-response model, the CS is viewed as eliciting opponent processes that counteract the effect of the US. This approach has significant application to understanding addiction. The Rescorla-Wagner theory accounts for certain conditioning phenomena (e.g., blocking) by proposing that a given US can support only so much conditioning, which must be distributed among the various CSs available.

The principles of classical conditioning are useful in understanding and treating phobias. This was first demonstrated by Watson and Rayner (1920), who conditioned an 11-month-old infant named Albert to fear a rat by associating presentations of the rat with a loud noise. True phobic conditioning, however, may involve several additional factors, including observational learning, temperament, preparedness, history of control, incubation, US revaluation, and selective sensitization.

One treatment procedure for phobias is systematic desensitization. This is a counterconditioning procedure in which a CS that elicits one type of response is associated with another stimulus that elicits a different response. Counterconditioning works through the process of reciprocal inhibition, in which one type of response can inhibit the occurrence of another incompatible response. The three components of systematic desensitization are: (1) training in deep muscle relaxation, (2) creation of a hierarchy of imaginary scenes that elicit progressively intense levels of fear, and (3) pairing each item in the hierarchy with relaxation. In one variant of this procedure, known as *in vivo* desensitization, the imaginary scenes are replaced by a hierarchy of real-life encounters with the feared stimulus. An alternative treatment procedure for phobias is flooding, which involves prolonged exposure to a feared stimulus, thus allowing the conditioned fear response to be extinguished. More recent exposure-based treatments for phobias often combine characteristics of both systematic desensitization and flooding as well as observational learning.

Aversion therapy attempts to reduce the attractiveness of a desired event by associating it with an aversive stimulus. Examples include associating nausea with alcohol ingestion or cigarette smoking and, in pedophiles, associating the smell of ammonia with the sight of young children. In a technique known as covert sensitization, aversion therapy is carried out with the use of imaginal stimuli rather than real stimuli.

Classical conditioning has been shown to have medical implications. For example, neutral stimuli that have been associated with an allergy-inducing substance can become CSs that elicit a conditioned allergic response. Research has also revealed that stimuli that have been paired with a drug that alters immune system functioning can become CSs that likewise alter immune system functioning. Related studies provide evidence that classical conditioning is involved in the creation of the placebo effect, with the placebo being a CS that elicits a drug-like response due to previous pairing with the actual drug.

SUGGESTED READINGS

Pavlov, I. P. (1941). *Conditioned reflexes and psychiatry*. (W. H. Gantt, Trans.). New York: International Publishers. Pavlov's attempt to apply the principles of conditioning to understanding various forms of human neuroses.

Wolpe, J. (1958). *Psychotherapy by reciprocal inhibition*. Stanford, CA: Stanford University Press. Wolpe's original book describing his development of systematic desensitization.

Spiegler, M. D., & Guevremont, D. C. (2010). *Contemporary behavior therapy* (*3rd ed.*). Pacific Grove, CA: Brooks/Cole. An excellent introductory text on behavior therapy describing many different treatment procedures, including some procedures not mentioned in this chapter.

STUDY QUESTIONS

1. Distinguish between S-R and S-S models of conditioning.
2. Describe stimulus-substitution theory. What is the major weakness of this theory?
3. Describe the preparatory-response theory of conditioning.
4. Describe the compensatory-response model of conditioning. How does the compensatory-response model account for drug overdoses that occur when an addict seems to have injected only a normal amount of the drug?
5. Describe the Rescorla-Wagner theory. Describe how the Rescorla-Wagner theory accounts for overshadowing and blocking.
6. Describe the overexpectation effect and how the Rescorla-Wagner theory accounts for it.

7. Briefly describe the Watson and Rayner experiment with Little Albert and the results obtained.
8. Assuming that the look of fear in others can act as a US, diagram an example of observational learning in the acquisition of a phobia. Be sure to include the appropriate abbreviations (NS, US, etc.).
9. Describe how temperament and preparedness can affect the acquisition of a phobia. Be sure that your answer clearly indicates the difference between them.
10. Describe how selective sensitization and incubation can affect the acquisition of a phobia.
11. What would be the likelihood of a child who had very little control over important events in her life of later acquiring a phobia (compared to a child who had more control over important events)? Also, describe how US revaluation can affect the acquisition of a phobia and give an example.
12. What is counterconditioning? Name and define the underlying process.
13. Outline the three components of systematic desensitization.
14. Define flooding. Be sure to mention the underlying process by which it is believed to operate. Also, what is the distinction between imaginal and *in vivo* versions of flooding?
15. Define aversion therapy. What is covert sensitization?
16. Diagram an example of a classical conditioning procedure that results in an alteration (strengthening or weakening) of immune system functioning. Diagram an example of a classical conditioning process involved in the creation of a placebo effect. Be sure to label each component with the appropriate abbreviations.

CONCEPT REVIEW

aversion therapy. A form of behavior therapy that attempts to reduce the attractiveness of a desired event by associating it with an aversive stimulus.

compensatory-response model. A model of conditioning in which a CS that has been repeatedly associated with the primary response (a-process) to a US will eventually come to elicit a compensatory response (b-process).

counterconditioning. The procedure whereby a CS that elicits one type of response is associated with an event that elicits an incompatible response.

flooding therapy. A behavioral treatment for phobias that involves prolonged exposure to a feared stimulus, thereby providing maximal opportunity for the conditioned fear response to be extinguished.

incubation. The strengthening of a conditioned fear response as a result of brief exposures to the aversive CS.

overexpectation effect. The decrease in the conditioned response that occurs when two separately conditioned CSs are combined into a compound stimulus for further pairings with the US.

preparatory-response theory. A theory of classical conditioning that proposes that the purpose of the CR is to prepare the organism for the presentation of the US.

preparedness. An inherited predisposition within a species to learn certain kinds of associations more easily than others.

reciprocal inhibition. The process whereby certain responses are incompatible with each other, and the occurrence of one response necessarily inhibits the other.

Rescorla-Wagner theory. A theory of classical conditioning that proposes that a given US can support only so much conditioning and that this amount of conditioning must be distributed among the various CSs available.

selective sensitization. An increase in one's reactivity to a potentially fearful stimulus following exposure to an unrelated stressful event.

S-R (stimulus-response) model. As applied to classical conditioning, this model assumes that the NS becomes directly associated with the UR and therefore comes to elicit the same response as the UR.

S-S (stimulus-stimulus) model. A model of classical conditioning that assumes that the NS becomes directly associated with the US, and therefore comes to elicit a response that is related to that US.

stimulus-substitution theory. A theory of classical conditioning that proposes that the CS acts as a substitute for the US.

systematic desensitization. A behavioral treatment for phobias that involves pairing relaxation with a succession of stimuli that elicit increasing levels of fear.

temperament. An individual's base level of emotionality and reactivity to stimulation that, to a large extent, is genetically determined.

CHAPTER TEST

8. The three steps in systematic desensitization are: (1) training in _____, (2) creation of a _____ of feared stimuli, and (3) pairing _____ with each item in the _____.

21. In the Little Albert study, the loud noise was the (CS/US) _____, while the white rat was the (CS/US) _____. Little Albert's fear of other furry objects illustrates the process of stimulus _____.

3. Lothar's job has recently become quite stressful. Interestingly, he is also developing a fear of driving through rush hour traffic. This is best described as an example of _____.

13. The _____ approach proposes that classical conditioning involves establishing a direct connection between an NS and a US.

25. Tara's original slight fear of spiders turns into a major phobia when she witnesses a friend become hospitalized after being bitten by a spider. This is an example of _____.

7. The procedure of pairing the frightening sight of a hornet with an appetitive stimulus such as candy is an example of _____. This type of procedure is effective due to the process of _____.

20. When Uncle Bob and Aunt Shirley were separated, they each gave Little Lucas great Christmas presents, with the result that he developed strong positive feelings for both of them. They then resolved their difficulties and moved back together. They now give Little Lucas one great present from the two of them. The Rescorla-Wagner theory predicts that Little Lucas's positive feelings for each will become (stronger/weaker/unaffected) _____. This is known as the _____ effect.

9. Desensitization and flooding procedures that utilize thoughts about the feared stimulus are known as _____ procedures, whereas procedures that involve exposure to the real stimulus are known as _____ procedures.

2. While playing with a spider, Suyen was frightened by the sound of a firecracker. As a result, she acquired a lasting fear of spiders, but not of firecrackers. This is an illustration of the concept of _____.

17. According to the Rescorla-Wagner theory, overshadowing occurs because the _____ stimulus picks up most of the associative value.

26. Many fatalities seemingly due to drug overdose appear to actually be the result of taking the drug in the presence of cues (associated / not associated) _____ with drug use thereby resulting in a (weaker/stronger) _____ compensatory response and a (higher/lower) _____ level of drug tolerance.

14. Whenever I see Attila, the neighbor's dog, I am reminded that he once bit me, which makes me quite nervous. This sequence of events fits best with an (S-R/S-S) _____ approach to classical conditioning.

10. In _____ therapy, one attempts to (decrease/increase) _____ the attractiveness of a desired event by pairing it with an (appetitive/aversive) _____ stimulus. An imagery-based form of this therapy is called _____.

6. Traditional advice has it that if you fall off a horse you should immediately get back on and keep riding until your fear has disappeared. This approach is similar to the therapeutic technique known as _____. Furthermore, getting back on immediately allows no opportunity for brief exposures to the feared stimulus that could result in _____ of the conditioned fear response.

24. Evidence for the role of conditioning in placebo effects includes the fact that such effects are more likely (following/preceding) _____ a period of treatment with (a fake / the real) _____ drug. Also, repeated administration of a placebo reduces its effectiveness, which suggests that a process of _____ is taking place.

12. The _____ approach to learning views classical conditioning as a process of directly attaching a reflex response to a new stimulus.

18. According to the Rescorla-Wagner theory, _____ occurs because the (CS/NS/US) _____ in the compound stimulus has already picked up most of the available associative value.

4. Bo was never afraid of bees until he saw his best friend, Emmet, react with a look of horror to the sight of a bee. Bo now becomes quite anxious each time he sees a bee. This is best described as an example of _____ learning.

15. A cat salivates to the sound of your alarm clock in anticipation of a breakfast feeding. It also freezes at the sight of another cat in anticipation of an attack. These examples are best accounted for by the _____ theory of conditioning.

23. Tika's slight fear of snakes turns into a major phobia when she suffers a serious illness. This is an example of the process of _____.

1. The ease with which an individual can acquire a conditioned fear response may be influenced by that person's base level of emotionality and reactivity to stimulation, which is known as _____. This may, to a large extent, be (genetically/environmentally) _____ determined.

11. Fionn experiences an allergic reaction whenever people even talk about dogs. In the terminology of classical conditioning, the talk about dogs appears to be a (use the abbreviation) _____ while the allergic reaction is a _____.

19. According to the _____ effect, if two fully conditioned stimuli are combined into a compound stimulus that is then subjected to further pairings with the US, the associative value of each member of the compound will (increase/decrease) _____.

5. Gina's parents are extremely concerned about her well-being, and as a result they do almost everything for her. By contrast, Sara's parents make sure that she does a lot of things on her own. Between the two of them, _____ may be less susceptible to the development of a phobia, insofar as a history of being able to _____ important events in one's environment may (reduce/increase) _____ one's susceptibility to acquiring a phobia.

16. Research on classical conditioning processes in drug addiction suggests that the withdrawal symptoms evoked by the sight of a desired drug are actually _____ reactions to the drug that have come to be elicited by environmental cues associated with the (drug/primary response to the drug) _____.

22. Tran's slight fear of rats turns into a major phobia when he is told by his parents that rats are much more dangerous than he previously suspected. This is an example of _____.

Visit the book companion Web site at http://www.academic.cengage.com/ psychology/powell for additional practice questions, answers to the Quick Quizzes, practice review exams, and additional exercises and information.

ANSWERS TO CHAPTER TEST

1. temperament; genetically
2. preparedness
3. selective sensitization
4. observational
5. Sara; control; reduce
6. flooding; incubation
7. counterconditioning; reciprocal inhibition
8. relaxation; hierarchy; relaxation; hierarchy
9. imaginal; *in vivo*
10. aversion; decrease; aversive; covert sensitization
11. CS; CR
12. S-R (or stimulus-response)
13. S-S (or stimulus-stimulus)
14. S-S
15. preparatory-response
16. compensatory (or opponent or b-process); primary response to the drug
17. more salient
18. blocking; CS
19. overexpectation; decrease
20. weaker; overexpectation
21. US; CS; generalization
22. US revaluation
23. selective sensitization
24. following; the real; extinction
25. US revaluation (in this case combined with observational learning)
26. not associated; weaker; lower

Compound Stimulus – Simultaneous presentation of 2 S's

   Overshadowing → Stronger CS more associated

CHAPTER 6

Operant Conditioning: Introduction

CHAPTER OUTLINE

"Hurry up," Joe growled as Sally carefully searched the selection of videos.

"Oh, don't be so grumpy," she said sweetly, hooking her arm into his.

"Just pick one, damn it!"

She quickly picked out a video, then gave him a hug as they walked to the checkout counter. (Based on a real incident observed in a video store.)

In the last few chapters, we focused on elicited behavior and the type of learning known as classical conditioning. Elicited behavior is controlled by the stimuli that precede it. Recall how in Pavlov's classic experiment food elicited salivation and how, after a tone had been paired with food, it too elicited salivation:

Tone: Food → *Salivation*
Tone → *Salivation*

Note how the target response in this type of learning always occurs at the end of the sequence. The preceding stimulus, by itself, is sufficient to elicit the response. In this sense, the process is very reflexive: Present the stimulus and the response automatically follows.

But is everything we do this reflexive? Does the sight of this text, for example, automatically elicit the response of reading? Obviously it does not (though students who tend to procrastinate might sometimes wish that it did). Rather, if you had to explain why you are reading this text, you are likely to say you are reading it in order to achieve something—such as an understanding of the subject matter or a high grade in a course. Reading the text is oriented toward some goal, a consequence, and this consequence is the reason for the behavior. Indeed, most behaviors that concern us each day are motivated by some consequence. For example, we go to a restaurant for a meal, we turn on a radio to hear music, and we ask someone out on a date hoping he or she will accept. When we fail to achieve the desired outcome, we are unlikely to continue the behavior. How long would you persist in asking someone out on a date if that person never accepted?

Behaviors that are influenced by their consequences are called *operant behaviors*, and the effects of those consequences upon behavior are called *operant conditioning*. They are called operant conditioning because the response *operates on the environment* to produce a consequence. This type of learning is also called *instrumental conditioning* because the response is *instrumental* in producing the consequence.

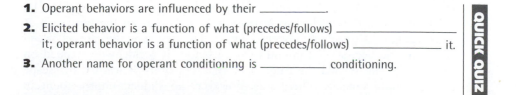

1. Operant behaviors are influenced by their _____.

2. Elicited behavior is a function of what (precedes/follows) _____ it; operant behavior is a function of what (precedes/follows) _____ it.

3. Another name for operant conditioning is _____ conditioning.

QUICK QUIZ A

Historical Background

Although people have used operant conditioning for thousands of years (e.g., in raising children, training animals, etc.), this kind of learning was not subjected to scientific analysis until the late 1800s when Edwin L. Thorndike investigated the learning ability of animals.

Edwin L. Thorndike
(1874–1949)

© Psychology Archives/The University of Akron

Thorndike's Law of Effect

The first experimental studies of operant conditioning were undertaken by Edwin L. Thorndike in the 1890s. As a graduate student, Thorndike was interested in animal intelligence. Many people at that time were speculating that animals were capable of higher forms of reasoning. Particularly impressive were stories about lost dogs and cats finding their way home over long distances. As Thorndike (1898) noted, however, "Dogs get lost hundreds of times and no one ever notices it or sends an account of it to a scientific magazine, but let one find his way from Brooklyn to Yonkers and the fact immediately becomes a circulating anecdote" (p. 4). Thorndike (1911) also said that such depictions did not provide "... a psychology of animals, but rather a *eulogy* of animals. They have all been about animal *intelligence*, never about animal *stupidity*" (p. 22).

Thorndike was not suggesting that animals could not be intelligent, but rather that we should not accept anecdotes as fact, nor should we assume that animals behaving in a particular way are doing so for intelligent reasons. It was not only the lay public that caused Thorndike to argue for caution in interpreting animal behavior. Some of his contemporary researchers were also guilty of noncritical analysis of animal intelligence. In particular, George John Romanes was known for interpreting the mental processes of animals as analogous to human thought processes, and he did so freely in his book, *Mental Evolution in Man* (Romanes, 1989). Thorndike, and others, were skeptical of this and rejected Romanes' anecdotal approach to the study of animal behavior. Thorndike's skepticism was driven by a belief that the intellectual ability of animals could be properly assessed only through *systematic investigation.*

Of the many experiments Thorndike (1898) conducted with animals, the most famous one involved cats. In a typical experiment, a hungry cat was enclosed in a puzzle box, and a dish of food was placed outside. To reach the food, the cat had to learn how to escape from the box, such as by stepping on a treadle that opened a gate. The first time the cat was placed in the puzzle box, several minutes passed before it accidentally stepped on the treadle and opened the gate. Over repeated trials, it learned to escape the box more quickly. There was, however, no sudden improvement in

Which of these workers is on a ratio schedule of reinforcement?

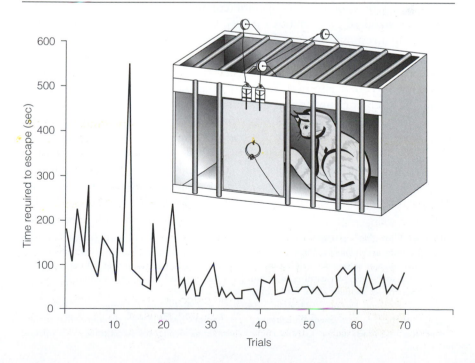

performance as would be expected if the cat had experienced a "flash of insight" about how to solve the problem. Rather, it seemed as though the response that worked (stepping on the treadle) was gradually strengthened, while responses that did not work (e.g., clawing at the gate, chewing on the cage) were gradually weakened (see Figure 6.1). Thorndike suspected that a

FIGURE 6.1 Thorndike's puzzle box. In a typical experiment, a hungry cat was enclosed in a puzzle box and a dish of food was placed outside the box. To reach the food, the cat had to learn how to escape from the box by stepping on a treadle that opened the gate. The graph illustrates the general decrease across trials in the amount of time it took the cat to escape. (*Source:* Nairne, 2000.)

similar process governed all learning, and on this basis he formulated his famous law of effect.[1]

Whether a behavior will be repeated (annoying or nice)

The **law of effect** states that behaviors leading to a satisfying state of affairs are strengthened or "stamped in," while behaviors leading to an unsatisfying or annoying state of affairs are weakened or "stamped out." In other words, the extent to which the *consequences* of a behavior are annoying or satisfying determine whether that behavior will be repeated. Thorndike's law of effect is a hallmark in the history of psychology. However, it was another young scientist by the name of Burrhus Frederick Skinner who fully realized the implications of this principle for understanding and changing behavior.

Skinner's Selection by Consequences   *Environment ——> Affects all*

Believed more on environmental consequences

Skinner came upon the study of operant conditioning by a somewhat different route. As a graduate student in the late 1920s, he was well aware of Thorndike's law of effect. However, like many psychologists of the time, he believed that behavior could best be analyzed as though it were a reflex. He also realized, like Pavlov, that a scientific analysis of behavior required finding a procedure that yielded regular patterns of behavior. Without such regularity, which could be achieved only in a well-controlled environment, it would be difficult to discover the underlying principles of behavior.

In this context, Skinner set out to devise his own procedure for the study of behavior, eventually producing one of the best-known apparatuses in experimental psychology: the operant conditioning chamber, or "Skinner box." In a standard Skinner box for rats, the rat is able to earn food pellets by pressing a response lever or bar (see Figure 6.2).

Skinner's procedure is known as the "free operant" procedure because the rat freely responds with a particular behavior (like pressing a lever) for food, and it may do so at any rate. The experimenter controls the contingencies within the operant chamber, but the animal is not forced to respond at a particular time. This contrasts with other procedures for studying animal learning, such as maze learning, in which the experimenter must initiate each trial by placing the rat in the start box.[2] Skinner demonstrated that the rate of behavior in an operant chamber was controlled by the conditions that he established in his experiments. Later, Skinner invented a variant of the operant chamber for pigeons, in which the pigeon pecks an illuminated plastic disc

---

[1]Although Thorndike's research led to a general tendency to reject anecdotal approaches to animal learning and behavior, some researchers believe that he may have overstated the case that animals do not experience sudden increases in learning. They claim that evidence is available for such "insight" learning, depending on the task and the species examined (see Wasserman & Zentall, 2006, for a comprehensive review).

[2]Although the terms *operant conditioning* and *instrumental conditioning* are often used interchangeably, the term *instrumental conditioning* is sometimes reserved for procedures that involve distinct learning trials, such as maze learning experiments, as opposed to Skinner's free operant procedure.

FIGURE 6.2 Operant conditioning chamber for rats. When the rat presses the lever (or bar), a food pellet drops into the food tray. Aversive stimuli can be presented by delivering an electric shock through the floor grids. [*Source:* Lieberman, 2000.)

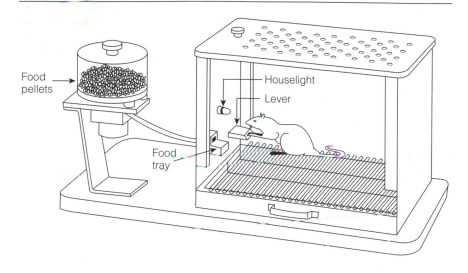

called a response key (named after the telegraph key) to earn a few seconds of access to food (see Figure 6.3). Many of the principles of operant conditioning, particularly those concerning schedules of reinforcement (discussed in Chapter 7), were discovered with the use of this key-pecking procedure.

FIGURE 6.3 Operant conditioning chamber for pigeons. When the pigeon pecks the response key (a translucent plastic disc that can be illuminated with different-colored lights), grain is presented in the food cup for a period of a few seconds. (*Source:* Domjan, 2000.)

With the evolution of the Skinner box, Skinner's beliefs about the nature of behavior also changed. He abandoned the notion that all behavior could be analyzed in terms of reflexes and, along with other learning theorists, came to believe that behaviors can be conveniently divided into two categories. One category consists of involuntary, reflexive-type behaviors, which as Pavlov had demonstrated can often be classically conditioned to occur in new situations. Skinner referred to such behavior as *respondent behavior.* The other category, which Skinner called *operant behavior,* consists of behaviors that seem more voluntary in nature and are controlled by their consequences rather than by the stimuli that precede them. It was this type of behavior that Thorndike had studied in his puzzle box experiments and upon which he had based his law of effect. It was this type of behavior that most interested Skinner as well. He spent the rest of his life investigating the basic principles of operant conditioning and applying those principles to important aspects of human behavior (see Bjork, 1993; Skinner, 1938, 1967).

1. Thorndike's cats learned to solve the puzzle box problem (gradually/ suddenly) _____.

2. Based on his research with cats, Thorndike formulated his famous _____ of _____, which states that behaviors that lead to a(n) _____ state of affairs are strengthened, while behaviors that lead to a(n) _____ state of affairs are weakened.

3. According to Thorndike, behaviors that worked were st_____ i_____, while behaviors that did not work were st_____ o_____.

4. The Skinner box evolved out of Skinner's quest for a procedure that would, among other things, yield (regular/irregular) _____ patterns of behavior.

5. In the original version of the Skinner box, rats earn food by p_____ a l_____; in a later version, pigeons earn a few seconds of access to food by p_____ at an illuminated plastic disc known as a _____ _____.

6. Skinner's procedures are also known as fr_____ o_____ procedures in that the animal controls the rate at which it earns food.

7. Skinner originally thought all behavior could be explained in terms of _____, but he eventually decided that this type of behavior could be distinguished from another, seemingly more voluntary type of behavior known as _____ behavior.

Operant Conditioning

Consequence effects behavior

Operant conditioning is a type of learning in which the future probability of a behavior is affected by its consequences. Note that this is essentially a restatement of Thorndike's law of effect. Skinner, however, was dissatisfied with Thorndike's mentalistic description of consequences as being either satisfying or annoying. Satisfaction and annoyance are internal states inferred from the animal's behavior. Skinner avoided any speculation about what the animal (or person) might be thinking or feeling and simply emphasized the effect of the consequence on the future *probability* of the behavior. The animal might be thinking, or feeling, but those behaviors are not explicitly measured or analyzed.

Note that Skinner's principle of operant conditioning bears a striking resemblance to Darwin's principle of natural selection (which forms the basis of the theory of evolution). According to the principle of natural selection, members of a species that inherit certain adaptive characteristics are more likely to survive and propagate, thereby passing that characteristic on to offspring. Thus, over many generations, the frequency of those adaptive characteristics within the population will increase and become well established. Similarly, according to the principle of operant conditioning, behaviors that lead to favorable outcomes are more likely to be repeated than those that do not lead to favorable outcomes. Thus, operant conditioning is sort of a mini-evolution of an organism's behaviors, in which behaviors that are adaptive (lead to favorable outcomes) become more frequent while behaviors that are nonadaptive (do not lead to favorable outcomes) become less frequent.

The operant conditioning process can be conceptualized as involving three components: (1) a response that produces a certain consequence (e.g., lever pressing produces a food pellet), (2) the consequence that serves to either increase or decrease the probability of the response that preceded it (e.g., the consequence of a food pellet increases the rat's tendency to again press the lever), and (3) a discriminative stimulus that precedes the response and signals that a certain consequence is now available (e.g., a tone signals that a lever press will now produce food). These components are examined in more detail in the next section.

3 component of OC

Operant Behavior

Voluntantary engagment

An *operant behavior* is a class of emitted responses that result in certain consequences; these consequences, in turn, affect the future probability or strength of those responses. Operant responses are sometimes simply called *operants*. Suppose, for example, that a rat presses a lever and receives a food pellet, with a result that it is more likely to press the lever in the future.

Lever press → **Food pellet**
The effect: The future probability of lever pressing increases.

Or Jonathan might tell a joke and receive a frown from the person he tells it to. He is now less likely to tell that person a joke in the future.

Tell a joke → **Person frowns**
The effect: The future probability of telling a joke decreases.

In each case, the behavior in question (the lever pressing or the joke telling) is an operant response (or an "operant") because its occurrence results in a certain consequence, *and* that consequence affects the future probability of the response.

In contrast to classically conditioned behaviors, which are said to be *elicited by stimuli* (e.g., food elicits salivation), operant behaviors are technically said to be *emitted by the organism* (e.g., the rat emits lever presses or the person emits the behavior of telling jokes). This wording is used to indicate that operant behavior appears to have a more voluntary, flexible quality to it compared to elicited behavior, which is generally more reflexive and automatic. (Does this mean that operant behavior actually is voluntary? Not necessarily. In fact, as we have pointed out, such behavior comes to be controlled by the consequences that follow the behavior, and it can be argued that the sense of voluntariness, or "freedom of choice", that accompanies such behavior is merely an illusion [Skinner, 1953].)

Note, too, that operant behavior is usually defined as a *class of responses,* with all of the responses in that class capable of producing the consequence. For example, there are many ways a rat can press a lever for food: hard or soft, quick or slow, right paw or left paw. All of these responses are effective in depressing the lever and producing food, and therefore they all belong to the same class of responses known as "lever presses." Similarly, Jonathan could tell many different jokes, and he could even tell the same joke in many different ways, all of which might produce a laugh. Defining operants in terms of classes has proven fruitful because it is easier to predict the occurrence of a class of responses than it is to predict the *exact* response that will be emitted at a particular point in time. For example, it is easier to predict that a hungry rat will press a lever to obtain food than it is to predict exactly how it will press the lever on any particular occasion.

QUICK QUIZ C

1. Skinner's definition of operant conditioning differs from Thorndike's law of effect in that it views consequences in terms of their effect upon the strength of behavior rather than whether they are s_atisfy___ing or a_nnoy_____ing.

2. Operant conditioning is similar to the principle of natural selection in that an individual's behaviors that are (adaptive/nonadaptive) _adaptive____ tend to increase in frequency, while behaviors that are _nonadaptive_ tend to decrease in frequency.

3. The process of operant conditioning involves the following three components: (1) a r_esponse___ that produces a certain _Consequence_, (2) a c_onsequence_ that serves to either increase or decrease the likelihood of the _response_ that preceded it, and (3) a d_iscriminative_ stimulus that precedes the _response___ and signals that a certain _consequence_ is now available.

4. Classically conditioned behaviors are said to be e_licited___ by the stimulus, while operant behaviors are said to be e_mitted___ by the organism.

5. Operant responses are also simply called _Operants_.

6. Operant behavior is usually defined as a(n) _Class___ of responses rather than a specific response.

Consequence

Operant Consequences: Reinforcers and Punishers

The second component of an operant conditioning procedure is the consequence that either increases (strengthens) or decreases (weakens) the frequency of a behavior. Consequences that strengthen a behavior are called reinforcers, and consequences that weaken a behavior are called punishers. More specifically, an event is a *reinforcer* if: (1) it follows a behavior, and (2) the future probability of that behavior increases. Conversely, an event is a *punisher* if: (1) it follows a behavior, and (2) the future probability of that behavior decreases.

Reinforcer — increases behavior

Punisher — Decreases behavior

Diagrams of operant conditioning procedures generally use the following symbols. Reinforcers are usually given the symbol S^R (which stands for *reinforcing stimulus*), and punishers are given the symbol S^P (which stands for *punishing stimulus*). The operant response is given the symbol R. Using these abbreviations, a diagram of a procedure in which a lever press is reinforced by the delivery of a food pellet looks like this:

> *Lever press* → **Food pellet**
> R $\qquad$ S^R

The food pellet is a reinforcer because it follows the lever press *and* increases the future probability of lever pressing. A diagram of Jonathan's failed attempt at humor, in which a frown punished his behavior of telling jokes, looks like this:

> *Tell a joke* → **Person frowns**
> R $\qquad$ S^P

The frown is a punisher because it follows the joke *and* the future probability of joke telling decreases.

Note that, from an operant conditioning perspective, we do *not* say that the person or animal has been reinforced or punished; rather, it is the behavior that has been reinforced or punished. Only the behavior increases or decreases in frequency. (There is actually a lesson in this. If you want a child to stop doing something, should you tell her that her behavior displeases you or that she displeases you? Similarly, when your roommate does something that bothers you, will it be more constructive to tell him that his behavior disturbs you or that he disturbs you? Is it easier for people to change their behavior or to change who they are?)

It is also important to differentiate the terms *reinforcer* and *punisher* from *reinforcement* and *punishment*. *Reinforcer* and *punisher* both refer to the specific

specific consequence

consequences used to strengthen or weaken a behavior. In the previous examples, the food pellet is a reinforcer for lever pressing, and the frown is a punisher for joke telling. In contrast, the terms *reinforcement* and *punishment* usually refer to the *process* or *procedure* by which a certain consequence changes the strength of a behavior. Thus, the use of food to increase the strength of lever pressing is an example of reinforcement, while the food itself is a reinforcer. Similarly, the process of frowning to encourage Jonathan to stop telling jokes is an example of punishment, while the frown itself is a punisher. In summary, the terms *reinforcer* and *punisher* refer to the actual consequences of the behavior; the terms *reinforcement* and *punishment* refer to the process or procedure of strengthening or weakening a behavior by instituting those consequences.

Note, too, that *reinforcers and punishers are formally defined entirely by their effect on behavior*. For example, a laugh is a reinforcer for the behavior of joke telling only to the extent that joke telling then increases. If, for some reason, joke telling decreased as a result of the laugh (maybe the person telling the joke delights in disgusting his listeners and does not want them to find his joke funny), the laugh would by definition be a punisher. It is important to remember this, because events that on the surface seem like reinforcers or punishers do not always function in that manner. We encountered this notion in Chapter 2 in our discussion of the distinction between appetitive and aversive events (and particularly in the cartoon depiction of Calvin ravenously eating what he believes to be a bowl of maggot soup). In similar fashion, a teacher might yell at her students for being disruptive, and as a result the students become *more* (not less) disruptive. Although the teacher is clearly trying to punish the disruptive behavior, the yelling is actually having the opposite effect. By definition, therefore, the yelling is a reinforcer because it is causing the disruptive behavior to increase in frequency (perhaps because disruptive students find that other students admire them if they upset the teacher).

Thus, the safest bet is to define consequences as reinforcers and punishers in relation to their effect on behavior and not in relation to how pleasant or unpleasant they seem. It is for this reason that many behaviorists prefer the term *reinforcer* rather than *reward*, the latter term being too strongly associated with events that are seemingly pleasant (e.g., affection, food, money). For example, the teacher's yelling is hardly what anyone would call a reward, but technically speaking it is a reinforcer for the students' disruptive behavior. Not all behaviorists are this strict in their terminology, however, and they sometimes use the terms *reward* and *reinforcer* interchangeably (e.g., Bandura, 1997; Herrnstein, 1997).[3] Moreover, because students often find

---

[3]Furthermore, some behaviorists use the term *reward* to refer to the effect of the consequence on the animal as opposed to the behavior (Rachlin, 1991). For example, a dog biscuit can be both a reinforcer for the dog's *behavior* of begging and a reward to the *dog* for having carried out such a behavior. Or, to put it somewhat differently, reinforcers strengthen our behavior, while rewards make us happy.

it helpful to think of consequences in terms of whether they are pleasant or unpleasant, we will sometimes make use of such terms in our discussion of consequences. In other words, to help you gain an initial grasp of this material, we will sometimes be rather informal in the terminology we use. (You should check with your professor, however, to determine if such informality will be acceptable in an examination on this material.)

Finally, you should be aware that punishment is not the only means of weakening a behavior. A response that has been strengthened through reinforcement can also be weakened by the withdrawal of reinforcement. *The weakening of a behavior through the withdrawal of reinforcement for that behavior is known as extinction.* For example, a child who has learned to whine for candy in the supermarket will eventually cease whining when behaving that way no longer results in candy. Likewise, a roommate who tells gross jokes because of the outraged reaction he gets from his religiously inclined roommates will eventually stop telling such jokes if the roommates stop reacting that way. Extinction is usually a much gentler process than punishment; one drawback to it, however, is that it is typically a much slower process. Extinction and the various issues associated with it are more fully discussed in Chapter 8.

1. Simply put, reinforcers are those consequences that s*trengthen* a behavior, while punishers are those consequences that w*eaken* a behavior.

2. More specifically, a reinforcer is a consequence that (precedes/ follows) *follows* a behavior and (increases/decreases) *increases* the probability of that behavior. A punisher is a consequence that (precedes/ follows) *follows* a behavior and (increases/decreases) *decreases* the probability of that behavior.

3. The terms *reinforcement* and *punishment* refer to the pr*ocedures* or pr*ocess* whereby a behavior is strengthened or weakened by its consequences.

4. Strengthening a roommate's tendency toward cleanliness by thanking her when she cleans the bathroom is an example of *reinforcement*, while the thanks itself is a *reinforcer*.

5. Eliminating a dog's tendency to jump up on visitors by scolding her when she does so is an example of *punishment*, while the scolding itself is a *punisher*.

6. Reinforcers and punishers are defined entirely by their *effect* on behavior. For this reason, the term *reinforcer* is often preferred to the term *reward* because the latter is too closely associated with events that are commonly regarded as pleasant or desirable.

7. When Moe stuck his finger in a light socket, he received an electric shock. As a result, he now sticks his finger in the light socket as often as possible. By definition, the electric shock was a *reinforcer* because the behavior it followed has (increased/decreased) *increase'd* in frequency.

8. Each time Edna talked out in class, her teacher immediately came over and gave her a hug. As a result, Edna no longer talks out in class. By definition, the hug is a(n) _Punisher_ because the behavior it follows has (increased/decreased) _decreased_ in frequency.

9. When labeling an operant conditioning procedure, punishing consequences (punishers) are given the symbol _S^D_ (which stands for _Punishing stimulus_), while reinforcing consequences (reinforcers) are given the symbol _S^R_ (which stands for _reinforcing stimulus_). The operant response is given the symbol _R_.

10. When we give a dog a treat for fetching a toy, are we attempting to reinforce: (a) the behavior of fetching the toy or (b) the dog that fetched the toy)? _A_

11. When we chastise a child for being rude, are we attempting to punish: (a) the child who was rude or (b) the child's rude behavior? _B_

12. Weakening a behavior through the withdrawal of reinforcement for that behavior is known as _extinction_.

13. Clayton stopped plugging in the toaster after he received an electric shock while doing so. This is an example of (punishment/extinction) _punishment_. Manzar stopped using the toaster after it no longer made good toast. This is an example of _extinction_.

Operant Antecedents: Discriminative Stimuli

The operant response and its consequence are the most essential components of the operant conditioning procedure. In most circumstances, however, a third component can also be identified. When a behavior is consistently reinforced or punished in the presence of certain stimuli, those stimuli will begin to influence the occurrence of the behavior. For example, if lever pressing produces food only when a tone is sounding, the rat soon learns to press the lever only when it hears the tone. This situation can be diagrammed as follows:

$$\text{Tone:} \quad \textit{Lever Press} \rightarrow \text{Food pellet}$$
$$S^D \qquad\qquad R \qquad\qquad\quad S^R$$

This sequence can be read as follows: In the presence of the tone, if the rat presses the lever, it will receive food. The tone is called a discriminative stimulus. Discriminative stimuli are traditionally given the symbol S^D (pronounced "es-dee"). A ***discriminative stimulus (S^D)*** is a stimulus in the presence of which responses are reinforced and in the absence of which they are not reinforced. In other words, a discriminative stimulus is a signal that indicates that a response will be followed by a reinforcer.

Stimulus that raising the Chance of a behavior to happen.

(not different around friends)

Another example: If Susan always laughs at Jonathan's jokes, then he is more likely to tell her a joke. Susan is an S^D for Jonathan's behavior of telling jokes. This can be diagrammed as follows:

Susan: *Tell her a joke* → She laughs
S^D R S^R

Discriminative stimuli are said to "set the occasion for" the behavior, meaning that the behavior is more likely to occur in the presence of those stimuli. Discriminative stimuli do not elicit behavior in the manner of a CS or US in classical conditioning. For example, the tone does not automatically elicit a lever press; it merely increases the probability that a lever press will occur. Whether or not lever pressing occurs is still a function of its consequence (food), and the S^D simply indicates that this consequence is now available. Similarly, the presence of Susan does not automatically elicit the behavior of joke telling in Jonathan; rather, he is simply more likely to tell a joke in her presence. Therefore, rather than saying that the S^D elicits the behavior, we say that the person or animal emits the behavior in the presence of the S^D. (Remember, it is only in classical conditioning that we say that the stimulus *elicits* the behavior. In operant conditioning, we say that the organism *emits* the behavior.)

The discriminative stimulus, the operant behavior, and the reinforcer or punisher constitute what is known as the *three-term contingency*. The three-term contingency can also be viewed as consisting of an *antecedent event* (an antecedent event is a *preceding* event), a *behavior*, and a *consequence* (which can be remembered by the initials *ABC*).

Event → behavior → consequence
notice → do → get

Antecedent	Behavior	Consequence
Susan:	*Tell her a joke* →	She laughs
S^D	R	S^R
Tone:	*Lever press* →	Food pellet
S^D	R	S^R

Another way of thinking about this sequence is that you notice something (Susan), do something (tell Susan a joke), and get something (Susan laughs at your joke). Similarly, you notice that it is 7:00 p.m., you turn on the TV, and you get to see your favorite sitcom. Or maybe your dog notices that you have popcorn, begs persistently, and gets some of the popcorn. Many students find this sequence easy to remember: Notice something, do something, get something. (As you will see later, however, the consequence in some cases involves losing or avoiding something rather than getting something.)

So far, we have dealt only with stimuli that are associated with reinforcement. Stimuli can also be associated with punishment. A stimulus that signals that a response will be punished is called a ***discriminative stimulus for punishment*** (which is sometimes given the symbol S^{Dp}). For example, if a

Stimulus that tells a punish will come if behavior happens

water bottle signals that meowing will result in being sprayed with water (rather than being fed), a cat will quickly learn to stop meowing whenever it sees the water bottle.

$$\begin{array}{ccc} \textbf{Water bottle:} & \textit{Meow} \rightarrow & \textbf{Get sprayed} \\ \text{S}^{\text{Dp}} & \text{R} & \text{S}^{\text{P}} \end{array}$$

Similarly, a motorist who receives a fine for speeding in the presence of a police car will soon learn to stop speeding in the presence of police cars.

$$\begin{array}{ccc} \textbf{Police car:} & \textit{Speed} \rightarrow & \textbf{Receive fine} \\ \text{S}^{\text{Dp}} & \text{R} & \text{S}^{\text{P}} \end{array}$$

For the speeding motorist, the presence of a police car is a discriminative stimulus for punishment.

A discriminative stimulus may also signal the occurrence of *extinction;* that is, the stimulus signals the nonavailability of a previously available reinforcer. If, for example, lever pressing is typically followed by the presentation of food, but only when a tone is sounding and not when a buzzer is sounding, then:

$$\begin{array}{ccc} \textbf{Tone:} & \textit{Lever press} \rightarrow & \textbf{Food pellet} \\ \text{S}^{\text{D}} & \text{R} & \text{S}^{\text{R}} \end{array}$$

$$\begin{array}{ccc} \textbf{Buzzer:} & \textit{Lever press} \rightarrow & \textbf{No food} \\ \text{S}^{\Delta} & \text{R} & \text{—} \end{array}$$

The buzzer in this case is a ***discriminative stimulus for extinction,*** which is a stimulus that signals the absence of reinforcement. As you can see in the example above, the discriminative stimulus for extinction is typically given the symbol S^{Δ} (pronounced "es-delta"). As noted earlier, the process of extinction is more fully discussed in Chapter 8.[4]

Finally, you should be aware that processes of operant and classical conditioning overlap such that a particular stimulus can simultaneously act as both a discriminative stimulus and a conditioned stimulus. For example, consider a tone that serves as an S^{D} for the operant behavior of lever pressing:

$$\begin{array}{ccc} \textbf{Tone:} & \textit{Lever press} \rightarrow & \textbf{Food} \\ \text{S}^{\text{D}} & \text{R} & \text{S}^{\text{R}} \end{array}$$

The tone is closely associated with food, and food, of course, elicits salivation. This means that during the course of our operant conditioning

---

[4]Note that the symbols for discriminative stimuli are not entirely standardized. Some textbooks use S+ (positive discriminative stimulus) to denote the discriminative stimulus for reinforcement, and S– (negative discriminative stimulus) to denote the discriminative stimulus for extinction or punishment.

procedure, the tone will also become a conditioned stimulus (CS) that elicits salivation as a conditioned response (CR). Thus, if we ignore the lever pressing and concentrate just on the salivation, then what is happening is this:

Tone: Food → *Salivation*
  NS **US**   **UR**

Tone → *Salivation*
  CS   **CR**

Whether the tone should be considered an S^D or a CS depends on the response to which one is referring. It is an S^D with respect to the operant response of lever pressing and a CS with respect to the classically conditioned response of salivation. (See Table 6.1 for a summary of the differences between classical and operant conditioning.)

QUICK QUIZ E

1. The operant conditioning procedure usually consists of three components: (1) a discrimative stimulus____, (2) an operant____ response, and (3) a consequence.

2. A discriminative stimulus is usually indicated by the symbol ___S^Ds___.

3. A discriminative stimulus is said to "_Set the Occasio_for the behavior," meaning that its presence makes the response (more/less) _More_ likely to occur.

4. A discriminative stimulus (does / does not) _does not_ elicit behavior in the same manner as a CS.

5. Using the appropriate symbols, label each component in the following three-term contingency (assume that the behavior will be strengthened):

Phone rings: *Answer phone* → Conversation with friend

_____   _____   _____

6. The three-term contingency can also be thought of as an ABC sequence, where A stands for _antecendent_ event, B stands for _behavior_, and C stands for _consequence_

7. Another way of thinking about the three-term contingency is that you _notice_ something, _do_ something, and _get_ something.

8. A stimulus in the presence of which a response is punished is called a _discriminative stimulus_ for _punishment_. It can be given the symbol _S^{DP}_.

9. A bell that signals the start of a round and therefore serves as an S^D for the operant response of beginning to box may also serve as a(n) (S^D/CS) _CS_ for a fear response. This is an example of how the two processes of _operant_ conditioning and _classical_ conditioning often overlap.

| **TABLE 6.1** | Differences between operant and classical conditioning. Note that these are *traditional* differences. As you will see in Chapter 11, the distinction between classical and operant conditioning is sometimes less clear than what is depicted here. |

CLASSICAL CONDITIONING	OPERANT CONDITIONING
Behavior is generally seen as involuntary and inflexible.	Behavior is generally seen as voluntary and flexible.
Behavior is said to be "elicited by the stimulus."	Behavior is said to be "emitted by the organism."
This type of conditioning typically involves innate patterns of behavior (URs).	This type of conditioning often does not involve innate patterns of behavior.
Behavior is a function of what comes before it; that is, the preceding stimulus is critical and the consequences are largely irrelevant.	Behavior is a function of what comes after it; that is, the consequences are critical and the preceding stimulus merely "sets the occasion for the behavior."
Conditioning involves a stimulus-stimulus-response (S-S-R) sequence.	Conditioning involves a stimulus-response-stimulus (S-R-S) sequence.

In general, to determine if operant or classical conditioning is involved, the most important question to ask is whether the behavior is mostly a function of what precedes it (classical conditioning) or what might follow it (operant conditioning).

Four Types of Contingencies

We have seen that there are two main types of consequences in operant conditioning: reinforcers and punishers. If the response is followed by a reinforcer, then we say that a *contingency of reinforcement* exists (meaning that the delivery of the reinforcer is contingent upon the response); if the response is followed by a punisher, then a *contingency of punishment* exists. However, contingencies of reinforcement and punishment can be further divided into two subtypes: positive and negative. This results in four basic types of contingencies (response–consequence relationships): positive reinforcement, negative reinforcement, positive punishment, and negative punishment. Because these are sometimes confusing to students, we describe them in some detail here.

As you learned previously, reinforcement is a procedure that strengthens a behavior, and punishment is a procedure that weakens a behavior. That part is pretty straightforward, but this next part can be tricky. When combined with the words *reinforcement* or *punishment*, the word *positive* means only that the behavior is followed by the *presentation* or addition of something (think of a + [positive] sign, which means "add"). Thus, the word *positive*, when combined with the terms *reinforcement* or *punishment*, does *not* mean good or pleasant; it means only that the response has resulted in something being added or presented. The event that is presented could either be pleasant (receiving a compliment) or unpleasant (getting yelled at).

Similarly, the word *negative*, when combined with the words *reinforcement* or *punishment*, means only that the behavior is followed by the *removal* of something; that is, something is subtracted from the situation (think of a – [negative] sign, which means "subtract"). The word *negative*, therefore, in this context, does *not* mean bad or unpleasant; it means only that the response results in the removal of something. The something that is removed could be an event that is pleasant (your dessert is taken away) or an event that is unpleasant (the person stops yelling at you).

To summarize, in the case of positive reinforcement and positive punishment, the word *positive* means only that the behavior has resulted in something being presented or added. In negative reinforcement and negative punishment, the word *negative* means only that the behavior has resulted in something being removed or subtracted. The word *reinforcement*, of course, means that the behavior will increase in strength, and the word *punishment* means that the behavior will decrease in strength.

Thus, to determine which type of contingency is involved in any particular instance, ask yourself the following two questions: (1) *Does the consequence consist of something being presented or withdrawn?* If the consequence consists of something being presented, then it is a positive contingency; if the consequence consists of something being withdrawn, then it is a *negative* contingency. (2) *Does the consequence serve to strengthen or weaken the behavior?* If it strengthens the behavior, then we are dealing with a process of *reinforcement;* if it weakens the behavior, then we are dealing with a process of *punishment*. Apply these two questions to any examples that you encounter, and you will generally have no problem sorting out these four types of contingencies in the following sections.

Finally, you will see in the examples below that we have used the generic symbols S^R and S^P for both the positive and negative versions of reinforcement and punishment. However, more specific symbols are sometimes used, such as S^{R+} for positive reinforcement, S^{R-} for negative reinforcement, S^{P+} for positive punishment, and S^{P-} for negative punishment. Your professor can let you know if he or she has any preferences in this regard.

1. The word *positive*, when combined with the words *reinforcement* or *punishment*, means only that the behavior is followed by the _presentation_ of something. The word *negative*, when combined with the words *reinforcement* or *punishment*, means only that the behavior is followed by the _removal_ of something.

2. The word *positive*, when combined with the words *reinforcement* or *punishment*, (does / does not) _does not_ mean that the consequence is good or pleasant. Similarly, the term *negative*, when combined with the words *reinforcement* or *punishment*, (does / does not) _does not_ mean that the consequence is bad or unpleasant.

QUICK QUIZ F

3. Within the context of reinforcement and punishment, positive refers to the (addition/subtraction) _addition_ of something, and negative refers to the (addition/subtraction) _Subtraction_ of something.

4. Reinforcement is related to a(n) (increase/decrease) _increase_ in behavior, whereas punishment is related to a(n) (increase/decrease) _decrease_ in behavior.

Positive Reinforcement

Positive reinforcement consists of the *presentation* of a stimulus (one that is usually considered pleasant or rewarding) following a response, which then leads to an increase in the future strength of that response. Loosely speaking, the behavior results in the delivery of something the recipient likes, so the person or animal is more likely to behave that way in the future. Some of the earlier illustrations have been examples of positive reinforcement. The standard rat procedure in which lever pressing produces food is an example of positive reinforcement because the consequence of food leads to an increase in lever pressing. It is reinforcement because the behavior increases in frequency, and it is positive reinforcement because the consequence involves the presentation of something—namely, food (which we would call a positive reinforcer). Here are some additional examples of positive reinforcement:

Turn on TV → **See the show**
   R   **S^R**

Smile at person → **The person smiles at you**
      R   **S^R**

Order coffee → **Receive coffee**
     R   **S^R**

Study diligently for quiz → **Obtain an excellent mark**
           R   **S^R**

Compliment partner → **Receive a kiss**
          R   **S^R**

Negative Reinforcement

Negative reinforcement is the *removal* of a stimulus (one that is usually considered unpleasant or aversive) following a response, which then leads to an increase in the future strength of that response. Loosely speaking, the behavior results in the prevention or removal of something the person or animal hates, so the subject is more likely to behave that way in the future. For example, if by pressing a lever a rat terminates an electric shock that it is receiving, it will become more likely to press the lever the next time it receives an electric shock. This is an example of reinforcement because the behavior increases in strength; it is negative reinforcement because the consequence consists of taking something away. Here are some additional examples:

Open umbrella → **Escape rain**
    R   S^R

Claim illness → **Avoid writing an exam**
    R   S^R

Take aspirin → **Eliminate headache**
    R   S^R

Turn on the heater → **Escape the cold**
    R   S^R

[margin handwritten note: Extinction → behavior ceases as a result of lack of rienforcement.]

The last example is interesting because it illustrates how it is sometimes a matter of interpretation as to whether something is an example of negative reinforcement or positive reinforcement. Does the person turn on the heater to escape the cold (negative reinforcement) or to obtain warmth (positive reinforcement)? Either interpretation would be correct.

[margin handwritten note: Switch my beh to stop a stimulus]

Negative reinforcement involves two types of behavior: escape and avoidance. *Escape behavior* results in the termination (stopping) of an aversive stimulus. In the example of the person getting rained on, by opening the umbrella the person stops this from happening. Likewise, taking aspirin removes a headache, and turning on the heater allows one to escape the cold. Avoidance is similar to escape except that *avoidance behavior* occurs before the aversive stimulus is presented and therefore prevents its delivery. For example, if the umbrella were opened before stepping out into the rain, the person would avoid getting rained on. And by pretending to be ill, a student avoids having to write an exam. Escape and avoidance are discussed in more detail in Chapter 9.

[margin handwritten note: Stopped a behavior prior to punishment.]

1. When you reached toward the dog, he nipped at your hand. You quickly pulled your hand back. As a result, he now nips at your hand whenever you reach toward him. The consequence for *the dog's behavior of nipping* consisted of the (presentation/removal) _presentation_ of a stimulus (namely, your hand), and his behavior of nipping subsequently (increased/ decreased) _increased_ in frequency; therefore, this is an example of _Positive_ reinforcement.

2. When the dog sat at your feet and whined during breakfast one morning, you fed him. As a result, he sat at your feet and whined during breakfast the next morning. The consequence for the dog's whining consisted of the (presentation/ removal) _____ of a stimulus, and his behavior of whining subsequently (increased/decreased) _____ in frequency; therefore, this is an example of _____ reinforcement.

QUICK QUIZ G

3. Karen cries while saying to her boyfriend, "John, I don't feel as though you love me." John gives Karen a big hug saying, "That's not true, dear, I love you very much." If John's hug is a reinforcer, Karen is (more/less) _More_ likely to cry the next time she feels insecure about her relationship. More specifically, this is an example of _negative_ reinforcement of Karen's crying behavior.

4. With respect to escape and avoidance, an _escape_ response is one that *terminates* an aversive stimulus, while an _avoidance_ response is one that *prevents* an aversive stimulus from occurring. Escape and avoidance responses are two classes of behavior that are maintained by (positive/negative) _negative_ reinforcement.

5. Turning down the heat because you are too hot is an example of an (escape/avoidance) _escape_ response; turning it down before you become too hot is an example of an (escape/avoidance) _avoidance_ response.

Positive Punishment

Positive punishment consists of the *presentation* of a stimulus (one that is usually considered unpleasant or aversive) following a response, which then leads to a *decrease* in the future strength of that response. Loosely speaking, the behavior results in the delivery of something the person or animal hates, so the subject is less likely to behave that way in the future. For example, if a rat received a shock when it pressed a lever, it would stop pressing the lever. This is an example of punishment because the behavior decreases in strength, and it is positive punishment because the consequence involves the presentation of something (i.e., shock). Consider some further examples of positive punishment:

$$\underset{\text{R}}{\textit{Talk back to the boss}} \rightarrow \underset{\text{S}^{\text{P}}}{\textbf{Get reprimanded}}$$

$$\underset{\text{R}}{\textit{Swat at the wasp}} \rightarrow \underset{\text{S}^{\text{P}}}{\textbf{Get stung}}$$

$$\underset{\text{R}}{\textit{Meow constantly}} \rightarrow \underset{\text{S}^{\text{P}}}{\textbf{Get sprayed with water}}$$

In each case, the behavior is followed by the presentation of an aversive stimulus, with the result that there is a decrease in the future probability of the behavior.

People frequently confuse positive punishment with negative reinforcement. One reason for this is the fact that many behaviorists, including Skinner, use the term *negative reinforcer* to refer to an aversive (unpleasant) stimulus and the term *positive reinforcer* to refer to an appetitive (pleasant) stimulus. Unfortunately, people with less knowledge of the field have then assumed that the presentation of a negative reinforcer is an instance of negative reinforcement, which it is not. Within the framework presented here, it is instead an instance of positive punishment.

Negative Punishment

Negative punishment consists of the *removal* of a stimulus (one that is usually considered pleasant or rewarding) following a response, which then leads to a decrease in the future strength of that response. Loosely speaking, the behavior results in the removal of something the person or animal likes, so the subject is less likely to behave that way in the future. Here are some examples of negative punishment:

> *Stay out past curfew* → **Lose car privileges**
>   R S^P
>
> *Argue with boss* → **Lose job**
>   R S^P
>
> *Play with food* → **Lose dessert**
>   R S^P
>
> *Tease sister* → **Sent to room (loss of social contact)**
>   R S^P

In each case, it is punishment because the behavior decreases in strength, and it is negative punishment because the consequence consists of the removal of something. The last example is known as "time-out" and is employed by many parents as a replacement for spanking. Removal of social contact is usually one consequence of such a procedure; more generally, however, the child loses the opportunity to receive any type of positive reinforcer during the time-out interval. Children usually find such situations to be quite unpleasant, with the result that even very brief time-outs can be effective.

Consider another example of negative punishment: Jonathan's girlfriend, who is quite jealous, completely ignored him (withdrew her attention from him) when she observed him having a conversation with another woman at a party. As a result, he stopped talking to the other women at the party.

> *Jonathan talks to other women* → **His girlfriend ignores him**
>   R S^P

Jonathan's behavior of talking to other women at parties has been negatively punished. It is punishment in that the frequency with which he talked to other women at the party declined, and it is negative punishment because the consequence that produced that decline was the withdrawal of his girlfriend's attention.

Question: In this scenario, Jonathan's behavior has been negatively punished. But what contingencies are operating on the girlfriend's behavior? When she ignored him, he stopped talking to other women at the party. Given that this occurred, she might ignore him at future parties if she again sees him talking to other women. If so, her behavior has been negatively reinforced by the fact that it was effective in getting him to stop doing something that she disliked. If we diagram this interaction from the perspective of each person, we get the following:

For Jonathan:
I talk to other women → **My girlfriend ignores me**
  R S^P

For his girlfriend:
I ignore Jonathan → **He stops talking to other women**
  R S^R

As you can see, a reduction in one person's behavior as a result of punishment can negatively reinforce the behavior of the person who implemented the punishment. This is the reason we are so often enticed to use punishment: Punishment is often successful in immediately getting a person to stop behaving in ways that we dislike. That success then reinforces our tendency to use punishment in the future, which of course can create major problems in the long run. We discuss the uses and abuses of punishment more fully in Chapter 9.

Many people mistakenly equate behaviorism with the use of punishment. It is important to recognize that behaviorists actually emphasize the use of positive reinforcement. Indeed, Skinner (1953) believed that many societal problems can be traced to the overuse of punishment as well as negative reinforcement. For example, teachers too often control their students by attempting to punish maladaptive behavior rather than by reinforcing adaptive behavior. Moreover, the educational system in general is designed in such a way that students too often study to avoid failure (a negative reinforcer) rather than to obtain knowledge (a positive reinforcer). As a result, schooling is often more onerous and less effective than it could be.

Similarly, in interpersonal relationships, people too often attempt to change each other's behavior through the use of aversive consequences, such as complaining, when positive reinforcement for appropriate behavior might work just as well or better. Marsha, for example, says that Roger forgets to call whenever he is going to be late, even though she often complains about it. Perhaps a more effective approach would be for her to express her appreciation when he does call.

Furthermore, although many people believe that the key to a great relationship is open communication, research has shown that a much more important element is the ratio of positive (pleasant) interactions to negative (aversive) interactions. In fact, one of the best predictors of a successful marriage is when the positives outweigh the negatives by a ratio of about five to one (Gottman, 1994). Even volatile relationships, in which there seems to be an enormous amount of bickering, can thrive if the number of positive exchanges, such as teasing, hugging, and praising, greatly outweigh the number of negative exchanges.

And Furthermore

Four Types of Contingencies: Tricky Examples

After learning about the four types of contingencies, students are sometimes dismayed when they encounter examples that suddenly confuse them. When this happens, the contingency typically has been worded in an unusual way. For example, suppose that a mother tells her son that *if he does not clean his room, then he will not get dessert*. What type of contingency is the mother specifying (think about this for awhile before reading further)? To begin with, it sounds like a negative contingency because the consequence seems to involve the threatened loss of something—namely, the dessert. It also sounds like reinforcement because the goal is to increase the probability of a certain behavior—cleaning the room. We might therefore conclude that this is an example of negative reinforcement. But does this make sense? In everyday terms, negative reinforcement involves strengthening a behavior by removing something that the person dislikes, while here we are talking about removing something that the person likes. So what type of contingency is this?

To clarify situations like this, it helps to reword the example in terms of the *occurrence* of a behavior rather than its *nonoccurrence*, because in reality it is only the occurrence of a behavior that is reinforced or punished. By doing so, and depending on which behavior we focus upon, this example can be interpreted as fitting either of two types of contingencies. On one hand, if we focus on the behavior of cleaning the room, it can be viewed as an example of positive reinforcement: *if the son cleans his room, he can have dessert*. On the other hand, if we focus on the behavior of "doing something other than cleaning the room" (or something other than following his mother's instructions), it can be viewed as an example of negative punishment: *if the son does something other than clean his room, he will not get dessert*. Thus, all behaviors other than room cleaning, such as watching television, will result in the loss of dessert. In fact, to the extent that the mother made her request in a threatening manner, she probably intended something like the latter. But note how she could just as easily have worded her request in the form of positive reinforcement—"If you clean your room, you can have some dessert"—and how much more pleasant that sounds. Unfortunately, many parents too often choose the unpleasant version, especially when they are frustrated or angry, which in turn helps to create a decidedly unpleasant atmosphere in the household.

To help strengthen your understanding of the four types of contingencies— positive reinforcement, negative reinforcement, positive punishment, and negative punishment—and deal with examples that are potentially confusing, see also "Four Types of Contingencies: Tricky Examples" in the And Furthermore box.[5]

---

[5]Note that the labels for the two types of punishment are not standardized. For example, positive and negative punishment are sometimes called *Type 1* and *Type 2 punishment* (e.g., Chance, 1994) or *punishment by contingent application* and *punishment by contingent withdrawal* (e.g., L. Miller, 1997).

1. When Sasha was teasing the dog, it bit her. As a result, she no longer teases the dog. The consequence for *Sasha's behavior* of teasing the dog was the (presentation/removal) _presentation_ of a stimulus, and the teasing behavior subsequently (increased/decreased) _decreased_ in frequency; therefore, this is an example of _positive_ _punishment_

2. Whenever Sasha pulled the dog's tail, the dog left and went into another room. As a result, Sasha now pulls the dog's tail less often when it is around. The consequence for pulling the dog's tail was the (presentation/removal) _removal_ of a stimulus, and the behavior of pulling the dog's tail subsequently (increased/decreased) _decreased_ in frequency; therefore, this is an example of _negative_ _punishment_

3. When Alex burped in public during his date with Stephanie, she got angry with him. Alex now burps quite often when he is out on a date with Stephanie. The consequence for burping was the _presentation_ of a stimulus, and the behavior of belching subsequently _increased_ in frequency; therefore, this is an example of _positive_ _____.

4. When Alex held the car door open for Stephanie, she made a big fuss over what a gentleman he was becoming. Alex no longer holds the car door open for her. The consequence for holding open the door was the _presentation_ of a stimulus, and the behavior of holding open the door subsequently _decrease_ in frequency; therefore, this is an example of _positive_ _punishment_

5. When Tenzing shared his toys with his brother, his mother stopped criticizing him. Tenzing now shares his toys with his brother quite often. The consequence for sharing the toys was the _removal_ of a stimulus, and the behavior of sharing the toys subsequently _increased_ in frequency; therefore, this is an example of _negative_ _reinforcement_

Positive Reinforcement: Further Distinctions

Because behaviorists so strongly emphasize positive reinforcement, let us have a closer look at this type of contingency. More specifically, we will examine various categories of positive reinforcement.

Immediate Versus Delayed Reinforcement

Better to reinforce immediately after behavior

A reinforcer can be presented either immediately after a behavior occurs or following some delay. In general, *the more immediate the reinforcer, the stronger its effect on the behavior.* Suppose, for example, that you wish to reinforce a child's behavior of playing quietly by giving him a treat. The treat should ideally be given while the quiet period is still in progress. If, instead, you deliver the treat several minutes later, while he is engaged in some other behavior (e.g., banging a stick on his toy box), you might inadvertently reinforce that behavior rather than the one you wish to reinforce.

The weak effect of delayed reinforcers on behavior accounts for some major difficulties in life. Do you find it tough to stick to a diet or an exercise regime?

This is because the benefits of exercise and proper eating are delayed and therefore weak, whereas the enjoyable effects of alternate activities, such as watching
television and drinking a soda, are immediate and therefore powerful. Similarly,
have you ever promised yourself that you would study all weekend, only to find
that you completely wasted your time reading novels, watching television, and
going out with friends? The immediate reinforcement associated with these
recreational activities effectively outweighed the delayed reinforcement associated with studying. Of course, what we are talking about here is the issue of self-
control, a topic that is more fully discussed in Chapter 10.

The importance of immediate reinforcement is so profound that some behaviorists (e.g., Malott, 1989; Malott & Suarez, 2004) argue that a delayed reinforcer does not, on its own, actually function as a "reinforcer." They point to
experimental evidence indicating that delaying a reinforcer by even a few seconds can often severely influence its effectiveness (e.g., Grice, 1948; Keesey,
1964; see also J. Williams, 1973). This finding suggests that delayed reinforcers,
to the extent that they are effective, may function by a different mechanism
from immediate reinforcement, especially in humans. Thus, receiving a good
mark on that essay you wrote last week does not reinforce the behavior of
essay writing in the same way that immediately receiving a food pellet reinforces
a rat's tendency to press a lever (or immediately seeing your mother's smile
reinforces your tendency to give her another compliment). Rather, in the case
of humans, behaviors that appear to be strengthened by long-delayed reinforcers are often under the control of rules or instructions that we have received
from others or generated for ourselves. These rules or instructions describe to
us the delayed consequences that can result from a behavior (e.g., "Gee, if I
work on that essay tonight, I am likely to get a good mark on it next week"),
thereby bridging the gap between the behavior and the consequence.

In this text, for simplicity, we will ignore some of the complexities associated with the issue of rules and delayed reinforcement, though we will briefly
discuss rule-governed behavior in Chapter 12. For the present purposes, it is
sufficient to note that delayed reinforcement is usually much less potent, and
perhaps even qualitatively different, than immediate reinforcement. This also
makes clear the crucial importance of immediate reinforcement when dealing
with young children (and animals) who have little or no language capacity,
since the use of rules is essentially dependent on language.

1. In general, the more _____ the reinforcer, the stronger its effect on
behavior.

2. It is sometimes difficult for students to study in that the reinforcers for studying
are _____ and therefore w_____, whereas the reinforcers for alter-
native activities are _____ and therefore s_____.

3. It has been suggested that delayed reinforcers (do / do not) _____ function in the same manner as immediate reinforcers. Rather, the effectiveness of
delayed reinforcers in humans is largely dependent on the use of i_____
or r_____ to bridge the gap between the behavior and the delay.

QUICK QUIZ I

Primary and Secondary Reinforcers

reinforcement fitting basic needs

Pizza

A *primary reinforcer* (also called an *unconditioned reinforcer*) is an event that is innately reinforcing. Loosely speaking, primary reinforcers are those things we are born to like rather than learn to like, and that therefore have an innate ability to reinforce our behavior. Examples of primary reinforcers are food, water, proper temperature (neither too hot nor too cold), and sexual contact.

Many primary reinforcers are associated with basic physiological needs, and their effectiveness is closely tied to a state of deprivation. For example, food is a highly effective reinforcer when we are food deprived and hungry but not when we are satiated. Some primary reinforcers, however, do not seem to be associated with a physiological state of deprivation. An animal (or person) cooped up in a boring environment will likely find access to a more stimulating environment highly reinforcing and will perform a response such as lever pressing (or driving to the mall) to gain such access. In cases such as this, the deprivation seems more psychological than physiological.

Something associated with a basic need.

Gift Card → Pizza

A *secondary reinforcer* (also called a *conditioned reinforcer*) is an event that is reinforcing because it has been associated with some other reinforcer. Loosely speaking, secondary reinforcers are those events that we have learned to like because they have become associated with other things that we like. Much of our behavior is directed toward obtaining secondary reinforcers, such as good marks, fine clothes, and a nice car. Because of our experiences with these events, they can function as effective reinforcers for our current behavior. Thus, if good marks in school are consistently associated with praise, then the good marks themselves can serve as reinforcers for behaviors such as studying. And just seeing a professor who once provided you with lots of praise and encouraged you to make the most of your life may be an effective reinforcer for the behavior of visiting her after you graduate.

Conditioned stimuli that have been associated with appetitive unconditioned stimuli (USs) can also function as secondary reinforcers. For example, suppose that the sound of a metronome has been paired with food to produce a classically conditioned response of salivation:

Metronome: Food → *Salivation*
    NS   US   UR
Metronome → *Salivation*
    CS   CR

The metronome, through its association with food, can now be used as a secondary reinforcer for an operant response such as lever pressing:

Lever press → Metronome
    R S^R

Because the metronome has been closely associated with food, it can now serve as a reinforcer for the operant response of lever pressing. The animal essentially seeks out the metronome because of its pleasant associations. Similarly, we might frequently seek out certain music that has been closely associated with a romantic episode in our life because of its pleasant associations.

Discriminative stimuli associated with reinforcers can likewise function as secondary reinforcers. Consider a tone that has served as an S^D signaling the availability of food for lever pressing:

Tone: *Lever press* $\rightarrow$ **Food**
$\quad S^D \qquad R \qquad\quad S^R$

This tone can now be used as a secondary reinforcer for some other behavior, such as running in a wheel:

Run in wheel $\rightarrow$ **Tone**
$\quad R \qquad\qquad S^R$

An important type of secondary reinforcer is known as a generalized reinforcer. A *generalized reinforcer* (also known as a *generalized secondary reinforcer*) is a type of secondary reinforcer that has been associated with several other reinforcers. For example, money is a powerful generalized reinforcer for humans because it is associated with an almost unlimited array of other reinforcers, including food, clothing, furnishings, entertainment, and even dates (insofar as money will likely increase our attractiveness to others). In fact, money can become such a powerful reinforcer that some people would rather just have the money than the things it can buy. Social attention, too, is a highly effective generalized reinforcer, especially for young children (though some aspects of it, such as touching, are probably also primary reinforcers). Attention from caretakers is usually associated with a host of good things such as food and play and comfort, with the result that attention by itself can become a powerful reinforcer. It is so powerful that some children will even misbehave to get someone to pay attention to them, even though the attention consists of people being angry with them. In fact, this is one of the ways in which punishment can backfire (other ways in which it can backfire are discussed in Chapter 9).

Generalized reinforcers are often used in behavior modification programs. In a "token economy," tokens are used in institutional settings—such as mental institutions, prisons, or classrooms for problem children—to increase the frequency of certain desirable behaviors, such as completing an assigned task, dressing appropriately, or behaving sociably. Attendants deliver the tokens immediately following the occurrence of the behavior. These tokens can later be exchanged for "backup reinforcers" such as treats, trips into the community, or television viewing time. In essence, just as the opportunity to earn money—and what it can buy—motivates many of us to behave appropriately, so too does the opportunity to earn a token—and what it can be exchanged for—motivates the residents of that setting to behave appropriately. (See Miltenberger, 2012, for an in-depth discussion of token economies.)

And Furthermore

Learned Industriousness

Some people seem to enjoy hard work while others do not. Why is this? According to *learned industriousness theory*, if working hard (displaying high effort) on a task has been consistently associated with reinforcement, then working hard might itself become a secondary reinforcer (Eisenberger, 1992). This can result in a generalized tendency to work hard. Experiments with both humans and animals have confirmed this possibility. For example, rats that have received reinforcers for emitting forceful lever presses will then run faster down an alleyway to obtain food (Eisenberger, Carlson, Guile, & Shapiro, 1979). Similarly, students who have received reinforcers for solving complex math problems will later write essays of higher quality (Eisenberger, Masterson, & McDermitt, 1982). Experiments have also confirmed the opposite: Rats and humans that have received reinforcers for displaying low effort on a task will show a generalized tendency to be lazy (see Eisenberger, 1992). (Something to think about if you have a strong tendency to take the easy way out.)

Note that an event can function as both a primary reinforcer and a secondary reinforcer. A Thanksgiving dinner, for example, can be both a primary reinforcer, in the sense of providing food, and a secondary reinforcer due to its association with a beloved grandmother who prepared many similar dinners in your childhood.

Finally, just as stimuli that are associated with reinforcement can become secondary reinforcers, so also can the *behaviors* that are associated with reinforcement. For example, children who are consistently praised for helping others might eventually find the behavior of helping others to be reinforcing in and of itself. They will then help others, not to receive praise but because they "like to help." We might then describe such children as having an altruistic nature. By a similar mechanism, even hard work can sometimes become a secondary reinforcer (see "Learned Industriousness" in the And Furthermore box).

QUICK QUIZ J

1. Events that are innately reinforcing are called p⎯⎯⎯⎯⎯⎯⎯⎯⎯⎯ reinforcers. They are sometimes also called un⎯⎯⎯⎯⎯⎯⎯⎯⎯ reinforcers.

2. Events that become reinforcers through their association with other reinforcers are called s⎯⎯⎯⎯⎯⎯⎯ reinforcers. They are sometimes also called ⎯⎯⎯⎯⎯⎯⎯⎯ reinforcers.

3. Honey is for most people an example of a ⎯⎯⎯⎯⎯⎯⎯ reinforcer, while a coupon that is used to purchase the honey is an example of a ⎯⎯⎯⎯⎯⎯ reinforcer.

4. A (CS/US) ⎯⎯US⎯⎯ that has been associated with an appetitive (CS/US) ⎯⎯CS⎯⎯ can serve as a secondary reinforcer for an operant response. As well, a stimulus that serves as a(n) ⎯⎯⎯⎯⎯⎯⎯⎯ for an operant response can also serve as a secondary reinforcer for some other response.

5. A generalized reinforcer (or generalized secondary reinforcer) is a secondary rein- forcer that has been associated with _several reinforcers_

6. Two generalized secondary reinforcers that have strong effects on human behav- ior are _____ and _____.

7. Behavior modification programs in institutional settings often utilize generalized reinforcers in the form of t_____. This type of arrangement is known as a t_____ e_____.

Intrinsic and Extrinsic Reinforcement

In the preceding discussion, we noted that operant behavior itself can some- times be reinforcing. Such a behavior is said to be intrinsically reinforcing or motivating. Thus, *intrinsic reinforcement* is reinforcement provided by the mere act of performing the behavior. We rollerblade because it is invigorat- ing, we party with friends because we like their company, and we work hard at something partly because hard work has, through experience, become enjoyable (though you are probably still not convinced about that one). Animals, too, sometimes engage in activities for their own sake. In some of the earliest research on intrinsic motivation, it was found that with no addi- tional incentive, monkeys repeatedly solved mechanical puzzles (Harlow, Harlow, & Meyer, 1950).

Internal process

Run for fun

Unfortunately, many activities are not intrinsically reinforcing and instead require additional incentives to ensure their performance. *Extrinsic reinforcement* is the reinforcement provided by some consequence that is external to the behavior (i.e., an "extrinsic reinforcer"). For example, perhaps you are reading this text solely because of an upcoming exam. Passing the exam is the extrinsic consequence that is motivating your behavior. Other examples of extrinsically motivated behaviors are driving to get somewhere, working for money, and dating an attractive individual merely to enhance your prestige.

Adding a stimulus to increase the frequency of that behavior

Money → Run

Unfortunately, the distinction between intrinsic and extrinsic reinforcers is not always clear. For example, is candy an intrinsic or extrinsic rein- forcer? In one sense, candy seems like an intrinsic reinforcer because eating it is an enjoyable activity; yet the candy exists external to the behavior that is being reinforced. In such cases, it often helps to focus on the behavior that is being strengthened. Imagine, for example, that we offer candy to a child to strengthen the behavior of being quiet in the supermarket. The candy is clearly an extrinsic reinforcer for the behavior of *being quiet*, but with respect to the behavior of *eating candy*, the candy is the critical compo- nent in an intrinsically reinforcing activity. In any case, do not fret too much if you encounter an example that seems confusing. The most impor- tant thing is to be able to distinguish situations in which the motivation is clearly intrinsic (taking a bath for the pleasure of it) from those in which the motivation is clearly extrinsic (taking a bath because you have been paid to do so).

Intrinsic > Extrinsic

Question: What happens if you are given an extrinsic reinforcer for an activity that is already intrinsically reinforcing? What if, for example, you love rollerblading and are fortunate enough to be hired one weekend to blade around an amusement park while displaying a new line of sportswear? Will the experience of receiving payment for rollerblading increase, decrease, or have no effect on your subsequent enjoyment of the activity?

Although you might think that it would increase your enjoyment of rollerblading (since the activity is not only enjoyable but also associated with money), many researchers claim that experiences like this can *decrease* intrinsic interest. For example, Lepper, Green, and Nisbett (1973) found that children who enjoyed drawing with Magic Markers became less interested following a session in which they had been promised, and then received, a "good player" award for drawing with the markers. In contrast, children who did not receive an award or who received the award unexpectedly after playing with the markers did not show a loss of interest. Similar results have been reported by other investigators (e.g., Deci & Ryan, 1985). However, some researchers have found that extrinsic rewards have no effect on intrinsic interest (e.g., Amabile, Hennessey, & Grossman, 1986) or actually produce an *increase* in intrinsic interest (e.g., Harackiewicz, Manderlink, & Sansone, 1984). Unfortunately, despite these mixed findings, it is the damaging effects of extrinsic rewards on intrinsic motivation that are often presented to the public (e.g., Kohn, 1993). But is this a fair assessment of the evidence? Are the harmful effects of reinforcement the rule or the exception?

Cameron and Pierce (1994) attempted to answer this question by conducting a meta-analysis of 96 well-controlled experiments that examined the effects of extrinsic rewards on intrinsic motivation. (A meta-analysis is a statistical procedure that combines the results of several separate studies, thereby producing a more reliable overall assessment of the variable being studied.) The meta-analysis by Cameron and Pierce indicates that extrinsic rewards usually have little or no effect on intrinsic motivation. External rewards can occasionally undermine intrinsic motivation, but only when *the reward is expected* (i.e., the person has been instructed beforehand that she will receive a reward), *the reward is tangible* (e.g., it consists of money rather than praise), and *the reward is given for simply performing the activity* (and not for how well it is performed). It also turns out that verbal rewards, such as praise, often produce an increase in intrinsic motivation, as do tangible rewards given for high-quality performance (see Deci & Ryan, 1985). Cameron and Pierce (1994) conclude that extrinsic rewards can be safely applied in most circumstances and that the limited circumstances in which they decrease intrinsic motivation are easily avoided. Bandura (1997) likewise has argued that the dangers of extrinsic rewards on intrinsic motivation have been greatly overstated. (See Cameron, 2001; Cameron, Pierce, Banko, & Gear, 2005; Cameron & Pierce, 2002; and Deci, Koestner, & Ryan, 2001a, 2001b, for further

And Furthermore

Positive Reinforcement of Artistic Appreciation

B. F. Skinner (1983) once described how two students used positive reinforcement to instill in their new roommate an appreciation of modern art. These students had several items of modern art in their apartment, but the roommate had shown little interest in them and was instead proceeding to "change the character" of the space. As a counterploy, the students first decided to pay attention to the roommate only when they saw him looking at one of the works of art. Next, they threw a party and arranged for an attractive young woman to engage him in a discussion about the art. They also arranged for him to receive announcements from local art galleries about upcoming art shows. After about a month, the roommate himself suggested attending a local art museum. Interestingly, while there, he just "happened" to find a five-dollar bill lying at his feet while he was looking at a painting. According to Skinner, "It was not long before [the two students] came again in great excitement—to show me his first painting" (p. 48).

contributions to this debate.)[6] (See also "Positive Reinforcement of Artistic Appreciation" in the And Furthermore box.)

QUICK QUIZ K

1. An _____ motivated activity is one in which the activity is itself reinforcing; an _____ motivated activity is one in which the reinforcer for the activity consists of some type of additional consequence that is external to the activity.

2. Running to lose weight is an example of an _____ motivated activity; running because it "feels good" is an example of an _____ motivated activity.

3. In their meta-analysis of relevant research, Cameron and Pierce (1994) found that extrinsic rewards decrease intrinsic motivation only when they are (expected/unexpected) _____, (tangible/verbal) _____, and given for (performing well / merely engaging in the behavior) _____ _____.

4. They also found that extrinsic rewards generally increased intrinsic motivation when the rewards were (tangible/verbal) _____, and that tangible rewards increased intrinsic motivation when they were delivered contingent upon (high/low) _____ quality performance.

---

[6]It is also the case that some consequences that appear to function as positive reinforcers might in reality be more aversive. For example, many years ago, a catcher for the Pittsburgh Pirates told one of the authors of this text that he hated baseball because there were so many young players trying to replace him. It seemed like the consequence that motivated his playing was no longer the love of baseball, nor even the desire to obtain a good salary; rather, it was the threatened *loss* of a good salary if he didn't play well. According to Skinner (1987), human behavior is too often controlled by these types of negative consequences—working to avoid the loss of a paycheck and studying to avoid failure (especially prevalent in students who procrastinate until they are in serious danger of failing). It is therefore not surprising that these activities often seem less than intrinsically interesting.

Natural and Contrived Reinforcers

The distinction between intrinsic and extrinsic reinforcers is closely related to the distinction between natural and contrived reinforcers. *Natural reinforcers* are reinforcers that are typically provided for a certain behavior; that is, they are an expected usual consequence of the behavior within that setting. Money is a natural consequence of selling merchandise; gold medals are a natural consequence of hard training and a great performance. *Contrived* (or *artificial reinforcers*) are reinforcers that have been deliberately arranged to modify a behavior; they are not a typical consequence of the behavior in that setting. For example, although television is the natural reinforcer for the behavior of turning on the set, it is a contrived reinforcer for the behavior of, say, accomplishing a certain amount of studying. In the latter case, we have created a contrived contingency in an attempt to modify the person's study behavior.

Although contrived reinforcers are often seen as a hallmark of behaviorism, behaviorists strive to utilize natural reinforcers whenever possible (Sulzer-Azaroff & Mayer, 1991). When contrived reinforcers are used, the ultimate intention is to let the "natural contingencies" eventually take over if at all possible. For example, although we might initially use tokens to motivate a patient with schizophrenia to socialize with others, our hope is that the behavior will soon become "trapped" by the natural consequences of socializing (e.g., smiles and pleasant comments from others) such that the tokens can eventually be withdrawn. Similarly, although we might initially use praise to increase the frequency with which a child reads, the natural (and intrinsic) reinforcers associated with reading will hopefully take over so that the child will begin reading even in the absence of praise.

Note, too, that natural contingencies tend to produce more efficient behavior patterns than do contrived contingencies (Skinner, 1987). Although a coach might use praise to reinforce correct throwing actions by a young quarterback, the most important factor in producing correct throws will be the natural consequence of where the ball goes.

To distinguish between intrinsic versus extrinsic reinforcers and natural versus contrived reinforcers, just remember that the former is concerned with the extent to which the behavior itself is reinforcing while the latter is concerned with the extent to which a reinforcer has been artificially imposed so as to manipulate a behavior. Note, too, that the extent to which a reinforcer has been artificially imposed is not always clear; hence, it is quite easy to find examples in which it is ambiguous as to whether the reinforcer is contrived or natural. Are grades in school a natural reinforcer or a contrived reinforcer? It depends on whether one's grades are considered as a typical aspect of the learning environment, at least within the school system, or as a contrived aspect. In any event, as with intrinsic versus extrinsic motivation, the important thing is to be able to distinguish those situations in which the reinforcers are clearly contrived—as often occurs in a behavior modification program—from those in which the reinforcers are considerably more natural.

1. A(n) _____ reinforcer is a reinforcer that typically occurs for that behavior in that setting; a(n) _____ reinforcer is one that typically does not occur for that behavior in that setting.

2. You flip the switch and the light comes on. The light coming on is an example of a(n) (contrived/natural) _____ reinforcer; in general, it is also an example of an (intrinsic/extrinsic) _____ reinforcer.

3. You thank your roommate for helping out with the housework in an attempt to motivate her to help out more often. To the extent that this works, the thank-you is an example of a(n) (contrived/natural) _____ reinforcer; it is also an example of an (intrinsic/extrinsic) _____ reinforcer.

4. In applied behavior analysis, although one might initially use (contrived/natural) _____ consequences to first develop a behavior, the hope is that, if possible, the behavior will become tr_____ by the n_____ c_____ associated with that behavior.

5. In most cases, the most important consequence in developing a highly effective slapshot in hockey will be the (contrived/natural) _____ consequence of where the puck goes and how fast it travels.

Shaping

Positive reinforcement is clearly a great way to strengthen a behavior, but what if the behavior that we wish to reinforce never occurs? For example, what if you want to reinforce a rat's behavior of pressing a lever but are unable to do so because the rat never presses the lever? What can you do? The solution is to use a procedure called shaping.

Shaping is the gradual creation of new operant behavior through reinforcement of successive approximations to that behavior. With our rat, we could begin by delivering food whenever it stands near the lever. As a result, it begins standing near the lever more often. We then deliver food only when it is facing the lever, at which point it starts engaging in that behavior more often. In a similar manner, step-by-step, we reinforce touching the lever, then placing a paw on the lever, and then pressing down on the lever. When the rat finally presses down on the lever with enough force, it closes the microswitch that activates the food magazine. The rat has now earned a reinforcer on its own. After a few more experiences like this, the rat begins to reliably press the lever whenever it is hungry. By reinforcing successive approximations to the target behavior, we have managed to teach the rat an entirely new behavior.

Another example of shaping: How do you teach a dog to catch a Frisbee? Many people simply throw the Frisbee at the dog, at which point the dog probably wonders what on earth has gotten into its owner as the Frisbee sails over its head. Or possibly the dog runs after the Frisbee, picks it up after it falls on the ground, and then makes the

[handwritten margin note: Cause a new behavior by providing a reinforcer.]

owner chase after it to get the Frisbee back. Karen Pryor (1999), a professional animal trainer, recommends the following procedure. First, reinforce the dog's behavior of taking the Frisbee from your hand and immediately returning it. Next, raise the criterion by holding the Frisbee in the air to make the dog jump for it. When this is well established, toss the Frisbee slightly so the dog jumps and catches it in midair. Then toss it a couple of feet so the dog has to run after it to catch it. Now gradually throw it further and further so the dog has to run farther and farther to get it. Remember to provide lots of praise each time the dog catches the Frisbee and returns it.

Shaping is obviously a fundamental procedure for teaching animals to perform tricks. During such training, the trainers often use a sound, such as a click from a handheld clicker, to reinforce the behavior. The sound has been repeatedly paired with food so that it has become a secondary reinforcer. The benefit of using a sound as a reinforcer is that it can be presented immediately upon the occurrence of the behavior, even if the animal is some distance away. Also, if food were presented each time the correct behavior occurred, the animal would quickly satiate, at which point the food would become ineffective as a reinforcer. By using a secondary reinforcer such as a click, with food delivered only intermittently, satiation will take longer to occur, thereby allowing for longer training sessions.

Most of our behaviors have, to some extent, been learned or modified through shaping. For example, when children first learn to eat with a knife and fork, parents might praise even very poor attempts. Over time, though, they expect better and better performance before offering praise. In a similar manner, we gradually shape the child's behavior of dressing appropriately, speaking politely, and writing legibly. And shaping is not confined merely to childhood. All of us are in the position of receiving constant feedback about our performance—be it ironing clothes, cooking a meal, or slam-dunking a basketball—thus allowing us to continually modify our behaviors and improve our skills. In such circumstances, it is usually the natural consequences of the behavior—the extent to which we are successful or unsuccessful—that provide the necessary reinforcement for gradual modifications of the behavior.

For further information on shaping as applied to both animals and humans, you might wish to obtain a copy of Karen Pryor's (1999) highly readable book, *Don't Shoot the Dog*. Pryor also has a Web site on "clicker training" (shaping through the use of clicks as secondary reinforcers) that can be accessed via the Internet (just search for "Karen Pryor" and "clicker training"). Clicker training has become increasingly popular with dog owners and is being used to shape behavior in everything from birds to horses and even llamas and elephants. Interestingly, Pryor observes that many animals greatly enjoy the "game" of clicker training. (See also "Training Ishmael" in the And Furthermore box.)

An excellent demonstration of the power of shaping.

ADVICE FOR THE LOVELORN

Dear Dr. Dee,

My boyfriend has a terrible tendency to boss me around. I have tried to counter this tendency by being especially nice to him, but the problem seems to be getting worse. He also refuses to discuss it or see a counselor. He says I am too sensitive and that I am making a mountain out of a molehill. What should I do?

Just About Hadenough

Dear Just,

You should first recognize that some people have a long history of reinforcement for being dominant or aggressive, and that it can sometimes be difficult to alter such tendencies. In fact, you might eventually have to bail out of this relationship, particularly because he refuses to discuss what seems to be an obvious problem.

Nevertheless, you might also wish to consider the possibility that you are inadvertently reinforcing his aggressiveness. Remember how, in the opening vignette to this chapter, the young woman reacted to her partner's angry demands by a show of affection. While this might reduce his anger in the short run, it might also reinforce his tendency to be aggressive. After all, not only was his anger effective in getting her to hurry up, it also resulted in a hug. The next time he wants her to hurry up or desires affection, what better way than to get angry?

As a first step, you might wish to take careful note of the situations in which your boyfriend becomes bossy. If it appears that you might be reinforcing his bossiness by being particularly nice to him when he acts that way, you could try offering him little or no attention when he behaves like that and lots of attention when he behaves more appropriately. Can this work? In her book *Don't Shoot the Dog*, Karen Pryor (1999) relates the following story about a woman who implemented just such a program:

> A young woman married a man who turned out to be very bossy and demanding. Worse yet, his father, who lived with them, was equally given to ordering his daughter-in-law about. It was the girl's mother who told me this story. On her first visit she was horrified at what her daughter was going through. "Don't worry, Mother," the daughter said. "Wait and see." The daughter formed the practice of responding minimally to commands and harsh remarks, while reinforcing with approval and affection any tendency by either man to be pleasant and thoughtful. In a year, she had turned them into decent human beings. Now they greet her with smiles when she comes home and leap up—both of them—to help with the groceries. (p. 30)

By reinforcing successive approximations toward decent behavior and not reinforcing bossy behavior (yet still responding minimally to their requests), this woman was apparently able to shape more appropriate behavior in her husband and father-in-law. Remember, though, such problems are often difficult to manage and may require professional help.

Behaviorally yours,

Dr. Dee

And Furthermore

Training Ishmael

Although the principles of reinforcement and shaping are easy enough to learn, applying those principles can be another matter. In this case, there is no substitute for the experience of shaping the behavior of a live animal. Dogs are ideal subjects for this, with cats and birds also being quite suitable. However, many people live in apartments where such pets are not allowed. Fortunately, apartment dwellers are often allowed to keep fish, and some fish are in fact surprisingly trainable. Goldfish, for example, have been trained to swim through hoops, push ping pong balls around, and (according to one report from an acquaintance who swore she saw it on television) pull a string to ring a tiny bell for food.

To illustrate the process of using reinforcement to train a fish, let us consider some training that I (Russ Powell) conducted with Ishmael, a 2-inch long, dark blue, male *Betta splendens* (Siamese fighting fish). Ishmael lived by himself in a 1-gallon acrylic tank with gravel and a few plants. It might seem to you that a 1-gallon tank is awfully small, but bettas have evolved to survive in small pools of water in their native Thailand. Isolation from other fish is also a natural state of affairs for a betta because the sight of another male, or something similar to it, often elicits the fixed action pattern of aggression that we discussed in Chapter 3. As it turns out, this natural proclivity for small living quarters and relative isolation is an advantage when it comes to training bettas, because this setup mimics some of the features of an operant conditioning chamber.

The interesting thing about training a male betta is that two types of reinforcers are available. One, of course, is food, and this generally works as well with bettas as it does with other animals (though bettas are sometimes fussy eaters). Unfortunately, being such small fish, they can be given only a few bites of food per day, which means that each training session must be kept quite short to prevent overfeeding. The other type of reinforcer is the presentation of a mirror that allows them to see a mirror image of themselves. This mirror image is often perceived as another male, which then elicits the fixed action pattern of aggression. Interestingly, the opportunity to aggress like this can serve as a positive reinforcer that can be used to strengthen some other behavior (Melvin, 1985; T. Thompson, 1963). Note that this is an excellent example of how positive reinforcers are not necessarily the kinds of events that one would classify as pleasant. If bettas had human-like feelings, one could only assume from their behavior that they hate the sight of another male; nevertheless, they will learn to perform a response in order to see that male.

As an informal demonstration of the effectiveness of mirror presentation as a reinforcer with Ishmael, mirror presentations were made contingent upon the behavior of turning a half-circle, first in a clockwise and then in a counterclockwise direction. A clockwise turn was defined as a clockwise movement from, at minimum, a left-facing position (from the observer's perspective) to a right-facing position in the tank. A counterclockwise turn was defined as a counterclockwise movement from, at minimum, a right-facing position to a left-facing position. Each training session lasted 10 minutes, which was measured with a kitchen timer.

(continued)

During an initial baseline period, Ishmael's clockwise and counterclockwise circling habits were recorded throughout the session with 10 mirror presentations presented noncontingently (independent of any behavior) at random points in time. (*Question: Why include mirror presentations in the baseline period?*) During this period, Ishmael showed a slight preference for turning in a counterclockwise direction (see Figure 6.4). A clockwise turn was selected for initial training beginning in session 5. Rather than simply waiting for a clockwise turn and then presenting the mirror, past experience with another betta suggested that the turning behavior could be established more rapidly by using a shaping procedure. Thus, mirror presentations were initially made contingent upon successive approximations to the required behavior (i.e., slight turns in the correct direction were initially reinforced, and progressively more complete turns were subsequently reinforced). Shaping proceeded rapidly, with Ishmael quickly establishing a pattern of clockwise turns. For the remainder of session 5 and for the following three sessions, he exhibited a clear preference for such turns.

Beginning in session 9, the requirement was reversed with counterclockwise turns reinforced and clockwise turns extinguished. Possibly due to the short length of each training session, counterclockwise turns did not become well established until session 13 (even with shaping), which was maintained for the following three sessions. A reversal was then attempted in which clockwise turns were again reinforced and counterclockwise turns were extinguished (hence, overall, this was an ABCB design). This time, three sessions were required before Ishmael developed a preference for turning in the newly reinforced direction. In session 20, however, the number of turns in either direction—as well as, it seemed, his general activity level—dropped sharply, especially toward the end of the session. During

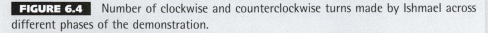

FIGURE 6.4   Number of clockwise and counterclockwise turns made by Ishmael across different phases of the demonstration.

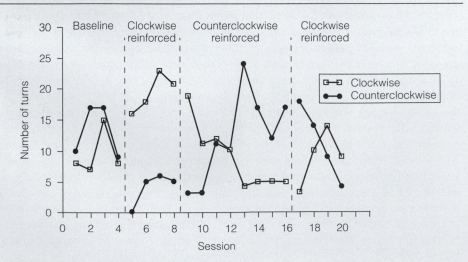

the first 5 minutes of the next session, he mostly sat at the bottom of the tank reacting minimally to the mirror. No circling behavior occurred. It appeared as though long-term habituation had set in such that the mirror was no longer sufficiently reinforcing to motivate the target behavior, and the session was therefore terminated. Ishmael showed a similar lack of interest in the mirror over the following 2 days as well.

Despite this less-than-ideal conclusion, the results generally confirmed that mirror presentation was an effective reinforcer for Ishmael's circling behavior. Most impressive was the initial learning of a clockwise turn, which occurred very rapidly. With food as a reinforcer, Ishmael also learned to bump, but not push, a ping pong ball—it was easy to get him to hover near the ball, but difficult to get him to contact it—and to swim through a wire hoop for food—which was relatively easy to accomplish. As for Ishmael, he easily trained his owner [me] to give him extra food by staring longingly and acting very agitated when I came home each evening—and then ceasing to act so agitated when I fed him. (Thus, my behavior of feeding him was being strengthened by which type of contingency?) If you are interested in training your own fish, a search of the web will likely reveal further information, including videos, on fish training, which seems to have become increasingly popular in recent years.

Now for the answer to the question about including mirror presentations in the baseline period: Intermittent presentation of the mirror by itself generates a lot of excitement and movement. Hence, noncontingent presentation of the mirror during the baseline period controls for the increase in circling that will likely occur simply due to the increased movement caused by mirror presentation alone. And as for the type of contingency that strengthened my tendency to feed Ishmael each evening: negative reinforcement.

1. Shaping is the creation of _____ operant behavior through the reinforcement of s_____ a_____ to that behavior.

2. In clicker training with dogs, the click is a s_____ reinforcer that has been established by first pairing it with f_____ which is a p_____ reinforcer.

3. The advantages of using the click as a reinforcer is that it can be delivered i_____. It can also prevent the animal from becoming s_____.

QUICK QUIZ M

SUMMARY

In contrast to elicited behaviors that are automatically evoked by the stimuli that precede them, operant behaviors are controlled by their consequences. Thus, in operant (or instrumental) conditioning, the future probability of a response is affected by its consequence. Reinforcers are consequences that increase the probability of (or strengthen) a response, whereas punishers decrease the probability of (or weaken) a response. In positive reinforcement and positive punishment, the consequence involves the presentation of a stimulus, whereas in negative reinforcement and negative punishment, the consequence involves the removal of a stimulus.

When a behavior has been consistently reinforced or punished in the presence of certain stimuli, those stimuli will begin to influence the occurrence of the behavior. A discriminative stimulus is a stimulus in the presence of which a response has been reinforced and in the absence of which it has not been reinforced.

Immediate reinforcers have a much stronger effect on behavior than do delayed reinforcers. Primary reinforcers are events that are innately reinforcing; secondary reinforcers are events that become reinforcing because they have been associated with other reinforcers. A generalized secondary reinforcer is a secondary reinforcer that has been associated with many other reinforcers. Intrinsic reinforcement occurs when performing a behavior is inherently reinforcing; extrinsic reinforcement occurs when the effective reinforcer is some consequence that is external to the behavior. Extrinsic reinforcement can undermine intrinsic interest in a task when the reinforcer is expected, tangible, or is made contingent on mere performance of the task. Extrinsic reinforcement can strengthen intrinsic interest when the reinforcer consists of verbal praise or is made contingent on high-quality performance. Natural reinforcers are reinforcing consequences that typically follow a behavior, whereas contrived reinforcers are reinforcing consequences that are artificially arranged in order to deliberately modify a behavior.

Shaping is the creation of novel behavior through the reinforcement of gradual approximations to that behavior. Effective shaping is often carried out with the use of a secondary reinforcer, such as the sound of a whistle or a click that can be delivered immediately following the occurrence of the appropriate behavior.

SUGGESTED READINGS

Thorndike, E. L. (1898). Animal intelligence: An experimental study of the associative processes in animals. *Psychological Review Monograph Supplement*, 2, 1–109. A classic work in the field.

Kohn, A. (1993). *Punished by rewards*. Boston: Houghton Mifflin. One of the harshest criticisms of the use of rewards to motivate people.

Pryor, K. (1975). *Lads before the wind: Adventures in porpoise training*. New York: Harper & Row. An engaging account of Pryor's experiences in becoming a dolphin trainer.

Pryor, K. (1999). *Don't shoot the dog: The new art of teaching and training* (Rev. ed.). New York: Bantam Books. Pryor's most popular book on the art of shaping behavior as applied to everything from dogs to horses to humans.

Cameron, J., & Pierce, W. D. (2002). *Rewards and intrinsic motivation: Resolving the controversy.* New York: Greenwood Publishing. An ardent defense of the use of rewards to motivate people.

STUDY QUESTIONS

1. State Thorndike's law of effect. What is operant conditioning (as defined by Skinner), and how does this definition differ from Thorndike's law of effect?
2. Explain why operant behaviors are said to be emitted and why they are defined as a "class" of responses.
3. Define the terms *reinforcer* and *punisher*. How do those terms differ from the terms reinforcement and punishment?
4. What is a discriminative stimulus? Define the three-term contingency and diagram an example. Be sure to include the appropriate symbols for each component.
5. Define positive reinforcement and diagram an example. Define negative reinforcement and diagram an example. Be sure to include the appropriate symbols for each component.
6. Define positive punishment and diagram an example. Define negative punishment and diagram an example. Be sure to include the appropriate symbols for each component.
7. What are similarities and differences between negative reinforcement and positive punishment?
8. How does immediacy affect the strength of a reinforcer? How does this often lead to difficulties for students in their academic studies?
9. Distinguish between primary and secondary reinforcers, and give an example of each.
10. What is a generalized reinforcer? What are two examples of such reinforcers?
11. Define intrinsic and extrinsic reinforcement, and provide an example of each.
12. Under what three conditions does extrinsic reinforcement undermine intrinsic interest? Under what two conditions does extrinsic reinforcement enhance intrinsic interest?
13. Define natural and contrived reinforcers, and provide an example of each.
14. Define shaping. What are two advantages of using a secondary reinforcer, such as a sound, as an aid to shaping?

CONCEPT REVIEW

avoidance behavior. Behavior that occurs before the aversive stimulus is presented and thereby prevents its delivery.

contrived reinforcers. Reinforcers that have been deliberately arranged to modify a behavior; they are not a typical consequence of the behavior in that setting. Also called *artificial reinforcers*.

discriminative stimulus (S^D). A stimulus in the presence of which responses are reinforced and in the absence of which they are not reinforced; that is, a stimulus that signals the availability of reinforcement.

discriminative stimulus for extinction (S^Δ). A stimulus that signals the absence of reinforcement.

discriminative stimulus for punishment (S^{Dp}). A stimulus that signals that a response will be punished.

escape behavior. A behavior that results in the termination of an aversive stimulus.

extrinsic reinforcement. The reinforcement provided by a consequence that is external to the behavior, that is, an extrinsic reinforcer.

generalized (or generalized secondary) reinforcer. A type of secondary reinforcer that has been associated with several other reinforcers.

intrinsic reinforcement. Reinforcement provided by the mere act of performing the behavior; the performance of the behavior is inherently reinforcing.

law of effect. As stated by Thorndike, the proposition that behaviors that lead to a satisfying state of affairs are strengthened or "stamped in," while behaviors that lead to an unsatisfying or annoying state of affairs are weakened or "stamped out."

natural reinforcers. Reinforcers that are naturally provided for a certain behavior; that is, they are a typical consequence of the behavior within that setting.

negative punishment. The removal of a stimulus (one that is usually considered pleasant or rewarding) following a response, which then leads to a decrease in the future strength of that response.

negative reinforcement. The removal of a stimulus (one that is usually considered unpleasant or aversive) following a response, which then leads to an increase in the future strength of that response.

operant behavior. A class of emitted responses that result in certain consequences; these consequences, in turn, affect the future probability or strength of those responses.

operant conditioning. A type of learning in which the future probability of a behavior is affected by its consequences.

positive punishment. The presentation of a stimulus (one that is usually considered unpleasant or aversive) following a response, which then leads to a decrease in the future strength of that response.

positive reinforcement. The presentation of a stimulus (one that is usually considered pleasant or rewarding) following a response, which then leads to an increase in the future strength of that response.

primary reinforcer (or unconditioned reinforcer). An event that is innately reinforcing.

punisher. An event that: (1) follows a behavior and (2) decreases the future probability of that behavior.

reinforcer. An event that: (1) follows a behavior and (2) increases the future probability of that behavior.

secondary reinforcer (or conditioned reinforcer). An event that is reinforcing because it has been associated with some other reinforcer.

shaping. The gradual creation of new operant behavior through reinforcement of successive approximations to that behavior.

three-term contingency. The relationship between a discriminative stimulus, an operant behavior, and a reinforcer or punisher.

CHAPTER TEST

31. Shaping is: (A) the reinforcement of a new operant behavior, (B) the gradual reinforcement of a new operant behavior, (C) the reinforcement of successive approximations to a new operant behavior, (D) the creation of new operant behavior through successive approximations to reinforcement, (E) none of the preceding. _____

20. A positive reinforcer is a stimulus, (A) the presentation of which increases the strength of a response, (B) the presentation of which follows a response and increases the strength of that response, (C) the presentation of which decreases the strength of a response, (D) the presentation of which follows a response and decreases the strength of that response. _____

2. Elicited behaviors are controlled by the events that (precede/follow) _____ their occurrence, while operant behaviors are controlled by the events that (precede/follow) _____ their occurrence.

14. An easy way to remember the three-term contingency is that you _____ something, _____ something, and _____ something.

25. Behaviors that are performed for their own sake are said to be _____ motivated; behaviors that are performed to achieve some additional incentive are said to be _____ motivated.

11. Reinforcers and punishers are defined entirely by their _____ on behavior.

8. An event is a punisher if it _____ a behavior and the future probability of that behavior _____.

23. Money and praise are common examples of _____ reinforcers.

12. If the rat does not press the lever, then it does not receive a shock. As a result, the rat is more likely not to press the lever. This is an example of (A) negative reinforcement, (B) negative punishment, (C) positive reinforcement, (D) positive punishment. _____ (*Think carefully about this.*)

28. At the zoo one day, you notice that a zookeeper is leading a rhinoceros into a pen by repeatedly whistling at it as the animal moves. It is

probably the case that the whistle has been paired with _____ and is now functioning as a _____.

1. Compared to most elicited behaviors, operant behaviors seem (more/less) _____ automatic and reflexive.

15. The three-term contingency can be thought of as an ABC sequence in which A stands for _____, B stands for _____, and C stands for _____.

27. The gradual development of new operant behavior through reinforcement of _____ to that behavior is called _____.

6. Operant behaviors are sometimes simply called _____. These can be contrasted with elicited behaviors, which Skinner called _____ behaviors or simply _____.

21. Each time a student studies at home, she is praised by her parents. As a result, she no longer studies at home. This is an example of what type of contingency? _____

17. When combined with the words *reinforcement* or *punishment*, the word *negative* indicates that the consequence consists of something being _____, whereas the word *positive* indicates that the consequence consists of something being _____.

10. The terms *reinforcer* or *punisher* refer to the specific _____ that follows a behavior, whereas the terms *reinforcement* or *punishment* refer to the _____ or _____ whereby the probability of a behavior is altered by its consequences.

24. Harpreet very much enjoys hard work and often volunteers for projects that are quite demanding. According to _____ theory, it is likely the case that, for Harpreet, the act of expending a lot of effort has often been _____.

3. According to Thorndike's _____, behaviors that lead to a _____ state of affairs are strengthened, whereas behaviors that lead to an _____ state of affairs are weakened.

30. A generalized secondary reinforcer is one that has become a reinforcer because it has been associated with: (A) a primary reinforcer, (B) a secondary reinforcer, (C) several secondary reinforcers, (D) several primary reinforcers, or (E) several reinforcers (either primary or secondary). _____

19. When Beth tried to pull the tail of her dog, he bared his teeth and growled threateningly. Beth quickly pulled her hand back. The dog growled even more threateningly the next time Beth reached for his tail, and she again pulled her hand away. Eventually Beth gave up, and no longer tries to pull the dog's tail. The dog's behavior of baring his teeth and growling served to (positively/negatively) _____ (punish/reinforce) _____ Beth's behavior of trying to pull his tail. Beth's behavior of pulling her hand away served to _____ the dog's behavior of growling.

32. Achieving a record number of strikeouts in a game would be a(n) (natural/contrived) _____ reinforcer for pitching well; receiving a bonus for throwing that many strikeouts would be a(n) _____ reinforcer.

5. Operant behaviors are usually defined as a _____ of responses, all of which are capable of producing a certain _____.

16. A stimulus that signals that a response will be punished is called a _____ for punishment. It is sometimes given the symbol _____.

22. Events that are innately reinforcing are called _____ reinforcers; events that become reinforcers through experience are called _____ reinforcers.

9. A reinforcer is usually given the symbol _____, while a punisher is usually given the symbol _____. The operant response is given the symbol _____, while a discriminative stimulus is given the symbol _____.

26. Steven has fond memories of his mother reading fairy tales to him when he was a child, and as a result he now enjoys reading fairy tales as an adult. For Steven, the act of reading fairy tales is functioning as what type of reinforcer? (A) primary, (B) secondary, (C) intrinsic, (D) extrinsic, (E) both B and C. _____

4. Classically conditioned behaviors are said to be e_____ by st_____; operant behaviors are said to be e_____ by the or_____.

18. Referring to this chapter's opening vignette, among the four types of contingencies described in this chapter, Sally's actions toward Joe probably best illustrate the process of _____. In other words, Joe's abusive behavior will likely (increase/decrease) _____ in the future as a result of Sally's actions.

7. An event is a reinforcer if it _____ a behavior and the future probability of that behavior _____.

29. Major advantages of using the sound of a click for shaping are that the click can be delivered _____ and the animal is unlikely to _____ upon it.

13. A discriminative stimulus is a stimulus that signals that a _____ is available. It is said to "_____" for the behavior.

Visit the book companion Web site at http://www.academic.cengage.com/psychology/powell for additional practice questions, answers to the Quick Quizzes, practice review exams, and additional exercises and information.

ANSWERS TO CHAPTER TEST

1. less
2. precede; follow
3. law of effect; satisfying; unsatisfying (or annoying)
4. elicited; stimuli; emitted; organism
5. class; consequence
6. operants; respondent; respondents
7. follows; increases
8. follows; decreases
9. S^R; S^P; R; S^D
10. consequence (event); process; procedure
11. effect
12. D (because *lever press* → shock" is the effective contingency)
13. reinforcer; set the occasion
14. notice; do; get
15. antecedent; behavior; consequence
16. discriminative stimulus; S^{Dp}
17. removed (or subtracted); presented (or added)
18. positive reinforcement; increase
19. positively; punish; negatively reinforce
20. B
21. positive punishment
22. primary (or unconditioned); secondary (or conditioned)
23. generalized (or generalized secondary)
24. learned industriousness; positively reinforced
25. intrinsically; extrinsically
26. E
27. successive (or gradual) approximations; shaping
28. food; secondary reinforcer
29. immediately; satiate
30. E
31. C
32. natural; contrived

CHAPTER 7

Schedules and Theories of Reinforcement

CHAPTER OUTLINE

"I don't understand why Alvin is so distant," Mandy commented. "He was great when we first started going out. Now it's like pulling teeth to get him to pay attention to me."

"So why do you put up with it?" her sister asked.

"I guess I'm in love with him. Why else would I be so persistent?"

Schedules of Reinforcement

has to meet specific criteria for reinforcement to occur.

In this section, we discuss schedules of reinforcement. A *schedule of reinforcement* is the response requirement that must be met to obtain reinforcement. In other words, a schedule indicates what exactly has to be done for the reinforcer to be delivered. For example, does each lever press by the rat result in a food pellet, or are several lever presses required? Did your mom give you a cookie each time you asked for one, or only some of the time? And just how persistent does Mandy have to be before Alvin will pay attention to her? As you will discover in this section, different response requirements can have dramatically different effects on behavior. Many of these effects (known as *schedule effects*) were first observed in experiments with pigeons (Ferster & Skinner, 1957), but they also help to explain some puzzling aspects of human behavior that are often attributed to internal traits or desires.

Continuous Versus Intermittent Schedules

Every response is reinforced.

A *continuous reinforcement schedule* is one in which each specified response is reinforced. For example, each time a rat presses the lever, it obtains a food pellet; each time the dog rolls over on command, it gets a treat; and each time Karen turns the ignition in her car, the motor starts. Continuous reinforcement (abbreviated CRF) is very useful when a behavior is first being shaped or strengthened. For example, when using a shaping procedure to train a rat to press a lever, reinforcement should be delivered for each approximation to the target behavior. Similarly, if we wish to encourage a child to always brush her teeth before bed, we would do well to initially praise her each time she does so.

Only some responses gets reinforced

An *intermittent (or partial) reinforcement schedule* is one in which only some responses are reinforced. For example, perhaps only some of the rat's lever presses result in a food pellet, and perhaps only occasionally did your mother give you a cookie when you asked for one. Intermittent reinforcement obviously characterizes much of everyday life. Not all concerts we attend are enjoyable, not every person we invite out on a date accepts, and not every date that we go out on leads to an enjoyable evening. And although we might initially praise a child each time she properly completes her homework, we might soon praise her only occasionally in the belief that such behavior should persist in the absence of praise.

There are four basic (or simple) types of intermittent schedules: fixed ratio, variable ratio, fixed interval, and variable interval. We will describe each one along with the characteristic response pattern produced by each. Note that this characteristic response pattern is the stable pattern that emerges once the organism has had considerable exposure to the schedule. Such stable patterns are known as *steady-state behaviors*, in contrast to the more variable patterns of behavior that are evident when an organism is first exposed to a schedule.

1. A s_____ of reinforcement is the r_____ requirement that must be met in order to obtain reinforcement.

2. On a c_____ reinforcement schedule (abbreviated _____), each response is reinforced, whereas on an i_____ reinforcement schedule, only some responses are reinforced. The latter is also called a p_____ reinforcement schedule.

3. Each time you flick the light switch, the light comes on. The behavior of flicking the light switch is on a(n) _____ schedule of reinforcement.

4. When the weather is very cold, you are sometimes unable to start your car. The behavior of starting your car in very cold weather is on a(n) _____ schedule of reinforcement.

5. S_____ e_____ are the different effects on behavior produced by different response requirements. These are the stable patterns of behavior that emerge once the organism has had sufficient exposure to the schedule. Such stable patterns are known as st_____-st_____ behaviors.

Four Basic Intermittent Schedules

Fixed Ratio Schedules On a *fixed ratio (FR) schedule*, reinforcement is contingent upon a fixed, predictable number of responses. For example, on a fixed ratio 5 schedule (abbreviated FR 5), a rat has to press the lever 5 times to obtain a food pellet. On an FR 50 schedule, it has to press the lever 50 times to obtain a food pellet. Similarly, earning a dollar for every 10 carburetors assembled on an assembly line is an example of an FR 10 schedule, while earning a dollar for each carburetor assembled is an example of an FR 1 schedule. Note that an FR 1 schedule is the same as a CRF (continuous reinforcement) schedule in which each response is reinforced (thus, such a schedule can be correctly labeled as either an FR 1 or a CRF).

FR schedules generally produce a high rate of response along with a short pause following the attainment of each reinforcer (see Figure 7.1). This short pause is known as a *postreinforcement pause*. For example, a rat on an FR 25 schedule

[handwritten margin notes: Reinforcement is fixed, predictable number of responses. Punch card → Free drink]

FIGURE 7.1 Response patterns for FR, variable ratio (VR), fixed interval (FI), and variable interval (VI) schedules. This figure shows the characteristic pattern of responding on the four basic schedules. Notice the high response rate on the fixed and variable ratio schedules, moderate response rate on the variable interval schedule, and scalloped response pattern on Lhe fixed interval schedule. Also, both the fixed ratio and fixed interval schedules are accompanied by postreinforcement pauses. (*Source:* Adapted from Nairne, J. S., PSYCHOLOGY: The Adaptive Mind 2nd Edition. Copyright © 2000 Brooks/Cole. Reprinted by permission of Cengage Learning.)

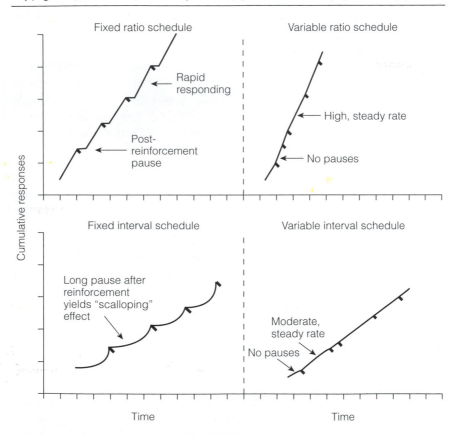

will rapidly emit 25 lever presses, munch down the food pellet it receives, and then snoop around the chamber for a few seconds before rapidly emitting another 25 lever presses. In other words, it will take a short break following each reinforcer, just as you might take a short break after reading each chapter in a textbook or completing a particular assignment. Note, too, that each pause is usually followed by a relatively quick return to a high rate of response. Thus, the typical FR pattern is described as a "break-and-run" pattern—a short break followed by a steady run of responses.

Similarly, students sometimes find that when they finally sit down to start work on the next chapter or assignment, they quickly become involved in it. Perhaps this is why just starting a task is often the most important step in overcoming procrastination; once you start, the work often flows naturally (Domjan, 2010). For this reason, it is sometimes helpful to use certain tricks to get started, such as beginning with a short, easy task before progressing to a more difficult task. Alternatively, you might promise yourself that you will work for only 5 or 10 minutes and then quit for the evening if you really do not feel like carrying on. What often happens is that once the promised time period has passed, it is actually quite easy to carry on.

In general, higher ratio requirements produce longer postreinforcement pauses. This means that you will probably take a longer break after completing a long assignment than after completing a short one. Similarly, a rat will show longer pauses on an FR 100 schedule than on an FR 30 schedule. With very low ratios, such as FR 1 (CRF) or FR 2, there may be little or no pausing other than the time it takes for the rat to munch down the food pellet. In such cases, the next reinforcer is so close—only a few lever presses away—that the rat is tempted to immediately go back to work. (If only the reinforcers for studying were so immediate!)

Schedules in which the reinforcer is easily obtained are said to be very *dense* or *rich*, while schedules in which the reinforcer is difficult to obtain are said to be very *lean*. Thus, an FR 5 schedule is considered a very dense schedule of reinforcement compared to an FR 100. During a 1-hour session, a rat can earn many more food pellets on an FR 5 schedule than it can on an FR 100. Likewise, an assembly line worker who earns a dollar for each carburetor assembled (a CRF schedule) is able to earn considerably more during an 8-hour shift than is a worker who earns a dollar for every 10 carburetors assembled (an FR 10 schedule).

In general, *"stretching the ratio"*—moving from a low ratio requirement (a dense schedule) to a high ratio requirement (a lean schedule)—should be done gradually. For example, once lever pressing is well established on a CRF schedule, the requirement can be gradually increased to FR 2, FR 5, FR 10, and so on. If the requirement is increased too quickly—for example, CRF to FR 2 and then a sudden jump to FR 20—the rat's behavior may become erratic and even die out altogether. Likewise, if you try to raise the requirement too high—say, to FR 2000—there may be a similar breakdown in the rat's behavior. Such breakdowns in behavior are technically known as *ratio strain*, a disruption in responding due to an overly demanding response requirement.

Ratio strain is what most people would refer to as burnout, and it can be a big problem for students faced with a heavy workload. Some students, especially those who have a history of getting by with minimal work, may find it increasingly difficult to study under such circumstances and may even choose to drop out of college. If they had instead experienced a gradual increase in workload over a period of several months or years, they might have been able to put forth the needed effort to succeed.

1. On a(n) _____ _____ schedule, reinforcement is contingent upon a fixed number of responses.

2. A schedule in which 15 responses are required for each reinforcer is abbreviated _____.

3. A mother finds that she always has to make the same request three times before her child complies. The mother's behavior of making requests is on an _____ schedule of reinforcement.

4. An FR 1 schedule of reinforcement can also be called a _____ schedule.

5. A fixed ratio schedule tends to produce a (high/low) _____ rate of response, along with a p_____ p_____.

6. An FR 200 schedule of reinforcement will result in a (longer/shorter) _____ pause than an FR 50 schedule.

7. The typical FR pattern is sometimes called a b_____-and-r_____ pattern, with a _____ pause that is followed immediately by a (high/low) _____ rate of response.

8. An FR 12 schedule of reinforcement is (denser/leaner) _____ than an FR 75 schedule.

9. A very dense schedule of reinforcement can also be referred to as a very r_____ schedule.

10. Over a period of a few months, Aaron changed from complying with each of his mother's requests to complying with every other request, then with every third request, and so on. The mother's behavior of making requests has been subjected to a procedure known as "s_____ the r_____."

11. Graduate students often have to complete an enormous amount of work in the initial year of their program. For some students, the workload involved is far beyond anything they have previously encountered. As a result, their study behavior may become increasingly (erratic/stereotyped) _____ throughout the year, a process known as r_____ s_____.

Variable Ratio Schedules   On a *variable ratio (VR) schedule*, reinforcement is contingent upon a varying, unpredictable number of responses. For example, on a variable ratio 5 (VR 5) schedule, a rat has to emit an *average* of 5 lever presses for each food pellet, with the number of lever responses on any particular trial varying between, say, 1 and 10. Thus, the number of required lever presses might be 3 for the first pellet, 6 for the second pellet, 1 for the third pellet, 7 for the fourth pellet, and so on, with the overall average being 5 lever presses for each reinforcer. Similarly, on a VR 50 schedule, the number of required lever presses may vary between 1 and 100, with the average being 50.

VR schedules generally produce a high and steady rate of response, often with little or no postreinforcement pause (see Figure 7.1). A postreinforcement pause is especially unlikely to occur when the minimum response requirement in the schedule is very low, such as a VR 50 schedule in which the requirement varies between 1 and 100 as opposed to a VR 50 in which the requirement varies between, say, 10 and 90 (Schlinger, Derenne, & Baron, 2008). This is understandable if you consider that each response on the former schedule has the potential of resulting in a reinforcer even if a reinforcer has just been obtained.

The real world is filled with examples of VR schedules. Some predatory behaviors, such as that shown by cheetahs, have a strong VR component in that only some attempts at chasing down prey are successful. In humans, only some acts of politeness receive an acknowledgment, only some residents who are called upon by canvassers will make a contribution, and only some CDs that we buy are enjoyable. Many sports activities, such as shooting baskets in basketball and shots on goal in hockey, are also reinforced largely on a VR schedule. As I am writing this passage, a colleague stopped by and joked that his golf drive is probably on a VR 200 schedule. In other words, he figures that an average of about one in every 200 drives is a good one. I (Russ Powell) replied that my own drives are probably on a much leaner schedule with the result that ratio strain has set in, which is fancy behaviorist talk for "I so rarely hit the ball straight that I have just about given up playing."

Variable ratio schedules help to account for the persistence with which some people display certain maladaptive behaviors. Gambling is a prime example in this regard: The unpredictable nature of these activities results in a very high rate of behavior. In fact, the behavior of a gambler playing a slot machine is the classic example of human behavior controlled by a VR schedule. Certain forms of aberrant social behavior may also be accounted for by VR schedules. For example, why do some men persist in using cute, flippant remarks to introduce themselves to women when the vast majority of women view such remarks negatively? One reason is that a small minority of women actually respond favorably, thereby intermittently reinforcing the use of such remarks. For example, Kleinke, Meeker, and Staneske (1986) found that although 84% of women surveyed rated the opening line "I'm easy. Are you?" as poor to terrible, 14% rated it as either very good or excellent!

Variable ratio schedules of reinforcement may also facilitate the development of an abusive relationship. At the start of a relationship, the individuals involved typically provide each other with an enormous amount of positive reinforcement (a very dense schedule). This strengthens the relationship and increases each partner's attraction to the other. As the relationship progresses, such reinforcement naturally becomes somewhat more intermittent. In some situations, however, this process becomes malignant, with one person (let us call this person the victimizer) providing reinforcement on an extremely intermittent basis, and the other person (the victim) working incredibly hard to obtain that reinforcement. Because the process evolves gradually (a process of slowly "stretching the ratio"), the victim may have little awareness of what is happening until the abusive pattern is well established. What would motivate such an unbalanced process? One source of motivation is that the less often the victimizer reinforces the victim, the more attention (reinforcement) he or she receives from the victim. In other words, the victim works so hard to get the partner's attention that he or she actually reinforces the very process of being largely ignored by that partner. Of course, it does not necessarily have to be a one-way process, and there may be relationships in which the partners alternate the role of victim and victimizer. The result may be a volatile relationship that both partners find exciting but that is constantly on the verge of collapse due to frequent periods in which each partner experiences "ratio strain."

1. On a variable ratio schedule, reinforcement is contingent upon a _____ un_____ _____ of responses.

2. A variable ratio schedule typically produces a (high/low) _____ rate of behavior (with/without) _____ a postreinforcement pause.

3. An average of 1 in 10 people approached by a panhandler actually gives him money. His behavior of panhandling is on a _____ schedule of reinforcement.

4. As with an FR schedule, an extremely lean VR schedule can result in r_____ s_____.

[handwritten margin note: reinforcement happens to the first response after a set period of time]

[handwritten margin note: pay check]

Fixed Interval Schedules   On a *fixed interval (FI) schedule*, reinforcement is contingent upon the first response after a fixed, predictable period of time. For a rat on a fixed interval 30-second (FI 30-sec) schedule, the first lever press *after* a 30-second interval has elapsed results in a food pellet. Following that, another 30 seconds must elapse before a lever press will again produce a food pellet. Any lever pressing that occurs during the interval, before the 30-second period has elapsed, is ineffective. Similarly, trying to phone a business that opens in exactly 30 minutes will be effective only after the 30 minutes have elapsed, with any phone calls before that being ineffective.

FI schedules often produce a "scalloped" (upwardly curved) pattern of responding, consisting of a postreinforcement pause followed by a gradually increasing rate of response as the interval draws to a close (see Figure 7.1). For example, a rat on an FI 30-sec schedule will likely emit no lever presses at the start of the 30-second interval. This will be followed by a few tentative lever presses perhaps midway through the interval, with a gradually increasing rate of response thereafter. By the time the interval draws to a close and the reinforcer is imminent, the rat will be emitting a high rate of response, with the result that the reinforcer will be attained as soon as it becomes available.

Would the behavior of trying to phone a business that opens in 30 minutes also follow a scalloped pattern? If we have a watch available, it probably would not. We would simply look at our watch to determine when the 30 minutes have elapsed and then make our phone call. The indicated time would be a discriminative stimulus (S^D) for when the reinforcer is available (i.e., the business is open), and we would wait until the appropriate time before phoning. But what about the behavior of looking at your watch during the 30 minutes (the reinforcer for which would be noticing that the interval has elapsed)? You are unlikely to spend much time looking at your watch at the start of the interval. As time progresses, however, you will begin looking at it more and more frequently. In other words, your behavior will follow the typical scalloped pattern of responding.

The distribution of study sessions throughout the term can also show characteristics of an FI scallop, which can again contribute to a student's tendency to procrastinate in their studying. At the start of a course, many students engage in little or no studying, given that the first exam is some distance away. This is followed by a gradual increase in studying as the first exam approaches. The completion of the exam is again followed by little or no studying until the next exam approaches. Unfortunately, these postreinforcement pauses are often too long, with the result that many students obtain much poorer marks than they would have if they had studied at a steadier pace throughout. (Note, however, that studying for exams is not a pure example of an FI schedule because a certain amount of work must be accomplished during the interval to obtain the reinforcer of a good mark. On a pure FI schedule, any responding that happens during the interval is essentially irrelevant.)

1. On a fixed interval schedule, reinforcement is contingent upon the _____ response following a _____, pr_____ period of _____.

2. If I have just missed the bus when I get to the bus stop, I know that I have to wait 15 minutes for the next one to come along. Given that it is absolutely freezing out, I snuggle into my parka as best I can and grimly wait out the interval. Every once in a while, though, I emerge from my cocoon to take a quick glance down the street to see if the bus is coming. My behavior of looking for the bus is on a(n) _____ (use the abbreviation) schedule of reinforcement.

3. In the example in question 2, I will probably engage in (few/frequent) _____ glances at the start of the interval, followed by a gradually (increasing/decreasing) _____ rate of glancing as time passes.

4. Responding on an FI schedule is often characterized by a sc_____ pattern of responding consisting of a p_____ p_____ followed by a gradually (increasing/decreasing) _____ rate of behavior as the interval draws to a close.

5. On a pure FI schedule, any response that occurs (during/following) _____ the interval is irrelevant.

Variable Interval Schedules On a ***variable interval (VI) schedule***, reinforcement is contingent upon the first response after a varying, unpredictable period of time. For a rat on a variable interval 30-second (VI 30-sec) schedule, the first lever press after an *average* interval of 30 seconds will result in a food pellet, with the actual interval on any particular trial varying between,

reinforcement to response after random period of time

paycheck
Day 1
Day 2
random Day 40
Day 56

say, 1 and 60 seconds. Thus, the number of seconds that must pass before a lever press will produce a food pellet could be 8 seconds for the first food pellet, 55 seconds for the second pellet, 24 seconds for the third, and so on, the average of which is 30 seconds. Similarly, if each day you are waiting for a bus and have no idea when it will arrive, then looking down the street for the bus will be reinforced after a varying, unpredictable period of time—for example, 2 minutes the first day, 12 minutes the next day, 9 minutes the third day, and so on, with an average interval of, say, 10 minutes (VI 10-min).

VI schedules usually produce a moderate, steady rate of response, often with little or no postreinforcement pause (see Figure 7.1). By responding at a relatively steady rate throughout the interval, the rat on a VI 30-sec schedule will attain the reinforcer almost as soon as it becomes available. Similarly, if you need to contact your professor with a last minute question about an assignment and know that she always arrives in her office sometime between 8:00 p.m. and 8:30 a.m., a good strategy would be to phone every few minutes throughout that time period. By doing so, you will almost certainly contact her within a few minutes of her arrival.

Because VI schedules produce predictable response rates, as well as predictable rates of reinforcement, they are often used to investigate other aspects of operant conditioning, such as those involving matters of choice between alternative sources of reinforcement. You will encounter examples of this when we discuss choice behavior in Chapter 10.

QUICK QUIZ E

1. On a variable interval schedule, reinforcement is contingent upon the _____ response following a _____, un_____ period of _____.

2. You find that by frequently switching stations on your radio, you are able to hear your favorite song an average of once every 20 minutes. Your behavior of switching stations is thus being reinforced on a _____ schedule.

3. In general, variable interval schedules produce a (low/moderate/high) _____ and (steady/fluctuating) _____ rate of response with little or no _____.

Comparing the Four Basic Schedules The four basic schedules produce quite different patterns of behavior, which vary in both the rate of response and in the presence or absence of a postreinforcement pause. These characteristics are summarized in Table 7.1.

As can be seen, ratio schedules (FR and VR) produce higher rates of response than do interval schedules (FI and VI). This makes sense because the reinforcer in such schedules is entirely "response contingent"; that is, it depends entirely on the number of responses emitted. For this reason, a rat on a VR 100 schedule can double the number of food pellets earned in a 1-hour session by doubling its rate of lever pressing. Similarly, a door-to-door salesman can double the number of sales he makes during a day by

TABLE 7.1	Characteristic response rates and postreinforcement pauses for each of the four basic intermittent schedules. These are only general characteristics; they are not found under all circumstances. For example, an FR schedule with a very low response requirement, such as FR 2, is unlikely to produce a postreinforcement pause. By contrast, an FR schedule with a very high response requirement, such as FR 2000, may result in ratio strain and a complete cessation of responding.

	FR	VR	FI	VI
Response rate	High	High	Increasing	Moderate
Postreinforcement pause	Yes	No	Yes	No

doubling the number of customers he calls on (assuming that he continues to give an adequate sales pitch to each customer). Compare this to an interval schedule in which reinforcement is mostly time contingent. For example, on an FI 1-minute schedule, no more than 50 reinforcers can be earned in a 50-minute session. Under such circumstances, responding at a high rate throughout each interval does not pay off and is essentially a waste of energy. Instead, it makes more sense to respond in a way that will simply maximize the possibility of attaining the reinforcer soon after it becomes available. On an FI schedule, this means responding at a gradually increasing rate as the interval draws to a close; on a VI schedule, this means responding at a moderate, steady pace throughout the interval.

It can also be seen that fixed schedules (FR and FI) tend to produce postreinforcement pauses, whereas variable schedules (VR and VI) do not. On a variable schedule, there is often the possibility of a relatively immediate reinforcer, even if one has just attained a reinforcer, which tempts one to immediately resume responding. By comparison, on a fixed schedule, attaining one reinforcer means that the next reinforcer is necessarily some distance away. On an FR schedule, this results in a short postreinforcement pause before grinding out another set of responses; on an FI schedule, the postreinforcement pause is followed by a gradually increasing rate of response as the interval draws to a close and the reinforcer becomes imminent.

1. In general, (ratio/interval) _____ schedules tend to produce a high rate of response. This is because the reinforcer in such schedules is entirely r_____ contingent, meaning that the rapidity with which responses are emitted (does / does not) _____ greatly affect how soon the reinforcer is obtained.

2. On _____ schedules, the reinforcer is largely time contingent, meaning that the rapidity with which responses are emitted has (little/considerable) _____ effect on how quickly the reinforcer is obtained.

QUICK QUIZ F

3. In general, (variable/fixed) _____ schedules produce little or no postreinforcement pausing because such schedules often provide the possibility of relatively i_____ reinforcement, even if one has just obtained a reinforcer.

4. In general, _____ schedules produce postreinforcement pauses because obtaining one reinforcer means that the next reinforcer is necessarily quite (distant/close) _____.

Other Simple Schedules of Reinforcement

Duration Schedules On a duration schedule, reinforcement is contingent on performing a behavior continuously throughout a period of time. On a ***fixed duration (FD) schedule***, the behavior must be performed continuously for a fixed, predictable period of time. For example, the rat must run in the wheel for 60 seconds to earn one pellet of food (an FD 60-sec schedule). Likewise, Julie may decide that her son can watch television each evening only after he completes 2 hours of studying (an FD 2-hr schedule).

On a ***variable duration (VD) schedule***, the behavior must be performed continuously for a varying, unpredictable period of time. For example, the rat must run in the wheel for an average of 60 seconds to earn one pellet of food, with the required time varying between 1 second and 120 seconds on any particular trial (a VD 60-sec schedule). And Julie may decide to reinforce her son's studying with cookies and other treats at varying points in time that happen to average out to about one treat every 30 minutes (a VD 30-min schedule). (*Question: How do FD and VD schedules differ from FI and VI schedules?*)

Although duration schedules are sometimes useful in modifying certain human behaviors, such as studying, they are in some ways rather imprecise compared to the four basic schedules discussed earlier. With FR schedules, for example, one knows precisely what was done to achieve the reinforcer, namely, a certain number of responses. On an FD schedule, however, what constitutes "continuous performance of behavior" during the interval could vary widely. With respect to wheel running, for example, a "lazy" rat could dawdle along at barely a walk, while an "energetic" rat might rotate the wheel at a tremendous pace. Both would receive the reinforcer. Similarly, Julie's son might read only a few pages during his 2-hour study session or charge through several chapters; in either case, he would receive the reinforcer of being allowed to watch television. Remember too, from Chapter 6, how reinforcing the mere performance of an activity with no regard to level of performance can undermine a person's intrinsic interest in that activity. This danger obviously applies to duration schedules. One therefore needs to be cautious in their use.

Response–Rate Schedules As we have seen, different types of intermittent schedules produce different rates of response (i.e., they have different *schedule effects*). These different rates are essentially by-products of the schedule. However, in a *response-rate schedule*, reinforcement is directly contingent upon the organism's rate of response. Let's examine three types of response-rate schedules.

In *differential reinforcement of high rates (DRH)*, reinforcement is contingent upon emitting *at least* a certain number of responses in a certain period of time—or, more generally, reinforcement is provided for responding at a fast rate. The term *differential reinforcement* means simply that one type of response is reinforced while another is not. In a DRH schedule, reinforcement is provided for a high rate of response and not for a low rate. For example, a rat might receive a food pellet only if it emits at least 30 lever presses within a period of a minute. Similarly, a worker on an assembly line may be told that she can keep her job only if she assembles a minimum of 20 carburetors per hour. By requiring so many responses in a short period of time, DRH schedules ensure a high rate of responding. Athletic events such as running and swimming are prime examples of DRH schedules in that winning is directly contingent on a rapid series of responses.

In *differential reinforcement of low rates (DRL)*, a minimum amount of time must pass between each response before the reinforcer will be delivered—or, more generally, reinforcement is provided for responding at a slow rate. For example, a rat might receive a food pellet only if it waits at least 10 seconds between lever presses. So how is this different from an FI 10-sec schedule? Remember that on an FI schedule, responses that occur during the interval have no effect; on a DRL schedule, however, responses that occur during the interval do have an effect—an adverse effect in that they *prevent* reinforcement from occurring. In other words, responding during the interval must *not* occur in order for a response following the interval to produce a reinforcer.

Human examples of DRL schedules consist of situations in which a person is required to perform an action slowly. For example, a parent might praise a child for brushing her teeth slowly or completing her homework slowly, given that going too fast generally results in sloppy performance. Once the quality of performance improves, reinforcement can then be made contingent on responding at a normal speed.

In *differential reinforcement of paced responding (DRP)*, reinforcement is contingent upon emitting a series of responses at a set rate—or, more generally, reinforcement is provided for responding neither too fast nor too slow. For example, a rat might receive a food pellet if it emits 10 consecutive responses, with each response separated by an interval of no less than 1.5 and no more than 2.5 seconds. Similarly, musical activities, such as playing in a band or dancing to music, require that the relevant actions be performed at a specific pace. People who are very good at this are said to have a good sense of timing or rhythm. Further examples of DRP schedules can be found in noncompetitive swimming or running. People often perform these activities at a pace that is fast enough to ensure benefits to health and a feeling of well-being, yet not so fast as to result in exhaustion and possible injury. In fact, even competitive swimmers and runners, especially those who compete over long distances, will often set a specific pace throughout much of the race. Doing so ensures that they have sufficient energy at the end for a last-minute sprint (DRH) to the finish line, thereby maximizing their chances of clocking a good time.

1. On a (VD/VI) _____ schedule, reinforcement is contingent upon responding continuously for a varying period of time; on an (FI/FD) _____ schedule, reinforcement is contingent upon the first response after a fixed period of time.

2. As Tessa sits quietly, her mother occasionally gives her a hug as a reward. This is an example of a _____ _____ schedule.

3. In practicing the slow-motion form of exercise known as tai chi, Tung noticed that the more slowly he moved, the more thoroughly his muscles relaxed. This is an example of d_____ reinforcement of _____ _____ behavior (abbreviated _____).

4. On a video game, the faster you destroy all the targets, the more bonus points you obtain. This is an example of _____ reinforcement of _____ _____ behavior (abbreviated _____).

5. Frank discovers that his golf shots are much more accurate when he swings the club with a nice, even rhythm that is neither too fast nor too slow. This is an example of _____ reinforcement of _____ behavior (abbreviated _____).

Noncontingent Schedules On a ***noncontingent schedule of reinforcement***, the reinforcer is delivered *independently* of any response. In other words, a response is not required for the reinforcer to be obtained. Such schedules are also called *response-independent schedules*. There are two types of noncontingent schedules: fixed time and variable time.

On a ***fixed time (FT) schedule***, the reinforcer is delivered following a fixed, predictable period of time, regardless of the organism's behavior. For example, on a fixed time 30-second (FT 30-sec) schedule, a pigeon receives access to food every 30 seconds regardless of its behavior. Likewise, many people receive Christmas gifts each year, independently of whether they have been naughty or nice—an FT 1-year schedule. FT schedules therefore involve the delivery of a "free" reinforcer following a predictable period of time.

On a ***variable time (VT) schedule***, the reinforcer is delivered following a varying, unpredictable period of time, regardless of the organism's behavior. For example, on a variable time 30-second (VT 30-sec) schedule, a pigeon receives access to food after an average interval of 30 seconds, with the actual interval on any particular trial ranging from, say, 1 second to 60 seconds. Similarly, you may coincidentally run into an old high school chum about every 3 months on average (a VT 3-month schedule). VT schedules there-fore involve the delivery of a free reinforcer following an unpredictable period of time. (*Question: How do FT and VT schedules differ from FI and VI schedules?*)

1. On a non_____ schedule of reinforcement, a response is not required to obtain a reinforcer. Such a schedule is also called a response i_____ schedule of reinforcement.

2. Every morning at 7:00 a.m. a robin perches outside Marilyn's bedroom window and begins singing. Given that Marilyn very much enjoys the robin's song, this is an example of a _____ _____ 24-hour schedule of reinforcement (abbreviated _____).

3. For farmers, rainfall is an example of a noncontingent reinforcer that is typically delivered on a _____ _____ schedule (abbreviated _____).

Noncontingent reinforcement may account for some forms of superstitious behavior. In the first investigation of this possibility, Skinner (1948b) pre-sented pigeons with food every 15 seconds (FT 15-sec) regardless of their behavior. Although you might think that such free reinforcers would have lit-tle effect on the pigeons' behavior (other than encouraging them to stay close to the feeder), quite the opposite occurred. Six of the eight pigeons began to display ritualistic patterns of behavior. For example, one bird began turning counterclockwise circles, while another repeatedly thrust its head into an upper corner of the chamber. Two other pigeons displayed a swaying pendu-lum motion of the head and body. Skinner believed these behaviors developed because they had been accidentally reinforced by the coincidental presentation of food. For example, if a pigeon just happened to turn a counterclockwise circle before food delivery, that behavior would be accidentally reinforced and increase in frequency. This would increase the likelihood of the same behavior occurring the next time food was delivered, which would further strengthen it. The eventual result would be a well-established pattern of turn-ing circles, as though turning circles somehow caused the food to appear.

Some researchers have argued that Skinner's evidence for superstitious behavior in the pigeon may not be as clear-cut as he believed. They claim that at least some of the ritualistic behaviors he observed may have consisted of innate tendencies, almost like fidgeting behaviors, that are often elicited during a period of waiting (Staddon & Simmelhag, 1971). These tendencies, which are discussed in Chapter 12, are known as *adjunctive behaviors.* Never-theless, other experiments have replicated the effect of noncontingent rein-forcement on the development of superstitious behavior. Ono (1987), for example, placed students in a booth that contained three levers and a counter. The students were told that "if you do something, you may get points on the counter" (p. 263). They were also told to get as many points as possible. In reality, the points were delivered on either an FT or VT schedule, so the students' behavior actually had no effect on point delivery. Nevertheless, most students developed at least temporary patterns of superstitious lever pulling; that is, they pulled the lever as though it were effective in producing points. Interestingly, one student started with lever pulling but then coincidentally received a point after simply touching the counter. This led to a superstitious pattern of climbing on the counter and touching different parts of the apparatus, apparently in the belief that this action produced the points. She then jumped off the apparatus at just the time that she received another point, which led to a superstitious pattern of repeatedly jumping in the air and touching the ceiling! After several minutes of this, she finally quit, apparently as a result of fatigue.

Professional athletes and gamblers are particularly prone to the development of superstitions, some of which may evolve in the manner that Skinner suggests. Under constant threat of losing their position to an eager newcomer, professional athletes are constantly on the lookout for anything that might enhance their performance. As a result, unusual events that precede a fine performance, such as humming a certain tune or wearing an unusual article of clothing, may be quickly identified and then deliberately reproduced in the hopes of reproducing that performance. Gamblers display even stronger tendencies toward the development of superstitions, probably because the activity in which they are engaged is even more uncertain in its outcome. Bingo players, for example, commonly carry lucky pendants, stuffed animals, or pieces of jewelry to each game, and they are often adamant (almost pathologically so) about obtaining cards that contain certain patterns or are drawn from the top or bottom of the stack. Many of these rituals probably evolved because they were at one time associated with a big win.

Herrnstein (1966) noted that superstitious behaviors can sometimes develop as by-products of contingent reinforcement for some other behavior. For example, a businessman might believe it is important to impress customers with a firm handshake—when in fact it is merely the handshake, and not the firmness of the handshake, that is the critical factor. (Unfortunately, such a superstition could have serious consequences if the businessman then attempts to branch out into the Asian market, where a firm handshake is often regarded as a sign of disrespect.) Similarly, some managers might come to believe that "pushing the panic button" is an effective way to deal with crises, simply because it is usually followed by a successful outcome. What they fail to realize is that a low-key approach might have been equally if not more effective—and certainly a lot less stressful.

Question: Although Skinner's (1948b) original demonstration of superstitious behavior involved the use of a fixed time schedule, you might wish to consider whether superstitious behavior in humans is more likely to develop under a fixed or variable time schedule. To answer this, think about the types of situations in which you are particularly likely to find superstitious behavior in humans. Is it in situations that involve predictable events or unpredictable events? Obviously, it is unpredictable events, such as games of chance, performance in sports, fishing ("Jana's lucky lure"), and so forth. In this sense, at least from a human perspective, superstitious behavior can be seen as an attempt to make an unpredictable situation more predictable.

1. When noncontingent reinforcement happens to follow a particular behavior, that behavior may (increase/decrease) _____ in strength. Such behavior is referred to as s_____ behavior.

2. Herrnstein (1966) noted that superstitious behaviors can sometimes develop as a by-product of c_____ reinforcement for some other behavior.

3. As shown by the kinds of situations in which superstitious behaviors develop in humans, such behaviors seem most likely to develop on a(n) (VT/FT) _____ schedule of reinforcement.

What happens if a noncontingent schedule of reinforcement is superimposed on a regular, contingent schedule of reinforcement? What if, for example, a pigeon responding on a VI schedule of food reinforcement also receives extra reinforcers for free? Will the pigeon's rate of response on the VI schedule increase or decrease? In fact, the pigeon's rate of response on the response-dependent schedule will decrease (Rachlin & Baum, 1972). Just as people on welfare sometimes become less inclined to look for work, the pigeon that receives free reinforcers will work less vigorously for the contingent reinforcers. Suggestive evidence of this effect can also be found among professional athletes. One study, conducted several years ago, found that major league pitchers who had signed long-term contracts showed a significant decline in number of innings pitched relative to pitchers who only signed a 1-year contract (O'Brien, Figlerski, Howard, & Caggiano, 1981) (see Figure 7.2). Insofar as a long-term contract or a guaranteed purse (as in boxing) virtually guarantees a hefty salary regardless of performance, these results suggest that athletic performance might suffer when the money earned is no longer contingent on performance. (*Question: Can you think of alternative explanations for this finding?*)

At this point, you might be thinking that noncontingent reinforcement is all bad, given that it leads to superstitious behavior in some situations and to poor performance in others. In fact, noncontingent reinforcement is sometimes quite beneficial. More specifically, it can be an effective means of reducing the frequency of maladaptive behaviors. For example, children who act out often do so to obtain attention. If, however, they are given a sufficient amount of attention on a noncontingent basis, they will no longer have to act out to obtain it. Noncontingent reinforcement has even been shown to reduce the frequency of self-injurious behavior. Such behavior, which can consist of head-banging or biting chunks of flesh out of one's arm, is sometimes displayed by people who suffer from retardation or autism; it can be notoriously difficult to treat. In many cases, the behavior appears to be maintained by the attention it elicits from caretakers. Research has shown,

FIGURE 7.2 Average number of innings pitched by major league pitchers in the years before and after signing long-term contracts. (*Source:* Coon, 1998. Data from O'Brien et al., 1981.)

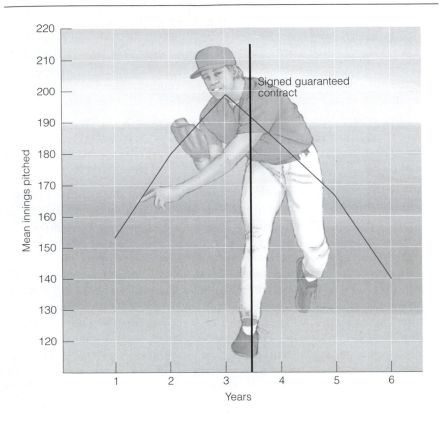

however, that if the caretakers provide the individual with plenty of attention on a noncontingent basis, then the frequency of their self-injurious behavior may be greatly reduced (e.g., Hagopian, Fisher, & Legacy, 1994). In a sense, such individuals no longer have to injure themselves to receive attention because they are now receiving lots of attention for free.

Interestingly, the beneficial effects of noncontingent reinforcement can be seen as providing empirical support for the value of what Carl Rogers (1959), the famous humanistic psychologist, called "unconditional positive regard." Unconditional positive regard refers to the love, respect, and acceptance that one receives from significant others, regardless of one's behavior. Rogers assumed that such regard is a necessary precondition for the development of a healthy personality. From a behavioral perspective, unconditional positive regard can be viewed as a form of noncontingent social reinforcement, which can indeed have beneficial effects. In fact, it seems likely that proper child rearing requires healthy doses of both noncontingent reinforcement, which gives the child a secure base from which to explore the world and take risks, and contingent reinforcement, which helps to shape the child's behavior in appropriate ways, maximize skill development, and prevent the development of passivity. Thus, Abraham Maslow (1971), another famous humanistic psychologist, argued that child rearing should be neither too restrictive nor too lenient, which in behavioral terms can be taken to imply that the social reinforcement children receive should be neither excessively contingent nor excessively noncontingent.

1. During the time that a rat is responding for food on a VR 100 schedule, we begin delivering additional food on a VT 60-second schedule. As a result, the rate of response on the VR schedule is likely to (increase/decrease/remain unchanged) _____.

2. In many mixed martial arts matches, each fighter typically receives a guaranteed purse, regardless of the outcome. In the Ultimate Fighter series, the winner of the final match is awarded a major contract in the UFC while the loser receives nothing. As a result, Dana is not surprised when he notices fighters in the latter event (more/less) _____ often fighting to the point of complete exhaustion, since the monetary reinforcer tied to the match is (contingent / not contingent) _____ upon winning the match.

3. A child who is often hugged during the course of the day, regardless of what he is doing, is in humanistic terms receiving unconditional positive regard. In behavioral terms, he is receiving a form of non_____ social reinforcement. As a result, this child may be (more/less) _____ likely to act out in order to receive attention.

Complex Schedules of Reinforcement

[handwritten: Combination of 2 or more simple schedules of reinforcement]

All of the schedules previously described are relatively simple in that there is only one basic requirement. On the other hand, a ***complex schedule*** consists of a combination of two or more simple schedules. There are a wide variety of such schedules, three of which are described here. Two other types of complex schedules—multiple schedules *and* concurrent schedules—are discussed in later chapters.

Conjunctive Schedules A ***conjunctive schedule*** is a type of complex schedule in which the requirements of two or more simple schedules must be met before a reinforcer is delivered. For example, on a conjunctive FI 2-minute FR 100 schedule, reinforcement is contingent upon completing 100 lever presses and completing at least one lever press following a 2-minute interval.

[handwritten: 2 or more schedules need to happen before reinforcement]

Many of the contingencies that we encounter in everyday life are examples of conjunctive schedules. The wages you earn on a job are contingent upon working a certain number of hours each week *and* doing a sufficient amount of work so that you will not be fired. Likewise, Jon's fiancée might have chosen to marry him because he is kind *and* humorous *and* interesting *and* drives a Porsche. With any one of these components missing, he would not have received the reinforcer of being engaged to her.

Adjusting Schedules   In an *adjusting schedule*, the response requirement changes as a function of the organism's performance while responding for the previous reinforcer. For example, on an FR 100 schedule, if the rat completes all 100 responses within a 5-minute interval, we may then increase the requirement to 110 responses (FR 110). In other words, because it has performed so well, we expect even better performance in the future.

In a similar fashion, when Seema displayed excellent ability in mastering her violin lessons, she and her parents decided to increase the amount she had to learn each week. And when Lily's high school students performed poorly on their exams, she gradually decreased the amount of material they had to learn each week. (It is, of course, in this manner that standards in school become gradually lowered, often to the detriment of the students.)

Note that the process of shaping also involves an adjusting schedule insofar as the criterion for reinforcement is raised depending on the animal's performance. As soon as the rat has learned to stand near the lever to get food, one raises the criterion to touching the lever, placing a paw on the lever, and so forth. The requirement for reinforcement changes as soon as the rat has successfully met the previous requirement.

QUICK QUIZ K

1. A complex schedule is one that consists of _____.

2. In a(n) _____ schedule, the response requirement changes as a function of the organism's performance while responding for the previous reinforcer, while in a(n) _____ schedule, the requirements of two or more simple schedules must be met before the reinforcer is delivered.

3. To the extent that a gymnast is trying to improve his performance, he is likely on a(n) _____ schedule of reinforcement; to the extent that his performance is judged according to both the form and quickness of his moves, he is on a(n) _____ schedule.

Chained Schedules   A *chained schedule* consists of a sequence of two or more simple schedules, each of which has its own S^D and the last of which results in a terminal reinforcer. In other words, the person or animal must work through a series of component schedules to obtain the sought-after reinforcer. A chained schedule differs from a conjunctive schedule in that the two component schedules must be completed in a particular order, which is not required in a conjunctive schedule.

As an example of a chained schedule, a pigeon in a standard operant conditioning chamber is presented with a VR 20 schedule on a green key, followed by an FI 10-sec schedule on a red key, which then leads to the terminal reinforcer of food. Thus, an average of 20 responses on the green key will result in a change in key color to red, following which the first response on the red key after a 10-second interval will be reinforced by food. The food is the terminal reinforcer that supports the entire chain. This chain can be diagrammed as follows:

$$\text{VR 20} \qquad\qquad \text{FI 10-sec}$$
$$\textbf{Green key: } \textit{Peck} \rightarrow \textbf{Red key: } \textit{Peck} \rightarrow \textbf{Food}$$
$$\text{S}^\text{D} \qquad \text{R} \qquad \text{S}^\text{R}/\text{S}^\text{D} \qquad \text{R} \qquad \text{S}^\text{R}$$

Note that the presentation of the red key is both a secondary reinforcer for completing the preceding VR 20 schedule and an S^D for responding on the subsequent FI 10-sec schedule. Note, too, that this is an example of a *two-link chain*, with the VR 20 schedule constituting the first, or initial, link and the FI 10-sec schedule constituting the second, or terminal, link. By adding yet another schedule to the start of the chain, we can create a three-link chain, for example:

$$\text{VI 30-sec} \qquad\qquad \text{VR 20} \qquad\qquad \text{FI 10-sec}$$
$$\textbf{White key: } \textit{Peck} \rightarrow \textbf{Green key: } \textit{Peck} \rightarrow \textbf{Red key: } \textit{Peck} \rightarrow \textbf{Food}$$
$$\text{S}^\text{D} \qquad \text{R} \qquad \text{S}^\text{R}/\text{S}^\text{D} \qquad \text{R} \qquad \text{S}^\text{R}/\text{S}^\text{D} \qquad \text{R} \qquad \text{S}^\text{R}$$

In this case, both the green and red keys function as secondary reinforcers that help maintain behavior throughout the chain.

1. A chained schedule consists of a sequence of two or more simple schedules, each of which has its own _____ and the last of which results in a t_____ r_____.

2. Within a chain, completion of each of the early links ends in a(n) s_____ reinforcer, which also functions as the _____ for the next link of the chain.

Once pigeons learn which schedule is associated with which key, they generally show the appropriate response patterns for those schedules. In the preceding example, this would be a moderate, steady rate of response on the white key, a high rate of response on the green key, and a scalloped pattern of responding on the red key. Nevertheless, responding tends to be somewhat weaker in the earlier links of a chain than in the later links. This can be seen most clearly when each link consists of the same schedule. For example, Kelleher and Fry (1962) presented pigeons with a three-link chained schedule with each link consisting of an FI 60-sec schedule:

$$\text{FI 60-sec} \qquad\qquad \text{FI 60-sec} \qquad \text{FI 60-sec}$$
$$\textbf{White key: } \textit{Peck} \rightarrow \textbf{Green key: } \textit{Peck} \rightarrow \textbf{Red key: } \textit{Peck} \rightarrow \textbf{Food}$$
$$\text{S}^\text{D} \qquad \text{R} \qquad \text{S}^\text{R}/\text{S}^\text{D} \qquad \text{R} \qquad \text{S}^\text{R}/\text{S}^\text{D} \qquad \text{R} \qquad \text{S}^\text{R}$$

The pigeons displayed very long pauses and a slow rate of response on the white key compared to the other two keys. The greatest amount of responding occurred on the red key.

Why would the earlier links of the chain be associated with weaker responding? One way of looking at it is that in the later links, the terminal reinforcer is more immediate and hence more influential; while in the early links, the terminal reinforcer is more distant and hence less influential (remember that delayed reinforcement is less effective than immediate reinforcement). Another way of looking at it is that the secondary reinforcers supporting behavior in the early links are less directly associated with food and are therefore relatively weak (e.g., the green key is associated with food only indirectly through its association with the red key). From this perspective, a chained schedule can be seen as the operant equivalent of higher-order classical conditioning—in which, for example, a tone (CS_1) associated with food (US) elicits less salivation than the food does, and a light (CS_2) associated with the tone elicits less salivation than the tone does. Similarly, in the example of the chained schedule, the red key associated with the food is a less powerful reinforcer than the food, and the green key associated with the red key is a less powerful reinforcer than the red key. (If you find that you can no longer remember the concept of higher-order classical conditioning, you should go back and review it.)

The difference in response strength between the early and later links in a chain is representative of a more general behavioral principle known as the goal gradient effect. The *goal gradient effect* is an increase in the strength and/or efficiency of responding as one draws near to the goal. For example, rats running through a maze to obtain food tend to run faster and make fewer wrong turns as they near the goal box (Hull, 1932). Similarly, a student writing an essay is likely to take shorter breaks and work more intensely as she nears the end. Dolphin trainers are well aware of the goal gradient effect. Dolphins who are trained to perform long chains of behaviors have a tendency to drift toward "sloppy" performance during the early parts of the chain, and trainers have to be vigilant to ensure that the dolphin's behavior is not reinforced when this occurs (Pryor, 1975). (Perhaps the most profound example of a goal gradient, however, is that shown by people who desperately need to urinate and become speed demons as they near the washroom.)

An efficient way to establish responding on a chained schedule is to train the final link first and the initial link last, a process known as *backward chaining*. Using the pigeon example, the pigeon would first be trained to respond on the red key to obtain food. This will establish the red key as a secondary reinforcer through its association with food. As a result, the presentation of the red key can then be used to reinforce responding on the green key. Once this is established, the presentation of the green key can be used to reinforce responding on the white key.

In these examples, each link in the chain required the same type of behavior; namely, key pecking. It is also possible to create behavior chains in which each link consists of a different behavior.[1] For example, a rat might

---

[1]Behavior chains that require the same type of response in each link are called *homogeneous chains*; behavior chains that require a different type of response in each link are called *heterogeneous chains*.

have to climb over a barrier and then run through a tunnel to obtain food. This can be diagrammed as follows:

Barrier: *Climb over barrier* → **Tunnel:** *Run through tunnel* → **Food**
S^D · · · · · · · R · · · · · · · · S^R/S^D · · · · · · · R · · · · · · · S^R

Note that the sight of the tunnel is both a secondary reinforcer for climbing over the barrier and a discriminative stimulus for then running through the tunnel.

As with the previous examples, backward chaining would be the best way to train this sequence of behaviors. Thus, the rat would first be trained to run through the tunnel for food. Once this is established, it would be taught to climb over the barrier to get to the tunnel, with the sight of the tunnel acting as a secondary reinforcer for this action. In this manner, very long chains of behavior can be established. In one reported example, a rat was trained to go up a ladder, cross a platform, climb a rope, cross a bridge, get into a little elevator box, release the pulley holding the box, lower the box "paw over paw" to the floor, and then press a button to obtain the food (Pryor, 1975). Of course, each of these behaviors also had to be shaped (through reinforcement of successive approximations to the target behavior). Shaping and chaining are thus the basic means by which circus and marine animals are trained to perform some remarkable feats (see Figure 7.3).

Most human endeavors involve response chains, some of which are very long. The act of reading this chapter, for example, consists of reading section after section, until the terminal reinforcer of completing the entire chapter has been attained. Completing each section serves as both a secondary reinforcer for having read that section as well as an S^D for reading the next section. Reading the chapter is in turn part of a much larger chain of behaviors that includes attending lectures, taking notes, and studying—the terminal reinforcer for which is passing the course. Fortunately, backward chaining

FIGURE 7.3 Through shaping and chaining, animals can be taught to display some remarkable behaviors.

© FogStock LLC/Newscom

© Keystone/Hulton Archive/Getty Images

is not required for the development of such chains, because language enables us to describe to one another the required sequence of behaviors (as is done by providing a course syllabus). In other words, for humans, response chains are often established through instructions.

Unfortunately, in the case of very long chains, such as completing a course, the terminal reinforcer is often extremely distant, with the result that behavior is easily disrupted during the early part of the chain (remember the goal gradient principle). This is yet another reason for why it is much easier to be a diligent student the night before the midterm than during the first week of the semester. Can anything be done to alleviate this problem? One possibility is to make the completion of each link in the chain more salient (i.e., more noticeable), thereby enhancing its value as a secondary reinforcer. Novelists, for example, need to write hundreds, or even thousands, of pages before the terminal reinforcer of a completed book is attained. To keep themselves on track, some novelists keep detailed records of their progress, such as charting the number of words written each day as well as the exact dates on which chapters were started and completed (Wallace & Pear, 1977). These records outline their achievements, thereby providing a much-needed source of secondary reinforcement throughout the process. Similarly, students sometimes keep detailed records of the number of hours studied or pages read. They might also compile a "to do" list of assignments and then cross off each item as it is completed. Crossing off an item provides a clear record that a task has been accomplished and also functions as a secondary reinforcer that helps motivate us (Lakein, 1973).

QUICK QUIZ M

1. Responding tends to be weaker in the (earlier/later) _____ links of a chain. This is an example of the g_____ g _____ effect in which the strength and/or efficiency of responding (increases/decreases) _____ as the organism approaches the goal.

2. An efficient way to train a complex chain, especially in animals, is through b_____ chaining, in which the (first/last) _____ link of the chain is trained first. However, this type of procedure usually is not required with verbally proficient humans, with whom behavior chains can be quickly established through the use of i_____.

3. One suggestion for enhancing our behavior in the early part of a long response chain is to make the completion of each link more s_____, thereby enhancing its value as a s_____ reinforcer.

Theories of Reinforcement

In this section, we briefly discuss some major theories of reinforcement. We begin with Clark Hull's early drive reduction view of reinforcement. This is followed by a brief description of a highly influential approach known as the Premack principle. This principle is of immense practical importance, and it has helped revolutionize the manner in which the process of reinforcement is now conceptualized. In fact, the two other theoretical approaches that we discuss—the response deprivation hypothesis and the bliss point approach—can be viewed as direct outgrowths of the Premack principle.

Drive Reduction Theory

An early approach to understanding reinforcement, and one that was strongly championed by Hull (1943), is drive reduction theory. In *drive reduction theory*, an event is reinforcing to the extent that it is associated with a reduction in some type of physiological drive. Thus, food deprivation produces a "hunger drive," which then propels the animal to seek out food. When food is obtained, the hunger drive is reduced. At the same time, the behavior that preceded this drive reduction, and led to the food, is automatically strengthened. In very simple terms (in actuality, the theory is more complex than this), if a hungry rat in a maze turns left just before it finds food in the goal box, the act of turning left in the maze will be automatically strengthened by the subsequent reduction in hunger.

We touched upon this theory in Chapter 6 when we noted that primary reinforcers are often those events that seem to reduce a physiological need. From this perspective, secondary reinforcers are events that have become reinforcers because they have been associated with a primary reinforcer and, hence, with some type of drive reduction. Thus, a person enjoys collecting cookbooks because cooking is associated with eating food, which in turn has been associated with a reduction in hunger. According to Hull, all reinforcers are associated, either directly or indirectly, with some type of drive reduction.

In Chapter 6, we also noted that a major problem with this physiological view of reinforcement is that some reinforcers do not seem to be associated with any type of drive reduction. A rat will press a lever to obtain access to a running wheel, a chimpanzee will press a button so that it can obtain a peek into another room, and teenagers will spend considerable amounts of money to be exposed to earsplitting, and potentially damaging, levels of rock music. It is difficult to see how such events are associated with a reduction in some type of physiological need. Instead, it seems as though the motivation for such behavior exists more in the reinforcing stimulus than in some type of internal state.

Motivation that is derived from some property of the reinforcer, as opposed to an internal drive state, is referred to as *incentive motivation*. Playing a video game for the fun of it, attending a concert because you enjoy the music, and working to earn enough money to buy a Porsche are examples of behaviors that are motivated by incentives. Even events that seem to be clearly associated with drive reduction can be strongly affected by incentive factors. For example, going to a restaurant for a meal might be largely driven by hunger; however, the fact that you prefer a restaurant that serves hot, spicy food is an example of incentive motivation. The spiciness of the food plays no role in the reduction of hunger; it is simply a form of sensory stimulation that you find highly reinforcing.

In conclusion, most theorists no longer believe that drive reduction theory can offer a comprehensive account of reinforcement, and this approach has now been largely abandoned. Some recent approaches have instead emphasized observable behavior patterns as opposed to hypothetical internal processes in their explanation of the reinforcement process. A major step in this direction was the Premack principle.

QUICK QUIZ N

1. According to drive reduction theory, an event is reinforcing if it is associated with a reduction in some type of p_____ drive.

2. According to this theory, a s_____ reinforcer is one that has been associated with a p_____ reinforcer.

3. A major problem with drive reduction theory is that _____ _____.

4. The motivation that is derived from some property of the reinforcer is called _____ motivation.

5. Research has shown that hungry rats will perform more effectively in a T-maze when the reinforcer for a correct response (right turn versus left turn) consists of several small pellets as opposed to one large pellet (Capaldi, Miller, & Alptekin, 1989). Chickens will also run faster down a runway to obtain a popcorn kernel presented in four pieces than in one whole piece (Wolfe & Kaplon, 1941). The fact that several small bites of food is a more effective reinforcer than one large bite is consistent with the notion of (drive reduction / incentive motivation) _____.

The Premack Principle

Remember how we earlier noted that Skinner defined reinforcers (and punishers) by their effect on behavior? This unfortunately presents us with a problem. In the real world, it would be nice to know ahead of time whether a certain event can function as a reinforcer. One way to do this, of course, would be to take something the person or animal seems to like and use that as a reinforcer. But it is not always easy to determine what a person or animal likes. Moreover, events that we might believe should be liked might not actually function as reinforcers. To a 5-year-old boy, a kiss from his mother is great if he needs comforting, but not when he is trying to show off to his friends. Fortunately, the Premack principle provides a more objective way to determine whether something can be used as a reinforcer (Premack, 1965).

The Premack principle is based on the notion that reinforcers can often be viewed as behaviors rather than stimuli. For example, rather than saying that lever pressing was reinforced by *food* (a stimulus), we could say that lever pressing was reinforced by the act of *eating food* (a behavior). Similarly, rather than saying that playing appropriately was reinforced by *television*, we could instead say that it was reinforced by *watching television*. When we

LPB = HPB

Chores → Watching TV   Eating Veges → Get desert

view reinforcers in this manner—as behaviors rather than stimuli—then the process of reinforcement can be conceptualized as a sequence of two behaviors: (1) the behavior that is being reinforced, followed by (2) the behavior that is the reinforcer. Moreover, according to Premack, by comparing the frequency of various behaviors, we can determine whether one can be used as a reinforcer for the other.

More specifically, the **Premack principle** states that a high-probability behavior can be used to reinforce a low-probability behavior. For example, when a rat is hungry, eating food has a higher likelihood of occurrence than running in a wheel. This means that eating food, which the high-probability behavior (HPB), can be used to reinforce the target behavior of running in a wheel, which is the low-probability behavior (LPB). In other words, the rat will run in the wheel to obtain access to the food:

Target behavior   **Consequence**
Running in a wheel **(LPB)** → **Eating food (HPB)**
     R S^R

On the other hand, if the rat is not hungry, then eating food is less likely to occur than running in a wheel. In this case, running in a wheel can be used as a reinforcer for the target behavior of eating food. In other words, the rat will eat to obtain access to the wheel.

Target behavior   **Consequence**
Eating food **(LPB)** → **Running in a wheel (HPB)**
     R S^R

By focusing on the relative probabilities (or relative frequencies) of behaviors, the Premack principle allows us to quickly identify potential reinforcers in the real world. If Kaily spends only a few minutes each morning doing chores, but at least an hour reading comic books, then the opportunity to read comic books (a higher-probability behavior) can be used to reinforce doing chores (a lower-probability behavior).

Do chores → **Read comic books**
    R S^R

In fact, if you want an easy way to remember the Premack principle, just think of Grandma's rule: First you work (a low-probability behavior), then you play (a high-probability behavior).

The Premack principle has proven to be very useful in applied settings. For example, a person with autism who spends many hours each day rocking back and forth might be very unresponsive to consequences that are normally reinforcing for others, such as receiving praise. The Premack principle, however, suggests that the opportunity to rock back and forth can be used as an effective reinforcer for another behavior that we might wish to strengthen, such as interacting with others. Thus, the Premack principle is a handy principle to keep in mind when confronted by a situation in which normal reinforcers seem to have little effect.

1. The Premack principle holds that reinforcers can often be viewed as _____ rather than stimuli. For example, rather than saying that the rat's lever pressing was reinforced with food, we could say that it was reinforced with _____ food.

2. The Premack principle states that a _____ _____ behavior can be used as a reinforcer for a _____ _____ behavior.

3. According to the Premack principle, if you crack your knuckles 3 times per hour and burp 20 times per hour, then the opportunity to _____ can probably be used as a reinforcer for _____.

4. If you drink five soda pops each day and only one glass of orange juice, then the opportunity to drink _____ can likely be used as a reinforcer for drinking _____.

5. If "*Chew bubble gum* → Play video games" is a diagram of a reinforcement procedure based on the Premack principle, then chewing bubble gum must be a (lower/higher) _____ probability behavior than playing video games.

6. What is Grandma's rule, and how does it relate to the Premack principle?

Response Deprivation Hypothesis

The Premack principle requires us to know the relative probabilities of two behaviors before we can judge whether one will be an effective reinforcer for the other. But what if we have information on only one behavior? Is there any way that we can tell whether that behavior can function as a reinforcer before actually trying it out?

The *response deprivation hypothesis* states that a behavior can serve as a reinforcer when: (1) access to the behavior is restricted and (2) its frequency thereby falls below its preferred level of occurrence (Timberlake & Allison, 1974). The preferred level of an activity is its baseline level of occurrence when the animal can freely engage in that activity. For example, imagine that a rat typically runs for 1 hour a day whenever it has free access to a running wheel. This 1 hour per day is the rat's preferred level of running. If the rat is then allowed free access to the wheel for only 15 minutes per day, it will be unable to reach this preferred level and will be in a state of deprivation with regard to running. According to the response deprivation hypothesis, the rat will now be willing to work (e.g., press a lever) to obtain additional time on the wheel.

Lever press → **Running in a wheel**
     R   S^R

The response deprivation approach also provides a general explanation for why contingencies of reinforcement are effective. Contingencies of reinforcement are effective to the extent that they create a condition in which the organism is confronted with the possibility of a certain response falling below its baseline level. Take Kaily, who enjoys reading comic books each day. If we establish a contingency in which she has to do her chores before reading comic books, her baseline level of free comic book reading will drop to zero. She will therefore be willing to do chores to maintain her preferred level of comic book time.

Do chores → **Read comic books**
    R S^R

You will notice that the diagram given here is the same as that given for the Premack principle, and in fact both approaches will often lead to the same type of contingency being established. But the interpretation of why it works is different. In this case, reading comic books is a reinforcer simply because the contingency threatens to push free comic book reading to below its preferred rate of occurrence. The relative probabilities of the two behaviors are irrelevant, meaning that it does not matter if the probability of reading comic books at the outset is higher or lower than the probability of doing chores. Even if Kaily is a workaholic who spends much of her time doing chores anyway, we could get her to do yet more chores by threatening to reduce her comic book time. The only thing that matters is whether comic book reading is in danger of falling below its preferred level if the contingency is not met. Thus, the response deprivation hypothesis is applicable to a wider range of conditions than the Premack principle. (Question 4 in the Quick Quiz will help clarify this.)

To help distinguish between the Premack principle and the response deprivation hypothesis, ask yourself whether the main point seems to be the frequency of one behavior relative to another (in which case the Premack principle is applicable) or the frequency of one behavior relative to its baseline (in which case the response deprivation hypothesis is applicable).

QUICK QUIZ P

1. According to the response deprivation hypothesis, a response can serve as a reinforcer if free access to the response is (provided/restricted) _____ and its frequency then falls (above/below) _____ its baseline level of occurrence.

2. If a child normally watches 4 hours of television per night, we can make television watching a reinforcer if we restrict free access to the television to (more/less) _____ than 4 hours per night.

3. The response deprivation hypothesis differs from the Premack principle in that we need only know the baseline frequency of the (reinforced/reinforcing) _____ behavior.

4. Kaily typically watches television for 4 hours per day and reads comic books for 1 hour per day. You then set up a contingency whereby Kaily must watch 4.5 hours of television each day in order to have access to her comic books. According to the Premack principle, this will likely be an (effective/ineffective) _____ contingency. According to the response deprivation hypothesis, this would be an (effective/ineffective) _____ contingency.

Behavioral Bliss Point Approach

The response deprivation hypothesis assumes there is an optimal level of behavior that an organism strives to maintain. This same assumption can be made for the manner in which an organism distributes its behavior between two or more activities. According to the ***behavioral bliss point approach,*** an organism with free access to alternative activities will distribute its behavior in such a way as to maximize overall reinforcement (Allison, 1983). For example, a rat that can freely choose between running in a wheel and exploring a maze might spend 1 hour per day running in the wheel and 2 hours exploring the maze. This distribution of behavior represents the optimal reinforcement available from those two activities—that is, the *behavioral bliss point*—for that particular rat.

Note that this optimal distribution of behavior is based on the notion that each activity is freely available. When activities are not freely available—as when the two activities are intertwined in a contingency of reinforcement—then the optimal distribution may become unattainable. Imagine, for example, that a contingency is created in which the rat now has to run in the wheel for 60 seconds to obtain 30 seconds of access to the maze:

$$\textit{Wheel running} \textbf{ (60 seconds)} \rightarrow \textbf{Maze exploration (30 seconds)}$$
$$\textbf{R} \qquad\qquad\qquad\qquad\qquad \textbf{S}^{\textbf{R}}$$

It will now be impossible for the rat to reach its behavioral bliss point for these two activities. When they are freely available, the rat prefers twice as much maze exploration (2 hours) as wheel running (1 hour). But our contingency forces the rat to engage in twice as much wheel running as maze exploration. To obtain the preferred 2 hours of maze exploration, the rat would have to engage in 4 hours of running, which is far beyond its preferred level for that activity. Thus, it will be impossible for the rat to attain its behavioral bliss point for those activities.

A reasonable assumption as to what will happen in such circumstances is that the rat will compromise by distributing its activities in such a way as to draw as near as possible to its behavioral bliss point. For instance, it might choose to run a total of 2 hours per day to obtain 1 hour of maze exploration. This is not as enjoyable as the preferred distribution of 1 hour of running and 2 hours of maze exploration; but, given the contingencies, it will have to do. Likewise, most of us are forced to spend several more hours working and several fewer hours enjoying the finer things in life than we would if we were independently wealthy and could freely do whatever we want. The behavioral bliss point for our varied activities is essentially unattainable. Instead, faced with certain contingencies that must be met in order to survive, we distribute our activities in such a way as to draw as near to the bliss point as possible.

The behavioral bliss point approach assumes that organisms attempt to distribute their behavior so as to maximize overall reinforcement. This, of course, is a very rational way to behave. In Chapter 10, you will encounter an alternative theory, known as melioration theory, which maintains that organisms, including people, are not that rational and that various processes often entice the organism away from maximization. Note, too, that none of the theories discussed in this chapter take account of an animal's innate tendencies toward certain patterns of behavior, which may affect how easily certain behaviors can be trained. In Chapter 11, you will encounter a theory that does take account of such tendencies.

1. According to the behavioral _____ _____ approach, an organism that (is forced to / can freely) _____ engage in alternative activities will distribute its behavior in such a way as to (optimize/balance) _____ the available reinforcement.

2. Contingencies of reinforcement often (disrupt/enhance) _____ the distribution of behavior such that it is (easy/impossible) _____ to obtain the optimal amount of reinforcement.

3. Given this state of affairs, how is the organism likely to distribute its activities?

ADVICE FOR THE LOVELORN

Dear Dr. Dee,

I recently began dating a classmate. We get along really well at school, so it seemed like we would be a perfect match. Unfortunately, once we started dating, our relationship seemed to lose a lot of its energy, and our lives seemed a lot less satisfying. Someone suggested that we must each have an unconscious fear of commitment. What do you think?

Less Than Blissful

Dear Less,

I suppose it is possible that you have an unconscious fear of commitment—if there is such a thing as an unconscious fear of commitment. On the other hand, it may be that the amount of time you spend interacting with one another at school is actually the optimal amount of time, given the various reinforcers available in your relationship. Spending additional time together (which also means spending less time on alternative activities) has, for each of you, resulted in a distribution of behavior that is further removed from your behavioral bliss point. Obviously, a good relationship should move you toward your bliss point, not away from it. Try being just friends-at-school again, and see if that restores some of the satisfaction in your relationship.

Behaviorally yours,

Dr. Dee

SUMMARY

A schedule of reinforcement is the response requirement that must be met to obtain a reinforcer. Different types of schedules produce different patterns of responding, which are known as schedule effects.

In a continuous schedule of reinforcement, each response is reinforced. In an intermittent schedule of reinforcement, only some responses are reinforced. There are four basic intermittent schedules. On a fixed ratio schedule, a fixed number of responses is required for reinforcement, while on a variable ratio schedule, a varying number of responses is required. Both schedules produce a high rate of response, with the fixed ratio schedule also producing a postreinforcement pause. On a fixed interval schedule, the first response after a fixed period of time is reinforced, while on a variable interval schedule, the first response after a varying period of time is reinforced. The former produces a scalloped pattern of responding, whereas the latter produces a moderate, steady pattern of responding.

On a fixed duration schedule, reinforcement is contingent upon responding continuously for a fixed, predictable period of time; on a variable duration schedule, reinforcement is contingent upon responding continuously for a varying, unpredictable period of time. Response-rate schedules specifically reinforce the rate of response. For example, on a DRH schedule, reinforcement is contingent on a high rate of response, whereas on a DRL schedule, it is contingent on a low rate of response. On a DRP schedule, reinforcement is contingent on a particular rate of response—neither too fast nor too slow. By contrast, on a noncontingent schedule of reinforcement, the reinforcer is delivered following a certain period of time regardless of the organism's behavior. The time period can either be fixed (a fixed time schedule) or varied (a variable time schedule). Noncontingent schedules sometimes result in the development of superstitious behavior.

A complex schedule consists of two or more simple schedules. In a conjunctive schedule, the requirements of two or more simple schedules must be met before a reinforcer is delivered; in an adjusting schedule, the response requirement changes as a function of the organism's performance during responding for the previous reinforcer. On a chained schedule, reinforcement is contingent upon meeting the requirements of two or more successive schedules, each with its own discriminative stimulus. Responding tends to become stronger and/or more efficient toward the end of the chain, which is an instance of the goal gradient effect. Behavior chains are often best established by training the last link first and the first link last.

According to drive reduction theory, an event is reinforcing if it is associated with a reduction in some type of internal physiological drive. However, some behaviors seem motivated more by the external consequence (known as incentive motivation) than by an internal drive state. The Premack principle assumes that high-probability behaviors can be used as reinforcers for low-probability behaviors. The response deprivation hypothesis states that a behavior can be used as a reinforcer if access to the behavior is restricted so that its frequency falls below its baseline rate of occurrence. The behavioral bliss point approach assumes that organisms distribute their behavior in such a manner as to maximize their overall reinforcement.

SUGGESTED READINGS

Ferster, C. B., & Skinner, B. F. (1957). *Schedules of reinforcement*. New York: Appleton-Century-Crofts. The seminal book on schedule effects. Not a book for light reading, but glancing through it will give you a sense of the history of behavior analysis and what real schedule effects look like.

Herrnstein, R. J. (1966). Superstition: A corollary of the principle of operant conditioning. In W. K. Honig (Ed.), *Operant behavior: Areas of research and application*. New York: Appleton-Century-Crofts. A discussion of the behavioral approach to superstitious behavior. The discussion of human superstitions at the end of the article would be of most interest to undergraduates.

Timberlake, W., & Farmer-Dougan, V. A. (1991). Reinforcement in applied settings: Figuring out ahead of time what will work. *Psychological Bulletin*, 110, 379–391. Reviews the Premack principle and the response deprivation approach to reinforcement and its usefulness in applied settings.

STUDY QUESTIONS

1. What is a schedule of reinforcement?
2. Distinguish between continuous and intermittent schedules of reinforcement.
3. Define fixed ratio schedule. Describe the typical pattern of responding produced by this schedule.
4. Define variable ratio schedule. Describe the typical pattern of responding produced by this schedule.
5. Define fixed interval schedule. Describe the typical pattern of responding produced by this schedule.
6. Define variable interval schedule. Describe the typical pattern of responding produced by this schedule.
7. Name and define two types of duration schedules.
8. What are three types of response-rate schedules?
9. Name and define the two types of noncontingent schedules.
10. What is a conjunctive schedule? How does a conjunctive schedule differ from a chained schedule?
11. What is an adjusting schedule? In what way does shaping involve the use of an adjusting schedule?
12. What is a chained schedule? Diagram and label an example of a chained schedule.

13. What type of reinforcer serves to maintain behavior throughout the early links in a chain? What is the best way to establish responding on a chained schedule in animals?
14. Define the goal gradient effect and give an example.
15. Describe the drive reduction theory of reinforcement. What is a major difficulty with this theory? What is incentive motivation?
16. Outline the Premack principle. Give an example of the Premack principle as applied to dealing with a classroom situation in which students are chatting to each other rather than focusing on their work.
17. Outline the response deprivation hypothesis. Describe how the response deprivation hypothesis differs from the Premack principle.
18. Describe the behavioral bliss point approach to reinforcement. Illustrate your answer with an example which shows how creating a contingency may prevent someone from reaching their bliss point.

CONCEPT REVIEW

adjusting schedule. A schedule in which the response requirement changes as a function of the organism's performance while responding for the previous reinforcer.

behavioral bliss point approach. The theory that an organism with free access to alternative activities will distribute its behavior in such a way as to maximize overall reinforcement.

chained schedule. A schedule consisting of a sequence of two or more simple schedules, each with its own S^D and the last of which results in a terminal reinforcer.

complex schedule. A schedule consisting of a combination of two or more simple schedules.

conjunctive schedule. A type of complex schedule in which the requirements of two or more simple schedules must be met before a reinforcer is delivered.

continuous reinforcement schedule. A schedule in which each specified response is reinforced.

differential reinforcement of high rates (DRH). A schedule in which reinforcement is contingent upon emitting at least a certain number of responses in a certain period of time—or, more generally, reinforcement is provided for responding at a fast rate.

differential reinforcement of low rates (DRL). A schedule in which a minimum amount of time must pass between each response before the reinforcer will be delivered—or, more generally, reinforcement is provided for responding at a slow rate.

differential reinforcement of paced responding (DRP). A schedule in which reinforcement is contingent upon emitting a series of responses at a set rate—or, more generally, reinforcement is provided for responding neither too fast nor too slow.

drive reduction theory. According to this theory, an event is reinforcing to the extent that it is associated with a reduction in some type of physiological drive.

fixed duration (FD) schedule. A schedule in which reinforcement is contingent upon continuous performance of a behavior for a fixed, predictable period of time.

fixed interval (FI) schedule. A schedule in which reinforcement is contingent upon the first response after a fixed, predictable period of time.

fixed ratio (FR) schedule. A schedule in which reinforcement is contingent upon a fixed, predictable number of responses.

fixed time (FT) schedule. A schedule in which the reinforcer is delivered following a fixed, predictable period of time, regardless of the organism's behavior.

goal gradient effect. An increase in the strength and/or efficiency of responding as one draws near to the goal.

incentive motivation. Motivation derived from some property of the reinforcer, as opposed to an internal drive state.

intermittent (or partial) reinforcement schedule. A schedule in which only some responses are reinforced.

noncontingent schedule of reinforcement. A schedule in which the reinforcer is delivered independently of any response.

Premack principle. The notion that a high-probability behavior can be used to reinforce a low-probability behavior.

ratio strain. A disruption in responding due to an overly demanding response requirement.

response deprivation hypothesis. The notion that a behavior can serve as a reinforcer when: (1) access to the behavior is restricted and (2) its frequency thereby falls below its preferred level of occurrence.

response-rate schedule. A schedule in which reinforcement is directly contingent upon the organism's rate of response.

schedule of reinforcement. The response requirement that must be met to obtain reinforcement.

variable duration (VD) schedule. A schedule in which reinforcement is contingent upon continuous performance of a behavior for a varying, unpredictable period of time.

variable interval (VI) schedule. A schedule in which reinforcement is contingent upon the first response after a varying, unpredictable period of time.

variable ratio (VR) schedule. A schedule in which reinforcement is contingent upon a varying, unpredictable number of responses.

variable time (VT) schedule. A schedule in which the reinforcer is delivered following a varying, unpredictable period of time, regardless of the organism's behavior.

CHAPTER TEST

21. On a _____ schedule, reinforcement is contingent upon the first response during a varying period of time. (A) fixed interval, (B) variable time, (C) fixed time, (D) variable interval, (E) none of the preceding.

6. On a _____ schedule (abbreviated _____), reinforcement is contingent upon a fixed, predictable number of responses. This produces a _____ rate of response often accompanied by a _____.

17. On a (use the abbreviation) _____ schedule, a minimum amount of time must pass between each response before the reinforcer will be delivered. On a _____ schedule, reinforcement is contingent upon emitting at least a certain number of responses in a certain period of time. On a _____ schedule, reinforcement is contingent on emitting a series of responses at a specific rate.

10. If Jason is extremely persistent in asking Neem out for a date, she will occasionally accept his invitation. Of the four basic schedules, Jason's behavior of asking Neem for a date is most likely on a _____ _____ schedule of reinforcement.

36. Russ is so impressed with how quickly his betta learned to swim in a circle that he keeps doubling the number of circles it has to perform in order to receive a reinforcer. This is an example of an _____ schedule of reinforcement (one that is particularly likely to suffer from r_____ s_____).

8. On a _____ schedule, a response *must not occur* until 20 seconds have elapsed since the last reinforcer. (A) VI 20-sec, (B) VT 20-sec, (C) FT 20-sec, (D) FI 20-sec, (E) none of the preceding.

28. Postreinforcement pauses are most likely to occur on which two types of simple intermittent schedules? _____ and _____.

16. On _____ schedules, reinforcement is contingent upon the rate of response.

31. Shawna often goes for a walk through the woods, but she rarely does yardwork. According to the _____, walking through the woods could be used as a _____ for yardwork.

5. On a _____ schedule (abbreviated _____), reinforcement is contingent upon the first response *after* a fixed period of time. This produces a _____ pattern of responding.

13. A _____ schedule generally produces a high rate of response with a short pause following the attainment of each reinforcer. In general, the higher the requirement, the (longer/shorter) _____ the pause.

29. On a(n) _____ schedule, a response cannot be reinforced until 20 seconds have elapsed since the last reinforcer. (A) VI 20-sec, (B) VT 20-sec, (C) FT 20-sec, (D) FI 20-sec, (E) none of the preceding.

37. Ahmed's daily routine consists of swimming without rest for 30 minutes, following which he takes a break. This most closely resembles a(n) _____ schedule of reinforcement.

3. If a dog receives a treat each time it begs for one, its begging is being maintained on a(n) _____ schedule of reinforcement. If it only sometimes receives a treat when it begs for one, its begging is being maintained on a(n) _____ schedule of reinforcement.

27. Dersu often carried a lucky charm with him when he went out hunting. This is because the appearance of game was often on a (use the abbreviation) _____ schedule of reinforcement.

32. Gina often goes for a walk through the woods, and even more often she does yardwork. According to the _____, walking through the woods could still be used as a reinforcer for yardwork given that one restricts the frequency of walking to _____ its_____ level.

26. On a fixed interval schedule, reinforcement is contingent upon the first response _____ a fixed period of time. (A) during, (B) before, (C) after, (D) none of the preceding.

9. Neem accepts Jason's invitation for a date only when she has "nothing better to do." Of the four basic intermittent schedules, Jason's behavior of asking Neem for a date is best described as being on a _____ schedule of reinforcement.

38. When Deanna screams continuously, her mother occasionally pays attention to her. This is most likely an example of a(n) _____ schedule of reinforcement.

30. Drinking a soda to quench your thirst is an example of _____ reduction; drinking a soda because you love its tangy sweetness is an example of _____ motivation.

4. On a(n) _____ schedule (abbreviated _____), reinforcement is contingent upon a varying, unpredictable number of responses. This generally produces a _____ rate of response (with/without) _____ a postreinforcement pause.

24. A pigeon pecks a green key on a VI 60-sec schedule, which results in the insertion of a foot-treadle into the chamber. The pigeon then presses the treadle 10 times, following which it receives food. To train this chain of behaviors, one should start with _____.

11. Neem accepts Jason's invitation for a date only when he has just been paid his monthly salary. Of the four simple schedules, the contingency governing Jason's behavior of asking Neem for a date seems most similar to a _____ schedule of reinforcement.

35. "If I'm not a success in every aspect of my life, my family will reject me." This is a severe example of a _____ schedule of reinforcement.

25. Dagoni works for longer and longer periods of time and takes fewer and fewer breaks as his project nears completion. This is an example of the _____ effect.

18. On a _____ schedule of reinforcement, the reinforcer is delivered independently of any response.

7. On a _____ schedule (abbreviated _____), reinforcement is contingent upon the first response after a varying interval of time. This produces a _____ rate of response.

15. Gambling is often maintained by a _____ schedule of reinforcement.

20. On a _____ schedule (abbreviated _____), the reinforcer is delivered following a varying period of time.

33. Anna ideally likes to exercise for 1 hour each morning, followed by a 30-minute sauna, in turn followed by a half hour of drinking coffee and reading the newspaper. Unfortunately, due to other commitments, she actually spends 45 minutes exercising, followed by a 15-minute sauna, and a half hour drinking coffee and reading the paper. According to the _____ approach, Anna's ideal schedule provides the _____ amount of overall reinforcement that can be obtained from those activities. Her actual distribution of behavior represents her attempt to draw as near to the _____ point as possible for these activities.

1. A _____ is the response requirement that must be met to obtain reinforcement.

22. A _____ schedule is a sequence of two or more component schedules, each of which has its own _____ stimulus and the last of which results in a _____ reinforcer.

34. The abbreviation DRL refers to _____ reinforcement of _____ rate behavior.

14. As noted in the opening scenario to this chapter, Mandy found that she had to work harder and harder to entice Alvin to pay attention to her. It is quite likely that her behavior was on a _____ schedule of reinforcement. As a result, she began experiencing periods of time where she simply gave up and stopped trying. Eventually, she stopped seeing him altogether. When her sister asked why, Mandy, having just read this chapter, replied, "_____ _____."

2. Different response requirements have different effects on behavior. For example, ratio schedules (FR and VR) tend to produce (higher/lower) _____ rates of behavior than interval schedules (VI and FI). Likewise, fixed (FI and FR) schedules tend to produce _____ whereas variable (VI and VR) schedules often do not. Such differences in response patterns are known as _____.

23. A pigeon pecks a green key on a VR 9 schedule, then a red key on an FI 20-sec, following which it receives food. The reinforcer for pecking the

green key is the presentation of the _____, which is a _____ reinforcer.

12. Eddy finds that he has to thump his old television set exactly twice before the picture will clear up. His behavior of thumping the television set is on a (be specific and use the abbreviation) _____ schedule of reinforcement.

19. On a _____ schedule (abbreviated _____), the reinforcer is delivered following a fixed interval of time, regardless of the organism's behavior.

Visit the book companion Web site at http://www.academic.cengage. com/psychology/powell for additional practice questions, answers to the Quick Quizzes, practice review exams, and additional exercises and information.

ANSWERS TO CHAPTER TEST

1. schedule of reinforcement (reinforcement schedule)
2. higher; postreinforcement pauses; schedule effects
3. continuous (or FR1 or CRF); intermittent
4. variable ratio; VR; high; without
5. fixed interval; FI; scalloped
6. fixed ratio; FR; high; postreinforcement pause
7. variable interval; VI; moderate, steady
8. E
9. variable interval
10. variable ratio
11. fixed interval
12. FR 2
13. fixed ratio; longer
14. variable ratio; ratio strain
15. variable ratio
16. response rate (DRL, DRH, and DRP)
17. DRL; DRH; DRP
18. noncontingent (or response independent)
19. fixed time; FT
20. variable time; VT
21. E
22. chained; discriminative; terminal
23. red key; secondary
24. treadle pressing
25. goal gradient
26. C
27. VT
28. fixed interval and fixed ratio
29. D
30. drive; incentive
31. Premack principle; reinforcer
32. response deprivation hypothesis; below; baseline
33. behavioral bliss point; optimal (maximum); bliss
34. differential; low
35. conjunctive
36. adjusting; ratio strain
37. FD
38. VD

Extinction and Stimulus Control

Poppea gained access to Nero, and established her ascendancy. First she used flirtatious wiles, pretending to be unable to resist her passion for Nero's looks. Then, as the emperor fell in love with her, she became haughty, and if he kept her for more than two nights she insisted that she was married and could not give up her marriage.

TACITUS, *The Annals of Imperial Rome*

Extinction

In the past few chapters, we have concentrated on strengthening operant behavior through the process of reinforcement. However, as previously noted, a behavior that has been strengthened through reinforcement can also be weakened through extinction. **Extinction** is the nonreinforcement of a previously reinforced response, the result of which is a decrease in the strength of that response. As with classical conditioning, the term *extinction* refers to both a procedure and a process. The *procedure* of extinction is the nonreinforcement of a previously reinforced response; the *process* of extinction is the resultant decrease in response strength.

Take, for example, a situation in which a rat has learned to press a lever for food:

$$\textit{Lever press} \rightarrow \textbf{Food}$$
$$\textbf{R} \qquad\quad \textbf{S}^{\textbf{R}}$$

If lever pressing is no longer followed by food:

$$\textit{Lever press} \rightarrow \textbf{No food}$$
$$\textbf{R} \qquad\quad \textbf{—}$$

then the frequency of lever pressing will decline. The act of withholding food delivery following a lever press is the procedure of extinction, and the resultant decline in responding is the process of extinction. If lever pressing ceases entirely, the response is said to have been *extinguished*; if it has not yet ceased entirely, then the response has been only *partially extinguished*.

Similarly, consider a child who has learned to whine to obtain candy:

$$\textit{Whining} \rightarrow \textbf{Candy}$$
$$\textbf{R} \qquad\quad \textbf{S}^{\textbf{R}}$$

If whining no longer produces candy:

$$\textit{Whining} \rightarrow \textbf{No candy}$$
$$\textbf{R} \qquad\quad \textbf{—}$$

the frequency of whining will decline. The procedure of extinction is the nondelivery of candy following the behavior, and the process of extinction is the resultant decline in the behavior. If the whining is completely eliminated, then it has been extinguished. If whining still occurs, but at a lower frequency, then it has been partially extinguished.

An important, but often neglected, aspect of applying an extinction procedure is to ensure that the consequence being withheld is in fact the reinforcer that is maintaining the behavior. You might believe that the consequence of candy is reinforcing a child's tendency to whine, when in fact it is the accompanying attention from the parent. If this is the case, and the parent continues to provide attention for whining (for example, by arguing with the child each time he or she whines), then withholding the candy might have little or no effect on the behavior. Of course, another possibility is that the whining is being maintained by both the candy and attention, in which case withholding the candy might only partially extinguish the behavior. Thus, determining the effective reinforcer that is maintaining a behavior is a critical first step in extinguishing a behavior.

QUICK QUIZ A

1. Extinction is the _____ of a previously _____ response, the result of which is a(n) _____ in the strength of that response.

2. Whenever Jana's friend Karla phoned late in the evening, she would invariably begin complaining about her coworkers. In the beginning, Jana listened attentively and provided emotional support. Unfortunately, Karla started phoning more and more often, with each call lasting longer and longer. Jana began to wonder if she was reinforcing Karla's behavior of phoning and complaining, so she decided to screen her late-evening calls and not answer any such calls from Karla. Eventually, Karla stopped phoning at that time, and they resumed a normal friendship that excluded lengthy complaints over the phone. Jana used the (procedure/process) _____ of extinction when she stopped answering Karla's late-evening calls, while the _____ of extinction is the eventual cessation of such calls.

3. In carrying out an extinction procedure, an important first step is to ensure that the consequence being withdrawn is in fact the _____ _____.

Side Effects of Extinction

When an extinction procedure is implemented, it is often accompanied by certain side effects. It is important to be aware of these side effects because they can mislead one into believing that an extinction procedure is not having an effect when in fact it is.

1. **Extinction Burst.** The implementation of an extinction procedure does not always result in an immediate decrease in responding. Instead, one often finds an *extinction burst*, a temporary increase in

the frequency and intensity of responding when extinction is first implemented. Suppose, for example, that we reinforce every fourth lever press by a rat (an FR 4 schedule of reinforcement). When extinction is implemented, the rat will initially react by pressing the lever both more rapidly and more forcefully. The rat's behavior is analogous to our behavior when we plug money into a candy machine, press the button, and receive nothing in return. We do not just give up and walk away. Instead, we press the button several times in a row, often with increasing amounts of force. Our behavior toward the machine shows the same increase in frequency and intensity that characterizes an extinction burst.

2. **Increase in Variability**. An extinction procedure can also result in an increase in the variability of a behavior (Antonitis, 1951). For example, a rat whose lever pressing no longer produces food might vary the manner in which it presses the lever. If the rat typically pressed the lever with its right paw, it might now try pressing it with its left paw. As well, if the rat usually pressed the lever in the center, it might now press it more to one side or the other. Similarly, when confronted by a candy machine that has just stolen our money, we will likely vary the manner in which we push the button, such as holding it down for a second before releasing it. And we will almost certainly try pressing other buttons on the machine to see if we can at least obtain a different selection.[1]

3. **Emotional Behavior**. Extinction is often accompanied by emotional behavior (Zeiler, 1971). The hungry pigeon that suddenly finds that key pecking no longer produces food soon becomes agitated (as evidenced, for example, by quick jerky movements and wing flapping). Likewise, people often become upset when confronted by a candy machine that does not deliver the goods. Such emotional responses are what we typically refer to as *frustration*.

4. **Aggression**. One type of emotional behavior that is particularly common during an extinction procedure is aggression. In fact, extinction procedures have been used to study aggressive behavior in animals. For example, research has shown that a pigeon whose key pecking for food is placed on extinction will reliably attack another pigeon (or model of a pigeon) that happens to be nearby (Azrin, Hutchinson, & Hake, 1966). Extinction-induced aggression (also called frustration-induced aggression) is also common in humans. People often become angry with those who block them from obtaining an important goal. For that matter, even uncooperative vending machines are sometimes attacked.

---

[1]Although we have treated them separately in this text, the increase in response variability during extinction is sometimes regarded as one aspect of an extinction burst. In other words, an extinction burst can be defined as an increase in the rate, intensity, and variability of responding following the implementation of an extinction procedure.

5. **Resurgence.** A rather unusual side effect of extinction is *resurgence*, the reappearance during extinction of other behaviors that had once been effective in obtaining reinforcement (Epstein, 1985). Hull (1934), for example, trained rats to first run a 20-foot pattern through a maze to obtain food, then a 40-foot pattern. When all running was then placed on extinction, the rats initially persisted with the 40-foot pattern, then returned to the 20-foot pattern before quitting. It was as though they were attempting to make the food reappear by repeating a pattern that had earlier been effective. Resurgence resembles the psychoanalytic concept of *regression*, which is the reappearance of immature behavior in reaction to frustration or conflict. Thus, a husband faced with a wife who largely ignores him might begin spending increasing amounts of time at his parents' house. Faced with the lack of reinforcement in his marriage, he returns to a setting that once provided a rich source of reinforcement.

6. **Depression.** Extinction can also lead to depressive-like symptoms. For example, Klinger, Barta, and Kemble (1974) had rats run down an alleyway for food and then immediately followed this with an assessment of the rats' activity level in an open field test. Thus, each session consisted of two phases: (1) running down an alleyway for food, followed by (2) placement in an open area that the rats could freely explore. When extinction was implemented on the alleyway task, activity in the open field test first increased to above normal, then decreased to below normal, followed by a return to normal (see Figure 8.1).

Klinger et al. (1974) noted that low activity is a common symptom of depression; moreover, depression is often associated with loss of reinforcement (Lewinsohn, 1974). For example, if someone dies, the people for whom that individual was a major source of reinforcement are essentially experiencing extinction, and they will likely become depressed for a period of time. And one symptom of such depression is a low level of activity. The fact that a similar process occurs in rats suggests that a temporary period of depression (accompanied by a decrease in activity) following the loss of a major reinforcer should be regarded as a normal aspect of disengagement from that reinforcer (Klinger, 1975).

These various side effects of extinction can obviously be an impediment to successfully implementing an extinction procedure. Note, too, how these side effects can be inadvertently strengthened if one suddenly gives in and provides the subject with the sought-after reinforcer. Imagine, for example, Bobbie has learned that by begging at the supermarket he can usually entice his mother into buying him some candy. One day, however, Bobbie's mother decides to withhold the candy, with the result that he becomes very loud and persistent (an extinction burst) as well as emotionally upset and aggressive. If Bobbie's mother now gives in and buys him some candy, what type of behavior has she reinforced? Obviously not the behavior of being polite and well mannered in the supermarket. In this way, parents sometimes inadvertently train their children into throwing

FIGURE 8.1   Changes in rats' activity level in an open field test as a function of extinction on a preceding straight-alley maze task. (*Source:* Adapted with kind permission from Springer Science + Business Media: *Animal Learning and Behavior,* "Cyclic activity changes during extinction in rats: A potential model of depression," 2, 1974, pp. 313–316, by E. Klinger, S. G. Barta, E. D. Kemble, copyright © 1974 by the Psychonomic Society.

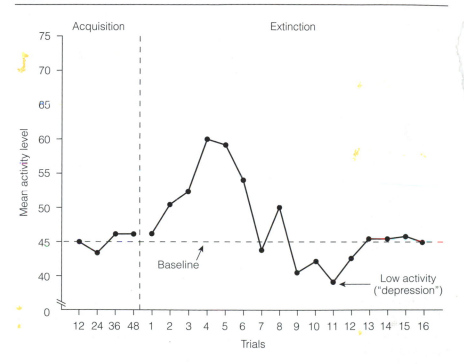

severe temper tantrums, a tendency that could have serious consequences if maintained later in life. After all, what the media calls "road rage"—or "air rage" when passengers become belligerent on airline flights—might, in many cases, be simply an adult version of a temper tantrum, a behavior pattern that was inadvertently established in childhood. (See also discussion of *partial reinforcement effect* later in this chapter.)

1. Krissy asked her father to buy her a toy, as he usually did, when they were out shopping. Unfortunately, Krissy's father had spent all of his money on building supplies and told her that he had nothing left for a toy. The first thing that might happen is that Krissy will (increase/decrease) _____ the frequency with which she asks for a toy and will ask for a toy with a (louder/softer) _____ voice. This process is known as an e_____ b_____.

QUICK QUIZ B

2. Krissy is also likely to ask for the toy in many different ways because extinction often results in an increase in the v_____ of a behavior.

3. Krissy might also begin showing a lot of e_____ behavior, including a_____.

4. When her father still refuses to buy her a toy, Krissy suddenly asks her dad to pick her up and carry her, something she has not asked for since she was much smaller. This could be an example of r_____ or what psychoanalysts call r_____.

5. On the trip home, Krissy, who never did get a toy, sat silently and stared out the window. This is not surprising, because extinction is sometimes followed by a temporary period of d_____.

ADVICE FOR THE LOVELORN

Dear Dr. Dee,

Why is it that I act so weird whenever I break up with a guy? One day I am intent on reestablishing the relationship, the next day I am so angry I don't ever want to see him again. Then I usually get all depressed and lie around in bed for days on end.

What a Rollercoaster

Dear What,

Sounds like extinction to me. The loss of a relationship is the loss of a major reinforcer in your life. You therefore go through many of the side effects that accompany extinction. You experience an extinction burst ("intent on reestablishing the relationship"), become angry ("don't ever want to see the guy again"), and eventually get depressed.

Solution: Extinction effects are a normal part of life, so don't expect that you shouldn't feel something. But you might be able to moderate your feelings a bit so they are not quite so painful. In particular, stay active as much as possible and seek out alternative sources of reinforcement. And try to avoid lying in bed for days on end, as this will only further reduce the reinforcement in your life. In fact, lying in bed for days on end will make just about anyone depressed, regardless of his or her relationship status!

Behaviorally yours,

Dr. Dee

FIGURE 8.2 Two hypothetical extinction curves. Following an initial period of reinforcement at the start of the session, the extinction procedure is implemented. This results in a brief extinction burst, followed by a decline in responding. The decline is more gradual in the top example than in the bottom example and hence illustrates greater resistance to extinction.

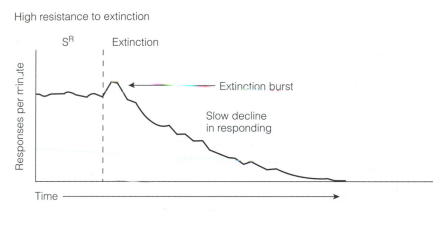

High resistance to extinction

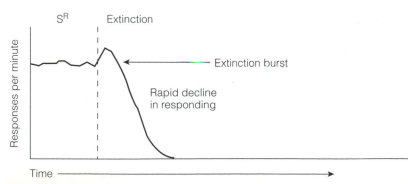

Low resistance to extinction

Resistance to Extinction

Resistance to extinction is the extent to which responding persists after an extinction procedure has been implemented. A response that is very persistent is said to have high resistance to extinction, while a response that disappears quickly is said to have low resistance to extinction (see Figure 8.2). For example, a dog that continues to beg for food at the dinner table for 20 minutes after everyone has stopped feeding it is displaying much higher resistance to extinction than does a dog that stops begging after 5 minutes.

Resistance to extinction can be affected by a number of factors, including the following:

Schedule of Reinforcement The schedule of reinforcement is the most important factor influencing resistance to extinction. According to the *partial reinforcement effect*, behavior that has been maintained on an intermittent (partial) schedule of reinforcement will extinguish more slowly than behavior that has been maintained on a continuous schedule. Thus, lever pressing that has been reinforced on an FR 10 schedule will take longer to extinguish than lever pressing that has been reinforced on a CRF (FR 1) schedule. Similarly, lever pressing that has been reinforced on an FR 100 schedule will take longer to extinguish than lever pressing that has been reinforced on an FR 10 schedule. Resistance to extinction is particularly strong when behavior has been maintained on a variable ratio (VR) schedule (G. S. Reynolds, 1975); thus, a VR 20 schedule will produce greater resistance to extinction than an FR 20 schedule.

One way of thinking about the partial reinforcement effect is that the less frequent the reinforcer, the longer it takes the animal to "discover" that reinforcement is no longer available (Mowrer & Jones, 1945). It obviously takes much longer for an animal to discover that reinforcement is no longer available when it has been receiving reinforcement on, say, a VR 100 schedule than on a CRF schedule. A less mentalistic interpretation is that there is a much greater contrast between a CRF schedule and extinction than between a VR 100 schedule and extinction. On a VR 100 schedule, the animal has learned to emit many responses in the absence of reinforcement; hence, it is more persistent in its responding when an extinction procedure is implemented (E. J. Capaldi, 1966).

The partial reinforcement effect helps account for certain types of annoying or maladaptive behaviors that are difficult to eliminate. Dogs that beg for food are often extremely persistent. Paradoxically, as mentioned earlier, this is sometimes the result of previously unsuccessful attempts at extinction. Imagine, for example, that all family members agree to stop feeding the dog at the dinner table. If one person nevertheless slips the dog a morsel when it is making a particularly big fuss, the begging will become both more intense and more persistent. This means that the next attempt at extinction will be even more difficult. Of course, the partial reinforcement effect also suggests a possible solution to this problem. If behavior that has been continuously reinforced is less resistant to extinction, then it might help to first spend several days reinforcing each instance of begging. Then, when extinction is implemented, the dog's tendency to beg might extinguish more rapidly (Lerman & Iwata, 1996).

History of Reinforcement In general, the more reinforcers an individual has received for a behavior, the greater the resistance to extinction. Lever pressing will extinguish more rapidly if a rat has previously earned only 10 reinforcers for lever pressing than if it has earned 100 reinforcers. Likewise, a child who has only recently picked up the habit of whining for candy should stop relatively quickly when the behavior is placed on extinction, as opposed to a child who has been at it for several weeks. From a practical perspective, this means it is much easier to extinguish an unwanted behavior, such as whining for candy, when it first becomes evident (hence the saying, "nip it in the bud"). There is, however, a limit in the extent to which further reinforcers will produce increased resistance to extinction. Furomoto (1971), for example, found that resistance to extinction for key pecking in pigeons reached its maximum after about 1000 reinforcers.

Magnitude of the Reinforcer   The magnitude of the reinforcer can also affect resistance to extinction. For example, large-magnitude reinforcers sometimes result in greater resistance to extinction than small-magnitude reinforcers. Thus, lever pressing might take longer to extinguish following a training period in which each reinforcer consisted of a large pellet of food than if the reinforcer were a small pellet of food. Lever pressing might also take longer to extinguish if the reinforcer was a highly preferred food item than if it were a less-preferred food item. From a practical perspective, this means that a dog's behavior of begging at the dinner table might extinguish more easily if you first spend several days feeding it small bites of less-preferred morsels (Lerman & Iwata, 1996). Unfortunately, one problem with this strategy is that the effect of reinforcer magnitude on resistance to extinction is not entirely consistent. In fact, researchers sometimes find that smaller reinforcers result in greater resistance to extinction (e.g., Ellis, 1962).

Degree of Deprivation   Not surprisingly, the degree to which an organism is deprived of a reinforcer also affects resistance to extinction. In general, the greater the level of deprivation, the greater the resistance to extinction (Perin, 1942). A rat that is only slightly hungry will cease lever pressing more quickly than a rat that is very hungry. This suggests yet another strategy for extinguishing a dog's tendency to beg at the table: Feed the dog before the meal.

Previous Experience with Extinction   When sessions of extinction are alternated with sessions of reinforcement, the greater the number of prior exposures to extinction, the quicker the behavior will extinguish during subsequent exposures (Bullock & Smith, 1953). For example, if a rat experiences several sessions of extinction randomly interspersed with several sessions of reinforcement, it will eventually learn to stop lever pressing soon after the start of an extinction session. The rat has learned that if it has not received reinforcement soon after the start of a session, then it is likely that no reinforcement will be forthcoming for the remainder of the session. Similarly, a child might learn that if he does not receive candy within the first 10 minutes of whining during a trip to the supermarket, he might as well give up for the day. It also leads to the prediction that people who have been through relationship breakups on numerous occasions will more quickly get over such breakups and move on to a new relationship.

Distinctive Signal for Extinction Extinction is greatly facilitated when there is a distinctive stimulus that signals the onset of extinction. As briefly noted in Chapter 6, such a stimulus is called a *discriminative stimulus for extinction*; it is more fully discussed later in this chapter.

1. R_____ to _____ is the extent to which responding persists after an extinction procedure is implemented.

2. According to the p_____ r_____ effect, responses that have been maintained on an intermittent schedule will show (more/less) _____ resistance to extinction than responses that have been reinforced on a continuous schedule.

3. Among the four basic intermittent schedules, the (use the abbreviation) _____ schedule is particularly likely to produce strong resistance to extinction.

4. In general, a behavior that has been reinforced many times is likely to be (much easier / more difficult) _____ to extinguish.

5. Resistance to extinction is generally greater when the behavior that is being extinguished has been reinforced with a (high/low) _____-magnitude reinforcer, though the opposite effect has also been found.

6. In general, there is a(n) (direct/inverse) _____ relationship between resistance to extinction and the organism's level of deprivation for the reinforcer.

7. Previous experience with extinction, as well as a distinctive signal for extinction, tends to produce a(n) (increase/decrease) _____ in resistance to extinction.

Spontaneous Recovery

Although extinction is a reliable process for weakening a behavior, it would be a mistake to assume that once a response has been extinguished, it has been permanently eliminated. As with extinction of a classically conditioned response, extinction of an operant response is likely to be followed by *spontaneous recovery* (Skinner, 1938). As you will recall, **spontaneous recovery** is the reappearance of an extinguished response following a rest period after extinction. Suppose, for example, that we extinguish a rat's behavior of lever pressing. The next day, when we place the rat back in the experimental chamber, it will probably commence lever pressing again. It is almost as though it has forgotten that lever pressing no longer produces food. Nevertheless, the behavior will likely be weaker than it was at the start of the extinction phase the day before, and will extinguish more quickly given that we continue to withhold reinforcement. Similarly, on the third day, we might again find some recovery of lever pressing, but it will be even weaker than the day before and will extinguish even more quickly. This process might repeat itself several times, with each recovery being weaker and more readily extinguished than the previous one. Following several extinction sessions, we will eventually reach the point at which spontaneous recovery does not occur (apart from a few tentative lever presses every once in a while), and

FIGURE 8.3 Graph of hypothetical data illustrating spontaneous recovery across repeated sessions of extinction.

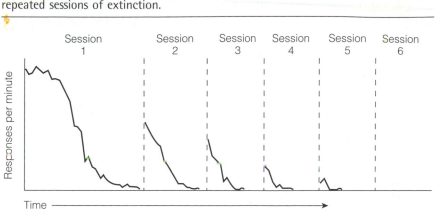

the behavior will have essentially been eliminated (see Figure 8.3). Likewise, a child's tendency to throw tantrums in the supermarket to obtain candy might require several visits to the supermarket during which a tantrum does not produce candy before the behavior is fully eliminated. In short, when applying an extinction procedure, you have to be persistent.

Skinner (1950) proposed that spontaneous recovery is a function of discriminative stimuli (S^{D}s) associated with the start of the session. For an experimental rat, the experience of being taken from the home cage, weighed, and placed in an operant chamber is itself a signal for the availability of food. ("Oh, goody, I'm being weighed. That means I'll soon be able to earn some food by lever pressing.") Only after repeated exposure to these events without receiving food does the rat at last fail to show the learned behavior. Similarly, for the child who has learned to throw tantrums in the supermarket to receive candy, entering the supermarket is itself an S^D for the availability of candy. The child will require repeated exposure to the sequence of entering the supermarket, throwing a tantrum, and not receiving candy before this cue becomes ineffective.

1. S_____ _____ is the reappearance of an extinguished response at a later point in time.

2. In general, each time this occurs, the behavior is (weaker/stronger) _____ than before and extinguishes (more/less) _____ readily.

3. Skinner believed that this phenomenon is a function of _____ that are uniquely associated with the start of the session.

Differential Reinforcement of Other Behavior

The process of extinction can be greatly facilitated by both extinguishing the target behavior *and* reinforcing the occurrence of a replacement behavior. This procedure is known as *differential reinforcement of other behavior (DRO)*, which is the reinforcement of any behavior other than the target behavior that is being extinguished. DRO procedures tend to be more effective than simple extinction procedures because the target behavior is weakened both by the lack of reinforcement for that behavior and by the reinforcement of alternative behaviors that come to replace it. Hence, it is easier to extinguish a child's habit of whining for candy at a supermarket if you not only withdraw the reinforcement for whining but also explicitly reinforce alternative behaviors, especially well-mannered behaviors.[2] Unlike a straight extinction procedure, in a DRO procedure the child is not being deprived of reinforcement within that setting, which will thereby reduce or eliminate possible side effects normally resulting from extinction. Note that the reinforcement for well-mannered behavior can include the very candy for which the child has been whining. He can therefore still obtain candy, but only if he exhibits an appropriate pattern of behavior. (The candy, of course, can then be gradually phased out—or replaced by a healthier treat—as the appropriate behavior becomes firmly established.)

A particularly useful type of differential reinforcement procedure is called *functional communication training (or differential reinforcement of functional communication)*. Many unwanted behaviors occur because the child is attempting to attain an important reinforcer, such as attention, but is doing so inappropriately. If the child is instead taught to communicate his or her need for the reinforcer in a socially appropriate manner ("Gee Mom, I'm really bored. Can you help me find something interesting to do?"), then the frequency of inappropriate behaviors (such as misbehaving to get mom's attention) is likely to decrease. So in *functional communication training*, the behavior of clearly and appropriately communicating one's desires is differentially reinforced (e.g., Durand, 1990).

As noted, differential reinforcement procedures can reduce many of the unwanted side effects of extinction, such as frustration and aggression. As a general rule, therefore, whenever one attempts to extinguish an unwanted behavior, one should also provide plenty of reinforcement for more appropriate behavior (Miltenberger, 2012).

1. The procedure of reinforcing all behaviors except the particular target behavior that you wish to extinguish is known as d_____ r_____ of o_____ behavior (abbreviated _____).

2. Giving a dog a treat whenever it does something other than jump up on visitors as they enter the house is an example of a (use the abbreviation) _____ procedure.

3. A DRO procedure is useful in that it tends to reduce many of the side effects of extinction, such as ex_____ b_____ and fr_____ .

---

[2]A precise type of DRO procedure in which the "other behavior" is specifically incompatible with the target behavior is *differential reinforcement of incompatible behavior (DRI)*. Thus, paying attention to a child if he is doing something other than fighting with his little sister is a basic DRO procedure, while paying attention to him only when he is interacting in a friendly manner with his little sister is a DRI procedure.

And Furthermore

Extinction of Bedtime Tantrums in Young Children

A common difficulty faced by many parents is training children to go to bed at night without fussing or throwing a tantrum. The problem often arises because parents pay attention to a child who is throwing a tantrum and getting out of bed, thereby inadvertently reinforcing the very behavior that is annoying them. Of course, the obvious solution to this problem is for the parents to place the child's tantrums on extinction by leaving the child alone in his or her room until he or she finally falls asleep. Research has in fact shown this to be a highly effective procedure. Rickert and Johnson (1988), for example, randomly assigned children to either a systematic ignoring condition (extinction), scheduled awakenings throughout the night (to comfort the child), or a control condition in which parents carried on as normal. In the systematic ignoring condition, the parents were told to initially check on their child's safety when the child made a fuss and then ignore all further cries. Results revealed that children who underwent the extinction procedure experienced considerably greater improvement in their sleep patterns than the children in the other two conditions.

   Thus, extinction seems to be an effective treatment for this type of problem. Unfortunately, it suffers from a major drawback. Many parents find it impossible to totally ignore their children's persistent heartfelt pleas during the night, especially during the initial stages of treatment when such pleas are likely to be magnified in both intensity and duration (the typical extinction burst). As a result, "graduated extinction procedures" have been devised that are more acceptable to parents and less upsetting to the child. Adams and Rickert (1989), for example, instructed parents to wait for a predetermined period of time, based on what they felt was an acceptable duration, before responding to the child's calls. The parents were also instructed to comfort the child for only 15 seconds or less. Combined with a consistent bedtime routine, this less-stringent procedure was quite effective in helping many parents, and children, finally to get a good night's sleep (see Mindell, 1999, for a review).

Stimulus Control

As previously noted, when a behavior has been consistently reinforced in the presence of a certain stimulus, that stimulus will begin to affect the probability of the behavior. This stimulus, known as a discriminative stimulus (S^D), does not automatically elicit the behavior in the manner of a CS eliciting a reflex; it merely signals the availability of reinforcement, thereby increasing the probability that the behavior will occur. Such behavior is then said to be under *stimulus control*, which means that the presence of a discriminative stimulus reliably affects the probability of the behavior.

For example, if a 2000-Hz tone signals that lever pressing will lead to food:

2000-Hz Tone: *Lever press* → **Food**
S^D R S^R

and the rat thus learns to press the lever only in the presence of the tone, the behavior of lever pressing is then said to be under stimulus control. Similarly, the sound of a ringing telephone has strong stimulus control over whether people will pick it up and say hello. People never answer phones that are not ringing and almost always answer phones that are ringing. Here are some other examples of stimulus control (with the S^D italicized):

- At *red lights*, we stop; at *green lights*, we proceed.
- If *someone smiles at us*, we smile at them.
- In an *elevator*, we stand facing the front rather than the back.
- When we hear an *ambulance siren behind us*, we pull our car over to the side of the road and stop or slow down.
- When your *email alert sounds*, you automatically open it up to read it (despite promising yourself that you wouldn't look at your email while working on your essay).
- When the *professor begins lecturing*, students cease talking among themselves (hint, hint).[3]

In this section, we will look more closely at discriminative stimuli and their effects on behavior. Note that some of the principles discussed, such as stimulus generalization, represent operant versions of principles discussed in earlier chapters on classical conditioning.

Stimulus Generalization and Discrimination

In our discussion of classical conditioning, we noted that stimuli that are similar to a CS can also elicit a CR, by a process known as *stimulus generalization*. A similar process occurs in operant conditioning. In operant conditioning, stimulus generalization is the tendency for an operant response to be emitted in the presence of a stimulus that is similar to an S^D. In general, the more similar the stimulus, the stronger the response. Take, for example, a rat that has learned to press a lever for food whenever it hears a 2000-Hz tone. If we then present the rat with a series of tones that vary in pitch, we will find that it also presses the lever in the presence of these other tones, particularly in the presence of a tone that is similar to the original S^D. Thus, the rat will display a higher rate of lever pressing in the presence of an 1800- or 2200-Hz tone, both of which are more similar to the original S^D, than in the presence of a 1200- or 2800-Hz tone, which are less similar.

---

[3]Some of these examples also represent a special type of stimulus control known as an instructional control ("Do not drive through red lights, or you will get a ticket!"). The concept of instructional control is discussed in the section on rule-governed behavior in Chapter 12.

   This tendency to generalize across different stimuli can be depicted in a ==**generalization gradient**, which is a graphic description of the strength of responding in the presence of stimuli that are similar to the S^D== and that vary along a continuum. As shown in Figure 8.4, gradients can vary in their degree of steepness. A relatively steep gradient indicates that rate of responding drops sharply as the stimuli become increasingly different from the S^D, while a relatively flat gradient indicates that responding drops

FIGURE 8.4   Two hypothetical generalization gradients depicting rate of lever pressing in the presence of tones that vary in pitch between 1200 and 2800 Hz ("Hertz" is the number of sound waves per second generated by a sound source). In both examples, tones that are more similar to the original S^D (a 2000-Hz tone) are associated with stronger responding. However, generalization is much greater in the bottom gradient, which is relatively flat, than in the top gradient, which is relatively steep.

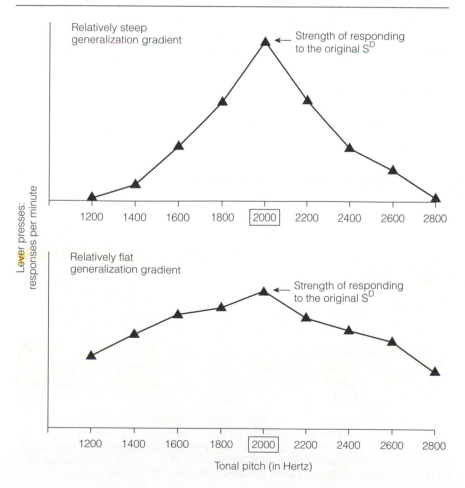

gradually as the stimuli become increasingly different from the S^D. In other words, a flat gradient indicates more generalization, while a steep gradient indicates less generalization.[4]

As in classical conditioning, the opposite of stimulus generalization in operant conditioning is *stimulus discrimination*, the tendency for an operant response to be emitted more in the presence of one stimulus than another. More generalization means less discrimination, and less generalization means more discrimination. Thus, a steep gradient indicates weak generalization and strong discrimination, whereas a flat gradient indicates strong generalization and weak discrimination.

1. A behavior is said to be under s_____ c_____ when it is highly likely to occur in the presence of a certain stimulus.

2. In operant conditioning, the term s_____ g_____ refers to the tendency for a response to be emitted in the presence of stimuli that are similar to the original _____. The opposite process, called s_____ d_____ refers to the tendency for the response to be emitted more in the presence of one stimulus than another.

3. In general, stimuli that are (more/less) _____ similar produce stronger generalization.

4. A g_____ g_____ indicates the strength of responding to stimuli that vary along a continuum.

5. In a graph that depicts a g_____ g_____, a relatively flat line indicates more _____ and less _____. A relatively steep line indicates more _____ and less _____.

6. When Jonathan looked at his watch and noticed that it was 12:30 p.m., he decided that it was time for lunch. Jonathan's eating behavior appears to be under strong s_____ c_____.

7. Jonathan always goes for lunch around 12:30, with the range being somewhere between 12:25 and 12:35 p.m. The generalization gradient for this behavior across various points in time would therefore be much (steeper/flatter) _____ than if the range was between 12:00 and 1:00. This indicates a pattern of strong (discrimination/generalization) _____ and weak _____ for Jonathan's lunch-going behavior across different points in time.

Discrimination training, as applied to operant conditioning, involves reinforcement of responding in the presence of one stimulus (the S^D) and not another stimulus. The latter stimulus is called a *discriminative stimulus*

---

[4]Generalization gradients are also used to indicate the extent of stimulus generalization in classical conditioning. Imagine, for example, that the 2000-Hz tone in Figure 8.4 is a CS that has been associated with food and now elicits a conditioned salivary response. A steep generalization gradient would indicate weak generalization of the CR across tones, while a flat gradient would indicate strong generalization of the CR across tones.

for extinction, which is a stimulus that signals the absence of reinforcement. As previously noted, a discriminative stimulus for extinction is typically given the symbol S$^\Delta$ (pronounced "es-delta"; remember that one can also use the symbol S+ in place of S^D and S− in place of S$^\Delta$). For example, if we wish to train a rat to discriminate between a 2000-Hz tone and a 1200-Hz tone, we would present the two tones in random order. Whenever the 2000-Hz tone sounds, a lever press produces food; whenever the 1200-Hz tone sounds, a lever press does *not* produce food.

> **2000-Hz Tone: Lever press → Food**
> S^D　　　　　　　R　　　　　S^R
>
> **1200-Hz Tone: Lever press → No food**
> S$^\Delta$　　　　　　　R　　　　　—

After repeated exposure to these contingencies, the rat will soon learn to press the lever in the presence of the 2000-Hz tone and not in the presence of the 1200-Hz tone. We can then say that the rat's behavior of lever pressing is under strong stimulus control.

In similar fashion, if the manager where you work complies with your requests for a day off only when he appears to be in a good mood and does not comply when he appears to be in a bad mood, you learn to make requests only when he is in a good mood. The manager's appearance exerts strong stimulus control over the probability of your making a request. In this sense, one characteristic of people who have good social skills is that they can make fine discriminations between social cues—such as facial expression and body posture—which enables them to maximize the amount of social reinforcement (and minimize the amount of social punishment) obtained during their exchanges with others. Likewise, college roommates are more likely to live in harmony to the extent that they learn to discriminate between each other's social cues and modify their actions appropriately.

1. In a discrimination training procedure, responses that occur in the presence of the (use the symbols) _____ are reinforced, while those that occur in the presence of the _____ are not reinforced. This latter stimulus is called a d_____ s_____ for e_____

2. An "Open for Business" sign is an (use the abbreviation) _____ for entering the store and making a purchase, while a "Closed for Business" sign is an _____ for attempting such behavior.

The Peak Shift Effect

An unusual effect often produced by discrimination training is the peak shift effect. According to the *peak shift effect*, the peak of a generalization gradient following discrimination training will shift from the S^D to a stimulus that is further removed from the S$^\Delta$ (Hanson, 1959). This constitutes an exception to the general principle that the strongest response in a generalization gradient occurs in the presence of the original S^D.

Suppose, for example, that we first train a rat to press a lever in the presence of a 2000-Hz tone. We then conduct a test for generalization across a range of tones varying in pitch between 1200 and 2800 Hz, and we find a generalization gradient like that shown in the top panel of Figure 8.5. We then submit the rat to a discrimination training procedure in which we reinforce lever pressing in the presence of a 2000-Hz tone (S^D) and not in the presence of a 1200-Hz tone (S$^\triangle$). When this has been successfully accomplished (the rat responds

FIGURE 8.5 Illustration of a peak shift effect following discrimination training. Prior to discrimination training (top panel), the gradient is relatively flat. Following discrimination training (bottom panel), in which a 1200-Hz tone has been established as an S$^\triangle$, the strongest response occurs not in the presence of the S^D (the 2000-Hz tone), but in the presence of a stimulus further removed from the S$^\triangle$. The gradient in the bottom panel therefore illustrates the peak shift effect.

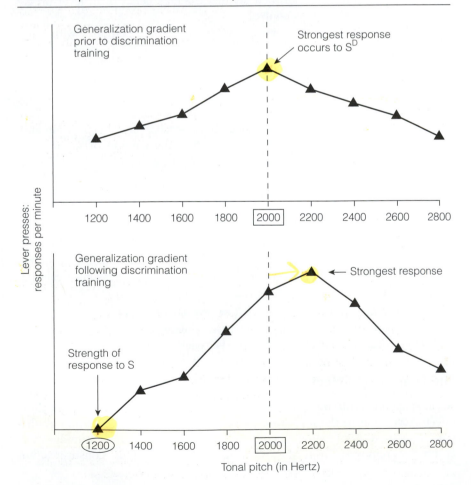

only in the presence of the 2000-Hz tone and not in the presence of the 1200-Hz tone), we again test for generalization across a range of tones. What we are likely to find with this rat is a generalization gradient something like that depicted in the bottom panel of Figure 8.5. Look carefully at this gradient. How does it differ from the gradient in the top portion of the figure, which represents generalization in the absence of discrimination training?

One obvious difference is that, with discrimination training, the gradient drops off more sharply on the side toward the $S^\triangle$, which simply means that this rat strongly discriminates between the $S^\triangle$ and the S^D. But what is the other difference between the two graphs? Before discrimination training (the top panel), the strongest response occurs to the S^D (the 2000-Hz tone). Following discrimination training (the bottom panel), the strongest response shifts away from the S^D to a stimulus that lies in a direction opposite to the $S^\triangle$ (in this case, it shifts to a 2200-Hz tone). This shift in the peak of the generalization gradient is the peak shift effect.

Perhaps a fanciful example will help clarify the peak shift effect. Suppose that Mr. Shallow identifies women entirely on the basis of how extraverted versus introverted they are. Jackie, with whom he had a very boring relationship, was an introvert (an $S^\triangle$), while Dana, with whom he had a wonderfully exciting relationship, was an extravert (an S^D). He then moves to a new city and begins touring the singles bars seeking a new mate. According to the peak shift effect, he will likely seek out a woman who is even more extraverted than Dana.

One explanation for the peak shift effect is that during discrimination training, subjects respond in terms of the relative, rather than the absolute values, of stimuli (Kohler, 1918/1939). Thus, according to this interpretation, the rat does not learn merely that a 2000-Hz tone indicates food and a 1200-Hz tone indicates no food; rather, it learns that a higher-pitched tone indicates food and a lower-pitched tone indicates no food. Given a choice, the rat therefore emits the strongest response in the presence of a tone that has an even higher pitch than the original S^D. Likewise, Mr. Shallow chooses a woman who is even more extraverted than Dana because greater extraversion is associated with a better relationship.

Another explanation for the peak shift effect is that, despite discrimination training, the S^D is still somewhat similar to the $S^\triangle$ and has acquired some of its negative properties (Spence, 1937). From this perspective, the 2000-Hz tone (the S^D) is somewhat similar to the 1200-Hz tone (the $S^\triangle$), making the 2000-Hz tone slightly less attractive than it would have been if the $S^\triangle$ had never been trained. Thus, a tone that has a slightly higher pitch than 2000 Hz, and is thereby less similar to the 1200-Hz tone, will result in the highest rate of responding. Likewise, Mr. Shallow seeks a woman who is very extraverted because he is attempting to find a woman who is even more dissimilar from Jackie, with whom he had such a poor relationship.[5]

---

[5]The peak shift effect is also found in classical conditioning following discrimination training between a CS+ and a CS−. For example, if the CS+ for a CR of salivation was a 2000-Hz tone and the CS− was a 1200-Hz tone, what would the peak shift effect consist of?

1. In the peak shift effect, the peak of a generalization gradient, following d_____ t_____, shifts away from the _____ to a stimulus that is further removed from the _____.

2. If an orange key light is trained as an S^D in a key pecking task with pigeons, and the pigeons are then exposed to other key colors ranging from yellow on one end of the continuum to red on the other (with orange in the middle), then the peak of the generalization gradient will likely be to a (yellowish-orange/orange/orange-reddish) _____ key light.

3. If a pigeon undergoes discrimination training in which a yellow key light is explicitly established as an S^Δ and an orange key light is explicitly established as the S^D, the strongest response in the generalization gradient will likely be to a (yellowish-orange/orange/orange-reddish) _____ key light. This effect is known as the _____ _____ effect.

Multiple Schedules and Behavioral Contrast

2 behaviors
affect the others
response strength

A → Bs

B → As

Reeses / Skittles

Stimulus control is often studied using a type of complex schedule known as a multiple schedule. A ***multiple schedule*** consists of two or more independent schedules presented in sequence, each resulting in reinforcement and each having a distinctive S^D. For example, a pigeon might first be presented with a red key that signals an FI 30-sec schedule, completion of which results in food. The key light then changes to green, which signals a VI 30-sec schedule, completion of which also results in food. These two schedules can be presented in either random or alternating order, or for set periods of time (such as 2 minutes on the red FI 30-sec schedule followed by 2 minutes on the green VI 30-sec schedule followed by another 2 minutes on the red FI 30-sec schedule, etc.). The following schematic shows the two schedules presented in alternating order:

FI 30-sec   **VI 30-sec**

Red key: Key peck → Food/Green key: Key peck → Food/Red key: etc.

S^D R S^R S^D R S^R S^D

Note that a multiple schedule differs from a chained schedule in that a chained schedule requires that all of the component schedules be completed before the sought-after reinforcer is delivered. For example, on a *chain* FI 30-sec VI 30-sec schedule, both the FI and VI components must be completed to obtain food. On a *multiple* FI 30-sec VI 30-sec schedule, however, completion of each component schedule results in food.

On a multiple schedule, stimulus control is demonstrated when the subject responds differently in the presence of the S^Ds associated with the different schedules. For example, with sufficient experience on a multiple FI 30-sec VI 30-sec schedule, a pigeon will likely show a scalloped pattern of responding on the red key signaling the FI component, and a moderate, steady pattern of responding on the green key signaling the VI component. The pigeon's response pattern on each key color will be the appropriate pattern for the schedule of reinforcement that is in effect on that key.

1. On a m_____ schedule, two or more schedules are presented (sequentially/ simultaneously) _____, with each resulting in a r_____ and having its own distinctive _____.

2. This type of schedule differs from a chained schedule in that a _____ is provided after each component schedule is completed.

3. On a multiple VI 50-sec VR 50 schedule, we are likely to find a high rate of response on the (VI/VR/both) _____ component(s).

[handwritten: Red button 1/10]
[handwritten: Green button 5/5]

An interesting phenomenon that can be investigated using multiple schedules is behavioral contrast. **Behavioral contrast** occurs when a change in the rate of *reinforcement* on one component of a multiple schedule produces an opposite change in the rate of *response* on another component (G. S. Reynolds, 1961). In other words, as the rate of reinforcement on one component changes in one direction, the rate of response on the other component changes in the other direction.

There are two basic contrast effects: positive and negative. In a **negative contrast effect**, an increase in the rate of *reinforcement* on one component produces a decrease in the rate of *response* on the other component. Suppose, for example, that a pigeon first receives several sessions of exposure to a multiple VI 60-sec VI 60-sec schedule:

[handwritten: 1/5 – 1/3   increases response strength]

VI 60-sec　　　　　　　　　**VI 60-sec**
Red key: Key peck → Food / Green key: Key peck → Food / etc.

Because both schedules are the same, the pigeon responds equally on both the red key and the green key. Following this, the VI 60-sec component on the red key is changed to VI 30-sec, which provides a higher rate of reinforcement (on average, two reinforcers per minute as opposed to one reinforcer per minute):

VI 30-sec　　　　　　　　　**VI 60-sec**
Red key: Key peck → Food / Green key: Key peck → Food / etc.

With more reinforcement now available on the red key, the pigeon will decrease its rate of response on the green key, which is associated with the unchanged VI 60-sec component. Simply put, because the first component in the sequence is now more attractive, the second component seems relatively less attractive. The situation is analogous to a woman whose husband has suddenly become much more affectionate and caring at home; as a result, she spends less time flirting with other men at work. The men at work seem relatively less attractive compared to her Romeo at home.

Decrease in A increases in B

5/5 → 1/10

5/5 → 5/5

In a **positive contrast effect**, a decrease in rate of *reinforcement* on one component results in an increase in rate of *response* on the other component. If, for example, on a multiple VI 60-sec VI 60-sec schedule:

VI 60-sec	VI 60-sec

Red key: Key peck → Food / Green key: Key peck → Food / etc.

the first VI 60-sec component is suddenly changed to VI 120-sec:

VI 120-sec	VI 60-sec

Red key: Key peck → Food / Green key: Key peck → Food / etc.

the pigeon will increase its rate of response on the unchanged VI 60-sec component. As one component becomes less attractive (changing from VI 60-sec to VI 120-sec), the unchanged component becomes relatively more attractive. The situation is analogous to the woman whose husband has become less caring and affectionate at home; as a result, she spends more time flirting with other men at work. The men at work seem relatively more attractive compared to the dud she has at home.

Positive contrast effects are also evident when the change in one component of the multiple schedule involves not a decrease in the amount of reinforcement but implementation of a punisher, such as a mild electric shock. As the one alternative suddenly becomes punishing, the remaining alternative, which is still reinforcing, is viewed as even more attractive (Brethower & Reynolds, 1962). This might explain what happens in some volatile relationships in which couples report strong overall feelings of affection for each other (Gottman, 1994). The intermittent periods of aversiveness seem to heighten the couple's appreciation of each other during periods of affection. Such relationships can therefore thrive, *given* that the positive aspects of the relationship significantly outweigh the negative aspects.[6]

---

[6]Similar contrast effects occur when there is a shift in the magnitude of a reinforcer (Crespi, 1942). For example, rats that experience a sudden switch from receiving a small amount of food for running down an alleyway to receiving a large amount of food for running down the same alleyway will run faster for the large amount (a positive contrast effect) than if they had always received the large amount. And those that are shifted from a large amount to a small amount will run slower (a negative contrast effect).

Warning

Remember that with positive and negative contrast, we are concerned with how changing the rate of reinforcement on the first component of a multiple schedule affects the rate of responding on the second component. The rate of responding will, of course, also change on the first component because the schedule of reinforcement on that component has changed, but that is not surprising. What is surprising is the change in response rate on the second component, even though the schedule of reinforcement in that component has remained the same. Thus, it is the change in response rate on the second component that is the focus of concern in behavioral contrast.

QUICK QUIZ J

1. In_____ behavioral contrast, an increase in reinforcement on one alternative results in a(n) (increase/decrease) _____ in (responding/reinforcement) _____ on the other alternative.

2. In _____ behavioral contrast, a decrease in reinforcement on one alternative results in a(n) _____ in _____ on the other alternative.

3. A pigeon that experiences a shift from a multiple FR 10 VI 60-sec schedule to a multiple FR 100 VI 60-sec schedule will likely (increase/decrease) _____ its rate of response on the VI 60-sec component.

4. When Levin (a lonely bachelor in Tolstoy's novel *Anna Karenina*) proposed to the beautiful young Kitty, she rejected him. Levin was devastated and decided to devote the rest of his life to his work. Kitty, in turn, was subsequently rejected by the handsome young military officer, Vronsky, whom she had mistakenly assumed was intent on marrying her. Kitty was devastated and deeply regretted having turned down Levin, whom she now perceived to be a fine man. A year later, they encountered each other at a social gathering. Relative to individuals who have not experienced such hardships in establishing a relationship, we would expect their affection for each other to be much (deeper/shallower) _____ than normal. This process seems most similar to which of the two types of contrast effects that you have just learned about: a _____ contrast effect.

An additional type of contrast effect is **_anticipatory contrast_**, in which the rate of response varies inversely with an upcoming ("anticipated") change in the rate of reinforcement (B. A. Williams, 1981). For example, Pliskoff (1963) found that pigeons increased their rate of responding for reinforcement when they were presented with a stimulus signaling that extinction was imminent. In other words, faced with the impending loss of reinforcement, the pigeons responded all the more vigorously for reinforcement while it was still available.

By anticipating a removal of something, rate increases before removal happens

Eat less for lunch to save room for Big Dinner

Anticipatory contrast seems analogous to what many of us have experienced—that things we are about to lose often seem to increase in value. For example, Lindsay views her relationship with Bryce as rather dull and uninteresting until she learns that Bryce might be romantically interested in another woman. Faced with the possibility that she might lose him, she now becomes intensely interested in him. Unfortunately, some people may use anticipatory contrast as a deliberate tactic to strengthen a partner's feelings of attachment. Read again the anecdote at the beginning of this chapter about Poppea's relationship with the Roman emperor Nero. In behavioral terms, Poppea first established herself as an effective reinforcer for Nero; then, to further increase her value, she intermittently threatened to withdraw herself from Nero's company. In anticipation of possibly losing her, Nero became even more attached.

The occurrence of these contrast effects indicates that behaviors should not be viewed in isolation. Consequences for behavior in one setting can greatly affect the strength of behavior in another setting. Consider, for example, a young girl who is increasingly neglected at home, perhaps because her parents are going through a divorce. She might try to compensate for this circumstance by seeking more attention at school (a positive contrast effect), perhaps to the point of misbehaving. Although the parents might blame the school for her misbehavior, she is in fact reacting to the lack of reinforcement at home. Thus, to borrow a concept from humanistic psychology, behavior needs to be viewed in a holistic manner, with the recognition that behavior in one setting can be influenced by contingencies operating in other settings.

1. An increase in the rate of responding for an available reinforcer when faced with the possibility of losing it in the near future is known as _____ contrast.

2. If Jackie hears her mother say that it is getting close to her bedtime, she is likely to become (more/less) _____ involved in the computer game she is playing.

3. Vronsky (another character in Tolstoy's *Anna Karenina*) falls deeply in love with Anna, who is the wife of another man. For several months, they carry on a passionate affair. When Anna, however, finally leaves her husband to be with him, Vronsky finds that he soon becomes bored with their relationship. The fact that his feelings for Anna were much stronger when their relationship was more precarious is in keeping with the _____ contrast effect.

Fading and Errorless Discrimination Learning

While discrimination training is an effective way for establishing stimulus control, it has its limitations. For example, during the process of learning to discriminate an S^D from an S^Δ, the subject will initially make several "mistakes" by responding in the presence of the S^Δ. Because such responses do

And Furthermore

St. Neots' Margin

The anticipatory contrast effect described by Pliskoff (1963) reflects the pigeon's reaction to a potential difficulty—namely, the impending loss of a reinforcer. According to British writer Colin Wilson (1972), such difficulties may provide our lives with a sense of meaning when more pleasant stimuli have failed. Wilson's description of how he discovered this concept provides an interesting illustration.

> In 1954, I was hitch-hiking to Peterborough on a hot Saturday afternoon. I felt listless, bored and resentful: I didn't want to go to Peterborough—it was a kind of business trip—and I didn't particularly long to be back in London either. There was hardly any traffic on the road, but eventually I got a lift. Within ten minutes, there was an odd noise in the engine of the lorry. The driver said: 'I'm afraid something's gone wrong—I'll have to drop you off at the next garage.' I was too listless to care. I walked on, and eventually a second lorry stopped for me. Then occurred the absurd coincidence. After ten minutes or so, there was a knocking noise from *his* gearbox. When he said: 'It sounds as if something's gone wrong,' I thought: 'Oh *no!* and then caught myself thinking it, and thought: 'That's the first definite reaction I've experienced today.' We drove on slowly—he was anxious to get to Peterborough, *and by this time, so was I.* He found that if he dropped speed to just under twenty miles an hour, the knocking noise stopped; as soon as he exceeded it, it started again. We both listened intently for any resumption of the trouble. Finally, as we were passing through a town called St. Neots, he said: 'Well, I think if we stay at this speed, we should make it.' And I felt a surge of delight. Then I thought: 'This is absurd. My situation hasn't *improved* since I got into the lorry—in fact, it has got worse, since he is now crawling along. All that has happened is that an inconvenience has been threatened and then the threat withdrawn. And suddenly, my boredom and indifference have vanished.' I formulated then the notion that there is a borderland or threshold of the mind that can be stimulated by pain or inconvenience, but not pleasure. (p. 27)

Wilson labeled the concept *St. Neots' margin* after the town they were driving through at the time. He proposes that such difficulties create "meaning" by forcing us to concentrate, and that the absence of such concentration makes life dull and uninteresting. But we can also view these difficulties as a type of contrast effect in which we are in danger of losing a reinforcer. As a result, we respond more vigorously for the reinforcer and value it more highly.

Contrast effects may therefore provide our lives with a sense of meaning that might otherwise be missing. Wilson describes, for example, how the writer Sartre claimed that he never felt so free as during the war when, as a member of the French Resistance, he was in constant danger of being arrested. In danger of losing his freedom, he truly appreciated his freedom. Consider too Balderston's (1924) play, *A Morality Play for the Leisured Class*, which recounts the story of a man who dies and finds himself in the afterlife. When a shining presence tells him that he can have any pleasure he desires by merely wishing it, he is overjoyed and fully indulges himself. He soon discovers, however, that things quickly lose their value when they are so easily attained. Facing an eternity of profound boredom (in which contrast effects are completely absent), he finally exclaims that he would rather be in hell—at which point the presence asks: "And wherever do you think you *are*, sir?"

not result in reinforcement, the subject is likely to become frustrated and display a great deal of emotional behavior. It would be helpful, therefore, if there were a method of discrimination training that minimized these effects.

Errorless discrimination training is a gradual training procedure that minimizes the number of errors (i.e., nonreinforced responses to the S^Δ) and reduces many of the adverse effects associated with discrimination training. It involves two aspects: (1) The S^Δ is introduced early in training, soon after the animal has learned to respond appropriately to the S^D, and (2) the S^Δ is presented in weak form to begin with and then gradually strengthened. This process of gradually altering the intensity of a stimulus is known as *fading*. (For example, one can *fade in* music by presenting it faintly to begin with and gradually turning up the volume, or *fade out* music by presenting it loudly to begin with and gradually turning down the volume.)

Terrace (1963a) used errorless discrimination training to establish a red–green discrimination in pigeons. The pigeons were first trained to peck a red key on a VI 60-sec schedule of reinforcement. As soon as this behavior was established, occasional 5-second periods of extinction were presented in which the key light was switched off. Since pigeons tend not to peck a dark key, the dark key was easily established as an effective S^Δ for not responding. The VI period and the extinction period were then gradually lengthened until they each lasted 3 minutes. Following this, the dark key was illuminated with a faint greenish hue that was slowly intensified. As the green key color was faded in (as an S^Δ) and gradually replaced the dark key, the pigeons emitted almost no responses toward it; that is, they made almost no errors. By comparison, pigeons that were exposed to standard discrimination training, in which the dark key was suddenly replaced by a brightly lit green key, made numerous responses on it before finally discriminating it from the red S^D. The pigeons exposed to the errorless procedure also showed few of the adverse side effects of discrimination training, such as emotional behavior.

Errorless procedures can also be used to transfer control from one type of stimulus to another. For example, Terrace (1963b) first trained pigeons to discriminate between a red key as the S^D and a green key as the S^Δ. He then gradually faded in a vertical line (the new S^D) on the red key and a horizontal line (the new S^Δ) on the green key, while at the same time fading out the colors. Eventually, the pigeons were pecking a colorless key that had a vertical line and not pecking a colorless key that had a horizontal line. With virtually no errors, stimulus control for pecking had been transferred from key color (red versus green) to line orientation (vertical versus horizontal).

Errorless discrimination training may have practical applications. For example, Haupt, Van Kirk, and Terraciano (1975) used an errorless procedure to enhance the learning of basic arithmetic skills. In their study, a 9-year-old girl who had a history of difficulties in basic arithmetic was given a series of addition problems using a standard drill procedure and a series of subtraction problems using an errorless procedure. The standard drill procedure for the addition problems consisted of presenting the problems on flash cards in which the answers were initially covered. If the child did not know the answer, the answer was uncovered and shown to her. The errorless procedure for the subtraction problems was similar except that the answer on each flash card was initially left exposed to view and then, over successive presentations, gradually blocked out by adding successive sheets of cellophane. The correct answer was thus initially available as a prompt for the correct answer and then gradually faded out. During a subsequent test, the girl made significantly fewer errors on the subtraction problems, for which the errorless procedure had been used, than on the addition problems, for which the standard drill procedure had been used.

Although errorless discrimination training might seem like the perfect answer to many unresolved problems in education, it has some serious drawbacks. Discriminations that have been established through errorless training are more difficult to modify at a later time. For example, Marsh and Johnson (1968) taught pigeons to discriminate between two key colors in which one color was the S^D and the other the S^Δ. Pigeons that had been taught to discriminate using an errorless procedure experienced extreme difficulty learning a new discrimination in which the meaning of the key colors was reversed (i.e., the color that had previously been the S^Δ now became the S^D, and vice versa). In contrast, pigeons that had learned the original discrimination in the normal error-filled way handled the reversal quite handily. Thus, although normal discrimination training has more adverse side effects compared to errorless discrimination training, it also results in greater flexibility when what is learned has to be modified later. For this reason, errorless procedures may be most useful in rote learning of basic facts, such as arithmetic and spelling, in which the substance of what is learned is unlikely to change. With material that requires greater flexibility, however, such as that typically found in most college-level courses, errorless learning might be a significant impediment (Pierce & Epling, 1999).[7]

1. In e_____ discrimination training, the S^Δ is presented (early/later) _____ in the training procedure, and at very (weak/strong) _____ intensity to begin with.

2. This type of discrimination training is likely to produce (more/less) _____ emotional behavior compared to the standard form of discrimination training.

3. This type of discrimination training is also likely to produce behavior patterns that are (easy/difficult) _____ to modify at a later point in time.

4. Gradually altering the intensity of a stimulus is called f_____.

QUICK QUIZ L

---

[7]This accords with the more general finding, briefly mentioned in Chapter 1, that experiencing a certain amount of difficulty during the learning process can enhance long-term retention and understanding (Schmidt & Bjork, 1992).

Stimulus Control: Additional Applications

There are many ways in which stimulus control can be used to manage behavior. Perhaps the most impressive use of stimulus control is by animal trainers, especially those who train animals for public performance. Dolphin trainers, for example, use a mere whistle or gesture to set off a dazzling array of leaps and twirls. Indeed, the control is so precise that the dolphins often seem like robots, an impression that probably contributes to the growing opposition to such shows. Not only has the animal been removed from its natural environment, it now appears to be a slave to the trainer's every whim. (Karen Pryor, 1999, however, contends that the reality is quite different, with such training—especially training through positive reinforcement—being much more a two-way process of communication than brute force control.)

A particularly useful form of stimulus control for animal management is *targeting*. In targeting, one trains an animal to approach and touch a particular object, as in training a dog to touch the end of a stick with its nose. Targeting is a key aspect of teaching dolphins to make their impressive leaps. The dolphin first receives reinforcement for touching a target stick with its snout, following which the stick is raised higher and higher, enticing the dolphin to leap higher and higher to touch it. Targeting is commonly used to manage animals in zoos. By simply moving the target stick, zookeepers can lead the animals from one cage to another or position them precisely for medical examinations. Animals can also be taught to target a point of light from a laser beam, which then allows the handler to send the animal to a spot some distance away. This can be a useful procedure for directing search-and-rescue dogs in disaster areas that are difficult for the handler to traverse (Pryor, 1999; see also "From TB to Landmines: Animals to the Rescue" in the And Furthermore box).

Stimulus control can also be used to eliminate certain types of problem behaviors in animals. Pryor (1999), for example, describes how she once experienced considerable difficulty in training a dolphin to wear suction cups over its eyes (as part of an intended demonstration of the dolphin's ability to swim solely by sonar). Although the cups did not hurt, the dolphin refused to wear them and would cleverly sink to the bottom of the pool for several minutes whenever it saw Pryor approaching with the cups. Initially stumped, Pryor finally hit on the idea of reinforcing the behavior of sinking by giving the dolphin a fish whenever it did so (which, she reports, seemed to greatly surprise the dolphin). Soon, the dolphin was sinking at high frequency to earn fish, at which point Pryor began to reinforce the behavior only after a cue had been presented. In short order, the dolphin was sinking only on cue, meaning that the behavior was now under strong stimulus control. Pryor found that she was then able to reintroduce the suction cups and place them on the dolphin without difficulty. In the absence of the cue for sinking, the dolphin no longer had a tendency to sink to avoid the cups. In similar fashion, a dog that has been trained to bark on cue may be less likely to bark at other times. In short, by putting a behavior "on cue," the behavior is less likely to occur in the absence of the cue.

And Furthermore

From TB to Landmines: Animals to the Rescue

Search-and-rescue dogs are an excellent example of discrimination training with animals that has had considerable benefit for humans. Dogs have a keen sense of both hearing and smell which, throughout history, have proven useful for a variety of tasks, ranging from hunting to search-and-rescue to drug detection. A particularly important manner in which dogs are being used these days is for detection of landmines (McLean, 2003). Landmines are an extreme hazard in former warzones, with large numbers of civilians being maimed or killed each year. Considerable effort is needed just to detect the mines, which is where the superior olfactory abilities of dogs have proven to be useful.

In an interesting twist, giant African pouched rats are now also being trained for landmine detection (Poling, Weetjens, Cox, Beyene, & Sully, 2010). As it turns out, these rats have some important advantages over dogs, such as: (1) they are less expensive and easier to maintain (a significant factor in the relatively poor nations that are commonly plagued by landmines), (2) they do not get attached to their handlers like dogs will and hence can be assigned to different handlers (high turnover rates among handlers being a major problem given the obvious stress involved in this type of work), and (3) last but definitely not least, the rats are so light that they can walk over mines without setting them off. It should be noted that training these animals (both dogs and rats) is extremely difficult and time consuming, requiring a highly accurate form of discrimination that will then reliably generalize across different settings. After all, landmine detection is an area of work in which "almost perfect" can be a disaster, and behavior analysts have an important role to play in devising optimal procedures for training these animals (Jones, 2011).

An even more unique setting in which the sensory capacities of animals may prove to be useful is the cancer clinic. Interest began in 1989 with a letter to the medical journal, *The Lancet*, which described a woman whose dog had essentially alerted her to the presence of a malignant tumor:

> The patient first became aware of the lesion because her dog . . . would constantly sniff at it. The dog . . . showed no interest in the other moles on the patient's body but frequently spent several minutes a day sniffing intently at the lesion, even through the patient's trousers. As a consequence, the patient became increasingly suspicious. This ritual continued for several months and culminated in the dog trying to bite off the lesion when the patient wore shorts. This prompted the patient to seek further medical attention [at which point the malignancy was discovered and removed]. (Williams & Pembroke, 1989, p. 734).

Similar reports followed, including one in which a dog was able to detect a malignant mole that had been incorrectly assessed by a doctor as nonmalignant (Church & Williams, 2001). Although mostly anecdotal, these reports strongly suggested that dogs have the ability to discriminate cancerous from noncancerous lesions. This in turn led researchers to wonder if dogs could be systematically trained to detect cancers. Several such studies have

(continued)

now been conducted, utilizing different types of cancer, somewhat different training procedures (many involving the use of clicker training as described in Chapter 6), and different stimuli (tissue versus breath versus urine) (Moser & McCulloch, 2010). For the most part, results have been very encouraging, and we can expect to hear more about this intriguing topic in the future. Interestingly, giant African pouched rats are now also getting in on the disease-detection act, only in this case with detection of tuberculosis by sniffing samples of patients' sputum (Poling, Weetjens, Cox, Beyene, Durgin, & Mahoney, 2011). Again, preliminary results are very encouraging.

But what about the behavior analyst's seemingly favorite animal, the pigeon? Well, pigeons do have excellent vision, and behavior analysts have tried to make use of this characteristic. In Chapter 1, we described Skinner's proposal in WWII to use trained pigeons to visually guide missiles to military targets. In similar fashion, in the late 1970s, an attempt was made to train pigeons for search-and-rescue missions at sea (Azar, 2002). Housed in a transparent bubble below a helicopter, pigeons that had been trained to respond to the sight of tiny objects in the seascape would peck at response keys that would then guide the pilot to the target. The pigeons were reportedly 93% accurate—whereas the flight crews were only 38% accurate—but the program was nevertheless cancelled when the need for budget cuts arose. As with Skinner's missile project, however, it seems that the "laugh factor" may have also played a role; it appears difficult for many people to take these pigeon projects seriously. Likewise, Verhave (1966) trained pigeons as "assembly line workers" to detect defective drug capsules for a drug manufacturer. Although the pigeons proved to be 99% accurate after only one week of training, the drug company never followed through on the project, one reason being a concern about publicity problems that might arise from using pigeons as "quality control inspectors." This is understandable, although for behaviorists who understand the power of conditioning, using pigeons as quality control experts would more likely be a selling feature!

Stimulus control is also an important aspect of human behavior, though we sometimes overlook it as a simple means for facilitating certain aspects of our behavior. Consider Stephanie, who promises herself that she will take vitamins each evening but so often forgets to do so that she eventually gives up. All she really needs to do is create a salient cue for taking vitamins, such as placing the vitamin bottle beside the alarm clock that she sets each evening. Likewise, the person who remembers to take her umbrella is the person who sets it beside the door when she hears on the news that it might soon be raining.

Stimulus control is also useful for creating an effective study environment. Too often students attempt to study in settings that contain strong cues for non-study behaviors, such as interacting with others or watching television. Most students do far better to study in a setting where such cues are kept to a minimum. For example, Heffernan and Richards (1981) found that students who isolated themselves from interpersonal distractions reported a major improvement in their study habits. More recently, Plant, Ericsson, Hill, and Asberg (2005) found that students who reported studying in quiet, solitary

Calvin and Hobbes

by Bill Watterson

environments had higher grade point averages (GPAs). Although the study was only correlational, the results are consistent with the possibility that students who study in such environments engage in higher-quality studying, which Plant et al. relate to the importance of high-quality, deliberate practice in the development of expert performance (see "Deliberate Practice and Expert Performance" in the And Furthermore box in Chapter 1). A particularly interesting result was that students who studied alone also tended to study fewer hours, which further supports the notion that they were engaging in high-quality studying such that they did not need to study long hours to do well.[8]

Likewise, Skinner (1987) recommends establishing a particular setting, such as a certain desk, that is used only for studying. Over time, the desk will become so strongly associated with the act of studying that just sitting at the desk will facilitate one's ability to study. Of course, this kind of stimulus control cannot be established overnight. Sitting at a desk for 3 hours at a time trying to study but daydreaming instead will only associate the desk with the act of daydreaming. Better to begin with short, high-quality study periods and then gradually progress to longer study periods (although, as the Calvin and Hobbes cartoon suggests, not too gradually).

An example of a procedure to improve study habits was reported by Fox (1962). The program began by first examining each student's schedule and finding a 1-hour period each day that was always available for studying. The students were instructed to spend at least part of that hour studying their most difficult subject matter. They were also told to conduct that studying only in a particular setting (such as a certain room in the library), to have only their study materials with them when they

---

[8]This is not to say that studying with others is necessarily ineffective. High-quality group studying can be of significant benefit; the problem is that most students studying with others do not engage in high-quality studying.

were in that setting, and not to be in that setting on other occasions. Most important, if they became bored or started to daydream, they were to complete just a bit more studying (such as reading one page) and then leave the setting. Finally, any studying done outside the special 1-hour period had to be done elsewhere. Initially, none of the students could study throughout the 1-hour period, but over time they gradually built up the ability to do so. A similar procedure was then carried out for each of their other courses. Soon the students were studying each of their courses for 1 hour per day, with a good level of concentration. The students were also given instruction in other academic skills, such as how to read a textbook and take lecture notes. Consequently, all of the students experienced considerable improvement in their grades.

Stimulus control procedures are also the treatment of choice for *sleep-onset insomnia*, in which people have difficulty falling asleep. For example, Bootzin, Epstein, and Wood (1991) recommend the following procedure:

1. Go to bed only when you are sleepy.
2. Use the bed only for sleeping (or sex). Do not lie in bed to read, study, or watch television.
3. If you cannot fall asleep within 10 to 20 minutes, get out of bed and go to another room. Go back to bed only when you feel sleepy.
4. Repeat the above rule as often as necessary. This rule should also be applied if you are unable to fall asleep after a middle-of-the-night awakening.
5. Use your alarm to get up at the same time each morning, regardless of how you slept the night before.
6. Do not take naps during the day.

The obvious goal of the program is to make lying in bed a strong cue for sleeping. Research has shown this to be an effective program, with many people reporting considerable improvement in their sleep habits both immediately following the program and at long-term follow-up (Lichstein & Riedel, 1994).

QUICK QUIZ M

1. Training a rhinoceros to touch the end of a stick with its nose is an example of a useful behavior management technique called t_____

2. Jaclyn's cat has a terrible habit of jumping up on the kitchen counter whenever Jaclyn is preparing food. How might Jaclyn use a stimulus control procedure to eliminate this behavior?_____

3. Briefly put, six rules for overcoming sleep-onset insomnia through the use of stimulus control are (chances are that you will have to check back to fill these out):

(1) _____
(2) _____
(3) _____
(4) _____
(5) _____
(6) _____

And Furthermore

Edwin Guthrie: Stimulus Control for the Practical Person

Edwin Guthrie (1886–1959) was a famous learning theorist who strongly emphasized the role of stimulus control. This is because, from his perspective, all learning is a function of one basic principle: If a behavior occurs in the presence of certain stimuli, then that behavior becomes automatically attached to those stimuli (Guthrie, 1952). Repeat those stimuli, and the person or animal must necessarily repeat the behavior. In other words, Guthrie's theory is an extreme version of an S-R theory.

Guthrie's theory makes a startlingly blunt prediction about behavior. Whatever you did the last time you were in a certain setting is exactly what you will do the next time you are in that setting. Suppose, for example, that the last time you walked down a certain hallway, you entered the first doorway to the right. Guthrie's theory predicts that the next time you walk down that hallway, you will again enter the first doorway to the right, *given that all the stimuli are the same as when you last walked down that hallway.* Of course, this last part is the catch. The stimuli that precede a behavior—and this can include both internal and external stimuli—are never exactly the same from one occasion to the next. Instead, they are only more or less similar, with the result that a behavior is only more or less likely to be repeated. Note also that the consequences of the behavior—for example, perhaps you entered the first doorway to the right because it leads to the cafeteria where you bought coffee—do not enter into the equation. Guthrie viewed consequences as having only an indirect effect on behavior, though his explanation for how this works is too complex to delve into here.

Guthrie himself did little research, and the research that was done provided only equivocal support for his theory. As a result, it receives relatively little attention from modern-day researchers. Nonetheless, Guthrie's approach still has its adherents and is still considered a major theory of learning (Hergenhahn, 1988). Perhaps one reason for its enduring attraction is the simplicity of the theory (scientists often find a parsimonious explanation quite attractive, possibly because they so often have to deal with complexities). Another reason is the engaging practicality of the theory. Guthrie by nature was a pragmatic individual and often used homey, practical examples for illustration.

One of Guthrie's most cited examples is that of a young girl who each day threw her coat on the floor when she arrived home and was each day scolded by her mother (Guthrie, 1952). On the surface, we might speculate that the girl repeated the behavior because it was rein-forced by the attention she received from her mother. From Guthrie's perspective, however, the mother's reaction had little effect on the behavior. Rather, the stimuli that the girl encountered when she entered the house had become so strongly connected to the response of throwing the coat on the floor that this response automatically occurred each time she entered. To solve the problem, the mother began to insist that the child pick up her coat, go back outside, and then practice the behavior of entering the house and hanging up the coat. The stimuli present when the girl entered the house then became associated with the act of

(continued)

hanging up the coat rather than throwing it on the floor, and the new behavior supplanted the old. Thus, from Guthrie's perspective, problem behaviors in a certain setting can often be rectified by deliberately practicing appropriate behaviors in that setting.

Another example is that of a student who was having difficulty studying because she was continually distracted by the sound of a neighbor's radio (Guthrie, 1952). Instead of trying to force herself to study, the student read mystery stories. The stories were so interesting that she was able to read them without being distracted by the sound of the radio. Within a week, the behavior of concentrating while reading had become so firmly established in that setting that she was then able to switch back to her study materials and concentrate well despite the radio.

This last example implies that students who have difficulty concentrating might sometimes do well to study something interesting before they study something boring. Starting with interesting material might establish a strong level of concentration that will then carry over to the less interesting material. This, of course, seems to contradict Grandma's rule—or the Premack principle, if you will—which contends that you should work before you play (applied to studying, this suggests that you should start with less interesting material and finish off with more interesting material). Guthrie, by contrast, seems to suggest that it might sometimes be useful to play before you work.

SUMMARY

Extinction is the nonreinforcement of a previously reinforced response, the result of which is a decrease in the strength of that response. Implementation of an extinction procedure is often followed by an extinction burst, which is a temporary increase in the rate and intensity of a behavior. Extinction is also followed by an increase in the variability of behavior and in emotional behavior, especially aggression. Extinction can also be accompanied by resurgence—the sudden appearance of a different behavior that had previously been reinforced—and depression.

Resistance to extinction is the extent to which responding persists during extinction. According to the partial reinforcement effect, an intermittent schedule of reinforcement, especially a VR schedule, produces greater resistance to extinction than a continuous schedule. Resistance also varies directly with the number of times the behavior has been reinforced, the magnitude of the reinforcers that have been used, and the extent to which the animal has been deprived of the reinforcer. Previous experience with extinction tends to lower resistance to extinction, as does the presence of a discriminative stimulus for extinction (known as an S^{Δ}).

Spontaneous recovery is the reappearance of an extinguished response following a rest period after extinction. With repeated sessions of extinction, however, the amount of recovery gradually diminishes. The process of extinction can be facilitated through differential reinforcement of other behaviors.

A behavior is said to be under stimulus control when the presence of an S^D reliably affects the likelihood of a behavior. The tendency to respond to stimuli similar to the S^D is called stimulus generalization; the tendency not to respond to such stimuli is stimulus discrimination. A graph that indicates the degree of generalization to similar stimuli is a generalization gradient. A flat gradient indicates strong generalization; a steep gradient indicates weak generalization. The peak shift effect is the tendency, following discrimination training, for the peak of a generalization gradient to shift to one side of the S^D, to a point that is further removed from the S^Δ.

A multiple schedule consists of two or more schedules presented in sequence, each resulting in reinforcement and each having a distinctive S^D. Multiple schedules are used to study contrast effects. In a negative contrast effect, an increase in reinforcement on one component of a multiple schedule produces a decrease in responding on the other component. In a positive contrast effect, a decrease in the reinforcement on one component produces an increase in responding on the other component. In anticipatory contrast, the rate of response varies inversely with an upcoming ("anticipated") change in the rate of reinforcement.

Errorless discrimination training is a procedure that minimizes the number of errors and reduces many of the side effects associated with discrimination training. It involves presenting the S^Δ early in training, beginning in weak form and then gradually strengthening it (known as a fading procedure). A drawback to errorless discrimination training is that behavior acquired in this fashion is later more difficult to modify.

Stimulus control procedures have been applied to a number of behavior problems, ranging from managing animals in zoos to facilitating the act of studying to treating insomnia.

SUGGESTED READINGS

Guthrie, E. R. (1952). *The psychology of learning* (Rev. ed.). New York: Harper & Row. (Original work published in 1935). Guthrie's very readable book outlines his provocatively simple theory of learning, backed up by plenty of down-home practical examples.

Lerman, D. C., & Iwata, B. A. (1996). Developing a technology for the use of operant extinction in clinical settings: An examination of basic and applied research. *Journal of Applied Behavior Analysis*, 29, 345–382. A nice overview of the use of extinction in applied settings.

Mindell, J. A. (1999). Empirically supported treatments in pediatric psychology: Bedtime refusal and night wakings in young children. *Journal of Pediatric Psychology*, 24, 465–481. Sleepless parents, or those who do not wish to become sleepless parents, will likely appreciate this overview of various methods for getting children to stay in bed at night.

STUDY QUESTIONS

1. Define extinction *as it applies to operant conditioning*. Be sure to distinguish between the process of extinction and the procedure of extinction.
2. What is an extinction burst? What is resurgence?
3. What are four side effects of extinction, other than extinction burst and resurgence?
4. What is resistance to extinction? Be sure to distinguish between low resistance and high resistance to extinction.
5. Define the partial reinforcement effect. Of the four basic intermittent schedules, which produces particularly strong resistance to extinction?
6. How is resistance to extinction affected by history of reinforcement, magnitude of reinforcement, degree of deprivation, and previous experience with extinction?
7. What is spontaneous recovery, and how is it affected by successive sessions of extinction?
8. Define a DRO procedure. To eliminate a behavior, why is a DRO procedure more effective than a straight extinction procedure?
9. Define stimulus control. What would be an example of stimulus control of behavior at a hockey game and at a church service?
10. Define stimulus generalization and stimulus discrimination as *they occur in operant conditioning*.
11. What is an S^Δ? Diagram an example of a discrimination training procedure (be sure to include the appropriate abbreviations for each component).
12. What is a generalization gradient? How does the shape of the gradient reflect the degree of generalization?
13. Define the peak shift effect. Illustrate your answer with a graph of a generalization gradient.
14. Define a multiple schedule. Diagram an experimental example involving the response of lever pressing for food on an FR 20 and VI 30-sec schedule, and the stimuli of tone and light. Be sure to include the appropriate label for each component (S^D, etc.).
15. Define positive and negative contrast effects, and give an example of each.
16. Define anticipatory contrast and give an example.
17. Describe errorless discrimination training and the two basic aspects of this procedure. What is a major drawback of such training?
18. How might a bird owner use stimulus control to eliminate a parrot's tendency to squawk for long periods of time? How might a novelist use stimulus control to facilitate the act of writing?

CONCEPT REVIEW

anticipatory contrast. The process whereby the rate of response varies inversely with an upcoming ("anticipated") change in the rate of reinforcement.

behavioral contrast. A change in the rate of *reinforcement* on one component of a multiple schedule produces an opposite change in the rate of *response* on another component.

differential reinforcement of other behavior (DRO). Reinforcement of any behavior other than a target behavior that is being extinguished.

discrimination training. As applied to operant conditioning, the differential reinforcement of responding in the presence of one stimulus (the S^D) and not another.

discriminative stimulus for extinction (S^Δ). A stimulus that signals the absence of reinforcement.

errorless discrimination training. A discrimination training procedure that minimizes the number of errors (i.e., nonreinforced responses to the S^Δ) and reduces many of the adverse effects associated with discrimination training.

extinction. The nonreinforcement of a previously reinforced response, the result of which is a decrease in the strength of that response.

extinction burst. A temporary increase in the frequency and intensity of responding when extinction is first implemented.

fading. The process of gradually altering the intensity of a stimulus.

generalization gradient. A graphic description of the strength of responding in the presence of stimuli that are similar to the S^D and vary along a continuum.

multiple schedule. A complex schedule consisting of two or more independent schedules presented in sequence, each resulting in reinforcement and each having a distinctive S^D.

negative contrast effect. The process whereby an increase in the rate of *reinforcement* on one component of a multiple schedule produces a decrease in the rate of *response* on the other component.

partial reinforcement effect. The process whereby behavior that has been maintained on an intermittent (partial) schedule of reinforcement extinguishes more slowly than behavior that has been maintained on a continuous schedule.

peak shift effect. Following discrimination training, the peak of a generalization gradient will shift from the S^D to a stimulus that is further removed from the S^Δ.

positive contrast effect. The process whereby a decrease in rate of reinforcement on one component of a multiple schedule produces an increase in the rate of response on the other component.

resistance to extinction. The extent to which responding persists after an extinction procedure has been implemented.

resurgence. The reappearance during extinction of other behaviors that had once been effective in obtaining reinforcement.

spontaneous recovery. The reappearance of an extinguished response following a rest period after extinction.

stimulus control. A situation in which the presence of a discriminative stimulus reliably affects the probability of a behavior.

stimulus discrimination. In operant conditioning, the tendency for an operant response to be emitted more in the presence of one stimulus than another.

stimulus generalization. In operant conditioning, the tendency for an operant response to be emitted in the presence of a stimulus that is similar to an S^D.

CHAPTER TEST

16. When Asha's parents won the lottery and bought her lots of neat playthings, she became (less/more) _____ interested in school. This is an example of a _____ contrast effect.

4. When Erin was babysitting Lucie, it took hours before Lucie would stop pestering her for a treat (Erin had been instructed to stop giving her treats). The next time Erin babysits Lucie, Lucie will (probably / probably not) _____ resume asking for a treat. This can be considered an example of an extinction effect known as _____. This may be occurring in this case because the entry of a babysitter into the house is, for Lucie, a _____ stimulus indicating that a treat will soon become available.

10. Lucie is ecstatic when Tamsen is her babysitter, and completely indifferent when Natasha is her babysitter. This is because Tamsen tends to give her treats, but Natasha does not. Thus, Tamsen is an (give the abbreviation) _____ for the availability of treats, while Natasha is an _____.

27. More persistent is to less persistent as (high/low) _____ resistance to extinction is to _____ resistance to extinction.

15. When Trish's friend Laura spread some nasty rumors about her, Trish stopped talking to her. Laura did not understand the reason for Trish's silence and initially (increased/decreased) _____ the frequency with which she attempted to talk to Laura. From the perspective of this being an extinction process, Laura's behavior can be seen as an example of a(n) _____.

9. Right after Gina was stung by a hornet, she was as likely to run away from houseflies as from hornets, which is an example of stimulus _____. One year later, we find that Gina runs away from hornets but not houseflies, which is an example of stimulus _____.

19. Lana finds that the children in her class are extremely unruly. To solve this problem, she announces that whenever she is holding up a flag, the children can run around and do whatever they want. Then, periodically throughout the day, she holds up the flag for a few minutes and lets the children run around like crazy. She also finds that when the flag is not

being held up, the children are now relatively (quiet/noisy) _____, insofar as the behavior of running around is now under _____.

5. When Charlene took her daughter, Lucie, to the store, it took hours before Lucie would stop making a fuss and pestering her for a treat. Charlene could likely have speeded up this process through the use of a (give the abbreviation) _____ procedure.

11. When Mehgan lived in Vancouver, she dated Mike, who was quite uneducated, and David, who was moderately educated. She had a boring time with Mike and a great time with David. She then moved to Dallas and set her sights on meeting someone new. According to the _____ effect, we would expect her to be most interested in meeting someone (as educated as / more educated than) _____ David.

21. In behavioral _____, a change in the rate of _____ on one component of a multiple schedule is followed by a(n) (similar/opposite) _____ change in the rate of _____ on the other component.

7. On a generalization gradient, the strongest response typically occurs to the _____.

13. The nonreinforcement of a previously reinforced response defines the _____ of extinction, while the resultant decrease in the strength of that response defines the _____ of extinction.

3. A dog whose begging for food has been reinforced 200 times is likely to show greater _____ to extinction than a dog whose begging has been reinforced only 10 times.

20. When Trish's friend Laura spread some nasty rumors about her, Trish stopped talking to her. Laura tried many different ways to get Trish to talk to her: phoning her, e-mailing, writing letters, and sending messages through mutual friends. The many ways in which Laura attempted to interact with Trish are indicative of an effect that often accompanies extinction, which is an increase in the v_____ of a behavior.

25. While teaching his daughter the letters of the alphabet, Vern would say each letter as he showed it to her and then encourage her to repeat what he said. He then began to say the letters more and more softly, with the result that she eventually said them on her own without any prompt from him. This can be seen as an example of _____ discrimination learning. One problem with this type of method is that the learning that results from this procedure tends to be (inflexible / too flexible) _____.

22. When Trish's friend Laura spread some nasty rumors about her, Trish stopped talking to her. Laura tried very hard to get Trish to talk to her. She also became emotionally (upset/distant) _____, which included becoming quite _____ with Trish.

2. When visiting a foreign resort last summer, you frequently encountered a group of children in the street who were trying to sell souvenirs. Although you always rejected their sales pitches, they were incredibly

persistent. Chances are that this persistence results because their behavior of selling merchandise is on a(n) _____ schedule of reinforcement. Another factor would be that the children seemed quite poor; hence, they were relatively _____ of the sought-after reinforcer.

8. A _____ indicates the strength of responding in the presence of stimuli that are similar to the _____ and that vary along a _____.

23. When Tamara first moved to the city, she went out each evening and had a great time. One evening at a nightclub, however, she had a frightening experience that really turned her off the club scene. Interestingly, she subsequently became (more/less) _____ interested in other activities, including her job. This may be an example of a (n) _____ contrast effect.

14. The first step in carrying out an extinction procedure is to identify the _____ that is maintaining the behavior.

18. When Trish's friend Laura spread some nasty rumors about her, Trish stopped talking to her. Laura tried to get Trish to talk to her but quickly gave up. Laura's behavior of trying to interact with Trish seems to have (low/high) _____ resistance to extinction.

24. Ahmed found school only slightly interesting. Unfortunately, his lack of studying led to some very poor marks one semester, with the result that he faced the real threat of being forced to withdraw for a year. Based on what you have learned in this chapter, throughout the rest of the semester, Ahmed probably became (more/less) _____ interested in his academic studies. This can be seen as an example of an _____ contrast effect.

12. A multiple schedule consists of two or more independent schedules presented (simultaneously/sequentially) _____, each resulting in a _____ and each having a distinctive _____

1. When Trish's friend Laura spread some nasty rumors about her, Trish stopped talking to her. Laura tried hard to get Trish to talk to her. She even asked Trish if she would like to go to the local video arcade, which had been one of their favorite activities when they first became friends. This may be an example of an extinction effect known as _____.

17. Yan lives in a very crowded city, so he teaches his little boy to stay in close contact with his right hand whenever they are walking in a crowd. This is similar to a behavior management technique known as _____ that is used to guide animals.

6. When the commander yells "Charge!", all of his troops climb out of the trench and start running toward the enemy. The behavior of these troops is obviously under strong _____ control.

26. When Trish's best friend Laura spread some nasty rumors about her, Trish stopped talking to her. Laura tried very hard to get Trish to talk to her. When Trish refused, Laura eventually became _____, one symptom of which was a relatively (low/high) _____ level of activity.

Visit the book companion Web site at http://www.academic.cengage.com/psychology/powell for additional practice questions, answers to the Quick Quizzes, practice review exams, and additional exercises and information.

ANSWERS TO CHAPTER TEST

1. resurgence
2. intermittent (VR); deprived
3. resistance
4. probably; spontaneous recovery; discriminative
5. DRO
6. stimulus
7. S^D
8. generalization gradient; S^D; continuum
9. generalization; discrimination
10. S^D (or S+); S^Δ (or S−)
11. peak shift; more educated than
12. sequentially; reinforcer; S^D
13. procedure; process
14. reinforcer
15. increased; extinction burst
16. less; negative
17. targeting
18. low
19. quiet; stimulus control
20. variability
21. contrast; reinforcement; opposite; response
22. upset; angry (or aggressive)
23. more; positive
24. more; anticipatory
25. errorless; inflexible
26. depressed; low
27. high; low

CHAPTER 9

Escape, Avoidance, and Punishment

James informed Misha, his new girlfriend, that he was once married to a woman who had been diagnosed with depression. He explained that she had stopped working, moped around the house all day, and would often break down and start crying. Despite his best efforts to be supportive, they finally got a divorce. Misha felt a lot of sympathy for James, who was obviously a very caring fellow. After several months, though, she noticed that she herself was becoming depressed. Although James was often quite affectionate, he would also become angry with her or, worse yet, grow coldly silent for no apparent reason. He also had a tendency to contradict her whenever she offered her opinion on some matter, and he took special pains to point out her mistakes (because, he said, he loved her so much that he wanted to be honest with her). Misha then learned that James' former wife had made a remarkable recovery soon after their divorce.

This chapter explores the effects of aversive consequences on behavior. We begin by examining the role of negative reinforcement in the development of escape and avoidance behaviors. As you will see, this process plays a critical role in the development and maintenance of phobic and obsessive-compulsive disorders in humans. We follow this with a discussion of punishment, in which the presentation or withdrawal of consequences serves to suppress a behavior. We discuss some of the undesirable side effects of punishment as well as some of the ways in which punishment can be effective. The chapter concludes with a discussion of the harmful effects of noncontingent punishment, in which the punishing stimulus is delivered independently of the individual's behavior.

Escape and Avoidance

As you will recall from Chapter 6, negative reinforcement consists of the removal of an aversive stimulus following a response, which then leads to an increase in the strength of that response. For example, if we wave our hands at a bothersome wasp and the wasp flies away, we will likely repeat that action with the next wasp that annoys us. Negative reinforcement is associated with two types of behavior: (1) *escape behavior*, in which performance of the behavior terminates the aversive stimulus, and (2) *avoidance behavior*, in which performance of the behavior prevents the aversive stimulus from occurring. Thus, we escape from the rain when we run indoors after it has started; we avoid the rain when we head indoors before it has started.

Typically, one first learns to escape from an aversive stimulus and then to avoid it. This process can be demonstrated using a *shuttle avoidance procedure*, in which an animal has to shuttle back and forth in a box to avoid an aversive stimulus. In a typical procedure, a rat is placed in a chamber divided by a low

FIGURE 9.1 Escape and avoidance in a shuttle avoidance task. As shown in the top panel, the animal first learns to escape from the shock by climbing over the barrier whenever a shock occurs. Later, as it learns that the light predicts the occurrence of shock, it climbs over the barrier whenever the light appears, thereby avoiding the shock (as shown in the bottom panel). (*Source:* Nairne, 2000.)

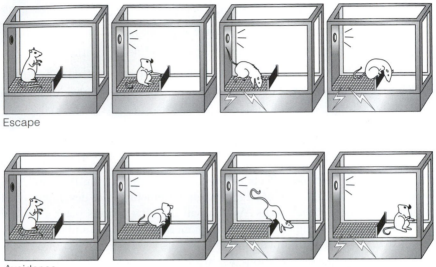

Escape

Avoidance

barrier. A stimulus of some sort, such as a light, is presented for, say, 10 seconds, followed by a mild electric shock. The rat can escape the shock by climbing over the barrier to the other side of the compartment, as it will quickly learn to do whenever it feels a shock (see top panel of Figure 9.1). Technically speaking, at this early point in the process, the presence of a shock is a discriminative stimulus that sets the occasion for the escape behavior of crossing the barrier. Crossing the barrier is then negatively reinforced by the removal of shock:

> **Shock:** *Cross barrier* → **Removal of shock**
> S^D **R** S^R

Now, remember that the shock is preceded by the presentation of a light, which is essentially a warning signal that a shock is about to occur. As the rat learns to associate the light with the shock, it will begin crossing the barrier whenever the light is presented and before the shock begins (see bottom panel of Figure 9.1). The light is now the effective discriminative stimulus for the avoidance response of crossing the barrier.

> **Light:** *Cross barrier* → **Avoidance of shock**
> S^D **R** S^R

In similar fashion, we might first learn to escape from an upsetting conversation with a racist acquaintance by inventing an excuse for leaving. After a few experiences, however, we might begin actively avoiding that individual before any encounter. By doing so, we avoid having to endure any exposure to that person's racist views.

1. Behavior that terminates an aversive stimulus is called _____ behavior, whereas behavior that prevents an aversive stimulus from occurring is called _____ behavior.

2. Typically, one first learns to _____ from an aversive stimulus, and then to _____ it.

3. Julio initially takes vitamin C whenever he has a cold, in the hope that it will shorten the duration of his symptoms. Feeling that this is effective, he begins taking it daily in the hope that it will keep him from getting a cold. Julio initially took the vitamin C to (avoid/escape) _____ the symptoms of a cold; he later took it to _____ the symptoms of a cold.

4. In the shuttle avoidance procedure described previously, the rat first learns to _____ from the shock, with the _____ acting as the S^D for the behavior. The rat later learns to _____ the shock, with the _____ acting as the S^D for the behavior.

Two-Process Theory of Avoidance

Researchers have generally shown more interest in studying avoidance behavior than escape behavior. This is because, from a theoretical perspective, escape behavior is relatively easy to understand. For example, when escaping from shock by climbing over a barrier, the rat moves from a clearly aversive situation to a nonaversive situation. But the motivation underlying avoidance behavior is less apparent. When climbing over a barrier to avoid shock, the rat seems to be moving from one nonaversive situation (no shock) to another nonaversive situation (no shock). How can a lack of change function as a reinforcer?

An early attempt to explain avoidance behavior was the *two-process theory of avoidance* (also known as the *two-factor theory of avoidance*) proposed by Mowrer (1947, 1960). According to this theory, two processes are involved in learning an avoidance response. The first process is classical conditioning of a fear response to a CS. For example, in the shuttle avoidance procedure described previously, the light that precedes the shock becomes a CS that elicits a conditioned fear reaction:

Light:	Shock	→	*Fear*
NS	US		UR

① Classical Conditioning

② Operant Conditioning

Light	→	*Fear*
CS		CR

Once this conditioned fear has been established, it then forms the basis of an operant conditioning procedure. If the CS generates a conditioned fear response, then moving away from the CS should result in a reduction of fear. This reduction of fear should in turn serve as a negative reinforcer for the response that produced it. In our experimental example, presentation of the light elicits a conditioned fear response, while climbing over the barrier produces a reduction in fear that serves as a negative reinforcer for climbing over the barrier.

(Level 1)

Light: *Climb over barrier* → **Reduction in fear**
S^D ^1R S^R

Fear is elicited by Classic Cond.

Thus, Mowrer's *two-process theory of avoidance* proposes that avoidance behavior is the result of two distinct processes: (1) classical conditioning, in which a fear response comes to be elicited by a CS, and (2) operant conditioning, in which moving away from the CS is negatively reinforced by a reduction in fear.

(Level 2)
Action emitted to avoid Fear

1. It is relatively easy to understand the process underlying (escape/avoidance) _____ conditioning because the organism moves from an _____ situation to a non_____ situation. By contrast, it is more difficult to understand _____ conditioning because the organism moves from a(n) _____ situation to another _____ situation.

2. According to Mowrer, avoidance is the result of two distinct processes: (1) _____ conditioning of a _____ response, and (2) _____ conditioning in which an avoidance response is n_____ r_____ by a reduction in _____.

Mowrer's two-process theory generated an enormous amount of study, with the result that researchers soon discovered several apparent difficulties with it. One problem was that avoidance responses are often extremely persistent. R. L. Solomon, Kamin, and Wynn (1953), for example, found that dogs would continue to jump a barrier to avoid shock for hundreds of trials even though the shock apparatus had been disconnected and avoidance was no longer necessary. One dog, for example, made more than 600 avoidance responses before the experimenters finally gave up and put a stop to the session.

Generally because persistant.

On the surface, it seems as though two-process theory cannot account for such persistence. If the animal repeatedly encounters the CS in the absence of the US, then fear of the CS should eventually extinguish—meaning that the animal should eventually stop jumping over the barrier. But it seemed as though the behavior would not extinguish. Why not?

A possible answer to this question is provided by a modification of two-process theory known as the *anxiety conservation hypothesis* (R. L. Solomon & Wynne, 1954). According to this approach, avoidance responses usually occur so quickly that there is insufficient exposure to the CS for the conditioned fear to fully extinguish—that is, a good deal of the conditioned fear is conserved because exposures to the CS are too brief for extinction to take place.[1]

happens so fast that it cannot be extinguished

---

[1] It is also possible, according to Eysenck's (1968) theory of incubation (discussed in Chapter 5), that such brief exposures might sometimes strengthen a conditioned fear response, which would further counteract the process of extinction.

For this reason, avoidance responses can be extremely persistent. In addition, supporters of two-process theory have pointed out that avoidance responses are not as persistent as sometimes claimed (Levis, 1989). If one continues to expose the animal to the aversive CS, extinction will often eventually occur given that there are no further pairings of the CS with the US. Thus, the fact that avoidance responses are extremely persistent might not be as damaging a criticism of two-process theory as was first assumed.

Researchers, however, also discovered a second, more serious difficulty with two-process theory. They found that, after repeated avoidance trials, animals appeared to show no evidence of fear but continued to make the avoidance response anyway (R. L. Solomon & Wynn, 1953). In other words, once the animals had become adept at making the avoidance response, they seemed to become almost nonchalant and relaxed while carrying it out. This constituted a major problem for two-process theory: If the animals were no longer afraid of the CS, how could avoidance of the CS have been negatively reinforced by a reduction in fear?

This was a pretty damaging criticism, and for a while it looked as though two-process theory was pretty much on the ropes. Levis (1989), however, has argued that although animals in avoidance experiments may become significantly *less* fearful with experience, there is no evidence that they become completely nonfearful. In fact, evidence suggests that if an animal completely loses its fear of the aversive CS, then, just as two-process theory predicts, the avoidance response ceases to occur. But as long as some fear remains, the avoidance response continues, suggesting that fear reduction is still functioning as a negative reinforcer for the behavior (Levis & Boyd, 1979).

Various other theories have been proposed to account for avoidance behavior. According to *one-process theory*, for example, the act of avoidance is negatively reinforced simply by the lower rate of aversive stimulation with which it is associated (Herrnstein, 1969; Herrnstein & Hineline, 1966). Thus, the rat in a shuttle avoidance task persistently climbs over the barrier when the light comes on because this action results in a decreased rate of shock, and not because it results in decreased feelings of fear. The attractive aspect of this theory is that it does away with any reference to an internal state of fear, the existence of which has to be inferred. The overall reduction in aversive stimulation that accompanies avoidance is regarded as a sufficient explanation for the behavior. By contrast, Bolles' (1970) *species-specific defense reaction theory* contends that many avoidance behaviors are actually elicited behaviors rather than operant behaviors. (This theory is described in Chapter 11.) Evidence exists both for and against each of these theories. (See Domjan, 2010, for an overview of these and other theories of avoidance.)

The debate over the processes underlying avoidance behavior will likely continue for some time, and it could well be that several processes are involved. At the very least, avoidance behavior is turning out to be more complicated than researchers originally suspected. Fortunately, the knowledge gained from all this theorizing and research is proving to have practical application, particularly in the analysis and treatment of anxiety disorders, a topic to which we turn next.

1. One apparent problem with two-process theory is that, even after hundreds of trials, the avoidance response does not seem to e_____.

2. However, according to the a_____ c_____ hypothesis, avoidance responses usually occur so (quickly/slowly) _____ that exposures to the (CS/US) _____ are too (long/brief) _____ for_____ to take place.

3. A second problem with Mowrer's theory is that after sufficient experience with avoiding the aversive CS, the animals no longer show any _____, yet continue to make the avoidance response. Levis, however, contends that such animals are nevertheless still (slightly/strongly) _____ fearful, otherwise the avoidance response would extinguish.

4. According to the one-process theory of avoidance, the avoidance response is negatively reinforced by a reduction in overall rate of av_____ st_____, as opposed to a reduction in _____.

5. According to species-specific defense reaction theory, avoidance responses are often (learned/innate) _____ reactions to aversive stimulation that are automatically (emitted/elicited) _____ in dangerous situations.

Avoidance Conditioning and Phobias

In Chapter 5, we noted that the basis of many phobias is the development of a classically conditioned fear response, which then fails to extinguish because the individual avoids the feared stimulus. At that time, we focused on the classical conditioning aspect of a phobia. Let us now examine the role of avoidance learning in phobic development.

As noted, avoidance learning appears to be a fundamental process in the development and maintenance of phobic behavior. This is no doubt one reason for the intense interest researchers have shown in studying avoidance. Indeed, demonstrations of avoidance learning in laboratory rats have often been regarded as applicable to phobic conditioning in humans. But is avoidance conditioning in the laboratory a true analogue of human phobic conditioning? Does a rat avoid shock in a shuttle avoidance procedure in the same manner that a person avoids dogs after being bitten? In fact, some have argued that there are considerable differences between avoidance conditioning in an experimental setting and human phobic conditioning.

Mineka (1985), for example, has claimed that there are two limitations in applying models of experimental avoidance to human phobias. The first limitation concerns the nature of what is being avoided. *In experimental avoidance conditioning, the animal avoids the aversive US.* For example, in the shuttle avoidance procedure discussed earlier, the rat avoids the shock (US) by climbing over the barrier whenever it sees the light (CS). *In human phobias, however, people avoid the CS.* A person who has been attacked by a dog and now has a severe phobia of dogs not only avoids being attacked by a dog but also avoids the possibility of even encountering a dog. A person who has a fear of elevators because he was once trapped in an elevator does not simply avoid being trapped in an elevator; he avoids elevators altogether, planning his day well ahead of time so that riding an elevator will not become an issue.

A second limitation of experimental avoidance is that the avoidance behavior seems to condition less readily and tends to be less certain than avoidance behavior in a phobia. Experimental avoidance typically requires at least a few pairings of the CS and the US (e.g., light and shock) before avoidance has been reliably established. And experimental avoidance is usually less than 100% certain, with the animal occasionally reencountering the aversive US. For example, in a shuttle avoidance task, the rat will occasionally be tardy in climbing over the barrier, with the result that it sometimes receives a shock. By contrast, human phobias often require only a single, brief conditioning trial to produce an avoidance response that is strong and persistent. For example, a very strong and persistent dog phobia may develop following a single dog attack.

1. According to Mineka, one limitation in applying experimental models of avoidance to human phobias is that the animals are usually avoiding the aversive (CS/US) _____ whereas human phobics are avoiding the aversive _____.

2. According to Mineka, a second limitation of applying experimental models of avoidance to phobias is that avoidance behavior in an experiment conditions (more/less) _____ readily than does avoidance behavior in a phobia.

3. Experimental avoidance usually requires (one / a few) _____ conditioning trial(s), while phobic conditioning usually requires _____ conditioning trial(s). Also, (experimental/phobic) _____ conditioning is less than 100% certain.

QUICK QUIZ D

In response to Mineka's (1985) concerns about the applicability of experimental avoidance conditioning to human phobias, Stampfl (1987) proposed that an adequate experimental analogue of a human phobia would require: (1) the reliable establishment of a fear response with only a single, brief pairing of the CS and US, (2) subsequent avoidance of the CS as well as the US, and (3) the occurrence of successful avoidance on 100% of trials. Stampfl acknowledged that when using these criteria the typical avoidance-conditioning procedure is an inadequate analogue of human phobic conditioning. He then devised an experimental procedure that produced avoidance conditioning that met all three criteria.

Stampfl's (1987) procedure focuses on the fact that human phobics typically make the avoidance response early in the chain of events leading up to the feared stimulus. For example, a person with an elevator phobia will plan his day well ahead of time so that he will not be faced with any pressure to take an elevator. He may, for example, arrange an appointment with a dentist whose office is on the main floor of an office building. This type of planning is important because not doing so could result in a direct encounter with a phobic stimulus, which in turn could greatly increase the cost involved in avoiding it (such as by having to climb the stairs to get to a dentist's office on the 23rd floor). Thus, *the phobic individual learns to make the avoidance response early on in the chain of events so as to minimize the effort of avoiding.*

The opportunity to make an early avoidance response is typically absent from most avoidance-conditioning procedures. Stampfl, however, designed an apparatus that provided just such an opportunity. As depicted in Figure 9.2, the apparatus consisted of an alleyway that was 5 feet in length and contained a dark compartment at one end. Each rat was first allowed to explore the alleyway at its leisure, during which time it came to strongly prefer the black compartment (rats generally prefer the dark). The rat was then given a foot shock while in the black compartment, at which point it fled to the far end of the alleyway. Three minutes later, a conveyor belt was turned on that began to slowly carry the rat toward the dark compartment. During this first trial, most rats waited until they reached the black sidewall area of the apparatus before running back to the far end. When they did run back to the far end, they broke a photobeam that stopped the conveyor belt for a 3-minute period. The conveyor belt then started up again, and the procedure was repeated. This initial session lasted 2 hours. During the second session, the response requirement for stopping the conveyor belt was increased from FR 1 to FR 10 (that is, the rat had to run back and cross the photobeam 10 times before the conveyor belt would stop).

Stampfl (1987) found that the rats soon learned to run back to the safe area immediately after the conveyor belt started up. In other words, rather than waiting until they reached the black sidewalls before running back, they began running back after traveling only a short distance. In this manner, they were able to minimize the effort involved in breaking the photobeam and stopping the belt. Moreover, under these circumstances, the rats completely avoided entering the black compartment on more than 1000 consecutive trials, thereby consistently avoiding the aversive CS that was

FIGURE 9.2 Illustration of a 5-foot automated alleyway similar to the one used by Stampfl (1987).

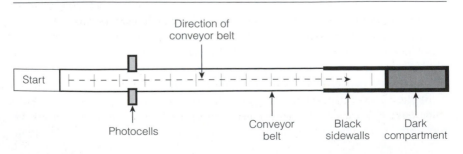

associated with shock. Furthermore, this persistent avoidance response resulted from only a single brief exposure to shock.

In summary, Stampfl's results confirm that a critical factor in the maintenance of phobic behavior is that the avoidance response occurs early in the sequence of events leading up to the phobic stimulus, thereby minimizing the effort involved in making the response. Such early responding greatly reduces the extent to which the avoidance response can be extinguished because the individual experiences little or no exposure to the aversive CS. In terms of the anxiety conservation hypothesis discussed earlier, exposure to the aversive stimulus is so minimal that the avoidance response is extremely resistant to extinction. It is therefore not surprising that phobic behaviors are often extremely persistent.

1. A critical aspect of Stampfl's experimental analogue of phobic conditioning is that the avoidance response can occur (early/late) _____ in the sequence of events leading up to the feared CS, thereby (maximizing/minimizing) _____ the amount of effort involved in making the response.

2. This results in (little/considerable) _____ exposure to the feared CS, thereby greatly (increasing/reducing) _____ the likelihood that the fear response will e_____.

QUICK QUIZ E

And Furthermore

Repression: Avoidance of Distressing Thoughts?

Repression is one of the most contentious concepts in present-day psychology. Simply defined (and ignoring some of the complexities), repression refers to the removal of anxiety-provoking thoughts from conscious awareness. Beginning in the 1980s, many therapists became intensely interested in this concept. In particular, they discovered that many clients were able to uncover seemingly forgotten memories of childhood abuse when encouraged to do so, and these memories seemed to be related to their symptoms (J. L. Herman, 1992). A controversy arose, however, when some memory researchers warned that such "recovered memories" might often be false memories of traumatic incidents that never occurred (e.g., Loftus, 1993).

Can the principles of conditioning offer us any insight into this controversy? As it turns out, repression can be viewed as a type of avoidance response. More specifically, the process of repression might be a covert form of avoidance conditioning in which the event being avoided is not an external event, such as a phobic object, but an internal thought. The memory of a childhood trauma is therefore an aversive stimulus that generates anxiety, which in turn motivates one to escape from the anxiety by thinking of something else. With practice, one eventually learns to think of something else before the memory even arises, thereby avoiding the memory (e.g., Levis, 1995; see also Skinner, 1953). To the extent that the memory is consistently avoided, never entering consciousness, then it meets the

(continued)

definition of being repressed. Indeed, Levis (1988) utilized this notion to devise a procedure for "reactivating" memories of traumatic events that had apparently been forgotten.

The process of repression is, therefore, consistent with some basic principles of conditioning. Principles of conditioning, however, also suggest that it may be possible to create false memories of abuse. If covert behavior is governed by many of the same principles as overt behavior, then it is conceivable that a therapist might inadvertently shape the production of novel thought patterns that depict a history of abuse and then reinforce the behavior of labeling such thoughts as memories. Consistent with this notion of shaping, some therapists admit that the process of uncovering repressed memories is often gradual, with the memories first appearing as fragmented images that are then strengthened and clarified by repeatedly thinking about them. As well, some therapists warn clients to discuss their recovered memories only with other survivors of abuse, who will reinforce the clients' belief that these memories are real. The overall result is that clients may become increasingly proficient at generating mental images of childhood trauma that they believe to be genuine memories (Pendergrast, 1995). Furthermore, even when it is claimed that memory recovery has occurred without any "suggestive influence" by the therapist (e.g., Levis & Brewer, 2001), it is possible that other factors, such as exposure to media stories about recovered memories, have played a role.[2]

Of course, the possibility that reinforcement and shaping may be involved in generating recovered memories does not prove that recovered memories are mostly false. It could be that by first uncovering and confirming a fragmented memory of abuse, a sort of desensitization occurs that then allows a more complete memory to emerge (Levis, 1995). On the other side of the coin, however, the fact that the process of repression is explainable in terms of avoidance conditioning does not constitute strong evidence that repression actually occurs and that recovered memories are often real. Thus, if our behavioristic analysis of recovered memories offers any insight into this controversy, it is simply that there are no easy answers. One would therefore do well to approach this issue with caution.

Finally, in an interesting aside to the controversy over recovered memories, L. S. Newman and Baumeister (1996) have proposed a cognitive-behavioral explanation for why some individuals become strongly committed to apparently false memories of UFO abductions. They point out that abduction memories share many of the characteristics of masochistic experiences (in which erotic pleasure is derived from pain and humiliation). In particular, stories of UFO abductions, like masochistic experiences, typically involve feelings of complete helplessness and the loss of one's normal identity. Newman and Baumeister also note that abduction accounts, like masochistic tendencies, are more common among individuals who are relatively successful, yet stressed out by their responsibilities. The act of "remembering" an alien abduction might therefore be a form of masochism that allows the "abductee" to temporarily escape from a stressful lifestyle, thereby negatively reinforcing the production of such memories.

---

[2]Such a claim may also reflect a tendency to underestimate the subtle ways in which a therapist can influence a client. It is said that one lesson learned by the "animal magnetists" in the early days of research into what is now called hypnosis was the extent to which the patient can detect and respond to very subtle cues emitted by the hypnotist. The cues were so subtle that people often missed them, resulting in speculation that hypnotism sometimes created a telepathic link between the patient and the hypnotist (Ellenberger, 1970).

Avoidance Conditioning and Obsessive–Compulsive Disorder

Phobia is one type of disorder in which avoidance conditioning plays a critical role. Another is *obsessive-compulsive disorder* (OCD), a disorder characterized by persistent thoughts, impulses, or images (called obsessions), and
repetitive, stereotyped actions (called compulsions) that are carried out in
response to the obsessions. For example, a person might have an obsessive
worry about contacting germs; this leads to a compulsive tendency to take a
shower and clean the house many times each day. Or a person might have an
obsessive worry about whether she locked her apartment door when she left
that morning, which leads to a compulsive pattern of returning to the apartment several times a day to check it. Note that the person recognizes that the
compulsive behavior is clearly excessive but nevertheless feels compelled to
perform the action. (Interestingly, cleaning and checking are the two most
common forms of compulsive behavior.)

[margin handwritten notes: Obsessions: - persistent thoughts / Fear. Compulsions - action help to reduce fear of persistence thoughts.]

OCD was once considered a particularly difficult disorder to treat.
This changed when clinicians began analyzing OCD in terms of avoidance
conditioning, especially Mowrer's two-process (Rachman & Hodgson,
1980). The applicability of this theory to OCD lies in the fact that obsessions
and compulsions have opposite effects on anxiety. In general, obsessions are
associated with an increase in anxiety, whereas compulsions are associated
with a decrease in anxiety. For example, a person who has a contamination
fear and is a compulsive cleaner usually experiences an increase in anxiety
after exposure to situations in which "contamination" might have occurred,
such as when taking out the garbage. Garbage elicits such a strong anxiety
response that any part of the body that has been exposed to garbage also
elicits an anxiety response. Taking a shower, however, results in the
removal of this anxiety. From the perspective of two-process theory, the
feeling of anxiety is a classically conditioned response elicited by contact
with the garbage, while showering is an operant response that is negatively reinforced by a reduction in anxiety.

The role of avoidance in OCD is virtually the same as in phobic behavior,
except that OCD typically involves an active avoidance response while phobic behavior typically involves a passive avoidance response. More specifically, a person with OCD will generally *do something* to reduce anxiety
(such as showering), whereas a person with a phobia will generally *not do
something to reduce anxiety* (such as not go near a dog). Nevertheless, individuals with OCD might also utilize passive avoidance responses (e.g., by
avoiding garbage whenever possible) such that some of their behavior patterns can also be characterized as phobic.

Two-process theory helped clarify our understanding of OCD and led to the
development of the first effective treatment for the disorder. If a compulsive
behavior pattern (such as excessive washing) is maintained by avoidance of an
anxiety-arousing event (such as contact with germs), then preventing the avoidance response from occurring should result in the eventual extinction of anxiety.
This treatment method is known as ***exposure and response prevention (ERP)***,

[handwritten note at bottom: Repression = avoiding thoughts that cause anxiety]

a method of treating OCD that involves prolonged exposure to the anxiety-arousing event while not engaging in the compulsive behavior pattern that reduces the anxiety (e.g., Steketee & Foa, 1985).

As with recent versions of exposure-based treatments for phobic behavior, ERP combines the graduated exposure of systematic desensitization with the prolonged exposure of flooding therapy. For example, a compulsive cleaner might be required to first touch objects associated with slight anxiety (such as door handles and hand rails), then objects associated with moderate anxiety (such as garbage cans and dogs), and finally objects associated with intense anxiety (such as dead birds and dog excrement). These graduated exposures are first carried out imaginally—given that the person has good imagery ability—and then *in vivo*—given that live exposure to the anxiety-arousing event is practical. The exposures are also relatively long, often 90 minutes or more, to ensure sufficient time for the anxiety to begin to extinguish. In addition to scheduled treatment sessions, the client is told to practice exposures at home. The client is also told not to perform any compulsive behavior patterns; for example, a compulsive washer might be instructed to avoid all nonessential showers except for one 10-minute shower every 5 days! Once the obsessive-compulsive pattern has been successfully eliminated, normal patterns of behavior are then reestablished (Steketee & Foa, 1985).

Mowrer's two-process theory has therefore proven quite useful in enhancing our understanding and treatment of OCD. Nevertheless, two-process theory does not provide an entirely adequate explanation for OCD (Steketee & Foa, 1985). For example, people with OCD are usually unable to recall any particular conditioning event that could account for the obsessional anxiety response. People who have a contamination fear, for example, typically do not recall, say, falling into a cesspool before the onset of the fear. On the other hand, onset of OCD does often coincide with a period of stress. One possibility, therefore, is that stress sensitizes certain individuals in such a way that normal concerns, such as those about cleanliness and safety, become greatly exaggerated. Thus, just as the process of selective sensitization might lead to the development of a phobia (as discussed in Chapter 5), so too it might lead to the development of OCD. Furthermore, just as genetic factors may predispose some people to develop a phobia (also discussed in Chapter 5), so too some people might have a genetic predisposition toward developing OCD (Billet, Richter, & Kennedy, 1998).

On a more cognitive level, people with OCD often hold the irrational belief that they should be in complete control of their thoughts—failing to realize that intrusive thoughts are not uncommon and that most people simply ignore them. In other words, they fail to realize that some thoughts are essentially respondents (reflexes) that are automatically elicited by certain stimuli, and that it is futile to try to control such thoughts (as though they were operants). People with OCD also have a tendency to feel personally responsible for events that are highly improbable. They therefore carry out various safety actions, such as rechecking doors and stoves, that other people would not bother with (Salkovskis, 1998). Given the involvement of cognitive factors in OCD,

"I THINK I WAS BETTER OFF WHEN I WAS OBSESSIVE-COMPULSIVE."

© ScienceCartoonsPlus.com

attempts have been made to combine ERP with cognitive therapy on the assumption that directly modifying these false belief systems might enhance treatment. However, the specific efficacy of these cognitive interventions has not yet been firmly established, and ERP by itself remains the treatment of choice for OCD (Foa, Franklin, & Kozak, 1998; Tolin & Steketee, 2007).

1. Janice continually worries that her alarm clock might not be set, and that she will wake up late for class. She therefore checks the alarm clock about 20 times each night before finally falling asleep. The persistent thoughts about the alarm clock not being set are classified as a(n) (compulsion/obsession) _____ while the frequent checking of the clock is classified as a(n) _____.

2. In general, (compulsions/obsessions) _____ are associated with an increase in anxiety, whereas _____ are associated with a decrease in anxiety.

3. From the perspective of two-process theory, this decrease in anxiety likely functions as a n_____ r_____ for the compulsive behavior.

4. Exposure and response prevention (ERP) therapy for OCD involves prolonged exposure to anxiety-arousing events while (engaging / not engaging) _____ in the (obsessive/compulsive) _____ behavior that serves to reduce the anxiety.

5. ERP is similar to systematic desensitization in that exposure to the anxiety-provoking event is usually (gradual/sudden) _____. It is similar to flooding therapy in that exposure to the anxiety-provoking event is (brief/prolonged) _____.

6. People with OCD are usually (able/unable) _____ to recall a particular conditioning event that was the cause of the obsessional anxiety response. The disorder often arises, however, during times of s_____. This suggests that a process of s_____ s_____ may exacerbate normal concerns about cleanliness and safety.

7. People with OCD fail to realize that intrusive thoughts are (common/uncommon) _____ and that such thoughts are often (controllable/uncontrollable) _____. They also (take / fail to take) _____ responsibility for highly (probable/improbable) _____ events.

8. Some evidence suggests that cognitive interventions for OCD, when combined with ERP, provide (much/little) _____ additional benefit.

Punishment

Escape and avoidance conditioning involves the strengthening of a behavior through the removal of an aversive stimulus. By contrast, punishment involves the weakening of a behavior through the application of an aversive stimulus or the removal of an appetitive stimulus. In this section, we discuss various types of punishment, as well various concerns about the application of punishment. We also briefly describe various theories of punishment.

Types of Punishment

Let us begin by reviewing the basic distinction between positive and negative punishment. *Positive punishment consists of the presentation of a certain event following a response, which then leads to a decrease in the future strength of that response*. In simple everyday terms, the behavior results in the delivery of something the person or animal hates, so the subject is less likely to behave that way in the future. Receiving a spanking for swearing and being reprimanded for talking back to the boss are both examples of positive punishment (given that these consequences result in a subsequent decrease in the frequency of these behaviors).

By contrast, *negative punishment consists of the removal of a certain event following a response, which then leads to a decrease in the future strength of that response*. In everyday terminology, the behavior results in the removal of something the person or animal likes, so the subject is less likely to behave that way in the future. A loss of employment for being obnoxious and a loss of dessert for complaining at the dinner table are both examples of negative punishment (again, given that the consequence results in a subsequent decrease in such behavior). Note that the events being removed are the types of pleasant events that can also serve as positive reinforcers; thus, negative punishment can also be defined as the loss of a positive reinforcer (a pleasant event) following a response.

There are two basic types of negative punishment: time-out and response cost. ***Time-out*** involves the loss of access to positive reinforcers for a brief period of time following the occurrence of a problem behavior. Time-out has become popular with modern-day parents, who frequently attempt to punish a child's misbehavior by sending the child to the bedroom or by making her sit in a corner for several minutes. Unfortunately, time-out procedures are often poorly applied, with the result that they have little effect on the problem behavior. For example, time-out is likely to be ineffective if the time-out setting is actually more reinforcing than the setting from which the child was removed. In fact, sending a child to her room for acting out at the dinner table might reinforce rather than punish the behavior of acting out if the child dislikes sitting at the dinner table. Another problem is that parents often use time-outs that are too long. The purpose of time-out is not to get the child "out of your hair" for a period of time but to facilitate the development of more appropriate behaviors. Those appropriate behaviors need to be reinforced, which cannot be done if the child is sitting in her room for hours on end. Time-out periods should therefore be quite brief, especially for young children. In fact, a time-out period as short as a minute may be all that is required to effectively suppress the unwanted behavior, especially if one immediately sets out to reinforce more appropriate behaviors as soon as the child is returned to the normal setting (Miltenberger, 2012).

The other type of negative punishment is *response cost*, which is the removal of a specific reinforcer following the occurrence of a problem behavior. Receiving a fine (which leads to loss of money) for speeding or taking a child's toys away for playing too roughly are examples of response cost. One advantage of response cost is that one can easily adjust the severity of the punishment to suit the behavior being punished. Slight aggression with a younger sibling could result in the loss of dessert, while more severe aggression could result in the loss of dessert as well as the opportunity to watch television that evening. A drawback to response cost, however, is that you must clearly identify a reinforcer that, if removed, will have an impact on behavior. It therefore requires a more careful analysis of the situation than a time-out procedure does. (See Miltenberger, 2012, for a more complete discussion of time-out and response cost procedures.)

Note that negative punishment is quite different from extinction, even though both involve the removal of reinforcers and both result in a decrease in the strength of a behavior. In the case of extinction, a behavior that used to produce a reinforcer no longer does, and the person therefore stops performing the behavior. If Jason used to receive cookies as a result of whining, but he no longer receives cookies by whining, then he will eventually stop whining. In the case of negative punishment, however, performing the behavior results in the loss of a reinforcer that the person would otherwise possess. Imagine, for example, that Jason has already received some cookies but then starts whining for a soda pop. If, each time he whines, one of his cookies is taken away, then he is likely to stop whining. Thus, to distinguish between extinction and negative punishment, ask yourself whether the behavior grows weaker because *performing the behavior no longer leads to something* (in which case, the process is *extinction*), or because *performing the behavior leads to the removal of something that you would otherwise possess (in which case the process is negative punishment).*

1. When the cat sat at your feet and meowed annoyingly during breakfast one morning, you sprayed it with water. As a result, the cat did not come near the table or meow the next time you sat down for a meal. The consequence for the cat's meowing consisted of the (presentation/removal) _____ of a stimulus, and the cat's behavior subsequently (decreased/increased) _____ in frequency. Therefore, this is an example of _____ _____.

2. Negative punishment involves the (presentation/removal) _____ of a stimulus following a response that subsequently results in a (increase/decrease) _____ in the likelihood of that response occurring again.

3. When Bobbi threw a temper tantrum, her mother turned off the television program that Bobbi was watching. Bobbi's mother is applying a (response cost/time-out) _____ procedure.

4. When Bobbi threw a temper tantrum, Bobbi's mother made her sit in the corner for a minute. Bobbi's mother is applying a (response cost/time-out) _____ procedure.

5. A(n) (advantage/disadvantage) _____ of a time-out procedure is that one (does / does not) _____ have to clearly identify a specific reinforcer before implementing the procedure. A(n) (advantage/disadvantage) _____ of a response cost procedure is that one (can/cannot) _____ easily modify the severity of the punishment to suit the behavior.

6. When Val began whining, her mother immediately stopped playing with her and left the room. Val quickly stopped whining. This is an example of (extinction / negative punishment) _____.

7. Val's mother used to play with Val whenever she whined but then stopped doing so. As a result, Val's whining soon ceased. This is an example of (extinction / negative punishment) _____.

8. If the frequency of a behavior decreases because performing the behavior no longer leads to something, the process involved is (extinction / negative punishment) _____. If the frequency of a behavior decreases because performing the behavior leads to the removal of something, the process involved is (extinction / negative punishment) _____.

Punishment can also be differentiated in other ways. For example, just as one can distinguish between intrinsic and extrinsic reinforcement, one can distinguish between intrinsic and extrinsic punishment. ***Intrinsic punishment*** is punishment that is an inherent aspect of the behavior being punished. In other words, the activity itself is punishing, such that the person performing the behavior is now less likely to repeat it. Doing push-ups is intrinsically punishing if you stop doing push-ups in the future because of the effort involved. ***Extrinsic punishment*** is punishment that is not an inherent aspect of the behavior being punished, but simply follows the behavior. In other words, the activity is followed by a separate event that serves to punish the activity. Being chastised after lighting up a cigarette ("Are you still indulging in that filthy habit?") is extrinsically punishing if it subsequently reduces how frequently you smoke.

One can also distinguish between primary and secondary punishers. A *primary (or unconditioned) punisher* is an event that is innately punishing. Loosely speaking, these are events that we are born to dislike. Electric shock, intense heat, and loud noise are examples of primary punishers. A *secondary (or conditioned) punisher* is an event that has become punishing because it has in the past been associated with some other punisher. For example, if shock is an effective punisher, then a tone that has been paired with shock in a classical conditioning procedure:

Tone: Shock → *Fear*
  NS   **US**   **UR**

Tone → *Fear*
  CS   **CR**

will become a conditioned aversive stimulus that can then be used as a secondary punisher. For example, presentation of the tone could now be used to punish wheel running:

Running in a wheel → **Tone**
              R S^P

Human behavior is often under the control of secondary punishers. A traffic ticket might effectively punish our tendency to speed, and an icy stare from our partner might effectively punish our tendency to drink too much at a party. Both the fine and the stare are punishing because they have been associated with other types of aversive events: loss of money in the one case and heated arguments in the other.

A special type of secondary punisher is a *generalized (or generalized secondary) punisher*, which is an event that has become punishing because it has in the past been associated with many other punishers. The icy stare is probably best categorized as a generalized punisher because disapproving looks have no doubt been associated with numerous unpleasant events such as reprimands as a child, marital arguments as an adult, and disciplinary action during one's stint in the army.

1. Exercising to the point of exhaustion is for many people likely to be an (extrinsically/intrinsically) _____ punishing event.

2. The bad taste of rotting food will likely, for most people, function as a (primary/secondary) _____ punisher, while a restaurant that has served such food will function as a _____ punisher.

3. Looking at an old photo album reminds you of your loneliness as a child, the loss of a favorite pet, and a childhood friend who died. As a result, you stop looking at it. The old photo album can be classified as a g_____ punisher.

QUICK QUIZ H

Problems with the Use of Punishment

Although many people are of the opinion that behaviorists promote the use of punishment, behaviorists in fact have a general bias against it. This bias results from several problems that are associated with punishment (e.g., Newsom, Favell, & Rincover, 1983; Van Houten, 1983):

1. **Punishment of an inappropriate behavior does not directly strengthen the occurrence of appropriate behavior, and may simply result in a generalized suppression of behavior.** A child who has been punished for playing aggressively will not necessarily begin playing more cooperatively, which is really the intended goal. She might instead simply stop playing with other children, which is not at all desirable.

2. **The person delivering the punishment could become an S^D for punishment, with the result that the unwanted behavior is suppressed only when that person is present.** The child, for example, might come to view the father as a discriminative stimulus for punishment and therefore continue to misbehave when the father is absent. The child has thus learned not to get caught misbehaving, rather than not to misbehave.

3. **Punishment might simply teach the individual to avoid the person who delivered the punishment.** A child who is severely punished by her father might begin minimizing the time spent with her father. This would obviously be less than ideal, especially if the father has much to offer the child.

4. **Punishment is likely to elicit a strong emotional response.** This is especially the case with the use of positive punishment, such as spanking or yelling, which is likely to result in crying or other displays of distress. These strong emotional responses are not only unpleasant but will also interfere with any subsequent attempt to teach the child more appropriate behavior. A child who is crying uncontrollably is not in an ideal state for learning anything new, such as how to play appropriately.

5. **Punishment can sometimes elicit an aggressive reaction.** Earlier in this text, we mentioned how a painful stimulus, such as electric shock, can elicit attack behavior in rats. Humans can also react with anger when subjected to aversive stimulation. This anger can be directed toward the individual responsible for the aversive event or, if there are inhibitions about doing so, can be directed toward a substitute target. Thus, a child who is severely punished for being noisy might not aggress toward the parent who spanked her but will instead aggress toward her younger sibling.

6. **The use of punishment, through the process of modeling, could teach the person that punishment is an acceptable means of controlling behavior.** The child whose behavior is being punished might come to believe that punishment is an appropriate method for controlling others. For this reason, children who are abused will sometimes (but not always) begin to abuse others. (The effect of modeling on aggression will be more fully discussed in Chapter 12.)

7. **Because punishment often has an immediate effect in stopping an unwanted behavior, the use of punishment is often strongly reinforced.** If hitting one's children has the immediate effect of getting them to stop making noise (an immediate negative reinforcer), then the behavior of hitting them has been strongly reinforced. The use of punishment can therefore be quite seductive, enticing the parent to use it more and more frequently, possibly to the point of being clearly abusive.

1. Punishment, especially (positive/negative) _____ punishment, can often elicit a strong e_____ reaction. This reaction might include _____ that, if not directed toward the punisher, might be directed toward a substitute target.

2. Punishment of an inappropriate behavior (will / will not) _____ directly strengthen the occurrence of an appropriate behavior. It might even result in a general s_____ of behavior.

3. The use of punishment could, through the process of m_____, teach the recipient that punishment is an acceptable means for modifying a person's behavior.

4. Yelling at your dog for chewing your slippers might teach the dog to avoid _____ rather than the slippers.

5. Yelling at your dog for chewing your slippers might also teach your dog not to chew the slippers only when _____.

6. If punishment has an i_____ effect in getting someone to stop annoying us, this result can then act as a strong n_____ r_____ for using punishment in the future.

Benefits and the Effective Use of Punishment

For the reasons outlined previously, most behaviorists tend to avoid or minimize the use of punishment. Nevertheless, there may be some circumstances in which punishment is judged appropriate, such as in quickly suppressing a potentially dangerous behavior in a young child (for example, stopping a child from jabbing at another child's face with a sharpened pencil). This is especially the case given that alternative interventions, such as extinction and reinforcement of other behaviors, often take considerable time to have an effect. In addition to quickly suppressing a particular behavior pattern, punishment can have some beneficial side effects (e.g., Newsom et al., 1983; Van Houten, 1983):

1. **Punishment can sometimes lead to an increase in social behavior.** For example, a young child who has been punished by a time-out period for playing aggressively with his sister may become more affectionate toward his sister when the time-out period has ended. Thus, although punishment does not directly teach more appropriate behaviors, such behaviors can sometimes arise as a side effect. Why would such increases

in social behavior occur? One possibility is that they represent innately determined appeasement gestures that are evoked by the punishment; in other words, when we are punished, we may have an innate tendency to become more sociable in an effort to restore our relationships with others.

2. **Paradoxically, punishment sometimes results in an improvement in mood, such as less crying.** This is the opposite of what one would usually expect, which is that punishment would lead to more emotional behavior, not less. In some cases, however, it may be that the child was misbehaving because he or she was in some way agitated; in such cases, the punishment might distract the child and disrupt the agitation.

3. **Punishment can increase attention to the environment**, as shown by increased eye contact and interest in ongoing activities. In other words, punishment, such as in the form of a shout, might motivate children to become more vigilant to what is happening around them. This can be especially valuable with children who tend to ignore the world around them, such as children who suffer from autism.

In summary, under some circumstances, the application of punishment may be justified and beneficial. If punishment is used, however, the following requirements should be met to maximize the possibility that it will be effective.

1. **As much as possible, punishment should be immediate rather than delayed.** Unfortunately, in the real world, delayed punishment is often the rule rather than the exception. A child's misbehavior is frequently discovered only several minutes or hours after its occurrence, and the delivery of a reprimand following such a long delay may have little effect. This is particularly the case with very young children and animals who, because they are unable to understand explanations, are unlikely to associate the punishment with the unwanted behavior. For example, yelling at a dog for making a mess on the carpet several hours after the incident has occurred will probably only upset the animal and do little to prevent future mishaps.

2. **At least at the outset, punishment should consistently follow each occurrence of the unwanted behavior.** Punishment tends to be less effective in suppressing a behavior when only some instances of the unwanted behavior are punished. In other words, unlike intermittent reinforcement, which has a strong effect on behavior, intermittent punishment tends to have a relatively weak effect on behavior. Nevertheless, once the behavior has been effectively suppressed, then intermittent punishment may be sufficient to maintain the suppression (Clark, Rowbury, Baer, & Baer, 1973).[3]

---

[3]One reason that intermittent punishment may be ineffective is that, particularly for intrinsically rewarding behaviors, it might produce a situation equivalent to intermittent reinforcement. In other words, to the extent that a behavior is reinforced on any nonpunished trial, then the behavior is being intermittently reinforced. And since intermittently reinforced behaviors tend to be quite persistent, this might counter the effects of the punishment being delivered on other trials. Needless to say, even when using continuous punishment, one should attempt to eliminate, so far as possible, any reinforcers for the unwanted behavior.

3. **Punishment should be intense enough from the outset to suppress the target behavior** (though—and this is the tricky part—not so intense as to be unnecessarily abusive). If one begins with a very mild punisher that is ineffective, and then gradually increases the intensity, it might require a very intense punisher to eventually suppress the unwanted behavior. For example, N. E. Miller (1960) presented rats with a very mild shock whenever they entered an alleyway, and then gradually increased the intensity of the shock until it effectively punished the rats' behavior. He found that these rats ceased responding only with very high levels of shock, far beyond what would normally have been required to suppress such a behavior. Likewise, a father who initially uses a very mild reprimand to try to get his daughter to stop teasing the dog, and then gradually increases the severity of the reprimand, might eventually have to deliver a very severe reprimand or worse before she will comply. But if the father had started with a moderately severe reprimand, the daughter might have immediately complied, thereby saving the two of them (as well as the dog) a lot of grief. By starting with such a mild intervention and then gradually increasing its severity, the father essentially allowed the daughter to adapt to the punishing stimulus.

4. **Negative punishment is generally preferable to positive punishment.** Negative punishment procedures, such as time-out and response cost, are generally less likely to produce many of the harmful side effects associated with punishment as opposed to positive punishment procedures such as spanking and yelling. Negative punishment can, nevertheless, become abusive, such as when children are forced to endure extremely long time-out periods or are exposed to severe response cost procedures, such as removal of sufficient food.

5. **With individuals who have language capacity, punishment is more effective when accompanied by an explanation.** A possible reason for this is that an explanation will help clarify the exact behavior that is being punished, thereby making it easier for the child to avoid punishment in the future. This accords with the more general recommendation that children should be given frequent feedback about their behavior, both good and bad, because this will greatly facilitate the children's attempts to learn appropriate behavior (Craig, Kermis, & Digdon, 1998).

6. **Punishment of inappropriate behavior should be combined with positive reinforcement for appropriate behavior.** This is perhaps the most important rule. As with extinction, punishment of unwanted behavior will be more effective if it is combined with differential reinforcement for other behavior, especially behavior that is incompatible with the target behavior. As the appropriate behavior is strengthened, it will come to supplant the inappropriate behavior. Thus, applying a time-out period to a child for playing inappropriately might have little effect if the child's behavior of playing appropriately has not been adequately reinforced. Time-out periods should, therefore, be followed by abundant reinforcement for appropriate behavior. In fact, differential positive reinforcement for appropriate behavior (which might include

functional communication training as discussed in Chapter 8) should always be considered the primary tool for eliminating unwanted behaviors. For a complete discussion of issues involved in the punishment of human behavior, see Axelrod and Apsche (1983).

1. Beneficial side effects of punishment include increases in s_____ behavior, improvements in m_____, and increased a_____ to the environment.

2. With verbally proficient humans, punishment tends to be more effective when it is accompanied by an e_____.

3. In general, when implementing a punishment procedure, one should begin with a punisher of sufficient i_____ to s_____ the behavior.

4. Unlike reinforcement, punishment tends to have a stronger impact on behavior if delivered (consistently/intermittently) _____.

5. In general, when attempting to punish a maladaptive behavior, one should also attempt to _____ more adaptive behavior.

6. If punishment is to be used, it should be im_____, since d_____ punishment tends to be relatively ineffective.

7. In general, n_____ punishment is preferable to p_____ punishment because the former is likely to have fewer side effects.

And Furthermore

Punishment and Procrastination

Do you procrastinate? If so, you are definitely not alone. In one survey, 83% of college students admitted to procrastinating on academic tasks, with 50% admitting to procrastinating at least half the time (L. J. Solomon & Rothblum, 1984). What you may not be aware of is that procrastination is also a problem for many professors. It is a particular problem for new faculty members who are under intense pressure to publish in order to obtain tenure but who, at the same time, are often given relatively heavy teaching loads. The result is that new faculty often spend too much time preparing for teaching and too little time writing articles, thereby running the risk of not obtaining tenure at the end of their probationary period.

Robert Boice (e.g., 1989, 1996) has conducted detailed analyses of the work habits of new faculty members, distinguishing those who are productive from those who are not. A major finding was that productive faculty tended to engage in regular, short writing sessions spread throughout the week, whereas nonproductive faculty tended to engage in occasional "binge" episodes of writing spread far apart—that is, they generally procrastinated in their writing, but when they did write, they wrote intensely for long periods of time. Although these procrastinators generally believed that long, intense writing sessions are necessary to be productive, and that they merely needed to increase the frequency of such sessions, Boice concluded that binge writing was itself part of the problem. However invigorated one might feel during an intense session of writing—and procrastinators often reported this—this pattern of work is so effortful that one soon starts to avoid it. In essence, *binge writing sessions are sufficiently aversive that they punish the act of writing.*

Based on these results, Boice has devised workshops for faculty members to help them overcome their tendency to procrastinate. A major component of these workshops is to learn to write in brief daily sessions, perhaps only 30 minutes per day at first, with the act of stopping on time considered as important as starting on time. The goal is to break the tendency to engage in binge writing sessions, and to begin to experience writing as less effortful and more enjoyable. Combined with other tactics, such as establishing a balanced lifestyle, arranging a comfortable writing environment, and seeking out mentors for feedback, these workshops have proven to be very effective in helping many faculty members become more productive.

Although Boice's advice is directed toward faculty, it also has obvious implications for students. In Chapter 7, we discussed how the tendency to take a break after accomplishing a certain amount of studying is similar to a post-reinforcement pause on an FR schedule of reinforcement, and that the trick in such cases is simply getting started again. But do you have trouble even getting started, perhaps because studying in your view has become associated with long hours of hard work? If so, you may wish to consider the benefits of shorter, more consistent study sessions. For example, suppose that you do most of your studying during, say, 5 weeks out of a 15-week term. During the other 10 weeks, when there are no exams or pressing assignments, you typically do little or no studying—although you do spend a lot of time feeling guilty about it. What if, during those 10 weeks, you consistently studied one extra hour per day, 5 days per week (perhaps even combining it with the stimulus control training described in Chapter 8)? Although 1 hour per day might seem minor, consider that it adds up to 50 extra hours of studying by the end of the semester! That is a whopping amount of studying that could have a significant impact on your grades (especially if it is high-quality studying), and it would very likely make the end of the semester less stressful for you. Something to think about.

The tendency to procrastinate represents a lack of self-control, an issue that we focus on in Chapter 10. The lesson for now, however, is that some of our self-control problems might arise from trying to do too much, thereby punishing the very behavior pattern that we are trying to nurture. In such cases, brief daily sessions may be the solution.[4]

---

[4]Another excellent (and very readable) book on how to become a more productive writer is *How to Write a Lot: A Practical Guide to Productive Academic Writing* by Paul J. Silvia (2007). Silvia is himself a psychologist and the book is directed specifically toward psychology faculty and graduate students, though undergraduates may also find the book to be of value. Silvia does a particular good job of demolishing (with fine humor) the typical excuses for not writing, such as needing to "find time" to write (nice try, but time is not lost and does not need finding; you need to *schedule time* for writing just like you schedule time for work and for school) or that you write best when feeling inspired to write (nonsense, you're working on a research report, not a novel—and even if it were a novel, most successful novelists stick to a writing schedule regardless of their level of inspiration). The book is also written from an explicitly behavioral perspective with practical advice on such things as the importance of establishing clear goals, the usefulness of tracking one's progress, and the benefits of self-reinforcement.

Theories of Punishment

Although a good deal of research has gone into investigating the effectiveness of punishment, less attention has been paid to developing and testing various theories of punishment. We will nevertheless briefly consider three theoretical approaches to punishment.

Conditioned Suppression Theory This theory is based on early work by Skinner (1938). He found that although punishment can quickly suppress a behavior, the behavior often quickly recovers to prepunishment levels when the punishment is withdrawn. What Skinner (1953) assumed was happening was that punishment generates an emotional response that tends to suppress any ongoing appetitive behavior. Crudely put, when the rat is shocked for pressing a lever that produces food, it becomes so upset that it loses interest in the food and therefore does not press the lever to obtain it. If, however, the shock is withdrawn, the rat resumes lever pressing as soon as it calms down enough for its interest in food to be revived. By analogy, if Tyler no longer teases his sister after being scolded for doing so, it is simply because he is too upset to pay much attention to his sister. Thus, the *conditioned suppression theory of punishment* assumes that punishment does not weaken a behavior but instead produces an emotional response that interferes with the occurrence of the behavior.

The temporary effect that Skinner (1938) found when he attempted to punish a rat's behavior led him to conclude that punishment is an ineffective means for producing a lasting change in behavior. Skinner's experiment, however, utilized a relatively weak form of punishment: a device that slapped the rat on the paw when it attempted to press a lever. Subsequent research revealed that more intense forms of punishment, such as strong electric shocks, are capable of suppressing behavior for much longer periods of time (Azrin & Holz, 1966).

Avoidance Theory of Punishment The *avoidance theory of punishment* holds that punishment actually involves a type of avoidance conditioning in which the avoidance response consists of any behavior other than the behavior being punished (e.g., Dinsmoor, 1954). In other words, just as the behavior of jumping over a barrier is strengthened by shock avoidance in a shuttle avoidance situation, so too is the behavior of doing "anything other than lever pressing" reinforced by shock avoidance in a punishment-of-lever-pressing situation. Thus, in carrying out the following punishment procedure:

$$\text{Lever press} \rightarrow \text{Shock}$$
$$\quad\text{R} \qquad\quad \text{S}^\text{P}$$

one is actually carrying out the following avoidance conditioning procedure:

$$\textit{Any behavior other than lever pressing} \rightarrow \textbf{No Shock}$$
$$\qquad\qquad\qquad \text{R} \qquad\qquad\qquad\qquad \text{S}^\text{R}$$

in which any behavior other than lever pressing is negatively reinforced by the absence of shock (e.g., Dinsmoor, 1954). Similarly, according to this theory, Tyler no longer teases his sister after being scolded for doing so because any behavior he carries out other than teasing his sister is negatively reinforced by the absence of a scolding. If correct, this means that punishment procedures are actually a form of negative reinforcement.

As with conditioned suppression theory, the avoidance theory of punishment assumes that punishment does not directly weaken a behavior. It simply replaces the punished behavior with an avoidance response of some sort. A disadvantage of this theory, however, is that it carries with it all of the theoretical difficulties associated with avoidance conditioning, some of which we discussed earlier in this chapter.

The Premack Approach to Punishment As you will recall from Chapter 5, the Premack principle holds that a high-probability behavior (HPB) can be used to reinforce a low-probability behavior (LPB). As it turns out, the opposite can be applied to punishment. According to the ***Premack principle of punishment***, an LPB can be used to punish an HPB (Premack, 1971a).

Take, for example, a rat that is both hungry and tuckered out from exercising. The rat in this condition is much more likely to eat food (an HPB) than to run in a wheel (an LPB). In terms of the Premack principle of reinforcement, this means that the behavior of eating can be used as a reinforcer for the behavior of running in a wheel:

$$\textit{Running in a wheel (LPB)} \rightarrow \textbf{Eating food (HPB)}$$
$$\textbf{R} \qquad\qquad\qquad \textbf{S}^{\textbf{R}}$$

Conversely, according to the Premack principle of punishment, one can also use running in a wheel to punish the behavior of eating:

$$\textit{Eating food (HPB)} \rightarrow \textbf{Running in a wheel (LPB)}$$
$$\textbf{R} \qquad\qquad\qquad \textbf{S}^{\textbf{P}}$$

If eating food is followed by the consequence of being forced to run in a motorized wheel, the rat will be less likely to eat than if this consequence did not exist. To bring this point home, imagine how much easier it would be for a person who hates exercising to stick to a diet if he were forced to run a mile each time he ate something not on the diet.

Note that this approach implicitly assumes that punishment is the opposite of reinforcement: If reinforcement strengthens behavior, then punishment weakens behavior. In this sense, it differs from the previous two theories in that it views punishment as the mirror opposite of reinforcement. (See Domjan, 2010, for an extended discussion concerning theories of punishment.)

1. According to the conditioned suppression theory of punishment, the application of punishment does not directly w_____ a behavior; instead, it produces an em_____ reaction that tends to interfere with ongoing behavior.

2. This theory was based on evidence that punishment tends to produce only a (temporary/permanent) _____ effect. This effect, however, probably results from using relatively (strong/weak) _____ forms of punishment.

3. According to the _____ theory of punishment, a rat stops lever pressing when lever pressing is followed by shock because the occurrence of any behavior other than lever pressing is n_____ r_____ by the nonoccurrence of shock.

4. According to the punishment version of the Premack principle, the occurrence of a _____ _____ behavior can be used to punish the occurrence of a _____ _____ behavior. This means that if Sally rarely washes dishes and often bites her nails, then the behavior of _____ _____ can be used to punish the occurrence of _____ _____.

5. According to the Premack principle, if running (an HPB) is followed by push-ups (an LPB), then running should (decrease/increase) _____ in frequency, which is an instance of (reinforcement/punishment) _____. If push-ups (LPB) is followed by running (HPB), then the push-ups should _____ in frequency, which is an instance of _____.

Noncontingent Punishment

In the typical escape/avoidance procedure, the aversive stimulus is controllable in the sense that the animal is able to make a response that significantly reduces its effect. Likewise, in a punishment procedure, the animal has some semblance of control because if it does not make the response, then it will not be punished. In both cases, some type of contingency exists. But what if such a contingency were absent? What if the aversive event was essentially uncontrollable (and even unpredictable), such that whatever you do, you are unable to influence your exposure to that event? In the same manner that noncontingent reinforcement has some unique effects on behavior (as discussed in Chapter 7), so too does noncontingent punishment. Let us therefore spend the remainder of this chapter examining some of these effects.

Learned Helplessness

Consider the following experiment by Seligman and Maier (1967). The experiment began with an initial phase in which dogs were suspended in a harness and exposed to one of three conditions. In an *inescapable-shock condition,* the dogs received a series of shocks but were unable to do anything about them. In an *escapable-shock condition,* the dogs received shocks but were able to terminate each shock by pressing a panel with their snout. Each dog in this condition was also *yoked to* (paired up with) a dog in the first condition, such that when it turned off the shock for itself, it also turned off the shock for its partner dog in the other condition. Thus, the only difference between these two dogs was that the dog in the escapable-shock condition had control over the shocks while the dog in the inescapable-shock condition did not. Finally, some dogs were in a *no-shock control condition:* These dogs were never shocked and simply waited out the session suspended in the harness.

In the next phase of the experiment, all of the dogs were exposed to a shuttle avoidance procedure in which the task was to learn to avoid shock by jumping over a barrier, each shock being preceded by a 10-second period of darkness. The dogs exposed to the no-shock control condition in the initial phase of the experiment soon learned to avoid the shock by jumping over the barrier during the period of darkness that preceded the shock. The dogs exposed to the escapable-shock condition also learned the avoidance task quickly. The dogs from the inescapable-shock condition, however, behaved quite differently. When shocked, many of them initially ran around in great distress but then lay on the floor and whimpered. They made no effort to escape the shock. Even stranger, the few dogs that did by chance jump over the barrier, successfully escaping the shock, seemed unable to learn from this experience and failed to repeat it on the next trial. In summary, the prior exposure to inescapable shock seemed to impair the dogs' ability to learn to escape shock when escape later became possible. This phenomenon is known as *learned helplessness*, a decrement in learning ability that results from repeated exposure to uncontrollable aversive events.

Seligman and Maier (1967) theorized that the dogs became helpless because they had learned during exposure to inescapable shock that any attempt to escape was useless—in other words, that there was a *lack of contingency* between making a response and achieving a certain outcome. As a result, when confronted with shock in a new situation, they simply gave up. Other researchers, however, have proposed alternative explanations. For example, one theory suggests that animals exposed to inescapable aversive stimulation are distressed, and because of this distress they have difficulty attending to the relationship between behavior and its outcomes. Evidence for this theory includes the fact that if animals are given a very salient feedback stimulus whenever they make a successful escape response, such as by sounding a loud bell, the learned helplessness effect may disappear and the animals may once more learn such tasks effectively (Maier, Jackson, & Tomie, 1987).

Learned helplessness may account for certain difficulties experienced by humans. For example, Dweck and Reppucci (1973) found that children who attempted to answer unsolvable problems later had considerable difficulty answering solvable problems. This suggests that children who have difficulty passing math exams in school, possibly because of poor teaching, might grow up to become "math-anxious" individuals who quickly give up when confronted by any sort of math problem. Learned helplessness has also been related to certain forms of depression (Seligman, 1975). People who suffer a series of uncontrollable aversive events—loss of a job, physical illness, divorce, and so on—may become extremely passive and despondent. Like animals exposed to inescapable shock, they show little interest in improving their lot in life. (See also the opening vignette to this chapter.)

Fortunately, researchers have discovered a way to eliminate learned helplessness. The helpless animal will eventually recover its ability to escape on its own if it is repeatedly forced to escape the aversive stimulus—for example, if it is repeatedly dragged from the shock side of the chamber to the no-shock side (Seligman & Maier, 1967; Seligman, Rosellini, & Kozak, 1975). In similar fashion, behavioral treatments for depression often involve encouraging the patient to accomplish a graded series of tasks, starting with relatively minor tasks, such as writing a letter, and progressing to more difficult tasks, such as seeking a new job (Seligman, 1975).

Research has also suggested a means for preventing the development of learned helplessness. Experiments have revealed that prior exposure to escapable shock often immunizes an animal against becoming helpless when it is later exposed to inescapable shock (Seligman et al., 1975); the animal will persist in trying to escape the shock rather than give up. This suggests that a history of successfully overcoming minor adversities might immunize a person against depression when the person is later confronted by more serious difficulties. As a tree is strengthened by exposure to winds strong enough to bend but not break its limbs, so too individuals seem to be strengthened by exposure to manageable amounts of misfortune.

1. The original experiments on learned _____ revealed that dogs that had first been exposed to inescapable shock had (no difficulty / difficulty) _____ learning an escape response when later exposed to (escapable/ inescapable) _____ shock.

2. It seemed as though these dogs had learned that there (is / is not) _____ a contingency between their behavior and the offset of shock.

3. This effect can be overcome by (forcing/enticing) _____ the dogs to make an escape response. As well, dogs that have had previous exposure to escapable shock are (more/less) _____ susceptible to becoming helpless when later exposed to inescapable shock.

4. Learned helplessness may account for various difficulties in humans, including the clinical disorder known as d_____.

Masserman's Experimental Neurosis

As you may recall, experimental neurosis is an *experimentally produced disorder in which animals exposed to unpredictable events develop neurotic-like symptoms*. We first encountered this phenomenon in our discussion of Pavlov's work on discrimination training in dogs (see Chapter 4). He and his colleagues discovered that dogs that had difficulty discriminating which cues predicted the delivery of food seemed to experience a nervous breakdown. Pavlov hypothesized that human neuroses might likewise develop as a result of exposure to unpredictable events.

A variation on Pavlov's procedure, involving the use of aversive rather than appetitive stimuli, was developed by Masserman (1943). He found that cats that experienced unpredictable electric shocks or blasts of air while eating often developed a pattern of neurotic-like symptoms. For example, normally quiet cats became restless and agitated, and normally active cats became withdrawn and passive—sometimes even to the point of becoming rigidly immobile (a symptom known as catalepsy). The cats also developed phobic responses to cues associated with feeding (since feeding had become associated with shock), as well as unusual "counterphobic" responses (for example, a cat might run to the goal box, stick its head inside the box, and then simply stare at the experimenter but not eat). It generally took only two or three presentations of the aversive stimulus to elicit these symptoms, which might then last several months.

More recent work (but with rats, not cats) has shown that many of these symptoms are similar to those found in posttraumatic stress disorder (PTSD) in humans (e.g., Foa, Zinbarg, & Rothbaum, 1992). PTSD is a disorder that results from exposure to unpredictable life-threatening events, such as tornadoes, physical and sexual assaults, and battlefield experiences. Symptoms include sleep difficulties, exaggerated startle response, intrusive recollections about the trauma, and nightmares. As well, victims often demonstrate fear and avoidance of trauma-associated stimuli (phobias), as well as a general numbing of responsiveness (for example, a restricted range of emotions). Although the subjective symptoms of PTSD, such as intrusive recollections, are impossible to replicate in animals (we have no idea what animals are actually thinking), many of the overt symptoms, such as phobic behavior, agitation, and passivity, are similar to those shown by animals subjected to noncontingent, unpredictable aversive stimulation.

Experimental neurosis is therefore proving to be a useful means for investigating the development of traumatic symptoms. For instance, as a general rule, traumatic symptoms are more easily induced in animals when the aversive stimulus is delivered in an environment that the animal has long associated with safety or some type of appetitive event. For example, unpredictable shocks delivered in a setting in which the animal typically eats food are especially likely to induce neurotic symptoms (Masserman, 1943). This suggests that symptoms of PTSD are more likely to arise when a person is, for example, unexpectedly attacked in the safety of his or her own home as opposed to a strange or dangerous area of town. The person who is attacked at home generalizes the experience and perceives the world at large as a dangerous, unpredictable place, with the result that he or she thereafter remains constantly vigilant (Foa et al., 1992).

You may be wondering how Masserman's experimental neurosis procedure differs from learned helplessness. The basic difference is that the typical learned helplessness procedure involves repeated exposure to aversive events that are predictable but uncontrollable. It is equivalent to being beaten up every day at 8:00 a.m. At first you try to escape from the beating, but eventually you give up any hope of escape. Masserman's experimental neurosis, on the other hand, involves infrequent but unpredictable exposure to aversive events. It is analogous to being unexpectedly dragged off every once in a while and beaten. The result is constant hypervigilance and an array of psychological and behavioral symptoms. But note that unpredictability also implies uncontrollability, so there is considerable overlap between the symptoms produced by learned helplessness and those produced by Masserman's experimental neurosis procedure (Foa et al., 1992).

ADVICE FOR THE LOVELORN

Dear Dr. Dee,

I am in a relationship that is starting to depress me, though most of what is happening is quite subtle. For example, when I am really excited about something, my partner will usually act quite disinterested. Similarly, when I suggest doing something that I believe will be fun, she usually turns it down and suggests something else. She also gets snippy with me (or worse yet, gives me the silent treatment) at the most unexpected moments.

I have tried talking to her about it, but she says that I am overreacting and then points to how affectionate she usually is (which is true).

So Am I Overreacting?

Dear So,

It sounds like you are in a relationship where much of your behavior is being subtly punished, some of it on a noncontingent basis. Thus, you are starting to perceive that whatever you do makes little difference. So it is not surprising that you are becoming depressed. You need to calmly point out to your partner the damaging effects of what she is doing, and the extent to which it is making you depressed.

First, however, you might wish to examine your own behavior to see if you are doing something to reinforce this pattern of behavior in your partner. Relationship problems are usually a two-way street, with neither party solely responsible for the difficulty. For example, perhaps you acquiesce to your partner's wishes so often that you are essentially reinforcing her for behaving this way. If that is the case, you may need to become a bit more assertive about your wishes. In fact, it could well be that she would be much happier if you were more assertive and your relationship with each other was more balanced.

Behaviorally yours,

Dr. Dee

QUICK QUIZ M

1. Experimental neurosis occurs when animals exposed to un_____ events develop neurotic-like symptoms.

2. Masserman (1943) found that normally quiet cats exposed to unpredictable shocks or blasts of air became (restless and agitated / withdrawn and passive) _____, whereas normally active cats became (restless and agitated / withdrawn and passive) _____.

3. When food was paired with unpredictable shock, the cats also developed p_____ and counter_____ responses to the food.

4. Evidence suggests that neurotic symptoms are more likely to develop when the traumatic event occurs in an environment that the animal (or person) generally regards as (safe/dangerous) _____ .

5. Learned helplessness can be viewed as resulting from repeated exposure to aversive events that are p_____ but un_____; experimental neurosis can be viewed as resulting from exposure to events that are u_____ .

And Furthermore

Dissociative Identity Disorder: A Behavioral Perspective

Some clinicians believe that the most severe disorder produced by exposure to traumatic events is dissociative identity disorder (DID; formerly called multiple personality disorder). The essential characteristic of this disorder is two or more personality states (or alter personalities) that repeatedly take control of behavior. Patients also suffer from extensive amnesia, with some personalities often unaware of the existence of other personalities. In the classic case of Eve White, for example (portrayed in the 1957 movie *The Three Faces of Eve*), the original personality of Eve White was reportedly unaware of an alter personality named Eve Black. Eve Black, however, was fully aware of Eve White and enjoyed making life difficult for her (Thigpen & Cleckley, 1957). This type of amnesia bears some similarity to repression, and in fact many clinicians prefer to conceptualize hidden memories of abuse as dissociated memories rather than repressed memories. Unfortunately, as with the concept of repression, the concept of DID is extremely controversial.

Behaviorists have traditionally viewed multiple personalities as distinct patterns of behavior (both overt and covert) that have arisen in response to distinctly different contingencies of reinforcement (Skinner, 1953). This reasoning has been carried a step further in the *posttraumatic model* of DID, which holds that DID usually results from childhood trauma (e.g., Ross, 1997). According to this model, an abused child can more easily cope with everyday life by usually forgetting about the abusive incidents and by pretending that the abuse is happening to someone else. In behavioral terms, this self-deception can be conceptualized as a type of covert avoidance response—"Nothing bad is happening to me"—that is negatively reinforced by a reduction in anxiety. As a result, the child learns to compartmentalize the distressing experience into a separate personality pattern that has its own dispositions and memories (Kohlenberg & Tsai, 1991; Phelps, 2000). This style of coping may become so habitual that it eventually results in the formation of dozens, or even hundreds, of separate personality states.

Others, however, have argued that DID is usually not the result of trauma but instead the result of suggestive influence (Lilienfeld et al., 1999; Spanos, 1996). According to this *sociocognitive model* (which can also be conceptualized as a cognitive-behavioral model), the patient's displays of alter personalities have been inadvertently shaped through

(continued)

processes of social reinforcement and observational learning. Supportive evidence for this model includes the following:

- The first clear observations of alter personalities are often obtained following exposure to a therapist who communicates to the patient that displays of alter personalities will be considered appropriate (and hence socially reinforced)—such as by asking the patient "if there is another thought process, part of the mind, part, person or force" within or who wishes to communicate with the therapist (e.g., Braun, 1980, p. 213).
- The number of alter personalities displayed by patients usually increases as therapy progresses, as does the patients' ability to quickly switch from one alter to another (Ross, 1997). This suggests that a process of shaping may be involved.
- The number of DID cases rose sharply following dramatic presentations of the disorder to the public during the 1970s and 1980s, such as the case of Sybil, which became a best-selling book (Schreiber, 1973) and a popular movie. This suggests that observational learning may have played a role in the increased prevalence of the disorder.
- In many (though not all) cases, patients' memories of childhood trauma are memories that were recovered during therapy (Kluft, 1998). As noted in our previous discussion of repression, recovered memories might sometimes be false.

Direct evidence for the role of behavioral processes in DID was reported by Kohlenberg (1973). He found that by manipulating the amount of reinforcement a patient received for displaying one of three alter personalities, he was able to change the amount of time that a particular personality was displayed. He then devised a successful treatment program that included reinforcing displays of the personality that acted normally and ignoring displays of other personalities.

Supporters of the posttraumatic model (e.g., Gleaves, 1996; Ross, 1997; Ross & Norton, 1989) and the sociocognitive model (e.g., Lilienfeld et al., 1999; Powell & Gee, 1999; Spanos, 1994, 1996) have each presented a series of arguments and counterarguments in support of their positions. The result has been some movement toward a middle ground. Ross (1997), for example, now acknowledges that at least some cases of DID have been artificially induced in therapy, while Lilienfeld et al. (1999) have acknowledged that a tendency toward developing DID-type symptoms might sometimes be the result of trauma. Likewise, Phelps (2000) has presented a behavioral account of DID, arguing that, although alter personalities could conceivably arise from a history of childhood trauma, therapists might also inadvertently strengthen displays of alter personalities through processes of social reinforcement.

SUMMARY

Negative reinforcement plays an important role in the development of escape and avoidance behaviors. A typical procedure for studying escape and avoidance is a shuttle avoidance task. In it, the rat first learns to escape shock by climbing over a barrier whenever it feels a shock; it then learns to avoid shock by climbing over the barrier in the presence of a cue that predicts shock delivery.

According to Mowrer's two-process theory, avoidance behavior results from: (1) classical conditioning, in which a fear response comes to be elicited by a CS, and (2) operant conditioning, in which moving away from the CS is negatively reinforced by a reduction in fear. One criticism of this theory is that the avoidance response is extremely persistent, even when the aversive US is no longer presented. According to the anxiety conservation hypothesis, however, avoidance occurs so quickly that there is insufficient exposure to the CS for extinction of the fear response to take place. A second criticism of the two-process theory is that once the animals become accustomed to making the avoidance response, they no longer seem fearful of the CS—hence, it seems that reduction in fear cannot serve as a negative reinforcer for avoidance. One answer to this criticism is that, although the animals may be significantly less fearful, they may still be slightly fearful.

Mineka pointed out that experimental avoidance conditioning in animals differs in several ways from phobic conditioning in humans. More specifically, the animals avoid the aversive US whereas phobic humans avoid the CS, and phobic conditioning in humans often requires only a single trial to produce extremely persistent avoidance. Stampfl, however, showed that phobic-like avoidance could be achieved in rats by providing them with the opportunity to make the avoidance response early in the chain of events leading up to the CS, thereby minimizing the amount of effort involved.

Avoidance conditioning plays a role in obsessive-compulsive disorders. Obsessions produce an increase in anxiety that is then reduced by carrying out the compulsive behavior pattern. Treatment procedures have been developed involving prolonged exposure to the anxiety-arousing event without engaging in the compulsive behavior pattern, thereby allowing the anxiety to be extinguished.

Positive punishment involves the presentation of an aversive stimulus, whereas negative punishment involves the removal of an appetitive stimulus. Two common forms of negative punishment are time-out, which involves the removal of access to all reinforcers, and response cost, which involves the removal of a specific reinforcer. Intrinsic punishment is punishment that is an inherent aspect of the behavior being punished, whereas extrinsic punishment is punishment that is not an inherent aspect of the behavior being punished. A primary punisher is one that is naturally punishing, and a secondary punisher is an event that is punishing because it has been associated with some other punisher. A generalized punisher has been associated with many other punishers.

There are several problems with the use of punishment, including a general suppression of behavior, avoidance of the person carrying out the punishment, elicitation of strong emotional responses, and an increase in aggressive behavior. Nevertheless, beneficial side effects can also occur, such as improvements in social behavior, mood, and attention to the environment. Punishment is more effective if delivered immediately, consistently, and at sufficient intensity to suppress the behavior. It also helps if punishment is accompanied by an explanation and if it is combined with positive reinforcement for appropriate behavior.

According to the conditioned suppression theory of punishment, punishment suppresses a behavior because it produces an emotional response that interferes with the behavior. According to the avoidance theory of punishment, punishment is a type of avoidance conditioning in which the avoidance response consists of doing anything other than the behavior that is being punished. The Premack principle, as applied to punishment, holds that low-probability behaviors can be used as punishers for high-probability behaviors.

Learned helplessness is a decrement in learning ability following exposure to inescapable aversive stimulation. Learned helplessness can be overcome by repeatedly forcing the animal to make the avoidance response, or can be prevented by providing an animal with prior exposure to escapable aversive stimulation. In Masserman's experimental neurosis procedure, animals are exposed to unpredictable aversive stimulation. This produces symptoms that are similar to those experienced by people who have developed posttraumatic stress disorder.

SUGGESTED READINGS

Newsom, C., Favell, J., & Rincover, A. (1983). The side effects of punishment. In S. Axelrod & J.Apsche (Eds.), *The effects of punishment on human behavior*. New York: Academic Press. A nice overview of the harmful, as well as beneficial, side effects of punishment.

Spanos, N. P. (1996). *Multiple identities & false memories: A sociocognitive perspective*. Washington, DC: American Psychological Association.

Lilienfeld, S. O., Kirsch, I., Sarbin, T. R., Lynn, S. J., Chaves, J. F., Ganaway, G. K., & Powell, R. A. (1999). Dissociative identity disorder and the sociocognitive model: Recalling the lessons of the past. *Psychological Bulletin, 125*, 507–523. This article and Spanos's book together constitute the most comprehensive presentation of the sociocognitive (or cognitive-behavioral) perspective on multiple personality disorder.

Sidman, M. (1989). *Coercion and its fallout*. Boston: Authors Cooperative. A strong indictment by a major behaviorist of the use of punishment to control human behavior.

STUDY QUESTIONS

1. Distinguish between escape and avoidance behavior.
2. Describe the evolution of avoidance behavior in a typical shuttle avoidance procedure.
3. Describe Mowrer's two-process theory of avoidance behavior.
4. Outline two criticisms of Mowrer's two-process theory of avoidance.

5. What is the anxiety conservation hypothesis? Outline Levis's answer to the problem of the "nonchalant" rat.
6. In what ways is experimental avoidance conditioning different from human phobic conditioning?
7. According to Stampfl, what is a critical factor in the development and maintenance of phobic behavior?
8. How can the two-process theory of avoidance account for obsessive-compulsive disorder?
9. Distinguish between time-out and response cost procedures.
10. What is the distinction between extrinsic punishment and intrinsic punishment? Give an example of each.
11. What is the distinction between a primary punisher and a secondary punisher? What is a generalized punisher?
12. Briefly outline at least five of the problems listed concerning the use of punishment.
13. What is the major advantage of punishment over extinction? What are three beneficial side effects of punishment?
14. Outline at least five of the characteristics of effective punishment.
15. Describe the conditioned suppression theory of punishment.
16. Describe the avoidance theory of punishment. Describe the Premack approach to punishment.
17. Describe the basic experimental procedure (with control group) that was first used to demonstrate learned helplessness in dogs and the outcome that was observed.
18. How can learned helplessness in dogs be eliminated? How can dogs be immunized against the development of learned helplessness?
19. Describe Masserman's procedure for inducing experimental neurosis in cats, and list some of the symptoms he observed.

CONCEPT REVIEW

avoidance theory of punishment. Punishment involving a type of avoidance conditioning in which the avoidance response consists of any behavior other than the behavior being punished.

conditioned suppression theory of punishment. The assumption that punishment does not weaken a behavior, but instead produces an emotional response that interferes with the occurrence of the behavior.

exposure and response prevention (ERP). A method of treating obsessive-compulsive behavior that involves prolonged exposure to anxiety-arousing events while not engaging in the compulsive behavior pattern that reduces the anxiety.

extrinsic punishment. Punishment that is not an inherent aspect of the behavior being punished but that simply follows the behavior.

generalized (or generalized secondary) punisher. An event that has become punishing because it has in the past been associated with many other punishers.

intrinsic punishment. Punishment that is an inherent aspect of the behavior being punished.

learned helplessness. A decrement in learning ability that results from repeated exposure to uncontrollable aversive events.

Premack principle of punishment. A low-probability behavior (LPB) can be used to punish a high-probability behavior (HPB).

primary (or unconditioned) punisher. Any event that is innately punishing.

response cost. A form of negative punishment involving the removal of a specific reinforcer following the occurrence of a behavior.

secondary (or conditioned) punisher. An event that has become punishing because it has in the past been associated with some other punisher.

time-out. A form of negative punishment involving the loss of access to positive reinforcers for a brief period of time following the occurrence of a problem behavior.

two-process theory of avoidance. The theory that avoidance behavior is the result of two distinct processes: (1) classical conditioning, in which a fear response comes to be elicited by a CS, and (2) operant conditioning, in which moving away from the CS is negatively reinforced by a reduction in fear.

CHAPTER TEST

11. According to Mowrer, the two processes that underlie avoidance behavior are: (1) c_____ conditioning, in which a _____ response comes to be elicited by a CS, and (2) _____ conditioning, in which moving away from the CS is _____ reinforced by a reduction in _____.

3. According to the _____ theory of punishment, if a rat is shocked for pressing a lever, then any behavior other than _____ will be _____ reinforced by the nonoccurrence of shock.

27. If a father punishes his son for being aggressive with his playmates, the son may learn not to be aggressive only when the father is _____.

8. Otto woke up one night to find an intruder standing over him in his bedroom. When the intruder saw that Otto was awake, he stabbed him and fled. Boyd was walking through a strange part of town one night when he too was stabbed. In keeping with certain research findings on experimental _____, the person most likely to suffer symptoms of PTSD is _____.

14. One criticism of Mowrer's two-process theory is that animals continue to make the avoidance response even though they no longer seem to

be _____ of the CS. One reply to this criticism is that although the animals may become significantly less _____ of the CS, they do not in fact become completely _____.

20. A person who checks her apartment door dozens of times each night to make sure that it is locked probably experiences a(n) _____ in anxiety when she thinks about whether the door is locked and a(n) _____ in anxiety when she checks it. This then acts as a _____ reinforcer for the behavior of checking.

15. According to the _____ theory of avoidance, I avoid bees simply because I am then less likely to be stung and not because I feel a reduction in fear.

9. Obert did not want to go to school one morning and so pretended that he was ill. Sure enough, his mother fell for the trick and let him stay home that day. Thereafter, Obert often pretended that he was ill so that he did not have to go to school. Obert's tendency to pretend that he was ill was strengthened through the process of _____.

28. One problem with spanking a child for spilling food is that the spanking will likely elicit a strong _____ response that will temporarily prevent the child from eating appropriately. The child may also become _____ as a result of the spanking, which might later be directed to his little brother or sister. He might also learn that an effective means of controlling others is through the use of _____.

19. Mowrer's two-process theory seems highly applicable to obsessive-compulsive disorder in that the occurrence of an obsessive thought is associated with a(n) _____ in anxiety, while performance of a compulsive behavior is associated with a(n) _____ in anxiety.

2. Skinner concluded that punishment generates a conditioned _____ reaction that then suppresses any appetitive behavior, and that the appetitive behavior (will / will not) _____ quickly recover once the punishment is withdrawn. Later research showed that this may be because Skinner had used a relatively (strong/weak) _____ form of punishment in his research.

13. One criticism of Mowrer's two-process theory is that an avoidance response often does not seem to _____, even after hundreds of trials. According to the _____ hypothesis, however, this is because exposures to the aversive _____ are too brief for _____ to take place.

4. According to the Premack principle, if Rick smokes a lot and rarely vacuums, then _____ can serve as an effective punisher for _____.

22. Losing your wallet by being careless is an example of a (negative/positive) _____ punisher, while getting a shock by being careless is an example of a _____ punisher (assuming in each case that the behavior subsequently _____ in frequency).

12. According to Mowrer, I go out of my way to avoid bees because behaving this way has been (positively/negatively) _____ (reinforced/punished) _____ by a _____ in fear.

29. One problem with spanking a child for being noisy while playing is that this will likely have an _____ effect in suppressing the behavior, which then serves as a strong reinforcer for the use of spanking on future occasions.

25. If you spank a dog for making a mess on the carpet, the dog might learn to avoid _____ rather than avoid making a mess on the carpet.

10. The theoretical difficulty with avoidance behavior, as opposed to escape behavior, is that the individual is moving from one (aversive/nonaversive) _____ situation to another, and it is difficult to see how a lack of change serves as a reinforcer.

31. The beneficial side effects of punishment can include increases in s_____ behavior, improvements in m_____, and increased a_____ to the environment.

21. One difference between OCD and a phobia is that a phobia usually requires a(n) (passive/active) _____ avoidance response, while OCD usually requires a(n) _____ avoidance response.

7. Pietro is having great difficulty sleeping, is easily startled, and has developed various phobias. Pietro's symptoms are similar to those shown by Masserman's cats that were exposed to _____ aversive stimulation. This set of symptoms in experimental animals is known as experimental _____; in humans, it is known as _____ stress disorder.

16. According to Mineka, there are limitations in the extent to which experimental demonstrations of avoidance are analogous to human phobias. For example, in an experimental demonstration of avoidance that involves a tone and an aversive air blast, the rat avoids the _____, which is a (CS/US) _____. By comparison, the bee-phobic person who was once stung avoids _____, which is a (CS/US) _____.

1. For children who are old enough to understand language, punishment should always be combined with an _____.

23. Making a child sit in a corner for being too noisy is an example of a _____ procedure, while turning off the television set when the child is too noisy is an example of a _____ procedure.

5. When Renee was in elementary school, she was cruelly teased by a classmate each recess. The teachers ignored her pleas for help, as did her other classmates. Seligman would predict that, as time passes, Renee is likely to (decrease/increase) _____ her efforts to stop the teasing. In other words, she will begin to suffer from learned _____. She may also become clinically _____.

17. According to Mineka, there are limitations in the extent to which experimental demonstrations of avoidance are analogous to human phobias. For example, in an experimental demonstration of avoidance that involves a tone and an aversive air blast, the rat will likely require

(one / more than one) _____ conditioning trial. By comparison, a bee phobia in humans may be acquired after _____ conditioning trial(s). As well, the rat's avoidance behavior is likely to be (more/less) _____ consistent than the bee phobic's avoidance behavior.

26. One problem with spanking a child for being noisy while playing with his friends is that he might not only stop being noisy but also stop _____.

30. A parent who wishes to punish her little girl for playing too roughly with the cat would do well to impose the punishing conse- quence _____ after the occurrence of the unwanted behavior and, at least initially, on a(n) (consistent/unpredictable) _____ basis. The parent should also _____ the behavior of playing appropriately with the cat.

6. According to learned helplessness research, Clint is (more/less) _____ likely to become depressed following a bitter divorce if his own parents divorced when he was a child and he later recovered from the experience.

24. Hugh got injured at work while goofing around, and as a result he became less likely to goof around. Eduardo got reprimanded by the boss for goofing around, and he also became less likely to goof around. Getting injured is a (primary/secondary) _____ punisher for the behavior of goofing around, while getting reprimanded is a _____ punisher.

18. Stampfl demonstrated that a critical factor in phobic conditioning is the possibility of making an (early/late) _____ avoidance response, thereby minimizing the amount of _____ involved in avoiding the feared event.

Visit the book companion Web site at http://www.cengage.com/search/showresults.do?N=16+4294922390+4294967274+4294949640 for additional practice questions, answers to the Quick Quizzes, practice review exams, and additional exercises and information.

ANSWERS TO CHAPTER TEST

1. explanation
2. emotional; will; weak
3. avoidance; lever pressing; negatively
4. vacuuming; smoking
5. decrease; helplessness; depressed
6. less
7. unpredictable; neurosis; posttraumatic
8. neurosis; Otto
9. negative reinforcement

10. nonaversive
11. classical; fear; operant; negatively; fear
12. negatively; reinforced; reduction
13. extinguish; anxiety conservation; CS; extinction
14. afraid; fearful; nonfearful
15. one-process
16. air blast; US; bees; CS
17. more than one; one; less

18. early; effort
19. increase; decrease
20. increase; decrease; negative
21. passive; active
22. negative; positive; decreases
23. time-out; response cost
24. primary; secondary (or generalized secondary)
25. you
26. playing
27. present (or nearby)
28. emotional; aggressive; punishment.
29. immediate
30. immediately; consistent; positively reinforce
31. social; mood; attention

Choice, Matching, and Self-Control

Mark was becoming quite frustrated by Jan's insistence that they were spending too much time together. He told her that if two people truly love each other, they should want to spend as much time together as possible. Jan countered that she did love him but that spending too much time together was making their relationship dull and boring. For her, life was more fulfilling when she interacted with a variety of people each day.

Operant conditioning in the real world is rarely a matter of being offered only one source of reinforcement. Instead, individuals typically choose between alternative sources of reinforcement. In this chapter, we examine some of the principles by which such choices are made—especially the principle of matching, which stipulates that the amount of behavior directed toward an alternative is proportional to the amount of reinforcement we receive from that alternative. We also examine the types of choices involved when people attempt to exert "self-control" over their behavior.

Choice and Matching

Concurrent Schedules

In operant conditioning experiments, investigations of choice behavior often make use of a type of complex schedule known as a concurrent schedule. A *concurrent schedule of reinforcement* consists of the simultaneous presentation of two or more independent schedules, each leading to a reinforcer. The organism is thus allowed a choice between responding on one schedule versus the other.

For example, a pigeon may be given a choice between responding on a red key that is associated with a VR 20 schedule of reinforcement and a green key that is associated with a VR 50 schedule of reinforcement (see Figure 10.1). We can diagram this situation as follows:

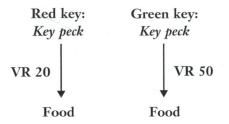

Which alternative would you choose? If you think of this situation as analogous to choosing between two slot machines, one of which pays off after an average of 20 quarters are plugged in and the other of which pays off after an average of 50 quarters are plugged in, the choice becomes easy. You would pick the better-paying machine, that is, the one that requires an

FIGURE 10.1 Illustration of a two-key operant procedure in which two schedules of reinforcement are simultaneously available, in this case, a VR 20 schedule on the red key and a VR 50 schedule on the green key. The two schedules thus form the two components of a *concurrent VR 20 VR 50* schedule of reinforcement. (*Source:* Domjan, 2003.)

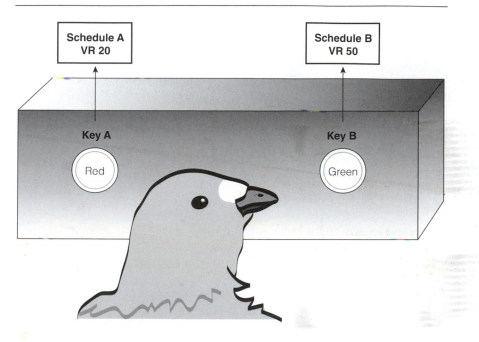

average of only 20 quarters to produce a win (if you can fight off everyone else who wants that machine). Similarly, the pigeon will come to develop an exclusive preference for the VR 20 alternative (Herrnstein & Loveland, 1975).

Choice between concurrent VR schedules is easy because an exclusive preference for the richer alternative clearly provides the better payoff. But what about concurrent VI schedules? What if, for example, a pigeon is presented with a concurrent VI 30-sec VI 60-sec schedule?

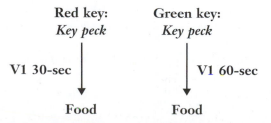

Remember that on VI schedules, reinforcers become available at unpredictable points in time (and any responses before that point will not result in reinforcement). Given this unpredictability, will the bird just randomly distribute its responses between the two alternatives, hoping to catch the reinforcers on each alternative as they become available (just as in trying to phone two friends at home, you might repeatedly dial each number in random order hoping to catch each person soon after he or she arrives home)? Herrnstein (1961) carried out just such an experiment using various schedule values and found that the pigeon's behavior under such circumstances is actually quite systematic. It is so systematic, in fact, that it led to the formulation of what is known as the matching law.

1. Many behaviors are reinforced on a c_____ schedule in which two or more in_____ schedules of reinforcement are s_____ available.

2. If a VR 25 and VR 75 schedule of reinforcement are simultaneously available, your best strategy would be to choose the _____ schedule (100/50/25) _____% of the time.

The Matching Law

The *matching law* holds that the proportion of responses emitted on a particular schedule matches the proportion of reinforcers obtained on that schedule (note that it is *proportion* of responses and reinforcers and not *number* of responses and reinforcers). Thus, a pigeon will emit approximately twice as many responses on the VI 30-sec schedule as on the VI 60-sec schedule because the rate of reinforcement on the former will be twice as great as on the latter (an average of two reinforcers per minute on the VI 30-sec schedule versus one reinforcer per minute on the VI 60-sec schedule). Similarly, a pigeon will emit three times as many responses on a VI 10-sec schedule as it will on a VI 30-sec schedule because the VI 10-sec schedule provides three times the rate of reinforcement (an average of six reinforcers per minute on the VI 10-sec schedule versus two per minute on the VI 30-sec schedule). *The matching law therefore predicts a consistent relationship between the proportion of reinforcers obtained on a certain alternative and the proportion of responses emitted on that alternative.* If a pigeon earns 10% of its reinforcers on a particular alternative, then it will emit 10% of its responses on that alternative; if it earns 60% of its reinforcers on an alternative, then it will emit 60% of its responses on it.

The matching law can also be expressed in the form of an equation:

$$\frac{R_A}{R_A + R_B} = \frac{S^R_A}{S^R_A + S^R_B}$$

where R is the number of responses emitted, S^R is the number of reinforcers earned, and the subscripts A and B refer to the two schedules of reinforcement. Thus, R_A is the number of responses emitted on schedule A, R_B is the number of responses emitted on schedule B, S^R_A is the number of reinforcers earned on schedule A, and S^R_B is the number of reinforcers earned on schedule B. Therefore, the term to the left of the equal sign:

$$\frac{R_A}{R_A + R_B}$$

indicates the proportion of responses emitted on schedule A. It is the number of responses emitted on schedule A divided by the total number emitted on both schedules. The term to the right of the equal sign:

$$\frac{S^R_A}{S^R_A + S^R_B}$$

indicates the proportion of reinforcers earned on schedule A. It is the number of reinforcers earned on schedule A divided by the total number earned on both schedules.

To illustrate how the equation works, let us look at some hypothetical data from an experiment involving a choice between a VI 30-sec and a VI 60-sec schedule. If the pigeon picks up most or all of the reinforcers available on each alternative in a 1-hour session, it should obtain about twice as many reinforcers on the VI 30-sec schedule as on the VI 60-sec. Imagine that this is essentially what happens: Our hypothetical pigeon obtains 119 reinforcers on the VI 30-sec schedule and 58 reinforcers (about half as many) on the VI 60-sec schedule. Plugging these values into the right-hand term of the equation, we get

$$\frac{S^R_{VI\ 30-s}}{S^R_{VI\ 30-s} + S^R_{VI\ 60-s}} = \frac{119}{119 + 58} = \frac{119}{177} = .67$$

which means that the proportion of reinforcers obtained from the VI 30-sec schedule is .67. In other words, 67% (about 2/3) of the reinforcers acquired during the session are obtained from the VI 30-sec schedule, and 33% (about 1/3) are obtained from the VI 60-sec schedule (meaning that twice as many reinforcers are obtained from the VI 30-sec schedule). As for responses, imagine that our hypothetical pigeon emits 2800 responses on the VI 30-sec schedule and 1450 responses on the VI 60-sec schedule. Plugging these values into the left-hand term of the equation, we get

$$\frac{R_{VI\ 30-s}}{R_{VI\ 30-s} + R_{VI\ 60-s}} = \frac{2800}{2800 + 1450} = \frac{2800}{4250} = .66$$

Thus, the proportion of responses emitted on the VI 30-sec schedule is .66. In other words, 66% of the responses are emitted on the VI 30-sec schedule (and 34% are emitted on the VI 60-sec schedule). In keeping with the matching law, this figure closely matches the proportion of reinforcement obtained on that schedule (.67). In other words, the proportion of responses emitted on the VI 30-sec schedule approximately matches the proportion of reinforcers earned on that schedule. (For results from Herrnstein's [1961] original matching experiment in which pigeons chose between several different combinations of schedules, see Figure 10.2).

FIGURE 10.2 Experimental results depicting the proportion of responses emitted by two pigeons on key A. Different combinations of schedules were offered on key A versus key B across the different conditions of the experiment, with the schedule values ranging from VI 90-sec to VI 540-sec to extinction (no reinforcers available). As the schedule combinations changed and the proportion of reinforcers earned on key A increased from approximately .1 to 1.0, the proportion of responses emitted on key A increased in similar fashion. (*Source:* Adapted from "Relative and absolute strength of response as a function of frequency of reinforcement," by R. J. Herrnstein, 1961, *Journal of Experimental Analysis of Behavior, 4,* pp. 267–272. Copyright © 1961 by the Society for the Experimental Analysis of Behavior, Inc. Reprinted with permission.)

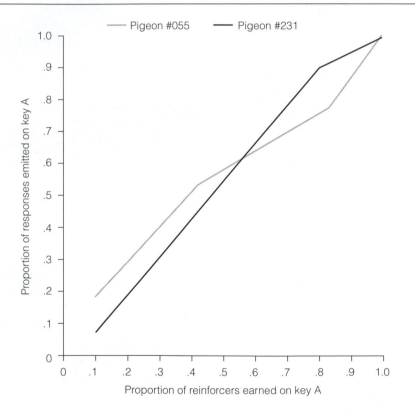

Matching appears to be a basic principle of choice behavior, applicable to a variety of situations and species. For example, Houston (1986) investigated the extent to which the pied wagtail, an insectivorous bird in Britain, distributed its foraging behavior between two separate patches of food: (1) a stretch of territory along the banks of the Thames River, which the territorial owner defended from other wagtails (and only some birds owned territories), and (2) an open meadow that any wagtail could visit and feed upon as part of the flock. Those birds that owned territories tended to walk circular routes within their territories, feeding off insects that were regularly washed up by the river. If, however, food along the river was scarce, the owner could fly over to the meadow and feed with the flock. (In a sense, finding nothing to eat at home, the bird had the option of eating out at the local restaurant.) Houston found that the proportion of time a bird spent in one food patch versus the other (its own territory versus the public meadow) approximately matched the proportion of food it obtained in that patch.

Matching is also applicable to human social behavior. For example, in a group situation, we must choose between directing our conversation to one person or another, each of whom provides a different rate of reinforcement (in the form of comments or acknowledgments). In one investigation, Conger and Killeen (1974) asked student volunteers to participate with three other students in a discussion session on drug abuse. Each volunteer was unaware that the other members of the group were actually confederates of the experimenter. During the discussion session, while the volunteer was talking, the two confederates sat on either side and intermittently expressed approval in response to whatever the volunteer happened to be saying at that time. The experimenters systematically varied the frequency of verbal approvals delivered by each of the confederates. They found that the relative amount of time the volunteer looked at each confederate matched the relative frequency of verbal approval delivered by that confederate. If one confederate delivered twice as many approvals as the other confederate, then that confederate was looked at twice as often. In general, these results suggest that the principle of matching may underlie various aspects of human social interaction.

1. According to the matching law, the (number/proportion) _____ of _____ on an alternative matches the (number/proportion) _____ of _____ obtained on that alternative.

2. On a concurrent VI 60-sec VI 120-sec schedule, the pigeon should emit about (half/twice) _____ as many responses on the VI 60-sec alternative as opposed to the VI 120-sec alternative.

3. If a pigeon emits 1100 responses on key A and 3100 responses on key B, then the proportion of responses on key A is _____. If the pigeon also earned 32 reinforcers on key A and 85 reinforcers on key B, then the proportion of reinforcers earned on key A is _____. This pigeon (did / did not) _____ approximately match pr_____ of r_____ to pr_____ of _____.

Deviations from Matching

Although matching provides a good description of behavior in many choice situations, exceptions have been noted. In general, there are three types of exceptions, or deviations, from matching (Baum, 1974, 1979). The first deviation, which is quite common, is called undermatching. In **_undermatching_**, the proportion of responses on the richer schedule versus the poorer schedule is less different than would be predicted by matching (to remember this, think of _under_matching as _less_ different). For example, the matching law predicts that the proportion of responses should be .67 on the richer VI 30-sec schedule and .33 on the poorer VI 60-sec schedule. If we instead find proportions of .60 and .40, respectively, then undermatching has occurred. There is less of a difference in responding between the richer and poorer schedules than would be predicted by matching.

Undermatching can occur when there is little cost for switching from one schedule to another. For example, in our previous description of a hypothetical matching experiment, we actually left out an important aspect of the procedure. Whenever the pigeon switches from one key to another, the act of doing so initiates a slight delay of, say, 2 seconds during which no response will be effective in producing a reinforcer, even if a reinforcer happens to be available at that time. It is as though, when the pigeon switches from one key to another, the first peck on the new key is simply a statement of intent that says, "I now want to try this key," following which there is a 2-second delay before any peck can actually earn a reinforcer. This delay feature is called a *changeover delay* or COD.

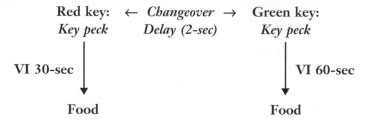

Without a COD, a pigeon will simply alternate pecks back and forth on each key, catching each reinforcer as soon as it becomes available. Only when a slight cost for switching is added to the situation does the pigeon spend more time on the richer alternative.

The COD can be thought of as the experimental equivalent of a foraging situation in which the animal has to travel a certain distance between food patches. If two food patches are extremely close together (say, each patch is separated by only a narrow stream), then undermatching is likely to occur. The animal will simply move back and forth from one side to another, looking for prey, even if one side is generally a much richer area in which to hunt. If, however, the two patches are more widely separated (say, the stream is somewhat broad), then the animal is more likely to match the amount of time it spends on one side of the stream to the number of prey that it obtains on that side. It will spend proportionately more time on the rich side of the stream, and less time on the poor side of the stream.

A second deviation from matching is called overmatching. In **overmatching**, the proportion of responses on the richer schedule versus the poorer schedule is more different than would be predicted by matching (to remember this, think of *over*matching as *more* different). For example, the matching law predicts that the proportion of responses should be .67 on the richer VI 30-sec schedule and .33 on the poorer VI 60-sec schedule. If we instead find proportions of .80 and .20, respectively, then overmatching has occurred. There is more of a difference in responding between the richer and poorer schedules than would be predicted by matching.

Overmatching can occur when the cost of moving from one alternative to another is very high. For example, Baum (1974) found that overmatching occurred when a pigeon had to walk around a partition and climb across a wooden hurdle to switch from one response key to another. The pigeon switched less often and spent more time on the richer alternative than the matching law would predict. Similarly, a predator that has to cross a mountain ridge to move from one food patch to another might make the trip only infrequently and spend considerably more time in the richer food patch than predicted by matching.

1. When the difference in the proportion of responding on richer versus poorer alternatives is greater than would be predicted by matching, we say that _____ has occurred.

2. When the difference in the proportion of responding on richer versus poorer alternatives is less than would be predicted by matching, we say that _____ has occurred.

3. In experimental studies of matching, the act of switching from one alternative to another results in a c_____ d_____: a short period of time that must pass before any response can produce a reinforcer.

4. This experimental procedure seems analogous to f_____ situations in which an animal has to t_____ a certain d_____ from one food patch to another.

5. In general, food patches that are separated by a very great distance will produce _____ matching, while food patches that are separated by a very short distance will produce _____ matching.

QUICK QUIZ C

The final deviation from matching is called bias. ***Bias from matching*** occurs when one response alternative attracts a higher proportion of responses than would be predicted by matching, regardless of whether that alternative contains the richer or poorer schedule of reinforcement. For example, suppose that our two schedules are VI 30-sec and VI 60-sec, and that we alternate which schedule is associated with red key versus green key. The matching law predicts that the proportion of responses on the red key should be .67 when the richer VI 30-sec schedule is presented on it, and .33 when the poorer VI 60-sec schedule is presented on it. But if the proportions instead turned out to be .77 when the VI 30-sec schedule is presented on it and .43 when the VI 60-sec schedule is presented on it, then bias has occurred (see Table 10.1). The pigeon is emitting 10% more responses on the red key than predicted by matching, both when it is the richer alternative and when it is the poorer alternative. (Of course, this also means that the pigeon is emitting 10% fewer responses on the green key.) In a sense, the pigeon seems to like red and therefore expends extra effort on the red key over and above the amount of responding dictated by the schedule of reinforcement. Similarly, in a conversation with a group of individuals, Erin might spend additional time directing her conversation toward Jason, whom she finds very attractive. For example, on one day, he provides 72% of the

And Furthermore

Basketball and the Matching Law

In an interesting application of the matching law to sports activities, Vollmer and Bourret (2000) examined the allocation of 2- versus 3-point shots made by male and female basketball players at a major university. The question of interest was whether the players would match the proportion of shots taken from the 3-point range to the proportion of reinforcers (baskets) they obtained from that range. The researchers found that such matching did indeed occur (particularly when the matching equation was altered somewhat to account for the greater value of 3-point shots). In other words, if a certain player obtained about 35% of his or her points from the 3-point range, then about 35% of his or her shots tended to occur from that range. The authors speculated that this ability to match the proportion of shots attempted from a certain range to the proportion of points obtained from that range may be a distinguishing characteristic of player excellence. One author, for example, described how he casually observed a local street game in which 3-point shots were frequently attempted even though they were almost never successful. In other words, it seemed as less-skillful players did not display the same tendency to match that the university players had displayed (this was a top-ranked university, by the way). In fact, subsequent research (e.g., Alferink, Critchfield, & Hitt, 2009) has confirmed that the matching law (with some deviations) is a good predictor of basketball shot selection by more successful players at both the college and professional level.

You may have noticed that this type of matching suggests that basketball shots are reinforced on a VI schedule, which contradicts the typical notion that shot-making in such activities is reinforced on a VR schedule (with rate of reinforcement largely dependent on the number of shots attempted). Vollmer and Bouret (2000), however, suggest that basketball shots may in fact be reinforced on a combination (conjunctive) VR–VI schedule, with reinforcement dependent both on the number of shots attempted (the VR component) and on defensive lapses by the opposition that occur at unpredictable points in time (the VI component). (See also Reed, Critchfield, & Martens, 2006, and Stilling & Critchfield, 2010, for an application of the matching law to play selection in National Football League games.)

reinforcers during a conversation, but she nevertheless looks at him 84% of the time; on another day, he provides only 23% of the reinforcers, but she nevertheless looks at him 36% of the time. In each case, she looks at him more than would be predicted by matching. His attractiveness is an additional factor, over and above the amount of conversational reinforcement he offers, that influences how much she looks at him.

Bias can be a precise way to measure preference. For example, on a concurrent VI 60-sec VI 60-sec schedule, the pigeon should respond equally on the two alternatives. But what if each alternative leads to a different reinforcer, perhaps wheat on one side and buckwheat on the other? Under these circumstances, the extent to which the pigeon biases its responding

| **TABLE 10.1** | Hypothetical results indicating bias from matching. More responses are emitted on the red key, both when it is the richer alternative (VI 30-sec) and when it is the poorer alternative (VI 60-sec), than would be predicted by matching. (Of course, this also means that fewer responses are emitted on the green key than would be predicted by matching.) |

CONDITION A (RICHER SCHEDULE ON RED KEY)	PREDICTED	OBTAINED
Red Key: VI 30-sec	.67	.77
Green Key: VI 60-sec	.33	.23
CONDITION B (POORER SCHEDULE ON RED KEY)		
Red Key: VI 60-sec	.33	.43
Green Key: VI 30-sec	.67	.57

toward the schedule leading to wheat indicates the extent of the pigeon's preference for wheat. In fact, Miller (1976) carried out just such an experiment and found that pigeons preferred wheat over buckwheat by a ratio of about 1.4 to 1.0. If we think of key pecks as equivalent to how much money pigeons would be willing to spend for one alternative versus the other, then the pigeons were willing to spend $1.40 on a bag of wheat compared to only $1.00 for a bag of buckwheat. Bias in matching can, therefore, be used to indicate degree of preference for different reinforcers.

In summary, undermatching occurs when the difference in responding between the richer and poorer schedules is less than predicted by matching. Overmatching occurs when the difference in responding between the richer and poorer schedules is more than predicted by matching, and bias occurs when one response alternative receives more responses than predicted by matching regardless of whether it contains the richer or poorer schedule. Each of these deviations has been incorporated into more complex versions of the matching law (Baum, 1974).

As with the phenomenon of behavioral contrast (discussed in Chapter 8), the matching law reminds us that operant behavior should often be viewed in context. The amount of behavior directed toward an alternative is a function of the amount of reinforcement available on that alternative as well as the amount of reinforcement available on other alternatives. This notion has important implications for everyday behavior. For example, although a child might spend little time reading, this does not mean that reading is not a reinforcing activity for that child. If other highly reinforcing activities, such as computer games and television, happen to be simultaneously available, reading may be losing out simply because it provides less reinforcement (especially immediate reinforcement) than those other activities. Thus, a simple but effective way to motivate the child to read might be to limit the amount of time those other activities are available. In the absence of such alternatives, the child might naturally gravitate toward reading as a source of reinforcement.

1. When greater responding is shown for a particular response alternative than would be predicted by matching, irrespective of the amount of reinforcement obtained from that alternative, we say that the organism has a b_____ for that alternative.

2. Food patches that differ in the type of prey found within them may produce the type of deviation from matching known as _____.

3. When a bear obtains 70% of its food from a nearby stream, it spends 80% of its time at the stream; when it obtains 30% of its food from the stream, it spends 25% of its time at the stream. When a cougar obtains 20% of its food in a particular canyon, it spends 35% of its time in that canyon; when it obtains 65% of its food from that canyon, it spends 80% of its time in the canyon. Among the 3 types of deviation from matching, the bear shows evidence of _____ while the cougar shows evidence of _____.

Matching and Melioration

The matching law describes how behavior is distributed across various alternatives in a choice situation. It does not, however, explain why this pattern of distribution occurs. You might think that it occurs simply because it somehow maximizes one's overall level of reinforcement, a proposition known as *maximization (or optimization) theory* (e.g., Rachlin, 1978). An alternative explanation, however, is called melioration theory (*to meliorate* means "to make better"). According to *melioration theory*, the distribution of behavior in a choice situation shifts toward those alternatives that have higher value regardless of the long-term effect on the overall amount of reinforcement (Herrnstein, 1990). For example, suppose that when a pigeon is first confronted with a concurrent VI 30-sec VI 60-sec schedule, it emits an equal number of responses on both alternatives. The responses emitted on the VI 30-sec schedule will result in twice as many reinforcers as those emitted on the VI 60-sec schedule. Thus, in terms of benefits (reinforcers obtained) versus costs (responses made), the VI 30-sec schedule will have a much higher value than the VI 60-sec schedule, because the bird will have obtained twice as many reinforcers on the VI 30-sec schedule for the same amount of work. This will make the VI 30-sec schedule a very attractive alternative to the pigeon, with the result that the pigeon will be tempted in subsequent sessions to shift more and more of its behavior in that direction. This shifting, however, will cease at the point of matching, because that is the point at which the two alternatives have about equal value. The pigeon will still be earning twice as many reinforcers on the VI 30-sec schedule, but in doing so it will be expending twice as many responses on that alternative. Thus, the cost of each alternative (in responses made) will now match the benefits obtained from that alternative (in reinforcers earned). Melioration in this situation is thus a sort of leveling-out process, in which behavior shifts until the two alternatives have about equal value in terms of costs versus benefits.

At this point, you might be thinking that melioration is rather trivial. Why would an animal or person not shift behavior toward the richer alternative? The problem is that this tendency to move toward the richer alternative can sometimes result in a substantial reduction in the total amount of reinforcement obtained. There are three ways in which this can occur.

First, an alternative may not require as much responding as one is distributing toward it to obtain all of the available reinforcers. Consider, for example, a pigeon that is presented with a concurrent VR 100 VI 30-sec schedule (note that the first alternative is a VR schedule). On the VR 100 alternative, 100 responses on average will result in a reinforcer, while on the VI 30-sec alternative, the first response after an average interval of 30 seconds will result in a reinforcer. What is the pigeon's best strategy in this situation?

The best strategy is for the pigeon to spend most of its time on the VR schedule in which the number of reinforcers obtained is directly tied to the number of responses made, and then briefly switch to the VI alternative about every 30 seconds or so to pick up any reinforcer that might have become available on that alternative. This strategy will maximize the amount of reinforcement obtained. In reality, pigeons tend to match the amount of time spent on the VI schedule to the number of reinforcers earned on that schedule, thereby spending more time on the VI schedule and less time on the VR schedule than they should (Herrnstein & Heyman, 1979). Thus, if a pigeon happens to obtain 60% of its reinforcers from the VI 30-sec schedule, it will spend 60% of its time responding on the VI 30-sec schedule and only 40% of its time responding on the VR 100 schedule—a distribution of behavior that greatly reduces the overall amount of reinforcement obtained during the session. Hence, the pigeon's tendency to match (meliorate) has the effect of producing an overall level of reinforcement that is suboptimal.

In similar fashion, Henry, a salesman with a large manufacturing company, might spend too much time courting clients who are relatively easy sells (in reality, he only needs to call on such clients once a month to make a sale), and too little time courting retailers who are relatively difficult sells (who need to be intensively courted before a sale can be made). If Henry shifted some of his time away from the easy clients and toward the difficult clients, he might experience almost no loss of business from the former and a substantial gain in business from the latter. Unfortunately, because the rich schedule of reinforcement provided by the easy clients is very attractive to him, he continues to spend too much time with his easy clients and too little time with his difficult clients.

As another example, consider the manner in which many students distribute study time between the courses they are taking. Students often spend the most time studying for their most enjoyable course and the least time studying for their least enjoyable course. Yet the least enjoyable course is probably the one on which students should spend the most time studying. The result is that they spend the least time studying those courses that require the most work.

1. According to _____ theory, the distribution of behavior in a choice situation shifts toward that alternative that has a (lower/higher) _____ value. This shifting will cease at the point where the two outcomes are (approximately equal / maximally different) _____ in terms of costs versus benefits.

2. A rat faced with a concurrent VR 60 VI 80-sec schedule will spend more time on the _____ schedule than necessary to pick up all of the available reinforcers on that schedule. This result is consistent with _____ theory but contradicts what is known as max_____ (or op_____) theory.

3. Shona spends a lot of time cleaning her apartment, which she quite enjoys, and little time studying, which she does not enjoy. Chances are that this distribution of behavior, which results from the tendency to _____, (will / will not) _____ maximize the amount of reinforcement in her life.

A second problem with melioration is that overindulgence in a highly reinforcing alternative can often result in long-term habituation to that alternative, thus reducing its value as a reinforcer. Suppose, for example, that you suddenly become so rich that you can eat as much as you want of whatever you want. Before becoming rich, you rarely ate lobster, which you absolutely loved. Now, with your newfound wealth, you begin eating lobster almost every day. The problem is that if you eat lobster this frequently, you will likely become habituated to it, such that, although still enjoyable, it is no longer the heavenly treat that it once was. For this reason, many people fondly remember those times in their lives when they had limited resources and had to struggle a bit to get by. The overall amount of reinforcement they experienced at that time, when highly valued items such as lobster could be experienced in only small quantities and truly enjoyed, actually may have been much greater than it is now.[1]

This same process can be a contributing factor to the development of substance abuse. If drinking in a bar is a highly enjoyable activity, you might begin shifting more and more of your behavior in that direction. Eventually, you will be spending so much time in the bar that the overall amount of reinforcement in your life is substantially reduced—both because drinking is no longer as enjoyable as when you drank less frequently, and because you are now in the bar so much that you are missing out on reinforcers from other, nonalcohol-related activities. You may in fact be fully aware that your alcohol-oriented life is not very satisfying (in fact, such awareness is a defining characteristic of an addiction) yet find it very difficult to break free and reject the pleasure of heading to the bar for another evening of positive reinforcement.

Many of the previous examples can also be seen as instances of a *third, more general problem, which is that melioration is often the result of behavior being too strongly governed by immediate consequences as opposed to delayed consequences.* The immediate reinforcement available from studying more enjoyable courses

---

[1]See also, "What Is Wrong With Daily Life in the Western World?" by Skinner (1987). Skinner does not use the term *melioration*, but many of the examples he provides can be interpreted as examples of this process.

ADVICE FOR THE LOVELORN

Dear Dr. Dee,

My boyfriend spends almost all his time with me, which I find depressing. I try to tell him that I need some breathing space, but he seems to think that if I truly loved him, I would want to be with me always. What is your opinion on this?

Smothered

Dear Smothered,

Sounds as if your love relationship may have fallen prey to the damaging effects of melioration. Although some people believe that being in love with someone means wanting to be with that person always, the reality is that too much togetherness may result in a severe case of habituation. Add to this the possibility that the two individuals involved are also spending much less time interacting with other people, and it could well be that the overall amount of reinforcement in their lives is actually less than it was before they met. This suggests that some relationships might improve if the couple spent a bit less time together and worked a bit harder at maintaining other sources of social reinforcement (given that this does not become a cheap excuse for having an affair!). So, behaviorally speaking, I agree with you.

Behaviorally yours,

Dr. Dee

tempts one away from working on less enjoyable courses and maximizing one's overall grade point average at the end of the term (a delayed reinforcer). And the immediate reinforcement available from going to the bar each evening tempts one away from moderating one's drinking and eventually establishing a more healthy and satisfying lifestyle (a delayed reinforcer). The difficulties that arise from the strong preference for immediate reinforcers over delayed reinforcers are described more fully in the following section.

1. One problem with melioration is that this tendency may result in (over/ under) _____indulgence of a favored reinforcer with the result that we may experience long-term h_____ to it. This means that our enjoyment of life may be greatest when we (do / do not) _____ have all that we desire.

2. Another problem is that melioration can result in too much time being spent on those alternatives that provide relatively i_____ reinforcement and not enough time on those that provide d_____ reinforcement.

QUICK QUIZ F

Self-Control

In our discussion of melioration, we noted that people often engage in sub-optimal patterns of behavior. Moreover, although people realize that these patterns are suboptimal, they seem unable to change them. They decide to quit smoking but do not persist more than a day; they are determined to go for a run each morning but cannot get out of bed to do so; they resolve to study each evening but spend most evenings either watching television or socializing. In short, they know what to do, but they do not do it. To use the common vernacular, they lack self-control.

Why people have such difficulty controlling their own behavior has long been a matter of conjecture. Plato maintained that people engage in actions that are not in their best interest because of a lack of education, and that once they realize that it is to their benefit to behave appropriately, they will do so. Aristotle disagreed, however, noting that individuals often behave in ways that they clearly recognize as counterproductive. Many people, at least in this culture, would probably agree with Aristotle. They would probably also contend that self-control seems to require a certain mental faculty called willpower. A person who behaves wisely and resists temptations is said to have a lot of willpower, whereas a person who behaves poorly and yields to temptations is said to have little willpower. But is the concept of willpower, as used in this manner, really an explanation? Or is it one of those false explanations based on circular reasoning?

Mental + behaviorial process

> "Sam quit smoking. He must have a lot of willpower."
> "How do you know he has a lot of willpower?"
> "Well, he quit smoking, didn't he?"

The term *willpower*, used in this way, merely describes what Sam did—that he was able to quit smoking. It does not explain why he was able to quit smoking. For this reason, telling someone that they need to use more willpower to quit smoking is usually a pointless exercise. They would love to use more willpower—if only someone would tell them what it is and where to get it.

In the remainder of this chapter, we discuss some behavioral approaches to self-control. These approaches generally reject the traditional concept of willpower and instead focus on the relationship between behavior and its outcomes. We begin with Skinner's rudimentary analysis of self-control.

Skinner on Self-Control

Believed willpower has nothing to do with self-control

Skinner (1953) viewed self-control, or "self-management," not as an issue of willpower but as an issue involving conflicting outcomes. For example, drinking alcohol can lead to both positive outcomes (e.g., increased confidence and feelings of relaxation) and negative outcomes (e.g., a hangover along with that idiotic tattoo you found on your arm the next morning). Skinner also proposed that managing this conflict involves two types of responses: a *controlling response* that serves to alter the frequency of a *controlled response*. Suppose, for example, that to control the amount of money you spend, you leave most of your money at home when heading out one evening. The act of leaving money at home is the controlling response, while the amount you subsequently spend is the controlled response. By emitting the one response, you affect the other.

Skinner (1953) listed several types of controlling responses, some of which are described here.

Physical Restraint   With this type of controlling response, you physically manipulate the environment to prevent the occurrence of some problem behavior. Leaving money at home so that you will spend less during an evening out is one example; loaning your television set to a friend for the rest of the semester so that you will be more likely to study than watch television is another.

Depriving and Satiating   Another tactic for controlling your behavior is to deprive or satiate yourself, thereby altering the extent to which a certain event can act as a reinforcer. For example, you might make the most of an invitation to an expensive dinner by skipping lunch, thereby ensuring that you will be very hungry at dinnertime. Conversely, if you are attempting to diet, you might do well to shop for groceries immediately *after* a meal. If you are satiated, as opposed to hungry, during your shopping trip, you may be less tempted to purchase fattening items such as ice cream and potato chips.

Doing Something Else   To prevent yourself from engaging in certain behaviors, it is sometimes helpful to perform an alternate behavior. Thus, people who are trying to quit smoking often find it helpful to chew gum, and people who are trying to diet often find it helpful to sip sugar-free sodas.

Self-Reinforcement and Self-Punishment   A self-control tactic that might seem obvious from a behavioral standpoint is to simply reinforce your own behavior. Although Skinner suggested that this might work, he also noted a certain difficulty with it. In the typical operant conditioning paradigm, the reinforcer is delivered only when the appropriate response is emitted. The rat must press the lever to receive food, the child must clean his room to receive a cookie, and the student must study and perform well on an exam to receive a high mark. In the case of self-reinforcement, however, this contingency is much weaker. You might promise yourself that you will have a pizza after completing 3 hours of studying, but what is to stop you from *not* studying and having the pizza anyway? To use Martin and Pear's (1999) terminology, what is to stop you from "short-circuiting" the contingency and immediately consuming the reward without performing the intended behavior?

A similar problem exists with the use of self-punishment. You might promise yourself that you will do 20 push-ups following each cigarette

smoked, but what is to stop you from smoking a cigarette anyway and not bothering with the push-ups? Note too that if you do perform the push-ups, it might punish not only the act of smoking but also the act of carrying through on your promise to punish yourself. As a result, you will be less likely to do the push-ups the next time you have a smoke. In fact, research has shown that people who attempt to use self-punishment often fail to deliver the consequences to themselves (Worthington, 1979).

Thus, some behaviorists believe that self-reinforcement and self-punishment do not function in the same manner as normal reinforcement and punishment (Catania, 1975). Rachlin (1974), for example, has proposed that self-reinforcement might simply make the completion of an intended behavior more *salient*, thereby enhancing its value as a secondary reinforcer. For example, eating a pizza after 3 hours of studying might simply be the equivalent of setting off fireworks and sounding the trumpets for a job well done. There is also some evidence that self-delivered consequences are more effective when the person perceives that other people are aware of the contingency, suggesting that the social consequences for attaining or not attaining the intended goal are often an important aspect of so-called *self*-reinforcement or *self*-punishment procedures (Hayes et al., 1985).

Despite these concerns, Bandura (1976) and others maintain that self-delivered consequences can function in much the same manner as externally delivered consequences, given that the individual has been properly socialized to adhere to self-set standards and to feel guilty for violating such standards. It is also the case that many people do make use of self-reinforcement and self-punishment procedures in trying to control their behavior. Heffernan and Richards (1981), for example, found that 75% of students who had successfully improved their study habits reported using self-reinforcement. Conversely, Gary Player, the senior golfer, is a staunch believer in the value of self-punishment for maintaining a disciplined lifestyle—such as by forcing himself to do an extra 200 sit-ups (over and above the normal 800!) after a game in which he has let himself become irritable (Kossoff, 1999). Self-delivered contingencies are, therefore, a recommended component of many self-management programs (D. L. Watson & Tharp, 2002).

QUICK QUIZ G

1. Behavioral approaches largely (accept/reject) _____ the concept of will-power as an explanation for self-control.

2. Skinner analyzed self-control from the perspective of a _____ response that alters the frequency of a subsequent response that is known as the _____ response.

3. Suppose you post a reminder on your refrigerator about a long-distance phone call you should make this weekend. Posting the reminder is the _____ response, while making the call on the weekend is the _____ response.

4. Folding your arms to keep from chewing your nails is an example of the use of p_____ r_____ to control your behavior.

5. A problem with the use of self-reinforcement is that we may be tempted to consume the _____ without engaging in the behavior. This problem is known as s_____-_____ the contingency.

6. This can also be a problem in the use of s_____- p_____, in which case we may engage in the behavior and not p_____ ourselves.

7. Some people believe that self-reinforcement is really a way of making the completion of a behavior (more/less) _____ salient, thereby enhancing its value as a s_____ reinforcer.

8. There is also some evidence that self-reinforcement is more effective when others (know / do not know) _____ about the contingency that we have arranged for ourselves.

9. Bandura believes that self-reinforcement and self-punishment can work for people who are likely to feel g_____ if they violate standards that they have set for themselves.

Self-Control as a Temporal Issue

Skinner recognized that self-control issues involve choice between conflicting consequences, but others have emphasized that a frequent, critical aspect of this conflict is that one is choosing between alternatives that differ in the extent to which the consequences are immediate versus delayed (e.g., Rachlin, 1974). As noted earlier, immediate consequences are generally more powerful than delayed consequences, a fact that can readily lead to suboptimal choices. Take, for example, a student who can either go out for the evening and have a good time (which is a relatively immediate or "smaller sooner reward") or study in the hopes of achieving an excellent grade (which is a relatively delayed or "larger later reward"). In a straight choice between having a fun evening and an excellent grade, she would clearly choose the excellent grade. But the fun evening is immediately available and hence powerful, and she will be sorely tempted to indulge herself in an evening's entertainment. Similarly, a pigeon who must choose between pecking a green key that leads to an immediate 2 seconds of access to grain (a smaller sooner reward) or pecking a red key that leads to a 10-second delay followed by 6 seconds of access to grain (a larger later reward) will strongly prefer the small, immediate reward. Thus, *from a temporal*

And Furthermore

B. F. Skinner: The Master of Self-Control

It is ironic that B. F. Skinner, the staunch determinist, was in fact very much an expert in the art of self-control. Of course, from his perspective, he was merely exerting "countercontrol" over the environmental variables that determined his behavior. Although he maintained that the ultimate cause of our behavior lies in the environment, he admitted that "to a considerable extent an individual does appear to shape his own destiny" (Skinner, 1953, p. 228). As it turns out, Skinner proved to be his own best example in this regard.

In behavioral terms, Skinner engineered his environment to be as effective and reinforcing as possible, particularly with respect to his academic work. In Chapter 8, for example, we mentioned how he recommended creating an environment devoted specifically to writing, thereby establishing strong stimulus control over that activity. In addition to this, Skinner (1987) wrote so regularly, at the same time each day, that it seemed to generate a kind of circadian rhythm. Evidence of this occurred when, upon traveling to a different time zone, he would experience the urge to engage in "verbal behavior" at his regular writing time back home! Moreover, in true behaviorist fashion (what is good for the pigeon is good for the behaviorist), Skinner carefully monitored the amount of time he wrote each day and plotted it on a cumulative record. He recognized that the most important factor in being productive was consistency. As he put it:

> Suppose you are at your desk two hours a day and produce on average 50 words an hour. That is not much, but it is about 35,000 words a year, and a book every two or three years. I have found this to be reinforcing enough. (Skinner, 1987, p. 138; see also Boice, 1996)

Although many people equate self-control with living a rigid and disciplined lifestyle, it was quite the opposite in Skinner's case. After he had once overworked himself to the point where he began to experience symptoms of angina, he resolved to lead a more relaxed and stress-free existence. He restricted his writing activities to a few hours each morning and devoted the rest of the day to less taxing activities, including watching football on television, listening to music, and reading mystery novels (R. Epstein, 1997). For Skinner, relaxation was not only enjoyable but also a critical factor in being an effective academic. In a paper entitled, *How to Discover What You Have to Say: A Talk to Students,* he described it thus:

> Imagine that you are to play a piano tomorrow night with a symphony orchestra. What will you do between now and then? You will get to bed early for a good night's rest. Tomorrow morning you may practice a little but not too much. During the day, you will eat lightly, take a nap, and in other ways try to put yourself in the best possible condition for your performance in the evening. Thinking effectively about a complex set of circumstances is more demanding than playing a piano, yet how often do you prepare yourself to do so in a similar way? (Skinner 1987, p. 133)

In a sense, Skinner very much lived his behaviorism. Just as Freud spent a few minutes each day analyzing his dreams, Skinner spent a few minutes each day analyzing the variables that controlled his behavior (R. Epstein, 1997). To all appearances, it was a successful endeavor. As former student Robert Epstein put it, "Fred was the most creative, most productive, and happiest person I have ever known. I cannot prove that his exceptional self-management skills were the cause, but I have no doubt whatsoever that they were" (p. 564).

perspective, lack of self-control arises from the fact that our behavior is more heavily influenced by immediate consequences than by delayed consequences.

Self-control can also involve choice between a smaller sooner punisher and a larger later punisher—only in this instance it is selection of the smaller sooner alternative that is most beneficial. In deciding whether to go to the dentist, for example, we choose between enduring a small amount of discomfort in the near future (from minor dental treatment) and risking a large amount of discomfort in the distant future (from an infected tooth). Unfortunately, the prospect of experiencing discomfort in the near future (from a visit to the dentist) might exert such strong control over our behavior that we avoid going to the dentist, with the result that we suffer much greater discomfort later on. Likewise, a rat given a choice between accepting a small shock immediately or receiving a strong shock following a 10-second delay might choose the latter over the former, with the result that it experiences a considerably stronger shock than it had to.

Of course, in many self-control situations, the full set of controlling consequences is a bit more complicated than a simple choice between two rewards or two punishers. Choosing not to smoke, for example, leads to both a smaller sooner punisher in the form of withdrawal symptoms and a larger later reward in the form of improved health; whereas continuing to smoke leads to a smaller sooner reward in the form of a nicotine high and a larger later punisher in the form of deteriorating health. Note, too, that later consequences are usually less certain than sooner consequences. There is no guarantee that you will become sick and die an early death if you continue to smoke (though you would be foolish to chance it), nor is there any guarantee that you will become radiantly healthy if you quit smoking (you might, after all, catch some disease that is not related to smoking). You can, however, be pretty certain that your next cigarette will be enjoyable, and that if you quit smoking you will soon experience withdrawal symptoms. Thus, delayed consequences often suffer from a sort of double whammy: Their value is weakened because they are delayed and because they are less certain. Given this combination of factors, it is easy to understand how delayed consequences sometimes have such weak effects on behavior (see Table 10.2).

Self-control issues in the real world therefore often involve a rather complex set of contingencies (e.g., Brigham, 1978). To investigate this issue, however, researchers have typically focused on relatively simple choices, most commonly a choice between a smaller sooner reward and a larger

TABLE 10.2 Full set of immediate and delayed consequences for the alternatives of quitting smoking versus continuing to smoke.		
	IMMEDIATE CONSEQUENCE (CERTAIN)	**DELAYED CONSEQUENCE (UNCERTAIN)**
Quitting smoking	Withdrawal symptoms	Improvement in health
Continuing to smoke	Nicotine high	Deterioration in health

later reward. The task of choosing between such alternatives is known as a *delay of gratification* task because the person or animal must forgo the smaller sooner reward (i.e., the subject has to "delay gratification") to obtain the larger later reward. Thus, in such tasks, **self-control** consists of choosing a larger later reward over a smaller sooner reward; the opposite of self-control, known as **impulsiveness**, consists of choosing a smaller sooner reward over a larger later reward.

1. From a temporal perspective, self-control problems arise from the extent to which we are (more/less) _____ heavily influenced by delayed consequences.

2. Self-control is shown by choice of a (smaller sooner / larger later) _____ reward over a _____ reward. It can also be shown by choice of a (smaller sooner / larger later) _____ punisher over a _____ punisher.

3. With respect to choice between rewards, the opposite of self-control is called i_____, which is demonstrated by choice of a (smaller sooner / larger later) _____ reward over a _____ reward.

4. An additional problem in self-control situations is that the delayed consequences tend to be (more/less) _____ certain than the immediate consequences.

5. Outline the full set of consequences involved in choosing between studying and not studying:

	Immediate	*Delayed*
Studying		
Not studying		

Mischel's Delay of Gratification Paradigm

Some of the earliest systematic research using a delay-of-gratification procedure was carried out by the social learning theorist Walter Mischel (e.g., 1966, 1974). In a typical experiment, a child was led into a room that contained two items (such as pretzels and marshmallows), one of which was clearly preferred. The child was told that he or she could attain the preferred item by simply waiting for the experimenter to return. If the child wished, however, the experimenter could be summoned by sounding a signal, at which point the child received only the smaller, non-preferred item. The question of interest was to see what sorts of strategies some children used to wait out the delay period and obtain the larger reward.

Researchers who conducted such studies quickly noted that the extent to which children avoided attending to a reward had a significant effect on their resistance to temptation. For example, one strategy employed by many children was to simply avert their eyes from the promised rewards or cover their eyes with their hands. Many children also adopted Skinner's tactic of "doing something else," such as talking or singing to themselves or inventing games. Children were also better able to wait out the delay period when the rewards were not present as opposed to when they were present. Thus, resistance to temptation was greatly enhanced by not attending to the tempting reward.

Later research revealed that the manner in which children thought about the rewards also made a difference. Children who were instructed to focus on the abstract properties of the rewards, such as viewing pretzels as tiny logs or marshmallows as clouds, did better than children who focused on the rewards as concrete objects (i.e., seeing pretzels for what they are). Note that all of these strategies are quite different from what one might suppose should happen from a "positive thinking" perspective, which usually recommends keeping one's attention firmly fixed on the desired outcome. In these studies, children who focused on the desired outcome, and conceptualized it as a desired outcome, generally became impulsive and were unable to wait long enough to receive the larger later reward. (See Mischel, 1966, 1974, for comprehensive reviews of this research.)

An interesting aspect of this research is the follow-up evaluations conducted on children who participated in some of the earliest studies (Shoda, Mischel, & Peake, 1990). These children were, on average, 4 years old in the original studies and 17 years old at follow-up. The children who, in the original study, had devised tactics that enabled them to wait for the preferred reward were, many years later, more "cognitively and socially competent"— meaning that they could cope well with frustrations, were academically proficient, and got along well with their peers. This suggests that one's ability to devise appropriate tactics to delay gratification is a basic skill that can enhance many areas of one's life.

1. Children who are (most/least) _____ successful at a delay of gratification task generally keep their attention firmly fixed on the desired treat.

2. While waiting for dessert, Housam imagines that the Jell-O looks like wobbly chunks of glass. By contrast, Ruby views the Jell-O as, well, Jell-O. Between the two of them, _____ is less likely to get into trouble by eating the Jell-O before being told that it is okay to do so. This is because delay of gratification can be enhanced by thinking about the desired reward in ab_____ rather than c_____ terms.

QUICK QUIZ I

The Ainslie–Rachlin Model of Self-Control

While the Mischel studies focused on some of the processes involved in resisting an immediately available temptation, the Ainslie–Rachlin model of self-control focuses on the fact that preference between smaller sooner and larger later rewards can shift over time (Ainslie, 1975; Rachlin, 1974). For example, have you ever promised yourself in the morning that you would study all afternoon, only to find yourself spending the afternoon socializing with friends? In the morning, you clearly preferred studying over socializing that afternoon; but when the afternoon actually arrived, you preferred socializing over studying. In other words, you experienced a reversal of preference as time passed and the smaller sooner reward (socializing) became imminent. The Ainslie–Rachlin model provides an explanation for this reversal of preference and suggests ways to minimize its occurrence and facilitate attainment of the larger later reward.

The Ainslie–Rachlin model is based on the assumption that the value of a reward is a "hyperbolic" function of its delay. In simple terms, what this means is that the delay curve for a reward—which describes the relationship between reward value and time delay—is upwardly scalloped (similar to an FI scallop) with decreasing delays producing larger and larger increments in value. In other words, the value of a reward increases more and more sharply as delay decreases and attainment of the reward becomes imminent (see Figure 10.3).

For example, think about a young child who has been promised a birthday party. When the party is still 3 weeks away, it is likely to be worth very little to him. Three weeks is a long time for a young child, and if you ask him if he would rather have the birthday party in 3 weeks or a chocolate bar right now, he just might prefer the chocolate bar. In other words, a birthday party at 3 weeks' delay is worth less than one chocolate bar available immediately. A week later, with the birthday party still 2 weeks away, you might find that little has changed and that he would still be willing to trade the birthday party for the chocolate bar. The value of the birthday party at

FIGURE 10.3 Graph indicating relationship between reward value and delay. Moving from left to right along the horizontal axis represents passage of time, with reward delivery drawing ever nearer. As delay decreases (reward draws near), reward value increases slowly at first and then more and more sharply as the reward becomes imminent.

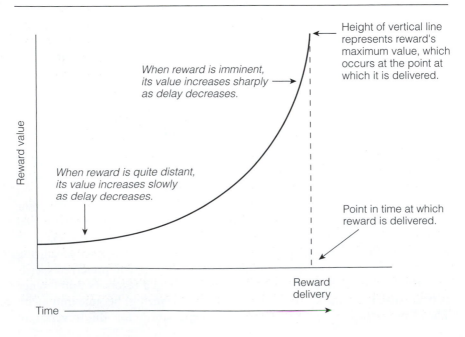

2 weeks' delay has increased very little, if at all, compared to its value the previous week. When the party is 1 week away, however, you might find that the value of the party has increased significantly and that you would now have to offer him two or three chocolate bars before he would agree to cancel the party. And by the time another week has passed and the day of the birthday party has arrived, he may be so excited that he would reject a year's worth of chocolate bars in order to have that party. The value of the party increased sharply as it became imminent.

Much of the experimental evidence for such upwardly scalloped delay functions is derived from research with rats and pigeons, for whom delays of even a few seconds have significant effects on preference. A hungry pigeon, for example, might show weak preference for a reinforcer that is delayed by 15 seconds, slightly stronger preference for one that is delayed by 10 seconds, moderately stronger preference for one that is delayed by 5 seconds, and very strong preference for one that is available immediately (0 second delay). The value of the reward increased only slightly between 15 and 10 seconds, moderately between 10 and 5 seconds, and greatly between 5 and 0 seconds. The delay curve for this pigeon would therefore be relatively flat between 15 and 10 seconds, moderately sloped between 10 and 5 seconds, and steeply sloped between 5 and 0 seconds, which is similar to the delay curve shown in Figure 10.3.

---

1. The Ainslie–Rachlin model is based on the finding that as a reward becomes imminent, its value increases more and more (slowly/sharply) _____, yielding a "delay curve" (or delay function) that is upwardly sc_____.

2. I offer to give people a thousand dollars. People are told that they will receive the thousand dollars in either 3 months, 2 months, 1 month, or immediately. Between which of the following conditions are we likely to find the largest difference in level of excitement about receiving the money: 3 months versus 2 months, 2 months versus 1 month, or 1 month versus immediately? _____. Between which conditions would we find the second largest difference in level of excitement? _____.

QUICK QUIZ J

The manner in which delay functions account for preference reversal is shown in Figure 10.4. At an early point in time, when both rewards are still distant, the larger later reward (LLR) is clearly preferred. As time passes, however, and the smaller sooner reward (SSR) becomes imminent, its value increases sharply and comes to outweigh the value of the LLR. Thus, the student who, when she wakes up in the morning, decides that she will definitely study that evening is at the far left end of the distribution, where the delay curve for the LLR (receiving a high mark) is still higher than that of the SSR (going out for an evening of socializing). As evening approaches, however, and the possibility of going out (the SSR) becomes imminent, the delay curve for the latter rises sharply, with the result that the student will be strongly tempted to socialize that evening. By doing so, however, she risks losing the LLR of an excellent grade.

FIGURE 10.4 Graph indicating relative values of a smaller sooner reward (SSR) and a larger later reward (LLR) as time passes. At an early point in time, before the SSR becomes imminent, its value is less than the value of the LLR. As time passes, however, and the SSR becomes imminent, its value increases sharply and comes to outweigh the value of the LLR.

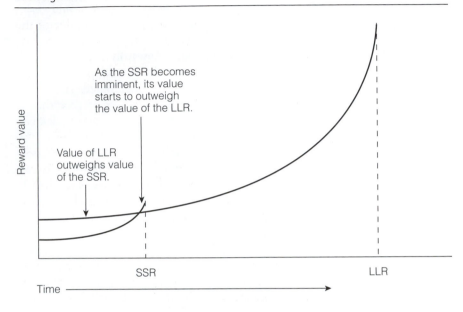

Such preference reversals have been demonstrated experimentally with pigeons. Green, Fisher, Perlow, and Sherman (1981) presented pigeons with a choice between two schedules of reinforcement. In one condition, a peck on the red key resulted in 2-sec access to grain following a 20-sec delay (the SSR), while a peck on the green key resulted in 6-sec access to grain following a 24-sec delay (the LLR). In this circumstance the pigeons strongly preferred the LLR; they selected it on more than 80% of the trials. In another condition, a peck on the red key resulted in 2-sec access to grain following a 2-sec delay, while a peck on the green key resulted in 6-sec access to grain following a 6-sec delay. This latter condition is equivalent to the first condition because the LLR still occurs 4 seconds later than the SSR; but it is different in that both alternatives are now much closer. Under this circumstance the pigeons strongly preferred the SSR, which was almost immediately available. Thus, just as the Ainslie–Rachlin model predicts, when the SSR reward was imminent, its value outweighed the value of the LLR. But when both the SSR and the LLR were further away, the pigeons strongly preferred the LLR. As the delay values changed, the pigeons displayed a reversal of preference between the two alternatives.

Human subjects making hypothetical choices have also demonstrated preference reversals. In one study by Ainslie and Haendel (1983), most participants said that they would prefer to receive a $100 certified check that can be cashed immediately to a $200 certified check that can be cashed in 2 years. However, when the delays for both alternatives were increased by 6 years—a $100 check that can be cashed in 6 years versus a $200 check that can be cashed in 8 years—subjects preferred the $200 alternative. Thus, with both alternatives quite distant, the LLR was preferred; with both alternatives closer, the SSR was preferred. (See Critchfield & Kollins, 2001, for a summary of research findings using this procedure.)

1. If confronted by a choice between one food pellet available in 10 seconds and two food pellets available in 15 seconds, a rat would likely choose the (former/latter) _____. But if 9 seconds are allowed to pass before the rat can make a choice, then it will likely choose the (former/latter) _____.

2. In the above example, as the (smaller sooner / larger later) _____ reward becomes imminent, its value comes to outweigh the value of the (smaller sooner / larger later) _____ reward.

QUICK QUIZ K

Given that this type of preference reversal occurs, the question arises as to whether anything can be done about it. Two alternatives suggest themselves: changing the shape of the delay function for the LLR and making a commitment response.

Changing the Shape of the Delay Function for the Larger Later Reward

The basic reason preference reversal occurs is because the LLR has low value at long delays; that is, its delay curve is deeply scalloped. If the delay curve were less deeply scalloped—meaning that the value of the LLR did not decline so drastically as a function of delay—then it would stand a better chance of outweighing any temptations that crop up along the way. This type of situation is illustrated in Figure 10.5.

Herrnstein (1981) suggested several variables that can affect the shape of a delay function. For example, *there appear to be innate differences in impulsivity between species.* Delays of only a few seconds can make a huge difference for rats and pigeons; such delays make little or no difference for humans, whose behavior is often directed toward consequences that will be delivered several hours, days, or even years in the future. (As noted earlier, humans' ability to use language to represent distant events may play a critical role in this behavior.) Thus, delay functions for humans are generally less deeply scalloped than they are for other animals.

There may also be differences between individuals, with some individuals more impulsive than others. People with antisocial personality disorder, which seems to have a strong genetic basis, are generally very impulsive (Kaplan, Sadock, & Grebb, 1994). Such individuals presumably have deeply scalloped

FIGURE 10.5 Graph indicating relative values of a smaller sooner reward (SSR) and a larger later reward (LLR) in which the delay function for the LLR is less deeply scalloped (somewhat flatter). Under such conditions, the value of the LLR will remain higher than the value of the SSR even as the SSR becomes imminent.

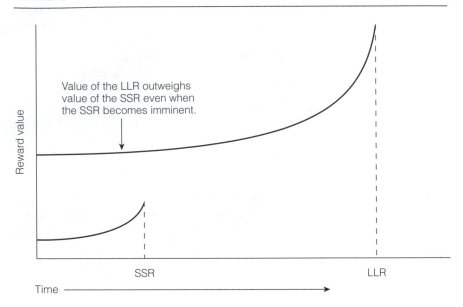

delay functions. Less extreme differences no doubt exist among normal individuals in the population. Some people may have an inborn temperament that predisposes them toward displaying the necessary patience to achieve long-term outcomes, whereas others have a temperament that predisposes them toward being rather impulsive.

Within individuals, age can make a difference. In general, *people become less impulsive as they grow older.* Although young children find it difficult to resist having a cookie before dinner, most adults are quite capable of doing so (well, at least more often than when they were kids). In fact, an increased ability to resist temptation and pursue long-term goals is considered a hallmark of maturity.

Related to age, another variable that affects impulsiveness is repeated experience with responding for delayed rewards. As children grow older, caretakers require them to display more and more patience—such as by forcing them to wait until after dinner to have a dessert—thereby gradually shaping their ability to delay gratification. Interestingly, in a scene from Skinner's (1948a) novel *Walden II,* which depicts a utopian community designed around behavioral principles, children are described as waiting in front of their meals for a short time before eating. With successive meals, the waiting period was gradually lengthened. Although such a procedure might sound frightfully authoritarian, it is probably not much different from what most parents carry out less formally as they expect their children to gradually display more and more patience as they grow older. Interestingly, the efficacy of Skinner's approach has been demonstrated experimentally. Research has shown that both pigeons (Mazur & Logue, 1978) and children (Newman & Kanfer, 1976) demonstrate an increased ability to resist the temptation of a smaller sooner reward after being exposed to large rewards that are systematically delayed for longer and longer periods of time.

The availability of other sources of reinforcement may be yet another factor that influences impulsiveness. Many people find that they are more impulsive during periods characterized by a lack of overall reinforcement. Thus, Kimberly experiences a strong urge to resume smoking after she loses her job, and Mike begins drinking heavily after his girlfriend leaves him. Under depressing or stressful circumstances, long-term goals seem to lose their relevance, and immediate temptations become quite powerful. This evidence suggests that, to maximize the possibility of resisting temptations, it helps if one's environment contains a plentiful supply of reinforcement. A student attempting to study for long periods of time in a dingy, cramped corner of the basement will likely find it extremely difficult to persist. Far better, as Skinner (1987) noted, is to arrange a study environment that is both pleasant and comfortable. Good lighting, a comfortable chair, and a well-organized desk (to eliminate the frustration of being unable to find things)—perhaps accompanied by some pleasant music in the background and a cup of coffee to sip on—will enable the act of studying to compete more effectively with such temptations as watching television or playing a computer game. Self-reinforcement procedures may also play a role here, in that they ensure that the person intermittently engages in some pleasant activities while attempting to complete a difficult task, for example by playing computer games for 15 minutes following every 2 hours of studying (the trick, of course, being to keep the game playing to only 15 minutes).

Finally, as noted in our discussion of behavior chains (Chapter 7), *we can more easily maintain responding for a distant goal by setting up an explicit series of subgoals.* The successful completion of each subgoal provides a salient form of secondary reinforcement that helps maintain progress toward a larger later reward. Additionally, because the secondary reinforcement from the completion of a subgoal is relatively immediate, it can compete more effectively with any temptations that crop up along the way. Note, however, that the subgoals should be relatively precise. Completing a vaguely worded goal such as "work on my term paper tonight" is likely to be considerably less reinforcing than completing the more explicit goal of "finish a comprehensive outline of my term paper tonight." The latter is a clearer indicator of progress and will therefore serve as a stronger reinforcer.

1. One strategy for increasing self-control is to make the delay function (or delay curve) for the larger later reward (more/less) _____ deeply scalloped.

2. The delay functions for a pigeon will likely be (more/less) _____ deeply scalloped than those for a human.

3. The delay functions for a 6-year-old child will likely be (more/less) _____ deeply scalloped than those for a 15-year-old.

4. Exposure to gradually increasing delays seems to make the delay function (more/less) _____ deeply scalloped.

5. A person is likely to be (more/less) _____ impulsive in a pleasant environment as opposed to an unpleasant environment.

6. From the perspective of the Ainslie–Rachlin model, the setting up and attainment of a subgoal related to a delayed reward serves to (raise/lower) _____ the delay function for that reward, making it (more/less) _____ deeply scalloped.

Making a Commitment Response Flattening out the delay gradient for the larger later reward (making it less deeply scalloped) is perhaps the ideal answer to problems of self-control. It seems unlikely, however, that this tactic will always be successful. For a person who smokes, the immediate reinforcement to be derived from having a cigarette (both positive reinforcement in the form of a nicotine high and negative reinforcement in the form of eliminating or avoiding withdrawal symptoms) is likely to be a powerful temptation. In such circumstances, the exercise of self-control might be facilitated through the use of a "commitment response" (Rachlin, 1974, 1991). A *commitment response* is an action carried out at an early point in time that serves either to eliminate or greatly reduce the value of an upcoming temptation.[2]

Early attempt to reduce a temptation

As an example of a commitment response, consider a student who, in the morning, decides that she definitely needs to study that evening. At this early point in time, the value of studying to ensure a good mark outweighs the value of alternate activities, such as going out with friends or watching television. Through experience, however, the student has learned that these early-morning preferences mean little when evening rolls around and more immediate reinforcement from other activities becomes available. To ensure that she studies tonight, she knows that she has to somehow eliminate ahead of time the various temptations that will arise. Thus, that morning, she gives her younger brother $20 and instructs him to keep it if she fails to study that evening. By making this monetary commitment, she has essentially locked herself into studying. As illustrated in Figure 10.6, the aversive consequence that would result from not studying (her obnoxious brother having a good time at her expense) has so reduced the value of any alternate activity that

---

[2]The commitment response is sometimes instead called a *precommitment response* (e.g., Logue, 1995).

FIGURE 10.6 Effect of a commitment strategy on preference between a smaller sooner reward (SSR) and a larger later reward (LLR). The commitment response needs to be made before the SSR becomes imminent. It will be effective to the extent that it reduces the value of the SSR, even when it is imminent, to below the value of the LLR.

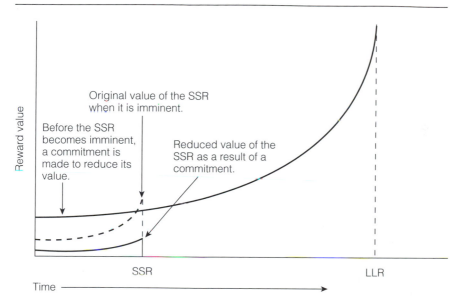

it no longer effectively competes with the value of studying and the larger later reward of obtaining a good mark.

Behavioral contracting, in which a person formally arranges to attain certain rewards for resisting temptation or receive certain punishers for yielding to temptation, essentially operates on this principle. The contract is negotiated with the therapist at an early point in time, before encountering the temptation. The contingencies outlined in the contract serve to reduce the attractiveness of the tempting alternative. Of course, in some circumstances, it might even be possible to completely eliminate the tempting alternative. A graduate student who is spending too much time watching television rather than working on his thesis—an unfortunately all too common difficulty— might solve the problem by giving his television to a friend for the rest of the semester.

Although the use of a commitment strategy might be seen as one that requires a certain amount of intelligence and foresight, experiments have shown that even pigeons can learn to make commitment responses. Rachlin and Green (1972) presented pigeons with a choice between a smaller sooner food reward and a larger later food reward. The pigeons invariably chose the SSR over the LLR. The pigeons were then given the option, several seconds before being presented with this choice, of pecking another key that would eliminate the SSR as one of the choices and leave the LLR as the only alternative. Many of the pigeons selected this option, thereby essentially removing the temptation ahead of time. The pigeons did the equivalent of giving away the television in the morning so that, when evening came around, they would be more likely to study.[3]

1. A _____ response is designed to either eliminate or reduce the value of an upcoming temptation.

2. Such a response is most likely to be carried out at an (early/later) _____ point in time when the temptation is quite (near/distant) _____ .

3. Gary would love to go running each evening but always feels so tired after work that he just plumps down in his favorite chair when he gets home and has a glass of wine. If Gary wishes to make a commitment to go running, such as arranging to go running with a neighbor, he is most likely to make this commitment (the day before / immediately before) _____ the run is supposed to take place.

The Small-But-Cumulative Effects Model

The basic delay of gratification paradigm, which both Mischel's early research and the original Ainslie–Rachlin model are built upon, involves a simple choice between a single SSR and a single LLR. This is, however, an extreme simplification of the full set of contingencies that we often face when trying to control our behavior. As mentioned earlier, many situations involve choosing between a combination of rewarding and punishing outcomes that vary not only in their value and delay but also in the certainty with which they are likely to occur. More importantly, in relation to the issue of certainty, many of the most difficult self-control issues cannot be resolved by a single choice; rather, they require an ongoing (often never-ending) series of choices, with any single choice having relatively little effect. Thus, according to this *small-but-cumulative effects model*, each individual choice on a self-control task has only a small but cumulative effect on our likelihood of obtaining the desired long-term outcome (e.g., Malott, 1989; see also Ainslie, 2001, and Rachlin, 2000).

Imagine, for example, that you have been following a program of healthy eating, but then find yourself choosing between a restaurant's world famous Greaze-Burger and their far healthier, but much less appetizing, Tofu Salad Supreme. In terms of achieving the larger later reward of good health, the choice might seem obvious. But is it obvious? That one

---

[3]Given the variety of items and services that can be purchased online these days, it should come as no surprise to learn that a behavior contracting service is also available online. Two economists, Dean Karlan and Ian Ayres, came up with the idea after successfully implementing a behavior contract with each other to lose weight. The story of their weight loss program—and how it cost one of them $15,000 when he once violated the contract!—can be found at the service's Web site: http://www.stickK.com.

Greaze-Burger, *by itself*, is very unlikely to make any significant difference in your quest to become healthy; in the same way, a single Tofu Salad Supreme will not, by itself, make you healthy. It is only by repeatedly selecting tofu salads over Greaze-Burgers that you will realize any significant, long-term effects on your health. So it is relatively easy, on any particular occasion, to talk yourself into making an exception to your healthy eating plan: "Hey, it's been a tough day, so why not indulge just this once?" The problem, of course, is that this same logic applies each time you encounter a tasty treat. Each single treat that you encounter will not, in and of itself, significantly affect your health. But to the extent that you are thereby seduced into frequently consuming those treats (and we very often are), you undermine the possibility of achieving good health.

This small-but-cumulative effects approach can be incorporated into the basic Ainslie–Rachlin model that we discussed earlier. The fact that each single choice of a smaller sooner reward has such little effect in the long run helps allow its value, when it becomes imminent, to rise above the value of the larger later reward. After all, would you really be tempted to eat a Greaze-Burger if you knew that one burger would, like a slow-acting poison, give you a heart attack in 20 or 30 years? Would you really smoke a cigarette if you knew that one cigarette would some day give you cancer? And would you really watch TV tonight rather than study if you knew that not studying tonight would result in obtaining a low grade in the course and completely ruin your chances of getting into law school? Not likely. It is only because that one burger, one cigarette, or one TV night is unlikely, by itself, to result in such punishing outcomes that its value can rise so sharply when it becomes imminent.

Each choice of an SSR versus LLR has only a small but cumulative effect, which helps explain why self-control is, for many of us, such a difficult task. Fortunately, the small-but-cumulative effects model also suggests ways to improve self-control. For example, it clarifies the importance of having a plan in place to handle occasional lapses (i.e., a relapse prevention plan), given that we will very likely be faced with an ongoing series of highly seductive temptations that we may not always be able to resist (e.g., Marlatt & Gordon, 1985; Watson & Tharp, 2002). This model also indicates the importance of establishing rules that clearly distinguish between acceptable and unacceptable behaviors, since the actual point when an impulsive behavior becomes harmful is often not clear. For some people or in some circumstances, the clearest rule might be total abstinence from a tempting event. For example, the Alcoholics Anonymous' rule of never, ever consuming alcohol seems to be an effective boundary for some recovered alcoholics. For other people or in other circumstances, it may be that total abstinence is too severe and they may do better to occasionally indulge themselves within clearly specified limits. For example, for many students, a flexible study plan that allows for some level of indulgence or interruptions may be more effective than a highly rigid plan that is difficult to maintain (see Ainslie, 2001).

We will return again to the issue of self-control, and especially the importance of establishing clear rules for our behavior, when we discuss rule-governed behavior in Chapter 12.

1. According to the _____ model, self-control is a difficult task because each temptation has only a _____ but _____ effect on our likelihood of obtaining the long-term goal.

2. This model highlights the potential usefulness of establishing clear r_____ for distinguishing between acceptable and unacceptable behaviors, since the point at which impulsive behavior becomes harmful (is / is not) _____ clear.

And Furthermore

Self-Control: How sweet it is! Or is it?

Although the emphasis in this chapter has been on behavioral approaches to self-control, which largely ignore internal constructs such as willpower, there are other approaches to self-control that do emphasize internal constructs. For example, according to the *strength model* of self-control (also referred to as the *limited resource* or *ego-depletion* model), self-regulatory behaviors are fueled by a type of limited internal resource (Baumeister, Bratslavsky, Muraven, & Tice, 1998). A key proposition of the model is that this internal resource—which is what most people would regard as "willpower"—is depleted by tasks that require mental or emotional effort, such as studying, solving puzzles, or resisting a temptation. This in turn results in a decrease in our ability to self-regulate, as indicated by a significant reduction in performance on subsequent tasks or by an increased likelihood of impulsive behavior. For example, in one study (Gailliot, Baumeister, DeWall, Maner, Plant, Tice, & Brewer, 2007), participants in the "ego-depletion" condition were asked to watch a short video with instructions to focus only on a woman's face and not look at the words appearing at the bottom of the screen (which many participants would find difficult to do). Participants in a control group were simply told to watch the video. Participants in both groups were subsequently given a Stroop test, which is a test of attentional ability. As predicted by the model, those who had been exposed to the ego-depletion task performed significantly worse on the Stroop test compared to those in the control group. Self-regulation, from this perspective, is therefore like a muscle which can become temporarily fatigued through intense use (but which can also be strengthened through repeated efforts).

   Interestingly, Baumeister and his colleagues have also identified glucose ("blood sugar") as the internal resource that underlies these effects (Gailliot et al., 2007). They reported that ego-depleting tasks had a significant impact on blood glucose levels, and that the usual decrement in performance following such tasks could be reversed by giving subjects a sugar solution to drink. These results suggest that glucose is therefore the underlying factor that fuels a person's willpower and self-control.

The strength model of self-regulation has proven to be very popular. Perhaps this is because it resonates so well with cherished notions of willpower and self-determination. Recently, though, evolutionary psychologist, Robert Kurzban (2010a, 2010b), has challenged the model, and especially the glucose hypothesis, arguing that it is based on outdated and simplistic notions about how the brain operates. For example, the idea that the brain burns up large amounts of glucose when engaged in cognitively effortful activity has been shown to be false; in reality, such activities require miniscule amounts of energy, making it extremely unlikely that cognitive processing would be significantly affected by the kinds of brief "ego-depletion" tasks often used. Kurzban also reanalyzed the original data from the Gailliot et al. (2007) study and found little evidence of an actual decrease in glucose levels following the effortful task, which is a logical requirement for the glucose model to be correct. Finally, Kurzban points out that the strength model in general has difficulty handling certain anomalous findings, such as when the receipt of a gift following an ego-depleting task somehow restores a participant's ability to perform well on a subsequent task (Tice, Baumeister, Shmueli, & Muraven, 2007). In such cases, it is insufficient to argue that the gift somehow releases internal reserves of energy, since such an argument could be made for almost any anomalous finding. It therefore remains to be seen how well the strength model can meet these challenges.

Whatever the long-term viability of the strength model of self-regulation, it does draw attention to some important phenomena. As noted earlier, Skinner carefully restricted the amount of writing he did on any particular day so as to ensure that he was well rested for his next writing session (R. Epstein, 1997). He fully recognized that there are limitations to the amount of effortful behavior that one can engage in, whether that behavior is overt or covert, but did not feel the need to speculate about the existence of a special internal resource that accounted for this limitation. He would have assumed instead that it involved a complex combination of internal biological processes that physiologists and neuroscientists have yet to fully elucidate. He was quite content to stick to what he could observe, both internally and externally, and what he could manipulate, such as the chair he sat on (ensuring that it was comfortable), the room he wrote in (ensuring that it was efficiently laid out), and the amount of sleep he got (by placing a "sleeping cubicle" nearby). Skinner appears to have lived a highly productive and satisfying life, and anyone wishing to do likewise would do well to pay serious attention to his emphasis on behavior and environment. But this doesn't mean that nonbehavioral models of self-control, such as the Baumeister's strength model or Kurzban's (2010b) evolutionary information-processing approach, might not also offer some unique insights. (We will revisit the issue of willpower, and how it might be accounted for from a more behavioral perspective, toward the end of Chapter 11.)

SUMMARY

On a concurrent schedule of reinforcement, the subject responds on two or more independent schedules of reinforcement that are simultaneously available. Choice behavior in such situations often obeys the matching law, which predicts that the proportion of responses emitted on an alternative will match the proportion of reinforcers received on that alternative. The matching law has been shown to have real-world applicability, ranging from predicting communication patterns in humans to foraging behavior in animals.

Researchers have also discovered certain deviations from matching. In undermatching, the difference in proportion of responses on the richer versus poorer schedules is less than that predicted by matching. In overmatching, the difference in proportion of responses on the richer versus poorer schedules is greater than that predicted by matching. Bias from matching occurs when one alternative receives more responses than would be predicted by matching, both when it contains the poorer schedule and when it contains the richer schedule.

According to melioration theory, matching results from the subject's tendency to shift behavior toward a better-paying alternative. This tendency can sometimes reduce the overall amount of reinforcement. For example, more behavior may be directed to a better-paying alternative than is needed to obtain the available reinforcers. Furthermore, overindulgence in a highly reinforcing alternative can result in long-term habituation to that alternative, so that it is no longer as enjoyable as it once was. Melioration also results in a tendency to be overly attracted to immediate reinforcers as opposed to delayed reinforcers.

Skinner viewed self-control as involving a choice between conflicting outcomes. He believed that self-control is facilitated by emitting a controlling response that then alters the probability of a controlled response. Specific techniques of self-control include physical self-restraint, self-deprivation, or self-satiation, and self-reinforcement and self-punishment. A major problem with the latter is that one can easily short-circuit such self-directed consequences.

Others have noted that self-control involves a choice between immediate outcomes, which are relatively powerful, and delayed outcomes, which are relatively weak. From this delay-of-gratification perspective, self-control can be defined as choosing a larger later reward (LLR) over a smaller sooner reward (SSR), while impulsiveness can be defined as choosing an SSR over an LLR.

Research has shown that children who are good at resisting temptation in a delay of gratification task try to distract themselves from the tempting reward. As well, children are better able to resist temptation when they think of the reward in terms of its abstract rather than concrete properties. Follow-up research has revealed that children who are successful in such delay of gratification tasks are, in later years, more academically and socially competent.

The Ainslie–Rachlin model of self-control is based on the assumption that the delay function for a reward is often deeply scalloped, so that its value increases sharply as it becomes imminent. This explains why preferences for LLRs and SSRs tend to shift over time. When both rewards are far away, the value of the LLR outweighs the value of the SSR. As the SSR becomes imminent, however, its value rises sharply, possibly exceeding the value of the LLR at that time.

Thus, one means for facilitating self-control is flattening the delay function for the LLR so that its value remains fairly high even at long delays. Factors that may affect the shape of a delay function include biological variables (including differences between species and between individuals within a species), age, experience with responding for delayed rewards, the presence of other sources of reinforcement, and the attainment of subgoals relating to the LLR. Another means for facilitating self-control is by making a commitment to the LLR at an early point in time, before the SSR becomes imminent. A commitment response is a response that serves to reduce the value of the SSR so that its value remains below the value of the LLR.

According to the small-but-cumulative effects model, each individual choice on a self-control task has only a small but cumulative effect on our likelihood of obtaining the desired long-term outcome. It is largely because of this factor that we are frequently tempted to make an exception to a self-control program insofar as each individual temptation has only an insignificant effect on our long-term goal. However, repeated violations of our program can eventually result in the collapse of the program. It is for this reason that relapse prevention programs, in which we create a plan for coping with the possibility of occasional lapses, are so important.

SUGGESTED READINGS

Epstein, R. (1997). *Skinner as self-manager. Journal of Applied Behavior Analysis, 30,* 545–568. An interesting discussion of Skinner's use of behavioral techniques to manage his own behavior.

Herrnstein, R. J. (1997). *The matching law: Papers in psychology and economics.* Cambridge, MA: Harvard University Press. For the serious student who wishes to acquire a more in-depth understanding of matching, melioration, and the behavioral approach to economics.

Watson, D. L., & Tharp, R. G. (2002). *Self-directed behavior: Self-modification for personal adjustment* (8th ed.). Pacific Grove, CA: Brooks/Cole. A good source book on various tactics of self-control for a wide range of everyday behavior problems.

STUDY QUESTIONS

1. What is a concurrent schedule? Diagram an example of a concurrent schedule that might be used in an operant conditioning experiment with pigeons.

2. Define the matching law. State the matching law as an equation, and define each of its terms.

3. Using the matching equation, show what the matching law predicts concerning the distribution of behavior displayed on a concurrent VI 10-sec VI 30-sec schedule of reinforcement. (Hint: What is the expected distribution of reinforcers on this schedule?)

4. What is a changeover delay (COD)? In what sense is a COD similar to a foraging situation with animals?

5. What is overmatching? Give an example of overmatching (with hypothetical proportions) that might occur on a concurrent VI 20-sec VI 30-sec schedule.

6. What is undermatching? Give an example of undermatching (with hypothetical proportions) that might occur on a concurrent VI 20-sec VI 30-sec schedule.

7. What is bias from matching? Give an example of bias (with hypothetical proportions) that might occur on a concurrent VI 20-sec VI 30-sec schedule, and response alternatives consisting of a green key and a blue key.

8. Describe melioration theory. Briefly describe three ways in which the tendency to meliorate can reduce the overall level of reinforcement.

9. Describe the major difficulty with the use of self-reinforcement and self-punishment.

10. What are the definitions of self-control and impulsiveness within the context of a delay-of-gratification task? Describe some of the strategies children use to facilitate success in a delay-of-gratification task.

11. With the help of a graph, describe the general effect of delay on reward value.

12. With the help of a graph, describe how the Ainslie–Rachlin model accounts for preference reversal between a smaller sooner reward and a larger later reward.

13. List four of the variables that can affect the shape of the delay function and hence the extent to which a person or animal is likely to display self-control.

14. With the help of a graph, describe how a commitment response serves to facilitate self-control.

15. Describe the small-but-cumulative effects model of self-control and impulsiveness. Explain how this accounts for the difficulty people often have in following an exercise program.

CONCEPT REVIEW

bias from matching. A deviation from matching in which one response alternative attracts a higher proportion of responses than would be predicted by matching, regardless of whether that alternative contains the richer versus poorer schedule.

commitment response. An action carried out at an early point in time that serves to either eliminate or reduce the value of an upcoming temptation.

concurrent schedule of reinforcement. A complex schedule consisting of the simultaneous presentation of two or more independent schedules, each leading to a reinforcer.

impulsiveness. With respect to choice between two rewards, selecting a smaller sooner reward over a larger later reward.

matching law. The principle that the *proportion* of responses emitted on a particular schedule matches the *proportion* of reinforcers obtained on that schedule.

melioration theory. A theory of matching that holds that the distribution of behavior in a choice situation shifts toward those alternatives that have higher value regardless of the long-term effect on overall amount of reinforcement.

overmatching. A deviation from matching in which the proportion of responses on the richer schedule versus poorer schedule is more different than would be predicted by matching.

self-control. With respect to choice between two rewards, selecting a larger later reward over a smaller sooner reward.

small-but-cumulative effects model. Each individual choice on a self-control task has only a small but cumulative effect on our likelihood of obtaining the desired long-term outcome.

undermatching. A deviation from matching in which the proportion of responses on the richer schedule versus poorer schedule is less different than would be predicted by matching.

CHAPTER TEST

12. According to the _____ law, if 25% of reinforcers are obtained on one of two simultaneously available schedules, then _____ of responses are likely to be emitted on that schedule.

6. The Ainslie–Rachlin model is based on the assumption that the value of a reward increases more and more sharply as delay _____ and attainment of the reward becomes _____.

17. The matching law predicts that on a concurrent VI 15-sec VI 60-sec schedule, _____% of responses should be emitted on the VI 15-sec schedule and _____% on the VI 60-sec schedule. In reality, you obtain 65% on the VI 15-sec schedule and 35% on the VI 60-sec schedule. This is an example of _____ matching.

9. A _____ schedule of reinforcement consists of the simultaneous presentation of two or more independent schedules, each of which leads to a _____.

13. The _____ law holds that the _____ of responses emitted on a particular schedule will match the _____ of reinforcers obtained on that schedule.

31. Hoa sometimes feels well and sometimes feels sick. If feeling healthy is a form of reinforcement, we would expect Hoa to be most impulsive when she is feeling (healthy/sick) _____.

20. The matching law predicts that on a concurrent VI 10-sec VI 30-sec schedule, _____% of responses should be emitted on the VI 30-sec schedule and _____% on the VI 10-sec schedule. In reality, you obtain 15% on the VI 30-sec schedule and 85% on the VI 10-sec schedule. This is an example of _____ matching.

3. From a temporal perspective, lack of self-control arises from the fact that our behavior is more heavily influenced by _____ consequences as opposed to _____ consequences.

18. When the cost of switching between schedules is quite high, then _____ matching is likely to occur. When the cost of switching is extremely low, then _____ matching is likely to occur.

30. Exposure to rewards that are presented at gradually increasing delays is likely to result in a(n) (increase/decrease) _____ in impulsiveness, which also means that the reward delay curve for these individuals has become (more/less) _____ deeply scalloped.

1. You always eat a full meal before going shopping, so that you will not be tempted (through hunger) to buy those chocolate cookies you are addicted to. From the perspective of self-control, Skinner would refer to the act of eating the meal as the _____ response and the subsequent decreased tendency to buy cookies as the _____ response.

27. In general, melioration is often the result of behavior being too strongly governed by _____ consequences as opposed to _____ consequences.

10. Given a choice between a VR 140 schedule and a VR 40 schedule of reinforcement, a rat is likely to show (exclusive/partial) _____ preference for the _____ schedule.

35. Given a choice between a VI 60-sec schedule and a VI 20-sec schedule, a pigeon is likely to emit _____% of its responses to the VI 20-sec alternative.

23. According to _____ theory, the distribution of behavior in a choice situation shifts toward those alternatives that have _____ value regardless of the effect on the overall amount of reinforcement.

14. Given a choice between a VI 40-sec schedule and a VI 20-sec schedule, a rat is likely to emit _____% of its responses to the VI 40-sec alternative.

5. From a behavioral perspective, self-control consists of preference for a _____ reward over a _____ reward, while the opposite of self-control, known as _____, consists of preference for a _____ reward over a _____ reward.

26. As soon as Mario retired, he moved to Florida and went for walks on the beach every day. Unfortunately, although going for walks continued

to be his most enjoyable activity, it soon became less enjoyable than it used to be. This appears to be an example of how the tendency to _____ can result in long-term _____.

33. A commitment response is most likely to be made at a(n) (early/later) _____ point in time before the (smaller sooner / larger later) _____ reward becomes imminent.

16. As Sal and his wife converse with the neighbor one evening, Sal is three times more responsive to the neighbor's comments than his wife is. Research evidence suggests that the neighbor will direct his conversation toward Sal, as opposed to his wife, (three times as often / exclusively) _____.

28. In general, humans have a (more/less) _____ deeply scalloped delay function than chickens. As well, a person who is very impulsive is likely to have a (more/less) _____ deeply scalloped delay function than a person who is very patient.

7. In keeping with the Ainslie–Rachlin model of self-control, I am most likely to choose $50 over $100 when the choice is between: (A) $50 now versus $100 a year from now, or (B) $50 a year from now versus $100 two years from now. The answer is alternative _____, which means that I tend to become impulsive when the smaller sooner reward is (imminent/delayed) _____.

11. According to the matching law, the proportion of _____ emitted on a certain schedule will roughly equal the proportion of _____ obtained on that schedule.

4. To the extent that Romano gets up early to study for his math test next week, as opposed to lying in bed an extra hour, he is displaying self-_____. To the extent that he chooses to lie in bed, he is displaying _____.

19. As Sal and his wife converse with the neighbor one day, Sal is three times more responsive to the neighbor's comments than his wife is. The neighbor, however, looks at Sal's wife about as often as he looks at Sal. During the next day's conversation, Sal's wife is three times more responsive to the neighbor's comments than Sal is. This time the neighbor looks at Sal's wife five times as often as he looks at Sal. This appears to be an example of the deviation from matching known as _____, which also suggests that the neighbor finds Sal's wife _____.

32. Maria announces to her parents that she is going to study all weekend, knowing that they will severely chastise her if she does not live up to her promise. Given that Maria hates being chastised by her parents, her announcement can be seen as a _____ response that will lower the value of any alternate activity that might interfere with studying during the weekend.

21. You tend to shop at two favorite clothing stores, Madison's Fine Fashions and Mike's Grubbies. Over time, you have learned that Mike's is twice as likely to have something in stock that you wish to buy. If the two stores are side by side, then you are likely to visit Mike's (twice/ equally) _____ as often as Madison's. This is an example of _____ matching.

8. According to the Ainslie–Rachlin model, one way to enhance self-control would be to raise the delay curve for the (smaller sooner / larger later) _____ reward.

24. On a concurrent VR 50 VI 10-sec schedule, a pigeon is likely to _____ the number of responses emitted on each schedule to the number of reinforcers obtained. By doing so, it (will / will not) _____ maximize the amount of reinforcement it obtains during the session. Such results support the _____ theory of matching.

25. Professor Huynh spends a lot of time reading articles, which she enjoys, but little time in the lab doing research, which she does not enjoy. Insofar as she needs to do research to maintain her position at the university, this appears to be an example of how _____ can lead to suboptimal patterns of behavior.

2. You decide to do your housework each evening at 7:00 p.m., and then reward yourself with 1 hour of playing your favorite computer game. A major problem with this kind of self-reinforcement procedure is that you might _____.
This problem is known as _____.

34. The _____ effects model of self-control helps emphasize the importance of establishing rules that clearly distinguish between acceptable and unacceptable behavior. It also makes clear the importance of having a _____ prevention plan to cope with situations in which we might violate our self-control program.

22. You tend to shop at two favorite clothing stores, Madison's Fine Fashions and Mike's Grubbies. Over time, you have learned that Mike's is twice as likely to have something in stock that you wish to buy. If the two stores are separated by a long and difficult drive, then you are likely to demonstrate _____ matching in your visits to Mike's versus Madison's, which means that you are (twice / more than twice) _____ as likely to visit Mike's than Madison's.

15. According to the _____ effects model, a student will often have difficulty studying on a particular night because the consequences for not studying that one night are (aversively significant / largely insignificant) _____.

29. In general, as people grow from childhood into adulthood, their delay curves will likely become (more/less) _____ deeply scalloped.

Visit the book companion Web site at http://www.academic.cengage.com/ psychology/powell for additional practice questions, answers to the Quick Quizzes, practice review exams, and additional exercises and information.

ANSWERS TO CHAPTER TEST

1. controlling; controlled
2. play the game and not do the housework; short-circuiting
3. immediate; delayed
4. control; impulsiveness
5. larger later; smaller sooner; impulsiveness; smaller sooner; larger later
6. decreases; imminent
7. A; imminent
8. larger later
9. concurrent; reinforcer
10. exclusive; VR 40
11. responses; reinforcers
12. matching; 25%
13. matching; proportion; proportion
14. 33%
15. small-but-cumulative; largely insignificant
16. three times as often
17. 80%; 20%; under
18. over; under
19. bias; attractive
20. 75%; 25%; over
21. equally; under
22. over; more than twice
23. melioration; higher
24. match; will not; melioration
25. melioration
26. meliorate; habituation
27. immediate; delayed
28. less; more
29. less
30. decrease; less
31. sick
32. commitment ("controlling" would also be correct)
33. early; smaller sooner
34. small-but-cumulative; relapse
35. 75%

Observational Learning and Rule-Governed Behavior

CHAPTER OUTLINE

"I don't care what Dr. Dee says!" Gina shouted in exasperation when Steve again pronounced judgment on some aspect of their relationship. "I am starting to wish you had never enrolled in that stupid course. Why don't you just listen to what I'm saying rather than acting like 'Mr. Behaviorist' all the time?"

Much of this text has been concerned with basic processes of conditioning in which new patterns of behavior are acquired through direct exposure to the relevant events. Ming fears dogs because she was once bitten by a dog, and Kyle goes to a particular restaurant because in the past he received good food there. However, not all behavior patterns are acquired this directly. Some people acquire a fear of dogs without ever being attacked by a dog, or they eagerly head off to a restaurant despite never having been there before. Such behaviors have somehow been acquired in the absence of any direct exposure to the relevant events.

In this chapter, we focus on two processes that allow us to alter behavior patterns through indirect means. We begin with observational learning (a process that was touched on in previous chapters), which plays a strong role in human learning but is also found in animals. We follow that with a discussion of how we use language to generate rules (or instructions) to control behavior, including the implications of "rule-governed behavior" for understanding and enhancing self-control.

Observational or Social Learning

Do you remember your first day of school? If so, you probably remember being a little afraid and unsure about what to do when you first arrived—where to stand, who to talk to, even where to go to the bathroom. After a while, though, it all became much clearer because you could watch what other people did and follow them. This type of learning is called *observational learning*.

In ***observational learning***, the behavior of a *model* is witnessed by an *observer*, and the observer's behavior is subsequently changed. Because observational learning is essentially a social process, and humans are social beings, we can quickly acquire new behavior patterns in this way (Bandura, 1986). In fact, observational learning is *often* referred to as *social learning* and, as discussed in Chapter 1, constitutes a significant aspect of Bandura's social learning theory. There is considerable evidence that people can improve their performance on many tasks, including sports, simply by *watching* others perform (e.g., Blandin, Lhuisset, & Proteau, 1999; Shea, Wright, Wulf, & Whitacre, 2000). In fact, this type of learning can occur without our even being aware that our behavior has been influenced in this way. For example, we may see television commercials showing attractive people modeling new, even undesirable, behaviors such as driving too fast in a new car. This subtle form of modeling might then affect our behavior when we find ourselves in a similar situation. Conversely, models need not be aware that their behavior is being observed, which means that we do not have to "teach'" someone for them to learn from us. This is another reason the term *social learning* is often used. Being in a social situation can change behavior, even if no one in the group realizes it.

Observational learning can be involved in both classical and operant conditioning. We begin, however, with two rudimentary forms of social influence, known as *contagious behavior and stimulus enhancement,* that are often confused with more sophisticated forms of observational learning.

Contagious Behavior and Stimulus Enhancement

Contagious behavior is a more-or-less instinctive or reflexive behavior triggered by the occurrence of the same behavior in another individual. For example, suppose you and your friends are sitting around a table in the library, studying for a quiz. You start to yawn. One by one, each of your classmates also yawns. Not a good sign for how your study session will progress, but it is an excellent example of contagious behavior.

Although yawning is one of the best-documented examples of contagious behavior in humans (see Provine, 1996, for a review), other behaviors in both humans and other animals are potentially contagious. All it takes to get a flock of ducks off and flying is one startled duck. The rest flee even if they do not detect any real threat. Fear responses of all kinds are quite contagious, which makes good adaptive sense. In a dangerous environment, you are more likely to survive and reproduce if you flee when you notice that someone else is fleeing, as opposed to taking the time to look around and ask a lot of questions such as "Hey Burt, why are you running from that bear?"

Behaviors that are important for social interaction and bonding are also often contagious. Have you ever noticed that you rarely laugh when you are alone? Even when watching a funny movie or reading a humorous novel (which, as media, could be considered quasi-social events), we laugh more in the presence of others than when we are by ourselves (Provine, 1996). Television producers know this, so they include laugh tracks or live (laughing) audiences in most comedy programs. Most of us have had the experience of starting to laugh with a friend and being unable to stop. Even when the laughing dies down, and even if you don't remember why you started in the first place, if the other person chuckles just a bit it will set you off for another bout of side-splitting laughter. A particularly powerful example of this type of emotional contagion can be seen in a case documented in Tanganyika, from a boarding school for 12- to 18-year-old girls (Rankin & Philip, 1963). The girls one day began to laugh uncontrollably, which subsequently spread through the entire district. Officials even had to temporarily close the school in order to contain the "epidemic"!

Orienting responses can also be contagious. Not only do we orient our-selves toward stimuli we have just sensed (like a sudden noise or movement in our peripheral visual field), but we also orient ourselves in the direction that *others* have oriented. For example, infants as young as 4 months of age will follow the gaze of others (Farroni, Johnson, Brockbank, & Simion, 2000), and adults will do likewise. To test this response, simply have a con-versation with someone, and then shift your gaze over his or her shoulder and widen your eyes a bit. See how quickly the other person turns to look. Interestingly, this effect also occurs across species. If you have a pet, you may have found yourself orienting in the direction of your pet's gaze, and becom-ing frustrated when you did not see anything! Because dogs and cats have somewhat different perceptual systems than humans, they can often hear, see, or smell things that we cannot detect. (*Question: Can you think of an evolutionary explanation for why orienting should be contagious, even across species?*)

Another rudimentary form of social influence, which is related to conta-gious orienting, is **stimulus enhancement**, in which the probability of a behavior is changed because an individual's attention is drawn to a particular item or location by the behavior of another individual. For example, imagine that you are sitting in a waiting room, reading a very old magazine, when a father and his daughter walk in. The girl emits a giggle of delight, so you look up and see that she is running toward a large bowl of candy in the corner that you had not previously noticed. Five minutes later, you help yourself to some candy. You do so, however, not because she took some candy (which as you will see would be an example of observational learning of an operant response), but simply because her behavior made you aware of the candy.

Stimulus enhancement is particularly effective for increasing the probabil-ity of a behavior associated with eating, drinking, or mating (although it can also be effective for other behaviors). These behaviors often have strong instinctive components; and in the presence of the appropriate triggers, the behaviors are highly likely to occur. Stimulus enhancement simply allows the triggers to be noticed. In the example of the candy, once your attention is directed toward the candy, the incentive value of the candy is sufficient to lead to its consumption whether or not the little girl actually took some candy (e.g., her father might have actually stopped her from having candy, but you would have taken some of it anyway).

A wide variety of cues can lead to stimulus enhancement. Animals will often use scent marking at food sites. When a conspecific (another animal of the same species) comes across the scent mark, that scent is sufficient to cause the animal to pay close attention to the location and find the food. The behavior of the model could happen hours or even days before the observer arrived, but the resulting stimulus enhancement of the location of food was a result of an observer utilizing a social cue to direct its behavior. Stimulus enhancement effects can also be generated by using learned symbols. One of the authors recalls an incident from her undergraduate days, when a

FIGURE 11.1 Young children learn many behaviors through observation. (Unfortunately for parents, this particular behavior pattern occurs much less readily when children reach their teens.)

Steve Mason/Getty Images

classmate put up large orange arrow signs in the hallway pointing toward an empty classroom where he waited. Within an hour, more than a dozen students and two professors wandered into the empty classroom to ask what was happening there. (It would likely be no surprise to you that the classmate was also a psychology major.)

Behavioral contagion and stimulus enhancement are clearly examples of social influence. But it can be argued that they are at best rudimentary forms of social influence in that they may result in only a momentary change in behavior (though subsequent processes, like being rewarded by candy for going to the candy bowl, could result in a more lasting change). More substantial forms of learning occur when observation of a model is involved in classical and operant conditioning (see Figure 11.1).

Observational Learning in Classical Conditioning

As mentioned earlier, observational learning is often involved in the development of classically conditioned responses. In such cases, the stimuli involved are usually *emotional* in nature. For example, imagine a young child walking into a daycare center. She sees other children laughing and smiling while playing with a new toy. The smiles and laughter of the other children can act as stimuli that elicit similar emotional responses in the observer. Such emotions, called **vicarious emotional responses**, are classically conditioned emotional responses that result from seeing those emotional responses exhibited by others. This type of conditioning is therefore called *vicarious emotional conditioning*.

Vicarious emotional conditioning can take place in two ways. First, as noted in Chapter 5, expressions of fear in others may act as unconditioned stimuli (USs) that elicit the emotion of fear in ourselves (Mineka, 1987). In other words, because we quickly need to learn which events are dangerous, we may have an inherited tendency to react fearfully whenever we see someone else looking fearful. For example, a young child could learn to fear jellyfish in the following way:

Jellyfish: Look of fear in others → *Fear in oneself*
    NS   US   UR

Jellyfish → *Fear in oneself*
    CS   CR

The more traditional way of viewing the process of vicarious emotional conditioning, however, is to construe it as a form of higher-order conditioning. In this case, the emotional reactions of others serve as conditioned stimuli (CSs) rather than USs. For example, because fearful looks in others are often associated with frightening events, they come to serve as CSs for the emotion of fear in ourselves:

Look of fear in others: Frightening events → *Fear in oneself*
    NS_1 US   UR

Look of fear in others → *Fear in oneself*
    CS_1 CR

This look of fear in others can now function as a CS in the higher-order conditioning of a fear response to a previously neutral stimulus (NS), such as a jellyfish:

Jellyfish: Look of fear in others → *Fear in oneself*
    NS_2 CS_1 CR

Jellyfish → *Fear in oneself*
    CS_2 CR

Thus, with respect to fear conditioning, the look of fear in others may function as either a US or a CS. Of course, it is also possible that both processes are involved, and they may even combine to produce a stronger fear reaction.

Higher-order conditioning no doubt plays a major role in the conditioning of other, subtler emotions. For example, because smiles are usually associated with pleasurable events—such as when a smiling mother feeds a baby—they quickly become conditioned to elicit pleasurable emotions. In diagram form:

Smiles in others: Pleasurable events → *Pleasant emotions in oneself*
    NS_1 US   UR

Smiles in others → *Pleasant emotions in oneself*
    CS_1 CR

As a result, through observing others' reactions to a novel event, we may now acquire the same type of emotional response through a process of higher-order conditioning:

Raw oysters: Smiles in others → *Pleasant emotions in oneself*
    NS_2 CS_1 CR

Raw oysters → *Pleasant emotions in oneself*
    CS_2 CR

Needless to say, vicarious emotional responses, once acquired, can motivate other types of new behavior patterns (e.g., Eisenberg, McCreath, & Ahn, 1988; Gold, Fultz, Burke, & Prisco, 1992). After watching happy children playing with a toy, the observing child may be eager to play with the toy herself. And once we have seen someone else react fearfully to a particular type of spider, we may go out of our way to avoid any encounter with that type of spider (Mineka & Cook, 1993). Also, as noted in Chapter 4, many advertisers use emotional conditioning to influence our view of their products. When we see a television family reunited by a long-distance phone call, with tears of joy flowing freely, the vicarious emotions elicited by the joy of the models can cause us to associate the phone company with that emotion. Thus, the phone company becomes a positive CS, and the likelihood of our subscribing to its service increases. (See "It's an Acquired Taste ..." in the And Furthermore box.)

QUICK QUIZ A

1. In observational learning, the person performing a behavior is the m_____; the person watching the behavior is the o_____.

2. From a classical conditioning perspective, smiles, giggles, and laughs are _____ that can elicit v_____ e_____ r_____ in observers.

3. In fear conditioning, the expressions of fear in other people may function as (CSs/ USs / both CSs and USs) _____ that elicit the same emotional response in ourselves.

4. David watches a television infomercial about a new product guaranteed to promote weight loss. The audience members are smiling, laughing, and enthusiastic in their praise for the product. Later, David decides that he will buy the product, even though he initially viewed it with skepticism. David's buying decision is probably motivated by v_____ e_____ conditioning that occurred during exposure to the infomercial.

Observational Learning in Operant Conditioning

Just as the observation of a model can influence the development of classically conditioned responses, it can also influence the development of operant responses. Descriptions of this process traditionally emphasize the distinction between *acquisition* and *performance* of a behavior. For example, you may have

And Furthermore

It's An Acquired Taste ...

In this chapter, we describe some of the ways we learn from those around us. One area of social learning that has been studied extensively is how we learn to eat and drink. Of course, eating and drinking are behaviors that occur very naturally, so we do not have to learn *to* eat and drink, but we do seem to learn *what* to eat and drink. Across the world, there are dramatic differences in flavor preferences, foods that are considered edible, and various practices associated with preparing and consuming food. Many North Americans, for example, have a hard time imagining how someone would enjoy the flavor and texture of various bugs, how it would feel to sit down to a dinner of dog or horse, or why anyone would eat something like haggis.

Much social learning about food and flavor preference is related to stimulus enhancement and social referencing, through which individuals (especially young children) attend to those things that others are attending to, and look to others for emotional cues about how to behave. If your niece is watching you eat a slice of pizza and sees the expression of pure joy on your face, she will be inclined to try the pizza as well. In general, children tend to eat the foods that are eaten around them, and these culturally or socially mediated preferences are strengthened over time, even for flavors that are very strong (see Rozin, Fischler, Imada, Sarubin, & Wrzesniewski, 1999, for a cross-cultural comparison of food preferences and attitudes).

In addition to food preferences, there is evidence for socially learned preferences for alcohol. In humans, it has been demonstrated that children like the smell of alcohol if they have been raised by parents who drink heavily (Mennella & Garcia, 2000). In fact, according to a longitudinal study that has been ongoing since 1974, exposure to alcohol early in life is a risk factor for alcohol use by adolescents (Streissguth, Barr, Bookstein, Samson, Carmichael, & Olson, 1999). This socially mediated preference for alcohol can even be found in animals. Rats that are raised with alcohol available, but that do not observe alcohol consumption by their mother or foster mother, drink very little alcohol when they are adolescents. In fact, most laboratory rats will not drink plain alcohol when it is available unless the concentration is very low. However, if they do observe their mother or foster mother drinking alcohol, those young rats will drink twice as much alcohol when they are adolescents (Honey & Galef, 2003; Honey, Varley, & Galef, 2004). This type of social learning is fairly powerful and long-lasting. With only a week of exposure and a delay of 1 month before having an opportunity to drink alcohol, young rats will still demonstrate an enhanced preference for alcohol (Honey & Galef, 2004). In fact, Hunt and Hallmark (2001) found that even as little as 30 minutes of exposure to an adolescent (rather than adult) rat can also lead to alcohol use.

We do not usually think of alcohol as an "odd" thing to consume; but alcohol is actually a relatively unpalatable substance, especially without the addition of various sugars and flavorings. Most people and animals initially dislike the flavor and smell of high

(*continued*)

concentrations of alcohol. However, once the rewarding, intoxicating aspects of alcohol have been experienced, it becomes more enjoyable. Observational learning is one way to enhance the likelihood that someone will try alcohol in the first place, which can then lead to a preference for alcohol and the possibility of alcohol abuse.

So here is something to think about: If we acquire all sorts of complex behaviors through social learning, is it not likely that we also learn *how* to drink from those around us? And just as some individuals might be learning maladaptive patterns of drinking from their families or peers, might others be learning to drink in a controlled or "responsible" way? Certainly there are multiple factors involved in the development of uncontrolled drinking, including genetic predisposition and one's ability to delay gratification as well as processes of social learning. But the next time you are in a bar or at some social event where alcohol is served, take a moment to watch the people around you and consider the roles of emotional contagion, stimulus enhancement, and observational learning in the drinking behavior you observe.

watched your parents driving a car for years, and you may have thereby *acquired* most of the basic information needed to drive the car—how to start it, how to shift gears, how to use the signal lights, and so on. However, until you reached legal driving age, you were not permitted to translate that acquired knowledge into the actual *performance* of driving.

Acquisition   Acquisition of an operant response (or, for that matter, a classically conditioned response) through observational learning first requires that the observer pay attention to the behavior of the model. After all, you cannot learn from someone unless you actually watch what that person does. So, what makes us attend to a model?

First, we are very sensitive to the *consequences of the model's behavior*. If a model's behavior is reinforced, an observer is more likely to attend to the behavior. For example, if you see a television commercial featuring a husband receiving lavish praise and affection for sending flowers to his wife, you are likely to learn that sending flowers may result in positive reinforcement.

A second factor that influences attention is whether the *observer receives reinforcement for the behavior of attending to a model* (e.g., Pepperberg & Sherman, 2000). Teaching is often based on this principle. Teachers demonstrate desired behaviors—something as basic as reading or as complex as writing a college essay—and reinforce their students' attention to their demonstrations. They may also use various techniques for drawing attention to their behaviors, including prompting ("Look here. See what I'm doing?") and physical modeling ("Hold the football like this, with one hand behind the other"). Teachers then provide verbal reinforcers when students pay attention ("Good!"). Reinforcing observer attention in these ways can greatly increase the amount of knowledge that an observer can acquire from a model.

A third determinant of whether we attend to a model depends on *whether the observer has sufficient skills to benefit from the modeling*. For example, if a model plays "Chopsticks" on the piano, even a musically inexperienced observer may be able to pick up the tune quickly and, with appropriate help, play it herself. However, if a model plays a complex Beethoven sonata, the observer may give up all hope of ever being able to play the piano. If you play computer video games, you have probably felt this way. Watching expert players in a video arcade is a humbling experience and may keep observers from trying the games themselves. Modeling works only when observers have the skills necessary to learn the behavior.

Finally, *the personal characteristics of a model can strongly influence the extent to which we will attend to their behavior.* We are much more likely to attend to models who resemble us—for example, if they are roughly the same age, dress similarly, and have similar interests (e.g., Bussey & Bandura, 1984; Dowling, 1984). We also attend to models we respect or admire, or who are noted authorities in that realm of activity. If the coach of your junior hockey team is a former NHL player and teammate of Wayne Gretzky's, you pay much more attention to what he tells you than if he is the local high school football coach who got pushed into coaching hockey because no one else is available.

Of course, you can acquire information about a behavior without ever translating that information into performance. Television exposes viewers to thousands of hours of violent scenes, yet only a few people ever "act out" those violent behaviors. How we move from knowledge to performance is the topic of the next section.

1. You may watch cooking shows on television and learn how to perform complex culinary feats. Translating that knowledge into a gourmet meal is the difference between a⎯⎯⎯⎯⎯ and p⎯⎯⎯⎯⎯.

2. An important aspect of gaining information about a modeled behavior is the extent to which we a⎯⎯⎯⎯⎯ to the model.

3. Teachers often directly reinforce the behavior of paying a⎯⎯⎯⎯⎯, sometimes accompanied by the use of pr⎯⎯⎯⎯⎯, such as "Look at what I'm doing."

4. The average person is unlikely to pay much attention to the precise moves of a grand master in chess simply because the average person does not have the sk⎯⎯⎯⎯⎯ to benefit from that type of modeling.

5. You are more likely to pay attention to a model whose behavior is (reinforced / not reinforced) ⎯⎯⎯⎯⎯, who is (similar/dissimilar) ⎯⎯⎯⎯⎯ to you, who is (admired/hated) ⎯⎯⎯⎯⎯, and who is a noted au⎯⎯⎯⎯⎯ in that activity.

Performance How does observational learning translate into behavior? As you might expect, it involves those familiar processes of reinforcement and punishment (e.g., Carroll & Bandura, 1987). Reinforcement and punishment work to modify our behavior in modeling situations in three ways. First, *we are more likely (or less likely) to perform a modeled behavior when we have observed the model experience reinforcement (or punishment) for that behavior* (e.g., Bandura & McDonald, 1994; G. R. Fouts & Click, 1979). The effect of such consequences on our behavior is technically known as *vicarious reinforcement (or vicarious punishment)*. For example, when a model is seen using a fragrance that appears to attract members of the opposite sex to her like flies to honey, that increases the likelihood that an observer will try that fragrance herself (assuming she desires the same effect!). And if you watch a comedian telling a joke that gets a big laugh, you may repeat that same joke to your friends. Conversely, if you see a comedian tell a joke that bombs, you are not likely to repeat it.

A second factor that influences performance is the consequence for the observer of performing the modeled behavior. *We are more (or less) likely to perform a modeled behavior when we ourselves will experience reinforcement (or punishment) for performing that behavior.* If you tell the same joke that got the comedian a big laugh and your friends love it, then you will continue to tell it; if you tell the joke and everyone frowns, then you probably will not tell it again. In general, the reinforcement or punishment of the *observer's* behavior ultimately determines whether a modeled behavior will be performed (e.g., Weiss, Suckow, & Rakestraw, 1999).

A third factor that influences our performance is *our own history of reinforcement or punishment for performing modeled behaviors.* Throughout our lives, we learn when it is appropriate to perform modeled behaviors as well as who is an appropriate model. Chances are that behavior modeled after that of teachers, coaches, and parents has been explicitly reinforced while behavior modeled after that of less exemplary individuals has been explicitly punished ("Don't be like that awful boy next door!"). As well, performance of a modeled behavior can be differentially reinforced in different contexts. The performance of some modeled behaviors—such as smoking or swearing—may be reinforced in the presence of your close friends but punished in the presence of your parents. Thus, over the years we gradually learn, through our own unique history of reinforcement and punishment, when it is appropriate to perform behaviors that have been modeled by others. (See also the discussion of *generalized imitation in the next section.*)

QUICK QUIZ C

1. Not only are you more likely to a_____ to a model's behavior if you see the model's behavior reinforced, you are also more likely to p_____ that behavior.

2. A second factor that influences whether we will perform a modeled behavior is the c_____ we receive for performing the behavior.

3. A third factor that influences our performance of a modeled behavior is our h_____ of r_____ for performing modeled behaviors.

4. When you repeat an off-color joke to your friends, they laugh heartily; but when you tell the same jokes to your parents, you are met with frowns. Due to d_____ reinforcement, you soon learn to tell such jokes only when you are with your friends.

Imitation

Imitation is a term that is often used interchangeably with observational learning. *True imitation*, however, is a form of observational learning that involves the close duplication of a novel behavior (or sequence of behaviors). For example, imagine that Chelsea is standing in a line outside an exclusive club when she sees a woman walk to the front of the line and begin flirting with the doorman. The doorman allows the woman to enter without standing in line. Chelsea gets out of line, walks up to the doorman, and also begins flirting with him. If she flirts in a different way from the other woman (using her own "flirting style"), this would be an example of observational learning but not true imitation. But if she flirts in virtually the same way as the other woman, which also happens to be quite different from the way Chelsea normally flirts (so it is a novel behavior pattern for her), then we would say that true imitation has taken place.

Children have a strong tendency to imitate the behaviors of those around them, hence the popularity of games like "Simon says." Interestingly, operant conditioning appears to play a major role in the development of this ability. In the earliest study along these lines, Baer and Sherman (1964) reinforced children's behavior of imitating certain behavior patterns that were displayed by a puppet. The researchers found that this process resulted in an increase not only in the frequency of the behaviors that had been reinforced but also in the frequency of other behaviors that had been displayed by the model but for which the children had never received reinforcement. In other words, the children had acquired a generalized tendency to imitate the model.

Generalized imitation is therefore a tendency to imitate a new modeled behavior with no specific reinforcement for doing so. This process has considerable real-world application. Applied behavior analysts make use of it when working with children who are developmentally delayed or have autism and who are often deficient in their ability to learn through observation (e.g., Baer, Peterson, & Sherman, 1967; Lovaas, 1987; Lynch, 1998). By deliberately reinforcing the imitation of some behaviors, therapists can produce in these children a generalized tendency to imitate, which then greatly facilitates subsequent training.

Can Animals Imitate? Although it is clear that humans are capable of true imitation, there has been considerable debate over the extent to which animals are capable of it (e.g., Galef, 1988; Tomasello, 1996). This is actually an old issue; early animal behaviorists and learning theorists, like Romanes (1884), Morgan (1900), and Thorndike (1911), debated whether animals could "intentionally" imitate (which could be construed as indicative of higher-level cognitive functioning) or whether any appearance of imitation was due to some lower-level, perhaps instinctive, mechanism. Now the controversy has again arisen, with a wealth of experimental studies examining the issue.

Most of these studies have examined the ability of animals, usually monkeys and apes, to solve novel problems such as how to obtain food locked away in a box. In a typical experiment, the animals watch a model perform a complex series of behaviors—such as getting a key, opening a lock, pulling a lever, and then using a stick to pull food out of a hole that has now been revealed in the side of the box. The observer animal is then given a chance to try opening the box. If the animal can imitate, it should be able to duplicate the actions performed by the model to obtain the food. What often happens, though, is that the animals do not copy the actions of the model exactly—they may pull the lever, for example, but not use the key; or they may turn the box over and shake it to remove the food rather than use the stick (e.g., Call, 1999; Call & Tomasello, 1995; Nagel, Olguin, & Tomasello, 1993; Whiten, 1998).

Further, when animals do show evidence of imitation in these types of studies, it is often not clear that the effects of stimulus enhancement and other potential confounds have been ruled out. For example, Chesler (1969) demonstrated that kittens more quickly learn to press a lever for food if they had observed their mothers pressing a lever than if they had observed a strange female cat pressing the lever. Although this study has been widely cited as providing evidence of imitation, Galef (1988) points out that the study might simply demonstrate that mothers are better stimulus enhancers than strangers are. Kittens are likely to pay more attention to their mother than to a stranger, and to attend to any item that she manipulates. This in turn makes it more likely that the kittens would themselves manipulate the lever and, through trial and error, receive food. Thus, simple stimulus enhancement could result in a duplication of behavior that looks a lot like imitation. Due to these kinds of difficulties, some researchers have suggested that nonhuman animals are incapable of true imitation (e.g., Tomasello, 1996).

Other researchers, however, have argued that sufficient evidence now exists, gathered from well-controlled studies, to indicate that at least some animals (especially birds and great apes) are capable of true imitation (see Zentall, 2006, for a review). For example, in a study by Nguyen, Klein, and Zentall (2005), demonstrator pigeons were trained either to peck at or step on a treadle and then push a screen either to the left or to the right to obtain food. Observer pigeons were significantly more likely to demonstrate the sequence they had observed (e.g., treadle step and screen push right) as opposed to a sequence they had not observed (treadle peck and screen push left).

It has also been argued that past research on this issue has sometimes utilized inappropriate criteria for judging imitative ability in animals. Horowitz (2003), for example, replicated a study using a task that had previously revealed greater evidence of true imitation in children than in chimpanzees, except that Horowitz also gave the task to human adults. He found that the adults' level of imitation was more similar to that of the chimpanzees than the children's level was! In other words, both human adults and chimpanzees displayed more flexible behavior patterns in solving the problem—as compared to the children, who had a stronger tendency simply to do what the model had demonstrated. The lower rate of imitation that had been shown by chimpanzees compared to the children in the previous study therefore seems like a poor basis for drawing inferences about their lack of imitative ability, insofar as one can hardly argue that human adults are also incapable of true imitation.

Finally, researchers have uncovered some impressive anecdotal evidence of true imitation. Russon and Galdikas (1993, 1995) observed orangutans living with humans in a camp designed to reintroduce the animals to the wild. They found that the orangutans regularly copied the complex actions of the humans with whom they interacted, including learning to hang hammocks, build bridges, and use boats. In one case, an orangutan even learned how to start a fire—something that the researchers did not expect and certainly did not demonstrate on purpose! (See "Can Animals Teach?" in the And Furthermore box.)

And Furthermore

Can Animals Teach?

We have so far discussed whether animals can learn by observing a model. An even more interesting question, perhaps, is whether animals can "deliberately" act as models for teaching another animal. This is not an easy question to answer, because people usually assume that teaching requires a "conscious intention" to demonstrate, or transfer knowledge from one individual to another, that is obviously difficult to assess in nonhuman animals. For example, consider an ape that seems to be calling her offspring's attention toward her tool use. By simply observing her actions, we may find it difficult to determine if she is trying to teach her young to use a tool to get food or simply trying to get food while at the same time keeping her offspring nearby. If her offspring do learn to use the same tool in the same way, were they intentionally taught by the mother? Or, did the offspring simply pick up the behavior on their own through observational learning or stimulus enhancement?

As with true imitation, some researchers have argued that teaching is a behavior performed only by humans (King, 1991). They contend that evidence that does suggest teaching by animals is often anecdotal and subject to *anthropomorphism* (assuming human motives or characteristics when observing animal behavior). Nevertheless, evidence has been gathered suggesting that at least some nonhuman animals, especially chimpanzees (Boesch, 1991) and bonobos (once known as "pygmy

(continued)

Kanzi with his trainer, Sue Savage-Rumbaugh.

Courtesy of www.GreatApeTrust.org

chimpanzees"; de Waal, 2005) do behave as teachers. A few anecdotes, in particular, are difficult to ignore. For example:

> At the Georgia State University Language Research Center in Atlanta, a bonobo called Kanzi has been trained to communicate with people. He has become a bonobo celebrity, known for his fabulous understanding of spoken English. Realizing that some of his fellow apes do not have the same training, Kanzi occasionally adopts the role of teacher. He once sat next to Tamuli, a younger sister who has had minimal exposure to human speech, while a researcher tried to get Tamuli to respond to simple verbal requests; the untrained bonobo didn't respond. As the researcher addressed Tamuli, it was Kanzi who began to act out the meanings. When Tamuli was asked to groom Kanzi, he took her hand and placed it under his chin, squeezing it between his chin and chest. In this position, Kanzi stared into Tamuli's eyes with what people interpreted as a questioning gaze. When Kanzi repeated the action, the young female rested her fingers on his chest as if wondering what to do. (de Waal, 2005, pp. 6–7)

In the quote, you may have noticed several assumptions, which may or may not be warranted, that were made about Kanzi's and Tamuli's motives. On the other hand, the behaviors Kanzi displayed are the types of behaviors that, with humans, we often use to infer the existence of an "intention." It is difficult, therefore, to witness a behavior like this and not have the impression that Kanzi is making some humanlike attempt at teaching or coaching. But it should also be noted that Kanzi is unique among bonobos in his demonstrated language and problem-solving abilities, and he may have skills that are not typical of other apes. (You will read more about language learning in animals in Chapter 13.)

1. If a young gorilla learns to gather tasty wild ginger plants by watching his mother forage, we can say that he has demonstrated o_____ learning.

2. Copying a new behavior to achieve a particular result is (true imitation / stimulus enhancement) _____; having one's attention drawn to a particular place or thing is (true imitation / stimulus enhancement) _____.

3. Jessica has just purchased a new computer and is trying to learn how to use the modem to access the Internet. She asks her friend Jill to show her how to do it. Jill performs a complicated series of clicks and keystrokes, and Jessica watches closely. If Jessica then connects to the Internet on her own using the same actions as Jill, Jessica's behavior is best described as an example of (true imitation / stimulus enhancement) _____.

4. Joe has also purchased a new computer and is trying to access the Internet. He watches his friend Daryl as he accesses the Internet and notices that he uses a couple of applications to do so. Joe opens those applications himself and then plays around with the settings until he figures it out. Joe's behavior is best described as an example of (true imitation / stimulus enhancement) _____.

Social Learning and Aggression

Bandura is well known for his studies on aggression, and he is particularly famous for what are now known as the "Bobo doll studies" (e.g., Bandura, 1965). In those studies, children observed adult models behaving aggressively toward a Bobo doll (an inflatable toy doll that pops back up when pushed over). The children were then tested to determine whether they also had learned to behave aggressively. The research involved various types of models, various forms of demonstrated aggression, and children of varying ages. In these studies, Bandura found some *striking* evidence concerning the social learning of aggression (pun intended).

Two images from Albert Bandura's famous Bobo doll study. The image on the left is from the film of the aggressive adult model that was shown to the children (the Bobo doll has bounced into the air from the force of the attack). The image on the right shows one of the children later attacking the Bobo doll.

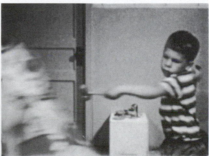

Courtesy of Albert Bandura

Courtesy of Albert Bandura

First, children who observed a model behaving aggressively toward the Bobo doll and other targets tended to replicate the same behaviors when they were allowed into the same room that the model had previously occupied (Bandura, Ross, & Ross, 1961; Bandura, Ross, & Ross, 1963; Bandura 1965). By *replicate*, we do not just mean that the children demonstrated an increase in general aggression (although that also occurred). The children in Bandura's studies were very precise in some of their aggressive behavior, performing many of the same movements toward the same targets, using the same weapons, and uttering the same hostile statements. In other words, these children demonstrated true imitation of the model's aggressive behavior.

The children were also influenced by the consequences that the model experienced while behaving aggressively. Although simply witnessing the aggressive adult often resulted in aggressive behavior in the child, the effect was even stronger if the child had observed reinforcement of the adult's aggression. Likewise, children who had observed models' aggressive behavior being punished were somewhat *less* likely to reproduce the behaviors spontaneously. However, if the researchers then offered the children incentives to behave aggressively, the level of aggression went back up; the children showed that they had in fact learned the behaviors very well (Bandura, 1965).

In a related study, children watched a televised fight in the presence of an adult male. The adult watched the film with the children and responded approvingly, disapprovingly, or made no comment. Children who had heard the disapproving comments produced far fewer aggressive behaviors upon testing compared to the other two groups—*but only when the disapproving adult was present*. In the absence of the disapproving adult, these children exhibited an increase in aggression (Hicks, 1968).

QUICK QUIZ E

1. The aggressive behavior of children in Bandura's studies was so similar to the model's behavior that it can be considered as an example of t_____ _____.

2. Watching a model demonstrate violent behavior has been shown to lead to an (increase/decrease) _____ in violence by observers; observing the reinforcement of violent behavior further (increased/decreased) _____ the amount of violence displayed by observers.

3. Although children in Bandura's study exhibited somewhat less violent behavior if the model's behavior had been p_____, their levels of violence increased again if they were later offered a(n) _____ for behaving violently.

Social Learning and Media Violence: From Bobo Doll to Grand Theft Auto In his research, Bandura found that filmed violence was as effective as live violence for inducing violent behavior in observers (Bandura, Ross, & Ross, 1963). Although this research was conducted before the extreme proliferation of mass media in the late twentieth century, these preliminary findings foreshadowed the concerns of modern researchers who examine the impact of violent media on the behavior of children and adolescents.

Children have always had opportunities to learn about violence, by observing violence at home and in the community. Children are often exposed to warfare and are sometimes even trained as soldiers. Social learning of violence by children is therefore nothing new, but the constant availability of aggressive or violent models is new and pervasive. Between 1950, when approximately 9% of American homes contained a television, and 2000, when virtually all North American families owned a television (Federal Trade Commission, 2000), there has been a substantial change in children's exposure to violent media. In addition to television, which is an essentially passive medium (one simply watches it), children are increasingly exposed to violent or aggressive video games that allow for a high degree of interaction and participation. Indeed, when looking at the hyperrealistic violent games now available—including the Grand Theft Auto™ series of games that depict violent criminal behavior such as theft, murder, and rape—it's hard to believe that in the 1980s, some parents complained that Pac-Man was too violent because Pac-Man went around eating the other characters!

Longitudinal studies and prospective studies are especially useful for isolating critical factors in violent behavior. Eron and his colleagues have studied a large sample of boys from 1960 until the present day. They have found that the amount of violent media viewed in childhood is significantly correlated with aggressive and antisocial behavior 10 years later, even after controlling for variables such as initial aggressiveness, social class, and education (Eron, Huesmann, Lefkowitz, & Walder, 1972). This early viewing of violence, and early aggression, has also been shown to be significantly related to adult criminality (Huesmann, 1986), although the relationship is weaker. More recently, Johnson and his colleagues have summarized the results of another 17-year study, in which they determined that the amount of television watched in childhood is positively correlated with amount of aggressive or violent behavior toward others (Johnson, Cohen, Kasen, & Brook, 2007). Although Johnson's team found a bidirectional relationship between viewing violence and aggressive behavior (in which those who are aggressive also tend to seek out violent media), the effect of violent media on later aggressive behavior was still robust.

Are there sex differences in the effects of media violence? Most studies find that males are more likely to express the effects of exposure to violent video games. C. A. Anderson and Dill (2000) report that male video-game players have a more hostile view of the world than do females, and some longitudinal studies suggest that males are more aggressive than females after exposure to violent media (Eron et al., 1972; Huesmann, Moise-Titus, Podolski, & Eron, 2003; Lefkowitz, Eron, Walder, & Huesmann, 1977). This conforms to results described by Bandura (1965) in his early Bobo doll studies. For example, he found that boys tended to produce more spontaneous acts of aggression than girls did. He also found that girls inhibited their aggression to a greater degree if the model had been punished. Once an incentive was provided for reproducing the aggressive acts, however, the sex differences disappeared. It appears therefore that girls learn violence as well as boys do, but girls have a greater tendency to inhibit violence unless there is an incentive for violence. Girls will also demonstrate a higher frequency of aggressive acts when the aggressive model is female as opposed to male (see review by Bandura, 1973). Since most violent models in the media and on computer games are male, this could account for some of the sex differences that we observe.

One troubling possibility is that, although exposure to violent media does not predispose females toward behaving aggressively as much as it does males, it might make females more vulnerable to being *victims* of aggression. Desensitization to violence may allow females to feel that violence and aggression are normal aspects of life, which could lead them to enter violent relationships. This may be related to the fact that, whereas most models of violent behavior are male, a high proportion of victims are female. Thus, in the same way that exposure to spousal violence in childhood increases the likelihood of becoming a victim of spousal abuse in adulthood (Ehrensaft et al., 2003), it is possible that females who watch violent media are more likely to become victims of violence.

Given all the evidence for the damaging effects of media violence, from both experimental and correlational studies, why do we rarely see this evidence clearly reported in the newspapers and other aspects of the popular press? Bushman and Anderson (2001) have proposed several reasons for why this is the case. For one thing, media sources are often interlinked. Thus, if the film or television industry wants to promote (or suppress) a particular viewpoint, they are likely to have connections at the level of newspapers and magazines that enable them to do so. Media outlets also tend to take a "balanced" approach to the topic of media violence by frequently including comments from researchers who believe that the effects of media violence have been overstated. On the surface, this appears to be a fair approach, since both sides of the debate are given equal representation. However, insofar as the vast majority of researchers agree that media violence is dangerous, then the "equal air time" given to the few naysayers tends to mislead the public into believing that the evidence linking media violence and aggression is much weaker than it is. Finally, researchers themselves have not been forceful enough in presenting their findings to the public. For example, media executives have sometimes argued that the correlations between media violence and aggression are so small as to be of little real significance, whereas in fact they are almost as high as the correlations between cigarette smoking and lung cancer—and they are higher than the correlations between passive smoking and lung cancer, exposure to asbestos and laryngeal cancer, and even condom use and sexually transmitted HIV! No one argues that these correlations are so small as to be of little real significance.

The comparison to lung cancer is particularly instructive. Smoking is an important cause of lung cancer—but it is not the only cause, and many people who smoke will never get lung cancer. On average, however, the risk of developing lung cancer if you are a smoker is substantially higher than if you are a nonsmoker. The same logic holds true for the effects of media violence on violent behavior. Watching violent TV is not the only contributing factor to personal violence. Some individuals who watch violent films or play violent video games will never demonstrate an increase in violent behavior. On average, however, those who view or interact with violent media have an increased risk of becoming violent themselves. As noted earlier, the possibility also exists that exposure to media violence can increase the likelihood of becoming a victim of violence. Therefore, although further research is warranted, it appears that media violence is very likely a significant contributor to violence in society.

QUICK QUIZ F

1. Longitudinal studies have shown that exposure to violent media is (strongly/weakly) _____ correlated with ag_____ and anti_____ behavior.

2. One troubling aspect of sex differences in response to media violence is that while (males/females) _____ are more likely to become violent as a result of such exposure, (males/females) _____ may be more likely to become _____ of violence.

3. The problem with the media giving equal air time to those who are (convinced/skeptical) _____ about the effects of media violence on violent behavior is that the public is then misled into thinking that the evidence for such effects is (stronger/weaker) _____ than it actually is.

Rule-Governed Behavior

Observational learning is one way in which we can learn appropriate behavior prior to directly experiencing the contingencies that actually control that behavior. Another means by which we can indirectly learn a behavior is through the use of language, which greatly enhances our ability to interact with one another and to adapt to the world around us. A prime example of this is the manner in which language allows us to influence each other, and ourselves, through the presentation of rules.

Definitions and Characteristics

A *rule* can be defined as a verbal description of a contingency. In other words, it is a statement telling us that in a certain setting, if we perform a certain behavior, then a certain consequence will follow: "If you drive through a red light, you will get a ticket"; "If you study hard throughout the semester, you will get a good grade"; and "If you are pleasant to others, they will be pleasant to you" are all examples of rules. Likewise, the course syllabus you receive at the start of a course is a set of rules about what you need to do to pass the course, and a guidebook to Paris is a set of rules about how best to find and enjoy the sites of Paris. Behavior that has been generated through exposure to rules, such as doing what the course outline tells you to do or touring Paris in the manner suggested by the guidebook, is known as **rule-governed behavior** (Skinner, 1969).

In its purest form, a rule is simply a statement about a contingency; it does not say anything about how we should respond with respect to that contingency. If it does say something about how we should respond, then it can also be called an *instruction* (Malott, Malott, & Trojan, 2000). Thus, "If you drive through a red light, you will get a ticket" is simply a rule, whereas "Don't drive through a red light, or you will get a ticket" (or "Don't drive through a red light!" in which case the consequence is implied) is an instruction. In this discussion, however, we will use the terms *rule* and *instruction* interchangeably given that many of the rules that concern us are offered in the form of instructions. (See Baldwin & Baldwin, 1998, for a further discussion of the different types of rules.)

Rules (or instructions) are extremely useful for rapidly establishing appropriate patterns of behavior. As with observational learning, we can learn how to behave effectively in a certain setting before we have any direct experience with the contingencies operating in that setting. We do not have to repeatedly drive through red lights to find out what happens if we do, and we do not have to fail a course repeatedly to figure out how to pass the course. We simply have to follow the rules that we have been given in order to behave effectively in those settings.

To illustrate the effectiveness of using rules to modify behavior, consider the task of teaching a rat to press a lever for food whenever it hears a tone. First, you have to shape the behavior of lever pressing by reinforcing closer and closer approximations to it. Then, once lever pressing is well established, you reinforce lever presses that occur only in the presence of a tone and not those that occur in the absence of the tone. Eventually, the rat learns to press the lever only when the tone is sounding. Now consider the task of teaching a person to press a button to earn money whenever a light is turned on (a common task in operant conditioning experiments with humans). All you have to do is sit the person down in front of the panel and provide the following instructions: "Whenever the light is on, you can earn money by pressing this button." Instantly, you have a button-pushing, money-earning human on your hands. What may require several hours of training with a rat requires only a few seconds of instruction with a verbally proficient human.

Learning to follow rules is so beneficial and important that parents devote considerable time to training this ability in young children. When Billie, for example, complies with his mother's request to pick up his toys, his mother praises him for doing so. Billie soon learns that people are pleased when he complies with their instructions, and he is therefore more likely to comply in the future. Billie later learns that following instructions can also be useful for completing a task. When, for example, he ignores the instructions that accompany a model airplane kit, he makes a complete mess of things; when he follows the instructions, he produces a great-looking model. Billie therefore learns that good things happen when he follows instructions; consequently, he acquires a generalized tendency to follow instructions. Of course, if bad things had happened when Billie followed instructions, or if good things happened when he did not follow instructions, he might instead have acquired a generalized tendency not to follow instructions and to be noncompliant. Thus, the extent to which we follow instructions—as well as the specific instructions we choose to follow— depends largely on the consequences we have received for following instructions (Baldwin & Baldwin, 1998).

1. A rule can be defined as a v_____ d_____ of a c_____.

2. Behavior that is generated through exposure to rules is known as r_____ g_____ behavior.

3. A rule that also indicates how you should behave with respect to a contingency is an _____.

4. Rules are extremely useful in that they allow us to learn about appropriate patterns of behavior in a setting (with/without) _____ direct exposure to the contingencies operating in that setting.

5. Children learn to follow instructions because they are often (praised/ignored) _____ for following instructions. As well, they learn that following instructions is usually a (good/poor) _____ way to actually accomplish a task.

6. The result is that most children acquire a (generalized/localized) _____ tendency to follow instructions.

7. In general, the extent to which we follow instructions—as well as the specific instructions we choose to follow—depends largely on the c_____ we have received for following instructions.

Some Disadvantages of Rule-Governed Behavior

As you can see, rules can be very useful. Unfortunately, they also have their drawbacks. One drawback is that rule-governed behavior is often less efficient than behavior that has been directly shaped by natural contingencies. For example, no matter how many books you read on how to play golf, you will undoubtedly be a poor golfer unless you devote considerable time to actually playing and practicing the game (see Figure 11.2). Instructions can give us only a rudimentary knowledge of how to play, and while this may be useful for getting started or for modifying certain aspects of an established game, nothing can replace the actual experience of hitting a golf ball and seeing where it goes (Baldwin & Baldwin, 1998).

FIGURE 11.2 Although golf lessons are a great way to get started in the game, the rules learned are, at best, general pointers that must then be modified through the actual experience of hitting the ball and seeing where it goes.

© Michael S. Yamashita/CORBIS

A second drawback of rule-governed behavior is that such behavior is sometimes surprisingly insensitive to the actual contingencies of reinforcement operating in a particular setting. This phenomenon has been demonstrated experimentally. For example, when human participants are told they can earn money by pressing a button, they will indeed begin pressing the button. Their button pressing may not, however, be very efficient given the schedule of reinforcement that is in effect. For instance, on an FI schedule of reinforcement, human subjects often do not display the scalloped pattern of responding that is typical of FI performance in rats and pigeons. Some subjects, for example, respond rapidly throughout the interval—as though continuous, rapid responding is necessary to produce the reinforcer (Lowe, 1979). Focusing only upon the rule they have been given—"Push the button

A good example of how the inflexible application of rules can get in the way of organizational efficiency.

to earn money"—some subjects never slow down enough to realize that such a high rate of response is unnecessary.[1] (See also Bentall, Lowe, & Beasty, 1985; Lowe, Beasty, & Bentall, 1983).

Likewise, a person who is taught to swing a golf club a certain way may persist with that swing for several years despite the fact that it is inappropriate for her build and level of flexibility. Because she is locked into the notion that she must follow the instructions she has been given, her golf game may never evolve to a more effective level. Similarly, a veteran businessman who has acquired a set of rules about how best to conduct business may have difficulty modifying his business practices to compete effectively in the new global economy. As the world of business changes, his old rules, highly effective in the old economy, are now an impediment. Thus, although rules are often extremely beneficial, we do well to recognize that they have their limitations and often require modification according to the particular circumstances in which we find ourselves. (See also "Psychopathology, Psychotherapy, and Rule-Governed Behavior" in the And Furthermore box.)

---

[1]The first author of this text directly experienced this phenomenon when, as a graduate student, he was conducting just such a button-pushing study. Because each session in the study lasted a couple of hours (and because the task was excruciatingly boring), subjects were given 10-minute breaks at regular intervals throughout each session. One subject, however, began spending almost all of her breaks in the washroom. Asked if she was okay, she explained that she was going to the washroom to run her arm under cold water to reduce the pain. As it turns out, having been told that pushing buttons would produce money, she assumed that faster button pushing produced more money. She therefore pushed the button at a blistering pace throughout each session, so much so that her arm muscles had begun to cramp. In fact, the money was being delivered on variable interval (VI) schedules of reinforcement, and she could have earned the full amount each session with a quite leisurely rate of response.

1. One problem with rule-governed behavior is that it is often (less/more) _____ efficient than behavior that has been shaped by natural c_____.

2. A second problem with rule-governed behavior is that such behavior is sometimes surprisingly _____ to the actual contingencies of reinforcement in a particular setting.

3. As an example of the above, experimental subjects who are told to press a button to earn money sometimes display a (scalloped pattern / high rate) _____ of responding on an FI schedule of reinforcement, which is (the same as / different from) _____ the type of responding typically shown on such schedules by animals.

And Furthermore

Psychopathology, Psychotherapy, and Rule-Governed Behavior

The fact that rule-governed behavior is sometimes insensitive to the actual contingencies has important implications, not only for everyday activities such as learning golf or conducting business, but also for understanding various forms of psychopathology. The starting point for this notion was the aforementioned finding that human subjects in operant conditioning experiments who are given instructions (rules) to "press the button" often behave in ways that are highly inefficient. This led to speculation that rule-governed behavior in general might often be insensitive to the actual contingencies, which in turn suggested that this insensitivity might even account for some forms of psychopathology. The outcome of this line of reasoning was an innovative form of therapy known as *Acceptance and Commitment Therapy* or *ACT* (Hayes, Strosahl, & Wilson, 1999).

The basic rationale that underlies ACT is that human verbal behavior has both advantages and disadvantages. Just as language allows us to reminisce about the past and plan for tomorrow, so too it allows us to relive painful experiences and catastrophize about the future. Thus, our ability to use language can sometimes be a serious drawback. (By comparison, your friendly neighborhood tree squirrel, with virtually no language, lives almost entirely in the present and seems largely immune to many of the forms of neurosis that plague humans.)

More specifically, according to Hayes et al. (1999), the culture that we live in engrains within us a particular set of rules about our psychological difficulties. These include:

- Psychological problems are indicated by unpleasant feelings, thoughts, bodily sensations, etc.
- These unpleasant experiences are "signals" that we have some type of deficiency (e.g., a lack of confidence) that needs to change for us to become healthy.
- This can be achieved by understanding or modifying the factors that caused the difficulty (e.g., "working through" our thoughts and feelings about a difficult childhood that resulted in low self-confidence).

In short, we must somehow get rid of our negative thoughts and feelings in order to live a satisfying life.

The main difficulty with these rules and the ways in which we try to deal them is that they are largely ineffective. For example, some symptoms are reflexive in nature and have been classically conditioned through exposure to upsetting experiences. Hence, attempting to alleviate the symptoms by deliberately suppressing them, as many people try to do, is unlikely to be effective. Thus, the basic goal in ACT is to enable clients to see the futility of their usual strategies for handling their symptoms. Through a diverse array of therapeutic techniques, clients are encouraged to "give up the struggle" and to "lean forward" into their symptoms. Once they learn to accept their thoughts and feelings as they are, they can then commit themselves to carrying out personally valued activities. This process by itself may result in a certain degree of symptom alleviation, insofar as clients will no longer be avoiding the events that elicit their symptoms (thereby allowing extinction to take place). More importantly, though, clients will come to understand that unpleasant thoughts and feelings are a normal part of everyday life, and that eliminating these events is not a prerequisite for engaging in appropriate and worthwhile behavior. (For examples of the therapeutic techniques used, see Hayes et al., 1999; see also Waltz & Hayes, 2010, for a recent overview of ACT.)

ACT is not the only type of therapy that preaches the benefits of focusing on behavior and accepting one's thoughts and feelings. Two other behaviorally-oriented forms of therapy, *dialectical behavior therapy* (Linehan, 1993) and *functional analytic psychotherapy* (Kohlenberg & Tsai, 1991), also include aspects of acceptance, as does an older Japanese form of therapy, known as *Morita Therapy*. Morita therapists, in particular, view psychological difficulties as arising from living a feeling-centered rather than behavior-centered lifestyle. Similar to ACT, clients in Morita therapy are taught to accept their feelings, to know their purpose, and to do what needs to be done. They learn that feelings are largely uncontrollable while actions are controllable, and that they must place greater emphasis on the latter if they wish to lead a satisfying life (see Reynolds, 1984, for a readable introduction to this style of therapy).

Personal Rules in Self-Regulation

Although rules have their drawbacks, their advantages obviously outweigh their disadvantages. For this reason, we use rules not only to influence the behavior of others but also to influence our own behavior. In other words, we often give ourselves instructions as to how we should behave: "I should study in the library rather than at home, because it is much quieter in the library"; "I should work out each day if I want to remain fit and healthy"; and "If I am polite to others, they will be polite to me." Such statements can be called *personal rules (or self-instructions)*, which can be defined as verbal descriptions of contingencies that we present to ourselves to influence our behavior (Ainslie, 1992).

ADVICE FOR THE LOVELORN

Dear Dr. Dee,

My boyfriend and I very much enjoy reading your columns. Unfortunately, Steve (my boyfriend) has begun using the ideas in these columns to analyze each and every aspect of our relationship. I know he means well, but it is starting to drive me nuts. Furthermore, I think his conclusions about our relationship are usually dead wrong. What is your opinion on this?

Going Nutty

Dear Going,

At the start of this book, we explicitly warned against taking these columns too seriously. For one thing, the advice given is usually quite speculative; it is not grounded in scientific research, nor is it based on a careful assessment of the relationship being discussed (which, in any case, is just a fictional relationship). Thus, our purpose in presenting these columns is simply to give students a sense of the *potential* ways in which behavioral principles *might* be applicable to some important aspects of human behavior.

It is also important to recognize that each relationship is unique, meaning there's no guarantee that advice that is appropriate for one relationship is relevant to another relationship. In fact, you can think of such advice as a rule for how to improve your relationship—and the act of following that advice as a form of rule-governed behavior. As we discuss in this chapter, such rules may not accurately reflect the actual contingencies that are in effect, and the person following the rule may become insensitive to the actual contingencies. This may be what has happened in your boyfriend's case. He seems to have concluded that the advice given in these columns is relevant to your own situation, which it might not be.

Tell him to lighten up a bit, pay less attention to what's being said in these advice columns (or, for that matter, anyone else's advice column), and pay more attention to what's going on in your relationship. And if you do need advice, there is often nothing better than some plain old common sense from one's close friends and family. These people often have a better knowledge of the type of person you are and the actual contingencies surrounding your relationship than any advice columnist could ever have.

Behaviorally yours,

Dr. Dee

Many of the personal rules that we use to regulate our behavior exert their effect as a function of "say–do correspondence." *Say–do correspondence* occurs when there is a close match between what we say we are going to do and what we actually do at a later time. If I say that I will go running at 4:00 in the afternoon and then actually go running at that time, my statement of what I intend to do matches the actual behavior that I later perform. As with rule-governed behavior in general, parents play a critical role in the development of this correspondence. If Billie promises that he will put his toys away when he is finished playing with them, and later he does put his toys away, his parents are quite pleased and praise him for carrying through on his promise. But when he does not carry through on his promise, they are annoyed. To the extent that Billie's parents apply these consequences consistently, Billie will likely grow up to display a strong level of say–do correspondence. He will become known as a reliable individual who can be trusted to carry through on his promises to others. Not only that, he may concurrently develop an ability to carry through on his promises to himself, which means that he will be able to use such promises as personal rules to guide his own behavior (Guevremont, Osnes, & Stokes, 1986).

Although personal rules can be useful in helping us manage our behavior, not all personal rules are equally effective. Ainslie (1986), for example, has proposed that personal rules are most effective when they establish a "bright boundary" between acceptable and unacceptable patterns of behavior. A bright boundary is a strategic concept stating that military leaders should make use of clearly specified landmarks, such as rivers, streams, or roads, to mark the limits of their territory. Such boundaries are easier to defend because they allow one to clearly determine when the enemy has intruded into one's territory. Similarly, in trying to carry through on rules for our own behavior, we are more likely to succeed when the rule specifically sets out the conditions under which it has been obeyed or violated. For example, the statement "I will study today" is so vaguely worded that we are at high risk for delaying the act of studying until it is too late to study. The point at which the rule has been violated is not easily determined until we have, in a sense, been overrun and lost the battle. By contrast, the statement "I will study from 7:00 p.m. to 9:00 p.m. this evening" is so specific that any violation of the rule—for example, it is now 7:10 p.m. and we are still watching television—will be readily apparent. This is related to the notion, discussed in Chapter 10, that each choice in a self-control situation often has only a small but cumulative effect upon the overall outcome. Each sugary soda that we drink will not, by itself, undermine our efforts at attaining good health; rather, it is only the repeated consumption of sodas that undermines our health. If we wish to occasionally indulge in such treats, it will help to clearly specify the level at which we will do so, since there is no natural boundary indicating the point at which further indulgence will significantly undermine our health.

The importance of clear, specific rules has been empirically supported. For example, Gollwitzer and Brandstätter (1997) asked college students to name two projects they intended to complete during Christmas break, one of which would be easy to accomplish (e.g., go skating) and the other of which would be difficult to accomplish (e.g., complete an English assignment). Students were also asked if they had made a decision about when and where the activity would be carried out. Following the Christmas break, the same students were asked if they had completed the project. For activities that were easy to implement, about 80% of the students said they had indeed completed them. With such easy projects, it seemed to make little difference if the students had also decided upon a time and place for implementing them. For difficult projects, however, students who had decided when and where their project would be carried out were significantly more likely to have completed it compared to those who had not made such a decision. In other research, participants who specified when and where they would take a vitamin supplement were significantly more consistent in taking the supplement than were those who merely intended to take the supplement (Sheeran & Orbell, 1999); likewise, patients who specified when, where, and how they would make a cervical cancer screening appointment were more likely to obtain such screening than were those who had not made such plans (Sheeran & Orbell, 2000).

More recently, Luszczynska, Sobczyk, and Abraham (2007) asked a group of Weight Watchers participants to formulate specific food and exercise plans for each day throughout the week (e.g., "This is my plan concerning the consumption of sweets for the next 7 days. I plan to eat ... [listing type and amount of sweets] at ... [indicating time at which it would be eaten] at ... [indicating place at which it would be eaten]"). The participants also made specific relapse prevention plans for how they would cope with temptations that might arise ("If someone offers me my favorite unhealthy food, then I will ... "). Compared to a control group of Weight Watchers participants who did not formulate such plans, those who did lost twice as much weight during a 2-month period.

Thus, the act of specifying when, where, and how a goal is to be accomplished can significantly affect the probability of accomplishing that goal. Gollwitzer (1999) refers to such when-where-and-how statements as *implementation intentions*. However, to be more consistent with Ainslie's (1992) terminology, they could also be called **personal process rules**, insofar as they are personal rules that indicate the specific process by which a task is to be accomplished. And a possible reason such rules are effective is that they establish a bright boundary between actions that conform to the rule and those that do not. (See also Schmitt, 2001, for a discussion of the issues involved in establishing instructional control over behavior that needs to occur at a later point in time.)

1. A p_____ rule is a description of a contingency that we verbalize to ourselves to influence our own behavior.

2. A close match between what we say we are going to do and what we actually do at a later point in time is called a _____-_____ c_____.

3. People who have been trained to display a high level of _____ _____ correspondence can more effectively use personal rules (or self-instructions) to influence their behavior.

4. P_____ p_____ rules indicate the specific process by which a task is to be carried out. The formulation of such rules tends to (increase/decrease) _____ the likelihood that the task will be accomplished. Such rules have also been called im_____ i_____.

And Furthermore

Say–Do Correspondence and Willpower

Using personal rules to regulate one's behavior represents a form of say–do correspondence. Moreover, to the extent that one displays a strong level of say–do correspondence, such personal rules might even function as a type of *commitment* response. As you may recall from Chapter 10, a commitment response is any response made at an early point in time that so reduces the value of a smaller sooner reward that it no longer serves as a temptation when it becomes imminent. One is therefore able to ignore the temptation and carry on working toward a larger later reward. Thus, handing your sister $10 with the understanding that she will return it only if you have completed a certain amount of studying that evening will reduce the value of any non-study activity to a level where you will in fact be quite likely to study (because any activity that interferes with studying will be associated with the loss of $10). Perhaps, however, people who display a very strong level of say–do correspondence do not require such artificial consequences to control their behavior; perhaps for them the mere act of promising to do something is by itself a sufficient form of commitment.

To what extent can self-promises serve as a strong form of commitment? Consider the following passage from a letter quoted by William James (1907) in his classic article, "The Energies of Men":

> My device [Prince Pueckler-Muskau writes to his wife] is this: I give my word of honour most solemnly to myself to do or to leave undone this or that. I am of course extremely cautious in the use of this expedient, but when once the word is given, even though I afterwards think I have been precipitate or mistaken, I hold it to be perfectly irrevocable, whatever inconveniences I foresee likely to result. If I were capable of breaking my word after such mature consideration, I should lose all respect for myself—and what man of sense would not prefer death to such an alternative? (p. 16)

The prince describes how, once he has vowed to perform or not perform an activity, he feels duty bound to carry out this vow. As a result, he is able to use this device to

(continued)

accomplish tasks that would otherwise be very difficult. He is also extremely careful in using this device, recognizing that its potency lies in the fact that he *always* keeps his word in such matters. In other words, a major consequence motivating adherence to his verbal commitments is that he always keeps these commitments, and to the extent that he does so they will remain a valuable tool (see also Ainslie, 1992). Note, too, how the prince pronounces these verbal commitments in a "most solemn" manner, thereby establishing a *bright boundary* between statements of intention that must be fulfilled ("I swear most solemnly that I shall complete this project by the weekend") and more ordinary statements of intention, which do not represent a commitment ("I should really try to complete this project by the weekend").

Another example of the power of verbal commitments can be found in the life of Mohandas K. (Mahatma) Gandhi, the famous statesman who led India to independence and whose philosophy of passive resistance strongly influenced Martin Luther King Jr. In his autobiography (1927/1957), Gandhi reveals that he made frequent use of verbal commitments to control his behavior and that the effectiveness of these commitments lay partly in the fact that breaking a commitment produced within him a tremendous feeling of guilt. At one point, for example, he was severely ill and was strongly urged by his doctors to drink milk (as a needed source of protein). As a committed vegetarian, he refused, maintaining that he would rather die than break his vow never to eat animal products. Only when his advisors pointed out to him that he had probably been thinking of cow's milk when he made his vow and not goat's milk did he acquiesce and drink goat's milk. He recovered from his illness

The great Indian statesman, Mahatma Gandhi, displayed a considerable degree of "say–do correspondence" during his illustrious life.

© Bettmann/CORBIS

but nevertheless felt considerable guilt over violating the spirit, if not the precise intention, of the vow he had made.

The strength of Gandhi's verbal commitments is also illustrated by the effect of his vow to remain sexually abstinent (despite being married). Before making the vow—and believing that it should be possible to practice abstinence without a vow—he had found the task extremely difficult. Making the vow, however, immediately resolved these difficulties. As he later wrote:

> As I look back on the twenty years of the vow, I am filled with pleasure and wonderment. The more or less successful practice of self-control had been going on since 1901. But the freedom and joy that came to me after taking the vow had never been experienced before 1906. Before the vow I had been open to being overcome by temptation at any moment. Now the vow was a sure shield against temptation. (Gandhi, 1927/1957, p. 208)

Gandhi's description indicates that the vow was such a strong form of commitment that it essentially eliminated the temptation to engage in sexual intercourse, thereby removing any sense of conflict.

You may remember how, in our discussion of self-control in Chapter 10, we questioned whether the concept of willpower was useful, noting that it was often no more than a descriptive term for the fact that a person had in fact been able to resist a temptation. But one way in which it might be useful is when it refers to an individual's ability to make use of a verbal commitment—derived in turn from a history of training in strong say–do correspondence—to exert control over his or her behavior. In this sense, some individuals may indeed have a considerable amount of willpower. Thus, as often happens when we examine traditional concepts from a behavioral perspective, the examination results not so much in a rejection of the concept but in a new and possibly useful way of understanding it.

Finally, are there lessons in this for those of us who wish that we could more often carry through on our own verbal commitments? Although we may not be capable of acquiring the same ability as Gandhi (nor perhaps would many of us even desire such an ability), most of us would probably agree that we are too often lacking in our level of say–do correspondence. In this regard, we might do well to close with yet another passage from William James (1890/1983), who wrote often on the concept of will (bracketed comments are ours):

> As a final practical maxim, relative to these habits of the will, we may, then, offer something like this: *Keep the faculty of effort alive in you by a little gratuitous effort every day.* That is, be systematically ascetic or heroic in little unnecessary points, do every day or two something for no other reason than that you would rather not do it [*and because you promised yourself you would do it*], so that when the hour of dire need draws nigh, it may find you not unnerved and untrained to stand the test. Asceticism of this sort is like the insurance which a man pays on his house and goods. The tax does him no good at the time, and possibly may never bring him a return. But if the fire *does* come, his having paid it will be his salvation from ruin. So with the man who has daily inured himself to habits of concentrated attention, energetic volition, and self-denial in unnecessary things. He will stand like a tower when everything rocks around him, and when his softer fellow-mortals are winnowed like chaff in the blast (p. 130; see also Barrett, 1931, and Assagioli, 1974; see Oaten and Cheng, 2006, for evidence concerning the extent to which repeated practice at self-control on one task can generalize to other tasks).

SUMMARY

In observational learning, an observer's behavior is altered as a result of socially interacting with or observing the behavior of a model. Two simple forms of observational influence are contagious behavior and stimulus enhancement. In the classical conditioning aspect of observational learning, the emotional cues exhibited by a model serve as CSs that elicit conditioned responses, called vicarious emotional responses, in an observer. The operant conditioning aspect of observational learning concerns the manner in which a model's operant behavior is translated into the behavior of an observer. First, the observer must acquire information from the model. Such acquisition depends on the consequences of the model's behavior, the personal characteristics of the model, whether the observer is capable of understanding and duplicating the modeled behavior, and whether the observer is explicitly reinforced for attending to the modeled behavior. Translating acquired knowledge into performance in turn depends on whether the observer's performance of the behavior is reinforced or punished.

Animals also learn by observation. However, unlike humans, many animal species appear to be unable to truly imitate the actions of another individual. Apparent examples of imitation can often be explained as examples of stimulus enhancement, which involves directing an animal's attention to a particular place or object, thereby making it more likely that the animal will approach that place or object. There is evidence, however, of true imitation in some species, and perhaps even intentional teaching.

Although much social learning is beneficial and positive, social learning of violent behavior is more controversial, especially in the context of exposure to violence through mass media and interactive games. Bandura (1965) initially warned of the power of social learning of violent behavior in his classic "Bobo doll studies." More recent correlational and experimental evidence suggests that exposure to media violence increases the likelihood that a person will behave violently, or perhaps become a victim of violence.

A rule is a verbal description of a contingency, and behavior that is generated as a result of such rules is known as rule-governed behavior. A rule that also includes information about how we should behave in a setting is an instruction. Rules are tremendously adaptive in that they allow us to learn about contingencies without having to directly experience those contingencies. Parents spend considerable effort training their children to follow rules, and children learn that following rules not only leads to praise but also facilitates accomplishing a task.

Nevertheless, rules have their drawbacks. First, rule-governed behavior is often less efficient than behavior that has been shaped by actual contingencies. Second, rule-governed behavior is sometimes surprisingly insensitive to contingencies. A personal rule (or self-instruction) is a description of a contingency that we verbalize to ourselves to influence our own behavior. The use of personal rules to regulate behavior is dependent on training in say–do correspondence, which occurs when there is a close match between what we say we are going to do and what we actually do at a later time. Personal rules tend to be most effective when they are stated in such a way that there is a clear distinction (a bright boundary) between when the rule has been followed and when it has not. In support of this, researchers have shown that specifying personal process rules (or implementation intentions) indicating the specific manner in which a project is to be carried out increases the likelihood that the project will be accomplished.

SUGGESTED READINGS

Bushman, B. J., & Anderson, C. A. (2001). *Media violence and the American public: Scientific facts versus media information. American Psychologist,* 56, 477–489. An interesting presentation of just how strong the evidence is for the harmful effects of media violence on viewers, and how this finding has remained hidden from the general public.

Malott, R. W., & Suarez, E. A. T. (2004). *Principles of behavior* (5th ed.). Upper Saddle River, NJ: Pearson. See Chapter 24, "A Theory of Rule-Governed Behavior", for a readable discussion of how behaviors that are directed toward delayed consequences, such as studying to obtain a good mark on an exam, is largely the result of instructional control. The authors theorize that, in such instances, the occurrence of guilt and anxiety for not following instructions—and the avoidance of guilt and anxiety by following instructions—may be the effective consequence that actually motivates the behavior.

STUDY QUESTIONS

1. Define observational learning, and give an example. Be sure to clearly differentiate the model from the observer.
2. Define contagious behavior and stimulus enhancement, and give an example of each.
3. Define vicarious emotional responses. Diagram the conditioning process by which a smile can become a conditioned stimulus for pleasant emotions.
4. Distinguish the roles of classical and operant conditioning in observational learning.
5. List three important features that determine whether an observer will attend to a model's behavior.
6. List three ways in which acquisition of information through observational learning translates into performance of the behavior.
7. Define true imitation. Describe evidence that some animals are capable of imitation.
8. Define stimulus enhancement. How does it differ from true imitation?
9. Use examples to illustrate the difference between stimulus enhancement and true imitation.
10. Describe Bandura's Bobo doll studies. What were the main conclusions from those studies?
11. Describe research which indicates that interaction with violent media increases the risk of violent behavior.
12. What are the sex differences associated with exposure to violent media and subsequent violent behavior?
13. Why has evidence about the relationship between violent media and violent behavior been underestimated or ignored?

14. Define the terms *rule and rule-governed behavior*. What is the distinction between a rule and an instruction?
15. Describe the main advantage of rule-governed behavior over contingency-shaped behavior. What are two disadvantages of rule-governed behavior?
16. What is a personal rule? What is say–do correspondence, and how is it related to the effectiveness of personal rules for controlling behavior?
17. What is a personal process rule (or implementation intention)? Why (in terms of bright boundaries) are personal process rules particularly effective?

CONCEPT REVIEW

contagious behavior. A more-or-less instinctive or reflexive behavior triggered by the occurrence of the same behavior in another individual.

generalized imitation. The tendency to imitate a new modeled behavior in the absence of any specific reinforcement for doing so.

observational learning. The process whereby the behavior of a model is witnessed by an observer, and the observer's behavior is subsequently changed.

personal process rule. A personal rule that indicates the specific process by which a task is to be accomplished. (Also referred to as an *implementation intention.*)

personal rule (or self-instruction). A verbal description of a contingency that we present to ourselves to influence our behavior.

rule. A verbal description of a contingency.

rule-governed behavior. Behavior that has been generated through exposure to rules.

say–do correspondence. A close match between what we say we are going to do and what we actually do at a later time.

stimulus enhancement. Directing attention to a particular place or object, making it more likely that the observer will approach that place or object.

true imitation. Duplicating a novel behavior (or sequence of behaviors) to achieve a specific goal.

vicarious emotional response. A classically conditioned emotional response resulting from seeing that emotional response exhibited by others.

CHAPTER TEST

11. Many animal species, when shown a sequence of actions designed to extract food from a locked box, (do / do not) _____ duplicate the sequence exactly. This suggests that few species exhibit true _____.

1. Improving your golf game by watching a video of an excellent golf player is a form of _____ learning.

25. At the start of each day, Victoria carefully plans out her studying for the day, writing down what she will study as well as when and where she will study. Although she is not always successful in fulfilling these plans, she usually accomplishes most of what she sets out to do. Her success is likely due to the fact that she is making use of personal _____ rules that establish a(n) _____ boundary between acceptable and unacceptable patterns of behavior.

6. If Claire observes her friend David laughing while enjoying a game of table tennis, she is (more/less) _____ likely to try the game herself. If Claire observes David frowning while he struggles over a math problem, she is (more/less) _____ likely to tackle the problem herself.

19. A rule that includes information about how we should respond is called a(n) _____.

26. "I should sit straight while working on the computer if I wish to prevent back problems." This is an example of a(n) _____ rule (or self-_____).

12. If a dog sees another dog eating at a particular location, it is more likely to visit that location later. This is an example of _____

5. The stimuli involved in the classical conditioning aspect of observational learning are often (emotional/rational) _____ in nature.

10. Tina tells herself each day that she will study, but she rarely succeeds in doing so. This illustrates a lack of _____ correspondence, which also means that, in general, she may have difficulty using _____ rules to control her behavior.

3. Smiling, yawning, laughing, and orienting when others do so are all examples of _____.

20. A big advantage of rules is that one (has to / does not have to) _____ directly experience a set of contingencies to behave appropriately with respect to those contingencies.

14. Bandura demonstrated that children who observed violent models were (more/less) _____ likely to behave violently themselves. Further, the behavior of the observers was so (similar/dissimilar) _____ to that of the models, it could be considered _____.

2. Observational learning can be involved in both _____ and _____ conditioning.

16. Longitudinal studies have demonstrated that exposure to violent media is _____ with violent behavior and criminality by observers.

22. Joel is very noncompliant. Chances are that he has received reinforcement for (following / not following) _____ instructions and / or punished for (following / not following) _____ instructions.

13. Directing a person's or animal's attention to an object or place is called _____; duplicating the actions of a model to obtain a goal is called _____.

4. Contagion of orienting responses is closely related to the process of s_____ e_____.

23. When Salima's mom became ill with a neurological disorder, Salima was assigned the task of giving her a daily massage to loosen up her tense muscles. By contrast, Byron has taken several massage workshops. Interestingly, Byron is much less skillful at massage than Salima, which may reflect the fact that _____ behavior is sometimes less efficient than behavior that has been shaped through direct exposure to natural _____.

17. Exposure to violent media may increase observers' violent behavior; it may also make some observers more likely to become _____ of violence. This is especially likely with (males/females) _____.

8. After training her daughter to imitate the manner in which she eats food with a knife and fork, Ashley noticed her daughter spontaneously imitating the manner in which Ashley uses a spoon to eat soup. This is an example of a process known as _____.

21. Children receive reinforcement for following instructions, both by their caretakers and by the fact that instructions can help them accomplish a task. As a result, most children acquire a (generalized/specific) _____ tendency to follow instructions.

9. If a juvenile rat watches its mother eat a novel food, like chocolate chips, the young rat is (more / less / neither more nor less) _____ likely to try the chocolate chips.

18. A(n) _____ can be defined as a verbal description of a contingency, while _____ behavior is the behavior that is generated by such verbal descriptions.

15. Bandura determined that children were affected both by live violence and _____ violence. Thus, Bandura was the first to demonstrate the potential influence of the mass m_____ on violent behavior.

24. Kent read somewhere that women are very attracted to a man who acts strong and dominant. Despite his efforts to appear strong and dominant, he is eventually dumped by every woman he meets. He nevertheless assumes that there must be something wrong with these women and persists in cultivating his heroic image. Kent's problem may reflect the fact that _____ behavior is sometimes surprisingly insensitive to the actual contingencies of reinforcement.

7. If a model receives reinforcement for performing a behavior, an observer is (more/less) _____ likely to perform the same behavior; if a model receives punishment for performing a behavior, an observer is (more/less) _____ likely to perform the same behavior.

Visit the book companion Web site at http://www.academic.cengage. com/psychology/powell for additional practice questions, answers to the Quick Quizzes, practice review exams, and additional exercises and information.

ANSWERS TO CHAPTER TEST

1. observational
2. classical; operant
3. contagious behaviors
4. stimulus enhancement
5. emotional
6. more; less
7. more; less
8. generalized imitation
9. more
10. say–do; personal
11. do not; imitation
12. stimulus enhancement
13. stimulus enhancement; true imitation
14. more; similar; true imitation
15. filmed; media
16. strongly (positively) correlated
17. victims; females
18. rule; rule-governed
19. instruction
20. does not have to
21. generalized
22. not following; following
23. rule-governed; contingencies
24. rule-governed
25. process; bright
26. personal; instruction

Biological Dispositions in Learning

Ken was worried about his girlfriend, Chantal, who had lost a lot of weight in recent months. As one of his friends noted, she was starting to look like a "hockey stick with hair." Nevertheless, Chantal maintained that she was still overweight and needed to lose a few more pounds. Ken had heard that anorexia is characterized by a distorted body image, in which people deny how thin they are. He wondered if Chantal was suffering from this type of denial. He had also heard that anorexia often results from growing up in an overcontrolling family—though on the surface, it seemed like her family was pretty nice.

Other than his concerns about her weight, Ken thought Chantal was terrific. He particularly loved the fact that she shared his enthusiasm for long-distance running. In fact, she was more addicted to running than he was.

By this time, you probably realize that the basic principles of conditioning have a surprising degree of generality and apply to a wide range of species and behaviors. But you may also recall how, at certain points in this text, we have noted some limitations in this regard. For example, people more readily learn to be afraid of events that have some type of evolutionary association with danger, such as encountering snakes and spiders, than they do of modern-day events, such as encounters with cars and electrical outlets. It is possible then that we have inherited a biological tendency to learn certain types of fears more readily than others. This innate tendency for an organism to more easily learn certain types of behaviors or to associate certain types of events with each other is known as *preparedness*. In this chapter, we further explore the role of biological preparedness in conditioning, as well as the manner in which such preparedness seems to produce an overlap between processes of classical conditioning and operant conditioning.

Preparedness and Conditioning

Preparedness in Classical Conditioning

Fear conditioning is one form of classical conditioning in which preparedness seems to play an important role. Another is *taste aversion conditioning*, a form of classical conditioning in which a food item that has been paired with gastrointestinal illness becomes a conditioned aversive stimulus. Simply put, an animal that becomes sick after ingesting a food item associates the food with the illness and subsequently finds it distasteful.

Conditioned taste aversions are quite common. In one survey of undergraduate students, 65% reported developing a taste aversion at some point in their lives (Logue, Ophir, & Strauss, 1981). Interestingly, and perhaps not surprisingly, many of these aversions involved an alcoholic drink of some sort. Most taste aversions are quite rational because the person believes that the food item was actually the cause of the illness. In some cases, however, the person knows that the food did not cause the illness and that the illness was instead caused by some other factor (such as the flu) with which the food was only coincidentally associated. Nevertheless, the person still finds the food item highly aversive—a convincing testament to the strength of this type of conditioning.

In a typical experiment on taste aversion conditioning, rats are first given some type of preferred food or drink to ingest, such as sweet-tasting (saccharin-flavored) water. The animal is then made to feel sick, either by injecting a nausea-inducing drug directly into the gut or through exposure to X-ray irradiation. After the rat recovers, it is given a choice of either sweet water or normal water. Although a rat typically prefers sweet water over normal water, it now strongly prefers the normal water. This indicates that the sweet water has become an aversive conditioned stimulus (CS) through its association with illness. This procedure can be diagrammed as follows:

Sweet water: X-ray irradiation → *Nausea*
     NS   **US**   **UR**
Sweet water → *Nausea* (as indicated by avoidance of the sweet water)
   CS   **CR**

Taste aversion conditioning involves many of the same processes found in other forms of classical conditioning (Schafe & Bernstein, 1996). For example, *stimulus generalization* often occurs when food items that taste similar to the aversive item are also perceived as aversive. Thus, a conditioned aversion to one type of fish might generalize to other types of fish. A conditioned taste aversion can also be *extinguished* if the aversive food item is repeatedly ingested without further illness. As well, *overshadowing* can occur in that we are more likely to develop an aversion to a stronger-tasting food item, such as onions, than to a milder-tasting item, such as potatoes, that was consumed at the same meal. And the presence of a food item that already has aversive associations can *block* the development of aversive associations to other food items. If you have already acquired a taste aversion to peas, but force yourself to eat them anyway, and then get sick because of some spoiled fish that was served at the same meal, you will probably *not* develop an aversion to the fish. The presence of the peas (already a CS for nausea) will likely block any conditioning occurring to the fish.

Of particular importance in taste aversion conditioning is the phenomenon of *latent inhibition*. We are more likely to associate a relatively novel item, such as an unusual liqueur, with sickness than we would a more familiar item such as beer (Kalat, 1974). Latent inhibition helps explain why it is often difficult to poison a rat. When a rat encounters a novel food item, such as rat bait, it will most likely eat only a small amount of the item before moving on to other, more familiar items. If the rat later becomes ill, it will associate the illness with the novel item rather than with any of the familiar items. The rat also has a high probability of recovering from the illness because it will have eaten only a small amount of the poisoned item.[1]

1. The term p_____ refers to an innate tendency for an organism to more easily learn certain types of behaviors or to associate certain types of events with each other.

2. Taste aversion conditioning is a type of _____ conditioning in which a food item that has been paired with gastrointestinal illness becomes a c_____ av_____ stimulus.

3. After recovering from a bad case of the flu, Robbie could not bring himself to eat oatmeal, which he had tried to eat during his illness. In all likelihood, Robbie has developed a t_____ a_____ to the oatmeal.

4. Robbie now dislikes other types of porridge as well, which appears to be an example of s_____ g_____.

5. Robbie's aversion to porridge would likely be e_____ if he repeatedly ate it without experiencing any further illness.

6. According to the o_____ effect, the strongest-tasting item in a meal is most likely to become associated with a subsequent illness. As well, a food item that was previously associated with illness will b_____ the development of aversive associations to other items in a meal.

7. In keeping with the process of l_____ i_____, Robbie would have been less likely to develop a taste aversion to oatmeal porridge if he had frequently eaten oatmeal before his illness.

Although taste aversion conditioning is in many ways similar to other forms of classical conditioning, there are also some major differences.

1. **The Formation of Associations Over Long Delays.** In most classical conditioning procedures, the neutral stimulus (NS) and unconditioned stimulus (US) must occur in close temporal proximity, separated by no more than a few seconds. By contrast, taste aversions can develop when food items are consumed several hours before the sickness develops. For example, Etscorn and Stephens (1973) found that rats could develop taste aversions to flavored water that had been ingested up to 24 hours before they were injected with an illness-inducing drug. The ability to associate food with illness after lengthy periods of time is highly adaptive in that poisonous substances often have a delayed effect. If animals

---

[1]This tendency to be wary of new food items, which is also present in humans and is especially strong in children, is known as *dietary neophobia* (a *neophobia* is a fear of something new). Neophobia is particularly important for rats, which are physically incapable of vomiting in order to purge toxins from the stomach. More generally, neophobia is an especially adaptive tendency for small animals and the young of most species because the dose–response relationships for many toxins are body-weight dependent. Simply put, small animals are more susceptible to food poisoning than large animals and have therefore evolved to be especially wary of food poisoning.

were unable to form such delayed associations, they would be at great risk of repeatedly consuming a poisonous food item and eventually perishing.

2. **One-Trial Conditioning.** Strong conditioned taste aversions can usually be achieved with only a single pairing of food with illness, particularly when the food item is novel (Riley & Clarke, 1977). One-trial conditioning sometimes occurs in other forms of conditioning, especially fear conditioning, but not as consistently as it does in taste aversion conditioning. As with the ability to form associations over long delays, one-trial conditioning of taste aversions is highly adaptive insofar as it minimizes the possibility of a repeat, possibly fatal, experience with a poisonous substance.

3. **Specificity of Associations.** When you feel nauseous following a meal, do you associate the nausea with that episode of *American Idol* you are watching (even though, given the quality of some of the singing, that might seem appropriate), or with the meal? Fortunately for the broadcast networks, you are more likely to associate the nausea with the meal. Similarly, the rat that receives an injection of a nausea-inducing drug several hours after drinking a sweet water solution does not associate the illness with the injection; it instead associates the illness with the sweet water. In other words, there seems to be a strong, inherited tendency to associate a gastrointestinal illness with food or drink rather than with any other kind of item (Garcia & Koelling, 1966). This type of preparedness is sometimes referred to as *CS-US relevance*, an innate tendency to more readily associate certain types of stimuli with each other.

An excellent example of the role of CS-US relevance in taste aversion conditioning was provided by Garcia and Koelling (1966) in their initial demonstration of this type of conditioning. In this experiment, the rats initially drank sweet water that was paired with a light and a noise (each time they licked the water tube, they heard a click and saw a light flash). This compound stimulus can therefore be described as "bright, noisy, sweet water." After consuming the water, some of the rats received a slight foot shock that elicited a fear reaction, while other rats received a dose of X-ray irradiation that made them nauseous. Finally, all of the rats were given a choice between two water bottles, one containing only "bright, noisy" water (i.e., regular water associated with the light and click) and the other containing only sweet water. Can you guess the results?

The rats that had been made nauseous by the X-ray irradiation avoided the sweet water and drank the bright, noisy water, which is consistent with the basic notion that nausea is more readily associated with taste than with other kinds of stimuli.

Conditioning trial:
Bright, noisy, sweet water: X-ray irradiation → *Nausea*
         NS   **US**   **UR**

Test trials:
Sweet water → *Nausea*
     CS   **CR**
Bright, noisy water → No nausea
     NS   —

But what about the rats that received a foot shock? It turns out that they avoided the bright, noisy water but not the sweet water. In other words, they developed a fear of the noise and lights associated with the water, but not the taste, and were quite willing to drink the sweet water.

Conditioning trial:
Bright, noisy, sweet water: Foot shock → *Fear*
           NS   **US**   **UR**

Test trials:
Bright, noisy water → *Fear*
     CS   **CR**
Sweet water → No fear
     NS   —

Thus, not only do rats have a predisposition to readily associate nausea with taste, they also have a predisposition to associate tactually painful events with visual and auditory stimuli. This makes sense from an evolutionary perspective in that tactile pain is more likely to result from something "out there" that a rat can see and hear, whereas nausea is more likely to result from something a rat ingests and can be tasted. Thus, for a rat to evolve in such a way that it could readily make such associations would facilitate its survival.

Further evidence for the role of biological dispositions in taste aversion conditioning has been revealed by comparative research on inter-species differences in the types of stimuli that can be associated. In one experiment, both quail and rats drank dark blue, sour-tasting water before being made ill (Wilcoxon, Dragoin, & Kral, 1971). The animals were then given a choice between dark blue water and sour-tasting water. As expected, the rats naturally avoided the sour-tasting water and strongly preferred the dark blue water. They associated the taste of the water with the nausea. The quail, however, were more likely to avoid the dark blue water than the sour-tasting water. This suggests that quail, which are daytime feeders and rely heavily on vision for identifying food, are more disposed to associate the visual aspects (rather than the taste aspects) of food with nausea. Rats, however, being nighttime feeders, rely more heavily on taste (and smell) than vision and are therefore generally disposed to associate the taste (and smell) aspects of food with nausea. (This is not to say that rats cannot learn to associate the visual aspects of food with nausea. They can, but additional conditioning trials are required to form such associations.)

In addition to between-species differences, there are often sex differences in taste aversion learning, which can be related to differences in sensory and perceptual processing. In humans, females are better than males at detecting odors and discriminating among odors. Because of this ability, women are more reactive to odors associated with the experience of nausea and are more prone to developing taste aversions (Chambers et al., 1997). As well, most women report that their sense of smell and taste is enhanced during the early stages of pregnancy, which often leads to the development of taste aversions (Nordin, Broman, Olafsson, & Wulff, 2004). Although experiencing these kinds of symptoms during early pregnancy might seem counterproductive, it is actually a highly adaptive mechanism. Fetal organ systems are developing during the first few months of pregnancy and are highly vulnerable to damage by toxins at this stage. A dislike of certain foods (especially bitter foods) and a propensity to taste aversions might prevent a woman from ingesting foods that contain dangerous bacteria (bitterness can indicate the presence of bacteria).

It should be noted that research on taste aversion conditioning has some practical applications. For example, cancer patients sometimes develop aversions to food items that have been inadvertently associated with the nausea resulting from chemotherapy (Bernstein, 1991). Because cancer patients often suffer from severe weight loss anyway, the development of taste aversions that lead to avoidance of certain food items could be serious. Fortunately, research has suggested ways to minimize this problem. One way is to serve meals that consist of highly familiar foods. In keeping with the latent inhibition effect, such familiar foods will be less likely to become associated with nausea. Along the same lines, the patient can be served a highly novel, yet trivial, food item just before a chemotherapy session. This novel item will then be associated with the nausea, preventing the development of taste aversions to other, more essential food items. For example, in one study, children about to undergo chemotherapy were given coconut- or root-beer-flavored candies following a regular meal. Compared to children who had not been given these candies, the children in the study later developed fewer aversions to their regular food items (Broberg & Bernstein, 1987).

Taste aversion conditioning also has implications for wildlife management. For example, if coyotes are given ground mutton (wrapped in sheep skin) that has been laced with a nausea-inducing chemical, they will subsequently refuse to attack sheep (Gustavson, Garcia, Hankin, & Rusiniak, 1974). Insofar as attacks upon livestock are not only costly to ranchers, but also a major impediment in efforts to protect certain predators from extinction, taste aversion conditioning would seem to be a potential solution to the problem. For example, if you seed an area with nausea-inducing packets of mutton or beef, you might soon have a pack of wolves that avoid livestock like the plague. Unfortunately, early field tests by wildlife officials in the United States were largely unsuccessful—the predators continued to prey upon livestock—as a result of which interest in the procedure soon dwindled. Some researchers, however, claim that the conditioning procedures used in these early tests were badly confounded, with cues being left on the meat packets that allowed the predators to discriminate "treated" meat from untreated meat. As a result, the predators learned to avoid the treated meat packets but continued to hunt livestock. However, renewed efforts are now underway to once again implement such programs, but this time with a greater focus on proper controls (Dingfelder, 2010). (See also "Predation Politics: The Sad Story of Wolves, Conditioned Taste Aversion, and the Wildlife Management Hierarchy" at http://www.conditionedtasteaversion. net/, for one researcher's perspective on the extent to which taste aversion conditioning has been neglected in wildlife management.)

1. Distinctive features of taste aversion conditioning, compared to other types of classical conditioning, include the fact that the associations can be formed over (short/long) _____ delays, typically require (one/several) _____ pairing(s) of the NS and US, and (are / are not) _____ specific to certain types of stimuli.

2. In the classic experiment by Garcia and Koelling, the rats that had been made ill avoided the (sweet/bright, noisy) _____ water, while the rats that had been shocked avoided the _____ water.

3. In the experiment on taste aversions in quail and rats, the rats avoided the (blue/sour) _____ water, while the quail avoided the _____ water.

4. To counter the possibility that chemotherapy-induced nausea will result in the development of taste aversions, patients should be fed meals that consist mostly of highly (familiar/unfamiliar) _____ foods. As well, just before the chemotherapy session, they can be given some trivial type of (familiar/unfamiliar) _____ food item, which will attract most of the aversive associations.

5. According to the concept of _____ _____, certain types of stimuli are more easily associated with each other.

Preparedness in Operant Conditioning

Biological preparedness also seems to play a role in some forms of operant conditioning. For example, Stevenson-Hinde (1973) found that the sound of recorded chaffinch songs (chaffinches are a type of bird) was an effective reinforcer for training chaffinches to perch in a certain spot, but not for training them to key-peck. Conversely, food was an effective reinforcer for training them to key-peck but not for training them to perch in a certain spot. Chaffinches seem to be biologically prepared to associate perching in a certain spot with the consequence of hearing songs, and to associate pecking with the consequence of obtaining food.

In a similar manner, rats will more readily learn to press a lever to obtain food pellets than to avoid shock (Bolles, 1970). But they readily learn to freeze or run to avoid shock. Once more, the explanation for these differences may reside in the animals' evolutionary history. Rats have evolved dexterous forepaws that are often used for eating; thus, pressing a lever for food is not far removed from the type of food-gathering behavior they display in the natural environment. However, avoiding painful events is, for a rat, more

And Furthermore

Conditioned Food Preferences

Just as conditioning processes sometimes make foods aversive, such processes can also make foods more appetitive. For example, a powerful way to increase our preference for a disliked food is to mix it with some food item or sweetener that we strongly prefer. This may be how some people grow to like black coffee: They first drink it with cream and sugar and then gradually eliminate the extra ingredients as the taste of the coffee itself becomes pleasurable. Similarly, in one study, college students developed increased preference for broccoli or cauliflower after eating it a few times with sugar (E. D. Capaldi, 1996). Unfortunately, few parents use such a method to improve their children's eating habits, possibly because they perceive sugar to be unhealthy and do not realize that the sugar can later be withdrawn (Casey & Rozin, 1989). Instead, parents often try to entice their children to eat a disliked food by offering dessert as a reward—a strategy that easily backfires in that the contrast between the disliked food and the subsequent dessert might result in the former becoming even more disliked. (See E. D. Capaldi, 1996, for other ways in which food preferences can be conditioned.)

naturally related to the response of freezing or running than it is to manipulating objects with its forepaws.

Biological dispositions for certain types of avoidance responses have also been found in pigeons. Bedford and Anger (cited in Bolles, 1979) found that pigeons will quickly learn to fly from one perch to another to avoid shock, but they will not learn to peck a response key to avoid shock. As with rats, the typical behavior pigeons use when fleeing danger provides an explanation: Flying is the usual way a pigeon escapes danger, while pecking is not. Thus pigeons, like rats, seem predisposed to learn certain types of avoidance responses more readily than others.

It may have occurred to you from the preceding examples that preparedness seems to play a particularly strong role in avoidance behavior. This observation has led Bolles (1970, 1979) to propose that some avoidance responses are actually not operants (in the sense of being controlled by their consequences) but are instead elicited behaviors (that are controlled by the stimuli that precede them). More specifically, he contends that aversive stimulation elicits a *species-specific defense reaction* (SSDR), which in the natural environment is often effective in countering danger. For this reason, a rat easily learns to run or freeze to avoid painful stimulation, simply because running and freezing are behaviors that are naturally *elicited* in dangerous situations. Indeed, a rat's tendency to freeze is so strong that it will sometimes freeze even when doing so results in a shock rather than avoid it. (Humans also have a tendency to freeze when feeling threatened, even when it is counterproductive to do so—as when giving a speech to a large audience or when being ordered about by a gunman.)

1. Chaffinches easily learn to associate (perching/pecking) _____ with the consequence of hearing a song and _____ with the consequence of obtaining food.

2. Rats are biologically prepared to learn to avoid a painful stimulus by (lever pressing / running) _____, while pigeons are biologically prepared to learn to avoid a painful stimulus by (pecking/flying) _____.

3. According to Bolles, these types of avoidance responses are s_____ -s_____ defense reactions that are naturally e_____ by the aversive stimulus.

Operant–Respondent Interactions

Bolles's concept of the SSDR is one example of how it is sometimes difficult to distinguish between operant behaviors and respondent (or elicited) behaviors. In this section, we discuss two further examples of the overlap between operants and respondents: instinctive drift and sign tracking.

Instinctive Drift

It was once assumed that an animal could be trained to perform just about any behavior it was physically capable of performing. Indeed, considering the remarkable array of behaviors that animals can be trained to display, this assumption does not seem all that unreasonable. There are, however, limits to such training, as two of Skinner's students discovered in the course of training animals for show business.

Marian and Keller Breland were former students of Skinner's who decided to put their knowledge of operant conditioning to commercial use. They established a business of training animals to perform unusual behaviors for television commercials and movies. In this endeavor, they were usually quite successful. Occasionally, however, they encountered some rather interesting limitations in what certain animals could be taught (Breland & Breland, 1961). For example, they once attempted to train a pig to deposit a wooden coin in a piggy bank. Using processes of shaping and chaining, the training initially proceeded quite smoothly. As time passed, however, a strange thing began to happen. The pig no longer simply deposited the coin in the bank, but started tossing the coin in the air and then rooting at it on the ground. Eventually, the tossing and rooting became so frequent that the coin never made its way to the bank. The Brelands also attempted to use a raccoon for this trick, but here too they ran into difficulties. As training progressed, the raccoon began rubbing the coin back and forth in its paws rather than dropping it into the bank. This stereotyped action sequence eventually became so dominant that this attempt too had to be abandoned.

Although these results were originally regarded as a strange anomaly and a serious blow to the generality of operant conditioning, it is now recognized that they merely represented situations in which a classically conditioned, fixed action pattern had gradually emerged to interfere with the operant behavior that was being shaped. With both the pig and the raccoon, the coin had become so strongly associated with food that it began to elicit species-specific behavior patterns associated with feeding. In the case of the pig, this meant that the coin was subjected to the type of rooting behavior pigs often display when feeding. In the case of the raccoon, the coin was repeatedly rubbed and washed in the way raccoons normally rub and wash their food (often shellfish). In both cases, the coin had become a CS that elicited a conditioned response (CR) in the form of a food-related, fixed action pattern.

Thus, in the case of the pig, the Brelands intended this:

$$\underset{S^D}{\text{Coin:}} \quad \underset{R}{\textbf{\textit{Deposit coin in bank}}} \rightarrow \underset{S^R}{\textbf{Food}}$$

which is an operant conditioning procedure. Initially, this worked quite well, but as the coin became more and more strongly associated with food, what happened instead was this:

$$\underset{NS}{\text{Coin:}} \quad \underset{US}{\textbf{Food}} \rightarrow \underset{UR}{\textbf{\textit{Rooting}}}$$

$$\underset{CS}{\textbf{Coin}} \rightarrow \underset{CR}{\textbf{\textit{Rooting}}}$$

Which is a classical conditioning procedure. And as the classically conditioned response increased in strength, it eventually overrode the operantly conditioned response of depositing the coin in the bank. Thus, **_instinctive drift_** is an instance of classical conditioning in which a genetically based, fixed action pattern gradually emerges and displaces the behavior that is being operantly conditioned.

QUICK QUIZ D

1. In the phenomenon known as i_____ d_____, a genetically based f_____ a_____ pattern gradually emerges and displaces the behavior being shaped.

2. In the experiment with the raccoon, the coin became a (CS/S^D) _____ that elicited a (R/CR/UR) _____ of washing and rubbing.

Sign Tracking

Pavlov once reported that one of his dogs, during a classical conditioning experiment, approached a light that had signaled the delivery of food and licked it (Pavlov, 1941). It seemed as though the light not only signaled food, but had acquired some of its appetitive properties. Little attention was paid to this finding, however, until recently. This phenomenon is now known as sign tracking.

In *sign tracking*, an organism approaches a stimulus that signals the presentation of an appetitive event (Tomie, Brooks, & Zito, 1989). The approach behavior seems very much like an operant behavior because it appears to be quite goal directed, yet the procedure that produces it is more closely akin to classical conditioning. Thus, sign tracking is yet another way in which classical and operant conditioning appear to overlap.

Take, for example, a hungry dog that has been trained to sit on a mat to receive food presented in a dish at the far side of the room. Suppose, too, that a light is presented just before the food, such that this light becomes a cue for food delivery (see Figure 12.1). A couple of things are liable to happen because of this arrangement. One is that the dog will probably start salivating whenever the light is presented. Through classical conditioning, the light will have become a CS for the conditioned response of salivation. But that is not all that will happen. Logically, when the light appears (which is a signal for food delivery), the dog should immediately walk over to the food dish and wait for the food. What happens instead is that the dog *walks over to the light* and starts displaying food-related behaviors toward it, such as licking it or even barking at it as though soliciting food from it. These behaviors are of course entirely unnecessary and have no effect on whether the food will appear. It seems as though the light has become so strongly associated with food that it is now a CS that elicits innate food-related behavior patterns (see Jenkins, Barrera, Ireland, & Woodside, 1978, for a description of a similar experiment).

FIGURE 12.1 Experimental setting for a sign-tracking experiment. The dog first learns to sit on the mat to receive food. A light is then presented before each food delivery.

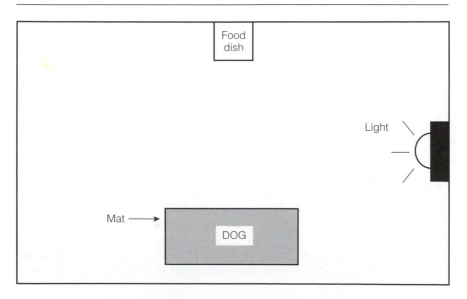

Sign tracking has also been found in pigeons, and in fact it helps to account for the ease with which pigeons learn to peck a response key for food. Brown and Jenkins (1968) presented pigeons with a key light for 8 seconds followed by the *noncontingent* delivery of food. Although the pigeons did not have to peck the key to obtain the food, they soon began doing so anyway. It was as though the pigeons automatically pecked the key, simply because it was associated with food. The pecking therefore seemed to be an elicited response, with the key light functioning as a CS through its association with food:

Key light: Food → *Peck*
  NS   US   UR
Key light: → *Peck*
  CS   CR

This procedure is known as ***autoshaping***, a type of sign tracking in which a pigeon comes to automatically peck at a key because the key light has been associated with the response-independent delivery of food. Rather than trying to deliberately shape the behavior of key pecking, the researcher merely has to put the pigeon in the chamber, program the equipment to present light and food in the appropriate order, and presto, within an hour or so, out pops a key-pecking pigeon. Once the pecking response has been established this way, the food can then be made *contingent* upon pecking (i.e., food appears only when the key has been pecked), at which point the pecking begins functioning as an operant:

Key light: *Peck* → **Food**
  S^D R S^R

Thus, a behavior that starts off as an elicited behavior (controlled by the stimulus that precedes it) becomes transformed into an operant behavior (controlled by its consequence). In other words, the pigeon initially pecks the key because the key light predicts the free delivery of food; later, it pecks the key because it has to do so to obtain food.

Autoshaping is one type of classical conditioning that fits well with Pavlov's stimulus-substitution theory (discussed in Chapter 5). Because of its association with food, the key light appears to become a substitute for food, with the bird attempting to consume it. Further evidence for this stimulus-substitution interpretation comes from an experiment that compared autoshaped key pecks toward a key light signaling water delivery versus a key light signaling food delivery (Jenkins & Moore, 1973). When the bird pecked a key associated with water, it did so with its eyes open and its beak almost closed—the standard pattern of behavior when pigeons drink water. But when the bird pecked a key associated with food delivery, it did so with its eyes closed and its beak open, which is the standard pattern of behavior when a pigeon pecks at food. (The eyes are closed possibly because, in the natural environment, pecking at food sometimes results in

ADVICE FOR THE LOVELORN

Dear Dr. Dee,

My old girlfriend, to whom I was very attached, recently moved away. I am now trying to get over her, but I still find myself going to our favorite restaurant, our favorite beach, and so on. Why do I torture myself like this?

What a Birdbrain

Dear Birdbrain,

Think of your behavior as similar to sign tracking. Your girlfriend was a powerful appetitive stimulus, with the result that you now approach stimuli that have been strongly associated with her. In fact (and somewhat in keeping with your signature), researchers have found similar behavior patterns in Japanese quail. Burns and Domjan (1996) found that if they lowered a block of wood into a chamber just before opening a door that allowed access to a female quail, male quail had a strong tendency to approach and stand near the block of wood rather than near the door. The block of wood had become a CS that elicited what was essentially a sexual sign-tracking response. In similar fashion, we may have a tendency to approach settings that are strongly associated with a person with whom we have had an intimate relationship. In any event, your "birdbrained" tendency to approach these settings should eventually extinguish.

Behaviorally yours,

Dr. Dee

dust or pebbles being thrown upward.) In other words, it seemed as though the bird was attempting to drink the key that was associated with water and eat the key that was associated with food.

Autoshaping procedures have powerful effects on behavior. For example, pigeons will peck a key associated with food even when doing so *prevents* the delivery of food (Williams & Williams, 1969). In other words, although the contingency requires the pigeons to refrain from pecking to actually obtain the food (they should simply wait for the food when the key light appears), they will nevertheless compulsively peck at the key. The key light exerts such strong control over the behavior that it essentially overrides the negative punishment (loss of food) associated with pecking. This phenomenon, in which sign tracking persists despite the resultant loss of a reinforcer, is known as *negative automaintenance*.

1. In s_____ t_____, an organism approaches a stimulus that signals the availability of food. In such circumstances, the stimulus is best defined as a (n) (CS/US/S^D) _____, while the approach behavior is best defined as a(n) (CR/UR/operant) _____.

2. In au_____, a pigeon will begin to peck a lit response key that is presented for 8 seconds before the non _____ delivery of food. The peck in this situation appears to be functioning as a(n) (elicited/operant) _____ behavior. Later, when a peck is required for the food to be delivered, the peck becomes a(n)_____.

3. In n_____ aut_____, pigeons will peck a lit response key that signals food delivery even when the act of pecking (prevents/facilitates) _____ the delivery of food.

Adjunctive Behavior

Instinctive drift and sign tracking represent two types of anomalous (unexpected) behavior patterns that can develop during an operant conditioning procedure. Yet another type of anomaly is adjunctive behavior. *Adjunctive behavior* is an excessive pattern of behavior that emerges as a by-product of an intermittent schedule of reinforcement for some other behavior. In other words, as one behavior is being strengthened through intermittent reinforcement, another quite different behavior emerges as a side effect of that procedure. Adjunctive behavior is sometimes referred to as *schedule-induced behavior*, and the two terms will be used interchangeably in this discussion.

Basic Procedure and Defining Characteristics

Falk (1961) was the first person to systematically investigate adjunctive behavior in animals. He found that when rats were trained to press a lever for food on an intermittent schedule of reinforcement, they also began drinking excessive amounts of water. During a 3-hour session, the rats drank almost three-and-a-half times the amount they would normally drink in an entire day. (To get a handle on this, imagine that a person who typically drinks 8 glasses of water a day instead drinks 28 glasses of water in a 3-hour period!) In fact, some of the rats drank up to half their body weight in water. These numbers are all the more remarkable because the rats were food deprived, not water deprived; and food deprivation typically produces a decrease, not an increase, in water intake. This pattern of excessive drinking—called *schedule-induced polydipsia* (polydipsia means "excessive thirst")—developed quite rapidly, usually beginning in the first session and becoming firmly established by the second session.

Studies of adjunctive behavior typically employ fixed interval (FI) or fixed time (FT) schedules of reinforcement (Falk, 1971). On such schedules, the delivery of each reinforcer is followed by a period of time during which another reinforcer is not available. It is during such *interreinforcement intervals* that adjunctive behavior occurs. For example, when schedule-induced polydipsia is generated by exposure to an FI schedule of food reinforcement, the rat usually drinks during the postreinforcement pause that is typical of such schedules. Thus, a short period of time during which there is a low probability or zero probability of reinforcement seems to be a critical factor in the development of adjunctive behavior.

Researchers soon discovered that schedule-induced polydipsia could be generated in other species, including mice, pigeons, and chimpanzees. They also discovered that it was possible to generate other types of adjunctive behaviors, such as chewing on wood shavings, licking at an air stream (presumably because of the sensory stimulation it provides), and aggression. In the latter case, it was found that pigeons exposed to an FI or FT schedule of food delivery soon began attacking a nearby target pigeon—or, more commonly, a picture or stuffed model of a pigeon—following each reinforcer (e.g., Flory & Ellis, 1973). Unlike extinction-induced aggression, which often grows weaker over time, this type of schedule-induced aggression tends to remain strong and persistent. (See Falk, 1971, 1977, and Staddon, 1977, for overviews of the findings on adjunctive behavior.)

Researchers also found that adjunctive behavior could be generated using reinforcers other than food delivery. For example, rats were found to eat excessive amounts of food (that is, they engaged in schedule-induced eating) when exposed to an intermittent schedule of electrical stimulation to the pleasure centers in the brain (J. F. Wilson & Cantor, 1987). Thus, rather than using food as a reinforcer to produce some other type of adjunctive behavior, these researchers used electrical stimulation of the pleasure centers as a reinforcer to produce an adjunctive pattern of eating. Interestingly, these rats gained considerable weight due to their compulsive tendency to snack between reinforcers, suggesting that schedule-induced eating may play a role in the development of obesity.

1. Adjunctive behavior is an excessive pattern of behavior that emerges as a_____ of an _____ schedule of reinforcement for (that behavior / a different behavior) _____.

2. Adjunctive behavior is also referred to as s_____-_____ behavior.

3. An excessive pattern of drinking that is produced by exposure to an intermittent schedule of food reinforcement is called s_____-_____ p_____.

4. Studies of adjunctive behavior typically use (fixed interval / variable interval) _____ or (fixed time / variable time) _____ schedules of food reinforcement. This is because adjunctive behavior tends to occur when there is a (high/low) _____ probability of reinforcement.

QUICK QUIZ F

According to Falk (1971, 1977), adjunctive behavior has several distinguishing features. These include the following:

1. As previously noted, *adjunctive behavior typically occurs in the period immediately following consumption of an intermittent reinforcer*. For example, in schedule-induced polydipsia, the rat will quickly eat each food pellet as soon as it is delivered and then immediately move over to the drinking tube for a quick bout of drinking. The start of the interval between food pellets, therefore, tends to be dominated by drinking. The end of the interval, however, as the next pellet becomes imminent, tends to be dominated by food-related behaviors, such as lever pressing for the food (Staddon, 1977).

2. *Adjunctive behavior is affected by the level of deprivation for the scheduled reinforcer. The greater the level of deprivation for the reinforcer, the stronger the adjunctive behavior that emerges as a by-product.* For example, with schedule-induced polydipsia, greater food deprivation not only produces a higher rate of lever pressing for food pellets, it also produces a higher rate of drinking between food pellets.

3. *Adjunctive behaviors can function as reinforcers for other behaviors.* This is in keeping with the Premack principle, which holds that high-probability behaviors can often serve as effective reinforcers for low-probability behaviors. Thus, with schedule-induced polydipsia, the rat will not only press a lever to obtain access to food pellets but, during the interval between food pellets, it will also press a lever to gain access to water so that it can engage in adjunctive drinking.

4. *There is an optimal interval between reinforcers for the development of adjunctive behavior.* For example, rats will engage in little drinking with an inter-reinforcement interval of 5 seconds between food pellets, progressively more drinking as the interval is lengthened to 180 seconds, and then progressively less drinking as the interval is lengthened beyond that. At an interreinforcement interval of 300 seconds, one again finds little drinking. The optimal interreinforcement intervals for other types of adjunctive behaviors tend to be similar, often in the range of 1 to 3 minutes.

QUICK QUIZ G

1. Adjunctive behavior tends to occur (just before / just after) _____ delivery of a reinforcer.

2. As the deprivation level for the scheduled reinforcer increases, the strength of the adjunctive behavior associated with it tends to (increase/decrease) _____.

3. The opportunity to engage in an adjunctive behavior can serve as a (reinforcer/ punisher) _____ for some other behavior. This is in keeping with the P_____ principle.

4. The optimal interreinforcement interval for the production of adjunctive behavior is often in the range of (a few seconds / a few minutes / several minutes) _____.

Adjunctive Behavior in Humans

The preceding discussion probably has you wondering about the extent to which adjunctive behaviors occur in humans. On an anecdotal level, Falk (1977) noted that a diverse range of human behaviors, from nail biting and talkativeness to snacking and coffee drinking, are commonly associated with periods of enforced waiting. Falk (1998) also noted that drug and alcohol abuse is frequently found in environments that provide sparse levels of economic and social reinforcement, suggesting that adjunctive processes (in addition to the physiological effects of the drug) contribute to the development of drug and alcohol abuse. This is supported by the fact that schedule-induced polydipsia has been used to induce rats to drink excessive amounts of water containing alcohol or other drugs. In other words, schedule-induced polydipsia can be used to create an animal analogue of drug and alcohol abuse (Falk, 1993; Riley & Wetherington, 1989).

On an experimental level, humans have produced adjunctive-type behavior patterns that are similar to, though not as extreme as, those found in animals. For example, Doyle and Samson (1988) found that human subjects exposed to FI schedules of monetary reinforcement for game playing displayed an increased tendency to drink water following each reinforcer. Similar to schedule-induced polydipsia in animals, the length of the interval between reinforcers was an important variable, with nearly twice as much drinking occurring on an FI 90-sec schedule as on an FI 30-sec schedule.

Experimental evidence for adjunctive drug use in humans has also been obtained. Cherek (1982) found high rates of cigarette smoking when monetary payment for button pushing was presented on an FI 120-sec schedule as opposed to FI 30-sec, 60-sec, or 240-sec schedules. And Doyle and Samson (1988) found high rates of beer sipping when monetary payment for playing a game was presented on an FI 90-sec schedule as opposed to an FI 30-sec schedule. In both cases, the drug-related behavior (smoking or beer sipping) was most likely to occur during the period immediately following delivery of the reinforcer, which is consistent with the notion that it was functioning as an adjunctive behavior. Studies such as these support the notion that adjunctive processes may play a significant role in the development of substance abuse in humans. Especially in the early phases of an addiction, adjunctive processes may encourage an individual to frequently consume an addictive substance, with the result that the person eventually becomes addicted to it (Falk, 1998).

1. Evidence that humans engage in adjunctive behavior includes the fact that studies of adjunctive-type behavior patterns in human subjects usually (find / do not find) _____ an optimal time interval between reinforcers for producing such behaviors.

2. Certain behavior patterns in humans, such as smoking and nail biting, are often associated with periods of (extreme activity / enforced waiting) _____, which (agrees with / contradicts) _____ the notion that these may be adjunctive behaviors.

QUICK QUIZ H

3. It has also been noted that alcohol and drug abuse is most likely to develop in environments in which economic and social reinforcers are (frequently/ infrequently) _____ available, which (agrees with / contradicts) _____ the notion that these may be adjunctive behaviors.

4. Adjunctive processes may play a particularly important role in the development of an addiction during its (early/later) _____ stages.

Adjunctive Behavior as Displacement Activity

Why would a tendency to develop adjunctive behaviors ever have evolved? What purpose do such activities serve, especially given how self-destructive they sometimes are? For example, it requires a considerable amount of energy for a rat to process and excrete the huge amounts of water ingested during a session of schedule-induced polydipsia. And drug and alcohol abuse is decidedly counterproductive for both rats and humans.

In this regard, Falk (1977) has proposed that adjunctive behaviors represent a type of ***displacement activity***, an apparently irrelevant activity sometimes displayed by animals when confronted by conflict or thwarted from attaining a goal. For example, a bird that is unable to reach an insect hidden

---

And Furthermore

Extreme Polydipsia: Not Just a "Rat Thing"

Schedule-induced polydipsia is a bizarre behavior pattern in which rats ingest enormous amounts of water in a short time. Experimental studies of schedule-induced drinking in humans have typically produced much lower rates of drinking, suggesting that rats and humans are quite different in their susceptibility to polydipsia (Klein, 1996). But extreme polydipsia does sometimes occur in humans. In fact, as a psychiatric label, the term *polydipsia* refers to a rare condition in which patients drink incessantly—so much so that they sometimes die from the disruption of electrolytes in their bodies. Although there are no doubt major differences between this psychiatric form of polydipsia in humans and schedule-induced polydipsia in rats, there might also be some similarities. If nothing else, schedule-induced polydipsia—and other adjunctive behaviors—are compulsive-type patterns of behavior and might therefore provide insight into the behavioral and neurological processes that maintain compulsive behaviors in humans. Psychiatrists have therefore shown considerable interest in schedule-induced polydipsia, in sorting out the neurological processes that underlie it, and in determining the effects of psychiatric drugs on alleviating it (Wallace & Singer, 1976). Research on adjunctive behavior could therefore have implications for furthering our understanding and treatment of some serious psychiatric conditions in humans.

between some rocks might begin pecking at some nearby twigs. This behavior seems completely unrelated to the goal of capturing the insect, which led early investigators to propose that displacement activities like this serve simply as a means of releasing pent-up energy (Tinbergen, 1951).

In contrast to this energy release model, Falk (1977) proposes that displacement activities serve two purposes. First, they provide for a more diversified range of behaviors in a particular setting, and a diverse range of behavior is often beneficial. Consider, for example, a bird that has a tendency to peck at twigs while waiting for an insect to emerge from its hiding place. By doing so, the bird may uncover another source of food or may even stumble upon using a twig as a tool for rooting out the insect. In fact, some species of birds do use twigs to root out insects—an evolved pattern of behavior that may have begun as a displacement activity. In similar fashion, an employee who grows restless and busies herself with some paperwork while waiting for an important phone call is apt to be a more productive employee than one who simply stares at the phone until the phone call arrives.

A second benefit of displacement activities is that they help the animal remain in a situation where a significant reinforcer might eventually become available. Periods of little or no reinforcement can be aversive—as any student knows when buckling down to study a boring subject matter—and anything that can alleviate the aversiveness of these intervals will heighten the probability of attaining the delayed reinforcer. Thus, pecking the ground gives the bird "something to do" while waiting for an insect to emerge from its hiding place, just as whittling a stick allows a hunter to patiently wait for a moose, and munching on licorice enables a student to sit still and study patiently throughout a study session.

Adjunctive behavior can therefore be seen as a natural tendency to do something else while waiting for a reinforcer. To the extent that it enhances the individual's ability to wait out the delay period, it thus constitutes a sort of built-in self-control device. This is a paradoxical notion in that adjunctive behaviors, such as smoking and drinking, are usually the kinds of behaviors that are viewed as indicating a *lack of self-control* (Tomie, 1996). But this depends on the specific consequence to which one is referring. Smoking is an impulsive behavior in terms of providing short-term pleasure at the risk of undermining one's long-term health, but it can also enhance self-control in terms of helping an individual work long hours so as to obtain a promotion. For this reason, students often find it particularly difficult to quit smoking during the academic year. Quitting smoking not only results in the temporary onset of withdrawal symptoms, it also undermines the student's ability to study for long periods of time.[2]

---

[2]As Freud once complained, if he could not smoke, he could not work. Interestingly, Freud was famous for his ability to work long hours, which is often attributed to his "self-discipline." Yet this self-discipline seems to have been at least partially dependent on the availability of an adjunctive activity in the form of smoking. Unfortunately, his 20-cigars-a-day habit resulted in cancer of the jaw, from which he eventually died (Gay, 1988).

Congruent with this notion, it has been shown that people who successfully overcome an addiction (such as alcoholism) are more likely to seek out a replacement for the addictive activity (such as coffee drinking) than those who are not successful in overcoming their addiction (Brown, Stetson, & Beatty, 1989). The moral of the story is that adjunctive behaviors sometimes serve a purpose, and we might do well to acknowledge that purpose and find other ways to fulfill it.

1. According to Falk, adjunctive behavior may be a type of d_____ activity, which is an irrelevant activity displayed by animals when confronted by c_____ or when they are (able/unable) _____ to achieve a goal.

2. One benefit of such activities is that it is often useful to engage in (just one type / a diverse range) _____ of behavior(s) in a situation.

3. The second benefit derived from such activities is that they may facilitate (moving away from / remaining near) _____ a potential reinforcer.

4. To the extent that adjunctive activities facilitate waiting for, or working toward, a(n) (immediate/delayed) _____ reinforcer, such activities may (facilitate/impede) _____ efforts at self-control.

Activity Anorexia

One type of behavior that can be generated as an adjunctive behavior is wheel running. When exposed to an intermittent schedule of food reinforcement for lever pressing, rats will run in a wheel for several seconds during the interval between reinforcers (Levitsky & Collier, 1968). A related type of procedure, however, produces even more extreme running. Known as *activity anorexia*, it has some important implications for people who are undertaking a diet and exercise program to lose weight.[3]

Basic Procedure and Defining Characteristics

The procedure for creating activity anorexia is as follows: If rats are allowed to access food for only a single 1.5-hour feeding period each day, and if they have access to a running wheel during the 22.5-hour interval between meals, they will begin to spend increasing amounts of time running during that interval. Not only that, the more they run, the less they eat, and the less they eat, the more they run. In other words, a sort of negative feedback

---

[3]Activity anorexia is considered by some researchers to be a type of adjunctive or schedule-induced behavior (e.g., Falk, 1994), and by other researchers to be a separate class of behaviors involving distinctly different processes (e.g., Beneke, Schulte, & Vander Tuig, 1995). For purposes of this discussion, we will adopt the latter position.

cycle develops in which the two behavioral tendencies, increased running and decreased eating, reciprocally strengthen each other. Within a week or so, the rats are running enormous distances—up to 20,000 revolutions of the wheel per day (equivalent to about 12 miles!)—and eating nothing. If the process is allowed to continue (for humane reasons, the experiment is usually terminated before this), the rats will become completely emaciated and die (e.g., Routtenberg & Kuznesof, 1967).

Thus, *activity anorexia* is an abnormally high level of activity and low level of food intake generated by exposure to a restricted schedule of feeding (Epling & Pierce, 1991). It is important to note that rats that are given restricted access to food, but with *no* wheel available, do just fine—they easily ingest enough food during the 1.5-hour meal period to maintain body weight. Rats that have access to a wheel, but without food restriction, also do just fine—they display only moderate levels of running and no tendency toward self-starvation. It is the combination of food restriction and the opportunity to run that is so devastating.

---

1. The basic procedure for the development of ac_____ an_____ in rats is the presentation of (one/several) _____ meal period(s) each day along with access to a running wheel during the (meal/between-meal) _____ period.

2. Thus, _____ _____ is an abnormally (low/high) _____ level of _____ and a (low/high) _____ level of food intake generated by exposure to a r_____ schedule of feeding.

Comparisons with Anorexia Nervosa

Activity anorexia was first investigated by Routtenberg and Kuznesof (1967). Two other researchers, Epling and Pierce (e.g., 1988), later noted its similarity to *anorexia nervosa* in humans. Anorexia nervosa is a psychiatric disorder in which patients refuse to eat adequate amounts of food and as a result lose extreme amounts of weight. People with this disorder often require hospitalization; and of those who do become hospitalized, more than 10% eventually die from the disorder or from complications associated with it (such as from a disruption of the body's electrolyte balance; American Psychological Association, *Diagnostic and Statistical Manual IV*, 2000).

Epling and Pierce (1991) contend that there are several similarities between activity anorexia in rats and anorexia nervosa in humans. For example, just as activity anorexia in rats can be precipitated by imposing a restricted schedule of feeding, so too anorexia nervosa in humans usually begins when the person deliberately undertakes a diet to lose weight. Even more significant, anorexia in humans, as with anorexia in rats, is often accompanied by very high levels of activity (Davis, Katzman, & Kirsh,

1999; Katz, 1996). This may consist of a deliberate exercise program designed to facilitate weight loss, or it may be displayed as a severe sort of restlessness. Although clinicians have typically regarded such high activity as a secondary characteristic of the disorder (e.g., Bruch, 1978), Epling and Pierce (1996) suggest that it is more fundamental than that. Thus, as with activity anorexia in rats, many cases of anorexia nervosa in humans might result from the combined effects of a stringent diet and high activity levels.

The importance of high activity levels in the development of anorexia nervosa is supported by several lines of evidence. First, even in humans who do not have anorexia, a sudden increase in activity is usually followed by a decrease in food intake, and a decrease in food intake is usually followed by an increase in activity (Epling & Pierce, 1996). Second, individuals who engage in high levels of activity appear to be at high risk for anorexia. For example, ballet dancers, who are under constant pressure to remain thin and are extremely active, show a higher incidence of the disorder than do fashion models who are under pressure only to remain thin (Garner & Garfinkel, 1980). Likewise, a surprising number of athletes develop symptoms of anorexia (Katz, 1986; Wheeler, 1996) or an "overtraining syndrome" that bears many similarities to anorexia (Yates, 1996).

In addition to high activity levels, there are other interesting parallels between anorexia in rats and humans. For example, just as anorexia nervosa in humans is more common among adolescents (*DSM IV*, 2000), activity anorexia is more easily induced in adolescent rats than in older rats (Woods & Routtenberg, 1971). Another similarity concerns the manner in which people with anorexia approach food. Although they eat little, they nevertheless remain quite interested in food (Bruch, 1978). For example, they often enjoy preparing food for others. As well, when they do eat, they often spend considerable time arranging the food on their plates, cutting it into pieces, and slowly savoring each bite. Anecdotal evidence suggests that anorexic rats might sometimes behave similarly (D. P. Boer, 2000, personal communication). Although the rats eat little or no food during each meal period, they do spend considerable time shredding the food with their teeth and spitting it out. And if allowed to do so, they will carry food with them when they are allowed to reenter the wheel following the meal period. In other words, like humans, rats seem to remain quite interested in food, even if they are not eating it.

Thus, activity anorexia in rats appears to be a rather close analogue of anorexia nervosa in humans. As with most analogues, however, the similarity is less than perfect. For example, the rat with anorexia is physically restricted from accessing food except during the meal period, whereas the person with anorexia is on a self-imposed diet with food still freely available. Epling and Pierce (1991) argue, however, that the free availability of food may be more apparent than real. Just as the researcher physically restricts the rat's supply of food, societal pressures to become thin may psychologically restrict a person's access to food. Women, of course, are more commonly subjected to such pressures, which probably contributes to the greater frequency of anorexia in women than in men. But medical biases probably also play a role; thin females are readily labeled "anorexic", but thin males are, well, thin.

A more substantial difference between humans and rats is that anorexia in humans is often accompanied by bulimia: a tendency to binge on food and then purge oneself by vomiting or taking laxatives. In fact, psychiatrists distinguish between two types of anorexia: the *restricting type*, which is characterized by simple food restriction, and the *binge-eating/purging type*, in which dieting is combined with episodes of binging and purging (*DSM IV*, 2000). Of course, anorexic rats do not binge and purge; indeed, it would be difficult for them to do so because rats are physically incapable of vomiting. Thus, activity anorexia in rats is most relevant to the restricting type of anorexia in humans. And, in fact, the restricting type of anorexia is most strongly associated with high activity levels (Katz, 1996).

1. As with the development of activity anorexia in rats, most instances of human anorexia begin with the person undertaking a d_____. As well, humans with anorexia tend to display (high/low) _____ levels of activity.

2. A sharp increase in activity is usually associated with a (decrease/increase) _____ in food intake, which in turn can result in a(n) (decrease/increase) _____ in activity.

3. Anecdotal evidence suggests that, as with anorexia in humans, rats suffering from activity anorexia are often quite (interested/uninterested) _____ in food.

4. Similar to anorexia nervosa in humans, activity anorexia in rats is more easily induced in (adolescent/adult) _____ rats.

5. Activity anorexia in rats is most similar to the r_____ type of anorexia in humans rather than the b_____-p_____ type of anorexia.

Underlying Mechanisms

Given the self-destructive nature of activity anorexia, what are the mechanisms underlying it? On a neurophysiological level, the processes involved are complex, involving several classes of hormones and neurotransmitters (Guisinger, 2003). Endorphins, for example, are a class of morphine-like substances in the brain that have been implicated in pain reduction. They have also been implicated in the feeling of pleasure that sometimes accompanies prolonged exercise, which is commonly known as "runner's high" (Wheeler, 1996). Significantly, drugs that block the effect of endorphins will temporarily lower the rate of wheel running in food-deprived rats (Boer, Epling, Pierce, & Russell, 1990).

Such evidence suggests that both activity anorexia in rats and anorexia nervosa in humans might be maintained by what is essentially an addiction to an endorphin high (Marrazzi & Luby, 1986). In support of this notion, patients with anorexia often report that the experience of anorexia is quite similar to a drug-induced high. To quote three patients: "[O]ne feels intoxicated, literally how I think alcoholism works" (Bruch, 1978, p. 73); "being hungry has the same effect as a drug, and you feel outside your body" (p. 118); and perhaps most disturbing, "I enjoy having this disease and I want it" (p. 2).

From an evolutionary perspective, it has been suggested that a tendency toward activity anorexia might have survival value (Epling & Pierce, 1988; Guisinger, 2003). An animal that becomes highly active when food supplies are scarce is more likely to travel great distances and encounter new food supplies. Under extreme circumstances, the animal might even do well to ignore small amounts of food encountered along the way—the gathering of which could be costly in terms of time and energy spent relative to the amount of energy gained—and cease traveling only when an adequate food supply has been reached. In support of this notion, research has shown that activity anorexia can be halted by suddenly providing access to a continuous supply of food (Epling & Pierce, 1991). When confronted with a plentiful food source, the rats cease running and begin eating. Evolutionary pressures may also contribute to the increased incidence of anorexia in women. When placed on a calorie restricted diet, female rats demonstrate increases in both activity level and learning ability more so than male rats, which may represent an evolutionarily-based tendency that enables females to compete effectively for resources in times of food scarcity (Marten et al., 2007).

QUICK QUIZ L

1. Endorphins are a class of morphine-like substances in the brain that are associated with p_____ reduction.

2. Congruent with the possibility that endorphins may be involved in activity anorexia, endorphins have been implicated in the feeling of p_____ that is sometimes experienced following prolonged exercise.

3. This finding suggests that both activity anorexia in rats and anorexia nervosa in humans may be maintained by an _____ high.

4. From an evolutionary perspective, increased activity in response to decreased food intake could (interfere with / facilitate) _____ contacting a new food supply.

5. This evolutionary perspective is supported by evidence that the activity anorexia cycle can be broken by suddenly providing (intermittent/continuous) _____ access to food.

Clinical Implications

The activity anorexia model has several clinical implications. From a treatment perspective, the model suggests that behavioral treatments for anorexia nervosa should focus as much on establishing normal patterns of activity as they do on establishing normal patterns of eating. As well, research into the biochemistry underlying this phenomenon could facilitate the development of drugs for treating anorexia. For example, it may be possible to develop long-lasting endorphin blockers that will effectively reduce the feelings of pleasure that help maintain the anorexic process.

The activity anorexia model also has implications for prevention. First and foremost, people should be warned that combining a stringent exercise program with severe dieting places them at risk for developing this disorder. The model thus calls into question those disciplines that traditionally combine dieting with intense activity. As already noted, one such discipline is ballet; another is amateur wrestling. Wrestlers are traditionally expected to lose several pounds before competition so as to compete in the lightest weight category possible. Many of the physical and psychological changes accompanying this process are similar to those found in anorexia nervosa— an indication that these athletes are at risk for developing symptoms of the disorder (Symbaluk, 1996).

The activity anorexia model also suggests that people who are dieting and may be susceptible to anorexia should eat several small meals per day as opposed to a single large meal, insofar as rats do not become anorexic when the 1.5-hour meal period is broken up into several shorter meal periods (Epling & Pierce, 1991). As well, people who are attempting to increase their exercise levels should do so slowly, because rats that become anorexic display the greatest reduction in food intake following a sharp increase in activity (Pierce & Epling, 1996). (Interestingly, the sharp increase in activity also has been shown to be most clearly associated with appetite suppression in humans.) And, finally, dieters should ensure that their meals are well balanced nutritionally. Research has shown that activity anorexia is more easily induced in rats that are on a low-protein diet as opposed to a normal diet (Beneke & Vander Tuig, 1996).

Of course, further research is needed to confirm the usefulness of these suggestions for preventing anorexia nervosa in humans. What is clear, however, is that a combination of severe dieting and exercise can have serious consequences and should not be undertaken lightly.

---

1. The activity anorexia model suggests that therapists should focus as much on establishing normal a _____ levels as they presently do on establishing normal eating patterns.

2. Specific suggestions (derived from activity anorexia research) for minimizing the risk of anorexia in humans include eating (several/one) _____ meal(s) per day, increasing exercise levels (rapidly/slowly) _____, and eating a diet that is (imbalanced / well balanced) _____.

QUICK QUIZ M

And Furthermore

The Healthy Side of the Diet–Activity Connection

We have so far discussed the negative aspect of the connection between food restriction and activity. There is also a positive side to this connection. Boer (1990) found that by adjusting the *amount of food* eaten by the rats, as opposed to the *length of the meal period,* he could precisely control the amount of wheel running. For example, rats that were given 15 grams of food once per day developed the typical activity anorexia cycle (see also Morse et al., 1995), whereas rats that were given 18 grams of food displayed only a moderate level of running (5–6 miles per day) with no tendency toward self-starvation. These rats were also quite healthy. Interestingly, the same effect was found using rats that had a genetic predisposition toward obesity (J. C. Russell et al., 1989). Raised on a regime of diet and exercise, these "genetically fat" rats remained incredibly lean and fit—an impressive demonstration of the healthy effects of a healthy lifestyle, even in subjects whose genetics are working against them.

It is also worth repeating that, as noted in Chapter 2, calorie restriction is currently the most reliable means known for slowing the aging process, at least in nonhuman animals. Lest the reader imagine, however, that this might be a good excuse for eating like a person with anorexia and quickly losing a lot of weight, the health-enhancing effects of low-calorie diets demand regular meals composed of highly nutritious foods—a far cry from the "two carrots and a cookie" diet of many people with anorexia. (See also Omodei & Fontana, 2011, for a recent overview of the effects of calorie restriction on age-related chronic diseases.)

Behavior Systems Theory

As seen throughout this chapter, biological dispositions appear to play a strong role in many aspects of conditioning. Needless to say, this evidence has led several researchers to propose various theories to explain these findings. The most comprehensive of these is behavior systems theory (e.g., Timberlake, 1993; Timberlake & Lucas, 1989). According to *behavior systems theory,* an animal's behavior is organized into certain systems or categories (such as feeding, mating and avoiding predators), with each system containing a set of responses that can become activated in certain situations. (The theory is actually more complex than this, but a simplified version will suffice for now.) Note that some of these responses may be very rigid, in the form of a reflex or fixed action pattern, whereas others may be more flexible and sensitive to the consequences of the response. Different systems may also overlap such that a response that is typically associated with one system may sometimes be instigated by another system.

As an example, let us consider the *feeding system* in the rat. When a rat is hungry, it becomes predisposed to engage in various food-related responses, such as salivating, chewing, food handling (with its paws), searching for food, and so on. Thus, during a period of hunger, all of these responses become primed, meaning that they can easily be set in motion. Which response is actually set in motion, however, will depend on the situation. For example, in a situation in which the delivery and consumption of food is imminent, behaviors such as salivating and food handling will occur. When food is slightly more distant than that, a focused search pattern will emerge, such as sniffing and looking about. When food is still more distant, a more general search pattern may dominate, such as running and exploring.

Interestingly, this theory helps explain the types of experimental procedures that have evolved to study learning in animals. It is no accident that the favorite methods for studying learning in rats have been maze running and lever pressing. These methods have become widely adopted because they work so well, and they work so well because they match the types of behaviors that rats are naturally predisposed to display in food-related situations. Thus, rats are great at running through mazes because they have evolved to run along narrow, enclosed spaces—such as through tunnels in a burrow—to find food. Similarly, rats have evolved dexterous forepaws that they use to pick up food and manipulate it. Therefore, manipulating something with their forepaws, such as pressing a lever, is for them a natural response associated with feeding.

Behavior systems theory also provides a comprehensive explanation for many of the unusual behavior patterns described in this chapter. For example, consider a sign-tracking experiment in which dogs approach a light that predicts food and begin to beg and whine as though they are soliciting food from it. Dogs are pack animals for which feeding is a social event; and subordinate animals often have to solicit food from the dominant leader who controls that food. Thus, the feeding situation that was set up in these experiments, in which a light strongly predicted the delivery of food, essentially elicited this social component of the dog's feeding system.

Although behavior systems theory assigns an important role to innate patterns of behavior, it assigns an equally important role to the environmental cues that determine which behavior will be activated. An illustration can be found in sign-tracking studies with rats. Timberlake and Grant (1975) devised a chamber in which a *stimulus rat* could be mechanically inserted and withdrawn (see Figure 12.2). When the stimulus rat was inserted just before the delivery of food, thus becoming a CS for food, the participant rat would approach the stimulus rat and engage in various forms of social behavior, including sniffing the mouth, pawing, and grooming. This behavior pattern becomes understandable when we consider that rats have evolved to pay close attention to what other rats are eating and will even steal food from the mouths of other rats. The stimulus rat that predicted the delivery of food therefore seemed to elicit this social component of the feeding

FIGURE 12.2 Illustration of the apparatus used by Timberlake and Grant (1975). The stimulus rat became a CS when it was inserted on a movable platform into the experimental chamber just before the delivery of food.

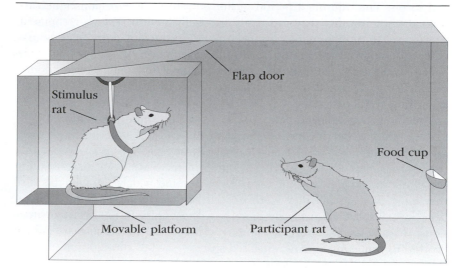

system in the participant rat. By contrast, a wooden block that predicted the delivery of food did not elicit social contact, with the participant rat merely orienting toward it. Likewise, in a different study, a rolling marble that predicted food delivery elicited a pattern of clawing, grasping, and gnawing, as though the rat was attempting to capture and consume the marble (Timberlake, 1983). Presumably, the moving marble activated the predatory component of the rat's feeding system, such as would naturally be activated by a small, moving insect (rats often hunt and devour insects). Such predatory behavior was not elicited, however, when the moving marble predicted the delivery of water.

The extent to which behavior systems theory can provide a comprehensive explanation for animal behavior has yet to be determined. According to Mazur (2002), neither does this theory undermine the importance of basic principles of conditioning, such as reinforcement and punishment, as powerful factors in learning and behavior. Behavior systems theory does, however, remind us of the need to pay attention to an animal's innate tendencies when attempting to modify its behavior. For example, the dog that habitually nips at your hand when you attempt to touch its food is not simply displaying a behavior that has been negatively reinforced by the removal of your hand. Rather, it might also indicate that the dog has assumed a position of dominance within the household, a naturally evolved pattern of behavior that is highly adaptive within a pack but rather a nuisance among humans. In a sense, the dog's tendency to be food aggressive reflects both the social component of its feeding system as well as the feeding component of its social system. Thus, a comprehensive attempt to modify this behavior might need to include strategies for signaling to the dog its subordinate status within the family—such as feeding the dog by hand rather than providing free food throughout the day (thereby clearly indicating to the dog that humans control the food supply). Fortunately, just as shaping is becoming a well-established technique among pet owners, so too is an appreciation of the need to understand a pet's innate tendencies (e.g., Coren, 1994; McConnell, 2003).

1. According to _____ _____ theory, an animal's behavior is organized into a number of s_____, such as feeding and mating, each consisting of a set of relevant responses that can be activated in certain s_____.

2. In terms of behavior systems theory, Bolles' notion of sp_____ -sp_____ d_____ reactions (SSDR) is concerned with responses that appear to be driven by the defense-against-predators system.

3. In the sign-tracking experiment with dogs, the light that predicted food seemed to activate the (predatory/consumatory/social) _____ component of the dog's feeding system.

SUMMARY

Animals appear to be biologically prepared to learn some things more readily than others. For example, in taste aversion conditioning, a food item that has been paired with nausea quickly becomes conditioned as an aversive CS. This type of conditioning is similar to other forms of classical conditioning in that processes such as stimulus generalization, extinction, and overshadowing can be found. It differs from other forms of classical conditioning in that strong associations can be formed over long delays and require only a single conditioning trial. As well, the nausea is specifically associated with a food item rather than some other stimulus.

Examples of preparedness in operant conditioning include how easily food can be used to reinforce pecking but not perching in chaffinches, while the sound of a chaffinch song can be used to reinforce perching but not pecking. As well, rats more easily learn to run or freeze to escape shock than press a lever to escape shock. The latter example suggests that many escape behaviors may be species-specific defense reactions elicited by the aversive stimulus.

Instinctive drift is a genetically based, fixed action pattern that gradually emerges to displace a behavior that is being operantly conditioned. Sign tracking is a tendency to approach (and perhaps make contact with) a stimulus that signals the presentation of an appetitive event. In both cases, the behavior superficially appears to be a goal-directed operant behavior, yet the procedures that produce it suggest it is actually an elicited (or respondent) behavior.

Adjunctive behavior, also known as schedule-induced behavior, is an excessive pattern of behavior that emerges as a by-product of an intermittent schedule of reinforcement. In schedule-induced polydipsia, for example, rats drink extreme amounts of water during the interval between food reinforcers that are delivered on an FI or FT schedule. Adjunctive behavior typically occurs in the period immediately following the delivery of the scheduled reinforcer, varies directly with the level of deprivation for the scheduled reinforcer, can function as a reinforcer for another behavior, and is most likely to occur when the interreinforcement interval is a few minutes in length. Examples of possible adjunctive behaviors in humans include smoking cigarettes, drinking alcohol, and using drugs. Adjunctive behavior may be a type of displacement activity that functions to ensure a diverse range of activities in a setting and to facilitate waiting for a delayed reinforcer.

Activity anorexia is a pattern of excessive activity and low food intake in animals as a result of exposure to a restricted food supply. It bears many similarities to certain forms of anorexia nervosa in humans, which is characterized by severe dieting and high activity levels. Evidence suggests that activity anorexia in animals as well as anorexia nervosa in humans may be maintained by an endorphin high that accompanies the process. From an evolutionary perspective, a tendency toward activity anorexia might induce an animal to travel long distances, thereby increasing the likelihood of encountering a new food supply. Clinical implications that have grown out of this research include the possibility of developing long-lasting endorphin blockers that could break the anorexic cycle. These findings also suggest that people should be cautious about combining a stringent diet with severe exercise.

According to behavior systems theory, an animal's behavior is organized into several motivational systems. Each of these systems encompasses a set of relevant responses; and in turn, each response can be activated by situational cues. This theory accounts for many of the unusual behavior patterns, including sign tracking, described in this chapter. It also accounts for the particular kinds of tasks that researchers have used to study animal learning.

SUGGESTED READINGS

Garcia, J. (1981). Tilting at the paper mills of academe. *American Psychologist, 36*, 149–158. Garcia's fascinating account of the difficulties he encountered in attempting to publish his early results on taste aversion conditioning simply because they violated certain assumptions of classical conditioning that were widely held at that time.

Epling, W. F., & Pierce, W. D. (1991). *Solving the anorexia puzzle: A scientific approach.* Toronto, Canada: Hogrefe & Huber. Epling and Pierce's overview of activity anorexia and its applicability to understanding anorexia nervosa in humans.

Timberlake, W. (1993). Behavior systems and reinforcement: An integrative approach. *Journal of the Experimental Analysis of Behavior, 60,* 105–128. For the serious student, a discussion of behavior systems theory and its applicability to operant behavior.

Coren, S. (1995). *The intelligence of dogs: A guide to the thoughts, emotions, and inner lives of our canine companions.* New York: Bantam Books. A fun and interesting guide for helping us better understand our canine companions, particularly from the perspective of their innate predispositions.

STUDY QUESTIONS

1. Define preparedness and CS-US relevance.
2. Define taste aversion conditioning and diagram an experimental example.
3. Outline three ways in which taste aversion conditioning differs from most other forms of classical conditioning.
4. Describe (or diagram) the results of the full experiment by Garcia and Koelling that illustrates the role of biological preparedness in classical conditioning.
5. Describe two examples of the role of preparedness in operant conditioning.
6. What is instinctive drift? Describe (or diagram) one of the Brelands' examples of instinctive drift.
7. What is sign tracking? Describe the experimental example of sign tracking in dogs.
8. Define autoshaping and describe the procedure used to produce it. Describe the research result that seems particularly supportive of a stimulus-substitution interpretation of autoshaping.
9. Define adjunctive behavior. What other term is used to refer to this class of behaviors?
10. What is schedule-induced polydipsia, and what is the specific procedure for experimentally inducing it in rats?
11. List four characteristics of adjunctive behaviors.
12. What are displacement activities? What are two benefits that may be derived from such activities?
13. Define activity anorexia. What is the basic procedure for inducing this behavior pattern?
14. List three similarities (other than low food intake) between activity anorexia in rats and anorexia nervosa in humans.
15. What type of chemical substance in the brain seems to play a role in the development of anorexia? Briefly describe the evolutionary explanation for the occurrence of activity anorexia.
16. List two implications for treatment and four implications for prevention that have grown out of activity anorexia research.
17. Define behavior systems theory. Describe the results of sign-tracking studies in rats that indicate the importance of environmental cues.

CONCEPT REVIEW

activity anorexia. An abnormally high level of activity and low level of food intake generated by exposure to a restricted schedule of feeding.

adjunctive behavior. An excessive pattern of behavior that emerges as a by-product of an intermittent schedule of reinforcement for some other behavior.

autoshaping. A type of sign tracking in which a pigeon comes to automatically peck at a response key because the key light has been associated with the response-independent delivery of food.

behavior systems theory. A theory proposing that an animal's behavior is organized into certain systems or categories (such as feeding, mating, and avoiding predators), with each category containing a set of relevant responses that can become activated in certain situations.

CS-US relevance. An innate tendency to easily associate certain types of stimuli with each other.

displacement activity. An apparently irrelevant activity sometimes displayed by animals when confronted by conflict or thwarted from attaining a goal.

instinctive drift. An instance of classical conditioning in which a genetically based, fixed action pattern gradually emerges and displaces a behavior that is being operantly conditioned.

preparedness. An innate tendency for an organism to more easily learn certain types of behaviors or to associate certain types of events with each other.

sign tracking. A type of elicited behavior in which an organism approaches a stimulus that signals the presentation of an appetitive event.

taste aversion conditioning. A form of classical conditioning in which a food item that has been paired with gastrointestinal illness becomes a conditioned aversive stimulus.

CHAPTER TEST

9. To prevent the development of anorexia nervosa, humans who are dieting might do well to eat (several small / one large) _____ meal(s) per day. And if they are exercising, they should increase the level of exercise (quickly/slowly) _____.

20. Taste aversion conditioning differs from other forms of conditioning in that associations can be formed over _____ delays, and in (many / a single) _____ trial(s).

2. According to the phenomenon of negative _____, a pigeon will compulsively peck at a key light that precedes the delivery of food even though the key peck (prevents / results in) _____ the delivery of food.

28. Displacement activities, including certain types of adjunctive behaviors, may serve as a type of self-_____ device in that they facilitate the act of waiting for a _____ reinforcer.

11. In general, a pigeon that is (more/less) _____ food deprived will display a greater tendency to engage in schedule-induced aggression.

1. When a key light is presented just before the noncontingent delivery of food, the pigeon will begin pecking at the key. This phenomenon is known as _____.

24. When a pig receives reinforcement for carrying a napkin from one table to another, it eventually starts dropping it and rooting at it on the ground. This is an example of a phenomenon known as _____ in which a _____ pattern gradually emerges and replaces the operant behavior that one is attempting to condition.

4. An excessive pattern of behavior that emerges as a by-product of an intermittent schedule of reinforcement for some other behavior is called _____ behavior.

12. In schedule-induced polydipsia, a rat likely (will / will not) _____ learn to press a lever to gain access to a (drinking tube / running wheel) _____ during the interval between food pellets.

19. Angie became sick to her stomach when she and her new boyfriend, Gerald, were on their way home after dining at an exotic restaurant. Fortunately for (Gerald / the restaurant) _____, Angie is most likely to form an aversion to (Gerald / the food) _____.

33. According to _____ _____ theory, the motivation to acquire a mate would constitute a system of behavior, whereas spreading one's tail feathers to attract a female would constitute a relevant response within that system.

26. A _____ activity is a (highly relevant / seemingly irrelevant) _____ activity sometimes displayed by animals when confronted by conflict or blocked from attaining a goal.

16. Following a turkey dinner in which, for the first time, Paul also tasted some caviar, he became quite nauseous. As a result, he may acquire a conditioned _____, most likely to the (turkey/caviar) _____.

31. Activity anorexia is more easily induced among relatively (young/old) _____ rats, which is (similar to / different from) _____ the pattern found with humans who suffer from anorexia.

8. Whenever a person combines a stringent exercise program with a severe diet, he or she may be at risk for developing symptoms of _____.

13. For the development of adjunctive behaviors, the optimal interval between the delivery of reinforcers is often about (3/6/9) _____ minutes.

22. My canary likes the sound of my whistling. Research suggests that my whistling will be a more effective reinforcer if I am attempting to train the bird to (perch in a certain spot / peck at the floor) _____.

29. An abnormally high level of activity and low level of food intake generated by restricted access to food is called _____.

6. From an evolutionary perspective, a tendency toward activity anorexia could (increase/decrease) _____ the likelihood of the animal encountering a new food supply. Indirect evidence for this includes the fact that the activity anorexia cycle can often be (stopped / greatly enhanced) _____ by suddenly presenting the animal with a continuous supply of food.

18. When Selma was eating oatmeal porridge one morning, she broke a tooth on a small pebble that accidentally had been mixed in with it. The next morning, after eating some bran flakes, she became terribly ill. If she develops aversions as a result of these experiences, chances are that they will be an aversion to the (look/taste) _____ of oatmeal and the _____ of bran flakes.

10. Adjunctive behavior tends to develop when a behavior is being reinforced on a _____ or _____ schedule of reinforcement. Also, adjunctive behavior is most likely to occur in the interval immediately (following/preceding) _____ the presentation of each reinforcer.

23. When a rat is shocked, it easily learns to run to the other side of the chamber to escape. According to Bolles, this is because the running is actually a(n) (operant/respondent) _____ that is (elicited / negatively reinforced) _____ by the (application/removal) _____ of shock.

7. The activity anorexia model suggests that behavioral treatments for anorexia nervosa should focus as much on establishing normal patterns of _____ as they do on establishing normal patterns of eating.

14. The tendency for many people to smoke while waiting in traffic can be viewed as an example of an _____ behavior in humans.

3. Adjunctive behavior is also known as _____ behavior.

27. One advantage of displacement activities is that they allow for a more (diverse/focused) _____ pattern of behavior, which is often advantageous.

32. According to _____ theory, an animal's behavior is organized into a number of motivational systems, with each system encompassing a set of relevant responses that are elicited in certain _____.

21. An innate tendency to more readily associate certain types of stimuli with each other is a type of preparedness that is known as _____.

17. Taste aversion conditioning most readily occurs to (familiar/unfamiliar) _____ food items, as well as to the (strongest/mildest) _____ tasting item in the meal. The latter can be seen as an example of the _____ effect in classical conditioning.

5. A class of brain chemicals that may play a particularly important role in the development of anorexia in both rats and humans is _____.

Evidence for this includes the fact that people suffering from anorexia often report that the feeling that accompanies the disorder is quite (unpleasant/pleasant) _____.

25. A behavior pattern in which an organism approaches a stimulus that signals the presentation of an appetitive event is known as _____.

30. As with the development of anorexia in rats, many cases of anorexia in humans might be the result of the combined effects of _____ restriction and high _____ levels.

15. Despite getting a shock when he plugged in his toaster one day, Antonio feels only slight anxiety when using it. On the other hand, he is deathly afraid of spiders, ever since one jumped on him when he tried to swat it. The difference in how easily Antonio learned to fear these two events seems to be an illustration of the effect of _____ on conditioning.

Visit the book companion Web site at http://www.academic.cengage.com/psychology/powell for additional practice questions, answers to the Quick Quizzes, practice review exams, and additional exercises and information.

ANSWERS TO CHAPTER TEST

1. autoshaping
2. automaintenance; prevents
3. schedule-induced
4. adjunctive
5. endorphins; pleasant
6. increase; stopped
7. activity
8. anorexia nervosa
9. several small; slowly
10. FT; FI; following
11. more
12. will; drinking tube
13. 3
14. adjunctive
15. preparedness
16. taste aversion; caviar
17. unfamiliar; strongest; overshadowing
18. look; taste
19. Gerald; the food
20. long; a single
21. CS-US relevance
22. perch in a certain spot
23. respondent; elicited; application
24. instinctive drift; fixed action
25. sign tracking
26. displacement; seemingly irrelevant
27. diverse
28. control; delayed
29. activity anorexia
30. food; activity
31. young; similar to
32. behavior systems; situations
33. behavior systems

Comparative Cognition

CHAPTER OUTLINE

Kary was very excited when her parents gave her a lovebird to keep her company while away at college. She named him Oscar, and what a great little guy he turned out to be. Mind you, he has been acting a little strange lately. He squawked like crazy when her new boyfriend dropped by the other night, which completely spoiled the mood. He also has a weird tendency to throw up on her sometimes. She wonders if he's in some way allergic to her.

What is Comparative Cognition?

As you learned in the last chapter, there are many species-specific differences in learning, with certain types of learning often dependent on a particular genetic predisposition. In this chapter, we will explore this topic in more detail by examining evidence from the field of research known as comparative cognition. *Comparative cognition* is the study of information processing across a variety of species, including humans. As noted in Chapter 1, comparative cognition is becoming an increasingly popular research area among many behaviorists these days, with research being conducted on such topics as memory, categorization, decision-making, problem solving, and even complex processes like language use and deception. The term "comparative" refers to the common practice of directly comparing these abilities across species to determine whether their skills are similar or different. This area is sometimes also called "cognitive behaviorism" or "animal cognition," but many researchers prefer the term "comparative cognition" because it recognizes that comparison is key to understanding a species' abilities. It also acknowledges that even when we study the cognitive abilities of just one species, we are often comparing that species to our own.[1]

Within comparative psychology, *Tinbergen's "four questions"* or *"four levels of analysis"* (Tinbergen, 1963) are traditionally used to categorize research findings (see Figure 13.1). The first two questions deal with the *ultimate cause* of a trait, which refers to *the reasons for which that trait evolved within a species*, while the last two questions deal with the *proximate cause* of a trait, which refers to *the more immediate causes for the expression of that trait in an individual* ("proximate" means nearer or more immediate). Listed below are Tinbergen's four questions, with the example of taste aversion learning included to help illustrate their meaning.

---

[1]As we mentioned in Chapter 1, not all behaviorists agree with the growing popularity of cognitive explanations of behavior, contending that noncognitive interpretations are in many cases equally viable. Such debates can be quite complicated, and hence are beyond the scope of this textbook. This chapter, being about comparative cognition, will be written from an explicitly cognitive perspective. But this is not to deny that some interesting arguments can be made for a noncognitive interpretation of certain findings, to which your professor, depending on his or her perspective, may refer.

FIGURE 13.1 Tinbergen's four "questions" (or levels of analysis)

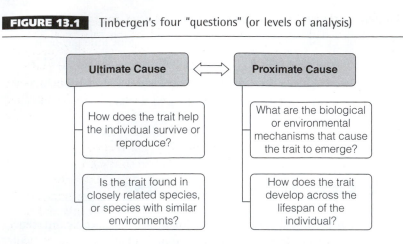

Ultimate Cause (relating to the evolution of the trait within a species):

1) *What purpose does this trait serve for survival or reproduction?*
   Example: One-trial taste aversion learning allows an organism to avoid poisonous food. This would lead to an enhanced rate of survival and reproductive success for members of that species.
2) *How is this trait distributed among various species?*
   Example: Taste aversions are quickly learned in most species with a varied (hence, sometimes risky) diet. Rats (that are unable to vomit when ill) learn it especially quickly. This suggests that individual species acquire taste aversions in ways that are adaptive for their ecological niches.

Proximate Cause (relating to the expression of the trait within an individual):

3) *What biological and environmental events lead to the expression of this trait in an individual?*
   Example: On a biological level, taste aversion learning appears to depend on having a functioning amygdala (Reilly & Bornovalova, 2005). On an environmental level, there must also be a conditioning experience in which a flavor was followed by nausea or illness.
4) *How does this trait emerge or change during an individual's development?*
   Example: Taste aversion learning begins around the time of weaning in mammalian species (Gubernick & Alberts, 1984), and can persist for years.

While any given study may examine only one of these questions at a time, you will generally find researchers working at each level of analysis. As you progress through this chapter, you may therefore find it useful to think about these four questions for each study that is described.

You might also be wondering why comparative psychology has become so popular in recent years. Obviously, many people find animal behavior fascinating, as indicated by the many television stations and programs devoted to this topic. But why the fascination? One suggestion is that humans may have an inherited predisposition to be drawn to or "bond" with nature, including other animals. This is known as the *biophilia hypothesis* (Wilson, 1984), in which biophilia means "love of nature". Thus, humans may find it innately satisfying to do such things as keep pets and build strong relationships with them, go to zoos and observe animals that they can't see in their everyday lives, and hang bird feeders outside their windows in order to draw wild animals close to them. Such curiosity by itself no doubt plays a role in the interest many researchers have in the behavior of different species, including in their cognitive abilities. More importantly, however, the well-researched and highly reliable techniques that behaviorists have developed for the study of animal behavior are in many ways ideal for testing different theories of cognition and for uncovering the different abilities that have evolved to help animals cope with their world. For example, the basic key pecking task with pigeons that has been used to uncover many of the basic principles of operant conditioning can also be an effective means for assessing a pigeon's ability to remember different kinds of events across a variety of conditions. In fact, it can even be used to assess whether a pigeon is more likely to "forget" something if you "tell it" that it needn't bother remembering what it just saw! As you will see, studies such as these have led to some rather remarkable findings, many of which demonstrate how little we know about the animals that surround us. That said, it is also important to remember that comparative researchers are, in keeping with Thorndike's (1911) concerns about the dangers of *anthropomorphism* (attributing human characteristics to animals), still careful to operationalize their variables in ways that can readily be replicated and define behavior in ways that can be precisely measured.

Finally, you may remember from Chapter 2 how experiments in this area often utilize comparative designs to compare the abilities of different species. (If you no longer remember what a comparative design involves, you should quickly go back and review it.) Be aware, however, that the comparative psychologists, biologists and primatologists (researchers who study primates) who work in this area also use a variety of other methods to test their hypotheses. Thus, in this chapter, you will find examples of correlational studies, observational studies, and case studies, as well as various types of experimental research, including comparative designs.

1. Comparative cognition is the study of i＿＿＿＿ p＿＿＿＿ across a variety of species.

2. Tinbergen's "four questions" are related to the u＿＿＿＿ c＿＿＿＿ of a trait and the p＿＿＿＿ c＿＿＿＿ of a trait.

3. Humans have a tendency to be interested in animals and nature. According to the b＿＿＿＿ h＿＿＿＿, this is an i＿＿＿＿ p＿＿＿＿.

QUICK QUIZ A

Memory in Animals

How to Study Animal Memory

Memory processes in animals have been an important area of study in comparative cognition, and one that might seem to present a rather unique challenge to assess. With humans, we closely identify memory with various kinds of verbal behavior. For example, your professor will likely assess your memory for the material you are now studying by giving you a quiz or an exam at some future time when you will be required to verbally respond (in writing) to various verbal stimuli (questions). Animals, however, do not have such verbal ability, so how then can we study their memory?

In answering this question, we need to consider that the act of remembering is, to a large extent, a matter of stimulus discrimination. For example, on a multiple-choice test, each question presents a series of statements (verbal stimuli), but only one of them corresponds to material that you studied earlier. To the extent that the material is well remembered, you will be able to clearly discriminate the correct statement from the other alternatives. If the material is not well remembered—an all too common occurrence, unfortunately—you could very well end up selecting a wrong alternative.

In studying animal memory, similar procedures are used; that is, at one time the animal is shown a certain stimulus and is then required to identify that stimulus at a later time in order to receive a reinforcer. One procedure often used for this these types of studies is called delayed matching-to-sample. In *delayed matching-to-sample*, the animal is first shown a sample stimulus and then, following some delay, is required to select that stimulus out of a group of alternative stimuli. The extent to which the animal is able to select the correct stimulus is regarded as an indicator of its ability to remember that stimulus.

An example of a matching-to-sample task for pigeons is shown in Figure 13.2. The chamber contains three response keys. In the basic procedure, the two side keys are initially dark while a sample stimulus, such as a triangle, is shown on the center key. When the pigeon pecks this sample (or target) stimulus—note that a response is required at this point to ensure that the pigeon has noticed the stimulus—a delay period is entered in which all three keys are dark. Following the delay period, a test period is entered in which the center key is dark and the two side keys are illuminated, one with a triangle and the other with a square. Pecking the triangle (which "matches the sample") is immediately reinforced with food, while pecking the square simply instigates a time-out period followed by the presentation of another trial. Thus, to earn food, the pigeon must select the correct alternative by remembering the sample stimulus that it was shown before the delay.

Using this procedure, one can investigate memory processes in pigeons by systematically altering various aspects of the procedure, such as the similarity of the stimuli during the test phase, the length of time the sample stimulus is presented, the length of the delay period, and the extent to which the delay period includes the presentation of other stimuli that could potentially interfere with the pigeon's memory for the sample stimulus. A particularly interesting capacity that has been investigated in this way is called *directed forgetting*. Directed forgetting occurs when you have been told to forget something—such as when your math professor makes a

FIGURE 13.2   The series of events in a delayed matching-to-sample task. The pigeon is first required to peck at the sample stimulus, which initiates a delay interval in which all keys are dark. Following the delay, a test phase occurs in which pecking at the stimulus that matches the sample results in food. The position of the correct stimulus randomly alternates across trials between the right and left keys; the sample stimulus randomly alternates between a square and a triangle.

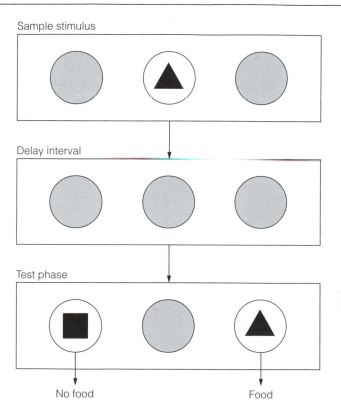

Sample stimulus

Delay interval

Test phase

No food   Food

mistake in a calculation and tells you to forget what he just wrote on the board (assuming that you understood what he was writing in the first place)—and as a result, you do indeed have poorer memory for that material than you would have had without the instruction to forget it. Figure 13.3 shows an example of a directed forgetting procedure for pigeons. The sample stimulus is presented as usual. During the delay period, however, the pigeon is shown either an O on the center key, which indicates that it must remember the sample stimulus, or an X, which indicates that it can forget the sample stimulus because the trial will be starting over again. In essence, the O tells the pigeon that everything is okay and that the test phase will be occurring as usual, whereas the X tells the pigeon something like, "Whoops, made a mistake; we'll be starting over again, so you may as well forget what you've just been shown."

FIGURE 13.3 A delayed matching-to-sample procedure for investigating directed forgetting. During a *remember trial,* the O (the "remember" stimulus) during the delay interval indicates that a test trial will be occurring as usual. During a *forget trial,* the X (the "forget" stimulus) during the delay interval indicates that a test phase will not occur and that the sample stimulus can be forgotten. Forget trials, however, occasionally end with a test phase.

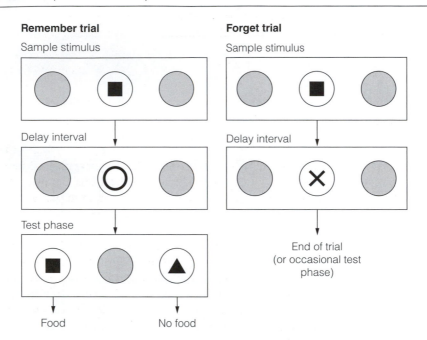

The question, therefore, is whether pigeons are actually less likely to remember the sample stimulus when they have been shown the X (the forget cue) as opposed to the O (the remember cue). The way to test this is to occasionally fool the pigeon by presenting the X and then proceeding to the test phase anyway (sort of like an evil professor who later tests you on lecture material that he explicitly said would not be on the exam). When this is done, it turns out that pigeons do in fact perform worse in the test phase following the forget cue than they do following the remember cue. In other words, when the pigeons are "told" that they need not remember a particular stimulus, they do in fact display poorer memory for that stimulus in the future (e.g., Maki & Hegvik, 1980; see also Kaiser, Sherburne, & Zentall, 1997).

Directed forgetting is only one of the phenomena that comparative psychologists have investigated in birds and is in a sense a demonstration of the potential similarities between birds and humans in the types of memory processes we exhibit. As you will see in the next session, a good deal of effort has also gone into demonstrating the kinds of differences that can occur in memory processes between species.

1. Memory is often a matter of s_____ d_____ in which one is first exposed to a stimulus and is then required to respond to that stimulus at a later time.

2. A useful procedure for studying memory is a d_____ m_____-to-s_____ task. In it, the animal is first shown a s_____ stimulus and then, following some d_____, is required to select that stimulus out of a group of alternative stimuli.

3. In a directed forgetting task, the pigeon is shown a cue during the _____ period, which signals whether the s_____ stimulus needs to be r_____ or can be f_____.

4. On directed forgetting tasks, pigeons are (less/more) _____ likely to select the correct stimulus following exposure to the forget cue.

Memory in Food–Storing Birds

As you may remember from Chapter 1, traits or features of a species that allow members of that species to survive or reproduce are called evolutionary adaptations. Different species have different adaptations because each species occupies its own niche in the environment. For example, a moth that is well camouflaged in its environment is well adapted to that environment. Moths without a camouflaged appearance are more likely to be eaten by predators, whereas moths that blend in with trees or grasses are less likely to be seen and eaten. Camouflaged moths, therefore, will have the opportunity to leave behind more offspring that carry the same genes, and subsequent generations will have more moths with the genes for camouflage and fewer moths without those genes. Predation is, in this case, the selective pressure that leads to the evolution of camouflage in our moth. This is an example of how a physical trait can evolve. But what about a cognitive trait like memory?

If you live in a location where the seasons change dramatically, then you have likely seen a variety of ways that bird species survive a harsh winter when food is difficult to find. Many bird species like geese and ducks migrate from colder areas to warmer areas in order to be able to access food and open water. Such species have therefore evolved rather impressive spatial navigation abilities (Mettke-Hofmann & Greenberg, 2005). Likewise, some birds are predators, and spend the winter hunting other birds or small mammals, in which case they have evolved keen vision and hearing abilities to facilitate hunting (Tucker, 2000). But many non-predators that don't migrate have a different solution; they store food in the fall which they retrieve over the winter. For example, Clark's nutcrackers and black-capped chickadees can store thousands of food items across hundreds of locations, and will retrieve most of them through the course of the winter (Shettleworth, 2010; Sherry & Hoshooley, 2009). For those of us who have difficulty remembering where we parked our car at the mall, this is an incredible feat of memory! However, in order to test whether this ability is specific to these birds, rather than an ability that all birds have (but only some birds make use of), it is necessary to bring both food-storing and non-storing birds into the lab for controlled tests of their memory abilities.

In a comparison of four species of corvids (Clark's nutcrackers, pinyon jays, scrub jays, and Mexican jays) that differ in their reliance on food storing, the Clark's nutcracker significantly outperformed the other three species in tests of retrieval accuracy (Balda & Kamil, 2006). This isn't surprising given that the Clark's nutcracker lives in a harsh, mountainous environment and only survives if it can successfully retrieve its food caches in the winter. Interestingly, the Clark's nutcracker was also better at learning certain types of mazes and at other tests of spatial memory, suggesting that it is a generalized ability that it possesses as opposed to one that is highly specific to one particular setting.

In another study, Brodbeck and Shettleworth (1995) compared the memory ability of black-capped chickadees (a food storing species) to that of dark-eyed juncos (a non-storing species) using a delayed matching-to-sample task, but one that was somewhat different from that described earlier. In the first condition of the experiment, each bird was shown two stimuli during the sample phase. The target stimulus (the one that the bird would have to peck during the test phase in order to get food) had a black circle around it, while the other (distractor) stimulus had no black circle around it. The black circle essentially served as a cue telling the bird which stimulus it had to remember in order to earn food after the delay period. Following the delay period, the bird was again presented with the same two stimuli but with no black circle and the bird could earn the reinforcer only if it pecked at the target. Thus, this task assessed whether birds could remember the target stimulus after a brief delay AND without a cue. As it turns out, in this condition of the experiment, both chickadees and juncos were equally capable of learning the task, which suggests that both species have good memories after a brief delay when having used a cue to identify the target stimulus.

The next condition of the experiment, however, involved a quite different task. During training, the bird was presented with, say, a blue stimulus on the left and a red stimulus on the right, with the blue stimulus on the left being the target. This means that there were two cues which the bird could learn to use to identify which was the correct target: color (blue) and/or position (left). Following training, however, the test phase was suddenly changed such that the bird was presented with a blue stimulus on the right (opposite side to training) and a green stimulus on the left (different color from training). The question of interest was, which stimulus would the chickadee versus the junco now select as the target? If you think about it, birds that are prone to remembering location should choose the green stimulus on the left, because even though it is the wrong color (it isn't blue), it is in the correct location (on the left). However, birds that are prone to remembering visual features should choose the blue stimulus on the right because it has the correct visual appearance (blue) even though it is in the wrong location (right). Now think about food-storing birds, like chickadees, and what features of a stimulus would be more important to them. Would it be more adaptive for them to remember what the tree looks like or where the tree is? Trees aren't likely to move, but they are likely to change in appearance as a result of losing leaves and being covered in snow. This means that chickadees would do best to remember where things are, and should therefore be more likely to choose the stimulus that is in the correct location—and this is precisely what they did. While juncos showed little preference for color or location in this task, chickadees showed a strong preference for location.

What is it about food-storing birds that lead them to preferentially recall the *location* of an item, rather than some other feature? For example, is it a result of social learning, or an innate tendency? In terms of biological factors, it has been discovered that the size of the hippocampus (an area of the brain strongly implicated in spatial memory) is positively correlated with the amount of food-storing that a species does (Pravosudov, 2009) as well as with the amount of practice that any individual within that species has had (Clayton, 2001). Thus, food-storing species of birds have a larger hippocampus than non-storing species, and individual birds with more food-storing experience have a larger hippocampus than those with less storing experience. In fact, chickadees actually grow new hippocampal neurons in fall, when it is time to start storing food for winter. Neurons also continue to be recruited throughout the winter, or die off quickly if they are not activated by appropriate experience (Sherry & Hoshooley, 2007). Thus, much like other arguments regarding the relative contributions of nurture and nature, experience and biology, the answer is that there is an interaction between the two factors.

The important thing to take away from all this is that similar species can have different abilities if they are subjected to different environmental demands; as well, different species can have similar abilities if they are subjected to similar environmental demands. Thus, chickadees and juncos are similar species, but only chickadees need to store food in the winter, and they are the ones with a strong tendency to remember location. Conversely, chickadees and nutcrackers are quite different species, yet they both have excellent spatial memory because both are food-storing species for whom location is critical. From an evolutionary perspective, the memory abilities of food-storing birds have been selected for because those individuals that were better able to retrieve food caches—and learn to retrieve food caches as a result of experience—left behind more offspring and those offspring inherited that ability.

1. When comparing Clark's nutcrackers to other corvids, the nutcracker has better sp_____ m_____, which is important for food storing.

2. In a test comparing chickadees to juncos, it was found that chickadees pay more attention to the l_____ of an item than to the c_____.

3. The h_____ is an area of the brain that is important for spatial memory, and food storing birds tend to have (greater/lesser) _____ volume in this area.

QUICK QUIZ C

Can Animals Count?

The Case of Clever Hans

Imagine that you've left four cookies sitting on a plate in the living room while you walk to the kitchen to get a drink. When you come back, would you notice if there were only three cookies left on the plate? Unless there is something very wrong with your human brain, you would likely perceive the difference immediately. But what about other animals? Are they aware of differences in numbers of items, or could you safely steal a cookie from them?

In the late 1800s, a German horse named Hans became a sensation when it was demonstrated that he could correctly answer mathematical questions by tapping his hoof on the ground. His owner was a math teacher who trained Hans in much the same way that he would teach young children to count and do simple arithmetic, only instead of answering verbally Hans was trained to respond by tapping. He could answer questions that involved adding and subtracting, as well as more complex operations such as fractions. He could even keep track of dates on a calendar. For example, if he were asked "Today is the 5th and it is a Wednesday, so what will the date be on Friday?" then Hans would tap the ground seven times to indicate that Friday would be the 7th. Pretty impressive, isn't it? The German board of Education even set up a commission of scientists (appropriately named "the Hans Commission') to investigate whether there was some trickery involved. But they ruled that Hans was answering questions legitimately with no obvious cues from his trainer. In operant conditioning terms, the commission believed that Hans had learned to do the following:

Question posed: *Tap out the correct answer* → **Earn a tasty treat**
S^D R S^R

Despite the commission's decision, a psychologist named Oskar Pfungst remained skeptical. A few years later, he systematically re-assessed Hans' abilities and determined that Hans was not quite as clever as he seemed. More specifically, Hans could not answer questions correctly if 1) he could not see the person asking the question or 2) the person asking the question did not know the answer to the question (Pfungst, 1911). Pfungst showed that Hans was instead attending to subtle changes in the posture and facial features of the questioner which would almost always change when Hans reached the correct number of taps. For example, if Hans was posed the question, "What is 5 plus 5?", he would simply begin tapping. In turn, the questioner would begin counting the taps, and when Hans reached the correct answer of 10, would almost invariably, on an unconscious level, alter some aspect of his features, such as by slightly dipping his head. In other words, Hans had simply learned to begin tapping on the ground until certain aspects of questioner's features changed. Of course,

Clever Hans only *appeared* to be capable of incredible feats of intellect. (*Source:* From http://www.skepdic.com/cleverhans.)

Das lesende und rechnende Pferd, mit seinem Lehrer HERRN von OSTEN (Berlin)

this by itself was an impressive ability for a horse. But it was also clear that what Hans was doing was not arithmetic, but rather exhibiting a very subtle form of stimulus discrimination. Essentially, from an operant conditioning perspective, what Hans had really learned was the following heterogeneous chain of behaviors:

Question posed: *Tap ground* → **Subtle facial change:**
$$S^D \qquad\qquad R \qquad\qquad S^R/S^D$$

Stop tapping → **Tasty treat**
$$R \qquad\qquad S^R$$

The case of Clever Hans provided an important lesson for researchers studying animal intelligence and cognition. It clearly indicated the need to have certain controls in place for differentiating a sophisticated "cognitive" skill like counting from more basic types of learned behavior. For example, it is often necessary to have experimenters that are *blind* to the purpose of the experiment or to the "expected" behavior of the animal in order to ensure that they are not somehow biasing or guiding the behavior. Unfortunately, another outcome of the Clever Hans case was that some people took it as evidence that only humans have numerical ability. But is that the case? As you will see, research has revealed that a variety of other species can in fact process information about numbers.

Beyond Clever Hans: Evidence for Numerical Ability in Animals

Otto Koehler was an early psychologist who was interested in animal intelligence. In order to test whether animals could count, he trained several species of birds, such as parrots, that were known for their "intelligence" to differentiate between numerical values (Koehler, 1951). For this he used a direct *matching-to-sample* task, similar to that described earlier, but without any delay in place between the presentation of the sample stimulus and the test stimuli. Whereas a delayed matching-to-sample task is used to test memory, a direct matching-to-sample task can be used for testing categorization. For example, a parrot might be shown a sample card with three dots on it along with two other cards that also have dots on them, one of which matched the number of dots on the sample. The parrot had to choose the *matching* card, such as by flipping it over, in order to earn the reinforcer. An important aspect of this procedure is that the dots could be of varying sizes and orientations, so the bird could not simply choose a card that was a replica of the sample. For example, the sample card might have two large dots and one small dot laid out in a line, whereas the correct response card could have three small dots organized in a triangle pattern. It was the *number* of dots that mattered and not their size or orientation. As it turns out, Koehler's research revealed that birds were particularly good at this task so long as the numbers remained relatively small. Some birds could match numbers as large as six or seven, but most failed beyond that point. Results like this therefore indicate that some animals can respond to stimuli in terms of their quantity and that they can differentiate quantity from volume or size.

Another type of procedure used to investigate numerical abilities in animals is borrowed from developmental studies with human infants, and hence allows for a direct comparison of animals' abilities with infants' abilities. Using a bucket with a false bottom, a researcher places items (grapes, toys, or some other valued commodity) into a bucket one at a time while the subject (animal or human infant) watches. On some trials, each item remains in the visible portion of the bucket while on other trials items are hidden in the false bottom. The subject is then given the opportunity to look into the bucket and retrieve the items. On the "visible" trials, the subject will find the exact number of items that had been placed in the bucket. On the "hidden" trials, the subject will find a number of items that is fewer than what it had seen being placed in the bucket. The independent variable is the amount of time the subject spends searching for items when allowed to retrieve the items from the bucket. Human infants even under one year of age will continue searching after retrieving 1 item if they saw 2 items go into the bucket. They will also keep searching if they retrieve 2 items after seeing 3 items go into the bucket. Once the quantity of items gets beyond 3, however, they don't seem to keep track (Feigenson & Carey, 2003).

How does this skill compare to that of other species? As it turns out, several species demonstrate a similar ability. Mongoose lemurs, for example, will keep searching after retrieving 1 item if they witnessed 2 or more items being placed in the bucket. Interestingly, they can also distinguish between larger quantities but only in a proportional sense. They can distinguish that 2 is more than 1 (as evidenced by their search time if they only find 1) and that 4 is more than 2, but they are not as good at distinguishing that 3 is more than 2 (finding 2 items they may not bother searching for the 3rd one) or that 8 is more than 6. This is the case even though the absolute difference between, say, 8 and 6 is actually larger than the difference between 2 and 1 and is equal to the difference between 4 and 2. What does this tell us about lemurs' ability to understand quantity? They don't seem to do it in terms of counting or absolute quantity, but rather in terms of proportion. (Two is readily distinguished from 4 because 2 is 50% less than 4, but 6 is not readily distinguished from 8 because 6 is 25% less than 8. Thus, they can distinguish a large proportional difference but not a small proportional difference.) Interestingly, this same species of lemur will also continue to search after retrieving a whole grape if they saw two half grapes placed into the bucket. This suggests they are tracking the number of food items as opposed to the volume of food items (Lewis, Jaffe, & Brannon, 2005).

Thus, a variety of studies with nonhuman species have provided evidence of ***numerosity***, which can be defined as an understanding of quantity. Primates have been repeatedly tested for this skill and all have demonstrated some capacity for distinguishing among small numbers. Larger numbers, however, seem to be well-understood only by older humans (Shettleworth, 2010).

QUICK QUIZ D

1. The case of C_____ H_____ reminds us that it is often important to have testers or experimenters who are b_____ to the conditions or expectations of the test.

2. Koehler used a direct m_____- to-s_____ task in order to determine whether parrots could match cards with different n_____ of items on them.

3. Results from Koehler's studies indicate that some birds can distinguish q_____ from vo_____ or s_____.

4. Using a bucket with a false bottom, researchers have determined that human infants will (continue / not continue) _____ to search if 3 items were placed in the bucket but only 2 items can be seen.

5. Using the same bucket task, lemurs seem to track differences between placed versus found items based on (proportion / absolute quantity) _____.

6. Although small numbers seem to be tracked and understood by a variety of species, larger numbers seem to be only understood by older h_____.

And Furthermore

When "Bird Brains" Outperform People

It's easy to assume that humans are cognitively superior to other species. Humans may not have wings, claws, or pretty stripes, but we do have wonderfully large brains! There are times, however, when our highly specialized intellect fails us, and other species beat us in complex tasks.

In an old TV game show called "Let's Make a Deal", contestants were asked to choose between three doors. Behind each door was a prize. One prize was valuable, such as a trip or a large sum of cash, whereas the other two were far less valuable (e.g., an old donkey or a month's supply of toilet paper). After the choice had been made, the host would open, not the chosen door, but one of the unchosen doors to reveal a worthless prize behind it. The contestant would then have the option of A) sticking with their original choice or B) switching to the other remaining door. What choice would you make?

If you are like most people, you would probably stay with your original choice because you would perceive that you started with a 1/3 probability of having chosen correctly (one of the three doors has a valuable prize behind it) and now that one door has been removed, the probability that you chose correctly has increased to 1/2. Thus, you may as well stay with your original choice. Another way of looking at it is that between the two remaining doors, there is now a 50% chance that you have chosen the valuable prize, so whether you switch or don't switch, the probability will remain the same.

Well, it turns out that you are wrong! In this logic problem (which is now known as the *Monty Hall dilemma*, after the host of the TV show), there is a higher probability of winning if you SWITCH after one of the doors has been eliminated! The reason is as follows. When you start out, there is a 1/3 probability that you chose correctly and 2/3 probability that you chose incorrectly. The 2/3 probability of being wrong DOES NOT CHANGE when one of the options is removed. So 2/3 of the time, sticking with your original choice will result in a loss. (If you are still confused by it, don't worry, even some matheticians are fooled by this problem [Vos Savant, 1990]. For further explanations of this puzzle, you can also search the web for *Monty Hall dilemma*.)

So how do pigeons do on a task like this? After playing this game several times (for food, rather than trips and cash), they begin to show evidence of *matching* and *overmatching* as described in Chapter 10. In other words, pigeons will match, or overmatch, the proportion of times they switch to the proportion of times switching leads to reinforcement. Because switching alternatives on this task leads to reinforcement two-thirds of the time, then pigeons will choose to switch two-thirds of the time (or, in the case of overmatching, more than that). This means that pigeons perform significantly better on this task than do humans who, with all their wondrous brain power, tend not to switch even after repeated trials (Hebranson & Schroeder, 2010)!

So why are humans so terrible at this task? One way of looking at it is that humans are using "*classical probability*" by looking at the problem and trying to calculate the likelihood that the prize is behind a given door. Thus, humans look ahead and attempt to rationally (if incorrectly) predict the probability of a certain outcome given the alternatives available. Most of the time, that would be a good strategy, but not in situations like this in which the outcome is tricky. Pigeons, however, appear to utilize "*empirical probability*" in which choices are made based on prior experience with a task (Herbranson & Schroeder, 2010). (It is as though they are asking themselves, what happened the last 10 times that I stayed versus the last 10 times that I switched?) Thus, while clever humans are trying to reason things out, independent of their experience, the pigeons are simply reacting on the basis on what has already happened. And in the same way that rule-governed learning is sometimes inferior to learning based on the actual contingencies of reinforcement (as discussed in Chapter 11), so too statistical reasoning is sometimes inferior.

But why don't human subjects learn to override this tendency when they are given repeated experiences with the task (which is an advantage the game-show participants never had)? It appears that humans have a strong bias toward trying to predict certain types of outcomes and basing their behavior on that prediction. It should be noted that children outperform adults on this task, so this appears to be a bias that develops as one grows older (DeNeys, 2006). On top of this, because of the one-third trials where our choice to stay turns out to be correct, we may to use this as evidence that our non-switching strategy is correct. In a sense, we are intermittently reinforced for non-switching, with instances of success being more salient than instances of failure. From a cognitive perspective, this is known as *confirmation bias*, in which we notice evidence that supports our strategy and ignore evidence that contradicts it, even though the contradictory evidence occurs more frequently than supportive evidence.

Of course, another way of looking at it is that people sometimes think they're a lot more clever than they are!

Category Learning and Relational Decisions

If various animals can determine how many items are in a group, can they also determine whether those items *belong together* or not? Learning a category involves being able to generalize and discriminate, two features of learning that are found across species. The training and testing procedures used to determine whether animals can learn to categorize are very similar to those used in studying basic processes of discrimination and generalization as outlined in earlier chapters. In other words, animals are subjected to a discrimination training procedure and then tested on the extent to which the learned response subsequently generalizes to other stimuli.

To start with a simple example, Herrnstein (1979) used standard discrimination training to get pigeons to categorize "trees" by presenting 40 pictures that contained trees and 40 pictures that did not contain trees. The birds earned reinforcement for pecking at a "tree" picture (an S^D), but not for pecking at a "non-tree" picture (an S^Δ). Not surprisingly, pigeons learned to discriminate trees from non-trees and would only peck at the tree photos. The next step in the process was to determine whether pigeons could generalize this training to novel pictures. As it turns out, the birds were very likely to peck at novel tree pictures, and very unlikely to peck at novel non-tree pictures. This demonstrates that pigeons can learn to group similar items together and then apply the "category" of *tree* to items they haven't seen before.

A more complicated ability involves organizing items or individuals in terms of how they relate to one another. For example, if you know that your friend is dating someone, then you know it would be risky to try flirting with that person. You understand that there is a social connection between those two people that affects the way you interact with them. It would also be useful to understand other social hierarchies that exist in your world. If you know that Helen is Richard's boss, but Stephen is Helen's boss, then you can infer that Stephen is more powerful than Richard. This second example requires a skill known as ***transitive inference***: a form of reasoning in which the relationship between two objects can be inferred by knowing the relationship of each to a third object. To use an abstract example, if A > B and B > C, then A > C (where > means "greater than"). Humans appear to be particularly good at this type of reasoning. However, many investigators are now convinced that other species are capable of this type of reasoning as well, but it seems to depend on the type of social structure that exists for that species.

Looking again at lemurs, it is interesting to note that some species of lemurs live in large social groups with clear dominance hierarchies while other species of lemurs live in small groups without a rigid hierarchy. It is theorized that living in a society, with all its rules and relationships, leads to an evolution of cognitive skills that would facilitate living socially. You can imagine how dangerous it would be if you were unable to identify the dominant individuals (or the bullies, or the friendly people) in your group. Thus, it is predicted that social species should have better skills at understanding things like hierarchies and hence at making transitive inferences.

In order to test this hypothesis, MacLean, Merritt and Brannon (2008) trained two groups of lemurs on a transitive inference task. One group consisted of ring-tailed lemurs, who are very social and live in large groups with a rigid social hierarchy. The second group consisted of mongoose lemurs, who are less social and live in small unstructured groups.

During training, the animals were presented a series of trials in which two images, (such as an image of *wavy lines* paired with an image of a *person*, or an image of a *star* paired with an image of *dots*), were simultaneously presented on a touch screen (see Figure 13.4). For each pair of items, one of the images was "higher ranked", which meant that selecting it resulted in reinforcement (it was an S^D), and the other item was "lower ranked", which meant that selecting it did not result in reinforcement (it was an S^Δ). But whether the item was higher ranked or lower ranked depended on which other image it was paired with. For example (going back to the use of letters which will be easier

FIGURE 13.4 Researcher Elizabeth Brannon with one of the lemurs working on a touch screen computer. (*Source*: Retrieved from: http://brannonlab.org.s84504. gridserver.com/wp-content/uploads/2010/06/Liz-with-Ringtail.jpg)

Courtesy of Brannon Lab

to follow), when images B and C were presented together, then selecting image B was reinforced (which we will indicate as B > C), whereas when images C and D were presented together, then selecting item C was reinforced (C > D). Training therefore consisted of having the lemurs learn the relative rankings of images within each of a number of pairs, such as: A > B, B > C, C > D, D > E, and E > F. During the actual training sessions, each image was randomly presented on either the left or right side of the screen, regardless of whether it was higher ranked on that occasion or lower ranked, to prevent the animal from learning to select on the basis of location rather than image. As it turns out, both types of lemurs learned this task quite readily, and selected the higher ranked image the majority of the time.

Following training, a test phase was conducted in which the lemurs were given 30 recall trials of familiar adjacent pairs (e.g., C and D, the same as during training) and 6 trials of novel, previously non-adjacent pairs (e.g., B and D, which were never paired during training). The question was whether, when presented with the novel pairings, the lemurs would transfer their understanding of the relative rankings to the novel pair. For example, would they transfer B's rank over C, and C's rank over D, into a choice of B over D? In fact, the ring-tailed lemurs (the social ones) performed quite well on this task and were able to use their previous training to make inferences about relationships among new pairs of items. Moreover, the farther apart the novel items were on the scale (e.g., B and F as opposed to B and D), the greater the accuracy that the ring-tailed lemurs displayed. The mongoose lemurs, on the other hand, responded at around chance level for all novel pairs. But when the researchers repeated this experiment using a correction procedure (all subjects were given more feedback on their performance and more systematic training about the hierarchy), both groups performed equally well. This suggests that both species are capable of learning the task, but that ring-tailed lemurs learn it more readily, with less explicit instruction. This supports the hypothesis that social hierarchy is an evolutionary pressure that enhances the acquisition of this type of skill (MacLean, Merritt, & Brannon, 2007).

1. Herrnstein (1979) trained pigeons to peck at pictures of trees, and not at non-trees. This is a d_____ t_____ procedure.

2. Herrnstein's study revealed that pigeons could g_____ their discrimination to novel pictures of trees, which suggests that they had learned the c_____ of tree.

3. Trevor is taller than Leah, and Leah is taller than Jeff. If you know that Trevor is taller than Jeff, then you have successfully made a t_____ i_____.

4. When lemurs are tested for their ability to understand relationships among items, the species with the rigid social hierarchy is (more/less) _____ skilled at relational decisions than the less social species.

Concepts of Tools, Self, and Others

Making and Using Tools

One piece of evidence that an animal has higher cognitive abilities is tool use. Using an item in a manipulative way demonstrates that the individual understands the relationship between objects and their effects. For example, imagine that you've dropped your keys into a tight spot that you can't reach. If you get a wire hanger and bend it so that you can use it to hook your keys and drag them out, then you have shown that you understand how to manipulate the environment to have a desired effect. You have solved a problem by utilizing a separate piece of equipment. Humans are great problem-solvers and tool-users, but a number of other species are capable of such skills also.

The simplest form of tool use involves the use of an existing item. For example, a sea otter will use rocks to crack open the shells of mussels or crabs (Hall & Schaller, 1964). Use of rocks to open nuts, shellfish, or eggs is also common among primates as well as some birds (Fragaszy et al., 2004; Shettleworth, 2010). Chimpanzees are known to use twigs to "fish" for termites by sticking the twigs into a termite mound. The termites swarm the invading tool, and then the chimp can withdraw the twig and slide a whole troupe of termites into her mouth at once (Sanz & Morgan, 2007). Chimps also use twigs to dip honey out of beehives (Boesch & Boesch, 1990), marrow out of bones, and water out of puddles (Sanz & Morgan, 2007). Sometimes tools are used for protection or for comfort. Chimpanzees have been observed laying down vegetation just to sit on and using leaves to cover their heads from the rain. They will also use leaves to clean wounds or wipe their faces (Sanz & Morgan, 2007). Bonobos (formerly named "pygmy chimpanzees" because they are so similar to chimps it was thought they were the same species) will sometimes use leaves and branches to cover their nests during bad weather (Kano, 1982) and dolphins will cover their snouts with sponges in order to prevent injury while hunting (Smolker et al., 1997).

Will just any rock or twig be sufficient for the task? For some species, there doesn't appear to be a great deal of selectivity but others are very picky. For example, black-breasted buzzards (Aumann, 1990) and Egyptian vultures (Thouless, Fanshawe, & Bertram, 1989) have been shown to prefer a particular weight and size of stone when selecting stones to crack open the eggs of other birds. New Caledonian crows also tend to be choosy about their tools, such as a twig to fetch food out of a hole. In laboratory studies, crows will preferentially select tools that are long enough to reach a desired item and some will select the appropriate tool even if it must be retrieved from another room (Chappell & Kacelnik, 2002). Tool use by itself seems to indicate a certain amount of intelligence and planning, but selectivity in tool use suggests a more sophisticated understanding of cause and effect.

---

1. Tool use by a species is evidence of understanding relationships between objects and their e_____.

2. The simplest form of tool is an ex_____ item like a stick or a rock.

3. Buzzards and vultures show (no/some) _____ preference for the weight of rocks they use to crack open eggs. This is evidence of (more/less) _____ cognitive complexity than basic tool use.

QUICK QUIZ F

Further evidence of planning is found among species that keep tools for more than one use. Saving or carrying a tool when there is no immediate need for it implies that the animal has the capacity to *expect* a future need for the tool. This prospective and proactive behavior is typical of chimpanzees, bonobos, and orangutans, all of whom can maintain a variety of tools for a variety of tasks (Mulcahy & Call, 2006). Some non-primates will also save tools for another time. For example, a sea otter will often keep a rock that has been previously used to crack open crustaceans, even when it is not currently feeding (Hall & Schaller, 1964). One of the most striking examples of saving an item for later use comes from an animal that one might not have expected to be capable of such foresight. Veined octopuses have been filmed using and transporting coconut shells, which they use as portable shelters and hiding places (Finn, Tregenza, & Norman, 2009). (Do a web search for *octopus* and *coconut shell* and you should easily find examples of the original videos taken by the researchers.) If you watch the video, you'll see that carrying your shelter around is not an easy task! The octopus finds a shell, wraps its tentacles around it and then "walks" with the shell tucked up under its body. When it encounters a predator, it then drops the shell and climbs underneath. One octopus was filmed using two half-shells and combining them to create a closed unit. But this is not the only example of clever behavior by octopuses. For example, at the Sea Star Aquarium in Germany, one problematic octopus is known for throwing rocks to smash glass, juggling the hermit crabs in its enclosure, and repeatedly short-circuiting a light by squirting a stream of water into the fixture (Otto the octopus wreaks havoc, 2008). Although this is anecdotal evidence, any animal that is rumored to juggle its cage-mates deserves further study!

Beyond tool use and tool carrying, it would seem to require even greater cognitive complexity to combine tools or to modify existing materials in order to create a new tool. The species that demonstrate this level of intelligence are very few indeed. Not surprisingly, though, chimpanzees have demonstrated this kind of ability. The chimpanzees of the Goualougo Triangle in the Congo use two or more types of sticks in order to fish for termites. One type of stick is harvested from a tree that produces straight, rigid twigs with smooth sides. These sticks are gathered and taken to the foraging site which may be more than 100 meters away. There, the sticks are broken to a particular length and the chimps sharpen the ends by chewing them. Once modified, the sticks are used to poke holes into termite mounds. Next, another type of tool is inserted into the mound. These have been harvested from a different type of plant, with long flexible stalks and fibres that can be frayed to create a brush-like effect on the end (Sanz & Morgan, 2007). As you can see, this is a multi-step process that requires harvesting of two different types of plants, at different points in time, and at locations that are not necessarily near the spot where they are modified or used. The chimpanzees that are successful at termite fishing in this way do seem capable of a rather sophisticated level of planning.

Where does the ability to use or create tools come from? Like many complex skills, animals can learn to use tools through observation and social interaction. For example, in the Tai forest in western Africa, chimpanzees use stone tools to crack coula nuts that are steadied or braced in tree trunks or other rocks. This hammer-and-anvil technique allows the chimp to focus a lot of force on a precise area, cracking the hard outer shell of the nut without pulverizing the softer seeds inside. It is a delicate task, and takes up to seven years to master the skill. Very young chimps sit and watch the nut-crackers work, and don't start using the nut-cracking tools until around three years of age. After that, practice makes perfect (with a bit of additional facilitation from role models) but the learning is slow (Boesch & Boesh-Achermann, 2000).

Although social learning may be the primary way in which animals acquire many of their tool using skills, there may also be a certain amount of insight or innovation involved. In the laboratory and in the field, crows and chimpanzees have demonstrated novel use of implements, novel modification of implements over time, and even modification of implements that have not previously been encountered (Yamamoto, Yamakoshi, Humle & Matsuzawa, 2008; Weir, Chappell, & Kacelnik, 2002). This suggests an ability to go beyond what one has been socially taught, and it is possible that tool use often involves both insight and social learning. (See Figure 13.5.)

1. Saving a tool for later use is common among p_____ including chimpanzees, gorillas, and bonobos, but is (also/not) _____ seen among other species.

2. Chimps have also shown the ability to cr_____ tools as well as mo_____ existing tools.

3. It appears that chimps learn to crack nuts through a long, gradual process of s_____ l_____.

4. In order for tool use to start, there is likely some form of in_____ that occurs where an item is used in a new way for the first time.

FIGURE 13.5 Betty the crow, who became famous for her discovery of how to fashion a tool to retrieve a "food bucket" from a "well". In the photo at left, Betty has just finished bending a wire into the shape of a hook. She then inserts the wire into the well to hook the handle of the bucket and retrieve it (Weir, Chappell, & Kacelnik, 2002, p. 981). Videos of Betty's performance can readily be found by searching the web for Betty the crow. (*Source:* Retrieved from http://users.ox.ac.uk/~kgroup/tools/crow_photos.shtml)

Oxford University – Dept. of Zoology

Theory of Mind

The creation, modification, retention, and use of tools demonstrates that a variety of species, including primates, birds, marine mammals, and even invertebrates, can evolve the cognitive capacity to understand cause and effect, and to plan ahead in order to manipulate the environment. Could these animals also have other abilities that we typically consider to be "uniquely human"? What about the ability to understand the mind of others, and use that information to achieve different types of goals? *Theory of mind* is the tendency to impute mental states to other individuals (Premack & Woodruff, 1978). This means seeing oneself as separate from others, and recognizing that the content of another's mind is different from one's own. If you have a theory of mind, then you can understand that someone else has information you don't (so you can ask questions of them), or that someone lacks information that you have (so you can conceal or share that information). As adult humans, we often take this ability for granted. We can ponder our own thoughts, and how others perceive us. We can share juicy gossip, or we can lie about an upcoming surprise party. As we discussed previously, however, the need to avoid anthropomorphism necessitates the use of very strict tests and cautious interpretation in assessing this kind of ability in animals.

QUICK QUIZ H

1. Camilla sees a spider near her sister Rory. Camilla knows that Rory is afraid of spiders, so she intentionally steps on the spider before Rory sees it. This intentional behavior could only occur because Camilla has t_____ of m_____.

2. Sharing or concealing information requires that you understand that you are s_____ from others, and that the c_____ of your mind is different from others'.

Self-Awareness and Differentiating Self from Others

One of the key features of a mind that can understand other minds is called *self-awareness*: the ability to see oneself as separate from others. It's difficult for a human to imagine what it must be like to not recognize oneself in the mirror or to not feel separate from others, but it seems as though many species do not have that ability. A classic test of self-awareness is known as the *mark and mirror task*. This test was developed independently by Gordon Gallup (1970), an animal behaviorist, and Beulah Amsterdam (1972), a clinical child psychologist. Both researchers were interested in the emergence of self-recognition and self-exploration that young primates (including humans) demonstrate when they have access to their own reflection. It was clear to both researchers that young apes and toddlers were interested in mirrors, but were they using mirrors in the same way? Were they seeing *themselves* or just an image?

Although different versions of the mark and mirror task have been used, the key features of the task are as follows: First, the subject is marked on the face with a noticeable bit of odorless paint or makeup. It is important that the subject not be aware of the mark when it is applied. Generally the mark is applied surreptitiously during another habitual activity, like when a mother cleans her child's face or when a zoo handler is petting the face of a young chimp during a daily interaction. Next, the subject is given access to a mirror and the subject's behavior is coded for his or her reaction to the image in the mirror. Evidence of self-recognition includes the subject touching the mark on its face while looking in the mirror, and other uses of the mirror to explore its body. For example, chimps will use the mirror to look at their teeth or get a very close look at their bottoms! Evidence of a lack of self-recognition includes reacting to the image as if it were another individual. In chimps this usually means aggression or fear. In infants, it may mean pointing to the image and saying "baby!" (if that is how the infant normally interacts with other infants). When both chimpanzees and human infants are tested in similar ways, it is clear that both species demonstrate self-recognition before the age of three years. Humans generally pass the test by around 24 months, and many chimpanzees pass the test by 28 months of age (Bard, Todd, Bernier, Love, & Leavens, 2006). Other species that pass the mark and mirror task include dolphins (Reiss & Marino, 2001), magpies (Prior, Schwartz, & Güntürkün, 2008), and elephants (Plotnik, de Waal, & Reiss, 2006), in addition to great apes like bonobos, orangutans, gibbons and gorillas (e.g., Heschl & Fuchsbichler, 2009). It has even been demonstrated in pigeons, though it took a considerable amount of training before it became evident (Epstein, Lanza, & Skinner, 1981).[2] Interestingly, even in species where self-recognition has been documented, it is not necessarily displayed by all members of the group. It appears that there is considerable variance within a species in terms of these cognitive abilities (Shettleworth, 2010).

---

[2]Not surprisingly, Epstein, Lanza, and Skinner (1981) interpreted these results as indicating that a cognitive interpretation of such constructs as "self-awareness" is unwarranted, and that researchers should instead focus on discovering the contingencies of reinforcement that lead a person or animal to display the type of behavior patterns that we interpret as self-awareness. In response, it has been argued that no pigeon has ever been found to spontaneously use a mirror for self-exploration, nor has any pigeon ever passed the mark and mirror task without explicit training (de Waal, 2008). Note that videos of the pigeon and self-awareness study can readily be found on the web by searching for such keywords as *Epstein, Skinner, pigeons* and *cognition*. The full video also includes a fascinating demonstration of training a pigeon to solve the classic "box-and-banana" problem that was famously used by Kohler (1959) to test for the occurrence of "insight" in chimpanzees (which Skinner and Epstein also argue is unwarranted).

1. The m_____ and m_____ task is a classic test of s_____- a_____ that has been used with a variety of species including humans.

2. Poppy the chimp is using a mirror to look at her teeth and her ears. Poppy is likely older than (24/28) _____ months.

3. Aside from primates, others species that show evidence of self-awareness include do_____, el_____, and mag_____.

4. There is considerable v_____ within a species for many high-level cognitive abilities. This means that (all / not all) _____ individuals within a species will show evidence of the ability.

Once you have the ability to see yourself as separate from others, what thoughts emerge from that ability? Can you then use information in different ways? (Or, to put it rather confusingly, do you know that they know that you know what they know?) In an attempt to determine whether children and other animal species can "understand the contents of another mind," researchers have used tasks where certain information is provided to the subject and then the subject is questioned or observed to see if that information is used to correctly infer what another individual knows. In the *false belief task*, children are told a story using props. For example, a researcher might tell the following story to a child: "Sally was playing with her teddy bear. Then it was time for dinner. Sally put her bear away in her toy box (here, the researcher would place the teddy bear into the toy box) and she went downstairs to eat. While she was gone, Sally's brother Billy came in and played with the teddy bear. Billy put the teddy bear under the bed (here, the researcher would place the bear under the toy bed). When Sally came back into the room, where do you think she looked for her teddy bear?" Children under the age of about four years typically say that Sally will look under the bed. This is where the bear is, and this is where the subject knows the bear to be. Children over the age of four typically respond that Sally will look in the box, because that's where Sally left it and she didn't know that the bear had been moved (see Baron-Cohen, Tager-Flusberg, & Cohen, 2000). This is an excellent task for verbal children, who can tell you where to look and also explain their choices. How could you test for this sort of ability in other species?

Chimpanzees live within a dominance hierarchy, and tend to be very competitive for food. If two chimps want the same food item, and one is more dominant than the other, then the dominant individual always takes the food or injures the lower-ranking chimp if there is conflict. Brian Hare and his colleagues used this situation to create a test that would determine whether low-ranking chimps could avoid punishment and still acquire food, by inferring what a dominant chimp knows (Hare, Call, & Tomasello, 2001). Two bananas were placed inside an enclosure. A dominant chimp could see into the enclosure from one end, and the subordinate chimp could see into the enclosure

FIGURE 13.6   In the *hidden banana task*, the subordinate chimp on the right can see both bananas, while the dominant chimp on the left is unable to see the banana on the other side of the barrier. If the subordinate chimp can infer what the dominant chimp can see, then, to minimize conflict, it should choose the hidden banana. (Although both bananas are placed closer to the dominant chimp, the subordinate chimp will be given a head start into the enclosure.) (*Source:* Reprinted with permission from Shettleworth, S. J., *Cognition, Evolution, and Behavior.* Figure 12.13 on page 444. Copyright © 2010 by Oxford University Press.)

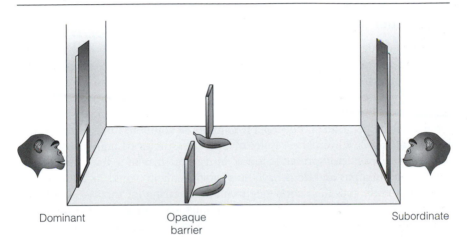

Dominant   Opaque   Subordinate
                                 barrier

from the opposite end. The chimps could see each other, and, if they were to take the perspective of the other, should also be able to know what the other is capable of seeing. One banana was placed in an area where it could clearly be seen by both chimps, but a second banana was placed behind a barrier where it could *only* be seen by the subordinate chimp. This *hidden banana* was put behind the barrier while the subordinate chimp was watching, but the dominant chimp was not watching. This meant that subordinate chimp could potentially retrieve the "hidden" banana without conflict, because the dominant chimp would be unaware of its presence (see Figure 13.6). But were the subordinate chimps actually capable of inferring what the dominant chimp did or did not know? In this and other variations of the task, subordinate chimps preferentially went for the hidden banana. This demonstrates that they were able to use information about what could be known by the dominant chimp to their advantage (Hare et al., 2001). These sorts of tasks, using differential information and competitive situations, reveal that other species, including jays, ravens, and baboons also act as if they are inferring the knowledge of another individual (Shettleworth, 2010).

1. The f_____ b_____ task is used to determine whether a child can use information correctly to i_____ what someone else would know.

2. Julie knows that someone placed Billy's teddy bear in a box, but Billy doesn't know. When asked where Billy would look, Julie says he will look in the box. Julie is likely (older/younger) _____ than 4 years of age.

3. Using the "hidden banana" task, it has been demonstrated that chimps (can/cannot) _____ use information about what dominant chimps know to make good decisions in a competitive task.

Cooperation and Deception

If I have unique information about a potential resource and about your abilities, there are two key ways that I could use that information. I could provide you with information that would allow us to cooperate and work together to acquire the resource, or I could mislead you in some way so that I acquire the resource for myself. Much like the tasks described in the last section, intentional cooperation and deception require the ability to infer what another individual knows. Given the results of previous studies of animal cognition, you might expect that primates, some birds, and maybe a few other social species like dolphins and dogs have these abilities. You would be correct!

Many species appear to cooperate in hunting, caring for infants, alarm calling, and other social activities. These examples of mutual action for mutual benefit are interesting, but because the behaviors are often acquired gradually over long periods of time, after considerable exposure to a variety of experiences, they are not necessarily evidence that animals are cooperating "intentionally", or with an "understanding" of how their actions affect other individuals (Shettleworth, 2010). However, animals that appear to have a theory of mind are sometimes able to cooperate in laboratory settings using novel tasks that require coordinated actions. One such task is the *rope task*, in which a rope is strung loosely through hooks attached to a board. On the board is food. If both animals pull the rope at the same time, the board will be pulled toward the animal's enclosure and the animals will get the food. But if only one animal pulls the rope, then the rope will simply slide through the hooks and detach itself from the board. The animal then has a rope, but no food.

So how do chimps fare in a cooperative task? Not well. Despite their intelligence at solving many other problems, chimpanzees are so competitive with one another that they seem to have a difficult time cooperating. In situations where they do cooperate, it is usually two individuals that have a history of sharing food (like a mother and daughter) or a pair comprised of one dominant individual and one subordinate (with the dominant one taking the entire prize most of the time) (Melis, Hare, & Tomasello, 2006). Bonobos, however, tend to do very well at this task. Chimps and bonobos are closely related, and the two species are our closest primate cousins, but bonobos tend to be less aggressive and more cooperative than chimps (Rilling et al., 2011). Bonobos engage in cooperative feeding, are very tolerant of one another, and will coordinate their actions by paying close attention to what their task partners are doing (Hare et al., 2007). Other species that tend to do well on the rope task include carnivores that are tolerant of one another, like spotted hyenas (Drea & Carter, 2009) and rooks, a bird species similar to ravens (Seed, Clayton, & Emory, 2008). As more species are tested using these sorts of procedures, we will likely find more evidence of animal cooperation. However, it is not expected to be particularly widespread.

If cooperation is rare, then what about *deception*? Which animals are most likely to use information *against* fellow members of their species for their own gain? When we use the term deception in this context, we are referring to either concealment of information or the presentation of misinformation. There are other, simpler forms of deception in the wild including the use of camouflage or evasion of predators, but those forms of deception are more mechanistic processes for which a theory of mind is unnecessary. For the purpose of making inferences about animal cognition, the type of deception described here requires more "thought".

Not surprisingly, chimps are capable of deceiving one another and also of deceiving humans. In one laboratory task, chimps were shown two containers, one of which contained a food reward. In some cases, chimps would interact with a *cooperative* trainer; if the chimp pointed to the container that held food, the trainer would retrieve the food and share it. In other cases the chimps would interact with an *uncooperative* trainer; if the chimp pointed to the container that held food, the trainer would retrieve the food and eat all of it himself. Chimps in this latter condition initially learned to share no information. In fact, they would turn their backs on the trainer and refuse to take part in the task at all (but they would still cooperate with the cooperative trainer). Eventually, though, after many trials, some of the chimps learned to point toward the empty container when interacting with the uncooperative trainer. This misinformation was only provided to the uncooperative trainer, which suggests those chimps were selectively providing misinformation to the uncooperative trainer (Woodruff & Premack, 1979).

Other, more complex examples of misinformation come from observations in the field and in large social groups of animals. Frans de Waal (1986) observed a chimp that limped for a week after a violent encounter with a rival, but only limped when the rival was watching! In another example, a low-ranking male would make an alarm call, which led other more dominant males to go investigate. Once the other males had left the area, the first male would take the opportunity to copulate with females, unharassed by the more dominant males. Although this appears to be an example of a clever ruse, it is important to remember that such reports are anecdotal with the behaviors occurring in uncontrolled situations. It remains possible that the alarm call was not an actual misdirection, and the low-ranking male simply took advantage of the absence of the dominant males. Then again, it could be as clever as it appears. Needless to say, further research is necessary to determine whether such behavior that *looks* intelligent really *is* intelligent.

1. Intentional cooperation or deception requires a t_____ of m_____.

2. In the r_____ task, two animals must c_____ by pulling at the same time in order to get food.

3. Bonobos are (more/less) _____ successful in cooperative tasks than chimps, which is likely related to that species being (more/less) _____ competitive over food.

4. Chimps can learn to point toward an empty container when interacting with an u_____ trainer. This is evidence that chimps are capable of d_____.

5. There is a great deal of a_____ evidence of misinformation among chimpanzees, but further controlled testing is necessary to determine whether this behavior is i_____.

Language

Since you have managed to make it this far in this book, it is a pretty safe bet that you understand language, and not only *written* language but *spoken* language and *symbolic* language—like road signs, gestures, and "body language"—as well. Language has often been used as the defining feature of human beings—the thing that makes our species unique. We use language, whether written, spoken, or symbolic, to communicate everything—meaning, motives, feelings, and beliefs. In fact, it is difficult to imagine how humans could exist without language.

If language is so basic to the human condition, you may wonder why we even discuss a topic like language in a textbook on learning. After all, many people believe language is not learned like other behaviors but rather is largely innate (e.g., Chomsky, 1988; Pinker, 1994). According to this view, humans are born with a "black box" that helps them to quickly acquire language, an ability not shared by other species. However, as you've likely noticed from earlier comparisons among species in this chapter, there is a continuity of cognitive ability across species. If this continuity applies to numerosity, categorization, and even self–awareness, it follows that we might also see examples of language capacity in other species. Is it possible, then, that animals can use language? This is a topic that behaviorists and ethologists have spent considerable effort attempting to answer, and in this section we summarize some of what they have discovered.

In order to discuss whether animals can use language, we must first define what we mean by language and distinguish it from the more general category of "communication." There is no question that animal species communicate with one another. *Communication* is the process of sending and receiving a signal of some sort. When a dog growls and another dog backs down, it can

Communication signals are often species-specific.

be said that the dogs have communicated with each other. When a female baboon's bottom swells and turns bright red, a male baboon notices this signal and will attempt to mate with her. She has communicated her receptivity and his behavior changed as a result. Communication does not need to be intentional (the baboon does not intentionally grow a large red bottom) and there is no need to invoke much cognitive function in order to explain the changes in behavior that result from these types of communication. There are a number of species-specific signals like this that elicit largely innate patterns of behavior.

Most animal behaviorists agree that *language* is a special category of communication which has some key features—symbols, syntax, and semantics—that distinguish it from other forms of communication (Fitch, 2005). Each of these features is described below.

1. **Symbols** In human language, we use discrete units of meaning to communicate with one another. Those units may be spoken words, specific gestures (as in sign language), an image (think of the shape of a stop sign or the simple figures used to indicate the men's and women's washrooms) or words written on a page. A *symbol* is therefore a cue that is used to represent

some experience or object that you can then share with someone else. An interesting thing about human language is that we can make up new symbols and change the meaning of existing symbols. Think of a word like "email" that didn't exist 20 years ago. Similarly, the word "web" has been modified to refer not only to a structure made by spiders, but also to the Internet. This ability to associate arbitrary symbols with objects or events is known as *reference*, and it is considered a particularly important characteristic of symbols used in language.

2. **Syntax** Another important aspect of language is *syntax*, which is the system of grammatical rules by which symbols are arranged, as well as how those symbols can be modified or interact with one another. Think about the word "email" again. I can use it in a sentence as a noun ("I just checked my email.") or as a verb ("I'll email you a copy of that file as soon as I get back to my office"). If I reordered the words in one of those sentences, then it would change or lose meaning ("I just emailed my check" or "Email just I checked my"). Understanding these rules, and using them to combine symbols, allows us to have an unlimited ability to communicate about things and ideas.

3. **Semantics** A critical aspect of language is the meaning associated with symbols, which is known as *semantics*. It is this meaning that allows us to refer to things that aren't currently visible or tangible. For example, you might talk about your friend who is out of the country or you might talk about an idea, like "truth," that has no real physical form. You can also talk about things that you subjectively experience but others are unable to perceive within you, like your emotions or thoughts about the future.

When we look at other species, we can see that they all communicate in some way. But in order for that communication to be called language, it must meet the standards that we use to define human language. This system of standards allows us to communicate with others *intentionally and with great specificity*. To be fair, not all human communication satisfies the criteria for language either. We respond to all sorts of cues in other people that don't involve symbols, syntax, or semantics. The communication system known as "body language" isn't really language at all, by these standards. If I bring my eyebrows together, cross my arms in front of my chest, and purse my lips together then I can signal my emotional state to you without using any arbitrary symbols. In fact, this form of communication is similar to the growling of a dog toward another dog. I may change your behavior and you may even have an awareness of my state of mind, but you don't actually know what I'm thinking about. If I were to say to you "I'm really frustrated with this project I'm working on, and I need you to turn down the music so that I can concentrate," then you are able to use all the complex information contained in my use of language to understand why I'm scowling, and also what you should do next. I was able to *intentionally* provide you with *specific information* that you can use. So language is special and is strong evidence of the complexity of human cognition.

There are, however, many examples of animal species that have evolved fascinating communication systems of their own. Vervet monkeys are small primates that live in Africa. Unfortunately for vervets, they are preyed upon by a wide variety of other species, including snakes, leopards, and eagles, each of which attacks the monkeys in a different way. Vervets are constantly on guard against predators and their system of communication incorporates alarm calls. When one vervet makes an alarm call as a result of spotting a predator, other vervets pay close attention and will often hide or escape the area. Alarm calling is not unique to vervets; many other animal species use alarm calls too. What *is* rather unique is that vervets have different calls for different predator types, and the different calls elicit different behavioral responses from the rest of the group. Thus, if a vervet monkey spots an eagle flying overhead, she sounds the "eagle" alarm, and the other vervets all dive for cover in the dense underbrush of the forest. If one of the monkeys sees a leopard, a different call is given, and the monkeys climb into the nearest tall tree (Seyfarth, Cheney, & Marler, 1980). This communication system (which seems extremely logical to us language-using humans) is very special, because it illustrates that animals can use a sound to symbolically refer to an object that exists in the world. As previously mentioned, this ability to associate arbitrary symbols with objects or events is called *reference*, and it is one of the important features of any language (e.g., Savage-Rumbaugh, 1993; Fitch, 2005). We take reference for granted because human languages are based on the idea that a combination of arbitrary sounds can stand for actual objects. For example, if I use the word "apple," you know what I am talking about. And when I learn a new language, such as French, I have to learn that the word "pomme" means the same thing as "apple" and that they both refer to the tasty round object found on trees. As it turns out, some animals, such as vervets, also seem capable of the referential use of symbols. (See the And Furthermore section, "A Border Collie is Worth a Thousand Words," for a remarkable example of the referential understanding of words by a dog.)

Does the existence of reference in animal communication mean that animals are using symbols in the same way that humans are? If I were to hear someone yell "snake!", not only would my behavior change (I would likely behave like a vervet by standing up tall and looking around my feet) but I might also have an image in my mind of a snake. Do vervets think of snakes when the snake alarm is sounded? We do not know. It seems that young vervets learn to behave in particular ways in response to alarm calls through a process of social learning. Initially, infant vervets are startled by the alarm calls but do not behave in a manner that suggests they "understand" the call. They pay attention to the behavior of their mothers and other adults, and only after multiple presentations of the alarm call do infants behave in a manner that is similar to the adults (Seyfarth & Cheney, 1986). The use of reference in animal communication *may* involve some sort of symbolic representation in the mind of the animal, but it is more pragmatic to explain it in operant conditioning terms. The various alarm calls act as clear discriminative stimuli for particular behaviors. "Eagle" calls signal that looking to the air or hiding under cover is appropriate; "leopard" calls signal that jumping into a tree is appropriate; and "snake" calls signal that the correct behavior is to stand up tall and scan the grasses. Thus, alarm calls clearly *influence* the behavior of other animals, but that doesn't mean that there is any identifiable *information* or *intent* contained in the signal itself (Rendall, Owren, & Ryan, 2009).

QUICK QUIZ L

1. The process of sending and receiving s_____ is known as c_____.

2. Shelly sees a door that has a sign on it with a stick figure wearing a skirt. She knows that this is a women's washroom because the picture is a s_____ that many people use and understand.

3. The phrase "the dog bit the man" differs in s_____ from the phrase "the man bit the dog".

4. If you change the word "happy" to "unhappy", you have altered the s_____ content.

5. The alarm calls of vervet monkeys provide evidence that they are (capable / not capable) _____ of r_____.

And Furthermore

A Border Collie is Worth a Thousand Words

If you have a dog, then you know that dogs learn to associate particular words with actions or objects. Hearing the command to "sit" is usually a strong discriminative stimulus for the behavior of sitting. Likewise, many dogs learn the names of the people around them and the items they regularly play with. It's fairly straightforward to train a dog to fetch a leash or a particular toy. Anecdotally, one of your authors needs to spell the word "WALK" when talking to other people at home if she doesn't want her dog to start barking and spinning in circles near the front door. How many words can a dog learn? To what extent can dogs learn words the way that people do, as symbols that represent other things?

Two researchers, John Pilley and Alliston Reid (2010), raised a female border collie named Chaser from the age of eight weeks. She was trained four to five hours per day on a variety of obedience tasks, herding skills that are typical for border collies, and word learning. This training continued for three years. This bright young dog learned the names for over 1000 toys and other items, in addition to a wide variety of commands and names for people. This performance is quite impressive, but Pilley and Reid did more than just determine Chaser's vocabulary. Using very controlled and systematic testing, they determined that Chaser's "verbal" abilities were evidence that a dog could learn the difference between nouns (toys) and verbs (commands), that she understood the words rather than merely responding to some subtle cue by the trainer, and that she could learn to categorize her toys based on particular features. They also demonstrated that Chaser could learn new words through a process of "exclusion". This means that if she was asked to retrieve an unknown item with a name she had never heard before, she could correctly select that item if it were placed among items she already knew. When tested two years after her official verbal training ended, Chaser still demonstrated nearly perfect retention of names and commands that hadn't been recently practiced. That's impressive!

Chaser in action. (*Source:* From http://newsfeed.time.com/2011/01/05/chaser-the-border-collie-the-smartest-dog-in-the-world/)

REUTERS/Manuela Hartling

    Before you decide to tackle this sort of training with your own puppy, keep in mind that border collies are known for their intelligence, their willingness to learn and follow commands, and their attention to auditory cues even when distractions are present. This is what makes them such excellent herding dogs, prized for their quick learning and responsiveness. Border collies and other dogs on the upper end of the canine intelligence spectrum (Coren, 1994) are ideal for this sort of study, but may not represent the word-learning abilities of all dogs. It's sort of like saying that not all humans are cut out to be physicists or Olympic athletes!

Can Animals "Talk"?

Now that we know a few important characteristics of language (symbols, syntax, and semantics), we can go back to our original question: Can animals use language? This question has intrigued people for generations. After all, who has not wished that a pet dog or cat could talk and wondered what the pet might say if it could? The most comprehensive research programs aimed at this question have attempted to teach animals a human-like language. Unlike Dr. Doolittle, who talked *to* the animals, many researchers have tried to teach the animals to talk to *us*.

The best-known research on language learning in animals involves our closest relatives, the great apes, including chimpanzees, gorillas, orangutans, and bonobos. The great apes share many characteristics in common with humans, from anatomy, blood chemistry, and DNA all the way to social behavior and cognitive skills (e.g., Begun, 1999). Because chimpanzees in particular are closely related to humans, the early experiments in this area focused on them. The first attempts to teach chimps language were based on the idea that wild chimpanzees did not use language simply because they had no motivation or encouragement to do so. This fits nicely with the *empiricist* approach described in Chapter 1. It was assumed that, with proper training, chimpanzees could learn and use human language. The first researchers, therefore, tried to train chimps to speak by raising infant chimps in a home environment reminiscent of that in which infant children are reared (e.g., Hayes & Hayes, 1951; Kellogg & Kellogg, 1933). Such studies are called *cross-fostering* experiments because the chimpanzees were raised in human foster homes. This research received considerable public interest, and one of the chimps, named Viki, became quite a celebrity. However, even though the chimpanzees thrived in the home environment, they never learned to talk. In fact, Viki only learned to produce four words: cup, up, mama, and papa. Watching old films of Viki, it is obvious that "speaking" is not something that chimps do naturally. Viki had to tortuously manipulate her mouth with her hand to produce those four short words.

Sign Language Experiments

Although chimps lacked the vocal apparatus to produce comprehensible speech, language experiments with chimpanzees eventually revealed that they might be capable of producing and understanding other forms of language. Thus, the next approach was to teach chimpanzees a different kind of language, one that relied on gestures instead of spoken words. In the wild, chimpanzees do communicate with each other using gestures—pointing, arm waving, and so on—so it seemed logical to assume that they might be able to learn a language that relied on hand gestures such as American Sign Language (ASL). Sign languages have been used by deaf people for many years, and there are many different such languages. ASL has existed for more than 100 years and is commonly used in North America. Contrary to popular belief, sign languages are not simply "finger spelling" of English words. They are complex, rich languages that share all the important features of any language including reference and grammar. Each signed "word" can convey different meanings, depending on the inflection, and some words can represent entire phrases. Sign languages are also learned in the same way that spoken languages are learned, through modeling, correction by adults, and learning the rules of grammar.

Experimenters conducted cross-fostering studies on chimps' ability to learn ASL in a natural home environment, thereby simulating the way human children learn language. This meant that the chimps were not taught by rote memorization or language drills but learned in day-to-day activities in a family group. Of course, the prospect of raising chimps like humans was a daunting one. The researchers had to devote years of their lives to the project because language acquisition is a long-term effort. The researchers also had to become fluent in ASL and to only use signs, not spoken English, in the presence of their foster "children." The first ASL cross-fostering study was named Project Washoe, after Washoe County in Reno, Nevada. An infant chimp named Washoe was raised by two scientists, Beatrix and Allen Gardner (e.g., Gardner & Gardner, 1969). Since Washoe, other chimps have been cross-fostered to replicate the findings of Project Washoe (and to give Washoe other chimps to "talk" to) (Gardner, Gardner, & Van Cantfort, 1989).

The researchers discovered that the best way to teach apes sign language is to use modeling—demonstrating the sign while performing the action that the sign refers to, such as signing "open" while opening a door. They also used a technique called *molding*, which involves placing the ape's hands in the correct signing position and associating that position with the object being "talked" about. Using these techniques, most ASL-trained chimps ended up with vocabularies of well over 100 signs. Both these procedures worked better than standard operant conditioning, which paired food reward with correct signing. The researchers found that rewarding each sign with food resulted in a very automatic or "reflexive" type of behavior that was oriented to the food reward. Interestingly, this process seems similar to the process of undermining intrinsic motivation through extrinsic rewards, which was briefly discussed in Chapter 6. Food rewards seemed to focus the chimps on producing the signs rather than on communicating with the researchers. Interestingly, though, Washoe (like other language-trained chimpanzees) often signed spontaneously, even when she was alone, which suggests that the signing behavior was rewarding in and of itself.

Strictly controlled tests of language use were performed with many of the chimpanzees trained in sign language (e.g., Fouts, 1973). All the chimps seemed to pass the test of *reference*; that is, they could all use the arbitrary ASL signs to refer to objects and could easily categorize novel objects using signs. For example, if Washoe was shown a photo of a kitten that she had never seen before, she immediately emitted the (correct) sign for "cat." Whether the ASL-trained chimps exhibited the other features of language—syntax and semantics—is much less clear. There is some evidence that Washoe did follow the grammatical rules of ASL. She responded to questions such as "What is that?" with, for example, "That apple" rather than simply "Apple" (Gardner & Gardner, 1975). However, there is only anecdotal evidence that Washoe and other language-trained chimps used signs in novel contexts or produced novel signs for unfamiliar objects. Further, ASL is not a rigid language. The syntax (or ordering of words) is relatively loose, so ASL speakers are not required to follow strict sequences of words. It is therefore extremely difficult to systematically assess chimpanzees' use of language when the language is a fluid, gestural language like ASL.

QUICK QUIZ M

1. Our closest relatives are chimpanzees, orangutans, and gorillas, known as the
   g_____ a_____.

2. Early attempts to teach chimpanzees to speak failed miserably, probably because chimps (have / do not have) _____ the v_____ apparatus to produce speech.

3. Studies by the Gardners and others looked at whether chimpanzees could learn a symbolic, gestural language called A_____ S_____ L_____.

4. In c_____-f_____ experiments, apes are raised in human environments.

5. W_____ was the first chimpanzee trained in ASL.

6. Researchers found that mod_____ was the easiest way to teach sign language to the chimpanzees. They also found mol_____, which involves physically placing the ape's hands in the correct position, to be an effective method.

7. Simply rewarding correct signs with f_____ tended to produce ref_____-type behavior that was oriented more toward producing signs than communicating with the researchers.

8. Almost all apes that have been trained in ASL can demonstrate r_____, the ability to associate particular signs with particular objects or actions.

Artificial Language Experiments

To get around the difficulties posed by the sign language cross-fostering studies, the next series of experiments designed to determine whether animals could use language were conducted in laboratory situations, using artificially constructed languages. These languages did not consist of spoken words or physical gestures; rather, they consisted of visual symbols, either plastic tokens placed on a magnetic board (Premack, 1971b; 1976) or symbols on a computer keyboard (Rumbaugh, 1977; Savage-Rumbaugh, McDonald, Sevcik, Hopkins, & Rubert, 1986). The chimps that participated in these experiments were not raised in human-like environments and did not interact with their caretakers in the same way that Washoe and the other ASL-trained chimps did. They lived in laboratories, and they conversed via the artificial language. A typical sentence in one of these languages—called "Yerkish" after the Yerkes Primate Research Center where it was created—is ? WHAT NAME OF THIS. You may notice that Yerkish grammar is *not* the same as English grammar. The question mark is placed at the beginning of the sentence and there are words missing. Nonetheless, it has its own grammar and is a language. The chimps that learned Yerkish could respond to questions and also ask for objects (e.g., PLEASE MACHINE GIVE BANANA). Although this type of language may seem restricted compared to ASL—and indeed it is, with a much smaller vocabulary and very rigid grammatical rules—it is constructed that way purposefully. The idea was to discover, once and for all, whether chimps could learn and use all the basic features of language. Also, the artificial and highly controlled surroundings made systematic assessment relatively easy. Everything the chimps "said" was displayed and recorded by a computer, so the way the chimps were using language was much clearer than in the ASL studies, which could often be interpreted differently by different observers.

Unfortunately, the artificial language experiments did not give the unequivocal answers that scientists were hoping for. The chimps in these experiments, like the ones in the ASL studies, did appear to use symbols to represent or categorize objects, so they seemed to have the ability to *reference* objects. However, whether the chimps had mastered the artificial *grammar* was less clear. Most of the chimps' sentences were of the form PLEASE MACHINE GIVE "X" (where "X" was usually a preferred food item, such as apples, bananas, or M&M candies). It can be argued that learning to produce a sequence of symbols like PLEASE MACHINE GIVE X is not the same as learning the underlying rules governing language production. In fact, pigeons can be readily trained to peck a sequence of four symbols to receive a food reward (Terrace, 1985), and very few people would say that those pigeons had learned language. It is clear, though, that the chimps in the artificial language experiments generally did not have much to talk about except obtaining food, so perhaps this type of study was not a fair test of their language ability after all. And although recent studies of ape language ability claim to have produced stronger evidence of language capacity (e.g., Benson, Greaves, O'Donnell, & Taglialatela, 2002; Savage-Rumbaugh, Shanker, & Taylor, 1998), some language specialists remain unimpressed (e.g., Pinker, 1994).

Taking the results of the cross-fostering ASL studies and the artificial language experiments together, it is difficult to draw a firm conclusion. Chimpanzees definitely can learn to use symbols to refer to objects, but they just as definitely do not use those symbols in the same way that adult humans do (Terrace, 1979; Terrace, Petitio, Sanders, & Bever, 1979). But how do other animals fare in this regard?

1. Studies of animals' ability to use symbolic languages created by researchers in a laboratory setting are known as (artificial/cross-fostering) _____ language experiments.

2. These studies allowed researchers to systematically assess the language abilities of chimpanzees in a (more/less) _____ controlled setting than was the case with the sign language cross-fostering studies.

3. One of the first artificial languages created was called "Yer_____."

4. Results of the artificial language experiments strongly suggest that many of the chimpanzees mastered (reference/grammar) _____, but there is less evidence that they mastered (reference/grammar) _____.

Although the language studies with chimpanzees received the most public attention, other researchers have focused on training language in other species, ranging from parrots (Pepperberg, 1999) to gorillas (Patterson & Linden, 1981) to dolphins (Herman, Pack, & Morrel-Samuels, 1993). That list of species might seem completely random to you, but in fact, animals that have been language-trained share some important features. First, they have relatively large, complex brains, which makes it likely that they have the cognitive capacity to represent concepts. Second, they are usually species that are extremely social. Social species, such as humans, generally evolve more complicated communication abilities simply because they have more neighbors to "talk" to and about. Dolphins are a good example of that because they have both large brains and a social system in which they regularly interact with members of their own and other species. In fact, although dolphins are far removed from primates in an evolutionary sense, they are often thought of as similar to primates in terms of cognitive abilities. (The alleged "mystical" qualities of dolphin-human interactions that have been reported also added to their cachet as potential language users.)

For almost 30 years, Louis Herman and his colleagues have been studying the cognitive abilities of dolphins and whales, and have trained dolphins to use symbolic languages (Herman, Richards, & Wolz, 1984; Roitblat, Herman, & Nachtigall, 1993). Two dolphins were each trained with a different artificial language. One dolphin, called Akeakamai, learned a gestural language, similar to ASL. The other dolphin, called Phoenix, learned a computer-generated language of acoustic signals, similar to Yerkish. Both dolphins "worked" on their language training in large tanks at the University of Hawaii (nice work if you can get it!). Although the languages are limited to describing things that the dolphins can see and do underwater, it is clear that the animals learned a vocabulary of symbols—ball, pipe, surfboard, spit, fetch, bottom, and so on—that *refer* to objects and actions (Herman & Forestell, 1985; Shyan & Herman, 1987). It is also clear that the dolphins understood rudimentary *grammatical* rules. For example, when given a sentence like FRISBEE FETCH BASKET, Phoenix would take the Frisbee and put it in the basket. When the sentence was given in the opposite order—BASKET FETCH FRISBEE—she would take the basket to the Frisbee. Both dolphins also showed very accurate performance on novel sentences, using new "words" (e.g., Herman, Kuczaj, & Holder, 1993; Herman et al., 1990). Interestingly, California sea lions, another sea mammal species, have also learned symbolic gestures and can respond accurately to three-word sentences like those used with the dolphins (Schusterman & Gisiner, 1988).[3]

So, back to our original question: Can animals use language? As you now know, this is not a simple question, and it certainly does not have a simple answer. It depends on how you define language, and whom you ask. Some animal species are clearly capable of learning some aspects of language and of using symbols in a variety of situations. Teaching animals to use language has also expanded the types of questions researchers are asking about the way animals think. Although we may never be able to sit down with a chimpanzee and have a deep discussion about the meaning of life, we have been able to study complex phenomena such as concept discrimination and categorization (Savage-Rumbaugh, Rumbaugh, Smith, & Lawson, 1980) and logical reasoning (Premack & Woodruff, 1978), which are very difficult to study without "words" of some kind. (See also "Alex Speaks" in the And Furthermore box.)

The evidence that animals are capable of some of the cognitive skills necessary for language production suggests that, much like for other complex cognitive skills, there is a continuum of abilities, and that different species with different social and physical environments have evolved specialized ways of dealing with those environments. Perhaps one day we will understand the extent of dolphin or bonobo communication and we will discover a language ability that humans lack, because it is an ability that is specific to the selective pressures faced by that species. It is unlikely that we will stumble across that skill by accident, because as humans we have a tendency to compare all other species to ourselves when it comes to cognitive abilities and we don't imagine things that are beyond our experience. Just like it is difficult to imagine how a dolphin can use sonar to "see" items that are hidden behind a barrier (Pack & Herman, 1995), it is also difficult to imagine a type of language that humans couldn't understand or use. Although this is merely a "what if" sort of thought, it is possible that we underestimate the abilities of some species due to a combination of necessary scientific skepticism and a bit of human self-centeredness. Fortunately, scientists will continue to investigate the various aspects of animal cognition and no doubt reveal the further similarities and differences among the species in their manner of communication.

---

[3]Akeakamai died in 2003, but she has been immortalized as a character in a science fiction novel, and in a number of videos for National Geographic and other nature programs. She even has her own Wikipedia page!

1. Dolphins, gorillas, and parrots are all (social/solitary) _____ species that have relatively (complex/simple) _____ brains, which makes them good candidates for studying language acquisition.

2. Dolphins have been taught to communicate acoustically as well as gesturally, which is evidence that they may be able to use sym_____ language.

3. Results of the dolphin language experiments suggest that the dolphins mastered the (reference/productivity) _____ aspect of language.

4. BALL FETCH BASKET means the opposite of BASKET FETCH BALL to language-trained dolphins. This suggests that, unlike many of the language-trained chimps, these dolphins can understand the gr_____ rules of a language.

And Furthermore

Alex Speaks

You know that someone is a celebrity when his death is announced on international news broadcasts including CNN and the BBC, and obituaries are published in the New York Times, the Economist, and a variety of other high-level publications. Alex was that kind of celebrity, and when he died at the age of 31 his death was mourned by the people who loved him as well as by scientists around the world. His last words were "You be good. I love you." Alex was a grey parrot. He was not, however, just any parrot. He was the focus of a 30-year research project conducted by Irene Pepperberg to determine whether a parrot could learn to speak. His name is actually an acronym for the study: **A**vian **L**earning **EX**periment.

Alex demonstrating his cognitive abilities. (*Source:* This is photo is from the NY Times http://www.nytimes.com/2007/09/10/science/10cnd-parrot.html, but other images can also be found on the web.)

Juniors Bildarchiv/Alamy

Grey parrots are great mimics, capable of reproducing a wide variety of sounds. Unlike apes, whose vocal apparatus is not suited to the production of human words, parrots can make most of the sounds associated with human speech and have a reputation for repeating phrases they have heard. Alex was purchased in a pet store when he was about a year old, and began his language training right away. Dr. Pepperberg used a training method known as the model-rival technique. This method uses a competitor for the subject being trained, and that competitor also acts as a model for the behavior to be learned. If Alex was learning to name colors, the trainer would hold up a color stimulus and ask "What color is it?" The competitor (usually a student in the lab) would answer the question correctly and be rewarded with a treat like an almond or a piece of banana. Gradually, Alex learned to name colors, to learn the names of items, and also the words for numbers (Pepperberg, 2009).

When he died, Alex knew over 150 words including 50 names for items, their colors, sizes, and other descriptors. Further, he used the words he knew to describe novel items that he had never encountered. His word for the newly-introduced "apple" was "bannerry', which was likely a combination of "banana" and "cherry', two fruits that were familiar (Pepperberg, 2007). If you search online for videos of Alex speaking, you'll see just how clear his speech was and how easy it was to communicate with him.

Was Alex using language? He certainly used words in a referential sense, as a result of the operant and social learning that he experienced. He seemed to be able to use the meaning, or semantic content, of speech. He also demonstrated the ability to create new words, and refer to items that were not present. What Alex could not do was to understand the grammar associated with language, including the use of verb tenses or many changes in syntax. Thus, according to the definition of language provided earlier in the chapter, Alex could not be described as truly using language. Dr. Pepperberg is therefore careful to describe his skills as communication using human words (Pepperberg, 2009).

Even more impressive than his verbal skills are the other cognitive skills that he displayed because of his verbal ability. For example, when shown an array of blue and green items including blocks, keys and toy cars, Alex could respond correctly to the question "How many green blocks?" This question requires Alex to count the number of items that are in two different categories. He couldn't just count the green items, and he couldn't just count the blocks. He had to count only the green blocks (Pepperberg, 1992). This sort of understanding of overlapping categories, as well as numerosity, would have been difficult to test without using language cues.

Alex died young (grey parrots can live to be 50), and likely did not reach his full potential. There are other birds being trained by Pepperberg's lab, and it is hoped that further studies will reveal the extent of parrot intelligence.

ADVICE FOR THE LOVELORN

Dear Dr. Dee,

My pet bird Oscar has been behaving very strangely! He is a lovebird, and I think he is taking his name a little too seriously. Ever since I got him, he has been very attached to me but recently this attachment has gotten a bit out of control. He's behaving like a possessive boyfriend. He needs to be near me at all times and gets very noisy and angry when I leave or when I'm too close to another person. One day while I was sitting outside on the patio, he pecked constantly at the window and made all sorts of noise until I came inside. What is really annoying is that when I finally let him perch on my lap or shoulder, he throws up on me! What's that all about? I know that you usually deal with all-human relationships, but could you please give me some insight about my lovestruck lovebird?

Oscar's Obsession

Dear Obsession,

You're in luck, because I know a thing or two about relationships in a variety of species! The lovebird is known for bonding with a single monogamous mate and forming a strong attachment. If another bird isn't available, then they do tend to act out their affections on their human companions. As for the vomit, that's actually a sign of his commitment to you because male lovebirds regurgitate food to feed their mates that stay on the nest!

You might consider getting Oscar another bird to bond with. It could be a girlfriend from his own species, or another parrot-type bird that can tolerate the aggressive wooing that lovebirds tend to display. If getting another bird isn't an option, then you should consider using some extinction techniques to reduce his possessive behaviors. If you give in to his demands, then you'll strengthen his needy behavior!

You should also realize that, although animals do show evidence of emotions, the experience of "love" that Oscar is feeling may not be at all the same thing that humans experience. There is much that we don't understand about animal emotion, even though it seems clear that there are similarities in basic emotions across species. Fear, contentment, anger, and even affection seem common in so many animals that it would be foolish to assume that animals don't "feel". We just can't be sure that they feel things in the same way that we do. So you should let poor Oscar down gently, and try to remember that his bird brain (and heart) functions somewhat differently than yours!

Behaviorally yours,

Dr. Dee

SUMMARY

Comparative cognition is the study of information processing in a variety of animal species, including humans. Research in animal memory often utilizes tasks developed by behaviorists to study discrimination and generalization. A typical procedure for studying memory in animals is a delayed matching-to-sample task, in which a subject receives reinforcement for selecting the correct match to a sample stimulus following a delay. As evidence of evolutionary adaptation, food-storing birds have better spatial memory than non-storing birds, and rely more on location cues than visual cues.

Numerosity is an understanding of quantity. The horse Clever Hans appeared to have an understanding of quantity, but it was later shown that he was actually responding to subtle visual cues inadvertently displayed by the questioner. Better controlled tests of numerosity have revealed that some species of birds can discriminate different numbers of items in a direct matching-to-sample task. Using a bucket task, lemurs have been shown to respond similarly to human infants in that they continue to search when they have seen more items placed in the bucket than are later found. In doing so, lemurs seem to be responding to differences in the proportion of items, as opposed to differences in the absolute number of items, that were placed versus found.

Evidence that animals can categorize stimuli includes pigeons that have been trained to discriminate photos of trees from photos of non-trees and then generalize this concept to new photos. Certain social species seem capable of transitive inference; for example, in a ranking task, if a ring-tailed lemur earns a reinforcer for selecting A over B and for selecting B over C, then when A and C are presented together, it is likely to select A.

The use of tools requires that animals understand that objects have effects and can be manipulated. Examples include chimps that use twigs, rocks, and other items from their environment as tools for foraging and for comfort. Octopuses, vultures, otters, and crows also use tools. At a more advanced level, some species have demonstrated selectivity about which items to use, and can even retain, combine, and modify objects for tool use.

A theory of mind is the ability to infer the existence of mental states in others. A step in this direction is self-awareness, which is recognizing that oneself is separate from others. Using a mark and mirror task, self-awareness is generally shown by human infants at 24 months of age and by chimps at 28 months of age. Other species that demonstrate self-awareness include dolphins, magpies, and elephants. The "hidden banana" task has revealed that chimps are capable of inferring what a dominant chimp knows and can then use that information to retrieve food in a way that will avoid conflict. A theory of mind is also necessary for intentional cooperation and deception. Apes and other social carnivores including hyenas and ravens have been shown to cooperate on the rope task, and apes have been shown to intentionally deceive.

Defining features of language include symbols, syntax, and semantics. The ability to use arbitrary symbols is known as reference. Research programs have attempted to teach animals, mostly chimpanzees, a human-like language. The first studies attempted, unsuccessfully, to teach chimps to speak. Later studies focused on teaching them to use gestural (sign) language. The chimps learned to use dozens of signs, although systematic assessment of their abilities was difficult. Later studies were conducted in better controlled laboratory situations with artificially constructed languages. The chimpanzees participating in these experiments readily used the symbols to refer to food items and behaviors, but evidence of grammatical ability was less clear. Other species have likewise demonstrated referential use of symbols and, in the case of dolphins, a rudimentary understanding of grammar. In general, however, only the referential use of symbols has been consistently found among a small number of animal species.

SUGGESTED READINGS

Boesch, C. and Boesch-Achermann, H. (2000). *The chimpanzees of the Taï Forest: Behavioural ecology and evolution*. Oxford: Oxford University Press. This is a fascinating exploration of tool use by chimpanzees, as well as the social learning and social behavior of a particular group of chimps.

de Waal, F. B. M. (2005). *Our inner ape*. New York: Riverhead Books. In this book, de Waal explains the differences between chimpanzees and bonobos, and describes the social behaviors and skills of these great apes.

Rendall, D., Owren, M. J., & Ryan, M. J. (2009). *What do animal signals mean? Animal Behavior*, *78*, 233–240. This article is an excellent summary of the current literature on animal communication, and explains what we know and don't know about whether animals are capable of actual language use.

STUDY QUESTIONS

1. Define the term comparative cognition. What are two alternative terms that are sometimes used for this field of study, and why is *comparative cognition* generally preferred?
2. Outline Tinbergen's four questions. Be sure to include the distinction between the ultimate cause and the proximate cause of a trait.
3. What is the biophilia hypothesis? What is anthropomorphism, and how do comparative researchers guard against it?
4. Using a diagram, describe the delayed matching-to-sample procedure used to study memory in pigeons.
5. Outline two research findings that are indicative of evolutionary adaptation in the memory abilities of food-storing birds.
6. Briefly describe the case of Clever Hans and its eventual outcome.

7. Define numerosity. Outline a research study in which animals were shown to display numerical ability.
8. Define transitive inference. Outline a research study in which transitive inference was displayed by animals.
9. Outline Herrnstein's (1979) experimental demonstration of concept learning in the pigeon.
10. What is the simplest form of tool use in animals? Give an example. Outline two examples of more sophisticated tool use in animals.
11. What is a theory of mind? Define self-awareness and describe how it is commonly assessed in children.
12. Describe the false belief task used with children and the hidden banana task used with chimps to assess their ability to infer the thoughts of others. What results have been obtained?
13. Describe an experimental task used for assessing cooperation in animals as well as a task used to assess deception. What results have been obtained?
14. Define communication. Define language.
15. Define three features of language and give an example of teach. What is reference?
16. Distinguish between ASL and artificial language studies. What was the reasoning behind trying to teach animals these languages?
17. What have been the general findings regarding attempted demonstrations of language learning in chimps and in dolphins? What is the overall conclusion regarding language learning in animals?

CONCEPT REVIEW

biophilia hypothesis. The inherited predisposition to be drawn to or bond with nature, including other animals.

communication. The process of sending and receiving a signal of some sort.

comparative cognition. The study of information processing across a variety of species.

delayed matching-to-sample. A memory task in which the animal is first shown a sample stimulus and then, following some delay, is required to select that stimulus out of a group of alternative stimuli.

language. A special category of communication which has some key features—symbols, syntax, and semantics—that distinguish it from other forms of communication.

numerosity. An understanding of quantity.

reference. The ability to associate arbitrary symbols with objects or events.

self-awareness. The ability to perceive oneself as separate from others.

semantics. The meaning associated with symbols.

symbol. A cue that is used to represent some experience or object that you can then share with someone else.

syntax. The system of grammatical rules by which symbols are arranged, as well as how those symbols can be modified and interact with one another.

theory of mind. The tendency to impute mental states to other individuals.

transitive inference. A form of reasoning in which the relationship between two objects can be inferred by knowing the relationship of each to a third object.

CHAPTER TEST

22. The _____ task is used to assess the capacity for self-awareness.

9. Although Clever Hans appeared to know how to count and do arithmetic, further testing revealed that he was actually responding to

_____

_____.

16. Highly social species are (better/worse) _____ at transitive inference tasks when compared to less social species.

4. A pigeon is shown a circle in a center key and then 10 seconds later must choose between a circle and a square on two side keys. Pecking at the circle will earn the pigeon a reinforcer. This is known as a _____ _____-to-_____ task.

25. Bonobos outperform chimpanzees on tasks that require (cooperation/deception) _____; this is likely because bonobos tend to be much (more/less) _____ competitive than chimps.

31. Both _____ language studies and _____ language studies provide evidence that chimps are capable of the _____ aspect of language but not necessarily the proper use of _____.

20. Chimpanzees' hammer-and-anvil technique of cracking nuts takes (several years / a few days) _____ to master and appears to be mostly the result of (insight/social learning) _____.

1. The study of information processing across a variety of species is most commonly referred to as _____ cognition.

23. Human infants tend to show evidence of self-awareness by about (12/24/36) _____ months of age; chimpanzees tend to show a similar ability (A) never, (B) at a slightly older age, (C) at a much older age. _____

27. If a bird avoids an area because it heard the territorial call of another bird, this is evidence that the birds are capable of _____ but not necessarily of _____.

14. A rat learns to press a lever each time some type of piano music is played, but not when some type of trumpet music is played. This is an example of (A) transitive inference, (B) category learning, (C) numerosity, (D) reference. _____

29. If a vervet monkey gives the _____ call, then the other vervets will dive for cover, but if the _____ call is given, then the others will jump up into the trees. Thus, vervets seem capable of using the _____ aspect of language in their communications.

28. If the phrase "hand on the snack" becomes "snack on the hand", then both the _____ and the _____ aspects of the sentence have changed.

2. If you are studying the brain mechanisms associated with learning, then you are focused on the (proximate/ultimate) _____ cause of a trait; if you are examining how learning allows a species to survive or reproduce, then you are focused on the (proximate/ultimate) _____ cause of a trait.

19. Chimpanzees (are / are not) _____ capable of creating new tools by modifying objects and combining objects.

5. In a directed forgetting task with pigeons, subjects tend to (recall / not recall) _____ a stimulus that had been followed by a "forget" cue.

30. Chaser the border collie has learned to identify by name more than _____ different toys.

8. In a direct matching-to-sample task in which the sample varies in both location and color, chickadees are most likely to match according to (location/color/either) _____ and juncos are most likely to match according to (location/color/either) _____. This is in keeping with the fact that chickadees, but not juncos, _____ in the winter.

21. In order to intentionally cooperate or deceive another individual, an animal must have a _____.

6. Migrating birds have excellent navigation abilities, which help them to survive their long journeys. Their navigation abilities are an example of a(n) _____ adaptation.

12. Numerosity is an understanding of _____.

11. A pigeon is shown a circle in a center key and must choose between a circle and a square presented at the same time on two side keys. Pecking at the circle will earn the pigeon a reinforcer. This is an example of a _____ _____-to-_____ task.

24. The "hidden banana" task indicates roughly the same ability in chimps as does the _____ belief task in verbal human children, which means that both chimps and children have a _____.

15. Tracy asked Elaine for advice about a problem with her boss, Chris. Elaine recommended that she speak to Maggie, because Maggie is Chris's boss. Elaine has used her understanding of _____ _____ to determine what advice to give.

10. After learning to discriminate the color green and also discriminate the shape of a block, Alex the parrot was able to correctly answer a question like, "How many green blocks?", when shown a number of objects of different colors and shapes. Thus, with the use of words, he was able to demonstrate that he understood the concept of (categorization/numerosity/both) _____.

18. A delayed matching-to-sample task is often used as a test of (memory / ability to categorize) _____; a direct matching-to-sample task can be used as a test of (memory / ability to categorize) _____.

3. Eli watched his new kitten pounce on a toy. He thought, "She must be practicing hunting because she knows it will make her better at it when she's an adult." This statement reveals Eli's tendency toward _____, which is something that animal researchers should avoid.

26. A mongoose lemur watches as you place a number of grapes inside a bucket. When it searches the bucket, it finds one less grape than you originally placed in the bucket. It is most likely to search for the missing grape, if you originally placed (3/5) _____ grapes in the bucket. This is because their perception of changes in quantity appears to be based on (proportional differences / absolute differences) _____.

13. To solve problems associated with the likelihood of an event, humans tend to use (classical/empirical) _____ probability, which is based on (experience/reasoning) _____, while pigeons seem to use _____ probability, which is based on _____. This results in better performance by (pigeons/humans) _____ in the Monty Hall dilemma.

7. When we compare food-storing birds to non-storing birds, food storing birds appear to have better _____ memory. On a neurological level, they also have a larger _____.

17. While bird-watching, Brian observed a crow use a twig to pry open a fast-food container that someone had left lying in the park. The crow's use of the twig is considered an example of _____.

ANSWERS TO CHAPTER TEST

1. comparative
2. proximate; ultimate
3. anthropomorphism
4. delayed matching-to-sample
5. not recall
6. evolutionary
7. spatial; hippocampus
8. location; either; store food
9. changes in features (or cues) inadvertently emitted by the questioner
10. both
11. direct matching-to-sample
12. quantity
13. classical; reasoning; empirical; experience; pigeons
14. B
15. transitive inference
16. better
17. tool use
18. memory; ability to categorize
19. are
20. several years; social learning
21. theory of mind
22. mark and mirror
23. 24 months; B
24. false; theory of mind
25. cooperation; less
26. 3; proportional differences
27. communication; language
28. syntax; semantic
29. eagle; leopard; reference
30. 1000
31. sign (or ASL); artificial; reference; grammar (or syntax)

Glossary

acquisition. The process of developing and strengthening a conditioned response through repeated pairings of an NS (or CS) with a US.

activity anorexia. An abnormally high level of activity and low level of food intake generated by exposure to a restricted schedule of feeding.

adjunctive behavior. An excessive pattern of behavior that emerges as a by-product of an intermittent schedule of reinforcement for some other behavior.

adjusting schedule. A schedule in which the response requirement changes as a function of the organism's performance while responding to the previous reinforcer.

anticipatory contrast. The process whereby the rate of response varies inversely with an upcoming ("anticipated") change in the rate of reinforcement.

appetitive conditioning. Conditioning procedure in which the US is an event that an organism approaches or seeks out.

appetitive stimulus. An event that an organism will approach or seek out.

applied behavior analysis. A technology of behavior in which basic principles of behavior are applied to real-world issues.

autoshaping. A type of sign tracking in which a pigeon comes to automatically peck at a response key because the key light has been associated with the response-independent delivery of food.

aversion therapy. A form of behavior therapy that attempts to reduce the attractiveness of a desired event by associating it with an aversive stimulus.

aversive conditioning. Conditioning procedure in which the US is an event that an organism avoids.

aversive stimulus. An event that an organism will avoid.

avoidance behavior. Behavior that occurs before the aversive stimulus is presented and therefore prevents its delivery.

avoidance theory of punishment. The theory that punishment involves a type of avoidance conditioning in which the avoidance response consists of any behavior other than the behavior being punished.

backward conditioning. Conditioning procedure in which the onset of the NS follows the onset of the US.

baseline. The normal frequency of a behavior before some intervention.

behavior. Any activity of an organism that can be observed or somehow measured.

behavior analysis (or experimental analysis of behavior). The behavioral science that grew out of Skinner's philosophy of radical behaviorism.

behavior systems theory. A theory proposing that an animal's behavior is organized into certain systems or categories (such as feeding, mating, and avoiding predators), with each category containing a set of relevant responses that can become activated in certain situations.

behavioral bliss point approach. The theory that an organism with free access to alternative activities will distribute its behavior in such a way as to maximize overall reinforcement.

behavioral contrast. A change in the rate of *reinforcement* on one component of a multiple schedule produces an opposite change in the rate of *response* on another component.

behaviorism. A natural science approach to psychology that traditionally focuses on the study of environmental influences on observable behavior.

bias from matching. A deviation from matching in which one response alternative attracts a higher proportion of responses than would be predicted by matching, regardless of whether that alternative contains the richer versus poorer schedule.

biophilia hypothesis. The inherited predisposition to be drawn to or bond with nature, including with other animals.

blocking. The phenomenon whereby the presence of an established CS interferes with conditioning of a new CS.

British empiricism. A philosophical school of thought which maintained that almost all knowledge is a function of experience.

case study approach. A descriptive research approach that involves intensive examination of one or a few individuals.

chained schedule. A schedule consisting of a sequence of two or more simple schedules, each with its own S^D and the last of which results in a terminal reinforcer.

changing-criterion design. A type of single-subject design in which the effect of the treatment is demonstrated by how closely the behavior matches a criterion that is systematically altered.

classical conditioning. A process whereby one stimulus that does not elicit a certain response is associated with a second stimulus that does; as a result, the first stimulus also comes to elicit a response. Also known as *Pavlovian conditioning* or *respondent conditioning*.

cognitive behaviorism. A brand of behaviorism that utilizes intervening variables, usually in the form of hypothesized cognitive processes, to help explain behavior. Sometimes called "purposive behaviorism." (As noted in Chapter 13, to the extent that it focuses upon research with nonhuman animals, it is also referred to as *animal cognition* or, more commonly, *comparative cognition*.)

cognitive map. The mental representation of one's spatial surroundings.

commitment response. An action carried out at an early point in time that serves to either eliminate or reduce the value of an upcoming temptation.

communication. The process of sending and receiving a signal of some sort.

comparative cognition. The study of information processing across a variety of species.

comparative design. A type of control group design in which different species constitute one of the independent variables.

compensatory-response model. A model of classical conditioning in which a CS that has been repeatedly associated with the primary response (a-process) to a US will eventually come to elicit a compensatory response (b-process).

complex schedule. A schedule consisting of a combination of two or more simple schedules.

compound stimulus. A complex stimulus that consists of the simultaneous presentation of two or more individual stimuli.

concurrent schedule of reinforcement. A complex schedule consisting of the simultaneous presentation of two or more independent schedules, each leading to a reinforcer.

conditioned response (CR). The response, often similar to the unconditioned response, that is elicited by the conditioned stimulus.

conditioned stimulus (CS). Any stimulus that, although initially neutral, comes to elicit a response because it has been associated with an unconditioned stimulus.

conditioned suppression theory of punishment. The assumption that punishment does not weaken a behavior, but instead produces an emotional response that interferes with the occurrence of the behavior.

conjunctive schedule. A type of complex schedule in which the requirements of two or more simple schedules must be met before a reinforcer is delivered.

contagious behavior. A more-or-less instinctive or reflexive behavior triggered by the occurrence of the same behavior in another individual.

contingency. A predictive relationship between two events such that the occurrence of one event predicts the probable occurrence of the other.

continuous reinforcement schedule. A schedule in which each specified response is reinforced.

contrived reinforcers. Reinforcers that have been deliberately arranged to modify a behavior; they are not a typical consequence of the behavior in that setting. Also called *artificial reinforcers*.

control group design. A type of experiment in which, at its simplest, subjects are randomly assigned to either an experimental (or treatment) group or a control group; subjects assigned to the experimental group are exposed to a certain manipulation or treatment, while those assigned to the control group are not.

counterconditioning. The procedure whereby a CS that elicits one type of response is associated with an event that elicits an incompatible response.

countercontrol. The deliberate manipulation of environmental events to alter their impact on our behavior.

covert behavior. Behavior that can be *subjectively* perceived only by the person performing the behavior. Thoughts and feelings are covert behaviors. Also known as *private behavior* or *private events*.

CS–US relevance. An innate tendency to easily associate certain types of stimuli with each other.

cumulative recorder. A device that measures total number of responses over time and provides a graphic depiction of the rate of behavior.

delayed conditioning. Conditioning procedure in which the onset of the NS precedes the onset of the US, and the two stimuli overlap.

delayed matching-to-sample. An experimental procedure in which the animal is first shown a sample stimulus and then, following some delay, is required to select that stimulus out of a group of alternative stimuli.

dependent variable. That aspect of an experiment that is allowed to freely vary to determine if it is affected by changes in the independent variable.

deprivation. The prolonged absence of an event that tends to increase the appetitiveness of that event.

descriptive research. Research that focuses on describing the behavior and the situation within which it occurs.

differential reinforcement of high rates (DRH). A schedule in which reinforcement is contingent upon emitting at least a certain number of responses in a certain period of time— or, more generally, reinforcement is provided for responding at a fast rate.

differential reinforcement of low rates (DRL). A schedule in which a minimum amount of time must pass between each response before the reinforcer will be delivered—or, more generally, reinforcement is provided for responding at a slow rate.

differential reinforcement of other behavior (DRO). Reinforcement of any behavior other than a target behavior that is being extinguished.

differential reinforcement of paced responding (DRP). A schedule in which reinforcement is contingent upon emitting a series of responses at a set rate—or, more generally, reinforcement is provided for responding neither too fast nor too slow.

discrimination training. As applied to operant conditioning, the differential reinforcement of responding in the presence of one stimulus (the S^D) and not another.

discriminative stimulus (S^D). A stimulus in the presence of which responses are reinforced and in the absence of which they are not reinforced.

discriminative stimulus for extinction (S^Δ). A stimulus that signals the absence of reinforcement.

discriminative stimulus for punishment (S^{Dp}). A stimulus that signals that a response will be punished.

dishabituation. The reappearance of a habituated response following the presentation of a seemingly irrelevant novel stimulus.

disinhibition. The sudden recovery of a response during an extinction procedure when a novel stimulus is introduced.

displacement activity. An apparently irrelevant activity sometimes displayed by animals when confronted by conflict or thwarted from attaining a goal.

drive reduction theory. According to this theory, an event is reinforcing to the extent that it is associated with a reduction in some type of physiological drive.

duration. The length of time that an individual repeatedly or continuously performs a certain behavior.

empiricism. In psychology, the assumption that behavior patterns are mostly learned rather than inherited. Also known as the nurture perspective (or, more rarely, as *nurturism*).

errorless discrimination training. A discrimination training procedure that minimizes the number of errors (i.e., nonreinforced responses to the S$^\Delta$) and reduces many of the adverse effects associated with discrimination training.

escape behavior. A behavior that results in the termination of an aversive stimulus.

establishing operation. A procedure that affects the appetitiveness or aversiveness of a stimulus.

evolutionary adaptation. An inherited trait (physical or behavioral) that has been shaped through natural selection.

excitatory conditioning. Conditioning procedure in which the NS is associated with the *presentation* of a US.

experimental neurosis. An experimentally produced disorder in which animals exposed to unpredictable events develop neurotic-like symptoms.

exposure and response prevention (ERP). A method of treating obsessive-compulsive behavior that involves prolonged exposure to anxiety-arousing events while not engaging in the compulsive behavior pattern that reduces the anxiety.

external inhibition. A decrease in the strength of the conditioned response due to the presentation of a novel stimulus at the same time as the conditioned stimulus.

extinction (in classical conditioning). The repeated presentation of the CS in the absence of the US (which is the "procedure" of extinction), the result of which is a decrease in the strength of the CR (which is the "process" of extinction).

extinction (in operant conditioning); The nonreinforcement of a previously reinforced response (the "procedure" of extinction), the result of which is a decrease in the strength of that response (the "process of extinction).

extinction burst. A temporary increase in the frequency and intensity of responding when extinction is first implemented.

extrinsic punishment. Punishment that is not an inherent aspect of the behavior being punished but that simply follows the behavior.

extrinsic reinforcement. The reinforcement provided by a consequence that is external to the behavior, that is, an extrinsic reinforcer.

fading. The process of gradually altering the intensity of a stimulus.

fixed action pattern. A fixed sequence of responses elicited by a specific stimulus.

fixed duration (FD) schedule. A schedule in which reinforcement is contingent upon continuous performance of a behavior for a fixed, predictable period of time.

fixed interval (FI) schedule. A schedule in which reinforcement is contingent upon the first response after a fixed, predictable period of time.

fixed ratio (FR) schedule. A schedule in which reinforcement is contingent upon a fixed, predictable number of responses.

fixed time (FT) schedule. A schedule in which the reinforcer is delivered following a fixed, predictable period of time, regardless of the organism's behavior.

flexion response. The automatic response of jerking one's hand or foot away from a hot or sharp object.

flooding therapy. A behavioral treatment for phobias that involves prolonged exposure to a feared stimulus, thereby providing maximal opportunity for the conditioned fear response to extinguish.

functional relationship. The relationship between changes in an independent variable and changes in a dependent variable; a cause-and-effect relationship.

functionalism. An approach to psychology which proposes that the mind evolved to help us adapt to the world around us, and that the focus of psychology should be the study of those adaptive processes.

generalization gradient. A graphic description of the strength of responding in the presence of stimuli that are similar to the S^D and vary along a continuum.

generalized imitation. The tendency to imitate a new modeled behavior in the absence of any specific reinforcement for doing so.

generalized (or generalized secondary) punisher. An event that has become punishing because it has in the past been associated with many other punishers.

generalized (or generalized secondary) reinforcer. A type of secondary reinforcer that has been associated with several other reinforcers.

goal gradient effect. An increase in the strength and/or efficiency of responding as one draws near to the goal.

habituation. A decrease in the strength of an elicited behavior following repeated presentations of the eliciting stimulus.

higher-order conditioning. The process whereby a neutral stimulus that is associated with a CS (rather than a US) also becomes a CS.

impulsiveness. With respect to choice between two rewards, selecting a smaller sooner reward over a larger later reward.

incentive motivation. Motivation derived from some property of the reinforcer, as opposed to an internal drive state.

incubation. The strengthening of a conditioned fear response as a result of brief exposures to the aversive CS.

independent variable. That aspect of an experiment that is made to systematically vary across the different conditions in an experiment.

inhibitory conditioning. Conditioning procedure in which the NS is associated with the *absence* or *removal* of a US.

instinctive drift. An instance of classical conditioning in which a genetically based, fixed action pattern gradually emerges and displaces a behavior that is being operantly conditioned.

intensity. The force or magnitude of a behavior.

intermittent (or partial) reinforcement schedule. A schedule in which only some responses are reinforced.

interval recording. The measurement of whether or not a behavior occurs within a series of continuous intervals. (The number of times that it occurs within each interval is irrelevant.)

intrinsic punishment. Punishment that is an inherent aspect of the behavior being punished.

intrinsic reinforcement. Reinforcement provided by the mere act of performing the behavior; the performance of the behavior is inherently reinforcing.

introspection. The attempt to accurately describe one's conscious thoughts, emotions, and sensory experiences.

language. A special category of communication which has some key features—symbols, syntax, and semantics—that distinguish it from other forms of communication.

latency. The length of time required for a behavior to begin.

latent inhibition. The phenomenon whereby a familiar stimulus is more difficult to condition as a CS than is an unfamiliar (novel) stimulus.

latent learning. Learning that occurs in the absence of any observable demonstration of learning and only becomes apparent under a different set of conditions.

law of contiguity. A law of association holding that events that occur in close proximity to each other in time or space are readily associated with each other.

law of contrast. A law of association holding that events that are opposite from each other are readily associated with each other.

law of effect. As stated by Thorndike, the proposition that behaviors that lead to a satisfying state of affairs are strengthened or "stamped in," while behaviors that lead to an unsatisfying or annoying state of affairs are weakened or "stamped out."

law of frequency. A law of association holding that the more frequently two items occur together, the more strongly they are associated with each other.

law of parsimony. The assumption that simpler explanations for a phenomenon are generally preferable to more complex explanations.

law of similarity. A law of association holding that events that are similar to each other are readily associated with each other.

learned helplessness. A decrement in learning ability that results from repeated exposure to uncontrollable aversive events.

learning. A relatively permanent change in behavior that results from some type of experience.

matching law. The principle that the *proportion* of responses emitted on a particular schedule matches the *proportion* of reinforcers obtained on that schedule.

melioration theory. A theory of matching that holds that the distribution of behavior in a choice situation shifts toward those alternatives that have higher value regardless of the long-term effect on overall amount of reinforcement.

methodological behaviorism. A brand of behaviorism which asserts that, for methodological reasons, psychologists should study only those behaviors that can be directly observed.

mind–body dualism. Descartes' philosophical assumption that some human behaviors are bodily reflexes that are automatically elicited by external stimulation, while other behaviors are freely chosen and controlled by the mind.

multiple-baseline design. A type of single-subject design in which a treatment is instituted at successive points in time for two or more persons, settings, or behaviors.

multiple schedule. A complex schedule consisting of two or more independent schedules presented in sequence, each resulting in reinforcement and each having a distinctive S^D.

nativism. The assumption that a person's characteristics are largely inborn. Also known as the *nature* perspective.

natural reinforcers. Reinforcers that are naturally provided for a certain behavior; that is, they are a typical consequence of the behavior within that setting.

natural selection. The evolutionary principle according to which organisms that are better able to adapt to environmental pressures are more likely to survive and reproduce than those that cannot adapt.

naturalistic observation. A descriptive research approach that involves the systematic observation and recording of behavior in its natural environment.

negative contrast effect. The process whereby an increase in the rate of *reinforcement* on one component of a multiple schedule produces a decrease in the rate of *response* on the other component.

negative punishment. The removal of a stimulus (one that is usually considered pleasant or rewarding) following a response, which then leads to a decrease in the future strength of that response.

negative reinforcement. The removal of a stimulus (one that is usually considered unpleasant or aversive) following a response, which then leads to an increase in the future strength of that response.

neobehaviorism. A brand of behaviorism that utilizes intervening variables, in the form of hypothesized physiological processes, to help explain behavior.

noncontingent schedule of reinforcement. A schedule in which the reinforcer is delivered independently of any response. Also known as a *response-independent schedule* of reinforcement.

numerosity. The understanding of quantity.

observational learning. The process whereby the behavior of a model is witnessed by an observer, and the observer's behavior is subsequently altered.

occasion setting. A procedure in which a stimulus (known as an *occasion setter*) signals that a CS is likely to be followed by the US with which it is associated.

operant behavior. A class of emitted responses that result in certain consequences; these consequences, in turn, affect the future probability or strength of those responses.

operant conditioning. A type of learning in which the future probability of a behavior is affected by its consequences.

opponent-process theory. A theory proposing that an emotional event elicits two competing processes: (1) an a-process (or primary process) directly elicited by the event, and (2) a b-process (or opponent process) that is elicited by the a-process and serves to counteract it.

orienting response. The automatic positioning of oneself to facilitate attending to a stimulus.

overexpectation effect. The decrease in the conditioned response that occurs when two separately conditioned CSs are combined into a compound stimulus for further pairings with the US.

overmatching. A deviation from matching in which the proportion of responses on the richer schedule versus poorer schedule is more different than would be predicted by matching.

overshadowing. The phenomenon whereby the most salient member of a compound stimulus is more readily conditioned as a CS and thereby interferes with conditioning of the less salient member.

overt behavior. Behavior that has the potential for being directly observed by an individual other than the one performing the behavior.

partial reinforcement effect. The process whereby behavior that has been maintained on an intermittent (partial) schedule of reinforcement extinguishes more slowly than behavior that has been maintained on a continuous schedule.

peak shift effect. Following discrimination training, the peak of a generalization gradient will shift from the S^D to a stimulus that is further removed from the S^Δ.

personal process rule. A personal rule that indicates the specific process by which a task is to be accomplished. (Also referred to as an *implementation intention*.)

personal rule (or self-instruction). A verbal description of a contingency that we present to ourselves to influence our behavior.

positive contrast effect. The process whereby a decrease in rate of reinforcement on one component of a multiple schedule produces an increase in the rate of response on the other component.

positive punishment. The presentation of a stimulus (one that is usually considered unpleasant or aversive) following a response, which then leads to a decrease in the future strength of that response.

positive reinforcement. The presentation of a stimulus (one that is usually considered pleasant or rewarding) following a response, which then leads to an increase in the future strength of that response.

Premack principle. The notion that a high-probability behavior can be used to reinforce a low-probability behavior.

Premack principle of punishment. The notion that a low-probability behavior (LPB) can be used to punish a high-probability behavior (HPB).

preparatory-response theory. A theory of classical conditioning that proposes that the purpose of the CR is to prepare the organism for the presentation of the US.

preparedness. An evolved predisposition (or innate tendency) for an organism to more easily learn certain types of behaviors or certain types of associations more readily than others.

primary (or unconditioned) punisher. Any event that is innately punishing.

primary reinforcer (or unconditioned reinforcer). An event that is innately reinforcing.

pseudoconditioning. A situation in which an elicited response that appears to be a CR is actually the result of sensitization rather than conditioning.

punisher. An event that (1) follows a behavior and (2) decreases the future probability of that behavior.

radical behaviorism. A brand of behaviorism that emphasizes the influence of the environment on overt behavior, rejects the use of internal events to explain behavior, and views thoughts and feelings as behaviors that themselves need to be explained.

rate of response. The frequency with which a response occurs in a certain period of time.

ratio strain. A disruption in responding due to an overly demanding response requirement.

reciprocal determinism. The assumption that environmental events, observable behavior, and "person variables" (including internal events) reciprocally influence each other.

reciprocal inhibition. The process whereby certain responses are incompatible with each other, and the occurrence of one response necessarily inhibits the other.

reference. The ability to associate arbitrary symbols with objects or events.

reflex. A relatively simple, involuntary response to a stimulus.

reflex arc. A neural structure that underlies many reflexes and consists of a sensory neuron, an interneuron, and a motor neuron.

reinforcer. An event that (1) follows a behavior and (2) increases the future probability of that behavior.

Rescorla-Wagner theory. A theory of classical conditioning that proposes that a given US can support only so much conditioning and that this amount of conditioning must be distributed among the various CSs available.

resistance to extinction. The extent to which responding persists after an extinction procedure has been implemented.

response. A particular instance of a behavior.

response cost. A form of negative punishment involving the removal of a specific reinforcer following the occurrence of a behavior.

response deprivation hypothesis. The notion that a behavior can serve as a reinforcer when (1) access to the behavior is restricted and (2) its frequency thereby falls below its preferred level of occurrence.

response-rate schedule. A schedule in which reinforcement is directly contingent upon the organism's rate of response.

resurgence. The reappearance during extinction of other behaviors that had once been effective in obtaining reinforcement.

reversal design. A type of single-subject design that involves repeated alternations between a baseline period and a treatment period.

rule. A verbal description of a contingency.

rule-governed behavior. Behavior that has been generated through exposure to rules.

satiation. The prolonged exposure to (or consumption of) an event that tends to decrease the appetitiveness of that event.

say–do correspondence. A close match between what we say we are going to do and what we actually do at a later time.

schedule of reinforcement. The response requirement that must be met to obtain reinforcement.

secondary (or conditioned) punisher. An event that has become punishing because it has in the past been associated with some other punisher.

secondary reinforcer (or conditioned reinforcer). An event that is reinforcing because it has been associated with some other reinforcer.

selective sensitization. An increase in one's reactivity to a potentially fearful stimulus following exposure to an unrelated stressful event.

self-awareness. The ability to perceive oneself as separate from others.

self-control. With respect to choice between two rewards, selecting a larger later reward over a smaller sooner reward.

semantic generalization. The generalization of a conditioned response to verbal stimuli that are similar in meaning to the CS.

semantics. The meaning associated with symbols.

sensitization. An increase in the strength of an elicited behavior following repeated presentations of the eliciting stimulus.

sensory preconditioning. In this phenomenon, when one stimulus is conditioned as a CS, another stimulus it was previously associated with can also become a CS.

shaping. The gradual creation of new operant behavior through reinforcement of successive approximations to that behavior.

sign stimulus (or releaser). A specific stimulus that elicits a fixed action pattern.

sign tracking. A type of elicited behavior in which an organism approaches a stimulus that signals the presentation of an appetitive event.

simple-comparison design. A type of single-subject design in which behavior in a baseline condition is compared to behavior in a treatment condition.

simultaneous conditioning. Conditioning procedure in which the onset of the NS and the onset of the US are simultaneous.

single-subject design. A category of research designs requiring only one or a few subjects in order to conduct an entire experiment. Also known as *single-case* or *small-n* designs.

situational freedom. Language can be used in a variety of contexts and is not fixed in a particular situation.

small-but-cumulative effects model. Each individual choice on a self-control task has only a small but cumulative effect on our likelihood of obtaining the desired long-term outcome.

social learning theory. A brand of behaviorism that strongly emphasizes the importance of observational learning and cognitive variables in explaining human behavior. It has more recently been referred to as "social-cognitive theory."

spatial contiguity. The extent to which events are situated close to each other in space.

speed. The amount of time required to perform a complete episode of a behavior from start to finish.

spontaneous recovery (in classical conditioning). The reappearance of an extinguished CR following a rest period after extinction has occurred.

spontaneous recovery (in operant conditioning). The reappearance of an extinguished operant response following a rest period after extinction has occurred.

S-R (stimulus-response) model. As applied to classical conditioning, this model assumes that the NS becomes directly associated with the UR and therefore comes to elicit the same response as the UR.

S-R theory. The theory that learning involves the establishment of a connection between a specific stimulus (S) and a specific response (R).

S-S (stimulus-stimulus) model. A model of classical conditioning that assumes that the NS becomes directly associated with the US, and therefore comes to elicit a response related to that US.

startle response. A defensive reaction to a sudden, unexpected stimulus, which involves automatic tightening of skeletal muscles and various hormonal and visceral changes.

stimulus. Any event that can potentially influence behavior. (The plural for stimulus is *stimuli*.)

stimulus control. A situation in which the presence of a discriminative stimulus reliably affects the probability of a behavior.

stimulus discrimination. In classical conditioning, the tendency for a response to be elicited more by one stimulus than another; in operant conditioning, the tendency for an operant response to be emitted more in the presence of one stimulus than another.

stimulus enhancement. Directing attention to a particular place or object, making it more likely that the observer will approach that place or object.

stimulus generalization. In classical conditioning, the tendency for a CR to be elicited by a stimulus that is similar to the CS; in operant conditioning, the tendency for an operant response to be emitted in the presence of a stimulus that is similar to an S^D.

stimulus-substitution theory. A theory of classical conditioning that proposes that the CS acts as a substitute for the US.

structuralism. An approach to psychology holding that it is possible to determine the structure of the mind by identifying the basic elements that compose it.

symbol. A cue that is used to represent some experience or object that can then be shared with someone else.

syntax. The system of grammatical rules by which symbols are arranged, as well as how those symbols can be modified and interact with one another.

systematic desensitization. A behavioral treatment for phobias that involves pairing relaxation with a succession of stimuli that elicit increasing levels of fear.

taste aversion conditioning. A form of classical conditioning in which a food item that has been paired with gastrointestinal illness becomes a conditioned aversive stimulus.

temperament. An individual's base level of emotionality and reactivity to stimulation that, to a large extent, is genetically determined.

temporal conditioning. A form of classical conditioning in which the CS is the passage of time.

temporal contiguity. The extent to which events occur close together in time.

theory of mind. The tendency to impute mental states to other individuals.

three-term contingency. The relationship between a discriminative stimulus, an operant behavior, and a reinforcer or punisher.

time-out. A form of negative punishment involving the loss of access to positive reinforcers for a brief period of time following the occurrence of a problem behavior.

time-sample recording. The measurement of whether or not a behavior occurs within a series of discontinuous intervals. (The number of times that it occurs within each interval is irrelevant.)

topography. The physical form of a behavior.

trace conditioning. Conditioning procedure in which the onset and offset of the NS precede the onset of the US.

transitive inference. A form of reasoning in which the relationship between two objects can be inferred by knowing the relationship of each to a third object.

true imitation. Duplicating a novel behavior (or sequence of behaviors) to achieve a specific goal.

two-process theory of avoidance. The theory that avoidance behavior is the result of two distinct processes: (1) classical conditioning, in which a fear response comes to be elicited by a CS, and (2) operant conditioning, in which moving away from the CS is negatively reinforced by a reduction in fear.

unconditioned response (UR). The response that is naturally elicited by the unconditioned stimulus.

unconditioned stimulus (US). A stimulus that naturally elicits a response.

undermatching. A deviation from matching in which the proportion of responses on the richer schedule versus poorer schedule is less different than would be predicted by matching.

US revaluation. A process that involves the postconditioning presentation of the US at a different level of intensity, thereby altering the strength of response to the previously conditioned CS.

variable. A characteristic of a person, place, or thing that can change (vary) over time or from one situation to another.

variable duration (VD) schedule. A schedule in which reinforcement is contingent upon continuous performance of a behavior for a varying, unpredictable period of time.

variable interval (VI) schedule. A schedule in which reinforcement is contingent upon the first response after a varying, unpredictable period of time.

variable ratio (VR) schedule. A schedule in which reinforcement is contingent upon a varying, unpredictable number of responses.

variable time (VT) schedule. A schedule in which the reinforcer is delivered following a varying, unpredictable period of time, regardless of the organism's behavior.

vicarious emotional response. A classically conditioned emotional response resulting from seeing that emotional response exhibited by others.

References

Adams, L. A., & Rickert, V. I. (1989). Reducing bedtime tantrums: Comparison between positive routines and graduated extinction. *Pediatrics, 84*, 585–588.

Ader, R. (2003). Conditioned immunomodulation: Research needs and directions. *Brain, Behavior, and Immunity, 17*, 51–57.

Ader, R., & Cohen, N. (1975). Behaviorally conditioned immunosuppression. *Psychosomatic Medicine, 37*, 333–340.

Ainslie, G. (1975). Specious reward: A behavioral theory of impulsiveness and impulse control. *Psychological Bulletin, 82*, 463–496.

Ainslie, G. (1986). Beyond microeconomics: Conflict among interests in a multiple self as a determinant of value. In J. Elster (Ed.), *The multiple self*. Cambridge, UK: Cambridge University Press.

Ainslie, G. (1992). *Picoeconomics: The strategic intervention of successive motivational states within the person*. Cambridge, UK: Cambridge University Press.

Ainslie, G. (2001). *The breakdown of will*. Cambridge, UK: Cambridge University Press.

Ainslie, G., & Haendel, V. (1983). The motives of the will. In E. Gottheil, A. T. McLellan, & K. Druley (Eds.), *Etiologic aspects of alcohol and drug abuse*. Springfield, IL: Charles C. Thomas.

Alferink, L. A., Critchfield, T. S., & Hitt, J. L. (2009). Generality of the matching law as a descriptor of shot selection in basketball. *Journal of Applied Behavior Analysis, 42*, 595–608.

Allison, J. (1983). *Behavioral economics*. New York, NY: Praeger.

Amabile, T. M., Hennessey, B. A., & Grossman, B. S. (1986). Social influences on creativity: The effects of contracted-for reward. *Journal of Personality and Social Psychology, 50*, 14–23.

American Psychiatric Association. (2000). *Diagnostic and statistical manual of mental disorders* (4th ed., text revision). Washington, DC: Author.

Amsterdam, B. (1972). Mirror self-image reactions before age two. *Developmental Psychobiology, 5*, 297–305.

Anderson, C. A., & Dill, K. E. (2000). Video games and aggressive thoughts, feelings, and behavior in the laboratory and in life. *Journal of Personality and Social Psychology, 78*, 772–790.

Anderson, C. M., Hawkins, R. P., Freeman, K. A., & Scotti, J. R. (2000). Private events: Do they belong in a science of human behavior? *The Behavior Analyst, 23*, 1–10.

Antonitis, J. J. (1951). Response variability in the white rat during conditioning, extinction, and reconditioning. *Journal of Experimental Psychology, 42*, 273–281.

Assagioli, R. (1974). *The act of will*. New York, NY: Penguin.

Aumann, T. (1990). Use of stones by the Black-breasted Buzzard. *Hamirostra melanosternon* to gain access to egg contents for food. *Emu, 90*, 141–144.

Axelrod, S., & Apsche, J. (Eds.). (1983). *The effects of punishment on human behavior*. New York, NY: Academic Press.

Axelrod, S., Hall, R. V., Weiss, L., & Rohrer, S. (1974). Use of self-imposed contingencies to reduce the frequency of smoking behavior. In M. J. Mahoney & C. E. Carlson (Eds.), *Self-control: Power to the person*. Monterey, CA: Brooks/Cole.

Azar, B. (2002, October). Pigeons as baggage screeners, rats as rescuers. *Monitor on Psychology, 33*(9), 42.

Azrin, N. H., & Holz, W. C. (1966). Punishment. In W. K. Honig (Ed.), *Operant behavior: Areas of research and application*. New York, NY: Appleton.

Azrin, N. H., Hutchinson, R. R., & Hake, D. F. (1966). Extinction-induced aggression. *Journal of the Experimental Analysis of Behavior, 9*, 191–204.

Baeninger, R., & Ulm, R. R. (1969). Overcoming the effects of prior punishment on inter-species aggression in the rat. *Journal of Comparative and Physiological Psychology, 69*, 628–635.

Baer, D. M., Peterson, R. F., & Sherman, J. A. (1967). The development of imitation by reinforcing behavioral similarity to a model. *Journal of the Experimental Analysis of Behavior, 10*, 405–416.

Baer, D. M., & Sherman, J. A. (1964). Reinforcement control of generalized imitation in young children. *Journal of Experimental Child Psychology, 1*, 37–49.

Baker, T. B., & Cannon, D. S. (1979). Taste aversion therapy with alcoholics: Techniques and evidence of a conditioned response. *Behaviour Research and Therapy, 17*, 229–242.

Balda, R. P., & Kamil, A. C. (2006). Linking life zones, life history traits, ecology, and spatial cognition in four allopatric southwestern seed caching corvids. In M. F. Brown & R. G. Cook (Eds.), *Animal Spatial Cognition: Comparative, Neural, and Computational Approaches*. Retrieved from http://www.pigeon.psy.tufts.edu/asc/balda/

Balderston, J. L. (1924). *A morality play for the leisured class*. New York, NY: Appleton.

Baldwin, J. D., & Baldwin, J. I. (1998). *Behavior principles in everyday life* (3rd ed.). Upper Saddle River, NJ: Prentice-Hall.

Bandura, A. (1965). Influence of models' reinforcement contingencies on the acquisition of imitative response. *Journal of Personality and Social Psychology, 1*, 589–595.

Bandura, A. (1973). *Aggression: A social learning analysis*. Englewood Cliffs, NJ: Prentice-Hall.

Bandura, A. (1975). Effecting change through participant modeling. In J. D. Krumboltz & C. E. Thoresen (Eds.), *Counseling methods*. New York, NY: Holt, Rinehart & Winston.

Bandura, A. (1976). Self-reinforcement: Theoretical and methodological considerations. *Behaviorism, 4*, 135–155.

Bandura, A. (1977). *Social learning theory*. Englewood Cliffs, NJ: Prentice-Hall.

Bandura, A. (1986). *Social foundations of thought and action: A social cognitive theory*. Upper Saddle River, NJ: Prentice-Hall.

Bandura, A. (1997). *Self-efficacy: The exercise of self-control*. New York, NY: W. H. Freeman.

Bandura, A., Blanchard, E. B., & Ritter, B. (1969). The relative efficacy of desensitization and modeling approaches for inducing behavioral, affective, and attitudinal changes. *Journal of Personality and Social Psychology, 13*, 173–199.

Bandura, A., & McDonald, F. J. (1994). Influence of social reinforcement and the behavior of models in shaping children's moral judgments. In B. Puka (Ed.), *Defining perspectives in moral development. Moral development: A compendium* (Vol. 1). New York, NY: Garland.

Bandura, A., Ross, D., & Ross, S. A. (1961). Transmission of aggression through imitation of aggressive models. *Journal of Abnormal and Social Psychology, 63*, 575–582.

Bandura, A., Ross, D., & Ross, S. A. (1963). Imitation of film-mediated aggressive models. *Journal of Abnormal and Social Psychology, 66*, 3–11.

Bard, K. A., Todd, B. K., Bernier, C., Love, J. & Leavens, D. A. (2006). Self-awareness in human and chimpanzee infants: What is measured and what is meant by the mark and mirror test? *Infancy, 9*, 191–219.

Barlow, D. H. (1988). *Anxiety and its disorders: The nature and treatment of anxiety and panic*. New York, NY: Guilford.

Baron, R. A., & Byrne, D. (1997). *Social psychology* (8th ed.). Boston: Allyn & Bacon.

Baron-Cohen, S., Tager-Flusberg, H., & Cohen, D. (Eds.) (2000). *Understanding other minds: Perspectives from developmental cognitive neuroscience*. Oxford: Oxford University Press.

Barrett, B. (1931). *The strength of will and how to develop it*. New York, NY: R. R. Smith.

Baum, W. M. (1974). On two types of deviation from the matching law: Bias and undermatching. *Journal of the Experimental Analysis of Behavior, 22*, 231–242.

Baum, W. M. (1979). Matching, undermatching, and overmatching in studies of choice. *Journal of the Experimental Analysis of Behavior, 32*, 269–281.

Baumeister, R. F., Bratslavsky, E., Muraven, M., & Tice, D. M. (1998). Ego depletion: Is the active self a limited resource? *Journal of Personality and Social Psychology, 74*, 1252–1265.

Baumeister, R. F., Gailliot, M. T., DeWall, C. N., & Tice, D. M. (1998). Self-control depletion: Is the active self a limited resource? *Journal of Personality and Social Psychology, 74*, 1252–1265.

Beck, H. P. (2010). The evidence supports Douglas Merritte as Little Albert. *American Psychologist, 65*, 301–303.

Beck, H. P., Levinson, S., & Irons, G. (2009). Finding Little Albert: A journey to John B. Watson's infant laboratory. *American Psychologist, 64*, 605–614.

Begun, D. R. (1999). Hominid family values: Morphological and molecular data on relations among the great apes and humans. In S. T. Parker, R. W. Mitchell, & H. L. Miles (Eds.), *The mentalities of gorillas and orangutans: Comparative perspectives*. Cambridge, UK: Cambridge University Press.

Beneke, W. M., Schulte, S. E., & Vander Tuig, J. G. (1995). An analysis of excessive running in the development of activity anorexia. *Physiology and Behavior, 58*, 451–457.

Beneke, W. M., & Vander Tuig, J. G. (1996). Effects of dietary protein and food restriction on voluntary running of rats living in activity wheels. In W. F. Epling & W. D. Pierce (Eds.), *Activity anorexia: Theory, research, and treatment*. Mahwah, NJ: Erlbaum.

Benjamin L. T., Jr., Whitaker, J. L., Ramsey, R. M., & Zeve, D. R. (2007). John B. Watson's alleged sex research: An appraisal of the evidence. *American Psychologist, 62*, 131–139.

Bennett, R. H., & Samson, H. H. (1991). Ethanol-related cues and behavioral tolerance to ethanol in humans. *Psychological Record, 41*, 429–437.

Benson, J., Greaves, W., O'Donnell, M., & Taglialatela, J. (2002). Evidence for symbolic language processing in a Bonobo (*Pan paniscus*). *Journal of Consciousness Studies, 9*, 33–56.

Bentall, R. P., Lowe, C. F., & Beasty, A. (1985). The role of verbal behavior in human learning: II. Developmental differences. *Journal of the Experimental Analysis of Behavior, 43*, 165–180.

Bernstein, I. L. (1991). Aversion conditioning in response to cancer and cancer treatment. *Clinical Psychology Review, 11*, 185–191.

Billet, E. A., Richter, M. A., & Kennedy, J. L. (1998). Genetics of obsessive-compulsive disorder. In R. P. Swinson, M. M. Antony, S. Rachman, & M. A. Richter (Eds.), *Obsessive-compulsive disorder: Theory, research, and treatment*. New York, NY: Guilford.

Binder, C. (1996). Behavioral fluency: Evolution of a new paradigm. *The Behavior Analyst, 19*, 163–197.

Bjork, D. W. (1993). *B. F. Skinner: A life*. New York, NY: Basic Books.

Blandin, Y., Lhuisset, L., & Proteau, L. (1999). Cognitive processes underlying observational learning of motor skills. *Quarterly Journal of Experimental Psychology: Human Experimental Psychology, 52A*, 957–979.

Boer, D. P. (1990). Determinants of excessive running in activity-anorexia. *Dissertation Abstracts International, 50(11-B)*, 5351.

Boer, D. P., Epling, W. F., Pierce, W. D., & Russell, J. C. (1990). Suppression of food deprivation-induced high-rate wheel running in rats. *Physiology and Behavior, 48*, 339–342.

Boesch, C. (1991). Teaching among wild chimpanzees. *Animal Behaviour, 41*, 530–532.

Boesch, C., & Boesch, H. (1990). Tool use and tool making in wild chimpanzees. *Folia Primatologica, 54*, 86–99.

Boesch, C., & Boesch-Achermann, H. (2000). *The chimpanzees of the Taï Forest: Behavioural ecology and evolution*. Oxford: Oxford University Press.

Boice, R. (1989). Procrastination, business and bingeing. *Behaviour Research and Therapy, 27*, 605–611.

Boice, R. (1996). *Procrastination and blocking: A novel, practical approach*. Westport, CT: Praeger.

Bolla-Wilson, K., Wilson, R. J., & Bleecker, M. L. (1988). Conditioning of physical symptoms after neurotoxic exposure. *Journal of Occupational Medicine, 30*, 684–686.

Bolles, R. C. (1970). Species-specific defense reactions and avoidance learning. *Psychological Review, 77*, 32–48.

Bolles, R. C. (1979). *Learning theory* (2nd ed.). New York, NY: Holt, Rinehart & Winston.

Bootzin, R. R., Epstein, D., & Wood, J. M. (1991). Stimulus control instructions. In P. J. Hauri (Ed.), *Case studies in insomnia*. New York, NY: Plenum Press.

Bouvier, K. A., & Powell, R. A. (2008, June). *A driven versus balanced approach to studying: The importance of rest and recuperation in academic performance*. Poster presented at the Annual Convention of the Canadian Psychological Association, Halifax, Nova Scotia.

Bovbjerg, D. H., Redd, W. H., Maier, L. A., Holland, J. C., Lesko L. M., Niedzwiecki, ... Hakes, T. B. (1990). Anticipatory immune suppression and nausea in women receiving cyclic chemotherapy for ovarian cancer. *Journal of Consulting and Clinical Psychology, 58*, 153–157.

Braun, B. G. (1980). Hypnosis for multiple personalities. In H. J. Wain (Ed.), *Clinical hypnosis in medicine*. Chicago: Yearbook Medical.

Breland, K., & Breland, M. (1961). The misbehavior of organisms. *American Psychologist, 16*, 681–684.

Brethower, D. M., & Reynolds, G. S. (1962). A facilitative effect of punishment on unpunished responding. *Journal of the Experimental Analysis of Behavior, 5*, 191–199.

Breuer, E., & Freud, S. (1955). Studies on hysteria. In J. Strachey (Ed. and Trans.), *The standard edition of the complete psychological works of Sigmund Freud* (Vol. 2). London: Hogarth Press. (Original work published 1895)

Brigham, T. A. (1978). Self-control. In A. C. Catania & T. A. Brigham (Eds.), *Handbook of Applied Behavior Analysis*. New York, NY: Irvington.

Broberg, D. J., & Bernstein, I. L. (1987). Candy as a scapegoat in the prevention of food aversions in children receiving chemotherapy. *Cancer, 60*, 2344–2347.

Brodbeck, D. R., & Shettleworth, S. J. (1995). Matching location and color of a compound stimulus: Comparison of a food-storing and a non-storing bird species. *Journal of Experimental Psychology: Animal Behavior Processes, 21*, 64–77.

Brogden, W. J. (1939). Sensory pre-conditioning. *Journal of Experimental Psychology, 25*, 323–332.

Brown, P. L., & Jenkins, H. M. (1968). Autoshaping of the pigeon's key-peck. *Journal of the Experimental Analysis of Behavior, 11*, 1–8.

Brown, S. A., Stetson, B. A., & Beatty, P. A. (1989). Cognitive and behavioral features of adolescent coping in high-risk drinking situations. *Addictive Behaviors, 14*, 43–52.

Bruch, H. (1978). *The golden cage: The enigma of anorexia nervosa*. Cambridge, MA: Harvard University Press.

Buckley, K. W. (1989). *Mechanical man: John Broadus Watson and the beginnings of behaviorism*. New York, NY: Guilford.

Bullock, D. H., & Smith, W. C. (1953). An effect of repeated conditioning-extinction upon operant strength. *Journal of Experimental Psychology, 46*, 349–352.

Burns, M., & Domjan, M. (1996). Sign tracking versus goal tracking in the sexual conditioning of male Japanese quail *(Coturnix japonica)*. *Journal of Experimental Psychology: Animal Behavior Processes, 22*, 297–306.

Bushman, B. J., & Anderson, C. A. (2001). Media violence and the American public: Scientific facts versus media misinformation. *American Psychologist, 56*, 477–489.

Buske-Kirschbaum, A., Kirschbaum, C., Stierle, H., Jabaij, L., & Hellhammer, D. (1994). Conditioned manipulation of natural killer (NK) cells in humans using a discriminative learning protocol. *Biological Psychology, 38*, 143–155.

Bussey, K., & Bandura, A. (1984). Influence of gender constancy and social power on sex-linked modeling. *Journal of Personality and Social Psychology, 47,* 1292–1302.

Byrne, D., & Clore, G. L. (1970). A reinforcement model of evaluative responses. *Personality: An International Journal, 1,* 103–128.

Call, J. (1999). Levels of imitation and cognitive mechanisms in orangutans. In S. T. Parker, R. W. Mitchell, & H. L. Miles (Eds.), *The mentalities of gorillas and orangutans: Comparative perspectives.* Cambridge, UK: Cambridge University Press.

Call, J., & Tomasello, M. (1995). The use of social information in the problem-solving of orangutans *(Pongo pygmaeus)* and human children *(Homo sapiens). Journal of Comparative Psychology, 109,* 308–320.

Cameron, J. (2001). Negative effects of reward on intrinsic motivation—A limited phenomenon: Comment on Deci, Koestner, and Ryan (2001). *Review of Educational Research, 71,* 29–42.

Cameron, J., & Pierce, W. D. (1994). Reinforcement, reward, and intrinsic motivation: A meta-analysis. *Review of Educational Research, 64,* 363–423.

Cameron, J., & Pierce, W. D. (2002). *Rewards and intrinsic motivation: Resolving the controversy.* Westport, CT: Bergin & Garvey.

Cameron, J., Pierce, W. D., Banko, K. M., & Gear, M. (2005). Achievement-based rewards and intrinsic motivation: A test for cognitive mediators. *Journal of Educational Psychology, 97,* 641–655.

Capaldi, E. D. (1996). Conditioned food preferences. In E. D. Capaldi (Ed.), *Why we eat what we eat: The psychology of eating.* Washington, DC: American Psychological Association.

Capaldi, E. J. (1966). Partial reinforcement: A hypothesis of sequential effects. *Psychological Review, 73,* 459–477.

Capaldi, E. J., Miller, D. J., & Alptekin, S. (1989). Multiple-food-unit-incentive effect: Non-conservation of weight of food reward by rats. *Journal of Experimental Psychology: Animal Behavior Processes, 15,* 75–80.

Carroll, W. R., & Bandura, A. (1987). Translating cognition into action: The role of visual guidance in observational learning. *Journal of Motor Behavior, 19,* 385–398.

Casey, R., & Rozin, P. (1989). Changing children's food preferences: Parent opinions. *Appetite, 12,* 171–182.

Catania, A. C. (1975). The myth of self-reinforcement. *Behaviorism, 3,* 192–199.

Catania, A. C. (1988). The operant behaviorism of B. F. Skinner. In A. C. Catania & S. Harnad (Eds.), *The selection of behavior: The operant behaviorism of B. F. Skinner: Comments and consequences.* New York, NY: Cambridge University Press.

Chambers, K. C., Yuan, D., Brownson, E. A., & Wang, Y. (1997). Sexual dimorphisms in conditioned taste aversions: Mechanism and function. In M. E. Bouton & M. S. Fanselow (Eds.), *Learning, motivation, and cognition: The functional behaviorism of Robert C. Bolles.* Washington, DC: American Psychological Association.

Chance, P. (1994). *Learning and behavior* (3rd ed.). Pacific Grove, CA: Brooks/Cole.

Chappell, J., & Kacelnik, A. (2002). Tool selectivity in a non-mammal, the New Caledonian crow *(Corvus moneduloides). Animal Cognition, 5,* 71–78.

Cherek, D. R. (1982). Schedule-induced cigarette self-administration. *Pharmacology, Biochemistry, and Behavior, 17,* 523–527.

Chesler, P. (1969). Maternal influence in learning by observation in kittens. *Science, 166,* 901–903.

Chomsky, N. (1988). *Language and problems of knowledge.* Cambridge, MA: MIT Press.

Church, J., & Williams, H. (2001). Another sniffer dog for the clinic? *Lancet, 358,* 930.

Cialdini, R. B. (1993). *Influence: Science and practice* (3rd ed.). New York, NY: HarperCollins.

Clark, H. B., Rowbury, T., Baer, A. M., & Baer, D. M. (1973). Timeout as a punishing stimulus in continuous and intermittent schedules. *Journal of Applied Behavior Analysis, 6,* 443–455.

Clark, L. A., Watson, D., & Mineka, S. (1994). Temperament, personality, and the mood and anxiety disorders. *Journal of Abnormal Psychology, 103*, 103–116.

Clayton, N. S. (2001). Hippocampal growth and maintenance depend on food-caching experience in juvenile mountain chickadees. *Behavioral Neuroscience, 115*, 614–625.

Colvin, G. (2008). *Talent is overrated: What really separates world-class performers from everybody else*. New York, NY: Penguin.

Conger, R., & Killeen, P. (1974). Use of concurrent operants in small group research. *Pacific Sociological Review, 17*, 399–416.

Cook, M., & Mineka, S. (1989). Observational conditioning of fear to fear-relevant versus fear-irrelevant stimuli in rhesus monkeys. *Journal of Abnormal Psychology, 98*, 448–459.

Coon, D. (1998). *Introduction to psychology: Exploration and application* (8th ed.). Pacific Grove, CA: Brooks/Cole.

Coon, D. J. (1994). "Not a creature of reason": The alleged impact of Watsonian behaviorism on advertising in the 1920s. In J. T. Todd & E. K. Morris (Eds.), *Modern perspectives on John B. Watson and classical behaviorism*. Westport, CT: Greenwood Press.

Coren, S. (1994). *The intelligence of dogs: A Guide to the thoughts, emotions, and inner lives of our canine companions*. New York, NY: Free Press.

Corsini, R. (2002). *The dictionary of psychology*. New York, NY: Brunner-Routledge.

Craig, G. J., Kermis, M. D., & Digdon, N. L. (1998). *Children today* (Canadian ed.). Scarborough, Canada: Prentice-Hall.

Crespi, L. P. (1942). Quantitative variation of incentive and performance in the white rat. *American Journal of Psychology, 55*, 467–517.

Critchfield, T. S., & Kollins, S. H. (2001). Temporal discounting: Basic research and the analysis of socially important behavior. *Journal of Applied Behavior Analysis, 34*, 101–122.

Danaher, B. G. (1977). Rapid smoking and self-control in the modification of smoking behavior. *Journal of Consulting and Clinical Psychology, 45*, 1068–1075.

Darwin, C. R. (1859). *On the origin of species by means of natural selection*. London: Murray.

Davey, G. C. L. (1992). Classical conditioning and the acquisition of human fears and phobias: A review and synthesis of the literature. *Advances in Behaviour Research & Therapy, 14*, 29–66.

Davey, G. C. L., De Jong, P., & Tallis, F. (1993). UCS Inflation in the aetiology of a variety of anxiety disorders: Some case histories. *Behaviour Research and Therapy, 31*, 495–498.

Davis, C., Katzman, D. K., & Kirsh, C. (1999). Compulsive physical activity in adolescents with anorexia nervosa: A psychobehavioral spiral of pathology. *Journal of Nervous and Mental Disease, 187*, 336–342.

de Waal, F. (2005). *Our inner ape: A leading primatologist explains why we are who we are*. New York, NY: Penguin.

de Waal, F. B. M. (1986). Deception in the natural communication of chimpanzees. In R. Mitchell & N. Thompson (Eds.), *Deception: Perspectives on human and nonhuman deceit*. New York, NY: SUNY Press.

de Waal, F. B. M. (2008). Putting the altruism back into altruism: The evolution of empathy. *Annual Review of Psychology, 59*, 279–300.

DeAngelis, T. (2010, January). Little Albert regains his identity. *Monitor on Psychology, 41*(1), 10–11.

Deci, E. L., Koestner, R., & Ryan, R. M. (2001a). Extrinsic rewards and intrinsic motivation: Reconsidered once again. *Review of Educational Research, 71*, 1–27.

Deci, E. L., Koestner, R., & Ryan, R. M. (2001b). The pervasive negative effects of rewards on intrinsic motivation: Response to Cameron (2001). *Review of Educational Research, 71*, 43–51.

Deci, E. L., & Ryan, R. M. (1985). *Intrinsic motivation and self-determination in human behavior*. New York, NY: Plenum Press.

Delk, J. L. (1980). High-risk sports as indirect self-destructive behavior. In N. L. Farberow (Ed.), *The many faces of suicide: Indirect self-destructive behavior*. New York, NY: McGraw-Hill.

DeNeys, W. (2006). Developmental trends in decision making: The case of the Monty Hall dilemma. In J. A. Ellsworth (Ed.), *Psychology of decision making in education*. Haupauge, NY: Nova Science Publishers.

Dingfelder, S. F. (2010, November). A second chance for the Mexican wolf. *Monitor on Psychology, 41*(10), 20–21.

Dinsmoor, J. A. (1954). Punishment: I. The avoidance hypothesis. *Psychological Review, 61*, 34–46.

Domjan, M. (2000). *The essentials of conditioning and learning* (2nd ed.). Belmont, CA: Wadsworth.

Domjan, M. (2010). *The principles of learning and behavior* (6th ed.). Belmont, CA: Wadsworth.

Dowling, J. E. (1984). Modeling effectiveness as a function of learner-model similarity and the learner's attitude toward women. *Dissertation Abstracts International, 45*(1-A), 121.

Doyle, T. F., & Samson, H. H. (1988). Adjunctive alcohol drinking in humans. *Physiology and Behavior, 44*, 775–779.

Drea, C. M., & Carter, A. N. (2009). Cooperative problem solving in a social carnivore. *Animal Behavior, 78*, 967–977.

Durand, V. M. (1990). *Severe behavior problems: A functional communication training approach*. New York, NY: Guilford.

Dweck, C. S., & Reppucci, N. D. (1973). Learned helplessness and reinforcement responsibility in children. *Journal of Personality & Social Psychology, 25*, 109–116.

Ehrensaft, M. K., Cohen, P., Brown, J., Smailes, E., Chen, H., & Johnson, J. G. (2003). Intergenerational transmission of partner violence: A 20-year prospective study. *Journal of Consulting and Clinical Psychology, 71*, 741–753.

Eikelboom, R., & Stewart, J. (1982). Conditioning of drug-induced physiological responses. *Psychological Review, 89*, 507–528.

Eisenberg, N., McCreath, H., & Ahn, R. (1988). Vicarious emotional responsiveness and prosocial behavior: Their interrelations in young children. *Personality and Social Psychology Bulletin, 14*, 298–311.

Eisenberger, R. (1992). Learned industriousness. *Psychological Review, 99*, 248–267.

Eisenberger, R., Carlson, J., Guile, M., & Shapiro, N. (1979). Transfer of effort across behaviors. *Learning and Motivation, 10*, 178–197.

Eisenberger, R., Masterson, F. A., & McDermitt, M. (1982). Effects of task variety on generalized effort. *Journal of Educational Psychology, 74*, 499–505.

Eisenstein, E. M., Eisenstein, D., & Smith, J. C. (2001). The evolutionary significance of habituation and sensitization across phylogeny: A behavioral homeostasis model. *Integrative Physiological and Behavioral Science, 36*, 251–265.

Ellenberger, H. F. (1970). *The discovery of the unconscious: The history and evolution of dynamic psychiatry*. New York, NY: Basic Books.

Ellis, N. R. (1962). Amount of reward and operant behavior in mental defectives. *American Journal of Mental Deficiency, 66*, 595–599.

Epling, W. F., & Pierce, W. D. (1988). Activity-based anorexia: A biobehavioral perspective. *International Journal of Eating Disorders, 7*, 475–485.

Epling, W. F., & Pierce, W. D. (1991). *Solving the anorexia puzzle: A scientific approach*. Toronto, Canada: Hogrefe & Huber.

Epling, W. F., & Pierce, W. D. (1996). An overview of activity anorexia. In W. F. Epling & W. D. Pierce (Eds.), *Activity anorexia: Theory, research, and treatment*. Mahwah, NJ: Erlbaum.

Epstein, R. (1985). Extinction-induced resurgence: Preliminary investigations and possible applications. *Psychological Record, 35*, 143–153.

Epstein, R. (1997). Skinner as self-manager. *Journal of Applied Behavior Analysis, 30*, 545–568.

Epstein, R., Lanza, R. P., & Skinner, B. F. (1981). "Self-awareness" in the pigeon. *Science, 212*, 695–696.

Epstein, S. M. (1967). Toward a unified theory of anxiety. In B. A. Maher (Ed.), *Progress in experimental personality research* (Vol. *4*). New York, NY: Academic Press.

Ericsson, K. A. (Ed.) (2009). *Development of professional expertise: Toward measurement of expert performance and design of optimal learning environments*. New York, NY: Cambridge University Press.

Ericsson, K. A., & Charness, N. (1994). Expert performance: Its structure and acquisition. *American Psychologist, 49,* 725–747.

Ericsson, K. A., Krampe, R. T., & Tesch-Römer, C. (1993). The role of deliberate practice in the acquisition of expert performance. *Psychological Review, 100,* 363–406.

Eron, L. D., Huesmann, L. R., Lefkowitz, M. M., & Walder, L. O. (1972). Does television violence cause aggression? *American Psychologist, 27,* 253–263.

Estes, W. K., & Skinner, B. F. (1941). Some quantitative properties of anxiety. *Journal of Experimental Psychology, 29,* 390–400.

Etscorn, F., & Stephens, R. (1973). Establishment of conditioned taste aversions with a 24-hour CS-US interval. *Physiological Psychology, 1,* 251–259.

Exton, M. S., von Auer, A. K., Buske-Kirschbaum, A., Stockhorst, U., Gobel, U., & Schedlowski, M. (2000). Pavlovian conditioning of immune function: Animal investigation and the challenge of human application. *Behavioural Brain Research, 110,* 129–141.

Eysenck, H. J. (1957). *The dynamics of anxiety and hysteria: An experimental application of modern learning theory to psychiatry*. London: Routledge & Kegan Paul.

Eysenck, H. J. (1967). *The biological basis of personality*. Springfield, IL: Charles C. Thomas.

Eysenck, H. J. (1968). A theory of the incubation of anxiety/fear response. *Behaviour Research and Therapy, 6,* 63–65.

Eysenck, H. J. (1976). The learning theory model of neurosis—A new approach. *Behaviour Research and Therapy, 14,* 251–267.

Falk, J. L. (1961). Production of polydipsia in normal rats by an intermittent food schedule. *Science, 133,* 195–196.

Falk, J. L. (1971). The nature and determinants of adjunctive behavior. *Physiology and Behavior, 6,* 577–588.

Falk, J. L. (1977). The origin and functions of adjunctive behavior. *Animal Learning and Behavior, 5,* 325–335.

Falk, J. L. (1993). Schedule-induced drug self-administration. In F. van Haaren (Ed.), *Methods in behavioral pharmacology*. Amsterdam: Elsevier.

Falk, J. L. (1994). Schedule-induced behavior occurs in humans: A reply to Overskeid. *Psychological Record, 44,* 45–62.

Falk, J. L. (1998). Drug abuse as an adjunctive behavior. *Drug and Alcohol Dependence, 52,* 91–98.

Fanselow, M. S., DeCola, J. P., & Young, S. L. (1993). Mechanisms responsible for reduced contextual conditioning with massed unsignaled unconditional stimuli. *Journal of Experimental Psychology: Animal Behavior Processes, 19,* 121–137.

Farroni, T., Johnson, M. H., Brockbank, M., & Simion, F. (2000). Infants' use of gaze direction to cue attention: The importance of perceived motion. *Visual Cognition, 7,* 705–718.

Federal Trade Commission. (2000). *Marketing violent entertainment to children: A review of self-regulation and industry practices in the motion picture, music recording, and electronic game industries*. Washington, DC: Author.

Feigenson, L., & Carey, S. (2003). Tracking individuals via object-files: Evidence from infants' manual search. *Developmental Science, 6,* 568–584.

Ferguson, E., & Cassaday, H. J. (1999). The Gulf War and illness by association. *British Journal of Psychology, 90,* 459–475.

Ferguson, E., Cassaday, H. J., & Bibby, P. A. 2004). Odors and sounds as triggers for medically unexplained symptoms: A fixed-occasion diary study of Gulf War veterans. *Annals of Behavioral Medicine, 27,* 205–214.

Ferster, C. B., & Skinner, B. F. (1957). *Schedules of reinforcement.* New York, NY: Appleton-Century-Crofts.

Finn, J., Tregenza, T., & Norman, M. (2009). Preparing the perfect cuttlefish meal: Complex prey handling by dolphins. *Public Library of Science, Biology, 4,* e4217.

Finn, J. K., Tregenza, T., & Norman, M.D. (2009). Defensive tool use in a coconut-carrying octopus. *Current Biology, 19,* R1069–R1070.

Fitch, W. T. (2005). The evolution of language: A comparative review. *Biology and Philosophy, 20,* 193–230.

Flory, R. K., & Ellis, B. B. (1973). Schedule-induced aggression against a slide-image target. *Bulletin of the Psychonomic Society, 2,* 287–290.

Foa, E. B., Franklin, M. E., & Kozak, M. J. (1998). Psychosocial treatments for obsessive-compulsive disorder: Literature review. In R. P. Swinson, M. M. Antony, S. Rachman, & M. A. Richter (Eds.), *Obsessive-compulsive disorder: Theory, research, and treatment.* New York, NY: Guilford.

Foa, E. B., Zinbarg, R., & Rothbaum, B. O. (1992). Uncontrollability and unpredictability in post-traumatic stress disorder: An animal model. *Psychological Bulletin, 112,* 218–238.

Fouts, G. R., & Click, M. (1979). Effects of live and TV models on observational learning in introverted and extroverted children. *Perceptual and Motor Skills, 48,* 863–867.

Fouts, R. S. (1973). Acquisition and testing of gestural signs in four young chimpanzees. *Science, 180,* 978–980.

Fox, L. (1962). Effecting the use of efficient study habits. *Journal of Mathematics, 1,* 75–86.

Fragaszy, D., Izar, P., Visalberghi, E., Ottoni, E. B., & De Oliveira, M. G. (2004). Wild capuchin monkeys (*Cebus libidinosus*) use anvils and stone pounding tools. *American Journal of Primatology, 64,* 359–366.

Franks, C. M. (1963). Behavior therapy, the principles of conditioning and the treatment of the alcoholic. *Quarterly Journal of Studies on Alcohol, 24,* 511–529.

Freud, S. (1955). Lines of advance in psychoanalytic therapy. In J. Strachey (Ed. and Trans.), *The Standard Edition of the Complete Psychological Works of Sigmund Freud* (Vol. 17, pp. 159–168). London: Hogarth Press. (Original work published 1919)

Furomoto, L. (1971). Extinction in the pigeon after continuous reinforcement: Effects of number of reinforced responses. *Psychological Reports, 28,* 331–338.

Gailliot, M. T., Baumeister, R. F., DeWall, C. N., Maner, J.K., Plant, E. A., Tice, D. M., & Brewer, L. E. (2007). Self-control relies on glucose as a limited energy source: Willpower is more than a metaphor. *Journal of Personality and Social Psychology, 92,* 2007.

Galef, B. G., Jr. (1988). Imitation in animals: History, definition and interpretation of data from the psychological laboratory. In T. R. Zentall & B. G. Galef, Jr. (Eds.), *Social learning: Psychological and biological perspectives.* Hillsdale, NJ: Erlbaum.

Gallup, G. G., Jr. (1970). Chimpanzees: Self-recognition. *Science, 167,* 86–87.

Gandhi, M. K. (1957). *An autobiography: The story of my experiments with truth.* Boston: Beacon Press. (Original work published 1927)

Garcia, J., & Koelling, R. A. (1966). Relation of cue to consequence in avoidance learning. *Psychonomic Science, 4,* 123–124.

Gardner, H. (1993). *Multiple intelligences: The theory in practice.* New York, NY: Basic Books.

Gardner, R. A., & Gardner, B. T. (1969). Teaching sign language to a chimpanzee. *Science, 165,* 664–672.

Gardner, R. A., & Gardner, B. T. (1975). Evidence for sentence constituents in the early utterances of child and chimpanzee. *Journal of Experimental Psychology: General, 104,* 244–267.

Gardner, R. A., Gardner, B. T., & Van Cantfort, T. E. (1989). *Teaching sign language to chimpanzees*. New York, NY: State University of New York Press.

Garner, D. M., & Garfinkel, P. E. (1980). Socio-cultural factors in the development of anorexia nervosa. *Psychological Medicine, 10*, 647–656.

Gay, P. (1988). *Freud: A life for our time*. New York, NY: Norton.

Gist, R., & Devilly, G. J. (2010). Early intervention in the aftermath of trauma. In G. M. Rosen & B. C. Frueh (Eds.), *Clinician's guide to posttraumatic stress disorder*. Hoboken, NJ: Wiley & Sons.

Gleaves, D. H. (1996). The sociocognitive model of dissociative identity disorder: A reexamination of the evidence. *Psychological Bulletin, 120*, 42–59.

Gold, S. R., Fultz, J., Burke, C. H., & Prisco, A. G. (1992). Vicarious emotional responses of macho college males. *Journal of Interpersonal Violence, 7*, 165–174.

Gollwitzer, P. M. (1999). Implementation intentions: Strong effects of simple plans. *American Psychologist, 54*, 493–503.

Gollwitzer, P. M., & Brandstätter, V. (1997). Implementation intentions and effective goal pursuit. *Journal of Personality and Social Psychology, 73*, 186–199.

Goodall, J. (1990). *Through a window: My thirty years with the chimpanzees of Gombe*. Boston: Houghton Mifflin.

Goodwin, C. J. (2005). *A history of modern psychology* (2nd ed.). Hoboken, NJ: Wiley.

Gottman, J. (1994). *Why marriages succeed or fail: And how you can make yours last*. New York, NY: Simon & Schuster.

Gray, J. (1999). Ivan Petrovich Pavlov and the conditioned reflex. *Brain Research Bulletin, 50*, 433.

Green, L., Fisher, E. B., Perlow, S., & Sherman, L. (1981). Preference reversal and self control: Choice as a function of reward amount and delay. *Behaviour Analysis Letters, 1*, 43–51.

Grice, G. R. (1948). The relation of secondary reinforcement to delayed reward in visual discrimination learning. *Journal of Experimental Psychology, 38*, 1–16.

Grosskurth, P. (1991). *The secret ring: Freud's inner circle and the politics of psychoanalysis*. London: Jonathan Cape.

Gubernick, D. J., & Alberts, J. R. (1984). A specialization of taste aversion learning during suckling and its weaning-associated transformation. Developmental Psychobiology, *17*, 613–628.

Guevremont, D. C., Osnes, P. G., & Stokes, T. F. (1986). Preparation for effective self-regulation: The development of generalized verbal control. *Journal of Applied Behavior Analysis, 19*, 99–104.

Guisinger, S. (2003). Adapted to flee famine: Adding an evolutionary perspective on anorexia nervosa. *Psychological Review, 110*, 745–761.

Gustavson, C. R., Garcia, J., Hankins, W. G., & Rusiniak, K. W. (1974). Coyote predation control by aversive conditioning. *Science, 184*, 581–583.

Guthrie, E. R. (1952). *The psychology of learning* (Rev. ed.). New York, NY: Harper & Row. (Original work published 1935)

Haggbloom, S. J., Warnick, R., Warnick, J. E., Jones, V. K., Yarbrough, G. L., Russell, T. M., … Monte, E. (2002). The 100 most eminent psychologists of the 20th century. *Review of General Psychology, 6*, 139–152.

Hagopian, L. P., Fisher, W. W., & Legacy, S. M. (1994). Schedule effects of noncontingent reinforcement on attention-maintained destructive behavior in identical quadruplets. *Journal of Applied Behavior Analysis, 27*, 317–325.

Hall, G. C. N., Shondrick, D. D., & Hirschman, R. (1993). Conceptually derived treatments for sexual aggressors. *Professional Psychology: Research and Practice, 24*, 62–69.

Hall, K. R. L., & Schaller, G. B. (1964). Tool-using behavior of the California sea otter. *Journal of Mammology, 45*, 287–298.

Hanson, H. M. (1959). Effects of discrimination training on stimulus generalization. *Journal of Experimental Psychology, 58*, 321–334.

Harackiewicz, J. M., Manderlink, G., & Sansone, C. (1984). Rewarding pinball wizardry: Effects of evaluation and cue value on intrinsic interest. *Journal of Personality and Social Psychology, 47,* 287–300.

Hare, B., Call, J., & Tomasello, M. (2001). Do chimpanzees know what conspecifics know? *Animal Behaviour, 61,* 139–151.

Hare, B., Melis, A. P., Woods, V., Hastings, S., & Wrangham, R. (2007). Tolerance allows bonobos to outperform chimpanzees on a cooperative task. *Current Biology, 17,* 619–623.

Harlow, H. F., Harlow, M. K., & Meyer, D. R. (1950). Learning motivated by a manipulative drive. *Journal of Experimental Psychology, 40,* 228–234.

Harris, B. (1979). Whatever happened to little Albert? *American Psychologist, 34,* 151–160.

Harris, B. (2011). Letting go of Little Albert: Disciplinary memory, history, and the uses of myth. *Journal of the History of the Behavioral Sciences, 47,* 1–17.

Haupt, E. J., Van Kirk, M. J., & Terraciano, T. (1975). An inexpensive fading procedure to decrease errors and increase retention of number facts. In E. Ramp & G. Semb (Eds.), *Behavior analysis: Areas of research and application.* Englewood Cliffs, NJ: Prentice-Hall.

Hayes, K. J., & Hayes, C. (1951). The intellectual development of a home-raised chimpanzee. *Proceedings of the American Philosophical Society, 95,* 105–109.

Hayes, S. C., Rosenfarb, I., Wulfert, E., Munt, E. D., Korn, Z., & Zettle, R. D. (1985). Self-reinforcement effects: An artifact of social standard setting? *Journal of Applied Behavior Analysis, 18,* 201–214.

Hayes, S. C., Strosahl, K. D., & Wilson, K. G. (1999). *Acceptance and commitment therapy: An experiential approach to behavior change.* New York, NY: Guilford Press.

Heffernan, T., & Richards, C. S. (1981). Self-control of study behavior: Identification and evaluation of natural methods. *Journal of Counseling Psychology, 28,* 361–364.

Herbranson, W. T., & Schroeder, J. (2010). Are birds smarter than mathematicians? Pigeons (*Columba livia*) perform optimally on a version of the Monty Hall dilemma. *Journal of Comparative Psychology, 124,* 1–13.

Hergenhahn, B. R. (1988). *An introduction to theories of learning* (3rd ed.). Englewood Cliffs, NJ: Prentice-Hall.

Herman, J. L. (1992). *Trauma and recovery.* New York, NY: Basic Books.

Herman, L. M., & Forestell, P. H. (1985). Reporting presence or absence of named objects by a language-trained dolphin. *Neuroscience and Biobehavioral Reviews, 9,* 667–681.

Herman, L. M., Kuczaj, S. A., & Holder, M. D. (1993). Responses to anomalous gestural sequences by a language-trained dolphin: Evidence for processing of semantic relations and syntactic information. *Journal of Experimental Psychology: General, 122,* 184 –194.

Herman, L. M., Morrel-Samuels, P., & Pack, A. A. (1990). Bottlenosed dolphin and human recognition of veridical and degraded video displays of an artificial gestural language. *Journal of Experimental Psychology: General, 119,* 215–230.

Herman, L. M., Pack, A. A., & Morrel-Samuels, P. (1993). Representational and conceptual skills of dolphins. In H. L. Roitblat, L. M. Herman, and P. E. Nachtigall (Eds.), *Language and communication: Comparative perspectives.* Hillsdale, NJ: Erlbaum.

Herman, L. M., Richards, D. G., & Wolz, J. P. (1984). Comprehension of sentences by bottle-nosed dolphins. *Cognition, 16,* 129–219.

Herrnstein, R. J. (1961). Relative and absolute strength of response as a function of frequency of reinforcement. *Journal of the Experimental Analysis of Behavior, 4,* 267–272.

Herrnstein, R. J. (1966). Superstition: A corollary of the principle of operant conditioning. In W. K. Honig (Ed.), *Operant behavior: Areas of research and application.* New York, NY: Appleton-Century-Crofts.

Herrnstein, R. J. (1969). Method and theory in the study of avoidance. *Psychological Review, 76,* 49–69.

Herrnstein, R. J. (1979). Acquisition, generalization, and reversal of a natural concept. *Journal of Experimental Psychology: Animal Behavior Processes, 5,* 116–129.

Herrnstein, R. J. (1981). Self-control as response strength. In C. M. Bradshaw, E. Szabadi, & C. F. Lowe (Eds.), *Recent developments in the quantification of steady-state operant behavior.* Amsterdam: Elsevier/North Holland Biomedical Press.

Herrnstein, R. J. (1990). Rational choice theory: Necessary but not sufficient. *American Psychologist, 45,* 356–367.

Herrnstein, R. J. (1997). *The matching law: Papers in psychology and economics.* Cambridge, MA: Harvard University Press.

Herrnstein, R. J., & Heyman, G. M. (1979). Is matching compatible with reinforcement maximization on concurrent variable interval, variable ratio? *Journal of the Experimental Analysis of Behavior, 31,* 209–223.

Herrnstein, R. J., & Hineline, P. N. (1966). Negative reinforcement as shock-frequency reduction. *Journal of the Experimental Analysis of Behavior, 9,* 421–430.

Herrnstein, R. J., & Loveland, D. H. (1975). Maximizing and matching on concurrent ratio schedules. *Journal of the Experimental Analysis of Behavior, 24,* 107–116.

Heschl, A., & Fuchsbichler, C. (2009). Siamangs (*Hylobates syndactylus*) recognize their mirror image. *International Journal of Comparative Psychology, 22,* 221–233.

Hicks, J. (1968). Effects of co-observers' sanctions and adult presence on imitative aggression. *Child Development, 39,* 303–309.

Hinson, R. E., & Poulos, C. X. (1981). Sensitization to the behavioral effects of cocaine: Modification by Pavlovian conditioning. *Pharmacology, Biochemistry, and Behavior, 15,* 559–562.

Hockett, C. D. (1960). The origin of speech. *Scientific American, 203,* 88–96.

Honey, P. L., & Galef, B. G., Jr. (2003). Ethanol consumption by rat dams during gestation, lactation and weaning increases ethanol consumption by their adolescent young. *Developmental Psychobiology, 42,* 252–260.

Honey, P. L., & Galef, B. G., Jr. (2004). Long lasting effects of rearing by an ethanol-consuming dam on voluntary ethanol consumption by rats. *Appetite, 43,* 261–268.

Honey, P. L., Varley, K. R., & Galef, B. G., Jr. (2004). Effects of ethanol consumption by adult female rats on subsequent consumption by adolescents. *Appetite, 42,* 299–306.

Horowitz, A. C. (2003). Do humans ape? Or do apes human? Imitation and intention in humans (*Homo sapiens*) and other animals. *Journal of Comparative Psychology, 3,* 325–336.

Hothersall, D. (1984). *History of psychology.* New York, NY: Random House.

Houston, A. (1986). The matching law applies to wagtails foraging in the wild. *Journal of the Experimental Analysis of Behavior, 45,* 15–18.

Huesmann, L. R. (1986). Psychological processes promoting the relation between exposure to media violence and aggressive behavior by the viewer. *Journal of Social Issues, 42,* 125–139.

Huesmann, L. R., Moise-Titus, J., Podolski, C.-L., & Eron, L. D. (2003). Longitudinal relations between children's exposure to TV violence and their aggressive and violent behavior in young adulthood: 1977–1992. *Developmental Psychology, 39,* 201–221.

Hull, C. L. (1932). The goal gradient hypothesis and maze learning. *Psychological Review, 39,* 25–43.

Hull, C. L. (1934). The rat's speed-of-locomotion gradient in the approach to food. *Journal of Comparative Psychology, 17,* 393–422.

Hull, C. L. (1943). *Principles of behavior.* New York, NY: Appleton-Century-Crofts.

Hunt, P. S., & Hallmark, R. A. (2001). Increases in ethanol ingestion by young rats following interaction with intoxicated siblings: A review. *Integrative Psychological and Behavioral Science, 36,* 239–248.

Jacobson, E. (1938). *Progressive relaxation* (2nd ed.). Chicago: University of Chicago Press.

James, W. (1907). The energies of men. *The Philosophical Review, 16,* 1–20.

James, W. (1983). *The principles of psychology*. Cambridge, MA: Harvard University Press. (Original work published 1890)

Jenkins, H. M., Barrera, F. J., Ireland, C., & Woodside, B. (1978). Signal-centered action patterns of dogs in appetitive classical conditioning. *Learning and Motivation, 9*, 272–296.

Jenkins, H. M., & Moore, B. R. (1973). The form of the autoshaped response with food or water reinforcers. *Journal of the Experimental Analysis of Behavior, 20*, 163–181.

Jensen, R. (2006). Behaviorism, latent learning, and cognitive maps: Needed revisions in introductory psychology textbooks. *The Behavior Analyst, 29*, 187–209.

Johnson, J. G., Cohen, P., Kasen, S., & Brook, J. S. (2007). Extensive television viewing and the development of attention and learning difficulties during adolescence. *Archives of Pediatric and Adolescent Medicine, 161*, 480–486.

Jones, B. M. (2011). Applied behaviour analysis is ideal for the development of a land mine detection technology using humans. *The Behavior Analyst, 34*, 55–73.

Jones, M. C. (1924). The elimination of children's fears. *Journal of Experimental Psychology, 7*, 382–390.

Kaiser, D. H., Sherburne, L. M., & Zentall, T. R. (1997). Directed forgetting in pigeons resulting from reallocation of memory-maintaining processes on forget-cue trials. *Psychonomic Bulletin & Review, 4*, 559–565.

Kalat, J. W. (1974). Taste salience depends on novelty, not concentration, in taste-aversion learning in the rat. *Journal of Comparative and Physiological Psychology, 86*, 47–50.

Kamin, L. J. (1969). Predictability, surprise, attention and conditioning. In B. A. Campbell & R. M. Church (Eds.), *Punishment and aversive behavior*. New York, NY: Appleton-Century-Crofts.

Kano, T. (1982). The use of leafy twigs for rain cover by the pygmy chimpanzees of Wamba. *Primate, 23*, 453–457.

Kantor, T. G., Sunshine, A., Laska, E., Meisner, M., & Hopper, M. (1966). Oral analgesic studies: Penzocine hydrochloride, codeine, aspirin, and placebo and their influence on response to placebo. *Clinical Pharmacology and Therapeutics, 7*, 447–454.

Kaplan, H. I., Sadock, B. J., & Grebb, J. A. (1994). *Kaplan and Sadock's synopsis of psychiatry* (7th ed.). Baltimore: Williams & Wilkins.

Karpicke, J. D., & Blunt, J. R. (2011). Retrieval practice produces more learning than elaborative studying with concept mapping. *Science, 331*, 772–775.

Katcher, A. H., Solomon, R. L., Turner, L. H., LoLordo, V. M., Overmier, J. B., & Rescorla, R. A. (1969). Heart-rate and blood pressure responses to signaled and unsignaled shocks: Effects of cardiac sympathectomy. *Journal of Comparative and Physiological Psychology, 68*, 163–174.

Katz, J. L. (1986). Long-distance running, anorexia nervosa, and bulimia: A report of two cases. *Comprehensive Psychiatry, 27*, 74–78.

Katz, J. L. (1996). Clinical observations on the physical activity of anorexia nervosa. In W. F. Epling & W. D. Pierce (Eds.), *Activity anorexia: Theory, research, and treatment*. Mahwah, NJ: Erlbaum.

Kawamura, S. (1963). The process of sub-cultural propagation among Japanese macaques. In C. H. Southwick (Ed.), *Primate social behavior*. New York, NY: Van Nostrand.

Kazdin, A. E. (2011). *Single-case research designs* (2nd ed.). New York, NY: Oxford University Press.

Keesey, R. (1964). Intracranial reward delay and the acquisition rate of a brightness discrimination. *Science, 143*, 702.

Keith-Lucas, T., & Guttman, N. (1975). Robust single-trial delayed backward conditioning. *Journal of Comparative and Physiological Psychology, 88*, 468–476.

Kelleher, R. T., & Fry, W. (1962). Stimulus functions in chained fixed-interval schedules. *Journal of the Experimental Analysis of Behavior, 5*, 167–173.

Kellogg, W. N., & Kellogg, L. A. (1933). *The ape and the child*. New York, NY: McGraw-Hill.

Kimble, G. A. (1967). *Hilgard and Marquis' conditioning and learning* (Rev. ed.). New York, NY: Appleton-Century-Crofts.

Kimble, G. A. (1967). *Foundations of conditioning and learning*. New York, NY: Appleton-Century-Crofts.

King, B. J. (1991). Social information transfer in monkeys, apes, and hominids. *Yearbook of Physical Anthropology, 34,* 97–115.

Kirsch, L. G., & Becker, J. V. (2006). Sexual offending: Theory of problem, theory of change, and implications for treatment effectiveness. *Aggression and Violent Behavior, 11,* 208–224.

Klein, S. B. (1996). *Learning: Principles and applications* (3rd ed.). New York, NY: McGraw-Hill.

Kleinke, C. L., Meeker, G. B., & Staneske, R. A. (1986). Preference for opening lines: Comparing ratings by men and women. *Sex Roles, 15,* 585–600.

Klinger, E. (1975). Consequences of commitment to and disengagement from incentives. *Psychological Review, 82,* 1–25.

Klinger, E., Barta, S. G., & Kemble, E. D. (1974). Cyclic activity changes during extinction in rats: A potential model for depression. *Animal Learning and Behavior, 2,* 313–316.

Kluft, R. P. (1998). The argument for the reality of delayed recall of trauma. In P. S. Appelbaum, L. A. Uyehara, & M. R. Elin (Eds.), *Trauma and memory: Clinical and legal controversies.* New York, NY: Oxford University Press.

Koehler, O. (1951). The ability of birds to 'count'. *Bulletin of Animal Behaviour, 9,* 41–45.

Kohlenberg, R. J. (1973). Behavioristic approach to multiple personality: A case study. *Behavior Therapy, 4,* 137–140.

Kohlenberg, R. J., & Tsai, M. (1991). *Functional analytic psychotherapy: Creating intense and curative therapeutic relationships.* New York, NY: Plenum Press.

Kohler, W. (1939). Simple structural function in the chimpanzee and the chicken. In W D. Ellis (Ed.), *A course book of gestalt psychology.* New York, NY: Harcourt Brace. (Original work published 1918)

Kohler, W. (1947). *Gestalt psychology: An introduction to new concepts in modern psychology.* New York, NY: Liveright.

Kohler, W. (1959). *The mentality of apes.* New York, NY: Vintage Books.

Kohn, A. (1993). *Punished by rewards.* Boston: Houghton Mifflin.

Kossoff, M. J. (1999, March/April). Gary Player: Swinging hard on life's course. *Psychology Today, 32,* 58–61, 78, 82.

Koubova, J. (2003). How does calorie restriction work? *Genes & Development, 17,* 313–321.

Kurzban, R. (2010a). Does the brain consume additional glucose during self-control tasks? *Evolutionary Psychology, 8,* 244–259.

Kurzban, R. (2010b). *Why everyone (else) is a hypocrite: Evolution and the modular mind.* Princeton, NJ: Princeton University Press.

Lakein, A. (1973). *How to get control of your time and your life.* New York, NY: New American Library.

Lang, W. J., Ross, P., & Glover, A. (1967). Conditional responses induced by hypotensive drugs. *European Journal of Pharmacology, 2,* 169–174.

LaRowe, S. D., Patrick, C. J., Curtin, J. J., & Kline, J. P. (2006). Personality correlates of startle habituation. *Biological Psychology, 72,* 257–264.

Lasagna, L., Mosteller, F., von Felsinger, J. M., & Beecher, H. K. (1954). A study of the placebo response. *American Journal of Medicine, 16,* 770–779.

Lefkowitz, M. M., Eron, L. D., Walder, L. O., & Huesmann, L. R. (1977). *Growing up to be violent: A longitudinal study of the development of aggression.* Oxford, MA: Pergamon.

Lepper, M. R., Green, D., & Nisbett, R. E. (1973). Undermining children's intrinsic interest with extrinsic reward: A test of the "overjustification" hypothesis. *Journal of Personality and Social Psychology, 28,* 129–137.

Lerman, D. C., & Iwata, B. A. (1996). Developing a technology for the use of operant extinction in clinical settings: An examination of basic and applied research. *Journal of Applied Behavior Analysis, 29,* 345–382.

Levis, D. J. (1988). Observation and experience from clinical practice: A critical ingredient for advancing behavioral theory and therapy. *Behavior Therapist, 11,* 95–99.

Levis, D. J. (1989). The case for a return to a two-factor theory of avoidance: The failure of non-fear interpretations. In S. B. Klein & R. R. Mowrer (Eds.), *Contemporary learning theories: Pavlovian conditioning and the status of learning theory.* Hillsdale, NJ: Erlbaum.

Levis, D. J. (1995). Decoding traumatic memory: Implosive theory of psychopathology. In W. O'Donohue & L. Krasner (Eds.), *Theories of behavior therapy: Exploring behavior change.* Washington, DC: American Psychological Association.

Levis, D. J., & Boyd, T. L. (1979). Symptom maintenance: An infrahuman analysis and extension of the conservation of anxiety principle. *Journal of Abnormal Psychology, 88,* 107–120.

Levis, D. J., & Brewer, K. E. (2001). The neurotic paradox: Attempts by two-factor fear theory and alternative avoidance models to resolve the issues associated with sustained avoidance responding in extinction. In R. R. Mowrer & S. B. Klein (Eds.), *Handbook of contemporary learning theories.* Mahwah, NJ: Erlbaum.

Levitsky, D., & Collier, G. (1968). Schedule-induced wheel running. *Physiology and Behavior, 3,* 571–573.

Lewes, G. H. (1965). *The life of Goethe.* New York, NY: Frederick Ungar.

Lewinsohn, P. M. (1974). A behavioral approach to depression. In R. J. Friedman & M. M. Katz (Eds.), *The psychology of depression: Contemporary theory and research.* New York, NY: Winston/Wiley.

Lewis, K. P., Jaffe, S., & Brannon, E. M. (2005). Analog number representations in mongoose lemurs (*Eulemur mongoz*): Evidence from a search task. *Animal Cognition, 8,* 247–252.

Lichstein, K. L., & Riedel, B. W. (1994). Behavioral assessment and treatment of insomnia: A review with an emphasis on clinical application. *Behavior Therapy, 25,* 659–688.

Lichtenstein, E., & Glasgow, R. E. (1977). Rapid smoking: Side effects and safeguards. *Journal of Consulting and Clinical Psychology, 45,* 815–821.

Lieberman, D. A. (2000). *Learning: Behavior and cognition* (3rd ed.). Belmont, CA: Wadsworth.

Lilienfeld, S. O., Kirsch, I., Sarbin, T. R., Lynn, S. J., Chaves, J. F., Ganaway, G. K., & Powell, R. A. (1999). Dissociative identity disorder and the sociocognitive model: Recalling the lessons of the past. *Psychological Bulletin, 125,* 507–523.

Lindsley, O. R. (1990). Precision teaching: By teachers for children. *Teaching Exceptional Children, 22,* 10–15.

Lindsley, O. R. (1991). Precision teaching's unique legacy from B. F. Skinner. *Journal of Behavioral Education, 1,* 253–266.

Lindsley, O. R. (1992). Why aren't effective teaching tools widely adopted? *Journal of Applied Behavior Analysis, 25,* 21–26.

Linehan, M. M. (1993). *Cognitive-behavioral treatment of borderline personality disorder.* New York, NY: Guilford.

Linnoila, M., Stapleton, J. M., Lister, R., Guthrie, S., & Eckhardt, M. (1986). Effects of alcohol on accident risk. *Pathologist, 40,* 36–41.

Loftus, E. F. (1993). The reality of repressed memories. *American Psychologist, 48,* 518–537.

Logue, A. W. (1995). *Self-control: Waiting until tomorrow for what you want today.* Upper Saddle River, NJ: Prentice-Hall.

Logue, A. W., Ophir, I., & Strauss, K. E. (1981). The acquisition of taste aversions in humans. *Behaviour Research and Therapy, 19,* 319–333.

Lovaas, O. I. (1987). Behavioral treatment and normal educational and intellectual functioning in young autistic children. *Journal of Consulting and Clinical Psychology, 55,* 3–9.

Lowe, C. F. (1979). Determinants of human operant behavior. In M. D. Zeller & P. Harzem (Eds.), *Reinforcement and the organization of behavior*. New York, NY: Wiley.

Lowe, C. F., Beasty, A., & Bentall, R. P. (1983). The role of verbal behavior in human learning: Infant performance on fixed-interval schedules. *Journal of the Experimental Analysis of Behavior, 39*, 157–164.

Lubow, R. E., & Gewirtz, J. C. (1995). Latent inhibition in humans: Data, theory, and implications for schizophrenia. *Psychological Bulletin, 117*, 87–103.

Luszczynska, A., Sobczyk, A., & Abraham, C. (2007). Planning to lose weight: Randomized controlled trial of an implementation intention prompt to enhance weight reduction among overweight and obese women. *Health Psychology, 26*, 507–512.

Lynch, S. (1998). Intensive behavioural intervention with a 7-year-old girl with autism. *Autism, 2*, 181–197.

MacLean, E. L., Merritt, D. J., & Brannon, E. M. (2008). Social complexity predicts transitive reasoning in prosimian primates. *Animal Behavior, 76*, 479–486.

Maier, S. F., Jackson, R. L., & Tomie, A. (1987). Potentiation, overshadowing, and prior exposure to inescapable shock. *Journal of Experimental Psychology: Animal Behavior Processes, 13*, 260–270.

Maki, W. S., & Hegvik, D. K. (1980). Directed forgetting in pigeons. *Animal Learning and Behavior, 8*, 567–574.

Malone, J. C. (1990). *Theories of learning: A historical approach*. Belmont, CA: Wadsworth.

Malott, R. W. (1989). Achievement of evasive goals: Control by rules describing contingencies that are not direct acting. In S. C. Hayes (Ed.), *Rule-governed behavior: Cognition, contingencies, and instructional control*. New York, NY: Plenum Press.

Malott, R. W., Malott, M. E., & Trojan, E. A. (2000). *Elementary principles of behavior* (4th ed.). Upper Saddle River, NJ: Prentice-Hall.

Malott, R. W., & Suarez, E. A. T. (2004). *Principles of behavior*. Upper Saddle River, NJ: Pearson.

Marks, I. M. (1969). *Fears and phobias*. New York, NY: Academic Press.

Marlatt, G. A., & Gordon, J. R. (Eds.). (1985). *Relapse prevention: Maintenance strategies in addictive behavior change*. New York, NY: Guilford.

Marrazzi, M. A., & Luby, E. D. (1986). An auto-addiction opioid model of chronic anorexia nervosa. *International Journal of Eating Disorders, 5*, 191–208.

Marsh, G., & Johnson, R. (1968). Discrimination reversal following learning without "errors." *Psychonomic Science, 10*, 261–262.

Marten, B., Pearson, M., Kebejian, L., Golden, E., Keselman, A., Bender, M., … & Mattson, M. P. (2007). Sex-dependent metabolic, neuroendocrine, and cognitive responses to dietary energy restriction and excess. *Endocrinology, 148*, 4318–4333.

Martin, G., & Pear, J. (1999). *Behavior modification: What it is and how to do it* (6th ed.). Upper Saddle River, NJ: Prentice-Hall.

Maslow, A. H. (1971). *The farther reaches of human nature*. New York, NY: Viking Press.

Masoro, E. J. (2005). Overview of caloric restriction and ageing. *Mechanisms of Ageing and Development, 126*, 913–922.

Masserman, J. H. (1943). *Behavior and neurosis: An experimental psychoanalytic approach to psycho-biologic principles*. Chicago: University of Chicago Press.

Masters, J. C., Burish, T. G., Hollon, S. D., & Rimm, D. C. (1987). *Behavior therapy: Techniques and empirical findings* (3rd ed.). New York, NY: Harcourt Brace Jovanovich.

Mayou, R. A., & Ehlers, A. (2000). Three-year follow-up of a randomized controlled trial: Psychological debriefing for road accident victims. *British Journal of Psychiatry, 176*, 589–593.

Mazur, J. E. (2002). *Learning and behavior* (5th ed.). Upper Saddle River, NJ: Prentice-Hall.

Mazur, J. E., & Logue, A. W. (1978). Choice in a self-control paradigm: Effects of a fading procedure. *Journal of the Experimental Analysis of Behavior, 30*, 11–17.

McConnell, P. B. (2003). *The other end of the leash*. New York, NY: Ballantine Books.

McCusker, C. G., & Brown, K. (1990). Alcohol-predictive cues enhance tolerance to and precipitate "craving" for alcohol in social drinkers. *Journal of Studies on Alcohol, 51*, 494–499.

McLean, I. G. (Ed.) (2003). *Mine detection dogs: Training, operations and odour detection*. Geneva, Switzerland: Geneva International Centre for Humanitarian Demining.

Melis, A. P., Hare, B., & Tomasello, M. (2006). Engineering cooperation in chimpanzees: Tolerance constraints on cooperation. *Animal Behavior, 72*, 275–286.

Melvin, K. B. (1985). Attack/display as a reinforcer in *Betta splendens*. *Bulletin of the Psychonomic Society, 23*, 350–352.

Mennella, J. A., & Garcia, P. L. (2000). Children's hedonic response to the smell of alcohol: Effects of parental drinking habits. *Alcoholism: Clinical and Experimental Research, 24*, 1167–1171.

Mettke-Hofmann, C., & Greenberg, R. (2005). Behavioral and cognitive adaptations to long-distance migration. In R. Greenberg & P.P. Marra (Eds.), *Birds of two worlds: The ecology and evolution of migration*. Baltimore, MD: Johns Hopkins University Press.

Michael, J. (1982). Distinguishing between discriminative and motivational functions of stimuli. *Journal of the Experimental Analysis of Behavior, 37*, 149–155.

Miller, H. L. (1976). Matching-based hedonic scaling in the pigeon. *Journal of the Experimental Analysis of Behavior, 26*, 335 347.

Miller, L. K. (1997). *Principles of everyday behavior analysis* (3rd ed.). Pacific Grove, CA: Brooks/Cole.

Miller, N. E. (1960). Learning resistance to pain and fear: Effects of overlearning, exposure, and rewarded exposure in context. *Journal of Experimental Psychology, 60*, 137–145.

Miller, N. E., & Dollard, J. (1941). *Social learning and imitation*. New Haven, CT: Yale University Press.

Miltenberger, R. G. (2012). *Behavior modification: Principles and procedures* (5th ed.). Belmont, CA: Wadsworth.

Mindell, J. A. (1999). Empirically supported treatments in pediatric psychology: Bedtime refusal and night wakings in young children. *Journal of Pediatric Psychology, 24*, 465–481.

Mineka, S. (1985). Animal models of anxiety-based disorder: Their usefulness and limitations. In A. H. Tuma & J. Maser (Eds.), *Anxiety and the anxiety disorders*. Hillsdale, NJ: Erlbaum.

Mineka, S. (1987). A primate model of phobic fears. In H. Eysenck & I. Martin (Eds.), *Theoretical foundations of behavior therapy*. New York, NY: Plenum Press.

Mineka, S., & Cook, M. (1993). Mechanisms involved in the observational conditioning of fear. *Journal of Experimental Psychology: General, 122*, 23–38.

Mineka, S., Gunnar, M., & Champoux, M. (1986). Control and early socio-emotional development: Infant rhesus monkeys reared in controllable versus uncontrollable environments. *Child Development, 57*, 1241–1256.

Mischel, W. (1966). Theory and research on the antecedents of self-imposed delay of reward. In B. A. Maher (Ed.), *Progress in experimental personality research* (Vol. 3). New York, NY: Academic Press.

Mischel, W. (1974). Processes in delay of gratification. In L. Berkowitz (Ed.), *Advances in experimental social psychology* (Vol. 7). New York, NY: Academic Press.

Monte, C. F. (1999). *Beneath the mask: An introduction to theories of personality* (6th ed.). New York, NY: Harcourt Brace.

Morgan, C. L. (1894). *An introduction to comparative psychology*. London: W. Scott.

Morgan, C. L. (1900). *Animal behaviour*. London: Arnold.

Morse, A. D., Russell, J. C., Hunt, T. W., Wood, G. O., Epling, W. F., & Pierce, W. D. (1995). Diurnal variation of intensive running in food-deprived rats. *Canadian Journal of Physiology and Pharmacology, 73*, 1519–1523.

Moser, E., & McCulloch, M. (2010). Canine scent detection of human cancers: A review of methods and accuracy. *Journal of Veterinary Behavior, 5*, 145–152.

Mowrer, O. H. (1947). On the dual nature of learning: A reinterpretation of "conditioning" and "problem-solving." *Harvard Educational Review, 17*, 102–150.

Mowrer, O. H. (1960). *Learning theory and behavior*. New York, NY: Wiley.

Mowrer, O. H., & Jones, H. (1945). Habit strength as a result of the pattern of reinforcement. *Journal of Experimental Psychology, 35*, 293–311.

Nagel, K., Olguin, K., & Tomasello, M. (1993). Processes of social learning in the tool use of chimpanzees (*Pan troglodytes*) and human children (*Homo sapiens*). *Journal of Comparative Psychology, 107*, 174–186.

Nairne, J. S. (2000). *Psychology: The adaptive mind* (2nd ed.). Pacific Grove, CA: Brooks/Cole.

Newman, A., & Kanfer, F. H. (1976). Delay of gratification in children: The effects of training under fixed, decreasing and increasing delay of reward. *Journal of Experimental Child Psychology, 21*, 12–24.

Newman, L. S., & Baumeister, R. F. (1996). Toward an explanation of the UFO abduction phenomenon: Hypnotic elaboration, extraterrestrial sadomasochism, and spurious memories. *Psychological Inquiry, 7*, 99–126.

Newsom, C., Favell, J., & Rincover, A. (1983). The side effects of punishment. In S. Axelrod & J. Apsche (Eds.), *The effects of punishment on human behavior*. New York, NY: Academic Press.

Nguyen, N. H., Klein, E. D., & Zentall, T. R. (2005). Imitation of a two-action sequence by pigeons. *Psychonomic Bulletin & Review, 12*, 514–518.

Nordin, S., Broman, D. A., Olafsson, J. K., & Wulff, M. (2004). A longitudinal descriptive study of self-reported abnormal smell and taste perception in pregnant women. *Chemical Senses, 29*, 391–402.

O'Brien, R. M., Figlerski, R. W., Howard, S. R., & Caggiano, J. (1981, August). *The effects of multi-year, guaranteed contracts on the performance of pitchers in major league baseball*. Paper presented at the annual meeting of the American Psychological Association, Los Angeles, CA.

O'Donohue, W., & Ferguson, K. E. (2001). *The psychology of B. F. Skinner*. Thousand Oaks, CA: Sage.

Oaten, M., & Cheng, K. (2006). Improved self-control: The benefits of a regular program of academic study. *Basic and Applied Social Psychology, 28*, 1–16.

Omodei, D., & Fontana, L. (2011). Calorie restriction and prevention of age-associated chronic disease. *FEBS Letters, 585*, 1537–1542.

Ono, K. (1987). Superstitious behavior in humans. *Journal of the Experimental Analysis of Behavior, 47*, 261–271.

Öst, L. (1989). One-session treatment for specific phobias. *Behaviour Research and Therapy, 27*, 1–7.

Otto the octopus wreaks havoc. (2011, August 10). *The Telegraph*. Retrieved from http://www.telegraph.co.uk/news/newstopics/howaboutthat/3328480/Otto-the-octopus-wrecks-havoc.html

Pack, A. A., & Herman, L. M. (1995). Sensory integration in the bottlenose dolphin: Immediate recognition of complex shapes across the senses of echolocation and vision. *Journal of the Acoustic Society of America, 98*, 722–733.

Patterson, F. G., & Linden, E. (1981). *The education of Koko*. New York, NY: Holt, Rinehart & Winston.

Pavlov, I. P. (1927). *Conditioned reflexes*. (G. V. Anrep, Trans.). London: Oxford University Press.

Pavlov, I. P. (1928). *Lectures on conditioned reflexes*. (W. H. Gantt, Trans.). New York, NY: International Publishers.

Pavlov, I. P. (1941). *Conditioned reflexes and psychiatry*. New York, NY: International Publishers.

Pendergrast, M. (1995). *Victims of memory: Incest accusations and shattered lives*. Hinesburg, VT: Upper Access.

Pepperberg, I. M. (1992). Proficient performance of a conjunctive, recursive task by an African Grey parrot (*Psittacus erithacus*). *Journal of Comparative Psychology 106*, 295–305.

Pepperberg, I. M. (1999). *The Alex studies: Cognitive and communicative abilities of grey parrots*. Cambridge, MA: Harvard University Press.

Pepperberg, I. M. (2007). Grey parrots do not always 'parrot': The roles of imitation and phonological awareness in the creation of new labels from existing vocalizations. *Language Sciences, 29*, 1–13.

Pepperberg, I. M. (2009). *Alex & Me*. New York, NY: Harper Collins.

Pepperberg, I. M., & Sherman, D. (2000). Proposed use of two-part interactive modeling as a means to increase functional skills in children with a variety of disabilities. *Teaching and Learning in Medicine, 12*, 213–220.

Perin, C. T. (1942). Behavior potentiality as a joint function of the amount of training and the degree of hunger at the time of extinction. *Journal of Experimental Psychology, 30*, 93–113.

Pfungst, O. (1911). *Clever Hans (The horse of Mr. von Osten): A contribution to experimental animal and human psychology* (Trans. C. L. Rahn). New York, NY: Henry Holt. (Originally published in German, 1907)

Phelps, B. J. (2000). Dissociative identity disorder: The relevance of behavior analysis. *Psychological Record, 50*, 235–249.

Pierce, W. D., & Epling, W. F. (1995). *Behavior analysis and learning*. Englewood Cliffs, NJ: Prentice-Hall.

Pierce, W. D., & Epling, W. F. (1996). Theoretical developments in activity anorexia. In W. F. Epling & W. D. Pierce (Eds.), *Activity anorexia: Theory, research, and treatment*. Mahwah, NJ: Erlbaum.

Pierce, W. D., & Epling, W. F. (1999). *Behavior analysis and learning* (2nd ed.). Upper Saddle River, NJ: Prentice-Hall.

Pilley, J. W. & Reid, A. K. (2010). Border collie comprehends object names as verbal referents. *Behavioural Processes, 86*, 184–195.

Pinker, S. (1994). *The language instinct: How the mind creates language*. New York, NY: William Morrow.

Plant, E. A., Ericsson, K. A., Hill, L., & Asberg, K. (2005). Why study time does not predict grade point average across college students: Implications of deliberate practice for academic performance. *Contemporary Educational Psychology, 30*, 96–116.

Pliskoff, S. S. (1963). Rate change effects with equal potential reinforcements during the "warning" stimulus. *Journal of the Experimental Analysis of Behavior, 6*, 557–562.

Plotnik, J. M., de Waal, F. B. M., & Reiss, D. (2006). Self-recognition in an Asian elephant. *Proceedings of the National Academy of Sciences, 103*, 17053–17057.

Poling, A., Nickel, M., & Alling, K. (1990). Free birds aren't fat: Weight gain in captured wild pigeons maintained under laboratory conditions. *Journal of the Experimental Analysis of Behavior, 53*, 423–424.

Poling, A., Weetjens, B. J., Cox, C., Beyene, N. W., Durgin, A., & Mahoney, A. (2011). Tuberculosis detection by giant African pouched rats. *The Behavior Analyst, 34*, 47–54.

Poling, A., Weetjens, B. J., Cox, C., Beyene, N. W. & Sully, A. (2010). Using giant African pouched rats (*Cricetomys gambianus*) to detect landmines. *The Psychological Record, 60*, 715–728.

Powell, R. A. (2010). Little Albert still missing. *American Psychologist, 65*, 299–300.

Powell, R. A. (2011). Research notes: Little Albert, lost or found? Further difficulties with the Douglas Merritte hypothesis. *History of Psychology, 14*, 106–107.

Powell, R. A., & Gee, T. L. (1999). The effects of hypnosis on dissociative identity disorder: A reexamination of the evidence. *Canadian Journal of Psychiatry, 44*, 914–916.

Pravosudov, V. V. (2009). Development of spatial memory and the hippocampus under nutritional stress: Adaptive priorities or developmental constraints in brain development? In R. Dukas & J. M. Ratcliffe (Eds.), *Cognitive Ecology II*. Chicago: University of Chicago Press.

Premack, D. (1965). Reinforcement theory. In D. Levine (Ed.), *Nebraska symposium on motivation* (Vol. *13*). Lincoln, NE: University of Nebraska Press.

Premack, D. (1971a). Catching up with common sense or two sides of a generalization: Reinforcement and punishment. In R. Glaser (Ed.), *The nature of reinforcement*. New York, NY: Academic Press.

Premack, D. (1971b). Language in a chimpanzee? *Science, 172*, 808–822.

Premack, D. (1976). *Intelligence in ape and man*. Hillsdale, NJ: Erlbaum.

Premack, D., & Woodruff, G. (1978). Chimpanzee problem-solving: A test for comprehension. *Science, 202*, 532–535.

Prior, H., Schwartz, A., & Güntürkün, O. (2008). Mirror-induced behavior in the magpie (*Pica pica*): Evidence of self-recognition. *Public Library of Science: Biology, 6*, 1642–1650.

Provine, R. R. (1996). Contagious yawning and laughter: Significance for sensory feature detection, motor pattern generation, imitation, and the evolution of social behavior. In C. M. Heyes & B. G. Galef. Jr. (Eds.), *Social learning in animals: The roots of culture*. San Diego, CA: Academic Press.

Provine, R.R. (2004). Laughing, tickling and the evolution of speech and self. *Current Directions in Psychological Science, 13*, 215–218.

Pryor, K. (1975). *Lads before the wind: Adventures in porpoise training*. New York, NY: Harper & Row.

Pryor, K. (1999). *Don't shoot the dog: The new art of teaching and training* (Rev. ed.). New York, NY: Bantam Books.

Rachlin, H. (1974). Self-control. *Behaviorism, 2*, 94–107.

Rachlin, H. (1978). A molar theory of reinforcement schedules. *Journal of the Experimental Analysis of Behavior, 30*, 345–360.

Rachlin, H. (1991). *Introduction to modern behaviorism* (3rd ed.). New York, NY: W. H. Freeman.

Rachlin, H. (2000). *The science of self-control*. Cambridge, MA: Harvard University Press.

Rachlin, H., & Baum, W. M. (1972). Effects of alternative reinforcement: Does the source matter? *Journal of the Experimental Analysis of Behavior, 18*, 231–241.

Rachlin, H., & Green, L. (1972). Commitment, choice and self-control. *Journal of the Experimental Analysis of Behavior, 17*, 15–22.

Rachman, S. (1977). The conditioning theory of fear-acquisition: A critical examination. *Behaviour Research and Therapy, 15*, 375–387.

Rachman, S., & Hodgson, R. J. (1968). Experimentally induced "sexual fetishism": Replication and development. *Psychological Record, 18*, 25–27.

Rachman, S., & Hodgson, R. J. (1980). *Obsessions and compulsions*. Englewood Cliffs, NJ: Prentice-Hall.

Rankin, A. M., & Philip, P. J. (1963). An epidemic of laughing in the Bukoba District of Tanganyika. *Central African Journal of Medicine, 9*, 167–170.

Rathus, S. A., Nevid, J. S., & Fichner-Rathus, L. (2000). *Human sexuality in a world of diversity* (4th ed.). Boston: Allyn & Bacon.

Reed, D. D., Critchfield, T. S., & Martens, B. K. (2006). The generalized matching law in elite sport competition: Football play calling as operant choice. *Journal of Applied Behavior Analysis, 39*, 281–297.

Reese, H. W. (2010). Regarding Little Albert. *American Psychologist, 65*, 300–301.

Reilly, S., & Bornovalova, M. (2005). Conditioned taste aversion and amygdala lesions in the rat: A critical review. *Neuroscience and Biobehavioral Reviews, 29*, 1067–88.

Reiss, D., & Marino, L. (2001). Mirror self-recognition in the bottlenose dolphin: A case of convergent cognition. *Proceedings of the National Academy of Sciences, 98*, 5937–5942.

Remington, B., Roberts, P., & Glautier, S. (1997). The effect of drink familiarity on tolerance. *Addictive Behaviors, 22*, 45–53.

Rendall, D., Owren, M. J., & Ryan, M. J. (2009). What do animal signals mean? *Animal Behavior. 78*, 233–240.

Rescorla, R. A. (1980). Simultaneous and successive associations in sensory preconditioning. *Journal of Experimental Psychology*: *Animal Behavior Processes, 6*, 207–216.

Rescorla, R. A., & Wagner, A. R. (1972). A theory of Pavlovian conditioning: Variations in the effectiveness of reinforcement and nonreinforcement. In A. H. Black & W. F. Prokasy (Eds.), *Classical conditioning II*: *Current research and theory*. New York, NY: Appleton-Century-Crofts.

Reynolds, D. K. (1984). *Playing ball on running water*. New York, NY: Quill.

Reynolds, G. S. (1961). Behavioral contrast. *Journal of the Experimental Analysis of Behavior, 4*, 57–71.

Reynolds, G. S. (1975). *A primer of operant conditioning* (2nd ed.). Glenview, IL: Scott, Foresman.

Rickert, V. I., & Johnson, C. M. (1988). Reducing nocturnal awakening and crying episodes in infants and young children: A comparison between scheduled awakenings and systematic ignoring. *Pediatrics, 81*, 203–212.

Riley, A. L., & Clarke, C. M. (1977). Conditioned taste aversions: A bibliography. In L. M. Barker, M. R. Best, & M. Domjan (Eds.), *Learning mechanisms in food selection*. Waco, TX: Baylor University Press.

Riley, A. L., & Wetherington, C. L. (1989). Schedule-induced polydipsia: Is the rat a small furry human? (An analysis of an animal model of human alcoholism). In S. B. Klein & R. R. Mowrer (Eds.), *Contemporary learning theories*: *Instrumental conditioning theory and the impact of biological constraints on learning*. Hillsdale, NJ: Erlbaum.

Rilling, J. K., Scholz, J., Preuss, T. M., Glasser, M. F., Errangi, B. K., & Behrens, T. E. (2011). Differences between chimpanzees and bonobos in neural systems supporting social cognition. *Social Cognitive and Affective Neuroscience*. Advance access.

Robins, L. N. (1974). A follow-up study of Vietnam veterans' drug use. *Journal of Drug Issues, 4*, 61–63.

Roediger, H. L., III, & Karpicke, J. D. (2006). Test-enhanced learning: Taking memory tests improves long-term retention. *Psychological Science, 17*, 249–255.

Rogers, C. R. (1959). A theory of therapy, personality, and interpersonal relationships, as developed in the client-centered framework. In S. Koch (Ed.), *Psychology*: *A study of a science* (Vol. 3). New York, NY: McGraw-Hill.

Romanes, G. J. (1884). *Animal intelligence*. New York, NY: Appleton.

Romanes, G. J. (1888/1989). *Mental evolution in man*: *Origin of human faculty*. London: Kegan Paul.

Ross, C. A. (1997). *Dissociative identity disorder*: *Diagnosis, clinical features, and treatment of multiple personality* (2nd ed.). New York, NY: Wiley.

Ross, C. A., & Norton, G. R. (1989). Effects of hypnosis on the features of multiple personality disorder. *American Journal of Clinical Hypnosis, 32*, 99–106.

Routtenberg, A., & Kuznesof, A. W. (1967). Self-starvation of rats living in activity wheels on a restricted food schedule. *Journal of Comparative and Physiological Psychology, 64*, 414–421.

Rozen, P., Reff, D., Mark, M., & Schull, J. (1984). Conditioned opponent processes in human tolerance to caffeine. *Bulletin of the Psychonomic Society, 22*, 117–120.

Rozin, P., Fischler, C., Imada, S., Sarubin, A., & Wrzesniewski, A. (1999). Attitudes to food and the role of food in life: Comparisons of Flemish Belgium, France, Japan and the United States. *Appetite, 33*, 163–180.

Rumbaugh, D. M. (Ed.). (1977). *Language learning by a chimpanzee*: *The LANA project*. San Diego, CA: Academic Press.

Russell, J. C., Amy, R. M., Manickavel, V., Dolphin, P. J., Epling, W. F., Pierce, W. D., & Boer, D. P. (1989). Prevention of myocardial disease in JCR:LA-corpulent rats by running. *Journal of Applied Physiology, 66*, 1649–1655.

Russell, M., Dark, K. A., Cummins, R. W., Ellman, G., Callaway, E., & Peeke, H. V. S. (1984). Learned histamine release. *Science, 225,* 733–734.

Russon, A. E., & Galdikas, B. M. F. (1993). Imitation in ex-captive orangutans. *Journal of Comparative Psychology, 107,* 147–161.

Russon, A. E., & Galdikas, B. M. F. (1995). Constraints on great apes' imitation: Model and action selectivity in rehabilitant orangutan (*Pongo pygmaeus*) imitation. *Journal of Comparative Psychology, 109,* 5–17.

Salkovskis, P. M. (1998). Psychological approaches to the understanding of obsessional problems. In R. P. Swinson, M. M. Antony, S. Rachman, & M. A. Richter (Eds.), *Obsessive-compulsive disorder: Theory, research, and treatment.* New York, NY: Guilford.

Sanz, C. M., & Morgan, D. B. (2007). Chimpanzee tool technology in the Goualougo Triangle, Republic of Congo. *Journal of Human Evolution, 52,* 420–433.

Savage-Rumbaugh, E. S. (1993). Language learnability in man, ape and dolphin. In H. L. Roitblat, L. M. Herman, & P. E. Nachtigall (Eds.), *Language and communication: Comparative perspectives.* Hillsdale, NJ: Erlbaum.

Savage-Rumbaugh, E. S., McDonald, K., Sevcik, R. A., Hopkins, W. D., & Rubert, E. (1986). Spontaneous symbol acquisition and communicative use by pygmy chimpanzees *(Pan paniscus). Journal of Comparative Psychology, 115,* 211–235.

Savage-Rumbaugh, E. S., Rumbaugh, D. M., Smith, S. T., & Lawson, J. (1980). Reference: The linguistic essential. *Science, 210,* 922–925.

Savage-Rumbaugh, E. S., Shanker, S. G., & Taylor, T. J. (1998). *Apes, language and the human mind.* New York, NY: Oxford University Press.

Schafe, G. E., & Bernstein, I. L. (1996). Taste aversion learning. In E. D. Capaldi (Ed.), *Why we eat what we eat: The psychology of eating.* Washington, DC: American Psychological Association.

Schlinger, H. D., Derenne, A., & Baron, A. (2008). What 50 years of research tell us about pausing under ratio schedules of reinforcement. *The Behavior Analyst, 31,* 39–60.

Schmidt, R. A., & Bjork, R. A. (1992). New conceptualizations of practice: Common principles in three paradigms suggest new concepts for training. *Psychological Science, 3,* 207–217.

Schmitt, D. R. (2001). Delayed rule following. *The Behavior Analyst, 24,* 181–189.

Schreiber, F. R. (1973). *Sybil.* Chicago, IL: Henry Regnery.

Schusterman, R. J., & Gisiner, R. (1988). Artificial language comprehension in dolphins and sea lions: The essential cognitive skills. *Psychological Record, 38,* 311–348.

Seed, A. M., Clayton, N. S., & Emory, M. J. (2008). Cooperative problem solving in rooks (Corvus frugilegus). *Proceedings of the Royal Society B: Biological Sciences, 275,* 1421–1429.

Seligman, M. E. P. (1971). Phobias and preparedness. *Behavior Therapy, 2,* 307–320.

Seligman, M. E. P. (1975). *Helplessness: On depression, development, and death.* San Francisco: Freeman.

Seligman, M. E. P., & Maier, S. (1967). Failure to escape traumatic shock. *Journal of Experimental Psychology, 74,* 1–9.

Seligman, M. E. P., Rosellini, R. A., & Kozak, M. J. (1975). Learned helplessness in the rat: Time course, immunization, and reversibility. *Journal of Comparative and Physiological Psychology, 88,* 542–547.

Seyfarth, R. M. & Cheney, D. L. (1986). Vocal development in vervet monkeys. *Animal Behaviour, 34,* 1640–1658.

Seyfarth, R. M., Cheney, D. L., & Marler, P. (1980). Monkey responses to three different alarm calls: Evidence for predator classification and semantic communication. *Science, 210,* 801–803.

Shea, C. H., Wright, D. L., Wulf, G., & Whitacre, C. (2000). Physical and observational practice afford unique learning opportunities. *Journal of Motor Behavior, 32,* 27–36.

Sheeran, P., & Orbell, S. (1999). Implementation intentions and repeated behaviour: Augmenting the predictive validity of the theory of planned behaviour. *European Journal of Social Psychology, 29*, 349–369.

Sheeran, P., & Orbell, S. (2000). Using implementation intentions to increase attendance for cervical cancer screening. *Health Psychology, 19*, 283–289.

Sherry, D. F., & Hoshooley, J. S. (2007). Neurobiology of spatial behavior. In K. A. Otter (Ed.), *The ecology and behavior of chickadees and titmice: An integrated approach*. New York, NY: Oxford University Press.

Sherry, D. F., & Hoshooley, J. S. (2009). The seasonal hippocampus of food-storing birds. *Behavioural Processes, 80*, 334–338.

Shettleworth, S. J. (2010). *Cognition, evolution and behavior*. New York, NY: Oxford University Press.

Shoda, Y., Mischel, W., & Peake, P. K. (1990). Predicting adolescent cognitive and self-regulatory competencies from preschool delay of gratification: Identifying diagnostic conditions. *Developmental Psychology, 26*, 978–986.

Shyan, M. R., & Herman, L. M. (1987). Determinants of recognition of gestural signs in an artificial language by Atlantic bottle-nosed dolphins *(Tursiops truncatus)* and humans *(Homo sapiens). Journal of Comparative Psychology, 101*, 112–125.

Sidman, M. (1960). *Tactics of scientific research: Evaluating experimental data in psychology*. New York, NY: Basic Books.

Siegel, S. (1983). Classical conditioning, drug tolerance, and drug dependence. In R. G. Smart, F. B. Glaser, Y. Israel, H. Kalant, R. E. Popham, & W. Schmidt (Eds.), *Research advances in alcohol and drug problems* (Vol. 7). New York, NY: Plenum Press.

Siegel, S. (1984). Pavlovian conditioning and heroin overdose: Reports by overdose victims. *Bulletin of the Psychonomic Society, 22*, 428–430.

Siegel, S. (1989). Pharmacological conditioning and drug effects. In A. J. Goudie & M. W. Emmett-Oglesby (Eds.), *Psychoactive drugs: Tolerance and sensitization*. Clifton, NJ: Humana Press.

Siegel, S. (2002). Explanatory mechanisms for placebo effects: Pavlovian conditioning. In H. A. Guess, A. Kleinman, J. W. Kusek, & L. W. Engel (Eds.), *The science of the placebo: Toward an interdisciplinary research agenda*. New York, NY: BMJ Books.

Siegel, S. (2005). Drug tolerance, drug addiction, and drug anticipation. *Current Directions in Psychological Science, 14*, 296–300.

Siegel, S., Hinson, R. E., Krank, M. D., & McCully, J. (1982). Heroin "overdose" death: The contribution of drug-associated environmental cues. *Science, 216*, 436–437.

Sijbrandij, M., Olff, M., Reitsma, J. B., Carlier, I. V. E., & Gersons, B. P. R. (2006). Emotional or educational debriefing after psychological trauma: Randomised control trial. *British Journal of Psychiatry, 189*, 150–155.

Silvia, P. J. (2007). *How to write a lot: A practical guide to productive academic writing*. Washington, DC: American Psychological Association.

Skinner, B. F. (1938). *The behavior of organisms: An experimental analysis*. Acton, MA: Copley.

Skinner, B. F. (1948a). *Walden II*. New York, NY: Macmillan.

Skinner, B. F. (1948b). "Superstition" in the pigeon. *Journal of Experimental Psychology, 38*, 168–172.

Skinner, B. F. (1950). Are theories of learning necessary? *Psychological Review, 57*, 193–216.

Skinner, B. F. (1953). *Science and human behavior*. New York, NY: Macmillan.

Skinner, B. F. (1956). A case history in scientific method. *American Psychologist, 11*, 221–233.

Skinner, B. F. (1967). B. F. Skinner. In E. G. Boring & G. Lindzey (Eds.), *A history of psychology in autobiography: Vol. 5*. New York, NY: Appleton-Century-Crofts.

Skinner, B. F. (1969). *Contingencies of reinforcement: A theoretical analysis*. New York, NY: Appleton-Century-Crofts.

Skinner, B. F. (1971). *Beyond freedom and dignity*. New York, NY: Vintage Books.

Skinner, B. F. (1974). *About behaviorism*. New York, NY: Knopf.

Skinner, B. F. (1983). *A matter of consequences*. New York, NY: Knopf.

Skinner, B. F. (1987). *Upon further reflection*. Englewood Cliffs, NJ: Prentice-Hall.

Skinner, B. F. (1989). *Recent issues in the analysis of behavior*. Columbus, OH: Merrill.

Skinner, B. F., & Vaughan, M. E. (1983). *Enjoy old age: A program of self-management*. New York, NY: Norton.

Skinner-Buzan, D. (2004, March 12). I was not a lab rat. *The Guardian*.

Slater, L. (2004). *Opening Skinner's box: Great psychological experiments of the Twentieth Century*. New York, NY: Norton.

Smolker, R. A., Richards, A. F., Connor, R. C., Mann, J., & Berggren, P. (1997). Sponge-carrying by Indian Ocean bottlenose dolphins: Possible tool use by a delphinid. *Ethology, 103*, 454–465.

Smoo, A. E., & Resnik, D. B. (2009). *Responsible conduct of research* (2nd ed.). New York, NY: Oxford University Press.

Soares, J. J., & Öhman, A. (1993). Backward masking and skin conductance responses after conditioning to nonfeared but fear-relevant stimuli in fearful subjects. *Psychophysiology, 30*, 460–466.

Sokolowska, M., Siegel, S., & Kim, J. A. (2002). Intraadministration associations: Conditional hyperalgesia elicited by morphine onset. *Journal of Experimental Psychology: Animal Behavior Processes, 28*, 309–320.

Solomon, L. J., & Rothblum, E. D. (1984). Academic procrastination: Frequency and cognitive-behavioral correlates. *Journal of Counseling Psychology, 31*, 503–509.

Solomon, R. L. (1980). The opponent-process theory of motivation: The costs of pleasure and the benefits of pain. *American Psychologist, 35*, 691–712.

Solomon, R. L., & Corbit, J. D. (1974). The opponent-process theory of motivation: I. Temporal dynamics of affect. *Psychological Review, 81*, 119–145.

Solomon, R. L., Kamin, L. J., & Wynne, L. C. (1953). Traumatic avoidance learning: The outcomes of several extinction procedures with dogs. *Journal of Abnormal and Social Psychology, 48*, 291–302.

Solomon, R. L., & Wynne, L. C. (1953). Traumatic avoidance learning: Acquisition in normal dogs. *Psychological Monographs, 67* (4, Whole No. 354).

Solomon, R. L., & Wynne, L. C. (1954). Traumatic avoidance learning: The principles of anxiety conservation and partial irreversibility. *Psychological Review, 61*, 353–385.

Solvason, H. B., Ghanta, V. K., & Hiramoto, R. N. (1988). Conditioned augmentation of natural killer cell activity: Independence from nociceptive effects and dependence on interferon-beta. *Journal of Immunology, 140*, 661–665.

Spanos, N. P. (1994). Multiple identity enactments and multiple personality disorder: A socio-cognitive perspective. *Psychological Bulletin, 116*, 143–165.

Spanos, N. P. (1996). *Multiple identities & false memories: A sociocognitive perspective*. Washington, DC: American Psychological Association.

Spence, K. W. (1937). The differential response in animals to stimuli varying within a single dimension. *Psychological Review, 44*, 430–444.

Spiegler, M. D., & Guevremont, D. C. (2010). *Contemporary behavior therapy* (5th Ed.). Belmont, CA: Wadsworth/Cengage.

Staddon, J. E. R. (1977). Schedule-induced behavior. In W. K. Honig & J. E. R. Staddon (Eds.), *Handbook of operant behavior*. Englewood Cliffs, NJ: Prentice-Hall.

Staddon, J. E. R., & Simmelhag, V. L. (1971). The "superstition" experiment: A reexamination of its implications for the principles of adaptive behavior. *Psychological Review, 78*, 3–43.

Stampfl, T. G. (1987). Theoretical implications of the neurotic paradox as a problem in behavior theory: An experimental resolution. *The Behavior Analyst, 10*, 161–173.

Steketee, G., & Foa, E. B. (1985). Obsessive-compulsive disorder. In D. H. Barlow (Ed.), *Clinical handbook of psychological disorders. A step-by-step treatment manual*. New York, NY: Guilford.

Stevenson-Hinde, J. (1973). Constraints on reinforcement. In R. A. Hinde & J. Stevenson-Hinde (Eds.), *Constraints on learning*. New York, NY: Academic Press.

Stilling, S. T., & Critchfield, T. S. (2010). The matching relation and situation-specific bias modulation in professional football play selection. *Journal of the Experimental Analysis of Behavior, 93*, 435–454.

Streissguth, A. P., Barr, H. M., Bookstein, F. L., Samson, P. D., & Olson, H. C. (1999). The long-term neurocognitive consequences of prenatal alcohol exposure. A 14-year study. *Psychological Science, 10*, 186–190.

Sulzer-Azaroff, B., & Mayer, G. R. (1991). *Behavior analysis for lasting change*. Fort Worth, TX: Holt, Rinehart, & Winston.

Symbaluk, D. G. (1996). The effects of food restriction and training on male athletes. In W. F. Epling & W. D. Pierce (Eds.), *Activity anorexia: Theory, research, and treatment*. Mahwah, NJ: Erlbaum.

Tacitus (Trans. 1956). *Annals of imperial Rome* (M. Grant, Trans.). New York, NY: Penguin.

Task Force on Promotion and Dissemination of Psychological Procedures. (1995). Training in and dissemination of empirically-validated psychological treatments. Report and recommendations. *The Clinical Psychologist, 48*, 3–24.

Terrace, H. S. (1963a). Discrimination learning with and without "errors." *Journal of the Experimental Analysis of Behavior, 6*, 1–27.

Terrace, H. S. (1963b). Errorless transfer of a discrimination across two continua. *Journal of the Experimental Analysis of Behavior, 6*, 223–232.

Terrace, H. S. (1979). *Nim*. New York, NY: Knopf.

Terrace, H. S. (1985). On the nature of animal thinking. *Neuroscience and Biobehavioral Reviews, 9*, 643–652.

Terrace, H. S., Petitio, L. A., Sanders, R. J., & Bever, T. G. (1979). Can an ape create a sentence? *Science, 206*, 891–902.

Thigpen, C. H., & Cleckley, H. M. (1957). *The three faces of Eve*. New York, NY: McGraw-Hill.

Thompson, R. F. (1972). Sensory preconditioning. In R. F. Thompson & J. F. Voss (Eds.), *Topics in learning and performance*. New York, NY: Academic Press.

Thompson, T. (1963). Visual reinforcement in Siamese fighting fish. *Science, 141*, 55–57.

Thorndike, E. L. (1898). Animal intelligence: An experimental study of the associative processes in animals. *Psychological Review Monograph Supplement, 2*, 1–109.

Thorndike, E. L. (1911/1965). *Animal intelligence*. New York, NY: Hafner.

Thouless, C. R., Fanshawe, J. H., & Bertram, B. C. R. (1989). Egyptian vultures *Neophron percnopterus* and ostrich *Struthio camelus* eggs: The origins of stone-throwing behaviour. *Ibis, 131*, 9–15.

Thyer, B. A. (1999). Was Carl Jung a behavior analyst? *Journal of Applied Behavior Analysis, 32*, 533.

Tice, D. M., Baumeister, R. F., Schmueli, D., & Muraven, M. (2007). Restoring the self: Positive affect helps improve self-regulation following ego-depletion. *Journal of Experimental Social Psychology, 43*, 379–384.

Timberlake, W. (1983). Rats' responses to a moving object related to food or water: A behavior systems analysis. *Animal Learning and Behavior, 11*, 309–320.

Timberlake, W. (1993). Behavior systems and reinforcement: An integrative approach. *Journal of the Experimental Analysis of Behavior, 60*, 105–128.

Timberlake, W., & Allison, J. (1974). Response deprivation: An empirical approach to instrumental performance. *Psychological Review, 81*, 146–164.

Timberlake, W., & Grant, D. S. (1975). Autoshaping in rats to the presentation of another rat predicting food. *Science, 190,* 690–692.

Timberlake, W., & Lucas, G. A. (1989). Behavior systems and learning: From misbehavior to general principles. In S. B. Klein & R. R. Mowrer (Eds.), *Contemporary learning theories: Instrumental conditioning theory and the impact of biological constraints on learning.* Hillsdale, NJ: Erlbaum.

Tinbergen, N. (1951). *The study of instinct.* Oxford: Clarendon Press.

Tinbergen, N. (1963). On aims and methods in ethology. *Zeitschrift für Tierpsychologie, 20,* 410–433.

Tolin, D. F., & Steketee, G. (2007). General issues in psychological treatment for obsessive-compulsive disorder. In M. M. Antony, C. Purdon, & L. J. Summerfeldt (Eds.), *Psychological treatment of obsessive-compulsive disorder: Fundamentals and beyond.* Washington, DC: American Psychological Association.

Tolman, E. C. (1932). *Purposive behavior in animals and men.* New York, NY: Appleton-Century-Crofts.

Tolman, E. C. (1948). Cognitive maps in rats and men. *Psychological Review, 55,* 189–208.

Tolman, E. C., & Honzik, C. H. (1930). Degrees of hunger, reward and nonreward, and maze learning in rats. *University of California Publications in Psychology, 4,* 241–275.

Tomasello, M. (1996). Do apes ape? In B. G. Galef, Jr., & C. M. Heyes (Eds.), *Social learning in animals: The roots of culture.* New York, NY: Academic Press.

Tomie, A. (1996). Self-regulation and animal behavior. *Psychological Inquiry, 7,* 83–85.

Tomie, A., Brooks, W., & Zito, B. (1989). Sign-tracking: The search for reward. In S. B. Klein & R. R. Mowrer (Eds.), *Contemporary learning theories: Pavlovian conditioning and the status of traditional learning theory.* Hillsdale, NJ: Erlbaum.

Tucker, V. A. (2000). The deep fovea, sideways vision and spiral flight paths in raptors. *Journal of Experimental Biology, 203,* 3745–3754.

Ulrich, R. E., & Azrin, N. A. (1962). Reflexive fighting in response to aversive stimuli. *Journal of the Experimental Analysis of Behavior, 5,* 511–520.

Valentine, C. W. (1930). The innate bases of fear. *Journal of Genetic Psychology, 37,* 394–420.

Van der Kolk, B. A. (1989). The compulsion to repeat the trauma: Re-enactment, revictimization, and masochism. *Psychiatric Clinics of North America, 12,* 389–411.

Van Houten, R. (1983). Punishment from the animal laboratory to the applied setting. In S. Axelrod & J. Apsche (Eds.), *The effects of punishment on human behavior.* New York, NY: Academic Press.

Vander Wall, S. B. (1982). An experimental analysis of cache recovery in Clarke's nutcracker. *Animal Behavior, 30,* 84–94.

Varady, K. A., & Hellerstein, M. K. (2008). Do calorie restriction or alternate-day fasting regimens modulate adipose tissue physiology in a way that reduces chronic disease risk? *Nutrition Review, 66,* 333–342.

Vargas, J. S. (1990). B. F. Skinner—The last few days. *Journal of Applied Behavior Analysis, 23,* 409–410.

Verhave, T. (1966). The pigeon as quality control inspector. *American Psychologist, 21,* 109–115.

Vollmer, T. R., & Bourret, J. (2000). An application of the matching law to evaluate the allocation of two- and three-point shots by college basketball players. *Journal of Applied Behavior Analysis, 33,* 137–150.

Vos Savant, M. (1990, September 9). Ask Marilyn. *Parade Magazine,* 15.

Wallace, I., & Pear, J. J. (1977). Self-control techniques of famous novelists. *Journal of Applied Behavior Analysis, 10,* 515–525.

Wallace, M., & Singer, G. (1976). Schedule induced behavior: A review of its generality, determinants and pharmacological data. *Pharmacology, Biochemistry, and Behavior, 5,* 483–490.

Waltz, T. J., & Hayes, S. C. (2010). Acceptance and commitment therapy. In N. Kazantzis & M. A. Reinecke (Eds.), *Cognitive and Behavioral Theories in Clinical Practice*. New York, NY: Guilford Press.

Wasserman, E. A., & Zentall, T. R. (Eds.). (2006). *Comparative cognition: Experimental explorations of animal intelligence*. New York, NY: Oxford University Press.

Watson, D. L., & Tharp, R. G. (2002). *Self-directed behavior: Self-modification for personal adjustment* (7th ed.). Pacific Grove, CA: Brooks/Cole.

Watson, J. B. (1913). Psychology as the behaviorist views it. *Psychological Review, 20*, 154–177.

Watson, J. B. (1919). *Letter to Frank J. Goodnow, December 5, 1919*. In the Ferdinand Hamburger, Jr., Archives of The Johns Hopkins University (Record Group 02.001/Office of the President/ Series 1/File 115, Department of Psychology, 1913–1919), Baltimore, MD.

Watson, J. B. (1925/1930). *Behaviorism*. New York, NY: Norton. (Original work published 1924)

Watson, J. B. (Writer/Director). (1923). *Experimental investigation of babies* [motion picture]. (Distributed by C. H. Stoelting Co., 424 N. Homan Ave, Chicago, IL).

Watson, J. B., & Rayner, R. (1920). Conditioned emotional reactions. *Journal of Experimental Child Psychology, 3*, 1–14.

Webster, R. (1995). *Why Freud was wrong: Sin, science and psychoanalysis*. New York, NY: Basic Books.

Weindruch, R. (1996, January). Caloric restriction and aging. *Scientific American, 274*, 46–52.

Weir, A. A. S., Chappell, J., & Kacelnik, A. (2002). Shaping of hooks in New Caledonian crows. *Science, 297*, 981.

Weiss, H. M., Suckow, K., & Rakestraw, T. L., Jr. (1999). Influence of modeling on self-set goals: Direct and mediated effects. *Human Performance, 12*, 89–114.

Welker, R. L. (1976). Acquisition of a free-operant-appetitive response in pigeons as a function of prior experience with response-independent food. *Learning and Motivation, 7*, 394–405.

Wells, A., & Papageorgiou, C. (1995). Worry and the incubation of intrusive images following stress. *Behaviour Research and Therapy, 33*, 579–583.

Wheatley, K. L., Welker, R. L., & Miles, R. C. (1977). Acquisition of barpressing in rats following experience with response-independent food. *Animal Learning and Behavior, 5*, 236–242.

Wheeler, G. (1996). Exercise, sports, and anorexia. In W. F. Epling & W. D. Pierce (Eds.), *Activity anorexia: Theory, research, and treatment*.

Whiten, A. (1998). Imitation of the sequential structure of actions by chimpanzees (*Pan troglodytes*). *Journal of Comparative Psychology, 112*, 270–281.

Wicks, S. R., & Rankin, C. H. (1997). Effects of tap withdrawal response habituation on other withdrawal behaviors: The localization of habituation in the nematode *Caenorhabditis elegans*. *Behavioral Neuroscience, 111*, 342–353.

Wilcoxon, H. C., Dragoin, W. B., & Kral, P. A. (1971). Illness-induced aversions in rat and quail: Relative salience of visual and gustatory cues. *Science, 171*, 826–828.

Williams, B. A. (1981). The following schedule of reinforcement as a fundamental determinant of steady state contrast in multiple schedules. *Journal of the Experimental Analysis of Behavior, 35*, 293–310.

Williams, B. A. (2010). Perils of evidence-based medicine. *Perspectives on Biology and Medicine, 53*, 106–120.

Williams, D. R., & Williams, H. (1969). Automaintenance in the pigeon: Sustained pecking despite contingent nonreinforcement. *Journal of the Experimental Analysis of Behavior, 12*, 511–520.

Williams, H. & Pembroke, A. (1989). Sniffer dogs in the melanoma clinic? *Lancet, 333*, 734.

Williams, J. L. (1973). *Operant learning: Procedures for changing behavior*. Monterey, CA: Brooks/Cole.

Wilson, C. (1972). *New pathways in psychology: Maslow and the post-Freudian revolution*. New York, NY: Taplinger.

Wilson, E. O. (1984). *Biophilia*. Cambridge: Harvard University Press.

Wilson, G. T. (1997). Behavior therapy at century close. *Behavior Therapy, 28*, 449–457.

Wilson, J. F., & Cantor, M. B. (1987). An animal model of excessive eating: Schedule-induced hyperphagia in food-satiated rats. *Journal of the Experimental Analysis of Behavior, 47*, 335–346.

Wolfe, J. B., & Kaplon, M. D. (1941). Effect of amount of reward and consummative activity on learning in chickens. *Journal of Comparative Psychology, 31*, 353–361.

Wolpe, J. (1958). *Psychotherapy by reciprocal inhibition*. Stanford, CA: Stanford University Press.

Wolpe, J. (1995). Reciprocal inhibition: Major agent of behavior change. In W. O'Donohue & L. Krasner (Eds.), *Theories of behavior therapy: Exploring behavior change*. Washington, DC: American Psychological Association.

Woodruff, G., & Premack, D. (1979). Intentional communication in the chimpanzee: Development of deception. *Cognition, 7*, 333–362.

Woods, D. J., & Routtenberg, A. (1971). "Self-starvation" in activity wheels: Developmental and chlorpromazine interactions. *Journal of Comparative and Physiological Psychology, 76*, 84–93.

Worthington, E. L. (1979). Behavioral self-control and the contract problem. *Teaching of Psychology, 6*, 91–94.

Yamamoto, S., Yamakoshi, G., Humle, T., & Matsuzawa, T. (2008). Invention and modification of a new tool use behavior: Ant-fishing in trees by a wild chimpanzee (Pan troglodytes verus) at Bossou, Guinea. *American Journal of Primatology, 70*, 699–702.

Yates, A. (1996). Athletes, eating disorders, and the overtraining syndrome. In W. F. Epling & W. D. Pierce (Eds.), *Activity anorexia: Theory, research, and treatment*. Mahwah, NJ: Erlbaum.

Zeiler, M. D. (1971). Eliminating behavior with reinforcement. *Journal of the Experimental Analysis of Behavior, 16*, 401–405.

Zelman, D. C., Brandon, T. H., Jorenby, D. E., & Baker, T. B. (1992). Measures of affect and nicotine dependence predict differential response to smoking cessation treatments. *Journal of Consulting and Clinical Psychology, 60*, 943–952.

Zentall, T. R. (2006). Imitation: Definitions, evidence, and mechanisms. *Animal Cognition, 9*, 335–353.

Index

To Seek America

We all go forth to seek America.
And in the seeking we create her.
And in the quality of our search
shall be the nature of the America
we create. Waldo Frank

TO SEEK

MAXINE SELLER

AMERICA

A History of Ethnic Life in the United States

Jerome S. Ozer, Publisher

Library of Congress Cataloging in Publication Data
Seller, Maxine S   1935-
To seek America.

Bibliography: p.
Includes index.
1. United States—Emigration and immigration—History.
2. Minorities—United States—History. I. Title.
JV6450.S44   301.32′4′0973   77-8248
ISBN 0-89198-117-9
ISBN 0-89198-118-7 pbk.

Manufactured in the United States of America

In memory of Annie Schwartz and Lena Wolk

Table of Contents

Preface

After four years of research and writing in the preparation of this book, I want to thank the many friends and colleagues who have contributed to its completion. I am particularly grateful to Professor Bill McNeill of Bucks County Community College, who gave me valuable insights into the sociology of minority groups, to Professor Murray Friedman of LaSalle College and the American Jewish Committee, who read the first chapter four years ago and encouraged me to continue, to Professor Warren Button of the State University of New York at Buffalo, who gave substantial advice on the colonial period and on the history of education, and to Professor John J. Appel of Michigan State University, who read the entire first draft of the manuscript and offered many useful suggestions. I am also grateful to the staff members of the libraries at the University of Pennsylvania and the State University of New York at Buffalo, who facilitated my research, and to my students at Bucks County Community College and the State University of New York at Buffalo, whose questions about ethnicity have helped shape this book. I also want to thank my publisher, Dr. Jerome S. Ozer, for suggesting that I undertake this project and for offering excellent advice on subject matter and style as well as on the technicalities of publication.

Finally, I want to acknowledge the contributions of my immediate family. My husband Bob and my sons, Michael, Douglas, and Stuart, served as an enthusiastic and discerning panel of critics for the testing of my ideas. Michael and Douglas reviewed portions of the manuscript from the student's point of view and helped with the unexciting chores of manuscript preparation. My youngest son, Stuart, showed maturity and a sense of humor in sharing his mother with a typewriter and, along with his father and brothers, helped me maintain my balance after long hours in the unreal world of the library stacks. I want to thank my sons and tell them that this book was written for them as well as my students. Most of all I want to thank Bob, whose understanding, encouragement, and support have been invaluable to me in this project as in everything else I have undertaken in the twenty-one years I have had the good fortune to be married to him.

To Seek America

CHAPTER 1

Ethnicity:

What Is It? Why Is It Important?

"Who am I?" The question is universal. We frame our own answers out of the uniqueness of our individual personalities and life experiences. But for most of us identity is more than this private sense of self. Identity has a communal, or group, dimension. Who am I? I am John or Jane Smith; but I am also a man or a woman, a member of a family, a church, a school, a business firm, a lodge, a political party, a neighborhood, a nation.

Most human beings crave the warmth and security of belonging to a group. We usually join a group because we want the comfort of feeling "at home" among others whose life styles, values, and interests are similar to our own. Some people have a strong need to define themselves as the insiders, "we," as opposed to the outsiders, "they," whose life styles, values, and interests are different. There are individuals who feel no need for identification with any group. They often discover, however, that society has made this identification for them. With or without their consent, they are classified as soldiers, taxpayers, Jews, underprivileged, or whatever other category, benevolent or malevolent, their society or its government finds useful.

Historically this human need for belonging and for classifying oneself and others has been met in many different ways. Primitive peoples usually identified themselves by membership in tribes or clans. In traditional China the extended family was the most important grouping, and in India one's fate was almost completely determined by the caste into which he or she was born. The ancient Greeks saw themselves primarily as members of the *polis*, or native city, with its own special gods and its own political and social institutions. In medieval Europe identity was based on a mixture of social and economic class; one's life style and sense of self depended upon whether one was a noble, a serf, a craftsman, or a member of a religious order.

In most cases governments recognized and reinforced these classifications by dealing with persons in terms of the groups to which they belonged. Even the relatively democratic city state of Athens denied political participation to people who were born in a different *polis*. In feudal Europe there were separate legal systems, even separate courts, for nobles, clergy, and commoners—a system which lasted in Western Europe until the French Revolution of 1789 and lingered on in Eastern Europe decades later.

In the United States we pride ourselves upon a tradition of dealing with persons as individuals, regardless of their group affiliations. Immigrants often came here to escape the rigid demands of class, sect, even family in the "old country," and to a large extent they were successful in doing so. The American Constitution recognized no collective orders or "estates," no classes, and after the abolition of slavery, no castes. The distinction or grouping which has survived the longest has been that of sex, and even this categorization seems to be fading. With few exceptions the law in the United States deals with each person as a discrete individual, standing alone.

Yet most Americans, like most other people, have felt the need to define themselves in terms of groups. As the French observer Alexis de Tocqueville pointed out over a century ago—and as any observer of contemporary American life can confirm—Americans are joiners. We join civic associations, fraternal orders, benevolent societies, political parties, bowling leagues, and labor unions. We come together in a host of changing organizations to pursue our passions for everything from bird watching to weight watching. While each of these voluntary associations has its own purpose and program, all share a common function; all bring like people together, creating, at least for the moment, a community of interest and a sense of belonging.

Yet when an individual asks himself, "who am I?" he or she is not likely to answer "an Elk," "a Rotarian," or "a member of the Garden Club." For most of us such voluntary associations are too limited in scope, too impersonal, and too transient to satisfy the human need for group identity. To satisfy so deep a need a grouping must be lasting, it must impinge upon many areas of a person's life (from infancy through adulthood), and it must provide a broad pool of people from whom one can choose a variety of associates. The ethnic community is such a grouping. Perhaps this is why throughout our history millions of Americans have responded to the question "who am I?" with an ethnic answer. I am a Polish-American. I am an Italian-American. I am a

To Seek America

Chinese-American. I am a Chicano. I am Puerto Rican. I am a Jew. I am black.

Ethnic identity may extend an entire life span and be passed down to the fourth generation or beyond. Americans who identify strongly as members of an ethnic community may live their entire lives in ethnic neighborhoods, attend ethnic schools, socialize in ethnic lodges, worship in ethnic churches, read ethnic newspapers, enjoy ethnic music and drama, earn their living in ethnic businesses, be ill in ethnic hospitals, and be buried in ethnic cemeteries. They may choose their friends, their doctors, their lawyers, their employees, their employers, and of course, their spouses from within the ethnic group. For most people such a totally enclosed ethnic life would no longer seem desirable, or even possible. Yet, as this book will show, many richly satisfying lives have been spent within the geographic and cultural confines of ethnic communities of the past. Equally important, ethnicity, recognized or unrecognized, remains a major factor in the lives of millions of Americans today.

What Is An Ethnic Community?

Ethnic communities in the United States are groups of people tied together by common national origin, common language, common religion, and perhaps common physical characteristics (such as skin coloring)—although not every community finds these factors equally important, or even necessary at all. Some ethnic communities are obviously based upon common national origin. Thus, Swedish-Americans are Americans whose families came originally from Sweden. Often, however, language has been more important than political geography in defining an American ethnic group. Sharing a common language led German-speaking immigrants from Bavaria, Hanover, and Westphalia to think of themselves collectively as German-Americans long before the separate political states from which they came were unified into modern Germany.

A common religion has been as important as a common national origin or language in defining ethnic loyalties in the United States. For the American Irish, for example, allegiance to the Roman Catholic Church has been as binding a cement as common origin on the Emerald Isle. Jewish families from Holland, England, Spain, South America, Germany, and many East European countries have been united by religion into what is in effect a single ethnic community. Religion can divide, however, as well as unite. The nineteenth century Irish-American and German-American communities subdivided into Protestant and Catholic segments, clearly defined and, in the case of the Irish, hostile to one another.

The idea of race as a distinctive set of biological characteristics has no scientific meaning. Still, as Chinese-Americans and Japanese-Americans, American Indians, Mexican-Americans, and blacks are acutely aware, many "white" Americans define these ethnic groups in terms of widely varying and overlapping physical characteristics such as the color of the skin, the texture of the hair, and the shape of the eyes. Because of their recognizable physical characteristics third generation American citizens whose ancestors had immigrated from Japan found themselves impounded as dangerous aliens after the bombing of Pearl Harbor.

While "race" used by hostile outsiders is a dangerous concept, a sense of biological kinship (vague and subjective as it may be) has been a unifying element within certain ethnic groups. Thus, Mexican-Americans proudly assert membership in *la raza* (the race), and blacks proudly claim that "black is beautiful." Yet many Mexican-Americans see *la raza* as a cultural, not a biological association. Similarly, many blacks find their identity more a matter of "soul" than of body.

The definition of ethnicity in the United States, then, is complex and varied. Still, significant generalizations can be made. First of all, the members of an ethnic group share the consciousness of a common historical past. For black Americans their shared historical experiences are mainly those of the New World, because slaveholders forcibly obliterated much (though not all) of the African heritage. For groups like Italian-Americans or Polish-Americans, who came to America more recently and who still maintain ties with relatives who stayed behind, there are vivid memories of shared experiences both in the old country and the new. In the case of American Jews, shared memories of the group's common historical past go back thousands of years and encompass every continent on the earth. However far back it extends and however accurately—or inaccurately—it is remembered, this sense of a common past helps to determine the life styles and values of the ethnic group in America today.

Second, the members of a given ethnic group do in fact share common life styles and common values. There are distinctive ethnic patterns in such important matters as child-rearing, marital relationships, career choices, political affiliations, and of course what goes on the table for dinner. Even in the fourth generation, the Irish "overchoose" careers in law and politics, the Germans in engineering, and the Jews in medicine. Italian-Americans remain close to their brothers and sisters in adult life, while Jewish-Americans are more likely to be close to their parents. Irish-Americans accept pain stoicly; Italian-Americans are more likely to complain. Of course not every member of an ethnic group will conform to all—or any—of these ethnic patterns, but the patterns do exist. This is why many people feel more comfortable with a clergyman, a physician, a political leader, and a wife or husband from within their own ethnic group.

Third, an ethnic community has aspirations for a common future, and these aspirations are focused upon the education of the young. A significant number of those who share memories of a common past and who participate in the common ethnic life style of the present are determined to pass on those memories and that life style (and the values they embody) to the succeeding generations. From the colonial era to the present, ethnic leaders have been convinced that education is crucial to the survival of the group and to the perpetuation of the values it holds dear. It is not surprising, then, that ethnic communities invest great emotional and financial resources in the education of their children. Some ethnic groups have built their own schools either to supplement or to replace totally the educational system of the Anglo-Saxon majority. Others have sought, through "community control" or political pressure, to make the public schools more supportive of their distinctive heritages. Whatever institutions they use, all ethnic educators have wrestled with the same problem—how to instill in the young a lasting loyalty to a minority culture while the majority culture with its powerful appeal impinges on every side.

If ethnic communities have been eager to use schools to perpetuate their distinctive heritages, the Anglo-Saxon majority has been equally eager to use the schools to enforce "Americanization." From Benjamin Franklin's time to the present, educators and political leaders (and more recently, sociologists and psychologists) have seen schools as places where minority group children would be taught the language, habits, and ideas considered appropriate by the majority. Generations of social reformers have counted upon the schools to save ethnic children—and with them American society—from poverty, crime, radicalism, sexual promiscuity, and other evil traits attributed to the unpopular minority communities of their day. That such utopian dreams went unrealized is not surprising. Nor is it surprising, given the conflicting hopes, fears, and expectations of majority and minority communities, that American schools have historically been on the front line of the many battles fought among ethnic communities and between ethnic minorities and the Anglo-Saxon Protestant majority.

Finally, ethnic communities in the United States have been and still are social, economic, and political interest groups. Because members of ethnic communities share a common history and often a common religious outlook, they may take a common position on an issue such as prayer in the public schools. Because they often cluster in the same socioeconomic level, sharing the same kinds of jobs and neighborhoods, they may take a common position on property taxes, labor unions, affirmative action quotas, or busing. Emotional and family ties to ethnic communities overseas may result in a common stand on a foreign policy issue. Even the almost assimilated may find themselves stirred to action when a sudden controversy—an outbreak of war in the Middle East, or a new abortion law—lays bare an ethnic nerve. As the older generations pass away, common interests may increasingly replace common memories as the cement that binds together American ethnic communities.

Origins of Ethnic Communities

One of the most heterogeneous nations on earth, the United States contains ethnic communities varying widely in numbers and historical background. Some were already well established when they were incorporated into the United States by conquest or by purchase. A vigorous Dutch community became part of the original thirteen colonies when the British seized New Amsterdam from Holland in 1664. The French and Creole communities of New Orleans became American ethnic groups with the Louisiana Purchase of 1803. A large Spanish-speaking minority entered our population when we annexed the Southwest, the fruits of military victory in the Mexican War.

Most ethnic communities, however, were the result of people leaving their original homelands to come to our shores. All Americans are immigrants or the descendants of immigrants. Even the American Indians, our oldest ethnic group, came originally from Asia in wave after wave of prehistoric immigration. No other country has attracted so many settlers of such diverse backgrounds.

The coming of large numbers of Europeans began in the seventeenth century as part of a world-wide migration of peoples. For reasons still not completely understood, the number of people on the earth increased fourfold between 1650 and 1950. In Europe the increase in population generally preceded the ability of agriculture and industry to feed and employ it. These "excess" Europeans abandoned their overcrowded homelands for the emptier areas of Africa, Australia, and North and South America. Of the more than seventy million people who left Europe after 1600, two thirds came to the United States. Here they were joined voluntarily by thousands of Asians and involuntarily by millions of Africans.

The immigration rate has varied with what historians have called the "push" of unfavorable conditions abroad and the "pull" of favorable conditions in the United States. Calamities such as the Irish potato famine of the 1840's and Russian pogroms (massacres) of Jews at the end of the nineteenth century sent immigrants flocking to the United States with little regard for the American business cycle. But usually the attraction of favorable economic prospects here exerted a greater influence upon immigration than problems overseas. Immigration has always increased in times of prosperity and decreased in times of recession.

Sometimes an individual man or woman came alone, worked, and sent for the rest of the family as soon as savings permitted. The younger and stronger members of a family, those at the peak of their earning power, immigrated first; and their labor in America supported aged parents overseas and financed the immigration of brothers, sisters, wives and children. Often husband, wife, and children came together, taking their chances, for better or worse, as a family unit. In still other cases an entire village or parish came, transplanting a whole community all at once. This kind of group immigration was often found among members of communitarian religious sects such as the Pennsylvania Germans.

Whether they came as individuals, families, or larger groups, immigrants quickly sought out others who spoke their language. Often a friend or a relative from their native village helped them to find jobs and places to live. People of similar national and linguistic backgrounds clustered together to relieve their loneliness and to help one another. Gradually these clusters of people formed institutions—churches, schools, banks, newspapers—to fulfill their needs and express their way of life.

The ethnic community—or ghetto—was the result not only of the internal needs of the ethnic group itself, but also of the external pressure of the outsider. Other Americans were often hostile to the newcomers. All ethnic minorities faced, to one degree or another, discrimination in housing, jobs, and social relationships. The prejudices of the outside world reinforced ethnic loyalty and helped perpetuate the ethnic community.

Just as all Americans were, at one time or another, immigrants, so all Americans were, at one time or another, members of ethnic communities. The white, Protestant, English-speaking immigrants, like the Polish, the Irish, and the Japanese, preferred to settle among people of similar background, married mainly within their own group, and set up institutions to perpetuate their particular life style. The neat, white Congregational churches built by New England Puritans were in reality as "ethnic" as the tiny synagogues built centuries later by East European Jews in New York City. Irish Catholic immigrants knew before the Civil War what blacks, Puerto Ricans, and Mexican-Americans have discovered in recent years—that the little red school house of the white Protestant majority is as committed to a particular pattern of behavior and system of values as is the more obviously ethnic parochial school in the Greek, Italian, or Jewish neighborhood.

The ethnicity of English-speaking immigrants has generally been unrecognized. Originally English, Scottish, Scotch-Irish, and Welsh immigrants were distinct from each other. But political, denominational, and other differences among these groups were quickly overshadowed by the fact that they all spoke English, the language that was politically and commercially dominant in the British colonies. Gradually historians came to view the English-speaking ethnic communities as one group and to identify that group with the nation. Thus English-speaking Americans became "real" Americans while others were defined as outsiders, or "ethnics."

Nineteenth century American historians—many of whom were of New England background—saw American history as a white, Protestant, Anglo-Saxon pageant, and enshrined this interpretation of the American past in their writings. Even today there is a strong tendency to view the group that produced George Washington, Thomas Jefferson, and Daniel Webster as the "real" Americans and to relegate the story of other kinds of Americans to the footnotes, the supplementary reading list, or at best, a special chapter on the "contributions" of minority groups.

Ethnicity–A "Neglected Dimension"

Why has ethnicity been, in the words of the historian Rudolph Vecoli, a "neglected dimension" in American history? The ethnocentricity of the traditional Anglo-Saxon historian is a part, but only one part, of the answer. Also at fault was the new generation of early twentieth century historians, many of whom were from non-English ethnic backgrounds. These historians felt until quite recently that it was not academically respectable to investigate the history of their own ethnic communities. They did not want to jeopardize their academic careers with charges of parochialism.

If the ethnocentricity and timidity of historians has hindered our appreciation of the ethnic factor in our history, the popular idea of the American "Melting Pot" has hindered it even more. Nineteenth century Americans believed that the free American environment, with its republican institutions, changed whoever came here into a totally new person. Even the early generation of historians who wrote about immigration, men like Carl Wittke, Theodore Blegen, and Marcus Lee Hansen, were convinced, as Hansen put it, that "it is the ultimate fate of every national group to be amalgamated into the composite American race." Until very recently scholars and most other Americans as well shared the assumption that the ethnic characteristics so apparent in new immigrants disappeared in a generation or two. The ethnic community was of interest only as a temporary way station for the individual along the rapid and inevitable road to "Americanization."

Since the 1960's such a view has become untenable. As the decade opened, Nathan Glazer and Daniel Moynihan suggested that "the point about the melting pot is that it did not happen." Ethnic identity not only survived, it seemed to be growing stronger. Black Americans were the pacesetters. The civil rights campaigns of the 1950's and 1960's were supplemented by a new emphasis upon black ethnicity. Black cultural centers were established and Black Studies programs emerged at major universities. Other ethnic groups followed the pattern set out by blacks. Mexican-Americans and Puerto Ricans demanded—and began to get—bilingual programs in the public schools. Despite some ambivalence toward blacks, white European ethnics followed their example and began to organize to call attention to their many social and economic problems. Responding to the demands of the ethnic constituencies, Congress passed the Ethnic Studies Heritage Act of 1971 to improve the opportunity of students in elementary and secondary schools to study cultural heritages of all the various ethnic groups.

Increasing self-consciousness and activism on the part of ethnic minorities forced scholars to rethink their earlier positions on the American melting pot. Massive European immigration was cut off by 1924, Oriental immigration decades earlier, and the importation of blacks as slaves much earlier still. Yet recognizable Irish, Italian, Chinese, black, and other ethnic communities remain throughout our country. In the 1970's the melting pot was being replaced by the idea of cultural pluralism as the key to an understanding of American society.

Why Ethnic History?

The ethnic activism of recent years has stimulated a new interest in ethnic history, but there are many other, equally valid reasons for taking a long overdue look at the ethnic experience in the United States. In the first place, America cannot be understood without it. At the time of the American Revolution over half our population was non-English in origin, and in 1920 one out of every five Americans was an immigrant or the child of an immigrant. Clearly any version of American history that excludes so many millions of people is not really American history at all. The continuing influx of Europeans, Africans, and Asians had an enormous impact upon the development of American institutions and culture. But even those groups that remained most aloof from the mainstream of American life, groups like the German religious sects, are worthy of study because their experience, too, is part of the total American experience.

Ethnic history has much valuable light to shed upon the gap—often tragically wide—between ideals and realities in American life. Traditionally we have pointed with pride to statements of our democratic principles, such as the Declaration of Independence, the Bill of Rights, and the Fourteenth Amendment. Ethnic history forces us to face our failures to live up to these ideals—black slavery, the ubiquitous "No Irish Need Apply" signs of the nineteenth century, police brutality against Slavs, Italians, and Jews in early twentieth century cities, and the imprisonment of Japanese-Americans during World War II. The struggle to earn a living and hold a family together in a hostile and depressing environment has loomed larger in the lives of millions of Americans than more traditional "textbook" issues such as the raising or lowering of the tariff and the constitutionality of the National Bank. A study of prejudice and discrimination against ethnic minorities is more than an exercise in moral indignation, however. It is an attempt to understand the social and personal pressures that increase friction between majority and minority groups and, hopefully, to identify the conditions that make better relationships possible.

The widely publicized "urban crisis" of the 1960's focused attention upon American cities and the problems of the people who live in them. How do we maintain the vitality of aging neighborhoods and cope with the turmoil of shifting populations? How do we curb the destructive activities of gangs? Because most American cities are patchwork quilts of ethnic populations, ethnic history may prove helpful in our search for the answers.

Ethnic history is of special interest to the contemporary educator trying to develop a public school system that will be acceptable and useful to all segments of our heterogeneous population. The immigrant's child was the "disadvantaged" child of the past. How did the schools respond to the challenge of such a child? Did the American educational system offer immigrant children an open door of opportunity, a path to upward social mobility? Or, as revisionist historians of education have suggested, did the schools program these children for manual labor, so that they would not compete with the children of the "advantaged" for the choicest positions in our society?

Ethnic ghettos are not new to our cities; nor are confrontations between ethnic groups. Local police shot striking Slavic mine workers in Pennsylvania, angry mobs lynched Italian-born murder suspects in New Orleans, and Lincoln used Union troops fresh from the battlefield of Gettysburg to restore peace to the Irish neighborhoods of New York City during the draft riots of 1863. The social problems and the violent confrontations of our urban, ethnic past may provide useful perspectives on the problems of megalopolis today.

If ethnic life in America has been difficult, even violent, it has also been warm, intimate, and intensely human. As our mid-twentieth century institutions became ever larger and more impersonal, many people feel increasingly cut off from meaningful contact with others. In the 1960's and 1970's interest in communal living and "encounter" groups demonstrated a hunger for the warmth and intimacy that, according to our writers, comedians, and grandparents, existed in their traditional ethnic communities. Undoubtedly some people found the intensity of family ties and group loyalties in their ethnic communities stifling; yet many look back upon these very qualities with longing and nostalgia. If ethnic communities have provided an acceptable alternative to loneliness and alienation for at least some Americans, they are worthy of serious attention by all.

Finally, ethnic history has relevance for Americans today because it is the story of people reacting to rapid and radical change. All non-English immigrants faced the shock of encountering the Anglo-Saxon society of majority America which differed in many ways from what they had known in their former homes. Early immigrants left age-old patterns of village life to make new beginnings in wild, untouched frontiers. Most traumatic of all was the adjustment of the late nineteenth century or early twentieth century peasants. Born and reared in the traditional, cooperative rural villages of Southern or Eastern Europe, they plunged abruptly into the rapidly changing, competitive, highly individualistic society of urban, industrial America. For such people the voyage across the ocean was a voyage across the centuries. The tremendous differences between immigrant parents and their American born children created a "generation gap" of unprecedented dimensions.

Anthropologist Margaret Mead has suggested that all Americans born before the end of World War II are immigrants, newcomers to a totally different America from the one in which they were born and reared. Alvin Toffler, in his 1970 best seller *Future Shock,* goes even further. He finds the rate of change in our society so greatly accelerated over anything man has known in the past that our main problem in the last three decades of the twentieth century will be learning to cope with rapid change. The experience of ethnic Americans in our past, people whose lives were often consumed by their efforts, successful and unsuccessful, to cope with change may well have new meaning for us now.

There are many compelling reasons, then, for a new interest in ethnic history—an interest which has led to the writing of this book. Hundreds of scholars are investigating the ethnic experience in America, and an ever expanding bibliography of titles appears each year dealing with individual ethnic groups, prominent ethnic personalities past and present, and the meaning of ethnicity itself. This relatively short volume does not attempt to reproduce such a vast and ever increasing quantity of information. Rather it is meant as an introduction to the field. It will delineate the main outlines of ethnic history, point out the significances of ethnicity in American life, past and present, and summarize some of the results of recent research.

Because of the vast scope of the subject, I have felt it necessary to place certain limits upon the material dealt with in this study. Although white, Protestant Americans of English background are as much an ethnic group as any other, I have included them only insofar as they have interacted with "minority" ethnic groups. The fact that they have been the numerical majority and the dominant political and cultural group makes their story different. Moreover, since the history of English America has come down to us as traditional "American" history, most readers will already be familiar with it.

Two other large ethnic groups whose experience will not be covered in this book are blacks and American Indians. Because blacks were subjected to slavery and unparalleled discrimination, and because American Indians were a "native" dispossessed population rather than immigrants, the experiences of these groups are unique. The story of blacks and American Indians constitute broad fields of scholarship in their own right, and the reader should consult the bibliography for suggestions about where to begin investigating them.

The ethnic communities which this study will focus upon are those of the immigrants from Europe (including Scotland and Ireland, but not England), the Spanish-speaking ethnic communities from Mexico and Puerto Rico, and the Chinese, Japanese, and Filipino communities. Despite the many differences among these groups, they have basic similarities that make it possible to treat them in a single volume. Most of the individuals in these groups came to America voluntarily. They came for very similar reasons and shared similar problems and experiences after their arrival.

The material available on even these groups is so vast that I have set up certain additional limitations—arbitrary, but, I hope, useful. Each ethnic group has produced its leaders, its famous sons and daughters of whom it is justly proud. I have chosen to focus attention not on these leaders (who by the nature of their leadership are exceptions) but rather on the experiences of the great numbers of ordinary ethnic Americans.

There are so many different ethnic communities that it will be impossible to deal individually with every one. The book is arranged chronologically, with most of the material about any one particular group given in the chapter dealing with the period in which most members of the group arrived. For example, although Italians and Jews were in America during the colonial period, most of them came in the late nineteenth and early twentieth centuries. Therefore, most of the material about them will appear in the chapters dealing with the late nineteenth and early twentieth centuries.

Ethnic history is difficult to write not only because there are so many different ethnic groups, but because there are wide variations within each group. Ethnic groups are divided by economic class, geographic distribution, political affiliation, and in many other ways. Any attempt to write their history must use generalizations. Therefore, the reader should remember that what was true for most Swedish-Americans, Japanese-Americans, or Puerto Ricans was not true of every individual within the group.

In conclusion, this book will attempt to introduce the reader to the story of ethnicity in America and to ask, if not to answer, the important questions ethnic history raises. It will deal with the traditional subjects of immigration history. Who came to America, and why did they come? How did immigrants react to America, and how did America react to immigrants? It will also deal with the creation and survival of the ethnic communities. How were their institutions established, and what functions did those institutions perform? Why did some ethnic communities disappear rapidly, while others survived generation after generation?

The book will also attempt to shed light on some less traditional but equally important questions. What was life like for the woman and the child as well as for the man within the ethnic community? What impact did ethnic Americans have upon the educational system of the United States, and what impact did the educational system have upon them? What factors have most influenced the upward mobility of minority individuals and minority communities? What circumstances have aggravated—or alleviated—tensions between ethnic communities? Finally, what role does ethnicity play in American life today?

CHAPTER 2

Beginnings:
Ethnic Communities in
the English Colonies

As every American school child "knows," our nation began with thirteen English colonies inhabited by Englishmen with names like Washington, Adams, Jefferson, and Lee. The story is more complicated, however. Long before the arrival of the English, the Spanish and French successfully planted settlements in Florida, the Southwest, and the Mississippi Valley—settlements that would eventually be incorporated into the United States. Nor were the so-called "English" colonies along the Atlantic seacoast exclusively English. Polish, German, and Italian craftsmen plied their trades in early Jamestown, the first permanent English settlement. When William Penn established his Quaker refuge in Pennsylvania in 1681, the area was inhabited by a Swedish settlement almost fifty years old. A large colonial population of American Indians, blacks, Swedes, Finns, Germans, French, Irish, Scotch, Poles, Italians, Welsh, Flemings, Jews, and others forshadowed the variety of humanity that would populate the United States in centuries to come.

Non-English immigrants faced many of the same problems in colonial America that immigrants have faced ever since. How much of their former life style could they maintain in the new American environment? How could they best adjust to changing conditions? As permanent residents of a predominantly English culture, should they try to maintain their traditional non-English language and life style? Should they pass this language and life style down to their children? If so, how?

There were so many ethnic communities in colonial America with such widely varying experiences that it is impractical to attempt a detailed account of each. Rather, this chapter will examine the experience of four representative groups—the Swedes, the Dutch, the Germans, and the Scotch-Irish. The Swedes and Dutch were relatively small groups. Arriving in the seventeenth century, they established colonies of their own which passed into the political control of the English several decades later.

Originally the majority in their respective areas, the Swedes and the Dutch gradually became minorities in an increasingly English society. Their responses to this situation differed, however. The Swedes assimilated so rapidly that a recognizable Swedish-speaking ethnic community had virtually disappeared by the time of the American Revolution. The Dutch maintained their language and life style generations longer. At the time of the American Revolution it was difficult to assemble an English speaking jury in Albany, New York. In the closing years of the nineteenth century many elderly people in rural New Jersey still spoke Dutch.

The Germans and the Scotch-Irish were the largest colonial ethnic communities. Both arrived mainly in the eighteenth century; and both come as unpopular minorities to pre-existing, predominantly English colonies. In other respects, their experiences were very different. Though they spoke English, the Scotch-Irish were a distinctive—and unpopular—group when they arrived. Yet they merged very quickly into mainstream America. The colonial Germans, on the other hand, survived as an ethnic community well into the nineteenth century. Thousands of their descendants, members of religious sects, retain a German dialect and a pre-industrial life style today.

Peopling the Colonies

"Emigration is a form of suicide because it separates the person from all that life gives except the material wants of simple animal existence," wrote a nineteenth century American journalist. Leaving family, friends, home, church, everything dear and familiar for an unknown future in America was a drastic step in the nineteenth century, but it was more drastic still in the seventeenth. Less was known about the New World, and one's future there, even one's survival, was uncertain. It is not surprising that the seventeenth century trading companies promoting New Sweden and New Netherland had trouble finding colonists.

New Sweden began as a Swedish trading post at the site of the future city of Wilmington, Delaware, and spread along the Delaware River valley into what would later be the states of Delaware, New Jersey, and Pennsylvania. Half the colonists were soldiers, sent by the

Swedish government; the other half included farmers, craftsmen, and a minister. Though the Swedish government was willing to send anyone who would go, including debtors, poachers, and other "undesirables," the colony numbered only a few hundred families when William Penn arrived fifty years later. Scattered thinly over a relatively wide area, the Swedes were absorbed in a few generations by the English newcomers who settled among them.

Both New Sweden and New Netherland had trouble attracting settlers because company policies made it difficult for persons of humble origin to become landowners. The Dutch colony soon became more populous than its Swedish counterpart, however, because it offered more varied economic opportunities. In addition to agriculture, settlers could also engage in commerce, using New Amsterdam (later New York City), the best natural harbor on the coast. The company's policy toward outsiders in New Amsterdam was a liberal one for the time. Settlers speaking at least eighteen different languages, Catholics and Jews as well as Protestants, came to this Dutch city.

New Amsterdam absorbed the energies of all comers—women as well as men. Women managed taverns, kept shops, and served on juries. As fur traders Dutch women made trips into the wilderness to negotiate with Indian suppliers. A particularly enterprising Dutch woman was Maria Provoost, who sold thirty pounds worth of merchandise in her store the day after delivering a baby daughter. Only two people in New Amsterdam had fancy coaches—the governor and Maria Provoost!

The coming of the Swedes and Dutch was primarily a response to the economic opportunities in America. The coming of the Germans and Scotch-Irish was due to a greater extent to harsh conditions in their homelands. The Germans, the largest non-English speaking community in the English colonies, came from a variety of German-speaking provinces, including parts of Switzerland. But most came from the Rhineland, a rich and strategically located area repeatedly devastated by war. The Thirty Years War, the Wars of Louis XIV, the War of the Spanish Succession, the War of the Austrian Succession—one followed so closely upon the heels of another that despondent German farmers refused to plant the crops experience had taught them they would be unlikely to reap. Even in peace time, poverty, high taxes, and oppressive rulers made life unbearable. In this atmosphere of despair dissenting religious sects proliferated, while alarmed officials tried in vain to suppress them with the most savage persecutions. Such were the conditions that led normally home-loving Germans to set out for America during the seventeenth century.

Even more numerous were the Scotch-Irish, immigrants who came in such numbers that a contemporary complained, "it looks as if Ireland is to send all its inhabitants hither." In a sense, the Scotch-Irish who came to America were double immigrants. Lured by the British government's promise of land at cheap rentals in northern Ireland (Ulster), their families had left the bleak, impoverished hills of Scotland in the seventeenth century. In Roman Catholic Ireland they maintained their Presbyterian faith and kept intact their religious and family ties to Scotland.

Thousands of these Scots in Ireland, or Scotch-Irish as they came to be called, moved to America in the eighteenth century. Like other Irish, they were subject to discriminatory British commercial regulations. Moreover, as staunch Presbyterians in an area where the official religion was the Church of England, they were considered religious dissenters and thus forbidden to vote, hold office, and maintain their own schools. But their most serious problem, the one that led most directly to emigration, was the sudden increase in the rents they paid for their farms. Originally attracted to Ulster by the low rentals, the Scotch-Irish found their first leases expiring and their absentee landlords doubling and tripling the rates.

Both German and Scotch-Irish immigration began slowly in the seventeenth century and increased in the eighteenth as conditions in the homelands grew worse. Immigration promoters, known as "newlanders," encouraged the flow with propaganda, often in the form of forged immigrant letters, praising the New World where "the maid had become a lady, the peasant a noble, the son of the artisan, a baron. . . ." A pamphlet published in 1734 described South Carolina as a utopia where the wolves were small and tame and the bison put their heads in the windows waiting for the hunters to shoot them. Exaggerated claims led to equally exaggerated counterclaims. The town council of Bern, Switzerland, hoping to keep its inhabitants at home, warned that America was a land without schoolmasters, blacksmiths, sickles, or spades, a land where crops were ruined by game and seed was unavailable.

Many prospective immigrants discounted the claims of both sets of propagandists. They were influenced, however, by authentic letters from fellow countrymen already in America who urged friends and relatives to follow. German immigrants wrote of the abundance of game and the fertility of the soil. Robert Parks, a Scotch-Irish immigrant, assured his sister in Ireland that America was "the best country for working folk and tradesmen of any in the world . . . a man will sooner earn a suit of clothes here than in Ireland, by reason of Workmen's labor being so dear."

We do not know whether Robert Parks' sister came, but so many others did that Scotch-Irish Ulster was stricken with "America fever."

In 1728 the Archbishop of Ireland complained that "the whole North is in a ferment at present; and people every day (are) engaging one another to go. . . . The humor has spread like a contagious disease. . . ." Although frightened authorities arrested ship captains on any possible pretext and confiscated the baggage of would-be emigrants, the America fever could not be stopped. In the half century before the American Revolution over a quarter of a million Scotch-Irish came to America, bringing with them a deep hatred for English authority.

From Europe to America

Never again would opportunity be so abundant; but, never again would it be so dangerous and so difficult to seize that opportunity. European families piled their belongings on carts or carried them on their backs as they trudged from farm to seaport. Unscrupulous agents often swindled them of what little money they had even before the voyage began. Families exhausted their resources waiting for a ship to sail. Once the ship did sail, its captain might deposit the passengers many miles from their original destination. Such passengers were more fortunate, however, than a group of Swedes recruited by the trading company in the seventeenth century and then left behind in Europe because the ship could not accomodate them.

> Here was seen such a lamentation and weeping, for the unfortunate ones have sold all they possessed, yea done away with home and ground for half of the value, journeyed such a long way at their own expense, and are now compelled to take up the beggar's staff, the one going here, the others there.

The mortality rate aboard ship was high. In 1745, for example, a ship left Germany with four hundred passengers and arrived in America with only fifty. Such a crossing was not unusual. Hunger as well as disease made long voyages lethal. Starvation led a shipload of Scotch-Irish immigrants to the verge of cannibalism. Their provisions gone, they had just picked Samuel Fisher, an elder of Londonderry parish, for the slaughter when a ship was sighted bringing help.

A German organist, Gottlieb Mittelberger, left a vivid description of his voyage to Pennsylvania, a description he hoped would discourage others from undertaking the trip. According to Mittelberger, the drinking water aboard the immigrant ship was "black, thick with dirt, and full of worms," and the ship's biscuit, was riddled with "red worms and spiders' nests." Inedible food was only the beginning, however. Mittelberger continued:

> During the journey the ship is full of pitiful signs of distress, smells, fumes, horrors, vomiting, various kinds of sea sickness, fever, dysentery,

headache, heat, constipation, boils, scurvy, cancer, mouthrot. . . . Add to all that shortage of food, hunger, thirst, frost, heat, dampness, fear, misery, vexation . . . there are so many lice, especially on the sick people, that they have to be scraped off the bodies. All this misery reaches its climax when, in addition to everything else, one must also suffer through two or three days and nights of storm, with everyone convinced that the ship with all aboard is bound to sink. . . .

Misery and malice are readily associated, so that people begin to cheat and steal from one another. And then one always blames the other for having undertaken the voyage. . . .

One can scarcely conceive what happens at sea to women in childbirth and to their innocent offspring. Very few escape with their lives, and mother and child, as soon as they have died, are thrown into the water. . . .

Children between the ages of one and seven seldom survive the sea voyage. . . .

Swedish and Dutch immigrants were transported to America by the trading companies that recruited them. The Germans and Scotch-Irish had to finance their own immigration. Lacking the necessary cash, many came as indentured servants. This meant that they sold their labor in America for a period of years to whoever would pay the ship captain the price of their passage. Young healthy adults, who had no trouble finding employers in labor-starved America, usually bound themselves for three to six years. Children aged five to ten served until they were twenty-one. Husbands were often separated from wives and children from parents. The work was hard, especially for the elderly, and discipline could be harsh. Runaways were commonly punished with a lengthened term of service.

Purchase by a kind master was no permanent assurance of good treatment, as indentured servants, like slaves, could be resold. Colonial newspapers frequently carried advertisements such as the following: August 24, 1766. "A German female servant is for sale. She has five years to serve," or February 10, 1754, "Rosina Dorothy Kost, nee Kaufmann, born in Waldenberg . . . desires to let her brother-in-law, one Spohr of Conestoga know through the medium of this paper of her sale at public auction."

Though Europeans denounced the indenture traffic as the "German slave trade," indenture was different from slavery. Indentured servants worked a limited span of years, were given some money or supplies on release, and were not subject to the social and racial stigma that plagued free blacks. Indeed, some Germans who could have paid their own passage chose indenture so as to save their own money and to have time to learn the new language before venturing out on their own.

There were relatively few runaways among German servants,

probably because of the language problem, but the Scotch-Irish were considered less reliable. Colonial papers frequently carried advertisements for the return of Scotch-Irish runaways. One master ran the following poetic announcement which embodies many of the negative stereotypes commonly associated with servants, Scotch-Irish or otherwise:

> Last Wednesday noon at break of day
> From Philadelphia ran away
> An Irishman named John McKeohn
> To fraud and imposition prone;
> About five feet five inches high
> Can curse and swear as well as lie . . .
> . . . take the rogue from stem to stern
> the hypocrite you'll soon discern
> and find tho' his deportment's civil
> A saint without, within a devil.
> Whoever secures said John McKeohn
> Provided I can get my own
> Shall have from me in cash paid down
> Five dollar bills; and half a crown.

Continuity—and Change

Life was difficult for the newcomers, whether they were indentured servants or whether they were fortunate enough to acquire their own land or independent employment from the beginning. Many Germans started out in lean-tos or caves, surviving the first months on game and wild fruits. By the mid-18th century, the established German community was organizing societies to aid its impoverished new immigrants, but this aid was inadequate to meet the enormous needs.

Cultural shock was often as great a problem as poverty, especially for the Germans. Accustomed to the rigid social stratification of the German states, conservative immigrants sometimes found American egalitarianism more upsetting than liberating. Because labor hungry employers did not require references, Mittelberger concluded that Pennsylvania was an ideal country for criminals. He was appalled that learned people working as indentured servants were treated "just as if they were common wage-laborers . . . beaten like cattle until they have learned hard labor." He was also appalled at the English (American) attitude toward their women who, according to his view, lived in pampered, luxurious idleness. Doubtless many immigrants agreed with Mittelberger that America was a land of "outrageous . . . rudeness" and "excessive freedom."

Cultural shock, like poverty, was usually a temporary problem. Some solved it by embracing as rapidly and completely as possible the life they found around them. One German Lutheran pastor, for example, sent his son to England for an education and had him ordained as a minister in the Church of England. Even more complete was the adjustment of a Moravian missionary, Christian Ferdinand Post. Post married an Indian woman and spent the rest of his days living like an Indian along the western frontier.

Most ethnic immigrants responded to cultural shock by recreating in the new environment as much as possible of their former life. Immigrants built farms and homes like the ones they had left in Europe. The Swedes burned trees to clear their land and used the ashes for fertilizer, a Scandinavian custom that proved equally useful along the Delaware. Accustomed to forest life, the Swedes and Finns built homes of logs plastered with clay, like the ones they had known at home—thus introducing the log cabin that would become the symbol of frontier America. The Dutch, on the other hand, reproduced the steep roofed lumber homes they had owned in the Netherlands. The interior of a typical New Amsterdam house had divided "Dutch" doors, built-in cupboards, and large, blue, tiled fireplaces customary in old Amsterdam. Traditional Dutch windmills appeared on the American landscape.

Ethnic immigrants sought out land similar to what they had known in their homelands. Germans settled in heavily wooded areas, where they raised livestock, flax, grain, and vegetables as they had in Germany. Unlike many other colonial farmers, Germans characteristically cleared their land completely, fenced in their livestock, and were careful (as in their impoverished homeland) to make the best possible use of all their resources. Though wood was plentiful, they preferred the more efficient iron stove to the American style open fire for heating and cooking. German farms were noted for their green fields, sleek livestock, and ample, well-built barns.

The Scotch-Irish, too, chose land similar to what they had known before—usually river bottom land, not as heavily wooded as that of the Germans. While German settlement was concentrated in the middle colonies, Pennsylvania in particular, the Scotch-Irish scattered more evenly from New England to Georgia. They flocked to the frontier where land was cheapest. Unable to purchase farms, some simply squatted on whatever land was available. In Pennsylvania Scotch-Irish immigrants settled "in an audacious and disorderly way" on tracts set aside for the Penns themselves, justifying their action on the grounds that "it was against the laws of God and nature that so much land should be idle while so many Christians wanted it to labor on it to raise their bread."

The Scotch-Irish found the American frontier not too different from what they had known in Ulster. In America, as in northern

Ireland, the Scotch-Irish built new farms in an unfamiliar and sometimes hostile environment. The Scotch-Irish frontiersman chopping down trees to form a little clearing for his cabin and planting corn among the stumps became the stereotype of the typical American pioneer.

All colonial families were relatively self-sufficient, but the frontier Scotch-Irish were more self-sufficient than most. The household grew its own food, manufactured its own clothing and tanned its own leather—just as it had in Ireland. Diversions were simple and often crude; they included heavy drinking, fighting, and gander pulling (players trying to pull the head off a live greased fowl while they gallop past on horseback). The reputation the Scotch-Irish enjoyed for being boisterous and unruly originated in Ulster but was reinforced in colonial America.

In many ways ethnic immigrants reproduced their European life styles in America. But they also adapted that way of life to the new environment. Dutch farmers, for example, had been accustomed to village life in Europe, but in America they soon learned to spread out in the ample countryside. Indian culture had an enormous impact on farming methods. Ethnic Americans acquired a taste for such American Indian foods as corn and squash. Dutch women learned to make Indian-style bark cradles for their babies.

Ethnic Institutions—The Family

Three important institutions limited change and preserved European traditions: the ethnic family, the ethnic church, and the ethnic school. The more effectively these institutions perpetuated Old World traditions, the longer the community preserved its distinctive cultural identity. The first stronghold of ethnicity was, of course, the family itself. Where no other institutions existed—no churches, no schools, no organized group life at all—parents taught their children to read in the mother tongue and to worship in the traditional way. Special foods, courting customs, funeral practices, holiday celebrations—all these strengthened ethnic identity within the family. Even with little or no outside reinforcement, the family could preserve the ethnic identity of its members at least for a generation or two.

Many factors influenced how well families succeeded in passing down their ethnic traditions from generation to generation. Density of settlement made a big difference. Swedish families were so thinly scattered over the Delaware Valley that they were soon outnumbered by the English who settled among them. When the English first arrived, they adopted pidgin Swedish. The existence of this Anglicized "Swedish" made it easier for second and third generation Swedes to shift from the language of their parents to that of the increasingly English society around them.

German families were so heavily concentrated in certain areas of Pennsylvania, Maryland, and Virginia that it was difficult for English newcomers to settle among them—even if they had wanted to do so. Many Germans lived near the frontier, where there was little contact with the English-speaking world. Transportation difficulties reinforced their isolation. Until 1733, there was no road between Philadelphia and the nearby German community of Lancaster. Where Germans shared the frontier with the Scotch-Irish, mutual hostility kept the two groups apart, socially as well as geographically.

The German family had a distinctive life style that differed in many ways from that of its Scotch-Irish or English neighbors. German families were large, even in a day of large families, and were unusually frugal and hard-working. As Mittelberger suggests, German women worked harder than their English counterparts. In addition to rearing large families and caring for the livestock and garden, they shared the field work of ploughing and harvesting with their husbands—a practice that was usual only among the most impoverished English-Americans. The German woman was expected to be more docile and submissive to her husband's authority than the "pampered" English woman who, according to the misinformed but opinionated Mittelberger, had received her great privileges from Queen Elizabeth. A news item from a 1775 German paper suggests that at least one German woman was far from docile. When the sheriff offered to pay someone to whip a farmer convicted of petty theft, his wife volunteered for the job. She whipped her husband soundly, adding an extra blow for the time he had boxed her ears, and walked away four dollars richer!

Such a case was, of course, exceptional. German family life was usually warm and close. Quilting bees, sleigh rides, barn raisings, and other celebrations provided a rich social life within the German community and often within the large family unit itself, making it unnecessary for the young to look elsewhere for amusement. Family and community ties were strong and lasting. Children typically settled on farms adjoining those of their parents, thus perpetuating the influence of the older generations upon the young and thereby strengthening ethnic as well as family ties. When overpopulation in a given area made it necessary for Germans to move, they usually migrated in groups, often taking their minister with them.

Family and community life was not as close and therefore not as effective in reinforcing ethnic identity among the Scotch-Irish immigrants. Unlike the more settled Germans, many Scotch-Irish families moved to a new farm every few years. As a result, friends and relatives were frequently separated. Unlike their German counterparts, Scotch-Irish young people often left the vicinity of the family farm to set up a homestead for themselves many miles away. Thus ties between the generations were severed, a pattern which made it difficult to transmit ethnic traditions. Finally, when they moved, the Scotch-Irish typically moved as isolated family units rather than in groups, thus making assimilation more likely.

The isolation and crudeness of Scotch-Irish frontier life was well known. What is less well known is that many Scotch-Irish, particularly the "better" sort, considered such conditions an undesirable makeshift. Their goal in America, as in Ulster, was to replace frontier isolation with a more settled village life, complete with church and school and court of law. Actually, the turbulent, rough frontier life style associated with the Scotch-Irish in colonial America was as much a function of economic circumstance as of ethnic origin. By moving up economically and settling down geographically, the English-speaking Scotch-Irish, unlike the Germans, could leave their ethnic stereotypes behind. Such upwardly mobile, settled, Scotch-Irish families rapidly blended into the English community, while frontier families disappeared—literally and ethnically—into the wilderness.

The Ethnic Church

Next to the family, the church was the most important ethnic institution in colonial America. Religion played a major role in the decision of many Europeans to come to America. Some groups were fleeing from religious persecution, others were looking for an ideal place to establish a particular kind of religious community, and still others considered the new world a fertile field for missionary effort.

Colonial America was still close chronologically and psychologically, to the Reformation and the religious warfare that followed it in Europe. In the seventeenth century, religious loyalties were intense, and religion played a major role in everyday life. Swedish and Dutch trading companies carefully provided for the establishment of their national churches in their colonies. Similarly, eighteenth century Germans and Scotch-Irish brought their accustomed churches with them when they immigrated.

Religion reinforced ethnicity in many ways. Ministers born and educated in Europe preached, prayed, and taught the catechism in their native language. Prayerbooks, hymnals, and catechisms encouraged literacy in the mother tongues. In areas with large ethnic populations, ethnic churches served as community centers. Where ethnic populations were sparse, itinerant ministers helped isolated families keep in touch with one another and with the homeland.

Ethnic churches were not transplanted to the United States without problems, however. Many groups found it difficult to raise money to build and maintain churches—a responsibility often assumed by the government in Europe. There was a shortage of ministers as well as money. With no mechanism for ordination in America, ministers had to be persuaded to immigrate from Europe. In no denomination were there enough ministers.

Church discipline as well as church personnel came from overseas—another source of difficulty. As early as 1737 Dutch ministers petitioned for a governing body of their own in America, but permission was not granted until 1771. With the passing of time, American born members of ethnic churches resented being dependent upon clergy and clerical governing bodies that were too far away to respond quickly to their needs.

The most serious problem in the long run, however, was that foreign-language churches were forced to operate in an increasingly English environment. Ethnic colonists often had the double expense of supporting the established church, the Church of England in New York and Virginia, for example, as well as their own churches. More important than expense was the growing language problem. By the early eighteenth century, American born Swedes wanted services in English. By the end of the century young people in the German and Dutch communities were making similar demands.

Ethnic communities met these problems with varying degrees of success. In the early seventeenth century, the Swedish colony in the Delaware Valley was supplied with ministers from Sweden, but after the English took control these aging pastors were not replaced. From 1648 to 1697, Swedish America was without effective leadership, secular or religious. In 1697 King Charles XI, responding to a colonial petition, sent three new ministers to Swedish America, but their struggle to save the tiny community from assimilating was unsuccessful. As English colonists joined Swedish parishes, the original Swedish churches were gradually Anglicized. In 1741 the old Swedish church at Penns Neck, New Jersey, voted to conduct its services in English and to change its doctrinal affiliation to the Church of England. In 1789 Archbishop Uno von Troil bade the American Swedish churches farewell in the name of King Gustavus III of Sweden; all church ties with the Swedish homeland were broken.

The Dutch Reformed Church was more successful than the Swedish both in maintaining its own ethnicity and in reinforcing the ethnicity of its community. Churches in New Netherlands served a variety of functions that gave them great importance to their communities. In the early years they were forts for protection against Indian attacks. They were also community centers and distribution outlets for public information. New laws were posted at the churches, as were notices of everything from political meetings to lost swine.

Charity for the sick, the old, and the poor was handled through the Dutch church. Money was collected at services in velvet bags, decorated with bells. When a Long Island minister attempted to substitute the mundane collection plate, irate congregants walked out. Often old people turned over all their assets to the church, which then paid a reputable family to board them for life and provide an elaborate funeral for them when they died.

Unlike its Swedish counterpart, the Dutch church was not disrupted by the transition to English rule. Dutch churches continued their active involvement in the life of the eighteenth century community, including the education of the children. Equally important, they solved the problems of leadership and governance. In 1766 members of the Dutch Reformed clergy established Queens College (later Rutgers) in New Jersey to educate a proper American ministry. Five years later they won permission from church authorities in the Netherlands to have a governing body of their own in America. In the nineteenth century English gradually replaced Dutch as the language of worship and other institutions took over many of the educational, social, and charitable functions the church had performed; but the church itself survived and was reinforced as new Dutch immigrants arrived in the succeeding centuries.

No ethnic community was more deeply religious than the colonial Germans. A small but significant minority, perhaps ten per cent, belonged to distinctive sects for whom religion was an all encompassing way of life. Sectarians immigrated in groups, bringing their ministers with them. Unlike Dutch and Swedish churches, the German sects had never enjoyed government support. As dissenters in Europe, they were accustomed to building and maintaining their own churches and appreciated the freedom from government harassment they found in the New World.

Years of persecution in Europe helped these sects develop such strong bonds of mutual support and group loyalty that they were highly successful in transplanting their religion-centered ways of life to America. The Seventh Day Baptists of Ephrata, Pennsylvania, lived celibate, cloistered lives of worship and study and created some of the earliest and most beautiful American church music. The Moravians established missions for the Indians, conducted schools, and expressed opposition to slavery. The Dunkers were probably the first Americans to preach and practice total abstinence from alcoholic beverages.

Of course the sectarians, like other immigrants, found it hard to resist the new environment altogether. A visitor to a vegetarian Dunker community in Virginia was surprised to find its members eating meat. The leader of the sect blamed the lapse upon a shortage of grain and roots. According to the visitor, however, "the plenty and deliciousness of the Venison and Turkeys has contributed not a little to this. . . ."

Lutherans and Calvinists—Germans who did not belong to the

nonconformist sects—had more difficulty then the sectarians in establishing and maintaining their churches. They missed the financial support they had enjoyed from their governments in Europe. Funds were scarce, and qualified ministers scarcer still. Poorly educated German immigrants sometimes fell under the influence of charlatans like John Martin, the spell caster, or Daniel Weisiger, an unscrupulous Pennsylvania fund raiser.

Eventually the Lutheran Church in Germany sent Reverend Henry Muhlenberg to America and the German Reformed (Calvinist) Church sent Reverend Michael Schlatter. Both men were talented, sincere, and generally successful in establishing ordered German worship in America. The prestige of their positions as well as their personal qualities made them influential leaders in the German community. These and other ministers from Germany renewed old links with the homeland, as did the continuation of sermons, prayers, and hymns in the native language.

Germans, more than either the Swedes or the Dutch, associated valid worship with the mother tongue and found it hard to conceive of one without the other. The struggle for the introduction of English into the German churches did not begin until well after the American Revolution and, unlike the parallel struggle among the Swedes and Dutch, did not result in a clear cut victory for the use of English. Lutheran and German Reformed congregations were torn by bitter conflict between pro-English and pro-German factions as the eighteenth century drew to a close. The Lutheran Ministerium of Pennsylvania, in the interests of peace, finally recommended that congregations divided on the language issue should split into two separate groups. Congregations did split, amidst court battles, riots, and even bloodshed as property and people were reapportioned.

"God is my witness," wrote the Lutheran minister Reverend Muhlenberg, "I worked against the English as long as I could. . . ." Eventually Muhlenberg and most other Lutheran and German Reformed ministers gave in to the demand for English, though German still survived in many rural churches. Among the sectarian Germans, sentiment for the preservation of the German language was even stronger. Many of the Dunkers and Mennonites successfully resisted the incursion of English, not only in their churches, but in their schools and in their daily lives as well.

The Scotch-Irish did not have an ethnic language, but they did have an ethnic church, the Presbyterian Church. They had succeeded in transplanting their church from Scotland to Ireland in the seventeenth century, but the move to America was more difficult. Here the scarcity of ministers, the scattered locations of their congregants, and the opposition of the Anglican Church in royal colonies such as New York made them much less successful. Moreover, in America, religious ties with other Presbyterians blurred ethnic boundaries; Presbyterians from Scotland and England cooperated with the Scotch-Irish in establishing the first American Presbytery in Philadelphia in 1692. Under this organizational structure, both Scotch-Irish and Scotch ministers were licensed and sent out to establish Presbyterian churches in the colonies.

Some of the early Scotch-Irish ministers were remarkably energetic and versatile, traveling hundreds of miles and preaching dozens of sermons every month. John Steels of Mercersburg, Pennsylvania, fortified his frontier church, led the local settlers in wars against the Indians, and arbitrated disputes over land on which his congregants had "squatted." Another interesting frontier minister was Charles Beatty, a one-time peddler, classical scholar, and, in 1755, chaplain to Benjamin Franklin's Pennsylvania militia. When Beatty complained that the Pennsylvania militiamen were not attending his services, the always practical Franklin made a suggestion:

> It is perhaps below the dignity of your profession to act as a steward of the rum; but if you were only to distribute it out after prayers, you would have them all about you.

Reverend Beatty liked the idea. According to Franklin, he became so efficient and generous in his new post of dispenser of the rum that "never were prayers more generally and punctually attended."

Despite its early ethnic flavor, the Presbyterian church was unable to provide an institutional framework strong enough to preserve Scotch-Irish ethnic identity. Possibly because of the high standards of classical scholarship demanded of its clergy, the church could never train enough ministers to serve its scattered constituency. Unhampered by language difficulties, the Scotch-Irish immigrants joined whatever existing church seemed most convenient. In remote frontier areas many lost contact with organized religion altogether. Under such circumstances, the church could not play the unifying, community building role among the Scotch-Irish that it had among the Germans and the Dutch.

Education and Assimilation

Recent minorities are acutely aware of the importance of education in preserving their ethnic identity. Colonial immigrants did not have this awareness—at least not at first. Like other colonial Americans, they considered education important, but for reasons that had nothing to do with ethnicity. Children were to be educated so that they could understand "the fundamental principles of the true Christian religion and salvation." Reading was a tool for learning the catechism, the prayers, and the hymns. Education, colonial ethnic parents hoped, would remove their children from occasions for sin and inculcate desirable habits of industry, modesty, thrift, and propriety. Literacy and some knowledge of basic arithmetic was considered useful for the sons of farmers, craftsmen, and merchants (though not nearly so useful for their daughters). Finally, living in a continent they perceived as savage, ethnic Americans considered education a bulwark to protect the young from being seduced into a life of barbarism. It was only after a generation or two in America that some, the Germans in particular, began to see education as a means of preserving the Old World tradition—ethnicity—and passing it on to succeeding generations.

There was no free public school system in colonial America. Parents educated their children at home or sent them to one of a variety of private schools ranging from the local "dame" school to the expensive Latin boarding school many miles away. In theory, ethnic Americans had a similar range of choices; in practice, their choices were narrowed by their distinctive languages and religious beliefs. Ethnic communities, therefore, set up schools of their own—or at least tried to do so.

If ethnic Americans shared the general American view that education, at least on the elementary level, was valuable, they also shared the difficulties of providing even that level of education to their children. Teachers, like ministers, were not attracted to the New World; there was always a shortage. Nor was the work of the teacher highly respected. Teaching was not even considered a full-time occupation; there were usually other duties. A Dutch schoolmaster in Long Island, for example, was expected to clean the church, ring the assembly bell, read psalms, furnish bread and wine for communion, serve as a messenger, and, when there was a death in the community, give out funeral invitations, dig the grave, and toll the bell. As might be expected, such a position did not always attract outstanding candidates. The first New Amsterdam schoolmaster, for example, had many brushes with the law, including a court conviction for "an attempt forcibly to violate Harch Sybalteen's wife in her own house."

Because of distance, lack of transportation, and the need for their labor on the farm and in the household ethnic children, like other colonial children, were irregular in their school attendance. Schools were only open a few months each year, and children attended three or four seasons at most, if they attended at all. Books were scarce, even in English; books in Swedish, Dutch, and German were scarcer still. Conscientious schoolmasters were hampered by lack of supplies of all kinds. "I am engaged in keeping school, with twenty-five children in it; but have no papers nor pens for the use of the children, nor slates and pencils," complained an early Dutch schoolmaster in New Amstel, Delaware.

When New Sweden and New Netherland were founded, the company instructed their respective governors to make provisions for the education of the colony's children. In both cases, the instruction tied education closely to religion. The Swedish authorities notified Governor Johan Printz that "all persons, especially the young, (should) be well instructed in the articles of their Christian faith." The Dutch West India Company gave teachers in its colonies, including New Netherlands, a broader charge:

> He (the teacher) is to instruct the youth in reading, writing, cyphering, and arithmetic, with all zeal and diligence; he is also to implant the fundamental principles of the true Christian religion and salvation, by means of catechizing; he is to teach them the customary prayers, and also accustom them to pray; he is to give heed to their manners and bring these as far as possible to modesty and propriety.

Under Governor Johan Printz (1642-1653) Swedish education made a promising beginning. Early ministers acted as both teacher and preacher. In 1654 the governor, Johan Rising, began plans for the construction of a school house. The colony fell to the Dutch in 1655 and to the English a few years later, and the proposed school was never built. In the second half of the seventeenth century the formal education of the young was neglected.

With few new immigrants arriving from Sweden, it was vital to the colony's survival that the ethnic tradition be passed intact to American-born children. This the 18th century Swedes were unable to do. The older generation made a valiant effort at least to preserve Swedish literacy, according to a letter written by the newly arrived Reverend Erik Bjork in 1697:

> . . . Not without wonder I can tell to the praise of this people that when there were scarcely three Swedish books here, they were nevertheless so anxious about their children that although they borrowed them (the books) from one another, all can nevertheless read a book fairly well . . .

The same colonists who petitioned the Swedish crown for ministers also asked for schoolbooks. The books arrived in 1697 and were distributed "according to the number of grownups and youths in the houses and their ability to read, in such a way that whoever would make the best use of this or that (book) received it."

Despite the arrival of the Swedish books in 1697 and despite the arrival of a dozen Swedish born and educated schoolteachers during the decades that followed, Swedish education did not take root in eighteenth century America. Swedish born ministers and teachers established a system of Swedish parochial schools, but they lacked community support. Provost Acrelius, one of the new ministers, tried to improve the schools, chided the young for staying away from them and from Swedish religious services, and made every effort to convince the adult parishioners of the importance of maintaining the mother tongue. But he was a leader without a following. As the Swedish colony became a smaller and smaller minority its people became increasingly Anglicized. Peter Kalm, a Finnish traveler, described the assimilation of the Swedish community as he observed it between 1748 and 1750:

> We had a Swedish guide along who was probably born of Swedish parents, was married to a Swedish woman, but who could not, himself, speak Swedish. There are many such here of both sexes; for since English is the principal language in the land all people gradually get to speak that, and they become ashamed to talk in their own tongue because they fear they may not in such a case be real English . . . Many Swedish women are married to Englishmen, and although they can speak Swedish very well it is impossible to make them do so, and when they are spoken to in Swedish, they always answer in English. The same condition obtains among the men . . . .

The assimilation of the colonial Swedes, like that of later Swedes and of most immigrant communities, was not the result of any visible coercion on the part of the English majority. No one was forced to give up Swedish and adopt English. But ethnic settlers received a message, unspoken but clear, that English was the language of "real" Americans. In the sparsely populated, scattered Swedish community neither family nor church nor school proved strong enough to resist this message.

Unlike the Swedes, the Dutch, with one of the best developed school systems in seventeenth century Europe, were successful in establishing ethnic schools in colonial America. Secular schoolmasters were licensed to teach in New Amsterdam as early as 1637. By mid century the Dutch had reading schools in half a dozen villages. There was a Latin grammar school for education beyond the elementary level in New Amsterdam in 1652. Though attendance was far from universal, especially in rural areas, a significant portion of the children (girls as well as boys) had some schooling, especially in the commercial community of New Amsterdam.

The earliest Dutch teachers were employees of the Dutch West India Company, chosen by the company and by officials of the Dutch Reformed Church in Amsterdam. Their pay was far from generous; at least one schoolmaster supplemented his salary by taking in washing. When the British took over the colony in 1664, they made no attempt to impose English schooling on the Dutch community. An English schoolmaster was licensed in Albany by the new British governor in 1664, but he provided little competition for his already well established Dutch counterparts.

Dutch schools were instrumental in preserving the ethnicity of the Dutch community of New York. Generation after generation, Dutch schoolmasters taught Dutch children in the language of their parents and grandparents. In the patriotic fervor that followed the American Revolution, many of the Dutch schools began a gradual transition to English as the language of instruction. This was especially true in New York City and other urban areas.

Even after English became the language of instruction, Dutch schools continued to survive as parochial schools. Since education for most New Yorkers, ethnic and otherwise, was organized along denominational lines until the coming of the public schools, such an arrangement was not considered unusual. Though the ethnic tongue was not used, Dutch Reformed parochial schools preserved a sense of social solidarity among the descendants of the colonial Dutch.

The early German sectarian communities were outstanding in their educational achievements. Germans established an excellent Quaker school in Germantown, Pennsylvania in 1701 and even ventured into the area of adult education. Their first schoolmaster, Francis Daniel Pastorius, a lawyer and a classical scholar, was well versed in natural science, philosophy, and at least eight different languages. Christopher Dock, a Mennonite schoolmaster, wrote what was probably the first book in the colonies on the management of schools. His system, innovative for its time, recommended the use of love and positive motivation in education rather than the more conventional reliance on the fear of physical punishment.

Even more innovative were the schools of the Moravians. They pioneered in opening cheerful nursery schools "to employ the little ones with short, easy lessons, and to awaken their faculties," and established excellent boarding schools for older children, some of which successfully combined vocational with academic training. While their educational system was originally intended for their own community, it attracted outsiders as well. In the early nineteenth century, the wealthiest planters of North Carolina educated their daughters in the Moravian academy at Salem. Colonial Moravian schools enrolled Germans of many religious denominations, girls as well as boys, Indians and mulattos as well as whites.

The Lutheran and Reformed (or Calvinist) German majority, who arrived in massive numbers in the eighteenth century, had more difficulty establishing schools. Poverty, geographic isolation, and a scarcity of teachers handicapped their efforts. When they could, they built schools, usually next door to their churches. Often they were unable to build either. Where schools established by the sectarian communities existed, the newer immigrants used them. Otherwise they educated their children at home. On the whole, the children of the impoverished eighteenth century German immigrants were about as well educated as other colonial Americans of comparable socioeconomic status. "There is scarcely an instance of a German of either sex in Pennsylvania that cannot read," wrote Dr. Benjamin Rush in 1789; "but many of the wives and daughters of the German fathers cannot write."

The early Germans, like other colonists, saw education as a means of teaching their children reading, religion, and manners. In the mid-eighteenth century, however, they were suddenly made acutely aware of the role education could play in the preservation—or destruction—of ethnicity. At that time an English charitable society tried to use free schools as a means of assimilating German children to the English language and life style. The German population rejected these schools indignantly and redoubled their efforts to build a school system of their own. The English charity school plan is important because it was the first—but by no means the last—attempt of the American majority to use schooling to impose cultural change on the children of an unpopular minority.

Ironically, the plan was set in motion by a Pennsylvania German minister, Reverend Michael Schlatter, who wrote the Calvinist synod in Amsterdam for funds to establish schools for the rapidly increasing numbers of Germans in Pennsylvania. Schlatter's letter, translated into English, came to the attention of the British Society for the Propagation of the Gospel in Foreign Parts. An American educator, Dr. William Smith, confirmed the "melancholy situation," of the Pennsylvania Germans for the Society adding grossly exaggerated warnings of "the approaching prospect of darkness and idolatry among them." The result was the organization of a missionary society in England and Pennsylvania to save the Germans for Protestant Christianity by establishing charity schools for their children.

Christianity was in no danger among the pious Germans, as Dr. Smith and other American supporters of the plan undoubtedly knew. Dr. Smith's correspondence suggests other motives for this educational venture:

> Without education it is impossible to preserve a free government in any country, or to preserve the spirit of commerce. Should these emigrants degenerate into a state little better than that of wood-born savages, what use could they make of English privileges?

> But further, education, besides being necessary to support the spirit of

liberty and commerce, is the only means of incorporating these foreigners with ourselves, in the rising generation . . . .

By a common education of English and German youth at the same schools, acquaintance and connections will be formed and deeply impressed upon them in their cheerful and open moments. The English language and a conformity of manners will be acquired . . . When once a few intermarriages are made between the chief families of the different nations . . . no arts of our enemies will be able to divide them in their affection; and all the narrow distinctions of extractions, etc., will be forgot . . . .

Dr. Smith, Benjamin Franklin, and other supporters of the charity school plan had concerns about the large German population, a third of the total of Pennsylvania, similar to the concerns subsequent generations have had about immigrant groups of their day. They were afraid that masses of impoverished Germans would perpetuate a low standard of living by accepting wages no respectable English worker could compete with. They were afraid that unassimilated Germans, ignorant of English tradition, would undermine their system of government. Finally, they were afraid that Germans would be disloyal in case of war with the French or the Indians.

Though the schools were designed to teach reading, writing, arithmetic, and religion, they had a "hidden curriculum"—Anglicization. According to one plan, German school boys would win impressive prizes by delivering orations in English or reading English authors with "nearest to the right pronunciation." The directors planned to educate girls in reading and sewing because "as mothers have the principal direction in bringing up their young children, it will be of little use that the father can talk English if the mother can speak nothing but Dutch [Deutsch, or German] to them. In that case the children will speak the mother tongue." Elementary education was to be free, but there would be a charge for all the more advanced subjects "to prevent the vulgar from spending more time upon them than is necessary." Clearly the main purpose of the charity schools was make the German children into good Englishmen, not good scholars.

The Germans themselves were given little to say about the schools being established supposedly for their benefit. Only one member of the board of directors was German. Teachers educated in Germany were not to be hired "for though they understand both languages, we could not be sure of their principles." The German community of Easton was not asked to help in the establishment of their school. Indeed, the Englishman in charge of this school considered the local German residents "so perverse and quarrelsome in all their affairs that I am sometimes ready to query with myself whether it be men or brutes that these most generous benefactors are about to civilize."

It is not surprising that the English charity school project and the persons connected with it aroused the hostility of the community they were trying to educate. Christopher Sauer, the leading German newspaper editor of the colonies, became the spokesman for German opposition to the controversial schools. Sauer denounced the entire scheme as "having only a political purpose and tendency." He questioned the religious motives of the educators, reminding them that "wicked men may preach in English as well as in German." Above all, he resented the suggestion that the German community would be disloyal in case of war with France, a suggestion that events would soon prove unwarranted.

About a dozen of these charity schools were built in the late 1750's and early 1760's. At their peak they enrolled about seven hundred students, not all of whom were German. By 1763 the schools were no longer in operation. They were discontinued because of Indian problems on the frontier, administrative difficulties, and, most important of all, the opposition of the community for whom they were intended.

The German community, having learned that schools could be used to destroy their children's ethnic heritage, now made a conscious decision to use schools to preserve that heritage. German leaders in Pennsylvania, Maryland, and Virginia worked with renewed zeal to build elementary schools of their own. Increased prosperity as well as increased determination made their efforts successful. The resulting schools taught generations of German-American children to read, write, sing, and pray in the tradition of their ancestors.

German elementary schools were successful because, unlike their Swedish counterparts, they were supported by large geographically concentrated German-speaking populations and by a flourishing German-language church. Equally important, they were supported by an influential and long-lived German press. Over two hundred publications, many of them religious or educational, were issued by the German press in America before 1755. German children had German primers from which to learn their alphabet. Between 1732 and 1800 there were thirty-eight German newspapers in Pennsylvania alone. German publications circulated in all thirteen colonies, creating a sense of unity and common interest throughout German-America. Children who learned to read in a German language school found German literacy important throughout their lives. Thus, home, church, press, and school worked together to preserve the ethnicity of the colonial German community.

In the rural communities of Pennsylvania, Maryland, and Virginia, German schools, and with them the German language, survived into the second half of the nineteenth century. Among the stricter sectarian

Germans, they still survive. A price was paid, however. Part of the price was the lack of opportunity for higher education.

A more serious price was that of social and cultural isolation. German-speaking Americans were cut off from the English intellectual heritage. At the same time, the eighteenth century rural German dialect preserved in their spoken language was also inadequate for the transmission of the German intellectual heritage. Nor was it adequate, as time passed, to meet the day-to-day needs of communication in an industrializing United States. A German vocabulary limited mainly to household, agricultural, and religious words isolated those who spoke it from the mainstream of modern life, both German and American. Some Germans tried to solve the problem by adding English words to the original German. The result was Pennsylvania Dutch, a new German-American dialect that developed a small literature of its own. The new dialect made daily life easier, but it did not alleviate the cultural or social isolation of its users.

For the stricter sectarians, however, isolation was not a problem. It was a goal. "To counteract the injurious influence of the time and to throw a safeguard about the children, the determined step was taken to have them taught in the German language only," explained a Mennonite bishop. A religious, German-language education for their children was a critical part of the sectarian's decision to reject the secular, industrial world for a simpler more spiritual life. In line with this decision, the stricter Mennonites have rejected all education beyond elementary school for the majority of their children—a decision bringing them into direct conflict with twentieth century compulsory education laws. But the Supreme Court upheld their view in 1972.

> We must not forget that in the Middle Ages important values of the civilization were preserved by members of religious orders who isolated themselves from all worldly influences against great obstacles. There can be no assumption that today's majority is 'right' and that the Amish and others like them are 'wrong.' A way of life that is odd or erratic but interferes with no rights or interests of others is not to be condemned because it is different.

Unlike most colonial ethnics, the Scotch-Irish took an early interest in higher education. Their Calvinist religion had developed a strongly disciplined intellectual tradition. Scotch-Irish ministers were scholars themselves and established schools to train their successors. The earliest was the Log College at Neshaminy, Pennsylvania, a crude cabin in which William Tennent, a graduate of the University of Edinburgh, educated his own sons and other future ministers in Latin, Greek, and Hebrew. Scotch-Irish ministers gave religious instruction to the elders of their congregations who, in turn, transmitted a sophisticated understanding of Calvinist theology to the average layman. The church that asked its clergy and elders to be well-grounded in ancient history, philosophy, and languages had a Scotch-Irish flavor, but the classical education it fostered did not. Thus while the Scotch-Irish established many schools, from one-room log huts to Princeton University, their schools did not reinforce a distinctive Scotch-Irish ethnicity.

Conclusion: On the Eve of the Revolution

Historians of the various ethnic communities have chronicled the "contributions" to colonial America made by individuals of their respective groups. There were many such individuals, of course, ranging from little known musicians, craftsmen, and physicians to better known figures such as Peter Zenger, the German-American journalist who helped to establish the principle of freedom of the press and Paul Revere, of French Huguenot origins. The idea that ethnic colonists made "contributions" to American life is misleading, however, because it implies that ethnic colonists were somehow separate from and outside colonial American life. Actually they were an integral part of every aspect of that life. In the cities and on the farms, along the seaboard or on the frontier, in schools, churches, and synagogues, in agriculture, commerce, or the beginnings of industry, ethnic Americans, along with their English-American counterparts, were building a new society.

By the outbreak of the Revolution, many ethnic individuals and communities, such as the Swedes and the Scotch-Irish, had become indistinguishable in language and life style from the dominant English majority. Others—including some Jews, some French Huguenots, many Dutch, and many more Germans, had not. Many factors influenced the survival of colonial ethnic groups as recognizable social and cultural entities—numbers, density of settlement, patterns of family life, degree of difference from the majority community, and strength of ethnic institutions such as the church, the school, and the press.

An additional variable, intangible but important, was the degree of commitment each group had to the perpetuation of its ethnicity. The Scotch-Irish appeared to have little. They did not experience the anguish of loss of a cherished mother tongue, for example, and their desire to seek new economic opportunities on the frontier was often stronger than their desire to build the settled group life that perpetuates ethnicity. The Germans, on the other hand, were determined to maintain their "German-ness," probably because it was closely linked to deeply felt values of religious faith and family life.

Even among the Germans, however, colonial ethnicity was cultural, not political. The German states had not yet been unified into a single nation, and German immigrants took little interest in the political affairs of the provinces that had been their homelands. "Our fathers lived under an Arbitrary Prince in Germany, a European Egypt," stated a German petition, "from whence they ventured to an American Canaan." The German-speaking residents of this new Canaan had strong attachments to the German language, religion, and life style, but none at all to the political interests of their "European Egypt."

Finally, the fate of colonial ethnic communities was influenced by the life around them. Even the most isolated communities felt the impact of the majority English society and of British political control. We have focused on the internal development of ethnic communities. But the development of ethnic communities was never purely an internal matter, as the episode of the English charity schools for German children suggests. The outside world did intrude. In the next chapter we will explore the interaction between colonial ethnic communities and the outside world.

CHAPTER 3

Interaction:

The Ethnics and the English to 1800

While ethnic minorities were adjusting to life in English America, the English-speaking majority was adjusting to them. They wondered whether they should keep the "aliens" out altogether, accept them with reservations, or actively recruit them? Should the British authorities grant the outsiders civil and economic rights? If so, to what extent, and how soon?

The English colonists and their governments faced these questions throughout the seventeenth and eighteenth centuries. Their answers varied from colony to colony and from year to year, depending upon circumstances and the persons involved. By the end of the colonial period definite attitudes and policies had emerged. Despite many prejudices against those who were different, the English community in America eventually decided, largely for economic reasons, that ethnic minorities should be accepted and even actively recruited. After the Revolution, the new United States government continued this hospitable policy for at least a century.

Prejudice and Discrimination

Europeans of the seventeenth and eighteenth centuries were far from tolerant. Commercial and political rivalries in Europe created animosity among the English, the French, the Spanish, and the Dutch in the New World as well as the Old. Religious hatreds stemming from the Protestant Reformation and the religious wars that followed were fresh and very bitter. Moreover, in an era of primitive transportation and communication, many people were hostile to anyone farther away than the neighboring village!

These fears and hates and suspicions came over as invisible baggage when European colonists began to settle the New World. The first impulse of the founders of each colonial empire was to keep the dangerous outsider away. The Spanish, for example, their own homeland only recently unified under the banner of militant Roman Catholicism, were most intent upon enforcing religious unity. The Inquisition followed the Spanish empire builders as far north as Mexico, effectively preventing settlement by Protestants. Spanish Jews fled to British possessions or practiced their religion underground. As late as the 1830's "Anglos" from the United States could become property owners in California or Texas only if they converted to Roman Catholicism.

The seventeenth century English, like the Spanish, tried to exclude religious nonconformists. The predominantly Puritan New England colonies outlawed Quakers, who were whipped and banished when they ventured within reach. Practically every English colony had laws to discourage the immigration of Catholics. Special duties on the importation of Irish servants, prohibition of public Catholic worship, and double taxation on the property of Catholic landowners are examples of such legislation. Jews seemed less threatening than Catholics, perhaps because there were so few of them. Moreover, English colonists associated Catholicism with France and Spain, their rivals for trade and territory in the New World. Still, Jews were also subject to political restrictions; indeed, Jews did not get full civil rights in North Carolina and New Hampshire until after the Civil War.

The restrictions on Quakers, Catholics, and Jews were religious in motivation, but ethnic prejudices were also evident in the English colonies. Ethnic prejudice clearly influenced the experiences of the French Huguenots, Protestant refugees from Louis XIV's France. When the British authorities gave these industrious people permission to settle in Virginia, the English colonists demanded that they be sent away. In the reputedly tolerant colony of Rhode Island, angry mobs attacked and destroyed a French Huguenot settlement forcing the inhabitants to flee to Boston. As these French Huguenots discovered, English colonists hated Frenchmen, Catholic and Protestant.

Economic factors also influenced English feeling and policy toward outsiders. In the early years, each colony lived at a near subsistence level. Any extra expense was to be avoided. Thus the authorities of Massachusetts objected to the landing of a group of Scotch-Irish in the early eighteenth century because of a shortage of provisions in the colony. The Pennsylvania colonial assembly was reluctant to appropriate funds for a "pesthouse" for sick immigrants, most of whom were German, because of the added tax burden. An English Calvinist mob destroyed a Scotch-Irish Calvinist church in Massachusetts to avoid paying taxes for the support of another church in their town!

Ethnic stereotypes were common among the English colonists. According to the *Pennsylvania Gazette* in 1729, "poverty, wretchedness, misery, and want are almost universal" among the Scotch-Irish. Worse yet, the Scotch-Irish were considered disorderly, intemperate, and ungovernable—"a pernicious and pugnacious people." The Germans, largely because of the language barrier, were considered stupid and uncultured. George Washington expressed the ethnocentricity of many English settlers when he said of the Germans in 1748, "I really think they seem to be as ignorant a set of people as the Indians. They would never speak English, but when spoken to they speak all Dutch."

Many English worried about the large concentrations of Germans. "May they not in time throw off their obedience to the British crown?" asked Benjamin Franklin, suggesting as a solution that they be scattered among the English and given English schoolmasters. The widespread prejudice against Germans was fed by two fears (neither grounded in reality)—that Germans would be disloyal in time of war with France, and that German culture would inundate and destroy "English culture."

Despite these fears and prejudices, the English attitude toward ethnic minorities grew increasingly liberal as the seventeenth century passed into the eighteenth. If fear and prejudice tended toward exclusionist policies in the colonies, economic needs pushed in the opposite direction. In an era of increasingly fierce international rivalry, European rulers were eager to use every possible source of wealth to finance their armies and navies. Colonies were a source of enormous wealth, but only if there was enough manpower to develop this wealth. The English colonies could be valuable to the mother country as suppliers of tobacco, sugar, indigo, rice, timber, and naval stores only if an adequate labor supply could be obtained.

It was so difficult to get this badly needed labor that the British government sent over tens of thousands of prisoners, people convicted of anything from vagrancy or debt to armed robbery or murder. Understandably, the overpopulated British Isles were glad to see such people go. Understandably, too, the American colonists were unhappy to see them arrive. "Our Mother (Great Britain) knows what is best for us," sarcastically noted the *Pennsylvania Gazette* in 1751. "What is a little House-breaking, Shop-lifting, or Highway-robbing; what is a son now and then corrupted and hanged, a Daughter debauched and Pox'd, a wife stabbed, a Husband's throat cut, or a child's brains beat out with an Axe, compared with this Improvement and Well peopling of the Colonies!"

Given the severity of the labor shortage, the ethnicity of a prospective immigrant seemed insignificant as long as that immigrant could work. William Penn actively recruited settlers from Germany in the late seventeenth century, and Queen Anne financed the immigration of thousands of Germans from the Rhineland in the early eighteenth century. Colonial landowners sometimes sent agents to Europe to recruit whatever labor they could, and ship captains filled their vessels with kidnapped victims when willing immigrants were not available. By 1660 Negro slavery had become institutionalized throughout the English colonies, but even the ever increasing importation of Africans failed to meet the insatiable demand for labor.

By 1700 the predominantly English settlers of the middle and southern colonies recognized the economic value of attracting non-English settlers. Within a few decades the less hospitable settlers of New England, outdistanced by the more rapid growth of the other colonies, did likewise.

Debates in the eighteenth century Pennsylvania legislature provide an excellent example of the conflicting and gradually liberalizing attitude of the English population toward non-English immigrants. Time and again legislation was proposed to cut off German immigration altogether. This restrictive legislation was always defeated, however, on the basis of the economic self-interest of the colony itself. In 1738 the lieutenant governor reminded the legislators that

> The present flourishing condition of it (Pennsylvania) is in a great measure owing to the industry of those people (the Germans); and should any discouragement direct them from coming hither, it may well be apprehended that the value of your lands will fall and your advance to wealth be much slower.

Ethnic immigrants did provide badly needed labor and, by their presence, did raise the value of the lands owned by the older, established colonists. Also, by settling along the frontier, they shielded the East from Indian attack. Thus, there were many reasons to encourage their coming. Recognizing this, the Pennsylvania legislators abandoned their policy of trying to restrict immigration and began to pass legislation to help immigrants. In 1742 the colony bought a 342 acre site for a "pesthouse" for the care of sick immigrants. Pressured by the *Deutsche Gesellschaft fur Pennsylvanien*, a German-American charitable society, Pennsylvania passed additional laws for the benefit of immigrants. Ship captains were directed to provide medical care, sanitary quarters, and a minimum of space for each passenger, "no more than two passengers in one bed unless parents want children with them." Immigrants were not to be separated from their baggage, an entire shipload was not to be held responsible for the profits of the captain, and, in case of disputes, new immigrants were to have the right to appeal to Pennsylvania courts.

Colony after colony passed similar regulations to protect non-English immigrants and to lure them not only from Europe, but also from their sister colonies. Pennsylvania and Maryland offered the inducement of religious toleration. Many colonies offered tax benefits, even bounties. The most powerful attraction of all, of course, was the offer of cheap land. Ownership of land in colonial America ensured economic independence. It was also the key to social respectability and, if the holding was large enough, to political enfranchisement. Property owners, whatever language they spoke, were eligible to vote. Easy access to land attracted new settlers of every ethnic background.

Laws of naturalization—or denization, as it was called at the time—varied from colony to colony, but the tendency was to make them increasingly liberal. A period of residence in the colony, from a few months to a few years, and an oath of allegiance to the English crown were all that was required. Often groups of non-English immigrants were given papers of denization, even before they embarked for the colonies. They were citizens upon their arrival. The ease with which they could become naturalized undoubtedly attracted many non-English settlers to the English colonies.

Population increase meant growth and prosperity. British authorities had recognized this even earlier than the colonists by encouraging settlement by ethnic minorities in the seventeenth and early eighteenth centuries, often in the face of local prejudice and opposition. The Stamp Act crisis and other acts of colonial insubordination in the mid-eighteenth century caused the British authorities to reverse their position. After 1764 royal governors were instructed to grant no new lands to settlers, to prevent settlers from buying Indian lands, and to refuse permission for all land surveying. All naturalization of aliens was forbidden. In 1774 Parliament stated that "the great increase of people in said colonies has an immediate tendency to produce independency," and levied a tax of fifty pounds on each person leaving England or Ireland for America. Parliament was afraid that the colonies, growing more populous and prosperous all the time, would be increasingly hard to control.

This last minute effort on the part of Great Britain to slow down the peopling of the colonies was too late. The vast migration of Germans had already taken place. The Scotch-Irish had already come, bringing with them their anti-British bias which, as Parliament recognized, did indeed contribute to the growth of the independence movement in the colonies.

By 1775 immigration had become one of the many issues over which the colonies and the mother country disagreed. Britain hoped to limit immigration and curtail westward expansion, both to make the colonies more easily governable and to avoid trouble with the Indians west of the Alleghenies. But by now immigration was so strongly identified in the colonists' mind with continued growth and prosperity that any effort to obstruct it was intolerable. Indeed, the new British policy was denounced by Jefferson in the Declaration of Independence as one of the reasons for dissolving the political bond with King George III.

The variety of languages, religions, and nationalities present in colonial America has had an enormous impact upon our subsequent history. The only possible way in which English, Dutch, Swiss, Germans, Swedes, Finns, Poles, Italians, Jews, Welsh, Irish, Scotch-Irish, and others belonging to an even longer list of churches and sects could survive in the same land was by developing a policy of "live and let live." There was prejudice, and political and economic advancement often depended upon a mastery of the English language and conformity to English ways. Still, the labor shortage of the colonies coupled with the great diversity of the population made a degree of tolerance a practical necessity. This tolerance was not extended to nonwhites—Indians and blacks were not embraced by it. Still, limited as it was, it was the beginning of an ideal powerful enough to make at least some Americans of every generation uncomfortable in its breach.

Common Experiences: The Great Awakening

Throughout the eighteenth century a series of common experiences drew many members of minority communities into increasing interaction with English America. The first of these experiences was the Great Awakening. The Great Awakening was a wave of emotional religious revivalism that swept through the English colonies in the first half of the eighteenth century.

The Great Awakening brought emotion and drama to American religion which had become too dry and intellectualized for many Americans. It offered the hope of heaven for all, not just for the chosen few who, according to orthodox Calvinist doctrine, were predestined for salvation. Traditional ministers were shocked by its methods and its content. By the 1740's the Great Awakening had caused many conflicts between its opponents, who were called the Old Light clergy, and its advocates, the New Light clergy.

As the Great Awakening reached out to people on the frontier and in the towns and villages throughout the colonies, the New Light preachers attracted many ethnic Americans. Some were convinced by these dramatic new ministers to abandon their ethnic religious affiliations—if, indeed, they had any—in favor of English-speaking evangelistic denominations such as the Baptists, the Methodists, and the New Light Presbyterians. Henry Crum, a German-American, left us a description of his conversion at a Methodist camp meeting:

> I prayed in Dutch (*Deutsch,* or German). I am Dutch and must get converted in Dutch .... These are all English people, and they get

converted in English. I prayed and prayed in Dutch, but could not get the blessing. At last I felt willing to get converted in English, as the Lord pleased. Then the blessing came, and I got converted in English.

Crum became a Methodist minister and spent many months traveling along the frontier to bring the message of salvation to others. Because frontier life was lonely, revivals attracted Americans of every ethnic background, people in search of human sociability as well as divine forgiveness. Crum's experience was not unique. Other ethnic Americans too moved into the majority community through the gates of the English churches, because, like Crum, they were influenced by the traveling evangelists of the Great Awakening.

Common Experiences: Politics

Politics was even more influential than religion in bringing eighteenth century ethnic Americans into the current of English American life. Prominent Dutch families who had been influential in the government of New Netherland continued to play an important role in the public life of New York. Jews were few in number and in many colonies were barred from holding office; hence they were not important politically. By the mid-eighteenth century, French Huguenots, Welsh, Swedes, and other Protestant ethnic groups who were well assimilated in other ways were also well assimilated politically. Individuals of French Huguenot background in particular played important roles in colonial political life.

The colonial Germans had a tradition of noninvolvement in public affairs. Many of the sectarian communities regarded all governments as instruments of the devil, institutions with which good Christians should have nothing to do. Bad experiences with government in the homeland had influenced many of their countrymen to adopt a similar attitude. The Germans of Pennsylvania were so hostile to participation in government that they were often fined in order to force them to serve as magistrates in their own communities. By the eighteenth century, however, even the Germans had begun to move in the direction of greater involvement in the public life of the colonies.

There were concrete reasons for this increasing involvement. German colonists, especially those on the frontier, found that they had needs which only government could satisfy—a new bridge, a new road, a fort for better protection, a court to enforce justice. Ethnic Americans joined their English neighbors to petition for these and similar improvements. Soon a sprinkling of ethnics, including the initially reluctant Germans, were seeking and holding local political positions. In sparsely populated areas of eighteenth century Virginia, German-speaking Lutherans served as officers of the parishes that constituted the units of local government.

Leaders emerged within the ethnic communities to help mold the political opinions and actions of their groups. Such a leader was Christopher Sauer, the German editor previously mentioned as the leader of opposition to the English charity schools. Sauer used his newspaper and his considerable personal influence to promote a political alliance between the Germans and the Quakers in Pennsylvania, an alliance which voted against the plans of the English proprietary government. In 1754 this alliance defeated Benjamin Franklin's famous Albany Plan for a unified colonial defense against the French and their Indian allies. Sauer convinced the frugal, peace-loving German farmers that the Albany Plan would crush them with taxes and make soldiers of their sons. German participation in politics remained slight as late as the middle of the eighteenth century, but, as the episode of the Albany Plan indicates, Germans could be stirred to political action when they believed their own interests to be at stake.

Unhampered by language barriers and by either fear of or deference to the existing authorities, the Scotch-Irish had a far greater impact on colonial politics. From their arrival, they plunged into public life to agitate two major issues—the question of military action against the Indians along the frontier and the relationship of the undeveloped West to the more established East.

It is surprising that the Scotch-Irish, with their insatiable land hunger and their tradition of frequent moves, did not come into conflict with the Indian population sooner. The absence of a large Indian population near the Virginia frontier and the tradition of fair dealings with the Indians followed by the Quakers and the Germans of Pennsylvania postponed the conflict in these areas. Eventually, however, the expansion of white settlement made the Indians realize that their way of life was endangered. They determined to resist.

By midcentury relations between Indians and whites along the Pennsylvania and Virginia frontier had degenerated into a series of raids and counterraids, atrocities and counteratrocities. The pacifistic German settlers often returned eastward rather than fight, but the Scotch-Irish remained to do battle. In their zeal they sometimes made no distinction between peaceful Indians and hostile ones, and they did not hesitate to move into the lands vacated by the Indians they had killed. From the vantage point of the twentieth century, the Scotch-Irish appear clearly as the aggressors, as it was they who were displacing the native inhabitants. Even their contemporaries condemned their brutality and their insensitivity to the rights of the Indians. As the historian James Leyburn pointed out, however, the Scotch-Irish pioneer had made a home in what, to him, had been wilderness and empty land, and "he had no intention of retiring supinely from what he had created with his own toil."

The Scotch-Irish population of Pennsylvania agitated constantly for military action against the Indians. They were instrumental in pressuring the governor and the council to declare war against them in 1754. Even after the French and Indian War, the pressure was maintained. In 1763 a group of five hundred frontiersmen, mostly Scotch-Irish, went to Philadelphia to demand continued protection from the Indians.

The Scotch-Irish who went to Philadelphia in 1763 had other grievances as well. They saw the failure of the colonial government to protect them from the Indians as part of the larger problem of western lack of influence in the eastern-dominated political structure. The Scotch-Irish of western Pennsylvania were angered by the unequal representation in the colonial government that made their interests secondary to those of the Philadelphia merchant gentry.

A similar situation existed in North and South Carolina, where the English tidewater planters looked down upon the Scotch-Irish frontier farmers. The Scotch-Irish of North Carolina protested against the abuse of eastern government power—disproportionate taxes, dishonest judges and lawyers, lack of paper currency, quitrents, abuse of land laws, and religious intolerance. The Regulators, as these protesters were called, caused so much disorder that Governor Tryon sent troops to defeat them in a pitched battle in 1771. Five Regulator leaders were hanged, and hundreds fled to new settlements in what would later be Tennessee. The remaining North Carolina Regulators were pardoned after taking a special oath of loyalty to the Crown.

In South Carolina the eastern authorities showed their indifference to the needs of the Scotch-Irish and other frontier people by refusing to provide them with courts, judges, or any local government whatsoever. In the resulting legal vacuum, gangs of outlaws terrorized the countryside. After petitioning in vain for help from the East, the Regulators formed vigilante groups that killed suspected outlaw leaders and burned their homes. In South Carolina the Regulators were more successful than they had been in North Carolina. In 1772 the Assembly finally agreed to bring local government with the long desired law courts to the troubled areas.

The French and Indian War

The French and Indian War drew ethnic Americans into the life of the general community from New England to Georgia. The war, which had long been brewing, was the great watershed for ethnic, particularly German, participation in American civic and political life. The Scotch-Irish, as has already been noted, were in favor of the war even before it began, as a move against the Indians. The Germans, on the other hand, were indifferent or even opposed. The pacifist sects refused to become involved in violence on religious grounds. Having always gotten along well with the Indians themselves, the Germans considered talk of Indian warfare an exaggeration. Indeed British authorities in the early stages of the war suspected the frontier Germans of being secretly allied with France because of their unusually peaceful relations with the Indians. The staunchly Protestant Moravians were suspected of being French Jesuit spies because of their robes, their crucifixes, and their concern with missions to the red men. The German community repeatedly voted against military appropriations.

When war came, Benjamin Franklin threatened and bribed indifferent German farmers into driving the supply wagons for General Braddock's disastrous march against Fort Duquesne in the summer of 1755. When Braddock's defeat seemed imminent, the German drivers headed their wagons for home as fast as they could. Later, much to Franklin's disgust, they not only demanded payment for their services but even pressed claims for damage to their crops caused by the fleeing British soldiers!

Braddock's defeat at Fort Duquesne in 1755 opened the entire frontier from New York to the Carolinas to a devastating series of Indian attacks. The Scotch-Irish and the Germans, living as they did in the western regions, bore the brunt of these attacks. The frontier settlements were devastated. Thousands fled their homes. Hundreds were killed or taken captive. Even the resolutely pacifistic Moravians were not spared; their missionary settlement at Gnadenhutten was attacked and destroyed.

Now for the first time the frontier Germans joined the Scotch-Irish and the English authorities in large-scale efforts to defend their homes. The Pennsylvania German press and clergy urged German-speaking communities from Massachusetts to Georgia to join the common cause. Many knew from their own tragic experience or that of relatives or friends how necessary such action was. Germans and other ethnic Americans flocked to the militia of every colony. The pacifistic sectarians supplied food and money and cared for the wounded. By the end of the war, German participation was active enough to assure even Benjamin Franklin, formerly their severest critic, of their loyalty and patriotism.

The impact of the French and Indian War upon the German community was enormous. For many German-Americans the war was their first close and sustained contact with their non-German countrymen. After the war the use of the English language, English dress, even English manners noticeably increased in areas of German settlement. Participation in colonial politics increased too. For the first time, Germans began to protest the necessity of paying taxes to support the established Anglican church in Virginia. When Indian problems reappeared with Pontiac's Rebellion many Germans joined the Scotch-Irish "Paxton Boys" march on Philadelphia to demand—and to get—better protection.

The French and Indian War created new traditions and new memories to bind ethnic Americans more closely to their new environment. After the war settlers taken captive by the Indians began to drift home. Their harrowing tales of life behind the enemy lines were told and retold around firesides for many years to come. A historian of the German community of Virginia suggests the cultural significance of these stories:

> Thus people who had come to Virginia from far-off lands, after enduring the pains and suffering the destructions, became attached to the soil they had chosen. The legends of the Black Forest and the Alps faded out of their memory. The tales of death on the New River and in Narrow Passage Creek now were their own legends in which the names of heroes and victims had a familiar ring.

The Revolution

The most far-reaching experience which the eighteenth century ethnic communities shared with their fellow Americans was, of course, the American Revolution. In the decade following the French and Indian War the increasing tension between the colonies and Great Britain was felt even in the most isolated ethnic enclaves. After the fighting began ethnic Americans, like other Americans, were forced to take sides. Some ethnic historians have emphasized the patriots within their respective groups, creating the false impression that each ethnic community was practically unanimous in its support of American independence. Actually ethnic Americans, like other Americans, were reluctant to sever their ties with Great Britain, ties which had been beneficial in many ways.

Each ethnic group produced its Tories as well as its Whigs. Many Scots fled to Canada, preferring the known prosperity of trade within the British Empire to an unknown economic future outside it. German sectarians had a double reason to hesitate before embracing the rebel cause; as pacifists they dreaded the bloodshed that revolution would bring, and as unpopular minorities they appreciated the tolerance and protection they had known under British authority. Would a new regime treat them as well?

Even the Scotch-Irish, who had ample cause to hate the British, were not unanimous in their support of independence. The upcountry Regulators of North Carolina had only recently sworn an oath of allegiance to the Crown, an oath which some were reluctant to break so soon. More important, the Scotch-Irish farmers of the Carolina Regulation were in no hurry to support the revolutionary cause of the tidewater planters who, to their way of thinking, were a closer and thus more dangerous foe than the British.

Even allowing for these exceptions, ethnic Americans supported the Revolution as enthusiastically as most other Americans. About a third of all colonial Americans were Whigs, another third were Tories, and the final third were ill-informed, indifferent, or undecided. Tory sentiment was strongest among office holders and others whose jobs depended upon British authority, and among the clergy and devout members of the Church of England. Few ethnic Americans were to be found in these categories. Having already rejected their original mother country in the act of immigration, ethnic Americans probably found it less difficult than their English countrymen to sever their ties with the Crown and the British Empire.

"Call this war by whatever name you may," wrote a Hessian captain in 1778, "only call it not an American rebellion; it is nothing more or less than a Scotch-Irish Presbyterian Rebellion." Many contemporary observers agreed that the Scotch-Irish were an important factor in the revolutionary equation. Horace Walpole is supposed to have remarked in Parliament, "There is no use crying about it. Cousin America has run off with a Presbyterian parson, and that is the end of it."

Undoubtedly many of the Scotch-Irish did seize the occasion to settle old scores with England. Some historians have claimed that Presbyterianism itself contained the ideals of self-government and resistance to authority. But the Scotch-Irish, like other Americans who supported the Revolution, were probably responding to immediate political and economic grievances rather than to elements within their national or religious background. Whatever the reason, the Scotch-Irish of Pennsylvania and Virginia were virtually unanimous in their support of the Revolution. Scotch-Irish soldiers constituted a large proportion of the Continental army, remaining loyally at Washington's side without pay during the gloomy winter at Valley Forge.

With a few exceptions, the Germans were also committed to the revolutionary cause. Franklin testified to an English investigating committee that the Pennsylvania Germans were even more strongly opposed to the Stamp Act than were their non-German neighbors. In 1772 leaders of the German community organized the "Patriotic Society of the City and County of Philadelphia" to prepare for the struggle ahead. A German Correspondence Committee set up in Pennsylvania in 1774 sent out a flood of letters and pamphlets to the German communities of other colonies, urging them to stand firm against the British. The same German farmers who could scarcely be persuaded to sell supplies to the British troops at the outbreak of the French and Indian War now filled their Conestoga wagons to overflowing with food for Boston when the Intolerable Acts closed the

Boston harbor. Throughout the war, the rich German farms of Pennsylvania and the Shenandoah Valley were the breadbasket of the colonial army.

Among the Germans as among the Scotch-Irish, religious leaders helped rally their congregations to the war effort. Reverend Peter Muhlenberg gave his last sermon in January 1776 and then, dramatically revealing a military uniform beneath his clerical garb, led the mustering of three hundred troops just outside the church. Despite their initial hesitation, most of the German sectarians eventually joined the Lutherans and Reformed in support of independence. Mennonites, Dunkers, Schwenkers, and Moravians furnished supplies and cared for the sick and wounded. The Moravians of North Carolina voted to pay triple taxes in lieu of military service. Most sectarian communities clung to their pacifism, however, causing serious conflicts for eager young patriots. Young men who enlisted were expelled from their church communities, a shattering experience for them, their families, and indeed, for the close-knit communities themselves.

The wartime emergency drew even the more isolated elements of the colonial population out of their accustomed orbits and threw them into the life of the wider community. Ethnic Americans served on a variety of local committees of safety and correspondence and participated in local political conventions. Even when these patriotic groups were organized within the ethnic community, their members soon found themselves cooperating or even merging with similar nonethnic organizations. Individual ethnic communities often recruited their own regiments and companies and served under their own officers. The fortunes of war soon mixed them with other ethnic groups and with their fellow Americans of English background. Differences within the colonial forces seemed less significant than the fact that they were united against a common enemy. Common hardships, common dangers, and a common victory did much to break down old barriers and suspicions and to hasten the acculturation of the minorities.

After the successful conclusion of the war a wave of patriotic pride swept over the new nation. Former Tories, who had not already fled to Canada or England left the country, were discreetly silent, or suddenly discovered that they had been in favor of independence all the time. Patriotic painters, sculptors, and writers glorified the new national heroes. The Fourth of July became the national holiday, and George Washington was canonized by his biographers and by a grateful people as the national saint. Noah Webster produced a new American spelling book to legitimize American spelling habits. Even language had to declare its independence of Old World ties.

Ethnic Americans joined their neighbors in celebrating the new national spirit and breaking their Old World ties. Old World mother tongues were the most obvious casualties. Languages already well on their way to extinction before the Revolution now vanished altogether. The use of Dutch and German in the cities declined sharply and even in rural areas began to give way to English. The German press reflected the trend. Before the Revolution New York, Philadelphia, and Baltimore had each supported two or three German newspapers, but in 1815 these cities could not boast of even one among them. The German language and German schools survived mainly in the small towns and rural communities of Pennsylvania and Virginia.

Ethnic Americans declared their religious as well as their linguistic independence from Europe. The gradual replacement of the ethnic language by English in the church services was given a definite boost by the patriotic fervor of the post Revolutionary years. In all ethnic churches local governing bodies were substituted for authority from across the sea. The Dutch Reformed churches now insisted that ministers ordained in Europe be approved by the new American governing bodies before being allowed to preach in American pulpits. Even the conservative German Lutheran Ministerium of Pennsylvania demanded a three year probationary period in America for German ministers from overseas.

Before the Revolution some ethnic Americans had begun to object to paying taxes for the support of the established church, usually the Church of England. Now, after fighting a war in which the slogan "no taxation without representation" figured prominently, they objected even more strongly. Ethnic minorities in Virginia joined the Baptists to campaign for complete separation of church and state. Jefferson and Madison spearheaded the successful drive and in so doing won the lasting support of many ethnic Americans in Virginia and elsewhere. Similarly, Benjamin Franklin won the gratitude of the sectarian Germans, his old enemies, when in 1785 he led the successful effort to eliminate the "Test Act" requiring certain religious oaths as prerequisites for the holding of office in Pennsylvania.

The loosening of religious restrictions after the Revolution made it easier for ethnic Americans to aspire to political careers. The military and political experience gained during the revolutionary period encouraged at least a few to move from leadership in their local communities to political activity on the national level. Michael Hillegas, a Pennsylvania German leader who served as treasurer for the Continental Congress, was elected to the United States Congress in 1789. A French Huguenot, James Bowdoin, president of the Massachusetts Constitutional Convention during the Revolution became governor of Massachusetts in the postwar years.

Ethnic communities as a whole maintained a much higher level of interest in politics than they had before the Revolution. Recognizing this, office seekers made special efforts to win the ethnic vote. One politician in Virginia even learned German to ingratiate himself with the German-American voters, most of whom were quite fluent in English. Robert Morris, Benjamin Rush, Benjamin Franklin, and other Pennsylvania politicians rallied German support for a revision of the Articles of Confederation by backing the establishment of the German-sponsored Franklin College. Franklin College itself was a testimonial to the growing political consciousness of the German community. In addition to training American born ministers, it had the specific mission of instructing German youth "in such languages and sciences as to qualify them in the future to fill public offices in the Republic."

The American Revolution also speeded up the acculturation of ethnic Americans by encouraging the breakup of ethnic enclaves. Mennonites and Dunkers left Pennsylvania for Virginia and elsewhere after the war, partly because of the pressure of natural population growth, and partly because their pacifism had made them unpopular among their militantly patriotic neighbors. Western lands given to American soldiers in lieu of cash stimulated many ethnic families to leave their old communities. Some headed for the frontier, away from their countrymen, where it was easier for them to become assimilated.

Immigration and the New Republic

An important factor in the increasing Americanization of ethnic communities was the slowing down of immigration between 1776 and 1815. The Old World languages and traditions were no longer reinforced by new arrivals from Europe. The unsettled conditions of the United States during and after the American Revolution, followed by the disruptive events of the French Revolution and the Napoleonic Wars, cut European immigration to a small fraction of what it had been earlier. Americans still wanted Europeans to come because labor was still in great demand. But immigration dwindled because European countries wanted to keep skilled laborers and young men of military age at home. In 1788 Britain forbade the emigration of artisans from Ireland as well as England, and in 1803 Britain sharply curtailed the number of passengers an immigrant ship could carry—two actions which effectively killed the trade in indentured servants from the British Isles.

After the Napoleonic Wars the German indentured servant trade revived, but only briefly. An epidemic aboard an overcrowded ship resulted in the restrictive Congressional Passenger Act of 1819. Although the Passenger Act was an attempt to protect the health and safety of the immigrants rather than to prevent their coming, its effect, like that of the earlier British laws, was to make traffic in indentured servants unprofitable.

Despite the political turmoil in Europe and America and the gradual disappearance of the indenture trade, there were significant, though numerically small, additions to the ethnic communities between 1776 and 1820. Thousands of German mercenaries, mainly Hessians, had been hired by the British during the Revolution. Christopher Ludwig, the Pennsylvanian German patriot who baked bread for Washington's army, suggested that captured Hessians be taken to Philadelphia, "Show them our beautiful German churches, let them taste our roast beef and homes. . . . You will see how many will come over to us." Ludwig conducted a group of captured Hessians on a personal tour of Lancaster county, and his tactic was amazingly successful. Many Hessians did come over to the American cause, and at least five thousand stayed after the war, settling permanently among the German communities of Pennsylvania and Virginia.

A second immigrant group, smaller but economically more significant, were the skilled artisans from Scotland, Ireland, and England who left for America regardless of governmental regulations aimed at preventing their emigration. Hoping to establish manufacturing in the United States, Secretary of the Treasury Alexander Hamilton launched a deliberate effort to attract such men. Even Washington participated until 1791, when he decided that "it would not carry an aspect favorable to the dignity of the United States for the President in clandestine manner to entice the subjects of another nation to violate its laws." Much of the technology of the fledgling New England mills came to America with these illegal immigrants from the British Isles, immigrants who blended almost immediately into the native-born population.

Some immigrants came as refugees from political and social upheavals. About twenty-five thousand French-speaking immigrants came to the United States during the 1790's. Exiles from all parts of the political spectrum fled their homeland during the French Revolution. The largest number of French-speaking immigrants, however, came from the French islands in the Caribbean rather than from France. Slave uprisings there caused an exodus of virtually the entire white population. American public opinion was warmly sympathetic to these refugees, perhaps a reflection of insecurity about America's slave population. Private individuals launched fund-raising campaigns for these Caribbean French, and in 1794 Congress appropriated $15,000 for their relief.

Some of the French refugees moved to New Orleans and St. Louis, where they became valuable additions to the older French communities already there. (They became part of the United States with the Louisiana Purchase of 1803.) Most, however, settled in the eastern seaboard cities of Charleston, Baltimore, Philadelphia, and New York. A general enthusiasm for French culture swept across the United States in the 1780's and 1790's, largely because of the friendship and invaluable aid the French government had provided during the American Revolution. Taking advantage of this enthusiasm, French immigrants became teachers of etiquette and dancing, fencing masters, wigmakers, and managers of elegant restaurants and boarding houses.

The most aristocratic "émigrés" produced a lively though short-lived adaptation of French court life—a miniature Versailles—in Philadelphia. Louis Philippe, later to become king of France, held court on Fifth Street. He was attended, among others, by the wily diplomat Talleyrand and the great epicure Brillat-Savarin, who did what he could to improve the quality of American cuisine. The French impact was as brief as it was colorful. When the conservative Directory came into power in France in 1798, many of the political refugees returned to their native land. Those who remained were rapidly assimilated.

Like the French, the Irish who came at the end of the eighteenth century were political refugees. In 1798 a major rebellion against British rule broke out in Ireland. The rebellion failed, and thousands of disappointed Irish patriots came to the United States. Rufus King, the American minister in London, protested that the United States wanted no more "wild Irish," a protest that, published in the Irish-American press, may have cost him the governorship of New York in 1816. Despite the opposition of King the "wild Irish" continued to come. By 1815 there were Irish fraternal lodges and Irish newspapers in all the major cities.

The first official policy of the United States on the naturalization of foreigners was generous: citizenship, with voting rights, could be obtained after only two years in the country. But as French and Irish immigrants began to cluster in urban communities, and to become increasingly vocal in the press and in the political arena, native-born leaders became apprehensive. In 1795 Congress revised the naturalization laws, lengthening the period of residency to five years.

A few years later President John Adams' administration introduced a bill to increase the residency requirement for citizenship from five to fourteen years. Although this bill was not passed, Congress did pass the Alien and Sedition Acts of 1798. The Alien Act, which was never used, gave the President the power to deport "dangerous" aliens at his discretion. The Sedition Act provided for the fining and imprisonment of persons criticizing the government. Among those arrested under its provisions were two foreign-born newspaper editors, William Duane of the Philadelphia *Aurora* and John Daly Burk, of the New York *Time Piece.*

The new Irish and French immigrants had become pawns in the political battle between the two American political parties—the Federalists, whose leader was President John Adams, and their Republican opponents, whose leader, Thomas Jefferson, was gaining adherents among the small farmers and the Irish and French. The Federalists were frightened by what they considered to be the excesses of the French Revolution, a revolution with which Jefferson and his followers sympathized. The Federalists were even more frightened by the prospect of losing office. Legislative measures against the foreign-born were a symptom of political panic on the part of the faltering Federalists, an attempt to silence the pro-Jefferson French and Irish.

The Alien and Sedition Acts may have temporarily stifled some attacks on the Federalist administration. In the long run, however, they rallied the new ethnic communities, and most other Americans, to the Jeffersonian cause. The French and Irish vote in New York City carried the state for Jefferson in the closely contested election of 1800. The episode is significant because it was the first, but not the last, case in which the foreign-born would become victims of domestic controversy.

American policy toward non-English immigrants at the opening of the nineteenth century was ambivalent. The Alien and Sedition Acts were repealed, and immigrants were welcomed as needed additions to the labor force, but there remained an undercurrent of fear and suspicion. Immigrants were welcomed, but with the tacit understanding that they would quickly become assimilated to a culturally Anglo-Saxon America. "They must cast off the European skin," said John Quincy Adams, "never to resume it. They must look forward to their posterity rather than backward to their ancestors; they must be sure that whatever their own feelings may be, those of their children will cling to the prejudices of this country."

The opening decades of the nineteenth century mark a watershed in the history of American ethnic communities. The era of the mass importation of indentured servants was over, and by 1820 the old colonial communities appeared to have taken John Quincy Adams' advice. The Dutch and large numbers of Germans were on their way to assimilation, as were the more recently arrived French and Irish. By 1820 the population of the United States was closer to Anglo-Saxon culture than it had ever been before, or would ever be again.

Within a single generation, however, this relative homogeneity would disappear. A new ethnic migration, more massive than any experienced in the colonial or early national era, would set out for the shores of the young republic. The lives of these immigrants would become enmeshed with the westward expansion, urbanization, and industrialization that changed the face of the country in the nineteenth century.

CHAPTER 4

New Frontiers:
Rural and Urban America

At the opening of the nineteenth century the United States was a quiet, slow-moving land not much different from the world the colonists had lived in for a hundred and fifty years. Forests still covered most of the land, minerals lay unmined beneath the earth, and two-thirds of the population clustered within fifty miles of the Atlantic Ocean. Most Americans were farmers. They tilled their acres with a technology similar to that of medieval Europe and lived in farmhouses that, according to the historian Henry Adams, were "hardly so well built, so spacious, or so warm as that of a well to do contemporary of Charlemagne." Yet within the span of one lifetime all this would change beyond recognition. By 1880 this quiet agrarian nation of modest size became an industrial giant, sprawling from coast to coast.

Change was rapid and all-encompassing. Between 1800 and 1880 the American population of five million exploded into fifty million. It spread so rapidly across the land that by 1890 the federal government announced that the frontier was no more. Cities increased tenfold in number, the population of many doubling every decade. The railroad, the telegraph, and the telephone brought New York City closer to Los Angeles in 1880 than it had been to Richmond in 1800. New technology revolutionized traditional farming and handicraft activities, abruptly quickening the pace of daily life for everyone. By 1880 Carnegie and Rockefeller had launched their careers, the United States was the world's largest producer of iron and steel, and the sky over Pittsburgh was black with smoke.

In each of these momentous changes—the settlement of the West, the rise of cities, the building of the transportation network, and the industrial revolution—ethnic Americans played a vital role. This chapter will explore that role. Like others, ethnic Americans were profoundly influenced by the changes they helped to create and were often the victims as well as the beneficiaries of their country's growth. This, too, will be explored. Finally, we will explore the problems of the ethnic newcomer trying to adjust to the new United States at a time when even the native-born were dizzied by the rapid changes in their nation and their lives.

Immigration Again

The resumption of large-scale, non-English immigration in the early nineteenth century was in itself a momentous new development on the American scene. Between 1815 and 1860 about five million immigrants came to the United States, a number equal to the entire population of the nation in 1790. By the eve of the Civil War, about thirteen per cent of the entire population was foreign born, a proportion never exceeded in the century that followed. In major cities as much as half of the population was composed of the foreign born and of their children.

The largest single source of this massive immigration was Ireland, which sent over two million people in the decades before the Civil War and continued to send sizable numbers well into the twentieth century. The second largest contingent, both before and after the Civil War, came from Germany, with smaller but significant groups coming from the Scandinavian countries, Holland, Switzerland, China, Scotland, and Wales.

This great new wave of ethnic Americans came as a surprise to a nation which, for about two generations, had experienced only a trickle of immigration. The ethnic communities of the mid-nineteenth century seemed, to the generation that greeted them, an entirely new phenomenon. The Irish and some of the Germans practiced what to many Americans seemed an alien religion, Catholicism. The brogue spoken by the Irish seemed almost as foreign as the unfamiliar languages of the Germans, Norwegians, Swedes, and Chinese.

The immigrants saw themselves as a new phenomenon, with little relation to anything or anyone in the American past. Norwegian immigrants had never heard of Leif Ericson, the Norwegian discoverer of America. Few nineteenth century Swedish immigrants knew of the existence of the earlier Swedish colony on the Delaware. To many nineteenth century German immigrants the remnants of the colonial German communities seemed quaint and old-fashioned.

Europeans in Motion

Why did millions of Irish, Germans, Scandinavians, Chinese, and others flock to our cities and scatter across our land in the decades just preceding and following the Civil War? The first Norwegians were Quakers who settled on farmland near Rochester, New York, to escape religious harassment in their homeland. Religious persecution was a factor in the immigration of thousands of Jews from Germany and thousands more Protestants from Germany and the Scandinavian countries. Political motives were also a factor. A few thousand disappointed political liberals left the German states after the failure of the Revolution of 1848; and these "forty-eighters," an unusually articulate and active group, had an impact in the United States far out of proportion to their numbers.

But the overwhelming majority of mid nineteenth century immigrants, like their colonial predecessors, did not come in search of the ballot or the Bill of Rights. They came in search of a better livelihood. Economic forces rather than political or religious repression set them in motion. The first of these economic forces was a rapid rise in population. Between 1750 and 1850 the population of Europe rose from 140 million to 260 million, and by the outbreak of World War I it approached 400 million. Even with the relief afforded by emigration, there were three persons in Europe in 1915 for every one that had been there in 1750.

Some scholars attribute the rise in population to a dramatic decline in infant mortality and that, in turn, to improvements in sanitation and public health. Others cite the sudden spread of the potato as the basic food crop. Easily cultivated, the potato provided a higher caloric yield per acre than traditional grain foods. A recent scholar has suggested still another explanation—a rise in freely chosen as opposed to arranged marriages, with a corresponding rise in sexual activity and births.

While the cause of the population rise remains unresolved, its results are clear—too many people trying to live off too little land. Where formerly one son survived to inherit the family farm, now there were two or three. The pressure of growing population on a limited land supply drove up the price of vacant land. It became increasingly difficult to buy farms for the younger sons (after the eldest inherited his father's) and to provide adequate dowries for the daughters. Farmers tried to provide for larger numbers of children by dividing their land among several sons instead of passing it intact to the eldest. This only increased the pressure on the next generation which had more mouths to feed on a smaller amount of land.

The situation was most critical in Ireland where the population, supported by the cultivation of the potato, increased sixty per cent between 1780 and 1840. "Every (potato) patch produces a new family," wrote an observer in 1822, "every member of a family, a new patch. . . . Hence a country covered with beggars . . . a complete pauper warren."

A member of the British Parliament further described the deteriorating conditions in Ireland:

> It is impossible for the able-bodied, in general, to provide against sickness . . . or against old age, or the destitution of their widows or orphans. . . . A great portion of them are insufficiently provided at any time with the commonest necessities of life. Their habitations are wretched hovels; several of a family sleep together upon straw or the bare ground. . . . Their food commonly consists of dry potatoes; and with these they are at times so scantily supplied as to be obliged to stint themselves to one spare meal in the day.

The failure of the potato crop in Ireland and parts of Germany increased the stream of emigration from these countries to a torrent by mid century. During the Great Potato Famine (1845 to 1851) a million Irish starved to death and a million more emigrated to England or to the United States. They took with them the memories of eating nettles, wild mustard seeds, and dogs, and of laying their dead in false bottomed, hinged coffins "to provide for more than one burial and yet preserve the decencies." Irish-Americans could not forgive the lack of assistance from the mother country, England, during the devastating famine. Some survivors had difficulty forgiving their own relatives for going so passively to paupers' graves. "They died like whipped curs awhinnin' under the lash—whimpering from the ditches and the bogs. Holy Mary—Mother of God—pray for us starvin' sinners now an' at the hour of our horrible death—Amen."

Other pressures compounded the basic problem of overpopulation. A rapid expansion of the population of cities in Western Europe increased the demand for agricultural products, encouraging landlords to evict their tenant farmers and consolidate their holdings for more efficient large-scale production. Reverend Michael Collins, reporting to a Parliamentary investigating committee in 1826, described the result of this policy in Ireland:

> As the leases fall in, they (the landlords) get rid of the surplus population by turning them out entirely from their lands. Those poor people, not getting employment, either erect temporary habitations like sheds on the highway, or they come into towns . . . perhaps four or five families will live in a garret or small hovel, huddled together there, without clothes or bedding, or food, living upon the chance of employment. . . . The men could get no employment, the women and children had no resource but to go to beg. . . .

Independent peasant farmers, as well as tenants, were hurt by economic change. The enclosure of the old common lands by landlords took away from these farmers important sources of firewood and grazing land. Moreover, as the large landowner consolidated his holdings and began to use the new farm machinery, the small farmer was unable to compete. These factors, plus a series of bad harvests in the 1840's and 1850's, made it increasingly difficult for independent peasant farmers to meet their obligations to family, church, and government. In a last desperate effort to save their independence, land-owning peasants supplemented their incomes by becoming itinerant laborers, traveling hundreds of miles each season in search of work.

Increasingly European peasants looked to emigration as a solution. Some fled from actual famine, aided by charitable societies or by the local gentry, who found it cheaper to finance their way to the next parish or the nearest seaport than to support them in the poorhouse. The majority did not wait until destitution left them no choice. Seeing that the future held nothing for them or their children, peasant families took the momentous step of selling land their families had lived on for centuries. As the farmers left, so too did the tailors, coopers, innkeepers, and other craftsmen and tradesmen whose livelihood depended upon them.

Many went to the nearest city to swell the growing ranks of urban industrial workers. Others set out to build a new life elsewhere. Emigrants from the British Isles sought refuge in Canada, Australia, and South Africa. Germans went to Brazil and Argentina. Chinese spread throughout southeast Asia, Hawaii, and Latin America. No destination beckoned so invitingly, however, as the United States, "the glorious country, the mountain of gold."

Despite economic pressures common to all, individuals decided to emigrate for immediate and personal reasons. Many fled oppressively rigid social structures. Young people left parental homes that denied them independence or the mate of their choice. Sometimes a jail sentence, an illegitimate child, or similar scandal made life in the old village unbearable. Young men left to avoid serving in the army. Some people went in search of adventure and excitement. Others were simply swept along by the outbreak of "America fever" that crossed their land, emptying entire villages as it passed.

Most of the emigrants were young, between the ages of fifteen and thirty-five, and the majority were male. Chinese emigration was almost entirely male, as strong tradition dictated that Chinese women remain at home to care for their husband's parents. Germans and Scandinavians usually came as family groups. Among the Irish and Scandinavians, single girls frequently came first, taking service in American homes to earn passage money for the rest of the family.

Except during the years of the potato famine, paupers were few among the immigrants to the United States, and criminals were fewer still. Those who traveled with the aid of charitable societies had to convince their benefactors of their good character and willingness to work. The Chinese were popularly believed to be "coolies," unskilled laborers imported under contract to mining or agricultural corporations. This was not the case, however. Those who came to the United States were usually free agricultural peasants fleeing areas devastated by the Taiping Rebellion. "Young, thrifty, and industrious . . . they possessed unusual independence of character," wrote Mary Coolidge, an early historian of the Chinese in the United States. As for the European immigrant, a German official echoed the observations of many:

> Those who are emigrating are the tillers in the fields and vineyards, men who are necessarily the largest contributors to our agricultural welfare, and who have generally some mechanical skill as well. They compose the element we can least afford to lose.

The most eloquent tribute to the value of the emigrants was their governments' efforts to keep them at home. An imperial decree banned emigration from China. Clergymen in the Scandinavian countries preached of the dangers to body and soul inherent in desertion of the fatherland. Many of the German states outlawed emigration.

All efforts to stop the stream of emigrants were futile, however. The Chinese bribed the local officials, who eased their conscience with the knowledge that remittances from California were enriching their provinces. The Scandinavian clergy eventually resigned themselves to the departure of their congregants, some even choosing to follow. Emigrants from the German states stole across the borders, embarking at seaports in Belgium, Holland, or France.

Folk songs of the era give insight into the mixed feelings of the emigrants. Songs from Norway complain bitterly of the hardships of life in the Old World: "Farewell, Norway, now I must leave thee. . . . All too sparing wert thou in providing food for the throng of thy laborers," said one. "Norway is a poor and wretched land . . . and now I am going to America. Here I have to save and suffer want; in America everyone can make a living. . . . Farewell," said another.

However difficult life in the old country had been, few could leave home and family and friends without the deepest of sorrow. This too was expressed in songs:

> Farewell, now, o Valley of Seljork; farewell to church and woods and home. Farewell to parson and parish clerk, to kith and kin, and the lovely gardens of home. Would to God this were undone! For the old home lies there grieving. . . .

The following song, taken from a popular Norwegian play, expresses the special sorrow of a woman looking for the last time at the home to which she had come as a bride:

> Farewell my old spinning wheel. How I shall miss you; the thought of leaving you breaks the heart in my breast.
>
> No more in the evening shall we sit by the fireside, old friend of mine, and gossip together.
>
> Ah, all that I see has its roots in my heart. And now they are torn out, do you wonder it bleeds?

The Magnetism of the United States

If "surplus" Europeans and Chinese were pushed out of their homes by economic and personal problems, many forces pulled them toward the United States. Still close to their own revolutionary origins, Americans enjoyed having their land play the role of the refuge of the oppressed. More important, the growing nation recognized its great need for labor. Special interests actively encouraged immigrants and tried to direct them to specific destinations.

Among the people in the United States who recognized the economic value of immigrants and made every effort to attract them were the ship owners. American ship owners sent bulky cargoes of raw materials to Europe, but the return cargoes of finished goods were less bulky. Immigrants filled the half-empty vessels coming from Europe to America, thus increasing the shipper's profit. Immigrant fares were an important source of income for ship owners in the Pacific as well as the Atlantic. Chinese embarking for San Francisco in 1852 alone paid a million and a half dollars in fares; and as many returned home within a few years, the profit was doubled. American ship owners found it profitable to open offices and keep agents overseas in the areas where emigration was common.

Railroad companies as well as shippers encouraged immigration. Immigrants were needed to perform the arduous labor of laying the track, work considered undesirable by most native-born Americans. Equally important, immigrants were good customers for the land the government had granted to the railroads. Having purchased railroad land, the immigrants would settle along the railroad and use it continuously to bring in supplies and to market their crops. Such an immigrant family could be counted on to provide two to three hundred dollars worth of business for the railroad every year.

Little wonder, then, that railroads competed fiercely with one another to attract immigrants. Some maintained agents who traveled to European countries to recruit new settlers. In American ports the agents of the various railroads provided food and other services for the new arrivals, hoping to win their confidence and their business. Railroad companies prepared handbooks in Swedish, Norwegian, German, Dutch, and Polish and offered special travel rates to attract immigrants to their areas.

The states were as zealous in their efforts as the ship companies and railroads. New population was an asset that increased their representation in Congress, swelled their tax receipts, brought in new skills, and increased the value of their land. As early as 1852 Wisconsin had a Commissioner of Emigration, assisted by German and Norwegian speaking deputies. Other states, particularly in the West and in the South, followed.

The states distributed thousands of pamphlets in many languages. They helped immigrants arriving in the eastern seaports by providing interpreters, food, shelter, and protection from the swindlers who were always at hand to prey upon the inexperienced newcomers. Not content with touting the advantages of their own states, "boosters" portrayed rival states in as bad a light as possible. Thus an enthusiastic Kansan warned newcomers to avoid Minnesota, "a land of ice and snow and perpetual winter where, if the poor immigrant did not starve to death, he would surely perish with cold."

Undoubtedly immigrants were intrigued by attractive leaflets and brightly-colored posters and by the blandishments of the various commercial and political agents. What really attracted them, however, was the economic opportunity America presented. In the first half of the nineteenth century the United States acquired the vast and fertile Mississippi Valley, Texas, Oregon, and the Southwest including California. Immigrants were attracted by this seemingly inexhaustible supply of cheap, fertile land. Immigrants were also attracted by the mineral wealth, especially the gold in California, and by wages that were many times what they could earn at home. Their knowledge of American business conditions was amazingly accurate. When jobs were scarce and wages low, as during the panics of 1837 and 1857, immigration slowed abruptly. When business recovered, immigration resumed its normal rate.

Obviously a great deal of information was flowing from ethnic Americans already in the United States to would-be immigrants. Some of it came from guidebooks written by travelers, ministers, journalists, and early settlers. These guidebooks set to rest many rumors (some Europeans feared that if they came to America they would be sold into slavery or eaten by wild animals) and gave details on practical concerns such as the price of land, the cost of salt, wages in different areas, and health hazards. Most guidebooks warned that immigration was for the young and strong and advised people to shun the eastern cities in favor of the Mississippi Valley, where wages were high and land was plentiful and easily cleared.

Another source of information was the successful immigrant, returned to visit relatives or perhaps marry a childhood sweetheart. As in the colonial period, immigration was considered a final parting; indeed, the Irish held wakes for friends and relatives going to America. Still, a few did return. People came from miles away to talk with such distinguished travelers, who often went back to the United States with friends and relatives in tow.

More important still was the flood of "America letters" written by immigrants already in America to the family and friends at home. Such letters were passed from hand to hand, read aloud in the village church, published in the local press, even printed and distributed as handbills. The letters told of the difficulties of the journey, of loneliness, of hard work, of monetary losses through fraud and natural disaster, and of the death of beloved members of the family, especially children. But the feeling in most of them was one of optimism, of promise fulfilled or soon to be fulfilled, of a land where life was better:

> Now for the first time am I able to breath freely. . . . No one is persecuted here because of his religious faith . . . everyone secures without hindrance the fruits of his own labor. . . . Norway can no more be compared with America than a desolate waste with a garden in full bloom.

> The hired man, maid, and governess eat at the husbandman's table. . . . On the street the maid is dressed exactly like the housewife.

> We are free to move at any time and to any place without a certificate from the employer or from the pastor.

> I am well pleased with my decision to come to this place. I believe I have achieved that which I desired: a higher welfare for all my children.

Moving West

Immigrants went immediately to the areas where opportunities could be found. Welsh miners went to the coal and iron centers of Pennsylvania where their specialized skills were needed. Scottish weavers settled in the textile producing areas of New England. Chinese headed for the farms and mines of California. Successful immigrants of every ethnic group served as a magnet attracting friends and relatives to their area of settlement, thus creating new ethnic communities.

A sprinkling of the Irish went as far west as San Francisco, where they were among the earliest and most prominent English-speaking settlers. Most of the immigrants who joined the westward movement, however, were Scandinavians and Germans. As in the colonial years, immigrants chose frontier areas that resembled as closely as possible the terrain of their native country. Scandinavians settled in the northern part of the Mississippi Valley, from Iowa to Minnesota, where the cold climate, lakes, and forests reminded them of home. Interestingly, they tended to occupy the same latitudinal positions relative to one another in America as they had in Europe, immigrants from Iceland settling furthest north, Danes furthest south, and Swedes and Norwegians in between.

A few Germans went to the edges of the frontier, like John Sutter, on whose land gold was first discovered in California. But most of the Germans who went west settled in Missouri, Wisconsin, Illinois, Indiana, and Texas, where they usually bought improved land, wooded and well watered. Wisconsin was highly favored because the traditional German crops of oats and hops could be grown there and because Milwaukee boasted a Roman Catholic bishop of German origin.

Ethnic Americans who settled the interior and western farmlands in the mid nineteenth century shared the hardships of their Anglo-Saxon neighbors, plus a few more distinctly their own. Like other frontier Americans, they suffered from lack of medical care. Because many immigrants were debilitated from the long ocean and overland journey, the bad housing, poor water, and inadequate sanitation of the new settlements were even more devastating to them than to the native born. Cholera, typhoid, pneumonia, and malaria were so common that immigrants declared the American air unwholesome and doubted that American food could nourish them as well as the familiar grains of their homeland.

Like other frontier Americans, ethnic immigrants came into conflict with the Indians in whose territory they took up residence. A German settlement at New Ulm, Minnesota, for example, was wiped out by the Sioux, angry at the broken promises and unfulfilled treaties foisted upon them by the American government. Ethnic Americans, particularly the Irish and the Germans, served in the American army in numbers greater than their proportion in the population and thus played a major role in the bloody Indian wars of the nineteenth century. Immigrants had no particular grudge against Indians. It was simply a job, well-paid and, unlike many other jobs, available to all without discrimination. Moreover, by serving under the Stars and Stripes, the immigrant could assert that he was, after all, a "real" American.

European knowledge and experience were not always relevant to American situations. In Europe farmers tilled small plots using the methods of their ancestors, and looked to the tightly-knit community of relatives and neighbors for assistance in time of need. In America, farms were larger and more isolated, soil and weather conditions were unfamiliar, and the supportive network of friends and relatives was often not available. Individual families were thrown back on their own resources.

Sometimes ethnic farmers tried to bring their European communities with them. Mennonite communities from Germany settled in Kansas, where they worked out a profitable blending of religious conservatism and agricultural innovation. Other attempts to transplant whole communities were less successful, especially when the enterprises were directed from Europe.

One such experiment was the German colony of New Braunfels, Texas, established as a profit-making enterprise by a company of German nobles who pooled their money to buy a tract of land. The company planned to sell the land in small parcels to German colonists, provide them with free schools, churches, and medical care, and sell them supplies. A handful of colonists did purchase land and actually went to New Braunfels to live, but poor choice of location, bad management, and misuse of funds crippled the settlement from the start.

New settlers brought in as reinforcements were left stranded on the Texas coast, many miles from New Braunfels, without jobs, shelter, or transportation to the interior. Those who finally reached their destination found the original colonists demoralized by Indian attacks, poor harvests, and disease. So many had died under the hand of the company physician, a Dr. Kester, that the cemetery was called "Kester's Plantation." According to an observer, the survivors decided to enjoy what they believed would be their last days. "Resorting to a wooden booth where there was dancing every night, the hale and the sick together raved in a dizzy reel of enjoyment to the shrill music of a clarinetist, an individual who was also the professional gravedigger of the place."

New Braunfels eventually recovered and even prospered. Not so the Norwegian settlement of Oleana in western Pennsylvania. Founded by Ole Bull, an eccentric violinist, Oleana was part of a plan to establish a "New Norway" in the United States. The plan was ill-conceived and ill-executed from the beginning. Bull purchased a tract of land from an unscrupulous speculator, paying a ridiculously high price. Not only was the land inaccessible and unsuitable for farming, but the sale itself proved fraudulent, for Bull did not have clear title to the land. After months of backbreaking toil, the settlers received only half the wages they had been promised. The once hopeful residents of Oleana abandoned their colony in disgust, leaving behind a wry ballad that has become part of the folk lore of both Norway and America:

CHORUS:

I'm off to Oleana, I'm turning from my doorway
No chains for me, I'll say goodby to slavery in Norway.

They give you land for nothing in jolly Oleana
And grain comes leaping from the ground in floods of golden manna.

The grain it does the threshing, it pours into the sack, Sir
And so you take a quiet nap a stretching on your back, Sir.

The crops they are gigantic, potatoes are immense, Sir
You make a quart of whisky from each one without expense, Sir.

The salmon they are playing, and leaping in the brook, Sir
They hop into the kettle, put the cover on, and cook, Sir.

REPEAT CHORUS

The cows are most obliging, their milk they put in pails, Sir
They make your cheese and butter with a skill that never fails, Sir.

Two dollars for carousing they give each day, and more, Sir
For if you're good and lazy, they will even give you four, Sir.

I'm off to Oleana, to lead a life of pleasure,
A beggar here, a count out there, with riches in full measure.

REPEAT CHORUS

Settlers who escaped fraud and incompetence had to contend with drought, blizzards, prairie fires, snakes, and hordes of locusts that consumed the crops before they could be harvested. Loneliness was a major problem. While some settled in communities, others, especially after the opening of the prairies and the passing of the Homestead Act, found themselves miles away from their nearest neighbors. Isolation, overwork, and early and frequent childbearing, took a heavy toll. Even the landscape could take on a hostile aspect. A Norwegian-American novelist recorded the frightened reaction of a woman accustomed to the hills, forests, and seas of Norway to her first encounter with the barren, silent plains of the Dakota territory:

> This formless prairie had no heart that beat, no waves that sang, no soul that could be touched, . . . Here no warbling of birds rose on the air, no buzzing of insects sounded. . . . Had they travelled into some nameless, abandoned region . . . empty, desolate wastes of green and blue. . . . How *could* existence go on. . . . ? If life is to thrive and endure, it must at least have something to hide behind!

Immigrants often had to cope with a strange and hostile moral landscape as well as a hostile physical landscape. Customs and values long honored in the old environment seemed out of place, even counterproductive in the new. In the relatively stable society of the European farming village, the family that behaved peaceably, cooperatively, and predictably, fulfilling its traditional obligations to its own members and others, was respected by all. Such a family was likely to be successful in its undertakings.

Not so in the rapidly changing, highly individualistic United States, particularly in the frontier areas in the mid nineteenth century. In the raucous, often violent, "boom or bust" world of the American West, population spread more quickly than legal institutions could follow. Cut loose from the moorings of family, church, and community back east, many of the new westerners felt free to make their way in the world at any cost. Under such conditions, might often meant right. It was the aggressive individual, unhampered by traditional morality, who seized the best mining claim or the well-watered homestead or who succeeded in getting the new railroad, canal, or county seat in the location most favorable to his interests.

Some ethnic Americans accepted, even thrived upon, the pragmatic, rough and ready frontier morality. "Just kick the dog that bites you, that's always the easiest way, and the simplest, too," said Per Hansa, the central character in Rölvaag's novel, *Giants in the Earth*. Others could not give up the traditional values taught them in an Old World childhood. Appalled by the changes she saw taking place in her husband, Per Hansa's wife worried that the entire family would desert the Christian decencies to become savages in a new and savage land.

If immigrants were more vulnerable than the native-born to the hardships of frontier life, they were also more appreciative of its rewards. Coming from a land of tiny farms that had been cultivated century after century, they rejoiced in the size and virgin fertility of their new American holdings. Their traditionally large families, liabilities in overcrowded Europe, became assets in labor-starved America. Of course, many ethnic homesteads were not successful. Thousands returned to the East, or even to Europe, defeated by loneliness, illness, or natural disasters. Agrarian America prospered, however, in the mid nineteenth century; and as it prospered, becoming the supplier of raw materials to America's growing cities and to the outside world, ethnic farmers prospered too. In time, sod houses and log cabins were replaced by sturdy frame and brick farmhouses, with large and well stocked barns and silos. Many humble families, heir to a few rocky acres in Europe, became the proud owners of the American manors that exceeded their wildest dreams. Oleana may have collapsed in failure, but private, less pretentious utopias materialized.

Other Occupations

Not all immigrants who headed west became homesteaders. Lacking the resources, skills, or inclination to become independent farmers, many turned to other means of making their livings. Young men from Germany, Ireland, and the Scandinavian countries became the badly needed "hired hands" to help other farmers with the planting, harvesting, land clearing, draining, and whatever other work had to be done. By 1884 at least half of the agricultural workers in California were Chinese. Five million acres of farmland at the mouth of the Sacramento and San Joaquin Rivers, including much of the present site of San Francisco, were reclaimed by Chinese labor, working without benefit of mechanical aids. The victims of intense prejudice, the Chinese had little choice but to accept such undesirable work. Similarly, Irish labor reclaimed swamp land in Virginia and other parts of the South, work considered too dangerous to be given to slaves. "If a Negro dies, it is a considerable loss, you know," explained a contemporary.

Ethnic Americans provided personal and commercial services to the newly opened West, and indeed, to the entire country. Irish, German, and Scandinavian women worked in American homes, where they cooked, cleaned, nursed the sick, and reared other people's children—invaluable services in a land where labor was scarce and women scarcer still. In the Far West Chinese men performed these traditionally "female" services in mining camps, hotels, and homes. Later they put this experience to good use by opening restaurants, laundries, and other services. This made them financially independent of the oppressive white community which monopolized better sources of income for itself.

An expanding nation needed commercial as well as personal services; and ethnic Americans played a major role here too. German immigrants, many of them Jews, traveled the roads in every corner of the land, from New England to the Sante Fe, bringing pins, needles, pots, pans, tools, news, and companionship to the most isolated homestead, logging camp, and mining village. One such peddler, Levi Strauss responded to frontier needs by inventing Levi's, the sturdy denim pants that still bear his name. The successful immigrant peddler settled down to become the proprietor of the dry goods or "general" store in many a crossroads town.

The skills and labor of ethnic Americans were instrumental in the development of many frontier industries. Scandinavians were important in dairying, lumbering, the manufacture of furniture, paper, and farm equipment; the most successful purchased grain elevators or became local bankers or wholesale commodities merchants. Germans were important as mining engineers and cattlemen and helped introduce crop-related industries such as cigar-making, wine-making, and sugar refining.

Nothing changed the face of nineteenth century America as radically as the building of the transportation network. Miles of new turnpikes, canals, and most important of all, the railroads, opened the West to settlement, supplied the growing urban areas, and provided the new industrialists with the largest tariff free market in the world. This revolutionary transportation network was built largely by ethnic Americans. German-trained engineers contributed much of the technology, and foreign capital, raised by the foreign-born, was indispensable. But the greatest contribution of ethnic Americans was, of course, their labor.

The work was backbreaking—too unpleasant and too poorly paid to appeal to any but the most desperate. In the East it was done by Irish, in the South by Irish and blacks, in the Midwest by Irish and Scandinavians, and in the Far West by Chinese. Railroad companies advertised in urban newspapers or sent agents to ports where immigrants landed to recruit gangs of workmen, a system used by mining and logging companies as well. The worker was offered what appeared to be good wages, with an advance for transportation to the work site, often hundreds of miles from his home. Upon arrival he found the work harder, the wages lower, and his supplies (available only at the company commissary) costlier than he had anticipated. Already in debt for his transportation, he had little choice but to stay.

Sometimes entire families followed the progress of the railroad as laborers for—and victims of—the corporations. In 1841 Charles Dickens described the plight of a colony of Irish families building railroads in upstate New York:

> With means at hand of building decent cabins, it was wonderful to see how clumsy, rough, and wretched its hovels were. The best were poor protection from the weather; the worst let in the wind and rain through the wide breaches in the roofs of sodden grass and in the walls of mud; some had neither door nor window; some had nearly fallen down, and were imperfectly propped up by stakes and poles; all were ruinous and filthy. Hideously ugly old women and very buxom young ones, pigs, dogs, men, children, babies, pots, kettles, dunghills, vile refuse, rank straw and standing water, all wallowing together in an inseparatable heap, composed the furniture of every dark and dirty hut.

Conditions were so bad in some of these labor camps that the state governments abandoned their usual hands-off policy to pass laws against the grossest abuses. From the point of view of the Irish, however, conditions in railroad towns were no worse than they had been in the old country—indeed, they were probably better. There was at least one beneficial side effect. The railroad shantytowns helped spread the Irish population out of the overcrowded eastern cities, creating little "Paddy's Quarters" in Indiana, Ohio, Illinois, and even west of the Mississippi.

On the west coast, railroad building was done by Chinese. Driven from the newly discovered gold mines by discriminatory taxes and by physical violence, Chinese immigrants were looking for employment while the first transcontinental railroad was being built. Chinese were considered too weak and unskilled for construction work, however, until Charles Crooker, an executive of the Central Pacific, pointed out that their ancestors had built the greatest piece of masonry in the world, the Great Wall of China. This convinced the company to give them a chance.

Crooker's Pets, as the new Chinese railroad workers were called, more than lived up to his expectations. With wives, children, and elderly parents in China depending upon their remittances, the Chinese went to work with amazing zeal. They chipped away at the sheer granite cliffs of the Sierra Nevadas, working suspended from ropes when they could find no foothold, until they had carved a shelf wide enough for the laying of the track. In winter they braved blizzards and avalanches, working in tunnels burrowed under fifteen feet of snow. The spring thaw uncovered Chinese corpses, shovels and picks still clutched in their frozen hands.

The Urban Frontier

At least half of the new immigrants never got to the rural frontier, either as homesteaders, hired hands, peddlers, or railroad workers. By choice or by necessity they settled in the mushrooming towns and cities instead. San Francisco had its famous Chinatown. Milwaukee, Chicago, St. Paul, Minneapolis, Cleveland, and Cincinnati had large German and Scandinavian colonies. Many Germans settled in the older eastern urban centers of New York, Philadelphia, and Baltimore. The largest ethnic community in the eastern cities, however, was the Irish.

A rural people in the Emerald Isle, ninety per cent of the Irish settled in cities in the United States, concentrating their population in New York, Boston, and Philadelphia. Many of the Irish lacked the skills and the capital to become farmers in America. By mid century the frontier was a thousand miles or more from the port of arrival. Even if land were cheap or altogether free, impoverished immigrants could not afford the cost of transportation, seed, and equipment, nor could they maintain themselves until the first crop was harvested. Moreover for many of the Irish, the isolation of rural life in the United States had no appeal. They preferred the city, where Catholic churches were available and where they could enjoy the sociability of being among their countrymen.

As immigrants poured into an expanding urban America, so too did the native-born. The cities were magnets, luring all kinds of people with their promise of adventure, excitement, and fortunes to be made.

As centers of commerce and transportation, the cities were, indeed, filled with opportunities. Moreover, as farms began to mechanize, proportionately fewer people were needed to produce the nation's food. Thus while the western farming frontier has often been seen as a "safety valve" for the excess population of the city, the opposite was closer to the truth. From mid-century on, the growing cities provided a safety valve for the excess farm population of both Europe and the United States.

Never before or since has urban growth taken place at such a rapid rate. The old eastern cities got larger, while whole groups of new cities in the Mississippi Valley, along the Great Lakes, and on the west coast made their sudden appearance. New York City grew from 60,489 in 1800 to 202,589 in 1830, to more than a million in 1860. St. Louis doubled its population every nine years; Buffalo, every eight; Cincinnati, every seven. In the two years following the completion of the transcontinental railroad, Los Angeles increased its population five hundred per cent!

Unprecedented growth presented unprecedented problems. How could the cities provide jobs and housing for so many newcomers? What about drinking water, waste disposal, transportation, and fire protection? How could law and order be maintained when neighborhoods changed in a matter of months and when people were strangers to one another? American cities were totally unprepared to solve such problems. Many had corrupt and antiquated forms of government and were unaccustomed to providing any but the most elemental services. At mid century New York City had no public police force or fire department. Such order as there was was kept by private guards, the militia being called out in case of dire emergency. Volunteer fire companies fought with one another while buildings burned. Disease, crime, and vice were rampant in an urban society growing too fast to meet its needs.

Foresight, planning, and the judicious use of regulations and public moneys might have alleviated some of the problems. Such policies were impossible, however, given the climate of opinion in the mid nineteenth century. Political leaders, like most of their constituents, were committed to "privatism," a government hands off policy in the area of social problems. Cities provided poorhouses and public hospitals, dreary institutions shunned by all but the most desperate, and committees of benevolent women dispensed food and fuel to "deserving" widows with small children. Beyond this, little was done. Poverty and other social problems were believed to be the result of vicious and improvident personal habits which the victims could correct if only they would try.

Because so many were concentrated in the poor and working

classes, ethnic Americans suffered proportionately more than the native-born from the growing pains of the city. Immigrants were coping with many changes at once. First they were moving from the European or Asian culture of their birthplace to the predominantly English culture of the United States, a change that often involved a totally different language and life style. In addition, most were moving from a rural to an urban environment—a formidable change in itself. And finally, the city to which they were coming was in itself in a state of constant change. Under these conditions, the urban frontier, like the rural frontier, offered problems as well as opportunities.

One of the most immediate and most difficult problems was finding a decent place to live. At no time in American history has the supply of urban housing kept pace with the demand, but in the pre-Civil War years the situation was especially acute. As newcomers poured into the cities, all hoping to live near commercial areas where jobs were available, there was simply no place to house them. Dwellings built for one family were divided and subdivided as the population doubled and doubled again. Sheds, stables, and warehouses were pressed into service, as were windowless garrets and underground cellars. By 1850, 29,000 people in New York City were living underground.

Recognizing the profits to be made from the housing shortage, landlords erected rows of tenements. The tenements often used every available foot of land on the building lot leaving many of the rooms without sunlight or ventilation. Outdoor privies in the alleys over-flowed, contaminating the water supply and seeping into the buildings. Still, the hapless tenants rarely complained, fearful of being put upon a "black list" and unable in any case to find other quarters. The prudent set aside the rent money before buying lesser necessities such as food, fuel, and clothing.

The impact of the tidal wave of new population (and the inability of the city to provide for it successfully) is illustrated by the history of the fourth ward in New York City. At the turn of the century the fourth ward was an elegant neighborhood of dignified family mansions shaded by blossoming cherry trees. John Hancock, signer of the Declaration of Independence had lived here, as had President Washington at the time of his inauguration. By 1840, however, the fourth ward had become a notorious slum. In one double row of tenements, Gotham Courts, sewer rats as big as cats swarmed freely. One third of the newborn children did not survive their first few weeks of life. Outsiders foolish enough to venture into Gotham Court were beaten, robbed, or worse; a murder a night was not uncommon. Police entered in groups of six—when they entered at all.

With the building of the trolley lines, those who could afford the fares—skilled workers and the middle class—moved out of the old, inner city neighborhoods, leaving them to immigrants, blacks, and others at the bottom of the economic ladder. Like blacks, immigrants could rarely afford to move and when they could afford better housing, discrimination prevented them from obtaining it.

The housing problems of ethnic immigrants were complicated by their inexperience in urban living. The European housewife had been poor in the old country, but she was at least accustomed to an adequate supply of sunshine, fresh air, open space, and clean water. In a cramped tenement five flights above the outhouse and the polluted well, the routine tasks of caring for a household and disposing of wastes became complicated and arduous chores.

As late as 1857 New York City had only 138 miles of sewers to serve five hundred miles of streets; twenty-four million gallons of sewage accumulated in the yards, gutters, and alleys of the city every day. In such an environment, it is scarcely surprising that bad health was a major problem. Dysentery, typhoid, cholera, tuberculosis, and smallpox were part of the price ethnic Americans paid for their participation in urban growth. Eighty-four per cent of the patients admitted to New York City's Bellevue Hospital between 1849 and 1859 were foreign-born. Throughout the country the Irish appeared to have the most illness, probably because they were the most debilitated upon arrival. Because of their poverty they were the most likely to be dependent upon public treatment facilities. The Chinese appeared to be the healthiest. If this was true, it was probably related to the fastidious care they took in the preparation of their food and the boiling of their drinking water. Moreover, Chinese rarely appeared in city hospitals, preferring—perhaps wisely—to die at home or in the streets.

Once they solved their housing problem (however unsatisfactorily) immigrants turned to their most important long-range concern, earning a livelihood. Contrary to popular opinion and stereotypes, many immigrants had valuable skills. They were brewers, weavers, printers, engravers, metalworkers, writers, manufacturers of musical instruments, and professionals of various kinds. Such people had no trouble finding their places and contributing to the expanding urban economy.

Less fortunate were the displaced farmers and peasants, who had no marketable urban skills. But they had muscle and an eagerness to work—commodities still needed in the nineteenth century city. The men found jobs at the docks, in shipyards, railroad depots, stockyards, sewers, and streets. They built, dug, lifted, carried, and packed whatever needed building, digging, lifting, carrying, packing. Such jobs were seasonal, poorly paid, and short-lived. Better paid employment and job training were frequently unavailable to the immigrants who needed them most because of the prejudices of employers. Help wanted notices commonly ended with the warning that "no Irish need apply."

Women had a double employment handicap; sexual discrimination compounded the problems of ethnic discrimination. The more personable young women, especially those who spoke English, could find work as domestics in American homes, but such work was hardly desirable. Irish "girls" (aged sixteen to sixty) in Boston or Philadelphia rose before dawn to work a sixteen hour day, six days a week, for a weekly salary of a dollar and a half! Less fortunate women took in washing or sewing at home for wages competitive with those paid to the women inmates of the public almshouses. The loss of husbands through sickness, accident, or desertion left many widows to support large families with few job opportunities open to them. During the years 1845 to 1850 the Boston Society for the Prevention of Pauperism received applications for employment from 14,000 female "foreigners" as opposed to 5,034 males.

Urban families worked together at the most menial and unpleasant tasks in order to survive. Impoverished Germans in New York City became scavengers. Men, women, and children gathered discarded bones from slaughter houses and filthy rags from hospitals and gutters. In their tenement apartments they boiled the rotting flesh off the bones, washed and dried the vile-smelling rags, bagged the products, and sold them to refuse dealers for a few cents a bag.

The earliest factory jobs were filled by native-born workers. New England's textile mill owners, for example, prided themselves on their carefully chaperoned work force of Yankee farm girls. By the mid 1850's, however, the farmers' daughters were becoming disillusioned with the low wages and drudgery of mill work. Irish and French Canadian immigrants began to take their places, establishing shanty towns and Catholic churches at the edges of neat New England villages, to the horror of the native-born inhabitants. In California, Chinese moved into the cigar, textile, and shoe making industries. As industry expanded in the decades after the Civil War, ethnic Americans moved into factory jobs in increasing numbers.

Life in Europe had been hard, but there were greater opportunities for relaxation and celebration in the traditional village than in the nineteenth century industrial city. Immigrants missed the singing, public games, festivals, and street dancing of the Old World. They complained that here "a gloomy, churlish, money-worshipping spirit" had "swept nearly all the poetry out of a poor man's existence." American employers had no time for poetry.

The new capitalists considered workers a commodity, like wood or iron, to be used as impersonally and as profitably as possible. They demanded long hours of work under unhealthful conditions, for which they paid as little as they could. Workers responded with absenteeism, alcoholism, even violence. Railroad workers protested company exploitation by destroying newly-laid track and attacking railroad personnel. Irish miners in Pennsylvania, working for their old ethnic enemies, the English and the Welsh, resisted the hated bosses with the organized terrorism (including murder) of the Molly Maguires.

Despite a generally expanding economy, periodic depressions caused serious urban unemployment. The groups who suffered most were those at the bottom of the economy—Irish and blacks. Sharing the worst housing and the most limited employment opportunities, Irish and blacks were forced into cutthroat competition for the same low-paid menial jobs. Economic competition combined with racial prejudice to produce the tragic Draft Riots of 1863 in New York City. The Irish community was angry because native-born liberal crusaders appeared more concerned about the plight of the southern slave than about economic evils closer to home. They were aroused still further by the injustice of a wartime draft that exempted the rich but took the immigrant poor. Anger boiled over into senseless violence. Burning and looting, Irish mobs vented their fury on the nearest blacks, hanging and mutilating dozens of people, even setting fire to the local black orphanage. Days of violence took a heavy toll in human life and in property before Federal troops fresh from Gettysburg restored order to the battlefield of New York City.

Pauperism, Crime, and Vice

As urban America grew, so too did pauperism, crime, and vice. Ethnic Americans were part of this as of all other aspects of the country's growth. When earning a living became too difficult, some immigrants sought refuge, temporary or permanent, in hospitals and almshouses. In 1860, eighty six per cent of the inmates of New York's poor house were ethnic Americans. A majority of the inmates of nineteenth century prisons were immigrants and their children. In the East the principal offenders were Irish (hence the nickname "paddy wagon" for the police van), while in Midwestern cities Scandinavian offenders were more numerous.

Because their living quarters were cramped and gloomy, immigrants spent much of their time on the streets. Here there was plenty of opportunity for people to get into trouble. Saloons, gambling establishments, dance halls, and houses of prostitution were common in ethnic neighborhoods; one did not have to go far to practice a favorite vice. Among the Irish, reputedly heavy drinkers even before immigration, alcohol all too often provided an escape from the dismal realities of daily life. Chinese brought their favorite vice, gambling, to America with them. Indeed, gambling had a wide appeal among immigrants. Only the miracle of winning the lottery could lift the unskilled laborer in an instant to the prosperity of his dreams.

About half of the prostitutes in the Eastern cities were foreigners, or the daughters of foreigners, a figure roughly equal to their proportion in the total population, and they were patronized by the foreign born and native-born alike. Gangs had a special appeal for the young men of the nineteenth century ethnic slums. At a time when advancement seemed beyond the reach of many, the gang offered opportunities to acquire money, status, and power. For some youths the gang leader served as a substitute father, teacher, and role model. For the young ethnic, uprooted from the culture of the Old World but not yet assimilated into that of the new, the gang offered companionship and the certainty of a set of rules. Finally, in the most violent neighborhoods, the gang was a practical response to the anarchy of the streets, a necessary means of survival.

Sometimes the ethnic gang was an offshoot of a similar organization in the old country. The notorious Chinese "hatchet men," for example, were an outgrowth of a secret political organization begun in China during the Taiping Rebellion. Consisting of criminals from China as well as native-born hoodlums, the hatchet men imported prostitutes, blackmailed respectable businessmen, engaged in street fighting, and served as paid assassins in San Francisco's Chinatown. In the East, gangs of young men (and occasionally women), many of them Irish, moved about with bludgeons, brickbats, and pistols, terrifying and sometimes even killing peaceful bystanders during bloody pitched battles that lasted for days.

While immigrant pauperism and crime did exist, much of the outcry against it was based upon exaggeration and misinformation. Immigrants outnumbered the native-born in urban public institutions because they were less likely to have friends and relatives who could help them through sickness, old age, or unemployment. Prejudice on the part of law enforcement officials contributed to the high arrest rate among some ethnic groups. Most of these arrests, moreover, were for minor offenses such as drunkenness, vagrancy, and petty theft of the necessities of life—food, clothing, tools, even laundry tubs. If human life was cheap in the worst immigrant slums, it was equally cheap in the mining and ranching towns of the Anglo-Saxon frontier.

Immigrant vice, like immigrant crime, was exaggerated by many of the native-born, who projected their own moral failings upon the foreigner. Saloons, gambling establishments, and brothels, for example, were not tolerated in "respectable" neighborhoods, but they could be located with impunity in ethnic ghettos, where they were patronized by the native-born. Excessive drinking was a universal American problem (the temperance movement predated the mass Irish immigration by decades) and the gambler is a classic Anglo-Saxon American stereotype. Prostitution thrived among predominantly male immigrant societies such as the Chinese, because a shortage of women made conventional family life impossible. But the same conditions produced the same results in Anglo-Saxon male communities. There was one prostitute for every one hundred and fifty men in the native-born white community of San Diego! Local politicians encouraged urban gangs, both native-born and immigrant, finding them useful for keeping "undesirable" voters away from the polls on election day.

Dismal living conditions, ill health, poverty, alcoholism, violence, loneliness—immigrants had many obstacles to surmount in the frontiers of nineteenth century rural and urban America. Some were defeated. Immigrant aid societies had many requests from individuals for money for return tickets to Europe. Unemployed men left their families in the cities to find work elsewhere and sometimes "forgot" to return. Scattered items in the contemporary press hint at the dimensions of the tragedy. "A Jewish young woman, having a healthy child about eighteen months old, would be greatly indebted to any religious family who might adopt it," ran an advertisement in the *Occident,* a Jewish periodical. The *New York Sun* reported that "a German . . . in a fit of desperation on account of pecuniary embarrassments . . . with a hair trigger pistol terminated his existence."

The overwhelming majority of the new ethnics were not defeated, however. Somehow they maintained their mental and moral balance in the midst of a dizzying world. Whenever possible they helped one another, bringing food to a sick neighbor, finding room in a cramped tenement for still another relative or unemployed friend. Gradually they established a variety of self-help organizations in which individuals pooled their resources to insure one another against sickness, death, or unemployment. Unfortunately such societies were often short-lived, because their resources were too limited.

There were other sources of assistance. The Catholic Church provided orphanages and, eventually, schools in major cities. Ethnic Americans who had been in the country for a number of years, or a generation or two, often helped new arrivals. German physicians gave free medical care to needy German immigrants in New York, for example, and Jews in the major cities provided fuel, clothing, and food for needy Jewish newcomers. Efforts by well established ethnics to help newcomers were most effective when the resources of the established community were great and the number of newcomers not overwhelmingly large. Such efforts were more successful among Germans and Jews, therefore, than among the Irish.

Clearly the new ethnic Americans were in many ways the victims of urban growth. But they were also its beneficiaries. As the economy expanded, the lot of the ethnic immigrant improved. Few followed in the footsteps of Andrew Carnegie, the Scottish immigrant boy who became a millionaire. Success was more likely to be measured in a move from a series of temporary, menial jobs to steady semiskilled or clerical employment—if not in the first generation, then perhaps in the second. Many immigrants never moved up the American socio-economic ladder. They worked at the same unskilled jobs and lived in the same tenements year after year, saving every spare penny to support aged parents abroad or to bring their families to the United States. This, too, was a kind of success.

CHAPTER 5

An American Style Emerges: The Common Man, the Common School, the Common Culture

In the years between 1820 and 1840, only a generation or two removed from colonial status, the citizens of the young republic had to define just what it meant to be an "American." What would "good" Americans believe in, how would they live, toward what goals should they strive? During the Jacksonian era, the "age of the common man," Americans explored these and similar questions.

Ethnic Americans participated in the definition of Americanism. But certain ethnic groups encountered problems when they got in the way of the new Americanism or deviated too far from its recently established norms. In the age of the common man there were great pressures to conform. What happened to immigrants who differed from the majority in language, religion, or life style?

Democracy and Protestantism

By the time the great wave of pre-Civil War immigration was well underway, the majority society had agreed upon two distinguishing principles of national identity—republican democracy and militant Protestantism. Americans saw their country as a unique experiment, "a city upon a hill." America was to be an example to the world of the blessings of republican institutions and Protestant Christianity. Nor were Americans modest in their view of what God had in mind for them. George Bancroft, the leading historian of the Jacksonian era, and indeed the most widely-read American historian of the nineteenth century, proclaimed the American Revolution the most momentous event since the birth of Jesus. It heralded "a new and most glorious era" in which the United States would bring the salvation of true liberty to all the world. In the opening decades of the nineteenth century, most Americans shared Bancroft's sense of a great and holy mission for their new nation.

Americans admitted that their country was not perfect—yet. Democracy must be expanded, institutions improved, and morality purified if the United States was to carry out its God-given mission. Such a task was sure to be accomplished—Americans were firm believers in the inevitability of progress—if only everyone put their minds to it. By 1850 the nation would be hopelessly divided on the most basic moral and political issues, slavery and the nature of the republic itself; but in 1828 Andrew Jackson's inaugural address expressed unbounded optimism and faith in the future.

> I believe man can be elevated; man can become more and more endowed with divinity; and as he does, he becomes more God-like in his character and capable of governing himself. Let us go on elevating our people, perfecting our institutions until democracy shall reach such a point of perfection that we can acclaim with truth that the voice of the people is the voice of God.

Manifest Destiny

Inspired by a missionary zeal for the spread of its own revolutionary ideology, nineteenth century America assumed the role of the champion of revolution all over the world. When Latin American nations declared their independence from Spanish rule, the United States issued the Monroe Doctrine, warning European powers against intervention in Spain's behalf. It was the opposition of the British navy rather than American declarations that prevented the recolonization of Latin America; nevertheless, Americans felt good about championing the independence of small nations whom they saw as following in their own footsteps.

Throughout the nineteenth century the United States assumed the role of verbal champion of freedom overseas, a role encouraged, or even initiated in many cases, by the immigrant population. In 1840 immigrant Jews enlisted the support of Protestants and Catholics to protest Turkish atrocities against the Jews of Damascus. As a result the State Department joined European governments in remonstrating, with eventual success, with the Sultan of Turkey. When revolutionary leaders, such as Louis Kossuth of Hungary, came to the United States after the unsuccessful revolutions of 1848 to raise money for the liberation of their homelands, recent immigrants from these countries welcomed them, contributed to their cause, and encouraged native-born Americans to do likewise. Similarly, Irish-Americans rallied themselves and their anti-British allies among the native-born population to the financial and verbal support of Irish freedom. Thus the concern of ethnic communities for their countrymen and coreligionists overseas reinforced America's concern for the rights of peoples all over the world. This concern, praised as humanitarian and condemned as meddling, has become a lasting part of our national heritage.

During most of the nineteenth century, the young nation usually limited its commitments to the spread of democracy to pious declarations and financial and moral support. In North America, however, Americans identified the spread of democracy with the spread of their own boundaries—a project to which they were willing to commit military as well as moral support. Most Americans were eager to spread the blessings of democracy and Protestantism—and acquire valuable real estate—by expanding across the continent. If peaceful means failed, force was used for the realization of expansionist goals.

Immigrants found it easy to identify with and to encourage the expansionist policies of their nation. The Irish in particular were enthusiastic; indeed, the term "manifest destiny," the watchword of the expansionists, was invented by an Irish journalist, John O'Sullivan. Long and bitter foes of Great Britain, the Irish joined American super-patriots in agitating for the annexation of Canada, which they saw as a blow to weaken the British Empire and thus free the Irish homeland. Indeed, several filibustering expeditions were launched against Canada by Irish American radicals, but to no avail.

Although European immigrants usually favored territorial expansion, some ethnic communities were victimized by this expansion. Native Americans—Indians—were driven from their lands, their way of life destroyed, their numbers decimated, the survivors confined to barren reservations.

Others found themselves in the path of an expanding United States. A French community had existed in the Mississippi Valley since the founding of such settlements as St. Louis and New Orleans in the early seventeenth century. Though never large in number, the French, like other settlers, had brought with them their own architectural preferences, their own churches (Roman Catholic), their own parochial schools, even their own theaters. The Louisiana Purchase incorporated this French community into the United States. French influence lingered on in the social life of the city, in the laws of the state, and in the Creole language and culture of the Mississippi Delta, but after a troubled transitional period, the old French America became little more than a tourist attraction.

More tragic still was the fate of the Spanish-speaking population of the American Southwest. "The Mexican, like the poor Indian, is doomed to retire before the more enterprising Anglo-Saxon," wrote an American soldier. Texas and the southwestern part of the United States had been settled as a military and religious outpost of the Spanish Empire in Latin America, an empire which boasted rich cities and universities before the landing of the Pilgrims. Some of the earliest English speaking settlers to venture into this Spanish realm were so favorably impressed that they converted to Catholicism, married Spanish speaking women, and settled down to farming or ranching in the Latin style.

By the fourth decade of the nineteenth century, however, the situation had changed. The Spanish had lost their empire, and the Southwest was now part of the struggling new nation of Mexico. Anglo-Americans no longer respected the Spanish speaking inhabitants; after all, they argued, their government was not democratic, their religion was not Protestant, and their skin was not even the proper shade of white! More important, their lands were attractive and poorly defended.

The Mexican-American residents of what were to become the southwestern states found themselves the victims of forces they could not control. The Mexican War placed them, against their will, within the territorial limits of the United States. Then the discovery of gold and other minerals, followed by the completion of the transcontinental railroad, brought in a flood of Anglo-Americans and European immigrants. Mexican-Americans were reduced to second class citizenship in lands they had considered their own for centuries. Discriminatory taxes and violence were used to drive them out of mining and other industries. Promises to protect their property rights were not honored. Though a few of the wealthiest landowners managed to hold on to their estates and their social positions, many Mexican-American families lost their lands to drought, taxes, foreclosures, and the "sharp" dealings of the aggressive new "Anglos." By 1890 most of the Mexican-Americans had become low paid laborers for the Anglo-American miners and growers of the Southwest. Denied opportunities for employment and decent living conditions, Mexican-Americans were stereotyped by the newcomers as lazy, shiftless, backward, and immoral.

The Age of the Common Man—The Democratization of Politics

The United States justified its expansionist policies with the dubious claim that it was spreading democracy to areas that would not otherwise know its blessings. Within the United States itself the expansion of democracy was indeed a basic tenet of the new American creed. Property qualifications for suffrage were dropped, so that all white males could vote. The aristocratic caucus system of nominating national officers was replaced by popular party conventions, and birth in a log cabin became a much sought after qualification for the highest office in the land. Finally, this became the age of the new, democratic political corruption—the age of the stuffed ballot box, the "boss," and the political machine.

Ethnic Americans were an important part of the new political democracy. With the exception of the Chinese (barred "forever" from citizenship under a racist ordinance of 1790) all male immigrants were voters or potential voters. In an era of white manhood suffrage, their numbers and geographic concentration, especially in the cities, made immigrants a valuable prize to aspiring politicians. Leaders of every political party ate sauerkraut, wore the green, and proclaimed that "some of their best friends" were Irish, German, or Swedish. More to the point, they passed ordinances giving immigrants the vote in local elections even before they became naturalized citizens. Hoping to win the Norwegian vote, legislators in Minnesota established a "professor-ship of the Scandinavian language" at the "State University," oblivious of the fact that there was neither a "Scandinavian language," nor an institution called the "State University"!

When Germans and Scandinavians arrived in the prairie states they were not usually interested in politics. Often their main motive for taking out "first papers" for citizenship was to qualify for government land. Later western immigrants were drawn into politics almost against their will. In isolated rural areas, they were often the only settlers, so they had no choice but to take up the task of naming and organizing the new townships, laying out roads, levying taxes, establishing schools and other services, and carrying out the first elections. After this rather thorough initiation into American political processes, they went on to hold county and state offices, even governorships.

The Germans were numerous enough and well enough organized to become influential in urban as well as rural politics. Typical of the first generation of German urban politicians was Philip Dorschheimer of Buffalo, New York. Dorschheimer had emigrated from Germany at the age of nineteen and was fluent in both German and English. He is said to have taken the entire German community of Buffalo with him from the Whig party to the Free Soil Party, and, eventually, to the Republican Party, where a grateful Lincoln appointed him a federal revenue collector. An example of acculturation at work, Dorsch-heimer's son broke away from his father's ethnic political base, established a "respectable" career independent of his father's machine, and eventually became the Democratic vice governor of New York.

No ethnic group entered the world of expanding democracy more enthusiastically or with more far-reaching consequences than the Irish.

When Jacksonian democracy opened the political door to the common man, the urban Irish rushed in and took over. Accustomed to political controversy and secret societies in their homeland, the Irish had developed great skill in political organization. Their American experiences—the family and neighborhood loyalties and the discipline imposed by boyhood gangs—gave them a good start, as did their numerical strength in particular wards. Building on these assets, they created political machines with precinct captains, neighborhood clubhouses, and a party hierarchy culminating in the city-wide leader, or "boss." After the Civil War Irish machines frequently took over the local Democratic parties. In many cities they functioned as shadow governments, more powerful than the legal bureaucracy.

The Irish political machines handed out jobs and lucrative government contracts to friends, relatives, and loyal supporters. In an era of rapid urban growth there were many such favors to be distributed. Cities governed by machines were notoriously corrupt; in six years the Tweed gang stole over thirty million dollars from New York City. Machine politicians had no qualms about accepting "kickbacks," protecting illegal businesses, buying votes, and using local gangs to terrorize their opponents.

Although the activities of the new political machines horrified the "good government" people, from the point of view of the Irish immigrant there was much to be said in their favor. The Irish had few financial and educational resources; their political cohesiveness was their chief asset in the struggle to survive and move up in nineteenth century America. Through the machine the Irish got jobs as firemen, policemen, construction workers, and, for those with education, jobs as civil servants and teachers. The machine provided picnics and excursions for recreation, and assistance in case of sickness, unemployment, fire, or other misfortune—person-to-person help with no embarrassing investigations or red tape.

"Good government" forces denounced the machines as evil, and urged civil service examinations for the selection of public employees. The continuing war between reformers and the machine was actually a cultural conflict between differing concepts of government. The reformers considered political office an exalted public service to be rendered as impersonally and impartially as possible. According to the political mythology of the reformers, office should not be sought. Rather it should be bestowed by the public upon a reluctant benefactor who would supposedly assume it unselfishly as a public service. The Irish, however, saw politics as the legitimate competition for power and the rewards to be gained therefrom. Individuals openly sought careers in politics in the same way they sought careers in law or business and for the same mixture of selfish and unselfish motives. Little wonder, then, that despite the constant exposure of corruption and graft, Irish voters did not "throw the rascals out." The machine meant power, and Irish immigrants needed power, both for the material benefits it could bring and as a compensation for centuries of powerlessness in Ireland. The urban Irish used the new democracy for their own ends, setting a precedent that other ethnic groups would follow as soon as they could.

Immigrants as Reformers

"What is the good of having a republic unless the mass of people are better off than in a monarchy?" asked an Irish American newspaper in 1878. "Does not a real republic mean that all men have an equal chance and not millions born to suffering and poverty?" Many Americans were beginning to ask whether the American dream had dimensions beyond the bounds of traditional political activity. Was white manhood suffrage and a republican constitution enough for the Promised Land? Or should America concern itself with further reforms—economic, social, and moral, as well as political—if it was really to be the "last best hope of man"?

Yes, answered many; more reform was needed. To perfect their "city upon a hill" Americans plunged into a variety of crusades in the decades preceding the Civil War, crusades whose goals ranged from the most noble to the most preposterous. Reformers organized and flooded the land with lectures, pamphlets, and petitions urging their countrymen to abolish slavery, improve education, give equal rights to women, humanize the treatment of convicts and the insane, end war and poverty, and ban alcohol, private property, marriage, coffee, tea, tobacco, sexual intercourse, Catholicism, and white bread flour!

Most ethnic Americans were too busy trying to survive in America to become involved in reform movements which, to a great extent, were the luxury of the Protestant, native-born middle class. A surprising number of ethnic Americans did become involved, however. Economic reforms interested them most of all, because these had a clear bearing on the problems of their lives, but political and social reforms were also of interest.

With the development of the new industrial capitalism and the widening of the gap between rich and poor, socialists in Europe and the United States began to question the free enterprise system itself. The earliest socialist organizations in the United States were heavily German in leadership and membership, including brilliant idealistic "forty-eighters" like Dr. Adolph Dounai, editor of the leading Marxist journal in the United States, and Wilhelm Weitling, founder of the Central Committee of United Trades in New York in 1850.

Unable to realize their revolutionary dreams in Germany, some political refugees transferred their hopes to the United States. Taking the American Declaration of Independence at face value, a small but highly articulate clique of German-born intellectuals shocked most Americans, foreign-born and native-born, by combining socialism with other causes such as the abolition of slavery and the radical democratization of the American government. Among the changes German radicals advocated were abolition of the Presidency, direct and universal suffrage for men and women (black and white), the abolition of all legislation regarding religious practices, the abolition of private ownership of land and utilities, the eight hour working day, free legal services, public care for the aged, progressive taxation, complete equality of the sexes, and the abolition of money.

The Irish, like the Germans, produced a small but articulate number of liberals intent upon solving the problem of poverty. John Boyle O'Reilly wrote poems such as "From the Earth, a Cry" and "City Streets," in which he described the plight of the poor and denounced "charity scrimped and iced in the name of a cautious statistical Christ." Patrick Ford, a liberal journalist, took a more doctrinaire approach. Ford blamed the depression of the 1870's, which put many Irish-Americans in bread and soup lines, on what to him was the immoral taking of interest for the use of money and rent for the use of land. In the pages of the widely-circulated *Irish World* he familiarized his many readers with the ideas of Henry George and the Land Reform League of California years before publication of George's internationally famous work, *Progress and Poverty*.

When Henry George ran for mayor of New York City in 1886 on a platform of social reform, free access to land for everyone, and the "single tax" on profits from the sale or rental of land, Irish liberals paraded in the streets in his support. George's ideas on conquering poverty through land reform were more appealing to the immigrant Irish than Marxism because their own experience with poverty had been agrarian rather than industrial. The Irish immigrant could well understand a reform philosophy in which the landlord was the villain! Irish-Americans took George's ideas back to Ireland, where they influenced attempts at land reform already underway.

Irish attempts to abolish rent and open land to all who wanted it met with staunch opposition from the Catholic Church both in Ireland and in the United States. Beleaguered by revolutionaries, the Pope took a strong stand against nationalism, socialism, liberalism, indeed, practically every reform "ism" of the mid nineteenth century. With a few exceptions, American churchmen followed the lead of Rome. The Bishop of Cleveland, for example, denounced the women's branch of the Land League as "destructive of female modesty," and warned Patrick Ford that inequalities in life are good because "some men must rise, others must fall; without this there would be no motive for individual effort."

The Irish women of Cleveland continued their activities in support of the Land League, and Ford suggested that the "ironhearted" bishop must be in the service of the monopolists. Moreover, if poverty were such a good thing, "why not distribute its blessings around?" But most Irish immigrants hoped to rise within the American system rather than to change that system. Taking their cue from their religious leaders, most of the Irish, like most of the Germans and Scandinavians, were socially and politically conservative. As for the Catholic Church, Protestants who had little good to say about it in any other context praised it as "an instrument of discipline and control over 'the dangerous classes'."

Immigrants and Utopias

Seeking alternatives to an increasing competitive and materialistic society, mid nineteenth century Americans produced experiments in group living—Brook Farm, Oneida, Hopedale, Deseret, and a variety of communes, phalanxes, and other utopias. "Not a leading man but has a draft of a new community in his waist-coat pocket," said Ralph Waldo Emerson. In these communities, social experimenters hoped to solve all social, sexual, and spiritual problems as well as all economic difficulties. What the utopias achieved on a small scale would then, it was hoped, spread everywhere.

Ethnic Americans, too, built utopian communities in which they hoped to solve all the problems of humanity. Some of these communities were completely secular in origin, like Icaria, created by the French socialist and author Etienne Cabet. Religiously motivated communities were more common, however. They were also more successful, as faith provided the discipline and unity of purpose necessary for a cooperative venture.

Thousands of Swedes, Norwegians, and Danes came to the United States because of the preaching of Mormon missionaries. They joined the great Mormon social experiment of Deseret, in the territory of Utah. Other Swedish religious dissenters built a utopian community at Bishop Hill in Henry County, Illinois. Their leader, Eric Jansson, was a charismatic prophet who claimed to represent the second coming of Christ. Founded in 1846, his theocratically ruled, communistic community flourished by growing flax and manufacturing linens and carpets. By 1851 it had grown to eleven hundred, about a third of the county's total population. Jansson's death, however, followed by the economic panic of 1857, brought Bishop Hill to financial ruin.

The most enthusiastic builders of ethnic utopias in nineteenth century America were Germans. In 1814 Father George Rapp of Württemberg, convinced that the end of the world was near, emigrated to the United States with seven hundred followers to build a godly new Jerusalem. Harmony, the colony he established in Indiana, was dedicated to celibacy and to communally organized, highly regimented labor. This colony and its successor, Economy (later Ambridge) Pennsylvania, were noted for their physical prosperity and their harsh discipline. Father Rapp was said to have executed his own son for breaking the ban he had imposed upon sexual intercourse, a ban so well observed that the colony literally died of old age in the early twentieth century!

Less bizarre and more permanent were the peaceful, industrious villages of the German pietist settlement at Amana, Iowa. When the original cooperative was dissolved in 1932 (ninety years after it was founded), Amana was operating thirty different commercial enterprises, including a winery and a woolen factory. Its tranquil, noncompetitive atmosphere still survives. Unlike Amana, most nineteenth century utopias were short lived. Their presence, however brief, indicates that some Americans were rejecting the new, competitive industrial society and seeking alternative ways to live.

Most people lacked the utopian commitment to a total restructuring of society. They tended to advocate one or more particular reforms—educational reform, abolitionism, or women's rights—as the key to the perfecting of American society. Ethnic Americans were involved in these humanitarian and democratic crusades in a variety of ways. German born educators played a major role in reforming American schools, for example, from the introduction of kindergartens and physical education to the establishment of graduate level university programs.

Though few ethnic Americans were active abolitionists—with the exception of some of the German "forty-eighters"—many played an indirect role in this vital reform. Scandinavian and German farmers in the midwest were staunchly opposed to the extension of slavery into the territories. Like other western settlers, they wanted to keep the frontier a white man's land of family farms and feared the introduction of a plantation system. In the 1850's the newly organized Republican Party gained popularity among Germans and Scandinavians both because it opposed the extension of slavery and because it favored free homesteads and federal aid for improved transportation. German-born Carl Schurz became a leading figure in the Republican party and helped bring in many other German-Americans. By voting in large numbers for Lincoln in 1860, Germans and Scandinavians in the midwestern states played an indirect role in the eventual ending of slavery throughout the country, though this had not been their intention.

Similarly, ethnic Americans played a role in the movement to improve the status of women. Most ethnic women were too busy rearing large families, earning a living, or both to be much concerned with the seemingly abstract issues of sexual equality raised by Lucy Stone, Elizabeth Stanton, and other pre-Civil War feminists. Moreover, their European ethnic and religious backgrounds reinforced the conventional American view that the only proper place for a woman was in the home, subordinate to a man, whether husband, father, or son.

For many immigrant women, however, reality dictated a lifestyle that departed from the conventional feminine stereotype. Sometimes illness, accident, or desertion eliminated the protective husband. Far from the help of fathers, uncles, or other supportive males, ethnic women became the sole breadwinners, parents, and decision makers for many families in the New World. In addition, thousands of young single women came to America on their own, showing by this act alone an unusual amount of supposedly unfeminine initiative and independence.

At least one ethnic woman, Ernestine Rose, was an active feminist. Ernestine Rose was born in a Polish Jewish community and educated by her father, a rabbi. Rejecting an unwanted arranged marriage (she later arranged her own), she emigrated first to England and then to the United States. Here she became known as an active freethinker and abolitionist, as well as a feminist. Soon after her arrival she began a campaign to give the women of New York State the right to control their own property and to become the guardians of their children. The campaign opened with a petition to the state legislature:

> After a good deal of trouble I obtained five signatures . . . . Some of the ladies said the gentlemen would laugh at them; others, that they had rights enough, and the men said the women had too many rights already. . . . I continued sending petitions with increased numbers of signatures until 1848, when the legislature enacted the law which granted women the right to keep what was her own. But no sooner did it become legal than all the women said: 'Oh, that is right. We ought always to have had that.'

Ernestine Rose became a close and active colleague of Susan B. Anthony and Lucy Stone. Although English was not her native language, she became one of the most effective orators of the women's movement.

Immigrants as Objects of Reform

If economic, social, and "humanitarian" reforms appealed to at least some ethnic Americans, "moral" reforms, such as temperance, sabbatarianism, and other religiously inspired "uplift" endeavors, had virtually no appeal at all. Not only were ethnic Americans unlikely to be participants in such reforms, they were likely to become their targets.

To many Protestant, native-born Americans, the new immigrants were sinners and their lifestyles were plagues to be eliminated.

Emotional, revivalistic religion which had lain dormant since the Great Awakening of colonial times, emerged again in the early nineteenth century. A new generation of zealous evangelists led the sons of the enlightenment freethinkers in a frenzied religious revival that spread from the college campuses to the country campgrounds throughout the land. The revivalist preached a simple, emotional, and democratic message: everyone must accept Jesus Christ as personal savior, and there was no time to lose. The Second Coming was imminent. One evangelist, William Miller, even set the date: October 22, 1844.

> Soon, very soon, God will arise in His anger and the vine of the earth will be reaped. See! See! . . . the clouds have burst asunder; the heavens appear; the great white throne is in sight! . . . He comes! He comes! Behold the Savior comes!—Lift up your heads, ye saints—He comes! He comes! He comes!

In this atmosphere church membership in Protestant evangelical sects soared. A variety of church-directed reform societies arose to make America worthy of the Second Coming. These societies distributed Bibles and religious tracts, sent out speakers, established Sunday schools and built homes for the wayward. They worked diligently to make America godly by converting Catholics and Jews to Protestantism, and by outlawing liquor, Sabbath breaking, and, in some cases, slavery (which churches saw as an institution fraught with sexual temptation for both master and slave).

Many of these reforms were directed at ethnic Americans, who responded with indifference or outright hostility. Efforts to convert immigrant Catholics and Jews met with virtually no success. Efforts to "uplift" ethnic slum dwellers through neighborhood preaching missions were equally unrewarding. A more promising approach was taken by Reverend and Mrs. Lewis Pease, who established a school and an industrial workshop in their mission at Five Points, New York, to fight sin by attacking poverty. The women's home missionary society that had engaged Reverend Pease relieved him of his post, furious that he had neglected his proper duty, preaching sermons to the poor.

The most popular campaign of the new militant Protestantism was the effort to outlaw the "demon rum." While there were advocates of temperance among the Scandinavians, and at least one temperance worker in the Irish Catholic clergy, most ethnic Americans (and many of the native born, as well) considered the effort to ban alcohol as unwarranted and outrageous interference with their lives. To the German-American, beer was as wholesome a drink as water (given the polluted condition of much of the urban water supply, it may often have been more wholesome) and the beer garden was a social center for the entire family. For many Irish-Americans, whiskey made a hard life more bearable, and the corner saloon was one of the few places a man could feel at ease. In addition, Catholics and Jews used wine as part of their religious ceremonies.

Sabbatarianism, strict Puritan observance of Sunday as a day of rest and prayer, had as little appeal as temperance. The Germans and Irish were accustomed to spending their Sundays in socializing and relaxing rather than in worship and meditation. For religious Jews, who observed the Sabbath by keeping their businesses closed on Saturday, Sunday "blue laws" were an economic hardship. They reduced the working week to five instead of six days.

Influenced by pressure from Protestant church groups, townships, counties, and states proposed laws against some or all alcoholic beverages and against Sabbath violation. In many communities the laws created hardships for dissenters. In some areas, people were arrested for working on their own farms on Sunday. Sometimes the laws were defeated because of the opposition of ethnic minorities, as well as other Americans who shared their views. The question of whether the majority can impose its concepts of morality and proper behavior on minorities was raised, debated, but not resolved, and remains controversial as ever.

Frustrated by immigrant resistance to their moral reforms, militant Protestants, including many ministers, were among the leaders of a movement against the "foreigner." Immigrants were associated in the public mind with many of the problems of nineteenth century society—poverty, crime, alcoholism, political corruption. As these were primarily the problems of rapid urbanization, concern about them focused on the urban immigrants, particularly the Irish.

The Scandinavians aroused the least hostility, probably because they were Protestants and because they tended to disappear into the vast prairies of the West. Prejudice against Germans was more common. Because they clung to their native language and, like the colonial Germans, enjoyed a social life of their own, they were considered clannish. They were criticized because of their drinking habits, and the political activities of a few led to the entire group being condemned as abolitionists, socialists, and atheists.

The Chinese bore the brunt of anti-immigrant feeling on the west coast, where their distinctive life style and their economic competition to whites made them immensely unpopular. Taxed, harassed, even lynched by the white population, the Chinese were eventually excluded by law from further immigration.

In most of the rest of the country it was the Irish who occupied the least favored position. Like the Germans, the Irish were condemned as clannish and intemperate. The activities of a few Irish nationalists, as well as the general Irish practice of remitting money to relatives in the old country raised charges of dual loyalty. In a country accustomed to associating virtue with rural living, the heavily urban Irish were associated with the crime, vice, and political corruption of the cities.

Most damaging of all, the Irish were Roman Catholics. To militant, nineteenth century American Protestants, Catholicism was the grossest of superstitions, associated with tyranny, immorality, and as in the colonial era, threats from overseas. Many Americans were convinced that Catholic monarchies were plotting to undo both the American Revolution and the Protestant Reformation and were sending masses of Roman Catholic immigrants to the United States as their instruments in pursuing these sinister aims.

Nativism, and hatred of Irish Catholics in particular, was the dark side of the nineteenth century effort to define Americanism. To some, the process of defining an American nationality required the existence of outsiders against whom they could measure their own qualifications as insiders, or "real" Americans. The existence of an Irish Catholic minority provided the necessary "outsiders."

For nativists, patriotism was heightened by the perception of foreign threats. European monarchies and the Papal States fulfilled this need in the mid nineteenth century. They did, at this time, represent repressive political ideologies hostile to the American democratic philosophy. In 1828 a conservative German scholar Friedrich von Schlegel gave a series of lectures connecting monarchy and Catholicism, while denouncing democracy and Protestantism. Calling the United States the "nursery of revolution," he urged Catholic missions for this troublesome country.

A few such missions were established, but they were of little importance. Certainly the massive immigration of Irish and German Catholics had nothing to do with them. Protestant superpatriots refused to believe this, just as they refused to believe that the social problems of their society could be indigenous, rather than caused by outsiders. Looking back at an idealized past, they blamed Irish Catholic immigration for all the ills of a rapidly changing, increasingly urban society. Samuel F. Morse, inventor of the telegraph, summarized this kind of thinking in his book *Imminent Dangers to the Free Institutions of the United States through Foreign Immigration*, published in 1835.

> How is it possible that foreign turbulence imported by shiploads, that riot and ignorance in hundreds of thousands of human priest-controlled machines should suddenly be thrown into our society and not produce turbulence and excess? Can one throw mud into pure water and not disturb its clearness?

Morse's dire warnings were followed in the 1830's and 1840's by a flood of anti-Catholic literature. Salacious tales of corrupt priests and immoral nuns were relished in the homes of Protestant churchgoers all over the country, serving as a kind of pious pornography. The most famous of such works was Maria Monk's *Awful Disclosures of the Hotel Dieu Nunnery of Montreal*, supposedly an eyewitness account of sexual licentiousness within the convent. According to the book, babies born of illicit unions between nuns and priests were thrown into a pit in a tunnel between the convent and the neighboring monastery. But no such tunnel or pit existed. Moreover, Maria Monk was a delinquent girl, neither a nun nor a Catholic. Her work was exposed as a fraud, and she ended her career in prison for picking the pocket of one of her clients in a house of prostitution. Nevertheless, her book continued to be circulated, read, believed—and profitably imitated.

The Schools as Battlegrounds

Anti-Catholic books, lectures, and sermons added to the cultural and economic tensions already present between the native-born and the ethnic communities. The results were often tragic. Mobs attacked Germans in Midwestern cities and rioting between the native-born and the immigrant was a common occurrence at election time. But no area aroused more emotion-laden conflict—and more violence—than the school.

The mid nineteenth century saw the beginnings of the public school system in most of the United States. The public elementary school—or common school, as it was called at the time—stood at the center of concurrent, and often conflicting social movements. Unlike traditional European societies, which looked reverently to the past, the United States was a new society whose members concentrated their attention upon the future. Immigrants and native-born, ethnic and nonethnics alike—everyone agreed that their best efforts and sacrifices were to be directed toward building for their children. In the nineteenth century, as today, observers from overseas noted that the United States was a child-centered society. In a future-oriented, child-centered society, the school became the focus of enormous hopes and expectations, and the object of enormous emotional as well as financial investment. Because different socioeconomic classes and ethnic groups had different hopes and expectations, no "common" school could possibly satisfy them all.

Urban working people hoped that the new common schools would offer social mobility for the next generation. In colonial America craftsmen had taught remunerative skills to their sons through the apprenticeship system. By the middle of the nineteenth century, however, factory-made goods were making many of these traditional skills obsolete. Skilled workmen realized that their children needed a new kind of education, a "book-learning" education, if they were to compete successfully in the world of commerce and industry. The same Jacksonian democrats who fought against the economic "monopolies" that deprived them of equal opportunity also fought against educational monopoly for the same reason. Unable to afford the private schooling available to the rich, they demanded public education as necessary to the realization of the American dream of equal opportunity and, more specifically, socioeconomic mobility for their children.

As revisionist historians of American education have recently pointed out, not all advocates of the common school were working people motivated by the desire for economic advancement. Many of the founders of common schools saw these institutions as instruments of social control rather than as avenues of social mobility. Linking urbanization with immigration, educators hoped to use schools as means of fighting crime and "turbulence" by providing urban children with the structured environment their families could not or would not provide. "As population increases, and especially as artificial wants multiply, the temptations increase, and the guards and securities must increase also, or society will deteriorate," wrote an educational reformer.

Schools were established to take young people away from the evil influences of the street—and of the slum home—and teach them "control," "self-discipline," "earnestness," and "restraint." Education was seen as a bulwark not only against crime, but also against sexual licentiousness (the "passions" of which middle class educators were so much afraid) and against labor disturbances, unions, and strikes. Diligence, docility, punctuality, cleanliness, and industriousness were the "hidden curriculum" of the new schools. These schools were designed to instill a Protestant, even Puritan, middle-class morality and life style in the children of the urban, often the immigrant, poor.

The founders of the common schools had patriotic as well as moral goals. Education was seen as the handmaiden of democracy. The electorate must be educated if it was to make wise decisions. Patriotic education it was hoped, would teach children the duty of changing laws and leaders by ballot rather than by rebellion. Moreover, it was believed, education would eliminate the political corruption of the cities. Horace Mann wrote:

> If the responsibleness and value of the elective franchise were duly appreciated . . . elections would be among the most solemn and religious days in the calendar. Men would approach them, not only with preparation and solicitude, but with the sobriety and solemnity, with which descreet and religious-minded men meet the great crises of life.

Education would end the practice of the urban working class, many of them Irish and German, of making election day an occasion for drinking and brawling as well as voting.

Finally, many of the early school reformers saw the common school as the place in which to forge a common American culture. In the common school children of varying denominations would come together to hear the Bible read and to worship together "a common Father." The debate over the use of German in Pennsylvania's common schools called forth comments such as the following: " . . . we ought no longer to be divided into separate races, and by distinct languages and habits. . . ." and "I think that the whole people of the state should be amalgamated as soon as that end can possibly be accomplished."

The new public schools were seen by their founders as crucibles of a common American culture—virtuous, Protestant, republican, and Anglo-Saxon. It was important, then, that the major threats to that culture—Catholics, the urban poor, immigrants from nonrepublican lands—become part of that system. Despite various stratagems to attract them, however, these very groups did not flock to the new common schools. Impoverished parents sometimes kept their children out of school because their meager earnings were vital to the immediate survival of the family. Because school was not compulsory, many children simply refused to attend. Besides, classrooms were usually grim, joyless places, offering little that could compare with the excitement of the street.

Parents and children resented the condescending attitude of school authorities who considered them inferior and tainted and who viewed their lives as devoid of beauty, culture, or virtue. Nor did immigrant parents share the optimism of the native-born working class that schools were in fact certain avenues to social mobility. Assessing their situation realistically, they saw that their children were unlikely to remain long enough to reap the much touted social and economic benefits, if indeed such benefits existed. Of what value was schooling in a society where "no Irish need apply"?

Finally, many immigrants resisted the public schools because they did not want their children absorbed in the Protestant Anglo-Saxon culture represented by the common school. To avoid this, Norwegians, Swedes, and Germans—Protestant and Catholic alike—set up schools in which their native language, religion, and historical traditions were preserved. The largest group to resist the common schools for religious and cultural reasons, were the Irish Catholics. Their resistance, which seemed especially sinister, led to bitter controversy and violence.

The earliest Catholic schools in the East were often private convent schools, patronized by the daughters of wealthy families, Protestant as well as Catholic. Such a school was the Ursuline convent in suburban Boston, forty of whose sixty pupils were the daughters of wealthy Unitarians. The failure of a rival Protestant school, the violently anti-Catholic sermons of ministers like Lyman Beecher, and recurrent friction between native-born and Irish-Catholic laborers touched off a riot in which anti-Catholic mobs burned the convent school to the ground. The nuns and their pupils barely escaped with their lives. Leaders of the mob were prosecuted, but their trial was a mockery; no one was convicted and no reparations were paid. Lyman Beecher continued to warn Protestant America in sermons and in writings of the dangers to republican institutions inherent in the sinister Catholic schools.

Private convent schools were only for the few, however. The vast majority of Catholics, especially the new immigrants, could not afford them for their children. Recognizing the need, urban parishes opened schools for the poor. These parish schools lacked the teachers, facilities, and above all the money to educate the masses of new children. For most children, the choice was between education in the new common schools or no education at all.

The choice was not an easy one. The Catholic clergy recognized the Protestant tone of the public schools, pointing out that the textbooks made derogatory references to Catholicism and that Protestant prayers, hymns, and Bible reading were part of the daily schedule. Irish priests discouraged parents from sending children to the public schools. Needless to say, this only heightened the suspicions of a Protestant population rapidly becoming committed to the public school as the cornerstone of Americanism. Could people who rejected the public schools be good Americans, it was asked?

In New York, Bishop John Hughes tried to solve the educational problems of his flock in 1840 by requesting money from the Public School Society for separate Catholic schools. He was encouraged by Governor Seward's public statement that

> The children of foreigners are too often deprived of the educational advantages of our system of public education in consequence of prejudice arising from differences of language or religion. . . . I do not hesitate, therefore, to recommend the establishment of schools in which they may be instructed by teachers speaking the same language with themselves and professing the same religion.

Seward's statement and Hughes' request touched off a storm of controversy. Catholics considered their request for part of the public school fund only fair, as their taxes contributed to that fund. Protestants worried that sectarian demands for public funding of parochial schools were unconstitutional and, worse yet, subversive of the whole idea of the "common" school. Already, other churches were requesting funds for their schools. If such requests were granted, could the public school system survive?

In New York the issue was resolved by the institution of local school districts, locally controlled. In their own neighborhoods, at least, Catholics could eliminate the most objectionable features of the Protestant public school system by secularizing the education offered and by appointing secular Catholic teachers. Bishop Hughes regarded this as a temporary makeshift, however. His goal was not secular education, but Catholic education taught by members of religious orders. With great financial sacrifice, the nineteenth century Catholic community in New York and indeed throughout the country, moved toward that goal. Meanwhile the public school system, recognizing its need to serve a heterogeneous population, became increasingly secularized.

Bishop Francis Kenrick of Philadelphia was faced with essentially the same problem as Bishop Hughes of New York. Rather than request public funds for parish schools, he asked that Catholic children be allowed to bring their own Bibles to public schools and be excused from religious instruction there. When the school board agreed, angry Protestant militants accused Catholics of trying to "kick the Bible out of the school." "Godless" schools could not be proper vehicles for real Americanism! In 1844 anti-Catholic "patriots" held a mass meeting in the Irish Catholic Kensington section. Rioting broke out. Catholic churches and schools were destroyed, several people killed, and many more wounded.

Nativism—Its Rise and Fall

The anti-Catholic violence begun during the school controversies escalated into institutionalized nativist activity. "A revolution has begun," announced a New York nativist publication, the *American Republican*. In the 1830's and 1840's nativists formed secret societies such as the Order of the Star Spangled Banner, the Order of the Sons of the Sires of '76, and the Order of United Americans, with a women's auxiliary, the United Daughters of America. Quasi-political from the beginning, these organizations united with local nativist political parties in the early 1850's to form the Native American, or Know Nothing, Party. Anti-foreign and anti-Catholic, the Know Nothings sought to deny political rights to immigrants, lengthen the naturalization period, and above all, close the doors to further immigration.

A strange collection of people took shelter within the Know Nothing Party. Native-born working men who were not rising as fast as they felt they should joined because they feared the competition of immigrant labor. Urban workers joined because they saw Catholics a threat to the existence of public schools, and hence to their children's futures. Southerners joined because they considered all foreigners abolitionists. In the North, on the other hand, abolitionists joined because they saw immigrants as stumbling blocks to their reforms, as did temperance workers and Sabbatarians. Though the party was rabidly anti-Catholic, French Catholics joined. As native-born Americans, they felt their position in the nation, and in the Church, threatened by the arrival of the Irish!

The Know Nothing Party had "as many elements of persistence as an anti-cholera or anti-potato-rot party would have," observed Horace Greeley, a contemporary editor. The party won control of the state legislatures of Rhode Island, New Hampshire, Connecticut, and Maryland in 1853 and of Kentucky, Texas, and California two years later, but its achievements were negligible. Know-Nothing legislators investigated convents and other Catholic institutions, usually as a pretext for junkets around the state at the taxpayers' expense, but did little else. In the presidential election of 1856 the party's candidate, Millard Fillmore, carried only the state of Maryland. Politically, the nativist movement was dead before the end of the decade.

It is significant that a nativist political party arose on the eve of the Civil War. Nativism was a last attempt to find an issue which would unite a divided nation by transcending increasingly bitter sectional disputes over slavery, tariffs, internal improvements, and the nature of the Union itself. These were the real issues confronting the nation in the 1850's, and a national outcry against the "foreigner" could not make them go away, any more than it could ease the stresses and strains of rapid social change.

Lack of relevance to America's real problems killed the Know Nothing Party, but other factors helped. Its following had always been a vocal but small minority. Native-born Americans opposed nativism and immigration restriction as denials of the principles of religious freedom and equal opportunity for which they believed their country stood. Many individuals, including Abraham Lincoln, rose to the defense of the newcomers.

Ethnic communities themselves fought nativism. Priests and rabbis explained their "alien" faiths in articles, lectures, and public debates with their Protestant detractors. Ethnic leaders appealed to economic expediency as well as to idealism in defense of continued immigration, pointing out fallacies in the nativist arguments and matching them statistic for statistic.

Faced with nativist attacks, German-Americans tended to withdraw into their own ethnic communities, strengthening them until they became bastions for survival. The Irish, on the other hand, took the offensive, seizing control of the machinery of urban governments whenever possible to guarantee their rights. The Plug-Uglies, Blood Tubs, Rip Raps, and other Irish gangs of New York fought nativism with their fists, defending Catholic churches from mobs and forcing Know Nothing voters away from the polls.

Irish intellectuals began the now time honored tradition in which minority groups write their own histories to prove what good Americans they are. When German, English, and American historians attributed all favorably viewed aspects of life to the inventiveness of the Teutons and Anglo-Saxons, Irish-American historians countered with the equally unrealistic "Celtic Myth." According to the Celtic myth, representative government, trial by jury, popular education, and other "American" traditions originated in Ireland. America was discovered by St. Brendan the Navigator, Columbus was rowed ashore by an Irishman, and Irish soldiers won the Revolutionary war almost singlehandedly. Native-born Americans were scarcely aware of the existence of the Celtic myth, but it boosted the confidence and self-esteem of the Irish newcomers.

The Civil War itself helped to kill the nativist movement. The great crusade to save the Union and abolish slavery swallowed up all other crusades—including the nativist movement. In the Union and in the Confederacy ethnic communities joined their neighbors in four years of tragic fighting. Most immigrants lived in the North, where they responded in large numbers to Lincoln's call for troops. However they felt about the issue of slavery—and most shared the antiblack prejudice of their society—they had suffered much to cast their lot with the United States and did not want to see it destroyed.

After the Civil War interest in nativism, like interest in many other prewar crusades, declined. Four years of bloodletting left the nation physically and emotionally exhausted. Though some individuals remained loyal to their favorite causes, the reforming zeal of the majority was spent. America entered a postwar period of materialism. Individuals devoted themselves to the pursuit of their own interests— and the main interest of almost everyone seemed to be making money. Ethnic Americans, whose main concern had, of necessity, been economic survival, fitted comfortably into this national pattern.

Contrary to the dire predictions of the nativists, ethnic Americans did adapt themselves successfully to the United States. In the postwar decades many moved up the socioeconomic ladder from poverty to solid working class, from unskilled to skilled occupations. Economic improvement brought with it changes in lifestyle, so that ethnic Americans no longer seemed threatening to the "American" way of life. While the Irish tended to advance more slowly than the Germans and Scandinavians, even they produced their millionaires. By the end of the century, this once-despised community had produced a large number of upwardly mobile "lace curtain" families whose obsession with the proprieties rivaled that of the native-born middle class.

In addition to their own hard work and determination, ethnic Americans in the middle decades of the nineteenth century had still another factor in their favor. They had arrived in a country that thought of itself as young with an unlimited potential for growth. In such a country there was ample room, geographically and psychologically for newcomers. Nativists worried that too many "outsiders" would destroy the nation, but most Americans did not agree. Firmly convinced that environment was stronger than heredity, they believed that their beneficent land, air, and institutions would make the immigrant a "new man"—an American. If, as the evangelists said, a man could be "born again," transformed from sinner to saint, then why couldn't the immigrant be transformed from foreigner to American? Despite the doubts and hesitations of some, nineteenth century America's unbounded optimism, its belief in the inevitability of progress, and its confidence in its own strength and rectitude made it secure enough to accept the new ethnic communities.

CHAPTER 6

The Urban Ghetto:
Immigrants in Industrial America,
1880-1924

By 1880 the Irish, German, and Scandinavian immigrants, once so alien and even frightening, were familiar figures on the American scene, their American-born children growing to adulthood. Soon, however, native-born Americans (including, often, the children of these earlier immigrants) would express alarm about a new group of "aliens" in their midst. Another wave of immigration was entering the country, a wave which began in the 1880's and peaked in the early twentieth century. The people it brought congregated in the great metropolitan areas, creating massive ethnic ghettos whose remnants are still visible. Who were these late nineteenth and early twentieth century immigrants? Why did they come? What conditions of life and work did they find in the great cities of a nation which was rapidly becoming the industrial, financial, and military leader of the entire world?

Immigration at the Turn of the Century

Contemporary observers were struck by the rapid increase in the number of immigrants. Total immigration in the three decades preceding the Civil War had numbered five million. Between 1860 and 1890 that number doubled, and between 1890 and 1914 it tripled. Over a million newcomers entered annually in the peak years of 1905, 1906, 1907, 1910, 1913, and 1914. By 1920 almost sixty per cent of the population of cities of one hundred thousand or more inhabitants were first or second generation ethnic Americans. Over three quarters of New York City's school children had foreign born parents.

As the century neared its close, there was a steady decline in immigration from the British Isles, Germany, and the Scandinavian countries. At the same time, immigration from eastern and southern Europe increased. By 1896 Italians, East European Jews, Poles, Ukrainians, Slovaks, Bohemians, Hungarians, Greeks, Portuguese, Armenians, Syrians, and Lebanese outnumbered western European immigrants, and by 1907 they constituted over eighty per cent of the total. They were joined by smaller numbers from Asia and the Western Hemisphere—including many Japanese, French Canadians, Mexicans, West Indians.

The religious backgrounds of the newcomers varied widely. The largest single religious group was Roman Catholic, but millions were Jews or members of Greek and Russian Orthodox churches, and some were Moslems and Buddhists. The cultural baggage they brought to America was equally varied. Slavic farmers came from traditional, closely knit peasant villages similar in many ways to those from which the earlier Irish, German, and Scandinavian peasants had come. Southern Italians were also tillers of the soil, but they lived in rural towns, often miles from the fields they tilled for their absentee landlords. Jews, too, were town dwellers. Forbidden for centuries to own land, they earned a precarious living in petty commerce and in crafts such as woodworking, capmaking, and tailoring.

The peasant village was the primary social and economic institution in the life of the Slavic farmer. For the southern Italian, this function was fulfilled by the family, a tightly knit unit in which the interests of the individual were subordinated to those of the group. The Japanese left a land in which nationalism, symbolized by devotion to the Emperor, was a strong unifying element. Jews, on the other hand, were scarcely touched by the emerging nationalism of the countries within which they lived. The unifying element in their lives was their age old religious tradition, an all-encompassing way of life. Clearly the cultural backgrounds of these immigrants varied widely and were radically different from the industrialized, secular, and individualistic society to which they came.

The newcomers varied just as widely in educational background and in skills. Half of the Italians were unable to read or write, but Jews, Bohemians, and Finns had a high literacy rate. Ninety-eight per cent of the Japanese who immigrated were literate, a percentage considerably higher than that of the total American population. Most of the early twentieth century immigrants had agricultural skills. But Syrians, Lebanese, and Jews often had commercial experience, which proved invaluable in the increasingly nonagricultural American economy.

Russian Jews and Scots had the highest percentage of skilled laborers of all immigrant groups.

The late nineteenth century marked the appearance of numerous "birds of passage," immigrants who spent a few years in the United States and then returned, permanently or temporarily, to their former homes. The great steamship lines, which made travel faster, cheaper, and safer than it had ever been before, made this possible. The movement of these "birds of passage" closely followed the ups and downs of the American business cycle, with some individuals shuttling back and forth many times as though unable to decide where they really wanted to live.

For every hundred immigrants to enter the country between 1900 and 1910, thirty eight left. Most of these were young single men—Italians, Slavs, Greeks, or Japanese—who had come to earn enough money to buy land or a small business in the old country. Many reached this goal; a majority of the small landowners in some south Italian villages were returned American immigrants. Others went home without reaching their goals, victims of tuberculosis, industrial accidents, or discouragement and disillusion.

Like earlier immigrants, most came to better themselves economically. By 1880 East European peasants were feeling the same pressures of too much population on too little land that had set their West European counterparts moving a generation or two earlier. As industrialization and urbanization moved from west to east, eastern European farmers had to compete with newly-consolidated large estates in supplying food to the growing cities. They also had to compete with the grain growers of Argentina, Canada, the United States, and Australia, whose products could now be shipped everywhere on newly constructed railroads and newly opened steamship lines. The following letter was written to an emigrant aid society by a Polish peasant in the early twentieth century. It could as easily have been written by an Irish, German, or Scandinavian immigrant a generation or two earlier.

> I have a very great wish to go to America. I want to leave my native country because we are six children and we have very little land. . . . So it is difficult for us to live. Father got me married and gave me . . . 200 rubles . . . my share (of the value of the family farm) and now I am alone with my wife. . . . Wages are very small, just enough to live, so I would like to go (to America) in the name of our Lord God; perhaps I would earn more there. . . . I am a healthy boy 24 years old. I do not fear any work.

Local problems set people in motion. Sometimes new transportation facilities brought in competition that ruined the livelihood of the local merchants and craftsmen. The McKinley Tariff of 1890 ruined the Bohemian button making industry, causing many Bohemians to come to the United States. French tariffs on Italian wines and Greek currants caused the emigration of Italians and Greeks from the wine and currant producing areas.

Many individuals made the decision to emigrate because of personal difficulties. Oscar Ameringer's autobiography, *If You Don't Weaken*, is a case study of such a decision. Even as a child, Ameringer did not fit into the life of his village in the Austro-Hungarian Empire. He outraged the staunchly Catholic school authorities by writing an essay favorable to Protestantism. An impulsive teenager, he plunged into a tavern battle to defend a peasant who was being abused by the emperor's soldiers. This incident led directly to his emigration. As Ameringer explained:

> I was already the town Pariah. In the opinion of its burghers and burghesses, all but mother, I was doomed and damned. There were only two courses for young hellions like me. The gallows and hell—or America. So to America I went. There were no tears shed at my departure, save mother's and mine.

As in earlier years "America letters" played a role in recruiting immigrants. Equally important, however, was the role of the "bird of passage," the former neighbor, returned from the "Golden Land" for a visit or to stay. The "Amerikanec" was an enviable character, glorious in his store-bought blue serge suit and gold watch, generously distributing gifts to friends and relatives from a bulging, imitation leather suitcase. Children listened wide-eyed to his tales of ranches as big as their entire province, of buildings as tall as mountains, of trees a thousand years old—and made up their minds to see these wonders for themselves.

Many immigrants were never quite sure why they came. They were the new victims of the old disease, "America Fever," which spread with industrialization and economic hardship. In his autobiography, *An American in the Making*, Marcus Ravage described how an emigration epidemic hit his Rumanian village. Prices plummeted as an entire village tried to sell its possessions all at once and headed for the local train station. "America had become, as it were, the fashionable place to go," wrote Ravage. "All my relatives and all our neighbors—in fact, everybody who was anybody—had either gone or was going to New York . . . and what took place in Vaslui was only typical of what had come to be the state of affairs everywhere in Roumania."

Political and religious oppression were important motives for emigration in the late nineteenth and early twentieth centuries. In the multinational empires (the German, the Russian, the Austro-Hungarian, and the Ottoman) the numerous ethnic groups were asserting their distinctive national identities. Intellectual and political leaders of these "subject nationalities" revived traditional languages, literatures, and religions and began to work for political as well as cultural independence. The rulers responded—sometimes with concessions, usually with repression. Poles within the German Empire were forbidden to teach their native language. The Russian Empire launched a program of forcible "Russification" of many minorities. Armenians and Greeks were constantly harassed, even massacred in the Turkish Empire.

The largest oppressed minority to come to the United States were the Jews of Russia. Wracked by the political and economic crisis that was to culminate in the Russian Revolution of 1917, the tottering Tsarist Regime adopted a policy of vicious anti-Semitism in order to divert attention from its own failures. Jews were segregated into the crowded "Pale of Settlement," denied access to education and employment, and systematically reduced to poverty by special taxes, fees, and the need to pay constant bribes in order to survive. The Russian government instigated periodic massacres, or pogroms. Mary Antin described these pogroms in her autobiography *The Promised Land* as times when ignorant peasants, filled with vodka and slanderous stories, invaded the Jewish quarters:

> They attacked them (the Jews) with knives and clubs and scythes and axes, killed them or tortured them, and burned their houses. . . . Jews who escaped pogroms came to Polotzk (Mary Antin's town) with wounds on them, and horrible, horrible stories of little babies torn limb from limb before their mothers' eyes. Only to hear these things made one sob and sob and choke with pain. People who saw such things never smiled any more . . . sometimes their hair turned white in a day, and some people became insane on the spot.

Millions of East European Jews fled to the United States, where they formed a new ethnic community second in size only to that of the Italians. Their immigration peaks were linked to outbreaks of persecution rather than to the American business cycle. Entire families left and rarely went back.

Entering the Economy

If most of the problems that drove immigrants from their homes between 1880 and 1924 were not new, neither were the attractions that lured them to the United States. The expansion of our transportation and manufacturing facilities and the building of our cities continued at a dizzying pace. This remarkable economic growth created an insatiable demand for unskilled labor, a demand which, as in the earlier decades, could not have been met without immigration. By the end of the nineteenth century the labor force of the western industrialized areas of Europe no longer wanted the unskilled and poorly paid jobs America had to offer. To the agricultural laborers of southern and eastern Europe, however, such positions were attractive.

Immigrants went where the jobs were—to the cities. By the turn of the century the frontier was gone, and the grain-growing prairies and other agricultural areas had fallen upon hard times. On the other hand, the cities which had been primarily commercial centers before the Civil War were now manufacturing centers as well, with a corresponding geometric increase in job opportunities. It is not surprising, then, that over three quarters of the new immigrants settled in the cities, creating foreign colonies of unprecedented size.

Many Americans were alarmed at the enormous concentration of immigrants in the cities. Uncomfortable with its giant new metropolitan areas (by the turn of the century over half the American population was urban), America believed that immigrants would assimilate faster in the presumably more wholesome environment of the farm. Charitable societies, churches, even foreign countries from which the immigrants came tried to encourage the newcomers to spread out, to go south or west, and to work the land. Such efforts met with very limited success.

One such effort was the campaign to bring Italian farmers to the southern states to supplement (or perhaps to replace) black farm labor. Thousands went but soon complained about working conditions and prejudice. Many southern states had severe laws requiring the poor to work off their debts or go to prison—laws originally passed to keep blacks "in their place," but which now victimized Italian labor as well. In some areas Italian workers were deprived of their civil liberties, even lynched. Between 1874 and 1915 twenty five were killed in Arkansas, Louisiana, Mississippi, and North Carolina.

Italians were more fortunate than blacks, however, because they had an outside government to speak for them. The Italian government protested and tried to get written guarantees from local authorities that Italian immigrants to the South would be protected. Because of the failure of local authorities to protect Italians or even to punish offenses against them, the Italian government soon refused to issue passports to immigrants bound for the southern states. The official campaign to get Italians to "spread out" as agricultural workers in the South came to an end.

Some immigrants did settle successfully on the land. Assisted by their own philanthropies, a small number of Jews established flourishing agricultural settlements in New Jersey. Italians and Slavs came to rural areas to build railroads and sometimes stayed to farm. The most successful specialized in one or two cash crops, perhaps peaches or lettuce or onions, and sold them in the nearby urban centers. Italian families sometimes peddled their own produce in the towns, beginning a long lasting and profitable connection with the urban food distribution industry. Poles bought the cheapest, least desirable land and coaxed it into productivity. According to Polish-American historian Joseph Wytrwal, the fact that Polish immigrants had practically to create the land they farmed made it especially dear to them. "They consider it a part of themselves and they love it as much as they formerly loved their own dear Polish land."

Immigrants from northern Italy established vineyards and orchards in California in a climate very similar to what they had known in Italy. On the west coast Japanese replaced Chinese as agricultural day laborers. Despite discrimination they were often able to acquire farms of their own. Like the Poles in the East, they purchased marginal land, arid and abandoned, and coaxed it into productivity with prodigious labor.

Most of the newcomers turned their backs on agriculture. Like the Irish a few decades earlier, the south Italians considered agriculture a "cruel stepmother," synonomous with "degradation, humiliation, and virtual starvation." In Italy rich landowners, lawyers, physicians, nobles—the people who counted—lived in the cities. Little wonder, then, that in a land of urban opportunities this is where the southern Italians went.

Most immigrants could not invest the time needed to make money from farming, even if they had wanted to. They needed cash immediately—to pay debts, to provide for themselves, and to send help to the families they had left behind. Cash would buy the farm or shop in the old country that would mean comfort and security for loved ones. A job in a factory or mine, street vending, construction work—these were the best means of obtaining ready money. "Cash, mobility, and the dream of going home at the earliest opportunity dominated his thoughts," says Theodore Saloutos of the Greek immigrant. The statement is applicable to many Italians, Slavs, and others as well.

The new steamship lines channeled most of the immigration into New York City, where Ellis Island became an assembly line for processing new arrivals. Many Poles and other Slavs moved inland to Buffalo, Pittsburgh, Detroit, Cleveland, and Chicago. The coal mines and iron and steel works of Pennsylvania and Ohio attracted Poles, Lithuanians, Ukrainians, south Slavs, and Italians. Working from bases in the northeast, Armenians, Lebanese, and Syrians peddled dry goods and notions from coast to coast.

Most ethnic groups, including the two largest, the Italians and the Jews, concentrated in the industrial Northeast—urban New England, New York, Pennsylvania, and New Jersey—where job opportunities were plentiful and varied. The Italians and Slavs did the pick and shovel work earlier done by the Irish. French Canadians and immigrants from the Middle East worked in New England's textile mills. Skilled in the needle trades before their arrival, Jews created and dominated the ready-to-wear garment industry of New York City. Jews, Italians, Bohemians, Hungarians, along with the Germans and Irish, made the clothing, costume jewelry, artificial flowers, suspenders, shoes, lamps, soap, cigars, candy, and an incredible variety of other items, large and small, that were produced in the dark workshops of the eastern cities.

Women worked as hard as men. Middle Eastern women helped their husbands peddle or managed small shops, as did women of virtually every ethnic group. Slovak and Bohemian women did domestic work, a highly undesirable job which other immigrant women considered "too heavy." Women did kitchen work and cleaning in hotels, restaurants, and office buildings. Jewish women were most commonly found in the clothing "sweatshops." Immigrant women of virtually every group worked in foundries, canneries, twine mills, tobacco factories, stockyards, and commercial laundries. Those who stayed at home often ran rooming houses for new arrivals. By cooking, cleaning, and washing for ten or more boarders, such women often earned as much or more than their husbands.

Sometimes immigrants came to live with friends or relatives, who took them to their own employers to find a job. But many were alone, penniless, unable to speak English, and therefore unable to get a job without outside help. Such people turned to the padrones or to the employment agencies, both of which provided needed services—at a price.

The padrone was a private labor broker of the same ethnic background as the group he served—Italian, Greek, Bulgarian, Turkish, or Mexican. He was a middleman who recruited laborers, sometimes in Europe, more often in ethnic neighborhoods in American cities, and delivered them, for a very high commission, to American employers who needed their services. Workers from the Northeast were sent as far south as Florida and as far west as Nebraska. Workers from midwestern cities were sent to New England or even to California. Gangs of immigrant labor organized by padrones worked on railroads, in mines, and on temporary construction sites. They harvested timber, farm products, and ice.

Some padrones stayed at the job with the laborers, acting as interpreters and as mediators between them and the English-speaking bosses or foremen. Often padrones provided lodging for their clients as well as the ethnic food they enjoyed and would not otherwise be able to obtain.

Because he spoke their language and provided services not otherwise available to the "green" immigrant, the padrone was able to compete successfully with private, government, and charitable employment agencies, despite the exorbitant fees charged by the more unscrupulous. In 1900 padrones controlled over half of the Italian laborers in New York City. The padrone system was most pervasive in the early years, when most immigrants were inexperienced. Greater sophistication on the part of the workers, the beginnings of unionization, and the labor shortage caused by World War I finally broke the power of the padrones.

Private employment agencies competed with the padrones. They recruited unskilled labor for seasonal or temporary employment in rural areas, or for construction, wrecking, or other unskilled jobs in the cities. Like the padrones, they sent large gangs of workers hundreds of miles for employment and were, if anything, more exploitive and less responsible than the padrones. Fees were erratic, but always high. "We charge all we can get," admitted one agency.

Agencies specializing in immigrant labor rarely investigated prospective employers and were often parties to deceit. Young girls were sent, under false pretenses, to work at "sporting houses" and similar institutions. Workers traveled many miles to misrepresented, even nonexistent jobs and were often stranded far from home. A young Slavic workman was sent from Chicago to Wyoming in midwinter for a nonexistent job. Penniless, he walked miles in deep snow to reach home, where his foot was amputated because of frostbite. Two Hungarian immigrants from Chicago were stranded in Arkansas by a disreputable agency. When they tried to board a freight train to get home, the local police shot them.

The Urban Ghetto

Immigrants from southern and eastern Europe concentrated in the largest American cities produced something new—the twentieth century urban ghetto. These were enclaves of ethnic Americans—little Italys, Polonias, little Syrias, "Jewtowns," and other foreign quarters— in the heart of the sprawling American metropolises. Each ghetto had its own distinctive national flavor, its own churches, its own games and amusements, its own newspapers, and its own "green ones," new arrivals in beards, kerchiefs, and other distinctive dress. "You could always tell which state you were in," reminisced journalist Mike Royko, "by the odors of the food stores and the open kitchen windows, the sound of the foreign or familiar language, and by whether a stranger hit you in the head with a rock."

Before the Civil War, the Irish had often settled in shantytowns on the outskirts of the growing cities, as well as in the cities themselves. By

1900, however, the outskirts were too far away from the industrial centers to attract immigrant settlement. The growing "streetcar suburbs" that surrounded the cities housed the middle class and the skilled workers. They were financially out of the immigrant's reach. New ethnic Americans crowded into the old housing near the commerical and industrial centers so that the various breadwinners in the family could be within walking distance of a variety of possible jobs.

Large ethnic ghettos developed for a number of reasons. Sometimes an ethnic group was heavily concentrated in one industry—Jews in the garment factories of New York, or Poles and Lithuanians in the stockyards of Chicago. Naturally the neighborhood nearest the job housed a heavy concentration of that particular ethnic group. There were other factors as well. Once a neighborhood had a large number of one ethnic group, it developed ethnic institutions to serve them—stores specializing in favored ethnic foods, churches similar to those they had known in the old country, parochial schools teaching the traditional language and history. The existence of these institutions attracted an even heavier concentration of this ethnic group into the neighborhood.

Prejudice played an important role in the creation and perpetuation of the ethnic ghetto. People who wanted to move elsewhere often found that they could not buy or rent housing at any price. An Italian-American minister and social worker, Constantine Panunzio, tells how the Italian vice consul, "a man of fine and keen intelligence, tall and pleasing in appearance, and a gentleman in every sense of the word," was unable to find decent housing in a major American city. Even the chairman of a Protestant Americanization committee turned him down because "the neighbors would object to having an Italian (pronouncing the "I" long) next door to them."

"Majority" Americans regarded the mushrooming ethnic ghettos with a mixture of fascination and horror. To some, they were quaint, romantic places where one went "slumming" to watch Sicilian church processions, Syrian ritual sword dances, and other "exotic" celebrations. Robert Woods, organizer of the National Foundation of Settlements, loved to wander through the Italian quarter of Boston, where "the lightheartedness of the Italians and their keen love of pleasure makes an atmosphere so full of gayety that a spectator . . . is led to overlook the many discomforts. . . ." In the Jewish quarter, Woods admired the fine old brass candlesticks and leather bound parchment books in the shop windows. He also admired the Jewish children, "all great lovers of music . . . who dance as if by instinct"—a stereotype usually reserved for blacks!

William Dean Howells, the best known novelist of the day, took a romantic view of New York's Jewish quarter:

Everywhere I saw splendid types of that old Hebrew world which had the sense if not the knowledge of God when all the rest of us were sunk in heathen darkness. There were women with oval faces and olive tints, and clear dark eyes, relucent as evening pools, and men with long beards of jetty black or silvery white, and the noble profiles of their race. I said to myself that it was among such throngs that Christ walked, it was among such people that he chose his disciples and his friends. . . .

Other American intellectuals, equally attracted by the color and vitality of the immigrant quarters, described them more realistically. In his famous novel, *The Jungle* Upton Sinclair wrote about the grinding poverty of Chicago's Slavs, who worked knee deep in blood and entrails in the grotesque demiworld of the stockyards. A group of urban artists, derisively termed the "Ash Can" school, found the ghettos excellent material for their socially conscious paintings. The Danish born writer and photographer Jacob Riis stirred the conscience of the comfortable with his photographs of ghetto life and his widely acclaimed exposé of immigrant (and native) urban poverty, *How the Other Half Lives.*

Cherry Street. Be a little careful, please! The hall is dark and you might stumble over the children. . . . Not that it would hurt them; kicks and cuffs are their daily diet. . . . The sinks are in the hallway, that all tenants may have access—and all be poisoned alike by their summer stenches. Hear the pumps squeak! It is the lullaby of tenement house babes. In summer, when a thousand thirsty throats pant for a cooling drink in this block, it is worked in vain. But the saloon whose open door you passed in the hall, is always there. . . . Listen! That short hacking cough, that tiny, helpless wail—what do they mean? . . . a sadly familiar story—The child is dying with measles. With half a chance it might have lived; but it had none. That dark bedroom killed it.

If intellectuals saw the ghettos as exotic, romantic, or tragic, most other people saw them as filthy and dangerous. To many, the ghettos were alien cesspools of alcoholism, crime, and vice. What was the early twentieth century ethnic ghetto really like? Obviously the answer would vary from ghetto to ghetto, from city to city, and from decade to decade. Some generalizations can, nevertheless, be made.

Ethnic ghettos were ugly. Immigrant quarters in mill and mining towns consisted of grim and grimy rows of ramshackle frame houses along trash-littered, muddy streets. Smoke, soot, and other industrial wastes made urban ghettos in industrial cities as unwholesome as they were ugly. Industrial Pittsburgh, as journalist Lincoln Steffens put it, "looked like hell, literally."

Ethnic quarters in late nineteenth century New York City were characterized by tightly packed rows of tenements as much as seven stories high in which only one room in four received direct air or light from outside. These were damp, foul smelling, rickety structures, lacking indoor plumbing or water supply, and, in the words of a little girl who lived in one, "so dark it seemed as if there weren't no sky." Ventilation was so bad that four hundred and twenty tenement dwellers died from intense and continuous heat in August of 1896.

As in the pre-Civil War era, housing was bad because the supply fell far short of the demand. Inadequate buildings quickly and cheaply constructed to meet temporary needs were pressed into service as permanent dwelling places, always for more families than they had been intended. Ghetto housing was bad; but because of the great demand, it was not cheap. Many immigrant families could not afford the rent—hence the widespread practice of taking in boarders. About half of all Hungarian households included boarders; among Lithuanians the number reached seventy per cent.

In the typical ethnic ghetto every building was crowded. People slept on fire escapes, on the roof, in stair wells, and within the apartments on rows of mattresses spread edge to edge across the floor. In mining and mill areas people slept as they worked—in a day shift and a night shift—so that each bed did double duty. In no place on the face of the earth was humanity packed as closely as the Lower East Side on New York City, where three thousand shared a single city block.

There were health problems in the ghettos, but surprisingly little correlation between population density and death rates. Death rates were high among the Italian born, perhaps because of dietary deficiencies or the difficulties of adjusting to the damp cold winters. Death rates in the Irish ghettos, where many of the residents were second generation, were even higher. Perhaps the more vigorous members of this group had moved elsewhere, leaving the older, more infirm behind. In the more densely populated Jewish neighborhoods, however, death rates were among the lowest in the city. The Jewish population was young and many Jews had already made their adjustment to urban life in Europe. Also, Jews had the advantage of many hygienic practices built into their religious ritual.

Generally, environmental factors had a greater impact upon immigrant health than ethnic background. Tuberculosis and other respiratory ills were common among all immigrants who worked at dust producing occupations, the manufacture of cigars, for example, and the packing of soap. Many immigrants were forced to live in housing sites that were unsuitable for human habitation—badly drained, swampy areas, or polluted areas bordering stockyards, slaughterhouses, steel mills, and similar industries. Such sites proved lethal to their inhabitants, regardless of ethnic background. Conversely, improvements in the water supply, sanitation, and drainage resulted in improved health, regardless of the population density or the supposed "slovenly" habits of the inhabitants. As New York City's ghettos increased in population density, sanitation and services were improved and death rates declined. Although the ghettos of Philadelphia and St. Louis were less crowded, structural defects and bad sanitation kept death rates there considerably higher.

"... the popular belief that the foreign born are filling the prisons has little foundation in fact ..." reported the United States Census on Prisoners and Juvenile Delinquents in Institutions in 1904. In survey after survey, the foreign born were shown to have lower arrest and conviction rates than the native born (and more recently arrived groups such as Jews and Italians had lower rates than groups that had been in the country longer). Nevertheless, the stereotype of the immigrant as a criminal persisted.

One reason for the persistent identification of the foreign born with crime, vice, and drink was the large number of saloons, brothels, and gambling houses located in their neighborhoods. As in the pre-Civil War period, such institutions were concentrated in ethnic neighborhoods because it was politically inexpedient to license them in "better" neighborhoods. "Tourists" from other parts of the city used the ghettos as convenient places to indulge in their favorite socially unacceptable behavior. Of 3,124 persons arrested for drunkenness in 1901 in the predominantly Jewish and Italian North End of Boston, for example, only 450 were residents of the area. Of these, only five or six were Italian and none was Jewish!

Crime and vice did, of course, exist among immigrants. While Italian and Jewish culture never condoned excessive use of alcohol, Irish and Slavic immigrants came from cultures that were more permissive in this area. For them, alcoholism was more likely to become a problem. Violence, promiscuity, desertion of families occurred among all ethnic groups.

Though the crime rate was low among the foreign born, it was high among their American-born children. Fleeing their cramped tenement apartments and their "old fashioned" parents, young people took to the streets, forming gangs and getting into trouble. Arrests for juvenile delinquency were alarmingly high in every ethnic group. A sympathetic social worker, Grace Abbott, pointed out that many ethnic youths were brought to court for offenses which, had they been committed by old-stock Americans in "better" neighborhoods, would have been dismissed as mischievous pranks. Off to a bad start, a small percentage of these children moved on to more serious offenses and even organized crime.

There were many misunderstandings between the newer ethnic communities and the police, most of whom were native-born or Irish-American. Called to quell disturbances in ethnic ghettos, bigoted policemen sometimes clubbed rioters and bystanders alike. The behavior of the New York police during a disturbance at Rabbi Jacob Joseph's funeral in 1902 was so outrageous that Mayor Seth Low appointed a committee "to investigate the incident and its wider implications of police inefficiency and brutality—particularly toward the Jews of the East Side."

The problems of the police were complicated by the fact that many immigrants, accustomed in Europe to regard every official as an enemy, gave them little cooperation. Language difficulties, too, created problems. Unable to understand policemen's instructions, immigrants sometimes seemed defiant when they were actually bewildered. A Slavic boy in Chicago was shot and killed by a policeman for disobeying a command that he had not even understood. When an immigrant woman in Chicago begged a policeman to protect her children from her abusive husband, the policeman, unable to understand her, jailed her overnight as an alcoholic. Such incidents did not endear the police to the ethnic community!

Older stock Americans feared that the inhabitants of the ethnic ghettos would never shed their "alien" ways and become part of American life. Such fears were based on misconceptions about the nature of the ghetto. First, ethnic ghettos were not homogeneous. Especially in the early years, predominantly Italian, Jewish, or Slavic neighborhoods rarely had more than half of their population composed of the dominant group. Italian produce peddlers served New York's Jewish ghetto, Jewish tailors served Italian neighborhoods, and Irish brogues could be heard in Boston's "little Syria." Throughout the southern and eastern European ghettos there were pockets of Germans, Scandinavians, and old-stock Americans who would not or could not move away and who mingled with the newer arrivals in the streets, the schools, the stores, and the settlement houses.

The Industrial Ghetto—a World of Change

Contrary to uninformed public opinion, ghettos were not stagnant pools of immobilized humanity. They were in a constant state of flux. Within any given year one third to one half of the families moved—by choice or because the landlord evicted them—sometimes to a house in the same block, sometimes to a different neighborhood, sometimes to a different city. Sometimes the entire ethnic composition of a neighborhood changed within a few years. Boston's "little Syria," which became Boston's Chinatown, had been Irish earlier.

From the moment they arrived in the ethnic ghettos, immigrants were caught up in many changes. Most of these immigrants were moving from agricultural to industrial work, from rural to urban living, from cooperative to competitive societies. The cultural shock was great and was made greater still by changes in language, religion, and life style.

Language was one of the first and most obvious changes. Their inability to speak English kept many skilled workers from getting jobs appropriate to their abilities. Immigrants stayed up late to memorize long lists of the English words needed for work or for personal convenience, spelling them phonetically in any alphabet they knew. Within a few days, a Slovenian or Croatian immigrant could ride a "subvej" (subway) to work, and buy a "lonc" (lunch) consisting of a "senvic" (sandwich) and "ajs krim" (ice cream). More important, he could ask his "bas" (boss) for his "paycheki" (paycheck).

Religion, like language, called for major adjustments. Many Syrians, Armenians, Serbians, and Japanese found no American churches with which they could identify. Roman Catholics from southern and eastern Europe often found Irish Catholic churches inhospitable, too far away from their neighborhoods, or too unfamiliar in ritual and tradition. Probably no group suffered so sharp a break in religious continuity as Orthodox Jews. In Eastern Europe they had lived in an isolated, all-Jewish world where dress, food, hygiene, marriage, indeed every detail of life, was prescribed by religious law and tradition. In America, even in the Jewish ghetto, that world was gone.

Some immigrants, Poles, Ukrainians, and other Slavs in particular, struggled to maintain as much of their old religion as possible. Others, like the main character in Abraham Cahan's novel, *The Rise of David Levinsky*, made compromises. Often they discovered, like David Levinsky, that "if you attempt to bend your religion to the spirit of your new surroundings, it breaks. It falls to pieces. The very clothes I wore, and the very food I ate had a fatal effect on my religious habits. . . ."

Sometimes change was motivated by the immigrant's desire to avoid embarrassment. People shaved off their beards and altered their style of dress rather than suffer the scorn or the pity of those less "green" than themselves. Sometimes change was dictated by the demands of American institutions. Hours for rising, eating, and going to bed were set, not by the sun and the farm routine as at home, but by the demands of the foreman of the mine, the mill, or the sweatshop. Chinese families altered centuries-old patterns of meal times to fit the schedules of the American public schools their children attended.

Perhaps the most radical change for the new immigrant was the change in the pace of everyday life. To the former inhabitant of a slow moving traditional village, the urban ghettos of New York, Chicago, Boston, and Detroit must have seemed like life run at double or triple speed. Many immigrants noted a change in the "feel" of life—an emotional as well as a physical quickening. David Levinsky describes his reaction to New York's lower East Side:

. . . The scurry and hustle of the people were not merely overwhelmingly greater, both in volume and intensity, than in my native town. It was of another sort. The swing and step of the pedestrians, the voices and manner of the street peddlers, and a hundred and one other things seemed to testify to far more self-confidence and energy, to larger ambitions and wider scopes, than did the appearance of the crowds in my birthplace.

Work

Work loomed large in industrial America at the turn of the century, and it loomed larger still in the ethnic ghetto. "Work! Serve! Or America beautiful will eat you and spit your bones into the earth's hole," shouts the foreman to an Italian construction crew in Pietro Di Donato's novel *Christ in Concrete*. A guidebook for immigrant Jews gave similar advice: "Forget your past, your customs, and your ideals . . . do not take a moment's rest. Run, do, work. . . ."

Ethnic Americans were fortunate that the period 1880 to 1924, with the exception of a depression in the mid 1890's, was one of prosperity. Still, the wages paid for unskilled and semiskilled labor in a country run largely by and for business interests provided such a marginal livelihood that women, children, the aged, and even the sick, were often forced into the labor market. The Massachusetts Bureau of Statistics estimated that a family of five needed $754 a year to live. Yet the average annual wage of the male South Italian was $368, the Pole $365, and the Syrian $321. Women earned about half as much, even when performing essentially the same jobs. At a time when the New York Bureau of Labor considered ten dollars a week inadequate for a working man with a family, working women received as little as three dollars a week. A married woman might use this to supplement her husband's earnings, but widows and single women with dependents could not live on it. Some turned to prostitution to escape starvation or the poorhouse.

Because of language problems and the prejudice of prospective employers, skilled workers often faced years of unskilled work. A skilled metalworker in Chicago committed suicide because he could not satisfy his strong craving to practice his art. Professional people such as lawyers, teachers, and writers, whose skills depended on language, were often unable to pursue the occupations for which they were trained. Sometimes their own communities no longer wanted their skills. Talmudic scholars, honored in Europe, were ignored in the Jewish quarter of New York. The suffering of such people, through poverty and loss of self-esteem, was enormous.

The typical working day in immigrant industries was twelve to sixteen hours, under conditions that were dangerous, even lethal. Soap powder, lacquer, and tobacco dust in unventilated workshops caused tuberculosis and other respiratory illnesses. "I never knew anyone who worked in a laundry long," said an immigrant woman, "the work is too hard and you simply can't stand the heat." Loss of limbs, eyesight, or life was common among the men and women who labored in laundries, foundries, factories, and mines.

Employers blamed the high accident rate entirely upon the carelessness of the workers. Crystal Eastman's carefully researched study *Work Accidents and the Law* (1910) indicated, however, that employers were more likely to be at fault. Although the injured workers were often young, new to the job and to the country, ill, or overtired, most accidents were caused by equipment malfunction, careless inspection of working areas, and the overzealousness of supervisors. Despite their responsibility for most accidents, employers rarely did more than contribute to medical or funeral expenses, after which the disabled workers or their dependents were left to fend for themselves.

Much late nineteenth and early twentieth century manufacturing was done in the home, where families huddled far into the night rolling tobacco into cigars, stitching garments, or twisting wires and papers into artificial flowers. In January 1907, *Cosmopolitan Magazine* estimated that over sixty thousand children worked in the garment industry of New York City alone.

> Nearly any hour on the East Side of New York City you can see them—pallid boy or spindling girl—their faces dulled, their backs bent under a heavy load of garments. . . . Once at home with the sewing, the little worker sits close to the inadequate window, struggling with the snarls of the thread. . . . Even if by happy chance the small worker goes to school, the sewing which he puts down at the last moment in morning waits for his return . . . (by) the sacrifice of all that should make childhood radiant, a child may add to the family purse from 50 cents to $1.50 a week. . . .
>
> Besides work at sewing, there is another industry for little girls in the grim tenements. The mother must be busy at her sewing or, perhaps she is away from dark to dark at office cleaning. A little daughter must therefore assume the work and care of the family . . . washing, scrubbing, cooking. . . .

After 1900 work in the factory increasingly replaced work in the home. Here, as in home labor, the system of paying for work by the piece led to enormous pressure and great abuse. Seeking to maximize profits by keeping labor costs down, employers and contractors frequently lowered the amount paid for each finished piece, thus forcing the employee to work faster and faster in order to receive the same meager wage. Each of the many thousands of mills and shops had its own horrors, but the most highly publicized industrial disaster was the Triangle Shirtwaist factory fire of 1911. The fire began on the eighth floor of a ten story building and spread rapidly, fed by the lacy fabrics and bolts of silk. Locked doors (so the workers could not leave early) and inadequate fire escapes compounded the tragedy. *The New York World* estimated the dead at 154:

> Screaming men and women and boys and girls crowded out on the many window ledges and threw themselves into the streets far below. They jumped with their clothing ablaze. The hair of some of the girls streamed up aflame as they leaped. Thud after thud sounded on the pavements . . . on both the Greene Street and Washington Place sides of the building there grew mounds of the dead and dying. And the worst horror of all was that in this heap of the dead now and then there stirred a limb or sounded a moan. When Fire Chief Croker could make his way into these three floors he found sights that utterly staggered him . . . bodies burned to bare bones . . . skeletons bending over sewing machines.

The Worker's Response

Individuals responded to the pressures and horrors of industrial life in ways that ranged from passive resistance and sporadic violence to trade unionism and the adoption of revolutionary philosophies. Accustomed to working at their own pace with time off for holidays of many kinds and breaks for refreshment and rest, immigrant workers from rural backgrounds sometimes refused to conform to the rigid and grueling time demands of the modern factory. With legislative prodding, employers eventually reduced the length of the working day and added vacations and "coffee breaks," thus institutionalizing the more humane (as well as more efficient) schedules their employees seemed determined to follow anyway. Meanwhile, many employers hoped that education would improve the work habits of their immigrant laborers. With this in mind, the International Harvester Corporation issued pamphlets teaching English and industrial discipline simultaneously. Lesson one reads:

> I hear the whistle. I must hurry.
> I hear the five minute whistle.
> It is time to go into the shop.
>
> The starting whistle blows.
> I eat my lunch.
> It is forbidden to eat until then.
>
> I work until the whistle blows to quit.
> I leave my place nice and clean.

Desperate immigrants sometimes turned to violence to express their frustration. Weavers, miners, and other workers stoned factories and burned equipment to protest their employers' use of the police against them. Italian railroad construction gangs tore up track to punish dishonest contractors. Jewish women in New York City paraded through the streets carrying chunks of meat on pointed sticks to protest the rising cost of kosher meat. One observer described how religious rituals were incorporated into labor battles. During a strike of Slavic steel workers in Hammond, Indiana, "The lights of the hall were extinguished. A candle stuck into a bottle was placed on a platform. One by one the men came and kissed the ivory image on the cross, kneeling before it. They swore not to scab."

The relationship between southern and eastern European immigrants and the rising union movement was complex. Employers skillfully exploited and even created hostilities between ethnic groups to prevent them from organizing. Newly-arrived Italians and Slavs were often used as strikebreakers, especially when the work force was predominantly Irish or native-born. Hoping to return to Europe as soon as they had saved enough money, many Italian and Slavic newcomers avoided unions fearing the loss of income during strikes or lockouts would delay their return. As their stay in America lengthened and showed signs of becoming permanent, these workers became more receptive to the long-range economic benefits offered by unions. On the eve of World War I one of the most important unions, the United Mine Workers, was composed largely of immigrants.

Religious tradition as well as previous experience with factory jobs in Europe predisposed Jewish immigrants to take the lead in unionizing New York's predominantly Jewish garment industry. "Ours is a just cause," said a striking vestmaker in 1898. "Saith the Law of Moses: 'Thou shalt not withold anything from thy neighbor nor rob him! . . .' So you see that our bosses who rob us . . . commit a sin." Tragedies such as the Triangle Shirtwaist fire led to massive demonstrations which engaged the sympathy of many middle class Americans.

A small percentage of immigrants turned from capitalism altogether to espouse one of many varieties of socialism or anarchism. While a minority of these believed that the destruction of the oppressive capitalist order required violence, most looked for peaceful change by means of the democratic process. Indeed, in the pre-World War I years socialism was in vogue throughout the nation, as muckraking journalists and other reformers exposed the abuses of the capitalist economy. In 1912 three quarters of a million Americans, native born and foreign born, voted the Socialist ticket.

Most ethnics, like most other Americans, were not involved in socialism, unionization, rioting, or even "passive" resistance to the new industrial order. Their goal was not to change American capitalism but to succeed in it. Their greatest fear was neither injury nor death, but unemployment, which would mean hunger and homelessness for their families. Work brought danger and grinding fatigue, but it also brought satisfaction and the hope of a better future. "Blessings to thee, O Jesus," says an Italian bricklayer in Pietro Di Donato's novel *Christ in Concrete.* "I have fought wind and cold. Hand to hand I have locked dumb stones in place and the great building rises. I have earned a bit of bread for me and mine."

The vast immigrant ghettos of the early twentieth century embraced all the evils characteristic of modern urban slums—dirt, disease, overcrowding, crime, vice, gang wars—but hope was more common than despair. Most immigrants earned more here, even in the worst jobs, than they could have earned at home. Poverty, after all, is relative. Immigrants evicted from tenement apartments in the United States piled store-bought chairs and couches on the sidewalk— possessions which in the old country would have marked their owners as wealthy indeed. "In Italy we were poor, always on the verge of starvation," explained an Italian immigrant. "We were not poor in America; we just had a little less than the others. In America no one starved, though a family earned no more than five or six dollars a week. . . ."

It was the age of the Horatio Alger story, the American rags-to-riches myth. Newcomers soon discarded naive ideas that the streets of America were paved with gold, and they had probably never heard of Horatio Alger. Still, most of them set to work with optimism and purposefulness. The Jewish family sewed pants sixteen hours a day in an airless tenement; but, they had escaped pogroms. With luck and perseverance they might see their children through high school, or even college. The Italian "shovel man," descending for the first time into the coal mines of Pennsylvania or the subways of New York, was already dreaming of the house and garden he would eventually buy with his carefully hoarded savings. In America he might attain the enviable status of landlord—a status beyond his wildest dreams in Calabria or Sicily.

CHAPTER 7

Progressive America:
Home, School, and Neighborhood

In America anything was possible—but nothing was easy! If some immigrants saw their dreams come to fruition, others met only with frustration and defeat. Every individual had his or her private difficulties, but certain kinds of problems were almost universal. Most immigrants had difficulties with language, religion, housing, and especially with earning a living. They were also confronted with the problem of interpersonal relations, for America had an impact upon the immigrant family. It affected the relationship between husband and wife and between parents and children.

Immigration and Family Life

For many immigrants, their journey to America meant the end of all normal family life. These were the people who came alone, leaving parents, spouses, children, brothers, sisters, and all other relatives behind. Men who came alone often worked in gangs, living in the crudest, cheapest dormitory arrangements. Saving every penny either to bring their families here or to return home themselves, they were often unwilling to spend the money or the time to establish churches, clubs, or other institutions. Such men led a lonely and drab existence, scarcely relieved by an occasional drinking or gambling spree.

Though the majority of immigrants who came alone were men, many women were in a similar situation. Between 1912 and 1917 half a million single women under the age of thirty came to the United States. Most of these were very young. Of 120,000 Polish women, 84,000 were under twenty-one. While a man without his family usually lived and worked with other men from the same background, the woman often found employment as a household servant, where she rarely met anyone who spoke her language. "I so lonesome, I cries all the time," said a Polish housemaid.

Loneliness was often intensified by guilt at having left elderly parents at home and anguish at not being able to send them the help they expected. ". . . says our Lord Jesus and the Holiest Mother Virgin Mary, do not abandon thy parents. . . ." a Polish immigrant wrote his parents in 1914. "I wear this in my heart and I remember. . . . Only dear parents, you demand too much . . . my work does not suffice for this." Immigrants did the best they could, often at great sacrifice to themselves, to satisfy the financial needs of those left behind; millions of dollars went from America to overseas relatives every year. But there were always letters asking for more.

Often young children were left with relatives in the old country while their parents came to America to earn money. The Yiddish poet M. Teitsch captures the yearning of immigrants who could not see their babies grow into toddlers, their sons and daughters enter young adulthood.

> There's a town in Lithuania on the shores of the Wilna—
> Whichever way my eyes look, that town meets my gaze.
>
> There's an alley there, and close by, a little house—
> Me thinks I would give away half my years for that little house.
>
> And a child lives in the little house, whom I love as my life—
> All my years I would give away for this child.

Husbands who came to America alone to earn passage for their wives often found the months of separation lengthening into years. Eagerly awaited letters sometimes brought more grief than comfort. Wives left behind complained that the work was too hard to do alone, that the hired hands were unruly and unreliable, and that the children were disobedient without their father to oversee them. "The wheelbarrow of life is too heavy for my shoulders . . . take me there, where you are. . . . Otherwise I shall perish," wrote a Polish woman.

Not all marriages were happy ones, and the desire to escape contributed to some men's decisions to emigrate. Such men were not in a hurry to send for their wives, especially if they had already found a desirable American substitute. "Klastor took his wife five weeks ago, Mania Pawlowska is going away presently. Only for me there is no place!" complains a suspicious wife. Sometimes the woman postponed joining her husband on one pretext or another, either from fear of the unknown land, or because she, too, had found someone else.

Husbands in America were often frantic with jealousy, justified or unjustified. Many an Italian husband refused to consummate a marriage that took place immediately before his departure; if his wife were unfaithful while he was gone, at least he would know about it!

In some cases love and trust survived the years of separation only to evaporate when the couple was reunited. "Once between us the Atlantic, yet I felt your hand in mine," wrote Israel Zangwill. "Now I feel your hand in mine, yet between us the Atlantic." After years of separation the Americanized husband might find his immigrant wife too drab and old fashioned. The newly arrived wife might be shocked to find that her husband had abandoned the traditional religion or life style. Such problems could put a strain on even the best marriages, and lead to separation or divorce.

In the old country—Europe, the Middle East, or Japan—a network of relatives and neighbors was always available to see that husband and wife fulfilled their obligations to each other and that children were respectful and obedient to their parents. In the United States, however, this network was absent, and such interference would not have been tolerated had it been available. The nuclear family—husband, wife, and children—were on their own. The result could be a new closeness, or, in times of stress, a rapid disintegration.

In a traditional European village each partner in the marriage had a socially recognized status, derived from the known qualities of their families going back for many generations. In the United States, no one knew or cared how prominent the husband's family had been or how large the wife's dowry. Status in the American community was more likely to depend upon how much money the couple could make. Visible signs of success—store-bought clothing and furniture, a larger apartment, ultimately a house, could become more important to the ethnic American family in the United States than they had been in the old country. Moreover, material success would justify the sacrifices and hardships of immigration.

The desire to succeed produced many conflicts, particularly in the husband. Now his status in the eyes of his family as well as his neighbors often depended on his ability to make money. Failure could lead to loss of self-respect so severe that the defeated man turned to the anesthetic of alcohol or deserted his family altogether.

The pressure on the male immigrant was intensified by the fact that behavior he had been brought up to accept as appropriate and effective did not bring the same satisfactory results in America as it had in Europe. Indeed, in this strange country success and status often came to those who would have scarcely been tolerated in the old country. An Italian immigrant complained that in Boston "it was the misfits of Italian society who were 'i *prominenti*' and held dominance;

... those who could 'bluff it through' ... the unscrupulous politician ... the quack ... the shyster lawyer. ...." Many new immigrants faced the same problem their predecessors had faced—the conflict between traditional rural values and the fiercely individualistic, competitive behavior apparently demanded by the new environment. Now that the United States was more heavily industrialized and more completely urbanized, the conflict was even more acute.

The Immigrant Woman

Women faced their own special problems of adjustment to the new environment, not the least of which was overwork. The grandmother or maiden aunt who had shared the burdens of housework and child care in the old country was no longer part of the household in America; the ethnic wife had to manage these things herself, often in addition to working for wages. Immigrant women often worked night shifts in the mills or cleaned office buildings at night so that they could care for children, household, and boarders during the day. Such a regime left little time for rest, recreation, or education.

Housework and child care were more burdensome in America because of the vastly different life style. In the old country a tiny hut with an earthen floor needed little care, and children could play safely in the fields under the watchful eyes of their parents. An American tenement, however, required endless scrubbing, and there was no place but the dangerous streets for young children to play.

In an agrarian economy, five and six year olds could be put to work at tasks that contributed to the family's welfare. In America there was little a young child could do to be useful, and after the turn of the century older children were kept in school by law until their early teens, or even later. Under such circumstances, the large family that religious and cultural tradition, as well as economic reality, defined as a blessing in the old country now became a source of endless anxiety. Even childbirth itself was newly complicated. The trained midwives immigrant women had used in the Old World were not generally available here, and many women were unwilling to use a male physician, even if they could afford the fee.

But there were advantages as well as disadvantages for the immigrant woman. The United States was far from egalitarian in its attitude toward women. Still, immigration often improved the position of the ethnic woman within her nuclear family. Economic and social conditions in the United States sometimes gave her more freedom of action than she had had in the old country. The most extreme example of such a change is that of women within the Arabic speaking immigrant community. In the Middle East women were carefully secluded from public life and rarely seen by any men but their own husbands or fathers on whom they were economically totally dependent. Functioning almost as servants, they exerted little independent influence even in the rearing of their children.

In the United States, many Arabic men were surprised to discover that their economic success—the reason for immigration in the first place—was dependent upon their wives. Men who sold dry goods from door to door, a common occupation for Arabic immigrants, found their wives welcomed into American homes from which they were turned away. Many wives began to peddle with their husbands, learned English, and eventually became equal partners in prosperous family businesses. Some went on to become leaders in their communities. Lebanese-born Mrs. Mantura Frangiea, of Springfield, Massachusetts, for example, a partner in her husband's wholesale dry goods business, became the advocate for the local Arabic community and was well known and respected as such by the politicians, judges, lawyers, social workers, and police.

Changes in the economic area brought other changes as well. The Mediterranean tradition of men socializing with other men in coffee houses while their wives stayed at home gave way rapidly to the American pattern of husbands and wives going out together. Similarly, the traditional pattern by which the Middle Eastern man assumed responsibility for school-aged children, disciplining them, supervising their recreation, even buying their clothes rapidly disappeared. In the United States, teachers, nurses, doctors, and school counselors consulted the woman, not the man, on matters concerning the children. The Arabic woman, like many other immigrant women, assumed increasing importance as the director of her children's social and academic lives.

Sometimes immigration speeded up changes that were already underway, as in the case of Jewish women. Though never secluded like Arabic women, Jewish women from Eastern Europe were expected to devote themselves entirely to home and family. Education was valued for men, but a third of the women who immigrated were illiterate. Even the most traditional Jewish woman, however, was often familiar with the world of the marketplace. Many a pious wife kept shop or did other paid work so that her husband could devote all his time to religious study.

During the era of mass immigration, the roles of Jewish women in Europe were already changing. Young women were beginning to participate in new secular movements such as socialism and Zionism, both of which included a strong commitment to the equality of women among their other ideological goals. Though Russian universities discriminated against Jews, a few women of unusual ability and determination were able to acquire a secular, even a professional education. These "new" Jewish women brought their nontraditional life styles to America with them.

A popular journalist, Hutchins Hapgood, described the "new" Jewish women of New York City in 1902:

> They have lost faith completely in the Orthodox religion ... read Tolstoy, Turgenev, and Chekov, and often put into practice the most radical theories of the new woman, particularly those which say that women should be economically independent of man. There are successful female dentists, physicians, writers, and even lawyers by the score in East Broadway who have attained financial independence through industry and intelligence.... They are ambitious ... and often direct the careers of their husbands.... There is more than one case on record where a girl has compelled her recalcitrant lover to learn law, medicine, or dentistry, or submit to being jilted by her....

Many of the "new" Jewish women became effective champions of causes such as trade unionism, woman's suffrage, and birth control. Their influence combined with the impact of the new environment, produced changes in traditional Jewish family life. Jewish women began to limit the size of their families, to enroll in night school in massive numbers, and to see that their daughters as well as their sons got higher education whenever possible.

"The man who does not beat his wife is not a man," says a South Slavic proverb. In Servia or Croatia it was not unusual to see women pulling plows while their husbands walked unencumbered beside them. In Southern Italy, women were subject to the authority of their fathers, brothers, husbands, male cousins, even teen-aged sons.

Slavic and Italian women did not gain the relative freedom of action achieved by Arabic and Jewish women in America. The subordination of women was an important part of the distinctive, centuries old South Italian family system, a system so strong and so functional that it survived immigration virtually intact. Because this system demanded close supervision and protection of women, South Italian women were more likely than other women to work within the home or, if employed outside, to work among people from the same Old World village or even the same family. Such women had fewer opportunities than their counterparts in other ethnic communities to achieve economic and social independence. Moreover, Italian and Slavic women were less likely than Jewish women to have abandoned religious orthodoxy, either before or after immigration. Traditional religion continued to play and enormous role in their lives. Thus the social philosophy of Roman Catholicism reinforced long established patterns of female subordination in the Italian and Slavic communities.

Even for the traditional Slavic and Italian women, America opened up new possibilities. Wife beating declined when women discovered that abusive husbands could be reported to the police! Ukrainian men complained American laws were made for women. Many Slavic and Italian women became active within their ethnic communities. Antonietta Pisanelli Alessandro, a South Italian wife and mother, founded Italian theaters in New York and San Francisco. Bohemian-born Josephine Humpel Zeman edited a nationally circulated Bohemian feminist newspaper. Polish, Lithuanian, Ukrainian, Slovakian, and other women developed national organizations that published newspapers and magazines and pursued educational and charitable work within the ethnic community. Members of religious orders established and ran much needed schools, hospitals, and orphanages. Nor were the activities of such women limited to their own communities. In Chicago, Slavic women helped organize a Woman's Civic League to register voters and campaign against a corrupt city administration. Women in other cities engaged in similar activities.

In most ethnic families the traditional authority of the male survived, in form if not in fact. It was not unknown for a woman to attribute important decisions she had made to her husband. Although he was often belittled in the outside world, the immigrant male had the satisfaction of being looked up to as the head of the household. Still, enough change had taken place that when immigrant families considered returning to Europe, it was the woman who most often did not want to go. Life was better for her in America.

The Immigrant Child

Children, like adults, had special problems adjusting to the new American environment. While adults might mingle primarily with those from within their own ethnic community, children were often forced into a school situation in which they were conspicuously "different." Eager to be accepted by their teachers and their peers, young people found minority status a devastating experience, as these childhood recollections of schooldays reveal:

I was nervous from nine o'clock until three. . . . I never spoke right, I did not walk right, my tie was atrocious, my mother did not take good care of me, and so it went. . . .

In elementary school I was often ridiculed for the clothes I wore until I began to believe myself that the dresses of other girls in school were by all means more proper than mine.

My mother gave me each day an Italian sandwich, that is, half a loaf of French bread filled with fried peppers and onions. . . . Such a sandwich would certainly ruin my reputation; I could not take it to school. . . . My god, what a problem it was to dispose of it. . . .

Timid and ill at ease in an "American" school, many ethnic children felt better in schools where their own group predominated. Undoubtedly this was one reason for the popularity of the parish parochial school. As immigration increased and ethnic ghettos grew, however, even public schools often acquired a predominantly ethnic population. "It made me feel at home. What a difference!" said an Italian boy after transferring from an Anglo-Saxon to a predominantly Italian school. "Even the cop in front of the school was an Italian." Segregated ghetto schools were often crowded, dark, and understaffed. There were other disadvantages to schools where most students were very poor. In the case of the Italian child quoted above, the new all Italian peer group reinforced his parents' view that earning was more important than learning. The boy lost interest in school work and dropped out at the age of thirteen because "everyone around me spoke of nothing but making dough."

Eager to "Americanize" their students, teachers often spoke disparagingly of the Old World language and traditions of their students. Children were torn between the old and the new. Some resolved the problem of conflict between the ethnic culture of their home and the American ways of the public school by dividing their lives into two separate compartments. Though dutiful and respectful within the home, they did not introduce their American school friends to their parents, thus avoiding exposure of their foreignness. Nor did they take their parents to functions at school; "that was our life, exclusively ours."

Other children devoted themselves with amazing patience and sensitivity to building bridges between the New World and the Old. Such children brought their parents proudly to their teachers, carefully translating what each said to the other to show them both in the best possible light. These children gave their teachers insight into their parents' lives, while introducing their parents to the mysteries of America. They were pioneers in breaking down parental resistance to American social customs, such as dating, and thus eased the path for younger brothers and sisters. Indeed, the oldest children were often surrogate parents to younger siblings, pleading their causes with the immigrant parents, helping them with their problems, even sacrificing their own higher education so that brothers and sisters could stay in school.

The realities of life in a new culture gave the child, like the woman, greater independence and status within the family. Children born in America or brought here at an early age learned English more rapidly than their parents, understood more of American life because of their American schooling, and could often earn money in their teens because of the job opportunities available in the American city. These new facts of life meant a reversal of the traditional family roles in which children were dependent upon adults for sustenance and for wisdom to cope with life. Now it was often the parents who were dependent upon the children—upon their earnings, and upon their ability to deal in English with teachers, social workers, doctors, and landlords.

Parents were proud of their children's achievements and appreciated their help, but many had mixed feelings. They worried that their Americanized children would lose respect for them and their way of life. Sometimes their fears were justified. Many Americanized children rejected their parents as totally old fashioned, rebelling against their authority, and against all other authorities as well. From among such children came the juvenile delinquents of the ethnic ghettos—and as police records indicate, there were many of these. Some parents were so painfully aware of their own "foreignness" that they accepted their children's version of what "everybody" did in America without question and did not attempt to control their children's behavior as they would have done in Europe. Other parents, equally unfamiliar with American life, reacted in the opposite way, imposing such severe restrictions that their children were driven into rebellion.

Journalist Lincoln Steffens described the extremes to which cultural and generational conflict could go and the anguish it could cause. He writes of the conflict between traditional Orthodox Jewish fathers, "parents out of the Middle Ages, sometimes out of the Old Testament days" and their sullen, rebellious sons, "the children of the streets of New York today":

> We would pass a synagogue where a score or more of boys were sitting hatless [traditional Jewish males keep their heads covered] in their old clothes, smoking cigarettes on the steps outside; and their fathers, all dressed in black, with their high hats, uncut beards, and temple curls, were going into the synagogue, tearing their hair and rending their garments [in mourning]. They wept tears, real tears. It was a revolution. Their sons were rebels against the law of Moses; they were lost souls, lost to God, the family, and to Israel of old.
>
> . . . If there were a fight—and sometimes the fathers did lay hands on their sons, and the tough boys did biff their fathers in the eye . . . the police would rush in and club now the boys, now the parents . . . bloodily and in vain. . . . I used to feel that the blood did not hurt, but the tears did . . . the old Jews were doomed and knew it. Two, three thousand years of continuous devotion, courage, and suffering for a cause lost in a generation.

Similar conflicts were acted out between the parents and children of virtually every ethnic group. The underlying problem was the children's desire to be "more American even than the Americans," as one school principal put it, and the parents' fear of indiscriminate change and of the consequent rejection of their values and way of life. In his study *Democracy and Assimilation*, Julius Drachsler summarized their fears:

> It is not merely the natural desire of parents to retain influence over the child. . . . It is a vague uneasiness that a delicate network of precious traditions is being ruthlessly torn asunder, that a whole world of ideals is crashing into ruins; and amidst this desolation, the father and mother picture themselves wandering about lonely in vain search of their lost children. . . .

Success and Failure—Two Case Histories

The crowded, unhealthful environment, the long, tedious hours of work, changes within the family relationships, conflicts between new ways and old—these problems touched the lives of all. Some families were unable to cope. Their unhappy stories can be found in the files of the newly organized urban charities. Many aspects of the social pathology of the ghetto are apparent in the story of the Judziewicz family, which came to the attention of the United Charities of Chicago in September, 1909. Mr. and Mrs. Judziewicz had immigrated from Poland in 1896. Mr. Judziewicz was unable to hold a steady job. He deserted his wife frequently, returning to live with her for brief periods, until she finally procured a divorce. At thirty, Mrs. Judziewicz was left with tuberculosis and five children under the age of eight. The youngest was a sickly infant, fathered by a boarder. The terse records of the social worker describe the situation shortly after the birth of the baby.

> *September 19, 1910.* Landlord in office to ask rent. . . . Says woman is a very untidy housekeeper and children do a great deal of damage about the premise.
>
> *September 21, 1910.* Woman in office asking help with funeral expenses as baby died 6:30 a.m. Her brother will buy [cemetery] lot. . . . The woman . . . says church will not help. Two teachers gave $5.00 and some friends $2.00. She had gone from house to house begging. . . . [the apartment] was extremely dirty and children playing in the room where the corpse was lying. Woman seemed utterly indifferent perhaps because she was so tired . . .

The future seemed bleak for the Judziewicz family. But for every family that fell apart under the stress of ghetto life, others, like that of

Mary and Martin Grubinsky, showed amazing strength and resource-fulness. According to Katherine Anthony, author of a study of working women in 1914, the Grubinskys immigrated from a remote corner of rural Hungary, stopping first in a Hungarian city for a few years before moving to New York. Perhaps this two-step immigration eased the shock of change for the Grubinskys and contributed to their ability to cope with urban America.

In New York the couple devoted themselves to one another and to the rearing of their eight children, four born in Hungary and four born in the United States. At the time Katherine Anthony described the family, Mr. Grubinsky had been working in the same furniture factory for seven years. He never missed a day and often took extra work home to finish on Sundays or in the evenings. He spent his free time doing things for his wife and children and entertaining his friends from the neighborhood. As for Mrs. Grubinsky:

> She helps her husband with the chair caning, makes the children's clothes, mends for her own family and also for hire, cooks, washes, irons, scrubs, tends her window boxes, minds the children of a neighbor who is doing a day's work, fetches ice from the brewery where it is thrown away, forages for kindling around warehouses, runs to school when the teacher summons her. . . . In her home nothing is wasted, nothing lost. Even the feathers from a Thanksgiving turkey were made into cushions and dust brushes.

Unlike the Judziewicz family, the Grubinskys have health, energy, a strong family commitment, and realistic plans for the future:

> . . . when Mary Grubinsky's parents die, she will have a small remittance from Hungary. Then, too, the children will be working and Mrs. Grubinsky will be able to go out [to work] more days. . . . When they get together $600 they will move to a little place on the other side of the Hudson. . . . It is a sustaining hope equally for the husband and the wife, and unites them through every other difference.

Outside Help

Immigrants struggling to cope with the changes in their lives in the early twentieth century ghettos had to depend primarily upon themselves, their own immediate families, and their ethnic communities (see Chapter Nine). But there was also help from the larger American community. Much of this help was motivated by the Progressive Movement, a broadly based attempt to improve American life. Progressives wanted to make the nation more efficient, more democratic, and more humane—goals which could be mutually contradictory. Progressive reformers tried to curb the excesses of the giant corporations, provide a better life for farmers and workers, and bring honesty, efficiency, and expertise to government, to industry, and to education.

Comprehensive national programs for economic relief did not exist until the Great Depression of the 1930's. The late nineteenth and early twentieth century did, however, see an increased understanding of the plight of the poor, an understanding that proved helpful to the immigrant. "Progressive" clergymen and social workers began to perceive that poverty might be caused by bad environment, poor health, or other unavoidable circumstances, rather than the innate depravity of the poor.

"... The man who cannot live on bread and water is not fit to live at all," proclaimed the traditional Reverend Lyman Beecher, who undoubtedly ate very well on his own salary of $20,000 a year. But other theologians, such as Washington Gladden, Walter Rauschenbusch, and Charles Sheldon disagreed, urging instead that Jesus' concern for the poor be translated into Christian efforts to solve the social problems of the day.

Influenced by this new "Social Gospel," the major Protestant denominations formed welfare organizations to work for such goals as the elimination of factory hazards to life and health, reduction of hours "to the lowest practical point, with work for all," and "a living wage in every industry," goals of obvious value to the immigrant poor. Instead of abandoning inner city parishes to follow congregants to the suburbs, some of the wealthier "Social Gospel" congregations maintained branches in the old neighborhoods to serve the new urban population. These "institutional churches" established soup kitchens, nurseries, libraries, gymnasiums, clubs, clinics, employment bureaus, and many kinds of classes. Church related organizations also planned programs of "outreach." The YMCA and YWCA offered recreation, education, and other services. The Salvation Army operated a comprehensive welfare program including emergency food and shelter, public nursing services, and special "rescue missions" for alcoholics, unwed mothers, prostitutes, and ex-convicts.

Several factors limited the effectiveness of these church-related programs. First, Protestant leaders often planned their programs without consulting the immigrant communities they sought to serve. Second, the tendency to use social welfare programs as missionary efforts to win converts for Protestant churches alienated the potential beneficiaries who were usually Catholics and Jews. Finally, many of the "helping" persons saw as their major goal the Americanization of their immigrant clients who must be persuaded to give up their ethnic language and habits both for their own benefit and for that of majority

America. "Business pleads for it, patriotism demands it, and social considerations require it," said one clergyman. However, even children resented help that was based on social manipulation and the belittling of their religious and cultural traditions. When the notice of the death of a prominent churchman was posted on a public bulletin board in a Jewish part of New York, "every boy of twelve or fourteen who stopped to read the notice deliberately spat upon it in the coolest and most matter-of-fact manner."

More acceptable to many of the new immigrant communities were the facilities provided by the better settlement houses. Many settlement houses were secular institutions. Jane Addams, a founder of the settlement house movement, understood that one could be as valuable a human being in a shawl as in a hat and that there was no danger to American life in the use of black bread instead of white! "Our aim is to work *with* the people rather than to work *for* the people," said James B. Reynold, head of the University Settlement on the Lower East Side of New York. Inspired by European examples and by the leadership of Jane Addams of Hull-House in Chicago, social workers, teachers, college students, and people of all ages who wanted to be "where idealism ran high" moved into large old homes, settlements, in the ethnic ghettos.

Responding to the needs and interests of the people among whom they lived, the settlement house personnel offered a variety of activities, such as social clubs for all ages, counseling services, employment agencies, and emergency relief. They offered classes in Shakespeare and Goethe as well as basic English, violin and ballet as well as sewing and woodworking. One of the strong points of the better settlement houses was their willingness to recognize the skills and the cultural heritages of the ethnic peoples they served. When the women who conducted cooking classes in a Milwaukee settlement published their still famous *Settlement Cook Book* as a fundraising project for the settlement, they included the treasured family recipes of the German, Bohemian, Jewish, and other immigrant women of their neighborhood. Hull-House in Chicago developed an industrial arts exhibit where residents of the neighborhood displayed their skills in weaving, spinning, woodcarving, and other traditional handicrafts. Evening entertainment at Hull-House featured ethnic costumes, dance, and song. Such programs gave American born children a new appreciation of their "foreign" parents and enhanced the self esteem of all who took part.

Many settlement houses worked closely with the public schools, suggesting programs, even sharing facilities. In Buffalo, for example, the kindergarten of Public School 41 met at Zion House, a Jewish settlement. Creative settlement workers in Boston, New York, and elsewhere used dramatics to teach immigrant children English and to help them "work through" their problems of adjusting to American life. This innovation led to the creation of some of the earliest children's theaters and was rapidly picked up by the public and parochial schools.

Responding to the needs of working mothers, settlement houses pioneered in quality comprehensive day care for young children. The goal of many settlement day care centers was to provide a complete program—education and medical and dental care for the child, educational and social services for the child's family, and special training for the teachers and other staff. By 1916, 695 settlement day care centers were in operation. Like many other Progressive reforms the day care movement declined in the conservative atmosphere of the 1920's. Ironically, the success of another reform, widow's pensions, helped kill the day care movement. As state legislatures enacted laws giving widows pensions to remain at home with their children, the day care clientele became stigmatized as the "undeserving" poor. There was a subsequent decline in the quality and the use of the day care centers.

Middle class women, including many second and third generation immigrants, staffed a variety of agencies that offered assistance to the population of the ethnic ghettos. Consumers Leagues worked to improve health and safety conditions in sweatshops and factories. The Women's Trade Union League assisted garment workers of New York in their attempts to unionize for better pay and working conditions. The Immigrant Protection League of Chicago helped immigrants reach their American destinations safely, protected them from fraud, and assisted them in their dealings with immigration officials, police, banks, and employers. Large cities established public charities, staffed by men and women social workers, new professionals to meet the emergency economic needs of the poor. These public charities were supplemented by ethnic or religious charities, often staffed by second generation Americans eager to help their more recently arrived countrymen.

Though good work was done by the settlement houses and by the various public and private charitable agencies, their resources were never adequate to their task. Only a small percentage, perhaps no more than five per cent, of the ghetto population were touched by their services. Moreover, like their religious counterparts, the secular agencies often approached their clients in a patronizing way, motivated more by a desire, conscious or unconscious, to preserve the "American" way of life than by a desire to help individuals solve their problems.

Too often aid was given grudgingly, with excessive investigation and red tape, and condescension. The immigrant paid a high price in self-respect for such assistance. An immigrant writer, Anzia Yezierska, left us vignettes of ghetto "caretakers" at their worst. The social worker: "By pictures and lectures she shows us how poor people should live without meat, without butter, without milk, and without eggs . . . why can't you yet learn us how to eat without eating?" The charity clinic: " . . . how that doctor looked on us, just because we were poor. . . . He only used the ends from his fingertips to examine us with. From the way he was afraid to touch us or come near us, he made us feel like we had some catching sickness that he was trying not to get on him." The unsympathetic school teacher: "She never perceived that I had a soul. . . . She could see nothing in people like me, except the stains on the outside." The truant officer: "What learning can come into a child's head when the stomach is empty."

Books, Schools, and "Progressive" Education

The two governmental agencies that did most to help the immigrant in the early twentieth century were the public libraries and the public schools, both of which expanded enormously during the Progressive era. The impact of the newly opened libraries can scarcely be overestimated.

> You can imagine my happy surprise when I found that here in this wonderful country are established free libraries, [wrote an immigrant] with thousands of books in many languages and everybody may take home a book or two. . . . With reverence I stepped into the Aguilar Library . . . and with a throbbing heart I told the girl what book I wanted and when I had the book in my hand, I pressed it to my heart and wanted to kiss it, but I was ashamed to do it.

Sympathetic librarians made their institutions community centers for classes, parties, meetings, and a variety of other activities. They befriended the local children, helping them select reading material for school and for leisure. Such librarians received smudged, misspelled thank you letters such as the following, quoted in the New York *Evening Post* of 1903: "My dear Miss Cheerin. Only God knows how much I love you. I send you as many kisses as there are pennies in the world." Perhaps the best thanks for Miss Cheerin and others like her was the knowledge that some people they helped, young adults as well as children, went on to higher education, pursuing careers in teaching, medicine, and other professions.

Ethnic newcomers were fortunate that they arrived at a time when public education in the United States was expanding. When the Irish and German immigrants arrived before the Civil War, public schools were just beginning and education was not compulsory. By the early twentieth century public school systems were well established everywhere and in most states education was compulsory at least to the age of fourteen. Educational reformers, the most famous of whom was John Dewey, were rethinking the entire purpose and process of education for a new urban and industrial society.

Reform was undoubtedly needed. The huge influx of new students, from rural America and from overseas, augmented pre-existing problems and created new ones. Overcrowding was so severe that classes were held in basements, attics, cloakrooms, corridors, and hastily built annexes. Buildings were old, dark, poorly ventilated and badly heated. Many teachers had less than a high school education themselves. Despite new pedagogical theories, memorization and rigid discipline were common. A journalist observing New York City schools a few years before World War I noted one in which "I did not once hear any child express a thought in his own words."

Progressive educational reformers spoke hopefully of changing all this—of creating self-governing, self-disciplined schools where "the teacher will float on the interest which the pupils manifest." The new educators urged classroom teachers to use "projects," dramatizations, and other innovative methods, to encourage students to express and pursue their own interests, and to create a democratic community in the classroom. Recognizing that many children, including many immigrant children, were not doing well in the traditional academic curriculum, educators urged that the curriculum be changed to meet what they saw as the needs of the "non-academic" child. Music, art, and physical and vocational education were to be stressed. Children were to be given the option of taking commercial or industrial rather than academic courses at the high school level, or even earlier. Teachers and counselors (a new educational professional) guided students into choices they considered appropriate for their socioeconomic background, assisted after World War I by a battery of newly developed, culturally biased psychological tests. In sum, the school was to concern itself with the social, physical, and vocational as well as with the mental development of the child.

Much of this program was constructed with the immigrant child in mind. In major cities two-thirds to three-quarters of the public school population was composed of immigrants or the children of immigrants. In the early twentieth century, as in the days before the Civil War, educators saw the public school as the answer to the social problems of rapidly growing polyglot cities. What Diane Ravitch found true of the situation in New York City was equally true in cities throughout the nation:

> In the early twentieth century the public school was transformed into a vast, underfinanced, bureaucratic social work agency, expected to take on single-handedly the responsibilities which had formerly been discharged by the family, community, and employer . . . the idea took hold that the public school was uniquely responsible for the Americanization and assimilation of the largest foreign immigration in the nation's history.

Though Progressive educational reform varied from one city to another, and indeed, from one classroom to another, certain general changes were widespread. New school buildings were constructed, some with showers, swimming pools, and laboratory or "shop" facilities for instruction in home economics and industrial arts. (Unfortunately, the urban population grew faster than the new facilities, so that overcrowding remained a problem.) Commercial and industrial curricula were offered and vocational guidance was introduced. Physical education was emphasized. Free physical examinations and medical and dental care were made available. Special classes catered to the needs of children with physical or mental handicaps. Hot lunches were provided for the undernourished. Playgrounds were built for school and neighborhood use. School buildings were opened to the community for evening activities. Kindergartens and summer schools were opened. Night schools taught English and citizenship to adults. In California visiting "home" teachers took education to immigrant women in the neighborhoods.

Critics of immigration pointed out that the children of Southern Italian, Slavic, and other immigrant communities lagged behind the children of the American born in school achievement and were more likely to be truant. Many factors influenced the school performance of ethnic children. Contemporary studies indicated that children from communities that had been in the United States longer, such as Germans and Scandinavians, performed better than those who had arrived more recently, such as Poles and Italians. Critics considered this evidence that the "new" immigration was inferior to the "old." What the studies really showed was that when groups had had time to become familiar with American language and culture and to move from poverty to a more acceptable living standard, the school performance of their children improved. Cultural background as well as economic status and length of time in America influenced school performance. Finns, Japanese, Jews, and other recently arrived immigrant groups from urban backgrounds or from cultures where schooling was widespread and learning highly valued performed better even than earlier, rural, English-speaking groups such as the Irish. Indeed, they often outperformed the native-born children of old American stock.

There were many causes for the "retardation" of some groups of immigrant children. Even those born in the United States were often handicapped by unfamiliarity with the language and with the middle class Anglo-Saxon cultural atmosphere of the public school. School districts were gerrymandered to keep immigrant children segregated, and more money was likely to be spent in "American" districts. Schools in immigrant ghettos were old, overcrowded, and lacking in facilities. In some ethnic neighborhoods the population turnover was so great that children rarely stayed in the same school more than a year or two. Immigrant parents were unable to help children with their school-work. Lack of proper clothing, illness, the need to earn money or to take care of younger brothers and sisters kept some children at home. Finally, some children were too tired and too hungry to pay attention to their teachers.

Cultural factors played an important role in determining how children of a particular ethnic group would react to the American public school. In the parts of Poland controlled by Russia and Germany schooling was either forbidden or used as a vehicle to force Russian and German culture on Polish speaking populations. Peasant children who went to school usually attended only for a few years to gain basic literacy along with a little Polish history, folklore, and catechism. They were not expected to go further, nor did their early education prepare them to do so. The pattern survived in the United States. Polish children attended elementary school, achieving about at the same level as most other children for the first four or five years. Then, as they approached the age of twelve, they were likely to fall behind and they rarely went to high school. As in Poland, they were expected to start work in early adolescence. It must be remembered, however, that fewer than ten per cent of all American children went through high school in the early twentieth century. The pattern within the Polish community was similar to that of the American urban working class in general.

In poverty stricken southern Italy it was essential for children to perform meaningful tasks such as tending animals, building fences, and helping with housework by the time they were six or seven and to make adult contributions to the family livelihood by the time they were twelve. Southern Italian parents found it hard to accept American laws that kept "big" boys and girls in school to the age of fourteen or longer when the family needed their earnings. Dutiful children sometimes dropped out of school before the legal age to go to work. Such behavior was labeled "bad" by school authorities who could not understand why the parents insisted that the truant was a "good" boy or girl!

Differences in educational philosophy caused further problems. To the Southern Italian peasant, education was a process by which children learned to respect and obey their elders, to perform their traditional family roles (the roles of males and females were sharply differentiated), and to do economically useful work. They had little sympathy for "progressive" American schools that stressed individualism and self-expression, permitted boys and girls to mingle freely and do many of the same things, and taught "useless" subjects such as drawing and physical education. In Southern Italy secondary schooling was a serious affair, leading to lucrative and prestigious occupations such as law, medicine, and the priesthood. Not so in the United States wrote an irate Italian parent!

> It is very, very bad that the little children are taught in school to do nothing else but play ball. But I cannot understand how it is possible for a high school to do the same thing. . . . When my boy went to high school, I was pleased that one in our family may become a learned man. But I was disappointed. . . . How can he learn when they compel him to play more than to study? I remember they called me to school to explain why my son does not want to attend his playing lessons! I did not go, because I brought up my boy well. I did not teach him to play. . . . This play business is the ruination of the family.

The complaints of this South Italian parent are ironic because physical education was added to the curriculum at least partly as a response to what educators mistakenly saw as the nonacademic interests, or low aspiration level, of immigrant children. Vocational education was added for a similar reason. In the early twentieth century, however, most vocations could be learned more effectively on the job than in school, especially with the added inducement of a paycheck. The automatic counseling of immigrant children into vocational rather than academic programs by guidance personnel with preconceived ideas of what was appropriate for such children was resented by many immigrant parents. Having come to America to improve the prospects for their families, they had higher aspirations for their children. The immigrant population of New York City indignantly rejected the "Gary Plan," a progressive reform in which children would spend half of their school day on the playground, in the shops, and in other nonacademic pursuits.

Because of language problems, immigrant children were often placed in classes with children many years their juniors, or with children who were mentally retarded. Inappropriate materials were another handicap to the education of the immigrant child. School books inherited from America's agrarian past pictured little blond Johnny skipping down the flower lined country lane to his slender, carefree mother—a world so far removed from that of the ghetto child as to be almost beyond belief. Many teachers were sympathetic and understanding; but others could be callous, even cruel. Well meaning teachers were sometimes so eager to instill love for America that they presented children a picture of their new country that was romanticized beyond recognition and that denied the reality of the child's own experience:

> The virtues of honesty and American courtesy which he (the teacher) recited so dutifully were forgotten by me as soon as I realized that my existence depended upon my own ability to get things by hook or by crook. . . . The teacher talked about civic beauty . . . the only civic beauty that appealed to me was the East River where . . . I could take a swim in summer. The teacher spoke of the officer at the street crossing as a "gentleman of peace." I realized soon that he was nothing but a big fat Irish bastard. . . .

Similar problems faced the tens of thousands of men and women, already overburdened with work and family obligations, who nevertheless found time to attend the "lighted schoolrooms" of the public night schools. Steel workers in Cleveland read juvenile stories about flowers and birds ("I am a yellow bird. I can fly.") and recited sentimental poems such as, "Oh baby, dear baby, Whatever you do, You are king of the home and we all bend to you." Students in English classes were forced to differentiate between the past, past perfect, and pluperfect tenses. Candidates for citizenship studied manuals that told them the dimensions of the Senate chambers and informed them that in 1916 the Bureau of Fisheries produced 4,800,000,000 fish and fish eggs! English speaking teachers often were unable to communicate with their students. Adult students in Passaic, New Jersey, and in many other cities as well, expressed a desire for teachers of their own nationality. "Then we will not get discouraged."

Undoubtedly preconceived ideas about the intellectual capacities, proper social stations, and interests of immigrants, as well as simple thoughtlessness, contributed to the inappropriate content and methods of immigrant education. Immigrant women were burdened with sexual as well as ethnic stereotypes. Though a million and a quarter foreign born women worked outside the home in a typical year, and though ethnic women like ethnic men had a wide range of interests, from art and music to politics, materials developed for the education of immigrant women were of the "I cook. I wash. I mop. I sweep." variety. A model English lesson on how to seek employment shows quite clearly what occupation was considered appropriate for ethnic women:

First pupil   — I want to work.
Second pupil— What can you do?
First pupil   — I can wash and iron.
Second pupil— What else?
First pupil   — I can wash windows and clean house.

Americanization—getting immigrants to adopt not only American loyalties, but also American food, dress, and life style—was an important part of education for children and adults. Immigrants who understood no English were drilled in the recitation of patriotic songs and poems. Los Angeles "home" teachers were instructed to maintain a model cottage and to give model tea parties and dinners so that foreign-born women would learn the American life style. "I am happy. I have money. I go to the store," said the Los Angeles English instruction manual, giving the immigrant woman training in her role as an American consumer as well as in English vocabulary!

Despite these difficulties, free public education had much to offer immigrants, and they flocked to take advantage of it. The desire for social mobility was the main reason for immigration in the first place, and most immigrants, even "birds of passage" soon realized that "to learn to speak and read English was to make their investment of time, expense, and money gilt-edged." Immigrant adults attended night schools at great personal sacrifice, petitioning the local authorities to establish them where they did not already exist. Parents of every ethnic group made enormous efforts to educate their children, sometimes leaving areas where jobs were better to move to cities where kindergartens and other special facilities were available. Among many groups the public school teacher was as revered as a priest or a rabbi. Recognizing the value of education in America, immigrant fathers wrote letters home insisting their children be sent to school in the old country even before immigration. Illiteracy was common among older immigrants, but the literacy rate among their American born children was higher than that of the old stock American population.

The public schools have received credit for the education and Americanization of the early twentieth century immigrants. Immigrants did become educated and Americanized, and public schools did contribute. They were able to do so because what they offered, the chance to become literate in English, supported the social and economic aspirations of the immigrant. But it must be remembered that public schools were only one of many institutions that helped immigrants adjust to the United States—and not necessarily the most important one. The job, the union, the political machine, the ethnic school, the ethnic press, indeed the ethnic community itself—these too, played significant roles in Americanizing and educating the immigrant.

The Immigrant and the Progressive

The relationship between the immigrant and the Progressive movement is a complex one. Progressive reformers were often middle class Anglo-Saxons who had their first experiences working with the immigrant poor through the institutional churches, settlement houses, and immigrant assistance leagues. Some social workers and reformers who began in those areas went on to become involved in political action. Recognizing the needs of the urban poor and the evils of unrestrained capitalism, they began to campaign for housing laws, factory inspection, child labor laws, compulsory education laws, workmen's compensation, widow's pensions, the ten (then the eight) hour day, and similar measures. Immigrants joined the Progressives in working for such changes.

Progressivism was an "umbrella" term which sheltered many different kinds of reforms, not all of which were supported by ethnic Americans. Many Progressives were intensely interested in the prohibition of alcoholic beverages, a reform which, then as in the pre-Civil War years, had little appeal to the ethnic voter. Even less appealing was the idea endorsed by some of the Progressives that the way to solve the social problems of the city was to cut off further immigration, especially immigration of "inferior" southern and eastern Europeans and Asians. Racism, directed at both immigrants and blacks, was a part of the "best" reform thinking of the day. Woodrow Wilson, a "Progressive" president, segregated all government agencies in Washington, D.C.!

Ethnic Americans were not usually sympathetic to Progressive appeals for political reform in the interests of efficiency or honesty. Political bosses opposed by good government reformers were often useful to the new ethnics, as they had been to the Irish, for reasons already discussed. They provided jobs and helped the party faithful in time of trouble. But when political bosses resisted factory inspection, sanitation improvements, or other "bread-and-butter" issues, immigrants joined with middle class reformers to unseat them. Unhampered by the old American tradition of hostility to active government, immigrants joined the wing of the Progressive movement that favored strong government action to limit the traditional freedom of landlords and business men to run their affairs as they saw fit. In states such as Massachusetts and New York, ethnic Americans were vital to the success of many economic and social reforms. Though most of the Progressive leadership was Anglo-Saxon, ethnic politicians like Robert Wagner and Fiorello LaGuardia began their careers as Progressive reformers.

Historians continue to debate the effectiveness of Progressivism and to question its motivation. From ethnic America's point of view Progressivism was a beginning, but only that. Parks, schools, and other facilities were built, but never enough to meet the need. Charities operated, but with limited effectiveness. Industrial states established health and safety regulations, forbade child labor, and extended compulsory education, but these laws were poorly enforced. Civil service and other "structural" reforms put many areas of government in the hands of trained experts, but in doing so they decreased the patronage power of the local ethnic politician. The substitution of "at-large" city wide elections for ward elections made it more difficult for ethnic communities to achieve any political representation at all.

Progressivism, then, was not the solution to ethnic America's problems. In the Progressive era, as in earlier years, ethnic Americans were essentially on their own. Success or failure depended less upon outside aid than upon the individual's own skills, health, determination, and luck. The most important source of help and support for virtually every ethnic American was the ethnic community itself.

CHAPTER 8

Building a Community:
Ethnic Institutions, 1820-1924

Even when outside help was not available, nineteenth and early twentieth century ethnic Americans did not face their problems alone. They joined together to share their experiences and their resources. Through this sharing, they created their own greatest asset, their "secret weapon" for entry into American life—the ethnic community. Arising from efforts to ease the shock of immigration for new arrivals, ethnic communities survived to meet the needs of subsequent generations and to become permanent features of the American social landscape.

An ethnic community was more than a ghetto, a geographic area in which a particular group was heavily concentrated. An ethnic community, like any other community, was a group of people who knew and cared about one another, enjoyed a common life, and shared common problems and concerns. The individuals in such a community related to one another in a variety of structured, or institutionalized, ways—some informal like the corner grocery or saloon, others formal, like the church, the school, or the fraternal lodge. Ethnic communities consisted of a network of such institutions, some as local as the nearby street corner, others as extensive as a national press.

The Neighborhood vs. the Community

The first step—but only the first—in the establishment of ethnic communities was the establishment of ethnic neighborhoods. Critics saw "foreign quarters"—little Italys, little Syrias, Polonias, Chinatowns, and the like—as evidence of the immigrants' clannishness and unwillingness to recognize that they were now living in the United States. This view was based on a lack of understanding of the nature and function of the ethnic neighborhood. Ethnic neighborhoods, like ethnic communities, were not "un-American." Rather they were the first step toward Americanization. Many immigrants arrived with little or no money, no job, no knowledge of English, in a land far different culturally and economically from the one they had left. The ethnic neighborhood met their immediate needs. Here they found information in their own language, familiar food, and lodging they could afford among people with whom they felt at ease. Here they got help in finding work, usually among coworkers who spoke their language and could help them learn the new occupation. Equally important, here they found the sympathy and friendship of others who shared their values and life experiences. These factors helped ease the cultural shock of immigration and made new beginnings possible.

In some cases ethnic neighborhoods were synonymous with ethnic communities—in small German, Scandinavian, or Dutch settlements in the Midwest, for example. Not every ethnic neighborhood grew into a true community, however. A community implies a degree of permanence and the institutionalization of interaction between its inhabitants. Sometimes immigrant neighborhoods were populated by members of so many different ethnic groups that no single group was numerous enough to establish its own institutions. Sometimes the inhabitants of an ethnic neighborhood did not remain there long enough to build a community. Immigrant enclaves at the edges of commercial or industrial areas were especially short-lived; as the cities grew, this property was quickly turned to more profitable commercial uses.

If some ethnic neighborhoods could not support even one ethnic community, others, Boston's South End, for example, and New York's Lower East Side, supported more than one. Several ethnic communities could coexist in the same immigrant neighborhood because an ethnic community was a network of interpersonal and institutional relationships, not a geographic location. By the beginning of the twentieth century, southern and eastern European immigrant groups had created communities that operated on a local, state, and national scale; northern and western European groups had created similar communities decades earlier.

To native-stock Americans the ethnic community, with its foreign language shops, churches, organizations, and publications seemed transported from an alien culture; but to the newly arrived immigrant it was an introduction to America. The familiar ethnic tongue spoken there was liberally seasoned with "Americanisms." "I was ten or twelve years old before I found out that such words as *pa tikkele* (particular), *staebel* (stable), and *fens* (fence) were not Norse but mutilated English words," wrote a Norwegian-American in 1900. The familiar tongue was used to express unfamiliar American ideas. Italian immigrants looked forward to the day they could purchase a *carro* (an automobile). Jewish immigrants found the new Yiddish vocabularly of their community a quick introductory course in American life: *blufferke* (hypocrite), *allrightnick* (an upstart), *next-doorige* (neighbor), and *consumptionick* (victim of tuberculosis).

What was true of language was equally true of virtually every institution within the ethnic community. Even the most familiar institutions, such as churches, were not the same; and new institutions existed that had no counterpart in the old country at all. The ethnic community was more American than foreign. Created on American soil to deal with American problems, the ethnic community was a halfway house between the old and the new. The familiarity of some aspects of life—language, food, religion—gave the immigrant the time, energy, and emotional security to concentrate on the many other things that were totally new. For some, the ethnic community was a temporary stop on the way to total assimilation into the life of the larger American community. For others, it became a permanent resting place.

Informal Institutions—Information and Companionship

In the European peasant community there were long established traditions about what should be done, by whom, and how. In America, on the other hand, obtaining work, keeping house, and rearing children raised troublesome new questions. In the European community there were well established places for people to get together to exchange ideas and information—the village tavern, the well or stream, or the job itself. In America, substitutes for these places had to be created. Informal institutions arose to meet the simple need for places to come together, share experiences, exchange information, and enjoy one another's company.

Even the earliest, most transient ethnic neighborhoods had at least a few of these "informal" community institutions. The first might be a boarding house where newcomers roomed with those who had been in America a little longer. Immigrants who ran such boarding houses often found that income from providing food, drink, and sociability to fellow immigrants exceeded their income from factory or mine and thus expanded into the operation of commercial taverns or saloons. In Irish, Polish, and other Slavic neighborhoods, the corner saloon was often the first important ethnic institution—the place where men came to meet their friends and talk of the old country, of jobs, of women, and the like. Among Syrian, Greek, and Armenian men, coffee houses played a similar role. Among German-Americans, the beer garden was a social and recreational center for the women and children as well as the men. In 1914 Mrs. Fernande Richter, a German-American from St. Louis, warned a Congressional committee that for Germans Prohibition—not alcohol—was a danger to family life!

In like manner, the local grocery store, the butcher shop, the bakery, even the dry goods store could serve as a social center where neighbors exchanged ideas and information. Indulging in gossip along with their shopping, people learned who among them was in trouble and thus were able to give help in the event of sickness, unemployment, or other catastrophe. Hearing how other people handled problems helped the listeners to solve their own. Even the good fortune of others was useful. Parents who bragged about the achievements of their children provided a "grapevine" of information about the opportunities available to the young.

The leaders of these informal institutions often became the leaders of their ethnic communities. In a Ukrainian neighborhood, for example, the owner of the tavern was often the most prosperous and influential man, the man who took the lead in building the first church and calling in the first priest. Other successful businessmen and sometimes businesswomen—undertakers, barbers, steamship agents, the owners of restaurants, physicians, and lawyers—played a similar role in other communities.

Young people as well as adults had their centers of information and recreation. The local poolroom, dance hall, or even a particular front stoop provided the recognized setting for such interaction. Among the boys, a special street corner might be the jealously guarded headquarters of an ethnic gang in which the strongest, shrewdest, or most charismatic boy instructed his fellows in the arts of urban survival. Though members of such groups sometimes got into trouble, often their activities were only mischievous, and the relationships they established survived a lifetime. Leaders trained in these neighborhood street corner gangs often graduated into careers of politics and community service or organized crime.

The home itself functioned as an informal community institution. People of all ages gathered in one another's kitchens to eat, to talk, to share—and by sharing to minimize hardships and maximize pleasures. Special celebrations like the wedding described in Di Donato's novel of Italians in New York, *Christ in Concrete,* became ritual events for the entire community. Traditional foods and familiar faces evoked common memories of the Old World, creating warmth and comfort in the New:

Annunziata and Cola passed the platters of antipasta as the paesanos found their seats. Bitter green Sicilian olives, sweet Spanish olives, whitings, and squid pickled in saffron, Genoese salami . . . pickled eggplants . . . soup with eggs, fennel, artichoke roots, grated parmesan and noodles that melted on the lips . . . boiled fat eels garnished with garlic and parsley . . . thick red wine. . . . The stuffing of the roast was rich with nuts, chopped squab, figs, cheese, eggs, and peppers, and hands that shoved it between wide lips were soaked in its flavors.

Ah, brother and sister, this is the life—cuddlingly arranged close to the flesh and smell and joy of them who are your own people. . . . I would this night last forever and more!

Five hours had they been at table, and now they sat back and in the strong tobacco clouds that nearly obscured the gaslight they talked of other days.

Remember the orange groves. . . .

The Campobasso where grazed the sheep of Don Pepe. . . .

And the Basilica of Saint Michael on All Soul's Day.

They reconstructed the beautiful terrain of Abruzzi and tenderly restored their youths and the times of Fiesta and Carnival.

The Lodge

As ethnic neighborhoods grew toward becoming ethnic communities, informal gathering places like the tavern, the shop, and the home were supplemented by more structured social organizations. The most common was the lodge, established by immigrants from the same county, parish, or district. As Italian immigrants often settled in the same blocks, even the same buildings, with their old neighbors from Calabria, Naples, or elsewhere, such organizations were natural in their communities. Eventually these local lodges were federated into a national network, the Sons of Italy. Similarly the Chinese of San Francisco formed the famous Six Companies, based upon the districts from which their members had emigrated. Japanese-Americans organized themselves into Kenjin-kai, again based upon common geographic origin. Jews from particular East European towns organized lodges known as landsmanschaften. Norwegians and others formed similar groupings.

The lodges usually began as social centers to supplement the cramped tenements, places to meet old friends, sing old songs, celebrate old holidays, and simply reminisce. They helped ease the shock and the loneliness of immigration for the newcomer. Though they were based upon common birthplace in the old country and their members spoke the same language, ethnic lodges were American in organization. They were voluntary associations with democratically elected officers and all the other trappings familiar to native-born "joiners" but perhaps unknown in the peasant village from which its members came. Their leaders were often men who had been of little consequence before immigration but who, because of luck or ability, had become influential in America.

Through the lodges, immigrants took on new tasks and learned to handle old tasks in new, American ways. Social life in the old country had taken care of itself. In America it was carefully fostered by the lodges which organized countless picnics, dances, parades, conventions, and other festivities for that purpose. Sometimes these activities were for men only, while branches, or even separate organizations, provided similar activities for women and children. Often the whole family participated together. As local lodges united into citywide, statewide, even national federations, the summer picnics, the New Year's Day parade, or the annual convention might involve thousands of people. Planning, publicizing, and handling the financial arrangements for such massive undertakings plunged many ethnic Americans into contacts with the general American community and its ways which they might not have known before.

Through the lodges, ethnic Americans took initiatives that would have been the responsibility of government officials in the old country. Lodges sponsored cultural programs and religious processions and established churches, synagogues, and schools. The Chinese Six Companies collected debts owed to Chinese immigrants by others within the community. The Japanese Kenjin-kai campaigned against gambling and other vices and served as an unofficial branch of the Japanese government, registering Japanese citizens at birth and doing other semiofficial business. Virtually every ethnic lodge became involved in economic self-help, acting as an informal employment bureau, lending small sums to help members buy farms or businesses, giving scholarships to deserving young people, and conducting insurance plans to cover funeral expenses, sickness, unemployment, and other needs.

Economic Self-Help

A variety of special institutions, some under the auspices of lodges, some independent, grew up to meet the very serious economic problems of the immigrants. Like the lodges, these organizations were essentially American solutions to American problems. In the old country close relatives or neighbors helped a family in need, and orphans and old people lived with the nearest kin. In an agrarian economy this system worked fairly well; there was always room for one or two more on the farm and always work they could do to help earn their keep. If the next of kin tried to shirk their duties to the unfortunate, the entire village would exert pressure to insure that responsibilities were met.

In the United States, as in Europe, tragedy was close at hand. Unemployment, illness or death of the breadwinner, a disabling accident, even another unplanned baby—such events could prove catastrophic when subsistence was precarious. But in America a family might be far from any relatives. When they were present, relatives were often unable to find room for the unfortunates in already crowded city apartments where they would take up space and contribute little. Nor was the old village social pressure available to force people to shoulder such obligations. New solutions had to be found.

When disaster struck, immigrants turned to neighbors who spoke their language. A collection might be taken up in the saloon, the bakery, the tenement house, or the lodge. Soon the idea arose that if everyone paid a small amount at regular intervals into a common fund, money would be on hand for emergencies. Thus arose the countless mutual benefit societies that provided funeral expenses, unemployment and sickness insurance, and even capital loans and college scholarships to large numbers of ethnic Americans. Most families were covered by one or more of these associations which existed in some form in every ethnic community.

From small beginnings, ethnic mutual aid societies sometimes grew into prosperous banks, building and loan associations, and insurance companies—a process which brought members of ethnic communities into the mainstream of American business life. The first Hungarian benefit society was formed by a group of miners pooling their resources to save a sick colleague from being evicted on a stormy night for nonpayment of rent. It began with a capital of $17.25. By 1945, the association had 364 chapters and assets of seven and a half million dollars.

An even greater success story is that of the Ukrainian National Association, which began as a mutual aid society in Shamokin, Pennsylvania in 1893. Founded by four clergymen, the association charged its members 50 cents a month for seven years in return for a small death benefit. Mutual benefit associations have become the most important institutions in the Ukrainian community. In the 1930's they insured over 137,000 Ukrainian-Americans, and had capital assets of close to twenty million dollars. In addition to their insurance activities, Ukrainian mutual benefit societies aided the poor, awarded scholarships, sent relief funds to the Ukraine, and held local and national meetings that were major events in the community.

Mutual aid societies were only one of many ethnic institutions that addressed themselves to economic problems. Because American banks were often reluctant to lend money to immigrants (who did not feel at home in these austere institutions anyhow), ethnic banks arose in every immigrant neighborhood. They provided badly needed services such as transmitting money overseas and making small loans. Japanese, West Indians, Chinese, and others with some commercial experience had informal "pools" for raising capital for prospective small businesses. Chinese trade guilds helped their members deal with American employers, provided aid to the unemployed, and, in the case of the laundries, divided the business territory among the competing firms to prevent cutthroat competition. Japanese farmers' societies disseminated information on improved farming methods and helped their members buy land, obtain supplies, and market their products. The activities of these and similar organizations in other communities were invaluable in helping newcomers secure a living.

Labor unions often functioned as ethnic organizations. In large cities unions were sometimes composed almost entirely of one ethnic group. There were Polish and Ukrainian unions near the Chicago stockyards, and Jewish unions in New York City's garment district. Though ethnically "segregated," these unions had an Americanizing effect. They taught their members about the American economy and about American politics. They encouraged their members to learn English, to become citizens, and to vote. Many sponsored classes, athletic events, parties, even theatrical activities for their members. The International Ladies Garment Workers Union owned a vacation resort and sent promising young workers to special labor colleges. Ethnic unions were often members of ethnic federations, such as the Hebrew Trade Unions of New York, but they were also integrated into the general American union structure through their craft affiliations. Unions dominated by a particular ethnic group were a bridge over which many workers passed into a fuller participation in American life.

Equally valuable as Americanizing agents were the ethnically mixed unions found in small mining or mill towns or in ethnically mixed urban neighborhoods. A study of Nanticoke, Pennsylvania during World War I noted a well integrated multiethnic population of 25,000 consisting of old stock Americans, second generation Welsh, Irish, and Germans, and immigrant Poles, Slovaks, and Lithuanians. The businessmen and their employees represented all of these ethnic groups. The tax collector was a Pole, the president of the Board of Health a Welshman, one of the appraisers a Slovak. Even "Quality Hill" had its foreign born residents. English was spoken everywhere. The cooperation among the various ethnic groups evident in all aspects of the town's life was the result of ties built up through the one organization common to all and central to the life of the entire town—the United Mine Workers local.

A similar role was played by the longshoreman's union in an ethnically mixed neighborhood in New York City. According to a union official, himself of Irish parentage:

> We understand one another, whatever the nationality. . . . Our meetingplace is open all the time and the men come here at any time when waiting for work. They read and discuss everything. . . . I know many a boy who has learned English because he had something to say at our meetings and he wanted everybody to understand him. . . . I have taken many a fellow up to naturalization court myself, and helped to put him through.

Though unions existed in Europe, the minority of immigrants who became union members did so for the first time in the United States. Because immigrants of every ethnic group were overwhelmingly working class, union membership was a unifying rather than a divisive force within each ethnic community. It was equally important as a force uniting the working classes of different communities and drawing them into a common American cause. The 1912 textile strike in Lawrence, Massachusetts, is an excellent example. Strike meetings were held at the Portuguese Center, the Franco-Belgian cooperative, and the Syrian Church. Issues were discussed in French, German, Italian, Polish, and Yiddish before Local 20 voted to begin the strike. Even though the strikers relief committees were organized along ethnic lines, all worked together in a common effort.

While most immigrants acquired their unionism in the United States, ethnic Americans brought another economic self-help institution—the cooperative—with them from abroad. More popular in Europe than in the United States, the cooperative movement was brought here mainly by Finns, although Russians, Lithuanians, Ukrainians, Poles, Italians, and other groups were also involved. Like unions, cooperatives were often located in ethnic neighborhoods. In 1920 the Finnish community of Fitchburg, Massachusetts, operated three successful cooperatives, a large grocery store, a boardinghouse-restaurant, and an apartment house. By purchasing shares, members of the cooperatives participated in the planning and management of these enterprises and shared the profits in the form of dividends. Meanwhile, outsiders as well as Finns enjoyed excellent products and services at the cheapest possible prices.

The Finnish Woman's Cooperative Home was begun in 1910 by a group of Finnish domestic servants in New York City who were looking for a place to spend their days off. They pooled their money to rent a few rooms for common use. The cooperative grew until its members, many of them young women still in their teens, owned and operated a commodious four story building with sleeping accomodations for forty, social lounges, club rooms, a library, a public dining room, and an employment bureau. The cooperative sponsored classes, provided music and other cultural programs, and held parties for the single young women of the Finnish community. The women who managed the cooperative learned a great deal about business, about America, and about their own capabilities.

Not all ethnic Americans were in a position to help themselves, either through mutual aid societies, unions, or cooperatives. Charities were needed for the sick, the disabled, the widow, the orphan, the aged. Through their lodges, churches, or independent organizations, ethnic communities made efforts to take care of the less fortunate among their numbers. Lack of resources and lack of experience in voluntary charitable organization limited the effectiveness of the efforts of some groups, the Irish, for example, and the southern Italians. Other groups, the Germans, the Japanese, the Chinese, the Syrians, the Lebanese, and the Jews were highly effective. Educated in the belief that charity is the obligation of every just person, Jews were particularly successful in this area. Accustomed to providing for their own poor in the hostile environments of Christian Europe, they built orphanages, old people's homes, hospitals, and other charitable institutions in the United States. The Jewish community pioneered new programs in social services, such as putting children in foster homes rather than orphanages whenever possible and devised fund raising techniques, such as the federation of charities idea, which were widely copied by other ethnic groups and by the larger American community.

Religious Institutions

Religious belief was part of the cultural baggage of every immigrant group; and every ethnic community reproduced, as far as possible, the religious institutions of its homeland. Catholic immigrants heard Mass in the United States just as they had in French Canada, Poland, or Austria. Jews sanctified the name of God in New York and San Francisco with the same prayers they had used in Russia and Rumania. Even Bohemian "freethinkers" established temples and Sunday schools to perpetuate their philosophy in the New World.

Religious belief did not survive immigration unchanged. In many cases an individual's religious faith and practice was weakened, even lost. Paradoxically, institutionalized religion, the church itself, was often strengthened. Visitors from Europe were often surprised to find that the institutionalized church had an influence far greater in the United States than in the old country. Pre-Civil War Irish immigrants, for example, grew up in Ireland where priests and nuns were in short supply, two thirds of the population never attended Mass, and "the ignorance of the people in matters of Religion is frightful." Yet the Irish became the staunchest and most devout supporters of the Catholic Church in the United States.

During the mid-nineteenth century, the Irish underwent what historian Emmet Larkin called a "devotional revolution." In their homeland pressures from their English rulers were causing them to lose their Gaelic language and culture. They became ardent Catholics because the Church provided them "a substitute symbolic language . . . a new cultural heritage with which they could identify and be identified and through which they could identify with one another." In like manner the Irish immigrants to the United States, finding other aspects of their Gaelic culture fast disappearing, made Roman Catholicism the touchstone of ethnic as well as religious identity.

Among other immigrant groups too the church increased in importance. It came to be not one ethnic institution among many, as in the old country, but the main bearer of ethnicity. The Polish Catholic parish became the American counterpart of the Old World communal village, for example; and the Greek Orthodox Church became the matrix of virtually all Greek ethnic life in the United States. To many immigrants the ethnicity of their church—its identification with their homeland and traditional culture and language—became more important than its religious content. This explains some of the difficulties immigrants faced in trying to transplant their old religious institutions to the New World. They were not just transplanting religion, they were transplanting ethnicity as well.

And there were difficulties. In theory the Roman Catholic Church was a universal Church, with services in a universal language, Latin. An immigrant from any European parish should have had no trouble fitting into any American parish. In practice this was not the case. Social and ethnic differences drove coreligionists apart. French and English stock Catholics were not enthusiastic about the waves of impoverished Irish Catholics who came in the mid-nineteenth century. The Irish, in turn, literally relegated the Italians and Poles to the church basement when they arrived, considering them scarcely human, much less Catholic. Nor were Catholics unique in this reaction. German Jews, settled and acculturated, were embarrassed by the arrival of impoverished, Orthodox Jews from Eastern Europe.

Part of the problem was the natural social snobbery shown by the newly respectable second or third generation toward their counterparts just off the boat. The newcomer presented a threat to a status won only recently and with much hard work! Other factors were also involved. The American Catholic Church experienced a struggle for leadership, a struggle won so decisively by the Irish that even in the mid-twentieth century Polish and Italian Catholics remain numerically underrepresented in the American hierarchy and are resentful of this situation.

There were ritual as well as social differences between ethnic coreligionists. East European Jews complained that the services of German Jews were cold and unfeeling, while German Jews considered the emotionalism of the newcomers undignified and improper. To Sicilian Catholics, the Catholicism of the Irish-dominated American church seemed puritanical, materialistic, and overly subservient to Rome. To the Irish, Italian Catholicism, with its devotion to local patron saints, its love of processions and pageantry, and its anticlerical tendencies seemed immoral and superstitious to the point of paganism.

In mixed parishes, Catholics fought over everything from the nationality of the priest to the name of the church. Ethnic groups that hated one another for political reasons in Europe could scarcely be expected to cooperate amicably in the same parishes in the United States. When Hungarians and Slavs, for example, or Poles and Ukrainians found themselves in the same parishes, Christian forbearance was rare. When a Ukrainian community in Pennsylvania left a Polish parish to establish its own church, the Polish priest urged his congregation to pray for its failure!

Such disputes led to the Cahenslyite movement, an attempt to divide the American Catholic Church, including its hierarchy, along ethnic lines. An enthusiastic Polish Cahenslyite took his case for a separate Polish church directly to President Grover Cleveland rather than the Pope. Perplexed, Cleveland referred the complaint to the Irish Cardinal Gibbons, who dismissed the Polish priest as "something of a crab." The Papacy, too, dismissed the idea of separate ethnic branches, considering it destructive of the unity of the American church. Undaunted, Polish dissidents seceded to form the still active Polish National Church. French Canadians fought the Irish dominated church fiercely, but in vain. Small groups of Italians, Czechs, and others turned to Protestantism. But most Catholic immigrants remained within the Church, establishing their own ethnic flavor in any parish in which they attained numerical dominance.

Ethnic churches in the United States were social centers as well as places of worship. This was especially important in rural areas, where the immigrant generation had few other outlets. Novelist O. E. Rölvaag described the reaction of a group of frontier Norwegians to the coming of the first minister, a reaction clearly more social than religious.

> It was so fun and jolly . . . the gathering together; now there would be some excitement in the settlement. . . . One was thinking about the congregation they would organize, another about the cemetery . . . men

would be needed to manage these activities . . . they would of course start a ladies aid, now that they had a minister; and that would be great fun, with meetings and cakes and coffee and sewing and all. . . .

In cities as well as rural areas, the church served as a social center for the ethnic community. A large urban parish included literally dozens of committees, religious fraternities, social clubs, and similar activities for men, women, children, and a new category scarcely recognized in the Old World, the teen-agers, or "youth."

While Christian and Jewish houses of worship had always recognized a "fellowship" function even in the Old World, the idea of the church as social center was new to Oriental religions. In Asia, Buddhism, Confucianism, and Shinto centered in home ceremonials and sacrifices at shrines; congregational worship was practically unknown. In the New World, however, Oriental immigrants either joined American missionary churches in their neighborhoods or established American style temples of their own—complete with women's committees and "youth" activities. Soon Oriental-American children were attending Sunday schools and singing, to the tune familiar to generations of American Sunday school children, "Buddha loves me, this I know. . . ."

With the church and synagogue changing from a place of worship to a community center also, the role of the priest, minister, and rabbi also changed. Religious leaders became administrators as well as spiritual leaders and took on additional responsibilities as fund raisers, educators, and social directors. Some clergymen established newspapers, insurance companies, even housing projects. Clergymen became counselors, helping their congregants adjust to America. At the same time, they became spokesmen for their community on the greater American scene, and were recognized as such by outside authorities. Thus when the participation of ethnic communities was needed in a charity drive, Fourth of July celebration, or other civic occasion, contact was made through the ethnic religious leader. As a result, one criteria in the selection of an ethnic clergyman was whether he would make a "good appearance."

Laymen also assumed new roles in America. In the early days of an ethnic community, religious services were often held in farmhouses, tenements, and storefronts. Laymen organized and conducted the services themselves, performing tasks reserved for officials and trained clergymen in the homeland. "We conducted our religious meetings in our own democratic way," said a Norwegian immigrant. "We prayed, exhorted, and sang among ourselves, and even baptized our babies ourselves."

In many European countries religion was supported by the

government. In the United States the lay community struggled, often for years, to build a house of worship and pay the salary of a minister when he was finally summoned. It is not surprising that laymen, accustomed in the early years to much independence, balked at relinquishing that independence to the clergy. There was constant bickering and factionalism in most of the Protestant denominations. The Catholic Church was shaken in the mid-nineteenth century by the controversy over control of church property—whether it should continue in the hands of lay trustees, as had become the custom in the United States, or whether it should be given to the hierarchy. The hierarchy was victorious, largely because it was supported by the increasingly numerous and influential Irish immigrants. Nevertheless, in most ethnic churches the move to America expanded the power of the laity.

When religious denominations moved to the United States, they often changed in content as well as in form. Protestant denominations moved away from their emphasis upon sin, judgment, and eternal damnation to a more optimistic emphasis upon salvation for all from a loving God—an evolution similar to that undergone by American Puritanism much earlier. Catholicism, too became more worldly, more optimistic, more "American," so much so that Pope Leo XIII warned American Catholics against overemphasis of the "active" virtues at the expense of traditional humility, charity, and obedience.

Similarly, age-old principles of Oriental religions were altered by the American environment. Filial piety, the absolute devotion and self-sacrifice of the young for the sake of their parents, was given a surprising redefinition by a Japanese bishop: "Parents may feel lonesome in some way or other and they will need your consolation," he told a group of young Japanese-Americans. "Tell them that good parents must think more of the future of their children than their own. To give in this life is to receive in another."

Beliefs and practices in Judaism changed as much as in any other faith. Reform Judaism, a movement to modernize traditional religion in the light of nineteenth century secular rationalism, came to America with mid-century German immigrants (although it had appeared independently in Charleston as early as 1825) and was successful almost immediately. Congregations split, factions took each other to court, and at least one rabbi was locked out of his synagogue as the battle between Orthodoxy and Reform raged. When the smoke cleared, the more radical reformers had abandoned the age-old authority of Jewish law, had dropped the Hebrew language from worship services altogether, had changed the traditional Sabbath from Saturday to Sunday, and were proclaiming the United States the new Jerusalem. The influx of East European Jews around the turn of the century led to a revival of Orthodoxy and to the growth of Conservative or Historical Judaism, a creative compromise that proved increasingly attractive to the second and third generations.

Ethnic churches were loved by their immigrant congregants because they preserved some of the ethnic feeling of the old country—the native language, the favorite saints, the special holidays. Church leadership was more deeply committed to preserving the religion, however, than the ethnicity. Thus when it became obvious that the traditional language was alienating the younger generation, many clergymen switched partly or completely to English over the vociferous objections of older congregants.

Recognizing that their denominations would survive in the United States only if they identified with the new land, ethnic churches soon began holding special services for American national holidays, participating in civic events and charity drives, and encouraging their congregants to do likewise. Thus even the most conservative churches became agents for change in the lives of their ethnic constituents, and that change was in the direction of greater involvement in American life. Many clergymen became skilled and trusted counselors for immigrants seeking help with problems of Americanization. Congregants who hesitated to use the settlement houses, night schools, and other public agencies took advantage of parallel services within their reassuringly familiar ethnic churches. Some immigrants accepted English lessons for themselves and mixed dances for their teen-agers only when these events were sponsored by their church. Thus the changing ethnic churches became effective agents of Americanization even though they maintained much of the Old World tradition—or perhaps *because* they did so.

The Ethnic School

Ethnic schools were an essential part of the life of most ethnic communities, especially Roman Catholic communities. Though the official goal of a parochial school education for every Catholic child was never realized, the nineteenth century Irish Catholic immigrant community built an extensive parochial school system at great financial sacrifice. German Catholics also built parochial schools in the nineteenth century, though they were perhaps less intensely committed to their use than the Irish. Twentieth century Catholic immigrants were more divided in their views. First generation Italian Catholics preferred public education for their children, because there was no tradition of church supported education in Southern Italy. Polish and other Slavic immigrants, on the other hand, were accustomed to church involvement in education in their homelands and were therefore more ardent in their support of parochial schools in the United States.

Parochial schools reflected the ethnicity of the sponsoring parishes. In Polish, Ukrainian, French-Canadian, and other parish schools, teachers from the mother country struggled valiantly to give their American born students a grasp of the language, traditions, songs, heroes, and holidays cherished by their parents. Many of these schools were bilingual, teaching religion and other ethnic subjects in the traditional language and "American" subjects such as American history, geography, and bookkeeping in English.

Parents, clergy, and community leaders spent untold money and emotional energy in building and maintaining parochial schools. To the devout, the parochial school was a religious necessity; the public schools were considered hotbeds of atheism. But most parents sent their children to parish schools for reasons that had more to do with culture, or ethnicity, than with faith. Parents and community leaders hoped that ethnic parochial schools would insure their children's loyalty to their ethnic heritage and the ethnic community and would encourage social relationships, including marriages, within that community. Finally, many parents disapproved of what they considered to be the lax discipline of the public school. Nuns, they believed, could be trusted more than public school teachers to teach their children proper manners and respect for their elders.

Catholics were not the only sponsors of ethnic education. Scandinavian and German Lutherans also built parochial schools. Of the 370 parish day schools in South Dakota in 1900, 213 used German or one of the Scandinavian languages for instruction. Norwegian and Swedish children who did not attend parochial schools during the school year often attended ethnic schools sponsored by their churches during the summer months. Chinese, Japanese, Greek, and Jewish parents supplemented their children's public school education with ethnic and religious schooling in the afternoons, or evenings, or on weekends. Here children studied the language, literature, philosophy, and religion of their ancestors.

A small percentage of ethnic schools were completely secular. Finnish socialists and Bohemian "freethinkers" conducted weekend schools to transmit their economic ideology as well as their national language and history to their children. Jewish groups such as the Workmen's Circle conducted secular Jewish schools. While synagogue schools concentrated upon the teaching of Hebrew, the traditional language of prayer, secular Jewish schools taught the East European vernacular, Yiddish, and its literature.

Stormy debates raged within ethnic communities and between ethnics and older stock Americans about the desirability and effectiveness of ethnic schools. Parochial schools, which enrolled as many as half of the eligible ethnic children in urban areas, undoubtedly relieved the pressure on the overcrowded public schools. Like the public schools, they ranged in quality from very good to very poor. Chronically short of money, ethnic schools, even more frequently than public schools, had poorly trained teachers and inadequate facilities. In parochial schools sixty or eighty children might be assigned to an enthusiastic but insufficiently trained teen-aged nun who had not yet finished her own high school education. Afternoon and weekend schools were conducted in makeshift quarters—the back of a store, or the basement of a church or synagogue—and were taught by anyone who could be persuaded to take a job with such meager financial and emotional rewards. Tired children rebelled at attending these unattractive and seemingly superfluous schools after a full day at the public school, and exasperated parents bribed, cajoled, and forced them to attend.

Contrary to the suspicions of their critics, ethnic schools transmitted a great love of the United States to their young pupils. Parochial schools taught American history and geography with great enthusiasm and held elaborate pageants to celebrate national holidays. Members of religious orders whose English was poor brought in special American born teachers to give the children a good English background and sent children to the public schools for high school or for vocational courses when this education was not available in the parochial system. The English part of the curriculum was the most successful part taught in the parochial schools, because parents and children both saw its relevance to American life. Bilingual education of the parochial school was especially valuable to the child who had just immigrated or who had had little or no opportunity to learn English. These children were frequently able to transfer to the public school system at their appropriate grade level after a few years of parochial school education.

The ethnic curriculum of both day and supplementary schools was less successful. Children who did not speak the mother tongue from birth rarely acquired more than a smattering of it—and in homes where it was no longer spoken, even this smattering was soon lost. Some of the children who attended these schools retained little of the ethnic history, literature, and language that was so laboriously taught them. What many did learn, however, was that their collective past extended beyond the squalid tenements to the glories of ancient civilizations and the achievements of great scholars, artists, and kings. Scorned by many of their Anglo-Saxon contemporaries, shabbily dressed immigrant children must have suspected that, like their illustrious ancestors, they too could achieve.

There were other benefits from ethnic education. The ability of ethnic teachers to maintain discipline and to communicate effectively with parents may have resulted in more years of education for at least some ethnic children. Good ethnic schools gave the American born generation a better understanding of their foreign born parents. By keeping lines of communication open, they enabled children to provide useful American information to their parents and parents to provide guidance and security to their children. Finally, loyalty to the local ethnic school was an important factor in building the cohesiveness of the ethnic community, both in the immigrant generation and in the generations that followed.

Cultural Institutions, Adult Education, and Athletics

Opportunities to enjoy their native culture, long established in the homeland, had to be created from scratch in the New World. Immigrants formed special associations—or used the auspices of lodges or churches—to bring artists, singers, actors, musicians, theatrical companies, and opera from the homeland. Culture was something one did as well as watched, however. From their earliest years in the United States ethnic Americans joined together to create their own folk dancing groups, musical ensembles, and drama companies which performed for the general American public as well as for the ethnic community itself.

The more highly educated ethnic Americans formed intellectual groups of various kinds. Bohemians, Germans, and Jews read and discussed classics and modern books. Arabic speaking intellectuals formed the Golden Link, a literary society, in 1918. Ethnic intellectuals did not always confine their activities to their own circles. The Hungarian Free Lyceum offered lectures to Hungarians and to the general public in Magyar (Hungarian) and in English. Topics included "Modern Hungarian Poets," "The Americanization of Hungarians," "The Discovery of America and Colonial History," "The American Revolution and the Civil War," "Industrial Hazards," and "The Influence of the Press." As the topics suggest, the Lyceum hoped to teach about the Hungarian heritage and also the United States.

Unlike the bilingual Hungarian Free Lyceum, the Polish University of Chicago held its sessions in the ethnic language only. It was begun by Polish socialists whose main aim was to educate the Polish working class, and its approach to learning was broadly humanistic. The scope of the Polish University's activities and their value to Polish immigrants and to the United States are suggested in this description by one of the University's moving spirits:

. . . we took up questions about the beginning of things . . . the creation of the world, the theory of evolution, primitive man, the development of language. . . . Almost all of our members could understand and speak ordinary English, but many others who attended the lectures could not. But obviously the use of Polish was necessary if such subjects, which are hard enough to grasp anyway and which involve many scientific terms and fine shades of meaning, were to be got across to our audiences.

. . . Gradually . . . we came to subjects connected with America and civil problems. But here we do more than have lectures. We go and see for ourselves how civic agencies work. At different times we have visited most of the public departments and institutions of this city. . . .

We hold our meetings at the public park center in the neighborhood . . . over a thousand people came to the last lecture. . . . We haven't preached "Americanization" . . . but practically all our members are citizens who take an active interest in civic affairs, and if what America wants is people who can think and act for themselves, then we're *doing* Americanization.

Athletic societies played a major role in the life of the American ethnic community. Groups such as the German *Turnverein*, the Scandinavian *Turners*, the Bohemian *Sokol*, and the Polish *Falcons* began with gymnastics and other kinds of physical training and branched out to include music, drama, and social and educational activities for the entire family. In Europe, these societies were often involved in politics; the Bohemian *Sokols* drilled their members for action against the Austrian rulers and the Polish *Falcons* did likewise against the Russians. In the United States such organizations took on an American patriotic flavor. They urged, even required, their members to learn English and become citizens, and encouraged them to serve in the American armed forces.

Of course, the young people played the traditional American team sports of baseball and football, often on ethnically mixed teams in their schools or neighborhoods. (A good ethnic athlete had access to American social circles, regardless of how hard the native born found his name to pronounce.) Adults came together to enjoy the sports of their homelands—wrestling, swimming, rowing, fencing, shooting, and gymnastics. Societies formed within an ethnic community for this purpose were soon in touch with one another and with their American counterparts. In 1920 the Amateur Athletic Union of New York included immigrant athletic societies representing Scandinavians, Jews, Hungarians, Finns, Bohemians, Scotch, Irish, Greeks, and Germans, who competed on even terms with a variety of native American teams. Similar arrangements existed throughout the nation. Athletic teans, like so many other ethnic institutions, functioned both to solidify the ethnic community itself and to bring that community in closer touch with the outside world.

Nationalist Societies

Many ethnic Americans maintained ties to their homelands, sending aid in time of war, famine, or other catastrophe. Ethnic communities institutionalized these ties in the form of nationalist societies. These societies encouraged interest in the traditional language, history, and culture of the homeland, defended its reputation (and at the same time, their own) and raised money for educational and charitable projects. Many of the nationalist societies worked to liberate the homeland from foreign domination. American Poles worked for the restoration of the Polish national state that had lost its independence in the late eighteenth century. The Irish and the south Slavs sought the establishment of free nations for peoples that had been ruled by outsiders for many centuries. Jews sought a Jewish state in Palestine after a lapse of almost two thousand years.

Nationalist societies might appear at first glance to be the ethnic institutions most foreign to American life, but such was not the case. Though intellectuals wrote and agitated for nationalist causes in nineteenth century Europe, most immigrants were simple people who acquired their ethnic nationalism after they arrived in the United States. Among rural Europeans, which included most of the immigrants, loyalties were parochial. "I never realized I was an Albanian," said one immigrant, "until my brother came from America in 1919. He belonged to an Albanian society over here." Immigrants from the Ukraine called themselves "Little Russians" or "Ruthenians" until World War I, when the most Americanized among them began to use the term "Ukrainian." Even the strong tradition of nationalism in Poland rarely reached the peasants until after they had emigrated. Polish nationalism in the homeland was strongest among the educated and well-to-do. "The lord was a Pole, he (the common man) was a peasant."

National consciousness in ethnic communities sprang largely from the American environment. Here for the first time some immigrants met a wide enough variety of people to be aware of the similarities and differences among them. Because there might be only a few people from a particular town or parish in an American city, ethnic colonies expanded to include countrymen who would have been considered "foreigners" at home.

American education gave many immigrants their introduction to the history and national aspirations of their homelands. American ideas about democracy, self-government, and freedom of expression made the political domination of their homelands seem even more oppressive than when they were living there. Sometimes an ethnic American began to identify with the plight of the oppressed mother country because of discrimination in the United States. Patrick Ford embraced the Irish cause after months of futile searching for a job in anti-Irish Boston. He concluded that, as an Irish-American, he was the victim of "conditions of poverty and enslavement" in Ireland and that his situation and that of all Irish-Americans would improve only when Ireland was regenerated. Nor was Ford's view without foundation. The fortunes of the homeland affected the way ethnic Americans saw themselves as well as how others saw them. The independence of Poland after World War I raised the status and self-esteem of Polish-Americans, and the establishment of the State of Israel in 1948 affected American Jews similarly.

The outbreak of World War I and the United States' entry on the side of the Allies was the event that did most to spark ethnic American nationalism. The war was widely interpreted as a struggle between the "good" western democracies (including Russia after the revolution of 1917) and the "bad" German, Austrian, and Turkish Empires. Because of the principle of the "self determination" of nations, one of Wilson's war aims, ethnic Americans from the "subject nationalities" suddenly found the larger American community in sympathy with the political aspirations of their homelands.

In this atmosphere old nationalist societies were revitalized and new organizations with mass support were created. One of the most effective of these new organizations was the Polish National Defense Committee, which collected fifty million dollars worth of goods and services for the homeland and helped raise the volunteer Blue Army to fight for Polish independence. The world famous pianist Ignace Paderewski toured the United States to raise funds for the Committee. Polish-Americans lobbied continuously to keep Congress, President Wilson, and later the League of Nations aware of their desire for the restoration of Polish independence. Similar activities were undertaken by Ukrainians and South Slavs, who held massive conventions, bombarded the government with telegrams and resolutions, and, at Wilson's invitation, marched through the streets of Washington in national costumes on July 4, 1918.

Some nationalist societies saw their objectives achieved, although not necessarily because of their efforts. Polish independence, for example, was restored because it suited the purposes of the Great Powers. New, independent Balkan states were carved out of the defeated Austro-Hungarian and Turkish Empires. The existence of at least one of them, Yugoslavia, has been attributed to the activities of south Slavs in the United States. Jewish nationalism achieved its first step toward success with the Balfour Declaration—Britain's promise of a Jewish "national home" in Palestine. Although Zionism attracted increasing support from American Jews in the years after World War I, it did not become a mass movement until the Nazi murder of six million Jews during World War II. A trickle of dedicated Jewish nationalists, including Golda Meir, a Milwaukee housewife and schoolteacher who became Premier of Israel, emigrated from the United States to help rebuild the Promised Land. The establishment of the Irish Free State in southern Ireland shortly after World War I was a partial victory for Irish nationalists here and abroad, though the struggle for the independence of Northern Ireland continued.

Ukrainian Americans were bitterly disappointed with the results of World War I. They had hoped for Ukrainian independence, but once again the Ukraine was swallowed up by rapacious neighbor states. Like the Irish, the Ukrainians refused to give up. The leading Ukrainian-American newspapers sent an investigating committee to document political atrocities in the Ukraine. The Ukrainian community sent telegrams to Congress and to the League of Nations. So much money was raised by the far from prosperous Ukrainian-Americans for the benefit of the homeland that, according to one Ukrainian-American historian, their own needs went unmet. At the New York World's Fair of 1940, the then politically nonexistent Ukraine had an impressive pavilion, sponsored by the Ukrainian-American community.

The plight of the homeland was one of the few concerns shared by the diverse religious and socioeconomic elements in every sizable ethnic community. Not all ethnic Americans joined nationalistic societies, but most supported their activities, attending their benefits and contributing money to their appeals. As Mr. Dooley, the Irish-American humorist observed, "Be hivins, if Ireland cud be freed by a picnic, it'd not only be free today but an empire." For many immigrants, working for a nationalist society was a constructive way of assuaging the guilt they felt over having abandoned family, friends, and fatherland to come to America. For their children and grandchildren, nationalist activities were a socially acceptable—and not too demanding—way of affirming an ethnic identity which, though still valued, was slipping away with time and Americanization.

In order to obtain citizenship, ethnic Americans had learned to describe America's political machinery. During World War I, through the political activities of nationalist societies, they learned how to use that machinery. Nationalist societies developed ethnic lobbies which soon became as much a part of the scene in Washington as farm lobbies, labor lobbies, and corporation lobbies. Ethnic nationalists became increasingly American in their ideology as well as their tactics. They often linked the struggle of their homelands against foreign rule to the revolt of the thirteen American colonies. "What the United States fought for in 1776 is what Serbia is fighting for today," said a Serbian-American leader in 1914.

The failure of some nationalist causes resulted in an intensified commitment of its followers to the United States. Continued poverty and political oppression in the Ukraine ended the dream many Ukrainian Americans had of returning to the Ukraine. Paradoxically, the success of other nationalist movements had a similar effect. The restoration of Poland and the creation of independent Slavic states in the Balkans gave ethnic Americans from these backgrounds a real option for the first time. They could go home to what seemed to be improved conditions, or they could stay in the United States and become Americans. Thousands did return to their former homes in the 1920's. But most discovered that they were already "home," that they did not really want to live in the foreign nations they had helped to create. Sentimental ties remained, but now they were unambiguously committed to the United States.

Contributions of the Ethnic Community

An ethnic community was more than the sum of its institutional parts. Each had its own values and priorities, its own social and political atmosphere determined by the cultural baggage its members brought from the Old World and the circumstances of their lives in the new. Southern Italians, accustomed to relating mainly to their own extended families, were most successful at first in forming small, localized institutions. Jews, on the other hand, accustomed to ties far beyond their own family and village, soon established citywide, statewide, even national organizations. Twentieth century Germans, rich in professional leadership and financial resources, had many institutions. Ukrainians, lacking both, had relatively fewer.

Some immigrants never affiliated with their ethnic communities, either by choice or because none was available. The majority did affiliate and reaped many benefits. Through the institutions of the ethnic community, formal and informal, they received information in their own language to help them find jobs, become citizens, establish households, and rear children. Self-help societies and charities mitigated their poverty, and social events eased their loneliness. Religious services alleviated their spiritual hunger, and nationalist organizations enhanced their self-respect. It is not surprising that immigrants who participated most fully in the life of their ethnic communities adjusted most rapidly to their new environment.

There were other benefits, less tangible but equally important. The ethnic community offered status and recognition to people who otherwise might have attained neither. Outstanding ethnic entertainers, athletes, and artists were acclaimed by the general American public, but people with less spectacular abilities went unnoticed. Most immigrants, with their broken English and their menial jobs, had few opportunities to feel important. But within their ethnic communities, as officers of the church, or lodge, or special committee, these immigrants received the recognition they needed and deserved. Through their ethnic communities, thousands of talented men and women whose abilities might otherwise have been wasted were helped to make significant contributions to American life. Many who received their "basic training" in the ethnic community went on to positions of leadership in the outside world as well.

Finally, the ethnic community helped fill the moral vacuum in the lives of immigrants who had left behind established patterns of "proper" behavior, and the social pressures of extended families and close-knit communities that had enforced these patterns.

Ethnic institutions—schools, churches, lodges, athletic associations—affirmed traditional religious, social and family values, reserving their offices, their honors, and their approval for people whose behavior was morally acceptable. Because the only weapon the American ethnic community had to enforce its standards was disapproval, chronic violators were more likely to be ostracized than reformed. The ethnic community was a positive force in support of stable, responsible living. In a bewildering new environment, it gave immigrants solid ground to stand on in determining what their priorities should be and how they should behave toward one another.

But there were negative sides to the ethnic community as well. Group pride could spill over into destructive chauvinism. The desire to favor one's own, in employment for example, could lead to discrimination against outsiders. Ethnic communities, the victims of prejudice, harbored many prejudices themselves. An important Irish-American newspaper, the *Catholic World,* denounced Italians as "totally devoid of what may be termed the sense of respectability." Ethnic theater often presented derogatory stereotypes of other ethnic groups. Polish, Jewish, Irish, and Italian gangs engaged in bloody battles in defense of ethnic "turf," and ethnic Americans sometimes joined old stock Americans in violent attempts to keep blacks out of neighborhoods and institutions they regarded as their own.

Factionalism within an ethnic community, even within a single ethnic institution, was a serious problem. Quarrels within ethnic institutions and communities could be bitter, even degenerating on rare occasions into physical violence. But violence could be spiritual as well as physical. In their zeal to preserve traditional values and standards of behavior, ethnic communities could be cruel to the nonconformist. New ideas were sometimes sacrificed to tradition, or, worse still, to pettiness or narrow-mindedness. Community organizations created bureaucracies with their attendant dangers of corruption and lack of responsiveness to the people they were meant to serve. Leaders sometimes became less interested in leading than in maintaining their own positions and enhancing their own fortunes. It is not surprising that young people—and mavericks of any age—often found the organized ethnic community more stifling than stimulating.

Like all human institutions, ethnic communities reflected the faults and the weaknesses of the people who comprised them. Their problems were magnified by the fact that they struggled to survive in a majority society that was often indifferent or even hostile. Moreover, their self-appointed task—preserving a foreign tradition while helping their members become Americans—was fraught with ambiguities. Whatever policy an ethnic institution followed, the one thing it could count upon was criticism. Yet despite these difficulties, ethnic communities served their members so well that subsequent generations continued to maintain at least some affiliation with them.

In serving their members, ethnic communities also served America. They gave financial aid and insurance to a large percentage of the American poor at a time when our national life provided little economic protection for anyone. Ethnic communities educated millions of children and adults. They brought stability to urban neighborhoods and enriched the cultural and social life of the entire nation. Finally, they embodied and fostered many of the traditional virtues of which the United States appears most proud—voluntarism, self-help, neighborliness, democracy, and community spirit.

CHAPTER 9

Words and Feelings:
The Ethnic Press, Theater,
and Literature, 1820-1924

Ethnic Americans seemed possessed by an irresistible compulsion to record their experiences and their feelings. Poorly educated or even illiterate in the lands of their birth, immigrants in America produced a prodigious number of newspapers, plays, poems, songs, stories, memoirs, autobiographies, and novels. Why was there such an explosion of words within ethnic America? What feelings did those words convey?

A Torrent of Words

A new and pressing need for information helped cause the explosion of reading and writing in ethnic America. Traditional wisdom handed down by word of mouth was inadequate to deal successfully with life in urban, industrial America, where the only thing certain was constant change. Immigrants needed access to a constant stream of new information provided by the printed word if they were to succeed in their new environment. Realizing this, people who might have been content to remain illiterate in the peasant village made heroic efforts to learn to read in America, or even before they arrived. They insisted that their children learn to read not only the mother tongue but English as well.

The need for information was equalled by the need for self-expression. Immigration was a shattering emotional experience, the equivalent, according to one ethnic writer, of being "born again." People who had undergone this upheaval in their lives needed to put into ordered and permanent form the chaotic feelings and experiences that, unexamined, threatened to overwhelm them. This need to articulate, understand, and thereby transcend their own experience led to ethnic theater, poetry, memoirs, and other forms of literature.

Finally, there was a great outpouring of writing in the mother tongues in America because many of these languages had been suppressed in Europe. Poles, Bohemians, Slovenes, Ukrainians, and other "subject nationalities" had been living under the cultural as well as the political domination of outside powers. In the Russian-controlled Ukraine, for example, it was illegal to publish a book, produce a play, deliver a sermon, or give a lecture in the Ukrainian language. Education from the village school to the university was conducted in Russian. Similar situations existed in many other areas. A ban against teaching Polish in German-controlled areas of Poland led to a strike of over 150,000 Polish school children.

In such an atmosphere, the use of the suppressed language became the symbol of the national survival of the people that spoke it. Bohemian patriots had a saying, "As long as the language lives, the nation is not dead." Nationalism and literacy spread from a few intellectuals and patriots to a wider population, a process that moved much more quickly in the free atmosphere of the United States than in the homeland. In the United States, as in the homelands, use of the native tongue became a self-conscious political program. In the mid nineteenth century Lithuanian was no longer spoken by the literate classes in Lithuania; yet between 1834 and 1895 at least thirty-four Lithuanian language periodicals were published in the United States. The revival of the ancient Irish language, Gaelic, flourished in Boston before it did in Dublin. Slovakian peasants read newspapers in their native language in New York and Chicago, a patriotic exercise not permitted in the Austro-Hungarian Empire. When the United States offered opportunities for self-expression in their native language, immigrants seized these opportunities.

The Ethnic Press

In little Italy, little Poland, little Syria, the Irish shantytown, the Jewish ghetto, Chinatown, and the Japanese colony—the ethnic press was visible everywhere. Educated immigrants debated its editorials. The semiliterate spelled out headlines and advertisements. The illiterate listened while a friend or relative read. In the sweatshops immigrants pooled their pennies to pay one of their number to read aloud while they worked. By 1920 over a thousand foreign language periodicals and newspapers were being published in the United States with their circulation running into the millions. In urban centers such as New York, Chicago, and Detroit, large ethnic communities supported dozens of newspapers while no group—the Letts, the Estonians, the Wends, the Spanish Catalons—was too small to have at least one.

Foreign language publications were as varied as the communities that produced them. There were dailies, weeklies, monthlies—and papers that came out whenever their editors could assemble the material and the money to print an issue. The smallest had a few dozen subscribers; the largest had circulations of over a hundred thousand. The four leading Yiddish newspapers in New York City alone sold over a third of a million copies every day. Many ethnic publications were local, serving a particular town or village or even a particular neighborhood or parish. Others were national and even international. In *Al Hoda*, for example, Arab-Americans advertised to locate missing relatives in Cuba, Brazil, and Mexico.

Most foreign language papers began as "shoestring" operations, often the work of unemployed immigrant intellectuals. Frequently the original owner was bought out by a businessman, who put the paper on a sound financial basis. The *Desteaptate Romane*, a leading Rumanian newspaper, is a good example. It was begun by an educated but sickly Rumanian immigrant who faced deportation because he had no prospects for employment. On the advice of a helpful immigration official, he collected a few dollars from each of his friends and set up the *Desteaptate Romane*. He was reputed to write well, but could not manage the paper financially. Eventually he was bought out by the owner of a steamship ticket agency.

A successful Japanese born journalist, Shakuma Washizu, left a colorful account of the early days of the Japanese-American press. Washizu's background before immigration was typical of that of many ethnic journalists—"middle class family, published a newspaper or two, ran for a political office or two, went into business, but was never successful. . . ." His first job in the United States was with a newspaper where "the editorial sanctum was at the same time kitchen, dining room, printing shop, parlor, and bedroom, all in one. The editor . . . unshaved face . . . shabby dress . . . gave me the impression of a tramp."

Washizu tried working first for one small paper then another. Finally he issued his own comic magazine called *Agahazushi* (*Open the Jaws*). "The magazine continued up to twelve numbers, but the total income . . . was not more than fifteen dollars. I did not eat more than once a day for several months." Eventually he became the manager of a larger paper with brighter prospects. "We got together a number of those press men at a building which became gradually a resort for the homeless and poverty stricken fellows. As I was manager of the paper, everybody called me a great king. I was a sad king indeed—I had to do all the cooking." This venture, too, almost ended in disaster. An unfortunate caricature resulted in a lawsuit. "As we could not hire a lawyer to defend the case, we lost it." Washizu and a colleague went to jail for nine months, not an unmitigated disaster. "During that time both of us really lived, as we had plenty to eat. . . ."

Despite this inauspicious beginning, Washizu's paper, later called the *Japanese-American News*, became the largest and most influential Japanese daily in the United States. Most ethnic newspapers were not so fortunate. Nine out of ten did not survive their first year of publication. The successful ones, however, the *Jewish Daily Forward*, the Italian *Il Progresso Italo-Americano*, the Spanish *La Prensa*, the German *Staats-Zeitung*, and similar papers lived on decade after decade exerting an enormous influence in their respective communities.

Ethnic newspapers reflected a variety of ethnic interests. Many were the organs of mutual aid societies, churches, or lodges. Others were commercial ventures. There were literary papers, humorous papers, and papers for farmers, musicians, socialists, anarchists, trade unionists, religious factions, and freethinkers. Special journals were published for young people and for women. The nationally circulated Bohemian *Zenske Listy* of Chicago was a feminist journal, printed and edited by women and devoted not to "beauty lessons" and "household hints" but to efforts toward women's suffrage and "the uplifting of the attitude of working women."

The contents of ethnic newspapers varied widely, but certain things were characteristic of most. The front page was usually devoted to news of the mother country, so that the press, like other ethnic institutions, served as a link between the Old World and the New. Here the immigrant could find out what the harvest had been like at home, what was happening in the old church, and what political or economic reforms were in the offing. Nineteenth century Irish-American papers, for example (English in language, but ethnic in content), included news of the Great Famine, of the various reform factions in Ireland, and of the arrival of immigrant ships to the United States.

News of the United States was also reported, often summarized and translated from the American press. The better papers taught their readers about American life through skillful coverage and interpretation of national and local news. The socialist press, important among Jews, Finns, and Bohemians, organized the news within a radical ideological framework. Previously uneducated laboring people were stimulated to read and think by a radical press interested in the problems of "workers" and "bosses"—their problems. According to

Robert E. Parks' study of the immigrant press, "socialism gave the common man a point of view . . . from which he could think about actual life. It [the socialist ethnic press] made the sweatshop an intellectual problem."

Even after they were able to read the American press, immigrants and their children turned to the ethnic press for news of their own communities. In local ethnic papers they could learn the news of the neighborhood available nowhere else—who had been married, who had died, who had had a new baby, who had been baptized, confirmed, or become a *bar mitzvah*, who had been honored with the chairmanship of the church committee, the presidency of the lodge. Here they could follow the progress of the organized community—the success of the latest fundraising drive, the building of the new ethnic school, the arrival of the new minister from overseas, the creation of a new national agency or political lobby. And here they could read about, and rejoice in, the success of their own people, in business, politics, education, or whatever, both within the ethnic community and in the larger world outside.

The editorial columns of the ethnic press aired the controversies of the day. Anarchists, socialists, nationalists, members of religious factions, and secularists debated ideology and tactics, the editors often talking more to one another than to their subscribers. Most readers were more interested in practical subjects that affected everyday life. They welcomed features on child rearing, cooking, health care, how to obtain American citizenship, and how to vote.

Catering to these interests, feature writers were effective agents of Americanization and of education in general. Julian Chupka of the leading Ukrainian paper *Svoboda*, was typical of many such feature writers. He published articles entitled "Pictures of America," "the Constitution of the United States of North America," and "Something about the Laws and Courts of the United States, Especially in Pennsylvania." Abraham Cahan, Abner Tannenbaum, and other Jewish journalists introduced the Yiddish reading public to Darwinism and other scientific ideas, and to the science fiction of Jules Verne. A Lithuanian radical paper introduced its public to the philosophy of Nietzsche with a translation of *Thus Spake Zarathustra*.

The most widely read features were poetry, fiction, and the letters to the editor. Much of the poetry and fiction was sent in by readers with more sentimentality than literary talent. Pulp novels ground out by "hack" writers were published in installments, to keep their following eagerly awaiting the next edition. Not all of the literature published in the ethnic press was the product of amateurs or hacks, however. The foreign language press introduced its readers to the works of many talented professional writers from within the community and outside.

Ordinary readers as well as professional writers and journalists contributed to the ethnic press. Rural subscribers wrote in news of the weather, the passing seasons, and the harvests. Often they voiced their concerns about the decline of religion among the young and expressed their nostalgia for the scenes and the faces of the homeland. Elderly people exchanged information about old friends and relived old times, as in the following letter published in *Swenska Amerikanaren* (a Chicago based Swedish paper).

> Thanks Carl Jonason of Britain, South Dakota, for your letter in the paper. Indeed, I remember you, even though it was a long time ago. . . . I was surprised to see a letter from you, Nelson, the miller of Hjulsnasis. . . . In the large village of Skarap, we had many happy occasions, as the man of Skane said when he buried his dead wife; 'I can't keep from laughing, when I think of the happy hours I had with that wife of mine.' If any acquaintances who know me see this, let us hear from you sometime.

Editors served as priests, psychiatrists, social workers, and friends to readers who had nowhere else to turn. Many papers had "advice" columns, but none was as famous as the "Bintel Brief," ("Bundle of Letters") of the *Jewish Daily Forward*. Through the "Bintel Brief," poverty stricken people found jobs, husbands were united with their wives, and parents located children from whom they had been separated many years. Everyone found sensible advice for problems ranging from the most trivial to the most overwhelming:

> My father does not want me to use face powder. Is it a sin?
> The editor assures a young girl that it is not.

> Since I do not want my conscience to bother me, I ask you to decide whether a married woman has the right to go to school two evenings a week. My husband thinks I have no right to do this.
> The editor states unequivocally that the wife "absolutely has the right to go to school two evenings a week."

> A long, gloomy year, three hundred and sixty-five days, have gone by since I left my home and I am alone on the lonely road of life. . . . My heart is heavy for my parents whom I left behind. I want to run back. . . .
> The editor tells this young man that all immigrants suffer similar loneliness and advises him to remain where he is, work hard, and bring his parents to America.

> I am one of those unfortunates who for many years has suffered from the workers' disease (tuberculosis). I am the father of a three year old girl. . . . All who know my child hug her and kiss her. But I may not. I know this all too well, yet I can't help myself. Every time I kiss the child I

feel my wife's eyes on me as if she wanted to shout, 'Murderer'! but she doesn't utter a word. . . . What can I do?

The editor warns the man not to kiss his child and holds out the hope that with good medical treatment he may live to enjoy her for a long time.

My husband deserted me and our three small children. . . . I am able and willing to work . . . but unfortunately I am tied down because my baby is only six months old. The local Jewish Welfare Agencies are allowing me and my children to die of hunger . . . because my 'faithful' husband brought me over from Canada just four months ago and therefore I do not yet deserve to eat their bread. I will sell my beautiful children . . . for a secure home where they will have enough food and warm clothing for the winter.

The editor asks "What kind of society are we living in that forces a mother to such desperate straits." He urges help for the mother, help which his readers will undoubtedly provide. As for the delinquent husband, "Who knows what's wrong with him. Perhaps he, too, is unhappy."

Glancing through the advertisements in an ethnic newspaper is like peering into the tenement windows of the community. The papers of the newer communities—Poles, Italians, Greeks, Armenians—advertised boarding houses, cheap restaurants, and local dry good stores. The papers of longer established communities, Germans, for example, contained the advertisements of ethnic professionals and of "downtown" as well as local merchants.

As food preferences are among the most long-lived ethnic characteristics, all papers carried ads for groceries and delicatessens. Gold watches, the status symbols of the successful immigrant, were also widely advertised, as were electric belts, trusses, and other items dealing with health care. Often professionals of one ethnic group developed specialties which they advertised in other ethnic presses. Thus Chinese physicians advertised syphilis cures in the Greek press of San Francisco, and a Jewish lawyer, Fannie Horovitz, offered her services on "civil and criminal cases" in *Il Progresso Italo-Americano*.

Advertisements for books and music varied with the interests and educational levels of prospective customers. The Spanish, Rumanian, Italian, and Portuguese press advertised books on religion, love, and magic. The Portuguese *Alvaorado* of New Bedford offered its readers a 35¢ library featuring such titles as *The Virgin and the Sinner*, *Perpetual Adoration*, and the *Rose of Granada*, while *Il Progresso Italo-Americano* tempted its readers with *Meditations on the Sexual Problem, the First Night of Matrimony*, and *Telepathy and Dreams*. The more radical or intellectual journals of all ethnic communities advertised substantial volumes on science, history, economics, and on literature with a tinge of social criticism, such as the works of Émile Zola and Upton Sinclair.

"Wanted—girl or childless widow, 19-27 years old, freethinker, agreeing to a civil marriage, knowing how to read and write in Lithuanian, wanted by a man 29 years old, photographer, using no intoxicants or tobacco," read an advertisement in *Kelevis*, a Lithuanian paper in Boston. Similar ads appeared in many ethnic papers, a symptom of the loneliness of the immigrant cut off from the traditional village matchmaking machinery.

According to the Jewish Communal Register of 1917-1918, "the election of any candidate on the East Side (of New York) is impossible unless the Yiddish press favors him." The impact of the ethnic press on public opinion in all ethnic communities was enormous, a fact which did not go unnoticed by politicians and other special interest groups. Louis Hammerling, an immigrant from Galicia, organized the American Association of Foreign Language Newspapers to dispense Republican party advertising during the political campaign of 1914. Hammerling made a successful business of influencing the foreign language papers' policies in return for the advertising accounts he could throw their way. Questioned by a Senate committee, he replied "I am simply doing what I learned in this country from the American newspaper people. . . . There is hardly an advertiser who is not asked if he wants something in that paper when he advertises."

During World War I Hammerling was suspected of selling influence in the ethnic press to "disloyal" parties. His organization was taken over by Frances A. Keller and used by her Inter-Racial Council for "Americanization" and "better understanding between capital and labor." Despite the special pleading of groups such as Hammerling's and Keller's, the ethnic press remained largely independent, responsive to the needs and interests of the readers. The ethnic press played many roles. By preserving the traditional language and reporting news of the old country it cushioned the shock of immigration and helped preserve the traditional heritage of the ethnic American. At the same time, it was an important force for educating immigrants and helping them adjust successfully to the New World.

A questionnaire sent out by a Russian paper, the *Russkoye Slovo*, in 1919 suggests the educational impact of the ethnic press. Of 312 immigrant readers surveyed, only sixteen had read newspapers in Russia! In the United States, all 312 were regular readers of the Russian press, two thirds were regular theatergoers (almost none had attended theater in Russia) and over a fourth were also regular readers of the American press. Russian-American journalist Mark Villchur concluded that "An interest in the (Russian-American) press creates an interest in the book, in the theater, and the whole outlook of the Russian in America widens. Not only his own interests, the interests of his family and of his circle become near and dear to him, but also the problems of his country, of the republic in which he resides, and, gradually, of the whole wide world."

Ethnic newspapers performed other important functions. Through the ethnic press, communities exchanged ideas and information and were able to take on projects on a scale that would otherwise have been impossible, establishing colleges and universities, seminaries for their ministers, and national charities. The nationalist societies could never have conducted their activities in behalf of the homeland without the ethnic press. The ethnic press also stood as a guardian against unfair treatment of its constituency. One example typical of many was the action taken by *Svoboda* to help 365 Ukrainians tricked into becoming contract laborers in Hawaii. *Svoboda* led a campaign of demonstrations and letter writing to American Congressmen that resulted in the voiding of the harsh contracts and the freeing of the laborers.

People did not read the ethnic press because they wanted to be Americanized or educated or molded into a community. They read the ethnic press because it reflected their interests, their problems, and their feelings. The intimate relationship between loyal readers and their favorite paper is suggested by Ruth Levine, a longtime employee of the Yiddish *Der Tog (The Day)*. According to Levine, readers felt free to come to the editors, day or night, when they needed help with a job, with the police or immigration authorities, or with a medical or personal problem. Readers argued with the columnists, expected to be answered when they wrote, and carried yellowed clippings of their favorite articles in their pockets for years.

Not long ago, an agent for the now defunct Yiddish *Der Tog*, traveling through the Middle West, stopped to call on an old subscriber he had not seen for a long time. The woman who greeted him introduced herself as the subscriber's wife and told the agent that her husband had been dead for a year. "But you never stopped the subscription," said the agent. "I know," she replied simply. "I'm not Jewish, but I know how much the paper meant to him. I bring it to his grave."

The Theater

The ethnic theater was not an occasional Saturday night amusement; it was a vital part of life. The Chinese immigrant would work a fourteen hour day in a restaurant or laundry and then sit in rapt attention to watch a four or five hour theatrical production. German shopkeepers, craftsmen, and farmers spent many hours rehearsing their parts in amateur productions. Sweatshop workers went without meals to buy tickets for the Yiddish theater. Among people hard pressed for time and money, theater was not a luxury, but a necessity.

"To the Jews from uptown who had achieved social standing and wealth in the new country, a visit to the Yiddish theater was a nostalgic return to the land and traditions of their fathers," writes David Lifson, a historian of the Yiddish theater. "To the poor and hard working laborers and artisans, it meant glamour and exultation; it was as a service in the synagogue . . . (but) more rewarding." As Lifson suggests, ethnic theater, like the ethnic press, filled many needs. It linked the young and the old, the newcomer and the old-timer, the rich and the poor. It provided education, excitement, and entertainment. But its greatest significance was that, like the ethnic press, it was the creation of the people themselves. It mirrored their experiences and their emotions. Through theater, even the illiterate and the inarticulate expressed themselves. In the theater, one's innermost feelings were turned outward and examined at the safe distance of the footlights where they suddenly became less fearsome, less overwhelming.

The ethnic theater, like the ethnic press, was as varied as the communities that created it. Hundreds of amateur theaters throughout the land were sponsored by cultural or athletic societies such as the *Turnvereins* and *Sokols*, ethnic churches, settlement houses, and schools. The *Circulo Italiano* used theater to create better understanding between immigrants and their children, and immigrants and the larger community. Finnish, German, Hungarian, and Jewish workers used theater to educate their fellow workers about industrial problems and the need for a new socioeconomic order. Finally, many ethnic communities such as the Chinese, German, Italian, Hungarian, Irish, and Jewish, supported commercial theaters with professional actors and actresses, directors, and playwrights. They performed regularly in metropolitan centers and went "on the road" to reach outlying communities.

Ethnic theater was a theater of the people, transcending the usual lines of class and education. An amateur German theater active in Hermann, Missouri as early as 1843 was led by a tanner and an architect; its actors included craftsmen and day laborers as well as lawyers, a doctor, and a saloon keeper. Professional theater attracted audiences ranging from the intellectual elite to the illiterate. No group was more devoted to its theater than the East European Jews of New York City. Hutchins Hapgood's description of Yiddish theater on the East Side in the early 20th century suggests the meaning of ethnic theater as "theater of the people:"

> In the three Yiddish theaters on the Bowery is expressed the world of the ghetto—that New York City of Russian Jews, large, complex, with a full life and civilization. . . . Into these three buildings crowd the Jews of

all the ghetto classes—the sweatshop woman with her baby, the day laborer, the small Hester Street shopkeeper, the Russian-Jewish anarchist and socialist, the ghetto rabbi and scholar, the poet, the journalist. The poor and ignorant are the great majority. . . .

Great enthusiasm is manifested, sincere laughter and tears accompany the sincere acting on the stage. Pedlars of soda water, candy, and fantastic gewgaws of many kinds mix freely with the audience between the acts. Conversation during the play is received with strenuous hisses, but the falling of the curtain is the signal for groups of friends to get together and gossip about the play or the affairs of the week.

Like newspapers, ethnic theaters often began with little financial support. Many closed, reopened, and closed again only to reappear, perhaps in another location or another town, with the same actors and directors. Financial difficulties were not their only problems. Theaters frequently ran into trouble with the local police for giving performances on Sunday, the day most convenient for working class audiences. In 1897 the sheriff seized the properties of a Chinese theater in New York because the theater had violated the Sunday "blue laws." During World War I many German theaters were forced to close because of the boycotts and threats of superpatriots.

Every ethnic theater had its own distinctive flavor, its own history and development. Because theater could be enjoyed by everyone, even the less well educated immigrant groups could bring a theatrical tradition with them from the Old World. Thus while most ethnic newspapers developed in the United States and copied American models, such as banner headlines, sensationalism, sports pages, and cartoons, ethnic theaters kept their "foreign" characteristics and traditions much longer.

One of the oldest immigrant theaters was the Chinese, which held two distinct types of performances. For the Caucasian community, the Chinese presented variety acts, including juggling and dagger throwing. For their own audiences they gave long, highly stylized productions consisting of hundreds of acts, often taking many weeks for a completed performance. The actors were all males, some of whom impersonated women with well cultivated falsetto voices. Costumes were elaborate. Scenery, on the other hand, was sparse and impressionistic. Placards indicated where the action was taking place—a desert, or forest, or town. Servants in plain dress walked on stage to hand the actor whatever he needed—a pen, a sword, a cup, a fan. Simple stools, boxes, and tables were the only properties, and actors not needed for a particular scene sat at the back of the stage, in plain view of the audience, smoking or eating while waiting to go on again.

Chinese theater included special conventions familiar to the

Chinese audience but bewildering to the outside observer. There was much use of pantomime. "To represent his entering a house and slamming the door in the face of another character, an actor had only to take a chair from a servant, slam it down on its side at the feet of the other actor, and then stand on it," wrote an observer. "With equally clear and convincing pantomime he could ride a horse, whipping a stool smartly on the rump." In historical dramas a whirl represented the passing of a generation, a somersault the passing of a century. A dynasty famous for its orators was suggested by a gorgeously dressed warrior who "strutted up and down for ten minutes, saying not a word but gesticulating powerfully, leaping aloft, smiting, striking . . . keeping time in all his gestures to the deafening gong beats."

Italian theater evolved from the *societe filodrammatiche*, informal amateur groups who assembled to play the mandolin, sing, perform pantomime, and in general to enjoy themselves entertaining one another. Often these groups gave public performances, charging a small fee which was donated to a community charity. Eventually some of these groups became professional theater companies.

One of the liveliest and most successful professional Italian theaters in America was the *Circulo Famigliare Pisanelli*, a combination theater and café which opened in 1905 in the Italian North Beach section of San Francisco. This theater, and its larger successor, the Washington Square Theater, became the social and entertainment centers of the North Beach Italian community due to the energy, business acumen, and talent of their founder, actress and impresario Antonietta Pisanelli Alessandro.

Alessandro's theaters performed translations of Broadway plays and of classics by Shakespeare, Goethe, and Dumas, but her audience was most enthusiastic about presentations of traditional Italian entertainment that reminded them of home. Alessandro's own renditions of regional Italian folk songs were always well-received, as were the *zarzuellas*, short comedy acts featuring the regional stock characters and humor of the traditional Italian *Commedia dell'arte*. As in *Commedia dell'arte*, actors usually worked without scripts, relying upon spontaneous wit and skill at improvisation. The audience recognized the costumes, characters, and situations portrayed in the *zarzuellas* as characteristic of particular districts in Italy. If the district was their own, their pleasure was undoubtedly increased.

The most popular productions in Alessandro's theaters, and perhaps in most Italian theaters, were operas. Whatever else was on the program (which often included several plays of one or more acts, with folk songs between the acts), the *Circulo* featured a different opera every night. *La Traviata, Rigoletto, La Boheme,* and *Otello* were favorites. The simplicity of staging necessitated by the small stage and budget did not dampen the enthusiasm of the audience. According to a contemporary observer:

> Italians look upon opera as a necessity and also strictly as an amusement, and they want it strong and good, artistically and musically. They care little for scenery—they want the acting, and upon this and the music everything depends. . . . This unique Circulo makes little effort at scenic effects—the artists are expected to make their own scenes and pictures in dramatic acting. At times the little stage is well crowded with characters, but there seems to be enough room for the most striking situations and dramatic scenes, and the auditors are satisfied without the aid of scenery.

If each stage had its own distinctive flavor, there were common themes in the material they produced and common satisfactions for the audiences they attracted. Ethnic theaters kept alive the language and culture of the mother country by producing its national classics. Italian theater produced the great Italian operas, which many immigrant laborers could sing from memory. German theaters produced works by Schiller and Goethe. Historical dramas were popular in many ethnic theaters. Yiddish theaters often performed plays based on Biblical themes.

Ethnic theater exposed its patrons not only to the past greatness of their native land, but also to its contemporary cultural developments. Ukrainian, Japanese, Italian, and other theater groups from the Old World performed on tour in American ethnic theaters, and individual actors, dancers, musicians, and singers from overseas made guest appearances in the United States. German language theater produced the best works of such modern German dramatists as Gerhart Hauptmann and Frank Wedekind. In 1896 the Irving Place Theater produced Hauptmann's controversial *Die Weber* (*The Weavers*), a story of a strike among Silesian weavers hailed by the *New York Dramatic Mirror* as "probably the most graphic picture of human misery ever written." The play was not produced for English speaking audiences until 1915.

The Jewish stage played Yiddish drama from Eastern Europe as well as translations and adaptations of the works of Moliere, Schiller, Tolstoy, Shakespeare, Zola, Gorki, Ibsen, Strindberg, and Molnar. In the late nineteenth and early twentieth centuries Yiddish speaking theatergoers had a better chance than their native born counterparts to become familiar with the best literature and drama of many lands. Like the ethnic press, ethnic theater was, in the broadest sense, educational.

People did not go to the theater to be educated, however; they went to be entertained. Serious drama by the best playwrights was less popular with general audiences than comedy, romance, and melodrama. Despite the harsh realities of their lives—or perhaps because of these harsh realities—ethnic audiences loved laughter, farce, and burlesque. The spirit of fun in mid nineteenth century German theater is captured in a report in the Missouri Hannibal *Tri-Weekly Messenger*:

> The German theater opened with a very 'talon-ted' company . . . on Bird Street. . . . The piece enacted on the occasion, we are informed, was the beautiful Tragedy entitled *The Butcher's Dog*, or the *Last Link of Sausage!* This beautiful and affecting piece was received with a handful of pea-nuts and a [sic] boquet of cabages! Their next presentation will be *The Strangled Codfish*, or the *Death of the Mad Mackerel*.

Such fare was played with great enthusiasm, for the sheer fun of it. But comedy had a practical function also. It provided emotional release for the immigrant struggling with loneliness, homesickness, family problems, and the dreariness of a life of hard work and uncertainty. Often the stock character in ethnic comedy was an immigrant, "green," stupid, ignorant, taken advantage of by those around him, comic in his daily tragedies. Such tragedies were only too familiar to the audience. This kind of comedy allowed ethnic Americans to laugh at their own problems and to rejoice in how far they had come. They watched the misadventures of the "greenhorn" on the stage with sympathetic recognition, and with the satisfying knowledge that they would not make such foolish mistakes—anymore.

This was the secret of Farfariello, a stock comedy character in the Italian-American theater. As the various districts and provinces of Italy had produced characteristic stock comedy figures, the Italian community in America produced Farfariello. Farfariello was the brain child of Eduardo Migliaccio, an Italian immigrant who became an actor after being fired from a sweatshop for burning a hole in the pants he was pressing. Farfariello was the "wop" of New York's Lower East Side. He was the garbage collector, the ice man, the fruit vendor, the pick and shovel man, the uneducated "greenhorn" who murdered the English language as well as the Italian. Much of his humor was based upon puns, parodies of famous people (Enrico Caruso, for example), or easily recognized Italian-American types such as the fruit dealer, the grocer, the school girl, and the nurse. His routines included shrewd satirical comments upon the class structure both of Italy and of the Italian-American community. Farfariello was a hero as well as a clown, exposing the weaknesses of the wealthier, pretentious people around him, and somehow triumphing over them.

The Irish theater, like the Italian, exposed the foibles of its own community and did so with broad farce and rollicking song. Masters of this kind of theater in the late nineteenth century were Harrigan and Hart, whose irrepressible productions included on-stage fights, fires, and explosions. In *Squatters Sovereignty,* a play about "shanty" Irish who decide to set up housekeeping in Central Park, two brawling clans appear on the stage, accompanied at various times by a goat, a donkey, and a flock of geese. Audiences mourned when the goat died on stage after cutting his throat on the sharp edge of a tin can.

Harrigan and Hart poked fun at the second generation as well as the first and especially at the social climbing "lace curtain" Irish. They also enjoyed satirizing the Irish political machine. In one play the main character, Mulligan, invites the Irish city aldermen to his home. The aldermen drink themselves into a stupor.

"Whatever will I do?" Cordelia Mulligan asks her husband. "The aldermen are all sound asleep."

"Leave them be," said Dan. "While they sleep, the city's safe."

Much ethnic theater was what the Germans called "kitsch," sentimental stories about everyday life in the Old World and the New. A historian of the Yiddish theater describes these "formula" plays which were common to all ethnic theaters but especially popular on the Yiddish stage.

> Plot counts for nothing compared with idiom and gesture; what matters is that the stock types . . . be put through their paces. The poor man (has) . . . a beautiful unmarried daughter and the rich man is outwitted by the peddler . . . true love will frustrate the marriage broker . . . the typical policeman will stroke his mustache. . . . The tradition is melodramatic, sentimental, and unsophisticated. It is also moving, funny, and intensely human.

Aside from being good entertainment, ethnic melodramas served many of the same functions as television "soap operas" of today. They provided insight into the problems, though in exaggerated form, that the audience met in their own lives. The unwed mother, the wayward son, the ungrateful daughter, the cold husband, the cruel stepmother, the faithless wife—such were the stock characters of ethnic melodrama. The audience recognized the shadow of reality, wept, yet felt somehow comforted. At least their spouse was not as cruel as the one depicted on the stage, their children not as heartless, their poverty not as hopeless.

The themes of the different ethnic melodramas suggest the problems in the lives of their respective ethnic groups. The Chinese theater in San Francisco, for example, featured a play about a husband separated from his wife for many years by the fortunes of war, just as the typical Chinese immigrant was separated from his wife. Undoubtedly the audience was heartened by the fact that the wife of the play rejects all suitors and remains faithful to the end. The husband's situation is more ambiguous. A beautiful princess falls in love with him and forces him to marry her. Like the immigrant, he is torn between the old and the new. The play has a happy ending. After many years and many obstacles, the husband is reunited with his faithful wife. The real life drama of the Chinese immigrant separated from his family did not usually end so happily.

The plays of Jacob Gordin, master of Yiddish melodrama, reveal much about the Jewish community for whom he wrote. His Yiddish adaptation of *King Lear* transformed the English king into a pious Jewish father in America abused and neglected by his Americanized —and heartless—daughters, a theme sure to bring tears to the eyes of an audience to whom it often represented reality as well as theater. *Minna*, a play similar in theme to Ibsen's *A Doll's House*, explores the dilemma of a woman whose husband neither understands nor appreciates her. Minna wants to be free to lead a life of her own. Unlike Ibsen's Nora, however, Minna cannot break away from her child and from the role of "faithful wife" she has been brought up to play. In desperation, she commits suicide.

One of Gordin's best plays was *The Slaughter*, which Hapgood described as "the story of the symbolic murder of a fragile young girl by her parents who force her to marry a rich man who has all the vices and whom she hates." The wife stays with her cruel husband—and his cold, curt mistress and half-witted son—to prevent her parents from being sent to the poor house. Life is misery for her and her parents until she discovers that she is pregnant. But this happiness only leads to further tragedy.

> There is a superb scene of naive joy in the midst of all the sordid gloom. The scene is representative of the way the poor Jews welcome their offspring. There is the rapturous delight of the old people, the turbulent triumph of the husband, the satisfaction of the young wife. They make a holiday of it. Wine is brought. They all love one another for the time. . . . But indescribable violence and abuse follow, and the wife finally kills her husband, in a scene where realism riots into burlesque, as it frequently does on the Yiddish stage.

Tears, like laughter, filled a need in the immigrant's life. The theater gave people a socially acceptable opportunity to express the anguish that so many had bottled up inside them. Harry Golden understood this when he observed, "Many of the immigrants had families in the old country. The Yiddish theater helped them to remember and to cry." This is why a famous soprano, Lucy Gherman, made a career out of one song, "Ebiga Mama" ("Eternal Mother"), and thousands of shopgirls wept through performance after performance of Jennie Goldstein singing "Ich Bin Ein Mama" ("I Am a Mother"). Immigrants who had left home, family, a whole way of life, unpleasant as some aspects of that life had been, experienced a deep sense of bereavement. They had lost much and like all who are bereaved, they needed to mourn. The melodrama of ethnic theater helped them express their grief at the passing of the old. In so doing, it helped prepare them to accept the new.

Poetry, Autobiography, Satire

Newspapers and theaters were institutions through which entire communities expressed themselves. Within each community, individuals also found means of self-expression—through poetry, autobiography, and fiction. Although the works of a few ethnic writers appeared in English, or were translated, and received praise from "American" critics, most immigrant writing was published in the mother tongue by ethnic presses and was, and unfortunately still is, inaccessible to the general reader.

The product of many hours of painstaking work, much immigrant writing was never published at all. It may never even have been read by anyone but its author, who put it carefully away in a box in a corner of a bureau drawer. Sometimes such work was lost forever. Sometimes it emerged years later, rediscovered by a curious relative cleaning out an attic or a basement—perhaps a child or grandchild unable to read or understand the language in which the work was written.

Because their folk traditions were rich in verse and song, immigrants turned naturally to poetry as a vehicle for their deepest emotions. The ethnic press was filled with poems of nostalgia for the old landscapes, faces, and songs. The following two poems, translated from German and Ukrainian, respectively, are typical of this popular genre:

> O, if I could hear again
>   In German forests, green and cool,
> The birds in May, and dream beside
>   The black wood pool.
>
> O, to find and smell again
>   Wood violets meek,
> To fall asleep on woodlawn mosses,
>   The Rhineland's breezes on my cheek.
>
> O, my Ukrainian song,
>   You sweeten my days.
> For I learned you
>   From my dear mother.
> My mother rests in the grave
>   Of her native land,
> But her songs still re-echo
>   From my lips.

Many immigrant poems are documents of the author's reactions to the new life of the United States. Such poems are often sad. The following poem was written in English by a young Italian immigrant who had studied the language only a few months. As the poem suggests, the young man was unhappy with his job in a mill and eventually returned to his homeland.

> Nothing job, nothing job,
> I come back to Italy;
> Nothing job, nothing job,
> Adieu, land northerly. . . .
>
> Nothing job, nothing job,
> O! Sweet sky of my Italy;
> Nothing job, nothing job,
> How cold is this country. . . .
>
> Nothing job, nothing job,
> I return to Italy;
> Comrades, laborers, goodbye;
> Adieu, land of "Fourth of July."

More sophisticated was the Yiddish poetry of Morris Rosenfeld, whose verses were sung in workers' meetings. Rosenfeld wrote of the dehumanizing pace of the factory. He described the men and women whose health and family life were ruined by the long hours of tedious, spirit-breaking labor demanded by the early twentieth century American industrial system.

A TEAR ON THE IRON

> Oh, cold and dark is the shop! I hold the iron, stand, and press;—my heart is weak, I groan and cough,—my sick breast scarcely heaves.
>
> I groan and cough, and press and think;—my eye grows damp, a tear falls; the iron is hot,—my little tear, it seethes, and will not dry up.
>
> My head whirls, my heart breaks, I ask in woe; 'Oh, tell me, my friend in adversity and pain, O tear, why do you not dry up in seething?'
>
> I should have asked more of the unrest, the turbulent tear; but suddenly there began to flow more tears, tears without measure, and I at once understood that the river of tears is very deep. . . .

After a collection of his poetry was published in English in 1898 under the title "Songs from the Ghetto," Rosenfeld was acclaimed by

critics and invited to read his works on tours of universities in the
United States and Europe.

The author of the following poem, a Chinese immigrant, was not so
"discovered." His poem, which appeared in an anthology of Chinese-
American verse published in 1927, describes the isolation of the
Chinese immigrant.

> He fought long years for life,
> For his daily bread,
> He, a Chinese, died in a strange land.
> In a little room where he lodged.
> No one knew, for a day, of his death,
> Then the landlady knocked at his door—
> She found him dead. . . .
> For seven years he worked throughout this land
> Doing good for others, not for self. . . .
> He knew so many persons,
> But he had none as friend.
> Buried in a lonely grave,
> He is gone! His work is finished! . . . .

While some immigrant poetry extolled the beauty and the
excitement of the new land, most of it like the examples just given had
at least a tinge of sadness. Like poetry, immigrant diaries and
autobiographies told of loneliness and hardship, but they usually
stressed the more positive aspects of the American experience—the
fertility of the land, the kindness of friends and neighbors, the
opportunities for education and advancement. In *Laughing in the
Jungle,* Louis Adamic, a Yugoslav journalist and intellectual, describes
the United States as an industrial jungle in which the strong young man
can make his way only by defying adversities and laughing at
hardships. In *The Promised Land,* on the other hand, Mary Antin finds
the urban ghetto flowing with the milk and honey of teachers and social
workers who offer encouragement and support to a talented
immigrant child. Most immigrant autobiographies are more sanguine
in their views of America than immigrant poems because their authors
were often looking back from positions of security and success.

Typical in many ways is Constantine Panunzio's *The Soul of an
Immigrant.* Panunzio traces his life story from his childhood in
Southern Italy through his difficult early years in the United States to
his later career as a minister involved in Americanization and social
work in the Italian-American community. A valuable aspect of this
autobiography is Panunzio's attempt to verbalize what he has gained in
ideas rather than in material advancement from his immigration to
America.

Panunzio begins by praising the American willingness to break with the past, to try something new—a new job, a new house, a new town, a new idea, in contrast to the Southern Italian way of staying with the familiar and the proven. "The mental outlook (in the United States) is one of free adventure and free movement," writes Panunzio. "I have adopted it as the first plank, I might call it, in my American philosophy of life." Other "planks" were to follow.

Panunzio remembered that his adult relatives in Italy had constantly worried about the children's overstepping the bounds of custom. He was glad to adopt the American system in which people paid attention "rather to the *right* or the *wrong* of an act, than to whether or not it is customary." He praised the American tendency to value a man not for his ancestors' achievements, as was often the case in Italy, but for his own achievements, or even for what he hoped to achieve in the future. One of the greatest things America did for him, Panunzio wrote, was to cure him of idle dreaming and make him a practical man. In America, according to Panunzio, even idealism was geared to action rather than to dreams.

Panunzio admired the native-born Americans for their pride, their self-reliance, and their refusal to ask favors as had been the custom in Italy. He resolved to adopt these virtues, too. Most important he learned "the power and value of optimism." Wars, poverty, uncertainty, "the morbidity of our religious teachings"—all had combined to create an atmosphere of "somber pessimism" in the home of his youth. In contrast, Panunzio found Americans indomitably cheerful.

> . . . the optimism of American life was first strikingly illustrated to me by the hilarious and exuberant cheering of men and women over a football game. What astounded me most was to see them cheer when their team was *losing* as well as when it was *winning*, as if to say, 'We will yet win' and thereby to overcome all obstacles to victory. . . . It may be that it is due in no small measure to the grandeur, the sunshine and the exuberance which God has showered in such abundance upon these vast and magnificent stretches! Whatever the reason . . . optimism grips the very soul of me. . . .

Ethnic Fiction

Every sizable ethnic community produced so large a group of short story writers and novelists that it is impossible to do more than suggest the scope of their work. Their subject matter was the entire range of ethnic life in the United States—the child growing up, the relationships between men and women, the sordidness of the ghetto, the world of work, satire, protest, success, and failure. Their style varied from stark realism to highly imaginative symbolism, from the matter-of-fact recording of outer actions to the psychological examination of inner feelings. To give examples of the range and flavor of ethnic fiction, the works of two writers will be considered in some detail—Anzia Yezierska, an East European Jew, and O. E. Rölvaag, a Norwegian. Both were immigrants and both wrote in the early decades of the twentieth century.

Anzia Yezierska was born in Russian Poland in 1885 and came to the United States as a girl of sixteen. She went to work immediately as a domestic in the kitchens of New York's Jewish quarter and then, for wages not much better, in the garment sweatshops. Meanwhile she struggled to get an education in the city's night schools. Her own experiences provided the material for many of her short stories, stories about immigrants "crazy to learn" and full of unarticulated hopes and ambitions. "I don't know what is with me the matter," says a girl in one of these stories, "I'm so choked. . . . My thoughts tear in me and I can't tell them to no one. I want to do something with my life and I don't know what."

By 1919, the publication date of *Hungry Hearts*, a collection of short stories about Jewish immigrants, Yezierska had decided what to do with her own life. She would record the experiences of her people, the East European immigrant Jews. This she did amazingly well. Though Yiddish was her native language, she wrote in English, skillfully capturing in this recently acquired tongue the rhythm and idiom of her community. Her writing lacks sophistication; but like the people it describes, it is full of color and emotion. Her short stories received favorable comment from American critics because of their undeniable "authenticity," and one of her novels, *Salome of the Tenements*, became a Paramount motion picture in 1925.

The theme of much of Yezierska's work is the inner beauty, the dignity, and the vitality of the immigrant Jews. Her characters live in the grim tenements of New York, haggle with the butcher and the grocer and do daily battle with the landlord, the truant officer, the social worker and the factory foreman. Despite the outward poverty of their environment, their inner lives are rich.

Typical of many of her stories is "The Lost Beautifulness." In this story an immigrant woman, Hannah, takes in extra washing at night and saves her pennies in order to paint her tenement kitchen shiny white. To her husband's ridicule, Hannah replies, "What do I get from living if I can't have a little beautifulness in my life?"

Hannah's yearning for beauty is misunderstood and abused by the outside world. Seeing the newly painted apartment so much improved, Hannah's landlord raises the rent beyond what she and her sick husband can pay. When Hannah's son comes home unexpectedly from the army, two wound stripes on his sleeve and a Distinguished Service

Medal on his chest, he finds the family evicted, the households goods piled on the sidewalk, and his mother mourning "so much lost beautifulness."

Like Hannah, many of Yezierska's characters are vicitimized by callous officials and landlords, by unfeeling teachers, social workers, and physicians. Their stories have great pathos. Yezierska does not want pity, nor even charity, either for her characters or for their real life counterparts. She wants the United States to live up to its stated ideals of fair treatment and equal opportunity for all. In "The Lost Beautifulness" Hannah takes her rapacious landlord to court; she puts America to the test. America fails; the court upholds the landlord in his eviction order. Hannah refuses an offer of money from the wealthy woman whose laundry she does, though this money would have enabled her to pay the higher rent. "You want to give me hush money to swallow down an unrightness that burns my flesh," she protests. "I want justice!"

Despite their troubles, Yezierska's characters are not defeated because, whatever their circumstances, they have a sense of their own worth. One of her best stories, "The Fat of the Land," tells of an impoverished widow whose four children escape the ghetto to become a fashionable hat designer, a factory owner, a football star, and a famous playwright. Completely acculturated, the children try to make their mother into a "proper" American lady or, all else failing, to keep her out of sight. But the mother will not be changed; nor will she be hidden. Into her daughter's elegant marble halled apartment house she stalks, her market basket giving off the familiar odors of herring and garlic, the scaly tail of a fresh carp protruding from its newspaper wrappings! Nor will she accept her children's negative evaluation of her:

> From where did they get the stuff to work themselves up in the world? Did they get it from the air. . . . Why don't the children of born American mothers write my Benny's plays? It is I, who never had a chance to be a person, who gave him the fire in his head. If I would have had a chance to go to school and learn the language, what couldn't I have been? It is I and my mother and my mother's mother and my father and my father's father who had such a black life in Poland; it is our choked up thoughts and feelings that are flashing up in my children and making them great in America.

While her work is deeply rooted in the life of the Jewish ghetto, much of what Yezierska writes is familiar to the immigrant of any background. In her partly autobiographical novel, *The Breadgivers*, she describes the bitter conflicts between immigrant parents and their American born children. Her work is filled with a sympathetic understanding of the plight of the poor. She recognizes, for example, that society has mechanisms for keeping the poor "in their place." One story tells of an immigrant girl who works her way through normal school in a commercial laundry and then finds herself unable to get any but the lowest paid, temporary positions because of her shabby appearance. "It was to the advantage of those who used me that my appearance should damn me," says the girl, "so as to get me to work for the low wages I was forced to accept."

Though many of Yezierska's characters are exploited and abused, they are not bitter. They believe in the United States as the place where miracles can and do happen. Their greatest wish is to be able to contribute. Yezierska's immigrants do a great deal of hard physical work; but they want to do other things too. "I got ideas how to make America better," says an immigrant girl in one of the stories to an uncomprehending trade school teacher. "Ain't thoughts useful? Does America want only the work from my body? . . . Us immigrants wants to be people—not 'hands'. . . . I came to help America make the new world." Yezierska's work is a plea for the native born Americans to recognize immigrants as fellow human beings and to allow them to make their contributions to their newly adopted homeland.

A Viking in America

Ole Edvart Rölvaag was born in Nordland, one of the most beautiful areas in Norway, in a fisherman's cottage on a rocky ledge forty feet above the sea. It was the same cottage that had been home to his great, great, great grandparents before him. Though he emigrated to South Dakota at the age of twenty, he never lost his love for the mountains and the sea of Norway. After attending Augustana Academy and St. Olaf College, Norwegian Lutheran schools, he returned to his homeland repeatedly to study Norwegian history and literature and to visit his family and friends. In the United States he became a professor of Norwegian literature, a novelist, and a lifelong activist in the struggle of Norwegian-Americans to preserve their language and culture.

Rölvaag was a literary artist with a highly developed and disciplined talent. His work is rich in symbols and images, much of which is lost in English translation, and reveals the inner as well as the outer life of its characters. While Yezierska excelled in the short story, Rölvaag needed a larger canvas. His most famous book, *Giants in the Earth,* is recognized as an epic of frontier life. This novel and its two sequels, *Pedor Victorious* and *Their Father's God* comprise a trilogy that explores the question central to all of Rölvaag's works: what were the costs of immigration?

Per Hansa, the hero of *Giants in the Earth* is a nineteenth century

Viking. He is bold, adventurous, ambitious. He navigates his covered wagon across the Dakota prairie as his ancestors had navigated their ships across the oceans. His motivation is the same; he will be the founder of a new kingdom. His labors are prodigious—and well rewarded. His grain ripens in the American sun, promising his children an even grander future than he had dreamed. There is a price to be paid, however—hardship, drought, locusts, fear of Indians. In the end the Viking kingdom in the New World, like its counterparts in the Old, must be purchased by blood. Per Hansa goes out into a blizzard to fetch a minister for his dying friend and becomes lost in the snow. His body is found the following spring, leaning against a haystack, facing west.

Rölvaag's novels explore the psychological as well as the physical costs of immigration. According to Rölvaag, there are some people who should never immigrate. Per Hansa's wife, Beret, is one of them. She cannot bear the loss of home; she misses the scenic beauty of Norway and the security of its traditions and institutions. Life without these things drives her to temporary insanity. When recognizable civilization arrives in the form of a Norwegian minister, she recovers. Like many frontier widows of every ethnic background, she successfully manages the farm and rears the children after the death of her husband. In Rölvaag's trilogy, Beret represents the strength of character, the almost intuitive wisdom of the person who is firmly rooted in tradition and in what Rölvaag meant by culture. His sympathies are with her, though he reveals her flaws—the pessimism and rigidity of her religious views, for example. In *Giants in the Earth,* Beret loses her home, her security, and finally her husband because of immigration. But there are other costs as well for Beret and immigrants like her, as Rölvaag reveals in *Pedor Victorious.*

> Hidden forces were taking the children away from her—Beret saw it clearly. And strangely enough, they were enticing the youngest first. Permand (Pedor) and Anna Marie would watch every opportunity to talk English to each other, surreptitiously; . . . . And never did she hear them so much as mention what pertained to them as Norwegians. . . . At times, as she listened to their talk, she would fall to wondering whether she actually was their mother—their language was not hers. Here, so it seemed, each did not bring forth after its own kind as the Lord ordained. Wheat did not yield wheat; nor cattle beget cattle. . . . Had nature's laws been annulled altogether in this land?

Pedor Victorious is a classic study of the gap between immigrants and their children. Unlike some immigrant parents who accepted the change in their children, even welcomed it, Beret marshals all her resources against it. Pedor, her youngest, is the focus of her efforts. She forces him to study nightly with her from a Norwegian primer, has him confirmed in the Norwegian church, and puts him in a "Norwegian" school—all to no avail. The rebellious Pedor rejects his mother's heritage. "When I am grown up I am going to go so far away that I'll never hear the word 'Norwegian' again," he says.

Rölvaag agonizes for Beret and the other Norwegian parents whose children, figuratively and often literally, no longer speak their language. "It is a tragedy for mother and child not to be able to converse intimately," writes Rölvaag. "Her songs he cannot understand. What her soul has found nourishment in, he cannot comprehend. She seems to him an anachronism, a senseless, unreasonable being. . . . Can you not feel the heartache of that mother . . .?"

The immigrant's American born children have the advantage of feeling at home in the new language and the New World; but, according to Rölvaag, they pay the price of being cut off from their roots. Rölvaag complained that the young Norwegian-Americans he taught were often shallow, lacking in character, ambition, ideals, and "resonance," because they had lost the Norwegian language and, through it, access to their ancestral culture. Mixed marriage is a frequent theme in ethnic literature, and Rölvaag handles it masterfully. In *Their Father's God,* the third volume of his trilogy, he shows the positive side of Pedor's marriage to Susie, a second generation Irish-Catholic, the real love and tenderness between the couple. But despite their apparently complete Americanization, the young people are not free of "their father's God." The centrifugal forces of different cultures, different religions, different family traditions, and different goals gradually pull them apart. The marriage does not last.

In *Their Father's God* Rölvaag speaks to his rapidly acculturating Norwegian-American readers through the character of Reverend Kahldahl. Reverend Kahldahl tells young Pedor about the adventurous deeds of his ancestors, pointing out that the achievements of the Vikings and of their American descendants, the immigrants, will live because "they are the visible token of a high creative courage, which has its roots in the cultural soil of their race."

Rölvaag believed that the United States needed the cultural richness of its immigrant cultures. He was a cultural pluralist who asked, "If richness of personal color is desirable in the individual, why should the monotonous gray be desirable as a national ideal?" While Yezierska was worried that prejudice on the part of the old stock Americans would prevent the newly arrived East European Jews from making their contribution to American life, Rölvaag was worried that too rapid assimilation would keep the Norwegian-Americans from making theirs.

Though Rölvaag wrote in Norwegian, his works were an attempt to show the native born Norwegian-Americans the beauty of their background in the United States. Convinced that young Norwegian-Americans needed an appreciation of their immigrant parents and grandparents if they were to feel "completely and wholeheartedly at home" in the United States, he advocated the study of Norwegian-American history as a means of inculcating American patriotism. "The homes that have been wrested from the prairies and forests of the Northwest have been bought with the sweat of their (the immigrants) brows and the agony of their souls, with many long years of toil and with their own warm blood," he told his students. "There is a strange glory over those homes. We desire that our own people shall be enabled to see that glory . . . the cultivation of love for home and history is the truest Americanization that any citizen may be taught." Like Yezierska, Rölvaag was deeply rooted in his own ethnic community. Also, like Yezierska, he was deeply American.

CHAPTER 10

Closing the Gates: Nativism and Restrictionism, 1880-1924

While ethnic Americans were building their communities and settling down to life in America, old stock Americans were becoming increasingly uneasy about their presence. By 1924 even the most recent immigrant groups were learning English, becoming citizens and contributing to the economy. Indeed the foreign born were more likely to own their own homes and to have their children in school than the native born. Paradoxically, however, the more Americanized the newer immigrants became, the more hostility they seemed to arouse. In 1924 Congress passed broad restrictive legislation to preserve America from further intrusions of "dangerous" aliens.

Between 1880 and 1924 a rising tide of nativism engulfed first the Oriental-Americans and then those who had come from Southern and Eastern Europe. Distrust of foreigners, it will be remembered, had been common during the colonial era and had risen to a national political movement before the Civil War. This early nativism had always been offset, however, by a tradition of hospitality to the poor and the oppressed, by the conviction that America had room for everybody, and by the belief that the American environment would transform the most debased foreigner into a "new man." Unlike earlier nativism, however, the nativist crusade of the early twentieth century was able to realize its goal—the closing of the gates for immigrants from Asia and from Southern and Eastern Europe.

The new nativists attributed their victory to the fact that the

Oriental and East European immigrants barred in 1924 were inferior to the Irish, German, and Scandinavian immigrants who had arrived in earlier years. However, objective observers noted then what recent historians have documented—that immigrants from Southern and Eastern Europe were similar to those from Western Europe in skills and motivations and in the problems they encountered. Why, then, were they perceived as sinister, and why did not the traditional American hospitality and optimism come to their rescue? The answer is that twentieth century nativism, like its earlier counterpart, was not so much an objective response to the qualities of the immigrants as it was an expression of problems within the nation as a whole. Now, for the first time, these internal problems included a loss of the youthful self-confidence and optimism that had made the nation so hospitable to newcomers in earlier eras.

New Doubts and Fears

As the nineteenth century reached its close, many Americans were haunted by a vague pessimism about their own and the nation's future; and the reasons for this pessimism somehow involved the massive immigration of the time. The government's announcement in 1890 that the frontier no longer existed contributed to this pessimism. Most Americans agreed with the historian Frederick Jackson Turner that the frontier had provided opportunity for the poor and had helped absorb and assimilate foreigners. With the frontier gone, where was the "safety valve" for the impoverished urban worker, and how could the increasing numbers of immigrants become Americanized?

Middle class Americans felt threatened by the growing concentration of wealth in agriculture and industry. By the end of the nineteenth century the best farm lands were in the hands of the railroads or of large corporations (agribusiness) with which family farms were unable to compete. Bewildered and angry, many farmers vented their fury on the growing cities which lured their children and held their mortgages—and which teemed with immigrants!

Exclusion of the Chinese and Japanese

The decline in the supply of good and inexpensive land, fear of the giant corporations, frustration of ambitions to get ahead, fear of the future—these and other elements played a part in the campaign against the Chinese, the first people to be legally excluded from the United States. Songs and poems from San Francisco, like the following, "Twelve Hundred More" demonstrate the fears of the Caucasian working man:

O workingmen dear, and did you hear
The news that's going round?
Another China steamer
Has been landed here in town.

Today I read the papers
And it grieved my heart full sore
To see upon the title page,
O just 'Twelve Hundred More!'

O, California's coming down
As you can plainly see,
They are hiring all the Chinamen
And discharging you and me.

Twelve hundred honest laboring men
Thrown out of work today
By the landing of these Chinamen
In San Francisco Bay.

This state of things can never last
In this our golden land,
For soon you'll hear the avenging cry,
'Drive out the Chinaman!'

When the Chinese first arrived in California at the time of the original Gold Rush, they were praised for their industriousness and usefulness. By the late 1870's, however, when the above song was popular, they were just as widely denounced for their servility and deceitfulness. The Chinese were still living in their own communities, running restaurants and laundries, working as agricultural laborers or as factory hands, and generally entering occupations considered undesirable by Caucasians. The Chinese had not changed. California had changed, however. Formerly a land of boundless opportunity for all, by the 1870's it was a state plagued by massive unemployment and political corruption.

The entire nation suffered a serious economic depression in the late 1870's, but its effects were particularly severe in California. A new transcontinental railroad had recently been completed. The railroad brought floods of immigrants from the east, refugees from the depression, seeking opportunities that were not available. Newcomers to California hoped to make their fortunes in agriculture or in mining—but their hopes were frustrated. As the population rose, so did the price of land, much of which was in the hands of the wealthy few. Newcomers from the East were unable to buy good land and were unwilling to work for others or reclaim waste areas, as Mexican-Americans and Orientals did. As for mining, the days when all one needed were a mule and a pan had vanished. Now mining was monopolized by big corporations that could afford the heavy initial investment in equipment. The large agricultural, mining, and railroad interests that dominated the economy also dominated an increasingly corrupt state government. Thus ambitious newcomers to California found themselves blocked wherever they turned.

It was in this atmosphere that Dennis Kearney, an Irish born sailor who had lost his money in mining stocks, began the anti-Chinese agitation. Kearney denounced the land, mining, and railroad monopolies for denying the masses their rightful opportunities to rise. He blamed the Chinese, many of whom worked for these large corporations, for depressing wages and causing the widespread unemployment.

In an earlier day Kearney's speeches might have gone unnoticed, but this was the era of sensational or "yellow" journalism. Cheap newspapers were building mass circulation among the newly literate reading public by printing the most lurid and emotion provoking stories and pictures they could find. The San Francisco *Chronicle* published Kearney's speeches and found them an instant circulation booster. A rival paper, the *Morning Call* countered by also featuring Kearney's speeches. Thus a newspaper circulation war helped catapult the little known agitator into a position of prominence.

Kearney became a popular demagogue and leader of a new antibusiness, anti-Chinese political faction, the Workingmen's Party. Kearney's followers vented their wrath on corporate monopolies as well as on the Chinese. Because local politicians found it easier to join the campaign against the defenseless Chinese than take up the cause of serious economic reform, they encouraged the anti-Chinese campaign.

Propaganda led to actions as a rash of anti-Chinese riots spread throughout the West. In 1871 rioters killed twenty-one Chinese in San Francisco. In 1877 rioters burned twenty-five Chinese laundries, shooting many of the owners as they attempted to escape the flames. In 1880 rioters destroyed every Chinese home and business in Denver. In 1885 twenty-eight Chinese were killed and hundreds wounded in Rock Springs, Wyoming, as rioters drove the entire Chinese community from their homes. Laws forbade the Chinese to send their children to "white" schools, to own land, to offer bail, even to wear the traditional queues (pigtails). A new expression—"not a Chinaman's chance"— reflected what it was like to be a Chinese-American in the closing decades of the nineteenth century.

Kearney's Workingmen's Party controlled enough votes to make its support necessary to either of the major parties that hoped to govern in California. Similarly, on the national scene California's electoral votes were eagerly wooed by the evenly matched Republican and Democratic Parties. Therefore the anti-Chinese forces received a favorable hearing disproportionate to their actual numbers both locally and in Washington. The results were the local anti-Chinese laws already mentioned, and on the national level, the Chinese Exclusion Act of 1882, the first immigration restriction in our history.

The original Exclusion Act was to be in force for ten years and was aimed at excluding only unskilled workers. The Act was renewed again and again, however, and was used to exclude virtually everyone. Chinese immigration. Like Indians, blacks, and Mexicans, Chinese measure, the Scott Act, denied Chinese-Americans the right to visit their families in China and then return to the United States. The Chinese, almost all of whom had left their families overseas, were faced with dismal alternatives. They could return to China permanently, in which case their families would sink once again into poverty, or they could resign themselves to indefinite exile in the United States and continue to send home the remittances that supported their families in China. Reared in a cultural tradition that emphasized family responsibility above individual desires, most chose to stay. A Chinese-American historian Betty Lee Sung suggests the costs:

> They were denied the joys and cares of seeing their children grow up. They no longer knew the feast days, the holidays when faces dear and close swarmed about to lend gaiety and festivity to the air. They were deprived of performing the thousand and one small gestures of gratitude and love to their parents. . . . Yes, these men were condemned to a life . . . shorn of love and warmth, of home and family in a land where prejudice surrounded them and fate was benign if one did not suffer bodily attack.

Racial prejudice undoubtedly played a role in the move to restrict Chinese immigration. Like Indians, blacks, and Mexicans, Chinese were considered to be less human than the Caucasian majority. Once the Chinese were excluded, it was easy to exclude the Japanese later. When Japanese immigrants began to arrive on the West Coast in the late nineteenth and early twentieth century, their physical appearance caused them to be placed in the same "inferior" slot that had already been reserved for the Chinese. The Japanese community in America was numerically much smaller than the Chinese and, unlike the Chinese, Japanese immigrants were almost always literate and represented a broad socioeconomic spectrum of their native society. However, most Californians recognized no such distinctions. "The Japanese are starting the same tide of immigration we thought we had checked twenty years ago," said Mayor James D. Phelan of San Francisco. "The Chinese and Japanese are not the stuff of which American citizens are made."

"The Japanese Invasion, the Problem of the Hour," screamed banner headlines in the San Francisco *Chronicle* on February 23, 1905.

Once again the press found resistance to the presence of Orientals a circulation booster. Once again the working classes, especially the skilled trade unions, took up the cry, and once again the issue was economic as well as racial. *Meat vs. Rice, American Manhood vs. Asiatic Coolieism, Which Shall Survive?* read the title of an anti-Japanese pamphlet issued by the American Federation of Labor. Once again, local politicians found it advantageous to pick up the issue. California passed a special law denying Japanese immigrants the right to own land, and the San Francisco School Board ruled that all Japanese children must go to school in Chinatown. Agitation to restrict Japanese immigration swelled.

Better educated than the Chinese, the Japanese were better equipped to fight back. Unlike the Chinese, they were supported by the government of their native land, a recently westernized and industrialized naval power which had just won the Russo-Japanese War. President Theodore Roosevelt respected Japan as a Great Power and did not want to alienate her. When Japan protested the treatment of its subjects in the United States (in the eyes of Japan, immigrants remained Japanese subjects), Theodore Roosevelt sent his Secretary of Commerce and Labor, Victor Metcalf, to investigate. Metcalf reported that Japanese children caused no problem in the schools and that Japanese-Americans were subject to violence and other unjustified harassment.

Because of Metcalf's report and the protests of Japan and the Japanese-American community, Japanese children in California were spared the indignity of racial segregation. To assuage the concern of Caucasian Californians, Roosevelt negotiated a "Gentlemen's Agreement" with the Japanese government whereby Japan would limit the number of immigrants granted visas for the United States. Hereafter only a few skilled Japanese and the immediate families of immigrants already here would be admitted.

While European, African, or Latin American born immigrants could become citizens after living in the United States five years, Chinese and Japanese immigrants were denied this privilege. According to a law passed in 1790, citizenship was available to "any alien, being a free white person," a clause meant to exclude Indians and blacks. The Fourteenth Amendment, passed after the Civil War, opened American citizenship to blacks, but Orientals, as nonwhites, were still excluded. In 1914 Japanese born Takao Ozawa applied for naturalization. The Supreme Court denied his application on the basis of the law of 1790. Ironically, the court assured him that "there is not implied—either in the legislation or in our interpretation of it—any suggestion of individual unworthiness or racial inferiority. These considerations are in no manner involved."

The Depression of the 1890's

The agitation against Oriental-Americans had been a local affair, concentrated on the West Coast where the Chinese and Japanese had settled. Similar economic and psychological pressures would soon operate nationwide to cause hostility to the far more numerous European immigrants as well. In the 1890's stock market manipulation, overproduction, and speculation plunged the nation into the most serious economic crisis it had ever experienced. In 1894 one out of every five workers was unemployed, and millions roamed the countryside looking for jobs or, in despair, sinking into a life of vagrancy. No fewer than seventeen "industrial armies" marched on Washington in 1894 to demand government help, thereby frightening President Grover Cleveland, and much of the nation, into the mistaken idea that mob rule was abroad in the land. When employers cut wages, workers struck and were ruthlessly suppressed by the police or by private armies. Like industrial workers, farmers found their economic situation worsening. Their revolt, known as the Populist Movement, spread quickly through the South and the West.

Meanwhile the government provided no help and the very rich continued their display of what the economist Thorstein Veblen called "conspicuous consumption," buying everything from private opera houses for their own amusement to titled European husbands for their daughters. People brought up to believe that honest labor and good character guaranteed success, or at least adequate food for their families, were bewildered to find that the system no longer seemed to function. In this atmosphere of class conflict, disillusionment, and bitterness, a new nativism arose.

At first the new nativism revived the old themes of the 1850's, directing its attacks against all immigrants indiscriminantly. According to the popular press, immigrants were "the very scum and offal of Europe," dirty, ignorant, and prone to crime and pauperism. The American Protective Association revived old slanders about the immorality of Roman Catholics and impending Papal invasion of the United States. Its members, close to a million at its peak, pledged to vote against all Catholic candidates, to oppose aid to Catholic schools, and to avoid participation in strikes "whereby the Catholic employees may undermine and substitute their Protestant co-workers."

An old nativist theme that seemed to be especially appropriate to the new conditions was the denunciation of immigrants as radicals. Native born Americans as well as immigrants participated in the strikes that rocked the nation in the closing decades of the nineteenth century, but frightened property owners blamed these "un-American" activities on the influence of foreigners. In 1886 someone threw a bomb at a labor rally in Chicago, killing a policeman and several bystanders.

Though no one could be certain who threw the bomb, during what came to be called the Haymarket Riot, a group of alleged anarchists, mostly German born, were tried and four were hanged. Many Americans agreed with a newspaper statement that "there is no such thing as an American anarchist." They blamed the Chicago bombing and, indeed, all labor unrest, on "long-haired, wild-eyed, bad-smelling, atheistic, reckless foreign wretches, who never did an honest hour's work in their lives. . . ."

At first, stereotypes of immigrant poverty, immorality, and radicalism were applied to those of western as well as eastern European origin. Gradually, however, nativism focused upon the latter. New stereotypes involving Slavs, Italians, and Jews reflected the new worries of the American community. Working class native born Americans began to depict Slavic and Italian laborers as tools of the giant corporations—imported strike breakers, degraded people who stole jobs from Americans by accepting wages no decent human being could live on.

This "degraded labor" stereotype of Italians and Slavs in the East was strikingly similar to attacks on Chinese and Japanese workers in the West. Like the anti-Oriental stereotype, it was part of the deeply felt anger toward the big industrialists and monopolists. And like the anti-Oriental stereotype, it was a distortion of the facts. Big corporations favored the open immigration policy as a means of guaranteeing an ample supply of labor, but they did not cause immigration. The movement to America was largely spontaneous. Like everyone else, immigrants worked for as much as they could get. Their wages were lower than those of the native born, because they were concentrated in unskilled occupations.

During the years of heavy immigration, small craft industries were being replaced by assembly line machine production. This mechanization did allow management to replace expensive skilled labor with cheaper unskilled labor, much of which was foreign born. In the long run, these technological changes created many new jobs. As immigrants took the unskilled positions, native born workers moved up to supervisory, clerical, or highly skilled positions. But these trends were not apparent to unemployed American born workers caught in the throes of the depression of the 1890's. Organized labor took an anti-immigration stand which it maintained until the restrictionist victory of 1924. Manufacturers, on the other hand, eager to keep a large supply of cheap labor, fought restriction until after World War I.

While the stereotype of the degraded Italian or Slavic worker reflected the anxieties of the American worker, the stereotype of the unscrupulous Jewish financier expressed the anxieties of the American farmer. As the depression deepened populism spread and among some of its adherents took on ugly anti-Semitic imagery. To the beleaguered farmer, the Jew was Shylock, the usurer, or worse yet, a representative of the mythological international money trust that was keeping him in financial bondage. To discontented farmers, the Jew, a traditionally urban figure, also symbolized the hated city which increasingly dominated American life.

Many of the populists lived in the West or South and may never have met a Jew. Less understandably, Easterners shared their view. "The Russian Jews and the other Jews will completely control the finances and government of this country in ten years," warned a New York worker, "or they will all be dead. The people of this country won't be starved and driven to the wall by Jews." The fact that the overwhelming majority of Russian Jewish immigrants were themselves poor and often unemployed during the depression was ignored.

To the older, privileged classes—men such as Henry Adams, the New England aristocrat, and Prescott Hall, founder of the Immigration Restriction League—the Jewish immigrant symbolized the aggressiveness and rapacity of the new American business culture, the domination of the monied interests at the expense of the "best" people. Jews were stereotyped as pushy, aggressive, unethical in business, and ostentatious in the display of their wealth. While a few of the older German Jewish families had acquired wealth, the far more numerous Russian Jews were poor. No Jews could compare in fortune to the corporate giants of Protestant America, giants whose sharp business practices and vulgar life styles were notorious. The old aristocrats ultimately had to make their peace with the new multimillionaires, but the Jewish "upstarts" could be excluded from "society." Thus a materialistic and aggressive American culture attributed its own least attractive qualities to one segment of its population, its Jews.

Violence Against Southern and Eastern European Ethnics

In the case of Southern and Eastern Europeans, as in the case of Orientals, negative stereotypes led to violence. Ukrainian miners imported into Pennsylvania as strikebreakers in the 1870's met with continued violence from the Irish miners already there. Union membership was as dangerous for immigrants as scabbing. When Slavic and Hungarian miners protested Henry Clay Frick's lowering of their wage scale, the Pennsylvania state militia killed ten and wounded fifty. In a similar incident in Hazelton, Pennsylvania, sheriff's deputies killed twenty-one immigrant "animals" and wounded forty more. Slavic miners were given the lowest paid positions because "it goes against the grain in an English-speaking man to fetch and carry for a Slovak or a Pole."

Italian immigrants often received even harsher treatment than Slavs. Their darker appearance contributed to their problems. "You don't call an Italian a white man?" a construction boss was asked. "No sir, an Italian is a Dago." Like Slavs, Italians were attacked both as strikebreakers and as strikers, but much of the violence against them stemmed from the stereotype of the Italian criminal flashing his stiletto. In 1895 six Italians suspected of murdering a Colorado saloon keeper were lynched, and three suspects in Louisiana met the same fate the following year. The most serious incident took place in New Orleans in 1891, when members of the Sicilian colony were blamed for the murder of the chief of police. When a jury found the evidence insufficient for conviction, a mob, backed by some of the city's leading citizens, lynched eleven Italian suspects.

In Northern cities Jews were commonly taunted and even assaulted in the streets. More serious violence took place in the South. The few East European Jews who went South usually made their livings as shopkeepers or in other commercial activities, as did German Jews who had been in the South since the early part of the nineteenth century. Jews often were attacked by Southern Populists who found in them the most convenient representatives of the nonproductive, monied "oppressors." In the late 1800's, debt-ridden farmers in Louisiana wrecked Jewish stores and threatened the lives of their owners. In 1893, Mississippi vigilantes burned dozens of farmhouses belonging to Jewish landlords.

However, the worst anti-Semitic outbreak in the South took place long after the depression of the 1890's had ended. It was the Frank case in Atlanta in 1914. The son of a New York manufacturer, Leo Frank managed a plant in Atlanta in which a young woman worker was found murdered. Frank was convicted of the murder on the flimsiest of evidence, probably because the angry working class community saw him as a northern capitalist exploiting southern womanhood. When Jewish organizations in the North tried to help Frank, southerners resented this "outside interference". When the governor commuted Frank's death sentence, angry Georgians boycotted Jewish merchants throughout the state. Leo Frank was abducted from prison and murdered.

Like the lynching of blacks, which was even more common in this troubled period, violence against immigrants generally went unpunished, but unlike the lynching of blacks, it was at least verbally deplored. Despite the violence of extremists and the lobbying activities of groups like the American Protective Association and the Immigration Restriction League, no government action was taken in the last decade of the nineteenth century to restrict European immigration. The South still hoped to attract immigrants and to use them as a base for industrialization. Businessmen appreciated the value of an imported labor force. And despite their economic problems, many Americans retained at least some faith in the traditional melting pot—the ability of English America to absorb all comers, improving them and perhaps even itself in the process.

The New Century

The violent nativism of the 1890's subsided during the first decade and a half of the twentieth century. The Spanish-American War restored America's self-confidence—expansion was still taking place. The acquisition of Puerto Rico and the Philippines encouraged an optimistic "larger America" mentality. The depression ended, and the discovery of gold in Alaska eased the currency problems that had so obsessed the Populists. Renewed prosperity in the city and on the farm quieted the rumblings of class war. Progressive reformers cleaned out at least some of the political corruption so distressing to the "better" people. Meanwhile, institutional reforms such as the direct election of Senators, the direct primary, and, eventually, woman's suffrage, gave ordinary people a feeling, however unjustified, that they, rather than the millionaires, controlled the country.

The major efforts of the nativists during these years were directed toward the adoption of a literacy test as a prerequisite for the admission of every immigrant. The literacy test, as its advocate Henry Cabot Lodge pointed out, would screen out immigrants from Southern and Eastern Europe while admitting those from Western Europe. Critics countered by noting that the ability to read and write was a measure of past opportunity rather than of character or ability. Congress passed the literacy test three times between 1896 and 1915, but Presidents Cleveland and Wilson vetoed each bill—partly on principles and partly, in Wilson's case, to maintain the support of the ethnic American voters who had helped elect him.

The federal government did pass new legislation against the admission of prostitutes, criminals, lunatics, anarchists, the feeble-minded, those suffering from "loathsome" diseases, and those considered likely to become public charges. At the newly opened embarkation center on Ellis Island millions of immigrants streamed by the federal health inspectors, dreading the white chalk mark that would single them out for a closer look, perhaps even for deportation. Sometimes one member of a family was quarantined or deported, while others were admitted. Inspectors tried to be fair, but injustices undoubtedly occurred. A Greek immigrant was deported after months in the United States on the grounds that a physical defect would make him a public charge, though he had been totally self supporting since his arrival! The percentage of immigrants turned away reached a high of 6.9% in 1915, an insignificant number compared to the masses that continued to be admitted.

Uneasiness about the entrance of foreigners did not disappear, however, and the restrictionist organizations continued their activities. Their ultimate success was due to the introduction of two new factors—"scientific" racism espoused by large portions of the academic community and "one hundred per cent Americanism" engendered by the passions of World War I.

Racism

The idea that one group of people was intrinsically inferior to another was all too familiar to American blacks, Indians, and Orientals. But earlier racism, though instrumental in determining how Americans behaved toward one another, had never enjoyed the official backing of the scientific community. Now for the first time racism emerged as an academically respectable, experimentally "proven" doctrine espoused by eminent biologists, sociologists, anthropologists, and psychologists. Beginning several decades earlier in Europe than in the United States, the new racists measured skulls, calculated comparative cranial volumes, and administered the first IQ tests. On the basis of carefully quantified evidence, white Anglo-Saxon and Germanic investigators concluded that lighter skinned peoples were inherently superior to Negroes and Orientals and that even among whites, Anglo-Saxons and Teutons were superior to the Alpine and Mediterranean races.

Nineteenth century American writers had long praised the virtues of the Anglo-Saxon race, especially its supposed talent for pioneering and for self-government. These writers had defined "race" loosely, as a group of people sharing a common cultural tradition, shaped by a common environment or historical experience. The early popularity of Darwin's ideas on evolution encouraged Americans to stress the importance of environment over heredity and the idea of "the survival of the fittest" seemed to guarantee the victory of Anglo-Saxons over all other cultural elements in the great American melting pot.

Twentieth century racism was different, however. It dwelled less upon Darwinism than upon Mendel's laws of heredity. To the new racists, race was not a common culture which could be changed by a favorable environment. It was a common genetic pool which was immutable. Bad genes were not overcome by good; they survived to pollute the stock, human or animal, to the thousandth generation. No longer confident that Anglo-Saxonism could conquer all, the new American racists proposed restriction of immigration as a necessary safeguard for the vigor of the superior American stock.

American nativists found racism a useful justification for their previously acquired anti-immigration sentiments. Henry Cabot Lodge defended the literacy test with dire warnings that the superior qualities of American civilization would be "bred out" by masses of racially inferior newcomers. According to Francis Walker, a leading economist and president of the Massachusetts Institute of Technology, the immigrants from Southern and Eastern Europe were "beaten men from beaten races . . ." having "none of the ideas and aptitudes which belong to those who are descended from the tribes that met under the oak trees of old Germany to make laws and choose Chieftains." Pessimistic about the direction of American society, Walker shared a fashionable melancholy which a German writer, Max Nordau, called "vague qualms about the Dusk of Nations." According to Walker, American workers, unwilling to compete with cheap European labor, were limiting their family size, failing to reproduce themselves, and thus committing racial suicide. (Actually, the falling American birth rate was due to increased urbanization, better education, easier access to birth control information, and a wider range of options for women.) To Walker, and others like him, immigration was the biological death warrant of the nation.

Between 1914 and 1924 a flood of articles and books popularized the new racism. Edward Alsworth Ross, a widely read and respected sociologist, started the vogue in *Century* magazine with a series of articles evaluating every immigrant group in terms of supposedly inborn racial characteristics. Lothrop Stoddard, a Massachusetts lawyer with a degree in history and an obsession with race, wrote two books, *The Rising Tide of Color Against White World Supremacy* and *The Menace of the Under Man*, both warning that the inferior brown and yellow skinned peoples of the world would soon outnumber and vanquish the superior whites. The most influential of the new racist books was *The Passing of the Great Race* by Madison Grant, a member of an old, patrician New York family, who had acquired a smattering of information on genetics and anthropology, and who was vehemently anti-Semitic. Grant's book glorified the tall, blond Nordic as the "white man par excellence" on whom American culture rested and warned that the American stock would be ruined if we continued to admit swarms of inferior Europeans such as the Alpines, the Mediterraneans, and, worst of all, the Jews.

These American writers, as well as the European investigators whose works they used, made the mistake of linking genetically caused physical characteristics—hair, skin coloring, and height—with environmentally produced cultural characteristics such as poverty and illiteracy. They were superficially correct in observing that Southern and Eastern Europeans in early twentieth century America were more likely to live in slums than older "English stock," but this was due to circumstances, not genes.

White skinned Americans and Western Europeans exercised political domination over the rest of the globe in the early twentieth century because of their superior technology. White, Western social scientists concluded from this fact that their group was inherently superior. A similar study of the world one thousand or two thousand years earlier might have concluded on the same kind of evidence that the Chinese, or the Mediterranean peoples, or Africans were superior —especially if Chinese, Mediterranean, or African experts had been conducting the study! Moreover, the assumption that the society with the most efficient tools and the deadliest weapons is "superior" is certainly debatable.

The ideas of the racists were apparently confirmed by the reports of school authorities and army psychologists during World War I that young people of Southern and East European background scored lower on intelligence tests than those of West European or native American parentage. The early IQ tests, however, were based upon familiarity with middle class Anglo-Saxon language and culture. The longer an ethnic group had lived in the United States and the more completely assimilated it had become, the higher its members scored. Thus old stock Americans tested better than Irish and German Americans, who in turn tested better than most members of the Oriental or Southern and Eastern European immigration. Studies showing that Italians and Jews sent far fewer of their members to poorhouses than the Irish, that Polish immigrants learned English more quickly than German immigrants, and that the foreign born produced fewer criminals than the native born were ignored. They did not fit the stereotype.

The new scientific racism legitimized old prejudices throughout the country, encouraging the blaming of every problem from political corruption to poverty upon the presence of blacks, Orientals, Jews, Italians, or whatever "inferior" group seemed most readily available. The new racism gave the South scientific justification for depriving blacks of their vote and subjecting them to total segregation. The new racism also guaranteed the success of the movement to restrict new immigration. First, by linking the inferiority of the Eastern European immigration to that of blacks and Orientals, it mobilized the support of the South and the West. Secondly, by including Irish, Germans, and Scandinavians in the "desirable" category of superior peoples, it flattered them and neutralized their opposition. After all, they were not to be restricted.

World War I and "100% Americanism"

The impact of the new racism was not felt all at once. From an inner circle of intellectuals it spread like a virus, gradually infecting much of the nation. In contrast, a new nationalism, equally damaging to the cause of open immigration, burst like a bombshell upon everyone. When Germany's unrestricted submarine warfare brought the United States into World War I, the country plunged into a frenzy of shrill, uncompromising, "one hundred per cent Americanism." A wave of superpatriotic conformity inundated the country. The Espionage Act of 1918 established a penalty of twenty years imprisonment for criticism of the armed forces, the flag, or even the military uniform!

German-Americans, many of whom still took great pride in the culture and language of their fatherland, were hardest hit by the war because Germany was considered the main enemy. The American press portrayed Germany as a barbarous nation whose soldiers delighted in raping Belgian women and bayoneting their babies. Between the outbreak of the European war in 1914 and our entry in 1917, some German-Americans protested our general anti-German orientation, especially our supplying of arms to Britain and her allies. After the United States entered on Britain's side, the overwhelming majority of German-Americans and the German-American press supported the war.

To many American patriots, however, "Huns" could not be trusted at home or abroad. Everything German was suspect. The anti-German furor became so irrational and intense that the German language was purged from the curriculum of many high schools and colleges, German names of individuals, firms, and even towns were changed, and restaurants substituted "liberty cabbage" for sauerkraut. As late as 1919 the *New York Times* reported two veterans organizations ready to use machine guns to stop a performance at the German Irving Place Theater.

A special act of Congress repealed the charter of the Alliance, a national federation of German-American organizations, and a damper fell upon German-American communal life at every level. Individual German-Americans who did not support the war warmly enough or buy enough Liberty Bonds to satisfy their neighbors could find themselves harassed, whipped, tarred and feathered, and in at least one case, lynched. Despite little evidence of disloyal activity, many Americans believed members of the German-American community to be responsible for every wartime shortage—when they were not too busy poisoning the war supplies with influenza germs or putting ground glass in Red Cross bandages!

While never subjected to the hatred reserved for German-Americans, ethnic Americans from the Austro-Hungarian Empire and the Turkish Empire were also identified with enemy powers and thus were objects of suspicion. Patriots pointed out that Slavic labor controlled the production of coal and steel, and that Slavic-Americans were numerous enough to control local elections in certain areas. In an article in *Everybody's Magazine* in March 1918, Samuel Hopkins Adams warned America about Slavic aliens. "Reckon each as a pound of dynamite—surely a modest comparison. . . . Not all these enemy aliens are hostile. Not all dynamite explodes."

The experience of being at war while large portions of the civilian population were culturally or even politically identifiable with the enemy was intolerable to many. It led to a clamor for immediate "Americanization" as the only way to defuse once and for all the foreign "dynamite." Churches and settlements had been working in the area of Americanization for years, but now large numbers of schools, business firms, civic groups, local and state governments, and even the federal government became involved. A few of the old settlement house personnel tried to revive the idea that ethnic cultures could make worthwhile contributions to American life, but these contributions were usually defined as folk dances, exotic foods, and other "quaint" and superfluous frivolities. The major thrust of wartime Americanization programs was toward immediate American citizenship for all who were eligible and toward total cultural conformity to the mores of the majority community. Ethnic Americans were pressured to abandon their own languages, customs and traditions, their loyalties, even their memories, as quickly as possible to become "one hundred per cent" American. A wartime English class in one of Henry Ford's factories acted out the new spirit. Outlandishly dressed workers carrying banners with the names of their native lands walked across the stage, entered a huge melting pot, and emerged identically dressed in neat American business suits, carrying neat little American flags.

The tactics of the Americanization crusaders were not subtle. The Governor of Iowa tried to ban the use of languages other than English in all public conversations and over the telephone. Industries refused promotions, or even employment, to aliens who had not begun citizenship applications. Some firms made attendance at English classes a condition of employment. The state of California sent "foreign language speakers" among immigrant communities to convince them to buy Liberty Bonds and give to the Red Cross because "the time had come for every foreign-born to make his decision." The most important duty of these state agents was to avert labor unrest and strikes, and to convince immigrant workers to stay patriotically on the job or "they themselves would suffer in the end."

Always seen as an instrument of Americanization, schools were heavily involved in the wartime push for loyalty and conformity. Teachers pressured immigrant children to support the Red Cross and gave them loyalty pledges for their parents to sign. School personnel were advised to use school plays, pageants and the like to instruct children and their parents in patriotism. Blatant wartime propaganda found its way into the classroom as in the following excerpt from Lesson 46, a model English lesson for immigrants.

father—mother . . . . . . .I have a father and a mother.
sister—brother . . . . . . .I have a sister and a brother.
relatives . . . . .I have other relatives.
babies . . . . .The Germans have killed many mothers and babies.
slaughter . . . . .The Germans have slaughtered many children.
butcher . . . . .The Germans have butchered many old men and women.
fight . . . . .I am going to fight the Germans.
protect . . . . .I shall fight them to protect my family.

The war hastened the assimilation of German-Americans and of many of the newer immigrants as well, though often this happened in spite of the efforts of the Americanization crusaders. The point is made in the following story that circulated in Washington during the war years. When a committee of ardent Americanizers paid a call on a Bohemian tenement family, the woman of the household suggested they come back later. The visitors demanded indignantly if this meant the family wanted to put off their entrance into American life. "No, no!" the Bohemian woman replied hastily. "We're *perfectly* willing to be Americanized. Why, we never turn *any* of them away. But there's nobody home but me. The boys volunteered, my man's working on munitions, and all the rest are out selling Liberty Bonds. I don't want you to get mad, but *can't* you come back next week?"

Obviously members of ethnic communities were Americanized by sharing a common patriotic effort with the larger American community. Though exempt from the draft, large numbers of noncitizens volunteered for the armed forces, and ethnic Americans in general furnished more than their numerical proportion of soldiers. Many more worked in war industries and took part in voluntary home front campaigns. Often ethnic Americans felt no affection for the Empires which had held their nationalities as unwilling subjects. Wilson's Fourteen Points, which included as American war aims self-determination for all subject minorities in central Europe and the restoration of an independent Poland, were greeted with great enthusiasm by Slavic-Americans. In some cities the Polish community bought more Liberty Bonds per capita than any other identifiable group, though they were by no means the most affluent.

Paradoxically the overwhelming interest in the war displayed by the ethnic communities hurt rather than helped them in their struggle against restrictionism. During and after the war ethnic communities lobbied for settlements most advantageous to their homelands. Austrians, Hungarians, and Germans wanted their homelands to retain as many of their former possessions as possible. Bohemians, Lithuanians, Ukrainians, Slovenes, Poles, Syrians, and Lebanese wanted autonomy or independence for their homelands. Jews wanted the end of anti-Semitic oppression in Europe and the establishment of a Jewish state in Palestine. Confident that one of the American war aims, "self-determination for all nations," legitimized their causes, ethnic organizations made increasingly sophisticated use of lobbying and other American political institutions in their support. When the first consulate of the newly restored Poland opened in New York City, crowds of cheering and weeping Polish-Americans surrounded it, blocking traffic in every direction.

Americanization crusaders were appalled. They did not see the activities of ethnic communities in behalf of their homelands as the old American tradition that it was, nor as evidence that the ethnic groups were willing and able to use American political processes. Instead, they saw these activities as evidence of the failure of Americanization, which they had unrealistically defined as the disappearance of all Old World ties. They failed to distinguish between political allegiance, which immigrants now fully gave to the United States, and emotional loyalties, which included the old as well as the new. Convinced that their efforts had been in vain, many of the Americanizers were now receptive to the racist ideas that "the leopard cannot change its spots"—that ethnic communities presented a permanent menace to the national well-being.

The Red Scare

The hand of the restrictionists was strengthened still further by the fact that a vocal minority, American born and foreign born, objected to the war. Old stock American socialists, such as Eugene Debs were imprisoned for their opposition. More conspicuous, but not more numerous, were ethnic pacifists such as the Italian-American poet Arturo Giovannitti and the Russian-Jewish anarchist and feminist Emma Goldman. Accustomed to advocating unpopular causes, Goldman ignored the wartime laws against expression of dissent. "I defy the police, when the lives of millions are at stake," she said.

In the long run Bolshevism rather than pacifism was the most damaging ethnic stereotype. When the Russian Tsar was overthrown in the spring of 1917, Americans were virtually unanimous in their approval. But when the Bolsheviks took over the following fall, ruthlessly carrying out a Marxist program of the abolition of private property, Americans shuddered. American socialists, already divided over the issue of the war, split again over their attitude toward the Russian experiment. This, together with conflicts over leadership and a widespread conservative reaction in the United States in the postwar years, led to mass defections of native born Americans from the ranks of the Socialist Party. In the early 1920's ethnic Americans, for the first time, constituted the majority of the Socialist Party (though the overwhelming majority of ethnic Americans were not socialists). The stereotype of the immigrant as radical took on a new and fearful life.

In the immediate postwar years the changeover to peace time production led to unemployment and temporary economic dislocations. Serious strikes broke out in the steel and textile industries, and in 1919 the Boston police force went on strike, opening the city to looting and violence. A rash of bombings and bomb threats, the work of a handful of criminal, perhaps insane, radicals terrified the nation. All the postwar unrest and violence was laid at the doorstep of Bolshevism, foreign and domestic, and a Red Scare swept across the nation. "Like a prairie fire, the blaze of revolution was sweeping over every institution of law and order," wrote Attorney General A. Mitchell Palmer, ". . . eating its way into the homes of the American workman . . . licking the altars of the churches, leaping into the belfry of the school bell, crawling into the sacred corners of American homes, . . . burning up the foundations of society."

Panicked middle class Americans did not stop to distinguish between trade unionists and philosophical radicals on the one hand and criminal or violently revolutionary elements on the other. All were lumped together as "un-American" and identified with the foreign population. In this atmosphere the notorious "Palmer Raids" took place.

On the orders of the politically ambitious Attorney General Palmer, police burst into homes and meeting places all over the country, loading "suspicious" aliens onto trucks or marching them handcuffed through the streets. On the flimsiest of evidence—possession of radical literature or guilt by association—over three thousand aliens were deported, often leaving their wives and children destitute and ostracized. Only when Palmer attempted to get a peace time law enabling him to punish citizens as well as aliens for their associations and opinions did the public turn against him. In 1924 the *Saturday Evening Post* looked back at the anti-Red hysteria as "nothing but the last symptom of war fever." Meanwhile the nation had been engulfed in a wave of intolerance that blighted the lives of native born and foreign born alike.

The Palmer Raids were not an isolated incident but were part of a pattern of postwar bigotry that affected all racial, religious, and ethnic minorities. Whites rioted against blacks in such cities as Chicago and

Washington. Henry Ford launched a vicious anti-Semitic campaign in the *Dearborn Independent*. The state of Oregon outlawed parochial schools. Two Italian anarchists, Sacco and Vanzetti, were executed for robbery and murder in a trial where their political views weighed as heavily as the evidence.

Racism converged with wartime fears and postwar insecurities to cause the rapid rise of a newly organized Ku Klux Klan. Unlike its Reconstruction predecessor, the new Klan was national in scope and added to its traditional hatred of blacks, newer hatreds of Catholics, Jews, socialists, the foreign born, and any person or group that did not conform to its own narrow definitions of Americanism and Christian morality.

Claiming three million members and many more sympathizers, the new Klan was, among other things, an expression of the distrust Americans born and reared in rural and small town America felt toward the new urban life styles and values of the "roaring twenties." Many Klan members saw the cities as dens of radicalism and sexual immorality, where Jews and Bolsheviks plotted the overthrow of the nation while young girls (perhaps their own daughters) painted their lips, drank bootleg whiskey, and brazenly wore their skirts above their knees. The Klan was eventually ruined by revelations of corruption among its own leaders. For several years, however, it functioned as a perverted continuation of the crusading spirit of the Progressive Era and the Great War, mounting vigilante attacks against alcohol, freer sex morality, "obscene" movies, socialism, atheism, Darwinism, blacks, Jews, Catholics, and similar evils—including immigration.

The National Origins Quota

In this atmosphere the postwar Congress began to work once again on the issue of immigration restriction. During the war the literacy test had finally become law, but as a device to keep out the "undesirables" it was obviously ineffective. Between 1918 and 1921, 1,487,000 immigrants entered the country and only 6,142 were excluded as illiterate. Clearly, the restrictionists concluded, a different type of legislation was needed. Their experts pointed out that immigration was increasing and warned, once again, of the harmful effects of Southern and Eastern Europeans, especially of "abnormally twisted Jews . . . filthy, un-American, and often dangerous in their habits." Equally important, the business interests that had favored immigration as a source of cheap labor no longer did so. The increasing mechanization of business meant that large numbers of unskilled workers were no longer needed, especially if such workers were suspected of radical tendencies.

In 1920 Senator William P. Dillingham introduced a bill to limit annual immigration for each ethnic group to five per cent of the number of foreign born of that group in the 1910 census. The House cut the percentage from five to three per cent, and in 1921 President Harding signed the bill into law. American immigration policy had taken a new course. Exclusionists soon found fault with the 1921 law, however. Though it gave the highest quotas to Britain and Germany, its allotments for Italy, Poland, Greece, and similar "undesirable" areas were too large. A new system would have to be found.

Representative Albert Johnson of Washington, Chairman of the House Committee on Immigration and a long-time advocate of restrictionism, realized that the quotas for Southern and Eastern European countries were sizable because they were computed on the basis of the number of foreign born people from those countries in a year of heavy "new" immigration, 1910. He proposed going back to the census of 1890, when most of the foreign born were still from Western Europe. The House agreed, but reaching back to a thirty year old census to make the figures come out right was too blatantly discriminatory for the Senate. Senator David Reed of Pennsylvania solved the problem. He suggested that the number of immigrants allowed to come in from any given country be tied, not to the number of foreign born persons from that country in the United States in any given year, but to the percentage of that nationality group in the makeup of the entire American population. This system, too, would keep immigration safely western.

In 1924 the Reed proposal was passed, to be put into effect as soon as statisticians computed what the ethnic breakdown of the American population actually was. A committee of "experts" worked for five years trying to determine the ethnic composition of the American population, using census records and immigration statistics. Reliable information for the period before 1790, or indeed, before 1850 was virtually nonexistent. Even after that time records were fragmentary. The quota system ultimately put into effect was based mainly on guesswork.

The final law provided for the admission of a total of 150,000 immigrants annually. Its restrictionist provisions gave Great Britain a quota of 65,721 and Germany 25,957. Southern and Eastern Europe fared less well. Italy had a quota of 5,802, the Soviet Union, 2,784, and Greece only 307. Most Asians were denied entry on the grounds that they could not become naturalized citizens, and African immigration was excluded outright.

The American Jewish Committee, the Knights of Columbus, the National Liberal League, and similar organizations fought the new legislation. Ethnic leaders issued fact sheets to counteract the racist charges of the restrictionists. Cultural pluralists such as Horace Kallen argued that true Americanism lay in the coexistence of many ethnic cultures rather than in their homogenization. Ironically, by the time the legislation was passed its pseudoscientific basis was being undermined. Anthropologist Franz Boas, himself foreign born, demonstrated that such supposedly immutable physical traits as the height and build of immigrants from Eastern Europe had changed after only one generation in the United States. In his classic work *The Mind of Primitive Man*, Boas condemned "the tendency to view one's own civilization as higher than that of the whole rest of mankind." He identified this behavior with that of the primitive person "who considers every stranger as an enemy and who is not satisfied until the enemy is killed." Despite mounting opposition, even within the Congress, the bill was passed, apparently because of the momentum it had been gathering over the years. Ironically, by the time it passed the public had lost interest in immigration restriction. Even the press did not consider the passage of the new bill a major event.

After the National Origin Quota Bill became law, immigration dropped sharply. Western European countries did not fill their quotas, and Southern and Eastern European and Asian nations lacked significant, if any, quotas to fill. Only Western Hemisphere immigration from Canada, Mexico, and other Latin American countries continued. Congress wanted the good will of Latin America, and the ranchers, farmers, and businessmen of the Southwest needed cheap Mexican labor.

The Commissioner of Immigration at Ellis Island was soon able to report that virtually all immigrants now "looked like Americans." Nativism had triumphed. It had triumphed because racism, superpatriotism, and fear of social change had caused many Americans to blame whatever they did not like in American life upon the "aliens." It triumphed also because, for the first time in our history, Americans lacked the confidence that they could successfully assimilate all comers. The era of unrestricted immigration had ended. Massive European and Asian ethnic communities remained, however. With infusions of fresh blood from overseas cut off, what would be their future—if any—in American life?

CHAPTER 11

Continuity and Change:
The Second and Third Generations,
1924-1960

The National Origins Quota Act ushered in a new era, but people disagreed on what the new era would bring. Restrictionists and advocates of the melting pot theory anticipated the rapid disappearance of ethnic communities. With most European immigration ended, they expected foreign enclaves to assimilate, that is, to blend indistinguishably with the rest of the population, perhaps enriching the new "American" nationality with the best of their traits in the process. Cultural pluralists, on the other hand, hoped that a variety of distinctive ethnic cultures would perpetuate themselves. Ethnic leaders shared this hope; surely the institutions they had built with so much sacrifice of time, energy, and money would continue to flourish!

Assimilation vs. ethnic survival, the melting pot vs. cultural pluralism—sociologists, journalists, and community leaders aired their conflicting theories in the literature of the day. But it was the immigrants, their children, and their children's children who would decide. The final verdict is not yet in; but by mid century some things were clear. In many ways the second and third generations had acculturated, that is, they had adopted the language, dress, technology, and general life style of majority America. But they had not assimilated. Recognizable ethnic communities remained and ethnicity continued to play an important role in the lives of millions of individuals. By 1960 it was apparent that neither the advocates of the melting pot nor the cultural pluralists had presented an accurate picture of the future of ethnic America. Scholars began to work toward a new conceptual framework.

Some Things Changed—Language and Life style

"For a man to speak one language rather than another is a ritual act," wrote cultural anthropologist E. R. Leach in 1954. " . . . to speak the same language as one's neighbors expresses solidarity with these neighbors; to speak a different language from one's neighbors expresses social distance or even hostility." If Leach is correct, the attitude of most second generation ethnics toward Anglo-Saxon society is clear. They wanted to merge with it as soon as they could. The children of the immigrants abandoned their parents' languages with scarcely a backward glance; and their children, the third generation, rarely knew enough of the ancestral tongues even to abandon them.

Immigrants' children sensed very early that English was the only language valued by the world in which they lived. English was the language of the public school (and usually the parochial school as well). English was the language of comic books, movies, radio, and eventually television, the language of the dance hall, the marketplace, and the political arena, the key to getting a good job, winning the right spouse, and becoming a "real" American.

"The trouble is, they don't want to use the Greek language," complained an immigrant father. "If I ask my boys to read me something in Greek, they don't want to do it. If I want (them) to write a letter in Greek to the old country, they don't want to. . . ." Many immigrants shared this father's complaint, as second generation children deliberately rejected the language of their parents. Adolescents "forgot" the language spoken in their homes since babyhood to avoid the embarrassment of being identified as "foreign", and, therefore, inferior. French-Canadian children reported making conscious efforts never to use French outside their own homes, even though it was the language they felt most comfortable with; they did not want to be labeled "ignorant Canucks."

Use of the traditional language survived in isolated pockets and in places where it was economically or socially necessary even to the second generation; in San Francisco's Chinatown, for example. The ethnic language also survived in areas adjacent to the native country, where constant travel could renew it—among Mexican-Americans in the Southwest, and among French-Canadians in New England. The state legislature of Iowa tried to maintain the old German speech of the nineteenth century town of Amana as a tourist attraction! More serious efforts at language maintenance were undertaken by ethnic churches, cultural organizations, and nationalist societies, but they made little headway against the prevailing conviction that English was the only acceptable speech for citizens of the United States. Elementary school teachers continued to erase children's knowledge of their parent's tongues, while university professors complained that American students had no language skills!

The second generation adopted a new life style as well as a new language. Symbolic of Americanization was the changing of many family names; Hershkowitz became Hersh, Bodinski became Boden, Rugero became Rogers. Edmund Sixtus Marciszewski became Ed Muskie.

Equally symbolic was the change in attitude toward money. Remembering the poverty of the old country, the insecurity of the early years in the United States, and the suffering of the Great Depression, the immigrant generation characteristically stressed the importance of saving. "I pay for the food, the coal, the rent, but other things, unless we need them, we don't buy them," said a Polish immigrant who had lived in the United States for many years. Among the immigrant Chinese, a person who spent freely on clothing, appliances, or cars was considered untrustworthy and immoral!

The children and grandchildren of the immigrants were much less cautious in their attitude toward money. This was partly a reflection of their greater economic security. Also, adopting the spending habits of their fellow Americans, like adopting their language, was a way of establishing solidarity with the majority society. Thus the children of thrifty Slavic and south Italian peasants filled their modest homes with draperies, furniture, and the latest appliances. Foreign born parents who never took a vacation in their working lives watched American born children flock to mountain and seashore resorts or, more recently, go backpacking along wilderness trails. In the prosperous post World War II years, the descendants of Italian, Polish, and Irish immigrants returned to Italy, Poland, and Ireland as tourists.

Less pervasive, but also widespread, was the religious revolution. Many second generation ethnics turned away from the religious practices of their parents. Most Jews gave up the strict observance of the Sabbath and of the dietary laws because they found them inconvenient. A few representatives of every ethnic religion abandoned not only the practices of their parents, but the faith as well—a far more painful break for all concerned.

National as well as religious ties were neglected by many second generation ethnics. Polish community leaders complained that the young were unmoved by any sense of Polish mission, and Irish old timers lamented the indifference of the young to the Irish heritage and national cause. "Stop calling me Chinese . . . I'm American, "insisted a typical Chinese-American college student of the 1950's. "My father happened to be born in China . . . but he's been here more than thirty years. . . . I have no interest in China."

Undoubtedly many aging immigrants looked at the new life styles of their Americanized children with dismay. "I feel like a chicken that has hatched a duck's egg," observed one. The differences between the first generation and their children should not be exaggerated, however. Immigrants, like their children, were moving toward the majority life style.

Although the rebellion of the young was a favorite theme in ethnic novels and autobiographies, it was neither universal nor irreversible. The religious life of the second and third generation illustrates this point. Second generation Catholics and Jews may have practiced their religion less meticulously than their parents, but they rarely converted to another faith. Their children, the third generation, experienced a widespread return to the traditional religion. Secure in their Americanism, the third generation did not need to avoid the church or synagogue as "foreign" or old-fashioned. During the 1950's, a religious revival swept the country. Church membership rose, especially among the middle class. For ethnics as for other Americans religious observance became a part of suburban conformity. Ethnic parents renewed old affiliations, revived half forgotten rituals, and created new rituals, believing that religion added warmth and color to family life and was "good for the children."

National loyalties were more submerged than religious loyalties, but given the proper circumstances they, too, could reappear. Thus when Germany invaded Poland in 1939 three generations of Polish-Americans huddled around their radios and wept. When Poland fell, a hundred thousand Polish-Americans of all ages marched mournfully through the streets of New York City. Similarly, American Jews of all ages and degrees of acculturation were swept into a new realization of their identity by the horrors of the Nazi slaughter of six million European Jews and by the drama of the reestablishment of a Jewish state, Israel.

Some Things Survived—Family Life, Neighborhoods, Jobs

"Men may change their clothes, their politics, their wives, their religions, their philosophies to a greater or lesser extent; they cannot change their grandfathers," observed Horace Kallen. In outward appearances, and in many of the routines of their daily lives, the children and grandchildren of the immigrants were indistinguishable from other Americans. Yet ethnicity survived as an ongoing set of attitudes and behaviors handed down, consciously and unconsciously, from generation to generation. Many immigrant parents could not pass on their ethnic language, literature, or even their folk songs and religious traditions. What they could and did pass on, however, were values and priorities, ways of expressing (or not expressing) emotion, subtle preferences, and unconscious practices that affected the texture of life in the home, on the job, and in the neighborhood. Ethnic patterns brought from the old country as "cultural baggage" survived in America if they were useful to the younger generations.

Distinctive patterns of family life were among the most lasting aspects of ethnicity. The continued survival of the close-knit Italian family is an excellent example. Second and third generation Italian-Americans, like their immigrant parents, invested an unusual amount of time and emergy in family life, sometimes limiting their social and even their business associations to members of their own extended families. This pattern originated in southern Italy, where life was hard, officials corrupt, and only family members could be trusted. It was reinforced in the United States by the hostility of the outside world toward Italian immigrants. Here, as in the old country, relatives were more reliable than outsiders, uncles hired young men when strangers would not, and aunts gave more reliable advice than social workers.

The Southern Italian pattern of unusually strong reliance on family survived in America because it was economically useful; and because it created a sense of warmth and belonging that was appreciated by both young and old. "I loathed Italian customs with all my heart," said a second generation Italian boy, "but I would never let anything stand between me and my family." When a correspondent complained to an Italian-American newspaper in the 1940's that he had few friends, the editor reminded him that friends were not important as long as he had his family.

Marriage continued to be affected by ethnic background. In many ethnic groups the relationship between the second generation husband and wife was less intense and less egalitarian than in the typical "American" marriage. Italian, Polish, and Greek women for example, were more likely to confide in their mothers, sisters, and women friends than in their husbands, who spent much of their leisure time in the company of other men. Among Greek and Italian Americans in particular the roles of the sexes remained more rigidly separated than in the general population. These women seldom worked outside the home after marriage (unless forced to do so by economic deprivation), took little part in community activities, and rarely challenged the authority of their husbands, at least not in public.

Traditional patterns tended to break down in the third generation in middle class families, which were more likely to adopt the American ideal of romantic love and companionship between husband and wife.

They survived longer, however, in working class families, where they were reinforced by religious traditions and economic realities. The jobs to which poorly educated working class ethnic women had access were so unrewarding, psychologically and financially, that there was little incentive to work outside the home and little opportunity in general to acquire a sense of independence.

Child rearing, like marriage, continued to be influenced by ethnic tradition. In many ethnic families, discipline was stricter than in the average "American" family and the authority of the parents more strongly maintained. "You don't see any joking or arguing in the Greek families as you do in others," remarked a Greek-American in the 1930's. Young people in Chinese and Japanese-American homes were less boisterous and more respectful of their elders than their nonethnic counterparts. In the mid 1950's a much larger proportion of young Japanese-American adults than the general population considered it shameful to send their parents to an old age home.

In Italian families children were expected to conform to the wishes and needs of the adults, while Jewish families were more likely to be "child centered." Adolescent boys in Italian families spent most of their time with their peers, whose influence upon them was very strong; Jewish children remained closer to their parents. Japanese-American mothers breast fed their infants longer than their American counterparts and were more protective of their young children, discouraging them from independent action at as early an age as their non-Japanese counterparts. Scandinavian and Oriental children were taught to control, even to hide their emotions, while Italian and Jewish children were taught to express theirs. Teaching of this kind was unconscious, by example rather than by precept, but effective nonetheless.

Research in comparative child rearing practices of the various ethnic groups has just begun, but it is clear already that significant differences did—and to a lesser degree still do—exist. Undoubtedly these differences contribute to the distinctiveness of adult ethnic communities.

Choices of neighborhoods, friends, and jobs are usually made at a more conscious level than choices about sex roles and the rearing of children. These areas, too, remained greatly influenced by ethnicity in the second and third generations and even beyond. Where people choose to live remains determined in part by their ethnicity. The ethnic map of the United States has changed very little in the past hundred years. The descendants of Scandinavian and German immigrants still cluster in the farms and small towns of the Midwest, and Irish, Polish, Italian, Jewish, and Arabic Americans remain heavily concentrated in the large cities of the Northeast and the Great Lakes states. French-Canadians remain primarily in New England, and Orientals primarily on the West Coast. Thus, despite the mobility of the American population, most ethnic Americans still live in the regions chosen by their immigrant predecessors.

Many ethnic individuals still live in ethnic neighborhoods, clearly identifiable by ethnic lodges, churches, and food stores and by the less visible but immensely important network of family relationships and lifelong friendships. In such neighborhoods, roots are deep and emotional attachments strong. When the residents of Boston's predominantly Italian West End were told that they would have to move because of an urban renewal project, their reaction was bitter. "The place you're born is where you want to die," said one young man. "I wish the world would end tonight. . . . I wish they'd tear the whole damn town down," said another. "I'm going to be lost without the West End. Where the hell can I go? . . . It pulls the heart out of a guy to lose all his friends."

When second or third generation ethnics moved out of their original neighborhoods to the suburbs, they often moved in identifiable groups. Major cities have newer neighborhoods and suburbs in which people of Irish, Italian, Polish, Jewish, and other distinctive backgrounds are heavily concentrated. The ethnic concentration in specific neighborhoods tends to decrease with succeeding generations, but it has not disappeared.

Ethnic neighborhoods have survived, not only because of the restrictive policies of real estate agents and the prejudice of the larger community, but also because many ethnic Americans enjoy living in them. Ethnic women in particular have often found the move to mixed suburbs a difficult one. Kept close to home by the needs of young children, they missed the tightly knit social group of family and friends in the old neighborhood and found it hard to adjust to the quick, and often shallow, friendships of suburbia.

Nostalgia for the city was common to second and third generation men and women of many ethnic groups. Suburban Chinese for example, continue to make regular Sunday pilgrimages to Chinatown because there "one can buy groceries, pick up the mail, visit Third Uncle, drop by the doctor's office, get some good food in the stomach and maybe catch the latest movie from Hong Kong, all in the same vicinity." When Jews moved to the suburbs after World War II, they passed over the more secluded country lanes for areas easily accessible to the cultural and educational facilities they had enjoyed in the city. When their children were grown, Jewish couples often moved back to the city again, though they were more likely to settle in newer apartment buildings than in their old neighborhoods. In many cities a hard core of Italians, Poles, Jews and other ethnics remained in their old neighborhoods as newer ethnics such as blacks, Puerto Ricans,

Mexican-Americans, or immigrants from Appalachia, moved in. Some did not want to move; others could not afford to move.

Ethnicity influenced the choice of jobs as well as neighborhoods. Like all Americans, the children and grandchildren of the immigrants wanted to "better" themselves, which meant a rejection of the occupation of their parents. Second generation women rarely worked as domestic servants, for example, an occupation common among their mothers; they were more likely to become sales clerks, factory operatives, teachers, or nurses.

Still, there was a surprising amount of continuity between the occupations of the first, second, and even the third generations of particular ethnic groups. The sons of German bakers, brewers, and cabinet makers took up similar but more highly skilled trades as upholsterers, metalsmiths, and bookbinders. The sons of unskilled Yugoslavian miners and industrial workers remained employed in these fields, moving up to skilled jobs as operatives, cranemen, and welders. Italians followed their parents into such trades as stone masonry, meat cutting, barbering, construction, and food distribution. Small private businesses continued to be popular among the second and third generation of Greeks, Jews, and Oriental Americans, as they had been among the first.

Some occupations, such as Italian skills in stone cutting, were brought from the old country. Others had been learned in the United States; there had been little heavy industry in the Balkan provinces from which Yugoslavian immigrants came. Sometimes young people chose their parents' occupations because they could be placed in a family business or sponsored for membership in a union dominated by their own ethnic community. The Irish capitalized on their early establishment of political power in the cities by remaining concentrated in civil service and other bureaucratic positions. Their favored profession was law. Individual career choices were undoubtedly influenced by the varying interests and abilities of the immigrant group. A recent study of ethnic school children indicated that Chinese-American children excelled in dealing with spatial relationships, a factor in their frequent choice of careers such as architecture and engineering.

In the third generation the upwardly mobile of every ethinc group began to break traditional occupational patterns. In the 1960's and 1970's the sons and daughters of Polish, Italian, and Irish laborers appeared in sharply increased numbers as scientists, physicians, university professors, and other professionals. For Jews, the move into academia and the professions took place a generation earlier. By the 1960's the children of second generation Jewish school teachers, social workers, and self-employed businessmen and professionals were entering more prestigious (though not necessarily more lucrative) fields, becoming college teachers, research scientists, lawyers in large firms, or entering occupations their parents had never been in, such as advertising and public relations. Since the hardest economic battles had been won by their parents, some members of the third generation could afford to be more concerned with prestige or leisure than with money. "My father's generation may have felt pressure to achieve success, but this generation is lazier," said one. "Sure I want money, but I don't want to work as hard for it as my father did," said another.

Still, prejudice and pragmatism led a surprising number of this successful, prestige and security oriented, third generation back to traditional ethnic occupations. In the mid 1970's Jewish organizations were still protesting the discriminatory practices that shut Jewish business school graduates out of top corporate positions. "Being Jewish doesn't help you when you want to advance as a metallurgist in industry," said a realistic university trained young man "so I gave up my salaried job to take over my father's scrap iron business." Chinese-American historian Betty Lee Sung writes of a young Chinese engineer who used his college training to renovate and mechanize a formerly despised family laundry business. Students and professionally employed Chinese, once eager to escape the family restaurant, found themselves returning there to work on weekends and holidays. "Now that they are no longer exclusively confined to restaurant work, they need no longer disdain it," wrote Sung. "Off hand I can name an architect, a vice president of a finance company, a welder in an aircraft factory, a medical student, and a dental student." Common occupations, like common neighborhoods and common family traditions, formed a social cement, helping to bind the second and third generations to one another and to the world of their parents and grandparents.

The Ethnic Community

The survival of ethnicity in the second and third generations was also encouraged by the continuing institutional life of the ethnic community. Despite increasing participation in the majority community life, most second and third generation ethnic Americans maintained at least some ties with their ethnic communities as well and many had deep commitments to particular institutions within that community. There were several reasons for this. Like the immigrants, they enjoyed the companionship and recognition they received in their own organizations and institutions. Like the immigrants, they had problems that could be understood and handled best by people with backgrounds similar to their own. Finally, like the immigrants, they were not welcomed in many of the activities of the Anglo-Saxon Protestant community.

Ethnic communities, as already described, consisted of a variety of institutions. Those that responded successfully to the changing needs of the second and third generations survived. Those that did not faded into insignificance. Ethnic churches were among the most successful in adjusting to the changes in language and life style that marked their more acculturated younger members. The churches continued the process begun even before 1924 of replacing the traditional language with English and supplementing worship with social and educational activities for all ages.

By midcentury ethnic churches were following their memberships to the suburbs, establishing impressive new buildings with gymnasiums and swimming pools for newly affluent congregations. Suburban churches and synagogues sponsored bowling leagues, chess tournaments, and classes in everything from Bible and ethics to child psychology and scuba diving. In the newer parishes Catholics of varying ethnic groups—German, Italian, Polish, Ukrainian, South Slav—worshipped together. In doing so they adopted a common "American" religious style—that of the Irish Catholics! By midcentury Italian Catholics were intermarrying with Irish Catholics and sending their children to Irish dominated parochial schools. Similarly, Russian Jews and German Jews were mixing in suburban synagogues and intermarrying with increasing frequency.

Changes in religious education reflected the changing needs and interests of the Americanized generations. Few parochial schools continued instruction in the traditional language, history and literature; parents no longer considered it important. In urban parishes the original ethnic children were gradually replaced by blacks and Puerto Ricans for whom the old ethnic curriculum was inappropriate. By midcentury Catholic parochial schools were teaching the ethnic tongues as foreign languages, where they were teaching them at all.

Though parochial schools no longer maintained the old languages, they kept their importance as centers of community loyalty and as repositories of ethnic values. Their tone, their discipline, and their constituency, if not their curriculum, remained distinct from that of the public schools. Though some Catholic intellectuals questioned their necessity, parochial schools were zealously maintained by second and third generation Catholic parents. Indeed, as urban public schools increasingly reflected the social problems of troubled cities, upwardly mobile families, including many blacks, sent their children to Catholic schools for educational rather than religious or even ethnic reasons. Enrollments in Catholic schools began to decline in the 1960's and 1970's because of a rise in cost, not because of a loss in confidence. By the 1970's, new efforts were underway to enlist public aid for parochial schools, many of which were on the edge of financial disaster.

Similarly, Greek, Jewish, and other supplementary, or "afternoon" ethnic schools did not disappear with the immigrant generation that had established them. They not only survived, they thrived, their enrollment even increasing with the emergence of the third generation. Like the Catholic parochial schools, these schools reflected the decline of the traditional language. Many chose to deemphasize language instruction because the parents thought it unnecessary and the children found it "too difficult." Increasingly, these schools taught a varied curriculum of ethnic history, religion, and customs in English. Many afternoon schools still tried to teach the traditional languages, but even their own teachers despaired of success.

In both the parochial schools and the afternoon and weekend schools, the ethnicity of the first generation was irretrievably gone by midcentury. Neither nostalgia, nor good intentions, nor the determination of "survivalist" educators appeared able to bring it back. For third generation children ethnic culture was a school subject to be self-consciously "studied," valued," "appreciated," and "believed in" rather than to be spontaneously experienced and lived.

Responding to this new situation, many ethnic schools tried to teach "identity," by offering courses in traditional ethnic dance, folk arts, music, and ethnic cooking. Another response was to turn from the teaching of religious or folk culture to the teaching of "high" culture, the classical literary and philosophical tradition of the mother country. The old language acquired new prestige, not as the everyday language of parents and grandparents, but as the language of Dante, or Sophocles, or Moliere. Using language skills acquired in ethnic or public schools, some third generation youth pursued the advanced study of the civilization of their ancestral country at an intellectual rather than an emotional level on the university campus. This abstract, intellectualized exploration of ethnic "high" culture indicated how far many members of the college educated third generation had moved from the spontaneous ethnic folkways of their grandparents.

Like the schools, other ethnic organizations changed to meet the needs of changing constitutencies, or gradually disappeared. Social lodges based upon their members' common birthplace in the old country declined both in number and importance. The original members grew old, and their children had no interest in joining. The depression of the 1930's depleted the resources of these lodges and of the mutual benefit societies associated with them, as did the increasingly heavy claims made by an aging membership.

Ethnic labor unions, on the other hand, often survived and enrolled the younger generation who, like their parents, found these organizations valuable aids in assuring adequate income and job security. Some ethnic unions changed over the years from one constituency to another. By 1960, for example, the formerly Jewish and Italian garment unions of New York were heavily Puerto Rican. Settlement houses, missions, and "Y's" also found their clients changing with the neighborhoods. Institutions that were unwilling or unable to make the adjustment necessary to be of service to the new populations did not survive.

Ethnic charities survived and even flourished as they changed to meet the needs of changing clientele. Many became recognized and highly respected components of their city's benevolent establishment. Syrian, Lebanese, and Jewish charity camps opened their doors to the poor of other groups when their own communities, now largely middle class, no longer sent enough needy children to fill them. Successful Y's and settlement houses phased out many of their welfare and "Americanization" activities, replacing them with social and cultural programs for constituencies who were no longer poor or "foreign." By the 1960's agencies such as the Jewish and Catholic Family Services were combating the ills of affluence as well as poverty, including the perplexing problem of drug abuse by the middle class young, and the effects of an increasing divorce rate. Chinese charities established "Golden Age" clubs for the growing number of foreign-born men who faced a lonely old age without relatives to care for them. Indeed, programs for the elderly occupied an increasing proportion of the attention of all ethnic charities.

Even when second and third generation ethnic Americans joined the organizations and institutions of the majority community, such affiliations often had an ethnic component. Many scout troops, for example, were sponsored by churches and synagogues or by public schools in strongly ethnic neighborhoods. Though nonsectarian and nonethnic in theory, such scout troops often functioned as ethnic institutions. Subtly or openly, second and third generation ethnics were frequently discouraged from joining clubs, charities, and other organizations which were in effect white, Anglo-Saxon preserves. In response, second and third generation ethnic Americans created an extensive network of parallel institutions for themselves—professional associations, lodges, resorts, summer camps, and even debutante balls for their daughters.

The most popular and broadly based second generation ethnic organizations were groups such as the Hellenic Progressive Association, the Chinese-American Citizens Alliance and the Japanese-American Citizens League. Like the old fraternal lodges which to some extent they replaced, these newer organizations fulfilled the need for "in-group" social life. Unlike many of the older lodges, however, they held their meetings completely in English, were totally secular, and focused on civic and political issues, especially on the fight against prejudice and discrimination. Still insecure in their Americanism, these second generation organizations were enthusiastic in asserting their devotion to the United States. In 1941, shortly before Pearl Harbor, members of the Japanese-American Citizens League recited the following creed:

> I am proud that I am an American citizen of Japanese ancestry, for my very background makes me appreciate more fully the wonderful advantages of this nation. Although some individuals may discriminate against me, I shall never become bitter. . . . I shall do all in my power to discourage such practices, but I shall do it in the American way . . . through courts of law, by education, by proving myself to be worthy of equal treatment and consideration.

In the 1960's, a more self-confident and militant third generation found much to criticize in what they regarded as the "Uncle Tom" organizations of their parents, organizations such as the Japanese-American Citizens League.

As the use of traditional non-English languages declined, so too did the foreign language press, theater, and literature. Foreign language newspapers decreased in number and in circulation. The number of German papers declined from 300 in 1920 to 60 in 1950, and by midcentury there were no Scandinavian language dailies left. Many of the foreign language papers that survived became increasingly conservative in their content. Catering to an aging clientele, and with few new subscribers, they took no chance of losing the readers they had.

Critics in every decade confidently predicted the imminent demise of the foreign language press. Nevertheless, it not only survived but in the 1950's and 1960's even began to grow again. Nonquota immigrants from Mexico, Puerto Rico, and Cuba revitalized the Spanish press and refugees from Eastern Europe had a similar effect on the Slavic presses. New weeklies, monthlies, and specialized journals were founded by well-educated ethnic refugees before and after World War II. In the 1960's there were eleven newspapers in Chinese alone. Every ethnic group continued to publish English language newspapers and magazines representing its ethnic churches, organizations, and political interests and recording its social and community news.

The foreign language theater declined after 1920, undermined by competition from the radio, movies, and television, as well as by the loss of the native language. The great ethnic theater traditions did not disappear, however. They merged with and enriched mainstream American entertainment. Actors such as Paul Muni and Jacob and Celia Adler of the famous Adler family moved from the Yiddish theater to Broadway, which added Yiddish expressions to its vocabulary and counted second and third generation Jews among its loyal audiences.

With the language barrier gone, theatrical figures of many ethnic backgrounds—Al Jolson, Eddie Cantor, Danny Kaye, Jack Benny, the Marx brothers, Bing Crosby, Gene Kelly, the Barrymores, Frank Sinatra, Perry Como, and Danny Thomas, to name only a few—became familiar to all Americans. Eventually, audiences no longer recognized the ethnicity of the performances they enjoyed—Jack Benny as the "cheap" Jew, or James Cagney as the tough little "fighting Irishman." "I'm a Yankee Doodle Dandy, Born on the Fourth of July," sang the very Irish George M. Cohan. Ethnic entertaining had taken out its citizenship papers.

In like manner, dozens of fine second generation ethnic authors became part of the American literary mainstream. Second generation novelists often wrote about their own ethnic communities. Writers representative of the "new ethnicity" of the 1960's and 1970's stressed the warmth, the vitality, and the emotional security to be found in ethnic life, but the "alienated" second generation writers of earlier decades presented a more negative view. James T. Farrell, for example, author of the controversial *Studs Lonigan* trilogy, described hard working but culturally impoverished Irish-American parents who bequeathed their children only "frustration, labor, and the bottle." Farrell's novels outraged many, not only because of their frankness in dealing with sex and violence, but also because of their unflattering portrayal of the Catholic Church, the family, and the Irish working class way of life. "I don't want to read any more of his books," an Irish-American said of Farrell. "He writes about the people I've spent all my life trying to get away from."

Like Farrell, many second generation intellectuals were alienated from their parent communities, yet not totally accepted by the general American society. Standing with one foot in each of two widely divergent cultures—and comfortable in neither—such people were referred to as "marginal men." Many of these "marginal" men and women became journalists, critics, sociologists, psychologists, historians, and economists. Taking advantage of the doubly rich perspectives of two cultural backgrounds, second generation ethnic intellectuals often became astute observers and commentators on the nature of American society.

Ethnicity and Social Mobility

American myth attributes economic and social success to the ability, or the luck, of the individual. But group identity—ethnicity—played an important role. Despite individual disclaimers, everyone assumes to some degree the status American society has assigned to his or her group. Thus the Italian physician shared the unfavorable status of the Italian gangster, while the lowliest white, Anglo-Saxon Protestant shared the favorable status of the WASP corporate executive. When a group considered "undesirable"—Italians, Jews, blacks, Orientals— moved into a neighborhood, previous residents considered the neighborhood to have gone "down," even though the value of its real estate may actually have risen.

According to another time-honored American myth, all immigrants arrived poor, worked hard, and were successful. While the myth contains elements of truth for some immigrants, it is oversimplified, even untrue, for many more. Between 1910 and 1950 foreign born males improved their economic status at a more rapid rate than the general American work force, but this does not mean that they got rich. Their rate of improvement was high because their starting positions had been so low! In most cases, success was modest. As late as the early 1970's, Polish, other Slavic Americans, Spanish-speaking Americans, and Irish Protestants were still heavily concentrated in low paying, low status occupations. Nor was economic mobility a steady rise when it did come. Gains made in the 1920's were wiped out in the depression of the 1930's. The World War II years were the first period of prosperity for most ethnic Americans. This taste of the "good life" was soon threatened, however, by a series of post war recessions and by an apparently unending inflationary spiral.

Ethnicity had an important impact upon a given individual's material success. Though individuals of every ethnic group achieved prominence in various fields, some ethnic groups were more successful, *as groups*, than others. Their members moved more rapidly and in greater numbers than others into the higher paid and higher status middle and upper middle class occupations, and into the more prestigious neighborhoods and community positions that accompanied these occupations. Using family income, education, and the relative prestige of occupations as criteria, the most successful groups by the mid 1960's were Jews, Orientals (especially Japanese), and Irish Catholics, all of whom were more successful than British Protestants. Germans and Scandinavians have done moderately well and Southern and Eastern Europeans generally less well (although Italians have average family incomes equaling those of British Protestants and appear to be rising rapidly). The least successful groups have been the Spanish-speaking minorities (many of whom are relatively recent arrivals), French-Canadians, and Irish Protestants.

While the newest immigrant groups were usually the poorest in the short run, economic status in the long run was not determined by length of residence in the United States. The Irish and the

French-Canadians arrived a generation or more before the majority of Jews who soon outdistanced them. Nor did language skills seem to matter for long. Jews, who came with no knowledge of English, moved ahead of the English-speaking Irish.

Discrimination and prejudice affected mobility, but the relationship was complex. Two of the most successful groups by midcentury were Jews and Japanese, yet discrimination against these groups was very strong. In the case of Jews, discrimination arose, at least in part, as an attempt to check their upward movement that began in the first and second generations. In the early twentieth century Jews were already enrolling heavily in the city colleges of New York and applying for positions in the more prestigious colleges and graduate schools in numbers greater than their proportion in the population. Anti-Semitic university administrators mouthed platitutes about maintaining "balanced" enrollments, while students complained that Jews were spoiling Harvard for "the native born Anglo Saxon young persons for whom it was really built." According to others, "in harmony with their policy of getting all they can for as little as possible," Jews were winning all the scholarships!

To keep Jews in what others considered "their place," academic institutions adopted quotas to limit the numbers admitted. In 1920, before the adoption of the quota system, about half the students at Cornell University School of Medicine were graduates of the heavily Jewish city colleges of New York. While the quota system was in operation, the number shrank to 1.4%. Nor was education the only area to adopt anti-Semitic policies. Hotels and resorts prided themselves on their "restricted" clientele, and major corporations hired Christians only. Half the advertisements for office help in the *Chicago Tribune* on July 6, 1941 specified "Gentiles only," or, more subtly, asked applicants to "state nationality or religion."

Prejudice and discrimination against Orientals was even more intense than against Jews. Popular literature such as Van Wyck Mason's Captain North stories and Sax Rohmer's tales of Dr. Fu Manchu portrayed all Orientals as vicious, depraved, and fiendishly cruel. In Mississippi, Chinese-American children, like Negro children, were segregated in separate and inferior schools. As for employment opportunities, in 1928 the Stanford University Placement Service reported that "it is almost impossible to place a Chinese or Japanese of either the first or the second generation in any kind of position, engineering, manufacturing, or business."

The most blatant act of discrimination against Orientals was the imprisonment of all Japanese-Americans, including American-born United States citizens, during World War II. Ordered by the military, approved by President Roosevelt, and later upheld by the Supreme

Court, this action was a response to widespread—but totally unfounded—fears of Japanese sabotage on the West Coast and reflected the long-standing anti-Japanese feeling of this area.

With virtually no advance notice, over 100,000 Japanese-American men, women, and children were evacuated from their homes, interned in "relocation centers" (race tracks, fairgrounds, stock exhibition halls), and then imprisoned in permanent camps, usually in the most desolate rural areas of the West and Midwest. Left-wing as well as right-wing commentators on American political life supported the internment of the Japanese. Carey McWilliams, then a member of the advisory board of the left-wing Japanese American Committee for Democracy, considered internment necessary for military and security reasons, and for the safety of the Japanese-Americans. In an article in *Harper's Magazine*, in September of 1942, he defended the policy with unintended irony.

> It would certainly not be accurate to characterize Santa Anita as a 'concentration camp.' To be sure, the camp is surrounded by barbed wire; it is guarded by a small detail of soldiers; searchlights play around the camp and up and down the streets at night; and the residents cannot leave the grounds. Their automobiles are all impounded; two roll calls are taken each day; . . . there is a military censorship on outgoing and incoming mail. . . . At Manzanar Camp, Hikaji Takeuchi, a twenty-two year old Nisei [second generation Japanese American] was shot by a guard, but the incident seems to have been the result of a misunderstanding. . . .

Family life was disrupted, old people and children were disoriented, and farms, shops, household property, and skills were lost. The Federal Reserve Bank estimated the financial losses at $400 million, less than ten per cent of which was ever repaid. By the time even this modest compensation was available, twenty years after the war, many of the original claimants were dead.

Length of residence in the United States, language barriers (or lack of them) and degrees of prejudice and discrimination then are not sufficient to explain why some groups were more successful in moving up the socioeconomic ladder than others. Other ethnic factors, such as educational and geographic background, skills, family and community structure, self image, and value system were important. As has already been discussed, immigrant groups from urban environments, groups who were accustomed to formal schooling and were aware of its value, and groups who were relatively less concerned that public schools would destroy cherished ethnic languages and cultures, were able to use the American public schools more effectively than others. The children of Japanese-Americans, and particularly of Jewish-

Americans, were often among the most highly motivated students, "overachievers" whose determination and hard work brought scholastic success.

As jobs for manual laborers declined in number and opportunities in service industries and professions expanded, "overeducated" Japanese and Jewish youth were able to move from the working class to the middle class. Mobility for Jews increased rapidly after World War II, when the revelation of Nazi atrocities made anti-Semitism less acceptable to American society. Ironically, the polarization of American society in the black-white confrontations of the 1960's helped Oriental Americans, who were able to successfully identify with the majority whites. Ironically, too, the World War II internment of the Japanese-Americans may have increased their mobility in the long run by producing a new generation of community leaders, and by breaking down old occupational and geographic patterns.

Skills as well as education gave some ethnic groups advantages over others. Groups with commercial experience—Lebanese, Armenians, Syrians, Jews, and West Indians, for example—were better able to function in the commercial society of twentieth century America than groups who came primarily with agrarian skills—South Italians, Irish, and Poles. Coming from cultures in which land was the major source of wealth and prestige, members of these ethnic groups often put their savings in a home and garden, or in elaborate church buildings, rather than in capital producing enterprises that paid dividends in future mobility. These culturally determined investment choices were often repeated by the second generation.

Other ethnic characteristics contributed toward socioeconomic mobility in the United States. Poor health and a high injury rate handicapped the Slavs, the Italians, and the Irish. Orientals and Jews appeared to be healthier. The Japanese, for reasons cultural, genetic, or both, were and still are the healthiest group in the United States, living on the average six or seven years longer than Caucasians. Certainly the fact that more breadwinners survived to assist their children into adulthood made upward mobility easier for these groups. Similarly, the fact that Protestant, Oriental, and especially Jewish immigrant groups limited their family size sharply as early as the second generation, while most Catholic groups did not do so until a generation later, enabled them to give each child a better economic start.

Ethnic family and community structures had an economic impact on comparative mobility. Strong families and tightly structured communities helped to increase economic mobility. While all immigrant families suffered some dislocations with immigration, Oriental, Jewish, and Italian families held together exceptionally well. Desertion and alcoholism, great handicaps to economic mobility, even survival, were relatively rare among these groups. Oriental children were brought up in a manner that encouraged close dependency upon family and community. Japanese children were taught that their misbehavior brought shame to their relatives and their entire ethnic group, while good performance reflected credit upon family and group. Family and group pride and community support for individual achievement served as powerful motivating factors.

Reflecting two thousand years of minority status, Jews often brought up their children to be unusually sensitive to the opinion of others about their behavior and their achievements. Jewish parents, like Japanese parents, were unusually protective. While the possessiveness of the Jewish mother has become an unpleasant cliché, her affectionate but manipulative behavior toward her children, especially her sons, contributed to their mobility. By keeping her children emotionally dependent upon her approval rather than upon the approval of peer groups, she was often successful in keeping them off the streets, in school, and thus on a track for socioeconomic advancement.

Of course every ethnic group had its "Jewish mothers"—and fathers—strong parents who dominated, protected, and directed their offspring and by doing so helped them escape the urban slums. John Pastore, the first Italian-American governor of Rhode Island, was such a child, and historian Samuel Lubell discovered that many of the more successful of Pastore's childhood acquaintances had similar upbringings.

> Those who have proven most successful—the doctors, lawyers, dentists, and the like—were all subject to the strictest discipline as children. To set them apart from the "tough" boys, the parents overdressed them to the point of having many considered sissies. As for the boy who had been the toughest kid on the block—he was now an iceman.

Obviously, "tough" kids did not always become icemen. Many school dropouts found very effective avenues to social mobility in the world of business. For some, the way to success was through illegitimate business, such as gambling, and bootlegging—the "rackets"—which American society generously patronized. In the 1920's and 1930's, ethnic bootleggers were aided by members of their own communities who considered Prohibition ridiculous and whose loyalties were with their friends and relatives rather than with the police.

Legitimate enterprises, too, found their own communities invaluable sources of support. One could—and still can—become financially successful by serving as shopkeeper, contractor, undertaker, doctor, or lawyer for the members of one's ethnic community. As sociologist Andrew Greeley pointed out,

> . . . in the large cities there are networks of intragroup client-professional relationships. The Italian doctor sees an Italian lawyer when he wants legal advice, both of them have their expensive suburban homes built by an Italian contractor, and all of them vote for an Italian political leader. . . . Thus an exchange of goods and services goes on within the religio-ethnic collectivity which may well have a multiplier effect in contributing to the economic well-being of this community as a whole.

The more tightly knit, or as critical outsiders saw it, the more "clannish" an ethnic community was, the more effectively this multiplier factor worked.

Unfortunately, however, business people and professionals serving their own communities usually had less prestige than those serving the total population. It was unusual for a businessman who attained wealth and prominence within his own community to be accorded comparable respect in the business world at large. Similarly, it was difficult for a professional person to move from a high position in an ethnic university, hospital, or other ethnic institution to a position of comparable status in a predominantly Anglo-Saxon institution.

Finally, socioeconomic mobility was influenced by the internal value systems of particular ethnic groups. Some groups brought with them, or quickly acquired, the so-called Protestant work ethic as they concentrated on moving up in American society. Other groups continued to place greater emphasis on noneconomic values such as family, leisure, friendship, and hospitality. For many first and second generation South Italians, for example, work was a means of survival; life's major satisfactions lay elsewhere. Among groups such as French Canadians and Mexican-Americans, individuals who advanced into the middle class sometimes did so at the risk of disapproval or, worse yet, isolation from their family and their community. To some extent these attitudes were a response to the realities of life—upward mobility was so illusive in the Mexican-American barrio that one avoided frustration by not pursuing it. On the other hand, these attitudes could also represent a conscious cultural choice, a rejection of the "rat race" and the materialism it represents, as well as an understanding that upward mobility often comes at a price. What Daniel Moynihan said of the Irish in *Beyond the Melting Pot* could apply equally well to members of other ethnic communities:

> Turning lower middle class is a painful process for a group such as the Irish who, as stevedores and truck drivers, made such a grand thing out of Saturday night. Most prize fighters and a good many saloon fighters

die in the gutter—but they have moments of glory unknown to accountants. Most Irish laborers died penniless, but they had been rich one night a week much of their lives, whereas their white collar children never know a moment of financial peace, much less affluence. A good deal of color goes out of life when a group begins to rise. A good deal of resentment enters.

The economic rise of ethnic Americans, whether it took place in one generation, two, or more, was not without its cost. Old-timers of every group complained that the children "nowadays" were spoiled by too many playthings and that the casual, noisy good times and human fellowship that once graced people's lives were gone. Still, as an elderly Jewish correspondent commented to the editor of the *Forward*, the people who longed for the "good old days" conveniently forgot the cold, the hunger, the sixteen hours of daily drudgery and all the other hardships of poverty in romantic nostalgia for their youth. There was no returning to the "good old days," and given the choice, few would really want to go back.

Ethnic America at Midcentury

European and Oriental ethnicity, then, did not disappear with the National Origins Quota Act. It survived in the private life of the individual and in the public life of the community. At midcentury millions of people, indistinguishable from the majority American society in all outward appearances, were living at least some parts of their lives in their own ethnic subcultures, separate from but parallel to the culture of the Anglo-Saxon majority. Ethnic subcultures of the second and third generations were not transplanted versions of overseas civilizations. They were "made in the U.S.A." by native born citizens who shared life styles, values, and interests based both on their common Old World heritage and their common New World experience.

People sharing an ethnic culture and community often shared common economic and political interests as well. Ethnic America never voted as a political bloc; it was neither sufficiently well organized nor sufficiently homogenous. On the other hand, common traditions from the Old World and common interests in the new gave particular ethnic communities distinctive political personalities. On some issues there were distinctive, even predictable, ethnic political positions. Legislation involving public school teachers in New York City evoked a Jewish political response because so many of the teachers were Jewish. Legislation involving the New York City police force, for the same reason, evoked an Irish response. Virtually every ethnic community had group responses to foreign policy issues involving their country of origin.

Sometimes a group of issues combined to evoke a broad ethnic response. During the presidential election of 1928, most Southern and Eastern European ethnics lived in northeastern urban centers, were Roman Catholics, and were opposed to Prohibition. Hence they voted *en masse* for the Democratic candidate, Al Smith, a Roman Catholic "wet" from the Lower East Side of New York City. Prohibition and Anglo-Saxon Protestantism, in the person of the "all-American" Herbert Hoover, defeated them.

Politicians of all parties tried to attract twentieth century ethnic voters as they had been doing since the days of Benjamin Franklin. But it was Franklin Roosevelt, president of the nation for four consecutive terms beginning in 1933, who cemented a long-term alliance between the Democratic party and ethnic America. Roosevelt's economic programs projected concern for the "little people," ethnics, blacks, and workers. His willingness to provide jobs and immediate relief during the depression, his support of the unionization of industrial workers, and his backing of measures such as Social Security won him the lasting gratitude of the largely working class ethnic population. Roosevelt's Democratic coalition, including the vast majority of the ethnic communities, ruled the country, with the exception of the Eisenhower years, from 1933 to 1968. The climax of that period for many ethnic Americans was the election of one of their own, Irish Catholic John F. Kennedy, to the highest office in the land in 1960. "Will you vote for Kennedy because he is a Catholic?" a campaign volunteer asked a working man in Buffalo, New York. "No," he replied. "Because I am."

Because ethnic Americans within each community had so much in common—jobs, neighborhoods, institutions, values, even political opinions, the second and, to a somewhat lesser extent even the third, generations continued to choose their friends and their spouses from within what sociologist Milton Gordon called their own "ethclass," people of their own ethnic group and social class. Among Orientals and South Italians, much socializing remained within the extended family and the immediate neighborhood. About eighty per cent of a sample of third generation Jews stated that their four closest friends were also Jewish. "I have no desire to avoid Gentiles, but I don't meet them." explained one.

The immigrant generation had been vehement in its disapproval of marriage outside the group. "He's better off dead," they said, or "She's no daughter of mine." While protesting against their parents' attitudes, the second generation usually conformed. Despite the shortage of Chinese women, three quarters of Chinese-American marriages from 1924 to 1935 were between members of the Chinese community. The

intermarriage rate among second generation French-Canadians of
Woonsocket, Rhode Island was only 8.8%. Young Japanese-Americans
boldly asserted their right to choose their own marriage partners as
they saw fit. In practice, however, they often used a mutual friend as a
"go-between" to be sure that the prospective marriage, usually to
another Japanese, was acceptable to their families.

The prevailing pattern of "in-group" marriages began to break
down in the third generation. While only 8.8% of their parents had
married outside the group, 35% of the third generation French-
Canadians in the Woonsocket sample were doing so. Studies showed
the Jewish intermarriage rate of the late 1960's was a third, or even
higher. Ethnic leaders were almost unanimous in their alarm at this
new trend. Yet if the "outsider" was successfully acculturated into the
group, the group was strengthened, at least numerically, by the
intermarriage. Long-term studies of the children and grandchildren
of such marriages will be necessary before any conclusions can be
drawn about their ultimate effect upon the survival of ethnic
communities.

Ethnicity was not, of course, the only factor affecting the lives of the
descendants of the European and Asian immigrants. Ethnic Americans were influenced by the variables affecting all Americans—
geographic regionalism had a great impact. A Jewish family living for
three generations in Savannah, Georgia, for example, acquired a
southern life style that set them apart from the "Yankee" Jewish family
of Brooklyn, New York. Similarly, the South Italian community of San
Francisco developed differently than the South Italian community of
Jersey City.

Social class, like geography, cut across ethnic lines, affecting the
choices ethnic Americans made and how they lived. The experiences of
the children of the wealthy Joe Kennedy, Ambassador to England,
were hardly the same as those of the children of the Irish policeman
from south Boston. Within each ethnic community individuals
associated mainly with those of their own social class.

As acculturation increased, ethnic individuals found they had
much in common with members of their own social class in other ethnic
groups and in the majority Anglo-Saxon community. Undoubtedly
this was one reason for the increase in ethnic intermarriage. Sociologist
Will Herberg, writing about ethnic America in the 1950's, felt that
religious cleavages were becoming more important than class lines or
even traditional ethnic boundaries. According to Herberg, all of
American society was moving toward organization into three supra-
ethnic religious communities, Protestant, Catholic, and Jewish.

By the 1960's experts were going beyond the earlier melting pot vs.
cultural pluralism dualism. They were beginning to describe ethnic

communities as evolving cultural and religious units, as social networks, and as political and economic interest groups. Ethnic communities remained distinct from the majority society, yet in constant and increasing interaction with that society. The acculturation—and in some cases even the complete assimilation—of individuals gradually increased. Yet ethnicity, recognized or unrecognized, remained an important factor in the lives of both individuals and groups. Its importance was enhanced by the two developments that will be discussed in the next two chapters—first, the immigration that continued throughout the twentieth century despite the National Origins Quota Act and, second, the rise of the "New Ethnicity."

CHAPTER 12

Still They Come:
Immigration After 1924

If the National Origins Quota Act of 1924 hoped to save America from further alien ethnic incursions, it did not achieve its goal. While the children and grandchildren of the controversial European and Asian immigrants were growing up, an even newer immigration was on its way. Since 1924 hundreds of thousands of "nonquota" immigrants have arrived. The majority have come from Mexico and the Caribbean Islands, areas excluded from the provisions of the restrictive laws of 1924. A significant minority were Europeans and Asians admitted by special acts of Congress as refugees from political upheavals and wars. Three and a quarter million of these refugees entered the country between 1945 and 1963 alone.

In 1965 the National Origins Quota Act was replaced with a new immigration law. Under this new law, over 400,000 persons from all over the world have entered the country annually in the last ten years. According to Leslie Aldridge Westoff, in the *New York Times Magazine* (September 16, 1973), an equal number of illegal immigrants have been discovered each year by the Immigration and Naturalization Service. "And this is only the tip of the iceberg," suggests Westoff. The United States has not lost its magnetic attraction for the peoples of the world.

Legally and illegally, people continue to come. Like their predecessors, immigrants who arrived after 1924 were looking for a better life and, like their predecessors, they found both problems and opportunities. This chapter will describe the major ethnic groups who arrived after 1924—Mexican-Americans, Puerto Ricans, other

Caribbean groups, and the various refugee immigrants. It will also describe the abandonment of the national origins quotas in 1965 and the adoption of a new immigration policy.

Mexican-Americans—One of the Oldest and Newest Ethnic Communities

Rodolfo "Corky" Gonzales was born in Denver, Colorado in 1928. The son of migrant laborers, he put himself through high school by working in a slaughterhouse, won the featherweight national boxing championship, and then retired from the world of sports to help his people, the Mexican-Americans. His poem "Joachim" suggests the experience of this old, yet new immigrant group:

JOACHIM

> I am still here!
> I have endured in the rugged mountains of our country
> I have survived in the toil and slavery of the fields
> I have existed
> In the barrios of the city
> In the suburbs of bigotry
> In the mines of social snobbery
> In the prisons of dejection
> In the muck of exploitation
> and
> In the fierce heat of racial hatred.

Mexican-Americans are the largest "foreign language" ethnic community in the United States, a minority group second in number only to blacks. One out of every three persons in New Mexico, one out of every six in Arizona and Texas, and one of every ten in California is a Mexican-American. More numerous and more clearly defined as an ethnic culture than most other immigrant communities today, Mexican-Americans are also the poorest, the least well educated, and the least socially mobile.

Long-established communities of Mexicans became part of the United States in 1848, against their will, with the annexation of Texas and the Southwest as a result of the Mexican-American War. They were joined by a trickle of Mexican immigrants throughout the nineteenth century. This immigration increased after 1910, as Mexicans fled the political turmoil of revolution and counterrevolution. The abolition of debt peonage made it easier for the peasants to leave, and the attraction of the more prosperous and more stable United States to the north was great.

As the twentieth century opened, a growing labor shortage in the

Southwestern United States stimulated the immigration of increasing numbers of Mexicans. The Reclamation Act of 1902 encouraged American farmers in the Southwest to replace the sparse population of sheepherders and cattlemen with agricultural laborers. Farmers were eager to hire low-paid Mexican agricultural workers. The need for Mexican labor was further intensified by the labor shortage created by World War I and by subsequent industrial expansion in the Southwest. Political pressure from this labor hungry region forced Congress to exempt Western Hemisphere immigrants from the provisions of the National Origins Quota legislation of 1924. Mexican immigration increased steadily. Between 1910 and 1930 one out of every eight Mexicans moved to the United States, "a hemorrhage from the Mexican nation."

Some of these immigrants found their way to cities such as Chicago and Detroit, where they worked side by side with East European immigrants and shared a parallel acculturation into American life. Most, however, remained in the rural Southwest, working as unskilled laborers, domestic servants, gardeners, and especially farm workers. Some settled permanently in small farming communities, known as "Mextowns"; others followed the crops, migrating with the seasons from planting to harvest. Families worked long hours in the fields to earn enough to survive the winter months until planting began again.

Migrant farm workers had no homes but the shacks erected for them by their employers and were often obliged to work without sanitary facilities or pure drinking water. The pace of life, the piecework systems, the callousness of foremen and employment agents, and the dehumanizing nature of the work itself created situations similar to those suffered by the European sweatshop worker decades earlier. In a short story, "The Plum Picker", Mexican-American Raymond Barrio describes the feelings of a fruit picker, Manuel, about his work, his life, and himself:

> It was the total immersion, the endless, ceaseless total use of all his energies and spirit and mind and being that tore him apart within. He didn't know what else he was good for or could do with his life. But there had to be something else. He had to be something more than a miserable plucking animal. Pluck, pluck, pluck. Feed, feed, feed, Glug, glug, glug. . . .
> Piecework. Fill the bucket, fill another, and still another. . . .
> The competition was not between pickers and growers.
> It was between pickers. . . .
> Between the poor and the hungry, the desperate and the hunted, the slave and the slave, slob against slob, the depraved and himself. You were your own terrible boss. That was the cleverest part of the whole thing. . . .
> You didn't even stop to take a drink, let alone a piss, for fear you'd get fined, fired. . . .

No matter which way he turned, he was trapped in an endless maze of apricot trees, as though forever, neat rows of them, neatly planted, row after row, just like the blackest bars on the jails of hell. . . .

Authorities discouraged Mexican immigration when jobs were scarce, resorting in times of stress to mass deportations. Mexican-Americans suffered greatly during the depression years of the 1930's. Faced with the prospect of paying relief funds to unemployed "greasers" when Anglo-Americans were also in need, authorities rounded up and deported at least a half million Mexican-Americans, many of whom were not aliens but American citizens. Families were divided, possessions lost. "They pushed most of my family into one van," remembers Jorge Acevedo. "We drove all day. The driver wouldn't stop for bathroom nor food nor water. Everybody knew by now we had been deported. Nobody knew why, but there was a lot of hatred and anger. . . . We had always known that we were hated. Now we had proof." In a similar operation in 1954, directed this time at illegal immigrants, 2.9 million Mexican-Americans were deported. Again, many local authorities paid little attention to the victims' citizenship or to the legality of their original entry into the country.

On the other hand, when cheap labor was needed, American authorities encouraged legal and illegal immigration from Mexico. The labor shortage of World War II and of the postwar boom years of economic development in the Southwest created a great demand for Mexican-American workers. In August 1942, the Mexican and United States governments instituted the "bracero" program which lasted, with the exception of a brief break in 1948, until December 1964. The Mexican word "bracero," from the Spanish *brazo* (arm), is a rough equivalent for the English "hired hand." The bracero program brought Mexicans to the United States under special immigration and contractual arrangements for temporary, seasonal employment. In addition to attracting many immigrants, both legal and illegal, the program brought millions of would-be participants to Mexican border towns where they created a formidable poverty problem for the Mexican government. The availability of a large pool of braceros and would-be braceros helped to keep wages low for Mexican-Americans already in the United States on a permanent basis.

In the 1950's and 1960's new industries, housing developments, shopping centers, and motels were springing up throughout the southwestern states. In these "boom" times, Mexican-Americans who would formerly have been farm workers found themselves changing tires at a Sears garage or sheets at a Holiday Inn, assembling automobiles at a Ford plant, or clerking at a J.C. Penney store. By 1960 over eighty per cent of the Mexican-American population was urban, whereas over half had been rural only a generation before. By 1970 the urban population was closer to ninety per cent and one third of all Mexican-Americans lived in Los Angeles, San Antonio, San Francisco, and El Paso. The attraction of the city can be summarized in one eloquent statistic; city dwellers had a per capita income double that of rural dwellers.

Every city in the Southwest has its Mexican-American quarter, or barrio. Some barrios were the original Spanish-speaking settlements around which the Anglo-Saxon city later grew. These barrios remained "downtown," in dilapidated inner city neighborhoods. Other barrios were originally rural farming or mining communities. Now they are located on the fringes of the Anglo-American city which has grown out to meet them. Where Mexican-Americans make up the majority of the population—in northern New Mexico, for example, or in the border towns of Texas—the barrio may be identical with the city.

Whatever their origin, today's barrios have certain things in common—substandard housing, littered streets, high unemployment rates, and frustrated residents. "When I came here, I wanted something better for my kids," said Ignacio Gonzales, a roofer's helper and relatively new resident of a Los Angeles barrio named, ironically "Maravilla," or Paradise. "But I don't know what to do. . . . Maybe we'll always live here. Who knows? It costs money to live like a gabacho (white-Anglo)."

Despite a small class of wealthy landowners, and a small, but growing group of white collar workers and professionals, most Mexican-Americans are poor. According to the University of California at Los Angeles Mexican-American Study Project, almost two thirds of rural Mexican-Americans live in poverty, as do one third of their urban counterparts. More than 1,700,000 Mexican-Americans live in substandard housing. In California they have an average per capita yearly income of $1380, which is $57 less than the black population and $700 less than the white population. Women, who head many barrio families, earn about half as much as men.

Nor does the situation appear greatly improved by time and acculturation. Whereas second generation European immigrants earned more than their parents and a mature third generation even more than the second, no such income progression is evident among Mexican-Americans. Exceptional individuals can and do advance their positions, but the statistical median income, according to the United States Census, remains about the same. Poverty is handed down from parents to children. The pathology of slum life—crime, gangs, prostitution, drugs, broken homes—infects every generation in the barrio.

The bitter side of barrio life was illustrated by the testimony of a nineteen year old Mexican-American girl at a recent national conference on poverty. The girl told how she had taken an overdose of sleeping pills at the age of thirteen because she was "tired of working and depressed." She was married at fifteen, her husband was sent to jail, and she was left to support their child alone:

> I got a car; the car broke down. I couldn't pay for it and they wanted to sue me, so I forged a check. . . . I started working the town. I got paid for it—they call it hustling—I needed the money . . . to go out and hustle, I had to be under the influence of narcotics.

A few weeks after the conference, the girl was dead of an overdose of narcotics.

The poverty and social problems of many Mexican-Americans have been rooted in at least three interrelated causes—prejudice on the part of Anglo-Americans, lack of education on the part of Mexican-Americans, and cultural differences between Mexican-American communities and the Anglo-American world in which they live and work. Most basic is the problem of prejudice. In the nineteenth century Mexican-Americans were considered inferior because they were a conquered people, dark-skinned, Catholic, and associated with a traditional American enemy, Spain. The twentieth century added new dimensions to this negative picture. American literature portrayed Mexicans as sly, cunning, and untrustworthy. Or, alternatively, as lazy, dozing in the sun and putting off worthwhile effort until "manana". As recently as 1970 a popular comic strip showed a fat, good-natured but sleepy Pancho, a sombrero over his space helmet, complaining to Flash Gordon that the space trip to Pluto was "Too short! Pancho never even slept!"

The darker-skinned Mexican-Americans have found themselves struggling against prejudices involving color as well as nationality and religion. California sociologist T. W. Parsons interviewed a group of Mexican-American teenagers in Castroville, California on this subject:

> The teenage boys said 'there wasn't much use of finishing high school if you are dark . . . you couldn't get a good job anyway.' Mexican girls who recently graduated from high school reported they had many difficulties in finding secretarial or clerical jobs. . . . They said that girls who looked 'almost white' got jobs first but that some of the Mexican-looking girls never did find the kind of employment they sought and finally had to go to work in the 'sheds' (local food packing companies).

After the removal of the Japanese-Americans to prison camps, Mexican-Americans became the scapegoats of a tense society during World War II. In a mass murder trial in California in January of 1943, seventeen Mexican-American youths were convicted and one served time in San Quentin prison before the District Court of Appeals dismissed the decision for lack of evidence. In the "Zoot Suit Riots" of June 1943, mobs of Anglo-American servicemen roamed the streets of Los Angeles assaulting young Mexican-Americans and blacks (who had taken to wearing the new "zoot suit" fashion). Civil and military authorities stood by for three days before intervening.

Professors as well as police showed the widespread prejudice against Mexican-Americans. "They are apparently of low mental caliber," wrote biologist L. L. Burlingame of Stanford University in 1940. In such an atmosphere of prejudice Mexican-Americans are often the last hired and the first fired. While working, they are subjected to discriminatory and degrading treatment, and they frequently receive "Mexican promotions"—more work, but no more money.

Educational disabilities have increased the difficulties of Mexican-Americans trying to succeed in Anglo-American society. According to an article by Philip Ortego in the *Center Magazine* (December 1970), Mexican-American children in the Southwest averaged only seven years of schooling (black children averaged nine, and Anglo children more than twelve). According to the National Advisory Committee on Mexican Education, "four out of five . . . fall two grades behind their Anglo classmates by the time they reach the fifth grade." In 1970, Mexican-American children were classified as retarded two and a half times as often as other children (on the basis of IQ tests geared to middle class, English-speaking children). In California, where Mexican-American students made up more than 14% of the public school enrollment, they constituted less than half of one per cent of the students at the University of California. Almost half the Mexican-Americans in Texas were functional illiterates.

Language problems were partially to blame for these shocking statistics. Spanish-speaking Mexican-American children were expected to learn English as a new language while mastering the regular first grade curriculum of reading and writing in English! In addition, many were handicapped by their family's poverty and by the cultural differences between home and school. Children of migrant workers usually did not stay in school in any one place long enough to learn.

While the goal of teaching English to Spanish-speaking children was certainly a valid one, the means used by many teachers to accomplish this did more educational harm than good. Young children were ridiculed, even punished, for using Spanish, the only language in which they could comfortably express themselves. The Anglo-American school scorned their mother tongue and belittled their cultural heritage. To succeed in such schools, children had to reject the things their families and communities held dear. Children who chose this course, who acceded to the demands and values of the Anglo-American school, still found themselves regarded as outsiders. Teachers ridiculed their Spanish accent, while peers shunned them as disloyal.

In the late 1960's school authorities began to experiment with bilingual and bicultural educational programs, hoping to improve the school experience of Mexican-American children, but progress was very slow. The dropout rate among Mexican-American children remained very high. Many Mexican-American children rejected the American school system because they felt it had rejected them. Stereotyped as stupid by teachers, they were shunted off into classes for the retarded or "tracked" into industrial education rather than college preparatory courses. One mother reported that a teacher actively discouraged her son from planning to be an engineer, suggesting that he take up carpentry instead because "he could start right away earning money." A California elementary school teacher made a practice of having "Johnny" lead five Mexican-American students in an orderly file out of the classroom. "His father owns one of the big farms in the area," she explained, "and one day he will have to know how to handle the Mexicans."

The problems of Mexican-Americans reflected not only the prejudice of teachers, employers, and other authorities, but also the cultural differences between the two communities. Recent studies indicated that Mexican-Americans have high aspirations, but that they often lack the knowledge of Anglo-American society to translate those aspirations into realities. Some sociologists have identified cultural patterns which they feel hinder Mexican-American upward mobility—large families, authoritarian rearing of children, a fatalistic acceptance of what life brings, and a dislike for aggressive, achievement oriented behavior.

Other scholars have pointed out that fatalism and similar traits are not characteristic of Mexican-American culture as such, but rather of all poverty cultures. The behavior patterns and values of middle class Mexican-Americans are close to those of their Anglo counterparts. The confusion about what is Mexican-American culture and what is "poverty" culture has created problems for contemporary Chicano (Mexican-American) leaders as well as for scholars. Some have warned their youth that in glorifying the life style of the barrio as being truly "Chicano" they are ignoring the rich heritage of upper class Mexican and Spanish culture. These leaders fear a false dichotomy will force young Mexican-Americans to choose between their Mexican ethnic identity on the one hand and social and economic mobility on the other.

Mexican-Americans in the Southwest have been able to preserve their distinctive language and life style (including ethnic preferences in music, food, family life, and recreation) longer than most other immigrant communities. Because some of their ancestors preceded the Anglo-Americans in settling the Southwest, many Mexican-Americans feel themselves a native rather than an immigrant population. Thus their motivation to become acculturated is less strong than that of European immigrants. Second, their relatively large numbers and high concentrations in the sparsely populated Southwest has helped them to preserve their own culture, as has the hostile attitude of the Anglo-American population. Finally, their proximity to the Mexican homeland, the constant flow of new immigrants, and the back and forth travel of residents of both nations have greatly strengthened Mexican-American ethnic identity.

Like all ethnic communities, however, Mexican-Americans have felt the pressures of change and have responded to those pressures. The younger generation have more formal education than their parents, are more likely to speak English, and are moving away from the unskilled jobs of their parents to higher status (if not higher paid) white collar positions. Social and occupational contacts between them and Anglo-Americans have resulted in an increasing rate of intermarriage.

Significant acculturation has taken place in family life. Like their European counterparts, Mexican peasants lived in closely knit villages in which the nuclear family received physical and emotional support from a network of relatives and friends. The first generation in the United States left this supportive network behind, as did their European counterparts. They suffered less from this, however, than comparable European groups, because as migrant workers they were able to maintain a strongly unified nuclear family. Husband, wife, and children traveled together and worked the fields together. At the end of the day, or week, or season, the husband collected and distributed the money earned by the entire family. The family stayed together, the children were closely supervised, and the authority of the father was maintained.

The urbanization of the Mexican-American family after World War II produced a radical alteration in these patterns. In the city the family no longer worked as a unit. Husband and wife were usually employed in separate factories and, according to writer and educator Ernesto Galarza, "the kids are out of sight and out of hand." Mechanization increased employment opportunities for women in low-paid factory work, while decreasing opportunities for men. According to Galarza, the result was disastrous for the traditional Mexican-American male. "The Mexican man today represents the bulk of the unemployment. He is no longer an economic or a moral factor in his family. Sometimes his kids can earn more pushing dope for an evening than he can in a month." Forty years ago young people addressed their fathers with respect as "el jefe" (the chief). Barrio youth today may refer to their fathers in deprecatory terms, such as "el viejo" (the old man).

In the traditional rural family, both in Mexico and the United States, women accepted a role of obedience, subservience, and sexual fidelity to their husbands, who protected and supported them. Men, on the other hand, were not supposed to assume any household responsibilities, but were expected to prove their virility by sexual exploits outside the marriage relationship. Recent studies of the better educated, English speaking third generation women show that they have adopted the dominant Anglo view of marriage as a more nearly egalitarian relationship. They expect their husband to assume some responsibility for home and children and consider sexual satisfaction within the marriage and not outside it as the ideal for both husband and wife.

Women have been increasingly active in the Mexican-American protest movements of the 1950's and 1960's, campaigning for school improvements and the unionization of farm and industrial workers. "These Mexican young women are taking very great advantage of their new opportunities," comments Galarza, "and they will not let any committee—whether it's to organize a confrontation or burn down a barn or talk back to the dean—they want to be there. This is a change and I think it's a change for the better. . . ."

A change has been taking place in the institutional as well as the family life of the Mexican-American. In rural Mexico there had been little role for the independent, voluntary associations so common in the United States. Whatever needs could not be met by the village community itself were referred to the Mexican government. Most Mexican immigrants, then, brought minimal organizational experience with them to the United States. Many were migrant workers who were rarely in one place long enough to establish the self-help institutions common to European immigrant groups. As a United States Government report of 1951 rather poetically put it,

> They pass through community after community, but they neither claim the community as home nor does the community claim them. . . . The migratory workers engage in a common occupation but their cohesion is scarcely greater than that of pebbles on the seashore. Each harvest collects and regroups them. They live under a common condition, but create no techniques for meeting common problems.

The Mexican-American community has not been completely destitute of organization, however. Nineteenth century New Mexico developed religious associations such as Our Lady of Light, the Poor Souls, and the secret religious order, Los Hermanos Penitentes. In the early twentieth century there were also small mutual aid and burial societies comparable to those developed by the early European immigrant communities. Unlike many European immigrant groups, however, Mexican-Americans did not convert these early societies into large-scale formal organizations. They preferred small, informal associations based upon family and kinship groups and held together by personal loyalties rather than by bureaucratic structures.

Between 1910 and 1941 the more acculturated middle class Mexican-Americans began to adopt the organizational style characteristic of second generation European and Asian ethnic Americans. In 1929 several local groups united to form the League of United Latin American Citizens, or LULAC. Similar in program to JACL (Japanese American Citizens League) and other second generation ethnic organizations, LULAC encouraged its members to conform to Anglo-American values, trained immigrants for citizenship, and defended as best it could the rights and the image of Mexican-Americans. Women's clubs such as the Pan American Round Table and the Good Neighbor Clubs shared LULAC's general aims of encouraging accommodation to the Anglo world.

Among working class Mexican-Americans short-lived local organizations sprang up to protest bad economic conditions. Field workers, pecan shellers, coal miners, and sheepherders organized local protests and strikes. The leaders often had more charisma than organizational ability, however, and the determined opposition of local authorities was hard to overcome. In the 1920's and early 1930's the American Federation of Labor tried to organize Mexican-American workers, but the unemployment of the depression years nullified their efforts.

After World War II, Mexican-American organizations began to move in new directions. A new generation began to question the goals of their parents. Young Mexican-Americans believed that accommodation with the Anglo world was neither possible nor desirable if it must be paid for with feelings of self-hate and neglect of one's own distinctive heritage. The new generation pursued their rights as Mexican-Americans more aggressively than had their parents. Under the leadership of Dr. Hector Garcia, veterans of World War II organized units throughout the Southwest. When a Mexican-American war hero, Félix Longoria, was denied burial in a Corpus Christi military cemetery, Dr. Garcia's veterans organizations took up the case. Longoria was eventually buried in Arlington National Cemetery. Ignacio Lopez, editor of a bilingual paper in California, organized the Unity Leagues. Unity League agitation resulted in the ending of school segregation for Mexican-American children in California in 1946 and in Texas in 1948.

By the end of the 1950's three new organizations represented the increasing political awareness of the community—MAPA (Mexican American Political Association) in California, PASO (Political Association of Spanish Speaking Organizations) in Texas, and ACCPE (American Coordinating Council on Political Education) in Arizona. The groups differed in matters of tactics—MAPA wanted only Mexican-American support, while PASO favored alliances with black civil rights groups, labor unions, and sympathetic Anglos. All agreed, however, on the importance of encouraging Mexican-Americans to register and to vote their own leaders into office.

Within the next few years candidates endorsed by MAPA and PASO were elected in California and in Texas. "After decades of political disenfranchisement and intimidation," wrote historian Ellwyn Stoddard, "at last there was evidence that a united Mexican American voting bloc could be victorious." Meanwhile, Cesar Chavez was beginning his activities among the farm workers of California. The Mexican American community was standing upon the threshhold of what Stoddard called "the period of ethnic autonomy and radicalism."

Other Nonquota Immigrants

Mexican-Americans constituted the largest group of nonquota immigrants, but they were by no means the only ones. A sprinkling of Spanish-speaking immigrants also arrived from South and Central America, from countries where extreme poverty was a powerful motivating push. A young immigrant from Guatemala recalls, "I remember that we only ate green bananas . . . green bananas, that's how poor our countries are . . . three out of five children die before they're five years old, back home. . . ."

Equally poor were the Filipino immigrants who entered free of any quota because the Philippine Islands were an American territory until 1946. Now that Chinese and Japanese immigration was forbidden, Filipinos joined Mexican-Americans to make up the agricultural and domestic servant supply of California. Like the Chinese and Japanese before them, the Filipinos who came were young, male—and enormously unpopular. Western Congressmen advocated independence for the Islands so that their population could be kept out of the United States!

Seeking better economic opportunities for themselves and their children, more than a hundred thousand immigrants from the Caribbean Islands entered the United States in each of the first three decades of the century. Until the post World War II period most were blacks from the British and French West Indies, Jamaica, Haiti, and Cuba. They settled in the Northeast, primarily in New York City, where they pursued a variety of occupations. Women utilized their needlecraft skills in the garment industry of New York. Highly trained cigar makers from Cuba and Jamaica practiced their craft in their new home. So many of these immigrants acquired professional training, either before immigrating to the United States or after their arrival, that by the 1930's a very high percentage of New York's black doctors, dentists, and lawyers were West Indians. Also, a high percentage of the city's black businessmen were West Indians, many of whom got their start through credit or loans extended to them by self-help societies within the West Indian community.

Salable skills, prior knowledge of English, and the ability to use community resources mitigated the rigors of economic adjustment for the most fortunate of the black immigrants, but social adjustment was difficult for all. West Indians had moved from islands where, as blacks, they constituted the majority of the population to a nation where they became identified with a historically despised minority. While darker color was often associated with lower social class in their homelands, West Indians were unprepared for the rigid and all encompassing color discrimination they encountered in the United States. Separated from American whites by an impenetrable color line, they were separated from American born blacks by significant cultural differences. Better educated and more self-confident than most American born blacks in the decades before World War II, their life styles had been influenced by the British and French traditions of their home islands. They were more likely to be Episcopalians or Catholics, than Baptists or Methodists, like most American born blacks, and their manners were more formal, their values more middle class. "Looking down upon American Negroes for their alleged ignorance and supineness," states immigration historian Maldwyn Jones, "the newcomers were cordially disliked in return for their supposed aloofness and aggressiveness."

One significant point of contact between American born blacks and West Indian immigrants was the career of Marcus Garvey. Born and educated in Jamaica, Garvey came to the United States in 1916. Struck by the deteriorated position of blacks in the United States and, indeed, all over the world (most of Africa was still under European control), Garvey asked himself: "Where is the Black man's government? Where is his King and kingdom? Where is his President, his country, and his ambassador, his army, his navy, his men of big affairs? I could not find them, and then I declared, I will help to make them."

Garvey founded the Universal Negro Improvement Association, which numbered its followers in the millions, and a variety of other black institutions, including a church, a newspaper, and a steamship line. He aroused the enthusiasm of millions of American born blacks, especially those of the lower socioeconomic strata, with his gospel of racial pride and black Zionism. "We are the descendants of a people determined to suffer no longer," he told an audience of 25,000, including delegates from Africa and Latin America. "We shall organize the 4,000,000,000 Negroes of the world into a vast organization to plant the banner of freedom on the great continent of Africa." While the post World War I Ku Klux Klan began its rapid rise, Garvey was among the first to proclaim that black was beautiful. His ideas aroused hostility among whites and among more conventional black leaders. In a proceeding that was political as well as judicial, Garvey was imprisoned for mail fraud and eventually deported.

The Puerto Ricans

Immigration from many islands in the French and British West Indies continued, but after 1945 the largest number of newcomers came from Puerto Rico. Like the Philippines, Puerto Rico had been an American territory since 1898, so its people could move freely between the island and the continental United States. American administration of the island aggravated the problems of poverty and overpopulation that led to immigration. One reason for poverty was the fact that the island's resources were controlled by absentee owners on the mainland. Public health improvements instituted by United States authorities cut the island's death rate, but not its birth rate, so a rapid population rise added to the poverty problem. Not even the American educational structure was an unmitigated blessing. The American government's vacillating policy as to whether to educate Puerto Ricans in English or in Spanish resulted in their being poorly educated in both.

In 1910 there were only about five hundred Puerto Ricans living in New York City; by 1940 there were 70,000. The great migration took place after 1945, however. In the early 1970's there were about a million and a half Puerto Ricans on the American mainland. Though still heavily concentrated in New York City, they also comprised sizable communities in New Jersey, Pennsylvania, Illinois, California, Ohio, and New England.

Under a new policy of self-government, Puerto Rico in the 1950's instituted "Operation Bootstrap," a massive attempt to solve the economic problems of the island through industrialization and education. The program was so successful that family income in Puerto Rico tripled in twenty years. Despite improving economic conditions on the island, Puerto Ricans continued to immigrate to the mainland. Improvement in Puerto Rico stimulated many to seek still further improvement in the United States. As early as 1948 over 85% of those who immigrated had been employed on the island. They did not come seeking *any* job; they came seeking a *better* job. They also came to join relatives already here and to enjoy the excitement they had heard was part of everyday life in New York City.

The earliest Puerto Rican immigrants were usually single males, farm workers who served as contract laborers in New Jersey and other agricultural areas. After 1945, however, immigrants usually came as family units and settled in New York and other urban centers. They took service jobs in hotels, restaurants, and laundries or became workers in urban industries such as steel, plastics, food processing, jewelry, and electronics. As Jews and Italians moved out of the garment industry, New York City's largest industry, Puerto Ricans took their places. According to a recent Harvard University study of the metropolitan region, Puerto Rican immigration has provided a supply of inexpensive labor that was instrumental in keeping this and other industries from leaving the city.

"Tidal Wave of Puerto Ricans Swamping the City," screamed a New York newspaper headline in 1946, when the net annual Puerto Rican immigration was only 40,000 people. As the last of the series of immigrant groups to enter New York City, the Puerto Ricans have aroused the same hatreds, fears, and suspicions as the Irish, Italians, Jews, and blacks who preceded them. Newspapers, even social workers, overestimated their numbers. Differences in language, skin coloring, and clothing gave Puerto Ricans high visibility and made them a natural target. Clarence Senior, author of a book friendly to Puerto Rican immigrants, received the following letter, quoted here with the original spelling and punctuation intact:

> So you are one of those—that are bring these monkey faced animals into this country. I consider a Puerto Rican lower than a pig. Those dirty black faced diseased dogs they are a menace to a decent people. I pray with all my might a violent death overtakes you. I am going to do everything in my power to fight them everybody I have spoken to hates there sight. Those knife carrying—. They loused up every neighborhood in New York.

The stereotypes of Puerto Ricans as neighborhood wreckers, criminals, and charges on the public purse evoke echoes of similar judgments about the ethnic groups that preceded them, and contain the same mixture of half truths and misconceptions. Puerto Ricans were undoubtedly associated with neighborhood decay. They had inherited the old brownstones and tenements that had housed Europeans and blacks before them and were now in a hopeless state of disrepair. Puerto Ricans were not surprised when the New York Health Commissioner announced that New York City had as many rats as it had people. Over half of the 565 people who reported rat bites in 1958 had Spanish surnames.

Nor were these rat infested quarters cheap. In 1960, according to

Senior, "the slum tenants on the west side of New York City, for instance, pay an average of $2.10 per square foot for their hovels while the inhabitants of the well-maintained elevator apartments within a block or two of Central Park West average $1.02." High rents and low salaries guaranteed that Puerto Ricans, like earlier immigrants, had to crowd many people into small spaces, resulting in still further deterioration of already poor housing.

Crime has risen rapidly throughout the United States in the past few decades and Puerto Ricans, like other "disadvantaged" citizens, have been part of this rise. Contrary to popular perceptions, their percentage of the crime rate in the 1950's, a time of heavy immigration, was only slightly above their percentage in the population. As in the case of earlier ethnic communities, delinquency is more often a problem among children born or reared on the mainland than among those born and reared in Puerto Rico. In recent years juvenile gangs have also become a problem in Puerto Rico. Puerto Ricans there blame them on the bad influence of young people returning from New York City!

More serious than crime (although crime is increasing among Puerto Ricans as among the rest of the American population) is the problem of drug addiction. Between 1964 and 1968, when Puerto Ricans constituted fifteen per cent of the population of New York, they accounted for almost a quarter of the heroin addicts. While Puerto Rican parents generally have the impression that the authorities could stop the drug traffic if they wanted to, the problem is not so simple. Puerto Rican youth turn to drugs to escape unpleasant life situations and because of powerful peer group pressures. "I used to see my friends doing it," reported a twelve year old Puerto Rican heroin addict, "and I didn't want to be left out. I started sniffing heroin, then skin-popping, and then mainlining." The youth supported his habit by stealing "anything I could find."

As late as the mid 1960's Puerto Rican adults had relatively little connection with organized crime, "the rackets," either because they were not interested or, more likely, because the tightly organized ethnic groups already in control would not let competitors in. As Dan Wakefield observed in his book on Puerto Ricans in New York, *Island in the City:*

> One of the few distinctions so far between the Puerto Ricans and the early immigrant groups to New York City is that the Puerto Ricans have developed no criminal gangs of adults as the Irish, Jews, and Italians did. This is perhaps a happy fact for the social workers but may in the long run be a sad one for the progress of the Puerto Ricans. Many old-time observers in the city believe this lack of an adult underworld is one of the reasons why Puerto Ricans have not yet achieved much power in politics.

Puerto Ricans arrived in New York in large numbers at about the same time—or shortly after—as the large influx of blacks from the rural South. Because many Puerto Ricans were more accustomed to urban life than rural blacks and because most Puerto Ricans were considered "white," a distinct advantage in American society, there was reason to believe that they would move ahead faster then the blacks and become adjusted to the city more rapidly. After surveying the census data of 1950, demographer Donald Bogue commented that " ... Puerto Ricans may become assimilated as fast as the Italians, the Polish, and the Czechs have, and much faster than the Negroes and Mexicans." Reverend David Barry, director of a social agency long active in work with immigrants, said in 1957:

> No previous immigrant group so quickly numbered among its members so many policemen and welfare workers, teachers and social workers, office workers and independent businessmen, and eventually doctors and lawyers—after barely a dozen years in New York.

Indeed, in the 1950's there were many signs of Puerto Rican success. Puerto Rican bar, medical, and teacher associations attested to the growing numbers of Puerto Rican professionals. A Philadelphia report commented on the "entrepreneurial superiority" of Puerto Ricans, and by the mid 1960's there were an estimated seven thousand Puerto Rican owned stores, barber shops, and restaurants, including almost four thousand *bodegas*, Puerto Rican groceries. By 1960 second generation Puerto Ricans were earning considerably larger incomes than the immigrant generation, and the 1960's saw a doubling of the number of Puerto Ricans living in the suburbs.

This prosperity and upward mobility was limited, however, to an educated minority; the majority did not share in it. In New York City the community as a whole did not improve its position as rapidly during the 1960's as observers had anticpated. In fact, relative to the black population, the situation of Puerto Ricans deteriorated. In 1970 Puerto Ricans were educationally and occupationally the poorest segment of the New York City population, with a median income considerably below that of other New York groups, black and white. In 1960 Puerto Ricans constituted 18% of the families living under the poverty level; by 1968 they constituted almost 40%. In that year it was estimated that about one third of the Puerto Rican population of New York City was receiving welfare under the Aid to Families with Dependent Children program.

Many factors contributed to this unfortunate situation. Though the Puerto Rican government tried to help prospective immigrants learn English, language presented many difficulties. About half of the Puerto Rican children entering school for the first time in the continental United States knew little English. Like Mexican-American children, they found their school experience so frustrating that many became early dropouts. Adults and children who knew a little English sometimes hesitated to use it. Coming from a culture with a strong emphasis upon "dignidad" (dignity), they preferred not speaking English at all to speaking it badly. Meanwhile, school officials argued the relative merits of various approaches—total immersion in English, the teaching of English as a second language, or the continued use of both Spanish and English in a bilingual and, perhaps, a genuinely bicultural education. This debate resembled that over the education of Spanish-speaking, Mexican-American children in the West.

Other cultural factors presented special difficulties for Puerto Ricans. Hurrying, for example, was seen as loss of dignity in Puerto Rican culture; yet hurrying was necessary for survival in New York City! Puerto Rican culture stressed personal relationships. Puerto Ricans were accustomed to dealing with school, government, and other authorities on an individualized person-to-person basis. They found it difficult to deal with the formal bureaucracies of cities on the mainland and saw even the best officials as "cold" and "uncaring." American attitudes on skin color have also caused difficulties. Ranging from very light to very dark, Puerto Ricans have paid less attention to color than to other kinds of social distinctions. In the United States, however, dark Puerto Ricans found it expedient to speak Spanish very loudly to separate themselves from American blacks—and some light skinned Puerto Ricans have become suddenly embarassed about the presence of blacks within their community.

Family life in the United States presented new problems for Puerto Ricans as for previous immigrants. A traditional love of children combined with nonuse of contraception meant a relatively large number of dependents for each breadwinner in the family—a handicap to a group seeking upward mobility. The highly protective system of childrearing practiced in Puerto Rico caused difficulties, too. On the island, "good" girls were carefully watched, indeed, reared largely inside the home until they escaped into early marriage. On the mainland, Puerto Rican girls often demanded freedom which their parents considered it unwise and immoral to give them. The boys were given more freedom, but after a few days on the streets of New York they often behaved in ways that their parents found puzzling and unacceptable.

In Puerto Rico consensual unions—couples living together on a long-term basis without a formal marriage—were common, especially among the poor, and the children they produced were not stigmatized. In the United States such unions were considered immoral and their children illegitimate. When such unions, or indeed, any marriages, broke up on the island, a network of relatives—sisters, cousins, "aunties," and godparents—were available to care for the children. In the United States this network might not be on hand.

Puerto Rican immigrants had problems in the job market as well as in the home. Those who came to the United States were, on the whole, better educated than those who remained on the island, but a sixth grade level Spanish education was of little value in New York City's job market. Moreover, automation had eaten away at the supply of low skilled jobs, the "pick and shovel" jobs that had been available to the unskilled of earlier immigrant groups. Unemployment was not uncommon.

There was more organized help available to Puerto Ricans than to earlier immigrant groups, but this could be a mixed blessing. Welfare regulations helped to undermine the already weakened family; women and children were given money only if there was no man present in the household. With public relief available, there was less necessity to establish the network of self-help institutions that proved so important to the earlier ethnic communities. Open housing legislation and subsidized housing projects were helpful, but, like the welfare system, they also had negative effects. By scattering Puerto Ricans throughout the city, they hindered the establishment of the geographic concentrations that had given earlier ethnic communities internal cohesion and political "clout." The most recent immigrants to the city, Puerto Ricans have had difficulty competing with blacks and other larger, better organized, and more firmly entrenched ethnic communities for money, services, jobs, and perhaps most critical, for political representation. Although the Civil Rights Act of 1965 eliminated the English language literacy test for voter registration, Puerto Rican registration has remained low. As late as 1970 there were no elected Puerto Rican officials in the New York City government and only four in the state government.

One reason Puerto Ricans have had difficulties in building a cohesive community is that many of their institutions were inherited rather than created from scratch. Unlike many earlier immigrant groups, Puerto Ricans usually did not have to build their own churches, or unions, or press. About 85% Roman Catholic, they usually moved into pre-existing parishes led by the clergy of other ethnic backgrounds. Similarly, their unions had often been founded by, and continued to be led by, Italians, Jews, and Irish. The era of the mass media had arrived, making it less necessary for this newest ethnic community to create its own culture and entertainment. American magazines were available in Spanish, thirty movie houses in New York City showed the latest films from all over Latin America, and direct contact with the culture of Puerto Rico was only a brief airplane trip away.

The Puerto Rican community has, nonetheless, begun to establish powerful institutions of its own. Two older Spanish newspapers recently merged to create *El Diario de Nueva York*, a popular paper which reflects many of the interests of the community. Aside from the professional groups already mentioned, there have long been athletic leagues, cultural societies, and clubs in which immigrants from particular towns in Puerto Rico get together for socializing and mutual help, similar to the clubs established by earlier European and Asian immigrant groups.

As in the Mexican-American communities new organizations have arisen in recent years, organizations intended to meet the needs of the wider community. The Puerto Rican Forum was established in the mid 1950's as a community wide service organization. From it came Aspira, founded in 1961, to identify and motivate promising Puerto Rican young people, to direct them toward higher education, and to instill pride in their heritage as Puerto Ricans. Also from the Forum came the Puerto Rican Community Development Project, which aimed at promoting ethnic identity, social stability, and political strength within the Puerto Rican community. This organization assumed the role of visible representative of Puerto Ricans in New York City, involving itself in job training, tutoring, fighting drug addiction, and establishing neighborhood youth corps and block organizations. Another relatively recent organization is the Puerto Rican Family Institute. Using the Puerto Rican tradition of personalized rather than institutionalized relationships, the Institute matches newly arrived families with well-established "helper" families in their own neighborhoods.

Puerto Rican adjustments to America were hindered by changes in the mid twentieth century city itself—the relative shortage of unskilled jobs, and the difficulty of breaking into already well-established political and economic institutions. On the other hand, a wider variety of government programs and services existed to help the newcomers who remained optimistic, seeing themselves as following the upwardly mobile path of earlier immigrant groups. This was the first airborne community, an ethnic group that could fly to its homeland in a few hours. The effect this will have on the survival of the Puerto Rican culture remains to be seen. Meanwhile Puerto Ricans, like Mexican-Americans, entered the 1970's with a heightened sense of ethnic identity and a growing number of community leaders and community institutions.

The Refugees

The millions of immigrants from the Western Hemisphere who poured into the country after the passing of the National Origins Quota Act were joined by smaller numbers from the more familiar immigrant areas of Europe and Asia. During the 1930's, the United

States took in about a quarter of a million refugees from the Nazi regime. Between 1945 and 1959 the number rose to three quarters of a million, including war brides, "displaced persons," and refugees from communist countries, such as Cuba and Hungary. While most of these people were fleeing political upheavals, a few were the victims of natural disasters, Portuguese refugees from earthquakes in the Azores, for example. Most of the refugees were nonquota immigrants, admitted by special acts of Congress. During these same years, however, two and a half million immigrants entered under regular quota procedures. Nor has the flow of refugees stopped. In 1975 over one hundred thousand South Vietnamese refugees were admitted to the United States.

The first large group of refugees were the people fleeing Nazi regimes in the 1930's and early 1940's. Heavily, though not completely, Jewish, this group included distinguished men and women who made immense contributions to the intellectual and cultural life of the nation—Albert Einstein, Enrico Fermi, Paul Tillich, Bela Bartok, Marc Chagall, Sigrid Undset, and others.

Less distinguished would-be immigrants, people with no credentials but their desperation to escape impending genocide, found American hospitality during the 1930's very limited. Efforts to overturn the quota system and save more fugitives from Nazism failed. Public opinion reinforced the view already held by most Congressmen that a nation in the throes of economic depression could not afford to offer sanctuary to people who might compete with the native born for jobs. An ugly current of anti-Semitism also played its role in the United States government's refusal to pass emergency legislation opening our doors to more of the Jewish refugees who sought admittance.

In 1939 a bill was introduced into Congress to admit 20,000 German-Jewish refugee children under the age of fourteen outside of the regular quota structure. Within a day after the plan was announced thousands of families of all religions offered to adopt the children, and the Quakers offered to supervise the resettlement procedures. Congressmen raised a host of objections ranging from the scarcity of jobs (for children under fourteen!) to the "iniquity" of separating the children from their doomed parents. Secretary of State Cordell Hull complained to the Congressional committee that admitting the children would not only set a bad precedent, but would also necessitate "increased personnel . . . as well as additional office space." The bill was not passed. Presumably these twenty thousand children took their places among the six million exterminated in Hitler's "final solution" to the Jewish problem.

The post World War II period ushered in a more humanitarian, less racist approach to immigration policy. The depression was over, jobs were available, and the revelation of Nazi genocide made it increasingly unacceptable to label whole categories of people "undesirable." In the new atmosphere, special legislation began to erode the older racist immigration policies. During the war Congress established an immigration quota for the Chinese, who were our allies; and shortly after the war a similar quota was established for Japan. The quotas were minuscule, a hundred immigrants a year from each country; but for the first time in many decades it was possible for Orientals to enter the country legally.

Additional special legislation admitted war brides and "displaced persons" in the immediate postwar years—though this legislation, too, was formed to favor immigrants from Western rather than from Eastern Europe. Additional acts of Congress opened the doors to anti-Communist refugees fleeing Fidel Castro's Cuba and the unsuccessful anti-Communist revolution in Hungary in 1956. It can be argued that the American response even to these popular refugees was niggardly in proportion to the magnitude of our resources. For every one hundred thousand of its own population, the United States admitted only 22 Hungarian refugees, while Israel admitted 111, and Canada admitted 214.

Twentieth century immigrants had tales to tell as harrowing as those of immigrants of the past. Families walked hundreds of miles through woods and over mountains, hiding in fields and cellars, eating wild animals and roots to escape capture by the Nazis. Refugees left Cuba in small boats, making their way across open seas to Florida. A young Hungarian officer told how he escaped from a communist hospital, where he was being treated for wounds received in the 1956 uprising:

> We knew the doctor . . . and trusted him. As the [Communists] watched
> . . . the doctor gave us each an injection which put us to sleep. He then
> ordered our bodies sent to the morgue. At the morgue we were revived
> and placed in private homes on the outskirts of Budapest.

Too weak to walk, the officer was carried across the Raba River to safety in weather so severe that his clothing froze on his body.

The Vietnamese refugees of 1975 were unique insofar as the American government assumed the responsibility of transporting them to their new home. Nevertheless, for many the journey was not an easy one. In the confusion of the rapid collapse of the South Vietnamese regime, families were separated and some individuals who were fleeing the battlefields found themselves unexpectedly on planes or ships bound for the United States. Between fifteen and twenty-five thousand refugees spent four days without drinking water in ninety degree heat on barges awaiting transfer to American ships. According to an eyewitness, the deck of one of the barges was strewn with the abandoned possessions of the refugees and at least seventy-five dead bodies, mostly of women, children, and babies.

Once in the United States, refugees faced additional problems. During the depression of the 1930's, even the most skilled found it difficult to find employment. Hans Morgenthau, a well-known political scientist, worked as an elevator "boy". His wife was forced to stay home from her job clerking at Macy's department store because she was covered with bedbug bites. Jewish immigrants in the 1930's were plagued by anti-Semitism as well as by economic problems. An adviser to the State Department was convinced that the new Jewish immigrants "are never to become moderate, decent American citizens." The National Patriotic Council opposed the admission of Albert Einstein as a "German Bolshevik," whose theory of relativity was "of no scientific value or purpose, not understandable because there was nothing there to understand." Nor did the racist reaction to refugees end in the 1930's. In 1975 high school children in Florida talked of starting a "Gook Klux Klan" to oppose the settlement in their area of refugees from South Vietnam. Economic considerations as well as racial prejudice dictated that Vietnamese refugees be dispersed rather than be allowed to form geographically concentrated communities. It was felt that they would not become an employment or a welfare burden on any single state.

On the other hand, many people all over the country welcomed and helped the various waves of refugee immigrants. Religious and civic organizations "adopted" individuals and families, supplying them with everything from food, clothing, and toys to job offers. Public interest in the newcomers was usually genuine and well meaning, but there was also exploitation. A woman offered to present dolls to Hungarian refugee children if the *New York Times* would publish a picture of the presentation. The Eisenhower Administration actually hired a public relations firm to "sell" the Hungarian refugees to the American people, like laundry detergent or breakfast cereal! The advertising campaign was successful. The refugees were soon in such demand that someone cynically paraphrased the old saying, "brother, can you spare a Hungarian."

Special categories of ethnic newcomers had special kinds of problems. War brides from abroad had many adjustments to make when they rejoined their husbands, now out of uniform, after months or even years of separation. Sometimes reality did not live up to the glowing picture the soldier had painted of his civilian job and home town. Husbands, as well as wives, could be disappointed; girls who had seemed desirable in Germany or Japan might seem less so in New York or Kansas. Women who had been submissive and deferential in Europe and Asia sometimes became "Americanized" too quickly to suit their husbands!

Similar problems plagued elderly Chinese-American men who took advantage of new immigration regulations to import young Chinese brides from Hong Kong. Young women from postwar Hong Kong were quite different from their husbands' idealized memories of the traditional Chinese women of their youth. Historian Betty Lee Sung tells the story, far from unique, of a young Hong Kong bride who gave her startled Chinatown husband a most untraditional ultimatum: "Move out of this dilapidated apartment by Tuesday, or I get a divorce!"

New laws enabled Chinese born sons to join elderly Chinese-American fathers and this, too, created problems. Brought up in China, these young men were often disappointed in their father's economic situation in the United States. Lacking skills and unable to speak English, the Chinese youths often found themselves jobless and rejected by both the American born Chinese and the Caucasian communities. Juvenile delinquency, formerly rare, made its appearance in San Francisco's Chinatown, as did divorce and a suicide rate four times that of the rest of the city.

Some refugees made a quick and relatively painless adjustment to American life. Many of those who fled the Nazis and the Communists were well-educated middle class or upper middle class people, often with professional training. Such people had little trouble overcoming the language barrier. Their main problems were the regulations of American professional societies, regulations that required them to repeat years of training or pass special examinations before taking up their professions in their new homes.

Most of the German, Hungarian, and Cuban refugees were soon self-supporting and, indeed, made important contributions to their adopted country. The economic adjustment of the Vietnamese refugees appears to be more of a problem, at least in the short run, even though the majority of the Vietnamese refugees are better educated than most of their countrymen. Unlike the anti-Communist Hungarians and Cubans, who had been hailed as heroes, the South Vietnamese are an embarrassing reminder of a politically divisive and militarily frustrating American war. To complicate their situation further, the Vietnamese refugees lack the economic and psychological support of an older established Vietnamese community. Arriving during a serious economic recession, they were practically pushed out of government supported refugee camps into jobs that are often low paid and menial, regardless of their previous education or employment experience.

Results of Twentieth Century Immigration

Post 1924 immigration established the Spanish-speaking community as the nation's largest foreign language group. Moreover, as the growing Mexican-American, Puerto Rican, and Cuban communities remained close, psychologically and geographically, to their homelands and seemed determined to preserve their own language, they presented a new kind of challenge to American ethnicity. For the first time, the United States was forced to consider the impact of an institutionalized, relatively permanent, non-English-speaking subculture—the Spanish.

The new challenge was reflected in a new school situation. In the past, American public schools had taught immigrant languages as foreign languages; the school curriculum as a whole was in English. If parents wanted educational equality for a non-English language, they had to set up their own schools, as many of the Slavic immigrant communities had done. By the 1960's, however, public school systems began to experiment with bilingual education for Spanish-speaking children.

Bilingual teachers had been hired in New York as early as the 1950's with the hope that they could facilitate the children's acquisition of English and help them adjust more quickly to the demands of the public school. Even when they learned English, Puerto Rican and Mexican-American children fell behind other children in school achievement. Some attributed this learning gap to social class differences. If this was the case then "compensatory education," giving lower class Hispanic children in the schools the advantages middle class children had at home, appeared to be the answer. Another interpretation was that Puerto Rican and Mexican-American children were not "disadvantaged" or deprived, but were culturally different. According to this theory, their education should not concentrate upon making up supposed deficiencies, but should emphasize the strengths within the child's background and build upon creative elements in the distinctive Puerto Rican and Mexican heritages. If the latter theory is adopted, bilingual education will not be a temporary tool to help the child adjust to the majority culture. Rather, bilingual education will be a permanent feature of the education of Puerto Rican and Mexican-American children. Whether the majority American society can accept the latter idea—and indeed, whether Puerto Ricans and Mexican-Americans will choose this course—remains to be seen.

Post 1924 immigration has had still other effects. For the first time in American history, midcentury immigration has been predominantly female. This large influx of women has helped to balance and thus "normalize" life in the formerly predominantly male Asian communities. Politically, the immigration of refugees from communist countries has contributed to anti-Soviet and anti-Communist feeling in the United States. Refugees from East Germany, Hungary, Cuba, and Taiwan have continued to agitate the "captive nations" issue, though they have had little actual influence on foreign policy. An impressive number of professionals and other talented individuals among the refugee groups and, indeed, among all post 1924 immigrants, has enriched the nation's cultural, scientific, and educational life. Immigrant intellectuals also have brought new vitality to older American ethnic communities, stimulating the continued use of ethnic languages, and sparking a revival of ethnic newspapers, theaters, schools, and cultural and nationalist associations.

Finally, the admission of refugees, displaced persons, and war brides under special legislative acts, as well as the admission of millions of nonquota immigrants from Latin America, gradually eroded the impact of the National Origins Quota Act of 1924. By midcentury it was clear that the Act was not achieving its original purpose—the limitation of immigration to persons from the British Isles and from Northern and Western Europe.

Increasingly, this very purpose was called into question. After World War II neither the scientific nor the political community could comfortably defend notions of the superiority and inferiority of races and nationalities. In the 1950's and early 1960's, the Cold War helped to kill the National Origins quota system. With the United States competing with the Soviet Union and the Peoples Republic of China for the good will of the "third world," the uncommitted African and Asian nations, discriminatory immigration policies, like racially segregated schools, were not only morally wrong but politically embarrassing. With the Russians launching "sputniks" an immigration policy that admitted an Irish housemaid while keeping out a scientist from Thailand could no longer be justified as serving the national interest.

The first major revision of the National Origins Quota Act was the McCarran-Walter Act of 1952. The new act, passed over President Truman's veto, maintained the essential provisions of the quota system based upon the census of 1920. The main proponent of the new bill, Senator Patrick McCarran, warned that anyone who opposed it "would wittingly or unwittingly lend themselves to efforts which would poison the bloodstream of the country." The McCarran-Walter Act was blatantly discriminatory in many of its provisions, but it differed from the earlier National Origins Quota Act in two significant ways. First, it did include quotas for Asian nations—tiny quotas, compared to those for western Europeans, but at least Asians were included. Second, the McCarran-Walter Act introduced the principle of considering skills as a criterion for the admission of immigrants. The first half of all quotas were to be assigned to people with "high education, technical training, specialized experiences, or exceptional ability."

Efforts to abandon the national origins system altogether met with opposition from southerners worried about racial mixture and from conservatives afraid of "subversive" activity. "If we transfer the pattern of our immigration to countries and peoples who have historically maintained a totalitarian concept of government, it will be only a matter of time until our Republic will veer from its traditions of freedom and democracy," warned Senator James Eastland of Mississippi. Despite this opposition, criticism of the old system swelled. In 1963 President John F. Kennedy, strongly conscious of his own immigrant origins, took up the cause of immigration law reform. "The use of a national origin system is without basis in either logic or reason," he wrote. "It neither satisfies a national need nor accomplishes an international purpose . . . such a system is an anachronism, for it discriminates among applicants for admission into the United States on the accident of birth."

After Kennedy's death, President Johnson took up the cause. A series of Congressional hearings highlighted the inequities in the existing system. Witnesses pointed out that while an unskilled laborer from northern Europe could enter the country in a few weeks, skilled immigrants (including parents, children, and siblings of American citizens) from Japan or Turkey faced waiting periods of up to 322 years! Opposition faded. On October 3, 1965 President Johnson signed Public Law 89-236, abolishing altogether the use of the national origins quota system.

Public Law 89-236 did not open the gates to unlimited immigration. There was general agreement that the nation, no longer a frontier country and no longer in the early stages of industrialization, could not absorb the large numbers it had absorbed in the past. An annual limit was set—120,000 immigrants from the Western Hemisphere and 170,000 from the Eastern Hemisphere, with a 20,000 person limit on the number that could come annually from any one country. Within these numerical limits, preference went to spouses and immediate relatives of American citizens, professional persons, persons of "exceptional ability in the sciences or the arts," and "qualified immigrants who are capable of performing specified skilled or unskilled labor, not of a temporary or seasonal nature, for which a shortage of employable and willing persons exists in the United States."

The new law, like the old, raised troublesome questions. Few would quarrel with the preferential treatment of relatives of American citizens, but the preference given to scientists and other professionals was more controversial. In practice, such a preference established a "brain drain," drawing trained personnel away from underdeveloped nations that badly need their services. While the national immigration laws encouraged the coming of foreign professionals, virtually every state has laws making it difficult or impossible for aliens to practice their professions. In several states one must be an American citizen to be an accountant, architect, attorney, dentist, nurse, optometrist, physician, or engineer. Finally, one might quarrel with the morality of an immigration system that turns away the tired, the poor, the lone, uneducated immigrant so characteristic of earlier years, to admit only the educated, the talented, and the brilliant. It can be argued that education and talent, as much as nationality or race, are accidents of birth.

Nevertheless, most Americans agreed with President Johnson's assessment of the new immigration bill. Speaking at the base of the Statue of Liberty, Johnson told the nation:

> This bill is not a revolutionary bill. It does not affect the lives of millions. It will not reshape the structure of our daily lives, or add importantly to our wealth and power.
>
> Yet it is still one of the most important acts of this Congress and this Administration.
>
> For it repairs a deep and painful flaw in the fabric of American justice. . . . It will make us truer to ourselves as a country and as a people. It will strengthen us in a hundred unseen ways. . . .
>
> The days of unlimited immigration are past. But those who come will come because of what they are—not because of the land from which they spring.

CHAPTER 13

The New Ethnicity

"Irish Power!" "Kiss me, I'm Italian." "Thank God I'm Polish!" In the early 1970's ethnic slogans blossomed on lapel buttons, on posters, and on automobile bumpers. From coast to coast, they decorated power boats, motorcycles, bicycles, and skis. "Every group is bragging about its heritage now," said an Armenian dentist from Long Island. "Today it's glamorous to be different."

A quick look at American life in the late 1960's and early 1970's supports the Armenian dentist's opinion. Clothes with an ethnic motif were fashionable. Ethnic restaurants were crowded, with more opening every day. Ethnic schools, churches, theaters, and summer camps seemed to have a new lease on life. Books poured off the press dealing with the history and culture of Italians, Jews, Poles, Irish, Puerto Ricans, Mexicans, as well as blacks and Native Americans. In *The Unmeltable Ethnics*, Michael Novak asserted that the "melting pot" was inoperable and cultural pluralism here to stay. Peter Schrag's *Decline of the Wasp* suggested that white Anglo-Saxon Protestant America had lost its traditional dominance; the ethnics were inheriting the land!

Some commentators took issue with the sweeping historical generalizations of Novak and Schrag. They worried that the "new ethnicity" was a dangerous upsurge of tribalism that would destroy the unifying bonds of a common American culture. Some felt that the new emphasis on ethnic differences would obscure what to them seemed more important realities of cleavages based on economic class. Others, pointing out the nation's addiction to novelty of any kind, declared "bumper sticker" ethnicity one more fad among many. Still, no one could deny that a revival of interest in ethnicity was taking place, both among ethnic Americans themselves and within the general community. This chapter will explore the origins of the new ethnicity and the problems and opportunities it opened up for all Americans.

Why the Ethnic Revival?

A variety of factors came together in the post World War II United States to set the stage for the new ethnicity. Many ethnic communities were roused into heightened self-consciousness by events originating overseas. The arrival of thousands of displaced persons and refugees from communist Eastern Europe for example, stimulated ethnic institutions and consciousness among American Slavic communities. Immigrants from Poland, Latvia, Czechoslovakia, and the Ukraine allied themselves with third generation Americans to lobby for the "captive nations."

The Six Day War of 1967 and the Yom Kippur War of 1973, which threatened the very existence of Israel, galvanized many of the most assimilated Jews, professionals and academics, for example, into a new affiliation with the Jewish community. American physicians left their practices to treat the wounded in Israeli hospitals, American college students brought in the harvest to free Israeli civilians for combat, and children gave their nickels and dimes and old people their social security checks to the Israel Emergency Fund. As the Middle East moved from crisis to crisis, support for the state of Israel became the touchstone of American Jewish ethnic identity.

Arab communities in the United States also reacted to the situation in the Middle East. Initial Arab military successes in the Yom Kippur War aroused a new sense of ethnic pride among Americans of Arabic descent, especially among the young. Nor was the Arab ethnic revival limited to politics. Recent immigrants from the Middle East, many of them students or young professionals, led their communities toward a new interest in traditional Arabic culture and in the religion of Islam.

The Irish were among the oldest and most nearly assimilated of the ethnic communities. Yet, terrorism in Northern Ireland, where a Catholic minority still chafed under rule by a Protestant majority, had repercussions in Boston, New York, and Philadelphia. According to a report in *Philadelphia Magazine*, over one hundred Northern Aid Committees in the United States were formed to collect funds for the Provisional Wing of the Irish Republican Army. Irish-American Mike Mallowe described the impact of such committees in the Philadelphia area:

> Typically, a local Northern Aid Chapter is composed of about 50 hard core sympathizers whose members are evenly divided between newly arrived immigrants . . . and native born Irish-Americans who feel as

deeply committed as their counterparts from the Ould Sod. . . . The immigrants gain a sense of American sophistication and efficiency while the Americans gain a fresh infusion of new blood and idealism. . . .

The best part of the IRA's greening of Philadelphia is the effect it is having on the Irish generation gap. Many young Irish are embracing the cause wholeheartedly. Their parents are suddenly discovering better ways to spend Sunday evenings and Saturday afternoons than on the golf course or at the country club, and grandparents, once forgotten on their geriatric shelves, are finding themselves celebrities simply because they recall the old days. . . . Unexpectedly, the Northern Aid Committees are helping to foster a sense of Irish family unity that had been rapidly disappearing as bank accounts grew.

Not all the impetus for the new ethnicity came from overseas. Many forces within American life of the 1960's and 1970's also contributed to it. The 1960's saw a revolt, especially among the young, against the conformity and blandness of the previous decade. The colorless "organization man," and the monotonous suburban subdevelopments were suddenly in disfavor. Individuality became increasingly important, and in this context cultural differences could be openly cherished rather than hidden or abandoned. Among people suddenly awakened to the pleasures of handicrafts and homemade bread, ethnic foods, traditions, and life styles took on a new attractiveness. The counterculture of the 1960's legitimized ethnicity.

An increasing number of people in the troubled 1960's turned their attention to the "urban crisis." City planners such as Jane Jacobs pointed out that the most livable urban neighborhoods were the stable, strongly organized, old ethnic neighborhoods. Here family, friendship, and institutional ties bound people together in orderly patterns of interdependent existence. Sociologists and other academicians in the 1960's were discovering what immigrant communities could have told them from decades of experience—the value of a sense of community, both in creating personal and family stability and in promoting safe and satisfying neighborhoods. Ethnic neighborhoods were often run-down areas, with poor and aging facilities, but their inhabitants could now take renewed pride in living in them.

Ethnicity had never really disappeared. It had remained a large factor in many lives, though, like an iceberg, much of it was submerged or invisible. Perhaps the newest thing about the "new ethnicity" was the new freedom people now felt to acknowledge its presence. The third and fourth generations were finally secure enough in American life to acknowledge their ethnicity, both to themselves and to others. "Twenty years ago, the Rumanian who came here didn't speak English, had a low-paying job, and was not accepted. Today none of this is true, and he is proud to be a Rumanian," said a Rumanian-American clergyman.

An active member of an Armenian dance group agreed, "Now the Armenians have made it; we're part of American life. What it really boils down to is that people aren't ashamed to be foreign any more."

Finally, the descendants of immigrants identified themselves as ethnics in the 1960's and 1970's in increasing numbers because fewer acceptable alternatives were available. In the depression years of the 1930's many of the second generation had found a sense of personal identity through radical political and social groups and through the newly active labor movement. During the religious revival of the 1950's, it appeared likely that religious identity would replace ethnicity as the main personal focal point.

Events proved otherwise. By the 1960's the working class ideologies of the "Old Left" were considered hopelessly out of date, by the "New Left" as well as by the Right. The industrial worker, once a motion picture hero played by John Garfield, had degenerated into the slowwitted television bigot, Archie Bunker. In 1935 it had been more acceptable to identify as a worker than as an Irish, Italian, or Polish-American, but by 1970 the reverse was true. By the 1970's the religious revival, at least among large traditional churches, was over. Neither economic ideology nor religious affiliation appeared likely to displace ethnicity, at least in the foreseeable future.

New Leadership, New Activism

While many factors made it easier for ethnic Americans to return to their backgrounds with new pride and interest, the most important stimulus for the new ethnicity was the black civil rights revolution. The civil rights marches of the 1950's and the exposés of black ghetto poverty in the 1960's were beamed into American living rooms in "living color." Ethnic Americans watched as blacks demanded their fair share of the American dream—civil rights, jobs, housing, education, and political recognition. They heard about black history, black culture, black pride, and saw the black community organizing to achieve its goals.

If black is beautiful, reasoned some ethnic Americans, is it not also beautiful to be Mexican, Puerto Rican, Polish, Italian, or Jewish? If black studies are valid and desirable, why not academic programs in the heritage of other ethnic groups as well? If blacks could organize to protest discrimination and fight for better living conditions, why should not other ethnic communities do the same? By the late 1960's new activist leaders were directing their ethnic communities along the paths laid out by blacks—toward pride in their cultural heritage and toward social and political activism.

One of the first groups to develop this new type of ethnic leadership was the Mexican-American community. Angered by what they perceived as the neglect of their community's acute needs and influenced by the example of black militance, Mexican-American leaders became increasingly militant. On September 16, 1965, Cesar Chavez launched the grape pickers strike at Delano, California, to unionize impoverished Mexican-American farm workers. After nationwide publicity, the strike was settled in 1970 when the last major grape grower signed a union contract granting a minimum wage.

Like Martin Luther King, Cesar Chavez believed in nonviolent protest and sought alliances with sympathizers everywhere. But as the black movement of the 1960's tended to move from moderate to more militant leadership, so too did the Mexican-American movement. Other leaders moved left of Chavez. The mystical Reies Lòpez Tijerina of New Mexico for example, led a drive for the return of the old communal lands of the Southwest to the Mexican-American community. Ambivalent toward broad coalitions and alliances, Tijerina used "direct action", such as his attempt at armed take over of the Rio Arriba Courthouse in 1967.

In the barrios of Los Angeles, David Sanchez founded the Brown Berets, an organization of young men who, like the Black Panthers, felt it necessary to defend themselves against the white police. The Brown Berets tried to instill pride and group unity among the ghetto youth. "Gang fights are going out," said their minister of public relations. "We're getting kids from all the different gangs into the Brown Berets. It's going to be one big gang. We try to teach our people not to fight with each other. . . ."

One of the most important new leaders of the urban community was Rodolpho "Corky" Gonzales. Having participated in federal poverty programs and become disillusioned with them, Gonzales complained that the best leadership of the community was being "bought out" by what he considered tokenism. Like the more radical blacks, he rejected integration as unlikely and undesirable. "Integration is an empty bag," he stated. . . . "it's like getting up out of the small end of the funnel. One may make it, but the rest of the people stay at the bottom."

By the late 1960's young Mexican-Americans were calling themselves Chicanos, a term formerly applied only to the poor and ignorant among their community. Activism spread, especially among the better educated. High school students in California and in Denver staged strikes protesting the neglect of their heritage in the public school curriculum. College students and professionals formed a variety of new organizations. "Chicanos, do not believe that the gabacho's (Anglo) life, values, and culture are better," admonished a college newspaper in 1969. "Be proud of what you are and demand what you have coming." But by the early 1970's, "direct action" was declining among Chicanos as it had among blacks. A more sophisticated Mexican-American community turned increasingly to political activity and community organization, focusing its efforts on specific problems such as education, housing, jobs, drug abuse, and police brutality.

The story of Edward J. Piszak illustrates the arrival of the new ethnicity among European ethnic communities. A second generation Polish-American who made his fortune in the frozen seafood business, Piszak grew up in a mixed working class neighborhood in Philadelphia with little awareness of his ethnic background. Unconsciously, he had internalized the American stereotype of the "dumb Polak." A trip to Warsaw in 1964 changed that. Piszak describes the impression the Polish capital made upon him:

> I remember, as the plane came down over Warsaw, thinking, 'My God! Who built this beautiful city?' I didn't know Polaks could do things like this, build these fine buildings and do all the engineering and design and construction. That's not what they teach you in America.

Involved in an employment program for the "disadvantaged" in his factories, Piszak began to compare the situation of the Pole in America with that of the black. "The Polish-American had much in common with the black," he said. "He was uprooted, found himself in a strange land, forfeited his identity and usually was undereducated, from the bottom of society. He didn't even know he had a cultural heritage."

To remedy this situation, Piszak launched Project Pole, patterned after the many black history and culture programs of the late 1960's. He placed ads in newspapers in Detroit, Chicago, Washington, Philadelphia, and Buffalo telling about the great people Poland has produced—Nicolaus Copernicus, Frederic Chopin, Joseph Conrad, Marie Curie. He distributed posters, art books, and other literature on Polish culture, encouraged tourism to Poland, and got a half million dollar appropriation from Congress to make the Kosciuszko House in Philadelphia a national Polish-American shrine.

Polish-American leaders in other cities took up similar projects. A Polish-American cultural group in Detroit opened the Adam Mickiewicz Library, which by 1974 had 8000 books, 1000 records, and over a hundred periodicals dealing with Poland or with Polish-America. In 1973, the group lined up Polish, Italian, and Ukrainian clubs to visit Detroit booksellers and protest the sale of a derogatory Polish and Italian joke book. Their efforts were successful; the booksellers took the offensive work off their shelves. The attitude of some of the newly aroused European ethnics such as these Polish-Americans is summed up by Mike Krolewski, curator of the Adam Mickiewicz Library: "Without our backgrounds, whatever nationality it happens to be, we are nothing."

The Cultural Renaissance

Italians, Armenians, Greeks, Rumanians, Jews, Chinese, Japanese, Puerto Ricans, and other ethnic communities underwent their own ethnic renaissances. The smaller ethnic churches reported increases in membership in the early 1970's, while larger, nonethnic churches reported declines. In Jackson, Michigan, the Rumanian Orthodox church had a waiting list for its summer camp, which taught Rumanian religion and church music as well as table tennis and swimming. New York's St. Nicholas Greek Orthodox Church reported that its afternoon Greek language school doubled its enrollment from 200 to 400 in five years. Armenians opened elementary schools in Michigan and Massachusetts, began an annual Armenian track and field meet in California, and started an Armenian golf tournament in Manhasset, New York.

Ethnic culture spilled out of ethnic schools into institutions serving the general public. Public high schools in various cities introduced courses in Polish, Italian, Hebrew, and Armenian. In the early 1970's, the University of California at Los Angeles enrolled 150 students a year in Armenian language and civilization courses and granted masters degrees and doctorates in Armenian studies. Leading universities established chairs of Jewish studies, and in 1973 a summer program in Yiddish language, literature, and culture had a larger enrollment than any other summer program at Columbia University.

Oriental-Americans shared in the ethnic revival. Japanese parents took their children to visit the internment camps of World War II. Japanese-American youth enrolled in university courses in their ancestral history and culture and in traditional arts such as flower arranging. Chinese teenagers flocked to Chinese language films from Hong Kong (with English subtitles!) "I worked all my life to get out of Chinatown and I finally got to Walnut Creek," said a successful second generation Chinese-American, "and my children want to go back to Chinatown. I don't understand this." Doubtless these children considered this bewildered parent a "banana,"—yellow on the outside, white on the inside!

The ethnic revival aroused an interest in ethnic culture among the general public as well as within the ethnic communities. Folk festivals in major cities displayed ethnic songs, dances, foods, and handicrafts. Foreign language radio stations multiplied, and ethnic television programming was introduced. Plays, books, and films about ethnic life became immensely popular, *Fiddler on the Roof* and *The Godfather*, for example.

Revivals of old Yiddish plays were attended by nostalgic audiences in New York and Miami, but the most vital ethnic theatre in the 1960's and 1970's was that of blacks, Puerto Ricans, and Mexican-Americans.

One of the most successful Puerto Rican plays was *The Ox Cart,* by Rene Marques. It described the deterioration of a simple farm family that moved first to San Juan and then to New York to "improve" itself. The play ends shortly after the death of the oldest son. The grief-stricken mother sets out for the mountains of rural Puerto Rico, hoping to recapture the lost traditions and values that had held the family together in earlier, happier times. Such a play must have had a powerful impact on Puerto Rican immigrants working out their own balance sheets on the positive and negative effects of urbanization and immigration.

Mexican-American activists of the 1960's and early 1970's used theater not only for entertainment, but also for education and social propaganda, much as European immigrant workers had done decades before. El Teatro Campesino, a bilingual farmworker's theater, borrowed from contemporary European theater as well as from traditional Mexican folk drama to produce *actos,* short plays explaining the plight of the pickers and the need for unionization. Luis Valdez, one of the founders of El Teatro Campesino, described its actors and productions:

> All our actors are farmworkers. . . . Starting from scratch with a real life incident, character, or idea, everybody in the Teatro contributes to the development of an acto. . . . We use no scenery, no scripts, and no curtain. We use costumes and props only casually—an old pair of pants, a wine bottle, a pair of dark glasses, a mask. But mostly we like to show we are still strikers underneath. . . . To simplify things, we hang signs around our necks, sometimes in black and white, sometimes in lively colors, indicating the characters portrayed.

El Teatro Campesino was valuable because it explored a social movement without asking its poorly educated, often foreign born participants to read and write. The existence of the theater itself condemned the loss of human talent caused by the deadening life farm workers were forced to lead. "More than that," said Valdez, "it affords us the opportunity to laugh as free men."

The Puerto Rican and Mexican-American communities produced increasing numbers of poets, novelists, and authors of short stories, autobiographies, and nonfiction. The works of such authors were varied, but they were often colored by their ethnic origins. Durango Mendoza, whose mother was Native American and whose father was a Mexican-American, explained:

> . . . being brown in a white culture, or Chicano in an Indian culture, gives a certain flavor to being a man that is unique. Propaganda and race—or culture—selling is not my bag. But being brown and springing from

brown roots is my reality—a reality that has shaped my life and given me a great concern for all people, a concern that I might not otherwise have known as strongly.

The variety of writing done within the framework of the new ethnicity is enormous, ranging from John Figueroa's vivid descriptions of the Puerto Rican barrio of East Harlem, to Jerre Mangione's reconstruction of Sicilian immigrant life in Rochester, to the widely read works of Jewish writers such as Saul Bellow, Bernard Malamud, and Chaim Potok.

Achievements

The new, activist leaders have been increasingly successful in fighting negative ethnic stereotypes in the American media. Italian-American protests eliminated the use of "Mafia" as a synonym for organized crime in the movies and on television. Offensive advertisements such as the Mexican "bandito" stealing cornchips on a television commercial and a bucktoothed, pigtailed Chinese on a powdered drink mix package were dropped because of organized ethnic protest. Newspapers and magazines featured articles on ethnic traditions, ethnic neighborhoods, and ethnic problems. Prime time television celebrated the new ethnicity with shows featuring comedians, detectives, and other central figures with recognizable ethnic identities.

More significant gains were made in civil rights. MALDEF, the Mexican American Legal Defense and Educational Fund, brought successful class action suits on behalf of Mexican-Americans seeking equal rights in education, employment, and political participation. Bilingual schools were begun on an experimental basis for Mexican-American and Puerto Rican children. Spanish speaking voters in New York City and Philadelphia were provided with ballots in Spanish. Affirmative action programs were designed to help Spanish surnamed individuals, as well as blacks and women, enter universities and professional schools and obtain good jobs. Much remains to be done, but at least a beginning was made.

For the first time, ethnicity was recognized as an important factor in many areas of American life. In health care, for example, research began on diseases encountered primarily in particular ethnic groups. Psychologists, psychiatrists, and social workers considered the impact of ethnic cultures upon behavior patterns, mental health, and social problems. In 1972 the medical school of Stanford University used skillfully prepared ethnic materials—a cookbook, a horoscope calendar, bilingual phonograph records, and radio and television dramatizations—to motivate Mexican-Americans toward habits that would reduce heart disease. Such constructive uses of knowledge about ethnicity are, unfortunately, still rare, but here too, beginnings were made.

Problems

If the new ethnicity made ethnic Americans more aware of their cultural heritage, it also made them more aware of their contemporary problems. Ethnic leaders were concerned that the new interest in ethnic culture was an "elitist" movement. They complained that the vast majority of their constituency cared less about history and literature than about their favorite ethnic foods. Would the new ethnic studies programs attract serious academic students, they asked, or would these programs degenerate into consciousness-raising sessions or exercises in nostalgia?

There were many other problems. Despite the public acceptance of many aspects of the new ethnicity, ethnic Americans were subjected to subtle forms of economic and social discrimination that would not go away. Affirmative action programs helped some with Spanish surnames, but it could be argued that these same programs worked against people with Italian, Slavic, or Jewish surnames. Covertly and overtly, ethnic groups continued to battle one another in many areas of American life. Polish and Italian Catholics still complained that the Irish shut them out of positions of influence in the American Catholic Church. Southern and Eastern European groups fought the Irish on the one hand and blacks and Puerto Ricans on the other for control of unions, jobs, neighborhoods, and political machines. Ethnic communities battled one another, and nonethnics as well, for control of lucrative underworld activities such as gambling, prostitution, and drug distribution.

Ethnic leaders found much to worry about within their own communities. Despite the new ethnicity, intermarriage and assimilation took an increasing toll. So too did the pressures and dislocations common to all Americans. In the 1960's and 1970's, for the first time, divorce became as common among Catholics and Jews as among Protestants. Groups that had prided themselves upon the stability of their family life found their social service agencies overwhelmed with cases of broken families and disturbed children. Poverty remained a major problem among Puerto Rican and Mexican-Americans, but even the most successful ethnic communities were dismayed to discover surprisingly large amounts of poverty among their members. Many of the ethnic poor were old people, left behind in decaying parts of the inner city where they struggled to survive on inadequate pensions or social security.

"Middle America"

The new ethnicity focused the attention of scholars on the formerly little noticed problems of a large group variously titled "white ethnics," "the silent majority," or "middle America". By whatever name, this group consists of the forty million children and grandchildren of the Southern and Eastern European ethnic communities. Most of them live in the major cities of the Northeast and the Great Lakes area, are Roman Catholic, and make their livings as industrial workers, clerks, or small shopkeepers. And most of them had increasing difficulties coping with the economic and social problems of the 1960's and 1970's.

The largest single problem was inflation, which ate away at already barely adequate paychecks. In 1969 the average industrial worker with three dependents took home $87.00 a week—less than the sum defined as necessary by the United States government to maintain an "adequate" standard of living and, surprisingly, a dollar less than the same worker had taken home in 1965! In the early 1970's prices rose faster than wages, so the "middle American" saw the purchasing power of his or her paycheck decline sharply. An electrician described the feelings of workers like himself:

> He gets a dollar raise and seventy cents of it goes to inflation. His wife says, 'Hey John, look, what's going on around here? We need more money.' He is confused. On his TV screen he sees angry blacks and browns getting it for themselves, and he thinks society is giving it only to them. He feels that he is supporting the poor and that the welfare and city budgets come off of his back. . . .

As the above quotation suggests, there were problems other than inflation. By the early 1970's working class white ethnics were filled with resentment. They watched affluent WASPS and more fortunate ethnics move to the suburbs, leaving them and blacks to cope with the long neglected problems of the cities—a shrinking tax base, antiquated schools, poor housing, inadequate services, unsafe streets. Though their wages were often little higher than welfare payments, they were excluded from many of the new social programs directed at the very poor. Many were too proud—or too ashamed—to accept help from such programs even when they qualified. Like the very poor, working class ethnics saw the American dream on their television screens—the luxurious suburban homes, the glamorous vacations, prestigious colleges for their children—and like the very poor, they knew that this dream was beyond their reach.

Working class white ethnics had other causes for resentment. Despite recent efforts of ethnic spokesman to correct the situation, they received little positive attention from the nation as a whole. In circles too enlightened to tolerate anti-black jokes, jokes derogatory to

Poles and Italians remained common. A technological society involved in putting a man on the moon had little respect for the unskilled, or even the skilled, manual laborer. "Who wants to be an electrician nowadays? If you are not a computer expert, you are nothing."

But middle Americans could rarely afford the specialized training their society valued, and were often dissuaded even from trying to get such training. Shunted into vocational or "general" high school programs rather than college preparatory classes, their youth were stigmatized as "fender benders" or "greasers" by contemptuous teachers, counselors, and classmates. Often young men of this group, lacking self-confidence, accepted routine, dead end jobs because they expected nothing better.

Working class white ethnic women also suffered from a negative self-image. Poorly educated, they marked time as sales clerks or office workers until marriage, which they had been brought up to consider the appropriate and satisfying career for a woman. Marriage was not a panacea, however. A study of working class women by Lee Rainwater, Richard Coleman, and Gerald Handel revealed that many regarded themselves as "little people" whose lives were "just dull." They did not believe that anyone cared what they thought. According to a paper given by Dr. Pauline B. Bart at the Radcliffe Institute Conference on Women in 1972:

> The question characteristically asked women is 'Are you a housewife or do you work?' implying that the seventy to ninety hour week women outside the labor force endure when they have children and a house to care for is not work. It is not surprising that their self-image may suffer. . . . Housewifery is menial work, and we do not regard our menials highly.

Economically insecure, lacking higher education, and low in self-esteem, many working class white ethnics found the political and social changes of the 1960's and early 1970's difficult to understand and to accept. Campus rebellions, urban riots, civil disobedience, hippies, yippies, draft resisters, and the antiwar movement were astonishing to people brought up to believe in hard work, respect for authority, and unquestioning patriotism. Faced with the civil rights movement, changing urban neighborhoods, busing, birth control, abortion, drugs, pornography, rising crime rates and inflation, many felt that "our lives were changing faster than our own self-image or basic values."

For people who had little, rapid social change—even positive, long overdue social change—could be a frightening experience. To make matters worse, traditional sources of support were less readily available. Civil service and political reform had destroyed much of the power of the old ethnic ward politician, whose influence had been a port in time of storm. "Affirmative action" plans appeared to advance racial minorities over white ethnics, even those with seniority. Automation, recurrent recessions, and a stubbornly unyielding unemployment rate made it hard to find new jobs when old ones were lost. Unions, a traditional source of help, seemed unresponsive, if not corrupt. The average working man was rarely active in his union and six out of seven working women were not union members at all. Even the Roman Catholic Church could not be counted on to provide the comfort of familiarity. In the wake of Vatican II "folk" masses were accompanied by rock guitar, nuns shed their habits, and priests campaigned for the abolition of celibacy.

Many of the problems of white ethnics were linked to the problems of the cities. The nation's tax structure resulted in the concentration of public monies in Washington, so that the amount available for local needs was limited. As the affluent moved to the suburbs, the cities were left with fewer and fewer resources to meet ever increasing needs. Industry, too, moved to the suburbs, and public transportation was poor, making access to jobs more difficult for blacks and whites who remained in the old neighborhoods.

Politically, many cities were securely in the hands of an Anglo-Saxon Protestant elite or the well-organized, firmly entrenched Irish. Before World War II, Southern and Eastern European communities usually lacked the affluence and the organization to gain control of the nation's cities. In the 1960's, when they were ready to assume positions of power, it was much harder to do so because the cities were declining. When the cities had been expanding, entrenched groups could move upward into more desirable positions, leaving vacancies for the newcomers to fill. But now, with few new positions available, the old guard was reluctant to yield what it had.

Finally, now that Southern and Eastern Europeans had served their time in the lower ranks of the urban structure and considered themselves entitled to political leadership and the jobs and other advantages that went with it, they faced a determined new competitor—an increasingly numerous and well-organized black community. Black Americans, too, were immigrants to the cities. While small communities had lived there since colonial days, most arrived from rural South in the twentieth century. Blacks felt that they, too, had served their time—three hundred years—and were entitled to the benefits of urban America.

Whites and Blacks—The Urban Battlefield

The new ethnicity bore a complex love-hate relationship to black America. As already described, much of the new ethnicity was imitative of the black civil rights movement. Irish, Slavic, and Jewish votes in the cities had supplied much of the political muscle for the civil rights revolution and antipoverty programs of the 1960's. Most ethnics were ardent supporters of John and Robert Kennedy, both of whom were considered liberal on social issues. In the conservative landslide of 1972, when 68% of Protestant America voted for Richard Nixon, George McGovern won over half of the Slavic vote and two-thirds of the Jewish vote.

Yet by the late 1960's white ethnics found themselves in city after city facing blacks in ugly confrontations over neighborhoods, jobs, schools, and often over political control of the city itself. Liberals, hoping to hasten the long overdue progress of black Americans, began to characterize working class white ethnics as mindless bigots. Television news cameras showed white ethnics stoning a school bus carrying black children to a formerly white school or vandalizing a home into which a black family was moving. These ugly scenes supported the view of white ethnics as bigots. So did the voting patterns of those white ethnics who backed candidates like Louise Day Hicks, opponent of school integration in Boston, Frank Rizzo, the "law and order" mayor of Philadelphia, and George Wallace, segregationist governor of Alabama.

While white America as a whole was riddled with racism, there is no evidence that ethnics were more bigoted than others. Many studies suggest that certain groups, Jews and Irish Catholics in particular, are less bigoted than most. In recent years working class white ethnics have appeared more bigoted than other Americans because their interests have clashed with those of blacks more frequently than the interests of the affluent and highly educated. Ethnic Americans realized what sociologist Peter Rossi pointed out:

> . . . without changes in social policy, the costs of producing racial equality are going to be borne more heavily by the white working class than by any other group in the society. The working class will have to share jobs, schools, neighborhoods, political posts, influence in city hall, and so on with blacks—types of sharing that come close to where people really live . . .

White ethnics, many of whom had little, resented being asked to shoulder so much of the burden of correcting the centuries old injustice of racism, while people with more advantages pointed accusing fingers from the shelter of affluent suburbs, private schools, and well-guarded luxury apartments. Also, to economically marginal but rigidly "respectable" white working class ethnics, the black stereotype represented the poverty, the social problems, and the lower class way of life which they had only recently escaped—and into which they were terrified of falling once again.

Racism was undoubtedly one cause of conflict between white ethnics and blacks in the cities, but it was not the only cause, nor perhaps even the most crucial one. Conflicts between groups entrenched in a given area and newcomers seeking a place there had been commonplace throughout America's past. Confrontations between white ethnics and blacks in America's troubled cities can be viewed in the context of other intergroup conflicts involving ethnic succession in jobs, neighborhoods, and politics. Catholics and Protestants had shed blood over school controversies in the nineteenth century. The first Polish family to move into an Irish neighborhood in the nineteenth century was scarcely more welcome than the first black family to move into a Polish neighborhood a hundred years later.

To many white working class ethnics, the neighborhood was not just a geographic place; it was a way of life, a community in which every shop, tavern, and street corner was a beloved institution. The residents of such a neighborhood therefore feared the influx of newcomers who they felt, rightly or wrongly, would change the pattern of community life. Moreover, having invested virtually all they possessed in their homes, many white ethnics were especially vulnerable to the warnings of unscrupulous real estate agents that if blacks move in, "property values will go down." Rapidly changing neighborhoods, regardless of the ethnic groups involved, often experienced rising crime rates. Racially integrated neighborhoods were often punished by banks that refused to extend credit for the improvements that would have prevented deterioration.

Jobs, like neighborhoods, were not impersonal, interchangeable positions to ethnic Americans, but rather a way of life to be handed down to future generations. A skilled craftsman charged with racial discrimination in his union, expressed this in a letter to the *New York Times*:

> Some men leave their sons money, some large investments, some business connections, and some a profession. I have only one worthwhile thing to give; my trade. I hope to follow a centuries old tradition and sponsor my son for an apprenticeship. . . . It is said that I discriminate against Negroes. . . . Which of us when it comes to a choice will not choose a son over all others?

In many cities political battles raged as conservative, working class white ethnics fought coalitions of liberal upper class Anglo-Saxons and blacks for control of the cities. Sometimes one side won, sometimes another. The stakes were high, for they included the distribution of jobs, patronage, and government funds. No conflict aroused as much bitterness, however, as the battles within the schools.

By the 1960's, many of the teachers and administrators in urban school systems were Irish, Jewish, and Italian; by the 1960's, the majority of the students in many of these systems were black. Politicians, teachers' unions, administrators, ethnic leaders, and parents became locked in heated conflict. White teachers and administrators wanted to maintain the existing seniority system in the schools, while blacks wanted representation, even control, at all levels. White teachers and administrators complained that blacks wanted to be promoted out of turn, to "change the rules of the game," and that too much political and parental influence on the schools would destroy the quality of education. Blacks charged that racially prejudiced white teachers and administrators were failing to educate black children, that black children needed role models of their own race in the schools, and that community control could lead to the improvement rather than to the deterioration of education. A declining birth rate and economic recession meant fewer job opportunities for teachers and administrators—black and white—thus compounding the difficulties.

The most explosive issue of all was the issue of busing as a means of ending de facto racial segregation in urban public schools. The federal judiciary had ruled that racially segregated schools were inherently unequal in the North as well as in the South. Most blacks favored integration as morally right and educationally sound. Many white ethnics, on the other hand, had strongly possessive feelings about "their" public schools which, like their neighborhoods and jobs, were seen as an integral part of a cherished way of life, a way of life that was being threatened from all sides and must be defended at all costs. The conflict was exacerbated by the poor quality of education in many black and white urban schools, and the scarcity of funds and ideas for improvements.

White ethnic resistance to the integration of neighborhoods, jobs, and schools was in part an attempt to deny unpleasant realities. White ethnic neighborhoods, like black neighborhoods, were old and in need of repair. White schools, like black schools, were antiquated, badly financed, and often ineffective. Crime was a growing problem throughout the cities in "Whitetown" as well as the black ghetto. Hostility to blacks was an effort on the part of some white ethnics to deny their own ever increasing difficulties by blaming them on "outsiders." Crime, neighborhood deterioration, poor schools, and unemployment were seen as *black* problems which could be kept away if only blacks were kept away.

New Directions

Of course the pressing problems of the cities were not black problems or white problems, but were human problems affecting everyone. Racism and social insecurity on the part of urban whites and bitterness and exasperation on the part of blacks obscured the fact that the two groups had many common interests. The two groups, both "have-nots" in American society, constituted the bulk of the remaining urban population. As such, they had a common stake in the improvement of housing, job opportunities, education, health care, and other services in the deteriorating cities.

Because of these common interests, the new ethnicity did not need to be anti-black. "I want something positive," said ethnic leader Barbara Mikulski of Baltimore. "I want to see a national movement developed to help American ethnics, but not at the expense of any other minority groups." In 1970, at the National Center for Urban Ethnic Affairs, Mikulski urged blacks and white ethnics to stop fighting and start cooperating:

> Government is polarizing people by the creation of myths. . . . The ethnic worker is fooled into thinking that the blacks are getting everything. . . . The two groups end up fighting each other for the same jobs and competing so that the new schools and recreation centers will be in their respective communities. What results is an angry confrontation for tokens, where there should be an alliance for a whole new Agenda for America.

The "New Agenda" for blacks and whites would include full employment, a greater allocation of the nation's resources to meet human needs, black and white, and quality education for everyone.

Tentative beginnings have been made toward creating the alliance of which Mikulski spoke—blacks and white ethnics working together for a "new agenda for Americans." Ethnic leaders such as Steve Adubo of Newark and Kenneth Kovach of Cleveland, and ethnic organizations have shown concern for the problems of blacks as well as of their own groups. In Detroit and Cleveland issue oriented coalitions worked for change in areas that affected both groups—urban renewal, education, the quality of city services, consumer and environmental problems. Most of these coalitions were short-lived, falling apart when the issue on which they were built was resolved. Under their auspices, however, court cases have been won and city ordinances passed.

The late 1960's and early 1970's also saw the opening of new political directions for ethnic America. Realistic politicians have always paid attention to ethnicity, attending ethnic banquets, acknowledging ethnic holidays, appointing some (but not too many!) ethnics to office, and, when necessary, "balancing" a ticket with candidates from powerful ethnic groups. Such efforts intensified in response to the new ethnicity.

Common experiences with poverty and discrimination had produced solid ethnic support for the Democratic Party from Franklin

Roosevelt's New Deal to Lyndon Johnson's War on Poverty. By the mid 1960's, however, ethnic Americans were rethinking their political positions. The affluent were moving toward suburbia and Republicanism, while working class whites were no longer convinced that the Democrats, whose programs now were for the very poor, had their interests at heart.

In the Presidential campaigns of 1968 and 1972, Richard Nixon made a determined effort to capture the votes of the formerly Democratic white ethnics, a large component of his "silent majority." His strategy was to appeal to the white ethnics' economic insecurities and to their fear of social change, particularly their fear of blacks, "hippies," and the "New Left". Though this strategy was not completely successful (Slavs and Jews voted for McGovern, as did the heavily Catholic, heavily ethnic state of Massachusetts), sufficiently great inroads were made in the old Democratic coalition of labor and minorities to produce Nixon victories in both elections.

By 1975, however, the ethnic vote was still "up for grabs." The ethnic votes Nixon had attracted to the Republican Party through appeals to traditional moral values, "law and order," and patriotism could hardly be expected to remain there after the exposure of the hypocrisy and corruption of Watergate. Patriotism and the "cult of gratitude" to the United States remained strong among ethnic Americans, however, as did a concern with traditional ethical values. Perhaps it was more than coincidence that many of the people prominent in efforts to uncover the Watergate scandal and bring honor back to America's public life—Judge John Sirica, Congressman Peter Rodino, special prosecutor Leon Jaworski—were the children of immigrants.

In the long run, ethnic Americans, like all Americans, would give their political support to the candidates and parties that met their needs. In an article in *Commonwealth* (September 1970), Michael Novak enumerated these needs:

> more self-determination and pride on the job, more prestige in the nation, more dignity—as well as better housing, a sharp control on inflation, full employment, more scholarships and welfare (so that nonwhites and whites don't have to compete for the same small piece of pie), more beauty and peace and easy transport and security in the cities and boroughs in which they live.

In the 1976 national elections, Jimmy Carter was able to reestablish the old Roosevelt coalition by convincing almost all black voters, over 70% of the Jewish voters, and 54% of urban Catholic voters that the Democratic Party was more likely than the Republican Party to provide jobs and improve the quality of their lives. The national political experience of the 1960's and 1970's indicated that white ethnics, like other voters, will support candidates who represent their interests, regardless of traditional party loyalties and affiliations.

Social as well as political trends opened new directions for ethnic Americans. The great expansion of educational facilities in the 1960's, including the community college movement, enabled young white ethnics—and older people as well—to pursue higher education in unprecedented numbers. Though community colleges, like high schools, could become traps tracking working class students into "dead end" vocational, rather than academic programs, new employment possibilities as well as new ideas about values and life styles have opened up to many of the students who have attended them.

Finally, the growing feminist movement of the 1960's and 1970's has also opened up new directions for ethnic Americans. In the late 1960's, ethnic women tended to consider the new feminists "bra burners," and wanted nothing to do with them. Working class women had little stake in middle class feminist issues such as the exclusion of women from corporate, academic, and political life. Rhetoric that called for freedom from male oppression alienated women brought up to depend upon their husbands for a sense of security. Nor did working class women want job equality with their blue-collar husbands. "We know that when they come home from work every day they feel they've been treated like the machines they operate."

By the mid 1970's, however, several factors were operating to bring ethnic women into the feminist movement. The movement itself made greater efforts to meet their needs, stressing such issues as equal pay for equal work, unemployment compensation for pregnant women, better medical care, better child care facilities, and social security for housewives. Often college educated daughters introduced their middle-aged ethnic mothers to feminist ideas and organizations. Finally, the rising rates of inflation and the increasing frequency of separation and divorce forced increasing numbers of ethnic women into the labor force, giving them firsthand experience with the kinds of discrimination the feminists were attacking.

Like their immigrant grandmothers, many poor and working class ethnic women have been drawn into the wider community and to the women's movement by efforts to improve their children's schools and to fight violence, drugs, and other problems in their neighborhoods. The recent activism of Puerto Rican and Mexican-American women raised serious questions about the "machismo" tradition of male superiority in their ethnic backgrounds. "The doctrine of Machismo has been used by our men to take out their frustrations on their wives and sisters," said a radical Mexican-American newspaper in Albuquerque, New Mexico. "We must support our women in their struggle for economic and social equality and recognize that our women are equals within our struggle for Liberation."

Asian and European ethnic women moved in the same direction. Labor union women, many of them ethnics, organized on a national basis to demand equality on the job. Radical caucuses of Catholic and Jewish women demanded sexual equality within these traditional ethnic religions. A study of white working class women in Chicago in 1972 stated that women who considered feminists "kooks" nevertheless agreed with them that women should have an equal voice in household decisions, that women were as capable as men of being leaders in science, education, and politics, and perhaps most surprising, that "a woman who does not marry can be a normal and adequate woman."

Like Mexican-American and Puerto Rican women, some European ethnics became involved in community improvement activities during the 1960's. Though these women might express no conscious interest in women's liberation, their activism had an impact upon the old life styles. "When a wife comes home after testifying at a city council hearing, she is fundamentally changing the balance of power in her marriage," said Nancy Seifer, author of a recent study of working class women. By the early 1970's, many working class women, the middle aged as well as the young, were convinced that they could "build a future different from the traditional path laid out by their mothers and grandmothers." The women's movement, like the black civil rights movement, and like the new educational opportunities, was opening new directions for ethnic America.

"To Seek America"

Accustomed to equating universalism with "good" and to identifying Americanism with the Anglo-Saxon heritage, many Americans in the mid 1970's were still uncomfortable with the concept of ethnicity. Critics of the "new ethnicity" worried that it would lead to a destructive fragmentation of American life, that it would cause difficulties for the individual who chose not to identify with an ethnic group, and that it would increase prejudice and intergroup conflict, particularly between blacks and whites. Swedish sociologist Gunnar Myrdal characterized the new ethnicity as "upperclass intellectual romanticism." According to Myrdal, emphasis upon unimportant cultural differences would divert attention from the real economic and social cleavages that threaten American society. Others were afraid that the traditional American ideology of individual rights would be replaced by one in which groups, rather than individuals, have rights and privileges—a "quota-ization" of American life.

Defenders of the new ethnicity countered that they were not

creating cleavages in American society, only recognizing diversities that already existed and had been ignored too long. They maintained that teaching young people about their ethnic heritages would confirm their own sense of self-worth, making them more, rather than less, tolerant of those who were different. "As I discover my own identity, I become more free and I want the same thing for all human beings," wrote an ethnic leader.

Though there were suggestions that the American political structure should be revamped to give ethnic and other groups institutionalized voting power *as groups,* most advocates of the new ethnicity did not support this. "All boundaries are understood to be permeable," suggested historian John Higham, describing his model for an ethnically diverse American society. "Ethnic nuclei, on the other hand, are respected as enduring centers of social action. If self-preservation requires, they may claim exemption from certain universal rules, as the Amish now do from the school laws in some states. Both integration and ethnic cohesion are recognized as worthy goals, which different individuals will accept in different degrees."

Advocates of the new ethnicity differed among themselves whether its emphasis should be the exploration of cultural uniqueness or the development of political and social action programs. If the latter, toward what goals should the program be directed and with what allies? Should the new ethnicity stress the real needs and problems of ethnic Americans so as to improve the material lot of its constituents? Or should it stress their equally real progress and achievements to combat destructive stereotypes and build group pride?

One thing that everyone interested in the new ethnicity agreed upon was the need for further investigation, both of the role ethnicity plays in the life of the individual and of the role ethnic communities play in the life of the nation. Scholars have just begun to describe the cultural characteristics of ethnic communities, communities which, like everything else in the United States, are constantly changing. They have also just begun to explore the dynamics of ethnic communities as economic and political interest groups competing for the rewards of American society and as nuclei for social relationships, emotional loyalties, and value systems.

Ethnicity is one of the oldest factors in American life; yet it has just begun to be explored. As the linguist Joshua Fishman pointed out in a study of foreign language loyalty in the United States, ethnicity in mid twentieth century America is not an all-or-nothing affair, nor is it logical, nor is it uniform from individual to individual or group to group:

> For some it is composed of half-forgotten memories, unexplored longings, and intermittent preferences; for others it is active, structured,

elaborated, and constant. . . . For some it is a badge of shame to ignore, fight, and eradicate; for others, it is a source of pride, a focus of initial loyalties and integration from which wider loyalties and wider integration can proceed . . . the varieties and variabilities of ethnicity in America are largely unknown. . . .

As Fishman points out, ignorance of ethnicity is self ignorance—for *all* Americans. All Americans are rooted in particular cultural backgrounds that affect how we see ourselves and others and how we behave, as individuals and as groups. All Americans have faced, and will continue to face, the problems most clearly seen in the lives of immigrants. They will have to work out their own relationships between the present and the past, between the individual and the group, between continuity and change. Like immigrants, all Americans enter every day into a society in the process of growth and change. Words written by Waldo Frank in 1919 during a great wave of foreign immigration remain pertinent today: "We go forth all to seek America. And in the seeking we create her. And in the quality of our search shall be the nature of the America we create."

Bibliographic Essay

The literature on immigrant groups and ethnic life in the United States is voluminous. The following essay will introduce some of the most important works, old and new; suggest the kinds of materials that have been used in the preparation of this book; and provide a starting point for the reader who wishes to investigate further.

Titles preceded by an asterisk (*) have appeared in a paperback edition.

I. General Works on the History of Immigration

The best single history is Maldwyn Allen Jones, *American Immigration* (1960), a comprehensive survey with a good bibliography. For a more recent, briefer treatment, see Leonard Dinnerstein and David Reimer, *Ethnic Americans: A History of Immigration and Assimilation* (1975), which concentrates on the late nineteenth and twentieth centuries and includes useful demographic statistics. The classic introduction to the more personal aspects of immigration is Oscar Handlin, *The Uprooted* (1951, 2nd edition 1973) which stresses the psychological and cultural alienation felt by the immigrants abruptly separated from familiar persons, places, and ways of living. Handlin's thesis has been challenged by Rudolph Vecoli, whose article "Contadini in Chicago: A Critique of *The Uprooted*," *Journal of American History*, LI (December 1964), 407-417, argues that Italian immigrants were able to bring their Old World traditions and institutions with them and thus did not suffer the psychologically devastating "uprootedness" described by Handlin.

Louis Hartz examines immigration to the United States in a comparative framework in *The Founding of New Societies: Studies in the History of the United States, Latin America, South Africa, Canada, and*

Australia (1964). Two excellent works on the "push" from Europe and the "pull" of the New World are Marcus Lee Hansen, *The Atlantic Migration 1607-1860: A History of the Continuing Settlement of the United States* (1940) and Philip Taylor, *The Distant Magnet: European Emigration to the U.S.A.* (1971), which covers the century from 1830 to 1930. See also Harry V. Jerome's older work, *Migration and Business Cycles* (1926). For details of the immigrant's journey to America, consult Maldwyn Allen Jones' anecdotal *Destination America: 1815-1914* (1976) and William Tefft and Thomas Dunne, *Ellis Island* (1971), both of which include photographs, and Terry Coleman, *Going To America* (1972). Thomas Monroe Pitkin's recent account, *Keepers of the Gate: A History of Ellis Island* (1975) chronicles the administration of Ellis Island and includes information on the controversy over immigration restriction.

There are a number of useful documentary collections on European immigration, including both primary and secondary materials. Two of the earliest and best, compiled by social worker and staunch opponent of restrictionism Edith Abbott, are *Historical Aspects of the Immigration Problem: Select Documents* (1926, reprinted 1969), which covers the period before 1882, and *Immigration: Select Documents and Case Records* (1924, reprinted 1969), which includes early twentieth century immigration as well. Both contain immigrant letters, diaries, government documents, and other primary historical, sociological, and legal sources. More recent compilations are Oscar Handlin, *Immigration as a Factor in American History* (1959) and the more comprehensive collection edited by Stanley Feldstein and Lawrence Costello, *The Ordeal of Assimilation: A Documentary History of the White Working Class* (1974), which includes documents on the "new ethnicity" of the 1960's and early 1970's. An attractive collection of essays on the Southern and Eastern European immigration of the early twentieth century is John J. Appel, *The New Immigration* (1971) with material on immigrant housing, community institutions, education, the exploitation of women, and the restrictionist controversy.

II. Ethnicity and Assimilation: Sociological Perspectives

Sociologist Andrew Greeley's lively *Why Can't They Be More Like Us?* (1971) is the best introduction to the concept of ethnicity and its importance in the behavior of ethnic Americans today. For a more sophisticated analysis of the impact of ethnicity on politics, family life, economic and educational mobility, and relations between white ethnics and blacks, see Greeley's later volume, *Ethnicity in the United States: A Preliminary Reconnaissance* (1974), which includes a bibliography and a list of provocative questions for further investigation.

Three early but still rewarding works introducing the theory of cultural pluralism are Horace M. Kallen's article "Democracy Versus the Melting Pot," in *The Nation,* February 18 and 25, 1915, reprinted in Horace M. Kallen, *Culture and Democracy in the United States,* (1924, reprinted 1970); Isaac B. Berkson, *Theories of Americanization: A Critical Study* (1920, reprinted 1969); and Julius Drachsler, *Democracy and Assimilation, The Blending of Immigrant Heritages in America* (1920).

Among the post World War II writers on the role of ethnic groups in American society, Will Herberg, *Protestant, Catholic, Jew: An Essay in American Religious Sociology* (1955), suggests that the United States was a "triple melting pot," where ethnic groups fused into three permanent and distinctive religious groupings. For a development of the theory of ethnic communities as political and economic interest groups, see Nathan Glazer and Daniel P. Moynihan, *Beyond the Melting Pot: The Negroes, Puerto Ricans, Jews, Italians, and Irish of New York City* (1963, 2nd edition 1970). Milton Gordon, *Assimilation in American Life: The Role of Race, Religion, and National Origins* (1964) explores the process of assimilation, pointing out that ethnic communities may adopt the life style of the majority society (cultural assimilation) while maintaining their own quite separate institutional and social structures. Other useful discussions of the nature of assimilation may be found in William Newman, *American Pluralism: A Study of Minority Groups and Social Theory* (1973) and John Higham, *Send These to Me: Jews and Other Immigrants in Urban America* (1975).

III. Works on Particular Ethnic Communities

A. BLACKS, NATIVE AMERICANS, ANGLO-AMERICANS

The most comprehensive text on blacks in the United States, with an excellent bibliography, is John Hope Franklin, *From Slavery to Freedom. A History of Negro Americans* (3rd edition 1967). For shorter accounts, see Lerone Bennett, *Before the Mayflower: A History of the Negro in America, 1619-1966* (1966) and Rayford Logan, *The Negro in the United States: A Brief History* (1966). Among the many useful documentary collections are *The Afro-Americans: Readings* (1970), edited by Ross Baker; *The Negro in America: A Documentary History* (1967), edited by Leslie Fischel and Benjamin Quarles; *A Documentary History of the Negro People in the United States* (1951), edited by Herbert Aptheker; and *Black Women in White America: A Documentary History* (1973), edited by Gerda Lerner. For listings of works on particular topics, individuals, or periods, consult Dorothy Porter, *The Negro in the*

United States: A Selected Bibliography (1970) and James McPherson, et. al., *Blacks in America: Bibliographical Essays* (1971).

For material on the Native Americans before the coming of the Europeans, see William T. Sanders and Joseph P. Marino, *New World Prehistory: Archaeology of the American Indian* (1970). Useful surveys are Edward Spicer, *A Short History of the Indians of the United States* (1969) and, by the same author, *Cycles of Conquest: The Impact of Spain, Mexico, and the United States on the Indians of the Southwest 1533-1960* (1962); William T. Hagan, *American Indians* (1961), which stresses the impact of Anglo-American governmental policies; and Murray L. Wax, *American Indians: Unity and Diversity* (1971), a sociological study with considerable historical background. Two interesting documentary collections are Francis Prucha, *The Indian in American History* (1971), selections from classic works on Indian history; and Joseph H. Cash and Herbert T. Hoover, *To Be An Indian* (1971), interviews with contemporary Indian spokesmen. For additional materials, see William T. Hagan's bibliography, *The Indian in American History* (1963, revised edition 1972).

The English "core culture" is treated as an ethnic group in E. Digby Baltzell, *The Protestant Establishment: Aristocracy and Caste in America* (1964), and Charles H. Anderson, *White Protestant Americans: From National Origins to Religious Group* (1970). For a negative assessment of this group compared to other European ethnic groups, see Peter Schrag's controversial *The Decline of the Wasp* (1973). Materials on specific English-speaking immigrant communities and their integration into American society include Rowland T. Berthoff, *British Immigrants in Industrial America, 1790-1950* (1953, reprinted 1968); Charlotte Erickson, *Invisible Immigrants: The Adaptation of the English and Scottish Immigrants in Nineteenth Century America* (1972); Alan Conway, *The Welsh in America* (1961); and John Rowe, *The Hard Rock Men: Cornish Immigrants and the North American Mining Frontier* (1974). Henry J. Ford's older work, *The Scotch-Irish in America* (1915, reprinted 1969), is especially valuable on Scotch-Irish religion and education in colonial America, while James Leyburn's newer and more comprehensive *The Scotch-Irish: A Social History* (1962) is excellent on the relationships between the Scotch-Irish and other ethnic groups, including the Indians, and on Scotch-Irish participation in colonial political life and in the Revolution.

B. EUROPEAN ETHNIC COMMUNITIES

For material on French-speaking immigrants in the seventeenth and eighteenth centuries, see Arthur Henry Hirsch, *The Huguenots of*

Colonial South Carolina (1928), and Elizabeth Huntington Avery, *The Influence of French Immigration on the Political History of the United States* (1890, reprinted 1972). The story of the French-speaking immigrants from Canada is told in Jacques Ducharme, *The Shadows of the Trees: The Story of the French Canadians in New England* (1943). For material on the colonial Dutch, see Maud W. Goodwin, *The Dutch and English on the Hudson* (1919). For a general survey, see Henry S. Lucas' exhaustive *Dutch Immigration to the United States and Canada, 1789-1950* (1955) and the briefer recent account by Gerald F. de Jong, *The Dutch in America, 1609-1974* (1975).

One of the first books to examine the social and political impact of immigrants upon American cities was Oscar Handlin's excellent **Boston's Immigrants* (1968) which deals primarily with the Irish. Other useful treatments of this ethnic group are George Potter, *To the Golden Door: The Story of the Irish in Ireland and America* (1960, reprinted 1974); William Shannon, *The American Irish* (1966); and Andrew Greeley, **That Most Distressful Nation* (1973). Two of the many specialized studies deserving attention are Edwin Levine's examination of the Irish in politics, *The Irish and Irish Politicians* (1966), and Thomas N. Brown's excellent study of Irish-American efforts on behalf of the homeland, **Irish-American Nationalism* (1966).

Albert Faust's monumental two-volume work, *The German Element in the United States with Special Reference to Its Political, Moral, Social, and Educational Influence* (1927, reprinted 1969) is short on interpretation but contains a wealth of information. More interpretive is John Hawgood's account of the attempts to create German states in the United States and of the German reaction to American nativism, *The Tragedy of German-America: The Germans in the United States of America During the Nineteenth Century* (1940, reprinted 1970). A particularly interesting specialized study is Frederick C. Luebke, *Bonds of Loyalty: German-Americans and World War I* (1974), which suggests that the wartime anti-German hysteria was the surfacing of long-standing hostility of English-Americans to German-Americans, a hostility engendered by cultural conflicts over such issues as public education, Sabbatarianism, and suffrage. See also William Parsons, *The Pennsylvania Dutch: A Persistent Minority* (1976).

Theodore C. Blegen's scholarly, *Norwegian Migration to America* (1931, reprinted 1969), and Carlton Qualey's, *Norwegian Settlement in the United States* (1938, reprinted 1970), provide an excellent introduction to Norwegian-American history. The comprehensive study of the Swedes in colonial America is Amandus Johnson, *The Swedish Settlement on the Delaware* (2 volumes, 1911, reprinted 1970). For the later periods, see Florence Edith Janson, *The Background of Swedish Immigration, 1840-1930* (1931, reprinted 1969), a superb study of the complex motivation in emigration, and Sture Lindmark, *Swedish-America 1914-1932* (1971), which emphasizes Swedish-American efforts to maintain ethnic life and institutions in twentieth-century America. For material on the Danes, see Kristian Hvidt's scholarly, *Flight to America: The Social Background of 300,000 Danish Emigrants* (1975), and Noel J. Choresman, **Ethnic Influence on Urban Groups: The Danish Americans* (1966, reprinted 1975), with information on family life, community structure, and economic activity in America. On the Finns, see William A. Hoglund, *Finnish Immigrants in America* (1960), and John Wargelin, *The Americanization of the Finns* (1924, reprinted 1972).

A brief statistical study by Francis M. Rogers, *Americans of Portuguese Descent: A Lesson in Differentiation* (1974), analyzes the impact of factors such as region of origin, time of immigration, and political affiliation on different waves of Portuguese immigrants. Also of interest on this little studied group is an older study of the problems of assimilation, Donald Taft, *Two Portuguese Communities in New England* (1923, reprinted 1969). Two older works on Greek-Americans, Henry P. Fairchild, *Greek Immigration to the United States* (1911), and J. P. Xenides, *The Greeks in America* (1922) contain useful information, but the definitive history of Greek America is Theodore Saloutos, *The Greeks in the United States* (1963). For the Armenians, see Malcolm H. Vartan, *The Armenians in America* (1919), and Aram Yeretzian, *A History of Armenian Immigration to America with Special Reference to Los Angeles* (1923, reprinted 1974).

For the story of Arabic speaking communities, see Philip K. Hitti *The Syrians in America* (1924); Habeeb Katibah, *Arabic-speaking Americans* (1946) and *The Story of Lebanon and Its Emigrants* (1968). The past decade has seen a surge of new writing on the Arab-American communities. See the two very useful collections, **Arabic Speaking Communities in American Cities* (1974), edited by Barbara C. Aswad, which includes studies of Christian and Moslem communities in Michigan, bilingual Arabic children, and occupational patterns, as well as a good bibliography; and *Arab Americans: Studies in Assimilation* (1969), edited by Elaine Hagopian and Ann Padan, which includes studies on Arab nationalism, community institutions, and the changing roles of women.

Two useful older works on Polish-Americans are Paul Fox, *The Poles in America* (1922, reprinted 1970) and W. I. Thomas and F. Znaniecki, *The Polish Peasant in Europe and America* (2 volumes, 1927; other editions available). The latter is a classic sociological study based mainly upon letters written by Poles and Polish-Americans during the peak immigration years of the early twentieth century. The study emphasizes the disorganization of personal and community life that sometimes resulted from immigration. For more recent histories see two books by Joseph Wytrwal, *America's Polish Heritage: A Social History of the Poles in America* (1961), especially good on institutions such as the Polish National Alliance and the Polish Roman Catholic Union of America, and *The Poles in America* (1969). The most recent general survey is the excellent **Polish Americans: Status and Competition in an Ethnic Community* (1976), by Helen Znaniecki Lopata. Many special studies have been written by the father of Polish-American historiography, Miecislaus Haiman, including *The Polish Past in America 1608-1895* (1975) and *Poles in New York in the 17th and 18th Centuries* (1938).

For information on other Central and Eastern European immigrant communities, see Wasyl Halich, *Ukrainians in the United States* (1937, reprinted 1970); Thomas Capek, *The Czechs in America* (1928, reprinted 1969); Emil Lengyel, *Americans from Hungary* (1948, reprinted 1975); Gerald G. Govorchin, *Americans from Yugoslavia* (1961); George J. Prpic, *Croatian Immigrants in America* (1971); Jerome Davis, *The Russian Immigrant* (1929, reprinted 1969); Maruta Karklis, Liga Streips, and Laimonis Streips, *The Latvians in America, 1640-1973* (1974); and Emily Balch, *Our Slavic Fellow Citizens* (1910, reprinted 1969).

The most useful recent synthesis of American Jewish history is Henry Feingold, **Zion in America: The Jewish Experience from Colonial Times to the Present* (1974). Among the earlier histories of value are Oscar Handlin, *Adventure in Freedom: Three Hundred Years of Jewish Life in America* (1954, reprinted 1971), and Nathan Glazer, **American Judaism* (1957, revised edition 1972), which stresses the impact of successive waves of immigration on religious life and thought. For an introductory sociology of the contemporary Jewish community, including material on education, family structure, institutional life, and ethnic identity, see Marshall Sklare, **America's Jews* (1971). Special characteristics of Jewish assimilation and acculturation are explored with insight and sophistication in C. Bezalel Sherman, **The Jew Within American Society: A Study in Ethnic Individuality* (1965), and Joseph Blau, *Judaism in America: from Curiosity to Third Faith* (1976). Among the excellent studies of particular periods and topics are Jacob R. Marcus' three-volume, *The Colonial American Jew: 1492-1776* (1970); Bertram Korn, *American Jewry and the Civil War* (1951); Irving Howe,* *World of Our Fathers* (1976), on the early twentieth century Eastern European immigration; and Melvin Urofsky, **American Zionism from Herzl to the Holocaust* (1975).

The classic introduction to Italian immigration throughout the Western Hemisphere is Robert Foerster, *Italian Emigration of Our Times* (1919, reprinted 1969). For a wealth of information on population, occupation, housing, health, education, and social welfare among

Italian immigrants in the United States in the early twentieth century, see John Horace Mariano, *The Italian Contribution to American Democracy* (1922, reprinted 1975), an early antirestrictionist study. Among the most useful of the many recent works on the Italian-American experience are Joseph Lopreato, **Italian Americans* (1970), which includes material on the Old World background, acculturation, education, and economic mobility, and Alexander DeConde, *Half Bitter, Half Sweet: An Excursion into Italian-American History* (1971). Two useful collections are Wayne Moquin, *Documentary History of Italian-Americans* (1974) and the volume of scholarly essays edited by S. M. Tomasi and M. H. Engel, **The Italian Experience in the United States* (1971). For a lively account of three generations of South Italian mores, see Richard Gambino, **Blood of My Blood* (1974).

C. ASIAN AND WESTERN HEMISPHERE IMMIGRANT COMMUNITIES

An early account of Chinese immigration which still has much valuable information is Mary R. Coolidge, *Chinese Immigration* (1909, reprinted 1969). For a lively, recent historical survey, see Betty Lee Sung, *Mountain of Gold* (1967), reprinted in a paperback edition as *The Story of the Chinese in America* (1971). For a sociological treatment of the contemporary Chinese community, see Rose Hum Lee, *The Chinese in the United States of America* (1960). In *Longtime Californ': A Documentary Study of an American Chinatown* (1975) edited by Victor G. and Brett de Barry Nee, a cross section of Chinese-Americans describe their hardships and achievements. The myth that Chinese-Americans have been universally successful in America is examined and shattered in Dean Lan's provocative study, *Prestige with Limitations: Realities of the Chinese-American Elite* (1976).

Yamato Ichihashi's early defense of Japanese immigrants, *Japanese in the United States*, (1932, reprinted 1969) is still valuable. For more recent treatments of the history and sociology of the Japanese-American community, see Harry Kitano, **Japanese Americans: The Evolution of a Subculture* (1969), and William Petersen, **Japanese Americans: Oppression and Success* (1971). Hilary Conroy and T. Scott Miyakawa have assembled an excellent collection of original scholarly essays, including material on education, Americanization, and economic life, in **East Across the Pacific: Historical and Sociological Studies of Japanese Assimilation and Immigration* (1972). Bill Hosokawa's study of second generation Japanese Americans, **Nisei: The Quiet Americans* (1969) emphasizes the impact of the relocation camp experience of World War II on the American born generation.

Literature on other Asian immigrant groups in the United States is scant. On the Filipinos, see Bruno Lasker, *Filipino Immigration to Continental United States and to Hawaii* (1931, reprinted 1969), and B. T. Catapusan, *The Filipino Social Adjustment in the United States* (1940, reprinted 1972). On the Koreans, see Hyung-Chan Kim, *The Koreans in America* (1974). Gail Kelly, *From Vietnam to America: Chronicle of the Vietnamese Immigration to the United States* (1977) is an excellent account of the immigration and resettlement of refugees from Vietnam. Based on government documents and extensive interviews with camp officials and refugees, Kelly's work highlights the contrast between Vietnamese needs and objectives and the American resettlement program, which was based on American political and economic imperatives.

For a general account of Canadian immigration, see Marcus Lee Hansen, *The Mingling of the Canadian and American Peoples* (1940, reprinted 1970). Twentieth century West Indian immigration is described by Ira de A. Reid in *The Negro Immigrant: His Background Characteristics and Social Adjustment, 1899-1937* (1939, reprinted 1969). For another aspect of black immigration from the Caribbean, see Glenn Hendricks, *The Dominican Diaspora: From the Dominican Republic to New York City, Villagers in Transition* (1974). The extensive literature on the midtwentieth century Puerto Rican migration includes Elena Padilla's anthropological study, *Up From Puerto Rico* (1958); Dan Wakefield's journalistic portrait of East Harlem, *Island in the City* (1959, reprinted 1975); Clarence Senior's plea for understanding, *The Puerto Ricans: Strangers—Then Neighbors* (1961, new edition 1965), which stresses the economic and educational progress being made by Puerto Rican immigrants; and Joseph P. Fitzpatrick's excellent sociological survey *Puerto Rican Americans: The Meaning of Migration to the Mainland* (1971), which covers education, family life, religion, health, and recent social and political movements within the community.

The first major survey of Mexican American history, the journalistic work of Carey McWilliams, *North from Mexico: The Spanish Speaking People in the United States* (1948) is a useful introduction. Two older works by Manuel Gamio, *Mexican Immigration to the United States* (1930, reprinted 1969) and *The Mexican Immigrant, His Life Story* (1931, reprinted 1969) provide information about Mexican immigration in the early decades of the twentieth century, including valuable first person accounts of the experiences of Mexican-American immigrants. An excellent historical survey incorporating recent scholarship is Rodolfo Acuna, *Occupied America: The Chicano Struggle for Liberation* (1972). For a contemporary sociological overview, especially good on the impact of urbanization and the problems of economic mobility, see Ellwyn Stoddard *Mexican Americans* (1973). Donald Meinig, *Southwest:*

Three Peoples in Geographical Change, 1600-1970 (1971) is a unique study of the interaction between peoples and an environment.

IV. Special Studies

A. IMMIGRATION AND IMMIGRANT GROUPS

For information on world migration patterns, consult Ragnar Numelin, *The Wandering Spirit: A Study of Human Migration* (1937) and Franklin D. Scott's anthology **World Migration in Modern Times* (1968). Two important works on immigrants who left the United States to return to their homelands are Theodore Saloutos' groundbreaking *They Remember America: The Story of Greek-American Repatriates* (1956) and Betty Boyd Caroli, *Italian Repatriation from the United States, 1900-1914* (1974). Caroli demonstrates that life in America profoundly changed those who experienced it even for a short period and suggests the importance of the American "safety valve" for Italy's excess population. For communication between immigrants who remained in America and those they left behind, see H. Arnold Barton, editor, *Letters From the Promised Land: Swedes in America, 1840-1914* (1975) and Theodore Blegen, *Land of Their Choice: The Immigrants Write Home* (1955).

The historical and sociological studies of ethnic communities at particular times or locations are too numerous to list. Among these, are such excellent works as Moses Rischin, **The Promised City: New York's Jews, 1870-1914* (1962); Selig Adler and Thomas Connelly, *From Ararat to Suburbia: The History of the Jewish Community of Buffalo* (1960); Frederick Bohme, *A History of the Italians in New Mexico* (1975); Humbert Nelli, **The Italians in Chicago, 1880-1930: A Study in Ethnic Mobility* (1973); Thomas Kessner, **The Golden Door: Italian and Jewish Immigrant Mobility in New York City, 1880-1915* (1977); Evans Wood, *Hamtramck, Then and Now* (1955), and Dennis Clark, *The Irish in Philadelphia: Ten Generations of Urban Experience* (1974). Of particular interest are a number of recent studies comparing the experiences of two or more ethnic groups. Among these are H. Brett Melendy, **The Oriental Americans* (1972); Josef J. Barton, *Peasants and Strangers: Italians, Rumanians, and Slovaks in an American City, 1890-1950* (1975), an example of the new quantitative social history dealing with Cleveland; Thomas Archdeacon, *New York City, 1664-1710: Conquest and Change* (1976), an analysis of how the English and the French Huguenots took social and political control of the city away from the Dutch; Eleanor C. Nordyke, *The Peopling of Hawaii* (1977); Elizabeth

A. H. John, *Storms Brewed in Other Men's Worlds: The Confrontation of Indians, Spanish, and French in the Southwest 1540-1795* (1975); and the collection edited by Allen F. Davis and Mark H. Haller, *The Peoples of Philadelphia: A History of Ethnic Groups and Lower Class Life, 1790-1940* (1973).

B. IMMIGRANT WOMEN, YOUTH, AND THE FAMILY

A rising interest in the history of women, youth, and the family is only beginning to be reflected in the literature on ethnic America. Many of the best materials on immigrant women are older works, usually written by women, such as Bessie Pebotsky, *The Slavic Immigrant Woman* (1925, reprinted 1971); Louise C. Odencrantz, *Italian Women in Industry* (1919); Caroline Manning, *The Immigrant Woman and Her Job* (1930, reprinted 1970); Elizabeth Beadsley Butler, *Woman and the Trades: Pittsburgh, 1907-1908* (1909, reprinted 1969); Grace Abbott, *The Immigrant and the Community* (1917, reprinted 1971), which includes material on health care, work, and the immigrant journey; and Sophonisba Breckinridge, *New Homes for Old* (1920, reprinted 1971), excellent on housework, child care, and family relations in the early part of the twentieth century. For studies of mid-twentieth century white, working class women, many of them second and third generation ethnics, see Lee Rainwater, Richard Coleman, and Gerald Handel, *Workingman's Wife* (1959); Mirra Komarovsky, *Blue-Collar Marriage* (1964); and Nancy Seifer, *Absent From the Majority: Working Class Women in America* (1973), which discusses the impact of the women's movement, the "new ethnicity," and other social and political changes of the late 1960's and early 1970's.

There is no single definitive history of immigrant women, but valuable material, which includes accounts of physicians, labor leaders, and other outstanding women of the past, can be found in Cecyle Neidle, *America's Immigrant Women* (1975); Linda Grant de Pauw, *Four Traditions: Women of New York During the American Revolution* (1974), about Iroquois, Afro-American, Dutch, and English women in the eighteenth century; Rosalyn Baxandall, Linda Gordon, and Susan Reverby, *America's Working Women: A Documentary History* (1976), a collection of excerpts from diaries, songs, and other documents; Charlotte Baum, et. al., *The Jewish Woman in America* (1976); and Barbara M. Wertheimer, *We Were There: The Story of Working Women* (1977).

Two particularly valuable works on the relationship between the feminist movement and contemporary ethnic women are Barbara Peters and Victoria Samuels, *Dialogue on Diversity: A New Agenda for*

Women (1976) and Elizabeth Koltun, editor, **The Jewish Woman: New Perspectives* (1976).

For a moving volume of oral history in which immigrant women describe the circumstances of their coming to America, their family lives, their work, and their feelings about themselves, see Sydelle Kramer and Jenny Masur, *Jewish Grandmothers* (1976). Another worthwhile oral history is Nancy Seifer, *Nobody Speaks for Me* (1976), in which black, Hispanic, and European ethnic women activists of the 1970's describe their personal and community lives. For information on new research directions and materials, see Maxine Seller, "Beyond the Stereotype: A New Look at the Immigrant Woman, 1880-1924," *Journal of Ethnic Studies,* Vol. 3 (Spring 1975) and Betty Boyd Caroli, "Italian Women in America: Sources for Study," *Italian Americana,* Vol. 2, #2 (Spring 1976).

Materials on immigrant and ethnic children can be culled from the recent three-volume work edited by Robert Bremner, *Children and Youth in America: A Documentary History* (1970, 1971, 1974); from the writings of Jane Addams, especially **The Spirit of Youth and the City Streets* (1909, reprinted 1972); and Grace Abbott's two-volume documentary collection, *The Child and the State* (1938, reprinted 1968), which contains valuable materials on child labor. For more recent material, see Francesco Cordasco and Eugene Bucchioni, *The Puerto Rican Community and Its Children* (1972), and Michael Novak's collection of essays, **Growing Up Slavic* (1975).

Arthur Calhoun's classic study, *A Social History of the American Family from Colonial Times to the Present* (3 volumes, 1917-1919, reprinted 1945) contains older relevant information on ethnic families. The best collection of recent scholarship on this topic is Charles H. Mindel and Robert W. Habenstein, **Ethnic Families in America: Patterns and Variations* (1976), with articles on the changing family structures of fifteen groups, including blacks and Native Americans as well as European and Hispanic peoples. For a useful overview of inter-marriage, see Milton L. Barron, **The Blending Americans* (1972).

C. EDUCATION AND AMERICANIZATION

For ethnic education in colonial America, see William Kilpatrick, *The Dutch Schools of New Netherland and Colonial New York* (1912, reprinted 1969) and James Pyle Wickersham, *A History of Education in Pennsylvania* (1885, reprinted 1969), which contains information on the education of the Germans. The quarrel between the Catholic Church and the Public School Society in mid-nineteenth century New York, as well as controversies surrounding the education of twentieth century ethnic communities, are ably described in Diane Ravitch, **The*

Great School Wars: New York City, 1805-1973: A History of the Public Schools as Battlefields of Social Change (1974). Revisionist interpretations that challenge the traditional view of public schools as promoters of immigrants' socioeconomic mobility are Michael Katz, *The Irony of Early School Reform: Educational Innovation in Mid-Nineteenth Century Massachusetts* (1968), and Colin Greer's provocative *The Great School Legend: A Revisionist Interpretation of American Public Education* (1973).

Among the many valuable studies of the educational experiences and problems of particular immigrant communities are Leonard Covello's classic study, *The Social Background of the Italo-American School Child* (1967), which includes material on South Italian family structure, and suggestions for an American school curriculum more responsive to ethnic communities; *Puerto Ricans and Educational Opportunity* (1972), an original Arno Pess anthology of reports and other documents on the educational problems of Puerto Rican children in the public schools; Alfred Castaneda, Manuel Ramirez III, Carlos E. Cortes, and Mario Barrera, editors, *Mexican Americans and Educational Change* (1974), a collection of papers focusing on the politics of educational change and on bicultural and bilingual education for Mexican-American children. See also Thomas P. Carter, *Mexican Americans in School: A History of Educational Neglect* (1970).

The literature on the education and Americanization of Europeans in the early twentieth century is extensive. For viewpoints of experts of the period, see Leonard Ayres, *Laggards in Our Schools* (1907), a national survey of immigrant "retardation" in public schools; Frank Thompson, *The Schooling of the Immigrant* (1920, reprinted 1971); and William Sharlip and Albert Owens, *Adult Immigrant Education* (1928), with a special chapter on the education of immigrant women. Recent accounts of immigrant education in the late nineteenth and early twentieth century can be found in Lawrence A. Cremin, *The Transformation of the School: Progressivism in American Education, 1876-1957* (1961); David Tyack, *The One Best System: A History of American Urban Education* (1974); Edward Hartmann, *The Movement to Americanize the Immigrant* (1948); John Bodnar, "Materialism and Morality: Slavic-American Immigrants and Education, 1890-1940," *Journal of Ethnic Studies*, Vol. 3 (Winter 1976); and Mark Krug, *The Melting of the Ethnics: Education of the Immigrants, 1880-1914* (1976). Two relevant recent studies are Gerd Korman, *Industrialization, Immigrants, and Americanizers: The View from Milwaukee, 1866-1921* (1967), which examines the role of business interests in Americanization and Robert Carlson, *The Quest for Conformity: Americanization Through Education* (1975), a concise survey of Americanization theory and practice from the colonial period through the 1960's with a good bibliographical essay.

The most stimulating work on education, broadly defined, within ethnic communities themselves is Joshua Fishman and Vladimir Nahirny, *Language Loyalty in the United States* (1966), a groundbreaking work which examines ethnic schools, newspapers, magazines, radio, and television as means of perpetuating ethnic languages and cultural traditions. For additional material on ethnic schools, see James A. Burns, *The Growth and Development of the Catholic School System in the United States* (1912, reprinted 1969); Andrew Greeley, William McCready and Kathleen McCourt, *Catholic Schools in a Declining Church* (1976), which emphasizes continuing Catholic commitment to the parochial school system; James W. Sanders, *The Education of an Urban Minority: Catholics in Chicago, 1833-1965* (1977); and Lloyd Gartner, **Jewish Education in the United States* (1970). For a view of a public school system with strong ethnic components, see Peter Schrag, *Village School Downtown: Boston's Schools, Boston's Politics* (1967).

D. THE IMMIGRANT IN THE CITY: LIVING CONDITIONS, SOCIAL PROBLEMS, ECONOMIC MOBILITY

The recent interest in urban history has produced many studies of immigrant life in the city, such as Robert Ernst, *Immigrant Life in New York City, 1825-1863* (1965); Stanley Lieberson, *Ethnic Patterns in American Cities* (1962), on immigrant neighborhoods; and David Ward's brief but important *Cities and Immigrants* (1971), which analyzes the relationships between ethnic neighborhoods, and changing economic conditions and transportation networks. For sociological studies of lower class and working class Italian neighborhoods, see William Whyte, **Street Corner Society: The Social Structure of an Italian Slum* (1943, revised edition 1955) and Herbert Gans, **The Urban Villagers: Group and Class Life of Italian Americans* (1962). See also Gerald D. Suttles' stimulating study, **The Social Order of the Slum: Ethnicity and Territory in the Inner City* (1968).

For glimpses into the social pathology of urban ethnic life, see Herbert Asbury, **The Gangs of New York* (1927, revised edition 1971), a social history of New York City's underworld in the nineteenth century and Joseph L. Albini, **The American Mafia: Genesis of a Legend* (1971). For sympathetic accounts of immigrants' difficulties in trying to find justice within the American legal system, see Kate Claghorn, *The Immigrant's Day in Court* (1923, reprinted 1969), and *The Mexican American and the Law* (1974), edited by Carlos E. Cortes, an anthology which includes case histories, petitions, and other documents. On health and safety problems, see Michael Davis, *Immigrant Health and the Community* (1921, reprinted 1971); Crystal Eastman, *Work Accidents and the Law* (1910, reprinted 1969); and Beatrice Bishop Berle, *Eighty*

Puerto Rican Families in New York City: Health and Disease Studied in Context (1958, reprinted 1975), a study suggesting that illness was related to the anxiety and frustration caused by "the discrepancy between an individual's aspirations and the limited employment opportunities open to him." *Italians in the City: Health and Related Social Problems* (1975), edited by Francesco Cordasco, contains special reports on the health of Italian women and the growth rates of Italian children in New York City in the early twentieth century. For a stimulating feminist perspective linking nativism with the response to immigrant health problems in the early twentieth century, see Barbara Ehrenreich and Deirdre English, *Complaints and Disorders: The Sexual Politics of Sickness* (1973). The authors attribute the success of the movement for the dissemination of birth control information in urban slums to nativist fear of immigrant fertility and point out that public health measures were adopted because the middle class feared "contamination" from the ethnic ghettos. On mental health and ethnicity, see Rita Stein, *Disturbed Youth and Ethnic Family Patterns* (1972).

Some of the best sources on social welfare are the works of the Progressive reformers, such as Jacob Riis, **How the Other Half Lives* (1890 and numerous reprints) and *The Battle With the Slums* (1902, reprinted 1969); John Spargo, **The Bitter Cry of the Children* (1908, reprinted 1969); Lillian Wald, **The House on Henry Street* (1915, reprinted 1969); and Jane Addams, **Twenty Years at Hull-House* (1910, reprinted 1966). For recent interpretations of the motives and achievements of Progressive reformers, see Paul McBride, *Culture Clash: Immigrants and Reformers, 1880-1920* (1975) and Allen F. Davis, **Spearheads for Reform: The Social Settlements and the Progressive Movement, 1890-1914* (1967). The most useful general history of nineteenth and twentieth century social welfare policy and attitudes is Robert Bremner, **From the Depths: the Discovery of Poverty in the United States* (1956).

Using census data, tax records, and other quantitative sources, recent historians have explored problems of socioeconomic mobility. Richard Hutchinson, *Immigrants and Their Children, 1850-1950* (1956, new edition 1976) analyzes the geographic and occupational patterns and distribution of major European ethnic populations throughout the nation over several generations. For mobility studies of particular cities, see Stephan Thernstrom, **Poverty and Progress: Social Mobility in a Nineteenth Century City* (1964), on the economic mobility of Irish laborers and their sons in Newberryport, Massachusetts, and **The Other Bostonians: Poverty and Progress in the American Metropolis, 1880-1970* (1973), comparing the mobility of major European communities in Boston. For similar studies of other cities, see

Nineteenth Century Cities: Essays in the New Urban History (1969), edited by Stephan Thernstrom and Richard Sennett.

E. INSIDE ETHNIC AMERICA: COMMUNITY LIFE, POLITICS, THE NEW ETHNICITY

One of the best descriptions of the various organizations and institutions in the immigrant communities, stressing their importance as agents of education and Americanization, is John Daniels, *America Via the Neighborhood* (1920, reprinted 1971), which includes a listing of many of the major ethnic organizations of the early twentieth century. Also useful are W. Lloyd Warner and Leo Srole, *The Social Systems of American Ethnic Groups* (1945, reprinted 1976) and Gerald Suttles, *The Social Construction of Communities* (1972). There are a number of useful studies of specific institutions, such as Odd Sverre Lovoll's study of Norwegian fraternal orders, *A Folk Epic: the Bygdelag in America* (1975); Borris Bogen, *Jewish Philanthropy: An Exposition of the Principles and Methods in Jewish Social Service in the United States* (1917, reprinted 1969); and Philip Gleason's history of the Central-Verein, a national federation of German-American Catholic Societies, *The Conservative Reformers: German-American Catholics and the Social Order* (1968). Victor Greene's *For God and Country: The Rise of Polish and Lithuanian Ethnic Consciousness in America, 1861-1910* (1975) explores the role of factionalism among the parish leadership in stimulating awareness of ethnic identity in the Polish and Lithuanian communities.

Among the many studies dealing with the role of religion in ethnic communities are William Mulder's account of the Norwegian, Swedish, and Danish Mormon immigrants, *Homeward to Zion: The Mormon Migration from Scandinavia* (1957) and George Stephenson, *The Religious Aspects of Swedish Immigration* (1932, reprinted 1969). The effort of Protestant missions to "uplift" the nineteenth century urban poor, many of whom were Catholic immigrants, is examined in Caroll Smith Rosenberg, *Religion and the Rise of the American City: The New York City Mission Movement, 1812-1870* (1971). The religious history of the same period from the Catholic immigrant point of view is described by Jay P. Dolan in *The Immigrant Church: New York's Irish and German Catholics, 1815-1865* (1975), stressing the rise of the Church as a tightly organized socially conservative bastion against Protestant America. Aaron Abell, *American Catholicism and Social Action: A Search for Social Justice, 1865-1950* (1960) emphasizes the material and educational assistance the Church offered the immigrant poor, while Richard M. Linkh, *American Catholicism and European Immigrants, 1900-1924* (1975) argues that the Church offered little aid to Southeastern

European immigrants before World War I and was halfhearted in its efforts to promote Americanization.

While studies of individual ethnic presses, such as Mordecai Soltes, *The Yiddish Press: An Americanizing Agency* (1925, reprinted 1969) and Carl Wittke, *The German-Language Press in America* (1953, reprinted 1972), can be located through specialized bibliographies, the best single comprehensive source on foreign language newspapers is Robert E. Park, *The Immigrant Press and Its Control* (1922, reprinted 1971). The author's concern about the loyalty of the ethnic press during World War I is less interesting than the valuable information he provides about the origins and circulation of ethnic newspapers and his extensive quotations of news, editorials, poetry, humor, and advertisements from ethnic papers. There is no general work on ethnic theatre, but information on this subject can be found in David Lifson, *The Yiddish Theater in America* (1965), which includes photographs; Henriette Naeseth, *The Swedish Theatre of Chicago 1868-1950* (1951), which covers other aspects of Swedish cultural life as well; and Maxine Seller, "Antonietta Pisanelli Alessandro and the Italian Theatre of San Francisco," *Educational Theatre Journal*, Vol. 28, #2 (May 1976); and J. Rosenberg, "The Emerging Chicano Drama," *Bulletin of the Cross Cultural Southwest Ethnic Study Center*, Vol. 3, #3 (September 1976).

Serious critical studies of immigrant and ethnic literature are still scarce, but the following works provide an introduction to this literature: Dorothy Burton Skardal, *The Divided Heart* (1974), a social history of Scandinavian-American life as reflected in its immigrant literature; Nona Balakian, *The Armenian-American Writer: A New Accent in American Fiction* (1958); Rose Basile Green, *The Italian-American Novel: A Document of the Interaction of Two Cultures* (1974); and Allen Guttman, *The Jewish Writer in America: Assimilation and the Crisis of Identity* (1971). For a vivid contemporary account of Yiddish literature and theatre, see Hutchins Hapgood, **The Spirit of the Ghetto* (1902, reprinted 1966 and 1976).

Ivan Light's **Ethnic Enterprise in America* (1972) compares the business activities of Chinese, Japanese, and blacks. Since the overwhelming majority of immigrants were members of the working class, there is a rich literature on labor activities and immigrant radicalism. See Wayne G. Broehl, Jr., *The Molly Maguires* (1964) on Irish labor violence in the coal mines of Pennsylvania; Victor Greene, *The Slavic Community on Strike: Immigrant Labor in Pennsylvania Anthracite* (1968); Malech Epstein's two-volume, *Jewish Labor in the United States: 1882-1952* (1950, revised edition 1969); and Edwin Fenton, *Immigrants and Unions, A Case Study: Italians and American Labor* (1975), a richly documented study demonstrating that when they were welcomed by the leadership, and when economic conditions were particularly favorable, Italians participated enthusiastically in unions and found this participation an important means of Americanization.

F. ETHNICS AND AMERICANS: THE POLITICS OF INTER-GROUP RELATIONS

In recent years historians have acknowledged that ethnicity as well as class affects voter allegiance. The political behavior of ethnic Americans has been explored in studies such as Samuel Lubell's pioneering *The Future of American Politics* (1952); John Allswang, *A House for all People: Chicago's Ethnic Groups and Their Politics, 1890-1936* (1971); and Thomas Pavlak, *Ethnic Identification and Political Behavior* (1976). Alex Gottfried's *Boss Cermak of Chicago: A Study of Political Leadership* (1962) examines the rise of an immigrant political boss who capitalized on his ethnic power base. In *Senator Robert F. Wagner and the Rise of Urban Liberalism* (1968), J. Joseph Huthmacher shows ethnic communities as agents of reform. The impact of ethnic communities on foreign policy in the twentieth century is traced in Louis Gerson, *The Hyphenate in Recent American Politics and Diplomacy* (1964) and in Joseph P. O'Grady, *The Immigrants' Influence on Wilson's Peace Policies* (1967), which suggests that on this issue the impact of immigrant lobbies was not a decisive one.

In *The White Ethnic Movement and Ethnic Politics* (1973), Perry Weed explores the effort of the major political parties to gain the white ethnic vote in the decades following World War II. Other works on the politics and other aspects of the "new ethnicity" of the 1960's and 1970's are Peter Schrag, *The Forgotten Americans* (1969); Michael Novak's controversial and stimulating *The Rise of the Unmeltable Ethnics* (1971); and Richard Krickus, *Pursuing the American Dream: White Ethnics and the New Populism* (1976), which explores neighborhood and school conflicts between white ethnics and blacks. Two excellent collections dealing with issues such as education, discrimination, urban renewal, affirmative action, employment, and the complex relationships between white ethnics, blacks, and WASPS are Murray Friedman, *Overcoming Middle Class Rage* (1971) and Michael Wenk, S. M. Tomasi, and Geno Baroni, *Pieces of a Dream: The Ethnic Worker's Crisis with America* (1972).

There are many studies of discrimination against individual ethnic communities, such as Chang-Tsu Wu's edited volume, *Chink! Anti-Chinese Prejudice in America* (1972) and Roger Daniels, *Concentration Camps USA: Japanese Americans and World War II* (1971). The best general histories of nativism, its intellectual and emotional origins, and its political consequences, are Ray Billington, *The Protestant Crusade,*

1800-1860 (1964) and John Higham, **Strangers in the Land: Patterns of American Nativism, 1860-1925* (1955), which has an excellent and comprehensive treatment of the background of the immigration restriction of the 1920's. For further insight into anti-immigrant feeling, see Robert K. Murray, **Red Scare: A Study in National Hysteria, 1919-1920* (1955) and Thomas Corran, *Xenophobia and Immigration, 1820-1952* (1975), which emphasizes Anglo-Saxon fear of being overwhelmed by other cultures.

For material on American immigration policy since the National Origins Quota Act of 1924, see Robert A. Divine, *American Immigration Policy, 1924-1952* (1957, reprinted 1972) and Marion T. Bennett, *American Immigration Policies, a History* (1963). America's failure to save significant numbers of European Jews from Nazi extermination by admitting them into the country has been chronicled and linked to anti-Semitism, indifference, and the economic depression of the 1930's in Henry Feingold, *The Politics of Rescue: The Roosevelt Administration and the Holocaust, 1938-1945* (1970) and Arthur Morse, **While Six Million Died* (1968). For the impact of post World War II changes in immigration laws, see D. S. North and W. G. Weissert, *Immigrants and the American Labor Market* (1973), which includes a discussion of the "brain drain," and S. M. Tomasi and C. B. Keely, **Whom Have We Welcomed?* (1975), which summarizes current policy, examines the question of illegal aliens, and considers proposed legislative and administrative changes.

V. Literary Sources

Though some immigrant writers undoubtedly exaggerated their hardships, their successes, or both, ethnic autobiographies, novels, short stories, poems, and plays provide valuable source material for the student of ethnic life. The following are a representative sampling of this vast literature.

A. IMMIGRANT AUTOBIOGRAPHIES

Short selections from autobiographies and memoirs can be found in collections such as Thomas C. Wheeler, **The Immigrant Experience: the Anguish of Becoming American* (1971); Cecyle S. Neidle, *The New Americans* (1967); and Oscar Handlin, *Children of the Uprooted* (1966), which deals with the second, or "marginal," generation. The National Council of Jewish Women in Pittsburgh has assembled a collective memoir based on oral histories of immigrant Jews in that city, *By Myself I'm a Book* (1972).

Among the many fascinating individual memoirs are the following: *Woman at Work* (1951, reprinted 1973), by Mary Anderson; *The Open Door* (1968), by Laurenda Andrade, a high school teacher of Portuguese who immigrated from the Azores; *Laughing in the Jungle* (1932, reprinted 1969), by Louis Adamic, who immigrated from Yugoslavia at the age of fourteen and found that survival in the United States depended upon brute strength and a sense of humor; *The Promised Land* (1912), by Mary Antin, a Russian Jew whose public school experience launched her career as a writer; *Son of Italy* (1924, reprinted 1975), by the poet Pascal D'Angelo; *The Americanization of Edward Bok: the Autobiography of a Dutch Boy Fifty Years After* (1921, reprinted 1972), by Edward Bok; *Living My Life* (1931, reprinted 1970), a two-volume memoir by the Russian-Jewish anarchist and feminist Emma Goldman; *Rosa: The Life of an Italian Immigrant* (1970) as told to Marie Hall Ets; *The Autobiography of Mother Jones* (1925, reprinted 1969), by Mary Harris Jones, Irish born labor organizer; *Mount Allegro* (1942, reprinted 1972) humorously written boyhood memories of Italian-American author Jerre Mangione; *The Soul of an Immigrant* (1928, reprinted 1969), by Italian born minister and social worker Constantine Panunzio; *The Woman Warrior* (1976), Americanization and intergeneration conflict as seen by second generation Chinese-American Maxine Hong Kingston; *Upstream* (1922) by Jewish journalist Ludwig Lewisohn; *Down These Mean Streets* (1967), growing up Puerto Rican, by Thomas Piri; *From Immigrant to Inventor* (1924), by Serbian physicist Michael Pupin; *Bread Upon the Waters* (1945) by Rose Pesotta, Russian Jewish immigrant elected four times to the vice presidency of the International Ladies Garment Workers Union; *Caste and Outcast* (1923) by Dhan Gopal Mukerji; and *A Far Journey* (1914) by Syrian minister Abraham M. Ribhany.

B. ETHNIC NOVELS

The following ethnic novels, a small sampling of the genre, present insights into first, second, and sometimes third generation ethnic life. For portraits of Greek-American life, see Harry Mark Petrakis, *Lion at My Heart* (1959), *The Odyssey of Kostas Volakis* (1963), and *A Dream of Kings* (1966); Peter Sourian, *Miri* (1957), and Mary Vardoulakis, *Gold in the Streets* (1945), about migration from Crete to a Massachusetts mill town. For Polish-American life see John Alexander Abucewicz, *Fool's White* (1969), about an immigrant's daughter who decides to become a nun and Richard Bankowsky's tetrology on the rise and fall of an immigrant family in New Jersey, *The Glass Rose* (1958), *After Pentecost* (1961), *On a Dark Night* (1964), and *The Pale Criminal* (1967). For other

East European groups see Thomas Bell, *Out of This Furnace* (1941), about the sufferings of Slovakian immigrant workers in the steel mills of Pennsylvania; Michael Novak, *Naked I Leave* (1970), the story of an upwardly mobile third generation Slavic immigrant's encounter with majority America, and Louis Adamic, *Grandsons: A Story of American Lives* (1935), *Two Way Passage* (1941), and *What's Your Name* (1942).

Pedro Juan Soto's **Hot Land, Cold Season* (1961) is a novel about a Puerto Rican immigrant who returns to the island in search of his identity. Hazel Lin, *The Physician* (1951) is a Chinese-American novel, and Jose Yglesias, *A Wake in Ybor City* (1963) tells of Cubans in Florida. For Armenian life, see Richard Hagopian, *Faraway the Spring* (1952) and Marjorie Housepian *A Houseful of Love* (1957). For the German experience, see Hermann Hagedorn, *The Hyphenated Family* (1960) and Elsie Singmaster, *The Magic Mirror* (1934). Working class Irish Catholic life is depicted by James Farrell in *Studs Lonigan* (1935) and *Danny O'Neill* (1936), each the first of a series. On Irish-American life, see also Tom McHale, *Farragan's Retreat* (1971) and Flannery O'Connor, **Wise Blood* (1962). For Norwegian immigration there is an outstanding trilogy by O. E. Rölvaag, **Giants in the Earth* (1927), *Peder Victorious* (1929), and *Our Father's God* (1931).

The Italian and the Jewish experiences are captured in many excellent novels. Among the best of the Italian are Pietro Di Donato, **Christ in Concrete* (1939) and *Three Circles of Light* (1960); Mario Puzo, *The Fortunate Pilgrim* (1964); Garibaldi Lapolla, *The Grand Gennaro* (1935); John Fante, *Wait Until Spring, Bandini* (1938); and Rocco Fumento, *Tree of Dark Reflections* (1962). For Jewish life see Abraham Cahan, **The Rise of David Levinsky* (1917) and *Yekl, A Tale of the New York Ghetto* (1896); Michael Gold, **Jews Without Money* (1930); Henry Roth, **Call It Sleep* (1934); Charles Angoff's series of novels beginning with *In the Morning Light* (1952); and Anzia Yezierska's *Bread Givers* (1925). For views of the contemporary Jewish community, see the works of Saul Bellow, Bernard Malamud, Chaim Potok, and Meyer Levin.

C. POETRY, SHORT STORIES, PLAYS

For Jewish immigrant poetry, see the anthologies by Irving Howe and Eliezer Greenberg, *A Treasury of Yiddish Poetry* (1969) and Jehiel and Sarah Cooperman, *America in Yiddish Poetry* (1967); and Morris Rosenfeld's moving poems on life in the Jewish ghettos of Europe and America, *Songs from the Ghetto* (1898). For Italian-American proletarian immigrant poetry, see Vincent Ferrini, *No Smoke* (1941), *Blood of the Tenement* (1944), and *Injunction* (1943) and Arturo Giovanitti, *The Collected Poems of Arturo Giovanitti* (1962). The Americanization of the

Italian immigrant is described in Joseph Tuccio's volume of poems, *My Own People* (1943). For traditional Polish poems and folklore see *The Wayside Willow* (1945) and *The Polish Land* (1943), collected by Klub Polski. For Hungarian-American poetry see Leslie Konnyu, *Collected Poems* (1968).

Short stories portraying ethnic life, most of them by ethnic writers, can be found in anthologies such as Myron Simon, *Ethnic Writers in America* (1972) and Abe C. Ravitz, **The American Disinherited: A Profile in Fiction.* (1970). Stories about particular groups include Anzia Yezierska, *Hungry Hearts* (1920) and *Children of Loneliness: Stories of Immigrant Life in America* (1923), and Max Rosenfeld's collection *A Union for Shabbos: Stories of Jewish Life in America* (1967), on the East European Jewish experience; James T. Farrell, *Short Stories* (1946) and Leo Rich Ward, *Holding Up the Hills* (1941) on the Irish; Harry Mark Petrakis, *Pericles on Thirty-First Street* (1965) and *Waves of Night and Other Stories* (1969) on the Greeks; Susie Hoogasian-Villa, *One Hundred Armenian Tales and Their Folkloristic Relevance* (1966) and Richard Hagopian, *The Dove Brings Peace* (1944) on the Armenians; and Monica Krawcyzk, *If the Branch Blossoms and Other Stories* (1950) and Nelson Algren, *The Neon Wilderness* (1947) on the Poles. **The Chicanos: Mexican American Voices* (1971), edited by Ed Ludwig and James Santibanez, contains stories, poetry, and essays. See also *AIIIEEEEE! An Anthology of Asian-American Writers* (1974), edited by Frank Chin, J. P. Chan, L. F. Inada, and S. Wong.

Examples of Yiddish drama in English translation can be found in *Three Plays by David Pinski* (1918) and David Lifson, *Epic and Folk Plays of the Yiddish Theater* (1975). Many of the works of Eugene O'Neill, such as *Anna Christie* (1973) and *Long Day's Journey Into Night* (1956) reflect aspects of Irish-American life. Recent plays about American ethnic life are collected in Francis Griffith and Joseph Mersand, **Eight American Ethnic Plays* (1974).

VI. For Further Investigation

For further information on specific topics or groups, consult bibliographies such as Richard Kolin, *Bibliography of Ethnicity and Ethnic Groups* (1973); Franklin Scott, *The Peopling of America: Perspectives on Immigration* (1972); Wayne Miller, *A Comprehensive Bibliography for the Study of American Minorities* (1977), a comprehensive two-volume reference work, and by the same author, the more concise guide, *A Handbook for the Study of American Minorities* (1977); and the bibliographical volume published by the National Council for the Social Studies, William H. Cartwright and Richard L. Watson, Jr., *The Reinterpretation of American History and Culture* (1973), with separately authored chapters on sources for the study of Native Americans, blacks, Mexican-Americans, Asian-Americans, and European ethnic groups.

Among the many useful bibliographies on individual ethnic groups are J. W. Zurawski, *Polish-American History and Culture: A Classified Bibliography* (1975); William Wong Lum, *Asians in America: A Bibliography* (1969); Francesco Cordasco and Salvatore J. LaGumina, *Italians in the United States: A Bibliography of Reports, Texts, Critical Studies and Related Materials* (1972); Paul McBride, *The Italians in America: An Interdisciplinary Bibliography* (1976); Luis Nogales, *The Mexican American: A Selected and Annotated Bibliography* (1971); Leo Pap, *The Portuguese in the United States: A Bibliography* (1976); D. H. Tolzmann, *German Americana: A Bibliography* (1975); and Irene P. Norell, *Literature of the Filipino-American in the United States: A Selective and Annotated Bibliography* (1976). Materials on the education of immigrant children are listed in Francesco Cordasco, *Immigrant Children in American Schools: A Classified and Annotated Bibliography, with Selected Source Documents* (1976). For listings of literary works on ethnic life, consult Louis Kaplan and James T. Coole, *A Bibliography of American Autobiographies* (1961); Otis Coan and Richard G. Lillard, *America in Fiction* (1967); Babett F. Inglehart and Anthony Mangione, *The Image of Pluralism in American Literature: The American Experience of European Ethnic Groups* (1974); and Daniel Weinberg, "Viewing the Immigrant Experience in America Through Fiction and Autobiography—With a Select Bibliography," *The History Teacher*, Vol. IX, #3, (May 1976), pp. 409-432.

Scholarly articles about various aspects of ethnicity and the experience of ethnic groups can be found in the academic journals of such disciplines as history, sociology, anthropology, and education as well as in various interdisciplinary periodicals. Some of the most useful specialized publications are *International Migration Review, Journal of Ethnic Studies, Ethnicity, American Jewish Historical Quarterly, Jewish Social Studies, Norwegian-American Studies, Polish-American Studies, Italian Americana, American-Hungarian Review, Amerasia Journal, Swedish Pioneer Historical Quarterly*, and the *Journal of Irish Studies*. For a listing of ethnic publications, popular and scholarly, see Lubomyr R. Wynar, *Encyclopedic Directory of Ethnic Newspapers and Periodicals in the United States* (revised edition 1976).

Primary source materials are limited only by the imagination and resourcefulness of the researcher. Among the varieties commonly used are census data, the reports of local, state, and national commissions on health, education, housing, employment, crime, and similar specific topics, the records of private and public welfare organizations, union, and political groups, and the documents of ethnic institutions such as churches, lodges, and cultural or nationalist societies. These and similar materials can often be located in large university or public libraries, and in specialized archival and resource centers such as the Balch Institute in Philadelphia; the Center for Migration Studies on Staten Island, New York; and the Center for Immigration Studies in St. Paul, Minnesota. Primary sources can also be found in local and state historical societies and in the archives of ethnic organizations and historical societies. For a listing of these ethnic societies, including their publications, see Lubomyr R. Wynar, *Encyclopedic Directory of Ethnic Organizations in the United States* (1975).

Index